A Second Modernism

A Second Modernism

MIT, Architecture, and the 'Techno-Social' Moment

Arindam Dutta, Editor

with

Stephanie Marie Tuerk

Michael Kubo

Jennifer Yeesue Chuong

Irina Chernyakova

SA+P Press
Department of Architecture
Massachusetts Institute of Technology

The MIT Press
Cambridge, Massachusetts
London, England

A publication by SA+P Press, Department of Architecture, MIT,
in collaboration with The MIT Press, Cambridge, Massachusetts, and London, England.

This book was set in Scala, ScalaSans, and Univers by SA+P Press.
Printed and bound in China by Four Colour Print Group.
Distributed by The MIT Press, Cambridge, Massachusetts, and London, England.

Library of Congress Cataloging-in-Publication Data:
A second modernism : MIT, architecture, and the 'techno-social' moment / edited by Arindam Dutta ; with Stephanie Marie Tuerk, Michael Kubo, Jennifer Yeesue Chuong, and Irina Chernyakova.
 pages   cm
Includes bibliographical references and index.
ISBN 978-0-262-01985-9 (hardcover : alk. paper) 1. Massachusetts Institute of Technology. School of Architecture and Planning. 2. Architecture—Study and teaching—History—20th century. 3. Education, Higher—Social aspects—History—20th century. 4. Architecture and technology—History—20th century. 5. Architecture and society—History—20th century. I. Dutta, Arindam, editor of compilation.
NA2300.M4S43   2013
720.71'17444—dc23
                        2013005441

Editor and Production Manager: Arindam Dutta
Research: Stephanie Marie Tuerk, Michael Kubo
Editing: Jennifer Yeesue Chuong, Arindam Dutta
Design: Chris Grimley for over,under (overcommaunder.com) and Irina Chernyakova
Reproduction Rights: Irina Chernyakova
Index: Arindam Dutta
SA+P Press liaison: Sarah Hirschman

Contents

Acknowledgments

Postwar America is not really my forte. Credit is due to Reinhold Martin and Felicity Scott for fashioning, early on in their graduate careers, a systematic critique of American technopolitics and its relationship to architecture. As a visiting instructor at Columbia University's architecture school in fall of 2007, somewhat an outsider to American Studies, it seemed to me peculiar that scholars elsewhere were pointing to MIT's key role in shaping key aspects of postwar discourse, while MIT faculty seemed either to be still unquestioningly eking out their 'humanist' careers of the 1960s-70s or – if younger – acutely at odds with its systems-laden past. Back in Cambridge late one evening, a short note to Dean Adèle Naudé Santos and Architecture Head Yung Ho Chang brought enthusiastic approval the very next morning. Adèle and Yung Ho allocated funds for the writers in this volume to travel to archives in Cambridge and the UK, as well as allow research assistants to compile thoroughgoing inventories of available archival material. Nader Tehrani, who stepped up as Head after Yung Ho, continued the strong support of his predecessor. Additionally, Nader and his partners at NADAAA, Katherine Faulkner and Daniel Gallagher, contributed a substantial sum of money to enable this book to be brought out in the lushly-illustrated form that you see it. I am deeply grateful to them for this generous, personal investment.

This book has been five years in the making, and many talented, dedicated people have contributed to bring it into being. Almost all of the production was done in-house at the Department of Architecture at MIT. Stephanie Tuerk, Michael Kubo, and Jennifer Chuong, all graduate students in the History, Theory, Criticism Program at MIT, served as equal partners with me in pulling together the huge swathes of information and data that went into the stories narrated in and the production of this book. Chris Grimley, Michael's partner at over,under, their interdisciplinary practice, produced the design template for the layout of this book. Irina Chernyakova, also an HTC student, did the final layout work and permissions, and is wholly responsible for the book in its current form. Irina chased down image rights down rabbit-holes and trails gone cold, and worked across the multiple formats that contributors worked in to deliver the final product to the printers. This book would not have happened without her extraordinary managerial and "closing skills". HTC students Alexander H. Wood produced the timeline, and Ann Lok Lui assisted with final details. Credit is also owed to Gary van Zante and Laura Knott at the MIT Museum for giving us unconditional access to their archives, in addition to giving us the rights to publish many of the images here presented gratis, thus significantly reducing costs. Sarah Hirschman, one of our design graduates, was a stellar leader at SA+P Press before she left, and she set up all the relevant contracts with printers and MIT Press. Jolene de Verges at the Rotch Library of Architecture & Planning provided library funds to document visual material in its collections. We also thank the MIT Institute Archives & Special Collections, and Jeremy Grubman and the Center for Advanced Visual Arts Archive for assisting us in our research and making their materials available for study. Roger Conover at MIT Press enthusiastically supported this book. His steady, sage advice was critical in the book's finishing stages, and is very much appreciated. Kathaleen Brearley rendered crucial administrative and logistical assistance in compiling printouts, writing letters, processing reimbursements, and organizing travel.

Lastly, a word of gratitude for the contributors to this volume: all of them enthusiastically took on this project, devoting time, travel, and labor to persevere in their writing even through what must have appeared as slowness on our end. It is to them that the book's scholarly edge is due. This volume is dedicated to them.

Arindam Dutta, February 2013.

Introduction

Linguistics, Not Grammatology:
Architecture's *A Prioris* and Architecture's Priorities
Arindam Dutta

ARINDAM DUTTA

Linguistics, Not Grammatology
Architecture's *A Prioris* and Architecture's Priorities

[Our work is] to refute the prejudice anchored in the reader by centuries of humanism and of "human sciences" that there is "man," that there is "language," that the former makes use of the latter for his own ends, and that if he does not succeed in attaining these ends, it is for want of good control over language "by means" of a "better" language.
—Jean-François Lyotard, *The Differend: Phrases in Dispute*

Globalization takes place only in capital and data. Everything else is damage control. Information command has ruined knowing and reading. Therefore we don't really know what to do with information. Unanalyzed projects come into existence simply because the information is there. Crowd sourcing takes the place of democracy. Universities become adjuncts to what is called international civil society; the humanities and imaginative social sciences bite the dust.
—Gayatri Chakravorty Spivak, *An Aesthetic Education in the Era of Globalization*

From the 1950s onwards, architectural discourse saw a tremendous upsurge of interest in linguistic, behavioral, psychological, computational, mediatic, communicational, and cybernetic paradigms. This "techno-social" tendency can be defined as much by its wariness towards what it considered the vagaries of aesthetic formalism as by its aspirations to what it considered "expertise" steeped in rule-based judgments and verifiability. This expertise premised much of its legitimacy in a universe where the State made the principal decisions related to investment and the distribution of social goods; this aspiration to legitimacy thus also vicariously aspired to the authority accorded to the legislators of the welfare and developmental state. The Thatcher-Reagan era would considerably upend that authority as well as its embedded epistemic priorities. That shift of the 1980s would eclipse the postwar age of the planner, with significant repercussions in the world of architects as well. Within the university, the tacit positivism nestled within these forms of expertise would come under severe censure from a set of critiques that came to be somewhat carelessly lumped together as "post-modernism." This book aims to examine some of the institutional contexts and histories of these particular forms of knowledge, the ambition of their purveyors to decision-making roles in society, their assumptions and experiments, and their eventual demoralization.

The techno-politics of the Second World War—its "scaled-up" mechanisms with vastly expanded modes of demographic control—and the Cold War that followed, had put paid to the old "liberal" order of institutionality: the patrician cadre of gentleman-scientists, the self-selective norm-breakers of the artistic avant-garde, the paternalist politicians given to "fireside chats," the cum laude administrator, the "renaissance" banker. The authority accorded to this patrician order—one still not completely eroded today—was deemed to draw from their connoisseurial ability to innately grasp the crux of a question: decisions would be affected as if the information driving them had been synthesized into an organic, qualitative, countermove whose resolution lay more in the powers attributed to intuition than the "mechanistic" processing of facts. John Maynard Keynes' *General Theory of Employment, Interest and Money*, with its dubious relation to data, might be said to signal the culminating crisis of the liberal order, an exercise in governmental "paradoxology" whose techno-political repercussions would spiral far beyond the jaunty and aesthetic "pluralism" of its author.[1] By contrast, the professionalization and "cult of the expert" that emerged in the aftermath of the war entailed a shift in the stances of epistemic authority. Paramount in the postwar framing of expertise, and the technologies propounded by it, was the emphasis on assembling, collating and processing larger and larger amounts of data. One immediate implication of this was the overwhelming emphasis on the systemic and mathematical elements of judgment. "Complex systems are counterintuitive . . . the intuitive processes will select the wrong solution much more often than not."[2]

The collation and processing of data inevitably affected the extant apparatus whose exceptional station it had been, since the turn of the nineteenth century, to vouchsafe the synthesis of knowledge: the university. "One of the characteristic aspects of the present epoch is that the major . . . disciplines have a tendency to expand into wider segments of the field of technology. The older patterns are changing, and it becomes increasingly difficult to find simple guides for the delimitation of these disciplines."[3] At the end of the Second World War, top American universities received federal monies for (military-related) R&D contracts that dwarfed those given to individual corporations: MIT, the highest in the list, received $117 million and Caltech $83 million, while Western Electric (AT&T), GE, RCA, Du Pont, and Westinghouse received no more than $7 million on average.[4] In his 1966

1 See Arindam Dutta, "Marginality and MetaEngineering: Keynes and Arup" in *Governing By Design*, eds. Daniel M. Abramson, Arindam Dutta, Timothy W. Hyde, and Jonathan Massey (Pittsburgh: University of Pittsburgh Press, 2012).

2 Jay W. Forrester, *Urban Dynamics* (Cambridge, MA: The MIT Press, 1969), 9.

3 MIT Report of the President, School of Engineering (1954), 61.

4 See Stuart W. Leslie, *The Cold War and American Science: The Military-Industrial-Academic Complex at MIT and Stanford* (New York: Columbia University Press, 1993), 6.

inaugural address, titled "The University of the Future," MIT President Howard W. Johnson spoke of the need to "reaffirm the vitality of the technological challenge for the universities, and especially for this one, in the continuing development of science and engineering that makes further advantage possible, and in the development of people to provide leadership in a technological society."[5] It is tempting to view these lofty expressions as a request for funds. In 1967, MIT's Vice President of Research Administration reported that of the sponsored research program, representing 55 percent of its operating budget, 90 percent came from the federal government, accounting for 30 percent of faculty salary and most of graduate student support.[6]

This book looks at the effects of this new "research-academic" complex on the American and transatlantic scenes as glimpsed through the archives of one particular institution: MIT's School of Architecture and Planning (SAP). The period demarcated in this story is roughly that between 1945 and 1981. The latter date may be characterized by the rise in currency of postmodernism in academic discourse, a turn that our actors would view with a good deal of discomfiture and indignation. 1981 was also the year of the submission of the voluminous *Architecture and Education Study* brought out by the Mellon Foundation-funded, MIT-led "Consortium of East Coast Schools of Architecture," a report that as much epitomizes the "techno-social" and systems-based currency (and torment) of the previous decades as it manifests its redundancy amongst an intellectual and institutional-funding conjuncture that had shifted elsewhere.[7]

What we call this era's "techno-social" impetus can be defined as follows: if architectural decision-making is seen to be encountering and involving a certain "complexity"—in confronting the multiple protocols of economy, technology, production, politics, etc.—then the protocols by which these decisions are seen to be made must acquire a concomitant air of complexity. The complexity must not be seen in institutional terms as an innocent one. Its power lies in a tendentious association: that the methodological protocols undergirding technological constructs bear analogies with the methodological protocols needed to understand "society."

5 Howard W. Johnson, "The University of the Future," *Technology Review* 69, no. 23 (November, 1966), 19. I am grateful to Alexander Wood for this reference.

6 MIT Report of the President, 1968, School of Architecture and Planning Report (henceforth MIT-PR; SAP) (1967), 565.

7 William L. Porter and Maurice Kilbridge (directors), *Architecture Education Study*, sponsored by the Consortium of East Coast Schools of Architecture (Cambridge, MA: Andrew W. Mellon Foundation, 1981).

The term "techno-social" may amount to a tautology. Michel Foucault had observed that "society" in the strict sense must be seen as nothing more than the effect of the technological in its widest arc, a rubric produced by biopolitical constructs such the census, hygiene, security apparatuses and so on.[8] The individual is manifestly a form of "political technology." Unlike Foucault's "specific intellectuals," who would presumably overturn the techniques of their specific expertise to work against the objectives of their controllers, it would be fair to say that if MIT's architects and planners had one ambition in common, it was the overwhelming ambition to be the designers and handlers—that is, the decision-makers—for this political technology.[9] To that end, they unquestioningly cast themselves—in their teaching, writing and curricula—as vicarious agents of the State, on the one hand inveterately cultivating the technocrat's ambition to improve efficiencies by which goods could be distributed in society, and on the other, affecting a deep social benevolence aimed at designing "fixes" for the social contract. This vicarious ambition would make them eager clients for the great technocratic institutions that would be built up in the postwar: the World Bank, the Ford and Rockefeller Foundations, HUD, the NSF, and so on, and also not ruling out, as we shall see in the case of Ciudad Guayana and others, Third World military autocrats. These institutions in turn solicited prestige from their association with the MIT experts.

In 1980, the United States Congress passed the Bayh-Dole Act, granting universities and other government research contractors substantial intellectual property control over the products of their research. This "subsidized privatization" would put paid to the entire era of postwar "Big Science," and with it, Big *Social* Science and the era of centralized governments. With that shift, the "techno-social" fervor of the postwar would find itself on the wane. The Consortium *Study* reads as a document patently out of joint with its time.

A Second Modernism

The episteme is the "apparatus" which makes possible the separation, not of the true from the false, but of what may from what may not be characterized as scientific. Michel Foucault, in interview[10]

8 See, for instance Michel Foucault, *Security, Territory, Population: Lectures at the Collège de France, 1977-1978*, trans. Graham Burchell (New York: Picador, 2007).

9 For Foucault's discussion on the specific intellectual, see Michel Foucault, "Truth and Power," in *Power / Knowledge: Selected Interviews and Other Writings 1972-1977*, ed. Colin Gordon, (New York: Pantheon Books, 1980), 126-133.

10 Michel Foucault, "The Confession of the Flesh," in conversation with Alain Grosrichard, Gerard Wajeman et al, in ibid., 197.

In describing the affairs of the School of Architecture and Planning at MIT, the very term "school" may be deceptive if the dominant association one has with the word is that of Raphael's painting: a panoply of conversations set off against a cohering dialectic and organized under a single roof. To some extent, this book implicitly argues that in the above-mentioned dispensations of funding no such unified horizon or dialectics of knowledge could be retained. For the architects and planners at MIT the primacy of funded research would thematize and reorganize academic work towards a "problem-solving" and relevance-seeking mentality, transforming the very sense of their discipline. What had been posed elsewhere at the end of the war as a training of the intuition—in the imported, Bauhaus system—was at MIT transformed into a subject for "research," whose expanded remit could count among its ancillaries the entire gamut of the social sciences: linguistics, information sciences, operations research, computer technology, systems theory. Aesthetics or the cultivation of virtuosity were here handily seen as inadequate—occasions for error—on their own grounds, requiring supplementation by multiple kinds of verificatory (the Popperian dogma of "falsifiability") paradigms. As SAP Dean Lawrence B. Anderson put it, architecture now demanded "a certain degree of structural hardness."[11] A *second*, "systems"-based modernism can thus be seen superimposing itself on the first one, affecting a "research" outlook to the outcomes of the art, one imbued with a strong anti-aesthetic impetus.

In expanding the compass of what can be reshaped under the heading of design, what appears to be at stake is architecture's very a priori: each new category of "object" thus encountered appears to occasion a revisiting of the terms of discursive agreement, requiring an entirely new frame of epistemic legitimation:

> There are sharp warning signals to indicate that the old idealization is too pat to survive new dynamics . . . the effectuating agencies are increasingly subject to the constraints of their own processes, and these tend to dictate solutions that often override the problem formulations. What one can do under these restraints often determines what one can have, independently of what is wanted. Thus the task of the designer is rendered far more difficult in regard to both ends and means. The entire train of events must be regarded as a complete

Richard Furm working in the Department of Architecture studio, MIT, n.d.. Photo: William Porter.

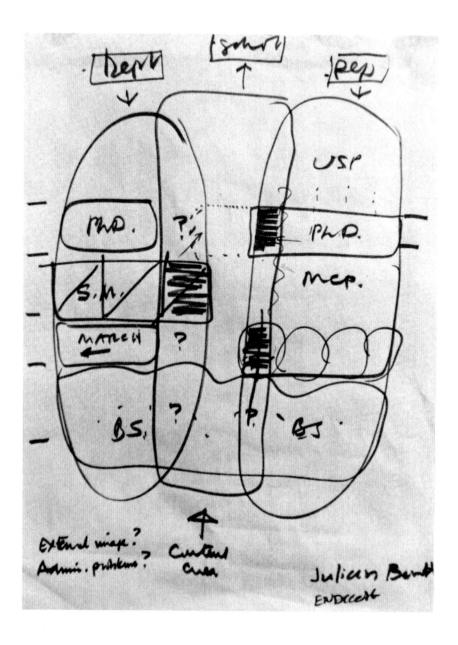

Julian Beinart, sketch of the curriculum for the School
of Architecture & Planning, MIT. *PLAN*, 1980.

system, and the role of the designer as catalyst in the system is being drastically revised . . . Under the growing dominance of total environment, the architect and planner is dispensable unless he himself can become more fully informed. Education for architecture and planning is in the process of increasing interaction with the disciplines that interpret urban social and political forces and also seeks deeper understanding and stronger links with industrial technology and the management arts.[12]

This is a *kind* of theory, to be sure, if one hallmark of theory is to peer into the abyss, into the maw of the Real. But one cannot avoid the sense that here theory is being posed as a stage-effect, given that what we are witnessing here is a routine bureaucratic exercise, an extract from the 1967 Department of Architecture's Annual Report written by then Head (and anagrammatically named) Donlyn Lyndon to the MIT President. It is in the nature of administrative speech to come equipped with an oft-used panic button, if only to be assured of adequate portions of the next round of funds. But in the above case, and as we shall see in this book, what is clear is that this professed interdisciplinarity also underscores a methodological trend: to re-describe design as a form of administration or governmentality. The "total design" aspired to in the "first" modernism has here become, in its second, "expertise-seeking" avatar, a totalitarian investment into systems-organization.

It is important to state that this investment could hardly be described in terms of some greater purchase on truths. Far from it, it speaks to an elaborate institutional mechanics of legitimation. Recent scholarship has suggested that the relationship between the interests of social scientists in the postwar to the research agendas laid out by the National Science Foundation amounted to what critics of federal government call "pork" or lobbying, replete as this was with full-fledged lobbying, "revolving door" appointments, and even occasional instances of blackmail by the professionals with the most clout within governmental corridors: the economists. The more severe the "crisis," the more entrenched the clout: "scholars in the social sciences were able to capture funding by offering to resolve environmental destruction, unemployment, economic inequality, a decline in worker productively, and social unrest."[13] Apprehensive of their own professional marginalization, architects and planners avidly embraced this culture of crisis-pronouncement for the

11 Anderson was appointed Dean of the SAP in 1965. MIT-PR; SAP (1968), 30.

12 MIT-PR; SAP (1967), 32.

13 Tiago Mata and Tom Scheiding, "National Science Foundation Patronage of Social Science, 1970s and 1980s: Congressional Scrutiny, Lobbying and an Advocacy Network" (n.d.), 7, <http://econ.duke.edu/uploads/assets/Workshop%20Papers/HOPE/Mata%20and%20Scheiding%20-%20NSF%20 70s%20and%2080s.pdf> Accessed December 20, 2011.

standing it could garner them; their desired parish of the distraught being, of course, "the city"—in the 1960s almost inevitably associated with poverty, race conflict, white flight, and perceptions of communal and infrastructural decay. As the Ford Foundation's Paul N. Ylvisaker wryly observed, "The approved way to talk about cities these days is to speak solemnly, sadly, ominously, and fearfully about their problems. You don't rate as an expert on the city unless you foresee its doom." [14] At the same time, as Lyndon's note above betrays, that traffic in Cassandraisms was seldom one in which the architects were given any speaking parts. By and large what devolved to them is the language of mimic men: the grandiose, world-making, world-dispensing tone—Charles Jencks would later call this "the tragic view"—that one discerns as so prominent in the architectural writing of this period, is markedly that of a derivative creole, peppered with stock phrases from the social sciences, from business administration, and from cybernetics and systems theory.

By the end of the 1970s, in his report on the future of the postwar university, Jean-François Lyotard had already foreseen "the predominance of the performance criterion [as] sounding the death knell of the age of the Professor."[15] In the second, postwar, modernism, the "researcher" marked a "post-modern" turn from master narratives to a pragmatics of knowledge. What Rachel Malik has written about the David Cameron government's restructuring of public education in the United Kingdom today might well be said to have been a model that institutions such as MIT were attempting to voluntarily forge five decades ago: the last half of the passage below holds particularly true for its architects and planners of the late 1970s, and as such offer us the complement to Lyndon's "pragmatic" arguments above:

> I am talking instead about the managerial embrace of a particularly degraded form of the modern. The management specialty is "radical" reorganizations: of teaching programs, organizational structures and research priorities, all of which must be achieved at absurdly accelerated rates. Such revolutions are always justified as a necessary response to external conditions and to a future whose only certain quality is its uncertainty. Emergency is our everyday: it is always wartime . . . In various forms of higher educational discourse, research is already starting to float free of "content," that tricky, highly specialized, fancy knowledge that presents such a challenge to institutions [professing an older, humanistic, model]. Education is becoming a training in learning. Students learn a good deal about how to "do" team-work and assess their peers, but rather less about the Victorian novel . . . These practices, increasingly generic and cross-disciplinary, are being taught to postgraduates, and increasingly to undergraduates, particularly those in what are now called "research-rich institutions" looking for ways to justify their fees. Just as the good manager takes pride in being able to manage anything, so the good researcher will take pride in being able to research anything. Not knowing much about a subject area will present no difficulty, rather it might be considered an advantage, for the researcher will be untroubled by disciplinary loyalty—just like the manager who comes in from outside.[16]

At MIT, for instance, reflecting as much external (federal and corporate) agendas in research as the initiative of individual faculty, a series of micro-institutions set up home within the School, turning out landmark pieces of polemic even as they over-determined the curricular agenda. "Research" entailed a kind of epistemic balkanization within the larger empire of the sciences, occasioning the formation of multiple sub-units whose acronyms run arabesques within the alphabet: the Harvard-MIT Joint Center for Urban Studies, the Urban Systems Laboratory, the Center for Advanced Visual Studies (CAVS), the History, Theory, and Criticism (HTC) Program, the Laboratory of Architecture and Planning, the Environmental Design Program, the Architecture Machine Group and the Media Lab, the Special Program for Urban and Regional Studies (SPURS), the list goes on. The exigencies for this proliferation lay, quite simply, in the disparate prerogatives of their funding bodies, federal or foundation-based—(D)ARPA, NSF, Fulbright, Ford, Rockefeller—as well as industry-based: Monsanto, the Tile Council of America, Sears-Roebuck, Pittsburgh Plate Glass, Du Pont. As Mary Lou Lobsinger points out in her essay in this book, these gambits for expertise groped around as much in the realm of nomenclature, occasioning a fervid traffic in boilerplate names—*Special, Joint, Center, Laboratory, Environment, Urban, Land, Unit, Planning, Studies, Built Form*—as well as personnel and knowledge paradigms.

In the event, shifts in nomenclature were happily accommodated to suit the vagaries of funding. Thus the Center for Urban Studies was renamed the Laboratory for Environment Studies, signaling a delicate balancing act between the different lines of legitimation: "laboratory" signaling a consanguinity with science-indexed sponsorship as much as "urban" and "environment" speak to the discursive stipulations generated by HUD and the Ford Foundation. Both internally and externally, this proliferation created an interminable array of extenuations for the "training of the architect," that boondoggle that remained the object of copious and captious histrionics both within departmental policy discussions and intramural publications such as the *Journal of Architectural Education.*

This book does not purport to present any kind of synthetic view as to what obtained or transpired in the history of the School, since the principal argument here is that such a synthesis was in fact unavailing, despite the routine frets and rants of the involved actors

14 Quoted in John A. Buggs, "Social and Political Realities in the City," in *The Engineer and the City* (Washington, D.C.: National Academy of Engineering, 1969), 32.

15 Lyotard, *The Postmodern Condition,* 53.

16 Rachel Malik, "Universities Under Attack," *London Review of Books* (16 December 2011 [online only]), accessed December 24, 2011, http://www.lrb.co.uk/2011/12/16/rachel-malik/universities-under-attack.

about the need for disciplinary agreement. While "synthesis" was very much in the air, in practice it was militated against in the School's continual search for institutional validation. Take for instance one of the projects undertaken by Aaron Fleisher through the Urban Systems Laboratory in the 1960s. The project was initiated as a HUD-sponsored study of the "urban mobility of the poor." However, making the problem pertinent to the academic context of the university entailed a particular framing of the problem—distinct from, say, how the legislature or the census would address these issues—since the problem-setting of "design" must also be shown to have pedagogical value. It was felt necessary, therefore, borrowing the social/architectonic frame of the "laboratory" as used by the engineering departments of the Institute, to set up an "Urban Data Laboratory," where narratives of poverty could be processed into analyzable fields of quanta. As data began to be compiled, the pressing task that emerged concerned "developing the use of the computer," since more important than the gathering of data, in itself mute, was the development of a specialized language to decipher it.[17]

As it happened, this shift in methodology did not owe only to cognitive challenges. In her essay in this volume, Felicity Scott presents the circumstances for this shift clearly, as in the following explanation provided in *The Tech*: "when the Urban Systems Lab was founded in 1968, 'there was the anticipation that urban problems would be approached on the basis of large scale, mission-oriented projects, as in the space program. These large scale projects never came about because of funding limitations. HUD never became the research equivalent of the Defense Department." The newfound interest in the computer drew from the fact that as HUD money ran out, IBM appeared as a new source of funds. However its interest lay in refining computational modes of input and output. All too coincidentally, we discover that the competence required to "read" poverty had little to do with the empirical outlines of the phenomenon per se,[18] but now consisted in the need to devise agreement amongst a diverse cadre of addressees or experts, a process which the putative reduction of data to computer code was presumed to assist. From "solving poverty," the problem now became one of devising code, a shift that could be rationalized as keeping faith with its original impetus since poverty—an inscrutable phenomenon at best—could always be described as a structure involving multiple genres of data. This triple shift, from designer to planner to programmer, also entailed a shift in temporalities: if poverty must be addressed with a "sense of urgency," the tools needed to address it on the other hand must have a long-term validity, one that "will go on for several decades or more," thus purchasing for the expert a perpetual legitimacy or decipherability, long after both the code's conceivers and its speakers would have disappeared from the scene. There is never this poverty or that poverty, your poverty or mine, only poverty in the global, abstract sense, a formal or model poverty computable down from its general prerequisites into its minutest, most diverse, manifestations. Expertise thrives on kicking cans down the road.

How then to write about this precocious and ongoing shift, a shift with no foreseeable end or conclusion even today, in a way that would run true to the kind of judgment that historians seek to capture, constrained as they are by the delimitation of finite epoch or era? The story here speaks to the continuous demoralization and new legitimacies of the sciences and the humanities in the second part of the twentieth century, and in the context of architectural departments it encompasses as much the erosion of curricular content as their new formulations. This book brings together a number of writers with strong expertise on the history of architecture and the "techno-social" impetus in post-war America. The subject matter—or "archive"—is MIT, but each writer addresses particular parts of that story through their own unique approach to what must be etched as a global scene. The aggregate outcome is designedly uneven, but this mirrors the intrinsic unevenness of the story that is being told: to have tried to produce greater coherence would have also meant producing an apologia in the shape of a story that wasn't.

Book Overview

This book is organized into six key sections, followed by Edward Eigen's excursus on the continuist traditions of history and science. Eigen's argument can be described as an apt response to the interpretive problems that beset this book. To a great extent, the stories told here also present tests for historians' ability to write about the inherent dysfunction that inevitably accompanies institutional functioning. Institutional histories tend to be written in the shadow of master narratives: institutional schisms or failures are routinely ascribed therefore to the *failure* to craft grand narratives. The fact that schism does not necessarily entail catastrophic failure, or that bureaucracies, departments, or institutional bodies can handily "muddle along" for decades, if not centuries, without evincible purpose or principle may appear inscrutable to some, but it may hew closer to the empirical picture. If anything, cohesiveness of narrative may well provide a compensatory mechanism to cover over what may in fact be an inscrutable set of factors—byzantine allegiances, pet peeves and ideological anathemas or obsessions, cabalistic rivalry, not to rule out erotic or sexual tensions—all of which may well thrive within an institution's "normal" functioning in a mode that may well otherwise defy simple rationalization.

17 This description is that of a project undertaken under Aaron Fleisher through the Urban Systems Laboratory at MIT in the 1960s. MIT-PR; SAP (1968), 492-4.

18 Indeed, IBM's own origins have been described as similarly incidental. "[MIT's Jay] Forrester started his own project, the Whirlwind Computer Project, and sold it to the Pentagon as the core of a system to build an "electronic radar fence," the "Star Wars" of the 1950s: the Semi-Automatic Ground Environment, or SAGE project. Forrester selected for the work a company, that—unlike Raytheon, Sylvania, and Remington Rand, the earliest major electronic firms—was not yet established in electronics. This new company was IBM, and it was chosen by pure chance. In June 1952, when Forrester was looking for a commercial manufacturer to build his iron core memory for the SAGE Project, he met at the Second Joint Computer Conference an IBM engineer, John McPherson, who seized the opportunity, convincing IBM's President Tom Watson to meet President Truman to offer the services of IBM. Having secured the contract,

MIT LABORATORY OF ARCHITECTURE AND PLANNING

**USERS AND INSTITUTIONS   SEMINAR: AUGUST 2-6   WORKSHOP/STUDIO: AUGUST 9-13, 1982
IN COLLABORATION WITH THE DEVELOPMENT PLANNING UNIT, UNIVERSITY COLLEGE, LONDON**

DESIGN AND HOUSING IN DEVEL-
OPING COUNTRIES: PROFESSION-
AL PRACTICE AND ALTERNATIVE
ROLES OF USERS AND INSTITUTIONS

K O E N I G S B E R G E R
C A M I N O S . . P O P K O
T U R N E R . P E A T T I E
D E M O N C H A U X . M I T
H A B R A K E N . S I L V A
H A R R I S . . M U M T A Z
H A M D I . G O E T H E R T

**SPECIAL PROGRAM: A One Week Seminar/
A One Week Workshop**

"What happens when accelerated urbanization occurs in a developing country? Usually it has a profound and detrimental impact on the living conditions of a majority of the population. The demands are unprecedented, the shortages are acute, and the problem is compounded by an ineffective administrative, financial, and management framework.

It is generally agreed that conventional housing approaches and attitudes are ineffective, and moreover, have hindered progress and compounded the waste of human and material resources. In response, an alternative attitude has arisen that focuses on the role of the users in management, design and construction, and in so doing, has redrawn the relative role of user and institution in the housing field. This issue is the basis around which the seminar is developed.

The seminar faculty includes a number of professionals who have been working on housing in many developing nations and development institutions. It will offer architects, planners, housing administrators and educators the opportunity to acquaint themselves with current practices, to discuss and work with distinguished guest faculty.

This program is organized as two related but autonomous one-week components. The first week's component, in a seminar setting, will explore the topical issues in presentations and case study discussions. The second week's component, in a studio and workshop setting, will focus on design and lab work. Participants can elect to attend Week One, Week Two or both. Enrollment in Week Two will be limited.

KEY TOPICS AND APPLICATIONS

- Introductory overview of the most critical general issues of rapid urbanization. Particular focus on common trends and

institutional responses. Review of policies and practices, past and present, of both successes and failures. Implications for the practicing design professional.

- An *alternative* view of the role of users, professionals, government and other institutions. Why the alternative view is necessary; what it means. Rational and philosophical bases. Focus on maximizing user inputs in the context of limited government/institutional capabilities. The most crucial existing dilemmas and alternative frameworks. The importance of an awareness of political realities, the fine line between awareness and cynicism.

- Consideration of the *social impacts* before design and decision-making. What practitioners should know about participation/roles in the housing process; values, aspirations, orientation; spontaneous settlement examples contrasted with a traditional project orientation; expected impacts on social structure of urban communities.

- Evaluating *economic factors* and housing policies; conventional and alternative interpretations. Critical choices in allocation of money in development and financing of housing. The relative contribution of public, private and other institutional funds.

- Identifying and assessing *physical alternatives* in process and design. Reevaluating shelter, land and services. Strategies in land subdivision and provision of utilities. Allocating user/institutional responsibilities. Housing options: sites and services, core housing, basan schemes.

SPECIAL FEATURES

Additional events throughout the two-week seminar will feature films and slide presentations.

Participants are invited to bring drawings and/or slides of their ongoing work for presentation, discussion and feedback.

Detailed case studies will illustrate concepts and provide a forum for analysis and discussion. Examples will include

projects developed through traditional forms of government/institutional involvement to site and services schemes and also to informal development processes.

The program is a part of a continuing series in Housing and Settlement Design Seminars; Seminar '85 is planned at the Development Planning Unit, London.

SEMINAR FACULTY

Reinhard Goethert: (Seminar Director) Research Associate, MIT.

Nabeel Hamdi: (Seminar Director) Assistant Professor of Architecture, MIT.

Horacio Caminos: Architect. Professor of Architecture, MIT.
John de Monchaux: Dean, School of Architecture and Planning, MIT.
N. John Habraken: Professor of Architecture, MIT.
Nigel Harris: Economist, DPU.
Otto Koenigsberger: Professor Emeritus of Development Planning, DPU.
Babar Mumtaz: Economist, Architect/planner, DPU.
Lisa R. Peattie: Professor of Urban Anthropology, MIT.
Edward Popko: Project Director, Harvard Computer Graphics Laboratory
Mauricio Silva: Former director of FSDVM, El Salvador.
John F.C. Turner: Architect and housing specialist, DPU.

REGISTRATION

The program will be held at MIT—Seminar: August 2-6, Workshop/Studio: August 9-13. The per person registration fee includes most lunches and all class materials. Each member will receive a Certificate of Participation.

The fee does not include lodging or travel. Lodging is available in MIT facilities or in various hotels nearby. Please check the appropriate box for further information. MIT athletic facilities (pool, track, tennis, sailing, squash) are available to seminar participants.

Please register early. To insure your place, the registration form must be accompanied by a non-refundable $50 deposit.

Name _____ Title _____

Organization _____ Phone (___) _____

Address _____ City _____ State _____ Zip _____

Please return this form to: Laboratory of Architecture and Planning   ( ) Fee enclosed $550. □ Seminar only   □ Workshop/Studio only
                               MIT, Room 4-209   ( ) Fee enclosed $975, both programs
                               77 Mass. Ave., Cambridge, MA 02139   ( ) Deposit enclosed $50   □ Seminar only   □ Workshop/Studio only
                               Tel: (617) 253-1350 for information   □ Both

                                                                        ( ) Send hotel list
                                                                        ( ) Send additional seminar information

( ) Send bill to: _____

To reserve a room at MIT's McCormick Hall, call (617) 253-1350. Please make checks payable to: MIT Laboratory of Architecture and Planning.

MASSACHUSETTS INSTITUTE OF TECHNOLOGY, CAMBRIDGE, MASSACHUSETTS

Poster for "Design and Housing in Developing Countries: Professional Practice and Alternative Roles of Users and Institutions," workshop/studio organized by the Laboratory of Architecture and Planning, Department of Architecture, MIT in collaboration with the Development Planning Unit, University College London, 1982.

The first section of the book, titled "Humanities," points to the manner in which the compensatory mechanisms of the humanities and the arts came—in the name of the "human"—to do duty in the postwar in providing narratives of civilization and enlightenment even as technologists and systems theorists were subverting these to seek more remunerative frames of "relevance." Reinhold Martin opens the discussion through his examination of the terms under which the "humanities" were given additional impetus in postwar MIT. Martin sees the doublet of religion and humanism, underscored by the simultaneous construction of Eero Saarinen's MIT chapel in 1955 and the establishment of the new School of Humanities and Social Studies[19] in 1950, as a quasi-theological effort to lend a *pastoral* air to and within the sciences. John Harwood's essay immediately following fleshes out the converse of that coin, giving us a glimpse into the kerfuffles by which that touted office of the humanities called "criticism" came to occupy a signal place in the education of the architect. Harwood situates the creation of the History, Theory, and Criticism program at MIT — America's first doctoral program in architectural history — as a key juncture in that national, if not international, debate. Anna Vallye looks at yet one more aspect of that trade-off between the humanities and the sciences, writing on György Kepes as the apt cross-over artist for the scientists. In gerrymandering the domain of "art" to the mechanics of "vision"—thus making it subject to the froth of behavioral, communicational and systems approaches being churned up at the Institute—Kepes's peculiarly high standing at MIT is here depicted as reflecting his uncanny felicity in producing the symbolic images to suit the engineers' sense of their own vanguardism.

The second section of the book, "Sponsorship," clubs together essays which particularly concentrate on the manner in which

IBM started moving from the punch-card business to computer manufacture. On the basis of the SAGE contract, IBM hired 8,000 engineers and workers, signaling its real head-start in computer manufacturing with its Model 650, delivered in December 1954." Manuel Castells and Peter Hall,

Technopoles of the World: The Making of 21st Century Industrial Complexes (New York: Routledge, 1994), 34. Forrester would then subsequently turn his computing expertise to addressing questions of urban planning. See Jay Forrester, *Urban Dynamics* (Portland: Productivity Press, 1969).

19 The School was renamed in its current form, the School of Humanities, Arts and Social Sciences, in 2000.

funding bodies or agendas organized or waylaid the interests of various actors within MIT, all under the guise of seeking their pragmatic "relevance" to real world problems. Matthew Wisnioski's essay looks at the fate of the Center for Advanced Visual Studies (CAVS)— originally created as Kepes's playpen—under Otto Piene in the context of the fraying contract between arts and sciences at the end of the 1970s. Wisnioski's essay is followed, later in the volume, by his interview with Piene. Avigail Sachs's essay on the Bemis Foundation—the name may ring a bell from your visits to the bathroom—offers a succinct account of how business entities such as Bemis and Monsanto drove a "pre-fabrication" agenda at the architecture school aimed at highlighting uses for their own products. Daniel Barber's ensuing essay outlines some of the fault-lines within funded research. He portrays the case of Maria Telkes' "failed" endeavor to build a working solar house at MIT. Her subsequent career can be compared to the Urban Systems Laboratory's meandering search for legitimacy that we have recounted above: fired from MIT, Telkes would nonetheless go on to have an influential career as a United Nations consultant, instructing Third World bureaucrats on questions of science and economy. Barber's implication is "environment" itself is such a "failed" concept, but a robust one in the sense that what admits of little falsifiability in the disciplinary realm may nonetheless have an enduring, and very different, life in the cult of expertise.

"The City," an ontological figure that stands in for an epistemological category, is the title of our next section, and might be said to be another one of those elusive, non-evincible, but overly feted rubrics. A similar instance to the USL's poverty study, described above, is that of Ciudad Guayana in Venezuela, presented here in Eric Mumford's and Ijlal Muzaffar's complementary essays—and in William L. Porter's memoir—on the MIT-Harvard Joint Center for Urban Studies. Muzaffar's work very closely analyzes the Joint Center's deft use and, with an eye to the main chance, deferral of one economic theory after another in an effort to perpetuate their own professional standing. Felicity Scott's blow-by-blow research into the policy dynamics of the department and the school shows the "urban" as lodged precisely in that cusp of disciplinary and professional uncertainty. We suggested earlier that the methodological preoccupations of our actors in question moved in tandem, "externally" towards developing codes that could do duty for complexity in the name of society and "internally" towards redacting the analytical languages in which these methodologies or codes were written. The section on "The City" and the following one on "Systems" represent, respectively, the two prongs of that doublet, the ontological and epistemological fronts of the sponsored-research complex. For a cadre of self-designated experts whose touted métier was managing complexity, the city became the epistemological object par excellence, at once an abstraction and a seething "real" laboratory of racial tensions, economic inequality, failing infrastructure, administrative (mis)management, and political drama. Hashim Sarkis's account of the legendary urbanist Kevin Lynch speaks as much to this political ferment as to his evident elision of this fraught terrain.

If "the city" propounded its own set of careers, computers and computational logic—specifically the mesmeric, alchemical incantations of Artificial Intelligence (AI)—became a pivotal edge on which the Institute staked its future. The section on "Systems" focuses on the multiple aspects in which these logics or metaphors appeared to find their suit, from design and landscape theory to art practice to graphic design. Alise Upitis looks at the particular kinds of computational machinery available to architects interested in systems, and the manner in which such machinery may have determined the logic deployed by designers, and then some: in the case of Christopher Alexander, she demonstrates how his use of the IBM 7090 mainframe entailed a particularly dogmatic adherence to a particular frame of reasoning. Catherine McMahon looks at the early beginnings of what is today called GIS (Geographic Information System) at MIT and Harvard and its intersections with language and landscape theory. Both fields, unsurprisingly enough, imply connections with the behavioral sciences, and McMahon, like Sarkis above, explains how projective systems were inherently based on particular behavioral models, and the manner in which the idiosyncratic assumptions embedded in those models inevitably carried over into the vaunted autonomy and the impersonal traits of those systems. Caroline Jones portrays the intellectual trajectory of Hans Haacke, a brief visitor at MIT, first an initiate into systems theory and then conscious dissenter. This early initiation was to linger, Jones argues, in a kind of systems theory at work in the gamut of Haacke's subsequent career, much of which lay out some kind of systemic or infrastructural substrate beneath the visible or the world of art. As *lingua franca* of the Institute, systems-thought did not belong only to those who espoused it, or who were signally adept in wielding it. Mark Jarzombek reports on the peculiar case of Maurice Smith, for whom the decipherment of a tectonic grammar in architecture descended into a dizzy whorl of idiosyncratic, solipsistic, and arcane maneuvers. Smith, an expatriate from New Zealand, cast a long shadow over relationships within the department, and to this day the recollections of those conversant with MIT in that period are riven by where one stood on the "Smith question"; one academic, for example, described him as the "man who single-handedly destroyed MIT," naming him as a key reason as to why many—the myriad legitimate and illegitimate offspring of the Texas Rangers, say—gave MIT a wide berth.

Going by Stanford Anderson's account, the antagonism was mutual, even if cordial. The next section, "Networks," lays out the premise that intellectual paradigms, despite their appearance of intellectual coherence, are driven by the relationship between certain sets of actors and their institutional berths. Anderson, apprehending fully the above perception of Maurice Smith, rises loyally to his defense, but this only as a foretaste of a thorough-going, magisterial recollection of the Conference of Architects for the Study of the Environment (CASE) and his own role, as MIT's representative and otherwise, within it. With the tireless provocateur Peter Eisenman at its center, CASE was to culminate in a collective study of housing for Harlem, involving architects and thinkers whose work would become seminal for the profession; its fractious career and eventual dissolution would nonetheless be capped by the establishment of the journal *Oppositions* as well as the Institute for Architecture and Urban Studies. Anderson's humorous, often self-deprecatory, writing offers us a stellar example of the fine art of memoir, taking us into the innards of what would prove to be a crucial pedagogical and research debate for the decades following. In more Latourian fashion, Mary Lou Lobsinger introduces us to yet another, but equally pertinent, network, the "Two Cambridge" circuit. Taking the September, 1969 issue of *Architectural Design* as her cue, in which MIT work was strongly represented, Lobsinger discerns an entire transatlantic and bicoastal regime at work. From Cambridge University to University College London to Harvard and MIT and then onwards to Berkeley and back again (Christopher Alexander's career straddles this entire circuit), Lobsinger outlines the manner in which "basic research" became the imprimatur of a host of institutions in this period, a veritable "geography of expertise" simultaneously pushing related agendas at multiple locations. Brendan Moran's insightful essay on the multiple determinations of "regionalism"—of which the School's first postwar Dean, William W. Wurster, is offered as exponent and proponent—looks at how terrestrial or cultural geography often came to stand in for what was in fact a network of expertise. In other words, rather that hark back to some "essential" regional constraints, Moran argues, regionalism was in fact tied to a game of recognition through which the smaller schools, dubbing themselves regionalist, could vie with the more prominent metropolitan schools, consequently trading in an equally distinct set of actors. (MIT and Berkeley's intermittent championing of this ideal, somewhat at odds with the Ivies, fits this model.)

The section on networks is followed by some of the actors themselves—Julian Beinart, William L. Porter, Nicholas Negroponte, N. John Habraken, Otto Piene—speaking to the reader in their own voices. These voices are gathered here in a variety of formats. Matthew Wisnioski rounds off his essay on CAVS and Piene above by interviewing the man himself; Alexander d'Hooghe and Arindam Dutta talk to Habraken about his career, and Molly Steenson does the same with Nicholas Negroponte.

As mentioned above, the book closes off with Edward Eigen's peregrine essay on the inscrutability—or illegitimacy—of making legitimate deductions in science. With the "shaggy dog story" of Tristram Shandy as its muse, Eigen dives into the suspect genealogy of an object that lurks under this very editor's window at MIT: the Newton tree, claimed to have descended from the tree whose falling apple is attributed with plummeting us into the modern era of science. Exploring this story of origins as opening up the cohesiveness of both science and history as epistemic vocations, Eigen's account brings up perhaps the "shaggy dog" premise of this book itself. It signally implies what we have been suggesting all along: that there is a disjunction between scientific modes of derivation or standardization and the narratives by which these authentications are authorized within a broader culture. The skepticism by which science examines statements seeking to enter its domain, and the reductionism by which it desires to collate its judgments into a continuous genealogy—the figure for which, we are reminded, is a tree—are at marked variance with the patch-worked historicism by which this continuity is produced.

Inevitably, there is much that is not covered in this book; what avails here is a patchwork. Institutions are peopled with a varied cast of characters, some more prominent than others, others deeper in shadow. Relative obscurity hardly dissuades cult following (the Maurice Smith case being an example) and there will be many who may well be annoyed by what has been included in or excluded from this volume. At best, we can offer the following disclaimer: this is a collection of multiple forays revolving around the question of the "techno-social," and the accounts presented here deliberately steer away from presenting, in their ensemble, any holistic or authoritative account of departmental events.

Legitimation

History is a Shandean tale to be sure, and institutional histories can invite a smorgasbord of approaches. The sparsely populated and, generally speaking, methodologically immature field of architectural history often tends to recounts institutional careers by exclusively foregrounding the travails of charismatic individuals (Gropius, Sert, the Texas Rangers). This is fine so far as it goes, and the MIT story certainly has a few impresarios (Lynch, Negroponte, Habraken), not to rule out, on the other hand, those for whom a self-regarding modesty or anti-charisma—in line with the anonymity required of the "expert"—came to serve as something like a calling card. Nonetheless, architectural historiography's inexorable, seemingly hapless, recourse to personification in recounting institutional histories offers us little insight into the regimens by which knowledge games are played by institutional players. A key deficiency that arises is that statements or enunciations are seldom read as situational or dialogical—set within a temporal, interactional matrix—and more as outward expressions of some otherwise elusive "self" or psychic tendency of the actors involved. Typically then, knowledge paradigms are seen as if wholly emergent from a circle of philosophical influence rather than as a hybridized system involving the infrastructural or regional contexts in which they are set—the availability of funds, of people, epistemic currents, disciplinary audience, and so on. In ignoring those parameters, there is a patent idealism in architecture's long-lingering and naïve dalliance with the premise of "autonomy." This self-serving stance is barely mitigated when, for not much else other than the need to appear "theoretically" conversant, it takes expedient appeal to that Kuhnian catchphrase called "paradigms." To set the record straight, paradigms are produced within the infinite aptitude of reason. As synthetic worlds, they appear replete with possibility, viability; they are internally consistent, defensible within their own idiom, even profess a certain realism; paradigms are overturned only when their synthesis begins to overtly slide into irreality. For all of these reasons, they seldom approximate the inconsistencies or finitude of this world, least of all the muddling, moldering, shambling structures that are institutions themselves.

Even if founded in the name of professing reason, there is nothing inherently rational in the manner in which institutions behave. At best they construct rationalities that appear to produce a certain unity or coherence in their functioning, but that is just, in Gayatri Spivak's words quoted above, "damage control."[20] Paradigms are at best worked within given epistemic parameters; to extend them to actual historical or institutional developments is to tantamount to arguing that lives and material histories move as if by some pre-ordained, narratological formula, in this case entirely coincident with the syllogisms of reason. This is, one would argue, tantamount to a mere idealism. Even within the Kuhnian narrative much happens as a matter of habit—bad habits even—or convention rather than as a literal shadow of the pure architectonic of argument.

I would like to argue that the thrust of the essays in this book tends rather towards the study of "legitimation." Rather than suavely posing some charismatic figure(s) or factional rivalries (Grays vs. Whites) as embodiments of institutional careers, or, in what amounts to the same thing, casting some supervening "idea" or principle as driving institutional practice, a study of legitimation entails that knowledge statements are made within a circuitry of power. Which is to say that knowledge or expertise is not the sum of unidirectional pronouncements issued from some preordained priesthood, upon the processing of whose content listeners efficiently carry out the requisite command. Legitimation primarily involves the question of audience: competence is staked as a territory where both sender and addressee of a message must come to some transactional import of whatever it is that is being said, as well as the manner in which it is said. Take for instance the above-mentioned Donlyn Lyndon's—Princeton classmate and business partner of Charles Moore—prescriptions for architectural pedagogy, published in the *Journal of Architectural Education* in February 1978:

> The interest in professional accountability is obviously related to the legitimization of plural interests. Accountability is a surrogate for trust and is a necessary condition for exchange between disparate interests. Accountability takes many forms in the profession, ranging from licensed responsibility to cost accounting. But most fundamentally one is called upon to explain the relative advantage of one decision or another. The notion of accountability has extended also to issues of methodology and has led schools to foster an articulation of both analytic and synthetic professes in an effort to make all activities explicable. Schools and government have—quite naturally—led the effort to make process explicit. Schools of architecture have generally been the home of design methods studies and government-sponsored research programs both in the universities and outside them have generated most of the explicit criteria by which environments may be measured.[21]

This, above all, lays out what within the MIT School would become a mantra, epitomizing its scientism as much as its technopolitics: that the codes by which architecture was "read" should be made explicit. The implications for legitimacy—"accountability"—are clear: design can no longer be left to aesthetics alone, that enigmatic Kantian traffic in the hierarchy between (organic) genius and (laborious) mimesis where the undetermined lines of taste seems only the prerogative of an unseemly esotericism. William L. Porter, Dean of the School, and Head following Lyndon, uses almost exactly the same language in his short memoir in this volume:

> What could be made explicit in design, and of that, what was describable in rational terms? I did not believe that design could or should be reduced to a set of logical propositions, nor that design should be revealed as the emperor unclothed. Instead I wanted to explore possibilities of harnessing the power of rationality to design intuition more effectively, of releasing the cavalry of thought (or intuition) when needed for important things, after having rested it when not really needed (to paraphrase Whitehead).[22]

The emphasis on rationality makes it clear that "explicitness" under no condition envisages a descent, on the other hand, into colloquialism. Common sense, in other words, is hardly commonsensical. The concept of legitimation rather entails that, in the context of knowledge production, all such subjective dynamics—whether person, faction or idea—in fact operate within a shared frame of competence: legitimation occurs when statements produced by a speaker receive agreement by its addressee not so much in its content as in terms of the protocol, code, or "phrase regimen" within which it is encrypted.[23] Agreement here does not indicate accord but a conditioned understanding, requiring particular modes of epistemic competence since statements are phrased within a code that is not identical to that of "natural" or colloquial language. In other words, in Lyndon's and Porter's formulation above, explicitness connotes less a question of transparency than the opening out of architectural deliberation to its decipherability by other experts: the social scientists, the policy Foundations, and the grant-making bodies that constituted their immediate clientele. The "explicitness" spoken of above, if anything, speaks to the architects' vulnerability within a technocratic field.

20 See Gayatri Chakravorty Spivak, *An Aesthetic Education in the Age of Globalization* (Cambridge, MA: Harvard University Press, 2012), 1.

21 Donlyn Lyndon, "Architectural Education Here," *Journal of Architectural Education* 31, no. 3 (February 1978), 3. If the import of poverty within epistemic legitimation entailed the refinement of input-output mechanisms, in the long run "environment"—and its fantasmatic "sustainability"—

would prove to be the research alibi that legitimized all potential codes and comers, the ultimate Babel in which all phrase regimens would come to be immediately transparent to each other.

22 William L. Porter, "Three Episodes, Three Roles," in this volume.

23 For a finessing of "phrase regimen," see Jean-François Lyotard, *The Differend: Phrases in Dispute*, trans. Georges Van Den Abbeele (Minneapolis: University of Minnesota Press, 1988).

On the other hand, legitimation cannot be seen as merely a shorthand or elite code shared amongst experts alone. To have authority, a code must be able to claim, within a finite set of rules, to describe the infinity of possible phenomena of the "world" in its totality, in other words, to simulate a certain empirical "realism." The economist must be able to model all social phenomena within her given set of tools; the linguist must evolve transformational grammars that can programmatically churn out every possible sentence in a given language, or better still, *all* language (in the singular); the architect must see social behaviors emanating from the make-up of the forms in which it is set. If the expert's competence is to be recognized, in an academic framework this relies, on the one hand, on the elegance of the model—its intuitive understandability—in simplifying the set of rules deployed, and, on the other hand, the use of this radical simplicity to explain the greatest possible complexity. "If culture must be explained in cultural terms, as anthropologists . . . have argued, then cultural systems must be explained in terms of themselves, in terms of their components, their structure."[24] As factory for knowledge production, the university's power—a legislative one—stems from this "censor's" role of stabilizing the protocols of agreement by staving off reason's descent into polysemia. This codifying, censoring, role does not imply a curtailment of "freedom," at least no more than codification such as that in a dictionary (we remember that universities were founded precisely to lexicalize) presents an obstruction to expression in any given language. In modernity, institutional legitimacy therefore inherently implies a *delegitimation* of unbounded natural languages in favor of the expert's synthetic language The university's specific mode of censorship is never to say "You cannot say that," but rather, "We do not know enough to make that statement," or "This is not how we would say this." Nothing to do with "freedom" or "unfreedom" then; the university is a device for the *stylization* of speech.

Again, by no means should this mode of control, this tendency towards simplifying or reducing the sets of grammatical rules, connote a constriction of speech or restriction on speech-types. Quite to the contrary, since on the other hand the success of stylization resides in its ability to encompass the greatest variety and complexity of phenomena, securing legitimation may in fact involve a multiplication of the *number* of possible and potential codes, and consequently, a simultaneous self-delegitimation or a proliferation of styles and knowledge games. Pitched at securing the totality of phenomena under the universal arc of reason, the university is inherently an "imperial" project, and like all good empires it affects a certain "multiculturalism" of rational styles. In the context of sponsored research, the very emphasis on functional outcomes can in fact produce in its wake a multiplication of speech-types, as the number of (contracted rather than waged) "researchers" and adjunct appointees multiply, with a kind of "freedom" or pluralism as a simulated effect.

Since utility-creation from knowledge obtains no benefit from hewing to the scholastic conventions of disciplinary insight, one sees in sponsored research the proliferation of more and more so-called "interdisciplinary" or exploratory fields. Both this democratizing air of proliferating the sites of inquiry and the emphasis on practical outcomes afford the sponsored research complex with a unique kind of rhetorical ardor which it must highlight in order to successfully supplant the social bonds it is replacing. The more stringent the terms on which research funds are provided, the more grandiose the scale of emancipation at which the research is directed. Science's continued fight against dogmatism, poverty and disease; the ongoing revelations about the secrets of matter; decoding the substance of life; these "grand narratives" and epic quests are continually invoked to elevate the sponsored research complex above mercenary appearance, the vulgar air of factionility, interest or mere profit. In the last forty or so years, "environment" and "sustainability" have been two such concept-metaphors peddled by the complex: they have the dual validity of providing the researcher's query with the urgency of practical necessity and imbuing their proclamations with a gravity that derives as if from the axiomatics of natural law. At the same time, since anything can be described as pertinent to "an" or "the" environment, irrespective of organic or inorganic domain, material or behavioral attributes, the indefinition of these concepts handily weighs in in the further disorganization and demoralization of disciplinary inquiry. It is indicative that, within the "Two Cambridge" research network described above by Mary Lou Lobsinger, both MIT and UC Berkeley, two sister concerns with the most faculty interchange, both considered renaming themselves as institutions of environmental design. MIT eventually demurred; at Berkeley, it was under William Wurster that the three schools devoted to architecture, landscape architecture and city planning were renamed as the College of Environmental Design in 1959.

Indeed, just as greater plurality and "freedom" in the above sense represent one apparition of this new topography of control, so do we find a proliferation of seemingly autarkic "personas" that continue to tether the system to the older, liberal kind of social readability. At MIT, a distinctive set of "experts" emerged, never quite central to the architectural field, but luminaries nonetheless at its penumbra, archaic "heroes" fronting the brave new world: Wurster, György Kepes, Kevin Lynch, N.J. Habraken, Nicholas Negroponte. Not that this did not present its own problems for the legitimacy of expertise: most of the "centers," "labs," and "programs" that proliferated through the post-war institution remained, in essence,

24 Leslie A. White, *The Concept of Cultural Systems: A Key to Understanding Tribes and Nations* (New York: Columbia University Press, 1975), 38.

structured around one or two charismatic individuals, often amounting to a kind of private sandbox to aid faculty retention. "The interdisciplinary nature of the Center, which is a vital asset, also results inevitably in a splintering of research funds among many departments and individuals."[25] Inevitably the "research" language game had to be supplemented by supervening organizational or "administrational" language games, necessitating "coordinating" bodies—with the requisite set of new administrative careers—such as the Urban Coordinating Group (overseeing urban research in all the pertinent disciplines at MIT— politics, economics, engineering, management, architecture, planning) or the Cambridge Project at MIT and Harvard ("to make computers more useful in the behavioral sciences").

The essays in this volume cut a narrative arc across these teeming, thriving sandboxes, stringing them together as heterogeneous components given recognition by their investment into—and by—the interstices of that broader system that some have christened Big (not to exclude Social) Science. For the most part, these studies examine disciplinary contexts— architecture, urbanism, arts, management—that are ancillary or parasitical to the sciences. At the same time, they beg the question of the "content" of science as such, since this can hardly be defined by a finite ontology. Distinctions between statements that are admissible and inadmissible to the domain of science concern more a matter of epistemic protocol.

The Ontology of Research

The Chomsky case bears mention in this regard, not only because so much of the conflict within the postwar sponsored-research complex can be epitomized by it, but also because his defense of science, often against extant science itself, appears to concern itself altogether with ontological distinctions. In 1999, looking back over developments in linguistics and the behavioral sciences, Noam Chomsky sought to defend the principles of a "minimalist" program in linguistics (and more generally science) against some of the more extravagant claims of latter-day behaviorism. The target of critique here was the inexorable characterization of language as the model or "optimal design" for "communication." Over the decades, Chomskian "universalism" has proved an expedient license for many a behaviorist to make global claims about optimal patterns in nature, and in his essay Chomsky's ire is particularly leveled at the grounds on which the behaviorists drew ontological inferences from empirical data.[26]

The context in question is the biological predisposition towards the acquisition of language. Compiled under the heading *On Nature and Language*, it is difficult not to descry Chomsky as bridling against a set of unconscionable claims that lay precisely in the realm that his "generative grammar" had sought to capture, but where it saw itself as necessarily falling short.[27] Although in "principle" biological disposition must be the presumption on which science proceeds, which is to say that whatever humans apprehend through the "unbounded" sphere of language and understanding *must* have some basis in the organism, the experimental data so far, Chomsky argued, had yielded little. At best what one had at the end of a century of behaviorist research was a potential not much improved since its beginning: an "ought." "Cautious speculation and confident pronouncement do not *show* anything, and the most that we learn is that there might be a useful path to follow. Perhaps."[28] By that standard, the irresistible itch of scientists to periodically announce overarching analogies between human society or linguistic structures on the study of rats or bees or songbirds should be seen as nothing but the "sheerest" kind of "dogmatism." At best, what one has is "largely a richly detailed variety of 'descriptive linguistics'"; the observation bears shades of his earlier attacks on the research program of the prewar, Bloomfieldian bias towards taxonomy. Of the actual correspondence between the social, even existential, impetuses of language and its basis in the organism, "we know nothing," for the moment, "and may never be able to find out." Chomsky's conclusive judgment is summary, if not damning,   and its tone harks back to his excoriation of the Skinnerians in the 1950s:

> Thus, it now seems possible to take seriously an idea that a few years ago would
> have seemed outlandish: that the language organ of the brain approaches a kind
> of optimal design... As far as I can see, the renewed call to pursue this approach,
> as advocated forty years ago in the critical literature on "behavioral science," leaves
> us about where we were.[29]

Pertinent to our discussion on ontology, the "disciplinary" evaluation of inferences across the nature-culture cusp is not left off without the requisite metaphysics. In a chapter reminding us of his genealogical study of the Port-Royal grammarians in *Cartesian Linguistics*, Chomsky attributes the inertia of these forty years, interestingly enough, not to the shortcomings or failings of his colleagues such as they are, but to the very premise of science itself, one that was, we are led to believe, scuppered at its very origin. The damning document in question is none other than Newton's *Principia Mathematica*, or more importantly, the "General Scholium" at its end. This is Chomsky at his sharpest, addressing what for him lay at the theoretical core of scientific scrutiny, whose only possible legitimacy lay in its reduction of the universe to mechanism. Paradoxically, Galileo and Descartes could entertain a conception of the world as mechanism, as pure matter,

25 MIT-PR; SAP (1963), 52-53.

26 Chomsky's comments on language here reprise the half century of his work on "transformational grammar" and its attempt to bridge the yawning gap between, on the one hand, the older, Bloomfieldian bias towards formal taxonomy and against "mentalism" (the link between structures of language and the biological mind's ability to acquire and decode them), and on the other the behaviorism—thinly covered Pavlovian experiments— propounded by the legatees of B.F. Skinner. Noam Chomsky, *On Nature and Language* (Cambridge: Cambridge University Press, 2002).

27 For two comprehensive historical accounts of the effects of Chomsky's theory on linguistic departments and debates, see Randy Allen Harris, *The Linguistics Wars* (Oxford: Oxford University Press, 1993); and Geoffrey J. Huck and John A. Goldsmith, *Ideology and Linguistic Theory: Noam Chomsky and the Deep Structure Debates* (New York: Routledge, 1995).

28 Chomsky, *On Nature and Language*, 79.

29 Ibid., 83.

because they presumed that design—God's scheme for the universe—resided outside
it: they were thus free to elucidate life as a machine since inferring teleology was simply
reverted to one of explicating God's "perfect" artisanal powers. Even with God out of
the picture, Chomsky argues, a properly Cartesian endeavor must nonetheless *assume*
this primary reduction, the lawfulness of the whole of the system to its parts, even
when it addresses questions of mind: otherwise "when mechanism fails, understanding
fails." On the other hand, if Newton's mathematical description thoroughly encompassed
the universe as a system, what Newton also proved unfalsifiable was the question of
cause. Gravity is constitutive of matter, but we have no idea *why* it is there. If Newton
rendered the question untenable, demonstrating—Chomsky quotes Koyré here—that "a
purely materialistic or mechanistic physics [is] impossible," the science of the subsequent
centuries had been little able to improve matters. Refuting God (i.e. teleology as
phantasmatic) thus remains an unresolvable problem: "Newton exorcised the machine; he
left the ghost intact." All that remained for science is an "epistemological modesty" that
veers on descriptivism—chemistry or taxonomy as opposed to a foundational physics—or
alternatively a kind of epistemological bluster that has no material counterpart. "Mind-body
dualism is no longer tenable, because there is no notion of body."[30] Consequently,

> on the factual side, there is no longer any concept of body, or matter, or the "physical."
> There is just the world, with its various aspects: mechanical, electromagnetic, chemical,
> optical, organic, mental—categories that are not defined or delimited in an a priori
> way, but are at most conveniences: no one asks whether life falls within chemistry
> or biology, except for temporary convenience. In each of the shifting domains of
> constructive inquiry, one can try to develop intelligible explanatory theories, and to
> unify them, but no more than that.[31]

Deprived of substance, all that is left for science is a move away from that originary
reduction into what Chomsky calls facetization, only somewhat leavened ("perhaps") with
the premise of eventual (metaphysical) unification. The disparagement of "communication"
as the original intent of language on the one hand and espousal of "mechanism"—we
notice in the paragraph above that another name for this is "life" itself—on the other

30 These quotes are all
taken from the chapter,
"Perspectives on language
and mind," in Chomsky, *On
Nature and Language.*
31 Chomsky, *On Nature and
Language,* 68.
32 Ibid, 76.

33 See Jean-Pierre Dupuy,
*The Mechanization of the
Mind: On the Origins of
Cognitive Science,* trans. M.
B. DeBevoise (Princeton:
Princeton University
Press, 2000); also see the
two volumes on *Artificial
Intelligence at MIT: Expanding
Frontiers* (Cambridge, MA:
The MIT Press, 1992).

34 Marvin Minsky, *The
Society of Mind* (New York:
Simon and Schuster, 1985);
Marvin Minsky, ed., Robotics
(New York: Garden City, 1985).
35 "We Were Bricoleurs,"
Nicholas Negroponte
in interview with Molly
Steenson, in this volume.

36 *The First Five Years, 1959
to 1964* (Cambridge, MA:
Joint Center for Urban Studies,
MIT, April 1964), 9-10.

indicates a fine but hard line drawn through the nature-culture cusp, such that "nature" firmly resides within the a priori. One cannot but notice that this talk of communication and mechanisms goes against the grain of the very different mobilization of these concepts by proponents of cybernetics or linguistics' other foundling, Artificial Intelligence (AI). At the very least, Chomsky's thinking patently exposes the "man-machine" analogies invoked by AI as in fact redrawing nature-culture boundaries: "in any useful sense of the term, communication is not *the* function of language, and may even be of no unique significance for understanding the functions and nature of language."[32]

Chomsky's methodological purism puts into relief the bulk of the sponsored research complex at MIT, most of which more or less imperviously disregarded any compunctions regarding the ontological delimitation of life as such. For the AI circle at MIT—J.C.R. Licklider, Marvin Minsky and Seymour Papert—as for the other diaspora of the Macy Conferences,[33] dissertations on the mind-body continuum were routine, even if the thrust of the work itself was rather to design various kinds of social optima. In books with indicative titles like *The Society of Mind* (featuring blurbs by Isaac Asimov and Michael Crichton), Marvin Minsky, AI's high priest at MIT, sallied forth into territory little perturbed by the biology of the body or of the organism, appealing to a smorgasbord of lay psychology, lay linguistics, and aw-shucks commonsense to model mental faculties such as "emotion," "memory," "reasoning," as already imputing a kind of logic, a self-serving logic in that these usually fit the premises from which the AI researcher usually framed the question.[34] Indeed, understanding the "body" may have been last on their minds; looking back, Negroponte, here in interview with Molly Steenson, lets the cat out of the bag: "we wouldn't sit down and have a conversation about cognition and perception, that's not what we'd discuss. It was doing things that were like magic. We'd discuss magic tricks."[35] When Moore's law began to take hold, the mind-body problem went out the window.

Urbanism might be said to be yet another, similar, bag of magic tricks, if anything a name simply for the evacuation of architectural substance. Much lip-service was paid to the new "structural hardness" demanded of the expert, on the other hand the "urbanists" were least interested in greater definitional focus. The thrust of legitimation in fact went quite the other way; the five-year report for the Joint Center explicitly acknowledged this "unifying" gambit:

> At the outset, the Faculty Committee was convinced that it ought not to commit its resources to a single research area or problem, despite the apparent advantages of a concentrated effort. No such effort would have been fruitful unless there had already been on the scene enough faculty members and graduate students who were absorbed in urban studies to provide intellectual strength. *Furthermore, it was by no means clear what the focus—if any—should have been*; the gaps in knowledge of urban affairs here and abroad were such that selecting research priorities would necessarily have involved considerable guesswork.[36]

As one Joint Center director put it: "One does not expect an aggregate product out of this kind of enterprise."[37] We could paraphrase Chomsky above: there is just the city, with its various aspects: political, infrastructural, economic, demographic, sociological, technological, administrational, each of these approaches being essentially, depending on faculty cultivation and the exigencies of funding, "conveniences." And where "urban" was seen as inadequate, there was always "environment"; today, we have "sustainability," "landscape urbanism," "ecological urbanism," "senseable [sic] cities," and so on: publicity copywriting for the movement of capital. As Janet Daley put it in a related context: "One is beginning to sense the presence of tail-chasing here: of definitions being established which require consent to other definitions which, in turn, refer to the first definitions."[38]

Propitiating the Ghost

To be sure, this affirmative obfuscation did not pass unscathed. If for Chomsky the "fall" towards glib functionalism lay in that original passage from metaphysics to physics, then within architecture, the encumbrances posed by this new "spirit of system," the thrust towards societal or governmental relevance, was deemed equally oppressive by thinkers schooled in the old, liberal order, where "spontaneity" or "initiative" could be espoused as signatures of aesthetic volition. Speaking on architectural education in 1974, Colin Rowe railed against what he considered "an entrenched establishment, . . . an establishment with a presumptive empiricist, naturalist, behaviorist, and technophile bias":

> That is, while for bohemian and liberal reasons, architectural education conveniently approves the so-called "counter-culture" (which is a not so implicit protest against both management and technology), architectural education becomes increasingly a compilation of courses devoted to the presentation of information designed to assist management and derived from technology, sociology, psychology, economics, cybernetics, etc., with the inference that no adequate, let alone valid, design decision is possible until all this information is digested, and with the even more tempting subliminal proviso that, once this information is digested, no design decision will be necessary anyway. Since, should it not be apparent that, given the "facts," these will automatically arrange themselves, will, presumably, promote their own hypotheses irrespective of any human intervention. That such a point of view should, in the end, extinguish or paralyze initiative should surely be obvious; but that, when its epistemological foundations are so very slight, when so painfully vulnerable, it yet remains predominant should not be considered strange.[39]

Writing to Stanford Anderson over the CASE meetings (the letter is reproduced in this volume) Rowe affected a similar, self-confessed "captiousness," this time about some of his own acolytes in CASE's Princeton group. "[They] use . . . the word 'total'—'total environment,' 'total architecture,'—etc. God knows how many times." Particularly irritating to him was the statement's political-sounding self-regard: its claims that the CASE magazine should "attempt to stem the flood" "[more appropriate for] a political meeting c. 1910." A flurry of vituperations follow in what amounts to a characteristic Roweian upbraid: "an old-fashioned nineteen twentyish manifesto . . . has a sentimental activistic vitalistic tone . . . both ungrammatical and boyscouty and therefore tacitly disimplying any possibility of rigor."[40]

In the talk on education above, Rowe declares himself—disingenuously enough for a tenured Ivy-League professor speaking at MoMA—as "skeptical of institutionalized objectives . . . skeptical of too much research." Sure enough, and soon enough, we find ourselves in the modus of the connoisseur: we are told that the values of architecture lie "very much in the virtues of confusion and the impromptu." As can be expected, this institutional defense of the impromptu against "system" and institutionality inevitably entails for Rowe, however indolently or unwittingly, a systemic proscription of the not-architecture that is the love of system. One receives good hints that Rowe had a clearer sense of the systemic than he was willing to let on. There is more than merely the flavor of the cultivated Canterbridgean here for one not to notice the string of throwaway mentions beyond the realm of architecture that appear if only to support this relegation: Bernard Berenson, Whitehead, "Gestalt psychology," neo-Positivism, and, with studied hand-waves, Russell and Wittgenstein.[41] A dichotomy presents itself, peculiar for the Cambridge-trained author of the "Mathematics of the Ideal Villa": under one heading there is "idealism" and aesthetics, unverifiable rubrics that cannot be acknowledged as products of institutional practice, under the other, there are institutions, with verifiability as their proper office, whose genealogy harks back to the mathematical "revolution" wrought by a certain Lucasian Professor of Mathematics at Cambridge:

> For, if the laws of statics can be safely assumed to be established beyond dispute, the laws of use and pleasure, of convenience and delight, have certainly not as yet been subjected to any Newtonian revolution; and, while it is not inconceivable that in the future they may be, until that time, any ideas as to the useful and the beautiful will rest as untestifiable hypotheses.[42]

37 Marion E. Bodian, "The Joint Center for Urban Studies: Unwilling, Unable, and Unsuited to Do Anything for Roxbury," *The Harvard Crimson* (June 13, 1968).
38 Janet Daley, "A Philosophical Critique of Behaviourism in Architectural Design," in *Design Methods in Architecture*, ed. Geoffrey Broadbent and Anthony Ward (London: Lund Humphries, 1969), 72.
39 Colin Rowe, "Architectural Education: USA," a statement first given at MoMA in 1974 and subsequently published in *Lotus International 27* (1980). Here cited from *As I Was Saying: Recollections and Miscellaneous Essays*, ed. Alexander Caragonne (Cambridge, MA: The MIT Press, 1996), 2:54.
40 Colin Rowe, letter to Stanford Anderson, June 18, 1965. Personal files of Stanford Anderson, MIT.
41 Take for instance the following assay in defense of Leon Krier: "For evidently, around 1900 such notions were very much in the air; and, if an entirely trivial reading of Russell and Wittgenstein will reveal their presence, and equally trivial survey of the visual world will disclose their important influence. And, of course, as these attitudes of mind became increasingly active and popular, a disintegration

The transition from a "computerized" environment to a "computer-aided" environment will enable designers to have a dialogue with their new design partners—for example, the architect with his Architecture Machine

Nicholas Negroponte
Assistant Professor of Architecture
M.I.T.

Towards a Humanism Through Machines

Nicholas Negroponte, "Towards a Humanism Through Machines." From MIT *Technology Review*, April 1969.

Mechanism has clear epistemological supremacy, but the task of architecture is to guard the ghost. For good measure, Rowe prefaced his MoMA talk with a sly invocation of God, professing his faith in Modernism as something like a fervid "pseudo-theological" belief after the death of belief, *a credo quia absurdum*. All-too unexpectedly, uncannily, we find ourselves, at this realization, exactly across the aisle from Chomsky's seat—two men regarding the ghost: one favors exorcism, the other wishes to savor the Eucharist, but both palpably aware of its presence. Around a dybbuk named Newton, "art" and "science," yin and yang, irreducibility and reduction, generality and specificity, come to impeccably define each other without remainder, chromosomally of the same Enlightenment but separated at conception by that scalpel or stigmata called verifiability.

The Uses of Humanism

The story, one may assume, is a little bit more complicated. In fact, educational policy documents pertaining to the sciences and technology are filled with a surfeit of concern about domains that lay well outside the verifiable. If "the old notion that science can discover universal "laws" is no longer [tenable, and if] its statements of theory are valid only within the range of data observed,"[43] there appears a good deal of worry that such a de-transcendentalized and disenchanted universe would also breed a deracinated, alienated culture. Postwar technopolitics thus resurrected a bifurcated spirit of humanism in order to counter its own tendency towards anomie, quite in line with the old, liberal dyad of "art" and "science": on the one hand, there was a heightened emphasis on "basic science," on the other there was an unprecedented institutionalization and professionalization of the humanities, whose mission was to lend to technocratic society its spiritual synthesis.

or decomposition, or a 'deconstruction' of the city began." "The Revolt of the Senses," *in As I Was Saying*, 3:277.

42 Rowe, "Architectural Education: USA," 60.

43 Hayward Keniston, "The Humanities in a Scientific World," *Annals of the American Academy of Political and Social Science* 249 (Jan. 1947), 160.

At MIT, the inauguration of the sponsored research complex was appropriately consecrated with two symbolic buildings. Reinhold Martin's essay on the Saarinen chapel at MIT highlights the building's conception as the hallowed placeholder for a chain of interchangeable "spirits"—science, nation, humanity, God—that were sung up in their venerability, as vocational school transformed itself into research institute. Paired with another Saarinen creation, the Kresge auditorium to create the "village church and the meeting house," the chapel was part of the broader, critical imperative to recast MIT as not just a pedagogical workshop for engineers but as a crucible for a redefined technology which would itself serve the cause of a so-called "humanity."

A common refrain in the MIT Presidential Reports of the three postwar decades is a kind of handwringing about intellectual and pedagogical autonomy of the scientists in the face of the conditions and stipulations imposed by federal research contracts. One reads a good number of homilies about the "independence of research," a theme that waxes into full-fledged piety as disruptive protests erupted on campuses at the end of the decade. In actuality, these homilies share a good deal of rhetorical substance with the denunciations to which they were a response, with the moral indignation of the critics who denounced the Institute as a mere contractor in hock to the "military-industrial complex"— Noam Chomsky's 1967 piece in the *New York Review of Books*, "The Responsibility of Intellectuals," might offer us a fair specimen—as Vietnam slid into imbroglio. Administrative piety and conscientious objector here both share a deeply-held topos: of science as expression of freedom, as nourishing truth to power, with the requisite hagiography of the noble scientist as free agent, knowledge activist and so on. The implication is that sponsored research, by the fact of being sponsored, entails the trivialization and constriction of a previously unencumbered, disinterested, sovereign remit. The sentiment has classical antecedents, dating back at least to the *Didascalion*, a twelfth century text by Hugh of St. Victor,[44] and it was also invoked by early modern aristocracies to distinguish their "disinterested" pursuit of knowledge from the economic compulsions embedded in the skill and knowledge of the lesser classes, e.g. artisans.

But in our context it has a very precise, although no less aristocratic, bearing, one that reverts back to the foundational document for the sponsored research complex, the 1945 report prepared by MIT president Vannevar Bush, as Director of the Office of Scientific Research and Development, to Franklin D. Roosevelt outlining the objectives of postwar national policy on the sciences. The report, while urging further attention to technological research as a critical tool in fighting the "war on disease"—apparently the major struggle that would remain for the sciences after the cessation of hostilities—put inordinate emphasis on the importance of "basic" science as against the government's emphasis on applications-led research. Basic science is science "without thought of practical ends," and such catholicity is critical to create the liberal range of skills which can then be purposively harnessed to "answer a large number of important practical problems."[45] Disinterest is here to be cultivated in the *interest of interestedness*; the surge towards economism proleptically reinstates liberalism as its foundational ground.

(It would be remiss not to point out the obvious. The rationalist dissenter replicates in the political sphere what was in fact the founding *alibi* of the sponsored research complex: that liberal morality - and all that it entails, freedom of speech, the radicalism of the arts, the cultivation of an "informed" citizenry—should establish its consensus in the same way that science produces agreement about truths, with all the appurtenant ramifications of deliberative "contingency" in the production of those truths. The objector's objection to "bad science" is typically less alert to the strictures that its adoptive methodology itself places on the modes in which political life is conducted—the scientist-contrarian's crusade against the instrumentalization and politicization of science asserts itself more as a scientization of politics.)

As for the humanities, the founding document for the new School of Humanities and Social Studies was prescriptively clear: it's role was "to emphasize the interrelation of the various humanities and social sciences as elements in human experience rather than as distinctive features which characterize them as different areas of academic study . . . [and] to introduce the student to the process of critical thought as applied in the humanities and social sciences."[46] In other words, basic science would provide epistemological generality on the plane where the humanities would provide conceptual critique. Hero of his own novel, striding the ambit from demographic number to demiurgic agency, the "human" almost appears as the sanctioning emblem—the allegory—corralling greater purposiveness amongst the disciplines. He is called to study science to free himself—and others that would hypnotically follow his blazon—from mechanism; he must learn literature and the arts to rid himself of dogma;[47] politics and philosophy, from despotism; economics, from mere wage slavery and hunger, and so on.[48] In cultivating the arts—critical as much for the scientist as for the artist, given the former's supposed tendency to think in mechanistic ways—he cultivates himself from primitive appreciation to true synthesis, transcending their disparate motifs and the trades involved in its production, to their "creativity." In the dawn of a new imperium, the human presents himself as an exemplar to the "savages,"

44 See Ivan Illich, *In the Vineyard of the Text: A Commentary to Hugh's Didascalion* (Chicago: University of Chicago Press, 1993).

45 Vannevar Bush, Science The Endless Frontier: A Report to the President, Director of the Office of Scientific Research and Development, July 1945 (Washington, DC: United States Government Printing Office, 1945).

46 *Report of the Committee on Educational Survey* (Cambridge, MA: The Technology Press, MIT, 1949), 101.

47 The immediate aftermath of the war saw a burst of declaratives about the uses of the humanities. A significant number of these specifically address the remit of the humanities in a technological age. The following titles are indicative: "Instrumentalism and the Humanities," "The Humanities in Engineering Colleges," "Post War Humanities," "The Humanities in a Scientific World," "Humanities in the Technological School," The Humanities and Defense," "The Humanities—Alternative to Orwell," "Synthesizing Science and the Humanities," "The Humanities and the Idea of Man," "The Western Tradition—Man and his Freedom," "Do the

not-yet-humans mired either by fear and ancient prejudices or by newer dogmatic creeds, by their denial of scientific truths and their inordinate reliance on charismatic leaders, by their tom-tomming creeds impenetrable to reason, and by their subjugation of women. The human is both subject and object of this civilizing venture, a prolepsis: both lifting and the one lifted into the techno-enlightenment.

Nothing could be more anathema to this office of reenchantment for the mechanists than the mechanistic reduction of the humanities to (mere) disciplines and departments; Rowe's repugnance towards "systemization" is well-echoed by the systems-thinkers themselves. If disciplinarity would be reductive for this imaginative office, on the other hand, it was critical that this office not overreach its brief or burden the students too much with its escape into imponderables; under no conditions should the work load be allowed to upset "the established ratio: 75 per cent technical skills and 25 per cent humanistic-social education."[49]

At MIT, since departmentalization of the humanities went so against the grain, it was also emphasized that their content be as loose as possible, that "the field need not . . . be strictly defined."[50] For some, this lack of definition would produce opportunities. It would provide an unsupervised space within the technical institute and outside the entrenched disciplinary politics of the established programs elsewhere, that could well translate into a circumscribed kind of freedom at the margins. Chomsky, for instance, had been passed up by the Bloomfieldian-dominated linguistics departments elsewhere; hired by the Research Laboratory of Electronics at MIT, he was required to teach German, French, philosophy, logic—i.e., the "humanities"—and linguistics. "Since there was no one there to tell him otherwise (MIT had no linguistics department), he taught *his* linguistics."[51] This definitional fuzziness produced a temporary refuge for an astonishing range of thinkers in their early careers: the philosopher Hilary Putnam, the historian Eric Hobsbawm, and of course those within the social sciences who remained at MIT to strongly define their nascent programs: Chomsky, Roman Jakobson, Paul Samuelson, Walter Rostow. Within the department of architecture, one can list a significantly impressive canon of visitors often at odds with the rest of the profession: the early Kahn (unknown enough at that time that Julian Beinart remembers being told a "Lewis Conn" was coming to teach studio), Bernard Rudofksy,

Humanities Humanize?" and so on.

48 George Boas, "The Humanities and Defense," *The Journal of Higher Education* 22, no. 5 (May, 1951), 229.

49 Boyd Guest, "The Humanities in Engineering Colleges," *College English* 6, no. 7 (April 1945), 402.

50 *Report of the Committee on Educational Survey*, 45.

51 Harris, *The Linguistics Wars*, 39.

52 "Proposal for a Ph.D. Program in History, Theory and Criticism of Art, Architecture and Urban Form," Massachusetts Institute of Technology, SAP (Winter 1972). Files shared by

Stanford Anderson.

53 *Report to the MIT Faculty on the Proposal for a Ph.D. Program in Art, Architecture and Environmental Studies* (March 13, 1975). Unsurprisingly, one encounters a prodigious number of conferences and edited volumes where the two founders, Henry A.

Millon and Stanford Anderson, perform "spiritual" duties as master of ceremonies or as editors, with little evidence as to their primary craft. John Harwood's essay in this volume recounts how the young Anderson saw architectural history's lack of "method" as occasion to turn to Popper, Lakatos and

Serge Chermayeff, R. Buckminster Fuller, Jane Drew, Hermann Hertzberger, Giancarlo de Carlo, Lewis Mumford, Herbert J. Gans, Cedric Price. This is equally true of the field of art and architectural history, the only "pure" humanities field allowed to establish a doctoral program at MIT, tellingly enough within the "purposive" remit of the School of Architecture. The list of names who began their careers there speaks as much to this fuzzy remit: Rosalind Krauss, Benjamin Buchloh, Donald Preziosi, Dolores Hayden.

The establishment of the History, Theory and Criticism Program in Art and Architecture (to go by its present, rebarbative, title) owed a good deal to this combination of mandated purposiveness and epistemological equivocation. The original proposal, drafted in 1972, as John Harwood lays out in his essay in this volume, spoke to the need to train specialists who would provide the "historical-critical-theoretical complement with studio and professional practice."[52] The historians were sent back to reconsider their premises. Three years later, the 1975 sequel to this document, the one finally approved by the faculty and dean, patently excised mention of History, Theory, or Criticism in its title: rather we have the more ecumenical and insipid, "Ph.D. Program in Art, Architecture and Environmental Studies." The document itself says little about the specific tools of historiography, now rather committing itself to examining architectural "claims which are constantly tested by man's involving [sic] understanding of himself and his world and . . . the limitations . . . and the possibilities it affords."[53]

If for the humanities this territorial limbo involved adopting a more muted, more equivocal voice, the career of the "arts" at MIT is equally stark as to its tendentious brief. Anna Vallye and Matthew Wisnioski provide almost mirroring accounts of the two driving personas behind the Center for Advanced Visual Studies (CAVS), György Kepes and Otto Piene. For Kepes, acquiring legitimacy in the domain of the technologists meant expressly moving art into the precinct of the "visual," handily subjugating aesthetics under the primacy of the behavioral or physiological sciences. The tendentious synthesis of art and technology could, at least for a while, acquire tokenist currency in a context where the technologists also sought to pass themselves off as exemplary humanists.

Feyerabend as prescriptions to get to a verifiable datum such that one can "improve one's guesses." (See Stanford Anderson, "The Context for Decision Making: Architecture and Tradition that isn't, Trad, Dad," AA Journal 80, no. 892 [May 1965].) The net result of this "critical history" in the 1960s and

1970s appears a shying away from historiography itself; a sizeable proportion of Anderson's work in the period focuses on analytical tasks or methodological prescriptions, the "systemic" modus by which architects and urban planners would verify their relations both to precedents and the tasks at

hand. Other than the well-known essays in Oppositions, he would return to his dissertation on Peter Behrens in its entirety only in the 1990s, the book appearing in 2002, a full four and a half decades after he joined MIT. See Stanford Anderson, Planning for Diversity and Choice: Possible Future

and their Relations to the Man-Controlled Environment (Cambridge, MA: The MIT Press, 1968); Form and Use in Architecture (Cambridge, MA: Laboratory of Architecture and Planning, MIT, 1969); Streets: Phases 1-2; Analysis/ Postulations (New York: Institute for Architecture and Urbanism, 1972); People in

This tokenism was not a matter of ideology alone. The principal concern undergirding the postwar emphasis on "basic science" was the felt need to graduate technological thought from mere instrumental problem-solving to a more projective, "synthetic" ability. A key reason for the emphasis on synthetic judgment was a hiatus perceived in the dominant philosophy of logical empiricism itself. The reasons as to why postwar Big Science would adopt the preoccupations of the Vienna Circle—the shibboleths of "falsifiability"—as a methodological aid may today appear both curious and abstruse, although the interwar passage from "*Wissenschaftliche Philosophie* to Philosophy of Science" has proved a tremendously rich area for historical study.[54] Within the tradition of logical empiricism (interchangeably called neo-positivism or neo-empiricism), figures such as W.V.O. Quine and Nelson Goodman had pointed to the uncertainty attributed to the senses as a nagging point of fallibility in the development of scientific logic: "Reception is flagrantly physical. But perception also, for all its mentalistic overtones, is accessible to behavioral criteria."[55]

The empirical tradition prior to the twentieth century—Hume, Berkeley, Mill—had steadfastly demarcated the boundaries of knowledge as those verifiable by the senses, "believing that even mathematics and logic must be empirically validated."[56] Although the neo-empiricists went against the obvious shortcomings of that tradition for scientific speculation, a shadow remained; it is here that we feel the appeal that Kepes's exertions on the "visual" may have held with the scientists. In the "physics paradigm" so-preferred by the philosophers of science, the problem of empirical validation remained at the core of whatever "truths" were to be garnered by science. Communications between scientists, no matter how exact and precise, were still subject to the vagaries of hearing, vision, smell, touch, in other words, the "sense receptors." Since these could be tricked (i.e. subject to "behavioral criteria"), how was one to ascertain that a truth ascertained by one practitioner of science and narrated to another does not become, in its content, an article of faith? Writing in Kepes's *Education of Vision*, for example, Harvard physicist Gerald Holton elucidated this by an incisive view into the dynamics of a science classroom or lab. In physics, a certain blindness has to be taken for granted. One does not "see" the phenomenon, only its effects registered on a given apparatus, tendentiously based on the experiment's original design. The description of "natural complexity"—entropic states for instance—inevitably tends towards a "demonstrable," and therefore conceivably deceptive if seductive, "simplicity":

the *Physical Environment:
the Urban Ecology of Streets*
(Cambridge, MA: Laboratory
of Architecture and Planning,
MIT, 1975); *Studies Toward
an Ecological Model of the
Urban Environment Streets*
(Cambridge, MA: Laboratory
of Architecture and Planning,
MIT, 1975); [ed.], *On Streets*
(Cambridge, MA: The MIT

Press, 1978).
54 See for instance Ronald N.
Giere and Alan W. Richardson,
eds., *Origins of Logical
Empiricism* (Minneapolis:
University of Minnesota
Press, 1996).
55 W. V. O. Quine, *The Roots
of Reference* (La Salle, IL:
Open Court, 1990), 4.

56 Victor Kraft, *The Vienna
Circle: The Origins of Neo-
Positivism*, trans. Arthur Pap
(New York: Philosophical
Library, 1953), 19.
57 Gerald Holton,
"Conveying Science by Visual
Representation," in György
Kepes (ed.), *Education of
Vision* (New York: George
Braziller, 1965, 54.

58 See Reinhold Martin,
"Pattern-Seeing," in his *The
Organizational Complex:
Architecture, Media, and
Corporate Space* (Cambridge,
MA: The MIT Press, 2005).
59 Mitchell P. Marcus, "A
Theory of Syntactic
Recognition for Natural
Language," in Patrick Henry
Winston and Richard Henry

The motion of an electric charge in a field cannot, to the uninitiated, be explained or demonstrated by actual examples where this conception counts, either in "real" nature or in the laboratory (. . . in the A. G. synchrotron). Instead, the lecturer might show the experiment of bending the fine beam of electrons in a large, evacuated globe placed in a magnetic field. It is a beautiful "experiment"—for the few students in the front rows who can see something of it—but, like most lecture demonstrations, it is of necessity and almost by definition a carefully adjusted, abstracted, simplified, homogenized, "dry-cleaned" case . . .[57]

It is towards the didactics of such "demonstrative beauty" that the "pattern-seeing" pedagogy of a György Kepes[58] could chime with the photographs of a Doc Edgerton. Kepes, for one, went further, pitching his "visual training" as less the prerogative of mere art, as nothing less than a training of the "sense receptors" themselves in order to better perceive the complexity being proposed within the sciences. Here Rowe's qualms might be said to have some basis: the "beauty" in question is expressly indexical insofar as it is used to produce a kind of communicational efficacy, as gleaning out noise between signs and their meaning—semantic closure rather than Kantian ambivalence. Conversely, this harnessing of the sensory through "pattern-seeing" took strands of nineteenth-century organicism right into the heart of the twentieth-century scientific establishment. For his efforts, Kepes became the only faculty ever from the SAP to be appointed Institute Professor, although there is more than enough reason to suggest that he was merely the right man for the right time. As Matthew Wisnioski points out in his essay here, the design of the new Wiesner building for the Media Lab, yet another sub-unit dedicated to the "synthesis" of art and technology and to the "creativity" vested in design, solicited absolutely no input from CAVS artists.

The "Creativity" of Machines

All current natural language parsers that are adequate to cover a wide range of syntactic constructions operate by simulating nondeterministic machines, either by using backtracking or by pseudo-parallelism . . . Since all physically existing machines must be deterministic, such a nondeterministic machine must be simulated by causing a deterministic machine to make "guesses" about what the proper sequence of actions for a given input should be, coupled with some mechanism for aborting incorrect guesses.[59]

One entanglement between humanism and technological research that is salient within the sponsored research complex is the question of "creativity." On the one hand, as the above problem-setting by an MIT-based AI researcher indicates, in the informatics domain this can be simply put down to the AI paradigm's search for an informational gestalt: the stage when intelligent machines could intelligently reframe the problems set for them by their programmers to produce results that in some senses exceed the domain of the original problem. In the Cartesian universe, humans were to be conceived as if machines: what would it mean to contemplate machines that could update themselves, "evolve", set problems rather than merely solve them? In Chomsky's thinking, there is no such utopian impulse. Creativity has a very precise meaning, quite distinct from the aesthetic one: it refers to the human ability to generate an infinite set of meaningful sentences—his transformational rules do not go beyond the "scale" of the sentence—from a finite set of grammatical rules. The work of science is to deliberate upon this grammatical finitude—*minimalism* –as if a universal mechanism that enables language to emerge everywhere as an already understandable, and learnable, construct. To establish the "physics" of behavior, a metaphysical assumption about the essential lawfulness of things has to be made. Otherwise, "understanding fails." "The property of having a grammar meeting a certain abstract condition might be called a *formal* linguistic universal, if shown to be a general property of natural languages."[60] This very emphasis on formal universality, on the other hand, presses Chomsky to paradoxically argue against both behaviorists and the AI theorists at the very points where that presumptive necessity of reduction is traduced to offer conclusive analogies between the ways that machines and humans behave. Thus on the one hand, the behaviorist looks for mechanical "order" in the chaotic compositions that are humans and societies; on the other, the AI theorist dreams of machines that can that can chaotically correct against the inhibited intelligence of the automaton. If reduction is a methodological necessity, in Chomsky's eyes, there is here a tendentiousness that reduces humans to functional archetypes of whatever task environment the researcher is interested in. The state of contemporary science remains far from discerning the totality of order in the universe, or for that matter, "life," language, or patterns of mind. Here is Chomsky eviscerating a "stimulus-response, billiard-ball model of language":

> A typical example of a *stimulus control* for Skinner would be the response to a piece of music with the utterance *Mozart* or to a painting with the response *Dutch*. These responses are asserted to be "under the control of extremely subtle properties of the physical object or event . . . Suppose instead of saying *Dutch* we had said *Clashes with the wallpaper, I thought you liked abstract work, Never saw it before, Tilted, Hanging too low, Beautiful, Hideous, Remember our camping trip last summer?* Or whatever else might come into our mind when looking at a picture . . . Skinner could only say that each of these responses is under the control of some other stimulus property of the physical object.[61]

Aesthetics and "creativity" are causal names for what empirically presents itself as random indeterminacy. As Randy Allen Harris writes, this is a Chomsky "on the side of the angels, all right, St. George to Skinner's dragon . . . on the side of free, dignified, creative individuals." The mechanisms of nature continue to lie in unfathomable deeps, whose mysteries are not easily yielded up to scientific prestidigitation.

For some, the problem was simply not so interesting. After all, the presumptive imputation of overlap between the natural and the technological or the artificial assumes that *there is* a separation, a "boundary," between them in the first place; this is itself a presumption. Herbert Simon's seminal book of 1969, *The Sciences of the Artificial*, denounced the tendency of those working within what he called the "boundary sciences" to pander to the widespread academic "movement toward natural science and away from the sciences of the artificial." The boundary sciences were fields where "systems-thinking" and applied research were dominant—engineering, business, medicine, and most importantly, *design*—involving the transformation or engineering of "found" states of matter into hybrid, usable ones. Given that overwhelmingly pragmatic, economic demand, bloviations on what nature is and what nature teaches us in Simon's view had little to do with the business at hand, and more with the "hanker[ing] after academic respectability." Epistemologically, he pointed out, isn't it the case that all science is boundary science? Which is to say, is not what we know of nature inevitably conditioned by the reflexive, *synthetic* premises of knowledge itself? It is because that what one knows of the "essences" of nature as thoroughly conditioned by the premises—the "task environment" in his language—that

> a science of artificial phenomena is always in imminent danger of dissolving and vanishing. The peculiar properties of the artifact lie on the thin interface between natural laws within it and the natural laws without . . . What is there to study besides the boundary sciences—those that govern the means and the task environment?[62]

There is no such thing as a "basic" science, no essential difference between a "pure" and an "applied" science, between artifice and what we can make of and out of nature. The epistemic limits for both, their driving "test"—and here Simon gives the game away—is not set according to truth or falsity but by "economic rationality": "The goal (profit maximization) fully defines the firm's inner environment, the cost and revenue curves define the outer environment to which it must adapt."[63] There are no angels here. It is *within* the "cost and revenue curves" of economic rationality—no matter the fervid professions of the aneconomy of the sciences, their dedication to a regime of facts, the religious affirmation of "basic science" and pedagogical autonomy, the fretting about the "independence of research" and

Brown, *Artificial Intelligence: An MIT Perspective* (Cambridge, MA: The MIT Press, 1979), 1:195.

60 Noam Chomsky, *Aspects of the Theory of Syntax* (Cambridge, MA: The MIT Press, 1965), 29.

61 Noam Chomsky, [review of Skinner], *Language* 35 (1959 [1957]), 26-258; excerpted in Harris, *The Linguistic Wars*, 56.

62 Herbert A. Simon, *The Sciences of the Artificial*, 2nd ed. (Cambridge, MA: The MIT Press, 1985), 130-132.

63 Ibid., 32.

the "responsibility of intellectuals"—that whatever is recalled in the name of the "human" and the natural must be placed. Creativity is determined by the task environment.

In complementary ways, both Chomsky and Simon may be seen as drawing lines in the sand over the access to "nature," although to quite different positions on the knowledge spectrum. For Chomsky, research inexorably remains a matter of relating truth to facts, where metaphysical entities such as nature or the human remain ever receding in the mechanistic presumptions of knowledge; for Simon, this "dissolving . . . disappearing" boundary was set less by some pristine, unmediated scrutiny of nature itself than the purposiveness embedded within the "task environment." Truths are contingent events in a domain overwhelmingly determined by use.

Ghosts in the Machine

Herbert Simon's arguments were directed towards the design of commodities, objects of use created within the market to satisfy demands; it was a short step for mainstream "economic rationality" to extrapolate this perspective to its natural conclusions and pose "society" itself as a dissolving boundary, tantamount to nothing more than a market. The commodity would likewise make the conceptual transition from utilitarian object to a "switch" within a libidinal economy, as stimulus and receptor of affect. At that point, information machines would no longer continue to be conceived merely as mimic men, as mechanical substitutes for whatever cognitive hierarchies theorists proleptically posed in the workings of mind; Google is a far cry from the manner in which the early cyberneticians and the Macy Conferences had seen mainframe computers aid in, say, master planning, the growth of the economy, or the prosecution of wars.[64] At MIT, the development of the Media Lab epitomizes that arc; in the long run, this entailed the waning authority and demoralization of the engineers themselves.

Postwar technological thought nonetheless remained entranced by that archaic metaphysics of mimicry, of the replication of nature by artifact. If we see a distinct fascination amongst CAVS fellows with the workings of systems—systems being the cross-over rubric between natural and artificial worlds—"cybernetics" could well be

64 See Siva Vaidhyanathan, *The Googlisation of Everything (and Why We Should Worry)* (Berkeley: University of California Press, 2011); Stephen Levy, *In the Plex: How Google Thinks, Works and Shapes our Lives* (New York: Simon and Schuster, 2011).

described as its counterpart in the scientific realm. Indeed, in its neuro-physiological models, cybernetics moved blithely into the empirical hiatus that Chomsky had so indignantly demarcated, a territory in which many careers were nonetheless forged. Kepes's "pattern-seeing" was one, paying lip-service to the imaginative vanity of the scientists; the continuisms asserted between inorganic and organic worlds by cyberneticians was another. If for Chomsky and Simon, the only path to understanding lay in the reduction of nature to machine, for Norbert Wiener the destiny of humans lay inexorably in guarding against the reduction of machines to mere mechanism.

> Thus, from the point of view of cybernetics, the world is an organism, neither so tightly jointed that it cannot be changed in some aspects without losing all of its identity in all aspects nor so loosely jointed that any one thing can happen as readily as any other thing. It is a world which lacks both the rigidity of the Newtonian model of physics and the detail-less flexibility of a state of maximum entropy or heat death, in which nothing really new can ever happen. It is a world of Process, not one of a final dead equilibrium to which Process leads nor one determined in advance of all happenings, by a pre-established harmony such as that of Leibniz.[65]

With little vested in the actual design of machines, "para-technological" fields such as architecture and the earliest exponents of the "gaming complex"[66] that would evolve into the Media Lab founded their legitimacy on precisely such a metaphysics of "process." Nicholas Negroponte attributes the origins of the Media Lab to the signal exertions of Steven Coons, an early pioneer in computer graphics and professor in the department of Mechanical Engineering: "It was 100% Steven Coons." Coons took a great deal of interest in cultivating relationships with the arts and architecture, appearing in several conferences on the subject of relationships between art and technology:

> ... I am *not* an artist... [but] I feel there is a common element in what we do. Artists, architects and scientists alike perform creative acts: it is our pleasure to be imaginative, intuitive, unpredictable and human; it is our agony that in the creation of our work, we are forced to do many things that are non-creative, that are drudgery, that are

65 Norbert Wiener, *I Am A Mathematician: An Autobiography* (New York: Doubleday, 1956), 328. Process, machine-organisms that abolish alienation and restore harmony: this reformism would paradoxically hold significantly more attraction for Soviet master-planners—

the reception of cybernetics in the Soviet Union has been described as nothing less than "euphoric"—than the more pecuniary and less-than-metaphysical interests of firms such as IBM. See Seymour E. Goodman, "Soviet Computing and Technology Transfer: An Overview,"

World Politics 31, no. 4 (July 1979), 544. Also see Slava Gerovitch, "'Mathematical Machines' of the Cold War: Soviet Computing, American Cybernetics and Ideological Disputes in the Early 1950s," *Social Studies of Science* 31, no. 2, Science in the Cold War (April 2001), 253-287; and Gerovitch, From

Viewspeak to Cyberspeak: A History of Soviet Cybernetics (Cambridge, MA: The MIT Press, 2002).
66 See Alexander R. Galloway, *Gaming: Essays on Algorithmic Culture* (Minneapolis: University of Minnesota Press, 2006).

decidedly uninteresting and that should be done by some kind of slave. Now, in 1966, an appropriate kind of slave exists: it is the computer. Therefore I will talk to you today about the emergent techniques that will enable human beings to do those things that are appropriate to them: and to leave those things that are not to the machine.[67]

The technopolitics of the computer pertains in fact to a political economy, the "socialism" promulgated by capital. Its task is to subsume all labor, effect the wholesale abolition of work *per se*. Humans will be left to appropriate only what is proper to them, which, we are led to assume, is the uncoerced labor of realizing their own "creativity," a labor that is no longer mere labor but play. What belongs to the technocrat is this excess of imagination, this supererogatory "free" ability released by the drudgery taken over by the machine. Constant Niewenhuys's *New Babylon*, its "massification of *homo ludens*," is not mere avant-gardist fantasy; in truth it only recapitulates the extant metaphysics and technocratic doxa of its own era. In his memoir here in this book, William L. Porter describes his own research as similarly "want[ing] to explore possibilities of harnessing the power of rationality to design intuition more effectively, of releasing the cavalry of thought (or intuition) when needed for important things, after having rested it when not really needed." And here is the SAP's 1964 President's Report, this time referring to planning itself, and the computer's promise of separating the "burdensome" task of collating data from the synthesizing essence of the discipline itself:

> The purpose is by no means to make city planning automatic—to surrender decision-making to the computer. On the contrary, it is two-fold: To free the time of planners as students and later as practitioners from the drudgery and limitations of manual methods of data analysis; [and] To free planning students' and professionals' minds for imaginative and creative innovation, by equipping planners with the methods both of better understanding the problems with which they deal, broadening the range of investigation of urban relationships, and of testing the consequences of alternative solutions and thus their validity as means to the intended goals.[68]

67 Stephen A. Coons,
"Computer Art & Architecture,"
Art Education 19, no. 5 (May,
1966), 9.
68 Italics added; MIT-PR; SAP
(1964), 67.

In other words, if, as in the Joint Center report, planning was simply a matter of "concentrated effort" without any clear delineation as to object, here we see a further definition of this "effort" as devoid of any "manual" burdens of organizing data itself. The implications of this multiple divestment are not hard to gauge. As Hashim Sarkis argues in his essay here, the exemplar of such fungibility might well be Kevin Lynch himself, whose "research" demonstrates a rather fuzzy attitude to both data and methodology. Something similar can be said about Carl Steinitz and the emergent field of "landscape urbanism," which Catherine McMahon characterizes in her essay as defined less by either strong epistemological reflection or particular sets of data "but rather [by] a series of products that fall into the category of reports, studies, and workshops—carrying the implication of action rather than reflection."

It is thus under the aegis of the technocrat's "creativity" in aid of more effective outcomes that the crimped parameters of fiscal viability can be reconciled with the "truths" of nature produced by the natural sciences. In the end, the supposed mismatch between the regime of facts and the regime of use is only an apparent one, and in the "creative," "process-dominated" universe one can handily support the other, albeit in the opposite direction than the mere "hankering for respectability" suggested by Herbert Simon. In putatively subsuming the "utilitarian" motivations of the boundary sciences under the catholic domain of basic science, the "task environment" set by the engineer/technocrat acquires the authority that is deemed to belong to the domain of nature alone; "design" can transpose itself into the world of facts. "Economic rationality" would have little currency in worldly affairs if it was not passed off as if natural rationality, as the adamantine and ineluctable will of the ghost, as therefore above any secular politics that could be directed from constituencies deemed less than competent no matter what their suit. Entangled in any professed liberalism is an inherently despotic technopolitics wherein the fantasmatic will of "natural law" is made available to adjudicate the politics by which technology produces and manages social demands.

Language Games

It is important to place Chomsky's reservations on inferences from language to communication within the epistemological context to which it spoke, since in a sense it concerns the dominant "paradigm" in which postwar science placed its queries. Writing almost at the end of the period addressed in this book, in 1979, in a report commissioned to speculate about the future of the university, Jean-François Lyotard described the scientific paradigm of the post-war as domineeringly defined by the rubrics of language:

> And it is fair to say that for the last forty years the "leading" sciences and technologies have had to do with language: phonology and linguistics, problems of communication and cybernetics, modern theories of algebra and informatics, computers and their languages, problems of translation and the search for areas of compatibility among

computer languages, problems of information storage and data banks, telematics and the perfection of intelligent terminals, paradoxology.[69]

If the study of language appears as the "boundary science" par excellence, at least some of its pervasive influence owes to the emphasis laid on it in the twentieth century as the armature of thought itself, encompassing not only organic behavior but also questions of expressivity and the social firmament. All of these lent to it an authority much aspired to by the sciences, the social sciences, and the humanities alike, not to rule out, for our purposes, architecture and urban planning as well. If language had always seemed positioned at the crossroads of multiple disciplines, the "descriptive" thrust of prewar linguistics had tended to actively cordon off epistemological reflection on the "causal" relationships between thought, biology and linguistic structure, limiting itself rather to developing a taxonomy of linguistic forms. By contrast, Chomsky's insistence on *models* whose verifiability stood above their immediate context of reference offered a much more pliable, cross-disciplinary pertinence across multiple arenas of investigation: in his words, "a formalized theory may automatically provide solutions for many problems other than those for which it was explicitly designed."[70] Linguistics would become, like the physics on which it was so explicitly modeled, an *imperial* science, pertaining to every realm of phenomena. Inasmuch as this prescription, coupled with strong Popperian injunctions about eradicating obscurity and so on, presented a *theory of theory* as such, Chomsky's formulation was also the cat out of the bag, so to speak. In the postwar emphasis on interdisciplinarity and "creative" translational between disciplinary models—Lyotard would call this paralogy—linguistics would be as if both methodological exemplar and investigative object par excellence, the very materiel on which these paralogies could be transported from one realm to the other. And despite Chomsky's own famed continence—often occasioning attacks on his own followers—Chomskian linguistics would provide the very stimulus that would foster forth these myriad, mongrel offspring.

The reasons for this fecund, "structural" influence of linguistics are worth speculating upon.[71] We could offer at least seven such reasons. 1) The availability of analytical models that allowed a given phenomenon to be parsed down into its morphological parts, into simpler and simpler sets of formal components (sememes, morphemes, phonemes, etc.), thus allowing systems to absorb more and more complex relationships between parts. 2) The homology afforded between the sequential nature of linguistic components, say, sentences, and the syllogisms inherent in machine-language code, a sequentiality that at the same time affords non-linearity or "parallel processing" between different constituents imbued with different functions (nouns, transitive and intransitive verbs, tenses); and so on. 3) The "structuralist" tendency within linguistics models emphasizing disjunctions or arbitrary relationships between aspects of given entities (between signifier and signified, for example), thus allowing phenomena to be reconstructed as synthetic, consequently tractable, entities.. 4) The methodological prerequisite of "defamiliarizing"

natural substrates—language, thought, behavior, etc.—providing the expert an epistemic
authority above that of the lay practitioners of the idiom. 5) The reduction to mechanism,
in Chomsky's words above, thus affording linguistics an additional, "imperalistic" vantage
by which expertise could be founded on devising generative frameworks from which a
minimum set of rules would produce the "unbounded" totality of a language. Turned on its
head, this in itself would become the experts's strongest nostrum: no matter how complex
or dynamic the phenomenon—cities, housing, poverty, the effects of environment—
expertise could always claim to be founded upon the possession of some finite set of
determining rules. 6) The grammatical emphasis on "transformational" rules, thus enabling
systems-thinking to attempt to account for, even predicate, change itself, and thus to
prognosticate the paths by which a system would metamorphose from one state to the
other. 7) Last, but not least, linguistics' claim to address the "unboundedness" of language,
thus authorizing an ambit for research that would amount to an ever-perpetuating "process,"
and thus providing a boundless field of legitimacy for the expert.

Within architecture, linguistics opened up an avenue to subsume the archaic craft into a
protean epistemological adventure. In postwar architectural thought, terms like "typology,"
"syntactic," "structure," "signification," (Stirling's) "quotations" appear as pervasive.
Architecture is sought to be "read" as if a language, allowing for both taxonomic and
theoretical treatises to resort to its common coin, but each often at great variance from
the other: Kepes's gestalt textbook was titled *The Language of Vision*; John Summerson's
transcript of his BBC talks was titled *The Classical Language of Architecture*, and in 1968
Paolo Portoghesi produced a tract on Borromini subtitled *Architecture as Language*. 1977
might be considered a banner year, producing three classics with "language" in the title:
Christopher Alexander's *A Pattern Language*, Charles Jencks' *The Language of Post-Modern
Architecture*, and Bruno Zevi's *The Modern Language of Architecture*. Peter Eisenman's 1971
essay in *Perspecta*, "From Object to Relationship," transparently carries out a vicarious shift
akin to the one in linguistics from Bloomfieldian morphology to Chomskian syntactics.[72]
Manfredo Tafuri's critique of this entire trend in *L'Architecture dans le boudoir* was
indicatively subtitled *The Language of Criticism and the Criticism of Language*.

69 Lyotard, *The Postmodern Condition*, 3-4.
70 Quoted in Harris, *The Linguistics Wars*, 39.
71 For a critical treatment and compendium on the "linguistic turn," see Richard M. Rorty, ed., *The Linguistic Turn: Essays in Philosophical Method* (Chicago: University of Chicago Press, 1972, 1992).

72 "There is a surface aspect essentially concerned with the sensual qualities of the object; that is aspects of its surface, texture, color, shape, which engender responses that are essentially perceptual. There is also a deep aspect concerned with conceptual relationships which are not sensually perceived; such as frontality, obliqueness, recession, elongation, compression, and shear, which are understood in the mind. These are attributes which accrue to relationships between objects, rather than to the physical presence of the objects themselves . . . It is here that the analogy to language and more specifically to the work of Noam Chomsky is important . . . This paper will concern itself first with exploring the nature of the relationship between the surface and deep aspects of architecture. If these deep aspects are to be made accessible, then second, there is a need to develop what will be called transformational

MIT was neither averse nor aloof to the trend: William Porter's dissertation was titled *DISCOURSE*; the urban theorist M. Christine Boyer's doctoral dissertation was likewise titled *The Language of City Planning*. One presumes that Donald Preziosi wrote his first book, *Architecture, Language and Meaning* during his tenure at MIT, and that at least some of the structuralist linguistics that underscores Rosalind Krauss's influential *Sculpture in the Expanded Field* (1979) was learned there. As late as the early 1980s, a series of studio exercises carried out under N.J. Habraken at MIT and submitted in the form of a report the National Science Foundation would be called *Concept Design Games*, with an explicit nod to Wittgenstein's conception of "language games." And as the disjunctive arguments of postmodernism gained ground everywhere else in the 1980s, MIT dug its heels into the positivist trenches by research appointments in the subject of "shape grammar."[73]

As with the sciences, the pell-mell impetus amongst architectural theorists to devise universal grammars and universal language (modernism was in any case inveterately historically predisposed towards minimalism)—in other words, an effort aimed at producing agreement between different experts and constituencies—would in fact produce its opposite. As opposed to the unique agreements forged in the prewar period, say, in the Athens Charter, the postwar period would generate a proliferation of grammars, as legion as there were actors, each with their own conception of minimal and generative logics, much of their so-called "universalism" simply amounting to idiosyncratic strangleholds exerted by particular individuals over their acolytes or schools. One need no more than simply remind the reader of the list: James Stirling's "quotations," Charles Moore's aedicules, the populist iconography of Venturi and Scott Brown, the purist iconography of the early Michael Graves, the cultural semantics deployed by Team X, Rossi and Kahn's evacuated signifiers, the iterative operations of Peter Eisenman. Manfredo Tafuri would later describe this referentiality as nothing more than "solipsism," the neo-avant-garde's way of circling back to its own comfortable idioms while the world tumbled, but this was patently missing the point. The analytics of language and of systems were crucial for a stylized modernism to conspicuously gain the didactic high ground in postwar institutions; they were the means by which modernism could affect a gravitas aimed at staving off the perception of architecture as mere excurses in taste.

methods for deriving and relating specific forms to formal universals. These transformational devices translate formal regularities into specific forms." Peter Eisenman, "From Objects to Relationship II: Casa Giuliani Frigerio: Giuseppe Terragni's Casa Del Fascio," *Perspecta* 13/14 (1971), 38-40.

73 This traffic went in both directions: one compilation of Chomsky's writing is titled *The Architecture of Language*, while a Worldcat database search reveals no fewer than five books with "architecture of grammar" in their title for every one book titled "grammar of architecture."

Maurice Smith House, Harvard, MA, begun in 1963. Photo: Mark Jarzombek, April 2010.

Compare with Peter Eisenman, House III, Lakeville, CT, 1969-71. Photo: Peter Eisenman.

Peter Eisenman could be offered here as example. In her scholarship on the Russian constructivists, Catherine Cooke, a scholar well familiar with the Cambridge architectural scene of the 1970s (having served as amanuensis to many of its actors), described the Constructivists' pedagogical forays, for instance Moisei Ginzburg's 1927 *kompleksynii* exercises, as "essentially today's 'systems' approach."[74] To a great extent, both Eisenman's dissertation at Cambridge and his work in the decade following can be seen as dressing up that older didacticism within the currency of the new jargon, with a declared debt to Chomsky. Much of the content of the dissertation rehearses a taxonomy of basic forms—Tafuri astutely labeled it "the worn signs of historical elementarism"[75] evinced in Malevich's Planits or Lissitzky's Prouns—but now imputing certain "mentalist" features, involving particular kinds of psychological responses relative to (but not determining) each formal composition. The "research" heft of this exercise, Eisenman tells us, rested on his effort to establish a "(universal) terminology for architectural form which might serve as a basis for communication, whether between teacher and pupil, architect and client, or critic and public."[76] Nonetheless, the only "universal" terminology that one can discern, if at all, subsists more or less in the borrowed linguistic terminology in the methodological prolegomena given in the initial chapters: the bulk of the remaining dissertation comprises a mind-numbingly—Tafuri is again a good aid here—"minute, pedantic, nearly insufferable [in its] step-by-step"[77] descriptivism.

There is one key difference with the elementarism invoked by the early modernists. In terms of reference, Constructivist or Purist didactic texts—or for that matter, those of the entire prewar avant-garde—inexorably use either Euclidean forms or what they considered generic type-objects, in other words, objects that were indifferent to cultural provenance. It was precisely to the point that the formal characteristics of steam-engines were considered at par with Greek temples; formal grammar was seen as a substrate that underlay all culture, high or low. By contrast, *every one* of Eisenman's examples cited in his dissertation, it turns out, is a modernist classic. Behind the veil of system, it turns out, is a tendentious attempt at clandestine canonizing, a return to the world of the connoisseur. The cloth of linguistics is handily cut according to the coat of *style*, with the mere qualification that, as Colin Rowe described it, "in default of that convenient anti-'art' entity of the Twenties

74 Catherine Cooke, *Fantasy and Construction—Iakov Chernikhov , Architectural Design* 59, no. 7-8 (1989).
75 Manfredo Tafuri, "Peter Eisenman: The Meditations of Icarus," in Eisenman, *Houses of Cards* (New York: Oxford University Press, 1987), 177.
76 Peter Eisenman, *The Formal Basis of Modern*

Architecture (Ph.D. Dissertation, Trinity College, Cambridge University, 1963), 87. Facsimile published Donauwörth: Lars Müller Publishers, 2006.
77 Tafuri, "The Meditations of Icarus," 180.
78 Colin Rowe, Introduction, in *Five Architects: Eisenman Graves Gwathmey Hejduk*

Meier (New York: Oxford University Press, 1975), 7.
79 K. Michael Hays' recent book on Eisenman et al. repeats the same conceit, only this time portraying the formal devices of Eisenman, Hejduk, and Tschumi as somehow evincing a basic language of architecture. See Hays, *Architecture's Desire:*

Reading the Late Avant-Garde (Cambridge, MA: The MIT Press, 2010).
80 Peter D. Eisenman, "Notes on Conceptual Architecture: Towards a Definition," *Design Quarterly* 78/79, Conceptual Architecture (1970).
81 Manfredo Tafuri, "L' Architecture dans le boudoir,"

called 'the machine,' we substitute the equally useful entities designated 'the computer' and 'the people' and that, if these two abstractions are absolutely at variance with each other, we will not indulge ourselves in too many scruples about this problem."[78] This is tantamount to a Chomsky, say, in a peer-reviewed article in *Language*, somehow seeking to establish Wordsworth's *Daffodils* as better evincing the basic structure of the English language.[79] If Eisenman and Rowe do not "scruple" themselves with the implications, lurking well underneath this stylistics is the determinism of a B.F. Skinner, of the passing off of contingent phenomena for universal ones. The machine here is at best a convenience, a prosthetic to reestablish, at the core of the research establishment, the *credo quia absurdum* so passionately defended by Rowe.

Indeed, by 1970, and the "Notes on Conceptual Architecture," the cycle is complete. Readers are presented with five pages, five pages of a supposedly scholarly article, complete with footnotes at the bottom. Only that the text has disappeared.[80] The footnote numbers drift like flotsam on the blank page, the absented argument leaving the footnotes as moves in a language game that has lost its rulebook, its code. Concept, the thumbprint of the Spirit, has manifestly occupied the place where the system, the research apparatus, had been. As we have suggested, Tafuri's charge of solipsism represents a patent failure to read this blank screen of legimation at its surface, mistaking a language game for the sentence's intent. Nonetheless, the following passage is worth quoting:

> to Nietzsche's question "Who speaks?" Mallarmé answered "The Word itself." This would seem to preclude any attempt to question language as a system of meanings whose underlying discourse it is necessary to "reveal." Therefore, whenever contemporary architecture ostensibly poses the problem of its own meaning, we discern the glimmering of a regressive utopia, even if it stimulates a struggle against the institutional functions of language. This struggle becomes evident when we consider how, in the most recent works, the compositional rigorism hovers precariously between the forms of "commentary" and those of "criticism" . . . Commentary takes the form a repetition desperately in search of the origins of signs; criticism takes the form of an analysis of the functions of the signs themselves.[81]

The Non-Architecture of Good Intentions

Two decades after his Cambridge stint, Eisenman described his doctoral work as an "infuriated" response to Christopher Alexander's dissertation, later published as *Notes on the Synthesis of Form*. It is conceivable that his fury may well have been directed at the entirety of the pedantic, plodding, positivist strand represented by the "Design Methods" group, by far the intellectually dominant trend in the Cambridge of the 1960s, a key spigot through which both the Frege-Wittgensteinian conception of language and the logical empiricism of the Vienna Circle spilled into the empty cup of the architects' institutional struggle for self-definition. Both Mary Lou Lobsinger's essay in this volume and Alise Upitis, in her research here and elsewhere, speak to the strong influence of the "Design Methods" movement at MIT.[82] There,

> words such as negative feedback, error correction, information and noise overran design discussions . . . [new] conceptual innovations, technological developments and metaphorical linkages [were made] between psychology and computer related media as these reconfigured thinking about approaches to designing. A new nature of humans and psychology emerged, reconfigured by the invention of new technologies for selection, storage, transmission and processing of information.[83]

If one aspect of Alexander's undertaking drew resolutely from the positivist impetus of reducing architectural propositions into logical or mathematical statements, a much more problematic aspect was the Skinnerian air of its inferential method, complete with stimulus-response model at its core, with a pointed—and unnerving—reference to "primitive" and unmodern societies as the stand-in for what behaviorism referred to as "natural" language. If Eisenman's lapsarianism covertly veered towards elite-connoisseurship, Alexander all-too patently lurched towards organicism, with nativism—complete with studies of Indian "village-structures"—as its inevitable accompaniment. The implications of prescriptions such as those in the following passage presented at the 1968 Design Methods conference in Cambridge, MA, despite their somewhat Chomskian air, are terrific, if not terroristic:

> We believe that all values can be replaced by one basic value: Everything desirable can be described in terms of freedom of people's underlying tendencies. Anything undesirable in life—whether social, economic, or psychological—can always be described as an unresolved conflict between underlying tendencies. Life can fulfill itself only when people's tendencies are running free. The environment should give free rein to all tendencies; conflicts between people's tendencies must be eliminated. In terms of this view, the rightness or wrongness of a relation is a question of fact.[84]

In a subsequent Design Methods conference, Janet Daley did not mince her words: she denounced Alexander's formulations as "insidious . . . fatuous . . . verging on a new intellectual fascism . . . so dazzlingly arbitrary as to approaching whimsy . . . betray[ing] a quite primitive and unfortunate theory of language."[85]

At MIT, behaviorism, coupled with a tendentious belief in organic grammars, remained at the core of faculty preoccupation. There is more than evidence within this book itself to suggest that the architecture department's "anthropological bent" was assiduously cultivated by its faculty as a way of distinguishing themselves from their institutional peers. Julian Beinart earnestly speaks of the department as "person-centered," and one discerns quite a bit of the proprietorial indignation of the self-appointed ecclesiast in Stanford Anderson's exclamation about MoMA and Eisenman's (the "Princeton group" alluded to earlier by Rowe) call for Harlem as the first design site for the CASE study group. "As implausible as it seems in hindsight, Drexler and Eisenman decided on projects for the radical transformation of Harlem as the content of the exhibition! Surely none of the participants were completely naïve about this venture, but I think it is fair to say that MIT as a school was more prepared to confront the issues of such a project."

One sees very little suspicion of the positivism owing to which the other east coast schools kept the anthropologisms and behaviorisms rife at MIT at arm's length. What made MIT faculty, in their vaunted identification with the downtrodden, think that they were on the side of "people" and others not? Is this merely a matter of—as Brendan Moran alludes to in his essay here—a self-fulfilling institutional "regionalism:" a market sequestration of touted good intentions posing as an epistemic problem? It is hard to say. If the archives are what we have to go by, however, the waft of righteousness is palpable, if not all-pervasive. As opposed to all the others who merely talked, they had slummed it in Harlem and with the squatters in Roxbury (while conveniently omitting the part of the story where they were kicked out). They had hired the anthropologists to leaven the self-confessed hard edges of their technocratism in Venezuela. They had recruited Peace Corps soldiers and gallivanted with the World Bank and United Nations missions to improve the lot of Third World *volk*. They *knew* about the poor and the blacks, about the wretched of the earth. They had held the portentous "shirt-sleeve" sessions where they had imagined "people" designing for themselves (while exponentially raising the level of complexity involved by framing the whole problem as a challenge for devising computer codes).[86] It was to their developmentalist preoccupations that indignant, upwardly-mobile Third World students applied in their journey as aspirant technocrats of their native countries. They had laughed off the hacking into and fornication inside the MIT President's Office, and they had built replicas of Dogon huts in front of Tang Hall, mulling over the semiotics of primitive and technological cultures in the wake of Aldo van Eyck and Fritz Morgenthaler.[87] They had celebrated counter-cultural initiative by lauding the maladroit "mezzanine" that the students had tacked up, practically overnight, in the design studios. They had embraced the democratic and anti-authoritarian zeitgeist of the counter-culture by letting the students set out the outlines of their own education. They just knew better about the blacks, about Harlem.

in *Sphere and the Labyrinth: Avant-Gardes and Architecture from Piranesi to the 1970s* (Cambridge, MA: The MIT Press, 1990), 268, 272.

82 Alise Upitis, "Nature Normative: The Design Methods Movement, 1944-1947" (Ph.D. Dissertation, MIT, 2008).

83 Upitis, *Nature Normative*, 8.

84 Christopher Alexander and Barry Poyner, "The Atoms of Environmental Structure," *Emerging Methods in Environmental Design and Planning: Proceedings of The Design Methods Group First International Conference,* Cambridge, Massachusetts, June 1968, ed. Gary T. Moore (Cambridge, MA: The MIT Press, 1970), 314.

85 Janet Daley, "A Philosophical Critique of Behaviourism in Architectural Design," in *Design Methods in Architecture,* ed. Geoffrey Broadbent and Anthony Ward (London: Lund Humphries, 1969), 71-75.

86 Edward Allen, ed., *The Responsive House: Selected Papers and Discussions from the Shirt-Sleeve Sesson in Responsive Housebuilding Technologies, held at Dept. of Architecture,* MIT, May 3-5, 1972 (Cambridge: MA: The MIT Press, 1974).

Model of a primitive Dogon grannery, constructed by MIT students to test water-storage capabilities, is dwarfed by the 24-story Tang Residence Hall, January 1974. Photo: Simon Wiltz.

Within the architecture department, one also gets the strong feeling that they were hard put to say much otherwise, and that ostentatious moralism may well have been the hobgoblin of functional disorganization, if not pedagogical confusion. A good instance here is that of Maurice Smith, unknown, certainly unmourned, outside MIT, but—in the absence of stronger figureheads—with an outsize footprint within the Department itself. Mark Jarzombek's sympathetic estimation of Smith and the house he built for himself in the village of Harvard, Massachusetts, nonetheless reveals a scattered sensibility significantly formed by the overall atmosphere of "systems-talk" and at the same time unable to acquire an authoritative voice within it. One notices the disjointed fragments, almost by hearsay as it were, of the disjunctions asserted in linguistics between signifier and signified, quite like Eisenman, in abstracting walls, columns, even gravity, as non-functional, and more as pure determinants of form. There is also the antipathy towards formal determinism, an antagonism given flesh by his personal acrimony against the "Brutalist" in the department, Eduardo Catalano. Smith's attempt to write out his pedagogical agenda, reproduced here, presents us with a strange kind of document: a twitchy, tetchy, raspy, spasmodic excursus into the mechanics of indecision.

clockwise, Ruth Dibble's sketchbook; Jan Wampler's studio; an assembled house; and examples of solutions to 4.01 problem using a kit of forms for short sketch problems; and wood patchwork from Wampler's house. *PLAN* 1980.

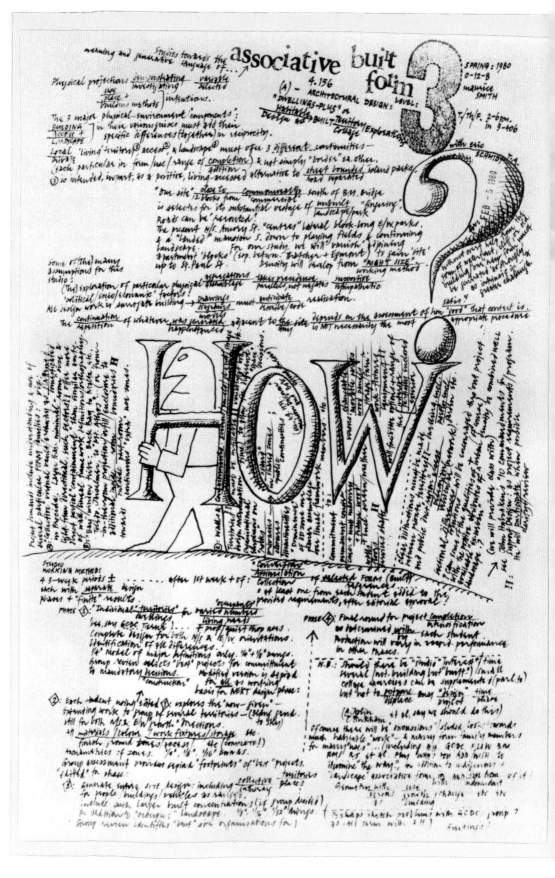

associative built form 3

Studies towards the meaning and generative language of...→

(a) – 4.156
ARCHITECTURAL DESIGN: LEVEL:
"DWELLINGS-PLUS" or Habitable
Design #3 → BUILT Tenure/Cottage Exploration

SPRING: 1980
0-12-8
maurice SMITH
T/Th/F. 2-6pm.
in 5-406

with eric SCHMIDT T.A.

FEB - 5 1980

Physical projections demonstrating variety investigating selected use place + building methods intentions.

The 3 major physical-environment "components": BUILDING / access + / LANDSCAPE. In these various guises must add their specific differences (together) in reciprocity.

Local 'living territories' access, & landscape must offer 3 different continuities — having particulars in form/use/range of completion) & not simply "bridges" ea. other.

③ is intended, in part, as a positive, living-accessed alternative to street bounded 'island parks' / fore separates.

"Our site" — close to Commonwealth south of B.U. bridge — is selected for its substantial vestage of unbuilt "fingering". Roads can be "recounted".

some of the many assumptions for this studio:
(The) exploration of particular physical 'political/socio/economic' factors!

All design work is surrogate building → drawings / models must participate realization.

The continuation of whatever was scanned happenstances adjacent to the site depends on the assessment of how good that context is / is NOT necessarily the most appropriate procedure.

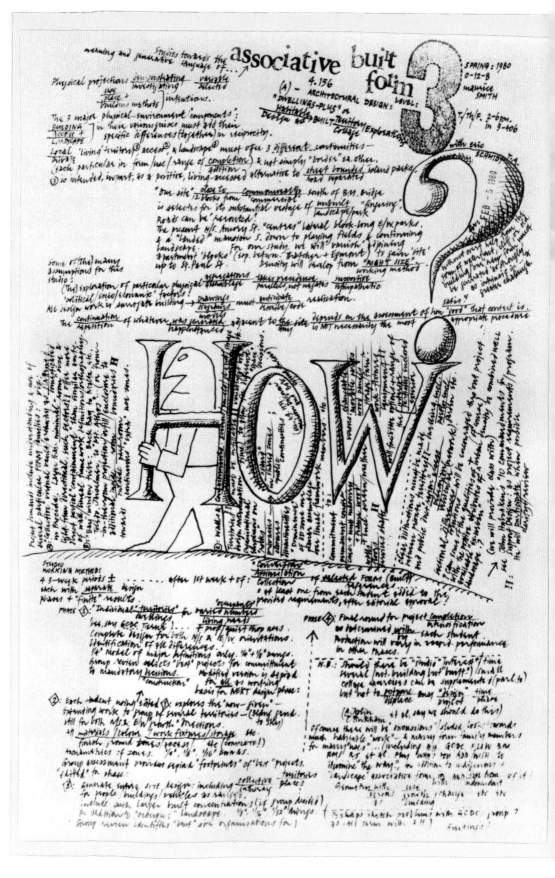
HOW?

STUDIO WORKING METHODS:
4 3-week periods ± each with separate design phases + "finite" results. . . . . . after 1st week + of: Collection of selected FORM (built) of at least one from each student added to the provided requirements, after external approval.

PHASE ① "Individual" territories for varied numbers dwellings / living units 'ee, say GEDE Tienes'). . . . . complete design for both N/S & E/W orientations. Identification of all differences. ¼" model of major definitions only. ¼" + ⅛" scales. group review selects "best" projects for commitment in mandatory decisions. Modified version is signed for all as working "construction" basis for NEXT design phase:

② Each student using settled ① explores this 'now-given'— extending work to group of several territories — (being freed still for both N/S & E/W growth "directions)...

③ Generate ...

PHASE ④ Final round for project completion intensification as determined with each student. Protection will vary in regard performance in other phases.

N.B.: Should there be "studio" interest of time several (not-building but "built") small cottage inquiries can be supplements of (part to) but not to postpone any "design" time displace project phases

(A John & Pinkham et al, say we should do this)

In the two decades previous to 2000, MIT's department of architecture did not make a single tenurial appointment in the field of architectural design. One gets a sense of a general dispiritedness, with the inevitable, internecine, idiosyncratic cycles of mutual recrimination (that other social characteristic of sandboxes). As the first postwar generation of "charismatic" figures—Lynch, Kepes—retired, their legacy was vested into a defensive tendency of the School to hire its own students. In 1980, graduating student (and later professor) Roy Strickland vented his anger at the lack of curricular clarity in these terms, in a piece indicatively titled "In Search of a School":

> I reacted against what I perceived to be MIT's structural determinism, its repeated references to "organic" Italian hill towns, its romanticized agrarianism, and its predilection for shed roofs. . . [we had come to MIT because we] shared a number of the School's goals and interests: the exercising of a socially responsive architecture . . . the recruitment of women and minorities into the profession, and research into the behavioral effects of design. And yet, looking about us, we saw things missing: . . . a core curriculum, a sense of contact with the architectural profession and with the profound changes in architecture proceeding outside the institutions's walls . . . we never won a new course in drawing . . . [eventually students] climbed into the niches and corners of the studios where they could struggle with their goals and problems privately . . . an ennui set in, the very ennui we had identified with the institution and had fought against just months before.[88]

N.J. Habraken's appointment in the 1970s signaled the department's lingering unease about its weaknesses on the front of formal didactics. Habraken's appointment at this critical juncture is indicative of the department's image of itself. His biographers suggest that at the time of Habraken's departure from the Netherlands, his work had been doubly discredited, first by the particular confluence of architectural firms and building industries that formed the basis for his research foundation, SAR, and then secondly by the wave of Marxism amongst students in the 1970s who declaimed this research as fundamentally corporate oriented.[89] In America, by contrast, deprived of that direct access to architectural practice or any potential for policy formulation, Habraken's work took on a distinctly more

Maurice Smith, "Studies towards the meaning and generative language of associative built form 3" for 4.156 Architectural Design: Dwellings Plus. *PLAN*, 1980.

87 See Aldo van Eyck, "The Interior of Time," in M*eaning in Architecture*, eds. Charles Jencks and George Baird (New York: George Braziller, 1970).

88 Roy Strickland, "In Search of a School," *Plan 1980: Perspectives on Two Decades* (Cambridge, MA: MIT School of Architecture, 1980), 139-143.

89 Koos Bosma, Dorine van Hoogstraten, and Martijn Vos, *Housing for the Millions: John Habraken and the SAR (1960-2000)* (Rotterdam: NAI Publishers, 2000).

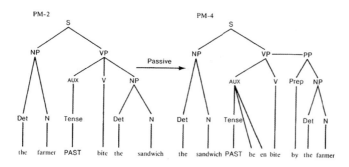

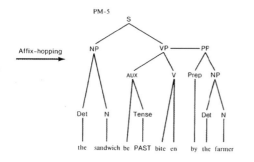

top, Noam Chomsky, phrase markers from "A Transformational Approach to Syntax" (Cambridge, MA, 1958).

middle, Christopher Alexander, tree of diagrams completed for "The Determination of Components for an Indian Village." Reprinted by permission of the publisher from *Notes on the Synthesis of Form,* by Christopher Alexander, p. 156-9, 173, Cambridge, MA: Harvard University Press, ©1964 by the President and Fellows of Harvard College. Copyright© renewed 1992 by Christopher Alexander.

bottom, N. John Habraken *Transformations of the Site,* (Cambridge, MA, Awater Press: 1988).

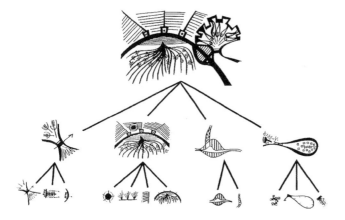

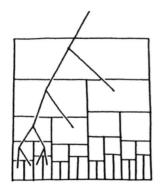

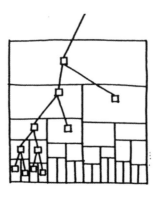

reflective—in Tafurian terms, solipsistic—turn. The new institutional and funding context wrought a greater fixation on Habraken's part with mathematical and rational modeling procedures, with the obligatory immersion in computational languages and logics. *Concept Design Games*, an NSF-funded project, took Habraken and his collaborators headlong, with a perfunctory nod to Wittgenstein, into game theory, where the architect is nothing more than an anthropological image for the probabilities and potentials of logic.

From the MIT perspective, however, nobody could have been more felicitous. Here finally was a pedagogue with impeccable Team X credentials, a European protégé of the post-war Dutch preoccupation with formal systems. Here was a scholar as willing to engage with Wittgenstein as the study of structural systems, as able to take on the funding imperatives presented by the National Science Foundation as to address himself to the didactics of form (at least the variant that was to result in the *Grunsfeld Variations*). And here, also, was a full-fledged organic intellectual of the welfare state, who had presided over an industry chamber—SAR—with "research" in its title. Most crucially, Habraken's adherence to the "structure-infill"—with its mechanical continuism between wholes and parts—concept finally presented a formal pedagogy as pertinent to the scale of the city as to building, promising therein a much more integrated conversation between the Schools' two departments. Likewise, the formal devices suggested by the SAR systems were equally applicable to the department's two theaters of formal conscience, the modern and the vernacular. His ongoing work in Holland, for instance the Matura system, seemed to speak precisely to the interactions between system thinking, architecture, and the broader social good which the department stood for. MIT seemed to have somewhat put its disparate pieces together.

Second Modernism / Post-Modernism

"Traditional" theory is always in danger of being incorporated into the programming of the social whole as a simple tool for the optimization of its performance; this is because its desire for a unitary and totalizing truth lends itself to the unitary and totalizing practice of the system's managers.
— Jean-François Lyotard, *The Postmodern Condition: A Report on Knowledge*

More likely, they were out of time. Habraken was invited to become head of the department in 1975. In 1977, Charles Jencks published *The Language of Post-Modern Architecture*, a chatty, cavalier broadside leveled as much at the experts' self-regard of their "second modernism" as the implicit social utopias they purported to engineer. As more and more humanities, art, and architecture departments gave vent to their long-brewing frustration with logical positivism, the "critique of humanism" advanced through the newly translated work of Foucault, Derrida, Deleuze and Guattari, and Lyotard appeared to take aim at the innate complicity between governmentality, the apparatuses of knowledge, and the transcendental entities—nature, man, structure, etc.—in whose names epistemic power was exercised. The passage by Lyotard quoted at the very beginning of this introduction as its epigram goes to the nub of that critique, and for those inclined to listen we can understand how it eviscerated the entire edifice that the postwar cult of expertise had stood on.

Having long shored up that crumbling edifice, mantra of "testability" in hand, MIT's architects and planners were signally undone by this turn. While, as we have seen, a certain anti-establishmentarianism does not go against the grain of what the technocrats construed as their activism, their motivation for action, what truly rankled for these practitioners was less the anti-technocratic brunt of these critiques as the postmodernists' insistence on the inherent disconnect between the world of facts and the betterment of practice: their antipathy to the notion, to paraphrase Lyotard, that devising "better languages" to better describe the human condition had little to do with the sphere of action, or more importantly, that the rationality employed to link these regimens could itself be the basis of its perversion.

In their writing, one observes amongst the MIT faculty a good deal of ire voiced against the intellectual trend towards postmodern "absurdities"[90] and "postmodern bullshit" (Chomsky). The implication that knowledge presented only contingent formations dependent on what Wittgenstein had called "language games"—not some continuous, perpetually self-improving, organic, edifice in the Cartesian mold—cut deep, as did the idea that social or natural phenomena did not transparently render themselves up to the expert, awaiting only more and more perfectible responses. For the cult of expertise, suspicion voiced against the deceptions of rationality was as if to break with the premise of social justice itself, and in Chomsky's acerbic phrasing, despite its assertions of epistemological modesty, in an essay from 1992 indicatively titled "Rationality/science and post-this-or-that," one finds a rousing, if flabbergasting, defense of the inherent agonistics of science. Legitimation is at the very heart of the question:

> I'm afraid I see only one way to proceed: by assuming the legitimacy of rational inquiry . . . It is not that scientists are inherently more honest, open, or questioning. It is simply that nature and logic impose a harsh discipline… [MIT scientists] have dedicated serious and often successful efforts to overcome traditional exclusiveness and privilege because they tend to agree with Descartes (as I do) that the capacity for understanding in the "profoundest sciences" and "high feeling" are a common human attribute, and *that those who lack the opportunity to exercise the capacity to inquire, create, and understand are missing out on some of life's most wonderful experiences.* . . . many scientists, not too long ago, took an active part in the lively working-class culture of the day, seeking to compensate for the class character of the cultural institutions through programs of workers' education or by writing books on mathematics, science and other topics for the general public . . . It strikes me as remarkable that their left counterparts today should seek to deprive oppressed people not only of the joys of understanding and insight, but also of tools of emancipation, informing us that the "project of the Enlightenment" is dead, that

we must abandon the "illusions" of science and rationality—a message that will gladden the hearts of the powerful, delighted to monopolize these instruments for their own use . . . One recalls the days when the evangelical church taught no-dissimilar lessons to the unruly masses as part of what E. P. Thompson called "the psychic processes of counter-revolution," as their heirs do today in peasant societies of Central America.[91]

No eyes, in other words, can be taken off of that primal, Cartesian, scene painted so fetchingly in the *Discourse on Method:* the illuminated world in front of a blind man, of his centuries-long effort at correcting for cognitive inadequacy, of his ever-perfecting ground of sensory and epistemic perception as abatement of misperception. It is "nature" itself, in its *erscheinungsform* as the demand of logic, that transparently confronts the scientist, the constraints posed by its unmediated cognition far outweighing the constraints of funding, institutional setting, genealogies of knowledge, or political knowledge. To be unappreciative of that primal scene is to lapse into dogma, into the obscurantism of religion, to "belong . . . to a different mentality: savage, primitive, underdeveloped, backward, alienated, composed of opinions, customs, authority, prejudice, ignorance, ideology . . . [prone to] fables, myths, legends, fit only for women and children."[92] As for the scientists' own inclinations, at most it is a matter of good or bad intentions, of honest or dishonest toil, the extent of which will only be judged in terms of their deviation from the Cartesian rubric.

Certainly the stymied cohort of "second modernists" at MIT put down their increased alienation from their contemporary academic currents to the eddies of what they "academic fashion," little acknowledging that they had blithely subscribed to their own only a generation before. Present-day explanations for the doldrums that set in within MIT-SAP in the 1980s and 1990s tend to attribute it to a noxious world of interpersonal conflict, but one may well argue that this was also the outcome of a defunct epistemic formation in a world out of joint. For the experts, blaming the critique of humanism would be convenient, a little bit like kicking the neighborhood dog after a bad day at work, but this vituperation also betrays their own idealism, their conception of the world as if ruled solely by ideas and so to be defended by the mere purity of ideas, as if the English professors had been suddenly allowed to take over the undespoiled ramparts of the NSF. In actuality, it would

90 "Interview: Donald Schön," Plan [Department of Architecture newsletter] (MIT, 1980).

91 Italics added. Noam Chomsky, "Rationality/science and post-this-or-that [October 1992]" in Chomsky, *Chomsky on Democracy and Education* (New York: RoutledgeFalmer, 2003), 88, 92-93, 96.

92 Lyotard, *The Postmodern Condition,* 27.

be the humanities, pawn in the postwar Great Game, despite their temporary rise to prominence in the culture wars of this period, that would be decimated in the postmodern turn. Nowhere, what with a disappearing job market, the erosion of tenure, and the millions of idealistically proferred, unpaid man hours of adjunct labor, would the post-human eclipse of the "age of the professor" be felt more deeply. Frank Donoghue has written of an unsparing, continuous arc of institutional decline in humanities appointments from the 1970s after the initial euphoria of the postwar years, an irrepressible trend towards greater emphasis on "developing a culture as steeped in the ethos of productivity and salesmanship as one might encounter in the business world,"[93] with even higher rates of attrition. At that point, undergraduate requirements in literature and the humanities would be pushed under the umbrella of "communication intensive" courses aimed at transforming tongue-tied engineers and other skill-based workers into velvet-tongued entrepreneurs.

Rachel Malik's present-day characterization of the "researcher" that we have read above has had a four decade history, and it is precisely that turn that Jean-François Lyotard, in the period of its inception, called the "postmodern." As we have suggested, the humanism dissembled by the sponsored research complex, its "second modernism," might be described as anticipating the postmodern, and to that extent the economic rationality nestled within systems-thought might be said to have underwritten its own eventual demoralization. It might be useful, in concluding this essay, to recapitulate the manner in which Lyotard's argument annotates that complicity in order to round out our discussion on legitimation, since it also annotates the shift in the institutional premises of research that would put paid to the era of Big Science.

Lyotard locates the origins of the modern—post-Kantian—university as inherently riven by an irreducible chasm—a differend—between two unrelated founts of knowledge, the first pertaining to truth and the second to ethics and the world of practice. A statement of the type "The door is open," is not of the same order as the type, "Close the door." The first is denotative; it refers to verifiability. The second is prescriptive, implying a pragmatics, a "morality," and efficiency (Close the door on whom? When? How? Is it to stay closed? How long? Under what constraints?) Legitimation in the first instance entails the competence of the addressee, not in the sense that they unconditionally affirm the "truth" of the message conveyed to them by the sender—on the contrary, skepticism must be their primary attribute—but rather in presenting the "legislative" authority that can evaluate if the message is admissible for evaluation by that epistemic community (for instance, scientists). A "proof" is in effect a petition. In principle, the competence of the addressee entails their corresponding competence as potential senders of like messages; the relationship between sender and addressee is therefore tantamount to a contract. As an "open system" that emphasizes competence, this dialectics also involves a didactics for those less competent;

the university is the institutional structure that negotiates this essential interlink between openness and censorship of what may or may not be attested to as authentic speculation. The second situation involves a different phrase regimen. It pertains to performatives: with what works, keeps things moving, defines successes in relation to failures, guarantees the legality of contracts, and assesses damages when contracts are broken. It therefore also pertains to an *ethikon*, to justice. To this second case belongs the question: what are the means and the techniques by which society, in the aggregate or in its parts, is to be managed or bettered? These questions encumber the university with a competing mission, the production of societal managers: civil servants, managers, technocrats, engineers, planners. Their statements do not refer back to denotative utterances but rather to imperative, prescriptive ones: "The minimum wage must be set at x dollars," or "The nation's engineers must devise alternative energy solutions to save the environment," or "(Where/Whom) Should we bomb to eradicate tyranny?" They are directed not to a sequestered community of authorized legislators but to an autonomous collectivity standing in for the practical subject, e.g. humanity. Moves in this regimen or "language game" are evaluated in relative terms, not as right or wrong but in terms of their being better or worse solutions for the purpose in question. Damages incurred in the course of activating these prescriptions are therefore assessed not according to some "essence" of a life that is being deprived or curtailed but as a negative—collateral—index of some efficient goal towards which the collective is being nurtured. Hence the new prevalence of tort—where injury is assessed by a price, a monetary restitution paid to the injured—the "crime" as it were is not seen as one of malevolence but of lapse of efficiency. An economy of reason already inheres within these prescriptions, including those that pertain to justice.

Inasmuch as Type 1 (scientific or denotative) statements distinguish themselves exclusively from Type 2 (prescriptives)—in Chomsky's words "[science's] intent is to understand, not to construct doctrine that accords with some ethical or other preferences..."[94] —the problem re-emerges when it concerns the relationship of science to society as a whole. This problem cannot be addressed by didactics alone, since it pertains also to addressees—"citizens"—whose legitimacy does not rest on the same competence. A scientist who has been invited to a television show to explain the implications of his newest finding will adopt a very different genre of narrative than the statements he uses to explain the same to his colleagues. Thus, the possible identification of the Higgs boson subatomic particle will be stated to have further clarified the Standard Model of subatomic behavior, but also restating a narrative of science as epic adventure, as, say, the finer appreciation of "some of life's most wonderful experiences." When it pertains to drawing funds, or executive power, science inevitably resorts to narrative or literary forms—"grand narratives"—that have nothing to do with verifiability or falsifiability. Humanism, enlightenment, modernity, etc., these are allegories, narrative effects, of science's valorization in society.

Generally speaking, no "facts" can be established in science without the appropriate equipment by which these facts can be measured; consequently those with the best equipment tend to have the best chance to be right. Science becomes a game increasingly corralled by wealthier and wealthier networks that are in the best place to devise more and more expensive sets of equipment. Hence the "market-effect" of the large space programs and seventeen-mile particle accelerators: a government that sponsors scientists' capacities to be "right" in their understanding of the atom or the weather on Mars does so precisely with the expectation that it will also be considered "right" in its treatment of debts. Science becomes a device for establishing market trust.

The reliance on investment makes "natural science" indistinguishable from "boundary science" not only, as in Simon's view, in theoretical terms but also in practice. A "boundary science"—systems thinking—expresses its viability in terms of Type 2 statements, in terms of relative efficacy and "economic rationality", but it nonetheless claims the sublimity, and the unimpeachability, traditionally accorded to Type 1. Humanism becomes the alibi for the system's economic ambitions; it infects it with the paranoia of its own incompletion, its "lack of progress". A system's success is premised on its tolerance of difference, of the atypical, of the outlier. What cannot be encompassed as a functional element of a system must be seen as grounds for the system's eventual dysfunction; what a system cannot tolerate must be catalogued or taxonomized as future tests for the system's ongoing morphogenesis.

"Creativity" thus has a precise role in the system. In the adjudicatory regime imposed by "innovation" it pertains to the systems' investigator's double responsiveness to the relationship between the system's own dysfunction and the given constraints posed by a particular market. Thus, a scientific move must be simultaneously expressed as an economic move. To possess or lack creativity has nothing to do with falsifiability; writing in 1979, Lyotard still cognized the economic in terms of an overt emphasis on the utilitarian. But the commodity no longer comprises merely the utilitarian, at least in its traditional sense of being measured against scarcity. An algorithm that allows you to place a "forward contract" on a price that will be determined on such and such a date, a handheld "app" that enables you to broadcast mundane details about your day to three hundred "friends" scattered across the globe; these represent expenditures, withdrawals, on the subject's relationship with time itself, a resource with the potentially infinite reserves of psychic interiority.

The "creative" person is therefore the counterpart of the paranoiac. If for the paranoiac the efficacy of a system conceals behind it the clandestine, ever-creative, influence and will-to-power of some malevolent spirit, then for the creative investigator all systems are condemned to be ever-failing mechanisms whose rigidity is seen to be mirrored in the rigidity of the social habits associated with them. Emancipation from the system can therefore only be construed as the emancipation *by* system. There are no longer machines in the sense that we construe them as a set of operations that expand the constraints of material behavior, but rather more and more sublime assemblages of circuits and social behavior. On the one hand, there is the acceleration in informational speed from the exponentially greater number of transistors that can be placed on integrated circuits, and on the other hand with this acceleration systems more and more run interference with the habits and temporal malaises that characterize the subject's inhabitance of time: boredom, anxiety, lassitude, exultation. Creativity then pertains not only to the primordial recesses of what used to be called "imagination" but also to the limitless accoutrements of psychic management. The everyday becomes the new front for the technosublime. One no longer buys a commodity in the sense of a "thing," but rather a contract that subjugates you to the system's morphogenesis, an ever-proliferating array of updates, prototypes, beta-tests, and versioning, all of which is couched in the idiom of "improvement" and betterment, but which are in fact are prolonged exercises in planned obsolescence. This applies as much to genomically engineered food as it does to healthcare and "smart" phones. (They are "smart" precisely to the extent that they are constantly monitored from some remote location: when they "lose network," they become "stupid".) Machines are cast off no longer because they "break down" in some unsalvageable sense but because of their inability to update.

The epitome of this recto and verso of paranoia and creativity is the "hacker." Conventionally, the hacker has been defined by a kind of erotic attachment to systems: a "person who delights in having an intimate [relationship with] a system."[95] The expression "hack" first originated at MIT, and there it speaks to a particular mode of institutional power relations. The hacker is, first of all, an apprentice, not an outsider to the game. (A hack from outside the student body will be treated as a crime and handed over to the police.) A good "hack", therefore, presents an instance not of machine-breaking but of exceptional competence, a precocious will-to-mastery in the game. In effect, then, a hack pays homage to the system, which is to say both to systems-thinking and to the experts pressing for the legitimacy of the system. Well-aware of this backhanded encomium, the administrators respond to the hack by a kind of noblesse oblige wherein the "success" of the hack is confirmed by its transmutation into an event for pleasure, an infantilizing bemusement. The legitimacy of the

93 Frank Donoghue, *The Last Professors: The Corporate University and the Fate of the Humanities* (New York: Fordham University Press, 2008), 26.

94 Chomsky, "Rationality/science and post-this-or-that," 92-93.

95 The Internet Engineering Task Force's (IETF –a cooperative body that lays out standards for the Internet) anthologized RFC 1392 defines it: "[a] person who *delights* in having an intimate understanding of the internal workings of a system, computers and computer networks in particular."

experts comprises here something like an upside-down police State: the hacker is like the "state approver" who fancies himself a criminal, while the masters happily countenance the juveniles with a get-out-of-jail-free license. The hacker develops the system's ability for control by exacerbating its tolerance; the larger a system, the greater its impetus to expand its cognitive reach in order to preempt, rather direct, precisely such "unruly" moves.

The hacker is, in other words, a managerial alibi. This at least comprised the substance of Mark Zuckerberg's letter to investors for his company's first IPO titled, indicatively, "The Hacker Way":

> As part of building a strong company [at Facebook]... we have cultivated a unique culture and management approach that we call the Hacker Way. The word "hacker" has an unfairly negative connotation from being portrayed in the media as people who break into computers. In reality, hacking just means building something quickly or testing the boundaries of what can be done... Hacking is also an inherently hands-on and active discipline. Instead of debating for days whether a new idea is possible or what the best way to build something is, hackers would rather just prototype something and see what works. There's a hacker mantra that you'll hear a lot around Facebook offices: "Code wins arguments."[96]

As for those who used to be called the "workers", humanism consequently supplements economic rationality by presenting additional grounds for summary dismissal. Since being right or wrong is no longer the criteria for success, and since the absence of creativity is itself associated with oppressiveness—bureaucracies, etc.—dismissing "uncreative" types deemed no longer useful may even carry an air of aesthetic or liberal discernment. Since this is no longer repression—denial of rights—in the old sense, protest against dismissal becomes more and more ineffective, and it risks finding itself on the wrong side of the "common humanity" in whose service the system claims to operate. "Rights do not follow from hardship, but from the fact that the alleviation of hardship improves the system's performance."[97] Those driven to desert the system in remonstration against its deemed "inhumanity" do not gain critical ground over the system; quite to the contrary, as

96 Mark Zuckerberg, "The Hacker Way," *CNNMoneyTech*, February 1, 2012. *http:// money.cnn.com/2012/02/01/ technology/zuckerberg_ipo_ letter/index.htm*, accessed March 12, 2012.

97 Lyotard, T*he Postmodern Condition*, 63.
98 Thomas Kuhn, *The Structure of Scientific Revolutions*, 2nd ed. (Chicago: The University of Chicago Press, 1970), 79.
99 Lyotard, *The Postmodern Condition*, 28.

100 Risa L. Lieberwitz, "Confronting the Privatization and Commercialization of Academic Research: An Analysis of Social Implications at the Local, National, and Global Levels," in Indiana Journal of Global Legal Studies, Vol. 12, No. 1, Winter 2005, 122.

101 Quoted in Leslie, T*he Cold War and American Science*, 14.

Thomas Kuhn puts it, "inevitably he will be seen by his colleagues as only 'the carpenter who blames his tools.'"[98] The "severity" of the system towards its workers legitimizes itself in the flexibility it provides to its users (or consumers). In Chomsky's "high-modernist" universe, scorn is reserved for those less inclined to savor for themselves the benefits of enlightenment; for those unable to do so, there simply remains the question of an appropriate education that would guide them to the requisite wellsprings. In the postmodern, systems-ruled domain, no such fealty towards process or tendency towards "synthesis" is required, only an acute nose for the "misfiring" nodes where a system may breed disaffection and occasion its users to look for alternatives. One need only demonstrate the capacity to "learn up" the localized, contingent determinants of a problem.

Conceptually, the Bayh-Dole Act had the "liberal" air of restoring the fruits of epistemic labor to its workers. Passed by the US Congress in 1980, it gave U.S. universities, small businesses and non-profits control over the intellectual property resulting from federal government-funded research. The actual, not unintentional, effect was to open up competitive rentierism in epistemic production. At its very conception, the separation between basic and applied science in the Vannevar Bush report had rested not on an ontological distinction but an economic one. We have suggested above that Type 1 statements can be discerned less from their level of facticity than the institutional context in which they are produced: their "disinterestedness" in essence is reliant on a set of institutions, financed by public revenues and philanthropic donations, whose operations play out a simulacra of detachment from the market. This air of detachment extends, in effect, even to those producing pronouncements on the market such as economists; conversely, the state's cultivation of this epistemic disinterestedness wins it an "abstract," sovereign omnipotence that appears to hover over and above the play of interests. In the modernist universe, "[t]he state spends large amounts of money to enable science to pass itself off as an epic: the State's own credibility is based on that epic, which it uses to obtain the public consent its decision makers need."[99]

Bayh-Dole would signally despoil that appearance of immunity: it opened up opportunities for universities to partner with third-party (business) concerns in order to exploit the commercial possibilities from research products resulting from federal funding. "This shift of presumptive title [to intellectual property] changes the public policy priority from using public funding to expand the public domain towards private control of federally funded research." The effect was one of university administrations "expand[ing] their technology transfer offices to provide the infrastructure and personnel to 'scour [university] labs' for commercially profitable discoveries."[100] In 1962, the physicist Alvin Weinberg, who coined the term "big science," remarked that it was increasingly hard "to tell whether the Massachusetts Institute of Technology is a university with many government research laboratories appended to it or a cluster of government research laboratories with a very good educational institution attached to it."[101] Over the 1980s and 1990s, as a new cycle of competitive patenting, start-ups, and venture capital took hold, the above statement could still hold, only one needs substitute "government research laboratories" with "product design firms."

The election of Reagan to power brought to the fore the 1981 "budget-crisis." One response to this from the ascendant "supply-side" faction was a proposal to cut federal research funding, including that of the NSF. These suggestions occasioned an official revaluation of the Vannevar Bush report, through a new report tabled by the National Academy of Sciences in 1983, accompanied by a companion volume from the NSF indicatively titled *Behavioral and Social Science Research: A National Resource.* Coddled by more than three decades of government largesse, the powerful clientele of social scientists and scientists, both within government and without—the "revolving door" appointments of the national foundations ensured that these threats were felt across the profession— fought back. Reagan's appointment of less-than-respected economists to his administration did not help matters, and the social scientists, led by the aforementioned Herbert Simon, vigorously mobilized to defeat of the proposed cuts.[102] As it were, funding actually increased in the Reagan-Bush administrations (in contrast, paradoxically, to the Carter and Clinton administrations) but these early confrontations set the tone for a particularly rancorous period of relations between government and the research community. The additional, sharp decline of philanthropic funds in this period hardly relieved the researchers' perception of a pervasive threat to their erstwhile status.

As aspirants to office as the State's decision makers, the urban planners' claim to authority had signally rested on the identification of the public domain with the cloistered preserves of Big Science. The demoralization of the sciences was not a crisis for the scientists alone; it scattered the entire chain of legitimation that had arisen in its wake, one link of which was the planners' own ambitions to graduate their administrative craft to a biopolitical science. For both them and the "systems"-obsessed architects who had sculpted themselves in their image, shadow apprentices of a shadow apprenticeship as it were, Jencks' powerful use of Pruitt-Igoe would hit hard, as would the jokes, whimsies, pastiches, and outright jibes that insidiously reverted their ambitions to a pseudo-science. The heroic age of the planner, with its dolorous psychodrama of identification between science and society, was over. A cadre of architects emerged whose interests seemed less in defining the behavioral or perceptual contours of "space"– deeming this the exclusive prerogative of the market—than in dressing up the skins around its aggregate volumes. Architecture here was passed off as wrapping rather than the thing in itself, and as a string of critical voices turned to examine the profundity of that shift, Robert Venturi, Robert Stern, Michael Graves, Charles Moore, Eisenman himself, Hans Hollein, and then the "masters" themselves, James Stirling, Aldo Rossi, the MIT architects appear bewildered by the frivolity aimed at the fuzziness that they had pursued so abjectly and seriously over the decades. Chomsky's exasperation at "post-this, post-that" may well stand in for the architects' and planners' sentiments on the matter, and one sees the familiar litany directed at the turn of ideas decried for its "lack of substance," its "superficiality" and its "trendiness," which in the case of postmodernism was apt and, paradoxically, to the point.

One reason for their frustration may have been that postmodernism zeroed in on an area where linguistics and systems-theory had remained most vulnerable: semantics or the field of meaning. Thirty years of linguistics and psychological investigations, with much harrumphing about falsifiability, the robustness of models, the testability of theory, and work on grammars had purchased precious little in that area. In response to criticism, Chomsky et al. had somewhat simplistically argued that transformation rules for grammar were intrinsically linked to meaning but would only be elaborated in the fullness of time. In any case, the distinction between syntax and semantics was more a founding, even enabling, device on which the science had rested, and one could argue "meaning" was only the justificatory abyss which the linguists kicked down the road, quite like urbanists and their claims to understand poverty. Julian Beinart's estimation of Kepes and Lynch in this volume inevitably subscribes to this very dualism: "While we acknowledged Kepes' association with gestalt psychology, some of us privately wondered if it plumbed the depth of the human visual experience enough . . . (Lynch's) optimism that future studies in environmental semiotics might illuminate the meaning quandary has so far remained an unrequited hope."

And yet, by one measure, what they perhaps could not perceive was the degree to which this turn of events was in fact a culmination of the processes which they had themselves been party to. Lyotard defined postmodernism as a shift in epistemological emphasis from games of truth to "performativity-that is, the best input /output equation";[103] thus on the one hand, the cynicism of a systems' logic would trump the "optimism" of its operators in favor of an emphasis on efficacy, on the other, the unguarded realm of what the modernists called "imagination" would be pressed into the service of that valorizing exploration called creativity. If practical reason would retire truth, creativity would kill art. Was it not, then, precisely the MIT architects who had cast off aesthetics—mere "formalism" in their lexicon—to the margins, on the one hand depreciated as susceptible to idiosyncratic

102 Mata and Scheiding, "National Science Foundation Patronage of Social Science" (see fn.13).

103 Lyotard, *The Postmodern Condition*, 46.

whimsy, and on the other, as surplus to be obtained after their informational machines had accomplished the objectives of economic rationality? Was it not they who, in favor of "substance" or deep strata of reason undergirding decision making, had deplored the avant-garde's assignation to pose the irrational, in favor of a cadre of professionals who would step to the beat of the economists and bankers and real estate developers? Why was it then that *that* postmodernism, or second modernism as we have called it, was so discomfited by *this* postmodern accent on making peace with those very forces, that what they had consigned to the margins had returned as "superficial" perorations on skin? Why was a cadre who had so assiduously reflected on the structural codes and languages that conceivably knit societies and technologies together so seamlessly, so put out by the inordinate emphasis on language as an inexhaustible terrain onto itself, from whose "prison house"[104] no entity could escape? Was it not Charles Jencks, in his long campaign for semantics against syntax, who had published Aldo van Eyck and Morgenthaler's research on the Dogon huts which MIT students had so faithfully constructed on campus? Was this not the inevitable outcome of a game that they themselves sought to play, with little demonstrable purchase on the order of things even as they saw it? Why then this indignation reserved for what they deemed capitulation when they themselves had long dreamed of marching in stride with the operators of the system?

Three generations, if not more, had inculcated themselves with "expertise" premised on the idea that the validity of knowledge games within the university rested on the presumed effects these could have on the decision-making games affecting "society." As opposed to the everyday pragmatism of society's "natives"—with whom they presumed both identification and solidarity—the superiority of their own, expert pragmatism had presumed to rest on their virtuosic ability to synthesize "formal universals" from the empirical data whose processing on the other hand they dreamed of consigning to machines. The postmodernism of Bayh-Dole and the spirit it embodied decimated the "modernist consensus" of the postwar: the university would no longer remain a privileged node within the decision-making games that affected the relationship of market to society. As the research and development universe scattered into indeterminate miscegenation

104 See Fredric Jameson, *The Prison-House of Language: A Critical Account of Structuralism and Russian Formalism* (Princeton: Princeton University Press, 1972).

105 Manuel Castells, *Technopoles of the World: The Making of 21st Century Industrial Complexes* (New York: Routledge, 1994).

106 Charles Jencks, *The Language of Post-Modern Architecture*, 4th ed. (New York: Rizzoli, 1977, 1984), 42.

between government stimulus, bank and venture capital, private enterprise, and university laboratories, the erstwhile monopolies accorded to knowledge production in the university would itself come under scrutiny for its inefficiencies. Rather, the value of the research-academic complex would be recouped in providing stimulus for real estate: as urban tethers for technology-intensive "technopoles"[105] whose success would be measured through their competition with other aspirant conurbations aspiring to the same status. If it was this postmodernism that would in actuality delegitimize the "second modernism" of the experts, it was one with which they were least inclined to resist given their own, deeply-held emphasis on pragmatic outcomes. It was after all they who had cast the role of the architect in the shadow of "creative innovation."

If on the other hand, if the exasperation of the experts was directed solely at those that called themselves postmodernists and those that they could accuse of being so, this speaks also to their sudden precariousness in the knowledge games within the university. It had been the postmodernist argument that no uncoercive agreements could be reached on the relationship of form to content, and that the recourse to formal universals marked not much else than a gambit for power in a condition of irreducible cognitive conflict. As Jencks put it, "The general point then is that code restrictions based on learning and culture guide a reading, and that there are multiple codes, some of which may be in conflict across subcultures."[106] With that move, the status of expert speech had been more or less relegated to a self-interested patois; for a cadre who had themselves long declaimed the "structural softness" of disinterested knowledge as an antiquated hangover, therein, perhaps, lay the rub.

The Duck-Rabbit Illusion.
From Joseph Jastrow,
The Mind's Eye, (New
York: Popular Science
Publication Co., 1872).

Humanities

REINHOLD MARTIN

The MIT Chapel
An Interdiscursive History

We begin on the afternoon of 31 March, 1949, in MIT's newly completed athletic facility, the Rockwell Cage, which had been designed by two members of the architecture faculty, Lawrence Anderson and Herbert Beckwith, and built of repurposed wartime aircraft hangars. The occasion is a two-day convocation held there to celebrate the inauguration of MIT's tenth president, James R. Killian. The architectural historian John Ely Burchard, who had been appointed Dean of Humanities in 1948, presides over the event and will later edit the published proceedings. The inaugural convocation begins with an invocation addressed to "God of our fathers" and delivered by Everett M. Baker, a Unitarian minister who had become MIT's Dean of Students in 1947.[1] In itself this is not unusual, though it does remind us of the non-secular origins of higher education in the United States.

More notable was the subject matter addressed by the pre-inaugural convocation itself, which explored "the social implications of scientific progress." Burchard's annotated collection of the presentations reveals a bias, not limited to its editor, toward "spiritual" matters as they impinge on scientific and technological research and education, particularly in the aftermath of the world war. Such matters were most explicitly addressed in a panel on "Science, Materialism, and the Human Spirit," which featured the philosopher and theologian Julius Seelye Bixler, the physicist Percy W. Bridgman, the Thomist philosopher Jacques Maritain, and the philosopher Walter Terence Stace. In his opening remarks for the convocation, Burchard suggested that this panel would also address, albeit indirectly, "the meaning of contemporary art." Given Burchard's vocation as an architectural historian, and other writings of his from the period, we can assume that "contemporary art" included architecture. Hanging over all of this was what Burchard called "the mushroom cloud of 1945," though his worries over the possibility of technologically-enabled thought control drew greater attention in press coverage of the event.[2]

Interior of Chapel
showing altar, 1957, MIT.
Photo: Ernest Hill.

Note: I am grateful to Stephanie Tuerk for her invaluable assistance with the research for this essay.

1 John Ely Burchard, ed. *Mid-Century: The Social Implications of Scientific Progress* (Cambridge, MA.: The Technology Press and Massachusetts Institute of Technology, 1950), 3.
2 Ibid., 8-10, 6.

Here already are the discursive figures within which the MIT chapel, which was completed in 1955, was inscribed. In 1938, William Welles Bosworth, the architect of the main campus, had in fact projected a campus chapel in the vicinity of the President's House on Memorial Drive. To the two domes that surmounted the central academic complex constructed between 1915 and 1930,[3] Bosworth's design would have added another neoclassical domed structure echoing that of McKim, Mead, and White's Low Library at Columbia University (1898). By the time Bosworth made this proposal, a number of monumental chapels had been built on campuses across the country, often in the recently formulated "collegiate Gothic." Other neoclassical American campus plans, including Columbia's, had also successfully integrated chapels into their fabrics, with the notable exception of Thomas Jefferson's University of Virginia, which added a neo-Gothic chapel beyond the perimeter of its colonnaded lawn in 1889. As evidenced even by Bosworth's unbuilt 1938 proposal, the chapel therefore came late to MIT, almost literally as an afterthought which awaited a subtle but important epistemological realignment, rather than as the fulfillment of a preordained plan.

As built, the chapel was part of an ensemble designed by Eero Saarinen and Associates, with the collaboration of the Boston architect Bruce Adams, that included the domed Kresge auditorium. The ensemble occupies an open site just across Massachusetts Avenue from the domed entrance to Building 7, and by extension the system of corridors which run through the main academic complex. Saarinen also projected a linear student center at the northern edge of the site and included it in his early plans; however, that building was eventually designed by MIT faculty member Eduardo Catalano and completed in 1965.

The small cylindrical brick chapel, which seats about 100, stands just slightly off-axis with the much larger auditorium, the top surface of which consists of one-eighth of a sphere connected to the ground only at its three apexes. Where the auditorium lobby opens onto the surrounding plaza with a transparent skin stretching down from the concrete roof shell, the chapel is separated from the plaza by a narrow, circular moat, across which spans an enclosed entry passerelle that connects the cylinder to a small rectangular service wing. As we shall see later, there are a number of formal and technical precedents and

3 On Bosworth's designs for the MIT campus, see Mark Jarzombek, *Designing MIT: Bosworth's New Tech* (Boston: Northeastern University Press, 2004); Jarzombek discusses the chapel proposal on p. 112. For a more general contextualiation of college and university chapels in the history of campus planning in the United States, see Paul Venable Turner, *Campus: An American Planning Tradition* (New York: The Architectural History Foundation and MIT Press, 1984).

accompaniments to both the auditorium and the chapel within the work of the Saarinen firm that help us situate the two buildings genealogically. However, it is the unresolved and ultimately aporetic relationship between the two otherwise distinct architectural types, the secular auditorium and the interdenominational chapel, that gives each its specific meaning.

As we shall also see, in both buildings this meaning is inflected by the apparently anomalous character of the chapel, to which the historical sketch that follows here is principally dedicated.[4] This overdetermination becomes intelligible only when the extant documentation is assembled in a manner that emphasizes the distinct yet overlapping spheres of discourse to which the chapel belongs: institutional, social, techno-scientific, and aesthetic. By reconstructing its history as a history of the partial overlap of these

MIT Convocation, looking to Killian Court from Building 10, MIT, 1949. Photo: William Porter.

4 The aporias discussed below are heightened by the chapel's relationship to scientific and technological education. For a comparison of Saarinen's MIT chapel and Ludwig Mies van der Rohe's chapel for the Illinois Institute of Technology (1952) in this context, see Margaret M. Grubiak, "Educating the

Moral Scientist: The Chapels at I.I.T. and M.I.T.," *Arris: Journal of the Southeast Chapter of the Society of Architectural Historians* 18 (2007): 1-14. Grubiak's thoroughly documented account accepts the category of the "moral scientist" conditioned by theology as an a priori against which to

evaluate the two buildings, and modern architecture in general, for their capacity to convey religious meaning as a counterbalance to scientific rationality.

spheres, we will be able to better understand the larger relationship between architectural discourse and practice and the historical "contexts" in which it takes shape. My hope is that this can be read as an object lesson in interdiscursivity that, if extrapolated back outward in any one of its several directions, disrupts but also complements those narratives concerning the secular character of modernity and by extension, of "enlightenment," which account for the devastations of the twentieth century by emphasizing the mythologization of technoscientific rationality. Our small historical sketch does just the opposite; it emphasizes the instrumental character of sacral or spiritual discourse and practice at a moment when modernity's two ideological poles, the rational and the spiritual, were in the process of trading places.

Returning to the MIT presidential inaugural of 1949 we note its humanistic overtones, which can be readily if not fully explained as a response to the traumas of war. Since its inception in the 1860s, MIT had made little room in its curriculum for what eighteenth and early nineteenth century pedagogy called "moral philosophy," a branch of humanistic learning descended from theology that proposed a universal ethics compatible with Christianity. Nor was a curricular or cultural role originally allotted to the newly defined "humanities," which by the turn of the century had emerged out of classical learning to supplant religious doctrine as a core component of the modern liberal curriculum.[5] Only in 1932 was a Division of Humanities created at MIT, with its mandate gradually expanded in the 1940s as faculty and administrators began to plan the Institute's postwar mission. The war itself was manifestly a turning point, and in 1947 a "Committee on Educational Survey" was set up to reevaluate curricular priorities in "a new era emerging from social upheaval and the disasters" brought on by the conflict.[6] Recognizing that "the world of 1940 is not the world of 1950," the committee observed in the foreword to their report, which appeared in December 1949 (nine months after Killian's inauguration) that "the release of nuclear energy is having a profound effect upon the course of human events, but other forces are also at work on society. They were beginning to modify our way of life long before the atomic bomb."[7] As a corrective, the report recommended broadening the Institute's curriculum especially at the undergraduate level, to require more thorough exposure to nonspecialized knowledge, particularly in the humanities.[8]

5 On "moral philosophy" and higher education in the American colonies and early republic, see George M. Marsden, *The Soul of the American University: From Protestant Establishment to Established Nonbelief* (New York: Oxford University Press, 1994), 50-64. On the role of the humanities, see

Jon H. Roberts and James Turner, *The Sacred and the Secular University* (Princeton: Princeton University Press, 2000), 75ff.

6 Ronald H. Robnett, C. Richard Soderberg, Julias A. Stratton, John R. Loofbourow, Warren K. Lewis, *Report of the Committee on Educational Survey to the Faculty of the*

Massachusetts Institute of Technology (Cambridge, MA: The Technology Press, 1949). http://libraries.mit.edu/archives/mithistory/pdf/lewis.pdf, 3.

7 Ibid., 4.

8 As the report puts it: "In the past [during which vocational training was unduly emphasized], the humanities

have necessarily been service fields concerned primarily with instruction at the elementary level. Now, however, there is a growing concern with human and social problems, an increased awareness of the interplay between science and technology on the one hand and the conduct of human affairs on the other,

Noting that steps taken in this direction by the administration of Karl T. Compton, president of MIT from 1930-1948, were interrupted by the war, the report asserted that a broadened educational mission at MIT would entail greater leadership in three primary areas in addition to engineering: the natural sciences, the humanities and social sciences, and architecture and planning.[9] The report also anticipated the conditions of 1950 when it foresaw "great opportunities for the field of architecture and planning at M.I.T., where it can be closely associated with engineering and science on the one hand and with the investigation of social and cultural problems related to science and technology on the other." Correspondingly, it proposed that architecture be more fully integrated into the Institute, where, as with the humanities, exposure to its traditions would expand the "cultural and general backgrounds" of engineers and scientists.[10] Much more specifically, however, the report recommended establishing a fourth school alongside the Schools of Engineering, Science, and Architecture and Planning: a School of Humanities and Social Science. The new School was intended as an integrated academic unit that would offer both undergraduate and graduate education based on current offerings in economics and other social sciences, history, modern languages and literature, and (somewhat incongruously) business and engineering administration.[11]

Largely as a result of this report, by the time of the 1949 inaugural convocation Burchard was poised to become (in 1950) the Institute's first Dean of Humanities and Social Studies, responsible for an independent school on equal footing with the scientific and professional schools.[12] In fact, during the first evening of that convocation Burchard's visibly anomalous position was noted by the event's keynote speaker, Sir Winston Churchill. Addressing an aside to Compton, the Institute's outgoing president, Churchill declared: "How right you are, Dr. Compton, in this great institution of technical study and achievement, to keep a Dean of Humanities and give him so commanding a part to play in your discussions! No technical knowledge can outweigh knowledge of the humanities in the gaining of which philosophy and history walk hand in hand."[13] But for our purposes, the passage immediately following this one in Churchill's speech is more revealing still. Several lines on, he suggests:

and an awakened realization of the fruitfulness of the techniques of the natural sciences in the study of human and social problems. We believe that these trends now make possible the study of the humanities and social sciences at advanced professional levels in the environment of a technological institution," Ibid., 27.

9 Although architecture had been taught at MIT since 1865, the first half of the twentieth century suffered from what the report politely calls an "emphasis on the aesthetic" that alienated a Beaux-Arts derived curriculum from an institutional milieu dominated by engineering. With the advent of modernism, this was no longer true. Thus the statement that "architecture as presently constituted derives much of its strength from the areas of engineering and science" would not have drawn much objection even in 1940.

10 *Report of the Committee on Educational Survey*, 43.
11 Ibid., 40-44.
12 Though Burchard was not a member of the Committee on Educational Survey, he did sit on an auxiliary committee set up to concentrate on the details of "providing undergraduates at the Institute with

James R. Killian Jr. presents a lectureship to Sir Winston
Churchill, Keynote Speaker at the MIT Convocation in
1949. Behind Churchill, *left to right*, are Karl T. Compton,
John E. Burchard, and Governor Paul A. Dever.

previous page, Model of the MIT Chapel and Kresge
Auditorium. Photo: Richard Shirk.

The problems of victory may be even more baffling than those of defeat. However much the conditions change, the supreme question is how we live and grow and bloom and die, and how far each human life conforms to standards which are not wholly related to space or time.

And here I speak not only to those who enjoy the blessings and consolation of revealed religion, but also to those who face the mysteries of human destiny alone. I say that the flame of Christian ethics is still our highest guide. To guard and cherish it is our first interest, both spiritually and materially. The fulfillment of Spiritual duty in our daily life is vital to our survival.[14]

The implications of this passage were apparently not lost on MIT's administrators, including its new president. Over the next few years, in the discourse surrounding the Kresge auditorium and chapel, Killian would repeatedly cite Churchill's phrase, "the flame of Christian ethics," to situate the new MIT chapel in the institutional context for which it was conceived. Churchill had, in effect, connected the dots in advance by associating the presence of a Dean of Humanities at a technical institute with the perceived need to attend to the "Spiritual duty" of all citizens in a nuclear age. Saarinen's buildings would add another set of statements to this developing discourse, while giving occasion for the repetition of others.

But we are still in the Rockwell Cage, on 31 March 1949. Churchill devoted the remainder of his speech to politics, building in crescendo to a characteristically dramatic *mise-en-scène*:

I must not conceal from you tonight the truth as I see it. It is certain that Europe would have been communized like Czechoslovakia, and London under bombardment some time ago but for the deterrence of the Atomic Bomb in hands of the United States.[15]

In that sense, just four months before the first successful Soviet atomic test, what Burchard had called in his opening remarks the "mushroom cloud of 1945" cast its shadow over the entire event. And there was no one in the room more suited than MIT's Dean of Humanities to resolve its contradictions on a campus newly populated with

broader and more effective cultural training," called the Committee on General Education (Ibid., 83). That committee's report, which is appended to that of its sponsoring entity, interprets the role of the humanities in a technical education more broadly still, recommending a series of

curricular reforms that build on the reorganization of humanities teaching at the Institute that began when a four-year humanities and social science requirement for all undergraduates was instituted for in 1944.

13 Sir Winston Churchill, "The Twentieth Century," in Burchard, ed. *Mid-Century: The Social Implications of Scientific Progress*, 60-61. In his otherwise enthusiastic annotations to the transcription, Burchard regretfully noted that most newspaper accounts of the speech had concentrated

on Churchill's subsequent remarks on nuclear armament rather than on the importance of humanistic knowledge (61).
14 Ibid., 62-63.
15 Ibid., 67.

returning veterans whose general education would now be extended, symbolically at least, toward those "spiritual matters" which science and technology, on their own, had been judged incapable of addressing.

This is not merely a way of setting the stage, so to speak, for the entry of Saarinen's strange pair of buildings onto the MIT scene. Since if anything, they were late arrivals to this scene, which by 1955 (the date of their completion) had been preoccupied for over a decade with smoothing over the roughest edges of technoscience with a humanistic polish. But nor is architecture here a mere mechanical expression of some pre-existing institutional ideology; it is part of a conversation that had been going on for some time. To get a better feel for this, we need to change venues and times, and move just south from the Rockwell Cage into the newly completed Kresge auditorium where, on 8 May 1955, the auditorium and the not-quite-complete chapel were dedicated.

Somewhat unwillingly, Burchard had organized the event, which was again (though not atypically) framed in religious terms. It began with an invocation by Rabbi Herman Pollack, advisor to the MIT Hillel Foundation, was punctuated by an affirmation by the Reverend Theodore P. Ferris, Rector of Trinity Church, Boston, and ended with a benediction delivered by Father Edward J. Nugent, Chaplain to the Technology Catholic Club.[16] If this combination emphasized the "nondenominational" (i.e. Judeo-Christian) program for the chapel (particularly resonant in the aftermath of the Holocaust), it also underlined an apparent conflict physicalized in the ambiguous space that separated Saarinen's brick cylinder from the concrete-domed auditorium. This was the conflict between secular and religious symbolization, and between the gathering of secular communities (in the auditorium) and the gathering of religious ones (around the chapel). This conflict shadows both buildings and their discourse. And just as Saarinen's site planning attempted to resolve it by staging, unsuccessfully, a compositional equilibrium in which the two elements would hang suspended, the dedication ceremony replayed the discrepancy between them in each of its parts.

16 "Dedication of the Kresge Auditorium and the M.I.T. Chapel, Massachusetts Institute of Technology, May 8, 1955," Karl T. Compton and James R. Killian Administrations (1930-1959), Records, 1930-1959; Institute Archives and Special Collections, Massachusetts Institute of Technology

(hereafter MIT Archives AC004), Box 131, Folder 10.
17 John E. Burchard to James R. Killian, Confidential report to President Killian, Subject: Aaron Copland, 29 December 1953, MIT Archives, Box 131, Folder 6.

18 James R. Killian, "Our Religious Program," in "Dedication of the Kresge Auditorium and the M.I.T. Chapel," n.p.

19 John E. Burchard, Q.E.D: M.I.T. in World War II (New York: Wiley, 1948).
20 See Julius A. Stratton, "Harold Eugene Edgerton (April 6, 1903-January 4, 1990)," Proceedings of the American Philosophical Society 135, n. 3 (1991): 447-448.

For example, at Burchard's suggestion the composer Aaron Copland was commissioned to prepare an overture suited to the occasion. Apparently in response to concerns regarding Copland's political affiliations, Burchard had compiled a confidential background check that contextualized Copland's testimony in 1953 before the Permanent Subcommittee on Investigations headed by Senator Joseph McCarthy.[17] Having been judged appropriate to represent the Institute publicly, Copland composed "Canticle of Freedom," a choral work that adapted the text of *The Brus* (1375) by the Scots poet John Barbour, which celebrated the Scottish wars of independence with England in the thirteenth and fourteenth centuries. The refrain—"Ah Freedom is a noble thing!"—and the orchestral accompaniment were ambiguous enough, and yet (during the McCarthy period) they were also precise enough to elicit a pious equivalence between religious "tolerance" and secular, political liberty. Such an equivalence was reinforced elsewhere in the event's rhetoric; indeed, its thematization in every aspect of the event, including the architecture itself, elevated a hackneyed formula to the status of a metaphysical axiom, in which the unity of secular and religious purpose acquired a distinctly theological cast.

This theologization parallels Killian's repeated citation of Churchill's 1949 speech. In remarks that were printed in the dedication pamphlet, it was as if Killian, whose presidency had been inaugurated with the symbolic, moral authority that Churchill's name bore after the war, was calling upon the full force of this authority when he cited Churchill's phrase, "the flame of Christian ethics." Killian did this not only to name MIT's "nondenominational" character, but also to name a principle that

> has lighted the institution throughout its history and given it direction and spirit. As a consequence we have a community held together by a humane and tolerant spirit of mediation, reconciliation and reverence for the individual, a community governed by a passion for truth, freedom of inquiry and a preoccupation with ideal aims. We have a community generous in its opportunities to live and let live; a community where men of many faiths and backgrounds are free to interact on each other; a community committed to the ideals of professional service, of ministering to the public, of advancing learning and creating beauty.
>
> These are the spiritual bonds that hold together our society of scholars. Our developing spiritual program, to be valid, must embrace them, exalt them and be consonant with the environment they have created.[18]

This was the same society of scholars whose wartime work Burchard himself had documented in a recently published book, *Q.E.D: M.I.T. in World War II* (1948).[19] Among them was Harold (Doc) Edgerton, an engineer who had invented stroboscopic photography. In 1947, Edgerton, together with two former MIT graduate students, set up the consulting firm of Edgerton, Germeshausen, and Grier to contract with the military on the design of

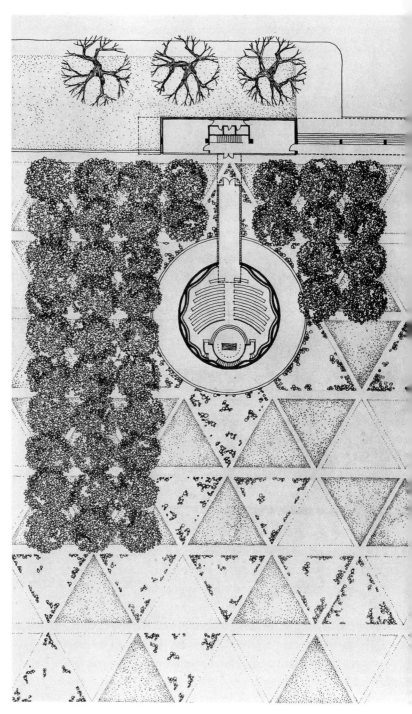

Eero Saarinen &
Associates, drawing for
Kresge Auditorium shows
the near-final scheme
of the cylindrical brick
chapel and three-pronged
auditorium positioned
on a diagonally-gridded
plaza, 1952.

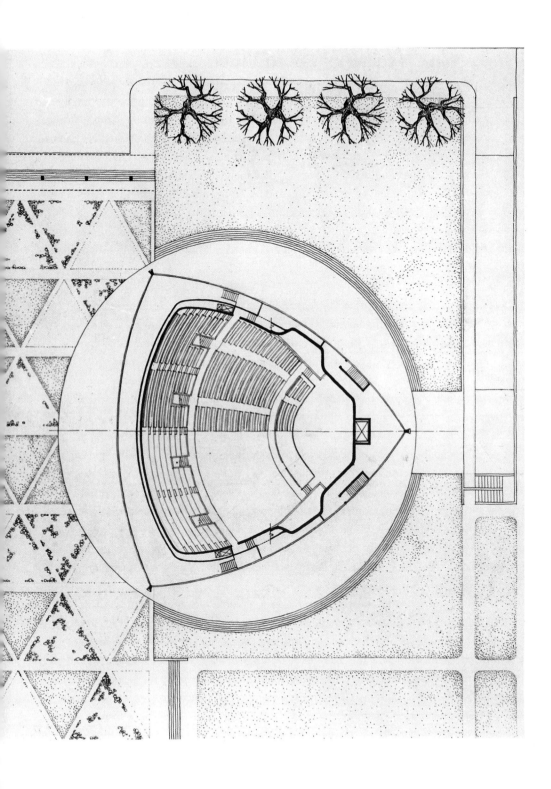

firing mechanisms for atomic bomb tests, adapting the high-speed photography techniques that they had developed during the war.[20] MIT, seeking to rebalance sponsored research with educational autonomy (another subject of the 1949 curricular report), had begun to recommend that faculty take on such work independently rather than through the Institute. In this case, the result was not only Edgerton's high-speed photographs of what we can call "the mushroom cloud of 1952" (the hydrogen bomb), but also the firing mechanism for the bomb itself. Rather than suggesting, however, that such work and the images it produced dismembered the academic community idealized by Killian into a cadre of guns for hire, the evidence we have compiled thus far suggests that it did just the opposite: it produced an instrumentally invaluable phantasm—the metaphysical union of the sacred with the secular under the sign of the bomb—in an environment previously thought to have been dominated by purely secular, instrumental reason.

To investigate further, we return to the Kresge auditorium that rainy Sunday afternoon in May 1955. The keynote speaker for the dedication ceremony was Eelco Nicolaas van Kleffens, the Netherlands minister to Portugal and President of the General Assembly of the United Nations. Van Kleffens was actually Killian's (and probably also Burchard's) third choice for keynote speaker, after *New Yorker* essayist E.B. White and the nuclear physicist and Washington University chancellor Arthur Compton, both of whom declined. In his consecutive letters of invitation to all three, Killian suggested that the dedicatory exercises would "emphasize the importance of human values and the 'human use of human beings.'" This last phrase directly quoted the title of a popular book published in 1950 by the MIT mathematician and originator of cybernetics, Norbert Wiener, an association that would have resonated with the respective addressees. Nor would the apparent conflict between secular and religious symbolization have been missed, prompting a preemptive apology from Killian that "[e]ven though we are dedicating a chapel along with the auditorium, we do not plan a conventional religious occasion but instead an academic festival which will stress our dedication here to those things which sustain and enrich the human spirit."[21]

Van Kleffens complied with a workmanlike speech, notable mainly for its repetition of themes that by then had been thoroughly developed in the MIT discourse. Praising the "Verities which are taught by religion," van Kleffens pleaded: "Let the new chapel, and also the auditorium, remain a constant warning that, just as technology cannot exhaust truth, it is not qualified, and therefore should not attempt, to monopolize belief."[22] He also joined his hosts in linking religion with the study of the humanities as he acknowledged MIT's recent investment in humanistic education as a source of "measure" and "reason" when applied to the "advanced technology [that] has found the means to split or fuse nuclei of certain atoms."[23] Reflecting further on the Institute's move to implement a religious program, van Kleffens celebrated the choice of a (nominally) "nondenominational" monument over a "state religion." This, said the UN official, was "Americanism at its best,"

an expression of "that broad tolerance which is one of the mainstays of your great Nation."
Again religious "tolerance" was conjoined with the "free" spirit of scientific inquiry: "We
breathe here the fresh, unstifled air of free thought, free inquiry, free expression, and we
are face to face with the care of scientific liberty, the essence of our Western tradition."[24]
This was the same sentiment that Copland's overture had promulgated, once its composer
had, unbeknownst to him, been granted the liberty to do so on the basis of a background
check conducted by Burchard, MIT's loyal custodian of the humanities.

In delivering this homily on the reciprocity of science, religion, and Cold War politics, van
Kleffens cited at length Killian's statement on religion, formulated in his presidential report
of 1954 and included in the dedication pamphlet, which had also been published separately
as a pamphlet titled "A Religious Program for the Massachusetts Institute of Technology."
Killian's 1954 report was one outcome of the curricular reorientation that we have already
noted, and it restated many of the programs elaborated by the Committee on Educational
Survey, including that of an enhanced commitment to general as well as professional
education. It is also, with respect to the discursive realignment of secular and religious
knowledge and practice, perhaps the most synthetic statement made by the Institute in
the aftermath of the war.[25] Though he had included it in earlier drafts, Killian only referred
to Churchill's phrase "the flame of Christian ethics" in the version of this report that was
excerpted in the dedication pamphlet and not in the published report itself.[26] Another
version of these remarks also appeared, in abbreviated form and without the Churchill
reference, in another, undated pamphlet titled "Religion at MIT," which was illustrated with
an interior photograph of the new chapel.[27]

These are the kinds of discursive networks into which Saarinen's two buildings were woven
even before they were complete, with their competing meanings produced and altered
at every step along the way. A particularly subtle instance of this is given in an exchange
between Killian and his new Dean of Students, William Speer, regarding an early draft of
Killian's statement on religion at MIT, titled "The Chapel and Its Use." Speer responded
favorably to the draft, which was substantially the same as the printed version. He took
issue, however, with a line from Killian's text that originally read: "In the twentieth century,

21 James R. Killian to E.
B. White 28 October 1954;
Killian to Arthur H. Compton
30 November 1954; Killian
to Eelco N. van Kleffens,
31 December 1954; MIT
Archives AC004, Box 131,
Folder 7.

22 Eelco N. van Kleffens,
"The Dedicatory Address," *The
Technology Review* 57, n. 8
(June 1955): 404.
23 Ibid., 405.
24 Ibid.

25 In his 1954 report, Killian
wrote: "…an institution
of science may well be an
environment favorable to
deeper spiritual insights.
More important than its
practical achievements are
the spiritual contributions of
science, its emphasis on the
importance of truth and of
the value of brotherhood and

its revelation of the beauty,
the order and the wonder of
the universe. Through these
contributions it shares with
the great faiths opportunities
for furthering man's spiritual
understanding; and creative
minds and spirits, availing
themselves of the resources
of both science and religion,
may advance men's search for

Sebastian S. Kresge, *left*, delivers scroll to J.R. Killian
Jr. at the dedication of the Kresge auditorium and
the MIT Chapel in May, 1955. From MIT *Technology
Review*, June 1955.

an institution of science may well be an environment especially conducive to new spiritual
insights and new religious syntheses."[28] Speer observed that (Christian) theologians might
interpret this statement as implying "that M.I.T. believes that science is going to provide
something necessary for man's salvation which God has not already supplied in the revelation
of himself in Christ." He therefore suggested changing "new spiritual insights and new
religious syntheses" to "deeper spiritual insights," which is the phrasing that Killian ultimately
adopted.[29] A technical matter, perhaps, but one that draws the fine line on which the MIT
chapel was balanced, while also reflecting the actual, quasi-political pressure that the self-
described "secular" Institute was under to incorporate religion in some formal way into its
campus. Metonymic discourse, in which the complex and often contradictory intentions of
the institution as a whole are collapsed into the statements of its representatives, circulates
and recirculates through the course of the project, culminating, in this instance, in a collection
of Killian's statements on religion at MIT upon the project's completion, but now addressed,
in a religious publication, to the same audience imagined in the above exchange.[30]

virtue and understanding with
new vigor and in new ways.
The chapel is in this sense but
a part of a broader spiritual
program long evolving at
the Institute. The future
direction and method of this
program must rest upon
community acceptance and
desire, and coordinate with
our developing program in

the humanities and social
studies. It should grow
naturally out of the spiritual
values which are inherent
in our institution." James R.
Killian, "A Religious Program
for the Massachusetts
Institute of Technology: A
Statement by Dr. James R.
Killian, Jr.," in *Annual Report
of the President of the*

*Massachusetts Institute of
Technology, 1954*, n.p.; MIT
Archives AC004, Box 131,
Folder 7.
26 Killian had actually added
this passage to another,
undated draft of his 1954
presidential report, "The
Chapel and Its Use" (MIT
Archives AC004, Box 131,
Folder 7, p. 3), and then

apparently deleted it. It did
not appear in the report's
final published version, but it
reappeared in the dedication
program for the auditorium
and chapel.
27 "Religion at M.I.T.," n.d.,
n.p.; MIT Archives AC004,
Box 131, Folder 10.
28 Killian, "The Chapel and
Its Use," 3.

A central document in this process was the application made by the Institute in April of 1950 to the Kresge Foundation "in support of a program in Development of Citizenship and Christian Character."[31] The Kresge Foundation, based in Detroit under the leadership of the entrepreneur Sebastian S. Kresge, was well known for its support of religious and educational institutions.[32] The MIT proposal was signed by former president Karl Compton, who was now serving as Chairman of the MIT Corporation, indicating continuity in the endeavor between successive MIT administrations across the war years. It was preceded about a month earlier by a rather urgent memorandum from the MIT Development Office to the recently inaugurated President Killian (who had previously served as Compton's vice president) which stated with conviction that "the proposal submitted to the Kresge Foundation should be for a project concerning humanities and character building. Mr. Kresge is not interested in buildings or equipment for the technical side of M.I.T."[33]

In probable recognition of this preference, the application submitted by MIT proposed a "Kresge School of Human Relations, which would enrich the existing program of technological education by increased emphasis on humanities, social sciences, character building activities, and religion."[34] Compton's cover letter to the application went on to refer to the 1949 report by the Committee on Educational Survey, which was then under internal review and had not yet been made public. He summarized the report's basic arguments, including its recommendation for a new School of Humanities and Social Sciences, and indicated that although some of the material needs for such an initiative were addressed in MIT's current development campaign, substantially greater funding would be required to support professorships, library acquisitions, and an "Auditorium-Chapel building."[35]

The application prospectus reproduces much of the language of the Committee on Educational Survey's report, which it sets against the background of MIT's overall effort, begun in 1944, to reassess its curriculum and needs in anticipation of the war's end. Four categories emphasized by this initial study are listed: enhanced resources to continue the advanced scientific research concentrated by the war; the opening of a new library (the Hayden Memorial Library, designed by Voorhees, Walker, Foley, and Smith, and supported by the Charles Hayden Foundation) and the founding of the Division of Humanities; increased

29 William Speer to James R. Killian, 29 July 1954, MIT Archives AC004, Box 131, Folder 7. Speer's emendations appear on the marked-up copy of Killian's text, referenced above.

30 James R. Killian, Jr., "The Scientist in the Community, the Classroom, the Chapel," *The Christian Register*

(January 1956): 10-11, 29; and "An Atmosphere of Religious Freedom," 12-13, 32.

31 "An Application to the Kresge Foundation from the Massachusetts Institute of Technology in Support of a Program in Development of Citizenship and Christian Character," 11 April 1950; MIT Archives AC004, Box 131,

Folder 12.

32 An internal MIT document summarizes the purpose of the Kresge Foundation as being the "promotion of eleemosynary, philanthropic and charitable mean of any and all of the means of human progress, whether they be for the benefit of religious, charitable,

benevolent or educational institutions or public benefaction of whatever name or nature." In "The Kresge Foundation," n.d.; MIT Archives AC004, Box 131, Folder 12. Killian had apparently first approached Kresge's son, who served as the foundation's vice president, in personal

endowment; and improvements in student life and extracurricular activities. This framework formed the basis for a $20 million development effort, which Compton admits had been more successful in raising funds from industrial sources in expectation of a technological "quid pro quo," than it had in supporting the "spiritual" components of the long-term program.[36]

MIT therefore proposed that the Kresge Foundation especially consider supporting those activities dedicated to "Education for Better Character and Citizenship" through a combination of 1) formal study within the new School of Human Relations, 2) endowed lectures similar to those currently arranged by Burchard on an ad hoc basis as Dean of Humanities, and 3) extracurricular activities (including religious ones). Specific requests were made for $2 million for endowed professorships in the humanities and social sciences; $250,000 for library acquisitions related to these fields; $100,000 for visiting lecturers; and $750,000 for the construction of an Auditorium-Chapel with an estimated seating capacity of 1,200. Plans are also mentioned for separating the smaller chapel (seating approximately 100), from the larger auditorium "which, though less distinctively religious in atmosphere, could be used for larger religious gatherings with some advantage of common facilities."[37]

But it was the chapel, and not the larger and more public auditorium or the expensive professorships, which carried the symbolic burden of the proposal, thus blending the secular and religious symbolizations associated with the two buildings, as well as the forms of academic community they supported. This impression is reinforced in the application by a reference to the mandate handed to MIT's recently appointed Dean of Students, Everett M. Baker who, as the application notes, was an ordained Protestant minister:

> The particular challenge which was put up to him, when the position was first discussed with him, was to develop a program and an attitude at M.I.T. which could supplement the natural interest of our students in materialistic things by an increasing attention to environment and activities which would develop civic responsibility and moral character.[38]

correspondence in late 1949, James R. Killian to Stanley S. Kresge, 7 November 1949, MIT Archives AC004, Box 131, Folder 4.

33 L. F. Lybarger to James R. Killian, Killian, 2 March 1950; MIT Archives AC004, Box 131, Folder 12.

34 Karl T. Compton to The Trustees of the Kresge

Foundation (cover letter to Kresge application), 11 April 1950, MIT Archives AC004, Box 131, Folder 12.

35 Ibid.

36 "Enclosure to Application to the Kresge Foundation from The Massachusetts Institute of Technology (Statement of Background and Details)," 8; MIT Archives

AC004, Box 131, Folder 12.

37 Ibid., 21.

38 Ibid., 18.

Two years earlier, in 1948, Baker had communicated to (then vice president) Killian a buildup of faculty and student requests for a campus chapel, which Baker recommended be located in some existing room on campus, possibly in proximity to the library's books on religion and philosophy. After Killian suggested that Baker discuss the chapel idea with Burchard and others, Baker replied with a memorandum, written in December 1949 to now-President Killian. This memorandum outlined "The Need for a Chapel Auditorium" several months prior to the Kresge proposal. In recommending that the Institute build an 1200-seat auditorium that contained within it a 75-seat chapel, Baker struck a chord that would resonate through the discourse: "It is difficult to think of America without the village church and the meeting house. It is equally difficult to imagine M.I.T. of tomorrow fulfilling its many responsibilities to our nation and our world without its chapel and its meeting house."[39] He followed this memorandum with another, more formal set of specifications for the auditorium chapel. Although these documents appeared three months after the application to the Kresge Foundation was submitted, it is most likely that the details of the request to Kresge reflected the ongoing discussions on the campus, coordinated and possibly encouraged by Baker, around the need for a combined auditorium/chapel.[40]

On 1 July 1950, Killian announced a $1,500,0000 grant from the Kresge Foundation for a "meeting house" (the image first conjured by Baker) dedicated to public gatherings and religious convocations.[41] In the meantime, Burchard had been preparing plans for a School of Humanities and Social Sciences, apparently in relation to the Kresge proposal. He summarized the details in a memorandum of 2 June 1950 that also reproduces the tensions between secular and religious educational activities inherent in the figure of the "meeting house" (which Baker had initially conjoined with a "village church") and in the hybrid auditorium/chapel. These appear most clearly in a jurisdictional distinction, wherein Burchard's new School of the Humanities would be responsible for the curricular dimensions of the enhanced spiritual education of MIT students, including courses in comparative religion, leaving the administration of extracurricular activities, including those of the chapel, to the Dean of Students (a post that Baker vacated in 1950).[42] Though this is easily understood as a conventional division of labor, the results of the Kresge grant application left Burchard's new school empty-handed. Instead, the entire $1,500,000 grant

39 Everett M. Baker, "Memorandum to James R. Killian Re: The Need for a Chapel Auditorium," 3; MIT Archives AC004, Box 131, Folder 5.

40 Everett M. Baker, "Specifications for Auditorium-Chapel for M.I.T.," 17 July 1950, MIT Archives AC004, Box 131, Folder 5. Although the Kresge proposal suggested two separate buildings, Baker's memo still contemplates a single building, but now with a separate entrance for the chapel. It also seems from this document that the site for the building had been decided by this time, since Baker suggests that the proposed building should have a secondary entrance from Memorial Drive, with a primary entrance from the "playing field side of the building" (4).

41 News Service, Massachusetts Institute of Technology, "For Release in the Morning Papers of July 1, 1950," MIT Archives AC004, Box 131, Folder 12.

42 John E. Burchard, "Objectives of M.I.T. School of Humanities," 2 June 1950, MIT Archives AC004, Box 131, Folder 12.

was devoted to the construction of what would eventually become two buildings which, accommodating extracurricular activities both secular and religious in nature, were meant to fulfill the initial program of enhanced spiritual education.

But the institutionalization of the humanities at MIT would continue to echo through the project in other ways. In 1951, with the design process well under way, Burchard delivered an address to the annual convention of the American Institute of Architects. Titled "Humanity: Our Client" and published in *Architectural Record*, the bulk of the talk consisted of a series of historical "lessons" concentrated in the earlier twentieth century. Burchard's main interlocutor was Sigfried Giedion, whom he interprets as having assigned to architecture the role of restoring "feeling" to a technocratic, atomic age.[43] But where Giedion's "feeling" was ultimately a form of aesthetic experience derived from the neo-Kantian tradition and redirected by the Hegelian *Zeitgeist*, Burchard's implications were more overtly theological in both tone and substance. One of the history lessons he offered to architects, which he amplified with words from André Malraux on the expressive character of church architecture, was that

> there have been agnostics in every culture, but no agnostic cultures until now. Even when great leaders of a time themselves were agnostic, they have not felt it prudent or wise or perhaps even comfortable to evade the responsibilities of the believer. Though Cesare Borgia may have blasphemed in his cups, he nonetheless continued to build St. Peter's. Thus living religions have, regardless of their absolute values, managed to afford a transcendent communion linking every man of the culture to the fellowmen of his culture and have created in this sense a sort of anonymity in which the individual was of minor consequence.[44]

Burchard's published text, which begins and ends with excerpts from Psalms, concludes with an image of what appears to be a New England village centered on a church spire, the very figure of the secular/religious "meeting house" and "village church" which was also circulating through the discourse around MIT's planned auditorium/chapel. And, especially given his references to religion as a binding agent for a unified "humanity" over and against

43 John E. Burchard, "Humanity: Our Client," *Architectural Record* 110, no. 1 (July 1951): 97. **44** Ibid., 95-96.

45 James R. Killian to Robert M. Kimball, 3 October 1950. MIT Archives AC004, Box 131, Folder 5.

Inside the MIT
Chapel, n.d..

isolated individuals, who better to deliver such a message to a professional assembly of architects than the new Dean of Humanities and Social Studies at MIT, a secular institution that, perhaps more than any other, was symbolically associated with the allegedly deleterious effects of an "agnostic" science, and now required a St. Peter's—or a New England meeting house and village church—of its own?

Meanwhile, it appears that Saarinen first visited the MIT campus to discuss the project sometime in the fall of 1950. In preparation for the architect's visit to the site (which also seems to have been selected by this time), Killian summarized his thoughts on what he still called the "auditorium-chapel" in a letter to the Institute's project manager, Robert Kimball. Here again it is worth noting that at the outset the secular and religious functions of the two building components were less distinct both symbolically and practically than they might now seem. Regarding the auditorium, Killian conjured for his project manager the image of a Cambridge University professor delivering a formal lecture, or an academic processional occurring there, or a performance of the London String Quartet, while also describing it as "a place where a distinguished minister might hold religious services." As for the structure itself, in Killian's description it still appeared more as a single building than an ensemble. Nevertheless, the auditorium and the chapel seemed to be drifting apart. Killian imagined the "devotional" chapel as perhaps "connected with the auditorium by an ambulatory or some similar architectural device," rather than, as in Baker's description a few months earlier, incorporated into a single volume. But he still associated the dual secular/religious function with the New England meeting house, by which he defined the building's overarching symbolic requirement: "to express the fact that we are interested in what a meeting house stands for and can accomplish."[45]

During the next few years, Killian frequently invoked this "meeting house" image in reference to the project, describing it at the dedication ceremony as a "house of many uses" in which "men and women went to worship God, to hold their town meetings, and to further their cultural and civic interests."[46] Earlier, in requesting that Burchard plan the dedication ceremony, Killian had written:

> I feel that the dedication of these two buildings can serve to call attention [sic] and demonstrate the humanistic aspects of our program at the Institute and the richness of our community life. I would like to see us build on the concept of the meetinghouse, where the community comes together to transact its business, to develop its solidarity, and to enrich its intellectual life.[47]

About a year later, an event-planning sub-committee assembled by Burchard recorded the underlying conflict (and, it seems, the internal debate) in the minutes of a meeting: "Is the dedication going to stress dependence on the creator, on a power greater than man, or not? The related question is: If we do not stress this dependence, do we silently affirm the opposite? Do we silently say that humanism is the answer?" In returning to the idea of "the auditorium as the New England Meeting House" and "the chapel as the one building on campus in scale with man" (both attributed to Killian), this committee essentially resolved the issue by converting the conventional opposition between theology and secular humanism into an uncomfortable identity.[48] Just as the imaginary of the "New England meeting house" also conjured the village church, so did the auditorium (which would eventually receive a plaque describing it as a "meeting house") require the chapel to complete its meaning. Correspondingly, just as the "human" scale and inwardness of Saarinen's chapel, juxtaposed with the monumental buildings surrounding it, implicitly reconciled the individual human with an encompassing, monotheistic deity, the "meeting house" extrapolated an only apparently secular community of human souls out of the anonymous corridors of "big science." In other words, coupled with the auditorium and read into the network of discursive practices woven around the institutionalization of the humanities and social sciences at MIT, Saarinen's little chapel actively participated in the desecularization—or sacralization—of humanism.

During this period, other American architects were grappling with the proposition that, far from being inherently secular, modern architecture was in fact capable of the sort of spiritual expression associated with historical styles like the Gothic, particularly as these were used in religious buildings. A telling instance of this was a roundtable discussion published in *Architectural Forum* in December 1955—with an interior photograph of the MIT chapel as its frontispiece—on "theology and architecture."[49] The *Forum* panel responded to a lecture by theologian Paul Tillich on artistic expression and theology and focused on "protestant Church architecture," which had recently become a object of architectural

Eero Saarinen &
Associates, rendering of
the interior of the Kresge
Chapel. From MIT
Technology Review, June
1952.

attention due in part to the commissions that many architects, including Saarinen, were receiving for such structures. Pietro Belluschi, who was the dean of MIT's School of Architecture and Planning for the duration of the chapel/auditorium project, and who acted regularly as an interpreter and friendly critic of Saarinen's project for the administration, was among the panel's participants. Responding to Tillich's talk, which emphasized the compatibility of modernism with Protestant theology, Belluschi, who had also completed a number of Protestant church commissions of his own, mentioned the heightened interest in symbolism among architects at the time.[50] In effect, the entire discussion turned on this problem, which articulated a version of the "new monumentality" proposed in 1943 by Giedion with Josep Lluís Sert and Fernand Léger.[51] As in the new monumentality debates then rippling through the field at large, the old problem of theology and architecture was recast by the *Forum* panel in terms of modern architecture's newfound capacity for symbolic communication.

46 Press Release, "Full text of an address prepared by James R. Killian, Jr., President of the Massachusetts Institute of Technology, for delivery at the Dedication of the Kresge Auditorium and M.I.T. Chapel at 3:30 o'clock on Sunday afternoon, May 8," 9 May 1955, 6; MIT Archives AC004, Box 131, Folder 8.

47 James R. Killian to John E. Burchard, 14 Aug 1953, MIT Archives AC004, Box 131, Folder 6.

48 Sub-committee on Actual Dedication Ceremony for Chapel and Auditorium, Meeting minutes, 23 July 1954, MIT Archives, Box 131, Folder 7.

49 Forum Paul Tillich, Pietro Belluschi, Darby Betts, Marvin Halverson, Morris Ketchum, Paul Weaver, "Theology and Architecture," *Architectural Forum* 103, n. 6 (December 1955) 130-136.

50 Ibid., 136

51 Sigfried Giedion, Fernand Léger, and Josep-Luis Sert, "Nine Points on Monumentality," reprinted in Giedion, *Architecture You and Me: The Diary of a Development* (Cambridge: Harvard University Press, 1958), 48-51. Burchard's own contribution to this discussion is summarized in John Ely Burchard, *Symbolism in Architecture: The Decline of the Monumental* (New York:

Mary Lynn Smoot and Pfc. Piet Bauke Bos. June, 1955.
Photo: Associated Press.

For related reasons, Saarinen's auditorium and chapel were much discussed and debated in professional circles, mostly for their departures from modernist orthodoxies in favor of symbolic expression, or, in the case of the auditorium, for their technical achievements.[52] In a brief, unpublished text composed in 1959, Saarinen acknowledges some of the criticism, while defining the challenge posed by the chapel as one of creating an atmosphere "derived ... from basic spiritual feelings," with all of the architectural devices—the lighting, the dark materials, the interior undulations—coordinated to produce an "other-worldly sense."[53] In contrast, amongst the several MIT communities we have been following, the auditorium and chapel were discussed primarily as symbols fraught with the tension between—and ultimately, the convergence of—secularism and religiosity. The discussion also concerned questions of aesthetic taste as it was associated with the popular imagery of church architecture. The buildings' controversial departure from the latter had caused representatives of MIT like Killian to respond by rhetorically assimilating the postwar renewal of "spiritual values" with the innovations of modern architecture.[54] The popular objection was such that it even prompted Albert Bush-Brown, then an assistant professor in the School of Architecture and Planning and later Burchard's co-author on an important survey of American architecture, to write an impassioned letter to the editor of *The Boston Herald*. In this response to published criticism of the chapel, Bush-Brown declared that the building "was in fact created according to God's law" by virtue of its evolutionary innovations, a response that drew an approving note from President Killian to the junior professor the day after its publication.[55]

Less discussed by either the architectural press or the reading public, however, was the ambiguous formal and programmatic relationship between the two buildings. Available evidence suggests that from the beginning Saarinen treated the auditorium and chapel components of the project as separate entities, with the principal design problem being one of establishing a syntactical relationship between the two. Implied was the hope that this relationship would sustain a distinction, which we can now interpret as ideological in nature, between secular and religious forms of monumentality, while assimilating both into what we can call a theological humanism. Such humanism is inter-discursive in that it relies on slippages from one symbolic register to another; where instrumental knowledge is not merely guided or mediated by moral-theological training, it depends on it.

Harper and Brothers, 1955).

52 The chapel and auditorium were widely covered in the architectural press in the United States and Internationally. See for example: "Saarinen Challenges the Rectangle," *Architectural Forum* 98 n. 1 (January 1953): 126-133; "Saarinen Dome a Year

Later," *Architectural Record* 115, n. 5 (May 1954): 20, 318, 320, 322; Edward Weeks, "The Opal on the Charles," *Architectural Record* 118, n. 1 (July 1955): 131-137; "M.I.T. Dedicates New Auditorium," *Architectural Forum* 103, n. 1 (July 1955): 128-129; "New M.I.T. Buildings Opened," *Progressive Architecture*

36, n. 7 (July 1955): 74-75; "Building in the Round: M.I.T. Completes Two of Today's Most Talked about Buildings," *Architectural Forum* 104, n. 1 (January 1956): 116-121; "Chapel: Interdenominational," *Architectural Record* 119, n. 1 (January 1956): 154-157; "New Chapel at M.I.T.," *Progressive Architecture* 37,

n. 1 (January 1956): 65-67; Bruno Zevi, J.M. Richards, Sigfried Giedion, "Three Critics Discuss M.I.T.'s New Buildings," *Architectural Forum* 104, n. 3 (March 1956): 156-157, 174, 178, 180, 182; "La cappella e l'auditorium el Massachusetts Institute of Technology," *Casabella* 208 (November-December 1955):

Saarinen's initial attempts at developing a syntax adequate to this task first show a small domed chapel attached to a larger, four-pronged, domed auditorium in an offset echo of Bosworth's earlier pair of domes on the central academic campus across the street. These studies are followed by a scheme that sets a vaulted chapel in front of a three-pronged auditorium dome and another scheme that offsets a rectangular chapel, designed as a glass box with an external ambulatory enclosed by solid brick walls, against the three-pronged dome. As published in *Architectural Forum* in January 1953, the near-final scheme shows a cylindrical brick chapel semi-connected to a three-pronged auditorium dome by an exterior breezeway. Both buildings are positioned on a patterned, diagonally-gridded plaza with parking below, and a pedestrian bridge connects back across Massachusetts Avenue to the main campus.[56]

Already, this first publication interprets the juxtaposition of brick cylinder and thin-shell concrete dome as solving the underlying stylistic problems associated with the demand for symbols of an ambiguously secular/religious nature:

> In the brick cylinder chapel Saarinen and his associates have out-traditionalized today's traditionalists just as conclusively as they out-modernized today's modernists in using a dome instead of the familiar wedge shape for the auditorium. More specifically, the chapel is as timeless as the dome is timely.[57]

Thus modern-versus-traditional is converted into a "timely," transparent, thin-shell concrete dome set against a "timeless," dense, and opaque brick cylinder. But, as interpreted several years later by the historian Bruno Zevi, this resolution was hardly satisfactory. In critical commentary on the project which also included remarks by Giedion and by J. M. Richards (the editor of *The Architectural Review*), Zevi referred to the "unhappy" experience of modern architects in Italy trying to adapt the traditions of church architecture to the expressive medium of modernism, which typically resulted in a compromise that was "half modern and half old." Zevi, who really was demanding nothing less than the full capitulation of the secular to the sacred, explained:

16-20.

53 Eero Saarinen, "Auditorium and Chapel, Massachusetts Institute of Technology, Cambridge, Mass.," January 1959, 2. Eero Saarinen Papers, Yale University Manuscripts and Archives, Box 28, Folder 121.

54 See, for example, Killian's remarks at the dedication

ceremony, op. cit.

55 Albert Bush-Brown, "M.I.T. Chapel Created According to God's Law," letter to the editor of *The Boston Herald*, 12 June 1955, and James R. Killian to Albert Bush-Brown, 13 June 1955; MIT Archives AC004, Box 131, Folder 8.

56 Ongoing discussion at MIT regarding the suitability of the chapel form was apparently concluded in late 1953, when Burchard wrote to Killian on behalf of the building committee endorsing the cylindrical brick form, which was approved shortly thereafter. John E Burchard, Memorandum to President

The bell tower and spire, designed by Theodore J. Roszak, being installed atop the MIT Chapel, January 1956.

The first christening in the
MIT Chapel, June 1955.

Modern religion is a problem that architects must cope with in a modern way. This chapel will not serve the purposes of religion or spiritual elevation; it will only provide an artificial escape.... To my mind, the mistakes of great architects are always significant. In the worst interpretation, Saarinen's M.I.T. group pictures the crisis of a generation too immodest to follow Wright or Le Corbusier, and too tormented to be as great as they are. But I am on the side of the positive interpretation: Saarinen will emerge from the present impasse, and his pseudomystical experiment will take its place in his biography as a chapter of insecurity and search, well symbolized by the dome carried on three points and by the vague, moving lights reflected from the water around the chapel.[58]

However, these two buildings were hardly exceptions in Saarinen's body of work. Nor were they merely the insecure products of a "generation" in crisis. Instead, it would be more accurate to say that they were typical of research within the firm which dated back to the work of Eliel Saarinen, beginning in the 1930s.

Take the question of lighting. The chapel's undulating brick interior surface moves in and out of the reflected light thrown up by the water passing beneath the arches, whose irregularity is matched by that of the interior undulations. The effect is a double pulsation: the undulating walls rhythmically blocking and revealing the indirect uplighting, and the gentle movement of the water itself. A counterpoint to this is given by the single skylight above the altar. Circular and focused, its light passes through a horizontal baffle and reflects off of the metal filigree screen designed by Harry Bertoia that is located behind the solid marble altar. By virtue of an artifice of the constantly changing wall section, light therefore enters mysteriously from below through the gap between two sets of curves: the vertical exterior arches and the horizontal interior undulations. Rising, it enters straightforwardly through a visible hole in the roof, only to pick up a mysterious flicker as it bounces off the Bertoia screen. In this theater of illumination, then, the Corbusian (and neo-Platonic) play of solids in light is not merely softened by the glow of an ambiguously meditative spirituality, as it was at Ronchamp (completed that same year). Light is made to appear in and of itself, as the product of a dynamic relationship between forms and materials. And the burden of

Killian, 18 December 1953, MIT Archives AC004, Box 131, Folder 6.

57 "Saarinen Challenges the Rectangle," 126.

58 Bruno Zevi, in Zevi, Richards, and Giedion, "Three Critics Discuss M.I.T.'s New Buildings," 157, 174.

mystification passes from the blinding glare of all-encompassing reason, to the apparent reasonableness, tolerance, and abstraction of the soft new spirituality.

Saarinen was well-equipped to stage this mystification. The equal and opposite structural and acoustical virtuosity of the auditorium, accomplished with much more evident artifice, heightens by contrast the effect of effortless, ambient theatricality within the chapel itself. Prior to the war the Saarinen firm, which had been founded by his father, Eliel Saarinen, had completed two notable auditoria: the Kleinhans Music Hall in Buffalo and the Berkshire Music Center at Tanglewood, both of 1938. Eliel Saarinen, who was himself the son of a Lutheran minister, had also designed two notable religious buildings: the Tabernacle Church of Christ in Columbus, Indiana (1940) and Christ Lutheran Church in Minneapolis (1950), both in collaboration with his son. When such precedents are taken into account, the "sublime" lighting effects that the Saarinen firm was simultaneously developing inside the General Motors styling dome, which were intended produce the artificial equivalent of a cloudy sky to bestow the latest automobiles with an otherworldly aura, are recognizable as only the most visible instance of a technical production of spirituality. Both the Tabernacle Church of Christ (1940) and its sequel, Christ Lutheran Church in Minneapolis (1950), wash a blank wall behind the altar with soft natural light. At the Tabernacle Church, as at MIT, water is used to frame the building and to set the brick volume in sharp relief; this is achieved with a circular moat at MIT and a flat, sheer reflecting pond at the Tabernacle Church (a device that was used to comparable effect at General Motors and elsewhere).

The refinement of these techniques only scratches the surface of Saarinen's own engagement with the problem of evoking of religious feeling, which (in unpublished comments on the work of Mies van der Rohe) he judged to be among the most important challenges for modern architecture "where the problem is to bring light in so it moves and plays dramatically."[59] Something similar can be said about campus planning, in which Saarinen saw the need for integration, and for the reconciliation of the singularity and originality of the modernist languages, in which his work was fluent, with the historical revivals typical of American collegiate architecture.[60] In a number of instances before and

Sculptor Harry Bertoia installing altarpiece in the MIT Chapel, n.d..

59 Undated transcript of remarks by Eero Saarinen on the work of Ludwig Mies van der Rohe, Eero Saarinen Papers, Yale Manuscripts and Archives, Box 28, Folder 17, 3-4.

60 Eero Saarinen, "Campus Planning: The Unique World of the University," *Architectural Record* 128, n.5 (November 1960): 123-130. For a summary of Saarinen's campus planning work and thinking, see Alan J. Plattus, "Campus Plans: Context and Community," in Eeva-Liisa Pelkonen and Donald Albrecht,

eds., *Eero Saarinen: Shaping the Future* (New Haven, Yale University Press, 2006), 308-321.

after the MIT commission, Saarinen would be given the opportunity to address these two problems simultaneously by designing chapels as part of a larger campus planning exercise: at Brandeis University (1949), Drake University (c. 1950), at Concordia Senior College (1957), and at Stephens College (1954). In each of these, aspects of the MIT "language" were either prototyped or refined—the undulating brick wall at Brandeis, the Protestant "village" (northern European, in this case) at Concordia, and the indirect illumination at Stephens. But at MIT, this research and the discourse to which it belonged acquired a specific cast as it intersected with the reorganization of the humanities, and with the sublimation of technoscience into a humanism no less instrumental in its functionalization of "spiritual" balance (as distinct from outright critique), as a binding agent holding the military-industrial-academic complex together.

Also at MIT, a problem that was typically formulated in architectural discourse as being one of simple opposition—abstract versus symbolic, modern versus traditional—acquired a good deal more complexity when it encountered the secular/religious conflict written into MIT's institutional realignments. The "new monumentality" had sought to resolve the opposition of non-symbolic (modern) to symbolic (traditional) by displacing symbolism in the secular, civic realm to a higher, more abstract level. But this type of resolution quickly became undone on the ground at MIT. Despite the strenuous efforts on the part of their architect to distinguish the chapel from the auditorium in all possible ways—spatially, formally, materially, and in terms of scale—there was no keeping these two elements and their meanings apart. But neither was one simply reducible to the other. Instead, they contaminated one another in a sort of incomplete dialectic. It would be inaccurate, however, to describe this dialectic as a microcosmic instance of a macrocosmic "dialectic of Enlightenment" dominated by instrumental reason.[61] In the soft light of the chapel, everything seems perfectly reasonable, perfectly in balance with the utilitarian environment from which the little round cylinder withdraws, its mystical theatricality finding a counterweight in the techno-theater of the auditorium. The threat this time comes from the inside rather than from the outside as the university rediscovers its human "soul." In doing so, it exchanges the "myth" of reason for the reasonable production of myth, in a theological humanism that is no longer in need of its dialectical, secular counterpart.

61 Max Horkeimer and Theodor W. Adorno, *Dialectic of Enlightenment: Philosophical Fragments*, trans. Edmund Jephcott (Stanford: Stanford University Press, 2002).

Interior of MIT Chapel with Harry Bertoia's altarpiece, n.d.. Photo: J.Ph. Charbonnier.

JOHN HARWOOD

How Useful?

The Stakes of Architectural History, Theory, and Criticism at MIT, 1945-1976

The influence a book has upon its readers is to a certain extent intangible and impossible to measure precisely . . .
—Rudolf Wittkower[1]

The best institutions can never be foolproof. . . . Institutions are like fortresses. They must be well designed and properly manned.
—Karl Popper[2]

"The task of criticism, has, in fact, changed," wrote Manfredo Tafuri in his halting but biting introduction to *Teorie e storia dell'archittetura* (1968). In the face of the successes and anxieties confronting the "third generation of the Modern Movement" (i.e. post-WWII architecture), architectural criticism needed to respond to new architectural designs and theories and reach out to new models of historical analysis; more importantly, Tafuri famously argued, it would have to forego its close bonds with this or that specific architectural ideology or risk "being blown to bits by the 'conscious negation' of principles."[3]

At first glance, Tafuri's ambitious attempt to reformulate the basic terms of architectural history, theory, and criticism seems to respond to a broad sweep of historical and political events. After all, he begins with the premise that "there is no doubt that the artistic avant-gardes of the twentieth century have fought for a revolution," "but when the revolution . . . has reached its goals, criticism loses the support it had found in its total commitment to the revolutionary cause."[4] Speaking of his and his contemporaries' "touchstones," Tafuri lists critics like "Pevsner, Behne, Benjamin, Giedion, Persico, Giolli, Argan, Dorner and Shand" who had, through their commitments to modernism, gone "beyond the thinking of

I wish to thank Stanford Anderson for his insightful and generous comments on an early draft of this essay, and Henry Millon for his remembrances of his interest in computer science in the mid-1960s while I was at CASVA in 2006. Andrew Leach, Mary Louise Lobsinger, Mary McLeod, and many others read drafts of this essay as well, with many helpful corrections and suggestions. Any remaining errors, of course, are my own.

1 Rudolf Wittkower, *Architectural Principles in the Age of Humanism*, 3rd ed. (London: Tiranti, 1962), preface.
2 Karl Popper, *The Poverty of Historicism* (Boston: Beacon Press, 1957), 157.
3 Manfredo Tafuri, *Theories and History of Architecture*, 4th ed., trans. Giorgio Verrecchia (New York: Harper & Row, 1976), 4.
4 Ibid., 1.
5 Ibid., 5.
6 Marcus Wiffen, ed., *The History, Theory and Criticism of Architecture: Papers from the 1964 AIA-ACSA Teacher Seminar* (Cambridge, MA: MIT Press, 1965).
7 Niklaus Pevsner, "Modern Architecture and the Historian, or the Return of

their time." But due to the new "advanced" questions posed by post-WWII architecture, the critic found him- or herself forced to uneasily "graft" new philosophical and scientific outlooks onto the works of their predecessors. The new engaged, *operative* criticism was a Frankenstein's monster—ugly, "whining," and "dangerous."

Thus, Tafuri's virulent critique was less a matter of identifying a new united front for architectural writing and more one of responding directly to the inconsistent methods of architectural writing in his own time. In short, as Tafuri concluded his introduction, the problem is one of how to back away from the model of the engaged architect-critic while moving toward a program of research conducted within the modern university: "Lately, architectural critics have shown a symptomatic interest in the researches that have introduced . . . methods analogous to those of the empirical and experimental sciences."[5]

This was no generalization. In fact, as the first chapter of the book—the infamous essay, "Modern Architecture and the Eclipse of History"—reveals, Tafuri was responding directly to a specific event, one which had occurred far from his vantage point in Rome, and his later perch in Venice: the 1964 AIA-ACSA Teacher Seminar on *The History, Theory and Criticism of Architecture* held at the Cranbrook Academy of Art.[6] This event, organized by Henry A. Millon, a recently appointed professor of Architectural History, Theory and Criticism at MIT, brought together a handful of the most influential architectural writers of the time to discuss the perceived crisis in architectural discourse. As Tafuri correctly summarizes (supported by lengthy quotations from participants such as Sibyl Moholy-Nagy, Reyner Banham and Bruno Zevi), the basis of the debate was the apparent truism, first articulated by Niklaus Pevsner,[7] that Walter Gropius's decision to exclude history courses from the curriculum at the Bauhaus constituted the 'original sin' of modernist architectural discourse. After 1919, any meaningful connection between progressive and revolutionary architectural practice and architectural history was decisively severed. Moreover, after WWII, the *re*-introduction of historical discourse in architecture had led to "the most absurd revivalist phenomena."[8] The Modern Movement had been betrayed, and moreover, the Judas was the architectural historian who, by representing history through inadequate means, had tempted the architect into an *a-historical* view of historicist and Modernist architecture alike.

Historicism," *Journal of the Royal Institute of British Architects*, 3rd series, 48 (April 1961): 230-240. In the lively discussion following the lecture, Pevsner's thesis— "when really original people in architecture start doing funny turns, then the less original people will imitate [them]" and be tempted to a banal historicism (235)—was

opposed by John Summerson in his "vote of thanks." Summerson held that this thesis was histrionic picture of a non-existent "chaos" that had been "cooked up" (237). Reyner Banham and Helen Rosenau, however, favored Pevsner's thesis (237-240). See Banham's strongest statement on this point in his "Neo-liberty: The Italian Retreat

from Modern Architecture," *Architectural Review* 122 (April 1959): 230-235.
8 Tafuri, *Theories and History*, 11.
9 Ibid., 14.
10 See note 3.
11 Tafuri, *Architecture and Utopia: Design and Capitalist Development*, trans. Barbara Luigia La Penta (Cambridge, MA: MIT Press, 1976).

12 The architectural history, theory, and criticsm journal of the IAUS, *Oppositions* (edited initially by Peter Eisenman, Kenneth Frampton, Mario Gandelsonas), offered a clear editorial statement regarding its publishing strategy, which explicitly identified the journal with Tafuri's critique:
In short, what we are striving for is the inducement

Tafuri was not very generous in his assessment of the outcome of this momentous seminar. Indeed, he ended his summary discussion rather abruptly:

> One could carry on with the quotations, but we think we have shown adequately the diffused attitude of architectural historiography: with the exception of Banham, paladin of technological orthodoxy, the historians are in revolt against the very sources of modern art. The Bauhaus and the masters of the avant-garde have been put in the dock; the new tasks are those left unsolved in the 'roaring twenties'; the anti-historicism of the Modern Movement is judged contingent and surmountable, and what is put forward is the hypothesis of history as a guide for a new type of experience.[9]

Needless to say, Tafuri's dismissal of "operative" architectural history, theory and criticism continued to animate discussions of method and politics in architectural discourse for decades, gathering particular momentum in the United States with the translation of the fourth edition of *Teorie e storia* into English in 1976.[10] This volume appeared in the US alongside another of Tafuri's works, the well-known, slender, but provocative tome, *Architecture and Utopia: Design and Capitalist Development*. Published in Italian in 1973, it was translated into English three years later and published in the United States by MIT Press.[11] Tafuri's polemic found a ready audience amongst American architectural intellectuals, most notably the membership of the Institute for Architecture and Urban Studies (IAUS), which cited Tafuri's works and provided further translations of his writings in its journal *Oppositions*.

This brief and circumstantial summary of the development of the critique of operative architectural discourse hardly offers any account of *why*, exactly, this concern became a central preoccupation during these years. Nevertheless it does point out that Tafuri's critique developed between two crucial historical moments: first, the AIA-ACSA seminar in 1964, which, despite the manifold disagreements between its participants, made a formidable case for placing architectural "research" at the center of architectural discourse; and second, the publication of Tafuri's work in English and the well-known institutionalization of American architectural theory under the auspices of the IAUS,

of a number of specific discourses; namely, the critique of built work as a vehicle for ideas; the reassessment of the past as a means of determining the necessary relations existing between built form and social values; the establishment of a spectrum of theoretical discourses linking ideology and built

form; the documentation of little known archival material as a means for advancing scholarship and thought in the field as a whole; and finally, the publication of reivews and letters that have a direct bearing on the discourses at hand. As to the last, they seem to us to be primarily twofold: firstly, an ongoing discourse on

the place of physical form in architecture and planning today; and secondly, the indivisible ideological and socio-political implications of architectural production as a whole. For us the sum total of these efforts constitutes a new polemical form which is dialectical in nature rather than rhetorical.

Moreover, the journal was

eventually reorganized into five sections: "Oppositions" (criticism), "Theory," "History," "Documents," and "Reviews and Letters," further underscoring the codification of architectural discourse into the tripartite structure of history, theory and criticism. In the years between 1973 and 1977, *Oppositions* published the following

primarily through MIT Press,[12] an effort which coincided with the founding of the first American Ph.D. program in the History, Theory and Criticism of Architecture at MIT in 1976.[13] In both instances, the institutional context within which the discourse took shape was dominated by MIT.

Several questions thus emerge, which have yet to be addressed by historians of architectural historiography in the post-WWII era, particularly after 1960.[14] How and in what context did the alignment of architectural discourse with natural- and social-scientific models of research take place? What role did MIT—its administration, faculty, and students—play in this alignment? A close look at the changing nature of architectural discourse at MIT in the post-WWII era provides many answers, some of them quite surprising.

Architectural History and the Imperative to "Research" at MIT, 1945-1960

Despite a "glorious" record in aiding the war effort with the provision of crucial research and development activities, manpower (civilian and military), and funding, MIT emerged in 1945 as an institution that "no doubt bears its scars."[15] Under the directorship of architectural historian and MIT librarian John Ely Burchard, Division 2 of the National Defense Research Committee (for "Structural Defense and Offense") had siphoned off architects from the MIT faculty to aid in "bomb selection" and "operations analysis" in the Bomber Commands.[16] Along with the rest of the Institute, student enrollment in the architecture school suffered during the war years, and the renewal of the program beginning in 1947 under the direction of the committed modernist William W. Wurster was marked by an effort to rebuild the curriculum almost from scratch.[17]

Amongst the three primary genres of architectural writing, it was history alone—not theory or criticism—that held a significant role and some degree of disciplinary autonomy within the School of Architecture during the immediate post-war period. From 1945 to 1954, architectural history courses were a regular element of the curriculum, even if the teachers were anything but constant fixtures. Moonlighting from his position as chair of the Department of Art at Wellesley College, Henry-Russell Hitchcock taught the survey of the history of architecture in 1945 and 1946, and was replaced on an *ad hoc* basis by

essays by Tafuri: "L' Architecture dans le Boudoir: The language of criticism and the criticism of language," trans. Victor Caliandro, 3 (May 1974): 37-62; "American Graffiti: Five x Five = Twenty-five," trans. Victor Caliandro, 5 (Summer 1976): 35-74; and "Giuseppe Terragni: Subject and 'Mask,'" trans. Diane Ghirardo, 11

(1977): 1-25.

13 Other American PhD programs in "Architecture" long predate the program at MIT (notable examples include those at Princeton University and Cornell University), but MIT's program was the first to be distinguished from programs based in technical research. See Stanford Anderson,

"Architectural History in Schools of Architecture," *Journal of the Society of Architectural Historians* 58, no. 3 (September 1999): 282-290. **14** See ibid., which offers an overview of each program up through the 1990s. Another article by Anderson, "The 'New Empiricism: Bay Region Axis': Kay Fisker and Postwar Debates on

Functionalism, Regionalism, and Monumentality," *Journal of Architectural Education* 50, no. 3 (February 1997): 197-207, which provides an account of changing formal and intellectual attitudes at MIT in the 1940s and '50s on more solidly historical grounds. A more recent assessment of the history of the discipline is given by another MIT

the architect, former MoMA curator of architecture, and fellow Wellesley architectural historian John McAndrew.[18] McAndrew was replaced in 1953 by an editor of *Architectural Review,* Marcus Whiffen, who, despite taking a post as architectural historian to Colonial Williamsburg (1954-59) and then a professorship at Arizona State University in 1960, continued to be associated with MIT intermittently as a visiting professor, historian, and critic into the 1980s.[19] The Dartmouth College art historian Hugh Morrison and Williams College architectural historian William H. Pierson temporarily split the post in 1954; they were followed by the Australian architect and critic Robin Boyd (1956-57), and then the historian and critic Lewis Mumford, who had taught several courses on urban history at MIT after WWII, and who returned to the campus for single terms in 1957 and 1958 to teach both architectural and urban history.

Stability only arrived in 1954, in the person of the art historian Albert Bush-Brown.[20] Holding both an A.B. and a master's degree in fine arts from Princeton University, Bush-Brown was brought in under the auspices of Dean of Humanities and Social Sciences, the previously mentioned John Ely Burchard, who was actively seeking to establish a consistent pedagogical approach to the visual arts within the Department of Architecture. In 1952, Burchard formed a committee—comprised of John Coolidge, Robert Inglehart, Bartlett Hayes, Jr., Charles Sawyer, and James Johnson Sweeney (all directors of museums or collegiate arts departments)—to make recommendations for a coherent arts curriculum. The committee's report, published by the Institute in 1957 as *Art Education for Scientist and Engineer*, recommended the creation of an elective course (in MIT's institutional jargon, a "course" identifies a suite of classes) in the visual arts.

The curriculum of this course, eventually named Field X ("Field Ten"), such as it was with only three faculty members to support it, was divided into two subjects: "drawing and painting" (with art history and criticism mixed in), taught by the painter Robert Preusser; and "history and criticism," taught by Bush-Brown. The latter aimed to "acquaint students with the great paintings, sculpture, and architecture of the past. The principal intent of this subject is to develop the capacity for making objective critical judgments upon quality in art and to relate the visual arts to the intellectual, emotional, and social disposition of their creators."[21]

professor, Mark Jarzombek, in "Postscript: The Rise of a New Architectural History," in his *The Psychologizing of Modernity: Art, Architecture and History* (Cambridge: Cambridge University Press, 2000), 205-207. Mardges Bacon has also provided a reassessment of some of the main lines of American architectural historiography

and criticism in the mid-20th century in her introduction to William H. Jordy, *"Symbolic Essence" and Other Writings on Modern Architecture and American Culture* (New Haven: Yale University Press, 2005), 1-52.

15 John Burchard, *Q.E.D.: M.I.T. in World War II* (Cambridge, MA: The Technology Press of the

Massachusetts Institute of Technology, New York: John Wiley & Sons; London: Chapman & Hall, 1948), 16. On the research and development collaboration between MIT, government, and industry before World War II, see Mark Jarzombek, *Designing MIT: Bosworth's New Tech* (Boston: Northeastern University Press,

2004), esp. chap. 1.

16 Ibid., 51-52, 63-64. In Division 2, architects and engineers were charged with evaluating the damage done to various types of buildings, building materials, and armor by a wide range of bombs and projectiles.

17 For insight into the importance of modernist architecture to the ideological

Under this new regime, art and architectural history were viewed less as an adjunct to the design curriculum and more as a means of providing a general humanistic education to a student body that was decidedly biased toward the physical and applied sciences. It also provided an opportunity to teach basic critical skills, and writing. As the School of Architecture and Planning reported to the President of the Institute in 1956, "Parenthetically, architectural history and related subjects provide wonderful opportunities for insistence on accurate and readable written composition."[22] Nonetheless, the creation of Field X greatly heightened the scholarly status of the history and criticism "area" within the Department of Architecture, and in 1957 Bush-Brown began offering graduate-level courses in "Theory of Architecture" and "Architectural Criticism."[23]

The need for graduate-level coursework was itself relatively new to the school. Bush-Brown's appointment at MIT coincided with a decision by the Dean of the School of Architecture, Pietro Belluschi, to offer a Ph.D. in Urban Planning. This was to be part of a massive expansion of the number of graduate degree programs at MIT over the years 1957 to 1963, under the auspices of Dean Harold L. Hazen. Although this expansion received much of its impetus from an influx of government funding in the wake of the Sputnik launch and the heightened tensions of the Cold War, it is interesting to note that the first program added—the one in Urban Planning—was announced in the spring of 1957 (Sputnik was not launched until October). In fact, the program had been in the works since 1955.[24] The others that followed—Political Science, Materials Engineering, Nuclear Engineering, Oceanography, Linguistics, Nutrition and Food Technology, Psychology and Group Psychology, Philosophy, Electrochemical Engineering and Petroleum Engineering—are perhaps more readily attributable as a response to the political economy of the period, but they also reflect something of Burchard's influence and agenda, who aggressively sought to expand the role of the humanities and social sciences at MIT.[25]

The real motivation for the creation of the Ph.D. program in Urban Planning was at once a perceived socio-economic crisis resulting from the rapid rate of urban growth in the post-WWII period, and an effort to mold planning education into the cooperative "basic research" model valued by the post-war technical institute.[26] Unlike programs in the arts and MIT

orientation of MIT in the immediate post-WWII years, see James R. Killian Jr., "M.I.T. Redeploys for Peace," in: ibid., 313-325, which includes photographs of the new campus plan and a model of the new dormitory design by Alvar Aalto. It is worth noting here that the Hungarian emigré artist and theoretician György

Kepes joined the MIT faculty in the Department of Architecture in 1946 and had an immediate impact upon arts education within the Institute. See Anna Vallye's essay on Kepes and the Center for the Advanced Visual Studies (CAVS) in this volume.
18 On McAndrew, see his capsule biography at

http://www.wellesley.edu/ Anniversary/mcandrew.html, accessed July 24, 2009. McAndrew also curated the exhibition series *What is Modern Architecture?* at the Museum of Modern Art in 1942.
19 On Whiffen, see the biographical note at the Arizona State University Archives site: http://lib.asu.

edu/architecture/collections/ whiffen, accessed October 16, 2009.
20 On Bush-Brown, see his *New York Times* obituary at http://www.nytimes. com/1994/07/25/obituaries/ albert-bush-brown-68-is-dead-historian-was-liu-president. html, accessed July 28, 2009. Bush-Brown eventually earned a PhD in Architecture

architects' nascent efforts at research, urban planning was seen as a critical ameliorative tool that could tame the excesses and oversights of unbridled capitalism. MIT had been one of the first institutions to offer a Master's degree in City Planning (which it had done since 1935), and it had numerous alumni in important bureaucratic and political positions on whose expertise it could draw.[27] As a result, the new Ph.D. program, established in a new Center for Urban and Regional Studies which was independent from but related to the Department of Planning within the School of Architecture, received ample funding from the Institute and foundations alike. Eventually, the Center was reincorporated as MIT's contribution to the Joint Center for Urban Studies with Harvard.

Key to this fundraising effort, and to laying out a clear agenda for the program, was a widely echoed emphasis on "basic research." In a press release announcing the establishment of the MIT Center, Chancellor Julius A. Stratton claimed that

> the central purpose of this new Center will be to try to determine what the physical form of the metropolitan region of the future should be and what we can do to bring it about. . . . The new approach at MIT will include the use of some of the sophisticated mathematical methods—such as network theory and information theory—which have been pioneered at MIT in mathematics, physics, and electrical engineering. These mathematical techniques provide the operating logic for such complex machines as giant digital computers, and the MIT men think they may prove equally useful in providing an understanding of the way various factors affect the growth of cities.[28]

Furthermore, the Center would make use of MIT's IBM 704 computer, "the largest and most versatile at any institution in the country," to model both actual and hypothetical urban phenomena. In short, the Center was an explicit effort to posit urban planning as an applied science on par with others by taking up theoretical models from the new hybrid disciplines of computer science, cybernetics, and information theory. Sociology, economics, and political science remained key components of the program, but the new technical emphasis of the program reinforced the discipline's claim to legitimacy both within the Institute and without.

from Princeton in 1958 with a dissertation on 19th-century campus planning titled *Image of a University*. Although nowhere near as prolific as Burchard, Bush-Brown was the leading scholar of art and architectural history within the School of Architecture and Planning until his departure for RISD in 1962, and was particularly vocal on pedagogical issues. See, for example: Bush-Brown, "This New Shell Game: Are the Ground Rules Function, Structure, Symbolism—or Art?" *Architectural Record* 121 (June 1957): 185-189; "College Architecture: An Expression of Educational Philosophy," *Architectural Record* 122 (August 1957): 154-157; "About Books not yet Written," *Journal of the American Institute of Architects* 34 (November 1960): 59; Louis Sullivan (New York: George Braziller, 1960); and John E. Burchard and Bush-Brown, *The Architecture of Modern: A Social and Cultural History* (Boston: Little, Brown, 1961).

21 MIT President's Report for 1957, 63-64.

22 MIT President's Report for 1956, 64.

23 Ibid.

24 The nascent program is mentioned prominently in Pietro Belluschi's report in *Massachusetts Institute of Technology; The Reports of the President and of the Deans of the School for the Year Ending October 1, 1955* (Cambridge, MA: MIT, 1955), 59-67.

The traditional emphasis on the "visual" aspect of cities was sustained most famously
by the group centered around Kevin Lynch (e.g. György Kepes, Donald Appleyard, Sidney
Brower and Michael Southworth), whose summation of five years' research in the book *The
Image of the City* (1960) was the most influential product of the MIT-Harvard collaborations
on urbanism. Although this aspect of the urban planning program gained a wide audience
in architectural circles, its research activities were only a small aspect of the center's
scholarly and practical life.[29] MIT's handful of architectural historians, theorists, and critics,
among them Henry A. Millon and Stanford O. Anderson, were able to take part in numerous
symposia and publication projects by the Center, but on the whole the theoretical apparatus
of the Center remained scientific and political, and not historical, in character.

Outside of ongoing research on construction methods (particularly the mass production
of prefabricated building components and "solar architecture"), efforts to establish a
reliable and comparable program of "architectural research" had met with generally poor
results. One proposal, floated by the architecture critic and curator Edgar Kaufmann Jr. in
the fall of 1956, called for a research project on "Fundamental Patterns of Large Group
Response to Esthetic Stimuli."[30] Kaufmann suggested working with a specialist in visual
symbolism (György Kepes), an industrial designer (Don Wallance or Charles Eames), an
architect (Belluschi or Eero Saarinen), a "philosopher expert in esthetics" (Susanne Langer
or Rudolf Arnheim), and an MIT faculty member who would use "electronic computers" to
map out the entirety of human aesthetic response to all environmental stimuli. Needless
to say, the proposal, filled with misused computer and social science jargon and largely
incomprehensible, was rejected out of hand.

Such laughable "research" proposals aside, the real reason for architecture's decline in
relative importance within the school was that, despite regular funding from the Alfred
Farwell Bemis Foundation (formerly directed by Burchard) for research into construction
technologies, no comparable institutional structure or intellectual apparatus existed within
the Department of Architecture. This remained the case despite the best efforts of the
Department Head, Lawrence B. Anderson (who would become Dean of the School
of Architecture and Planning after the departure of Belluschi), who saw enrollments in

25 See ibid.; and "The
Corporation," Report
(November 1966): 1-6, MIT
Institute Archives, AC400 Box
4, Folder: Graduate School
Study Committee 1 of 2.
See also John E. Burchard
to Lawrence B. Anderson,
28 January 1955, in which
Burchard lays out a case for
expanding the upper level
courses in the arts. By 1962,

despite Burchard's efforts,
arts course offerings were
even rarer than they were in
1955, due to fundraising and
staffing problems. This is also
discussed in Robert Preusser
to John E. Burchard, 19
November 1962 (AC400 Box
4, Folder "Visual Arts").
26 See James R. Killian Jr.,
"M.I.T. Redeploys for Peace,"
in Burchard, *Q.E.D.: M.I.T. in*

World War II, esp. 318-319:
"One of the devices which we
are using to handle group
research—and to stimulate
individual work—is what
we call 'centers of research.'
These are interdepartmental
organizations which
coordinate the cooperative
activities of various
departments in important
fields of overlapping interests

... especially by providing
superior opportunities for
senior and graduate student
thesis work." See also
*Report of The Committee on
Educational Survey to the
Faculty of the Massachusetts
Institute of Technology*
(Cambridge, MA: The
Technology Press of the
Massachusetts Institute of
Technology, December 1949)

the architecture programs decline alarmingly even as enrollments in the Department of Planning climbed rapidly.

In a long series of memoranda and studies dating from the late 1950s, Anderson decried this state of affairs and actively sought solutions. Much of this material is limited to hand-wringing about MIT admissions policies, which Anderson saw as expressing a bias towards students with high aptitudes for math and science and against students with potential in the arts and humanities. However, Anderson did take action at the level of the curriculum as he sought to expand the humanistic and intellectual basis of architectural study at both the undergraduate and graduate levels. He prepared a series of charts of the undergraduate curriculum that proposed doubling coursework in the "history, theory and criticism area" and expanding course offerings in the visual arts.

Thus, even before Belluschi stepped down as dean in 1963 (with the expected shifts in staff that accompanied this change), Anderson had established the grounds upon which architecture would stake its claim to disciplinary and intellectual legitimacy within the research institute. One area in which it would be possible to do this was the history of art and architecture; and in particular Anderson cemented the school's commitment to the history of art by orchestrating the appointment of the art historian Wayne V. Andersen in 1964.[31] As Anderson wrote to Belluschi in 1959, the former role of architecture at MIT as an adjunct to engineering was obsolete. Objecting to the notion that architecture was a "profession nourished by science and technology, and therefore to be included among the first courses to be offered" at MIT, Anderson argued that

[O]ne has only to consider how completely 19th Century ideas have become dissolved to realize the impossibility of reaching a full solution of our problems with this particular premise. There may have been a time during the early decades of M.I.T. when it was useful to consider the architect to be a kind of engineer under a different name, a builder and designer with an educated visual taste. Engineers and architects then shared the joyful task of adapting the fruits of the industrial revolution to the first building of our big cities.

[also available at: http://libraries.mit.edu/archives/mithistory/histories-offices/lewis-com.html].

27 Memorandum from Carl Feiss, Joseph L. Fisher, T.J. Kent Jr., Arthur D. McVoy, Clarence S. Stein, Edwin S. Burdell [Chairman] to James R. Killian Jr. [MIT President], 20 January 1956, with attached pamphlet "City

and Regional Planning at M.I.T.," MIT Institute Archives, AC400 Box 3, Folder: Burdell Committee on City Planning. A key player in establishing the Center was McVoy, an MIT alumnus who was then the Director of the Department of Planning in Baltimore.

28 Undated press release [1958], MIT Institute Archives,

AC400 Box 3, Folder: MIT-Harvard Joint Center [for Urban Studies], 1959-63, 3/4," p. 1-2.

29 Indeed, the work of architects in urban planning was often viewed with disdain by the planners and administrators of the Center. In a letter to Pietro Belluschi dated 27 April 1961, Burchard wrote an informal

review of Serge Chermayeff and Christopher Alexander's manuscript *Community and Privacy*, which the two architects had submitted for publication by the MIT-Harvard Joint Center: *My informal opinion is that there is probably absolutely nothing in it that ought to be published, either by a commercial publisher or a*

This time and these ideas are gone. Science has progressed to where the non-scientist can no longer delve deeply. Engineering has taken up tasks that are unrelated to building problems. The challenges of techniques in architecture have for the time being [sic] somewhat abated, in the face of greater challenges involving social, philosophical, and aesthetic issues. It is now clear that we must share the destiny of the creative arts, which in our time are more and more a spiritual refuge, tinged often with a strong element of revolt against much that technology has brought to our culture. Architecture, even in a "university polarized about science" must stand apart as having the program and the temperament of a high art, and cannot masquerade as an aberrant kind of engineering.[32]

The language of Anderson's letter is borrowed almost directly from a series of articles that Burchard had published in *Architectural Record* on the changing nature of the relationship between architecture and the arts and sciences. In one notable article which formed part of a debate with Sam T. Hurst, Dean of the School of Architecture at the University of Southern California, Burchard rejected Hurst's call for a new holistic scientific theory of rational design on the grounds that theory had yet to produce architecture in any meaningful way.[33] "The architectural times are surely out of joint but I do not believe that theory will set them right. . . . Thus it is rather purpose than theory that is needed—and architects cannot create purpose all by themselves."[34] On the face of it, Burchard's rejection of Hurst's faith in techno-scientific systematicity—shared by a generation of architects and critics which included luminaries like Reyner Banham, Charles Eames, Richard Llewellyn-Davies, and Geoffrey Broadbent—would seem to be a rejection of theory *tout court*. Yet the caveat with which Burchard concludes is an appeal to a para-architectural discursive project, one which, articulating "purpose," would run in parallel with the efforts of the architect. Burchard, much like Mark Jarzombek responding decades later to the "professionalization of architectural theory,"[35] rejected not theory but rather the idea that architectural theory was the exclusive province of the architect and should be limited to matters of technique; for both men the architectural writer's real project was a *critique* of the nature of the architectural project in its entirety.

university press. Most of it is banal, tired, and has been much better said by others earlier, and at the same time no additional data of any concrete sort has been upplied to bolster for example the polemic part; while the use of the Steinberg cartoons and blown-up pictures of cancer tissue are equally unoriginal.

It is barely possible that in the last fifty pages or so, where Chermayeff finally gets down to what it seems he did with his research project, namely the listing of a few requirements for a good modern dwelling, a comparison of a number of plans against the requirements, etc., there is material for a slender

monograph. I myself tend to doubt this, but I would not object to a fifty-page thing devoted mostly to the report on Chermayeff's work with a page or two of summarized polemic if he still thinks this is necessary. Anything more than this I would regard as a waste of time and money, and extremely bad judgment on the part of the Center and

of the presses if they went along with the judgment . . . I may say also that I hope the Center did not invest much money in this piece of 'research.'

Burchard's and others' vociferous objections caused Chermayeff and Alexander to look elsewhere for help; the book was eventually published as *Community*

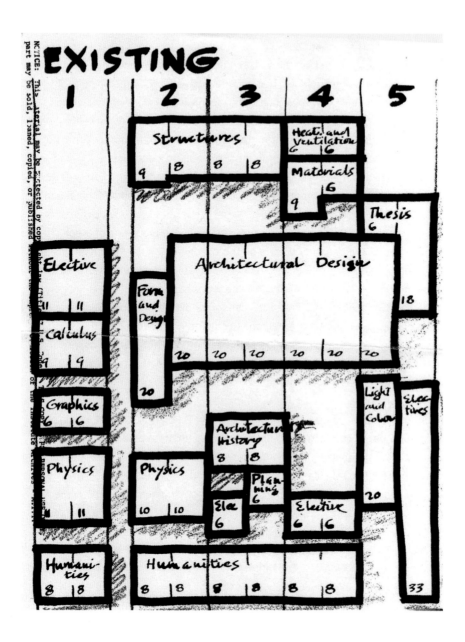

Lawrence B. Anderson,
Diagrams of "Existing"
and "Proposed"
curricula in the B.Arch.
curriculum at MIT. From
"School of Planning
Arts: Undergraduate
Curricular Structure,"
Report, November 21,
1961.

*and Privacy: Toward a New
Architecture of Humanism*
(Garden City, NY: Doubleday,
1963). See MIT Institute
Archives, AC400 Box 3,
Folder: M.I.T.-Harvard Joint
Center [for Urban Studies],
1959-63, 2/4.
30 See memoranda between
Edgar Kaufmann, Pietro
Belluschi, György Kepes,
September-October 1956,

MIT Institute Archives, AC400
Box 4, Folder: Research
Misc. 2/2.
31 Stanford Anderson
to author via e-mail, 23
September 2009.
32 Lawrence B. Anderson
to Pietro Belluschi, 22 July
1959; see also Lawrence
B. Anderson, Eduardo
F. Catalano, Jane Drew,
Roland B. Greeley, Lloyd

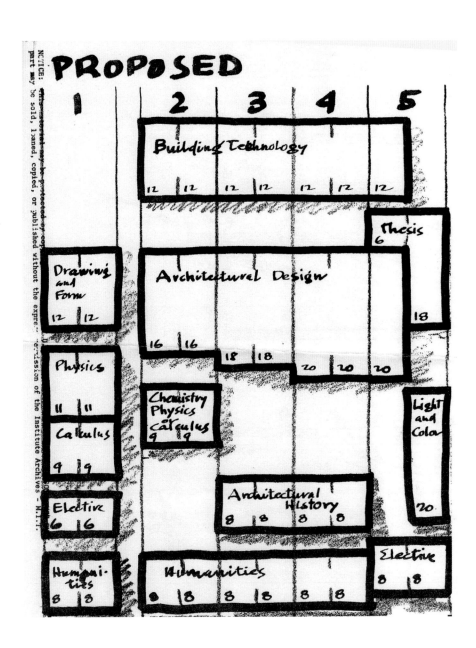

PROPOSED

1   2   3   4   5

Building Technology
12 | 12 | 12 | 12 | 12 | 12 | 12

Thesis 6

Drawing and Form
12 | 12

Architectural Design
16 | 16
18 | 18
20 | 20 | 20
18

Physics
11 | 11

Chemistry Physics Calculus
9 | 9

Calculus
9 | 9

Light and Color
20

Elective
6 | 6

Architectural History
8 | 8 | 8 | 8

Humanities
8 | 8

Humanities
8 | 8 | 8 | 8 | 8 | 8

Elective
8 | 8

Rodwin, memorandum re: "Special Graduate Program for Problems in Developing Areas," 20 June 1961, p. 4, MIT Institute Archives, AC400 Box 3, Folder: School of Architecture and Planning Policy 1/3.

33 Sam T. Hurst, "In Search of Theory (Parts I and II)," *Arts and Architecture* 80 (June 1963), 17; 80 (November 1963): 19, 39-40; John E. Burchard, "In Search of Theory (Part III)," *Arts and Architecture* 81 (March 1964): 22-23, 32-34.

34 Ibid. 34.

35 See Mark Jarzombek, "The Crisis of Interdisciplinary Historiography," *Journal of Architectural Education* 50, no. 3 (September 1991): 311-313. The contributions to this issue were solicited by Stanford Anderson for a session at the Annual Meeting of the Society of Architectural Historians, and were [this correction seems to me to be grammatically incorrect (i.e. redundant), since "were" is part of the previous clause] edited by Anderson.

36 "Report on the Summer Space Study of the School of Architecture and Planning, August 1973, Revised November 1973, Final Report November 1973," p. 7-8, MIT Institute Archives, AC400 Box 48, Folder: Report on the Summer Space Study of the School of Arch and Planning, November 1973.

Lawrence B. Anderson, Diagram of "University Curricular Structures," in "School of Planning Arts: Undergraduate Curricular Structure" Report, November 21, 1961.

37 The following information on Millon's early life is summarized from Millon, *A Life of Learning: Charles Homer Haskins Lecture for 2002* (Washington, DC: American Council of Learned Societies, 2002): Born in Altoona, PA in 1927, Millon attended Tulane University on a US Navy ROTC scholarship. After a year of active service in 1946, he returned to Tulane to earn two undergraduate degrees, in English and Physics. After his second graduation, a visit to his "grandmère," who ran a shop selling tools and equipment to sculptors in Paris, galvanized his interest in the arts. He returned to Tulane in 1950 to study architecture. At the time, the school was run by "a converted modernist, Buford Pickens, who implemented the reforms instituted at Harvard by Walter Gropius in the late 1930s, and had brought in young designers who taught modern architecture with a missionary zeal. For the most part they were educated at Columbia and Harvard." This was his first exposure to the history of art and architecture, which he studied under Bernard Lemann, who had earned his PhD at Harvard. (Lemann is editor, with Malcolm Heard Jr. and John P. Klingman, of *Talk About Architecture: A Century of Architectural Education at Tulane* [New Orleans: Tulane University School of Architecture, 1993].) Another

For all of his postulation, however, Burchard himself was largely powerless to effect this change in the production of architectural knowledge—i.e to create a semi-autonomous institution within the architecture school that would elevate not only history, but theory and criticism, to the status of serious academic research. A prolific writer on architecture, he single-handedly outpaced the scholarly production of the entire architecture school, but his institutional position, responsibilities outside of the school, and conservative critical temperament proved insurmountable obstacles to his fulfilling his ultimate and stated aim.

Despite Burchard's failings in this regard, by 1973 research appeared to be thriving in the department. According to a report on space needs within the school announced in November of that year, the "School has a rapidly growing research program . . . [varying] from building technology research . . . to computer programming, to standard office/library activity," and that "[e]ven in the Architecture Department, some of the education is being directed away from the drafting board to research-centered studies."[36] But especially given the anxious formulation of the latter, none of this work seemed to fit the bill as part of dream of a specifically *architectural* research. How did this dream become fulfilled?

The Stakes of Architectural Research, 1960-1976

In fact, the problem of mobilizing the institution to establish a meaningful agenda and structure for architectural research at MIT fell to a new assistant professor, Henry A. Millon. Millon had taught architectural history at MIT as Bush-Brown's assistant in 1956, and, before his arrival as Assistant Professor, had participated actively in the life of the School of Architecture and Planning at MIT as a student at Harvard.[37]

Millon's long early education, which included three undergraduate degrees (one in architecture) from Tulane University, had not galvanized his commitment to architectural history, and in the early 1950s he must have seemed an unlikely candidate to spearhead the reform of architectural research. A pair of seminars with Rudolf Wittkower at the Fogg Museum of Art during his graduate pursuits (another degree in architecture and a PhD in art history) in 1954 and 1955, however, made a much deeper impression. The first seminar was on 15th- and 16th-century Italian architectural treatises, the second on those

visiting scholar, Mervyn Frederick Henry Roe, taught Renaissance and Baroque architecture, with particular emphasis on the works of Geoffrey Scott and Rudolf Wittkower.

By his own account, Millon was an "unremarkable" student of architecture, but he nonetheless earned himself a spot in the Department

of Fine Arts at Harvard University. There he studied with Jacob Rosenberg, John Coolidge, Sydney Freedberg and George Hanfmann; he also took courses in the Graduate School of Design with Fred Deknatel, Leonard Opdycke, Kenneth Conant and Sigfried Giedion. He also spent a year earning a master's degree in the

GSD taking studio courses with Josep Lluis Sert, Jean Paul Carlhian, Wells Coates, and Jacqueline Tyrwhitt, "with occasional crits from Joseph Zalevsky and Eduard Sekler, [which] reinforced a continuing interest in contemporary architecture."

38 Henry A. Millon, "The Architectural Theory of Francesco Di Giorgio," *Art*

Bulletin 40, no. 3 (September 1958): 257-261.

39 John Coolidge was trained as an architect at Columbia University during Hudnut's tenure there as dean and then completed a PhD in art history at the Institute of Fine Arts at New York University. He returned to Harvard's Department of Fine Arts as a professor, and

of the 17th and 18th centuries. Millon's seminar report on Francesco di Giorgio led to the publication of a short article in *Art Bulletin*—his first publication.[38] Upon completion of his coursework, Millon embarked upon a dissertation under the supervision of John Coolidge.[39]

It is likely that the *Art Bulletin* essay—which is largely a reconfirmation of the thesis proffered in Wittkower's *Architectural Principles in the Age of Humanism*, of 1949—and Coolidge's and Wittkower's support played key roles in securing Millon two fellowships. The first was a Fulbright, granting Millon a year in Turin "where British historian Stuart Woolf . . . guided [him] through the intricacies of archival holdings, provided counsel in [his] searches, and supplied building costs as he noted them in family archives." While in Turin, Millon met and befriended all of the architects and historians then teaching at the Politecnico, as well as visiting speakers Francis Haskell and Paolo Portoghesi. Millon's meeting with Portoghesi, in particular, was the beginning of a long friendship and alliance. In the summer of 1958, before beginning two years at the American Academy in Rome, Millon took a seminar on Piedmontese art and architecture of the 17th and 18th centuries. As he put it: "Long-term interest was assured."[40]

His time in Rome was no less influential on his outlook: "From the policies and activities of the director, Laurance Roberts, I learned the signal importance for most scholars of a support system with adequate resources, a staff dedicated to facilitating each fellow's endeavor, and a director interested in scholarship."[41] Moreover, he met an even wider circle of mentors and future colleagues, including

> Ralph E. Griswold and Thomas Church (landscape architects), Francis Comstock, Nathaniel Owings, Jean Labatut, and Edward Durell Stone (architects) . . . Craig Hugh Smyth, colleague and mentor, and H.W. Janson (art historians) . . . and among the art historians, Howard Hibbard, Milton Lewine, and Donald Posner . . .

> Short- and longer-term visitors were . . . Gisela M.A. Richter; Richard Krautheimer . . . G.E. Kidder-Smith; George Kubler . . . and Lewis Mumford.[42]

was soon tapped to become the Director of the Fogg Museum, a post he held for more than two decades. See John Coolidge, "Harvard's Teaching of Architecture and of the Fine Arts, 1928-1985," in Margaret Henderson Floyd, ed., *Architectural Education and Boston: Centennial Publication of the Boston Architectural Center,*

1889-1989 (Boston: Boston Architectural Center, 1989), 59-66. Millon's dissertation was eventually completed under the supervision of Wittkower: Millon, *Guarino Guarini and the Palazzo Carignano in Turin* (Ph.D dissertation, Harvard University, 1964).

40 Millon, *A Life of Learning*, 8.
41 Ibid., 9.
42 Ibid.
43 Anecdotes and reflections on their collaborations can be found in Millon, *A Life of Learning*, 8-9. The highly detailed scholarly outcome of their work is documented in the following: Millon and Smyth, "Michelangelo and St. Peter's, I: Notes on a Plan

of the Attic as Originally Built on the South Hemicycle," *The Burlington Magazine* 111, no. 797 (August 1969): 484-499, 501; Millon and Smyth, "Michelangelo and St. Peter's: Observations on the Interior of the Apses, a Model of the Apse Vault, and Related Drawings," *Römisches Jahrbuch für Kunstgeschichte* (1976); Millon and Smyth, "A

It was also at this time that Millon and Smyth embarked upon a decades-long project on Michelangelo's designs for St. Peter's, a project which would ensure that Millon became anything but a narrowly focused scholar of the Piedmontese baroque.[43] In addition to generating a lifetime's worth of scholarly production, this project spurred in Millon an intensive interest in models and modeling. This interest inspired his broad and sustained collaborative projects with contemporary architects at MIT and elsewhere in the 1960s, some of which are discussed below.

Upon returning to Cambridge in the summer of 1960, Millon took a post as an Assistant Professor in the Department of Architecture alongside his former professor Bush-Brown, who would leave MIT in 1962 to become the president of the Rhode Island School of Design. The impact of Millon's arrival was immediate: in December of 1960 he published an editorial in *Architectural Record*—titled "History of Architecture: How Useful?"—which laid out, in very concise terms, a coherent theory of the role of architectural history within architectural culture with specific reference to the instruction of architects. Were the editorial not so modestly phrased, it could be characterized as a manifesto for architectural history and architectural education in general. In truth, it is more a counter-manifesto, written in rebuttal of Bruno Zevi's 1957 call—on the editorial page of his journal, *L'architettura, cronache e storia*—for an aggressively engaged architectural history. Under the direct heading "Architectural history for modern architects," Zevi had argued passionately that "the history of ancient architecture should be taught with a modern critical mentality: it must serve to create better architects, not only specialized historians of art. The study of history creates a critical consciousness whose usefulness can be checked at the drawing table better than in the library."[44]

Zevi went even further, proposing that *every* course in Italian architectural curricula should be regarded as first and foremost a course in critical history:

all the courses with their various emphases, will be courses of architectonic history, especially those concerning the materials of construction, which in the most advanced schools, are already oriented in that direction. From a coherent historical-critical direction

Design by Michelangelo for a City Gate: Further Notes on the Lille Sketch," *The Burlington Magazine* 117, no. 864 (March 1975): 162-166; Millon, "A Note on Michelangelo's Façade for a Palace for Julius III in Rome: New Documents for the Model," *The Burlington Magazine* 121, no. 921 (December 1979): 770-777. Millon and Smyth

also produced the exhibition catalogue, *Michelangelo Architect: The Façade of San Lorenzo and the Drum and Dome of St. Peter's* (Milan: Olivetti, 1988), in conjunction with the exhibition *Michelangelo Draftsman/ Architect* at the National Gallery of Art, Washington DC, in the same year.

44 Bruno Zevi, "La storia dell'architettura per gli architetti moderni" [Architectural history for modern architects], *L'architettura, cronache e storia* 3, no. 23 (September 1957): 292-293, p. 292.
45 Ibid., 292-293. The English translation is Millon's, quoted here from Henry A. Millon, "History of Architecture: How

Useful?" *AIA Journal* 34, no. 6 (December 1960): 23-25, p. 24.
46 See Gwendolyn Wright and Janet Parks, eds., *The History of History in American Schools of Architecture, 1865-1975* (New York: Temple Hoyne Buell Center for the Study of American Architecture; Princeton: Princeton University Press,

the entire teaching of architecture, now split into half-a-score of closed compartments, will draw the motive of its dynamic unity. Many professors, with the most varied artistic and technical inclinations teaching only one subject: architecture in its history, acting on the problems of man in forging its modernity.[45]

Looking to the "most advanced" architecture schools of the period, it is difficult to understand Zevi's proclamation that "historical-critical" courses in tectonics were central to architectural curricula.[46] Nonetheless, in Italy he continued to press for curricular reforms that would more fully integrate history into architectural education. As he put it in *Archittetura e storagrafia* (1951; 2nd ed. 1974), his lengthy manifesto for an on-going renewal of architectural modernism, history had been neglected as the prime conceptual mover in the development of modern architecture: "The development of modern architecture, therefore, progresses hand in hand with a cultural excavation, speaking figuratively, which drastically altered the methods adopted by traditional historiography and the results it had achieved . . . The historiographical revolution is an indispensable accomplice of the architectural revolution."[47]

Millon found Zevi's brand of engaged criticism and history, whose rhetoric he no doubt encountered often enough during his time in Italy, to be at once redundant and dangerous. With regard to Zevi's insistence that architectural history shake off its static, "closed" traditions and become "dynamic," the young Millon chided the senior scholar, noting that

> there are many different "true" histories and it will be difficult to decide which one the schools should espouse. As to the term 'dynamic history,' Zevi should be aware of his great fellow Italian Benedetto Croce who said that historians both write and create history. The implication is clear—historians, in their process of selection, organization, and presentation, interpret the past for the present and in so doing mould the present. Is this not dynamic? How could it be otherwise?[48]

Pushing back harder against Zevi's injunction, Millon emphasized a fundamentally conservative approach to architectural history within architectural education as a whole. For

1990); more relevant to the current discussion, but a non-scholarly source, is Margaret Henderson Floyd, ed., *Architectural Education and Boston*, which covers aspects of the curricula at Harvard and MIT (see note 41).

47 Bruno Zevi, *The Language of Modern Architecture* (Seattle: University of Washington Press, 1978), 112.

Part II, "Architecture versus Architectural History," is a translation (uncredited) of the 2nd ed. of *Architettura e storiografia* (Turin: Einaudi, 1974).

48 Henry A. Millon, "History of Architecture: How Useful?"

49 Henry A. Millon, "History of Architecture: How Useful?," 25. See also the discussion of Millon's and Zevi's debate

in Andrew Leach, *What is Architectural History?* (London: Polity, 2010).

50 Henry A. Millon, "Rudolf Wittkower, *Architectural Principles in the Age of Humanism*: Its Influence on the Development and Interpretation of Modern Architecture," *Journal of the Society of Architectural Historians* 31, no. 2 (May

1972): 83-91, p. 87.

51 Millon, "Rudolf Wittkower, *Architectural Principles in the Age of Humanism*," 88.

52 Ibid., 89. However, the Smithsons' and other English modernist architects' admiration for Wittkower's book may also spring from Wittkower's claim at the conclusion of his famous book that: *it was . . . in England*

Millon, the success of any particular architectural history curriculum hinged upon, on the one hand, the "individual talent and predilections" of the instructor, and on the other the "awareness" and "maturation" of the student. In Millon's charismatic and pluralistic view, the only consequences of forcing a particularly engaged critical historical practice onto the would be an undue distortion of the historical record and would even risk denaturing the design process itself:

> The real danger to the student is from the historian who strips down or soups up his presentation to get a little more mileage out of the Art Nouveau or the Space Frame. Denatured or overvitalized presentations will give the alert student architectural indigestion, while a spirited, sincere exposition by a competent scholar may offer sustaining nourishment . . . developing in him a sophisticated confidence.[49]

In short, for Millon architectural history was a means of providing a humanistic intellectual grounding for the architecture professional of whatever stripe, and not—as Millon reads Zevi—as a means to correct, politicize, or dominate architectural culture as a whole. The conceptual and instrumental linkages between historical practice and design practice were as yet unarticulated, and to exploit them blindly was to risk the very nature and autonomy of each discipline. Much as Manfredo Tafuri would do six years later in *Teorie e Storia*, Millon offered a decisive critique of the engaged historian; this targeted not just Zevi, but also Hitchcock, Pevsner, Giedion, and Banham. However, unlike Tafuri, Millon's views were based not upon a structural-Marxist approach, but on the selectively discursive approach of his mentor Wittkower.

In an illuminating article regarding Wittkower's influence on modern architectural historiography from 1972, Millon reflected on the legacy of that scholar's influential book, *Architectural Principles in the Age of Humanism* (1949) For the most part, the article is an effort to assess what Millon identifies as the "positive" impact of the book on modernist architects and architectural historians, and in particular the credence it lent to contemporary debates on modular construction, proportions, architectural composition, and architectural historiography. In the end, however, Millon argues that rather than having a positive

that the whole structure of classical aesthetics was overthrown from the bottom . . . 'Les proportions, c'est l'infini'—this terse statement is still indicative of our approach. That is the reason why we view researches into the theory of proportion with suspicion and awe. But the subject is again very much alive in the minds of young

architects to-day, and they may well evolve new and unexpected solutions to this ancient problem. *Architectural Principles in the Age of Humanism*, 2nd ed. (London: A. Tracanti, 1952), p. 131, 135. The phrasing of this last paragraph remained unchanged in later editions.

53 Sibyl Moholy-Nagy, Review of *Key Monuments of the History of Architecture* by Henry A. Millon, *The Beginnings of Architecture* by Sigfried Giedion, *Journal of the Society of Architectural Historians* 19, no. 3 (December 1964): 41-43.

54 For a summary of his position vis-à-vis the audience and his fellow participants, see Chermayeff's contribution to the seminar, "Random Thoughts on the Architectural Condition," in Marcus Wiffen, ed., *The History, Theory and Criticism of Architecture*, 23-36, esp. p. 23: "I don't like much what you do, I don't like very much *how* you do it, and

influence on the interest in proportion in modern architecture, the book had quite the opposite effect. Drawing architects towards "the integral societal or cultural significance of the forms, methods, and proportions employed by architects in the Renaissance," the book, Millon contends, "contributed substantially to a new examination of Modern Architecture in terms of its cultural, social, and political intent."[50]

Per Millon, "Rowe, Banham, Jordy, Frampton, Colquhoun, Eisenmann, Rykwert, and Anderson" all owed something to "Wittkower's exposition of the relationship between architecture and society . . . as an apt methodological model for a revision of views about twentieth-century architecture." With only circumstantial evidence, Millon goes so far as to claim that "what Wittkower did to correct Wölfflin's and Geoffrey Scott's interpretations, his pupils and others, following the same model, were to do to correct Hitchcock and Johnson, Pevsner, and Giedion."[51]

Although this argument has its own inherent interest to the student of the mid-twentieth-century's debates over architectural historiography, of greater interest here is a small paragraph near the conclusion of the argument, where Millon once again outlines his firmly held belief that the ideal architectural historian is one disengaged from instrumental criticism and practice; for Millon, the ideal architectural historian is instead devoted to maintaining a critical *distance* from contemporary practice. He insinuates—indeed, he seems almost to provide a caveat—that what made it possible for Wittkower to achieve this wide-ranging influence was his refusal (with one notable exception) to write engaged criticism or history on modernist architects or architecture.

Millon's noted disagreements with Zevi do not, however, necessarily lead to the conclusion that Millon's view was fully closed to engagement with contemporary practitioners. In the same essay on Wittkower, Millon quotes a letter to the editor of the *RIBA Journal* from Alison and Peter Smithson, in which they complain that a review of Wittkower's book by A.S.G. Butler was unfair in the extreme: "Dr. Wittkower is regarded by the younger architects as the only art historian working in England capable of describing and analyzing buildings in spatial and plastic terms, and not in terms of derivations and dates. . . ".[52]

I don't believe what you are doing serves any good." **55** See Marcus Whiffen, ed., *The History, Theory and Criticism of Architecture*. The questions are reprised in Stephen W. Jacobs's essay in this volume, "History: An Orientation for the Architect," p. 47-70.

56 The language quoted here, although characteristic of all of the lectures, is borrowed from Peter Collins, "The Interrelated Roles of History, Theory and Criticism in the Process of Architectural Design," in Marcus Whiffen, ed., *The History, Theory and Criticism of Architecture*, 1-10, p. 1-2.

57 Anderson studied architecture at the University of Minnesota and at the University of California at Berkeley, where he earned a master's degree. He was appointed assistant professor at MIT in 1963 while still pursuing his Ph.D. at Columbia University with the justly famous dissertation *Peter Behrens*

and the New Architecture of Germany, 1900-1917 (1968). This was published, much revised and thirty-two years later, as *Peter Behrens and a New Architecture for the Twentieth Century* (Cambridge, MA: MIT Press, 2000). See also Kathleen James Chakraborty's excellent review of the published book in the *Journal of the Society*

For Millon, this was evidence of the viability of Wittkower's scholarly attitude towards contemporary practice: through a combination of art historical acumen and acute disciplinary awareness of the way in which architects think and work, architectural history may become both a living document and a "useful" practice.

In this way, Millon in fact left the door open to the historian's engagement with contemporary practitioners, and especially to collaboration with researchers in various disciplines ranging from the arts and humanities to the sciences. The surprising degree to which Millon tolerated Zevi's point of view--and eschewed a decisive statement regarding the role of architectural history, theory, and criticism in favor of articulating all of them as little more than a series of open questions--is reflected in Millon's leadership of the 1964 AIA-ACSA Teacher Seminar at the Cranbrook Academy of Art. The seminar's leadership was dominated by representatives of MIT: Burchard was a member of several important AIA committees and a frequent speaker at conferences; Lawrence B. Anderson, Dean of the School of Architecture and Planning, was chair of the steering committee; and Millon was appointed both as a member of the scholarship committee and as chair of the program committee. Nevertheless, the seminar was hardly a closed forum. The invitees were a who's-who of Millon's opponents in contemporary debate over the stakes of architectural history, theory, and criticism: Zevi, who at the conference presented the reforms he had announced in 1957 as a *fait accompli*; Sibyl Moholy-Nagy, who later that year mercilessly dismissed Millon's pictorial survey of the history of world architecture, *Key Monuments of the History of Architecture*;[53] Serge Chermayeff, who had vocally denounced the possibility of a purpose of any kind for architectural history;[54] Peter Collins, also on the program committee, who professed an ethos of teaching architectural history, theory, and criticism as a means to improve "the process of architectural design"; Stephen W. Jacobs, of Cornell University, a proponent of a vernacular and socially engaged architectural history, and an early preservationist; and Reyner Banham, not yet in his chair at the Bartlett, but already well known for his partisan criticism in *Architectural Review* and his controversial *Theory and Design in the First Machine Age* (1960).

of *Architectural Historians* 62, no. 3 (September 2003): 398-400.

58 Although it was recorded on audio tape, Charles Eames's Annual Discourse (14-15 April 1958) at the Royal Institute of British Architects was never published, probably due to a printer's strike in mid-summer 1958; nevertheless, its

contents are familiar through Reyner Banham's famous response to it in his series of articles, "Architecture after 1960," in *Architectural Review* 127 (February-June 1960). Eames's discourse (and Banham's boosterism) helped to unite a generation of young architects and critics in a firm commitment to technology as the means of renovating

modern architecture and preserving a role for the architect. See note 61 below. See *RIBA Journal* 66, no. 7 (May 1959): 226.

59 Reyner Banham, "Coventry Cathedral—Strictly 'Trad, Dad,'" *New Statesman* 63 (25 May 1962): 768-769; reprinted in *Architectural Forum* 117 (August 1962): 118-119.

60 See William Jordy, "The Symbolic Essence of Modern European Architecture of the Twenties and Its Continuing Influence," *Journal of the Society of Architectural Historians* 22, no. 3 (October 1963): 177-187.

61 *Architectural Review* 127 (February-June 1960). See especially Banham, "Architecture after 1960. 1.

In preparation for the seminar, Millon distributed a list of five questions that he desired the participants to answer, more or less directly, in their presentations:

What place should the history of painting and sculpture have in the curriculum?
Is the history of architecture the same discipline as the history of art?
Is it desirable or necessary that a historian of architecture be an architect?
Is contemporary architecture a legitimate subject of historical research?
Do historians influence the development of contemporary architecture? [55]

No one but Jacobs bothered to respond directly to these questions; each participant preferred instead to press his or her own agenda. Even a cursory reading of the gathered lectures immediately raises several key issues. The most prominent of these is that of vocabulary: the participants did not share functional definitions for the three key terms ostensibly at the center of the debate—"history," "theory," and "criticism" were protean subjects, and each thinker deployed them as they liked.

More surprising is the near-universal agreement amongst the participants that a "gap" had somehow appeared in the space between architectural thought and practice. In almost every case, the culprit was Walter Gropius, who had "banned" lectures on architectural history from the Bauhaus in order to "innoculate" students against the "evils of architectural historicism."[56] Several speakers intimated that it was this gap that was responsible for the Babel-like dispersion of descriptive vocabulary; even if history seemed to be a relatively stable term, the meanings of the terms "theory" and "criticism" could not be easily pinned down.

Characteristically, Millon stayed to one side of the debate, moderating discussion and allowing his former dean at Tulane, Buford Pickens (now teaching at Washington University in St. Louis), to offer summary statements; however, he did enlist one ally not yet mentioned: the young architectural historian and recently appointed MIT Assistant Professor of architectural history Stanford O. Anderson.[57] Anderson's talk, originally delivered a year earlier at the Architectural Association in London (where, one imagines, it was an even more unsettling attack),[58] was titled "Architecture and Tradition that isn't 'Trad, Dad,'" a direct reference to a well-known

Stocktaking" (February 1960): 93-100; Banham, "Science for Kicks" (June 1960): 387; and the response to Banham's series by J.M. Richards, Hugh Casson, Nikolaus Pevsner, and H. de C. Hastings, "1960: Propositions 5" (June 1960): 381-388.
62 Anderson, "Architecture and Tradition that isn't 'Trad, Dad,'" in: Marcus Whiffen,

ed., *The History, Theory and Criticism of Architecture* 71-89, p. 71.
63 Ibid., 74.
64 Ibid., note 15. Anderson claims that he and Colin Rowe came independently to their study of Popper and Imre Lakatos—see "Architectural History in Schools of Architecture," *Journal of the Society of*

Architectural Historians 58, no. 3 (September 1999): 282-290, p. 284. In his years at Berkeley, he was also deeply marked by his engagement with the work of Ernst Gombrich, especially the summaries of Gombrich's method as given in the lecture *Art and Scholarship* (London: H.K. Lewis, 1957) and his chef d'oeuvre *Art*

and Illusion: A Study in the Psychology of Pictorial Representation, 2nd ed. (New York: Bollingen Foundation/ Pantheon Books, 1961); for Anderson's acknowledgment of this debt, see ibid., 23. See also Paul Feyerabend, *Against Method: An Outline of an Anarchistic Theory of Knowledge* (London: Verso, 1978).

article by Reyner Banham on the controversies surrounding the rebuilding of Coventry Cathedral.[59] In fact, the paper was devoted to a much broader critique of—or really, an all-out assault on—Banham's positions on both the relationship between architectural criticism and architectural history and what Anderson called Banham's "scientific determinism."

The crux of Anderson's critique was the too-easy distinction that Banham (along with other historians like Zevi and Brown University architectural historian William Jordy[60]) had made between historicist ("traditional") architecture and avant-guardist architecture. Citing both Banham's landmark *Theory and Design in the First Machine Age* (1960) and the well-known and controversial set of articles he wrote and edited in *Architectural Review* on "Architecture after 1960" in the same year,[61] Anderson sought to "establish an interpretation of tradition [in architectural theory] that will recognize our debt to the past without establishing the past as an authority."[62] This, however, would be impossible without a wholesale reevaluation of both received architectural knowledge and the bases of architectural research. As he asked with rhetorical fervor:

> Even if we were to accept that such a thing as a qualitative change distinguished modern architecture from that which preceded it, does this liberate us from the past? Is the traditional operational lore of architecture categorically superseded? Or is the situation of architecture similar to that of physics, where older hypotheses—Democritean atomism or Newtonian physics, for example—remain theoretically suggestive or pragmatically operative? . . . Is [Banham's] concept of a "scientific surf-ride" which demands little more from the architect than daring and a sense of balance the most rational or, indeed, the most radical possible adaptation of science by architecture?[63]

In short, Anderson argued, architectural historians had as yet little by way of *method*. Without a consistent means with which to critique past architecture and architectural theories—without a scientific approach to the "problem" of architectural history—the contemporary architect's relationship to both tradition and advanced technology would be idiosyncratic, irrational, and left to chance.

65 Karl Popper, "On the Sources of Knowledge and Ignorance," in Popper, *Conjections and Refutations*: 3-43, quoted in Anderson, "Architecture and Tradition," p. 81.

66 See Imre Lakatos, "Falsification and the Methodology of Scientific Research Programmes," in *Criticism and the Growth of* *Knowledge* (Proceedings of the International Colloquium in the Philosophy of Science, London, 1965, volume 4), eds. Imre Lakatos and Alan Musgrave (Cambridge: Cambridge University Press, 1970): 91-196.

67 See ibid., 79: "The radical step would be to formulate problems and hypotheses within our own architectural problem situation, and then to criticize and test them as rigorously as our current information and methods permit. As science and technology have been known to profit from science fiction, so architecture could profit from a form of 'architectural fiction.' But architects must learn not to take such writings and projects as either predictive history or as established theory. Like science fiction, it would bear fruit only when it had been critically assimilated into the problem situation."

68 Here it may be useful to point out that it is in this articulation of the scientific method that Anderson decisively distinguishes himself from other

The model with which Anderson sought to supplant the art historical methods of Banham was, as the above quotation suggests, taken from the history and philosophy of science as outlined by Karl Popper. While still an architecture student at Berkeley, he had been introduced to Popper's work by Popper's disciple and later critic Paul Feyerabend.[64] Taking advantage of a felicitous architectural metaphor in Popper's "On the Sources of Knowledge and of Ignorance"—"blue prints have no meaning except in a setting of traditions and institutions—such as myths, poetry and value—which all emerge from the social world in which we live . . . You may create a new theory, but the new theory is created in order to solve those problems which the old theory did not solve"[65]—Anderson identified a new attitude towards *criticism* that could reanimate and reorganize history and theory alike: the school of thought known as "fallibilism," of which Anderson remains a devoted student and proselytizer.

The historian of architecture, following Anderson following Popper (and later Imre Lakatos[66]), should thus endeavor to *test systematically* past "conjectures" in architectural practice, measuring accomplishments against stated theoretical aims, and in so doing serve the profession by providing an index of what remains to be done.[67] The historian's task is even broader when it encompasses the work of theory and criticism; the project here is to look outwards, beyond the disciplinary confines of architecture, to a scientific critique of architectural conjecture. Otherwise, Anderson argues, one is limited to a "conspiracy theory of society," in which some unknown and unknowable force accounts for the failure of the architectural project.[68] Anderson concluded his lecture forcefully with a lengthy quotation from Popper's essay, "Towards a Rational Theory of Tradition": "Try to learn what people are discussing nowadays in science. Find out where difficulties arise, and take an interest in disagreements. These are the questions which you should take up . . . In this way we make progress."[69]

These exciting methodological innovations were the core of the young Anderson's thought (and, we can assume, of Millon's); however, it would be criminal to miss the emphasis that Popper places not only on traditions, but on *institutions*. Here, at last, in Anderson's "radical adaptation of the methods of scientific discovery with neither the implication of a

architectural historians engaged in the critique of architectural ideology, especially Manfredo Tafuri and Francesco Dal Co. The *a priori* Freudian-Marxist convictions of Tafuri and Dal Co can find little place in the Popperian model of historical progress, and no place at all in the models offered by Popperians who also

became crucial to Anderson's theoretical approach. On this matter, see Anderson's later articles on critical historical method, especially "Critical Conventionalism: Architecture," *Assemblage* 1 (1986): 6-23; and "Critical Conventionalism: The History of Architecture," *Midgård* 1, no. 1 (1988): 33-47.

69 Popper, "Towards a Rational Theory of Tradition" (1948), in Popper, *Conjectures and Refutations*, 161-189, quoted in Anderson, "Architecture and Tradition," 88. **70** In fact, the majority of Anderson's scholarly output was devoted to such methodological concerns, rather than with empirical research. See the selected

bibliography of Anderson's work in Martha Pollak, ed., *The Education of the Architect: Historiography, Urbanism, and the Growth of Architectural Knowledge, Essays Presented to Stanford Anderson* (Cambridge, MA and London: MIT Press, 1997), 453-455.

scientific determinism nor the advocacy of leaping on the latest bandwagon," coupled with an institutional structure that would support such a project over the required *longue durée*, was the seed of a coherent yet flexible program for architectural research.

To judge from Millon's and Anderson's subsequent scholarly writing, however, it proved ambitious to integrate directly architectural history methods with those drawn from disciplines other than art history and historiology.[70] Millon and Anderson therefore wasted little time in attempting to explore the potential of their new historical, theoretical and critical attitude, and the bulk of this exploration occurred through a series of experimental engagements with architectural and extra-architectural disciplines alike. Throughout the 1960s and early 1970s, Millon participated in a broad array of projects outside the traditional bounds of architectural history, ranging from conferences on computing technologies to large-scale urban planning schemes. During this period, Anderson continued his study of the philosophy of science, eventually branching out to consider ecology, sociology, and—most importantly—architectural criticism. Anderson's particular approach to criticism was distinctive, however, from that of his contemporaries, for through it Anderson pushed beyond his polemical exchange with Banham to articulate a new agenda for what would eventually become the Ph.D. program in History, Theory and Criticism at MIT.

Millon and Anderson both took vital impetus for their project from their immediate institutional surroundings. Alongside on-going research into urbanism, the Department of Architecture also drastically expanded its research apparatus by adding Nicholas Negroponte to its faculty in 1967. While studying as an undergraduate and an M.Arch. student at MIT in the early 1960s, Negroponte had become interested in computer science. He took courses and collaborated with several MIT faculty and graduate students then making important first strides in the articulation of the modern contours of the discipline: Daniel Bobrow, a pioneer in artificial intelligence; Ivan Sutherland, who produced the first graphic software for computer-aided design (Sketchpad); and the nuclear physicist Norman Rasmussen, who directed a section of the IBM Cambridge Scientific Center in which Negroponte worked on early computer design software (URBAN5). Negroponte's MArch thesis—which, according to Negroponte, was "controversial" in the eyes of the School

71 Nicholas Negroponte, "Introduction," in Negroponte, ed., *Reflections on Computer Aids to Design and Architecture* (New York: Petrocelli/Charter, 1975): 1-13, p. 8.

72 Funding statistics are detailed in The Department of Architecture, Massachussetts Institute of Technology, "Educational Development Plan...submitted to National Architecture Accrediting Board, March 1978," MIT Institute Archives Folder "Educational Development Plan....," Section II, p. 43ff. Negroponte is listed with the largest number of external sponsors: IBM sponsored "Television Based Animation," $43,951; the National Science Foundation sponsored "Machine Recognition and Inference Making" $622,400; ARPA sponsored "Aug of Human Res Command and Control," $82,334 and $367,666; and the US Army, Navy and Air Force also sponsored large block grants over several-year spans.

Architecture and the Computer, proceedings of the first Boston Architectural Center Conference, December 5, 1964. (Cambridge, MA: Boston Architectural College, 1965).

right, Henry Millon moderating the evening panel discussion, "Computers and Creativity." *Architecture and the Computer*, 1964. Photo: Phokion Karas.

of Architecture and thus had a significant impact on the culture of the school even before he joined the faculty in 1966—"on the [machinic] simulation of perception" was the first such project to integrate successfully the relatively young field of computer science into the even younger one of architectural research.[71] As an assistant professor, Negroponte quickly expanded the Department of Architecture's efforts in this direction, establishing the Architecture Machine Group (AMG) in 1967 to develop "man-machine design systems." Drawing on ample sources of funding from the government, IBM, and the architecture and engineering firm SOM, the AMG soon became the most richly endowed portion of the School of Architecture, outstripping even the Joint Center in funds by nearly a million dollars by the early 1970s.[72]

Without prior knowledge of the theoretical and critical issues he was exploring at this period, and without attention to his shifting institutional surroundings, it would perhaps be surprising to learn that Millon, the scholar of the Italian Renaissance and Baroque, participated prominently in perhaps the first ever conference on the emergent relationship between architecture and computer sciences and technologies. Titled *Architecture and the Computer* and held in Boston, the 1964 conference was sweeping in scope, exploring what

the participants—computer scientists as well as architects and engineers—considered to be the full range of possibilities for the use of computing technology in architecture.[73]

Following a day of academic papers and lectures, Millon moderated the summary evening panel, reading a statement on "Computers for Architectural Design" by Walter Gropius and then offering some telling remarks of his own. Frankly skeptical about the potential of the computer to serve as anything more than a statistical aid to the designer, Millon nonetheless proceeded to press the panelists with questions regarding the computer's potential to reform the discipline at a fundamental level. As he asked Marvin Minsky, prominent cognitive scientist, cybernetician and computer scientist (and founder of MIT's Artificial Intelligence Laboratory), "Will the architect's time honored role as 'image maker of a new society' be affected by new analytical techniques?"[74] That is, would the computer replace or fundamentally change the modernist self-image of the architect? Minsky replied in ingenuously historical terms:

> Architects will have to face the automation of design. Eventually, I believe computers will evolve formidable creative capacity . . .

Henry A. Millon regarding an I/O device for MIT
Department of Architecture's IBM 7094 computer.
From *Architecture and the Computer*. Photo: Phokion
Karas.

. . . You can look ahead from one year to the next and predict normal progress. On the other hand, if you look back ten years, computers couldn't do anything intelligent; now they solve quite difficult problems. If you look ahead two or three more intervals of ten years, you can imagine the face of the world as entirely different with machines competing in creativity and intelligence with me. It depends on how far you look ahead.[75]

In short, the answer was yes; however, and more importantly for Millon's on-going discursive concerns, the general implication was that historical analysis of increasingly imbricated fields of architecture and computer science would yield an inevitable result. Millon thus probed further in this direction, again asking not his architect colleagues but rather Minsky, "Now, if one addressed himself to the design of a theory of criticism of which architectural criticism would be a part, how should one go about doing this?" Minsky hedged, admitting that machines could not yet replace the human faculty for what Millon called "value judgment"; however, he did suggest that "[w]e can give you what you want; the trouble is you can't afford it."[76] That is, for Minsky the problem of resolving the application of decision-making by computers to *architectural design and criticism alike* was simply one of labor—with sufficient hardware, data entry and research capital, "in a few years . . . a computer's memory could hold a lifetime of experience . . . Eventually we will have programs able to draw on a large body of experience, the value judgments of a large number of people who have contributed to its memory."[77] Exchanges like this one—direct engagements with computers and computer scientists—allowed Millon and Anderson to formulate what they considered to be rigorous questions regarding the nature of the architectural discipline, and these questions provided additional contours to their nascent theory of architectural history, theory, and criticism. If critical practice could be reduced to logical practice, then it followed that it was possible to develop a rigorous curriculum in history, theory, and criticism could—in theory—serve as a crucial adjunct to design research within the architecture school.

Following through on Millon's engagement with computer science, Anderson contributed to a report by researchers in the Department of Architecture at MIT, which was published

73 See *Architecture and the Computer* (Proceedings of the First Boston Architectural Center Conference, December 5, 1964, Boston, MA) (Boston: Boston Architectural Center, 1965), esp. the discussion on "Computers and Creativity" moderated by Millon, 42-51.

74 Ibid., 42.
75 Minsky in ibid., 45.
76 Henry Millon and Marvin Minsky in "Panel Discussion," in *Architecture and the Computer*, 46-49.
77 Ibid. 47.

78 Stanford Anderson, "Commentary" on "Experiments in Computer Aided Design: Report from the Department of Architecture, Massachusetts Institute of Technology," *Architectural Design* 39 (September 1969): 509-514, p. 514; this was part of a special issue guest edited by the architect Roy Landau titled

"Despite Popular Demand AD is Thinking about Architecture and Planning," which focused on efforts to coordinate contemporary scientific and technical research with design methods. Anderson's favored philosopher, Imre Lakatos, was also a contributor.

in *Architectural Design* in 1969.[78] Titled "Experiments in Computer Aided Design," it chronicled recent projects—"Space Arrangement," led by Tim Johnson; "Discourse and Choice," led by William Porter, John Boorn and the Urban Systems Laboratory at MIT and IBM; and "Architecture Machine," led by Negroponte and Léon Groissier of the AMG—within the department that had attracted significant funding from major foundations and corporations to study the potential for using computers as design tools. In a short commentary at the end of the three groups' reports, Anderson offered guidance to these putatively scientific researchers with his first fully articulated agenda for the adaptation of Popper's and Lakatos's method to architectural concerns:

> Architecture structures man's environment to facilitate the achievement of human purposes (intellectual, psychological and utilitarian) where those purposes are incompletely known and cannot be extrapolated from what is given in the situation. Rather, human purposes are altered by the very environment that is created to facilitate them. The structuring of the environment must be accomplished, then, through the exercise of tentative foresight and the critical examination of that foresight and the actions to which it leads . . . In logical terms, universal theories cannot be derived from reports of finite number of observations.[79]

To the extent that Negroponte et al considered this principle the logical core of their on-going research, Anderson offered his cautious praise. Over the next four decades, Anderson has continued to publish similar critiques of on-going "architectural research programmes" by contemporary practitioners and educators.[80]

Stanford O. Anderson, Robert Goodman, Henry A. Millon and MIT students, "Model of view to the northeast:" Urban Plan for New York City proposal to link Randall's Island and Ward's Island to Manhattan through landfill operations, in *The New City: Architecture and Urban Renewal*, ed. Arthur Drexler (New York: MoMA, 1967). Digital image ©The Museum of Modern Art/ Licensed by SCALA/Art Resource, NY.

---

79 Stanford Anderson, "Commentary" on "Experiments in Computer Aided Design."

80 See Anderson, "Environment as Artifact," *Casabella* 35, no. 359-360 (December 1971): 71-77; Anderson, "Architectural Design as a System of Research Programmes," *Design Studies* 5 (July 1984): 146-150.

81 Henry Millon and Stanford Anderson, "Proposal for a Ph.D. Program in History, Theory and Criticism of Art, Architecture and Urban Form," Spring 1971, n.p., MIT Institute Archives, Series VII, Departments 1965-85, Box 175, Folder: Dept. of Architecture and Planning, 1969-76 2/4.

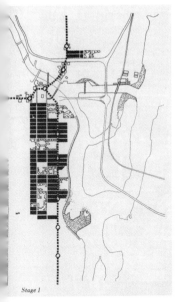
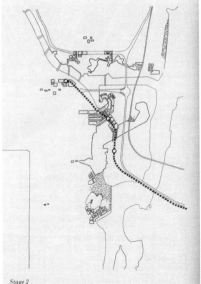
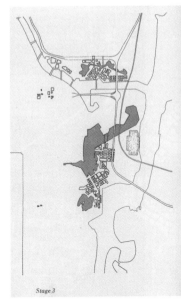

Stage 1 *Stage 2* *Stage 3*

In the year following the Boston computer conference, Millon and Anderson succeeded
in establishing a new undergraduate major in the History, Theory and Criticism of Art and
Architecture, leading to the BASD degree (offered for the first time in 1966).[81] Wayne V.
Andersen, who had studied under Wittkower and modern art historian Meyer Schapiro at
Columbia University (producing a dissertation and later a book on Cézanne), was added
on a permanent basis as a historian of modern art in 1964, and he was joined by Rosalind
Krauss in 1967.[82]

In 1966, Anderson and Millon had both begun working with the Conference of Architects
for the Study of the Environment (CASE), an inter-institutional group of architects formed
in 1964, which was committed to expanding architectural study to embrace urban planning
issues and explore alternative design methodologies. As a result of their involvement,
Anderson and Millon, along with Robert Goodman and several MIT students, were invited
to submit an urban planning project for New York alongside similar proposals from Cornell,
Princeton, and Columbia. The projects were exhibited as part of the exhibition, *The New
City: Architecture and Urban Renewal*, in 1967.[83] Given the problem of developing "new
land out of relatively under-used, or mis-used, peripheral areas" to provide "important
new amenities," the MIT team proposed expanding landfill operations then taking place
as part of the construction of the Triboro Bridge, connecting Randall's and Ward's islands
to provide space for parks, transit, mixed-use high-density developments, and water
purification systems. It should be noted here that we once again find Anderson and Millon
situated at the crux of major moment in the development of American architectural theory.
After their own CASE experiments, Peter Eisenman and Michael Graves turned away (in

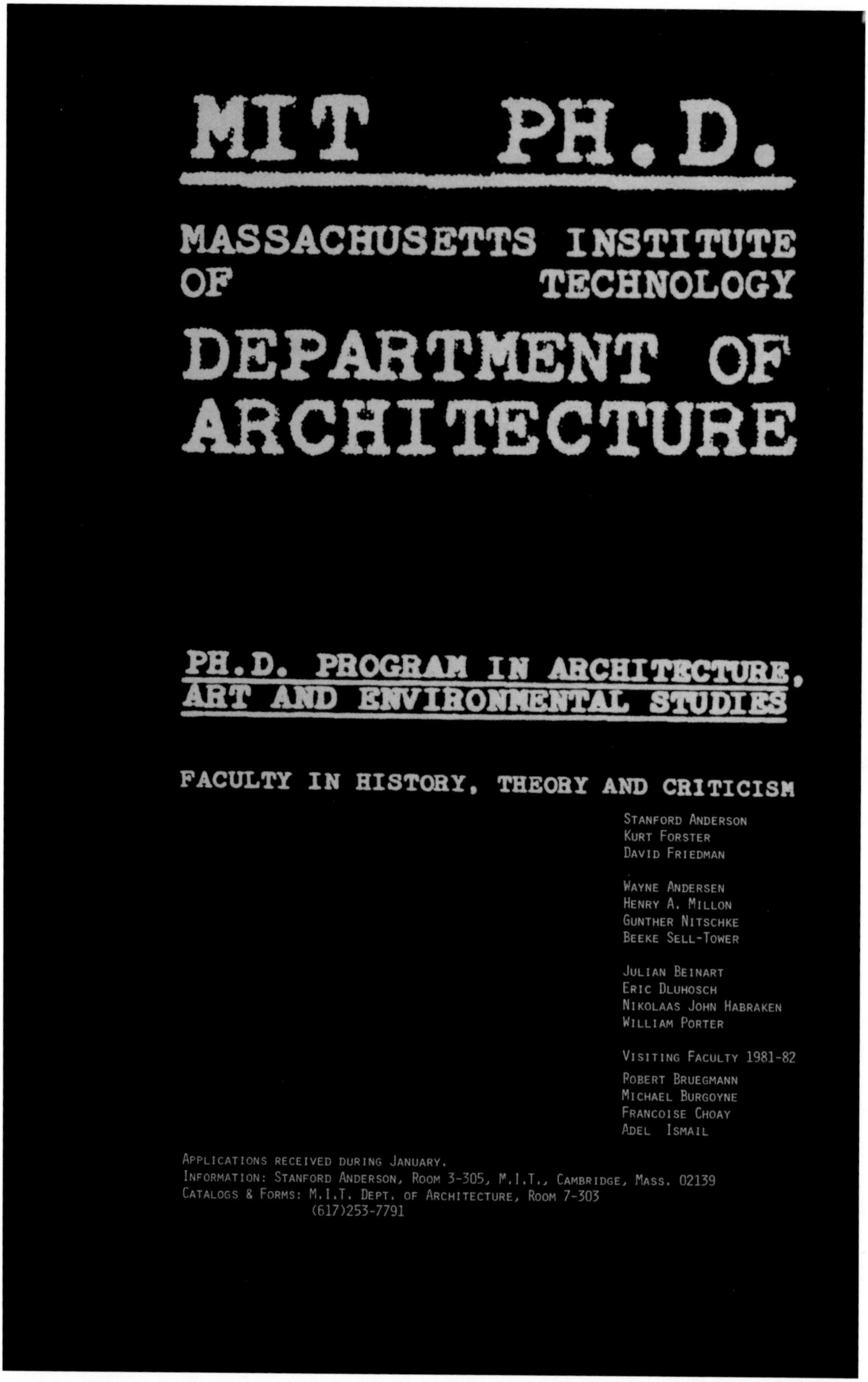

MIT   PH.D.

MASSACHUSETTS INSTITUTE OF   TECHNOLOGY

DEPARTMENT OF ARCHITECTURE

PH.D. PROGRAM IN ARCHITECTURE, ART AND ENVIRONMENTAL STUDIES

FACULTY IN HISTORY, THEORY AND CRITICISM

STANFORD ANDERSON
KURT FORSTER
DAVID FRIEDMAN

WAYNE ANDERSEN
HENRY A. MILLON
GUNTHER NITSCHKE
BEEKE SELL-TOWER

JULIAN BEINART
ERIC DLUHOSCH
NIKOLAAS JOHN HABRAKEN
WILLIAM PORTER

VISITING FACULTY 1981-82

ROBERT BRUEGMANN
MICHAEL BURGOYNE
FRANCOISE CHOAY
ADEL ISMAIL

APPLICATIONS RECEIVED DURING JANUARY.
INFORMATION: STANFORD ANDERSON, ROOM 3-305, M.I.T., CAMBRIDGE, MASS. 02139
CATALOGS & FORMS: M.I.T. DEPT. OF ARCHITECTURE, ROOM 7-303
        (617)253-7791

different directions!) from putatively politically engaged urban
planning to explore alternative approaches to design—Eisenman to
his series of "syntactical" house designs, Graves to his ambiguous
house designs.[84] In Eisenman's case, this led to a well-known
series of texts defending his "Cardboard Architecture" that form
some of the foundational texts of 1970s architectural theory.

In the case of Anderson and Millon, their CASE activity led to
Anderson's involvement in a wildly ambitious project, funded
by the AIA, Graham Foundation for the Arts, and the Princeton
University Educational Research Project, to explore "the societal
context within which architects will work in the near future."[85]
*Possible Futures and their Relations to the Man-Controlled
Environment*, the first conference organized under this project in
October of 1966, was a far-reaching affair, with contributions from
philosophers (including, significantly, Feyerabend), economists,
historians, sociologists, architects, and urban planners. This
presentation of research led to a long, multifaceted history and
design project headed by Anderson and funded by the IAUS and
the Graham Foundation for Advanced Studies in the Fine Arts,
which was eventually documented in the volume *On Streets*
(1978).[86] Millon, for his part, withdrew from the field of urban
design, choosing instead to devote his energies to institution-
building and historical research.

82 Anderson, "Architectural
History in Schools of
Architecture," 285.
83 Arthur Drexler, ed., The
*New City: Architecture and
Urban Renewal* (New York:
Museum of Modern Art,
1967), esp. p. 42-47.

84 See Manfredo Tafuri,
"European Graffiti: Five x Five
= Twenty-five," *Oppositions*
5 (Summer 1976): 35-74, esp.
p. 45-57, along with related
citations therein.

85 The proceedings of this
conference were published
in Stanford Anderson, ed.,
*Planning for Diversity and
Choice: Possible Futures
and their Relations to the
Man-Controlled Environment*
(Cambridge, MA: MIT Press,
1968).

History, Theory and Criticism at MIT, ca. 1975

Despite all of these efforts, by 1970 the exact contours of a consequent advanced curriculum in architectural history, theory, and criticism were as yet unclear. While course offerings and scholarly production amongst young art and architectural historians in the Department of Architecture gathered momentum throughout the 1960s, the Department of Planning[87] remained the dominant scholarly force within the School of Architecture and Planning. But the critical investigations—one might almost say experiments—of Millon and Anderson had produced the conceptual groundwork for a new institution within the Department of Architecture, and sometime in late 1970 they turned their full attention to developing it.

To judge from one letter surviving in the MIT Institute Archives,[88] it appears that Millon took the lead in securing both intra- and extra-institutional support for a PhD program in "History, Theory and Criticism of Art, Architecture and Urban Form." Anderson is silent on the matter in his own account of the program's foundation, except to note that the proposal was submitted to a "rigorous external examination."[89]

Unsurprisingly, the proposal—apparently coauthored by Millon and Anderson, with contributions from Wayne Andersen and Krauss[90] —for a PhD program in History, Theory and Criticism within the Department of Architecture began with an historical account of arts education at MIT since World War II. A relatively detailed summary of internal developments included an account of the expansion of Hayden Gallery, MIT's art museum, since its founding in 1948, and the establishment of the Center for Advanced Visual Studies (CAVS) in 1968.[91] More significantly for this account, the MIT art and architectural historians stressed the changing nature of architectural scholarship in the immediate post-war era, citing work at the Warburg Institute, Columbia University, Princeton University, and the Institute of Fine Arts at New York University. Yet despite this scholarship's success in getting "architecture . . . to yield some of its meaning," there remained a significant problem. It has already been rehearsed in this essay but is worth quoting in length for the way in which it establishes the stakes of the new program at MIT:

86 Anderson, ed., *On Streets* (Cambridge, MA: MIT Press, 1978). One of Anderson's two contributions to the volume, "People in the Physical Environment: The Urban Ecology of Streets," demonstrates his growing intellectual and political commitment to "cultural ecology" as a system of thought that avoided "blind

commitment to the status quo while defining the conditions and rates of non-catastrophic or more protectively defined change" (2). Anderson identified, somewhat idiosyncratically, this approach with that of Tafuri (13); however, it is plain that this outlook was not shared by the leading members of IAUS, especially

Eisenman, who moved further away from urban planning and towards other modes of design research. On Eisenman's changing attitude towards IAUS during this period, see Lucia Allais, "The Real and the Theoretical, 1968," *Perspecta 42: The Real* (Cambridge, MA: MIT Press, 2010), 27-40 and Kim Förster, "The Institute for Architecture

and Urban Studies, New York (1967-1985): A Cultural Project in the Field of Architecture" (D.Arch. Dissertation, ETH Zürich, 2011).

87 Between 1959 and 1963, the Joint Center published seven volumes on urban planning and related issues— Edward C. Banfield and James Q. Wilson, *City Politics*, 1963; John E. Burchard and

Studies of form and meaning, however excellent, nevertheless, failed to serve the immediate needs of the modern architects who sensed a need to polarize their own position relative to the traditionalism they found in their potential clients and in the curricula of the schools. A historian writing critically about either modern or pre-modern works would inevitably introduce unwanted nuance in the desired black and white image. The architects propagandizing for an open-minded development from modern conditions, thus found an aggressive stance against historical studies more effective than any critique or reorganization of historical studies. With few exceptions only those historians (e.g. Pevsner, Giedion) who would put their work in the service of the modern movement could play more than a minor role in the reformed schools of architecture. The difficulty of reform had understandably encouraged partisan historiography, and some of the work of this reform movement will easily outlive any propagandistic use it may have served. Nevertheless, the success of the reform quickly dramatized the inadequacies of the situation in architectural history.[92]

A generational shift had followed this reform, with the disciples of Wittkower and others issuing meaningful correctives to the excesses of the "propagandistic years;" nevertheless these architectural historians were all too often art historians rather than architects. The MIT program would change this:

The art historians presently on the MIT faculty . . . have chosen to teach in the Architecture Department at MIT out of the conviction that they have the most to give to and to learn from students actively engaged in extending their own sense of mastery over the problems of making art. They feel, as well, that such an atmosphere would have a liberating and envigorating effect on those graduate students who share their feeling that studio-oriented contemporary art historical studies have a creative role to play . . .

Since 1956, MIT has been unique in sustaining the nucleus of a professional department of the history of art within the department of architecture. Its two architectural historians in particular are committed to a close association between their efforts and the school as a whole; a critical and theoretical grasp of history shares a natural and mutual growth with

Oscar Handlin, ed., The Historian and the City [edited papers from the conference, "The City in History," summer 1961], 1963; Nathan Glazer and Daniel Moynihan, Beyond the Melting Pot, 1963; Kevin Lynch, The Image of the City, 1960; Lloyd Rodwin, Housing and Economic Progress, 1961; Sam B. Warner, Jr., Streetcar Suburbs, 1962; and

Morton and Lucia White, The Intellectual Versus the City: From Thomas Jefferson to Frank Lloyd Wright, 1962—whereas the history, theory, and criticism area could only claim the publication of Burchard and Bush-Brown's The Architecture of America, Millon's pictorial survey (see note 44), and Millon's survey of Baroque

and Rococo Architecture (New York: Braziller, 1961). For the initial period of the Center's publishing endeavor, from 1959-1963, MIT Press and Harvard University Press published titles jointly. Thereafter, the Center's publications were produced by one press or the other. As a result, in the late 1960s, the gap between

the publications of the Joint Center and the History; Theory, and Criticism group only widened. According to a capsule biography in Stanford Anderson, ed., Planning for Diversity and Choice: Possible Futures and their Relations to the Man-Controlled Environment (Cambridge, MA: MIT Press, 1968), Millon and Anderson attempted a "book

the criticism which is the core of the design studio. The strengthening of this program would . . . graduate the kinds of studio-oriented professional historians that are still rare in schools of architecture.[93]

Because of various shifts in staffing, the curriculum had a something of a false start, but was soon up and running.[94] Despite a relatively small faculty, the breadth of the curriculum was impressive. The Educational Development Plan submitted by the Department of Architecture to the National Architecture Accrediting Board in March 1978 lists a steadily growing enrollment of Ph.D. candidates, reaching ten by 1977. Within the PhD curriculum, Millon and Anderson assumed primary responsibility for seminars on theory and criticism, with Millon teaching courses on perceptual psychology as applied to understanding architectural form. Millon and Anderson shared responsibility for seminars on contemporary theory and invited numerous internationally prominent architects and historians to campus as part of the seminar (over the years the impressive list grew to include Manfredo Tafuri, Werner Oechslin, Colin St. John Wilson, James O'Gorman, and Rem Koolhaas). Anderson taught "Meaning in Architecture," an advanced seminar on various methodologies, including the philosophy of science. Anderson also taught "Modern Architecture in Europe from 1895 to the Bauhaus," "Selected Topics in Architecture 1750 to the Present," "Origins of Contemporary Architecture in the 18th Century," "Selected Topics in Architecture in the Middle Ages," and a "Seminar in Urban Communal Space."

In anticipation of Millon's 1974 departure for Rome, where he was to take up the directorship of the American Academy, the department hired two additional historians, Dolores Hayden and Donald Preziosi, who began teaching in 1973. The architect and theorist Hayden[95] taught advanced courses in history—including "History of the Architectural Profession," "American Landscapes, Towns and Buildings," "The Architect as Activist," and "The Architecture of American Socialist Communities"—as well as several courses on feminist theories of architecture and introductory courses in the history of architecture. Art historian and semiotician Preziosi taught a wide array of courses on critical theory and art historical method. Urban and landscape designer Günter Nitschke taught East Asian art and architectural history courses, and the sole tenured art historian,

on architecture in the United States since the Second World War" (vi), but this volume never appeared.
88 Henry A. Millon to Mary Davis [Samuel H. Kress Foundation], 1 April 1971, with enclosed copy of proposal for Ph.D. in Art History at MIT, MIT Institute Archives, Series VII, Departments, 1969-1980,

Box 175, Folder: Department of Architecture and Planning, 1969-76 2/4.
89 Stanford Anderson, "Architectural History in Schools of Architecture," *Journal of the Society of Architectural Historians* 58, no. 3 (September 1999): 282-290.
90 Stanford Anderson written comments to author, 23 September 2009.

91 On CAVS, see Anna Vallye's essay in this volume.
92 "Proposal for a Ph.D. Program in History, Theory and Criticism of Art, Architecture and Urban Form," n.p. (see note 81).
93 Ibid.
94 Millon left MIT to become the Director of the American Academy in Rome from 1974 to 1977; following this he

became the first Dean of the Center for Advanced Study in the Visual Arts (CASVA) at the National Gallery of Art in 1979, a post he held until his retirement in 2001. Millon resigned his post at MIT in 1980, but would return to the Institute regularly as a visiting professor, teaching numerous seminars for graduate students between

Wayne V. Andersen, taught courses for Ph.D. students on "Environmental Symbolism" and "Advanced Studies in Iconography and Symbolism." Rosalind Krauss (who departed for Princeton in 1972), Judith G. Wechsler, Whitney Chadwick, and Nan Freeman Arghyros taught art history subjects before the program was approved, with Wechsler and Chadwick continuing to teach after approval. The first person to enroll in the Ph.D. program before it was officially approved by the Institute, was Hong-Bin Kang, although Arghyros, having transferred from Harvard, was the program's first graduate.

Despite the rapid changes that followed the approval of the program in 1975, the institution-building imperative that motivated its founding continued to reap benefits for the discipline. Anderson and Millon collaborated with Harriet Ritvo to produce a report on the need for English translations of important works in architectural history,[96] and MIT's art and architectural historians benefited from numerous collaborations with the Aga Khan Program for Islamic Architecture at Harvard and MIT, particularly with Oleg Grabar (Harvard's Aga Khan professor). Millon went on to a long career in institution building, most notably as the first Dean of the Center for Advanced Study in the Visual Arts at the National Gallery of Art and as a member of the working group *Thesaurus Artis Universalis* (dedicated to producing comprehensive international digital databases of art and architectural historical materials); he also helped to found the Association of Research Institutes in Art History (ARIAH) and the Council of American Overseas Research Centers (CAORC).[97] At MIT, Millon was replaced by David Friedman.

Although the IAUS is often given credit for spurring the academicization of architectural history, theory and criticism in the United States, the events leading to the foundation of the PhD program in History, Theory and Criticism constitute an alternate and parallel trajectory in the institutionalization of theory within the American academy. Rather like two parallel curves marking turns of the same degree at different radii from a single center (in this case the fiction of architectural autonomy and facticity), the "linguistic turn" in architectural theory and the critical turn in historiography constitute a way around Tafuri's damning assessment of the neo-avant gardes of the late 1960s and early 1970s. If "[t]he return to language is a proof of failure," as Tafuri had argued regarding what he

1980 and 2001. Between the initial proposal in 1970 and the realization of the program in 1976, Rosalind Krauss had departed for Princeton; according to Anderson, from 1977 "Andersen shifted his attention to external activities and left MIT in 1986" (Anderson, "Architectural History in Schools of Architecture," 286). Anderson

took a research leave in the 1976-1977 school year as well, which meant that the program did not really gather full momentum until 1978.
95 Despite not holding a PhD, Hayden made an immediate impact upon the research profile of the Department of Architecture, publishing *Seven American Utopias: The Architecture of*

Communitarian Socialism, 1790-1975 (Cambridge, MA: MIT Press, 1976) and *The Grand Domestic Revolution: A History of Feminist Designs for American Homes, Neighborhoods and Cities* (Cambridge, MA: MIT Press, 1981), in addition to numerous articles.

96 Millon, Anderson and Harriet Ritvo, *Report of the Survey of Translation Needs in the History of Architecture* (Boston: Academy of Arts and Sciences, 1979).
97 See Millon, *A Life of Learning*, 27-34.

viewed as the retreat of so-called post-modern architects to the "boudoir,"[98] the same cannot be said of the discursive developments within MIT. There, instead, history, theory and criticism were allowed to develop as putatively logical *legitimations* of architectural practice considered as an intellectual endeavor by considering architecture and its history as the objects of a systematic program of research. Any "failure" would be contingent, the negative outcome of a program of experimentation, rather than as an irreversible collapse of a revolutionary program. Although Tafuri would likely (and correctly) criticize such a development as patently ideological in its own right, he did not have much say in the matter as he is often credited with in shorthand histories of the rise of American architectural theory; nor, for that matter, did Eisenman and the IAUS. More than three decades of scholarly production later—including 86 dissertations, at last count—and following the growth of subsequent programs at tens of other institutions since, the architectural Ph.D. program has at any rate outlasted the prediction that it would be "blown to bits by the 'conscious negation' of principles."

The last illustrations in Millon's pictorial survey, *Key Monuments in the History of Architecture*, which appeared in the same year as the AIA-ACSA conference, are Mies van der Rohe and Philip Johnson's Seagram Building and I.M. Pei's Earth Sciences Center at MIT (1963). No textual or historiographic framework offers a justification for placing them in juxtaposition, still less for placing Pei's skyscraper for scientific research as the terminus of the whole of architectural history to that point. Yet viewed from the vantage point offered here—the gradual re-institutionalization of architecture as a research discipline on par with the pure and applied sciences—this final image marks an only thinly veiled statement of ambition.

98 Tafuri, "L'architecture dans le boudoir: The language of criticism and the criticism of language," trans. Victor Caliandro, *Oppositions* 3 (May 1974): 37-62, p. 47.

I.M. Pei, Earth Sciences Center, Massachusetts Institute of Technology, Cambridge, MA. From Henry Millon, *Key Monuments in the History of Architecture*, (New York: Abrams, 1963). Photo: Nishan Bichajian.

[529]

I. M. Pei. Earth Sciences Center, Massachusetts Institute of Technology,
Cambridge (Mass.). 1963. *Exterior View*

ANNA VALLYE

The Middleman
Kepes's Instruments[1]

Unlike engineering, the natural sciences are not motivated by immediate utility. But when science ranges from the abstract toward the applied, and when engineering shifts its focus from immediate applications to underlying principles, the two fields merge in a borderland area in which it is impossible to distinguish one from the other. . . . In order for science to contribute to the borderland area, and thus for engineering to progress as a result of the progress of science, it is essential that the more creative and abstract aspects of science continually forge ahead in the direction of the new, original, and hitherto unexplored.
—Report of the Committee on Educational Survey to the Faculty of the Massachusetts Institute of Technology, 1949.

Among the allegorical murals housed at the Walker Memorial, there is one that presciently captures MIT's postwar gambit of instrumentality. Titled *Good and Bad Uses of Science*, the mural conveys, catechistically, the premise of *scientia* guiding the labors of the Institute: "Ye Shall Be as Gods Knowing Good and Evil."[2] The passage from Genesis hems a tableau in which a scientist, white-haired, clad in a lab-coat, releases with an impartial gesture symmetrical spirits of beneficent and maleficent nature from two identical jars. The dogs of war and the cherubim of peace counter-align. A group of statesmen and military officers gathered around a conference table contemplates the scene. The consequential decision is theirs to make.

This breach between knowing and doing was rehearsed by countless MIT spokesmen in the postwar period under the motto of "service to the nation." Take, for example, the words of MIT President Julius Stratton: "Knowledge itself is neither intrinsically good nor evil; but the power that knowledge gives can be turned to evil purpose. . . . [Science] tells us what we *can* do; we must turn elsewhere to learn what we *ought* to do."[3] In thus charting a strategic

1 An expanded version of this article appears in my dissertation *Design and the Politics of Knowledge in America, 1937-1967: Walter Gropius, György Kepes* (Ph.D. dissertation, Columbia University, 2011). I am grateful to David Kaiser for sharing his thoughts on postwar MIT and the manuscript of

his essay "Elephant on the Charles: Postwar Growing Pains," subsequently published in David Kaiser, ed., *Becoming MIT: Moments of Decision* (Cambridge, MA: MIT Press, 2010).

2 The mural by Edwin Howland Blashfield is part of a cycle the artist executed at the Walker Memorial between 1924 and 1930. The other murals in the cycle are *Alma Mater* and *Humanity Led from Chaos into Light by Knowledge and Imagination*, as well as representations of learning through the written

word and through experiment, and groups of figures symbolizing various fields of study. See Mina Rieur Weiner, ed., *Edwin Howland Blashfield: Master American Muralist* (New York: W.W. Norton & Company, 2009), 99-103.

topography in the relationship of knowledge to governance, a contiguous distribution of roles between scientist and statesman, MIT was, moreover, elaborating a new meaning for scientific knowledge as deferred agency. That latter postulate was perhaps most famously announced by the 1945 Vannevar Bush report to President Franklin Delano Roosevelt, titled *Science: The Endless Frontier,* which opened up the postwar era of federal investment in the scientific research enterprise. "[N]ew products and processes are not born full-grown," wrote the President's scientific advisor, "They are founded on new principles and new conceptions which in turn result from basic scientific research." Bush's innovation was to champion the utility to the state of basic rather than applied science. The instrumentality of scientific knowledge, he proposed, was indirect, a catalyst acting through a set of mediations: "basic scientific research [was] scientific capital."[4] A caesura was thus instituted between the agency with which knowledge was fertile and its economic or political manifestation. It produced a space of contingent autonomy in which science was free to explore the full dimensions of its new frontier, bounded only by the requirement of creating potential utility, and otherwise endless.

Edwin Howland Blashfield, *Ye Shall Be as Gods Knowing Good and Evil*, part of a series, 1924 - 1930. Walker Memorial, MIT. Photo: Ann Day.

3 Julius A. Stratton, "The Fabric of a Single Culture," The Centennial Convocation Address Delivered at MIT on April 9, 1961, in *Science and the Educated Man: Selected Speeches of Julius A. Stratton* (Cambridge, MA: MIT Press, 1966), 69, 73. Emphases in the original.

4 Vannevar Bush, *Science: The Endless Frontier* (Washington, DC: National Science Foundation, July 1945), 6.

From around 1930 and through the immediate postwar period, MIT underwent momentous changes in institutional identity. Postwar president James Killian fulfilled and expanded the reforms initiated by his predecessor Karl Compton with the intent to transition the Institute from an established engineering school to an entirely new model of a science-based research university.[5] Rejecting a focus on immediate industrial applications, MIT assimilated the liberal arts educational model at the undergraduate level and promoted basic science in graduate and post-graduate research. No longer a practical servant to industry, the Institute would dedicate itself to the broader and more abstract purpose of service to the nation. The transition involved the development of a new logic of instrumentality capable of articulating relationships between knowledge production and citizenship.

During his long tenure at the MIT School of Architecture, on the faculty of which he served from 1946 to 1977, the artist, intellectual, and cultural impresario György Kepes established himself as a spokesman and innovative practitioner of the deferred instrumentality that anchored the Institute's regime of knowledge production. Kepes's Visual Fundamentals program as applied to the professional education of architects offered one way—among the multiple ways pursued at the School of Architecture—to articulate design as a discipline of intellectual research, analysis, and invention parallel to that practiced in Institute laboratories and seminar rooms. His courses accomplished this by advancing a cognitive and perceptual technology which aimed to give the arts access to the relative social agency of the sciences. But Kepes's project carried him well beyond the problems of professional education. His real energy was directed toward inventing a discourse of the aesthetic image as both analogue and catalyst for communities of knowledge—tentative, exploratory and allusive structures dedicated to the production of the ultimate postwar desideratum: social potential, aleatory and opportunistic.

Kepes's appointment at MIT came on the heels of curricular reform affecting both the School of Architecture and the Institute as a whole. In 1944, MIT completed an Institute-wide "simplification of curricula," which determined a line-up of first-year undergraduate core subjects and outlined a four-year program of required electives. Under the banner of simplification, a program of "fundamentals" and an influx of "non-professional" courses announced the Institute's ambitions for a changed profile as a research university "polarized around science," to borrow a standard postwar expression.[6] The merger of professional and liberal arts education was inaugurated at MIT in 1932 by President Compton, who reorganized the Institute into three schools (Engineering, Science, and Architecture) and two supporting Divisions (the Division of Humanities and the Division of Industrial Cooperation), which were conceived of as "service" adjuncts to the schools. A Committee on Educational Survey, (commonly referred to as the Lewis Committee), established in 1947 with the task to define MIT's educational philosophy for the postwar period, traced its lineage to Compton's reforms, which it understood to have "enlarge[d] the purpose and meaning of an MIT education."[7] Expanding on that heritage, the Lewis Committee

György Kepes, 1977.
Photo: Béla T. Kalman.

proposed an "integral plan" intended to suffuse professional education with the goals of general education "to develop the character traits, the intellectual habits and skills, and the understanding of nature and man that an educated person should have, regardless of the kind of work he does."[8] The basis for such a policy was found in the assertion that "in our increasingly complex society, science and technology can no longer be segregated from their human and social consequences."[9] The Committee offered as evidence a series of ongoing trends, including shared methodologies between the natural and social sciences, the merging of basic science with engineering "in a borderland area," and finally, the

5 See Christophe Lecuyer, "The Making of a Science Based Technological University: Karl Compton, James Killian, and the Reform of MIT, 1930-1957," *Historical Studies in the Physical and Biological Sciences 23* (1992): 153-180.

6 "President Compton Announces Post-War Curriculum Changes; Tells of Institute's War Service," *The Tech 64*, no. 21 (June 9, 1944), 4.

7 *Report of the Committee on Educational Survey to the Faculty of the Massachusetts Institute of Technology* (Cambridge, MA: Technology Press, 1949), 13. See also Karl Taylor Compton, *MIT Bulletin, President's Report Issue 68, no. 3* (October 1932).

8 *Report of the Committee on Educational Survey*, 19.

9 Ibid., 42.

growing emphasis in architecture on scientific and engineering expertise in the "solution of environmental problems arising from the impact of science and technology upon everyday living and working."[10]

In fact, under such new institutional conditions of knowledge production, Compton's pre-war policy was obsolete in one key respect. The basic sciences and the humanities could no longer be thought of as "service" adjuncts to engineering expertise, intended to provide a compensatory cultural and scientific grounding. Instead, they had to be at once independently strengthened and deeply integrated with engineering methodology. Thus, the humanities and basic sciences were to be professionalized and instrumentalized, while engineering, symmetrically, was to be reoriented to the imperatives of general education. According to the Committee, the Institute had to recognize that "the method of learning typical of technological education also has a general educational value" on par with the methods of the basic sciences and the humanities. Likewise, the humanities and basic sciences should have "full *professional* status," equal to that of the applied sciences.[11] All four main branches of knowledge that now defined the work of the Institute (basic science, engineering, architecture, humanities) would submit to the single primary educational objective of "developing intellectual power rather than knowledge of routine procedures; mastery of basic principles rather than accumulation of information; and sensitivity to a variety of values and broad understanding of nature and man rather than specific competence in a narrow field."[12]

The pedagogical focus on "fundamentals" of an integrated knowledge, premised upon a balance of the humanities with the natural and social sciences, was the basis of a widespread postwar "liberal arts" program, outlined most famously in the 1945 Report of the Harvard Committee on the Objectives of a General Education in a Free Society.[13] Intended as a counter to the unavoidable "centrifugal forces" of specialization, general education in the liberal arts was conceived here as a "concurrent, balancing force" that would enable the student to "grasp the complexities of life as a whole."[14] Notably, the Harvard Committee saw specialization concurrently as a source of intellectual fragmentation and as a disjunctive *social* force—and therefore its prescription for a focus

10 Ibid., 27, 40, 43.

11 Ibid., 22, 35. My emphases.

12 Ibid., 25. The four equal, degree-granting subsets of the Institute after 1948 were: School of Engineering, School of Science, School of Architecture and Planning, School of the Humanities and Social Sciences.

13 For a discussion of Kepes's relationship to the postwar general education movement, see "Vision's Value in Democracy: Kepes and the Education of the Creative Intellect" in my *Design and the Politics of Knowledge*, 196-267.

14 *General Education in a Free Society: Report of the Harvard Committee* (Cambridge, MA: Harvard University Press, 1945), 56.

15 Bruce A. Kimball, *Orators and Philosophers: A History of the Idea of Liberal Education* (New York: Teachers College Press, 1986), 233.

16 "Liberal" knowledge, therefore, was taken here to mean "that which befits or helps to make free men"; and a free man was one who was "able to judge and plan for himself, so that he [could] truly govern himself." General education was essential to the production of a "social freedom" premised upon

on fundamentals was weighted with both knowledge-acquisition and socio-political imperatives. On the one hand, liberal education was defined as education for the "free person," the liberal-democratic citizen.[15] The capacity to understand "life as a whole" was understood to be essential to the student's formation as citizen and participant in the political life of the nation.[16] On the other hand, education had to sustain the task of "freeing the person" for a life of ongoing self-directed inquiry, the free pursuit of truth.[17] A training in "fundamentals" entailed the acquisition of skills in the conduct of certain key thought processes, an intellectual "method and outlook"—as opposed to specialized "subject matter."[18] In that respect, however, the need to "become an expert . . . in the general art of the freeman and the citizen" also had an economic rationale. As recognized by the Harvard Committee, an independent mind was a prerequisite for success in a rapidly changing knowledge economy:

> Specializing in a vocation makes for inflexibility in a world of fluid possibilities. Business demands minds capable of adjusting themselves to varying situations and of managing complex human institutions. Given the pace of economic progress, techniques alter speedily; and even the work in which the student has been trained may no longer be useful when he is ready to earn a living, or soon after.[19]

Thus, the Harvard report conceived of general education as the simultaneous cultivation of liberal-democratic political man and post-industrial knowledge worker.

This coupling would be paradigmatic of the general education platform that was favored not only at MIT, but nationwide, in the postwar period. Its persistence may be witnessed, for example, in a 1965 observation by Stratton that engineering calls for "such an understanding of fundamentals as to resist obsolescence . . . [a] requirement of commanding knowledge and adaptability to change and innovation . . . in sum, a human perspective."[20] In 1945, however, Harvard sought to educate not only the liberal-democratic political man and contemporary knowledge worker in general, but specifically, a socio-political elite. In borrowing that conception of general education, MIT inflected it with its own brand of instrumentality, reflecting the increasing political prominence of science and technology.

the possession of an "inner freedom." *General Education in a Free Society*, 53. The postwar history of the ethico-political notion of general education as the cultivation of mental traits associated with democratic citizenship, and expressed in the link between democratic freedom and the freedom of the mind,

is also outlined in Jamie Cohen-Cole, *Thinking About Thinking in Cold War America* (Ph.D. dissertation, Princeton University, 2003), 74-95.
17 Kimball, *Orators and Philosophers*, 233-4.
18 *General Education in a Free Society*, 52-56.
19 Ibid., 53.

20 Julius Stratton, "The Humanities in Professional Education," An address given on the occasion of the inauguration of Dr. H.G. Stever as President of the Carnegie Institute of Technology, October 21, 1965, in *Science and the Educated Man*, 130. The Lewis Committee, likewise, wrote

that a general education offers preparation "for a wide variety of occupations" by investing the student with "a knowledge of basic principles and a capacity for learning rather than specialized knowledge or skills. It is this thorough grounding in fundamentals and this adaptability that make a man

"All education should prepare men for social responsibility," wrote the Lewis Committee:

> All education should concern itself with ends as well as means, with value as well as
> technique. We reject the view that there is one particular curriculum suitable to prepare
> men to be the leaders of society, and another distinct type suitable for specialists in
> techniques who are to be the servants of the policy makers. We believe that if the
> problems chosen for study are alive and complex, with social and ethical dimensions,
> the curriculum of the technological school can be an excellent medium for the
> development of leaders competent to handle the urgent social and political problems
> that now confront the world.[21]

The Institute's bid for a new status as a research university involved colonizing the
domains of social and political agency that had traditionally been associated with the elite
universities and their graduates—most immediately, those of MIT's Cambridge neighbor.[22]
MIT would not simply absorb, but further reconfigure the liberal arts, investing them with a
form of knowledge structured by "techniques" to produce a new generation of leaders.

The notion of a compensatory, ameliorative, or even public relations role assigned to the
arts and humanities within an institution driven by the imperatives of large-scale sponsored
techno-scientific research and development has frequently shaped discussions of Kepes's
contribution at MIT.[23] It is a position readily sustained by an ideology dominant in both
public and critical discourses on the relationship between the sciences, on the one hand,
and the arts and humanities, on the other, in the American academy. According to this
view, the sciences are bearers of social utility, measured by the inventions they contribute
to the life of the nation, while the arts have no pragmatic purpose, but are important as
the carriers of moral and political value, which serve to temper the indifferent advance of
science.[24] This rationale was frequently invoked in postwar formulations of the art-science
dialectic, and it can also be found in Kepes's own writings. However, the history of MIT's
reinvention as a research university, and especially the history of Kepes's role in that
process, suggests that the rhetoric of "humanization" was a screen that obscured more
complex transitions marking all forms of disciplinary knowledge at the Institute. Whatever

valuable to industry despite
fluctuations in the demand
for specialists." *Report of the
Committee on Educational
Survey*, 23.
21 Ibid., 23.
22 Compton's reforms took
Yale, Harvard, and Princeton
as models for creating
educational distinction and
increasing selectivity at

both the undergraduate and
graduate levels. See Lecuyer,
"Science-Based Technological
University," 162. In addition,
MIT's ambitions had an
undercurrent of long-standing
rivalry with Harvard, the
identification of which with
"literary culture," counterposed
to the "vocational training"
of MIT, had obvious social

class connotations. See
Fred Hapgood, *Up the
Infinite Corridor: MIT and
the Technical Imagination*
(Reading, MA: Addison-
Wesley Publishing Company,
1993), 47-62.
23 See, for example,
Elizabeth Finch, "Languages
of Vision: György Kepes
and the 'New Landscape'

of Art and Science" (PhD
dissertation, The City
University of New York, 2005).
24 See, for example, Mark
Slouka, "Dehumanized: When
Math and Science Rule the
Schools," *Harper's Magazine*
319, no. 1912 (September
2009): 32-40.

the relative significance of the arts measured against the sciences to the MIT enterprise, both forms of practice were shaped in a liminal area not accessed by oppositions of value and utility, autonomy and instrumentality. Rather, a logic of deferred agency and enhanced potential, which forged and strengthened links between knowledge production and the state, was cardinal to both.

Visual Design for the MIT Architect

Kepes would often claim that he discovered his life project to unite art and science at MIT, but it would be more correct to say that the evolving Institute provided him with fertile ground on which to implement his long-developing reflections on art as a form of instrumental knowledge. Already in the mid-1940s, the School of Architecture must have seen in him a potential philosopher and activist of its own role within the emergent institutional episteme. Postwar MIT needed Kepes just as much as Kepes needed postwar MIT. Shortly before his appointment to the position of Associate Professor of Freehand Drawing, the School of Architecture had undergone a set of curricular reforms in line with those taking place within the Institute at large. In 1942, a Committee on the Curriculum appointed by the School had arrived at two interdependent conclusions: first, that the curriculum had to be modernized, and second, that the School must "pursue to its utmost the integration of [its] courses with the Institute environment."[25] The 1943 President's Report summarized those twinned premises: "[I]t is abundantly clear that the ["modern"] movement is having a profound effect upon architectural thinking and practice. The trends emphasize the value of a technological environment around an architectural school."[26] The Curriculum Committee stressed the growing importance of technology and "scientific method" to contemporary architectural practice and noted as problematic that a lack of sufficient basic math and science prerequisites precluded architecture students from access to higher-level electives in science and engineering. Accordingly, on the one hand, the restructured curriculum would include a rebalancing of the overall course load in favor of mechanical engineering, building industry economics, and city planning—with a proportional reduction of offerings in Graphics, Shades and Shadows, Perspective, and Abstract Design.[27] ("We do not consider architecture as a field for unbridled personal expression" was the terse conclusion of the Committee, and a fine index of its "functionalist" ethos.[28])

25 "The design staff, ca. 1942," MIT Archives, AC 400, Box 2, Folder 1.

26 *Massachusetts Institute of Technology, President's Report*, 79, no. 1 (October 1943): 21.

27 See Walter R. MacCornack, "*School of Architecture*," President's *Report* (1943): 122-123; Anderson, et.al., *Preliminary Report*.

28 Architectural Design Staff to Karl Compton (11 December 1942), MIT Archives, AC 4, Box 16, Folder 9, p.11.

György Kepes and physicist Philip Morrison, n.d..

On the other hand, the School of Architecture would embrace the first year core curriculum being concurrently proposed for the Institute as a whole.[29] This latter resolution would achieve the desired "breakdown of the isolation of [the architecture school] from the Institute."[30] In the first year of Kepes's appointment, accordingly, the architecture curriculum featured a first-year core of Chemistry, Physics, Calculus, and Descriptive Geometry, in addition to English, Military Science, and Drawing; this was followed by a heavy course-load in mechanical engineering, and required electives in the areas of history, urban sociology, economics, psychology, labor relations, history of thought, Western world literature, international relations, fine arts, and music in the subsequent four years.[31] In "almost completely de-professionaliz[ing]" the core, architectural education was aligned to the transitions taking place within MIT as a whole.[32] The architectural student, on par with the science and engineering student, was provided with what the design staff considered to be "a broad general education" and "a certain mastery of the fundamentals of the larger fields of human knowledge," and was thus informed "with the sense that all fields are related by a common basis of understanding."[33] Drawing, "an all-important means of expression" for the architect, was merged into this pattern.[34]

Drawing belonged among the "fundamental" disciplines of the core because, framed as a basic technique or method, it was understood to be a specifically architectural expression of instrumental knowledge advanced at the Institute. Echoing the Lewis Committee, the architecture faculty observed that, due to the rapid obsolescence of technical expertise with ongoing technological innovation, method should take precedence over information in the education of the architect; in other words, "more science, less technology."[35] In architecture, drawing was an expression of design method as organized thought process. "[D]rawings," wrote the design staff, "like words, are only an expression of thought." Rather than being "pictorial" end-products of design activity, drawings were made "during the evolution of a design . . . [as] illustrations to logical arguments . . . [and as aids to the architect in] the outline of his research and his reasoning."[36] "[U]npretentious diagrams which the architect makes in search of a general directive," drawings were indexes of a cognitive and research-based design process.[37] Skill in drawing was accordingly conceived, in the words of John Burchard, as a "tool" or a "means to an end," comparable to the physicist's laboratory practice.[38] As such, drawing was a metonym for the architectural design process in general, given that the latter was defined as "the ability to analyze the requirements of a proposed building and to synthesize them into a smoothly working plan."[39] Both architectural design and drawing as its graphic record, in mutually reinforcing fashion, were defined as cognitive techniques at the juncture of general or fundamental knowledge and instrumental methodology.[40]

Kepes was hired to teach this renewed discipline, administratively expressed in the filtering of the component techniques of Beaux-Arts rendering (Shades and Shadows, Perspective) into a single unit of Freehand Drawing, which would be threaded through the five-year curriculum. He was to replace the categorically Beaux-Arts approach of previous instructor Johan Selmer-Larsen ("basic figure construction and anatomy; rapid drawing direction from the human figure.")[41] The term "drawing", however, was clearly inadequate to the visual technology of knowledge Kepes's contribution was to embody. Already in his appointment correspondence with Kepes, architecture dean William Wurster referred to the subject at issue as "'drawing' . . . for lack of a more complete word," and expressed his eagerness to "confer with [Kepes] about photography, typography, etc., which

29 Anderson, et.al., *Preliminary Report*, 4.

30 Architectural Design Staff to Karl Compton, 2.

31 William Wurster to E.B.Millard (15 January 1945), MIT Archives, AC 4, Box 241, Folder 10.

32 Architectural Design Staff to Karl Compton, 2-3.

33 Lawrence B. Anderson,

et.al., *Preliminary Report of Curriculum Committee* (1942), MIT Archives, AC 4, Box 16, Folder 9, p. 6-7.

34 Architectural Design Staff to Karl Compton, 2-3.

35 "A frequent objection," wrote the design staff, "made to teaching an architect anything about mechanical equipment is that these

techniques are in process of rapid development and his knowledge will soon be out of date, or likely is even at the moment of instruction. [Therefore] a thorough grounding in science provides the basis for understanding what any piece of equipment, choice of material, or method of assembly can do or can

not do in a building, even though the situation may be encountered for the first time in the field." Anderson, et.al., *Preliminary Report*, 9.

36 Architectural Design Staff to Karl Compton, 7.

37 Ibid.

38 John E. Burchard to James R. Killian, Jr., (6 January 1942), MIT Archives,

would replace some of the courses as [currently] described."[42] By 1948, Kepes was teaching a five-term sequence, consisting of a rotating set of subjects, which included Visual Fundamentals, Structure of the City, Form and Design, Light and Color, Graphic Presentation, Painting, and Advanced Visual Design.[43]

The educational program Kepes was invited to establish at MIT under the placeholder of "drawing" was developed during his years teaching at the New Bauhaus in Chicago as a course in Visual Fundamentals, and it was encapsulated in his *Language of Vision* (1944). Wurster clearly had the book in mind in hiring Kepes, pointing out that it had brought the latter "into certain national prominence."[44] *Language of Vision* advanced a philosophy of the image as both index and instrument of a visual technology of knowledge. Although Kepes's discussion was bracketed by a concern with the aesthetic properties of the material environment, at the heart of his project was a shift of attention from the exteriority of visible forms to the interiority of the viewing subject; and specifically, the viewing subject as a *thinking* subject. "The experiencing of every image," Kepes wrote,

> is the result of an interraction [sic] between external physical forces and internal forces of the individual as he assimilates, orders, and molds external forces to his own measure. . . . As soon as [light rays] reach the retina, the mind organizes and molds them into meaningful spatial units.[45]

This conception of vision as the relation between "external" physical stimuli and "internal" cognitive schemas was a basic tenet of Gestalt perceptual psychology, which Kepes cited as the primary source of his insight into the "laws of visual organization."[46] Equating formal organization with intellectual comprehension, Gestalt psychology activated vision as a creative process, rather than a static reflection of physical reality. The premise that to see an order *in* the world was at once to give an order *to* the world also grounded the particular agency that Kepes assigned to the image. Unlike the Gestaltists, however, he compounded the natural and the social modalities of stimulus, investing his conception of vision's agency with an explicitly social dimension. If vision's cognitive patterning was "a creative act of integration," Kepes's goal was to "mobilize the creative imagination for positive social action."[47]

AC 400, Box 2, Folder 1, p. 3. John Ely Burchard, Director of the Albert Farwell Bemis Foundation, an independent division within MIT dedicated to research on the building industry, had a degree in architectural engineering. Although on leave from MIT during WWII, Burchard remained involved in curricular reform at the School of Architecture, as evidenced by this letter of response to the proposals of the curriculum committee he addressed to Killian, the acting president of MIT during the war. In 1948, Burchard would become the first dean of the School of Humanities and Social Sciences.

39 Ibid.

40 By 1962, the cognitive conception of design was articulated even more forcefully at MIT. "Architectural education," wrote the faculty, "tends to emphasize the acquisition of insights and skills more than the creation of new knowledge. . . . The aims of [architectural design courses] are: a.) to foster a capacity for observation, understanding, analysis, synthesis and creation; b.) to develop a mental discipline to face and solve an architectural problem. The design courses are essentially laboratory courses where problems are presented to

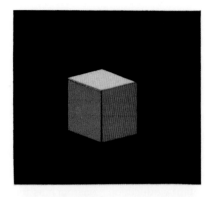

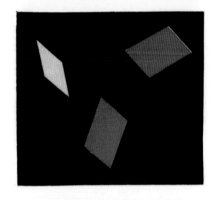

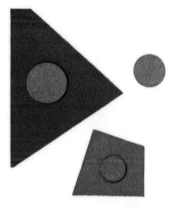

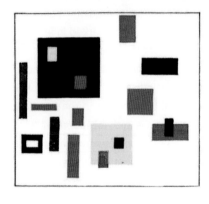

the students. The solution of these problems are [sic] not a mechanical or mathematical process but rather a process of selection; therefore the question of a mental discipline becomes of prime importance in the education of a designer." *The Professional Curriculum in Architecture* (7 December 1962), MIT Archives, AC 134, box 13, folder IV, pp. 1, 4. See also Hyungmin Pai's discussion of the epistemology of architectural drawing from the Beaux-Arts to the modern paradigm in Pai, *The Portfolio and the Diagram: Architecture, Discourse, and Modernity in America* (Cambridge, MA: MIT Press, 2002).

41 "Freehand Drawing," *MIT Bulletin, Catalogue Issue* 81, no. 3 (February 1946): 91.

42 William Wurster to György Kepes (30 August 1945); William Wurster to György Kepes (14 July 1945), MIT Archives, AC 4, Box 241, Folder 10.

Interaction of colors studies. From György Kepes, *Language of Vision*, (Chicago: P. Theobald, 1944; New York: Dover, 1995).

At MIT, Kepes proceeded to adapt this platform to the concrete task of educating the professional architect according to the precepts of the new curricular program. As indicated in a number of his preparatory teaching notes, Kepes approached this task by positioning design processes and outcomes as functions of the social subjectivity envisioned by general education philosophy, and by further establishing his own technology of vision as vital to the promotion of that subjectivity. In an undated note for a speech, Kepes summarized his activities at MIT as driven by a "dedication to fundamentals—faculties, sensibilities—and not professional... vocational shortcuts."[48] "Architecture," he concluded in a teaching note, "is made of architects—their vision, [their] ability to form."[49] The visual arts, further, are "an important discipline in [the] architect's education" inasmuch as they are able to provide a "sense of organic relatedness," integrating the "structural, biological, technical, . . . psychological, . . . sociological [and] intellectual . . . frames of reference." In cultivating overall cognitive faculties, rather than specific vocational skills, Kepes's visual training would respond to the goals of MIT curricular reform by making the professional architect a "full man sensitive to issues of [the] present."[50]

While *Language of Vision* was oriented to a generalized cognitive-perceptual social subject, rather than the visual arts professional, Kepes nevertheless assigned a privileged role in the cultivation of that subjectivity to artistic vision broadly conceived. Professionals of the image – "painters, sculptors, . . . photographers, advertising designers"—were invested with the task of "teach[ing] to see" the rest of society.[51] The MIT architect, positioned within the new knowledge regime, was perhaps an ideal mediator between the general social and the specific artistic subjectivity. "Today," Kepes remarked in another teaching note, "the needs of the eye, the human spirit, are not [fulfilled], mainly because of [the] lack of visual sensibilities. The education of architects must, therefore, include the education of the eye."[52] Kepes's strategy focused on articulating the products of architectural design as functions of their psycho-perceptual reception, and the architectural design process as a function of the architect's ability to mediate in that reception. "[T]he goal" of his teaching program, in other words, was "to synchronize physical structure and visual structure."[53] Judging by the content of his teaching notes, the substance of Kepes's courses consisted in the detailed elaboration of that principle through the

43 See, for example, *Massachusetts Institute of Technology Bulletin, Catalogue Issue* 81, no.4 (June 1946) - 91, no. 6 (July 1956).

44 William Wurster to James R. Killian, Jr. (10 July 1945), MIT Archives, AC 4, Box 241, Folder 10. See György Kepes, *Language of Vision* (Chicago:

Paul Theobald, 1944).

45 Kepes, *Language of Vision*, 31.

46 Ibid, 4.

47 Ibid.,13, 14. See also my "Vision's Value for Democracy."

48 György Kepes, [handwritten undated note], György Kepes Papers, Archives of American Art, Smithsonian Institution,

Washington, D.C., Reel 5312, frame 867. From here on: Kepes Papers.

49 György Kepes, [handwritten undated note], Kepes Papers, Reel 5312, frame 461.

50 György Kepes, "Introduction" [handwritten undated note], Kepes Papers, Reel 5312, frame 441.

51 Kepes, *Language of Vision*, 67.

52 György Kepes, [handwritten undated note], Kepes Papers, Reel 5312, frame 446.

53 György Kepes, [handwritten undated note], Kepes Papers, Reel 5312, frame 455. Punctuation added.

systematic translation of spatial properties into the terms of perceptual experience. For example, a Visual Fundamentals class dedicated to the analysis of "expansion and contraction of color" focused on the exploration of the general rule that "light rooms appear larger [and] wider than dark rooms."[54] Kepes then asked his students to "study the effect of color on the relative illusory size of a closed and an open space" through a series of graphic exercises.[55] Another class dedicated to the study of color effects involved students in working to "induce consciously [the perception of] border contrast" by making models of rooms with a single window covered by a color filter and photographing these "against strong light."[56]

The 1946 MIT course catalogue enumerated "point, line, shape, value, form, [and] texture"[57] as the aesthetic expressions of "visual fundamentals," the same markers described by Kepes in *Language of Vision* as constituent elements of perceptual "event[s]."[58] "The picture-surface," Kepes wrote in the latter text, "becomes a vital spatial world, not only in the sense that the spatial forces are acting on it—moving, falling and circulating—but also in the sense that between these movements

54 György Kepes, "Visual Fundamentals: Expansion and Contraction of Color" [handwritten undated note], Kepes Papers, Reel 5312, frame 771.
55 Ibid. Punctuation amended.

56 György Kepes, "Education of Vision: Contrast—Positive Negative—Color," handwritten undated note, Kepes Papers, Reel 5312, frame 760.
57 *Massachusetts Institute of Technology Bulletin, Catalogue Issue* 81, no. 4 (June 1946): 99.
58 Kepes, *Language of Vision*, 24.

"Each unique interrelationship yields a unique spatial feeling... The spots move away from or toward each other, receding or advancing, and seem to have weight or a centripetal or centrifugal direction. A still more vital spatial event is created when these surface areas are articulated in size, color." From György Kepes, *Language of Vision* (1944, 1995).

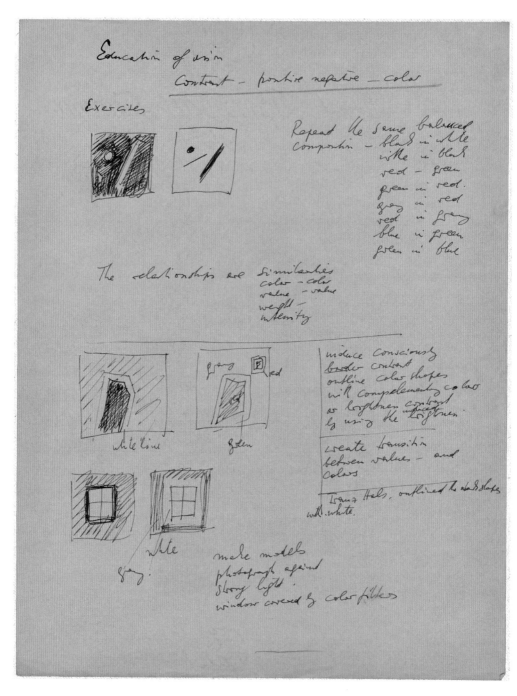

Notes on "education of vision" and "visual
fundamentals", 1940-1951 / György Kepes, creator.
György Kepes papers. Archives of American Art.
Smithsonian Institution.

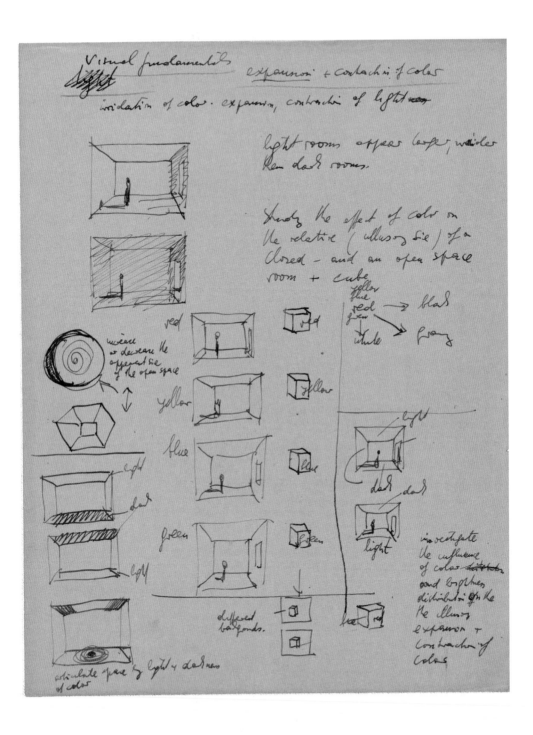

the field itself is charged with action."[59] He understood such graphic units or qualities to be indexes of the perceiving mind's dynamic "creative act."[60] Kepes's MIT courses for architects extended that concept outward from the "picture-surface" to the spatial environment. At the most basic level, "graphic elements"—such as "point, line, shape"—could be analogically linked to structural elements—such as "trusses, beams, arches, cantilever[s]"—understood "in a visual plastic illusory sense."[61] But the larger point was to translate those perceptual properties of the environment as psycho-cognitive attributes of the socially-situated subject. "Every visual structure," Kepes explained, "is more than [an imprint] of the outside . . . material environment.

> Each visual perception . . . stands for corresponding human attitudes.
> *Extension*—is lived as [a] need to extend beyond individual enclosure, [as a] search for connectedness . . .
> *Figure-shape*—stands for cohesion of individual completeness . . .
> *Solidity*—also for inner cohesion, strength, vigor, inner fiber, security, integrity.
> *Gravity*—bondage to nature . . .
> *Motion*—growth, flexibility, contact, variety, enrichment, change.
> *Rest*—harmony, repose, recovery of strength, etc.
> With disciplined vision, one [derives] orderliness from the visual ordering of the surroundings. The greater the ability to see intensely, the greater the possibility to make [one's] life richer [and] stronger.[62]

The correspondence between the physical and the psycho-cognitive environment that Kepes focused on articulating at MIT was essential to the translation of professional skill into social value in the training of the citizen-architect.

59 Ibid., 29.

60 Ibid., 13.

61 György Kepes, "Visual Fundamentals: General Introduction," handwritten undated note, Kepes Papers, Reel 5312, frame 535.

62 György Kepes, "Education of Vision: General Introduction," handwritten undated note, Kepes Papers, Reel 5312, frame 503.

Ruth Robbins, *Study of dynamic equilibrium in texture values*, work done for the author's course in Visual Fundamentals, The New Bauhaus, Chicago.

below, R.B.Tague, *Analysis of the Receding and Advancing Planes of a Frank Lloyd Wright House.*

From Kepes, *Language of Vision*, (1944, 1995).

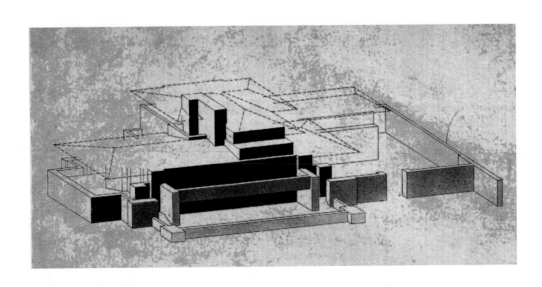

Instrumental Collectivities Of Knowledge

The architectural elaboration of social instrumentality was, however, only a small part of Kepes's overall activities at MIT. He also developed other practices of "interdependence," in response to another set of conditions encountered at the Institute. MIT's postwar educational philosophy was a claim to institutional status on par with that of established major universities, but it was equally motivated by the dramatic impact made by the influx of defense funding on campus—the largest share of any US university in the postwar period.[63] In fact, MIT's ambitions for a higher profile were both prompted and justified by its ballooning growth in faculty, students, and physical plant.[64] At the same time, the Institute's model of instrumental knowledge linking "techniques" and "fundamentals" was equally applicable to its new graduate research structures.

Defense R&D spending privileged approaches that blurred boundaries among academic disciplines and between basic and applied research. Writing at the time of the Lewis Committee deliberations, Killian linked the Committee's activities in general education to concurrent administrative experimentation with so-called "centers of research" intended to accommodate "those interests which reach outside the traditional departmental boundary lines and require the cooperation of the specialists from several disciplines."[65] Independent organizations jointly operated by two or more departments within the Institute, these centers were a concrete manifestation of "integration" in their mobilization of disparate disciplinary representatives "into a cooperative whole" and their "full coordination" of the functions of research and education.[66] By 1948 there were already five such "centers" at MIT, and interdisciplinary institutions continued to proliferate in the humanities and social sciences as well as the natural sciences. In 1967, the Center for Advanced Visual Studies (CAVS) founded by Kepes would extend the research center model to the MIT visual arts. The Center's roots, however, can be discerned in Kepes's last major published statement of philosophy—*The New Landscape in Art and Science* of 1956.

Upon his arrival at MIT, Kepes later recalled, he had discovered "a new cosmology [opened up by the sciences], a new broad vista of the world that for . . . artists was not given."[67] This other-than-human landscape composed of phenomena beyond the threshold of "sense

63 In the academic year 1944-45, MIT's annual budget was $44,354,800, or nearly fourteen times the 1938-39 figure, with $44,354,000 of it derived from sponsored research monies received ($39,970,900 was budgeted for defense research, with the rest used for general operations, a pattern that would persist into the postwar period). By 1969-70, sponsored research funds stood at $171,294,000, or 51% of the university's total budget. Throughout this postwar period, MIT was the largest university defense contractor in the country. See John Burchard, *Q.E.D.: M.I.T. in World War II* (Cambridge, MA: the Technology Press, 1948), 8; Dorothy Nelkin, *The University and Military Research: Moral Politics at M.I.T.* (Ithaca: Cornell University Press, 1972), *18*; Stuart W. Leslie, *The Cold War and American Science: the Military-Industrial-Academic Complex at M.I.T. and Stanford* (New York: Columbia University Press, 1993).

64 See David Kaiser, "Elephant on the Charles: Postwar Growing Pains" in David Kaiser, ed., *Becoming MIT: Moments of Decision* (Cambridge, MA: MIT Press, 2010), 103-121.

experience" revealed with the aid of advanced imaging technologies—"invisible viruses, atoms, mesons, protons, cosmic rays, supersonic waves"[68] —would inspire a significant new departure in the "language of vision." Collected in large part during the period between 1947 and 1952 from various laboratories in the burgeoning complex of MIT's research centers, these photographic records combined to form the central visual and conceptual argument of *The New Landscape*.[69] At once a definitive theoretical statement and a practical experiment in the production of instrumental knowledge, the book was articulated through a matrix composed of the visual products of the new knowledge economy crystallizing at the Institute.

By his own admission, Kepes's interest in "images from the scientific world" actually pre-dated his arrival at MIT.[70] His first reported encounter occurred in Weimar-era Berlin, when a metallurgist friend introduced Kepes to photomicrographs taken in his laboratory. The role of scientific images like the x-ray and the photomicrograph in the work of Kepes's colleague and mentor László Moholy-Nagy is well-known, and Kepes must have shared the latter's enthusiasm for a technologically-mediated "new vision" presumably accessed through such imagery. Rediscovered at MIT, however, was an entirely new generation of scientific images, and these entailed a conceptual shift in approach. For Moholy-Nagy, the microphotograph signified an expansion of time achieved in space through technological means—"our substitute for the longer period of time that primitive man could devote to observation." Analogously, its opposite, the aerial view or "macrophotograph," represented a compression of space in time.[71] Such images, therefore, were indexes of an existing natural-historical—or bio-technological—condition of space-time. *The New Landscape* also had its share of images of the new "scale," from the micro to the macro; but they were shuffled in with others, like a spark photograph of model projectiles in flight, a high-speed photograph of a falling drop of water, or photo-elasticity records of the effects of shear forces. Such latter images were records of experimental manipulations of material conditions, enabled by imaging devices developed for the purpose of tracing the effects of processes unfolding in time.

The products of the oscilloscope, stroboscope, and interferometer, the images on radar screens, radiographs, and spectrographs, were diagrams of *events*, rather than descriptions

65 James R. Killian, Jr., "M.I.T. Redeploys for Peace" in *Q.E.D.: M.I.T. in World War II*, 318.

66 Ibid.

67 György Kepes, "A Painter's Response to the Idiom of Science," Minutes of the Columbia University Seminar on Technology and Social Change, New York, NY (December 9, 1965), 4.

68 György Kepes, *The New Landscape in Art and Science* (Chicago: Paul Theobald, 1956), 19.

69 György Kepes in Robert C. Morgan, "Sermon for Tranquility: an Interview with György Kepes," *Afterimage* 10, no. 6 (January 1983): 8.

70 Ibid., 7.

71 László Moholy-Nagy, *The New Vision*, 1928, fourth rev. ed. (New York: George Wittenborn, Inc., 1947), 25-26.

Records photographs tracing the effects of processes unfolding in time enabled by imaging devices, *clockwise from top:* Photo-elasticity record of strain forces; Spark photograph of a model projectile in flight; High-speed photograph of a waterdrop. From György Kepes, *The New Landscape in Art and Science,* (Chicago, P. Theobold, 1956).

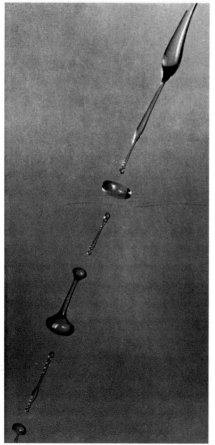

of "things" or "properties." "The path of a cosmic ray," wrote Kepes, "the growth of a crystal, the stroboscopic record of a raindrop are meaningful only as interrelations. We are compelled to interpret them as intersections of events."[72] Because, in practice, these images functioned as experimental data in research and development applications, the "events" they chronicled were exposed to vision not as preexisting natural conditions but as outcomes of interventions, at once purposeful and open-ended. Inasmuch as they necessarily showed nature as a medium of transformation and manipulation, their content was both operative and descriptive—a point emphasized throughout the book: "The patterns of structure are also patterns of action!"[73] Here was an empirical parallel to the cognitive intervention in the material world that Kepes had earlier identified with the process of perception when he described the mind's creative act transforming visual data into "vital spatial event[s]."[74] However, the scientific photographs now collected by Kepes register most directly as epistemological traces of the blurring of pure and applied research carried out at the Institute.

Following his initial encounter with photomicrographs in the 1930s, Kepes invented an artistic technique he called "photo-drawing" or "photo-painting."[75] In his works employing this technique, Kepes later recalled, he "almost tried to imitate scientific data, or scientific images, without having a justification."[76] He would place an ink drop on a glass plate and press down on top of it with another plate, creating "really beautiful patterns, which [sic] were really an expression of the logic of nature." Reflecting in retrospect, Kepes saw in those patterns the same "inevitability of texture" that was revealed in photomicrographs and electromicrographs. Before putting the plate into a negative enlarger to produce the final photogram, he would draw directly on the ink pattern to nudge it towards abstract or figurative forms in what he described as a "dialectical process, a dialogue with the material." Through this process, a "hidden [natural] image" exposed through the force of pressure between the two glass plates would emerge invested with signification, to reveal "a hidden symbolic image." Kepes would thus act as the "midwife" of that symbolic image, facilitating the emergence within natural processes of what his interviewer perceptively called a "latent moral condition." "It's not really me who is doing it," Kepes quipped, "I'm just the middleman."[77] The scientific images of natural processes set in

72 Kepes, *New Landscape*, 206.

73 Ibid., 204.

74 Kepes, *Language of Vision*, 24.

75 Elizabeth Finch identifies the technique described by Kepes as the *cliché-verre*, a nineteenth-century invention, in which a hand-rendered image on a transparent matrix is replicated by light projection onto a photosensitive surface. See Finch, "Languages of Vision," 150-151. For a detailed description and nineteenth and twentieth-century examples, see also Elizabeth Glassman and Marilyn Symmes, eds., *Cliché-Verre: Hand Drawn, Light Printed* (Detroit: Detroit Institute of the Arts, 1980).

76 Kepes in "Sermon for Tranquility," 8.

77 Ibid.

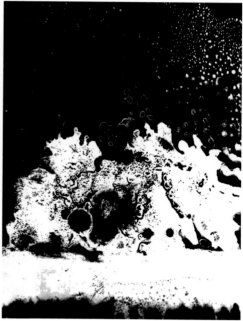

Hans Arp cut out bits of colored paper and, with deliberate abandon, tossed them on a piece of cardboard, threw them around, and finally turned them over and pasted on the cardboard the pattern that they formed by chance. Such chance has in it, however, more reason than we, with our present blinkers and confused senses, can see. The resulting order shows an organic understanding far more embracing than the formal logic-sharpened-in-static-object concept. It is natural that these automatic expressions resemble the biomorphic realms of nature. They have the same order as the visible forms of mutations, transformations, the perpetual asymmetric rhythm of the processes not yet fossilized in terms of things.

Hans Arp. Mountain, Table, Anchors, Navel 1925
Courtesy of The Museum of Modern Art

Microphotograph
of Sponge Spicules

195

Comparison between (left) a microphotograph of sponge spicules and (right) Hans Arp, *Mountain, Table, Anchors, Navel*, 1925. Spread from Kepes, *Language of Vision* (1944, 1995).

György Kepes, *Monument,* photo-drawing, 1937 and *Untitled,* photo-painting, 1941. CAVS, MIT.

motion through experimental manipulation, gathered by Kepes in *The New Landscape,* shared with his own earlier photograms this constitutive mixture of indexicality and instrumentality.

In fact, Kepes had used the metaphor of the artist as middleman or "midwife" in one other prior context. Writing of artists affiliated with Dada and Surrealism in *Language of Vision,* he had described their practices as "reduced only to a sheer assistance of chance happenings." The artist, Kepes had explained,

> acts the role of the midwife. He only assists at the birth of a living form that grows from deeper strata than his conscious efforts could reach. He invents techniques that give the fewest obstacles to the free flow of organic formation.[78]

Notably, Kepes reproduced a photomicrograph as illustration to this part of the text, juxtaposing it with a Hans Arp cutout, in the only identified example of the former medium included in the book.[79] When Kepes later spoke of his own light-based art installations he similarly emphasized "acceptance of randomness" and the "creative invocation of chance events" as crucial design elements.[80] With respect to his own work, however, he also insisted on the presence of conscious control as an important counterweight. For example, his *Kinetic Light Mural* of 1959, a site-specific design for the New York offices of KLM Royal Dutch Airlines, consisted of an aluminum screen with "some sixty thousand random perforations," behind which were placed multiple artificial light sources controlled by switching devices.[81] The purpose," Kepes wrote, "was to create . . . a fluid, luminous pattern with random changes, alive through the continuous transformation of color, intensity, direction, and pattern."[82] Thus, the viewer would sense at once the persistence

---

78 Kepes, *Language of Vision,* 194.
79 An image of a magnetic field on page 28 might also be a photomicrograph, but it is not identified as such.

80 György Kepes, "Kinetic Light as a Creative Medium," *Technology Review* 70 (December, 1967), 26.

81 György Kepes, "Light—Art on a New Scale," *The Structurist* 13/14 (1973-1974), 79.
82 Ibid.

György Kepes, *Kinetic
Light Mural* (detail), KLM
Office, New York, 1959.

of structure and its continuous disruption through chance events. Designed to invoke "the visual richness of the city seen from the air by night,"[83] the mural employed "random, chance movement as against a rhythm of the mechanical environment."[84] Interstitially situated between natural contingency and human purpose, the mural too was an indexical-instrumental image.

If Kepes identified his creative persona as that of the "middleman" in the sense outlined above, it was also a fitting description of the role he sought to occupy within the new knowledge regime advanced at the Institute. The link between image and knowledge was asserted in no uncertain terms already in the second paragraph of *The New Landscape*: "vision is itself a mode of thinking."[85] *The New Landscape*, Kepes hoped, would mobilize a "pattern-seeing" that would enable one to "trace the interplay of processes in the world."[86] The notion of "pattern" now served to translate into perceptual terms what Kepes understood to be the epistemological conditions of the contemporary world marked by "rapid expansion of knowledge and technical development."[87] This world of knowledge was a result of scientific production that specifically merged instrumentality and indexicality. Science has produced a "vast and constantly expanding armory" of "powerful tools and ideas with which we may either create or destroy," Kepes wrote, which are at the same time "resources for new sights and sounds, new tastes and textures"—perceptual markers of an already existing "new landscape."[88]

It is not surprising that the MIT environment fueled Kepes's interest in the cognitive investment of the image and directed his attention to visual documents of scientific research as ideal manifestations of the image as bearer of potential knowledge. The postwar period witnessed a wide-spread use of images as aides in the scientific laboratory in general.[89] Some of the very same stroboscopic photographs that inspired Kepes's awe as examples of "tools and ideas" for creation and destruction figured as sources of more didactic "mystery" in a regular "Strobe Probe" column of MIT's *Technology Review* journal. Here, a split-second image of a bullet's impact, for example, could be reproduced as a conceptual problem for the student to solve by identifying the physical processes it documented.[90] Poetically translating the rationale motivating such exercises, Kepes too identified the scientific image as both new knowledge product and new pedagogical tool.

83 Ibid.

84 Kepes also continued to associate this principle with the work of Arp, among others. "Randomness," Kepes wrote in 1967, "was the goal of a generation of artists who tried to put into their images of movement the freedom and spontaneity of nature: the paintings of Arp, Miro, and Pollock evoke man and nature's common rhythm." Kepes, "Kinetic Light as a Creative Medium," 35.

85 Ibid., 17.

86 Kepes, *The New Landscape*, 205.

87 Ibid., 19.

88 Ibid.

89 See Peter Galison, *Image and Logic: A Material Culture of Microphysics* (Chicago: University of Chicago Press, 1997).

90 "Strobe Probe," *Technology Review* Vol. 72 (July-August 1968).

but if successful he would undoubtedly become the cynosure and admiration of the "lay" world of ordinary humans who, like the Eighteenth Century peasants in Oliver Goldsmith's *Deserted Village* were awestricken by the erudition of their Schoolmaster:

"And still they gaz'd, and still the wonder grew
That one small head could carry all he knew."

Is the worthy Dr. Hutchins still trying, as he did in his earlier days, to "astonish the natives"? Or were his and the Florman articles "planted" to stimulate discussion, hence circulation for *Engineer*?

G. M. Rollason, '13
Plainfield, N.J. 07060

To Pay the Piper

To the Editor:
I want to congratulate Robert C. Cowen on both his subject and style in "Man's Fingerprints on His Environment" (*see* Technology Review, *Apr., 1968, pp. 8-9*).

Personally, I have a deep, growing, and long-standing concern with our entire ecological mess. I applaud the necessity and supreme relevance of articles such as his, but see all sorts of signs that we must increasingly pay the piper for what we have already done, not to mention for the continuation of the trends now in force. Our ecological ignorance and *hubris* I both fear and hope will appall those who come after us. Nor is it anything but inevitable that many of the more subtle and far-reaching implications of our present behavior will not be recognized for some time and that the imbalances involved will, consequently, continue for years.

I have many times asked myself what kind of ecologic imbalance will bring our society to its senses. For whatever it is worth, it seems to me that articles such as Mr. Cowen's are absolutely essential and that they are beginning to penetrate to some extent. Nonetheless, since the public has not really generated much of a reaction to the most immediately pressing symptoms of ecological decay, such as air pollution, traffic jams, shortages of capital for school construction and the like, power failures, water shortages, and the destruction of the pleasantness of our surroundings, we may need far more acutely embarrassing imbalances.

Dr. William Haddon, Jr., '49
Washington, D.C. 20591

Dr. Haddon is Director of the National Highway Safety Bureau in the Department of Transportation. This letter was written on May 2 as a personal communication to Mr. Cowen and is published here with Dr. Haddon's permission.—Ed.

Strobe Probe

Harold E. Edgerton, Sc.D.'31

Mystery Photograph

This silhouette photograph shows a 30-caliber bullet (900 meters per second velocity) after it has impacted a Plexiglas bar.

1. The microphone (black box) is supposed to trigger the lamp when excited by the shock wave from the bullet. Obviously the flash has occurred before the bullet shock wave has reached the microphone. Why?

2. There is a white ghostlike exposure on the left-hand side of the Plexiglas. Why?

Answers are on p. 90.

"Strobe Probe" spread.
From MIT *Technology Review*, July-August 1968.

325
Wassell Ridge Moraine
Photograph: Bradford Washburn

When the frost comes out in the Spring, and even in a thawing day in the winter, the sand begins to flow down the slopes like lava, sometimes bursting out through the snow and overflowing it where no sand was to be seen before. Innumerable little streams overlap and interlace one with another, exhibiting a sort of hybrid product, which obeys half way the law of currents, and half way that of vegetation. As it flows it takes the forms of sappy leaves or vines, making heaps of pulpy sprays a foot or more in depth, and resembling, as you look down on them, the laciniated, lobed, and imbricated thalluses of some lichens; or you are reminded of coral, of leopards' paws or birds' feet, of brains or lungs or bowels, and excrements of all kinds. It is a truly *grotesque* vegetation, whose forms and color we see imitated in bronze, a sort of architectural foliage more ancient and typical than acanthus, chicory, ivy, vine, or any vegetable leaves; destined perhaps, under some circumstances, to become a puzzle to future geologists.

What makes this sand foliage remarkable is its springing into existence thus suddenly. When I see on the one side the inert bank,—for the sun act on one side first,—and on the other this luxuriant foliage, the creation of an hour, I am affected as if in a peculiar sense I stood in the laboratory of the Artist who made the world and me,—had come to where he was still at work, sporting on this bank, and with excess of energy strewing his fresh designs about. I feel as if I were nearer to the vitals of the globe, for this sandy overflow is something such as the fluous mass as the vitals of the animal body. You find thus in the very sands an anticipation of the vegetable leaf. No wonder that the earth expresses itself outwardly in leaves, it so labours with the idea inwardly. The atoms have already learned this law, and are pregnant by it. The overhanging leaf sees here its prototype. *Internally*, whether in the globe or animal body, it is a moist thick *lobe*, a word especially applicable to the liver and lungs and the *leaves* of *fat* (λείβω *leibo*, *labor*, *lapsus*, to flow or slip downward, a lapsing; λοβός *globus*, lobe, globe; also *lap*, *flap*, and many other words); *externally*, a dry thin *leaf*, even as the *f* and *v* are a pressed and dried *b*. The radicals of *lobe* are *lb*, the soft mass of the *b* (single-lobed, or *B*, double-lobed), with the liquid *l* behind it pressing it forward. In globe, *glb*, the guttural *g* adds to the meaning the capacity of the throat. The feathers and wings of birds are still drier and thinner leaves. Thus, also, you pass from the lumpish grub in the earth to the airy and fluttering butterfly. The very globe continually transcends and translates itself, and becomes winged in its orbit. Even ice begins with delicate crystal leaves, as if it had flowed into moulds which the fronds of water-plants have impressed on the watery mirror. The whole tree itself is but one leaf, and rivers are still vaster leaves whose pulp is intervening earth, and towns and cities are the ova of insects in their axils.

Henry David Thoreau
Walden
W. W. Norton & Co., Inc., New York, 1951

326
Marblehead Dish. Sung Dynasty. Hoyt Collection, Museum of Fine Arts, Boston.

327
Blood Vessels
Photomicrograph: Carl Strüwe

The scientific image, however, was not the only type of instrument collected in *The New Landscape*. The book interspersed a compendium of scientific photographs with reproductions of works of art from different cultures and eras, as well as short textual quotations from various sources, and essays by invited contributors—all set within the framework of a master narrative, written by Kepes himself. The "method" driving this presentation of material, Kepes explained, was "a kind of laboratory experiment [that]

> fuses visual images and verbal communication in a common structure . . . [T]he visual and verbal statements neither parallel one another in exact correspondence nor follow one another in a strict causal chain. They complement one another in an interwoven sequence. The structure builds, then, as the observer proceeds from one experience to another, and finally a new aspect of perception is outlined.[91]

In a sense, the book functioned as a collage of instruments and agents, a subjects-objects collectivity within which "pattern-seeing" would spring forth from multiple sources, including the viewer's own active participation. This strategy of facilitating the formation of instrumental collectivities of vision and knowledge is traceable in every major endeavor Kepes would pursue from this point forward.

In 1956, Kepes started a series of themed interdisciplinary seminars at MIT that brought together specialists in the arts and the sciences to discuss such issues as "structure" or "the man-made object." The intellectual products of those seminars were gathered in 1965-66 into the six-volume *Vision and Value* book series.[92] The books modified the *New Landscape* precedent, consisting of more conventional anthologies of essays by seminar participants, augmented with short introductions by Kepes, as well as consolidated segments of scientific and artistic images, which were titled "visual documents." In 1960, Kepes was invited to edit an issue of the interdisciplinary academic journal *Daedalus* on "The Visual Arts Today," which he executed on much the same model. *Education of Vision*, one of the Vision and Value books, substituted the "visual documents" section with a documentation of student work from MIT visual design courses—their remarkable similarity to scientific images qualified these explorations of fledgling MIT architects to enter the

Two-page spread showing the collage strategy of juxtaposing text and images from disparate sources. From György Kepes, *The New Landscape in Art and Science* (1956).

91 Kepes, *New Landscape*, 17.

92 The full series included: *Education of Vision; Structure in Art and in Science; The Nature and Art of Motion; Module, Proportion, Symmetry, Rhythm; The Man-Made Object; Sign, Image, Symbol.*

93 *MIT Art Committee Meeting*, minutes (18 March 1965), p. 1, Kepes Papers, Reel 5304, frame 454.

94 Ibid., 2-3.

95 [György Kepes], "Center for Advanced Visual Studies," [ca. 1967], Center for Advanced Visual Studies, uncatalogued archival collection, file:

"Miscellaneous re: opening July, 1967 & other," p. 2. From here on: CAVS Archives.

96 György Kepes, *The Center for Advanced Visual Studies*, brochure produced for the opening, [ca. 1967], CAVS Archives, n.p.

97 György Kepes, "The Visual Arts and the Sciences: A Proposal for Collaboration,"

proliferating knowledge collectivities orchestrated by Kepes. By 1965, he was advancing plans for an MIT "Expanded Visual Arts Program," to be jump-started with a series of seminars intended to "produce new patterns [of] concepts and inter-relationships."[93] The rest of the program would include artist residencies, curricular programs for "studies in seeing anew," exhibitions, and even a "common cafeteria where people working in different disciplines [could] meet." The key, Kepes stressed, was to "involv[e] the total community in this new approach."[94] Finally, in 1967, a major milestone in this ongoing project was reached with the establishment of CAVS.

In describing the new institution, Kepes referred to it, variously, as a "research center . . . for new creative objectives,"[95] a "research laboratory,"[96] or a "small work community" that would produce "interthinking between different disciplines in the visual arts and scientific and technical fields."[97] "[M]ajor creative achievement," he maintained, "comes from the confluence of many types of creative personalities." The proposed "small work community," therefore, "by recognizing common problems of adjoining or related fields, could accomplish the dovetailing . . . of knowledge and knowledge."[98] CAVS is typically identified by historians as an effort to bridge the cultural divide between the arts and the postwar techno-sciences, and is linked as such to other contemporaneous initiatives claiming the same ideological banner—such as Experiments in Art and Technology (E.A.T.).[99] Kepes, however, dwelled less on the antimonies of art and science than he did on the artist's cultural isolation from "the total contemporary world."[100] Likewise, his efforts focused on overcoming a generalized condition of isolation or fragmentation, which he read at once in epistemological and societal terms.

Student work from the course *Form and Design*, MIT, n.d.. From György Kepes, ed., *Education of Vision* (New York: George Braziller, 1965).

Architectural Record 137 (May 1965): 149-150. The term "interthinking," used by Kepes to describe the key characteristic of the collectivity he sought, was derived from the writings of evolutionary paleontologist George Gaylord Simpson, who predicted that "interthinking" would succeed

"interbreeding" as the catalyst for human evolution. See George Gaylord Simpson, *The Meaning of Evolution* (1949). See also John C. Greene, *Science, Ideology and World View: Essays in the History of Evolutionary Ideas* (Berkeley: University of California Press: 1981), 172.

98 Kepes, "The Visual Arts and the Sciences," 149-150. **99** See for example Anne Collins Goodyear, *The Relationship of Art to Science and Technology in the United States, 1957-1971* (PhD dissertation, The University of Texas at Austin, 2002), which discusses CAVS as one of five "case studies," alongside

E.A.T.; the NASA Art Program, established in 1962; and "Art and Technology," an exhibition program carried out at the Los Angeles County Museum of Art between 1966 and 1971. **100** "Lacking orientation in the total contemporary world," Kepes wrote, "many artists have inevitably withdrawn into themselves. Their only

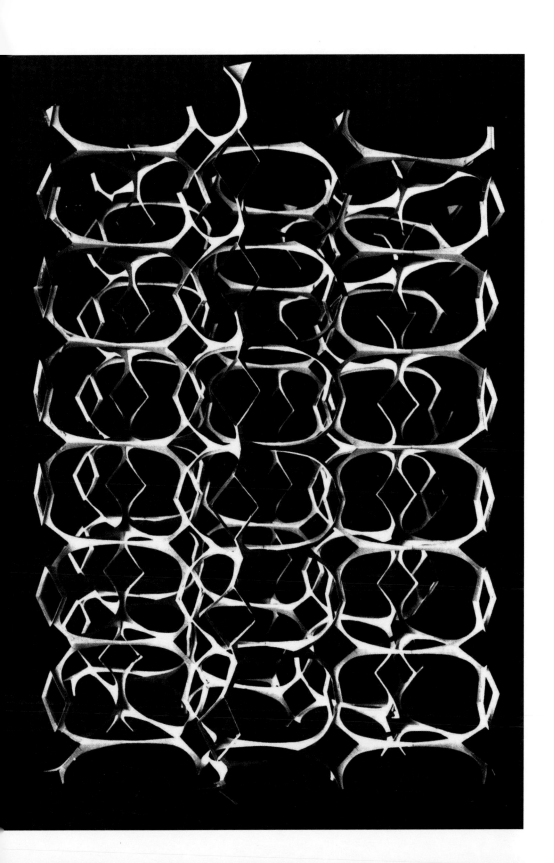

Student work from
Light and Color Course,
Professor Richard
Filipowski, MIT, n.d.
From György Kepes,
Education of Vision (1965).

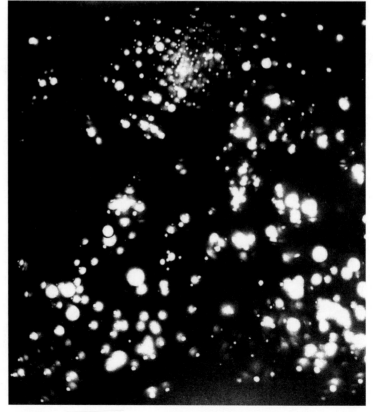

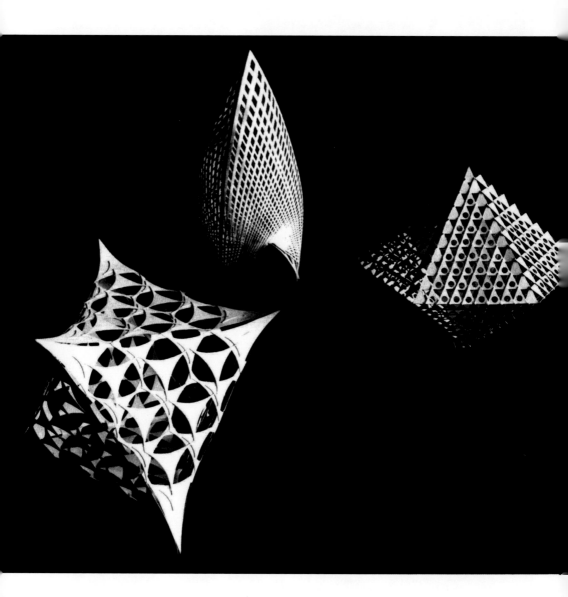

Student work from Form and Design Course.
From György Kepes, *Education of Vision* (1965).

He wrote, for example, that the "common life of society" is "frozen into separate compartments each with its specialized interests and jargon," thus proceeding seamlessly from a vision of disciplinary specialization to that of social disintegration. Kepes's overriding goal was the creation of a cultural community based on established channels for communication and the exchange of knowledge—a social-discursive zone where all involved could "communicate . . . in the same language and could pool their feelings and knowledge in a common cultural stream."[101] So much was this the dominant idea that Kepes tried to select CAVS artists primarily for their ability to successfully collaborate or "interact" with others, and only secondarily for their interest in engaging with scientific or technological practices. He frequently reiterated this point in letters to current and potential CAVS fellows. "The choice I have to make when I ask people to work at the Center," he wrote to artist Keiko Prince for example,

> is not guided by my liking for them nor by my estimation of their creative qualifications. To be at the Center . . . means more than just being there. There should be an interaction which produces a vital, creative 'gestalt' and not merely a co-existence of gifted, sensitive, human humans. . . . [T]he people working here have to have, aside from their creative gifts, . . . a quality that . . . could create a relationship that opens up in collaboration—in the exchange of ideas with other people—a new climate which could generate new ideas and new insights.[102]

The ideal of a tightly-knit small-scale intellectual association, linking heterogeneous forms of knowledge by means of a shared language of communication, and dedicated to creative innovation, was widely shared in postwar academic circles. As historian Jamie Cohen-Cole has argued, the evident success of interdisciplinary research practices in the postwar academy gave rise to an ideology of interdisciplinary communication as a paradigm of social cohesion.[103] Based less on the knowledge of several fields than on "the ability, cognitive skills, and personality to get along with people of other disciplines," interdisciplinary communication was in itself a function of social subjectivity.[104] It was likewise precisely a communicative and cooperative capacity—an intellectual, ethical, and aesthetic disposition—that Kepes sought to cultivate at CAVS.

honest response to this world has been the expression of complete isolation." See Kepes, "The Visual Arts and the Sciences," 150.

101 Ibid., 150.

102 György Kepes to Keiko [Prince], 17 July 1973, Kepes Papers, AAA, Reel 5309, frame 456.

103 Jamie Cohen-Cole, "The Creative American: Cold War Salons, Social Science, and the Cure for Modern Society," *Isis* 100, no. 2 (June 2009): 246-249.

104 Cohen-Cole, *Thinking About Thinking*, 195. See also Cohen-Cole, "The Creative American," 253.

105 Cohen-Cole, "The Creative American," 256-7.

106 For the impact of the Macy conferences on Kepes's work, see Reinhold Martin, *The Organizational Complex: Architecture, Media, and Corporate Space* (Cambridge, MA: MIT Press, 2003); for a history of the Macy conferences, see Steve

J. Heims, *The Cybernetics Group: Constructing a Social Science for Postwar America* (Cambridge, MA: MIT Press, 1991).

107 See, e.g., *MIT Art Committee Meeting*, minutes, 18 March 1965, p.1.

Although this ideological tendency was widespread in postwar academic intellectual culture at large, Cambridge was a particularly important hub. The Cambridge academic world, Cohen-Cole writes, was "a web of intimate intellectual exchange" woven in dinner clubs, discussion groups, academic societies, and research centers that both grew out of high-level interdisciplinary conversations taking place in such settings and had the continuation of those conversations as their primary *raison d'être*.[105] Kepes must be considered a member of that discursive society. He participated in the interdisciplinary Macy conferences on cybernetics and the regular meetings of the Cambridge-based American Academy of Arts and Sciences (AAAS), which he joined in 1952.[106] The series of themed interdisciplinary seminars he organized, discussed earlier in this essay, were certainly based on the same model; and the interdisciplinary conference in general remained an important site for the articulation of Kepes's vision.[107]

AAAS, for example, is a good prism through which to view the development of the intellectual-social community ideal. Discussion of the social value of interdisciplinary communication pervaded its publications.[108] In fact, its house organ, the journal *Daedalus*, was launched in 1955 under the auspices of Burchard, at the time Dean of the MIT School of Arts and Sciences and Kepes's friend, to enable the Academy to "make its mark on the whole nation or even the world" specifically by organizing and publishing "vigorous conferences on topics of cross-disciplinary interest."[109] In a 1959 issue of *Daedalus*, the anthropologist Margaret Mead, who appeared in Kepes's anthologies and was an active voice in the discourse of intellectual-social community, wrote on the relationship between scientific and general cultures.[110] Her solution to "closing the gap between the scientists and the others" focused on the "intoxicating" process of "face-to-face . . . specialized communication" characteristic of the scientific "working conference." In a passage that could have been written by Kepes, Mead extended that emphasis on communication to the fine arts, asserting that

> [s]o long as the arts fail to come to grips with the findings of those sciences that are changing the face of the world, there is a danger that the group within which communication is really possible will become narrower and narrower. Thus it is

108 See Cohen-Cole, "The Creative American," 256, fn. 115.

109 John E. Burchard, "Imperium Sine Fine: Presidential Valedictory Delivered at the One Thousand Three Hundred and Ninety-Eighth Meeting of the Academy on 10 April 1957," *Daedalus* 86 (May 1957): 179.

110 Margaret Mead, "Closing the Gap Between the Scientists and the Others," *Daedalus* 88 (Winter 1959): 139-146. On Mead and the interdisciplinary community model, see Cohen-Cole, "The Creative American," 247-249.

111 Ibid., 142-143.

112 "Science and Culture," *Daedalus* 94 (Winter 1965). Later published in book form as Gerald Holton, ed., *Science and Culture: A Study of Cohesive and Disjunctive Forces* (Boston: Beacon Press, 1967).

113 See György Kepes, "The Visual Arts and the Sciences: A Proposal for Collaboration,"

Daedalus 94 (Winter 1965): 117-134.

114 Gerald Holton, "Introduction to the Issue 'Science and Culture,'" *Daedalus* 94 (Winter 1965): xii.

115 Ibid., vii.

116 György Kepes, [undated handwritten note], Kepes Papers, AAA, Reel 5312, frame 902.

imperative for the arts to come to terms with the physical, biological, and social sciences, so as to preserve and enhance their own powers of communication.[111]

The same themes were again replayed in an AAAS conference on the relationship between science and culture, the proceedings of which were published in a 1965 *Daedalus* special issue.[112] Kepes participated in the conference, dedicating his remarks to the announcement of his initial plans for CAVS.[113] After rehearsing the well-worn "two cultures" idea, the conference focused more generally on the possibility of communication in an age of specialized knowledge. "[D]etailed professional knowledge of the other's specialty," it was agreed, "is not necessary for acknowledging common elements in science and scholarship . . . [there will always be an inescapable] tension between recognized commonalities and . . . necessary differences."[114] Thus perhaps the clearest, and most frequently invoked in the proceedings, expression of the conference's ideal was the art historian James Ackerman's definition of *scientia*—a "single, evolving structure of ideas and of images that characterizes [the culture of a given time, and thus] pervades the attitudes of scientist, artist, and humanist-scholar alike, even though they are working on very different materials and in different languages."[115] It was also Kepes's goal to access this *scientia*.

The idea of CAVS was in so many ways the ultimate expression of Kepes's career trajectory that it is difficult to date its origin. Already in Chicago during the war, Kepes had tentatively sketched out a plan for a University of Vision.[116] Around 1964, the MIT School of Architecture had on file a proposal he made for an MIT Institute of Vision.[117] Kepes himself has asserted that he had been pressing for the establishment of a visual arts center at MIT since the mid-1950s.[118] Nevertheless, it appears that it was not until 1963 that he started to make headway with the MIT administration in his plans to develop a "work center [that would be] a complementary part of the general education program."[119] By the start of 1964, President Stratton had been converted to "the concept of a Center for the Visual Arts, modeled after the pattern of [the Institute's] other interdisciplinary centers, such as the Center for International Studies."[120] The brochure produced for the opening of the Center would explain that CAVS was established "to be the common focus of . . . a continuing, Institute-wide, interdisciplinary program," conditioned by the structure of "scientific enterprise, [which] has been losing its own sharply defined boundaries, [with] specialties . . . become less distinct and frontiers interdisciplinary."[121] The administrative extension to CAVS of the research center model was clearly premised on the conceptual extension of the interdisciplinary research science paradigm to the visual arts accomplished by Kepes. Indeed, the proximity was so tight that, in its early years, CAVS was frequently assumed to be a research center in perceptual psychology.[122]

A CAVS "work community," ca. 1977. Around the table clockwise, beginning second from left:

O. Piene, A. Hiemer, H. Casdin-Silver, E. Goldring, L. Burgess, J. Brigham, K. Kantor,   A. Sina, M. Chow, K. Bacon, N. Doll, W. Ahrens, M. Moser, P. Earls, B. Cadogan, M. Mendel. Photograph by Nishan Bichajian.

117 See Lawrence Anderson to György Kepes, 2 July 1964, Kepes Papers, AAA, Reel 5304, Frame 201.

118 See Benthall, "Kepes's Center at M.I.T.," 29. Certainly, any such possibility would have been tied to the question of funding. Kepes makes reference to a Ford Foundation grant proposal

in György Kepes to Julius A. Stratton, August 21, 1963, Kepes Papers, AAA, Reel 5303, frame 1179. In 1957, Killian made a pitch to the Ford Foundation for a grant to further engineering education in the liberal arts context, including "an array of cultural activities." (James R. Killian to Henry T. Heald, President, The

Ford Foundation, [1957], MIT Archives, AC 4, Box 90, Folder 1, p. 3.) At the same time, Killian was absorbing *The New Landscape* "with delight, stimulation, and satisfaction," as he reported to Kepes. (James R. Killian to György Kepes, January 4, 1957, MIT Archives, AC 4, Box 128, Folder 12.) It is plausible that

Kepes broached the question of a visual arts center with Killian at this time and in this context.

119 György Kepes to Julius A. Stratton, August 21, 1963, Kepes Papers, AAA.

120 Julius A. Stratton to Jeptha H. Wade, III, January 8, 1964, MIT Archives, AC 66, Box 1, Folder 14, p. 1.

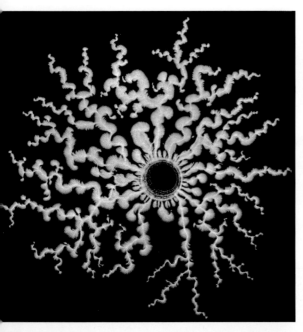
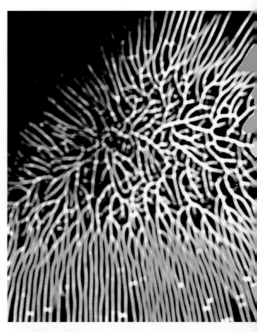
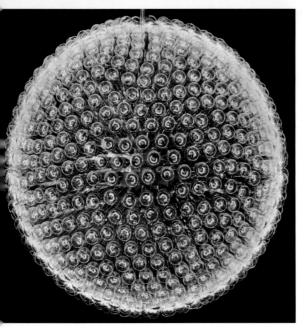

Clockwise from top left: Lichtenberg figure of electric
discharge, photograph taken under the direction of
Professor Arthur R. von Hippel, MIT; György Kepes,
Light Projection, 1953; Otto Piene, *Onion Flower*, 1964-
65; Takis, *Electronic Flower*, 1957. From MIT CAVS
brochure (1967).

The interdisciplinary center structure, explained Max Millikan, head of the MIT Center for International Studies, was "focused around problems rather than disciplines."[123] A similar concept of gathering collectivities around problems was evident in all of Kepes's post-*New Landscape* projects. CAVS would become one more mode in this ongoing production of "a collective vision born of pooled feelings, ideas, and knowledge"—"the vector, as it were, of the creative impulses of artists, city planners, scientists, and engineers, all working together."[124] Practically, this was accomplished by appointing artist fellows to engage in "a sequence of major collaborative projects" with each other as well as with Institute scientists and engineers, and with groups of graduate students and postdoctoral fellows in architecture, painting, sculpture, and film-making.[125] The inaugural CAVS brochure collated the work of the first set of artist fellows—Otto Piene, John Whitney, Takis, and Harold Tovish—with the already established members of Kepes's visual-cognitive collectives—scientific images and Kepes's photograms. Their integration was emphasized through the use of a uniform format—black-and-white—and scale for all. A set of studio photographs taken in the Center's first years re-stages the deskilling implicit to the visual collectivity: a pair of scissors in the foreground of one photograph is the lone and feeble evidence of manual craft in an environment set up largely for the production of texts and images. CAVS fellows, Kepes's visual design students, MIT postdocs—all would be engaged in the production of devices whose ur-form, the instrumental-indexical scientific photograph, was the epistemological record of postwar academic knowledge as it was shaped at the Institute.

The Center's inaugural brochure emphasized the "reinforcement" CAVS would give to the Institute denizen in the carrying out of "the present extremely significant role of the scientist-citizen."[126] Thus CAVS could be traced back to Kepes's initial activities at the School of Architecture, which were in turn an expansion and realization of the fundamental social goals of *Language of Vision*: the formation of cognitive-perceptual social leadership. CAVS was established to undertake an "education of the educators of sensibilities," Kepes wrote, echoing *Language of Vision*.[127] Only now, from within his mature conception of vision that no longer admitted any substantive distinctions between aesthetics and advanced knowledge production, the ranks of the "educators of sensibilities" would expand to include the "scientist-citizen" as well as the artist and the architect.

121 György Kepes, *The Center for Advanced Visual Studies*, n.p.

122 The suggestion of changing the name to avoid this confusion was repeatedly considered (and, significantly, dismissed). See Jonathan Benthall, "Kepes's Center at M.I.T.," *Art International* 19 (January 1975): 29.

123 Cited in Christopher Rand, *Cambridge, USA: Hub of a New World* (New York: Oxford University Press, 1964), 101. See also the discussion of "problem oriented" as against "discipline oriented" research strategies in Cohen-Cole, *Thinking About Thinking*, 161.

124 György Kepes, *The Center for Advanced Visual Studies*, n.p.

125 Ibid.

126 György Kepes, *The Center for Advanced Visual Studies*, n.p.

127 György Kepes, [untitled manuscript], 1966, CAVS Archives, Folder: "Miscellaneous re: opening July, 1967 & other," p. 1.

Interior photographs of CAVS Studios, ca. 1967.

Sponsorship

Centerbeam: Art of the Environment
Matthew Wisnioski

The Pedagogy of Prefabrication:
Building Research at MIT in the Postwar
Avigail Sachs

Experimental Dwellings: Modern Architecture
and Environmental Research at the MIT
Solar Energy Fund, 1938-1963
Daniel A. Barber

Centerbeam
Art of the Environment

> How, then, is the much-yahooed copulation of artists, scientists,
> and engineers working at all?
> —Otto Piene, 1979

The story of *Centerbeam*, the most successful collaborative project of the Center for
Advanced Visual Studies (CAVS), opens on November 20, 1969 with a "fuck you" and
closes a decade later with a realignment of aesthetic virtue that amounted to the same
sentiment. At the start, the Institute is on edge. It is feeling the heat of what the Rosa
Luxemburg chapter of Students for a Democratic society (SDS) has dubbed its November
Action, and MIT's disorder has become a national referendum on out-of-control technology.
CAVS is doing its part to restore harmony. Artists open their studios to the public with
participatory events that convey the humane potential of the technological environment.
Since his arrival in 1968, no one has contributed more to this effort than Otto Piene. His
Sky Art—temporary helium sculptures reaching 1,000 feet in length—has brought students,
faculty, and community volunteers together in monumental collaborative celebrations. In
October 1969, when 100,000 antiwar protesters formed the largest crowd to ever occupy
Boston Common, MIT's contingent stood out because of Provost Jerome Wiesner's
solidarity and Piene's "insane balloons."[1] During the CAVS open house, Piene again is at
the forefront, organizing seminars that MIT's Annual Report of the President argues "were
lively and received exceptionally positive response."[2]

Sid Lewis, representing an outfit called the Council for Conscious Existence, begs to
differ. He leaves behind a pamphlet at Piene's workshop that declares CAVS' ambitions
to be "nothing but the first step in transforming the spectators of empty culture into
its organizers." Depicted as a Strangelovian balloon vendor, Piene is castigated as "the
advanced guard of the cybernetic welfare state, the reconsecration of order, no longer with
God as ruler, but with technology raised to myth in the perfect order of zombies."[3]

Note: I owe my thanks to   1 Bruce Schwartz, "If Two and   2 György Kepes, "Center   Otto Piene, CAVS, *Sky*
Otto Piene for sharing his   Fifty Make a Million," The Tech   for Advanced Visual Studies,"   *Art*, in front of MIT,
recollections with me and to   (October 17, 1969): 12, 15.   Massachusetts Institute of   November 15, 1969. From
Meg Rotzel and Alise Upitis   Technology Annual Bulletin   MIT *Technique*, vol. 86,
for invaluable assistance in   106, no. 2 (September, 1971),   1970.
the CAVS Archives.   35.

CAVS, *Centerbeam*,
National Mall,
Washington D.C.,
1978. From Otto Piene
Retrospektive, 1952-1996.
Photo: Dietmar Loehrl.

Piene, Kepes, and Ted Kraynik, an illustration from a pamphlet for The Council for Conscious Existence, 1969/ The Council for Conscious Existence, creator. György Kepes papers, Archives of American Art, Smithsonian Institution.

Ted Kraynick, Otto Piene, and Gyorgy Kepes pretend to organize the participation of spectators. This is nothing but the first step in transforming the spectators of empty culture into its organizers, to refill the inanity of the spectacle through the obligatory participation of the spectator, the passive agent par excellence.

22   November 20, 1969

In a now familiar narrative, this missive from one of Central Square's innumerable cranks portends a historic reversal. On one side, there is genuine enthusiasm for cybernetics, lasers, and strobes in collaborative works by artists, scientists, and engineers. According to participants and critics, these interdisciplinary projects are "essential in a crumbling democracy."[4] On the other side, gleefully reported calamities, including the tribulations faced by artists and corporations alike in the Los Angeles County Museum's *Art & Technology* show and the rapid decline of Experiments in Art and Technology (E.A.T.), sparked by a clash with Pepsi, Co. over authorial rights to its environment of fog and mirrors at the 1970 World Exhibition.[5]

At MIT itself, evidence for a shift from technophila to technophobia abounds. Throughout the Cold War era, MIT provided the technological arts with credibility and economic security, while the arts bestowed creative authority on the Cold War defense institute. Driven by György Kepes' ideal of a unity between visionary artists and scientists, the establishment of CAVS—dually christened in 1968 with the Center for Theoretical Physics—marked

3 Sid Lewis and CAVS correspondence (November 1969). György Kepes papers, 1925-1989, Archives of American Art, Smithsonian Institution, Reel 5306 items 0801-0807.
4 The quote describes E.A.T.'s inaugural event 9 Evenings: Theater and Engineering. Jill Johnson, "Post Mortem,"

Village Voice, 15 December 1966: back cover.
5 Anne Collins Goodyear, "From Technophilia to Technophobia: The Impact of the Vietnam War on the Reception of 'Art and Technology,'" *Leonardo* 41 (April 2008): 169-173; Jack Burnham, "Art and Technology: The Panacea That

Failed," in *Video Culture: A Critical Investigation*, ed. John G. Hanhardt (Rochester, NY: Gibbs M. Smith, Inc., 1986): 232-248.
6 C.P. Snow, *The Two Cultures and the Scientific Revolution* (New York: Cambridge University Press, 1959)
7 David Curt Morris, Tape 9; Otto Piene, Tape 11;

Robert Preusser, Tape 12. Massachusetts Institute of Technology. Committee of the Visual Arts. AC 48, Box 1, Institute Archives and Special Collections, MIT Libraries, Cambridge, Massachusetts.
8 William Thompson, "Art and Science: Shotgun Wedding," *Thursday* (May 1, 1969), 4.

an apogee among efforts to bridge C.P. Snow's "two cultures" divide.[6] However, CAVS seemed compromised in the very moment of its inception. Supported by short-term grants, funding was uncertain. The civic commission for the nation's Bicentennial that Kepes anticipated never materialized. In the midst of preparations for one-man exhibitions, Fellows struggled to collaborate.[7] The failure was noted by outsiders and insiders alike. In MIT's alternative newspaper, *Thursday*, humanities lecturer William Thompson described CAVS as a "shotgun wedding" arranged to make artists "new apologists for the system,"[8] and Jack Burnham, one of CAVS' first Fellows, later infamously judged it a "panacea that failed."[9]

And yet, CAVS did not fold under these pressures. Witness the summer of 1978, when, through its productions, five hundred thousand people experience an almost indescribable accretion of sensations generated by a 144-foot water prism on the National Mall in Washington, D.C. Those who brave solar-powered holographic forks are able to draw video images with their eyes. Children trigger electronic sounds as they dance on illuminated squares. Hand-rotated mirrors cast poems of light. Steam plumes erupt sixty feet into the air, penetrated by a twelve-color laser. In addition to patches of seasonal vegetation, the structure sprouts 250-foot polyethylene flowers. As summer ends, the temporary sculpture becomes a Minotaur, clanging and booming while a helium-filled Icarus floats in concert with a flying violinist. Wiesner again enters the picture—now as Institute President—to declare that *Centerbeam's* visitors are "moved to understand that MIT is a place where new ideas meet new means, thus inspiring new art of an environmental scale."[10]

Originally built for the quadrennial arts festival *documenta 6* in Kassel, Germany, *Centerbeam* was conceived as a 10th Anniversary celebration of CAVS: the first realization of its founding mission of "collaborative daring."[11] Supported by funds and equipment from over twenty corporations, foundations, and government agencies, *Centerbeam* was planned as a "participatory drama" that would represent society's collective need to "respond humanly, creatively, unexpectedly and with a shared sense of wit to the bundle of energy and communication lines that have become our network of existence."[12]

9 Burnham, "Art and Technology," 239-241.

10 Jerome Wiesner, "Preface" in *Centerbeam*, ed. Otto Piene and Elizabeth Goldring (Cambridge, MA: MIT, 1980), 9.

11 György Kepes, "The Visual Arts and the Sciences: A Proposal for Collaboration," *Daedalus* 94, no. 1 (1965):

117-134.

12 Elizabeth Goldring, "'Centerbeam'—Description and Plan for documenta 6, 1977" in *Centerbeam*, ed. Piene and Goldring, 54.

13 Manfred Schneckenburger, "An Aqueduct to the 21st Century," in *Centerbeam*, ed. Piene and Goldring, 27-29.

14 Lowry Burgess, "'Centerbeam,'" in *Centerbeam*, ed. Piene and Goldring, 26.

15 Otto Piene, "'Centerbeam,'" in *Centerbeam*, ed. Piene and Goldring, 20-24; Otto Piene, "Recognition (in Praise of 'Centerbeam')," in *Centerbeam*, ed. Piene and Goldring, 10.

16 The mapping in Chart 1 is informed by Adele E. Clarke, *Situational Analysis: Grounded Theory after the Postmodern Turn* (Thousand Oaks, CA: Sage, 2005), 262-289.

But even as they praised *Centerbeam*, its contributors found it difficult to provide a unitary account of their achievement. For curator Manfred Schneckenburger, who invited CAVS to *documenta 6*, the device was "an aqueduct to the 21st century," an encyclopedia of human advancement from the industrial revolution to the present that settled tired polemics about the technological arts.[13] For CAVS Fellow Lowry Burgess, who proposed the core design, it represented the outcome of scaling "human and environmental relationships not readily available in our individual work."[14] For Piene, then in his fourth year as Director of CAVS, *Centerbeam* was a model of what could be achieved beyond the "the coterie of artists-for-art-for art-world associations" and "classroom intellectualism." He varyingly described it as the "beast"; "the community of volunteers forming daily symbioses"; and "a house . . . a place to live, to rest, to entertain guests, to go through generations of human life."[15]

In this chapter, I investigate the making and unmaking of *Centerbeam* in order to map the entangled politics of artistic collaboration at MIT between the heyday of the 1960s and the sponsored media research of the 1980s. Both in its material instantiation

top to bottom, Detail of Derith Glover's *Drawing With Your Eyes* device. Photo: Jeanne Coffin. Detail of Chris Janey's *Water Prism* and *Soundshuffle/Light Walk*. Photo: Calvin Campbell. From *Centerbeam*, (Cambridge, MA: MIT Press, 1980).

facing page, CAVS, Harriet Casdin-Silver hologram, *Equivocal Forks* for *Centerbeam documenta 6*. Photo: Dietmar Loehrl. *Centerbeam* with Otto Piene, *Brussels Flower*. Photo: Elizabeth Goldring. From *Centerbeam* (1980).

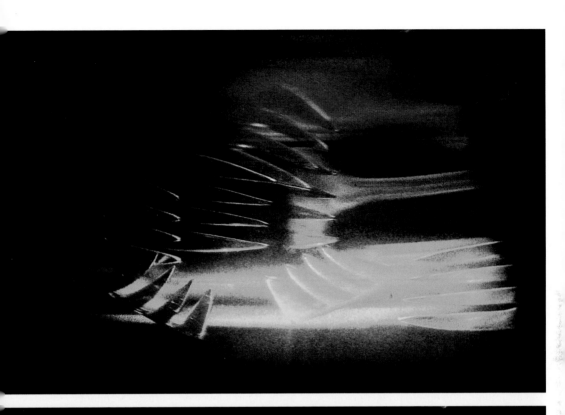

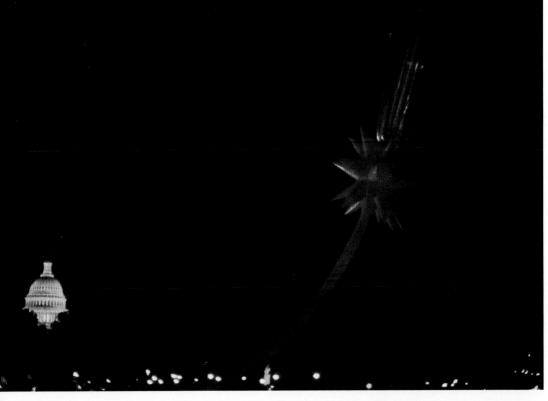

and in the networks that gave it life, *Centerbeam* encapsulates CAVS' ambivalent position in MIT's environment for the arts. Simply tallying its human and nonhuman elements, however, taxes narrative capacity.[16] The installation had distinct lives with differing audiences in two countries. In the process of its making it shed and accumulated both designers and capabilities. *Centerbeam's* contributors ranged in age from 21 to 75 years old. Some had collaborated for decades. Others joined the project when it arrived on the Mall. Working in no less than fifteen distinct media, team members consisted of artists from four continents, astronomers, industrial scientists, electrical engineers, graduate students in the School of Architecture, and a bevy of skilled undergraduates. Full deployment of *Centerbeam's* devices required permission from the Federal Aviation Administration, the Bureau of Radiological Health, the National Park Service, and the Secret Service. All this says nothing of the rift set in motion by a bargain struck by President Wiesner while *Centerbeam* performed on the Mall.

In his introduction to *Centerbeam's* catalogue, Lawrence Alloway described the structure as a "path-node diagram—a graph of processes."[17] Reconstructing its history bears a similar quality. Beginning far afield of the event itself, I document the situational networks from which *Centerbeam* emerged, tracing its paths of energy as they merged and branched. In a shifting landscape of leadership changes, hybrid professional identities, evolving funding structures, and emerging technologies, all of the figures involved—artists, architects, administrators, engineers, and scientists—pursued overlapping and often competing visions of "humane technology" through aesthetic acts. As such, *Centerbeam* forces an inter-textual reading of MIT's "second modernism" that puts into conversation its "clean" and "dirty" ideals. What follows is the biography of a transitory entanglement of virtues.

Aesthetic Virtue in the Defense Institute

Though Kepes served only as a consultant for the project, *Centerbeam* is inexplicable without an appreciation of how he made artist/scientist collaboration fundamental to the "wholeness" of postwar society by promising "epic tasks" of civic transformation, how he institutionalized that vision, and what was lost when it faltered.[18]

17 Lawrence Alloway, "Introduction," in *Centerbeam*, ed. Piene and Goldring, 5.
18 György Kepes, *Center for Advanced Visual Studies* (Cambridge: MIT, 1967). For an analysis of Kepes' ideal of "wholeness" see Elizabeth Finch, *Languages Of Vision: György Kepes and the "New Landscape" of Art and*

Science (Ph.D. Dissertation, City University of New York, 2005).
19 See Anna Vallye, "The Middleman," in this volume.
20 *Massachusetts Institute of Technology Committee on Educational Survey, Report to the Faculty of the Massachusetts Institute of Technology* (Cambridge, MA:

The Technology Press, 1949); Robert Preusser, "Visual Education for Science and Engineering Students," in *Education of Vision*, György Kepes, ed. (New York: George Braziller, 1965), 208-219. By the early 1960s, Field 10 had become a national selling point for MIT, with student work appeared in no less than

Otto Piene, CAVS, *Icarus*, 1978. From *Centerbeam*, (1980). Photo: Elizabeth Goldring.

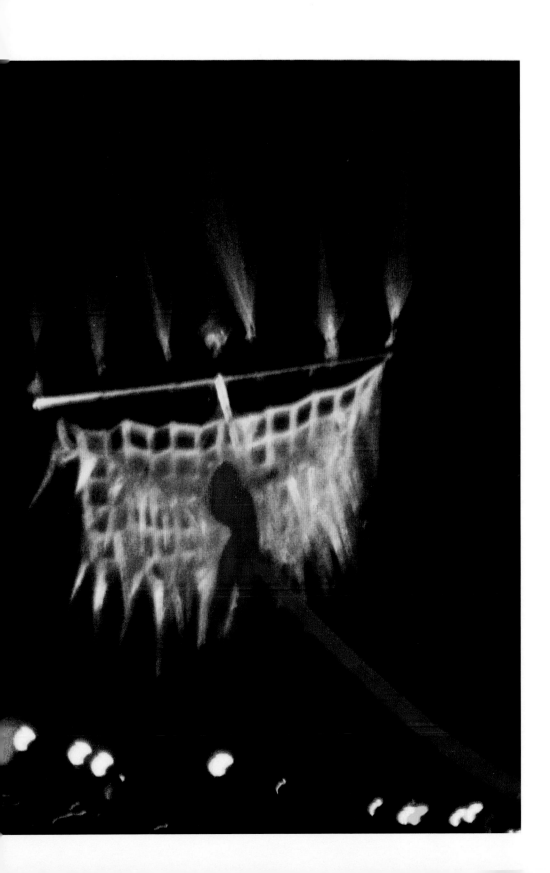

Partial List of Elements in the Making and Unmaking of Centerbeam

Human Actors

Centerbeam Artists
Joan Brigham, Lowry
Burgess, Harriet Casdin-
Silver, Mark Chow, Betsy
Connors, Alva L. Couch,
Paul Earls, Derith Glover,
Elizabeth Goldring, Michio
Ihara, Christopher Janney,
Kenneth Kantor, Harel Kedem,
György Kepes, Paul Matisse,
Mark Mendel, Michael Moser
Muntadas, Carl Nesjar, Otto
Piene, Alejandro Sina, Aldo
Tambellini, Don Thornton

Centerbeam Technologists
Werner Ahrens, Edward Blair
Allen, Jim Ballintine, Stephen
Benton, Patricia Downey,
William Cadogan, Harold
Edgerton, Walter H.G. Lewin,
Charles E. Miller, Michael
Naimark, Marc A. Palumbo,
Brian Raila

Other Actors
Lawrence Alloway, Jack
Burnham, Muriel Cooper,
Kathy Halbreich, Richard
Leacock, Abe and Vera
List, Donlyn Lyndon, Nick
Negroponte, Jerome
Wiesner, Starr Ockenga,
Robert Preusser, Jon Rubin,
M. Schneckenburger, Peter
Spackman

Administrators
Michael Collins, Paul
Gray, John de Monchaux,
William Porter, Walter
Rosenblith

Broader Publics
art critics, students, National
Mall goers, documenta 6
attendees, MIT alumni

Institutions

*Massachusetts Institute of
Technology:* Architecture
Machine Group, CAVS,
Committee on Visual Arts,
Council for the Arts, Creative
Photography Laboratory,
Department of Architecture,
Film and Video Section,
Media Lab, Masters in Visual
Arts Program, School of
Architecture, Visible Language
Workshop

Corporations
Alcoa Foundation, American
Speaker Company, Aries
Music Company, Carpenter
Division of Gardner
Cryogenics, Coherent
Radiation, Comsat, The
Computer Factory, Inc.
Corning Glass Works
Foundation, Crown
International, Electro-Voice,
General Electric Company,
Infodex, Inc., International
Telephone and Telegraph,
Laser Creations, Inc., Lubing
Maschinenfabrik,

Philips Petroleum Company,
Pittsburgh Plate Glass,
Spraying Systems, Inc.,
Steam Rent, Inc., Sylvania
GTE, Tapco, Inc., Thyssen
Henschel

Museums and Art Agencies
Documenta GmbH, Federal
Council on the Arts &
Humanities, Fine Arts
Commission, Hirshhorn
Museum, Milwaukee Art
Center, Museum of Art,
Carnegie Institute, National Air
and Space Museum,

National Collection of Fine
Arts, National Endowment
for the Arts, National Gallery,
Smithsonian Institution

Government Agencies
Bureau of Radiological Health,
HEW, D.C. Architectural
Commission, Federal Aviation
Administration, Goddard
Space Center, Government
Service Administration,
National Park Service, Secret
Service, US Embassy, Bonn,
Germany, United States
Information Agency

Non-Human Elements

brine, computers, electricity,
glass, helium, holograms,
hydroponics, kalliroscope,
lasers, mirrors, neon-argon,
nozzles, polyethylene,
speakers, steam, steel,
strobes, synthesizer tubes,
video, violins, water, weather

Significant Discourses

art: height of human creativity,
source of pleasure and
expression, visual inquiry
equivalent to research
commodified window
dressing beyond common
understanding force for moral
good

technology: height of human,
creativity out-of-control force,
environment in which we
live, source of pleasure and
expression, militaristic and
artificial

science: height of human
creativity, source of
human destruction, moral
rationality, beyond common
understanding, beautiful,
pleasurable act

artists: society's heroic seers,
participatory interpreters,
experts equivalent to
scientists, romantics,
unnecesary expenses

scientists and engineers
society's heroic seers,
creative entrepreneurs,

"doers" and "makers,"
organization men, rationality
incarnate

architects: see *artists,
scientists and engineers)*

collaboration: source of
societal wholeness, basis
of new creative knowledge,
cooptation/ compromise of
vision

Matthew Wisnioski,
Chart 1: Partial List of
Elements in the Making
and Unmaking of
Centerbeam.

The resources Kepes tapped to create CAVS were more diverse
than even his *Vision and Value* series let on. During Kepes'
tenure, there were five distinct movements in support of the
arts at MIT. The first and longest standing centered around the
professional training of architects. The School of Architecture's
desire to modernize its curricula by emulating changes in the
sciences contributed to Kepes' appointment in 1945 and his
subsequent replacement of "freehand drawing" with "visual
design."[19] The second movement concerned the "integral plan"
of general education; intended to prepare students for leadership
in a nuclear age, it gave rise to Field 10 (under the direction of
Robert Preusser).[20] The third movement stemmed from a related
desire among alumni and the wives of MIT administrators to
"humanize" MIT by beautifying the campus and providing outlets for
experiencing master works, a desire made manifest in the founding
of Hayden Gallery. The fourth was a complicated mix of ideologies
and practices by which MIT scientists and engineers themselves
laid claim to artistic vision, a position Kepes himself cultivated to
great effect. The fifth movement, by far the most tenuous, was the
idea that MIT should aspire to professional art-making on par with
its achievements in science and engineering.[21]

MIT, moreover, was not a universe unto itself. Its conceptions of
the arts were co-produced with a range of activities in American
science and industry. Informed by a highly theorized notion of
"interdisciplinarity," psychologists, art historians, and sociologists
identified the scientist and the artist as emblems of the most
innovative and least conformist individuals who provided the
principal source of innovation and social cohesion in a modern
age.[22] For government and industrial research laboratories, art was
a marker of disinterested purity, the pursuit of truth by cultured
employees dedicated to their task. Los Alamos, for example, ran
a series of recruitment advertisements with abstract paintings
inspired by scientific phenomena. Titled with the adage "From
Diversity Comes Unity," these advertisements trumpeted
collaboration while implying that researchers did not dirty their
hands in weapons design.[23] Inside America's corporations,
there was also a veritable "creativity" boom among engineers,
managers, and industrial scientists aimed at enhancing productivity
and dispelling the anxiety that postwar expansion had turned
employees into organization men.[24]

The Airborne Instruments Laboratory (AIL) of Cutler Hammer, for instance, showcased employee artwork that included paintings of a Siamese cat, a pastor, and covered bridges to demonstrate that its employees were a "broad-gauged group of humans" who were "civic-minded" and "artistic"—the sort "the world needs."[25] Finally, in the late 1960s and early 1970s, nearly two hundred of the nation's engineering colleges revised their curricula, adding humanities, social sciences, and art courses to "humanize" technologists.[26]
A similar range of normative aims existed among artists drawn to new media and scientific themes. Between the mid-1960s and early 1970s, artists and critics debated the eroding meaning of the "art object" and the identity of the "artist" as its authorial maker. Video art, computer art, electronic art, light works, cybernetic environments, and holography proliferated as artists simultaneously praised, condemned, and appropriated the tools of the technological order.[27]

Throughout the Cold War era, in short, "the art of science" and "technological art" conjured contradictory values: hybridity and purity, elite expertise and participatory democracy the neutrality of knowledge and its inherent politics. Nonetheless, these visions shared a set of common ideals. Throughout a technological society, art always signified an intellectual, professional, and social good which promised to repair societal divisions through *creativity and collaboration*.[28]

Kepes united these diverse energies at MIT by enfolding everyone else's worldview into his own. Externally, he embraced the persona of interdisciplinarity incarnate. Time Life Books used MIT's art programs to lionize scientists and engineers as fonts of "Poetic Vision."[29] Kepes' paintings lined the offices of Route 128 executives. He spoke at events ranging from a symposium on "hierarchical structure" at McDonnell Douglas's Advanced Research Laboratories to "Ladies Night" at the local chapter of the American Institute of Mining, Metallurgical, and Petroleum Engineers (AIME).[30] Internally, he cultivated a patronage relationship with Julius and Catherine Stratton familiar to any Renaissance courtier. To broaden support for the arts, Kepes encouraged the efforts of Ida Rubin and other MIT matrons to develop a permanent collection. He welcomed a faculty-directed Committee on the Visual Arts (CVA), ensuring that MIT would collect and exhibit contemporary works.

25 magazines ranging from Art in America to Fortune, between 1961 and 1969.
21 I am grateful to Meg Rotzel for this delineation, used in similar fashion in her adept analysis of MIT's Wiesner Building, "The Media Lab that Wasn't" (2009). Unpublished manuscript cited with permission of the author.

22 Jamie Cohen-Cole, *Thinking about Thinking in Cold War America* (Ph.D. dissertation, Princeton University, 2003); Peter Galison, "The Americanization of Unity," *Daedalus* 127 (1998): 45-71.
23 Los Alamos, "From Diversity Comes Unity," *Mechanical Engineering* 83,

no. 12 (December 1961): 155.
24 See e.g.: *Company Climate and Creativity* (New York: Industrial Relations News, 1959); Eugene K. Von Fange, *Professional Creativity* (Englewood Cliffs, NJ: Prentice-Hall, 1959). J.H. McPherson, "How to Manage Creative Engineers," *Mechanical Engineering* 87

(February 1965): 32-36.
25 Cutler Hammer, "Art at A.I.L.," *IEEE Spectrum* 4, no. 5 (1967).: 5.
26 Matthew H. Wisnioski, "'Liberal Education Has Failed': Reading Like an Engineer in 1960s America," *Technology and Culture* 50 no. 4 (2009): 753-782.
27 For contemporary

Most importantly, to appeal to the School of Architecture's desire to emulate the sciences, Kepes adopted the "Center" rhetoric and cast artists as experimental researchers. But in the upheaval of the late 1960s, Kepes struggled with the negative connotations of collaboration. The failed Boston Harbor project was followed by the similarly compromised *Explorations* exhibit.[31] As "The System" took on sinister meaning, Kepes did his best to adopt anti-technology tropes while maintaining optimism about the humanizing power of art. "What we face," he offered, "are destructive forces of a completely new kind—man-generated, cumulative, and of almost cosmic proportion."[32] On the brink of retirement, Kepes questioned the viability of his dream.[33]

Cutler Hammer, "Art at A.I.L.," Airborne Instruments Laboratory, *IEEE Spectrum* 4, no.5, 1967.

right, Los Alamos, "From Diversity Comes Unity," recruitment advertisement, Los Alamos Scientific Laboratory, 1961. From *Mechanical Engineering*, December, 1961.

Otto Piene, *Sky Art*,
Olympic Rainbow test
flight, Minneapolis 1972.
From *Sky Art, 1968-1996.*
Photo: Winzen Research
Inc.

Art Transition

At this point, two of *Centerbeam's* principal agents—Piene and Wiesner—began rearranging Kepes' network. As they assumed new positions of leadership at MIT, they directed existing energies and sparked new ones that would be vital to *Centerbeam's* construction. They also made choices that assured its singularity.

Shortly after Wiesner was appointed President in 1971, he declared his intention to "transform MIT into a large multi-purpose arts center."[34] In front of nine hundred alumni at the Metropolitan Museum of Art he announced a new Council for the Arts designed to raise funds and integrate the arts through centralized management. He explained to the Council's first chairman, real estate developer Paul Tishman, that the "humane arts" were "illuminators of human potential, genius and uniqueness" and thus should be at the core of a scientific education designed to meet the inner needs of technologists and improve "the quality of the environment on the scale of the city or even the world ecosystem."[35] In 1974, Otto Piene was chosen to inherit CAVS' directorship from its seemingly irreplaceable founder at a moment of skepticism about its mission. Like Kepes, Piene's art had evolved from painting to light works to interactive environments. He had been incredibly prolific during his six years as a Fellow. Along with Nam June Paik and Aldo Tambellini, he participated in the first video art broadcast, WGBH's *Medium is the Medium*. He presented his second solo exhibition at New York's Howard Wise Gallery, published a collection of sky art lithographs, and wrote a book outlining his tenets of environmental art. Piene's sky events grew in scale and frequency, unfolding across the Charles River and over rooftops in Pittsburgh, beaches in Hawaii, city streets in Germany, the National Mall in Washington, DC., and finally culminating with the 1500-foot illuminated helium rainbow at the Munich Olympics.[36]

Piene was an evangelist for technologically-mediated collaboration. When he arrived at MIT, he was already an acclaimed organizer of Group Zero, an avant-garde collective formed in Düsseldorf when he was just twenty-nine. Celebrating scale and change, Group Zero defined artistic collaboration as a balanced process of teamwork and individuality.[37] Of the Fellows chosen by Kepes, Piene actualized the artist/scientist partnership to greatest

explanations of the phenomena see: Jonathan Benthall, *Science and Technology in Art Today* (New York: Praeger, 1972); Douglas Davis, *Art and the Future: A History-Prophecy of the Collaboration between Science, Technology and Art* (London, 1973). For historical analysis see: Caroline A.

Jones, *Machine in the Studio: Constructing the Postwar American Artist* (Chicago: University of Chicago Press, 1996); Marga Bijvoet, *Art as Inquiry: Toward New Collaborations Between, Art Science, and Technology* (New York: Peter Lang, 1997); Oliver Grau, ed., *MediaArtHistories* (Cambridge, MA: MIT Press,

2007); Edward A. Shanken, *Art and Electronic Media* (London: Phaidon Press, 2009).

28 Matthew Wisnioski, *Engineers for Change: Competing Visions of Technology in 1960s America* (Cambridge, MA: MIT Press, 2012), 125-128, 140.

29 Henry Margenau, David

Bergamini, and the Editors of LIFE, *The Scientist* (New York: Time Incorporated, 1964): 16-27. C. C. Furnas and Joe McCarthy, *The Engineer* (New York: Time Incorporated, 1966), 91.

30 I.S. Servi, "Dear Professor Kepes" August 21, 1969; Albert F. Wilson, "Dear Professor Kepes," October

Otto Piene, X-ray
Telescope Launch,
Mildura, Australia, 1967.
From *Sky Art*, 1968-1996.
Photo: Walter Lewin.

effect. He arrived at MIT with the intention of using the sky as an expansive medium. A
call for volunteers attracted Walter Lewin, perhaps the one person alive best suited to help
him.[38] A young Dutch astrophysicist, Lewin would became famous for discovering X-ray
Burster stars, and, in an era before ubiquitous satellites, his detectors reached the outer
atmosphere attached to the world's largest helium balloons.[39]

Piene's understanding of collaboration, however, differed from Kepes' in important ways.
Piene was a maker rather than a theorist. In *More Sky*, he called for the proliferation
of "Integration Departments" in technical and artistic institutions, but criticized the
academicism of "paper projects":

> Given the advanced age of technology, it is deeds that count, not babble . . . You hang
> a sculpture in the wind, and the wind becomes visible. You talk about the wind, and the
> wind becomes a word. You talk about art and technology, and they turn it into a phrase
> easily overcome or neutralized at least by words, a process also known as sloganeering.[40]

8, 1968. György Kepes
papers, 1825-1989, Archives
of American Art, Smithsonian
Institution, Reel 5306 item
609 and Reel 5305 item 1124.
Additional requests came
from Bell Labs, Univac, AT&T,
and the Lincoln Laboratory.
31 Finch, Languages Of
Vision, 296-308.
32 György Kepes, "Art and

Ecological Consciousness"
and "The Artist's Role
in Environmental Self-
Regulation," in *Arts of the
Environment*, ed. György
Kepes (New York: George
Braziller, 1972), 1-12, 167-197.
33 György Kepes to Dean
William Porter (May 2, 1972)
György Kepes papers, 1825-
1989, Archives of American

Art, Smithsonian Institution,
Real 5308 items 294-298.
34 "Wiesner Announces
Formation of MIT Council for
the Arts," *Tech Talk*, November
1971.
35 Jerome Wiesner,
"Building a Shared Culture."
Massachusetts Institute
of Technology. Office of
the Arts. AC 230, Box 2,

Institute Archives and Special
Collections, MIT.
36 The best survey is Otto
Piene, ed., *Sky Art*, 1968-
1996 (Köln: Wienand, 1999).
37 Otto Piene, "Group Zero,"
Art Education 18 no. 5 (May
1965): 20-23.
38 Piene's fascination
with the sky as a medium
was rooted in his teenage

Though not a political radical, Piene's sensibilities leaned much more towards participatory democracy than Kepes'. His most focused critical insights, moreover, were directed at artists rather than scientists or engineers. Piene railed against the commoditization and objectification of collectors and museums. At the same time, he argued that the professional artist had a unique responsibility to interpret the technological world for broader publics that could not be achieved by amateurs. These positions would prove crucial in his interactions with other MIT stakeholders.

When he became director, Piene also faced a different institutional landscape than Kepes had. The utopian sheen that had attracted scientists, artists, and the press to Kepes' project had been severely dampened. Nevertheless, the 1970s were a period of growth for the arts at MIT. Wiesner and the Council for the Arts gave CAVS financial stability in exchange for a teaching mission that reconnected a thread Kepes had severed.[41] Simultaneous with Piene's appointment, Preusser was made CAVS director of educational programs. In 1973-1974, CAVS served eleven students in an informal capacity; the following year 133 enrolled in six new course offerings; in 1975-1976 there were 240 students.[42] To accommodate the surge, CAVS converted one of its five studios into a lecture/exhibition room, and Lobby 7, a short distance across Massachusetts Avenue, became its *de facto* exhibition space.

CAVS' education program created pockets of appreciation for environmental art among MIT students and provided Fellows with access to a pool of skilled technical assistants. This was a relationship that Piene had already found productive; for example, Piene would develop a near decade-long collaboration with William Cadogan, a one-time engineering student who later became *Centerbeam's* chief engineer. Students discovered, however, that the audience that enthusiastically supported Field 10's scientific modernism in the 1960s responded less kindly to environmental art. In 1975, CAVS held its Food exhibition in Lobby 7, which included a giant inflated apple with an internal slide, piles of rotting fruit, and a spaghetti-like net hanging above the atrium. The show was conducted with understandable amateurism and committed the cardinal sin of obstructing the infinite corridor. In addition to negative letters to the editor, MIT's student newspaper, *The Tech*, published a satirical review of a "Trash" show consisting of "three tons of garbage, litter, and sewage," anchored by a 200-foot inflatable plastic can.[43] *Food*, however, had a formative impact on at least four participants who later became part of the *Centerbeam* crew. Kenneth Kantor, for example, a freshman contributor to *Food*, served as *Centerbeam's* electronics engineer and went on to a distinguished career as an audio speaker inventor.

From CAVS' perspective, the Council for the Arts made judgments not far removed from *Food's* detractors. The Council, which had no practicing artists on its executive board, empowered alumni, who were typically much more conservative in their conception of "art" than CAVS. The Council's inaugural event, for example, was a national fundraising tour by the Institute's Symphony Orchestra intended to showcase the well-rounded talents of MIT students. Art/science/technology collaborations had an ambiguous status among Council activities, a situation that Piene did not seek to improve through the sort of patron outreach that had earned Kepes respect among businessmen, engineers, and industrialists.

In addition to the Council, CAVS had to negotiate with new programs in the School of Architecture which were also staking claims to art/science/technology collaboration as professional practice: Richard Leacock's Film and Video Section, Muriel Cooper's Visible Language Workshop, Starr Ockenga's Creative Photography Laboratory, and Nicholas Negroponte's Architecture Machine Group (AMG). In general, these programs were mutually reinforcing, but they were spread across the campus, competed for resources, and their directors were each interested in fashioning MIT's arts in their own image. Negroponte emerged as Piene's chief sparring partner. As an undergraduate, his Field 10 coursework had been reprinted in *Technology Review* and *Mechanical Engineering* as prime examples of the art program's benefits.[44] Later, his mixed media contribution "SEEK" at the Jewish Museum's *Software* exhibit—which involved gerbils interacting within a computer-controlled landscape of aluminum blocks—was heralded by critics.[45] But Negroponte's product-oriented computer graphics research was heavily funded by defense contracts. Moreover, while he shared Piene's desire to encourage art observers to become participants, he believed that technology itself would facilitate the transformation.[46]

top, CAVS "Food Show," Lobby of Building 7, MIT, 1975. Photo: Roger N. Goldstein.

bottom, Nicholas Negroponte, "SEEK" at the Jewish Museum's *Software* exhibit. From Douglas Davis, *Art of the Future* (Praeger, 1973).

Pooling their resources, these programs developed a new Masters in Visual Studies (SMVisS) within the Department of Architecture. Divided into five concentrations with different admission requirements and plans of study, the program was a fraught alliance in which students were expected to chart their own paths. The mix, however, had impressive results. Michael Naimark, who would contribute to *Centerbeam's* holography line, for example, earned his degree from Piene's Environmental Art concentration but worked as an assistant in Negroponte's AMG.[47] The SMVisS program, moreover, immediately became CAVS' lifeblood. Students worked in apprentice-like relationships with Fellows, and upon graduation were given fellowships at the Center to further develop their work and professional reputation.

Bolstered by its graduate and undergraduate programs, CAVS expanded its community to involve over twenty Fellows a year. Many were supported by external foundations or had complementary positions in Boston's art world. Burgess, for example, came to CAVS in 1972, but was also chairman of the MFA Program at the Massachusetts College of Art. Fellows invited by Piene had typically worked with scientists and engineers prior to their arrival at MIT. Some were technical adepts in their own right. Harriet Casdin-Silver, who became a Fellow in 1976, evolved from an environmental artist into a holographer. She first began working with industrial physicists in 1968, gaining her own laboratory space at American Optical Research. This led to further collaborations with Stephen Benton, inventor of white light holography. She then became a visiting researcher in the physics department at Brown University, simultaneously performing technical and aesthetic research, a position that overlapped with her time at MIT.[48]

In sum, during his first years as director, Piene cultivated a diverse community of undergraduates, SMVisS graduate students, emerging talent, and established artists that virtually defined what it meant to be a "technological" artist in the 1970s. In October 1975, he publicly announced CAVS' expanded mission by co-organizing the international *ArtTransition* conference.[49] For Piene, *ArtTransition* was an effort to stake CAVS' position as a leader in the environmental and new media arts. With collaboration as the central theme, it also set the tone for future events under his tenure. He appointed Wiesner

experiences as a flak gunner during World War II. Conscripted at the age of 15, he remembers how gymnasium teachers gave lessons on Tacitus while children manned the guns. Robert F. Brown and Otto Piene, "Oral history interview with Otto Piene, 1988 Aug. 4-1990 Feb. 22) Archives of

American Art, Smithsonian Institution. Tape 1, Side A. **39** Walter HG Lewin, "Three Decades with Otto Piene," in *Sky Art*, 1968-1996, ed. Otto Piene, 37-53. **40** Otto Piene, *More Sky* (Cambridge: MIT Press, 1973), 37, 108. **41** Otto Piene to Jerome Wiesner, October 3, 1974.

Folder 301. Center for Advanced Visual Studies Archive. **42** Otto Piene, "Center for Advanced Visual Studies," in *Massachusetts Institute of Technology Annual Bulletin* 111, no. 4 (November 1975), 76-79; Otto Piene, "Center for Advanced Visual Studies," in *Massachusetts Institute of*

right, CAVS Course Offerings, Fall semester 1977/78.

Center For Advanced Visual Studies

SUBJECTS, FALL SEMESTER, 1977/78

CENTER FOR ADVANCED VISUAL STUDIES
IN ASSOCIATION WITH THE DEPARTMENT OF ARCHITECTURE,
SCHOOL OF ARCHITECTURE AND PLANNING,
MASSACHUSETTS INSTITUTE OF TECHNOLOGY,
BUILDING W11, 40 MASSACHUSETTS AVENUE,
TELEPHONE: 253-4415, 253-6849

PROFESSOR OTTO PIENE, DIRECTOR
PROFESSOR GYORGY KEPES, DIRECTOR EMERITUS
PROFESSOR ROBERT PREUSSER, DIRECTOR OF EDUCATION

ELIGIBLE FOR REGISTRATION IN THESE SUBJECTS ARE UNDERGRADUATE
AND GRADUATE STUDENTS FROM ALL SCHOOLS AND DEPARTMENTS
AT M.I.T. AND OTHER SCHOOLS WITH WHICH THE INSTITUTE HAS CROSS-
REGISTRATION ARRANGEMENTS (MASSACHUSETTS COLLEGE OF ART
STUDENTS CONSULT THE C.A.V.S. OFFICE).

4.801   ART AND THE ENVIRONMENT (3-0-6)
Otto Piene, Paul Earls, Elizabeth Goldring

Contributions by Dr. Harold Edgerton, Derith Glover, Chris Janney, Maggie
Lettvin, Donlyn Lyndon, Mark Mendel, Carl Nesjar, John Newman, Jen Rubin,
Judith Wechsler, John Wynne.

Continuation of lecture and investigation series on the history, theory and
practice of environmental art; assignments for environmental investigations in
various media by students.

Tuesday evenings, 7-10 p.m., 3-133.

4.831   ENVIRONMENTAL ART (0-4-8)
Otto Piene

Design, planning and building of environmental art installations in given and
chosen existing settings, e.g. Staircase 7 and sites and conditions from
commissions. Emphasis on integration of urban elements, nature and sculptural
architecture. Further emphasis on possibilities for execution.

Thursdays, 9 a.m.-1 p.m., W11 and by arrangement. Subsequent classes
may also meet in 7-437.

4.841   ENVIRONMENTAL LIGHT AND COLOR(A) (2-4-6)

4.842   ENVIRONMENTAL LIGHT AND COLOR(A) (2-9-9)
Robert Preusser, Nishan Bichajian

A study of the dynamic and qualitative attributes of light and color within the
context of architectural and urban settings. Emphasis on innovative alternatives to prevailing practice in the illumination of man-made environments and
the use of light as an environmental art medium. Projects include additive and
subtractive color interaction, minimal lighting, reflected color, complementary
color shadows and the coordination of light and movement. Photography
utilized as an analytical tool and for recording experiments.

Mondays and Wednesdays, 2-5 p.m., E21-204.

4.845   ADVANCED VISUAL DESIGN(A) (0-8-12)
Otto Piene, Dan Dailey, Alejandro Sina

Theory and practice of some aspects of kinetic, light and media art, environmental art and celebrations; planning of public art complexes: sculptural
architecture and architectural sculpture. Work on public commissions and
exhibitions of environmental scale. Mostly individual assignments and tasks.
General art and workshop experience required.

First meeting, Thursday, September 15, 9 a.m.-1 p.m., W11 (same as 4.831 for
organizational reasons; subsequent meetings will be scheduled individually).

4.861   GRAPHICS LABORATORY (0-3-2)
Nishan Bichajian, John Newman, Harel Kedem

Free hand drawing for beginners and advanced students. Students may choose
to draw from live models to develop skill in observation of action, proportion,
line, texture and form using conte crayon, pen and brush. Kinetic drawing as well
as detail and perspective rendering with emphasis on technique and
spontaneity. Optical anatomy instruction will also be given. Or, students may opt
to draw from still life forms from simple lines to light and shadow modeling from
varied subject matter. May be repeated for credit.

New students consult instructor, Monday, September 12, between 10 a.m. and
3 p.m., W11; first meeting Wednesday, September 14, 12 noon-1 p.m., W11.

4.895   SPECIAL PROBLEMS IN ENVIRONMENTAL ART(A):

VIDEO AS AN ART MEDIUM (0-12-0)
Peter Campus

Seminar on video with emphasis on individual student projects. Each meeting
there will be viewing and discussion of the students' videotapes as well as those
of established artists. All student work will be done outside the class. The
seminar will meet every other week.

First meeting, Thursday, September 12, 2-5 p.m., W11.

4.897   SPECIAL PROBLEMS IN ENVIRONMENTAL ART(A):

VIDEO IMAGE PROCESSING AND MANIPULATION (0-9-0)
Aldo Tambellini

A course for the production of videotapes and cable programs. Emphasis on
innovative ways for processing visual images and the relationship of sound to
image. Students will work on various exploratory aspects of images generated
by a camera or synthetic means. They will be exposed to the language of
computer graphics, film, photography, holography and the video synthesizer.
The course will be conducted in the C.A.E.S. television studio and through
outdoor video workshops.

Video will be approached as a concept of manipulation with an awareness that
an image can be generated and manipulated through many sources with each
source having its own characteristic and influence on the structure of video.
Several of the projects will be used for cable programs.

First meeting, Thursday, September 15, 4-6 p.m., W11.

4.898   SPECIAL PROBLEMS IN ENVIRONMENTAL ART(A):

HOLOGRAPHY AS AN ART MEDIUM (0-9-0)
Harriet Casdin-Silver

Concept, design, technique. Consideration of the present state of the art of
holography and its developmental potential. Hologram actualization. Media
interaction: experimental projects integrating holography and video, film,
computer graphics, etc.

First meeting, Thursday, September 15, 2-5 p.m., W11. Subsequent meetings to
be scheduled.

4.938   SPECIAL PROJECTS IN PHOTOGRAPHY (0-9-0):

EXPLORATION OF LIGHT IMAGES AND PHOTO IMAGE MANIPULATION
Aldo Tambellini

The course will explore the property of light sensitive emulsion and the process
which produces the photographic image as a basic element. It will deal with
direct visual sensory impact derived from light and the manipulation of
photographic images rather than a straight recording or rendering of nature.
Emphasis will be on images produced by camera-less photography and other
experimental forms — photograms (producing photographs by placing objects
directly on film emulsion), solarization, photomontage, working with various
media under glass to produce slides, reworking negatives, and fun prints.

The course will include a series for cinematic like sequences, videograms
(images printed from television as a light source), and painting directly with
chemicals on paper. Throughout the course inventiveness will be encouraged.

All students registering for a basic photography course will meet to determine
their appropriate sections on Monday, September 12, at 5 p.m., W31-310.
Subsequent class meetings for 4.938 on Mondays, 1-5 p.m.

4.921   CREATIVE PHOTOGRAPHY I (2-5-5)

Two sections of Creative Photography I are being offered, one by CAVS Fellow,
Mike Moser. Consult the Creative Photography Lab for description.

All students registering for a basic photography course will meet to determine
appropriate sections on Monday, September 12, at 5 p.m., W31-310.

4UR   UNDERGRADUATE RESEARCH IN ARCHITECTURE

MULTI-MEDIA RESEARCH (UNITS TO BE ARRANGED)
Paul Earls, Robert Preusser

Research in multi-media techniques and production. Independent or collaborative work. Consult instructors for more details and to initiate individual
proposals.

"CENTERBEAM" at documenta 6, Kassel, Germany
Center for Advanced Visual Studies, 1977
Photo: Dietmar L9hrl

as conference Chairman. Instead of showcasing a delicate balance of artists, scientists, and essayists, however, the emphasis was decidedly on artists. According to Piene, it was artists who were responsible for fostering human uses of technology and guiding the "'archaic stages of the information industry." This was a democratic task that would preserve the "artist's identity" as he or she engaged technologists and politicians. The result, he argued, would not be "ultimate solutions to perennial problems," but rather "momentary psychic energy."[50]

CAVS' statement of purpose at *ArtTransition* offers a convenient place to regain our bearings. Throughout the 1970s, CAVS, Wiesner, the Council for the Arts, the School of Architecture, and other groups had all debated what counted as "art" and how the diverse energies of art could be brought together at MIT. There was a persistent hope for an architectural solution to integration, and, as early as 1973, the Council began planning for new facilities.[51] Discussion accelerated with the formation of the SMVisS degree. In 1976, Architecture Professor Donlyn Lyndon conducted an *Arts Environments Study* at the request of the Council; the Study emphasized that facilities along MIT's main corridor were needed to maximize informal interaction.[52] Late in 1977, the discussion ceased

A Revised Mission for CAVS, 1975

Environmental Art & Design	"enhance the physical environment's psychological economy by means of beauty which is both expressive and practical"
Developmental Media	"find the expressive artistic language which can reach a large audience with human dignity and *without commercial stimulation*"
Art/ScienceTechnology	"use every chance for interaction between artists, scientists, engineers and scholars to master the increased scale of communication"
Celebrations	"an oft-neglected art form presumably earlier than painting, which is obviously communal and most inviting to people of all ages, denominations and professional commitments"
Education	"toward the new arts and general education towards a broader understanding of our 'modern' world"

above, Matthew Wisnioski, *Chart 2: A Revised Mission for CAVS, 1975.*

Technology Annual Bulletin 112, no. 4 (November 1976), 67-69.

43 USC, "The ultimate in environmental art . . ." *The Tech* (Friday, April 11, 1975), 5; Otto Piene, "To the Editor," *The Tech* (Tuesday, May 6, 1975), 4.

44 Jane H. Kay, "A Gallery of Visual Design," *Technology Review* (April 1967): 96-97. "Art and the Engineer," *Mechanical Engineering* 89 (December 1967): 48-49.

45 Davis, *Art and the Future,* 100-102, 168; Benthall, *Science and Technology in Art Today,* 50, 75-78, 166-167.

46 Nicholas P. Negroponte, "The Return of the Sunday Painter," in *The Computer Age: a Twenty-Year View,* ed. Michael L. Dertouzos and Joel Moses (Cambridge, MA: MIT Press, 1979), 21-37. Negroponte found ample support beyond MIT, as entrepreneurs and former counterculturalists fashioned themselves as socio-technical visionaries. Fred Turner, *From Counterculture to*

to be academic when Abe and Vera List announced their intention to make a major donation for the construction of an arts complex. At the same time that Wiesner's vision was becoming reality, Piene also was on the brink of actualizing the civic art that had eluded Kepes.

Assembling *Centerbeam*

Having established the institutional and discursive groundwork and introduced the main players, we can finally approach *Centerbeam* with an eye toward its proximate aesthetic and organizational meanings. Late in 1976, Schneckenburger, who had been a panelist at the *ArtTransition* conference, invited CAVS to present a group project at *documenta 6*. The result was an accumulation of agents and resources dating from Piene's arrival in 1968.

ARTTransition, Jerome Wiesner depicted on TV Cello by Nam June Paik and Charlotte Moormon. *Left to right*, Moorman, Wiesner, Piene, and Paik, 1975. Photo: Nishan Bichajian.

Centerbeam's organizing form was established by democratic vote. Among three ideas—one from Piene, one from Burgess, and one from Harel Kadem (an SMVisS graduate student)—the group chose Burgess' concept of "bundled energy and communications lines from the well springs of an urban environment to extend into the natural landscape, where they would become visible interactive transmissions."[53] Burgess, Piene, and Michio Ihara (a sculptor of modernist architectural spaces invited by Kepes in 1970) then worked out the structural base, which was intended to convey infinite length, but was which was pared down to 128 feet to accommodate the Baroque courtyard at Kassel. The water prism—its dimensions calibrated to maximum visual effect by Lewin—was the first component to stabilize. It was to be raised four feet from the ground on stanchions carrying fifteen distinct media "lines."

Cyberculture: Stewart Brand, the Whole Earth Network, and the Rise of Digital Utopianism (Chicago, 2006).
47 He later established Atari Research, earned an international reputation as a video artist, and now leads a similar academic unit at the University of Southern California. His personal

website is located at http://www.naimark.net/.
48 Harriet Casdin-Silver, "My First 10 Years as Artist/Holographer (1968-1977)" *Leonardo* 22, no. 3/4 (1989): 317-326. For an analysis of the hybrid artistic/technical character of holography see: Sean F. Johnston, *Holographic Visions: A History of New*

Science (New York: Oxford University Press, 2006).
49 The event was prompted by an invitation from the University Film Stud Center, whose director Peter Feinstein wanted to draw attention to art forms that fell between mass culture and the collector's market. Peter Feinstein, "Film," in

Artransition (Cambridge, MA: MIT Press, 1975), 67.
50 Otto Piene, *Artransition*, x-xi.
51 "Background: Arts and Media Technology Program." Folder 229, "Arts Building Facility." Center for Advanced Visual Studies Archive.
52 Arts Advisory Group and the Arts Environments Study

After the senior group had established the modernist steel scaffolding, the CAVS community adopted a fluid process for integrating elements of individual expression. In December 1976, they met in the alley of building W-11 with an "impromptu changing collage" consisting of a three-foot prism, a steam generator, a hologram, a laser, and neon rods. Biweekly meetings addressed problems of technical integration and aesthetic sensibility.

The most complicated element of *Centerbeam* was Casdin-Silver's white-light transmitted solar holograms. From 12" x 16" plates, they projected images at a frontal distance of roughly three feet.[54] To assure a consistent light source for her forks, Casdin-Silver worked with a team composed of Lewin, his graduate students, Kantor, Naimark, Brian Raila (an Art and Design undergraduate), and Benton. When completed, the solar tracking mirrors automatically determined the position of the sun from "anywhere on Earth."[55] All the while, Piene and Elizabeth Goldring worked the phones and travelled to companies and government agencies in Washington, New York, and Pittsburgh. President Wiesner assisted as a critical fundraiser and ideas man. Corporate and government sponsors were enthusiastic, but unwilling to support a one-off event in Germany. To enroll American foundations and government agencies, CAVS promised a traveling sculpture. The majority of funding for *documenta 6* came from the United States Information Agency (USIA), which at first imagined that *Centerbeam* would be reconstructed in Eastern Europe and Moscow as a symbol of political reconciliation. Vice President Walter Mondale's office, however, wanted it shown in Washington to represent Carter's energy policies and his administration's willingness to work together with industry.[56]

The team arrived in Kassel a month prior and began assembly. Following the release of one of Piene's fifty-foot flowers, *Centerbeam* was turned on for a duration of roughly one hundred days. With additional funding from the USIA, Piene invited Leacock and Jon Rubin of Architecture's Film/Video Section to document the "developing art and technology relationship."[57]

While *documenta 6* deserves further attention, *Centerbeam's* incarnation in Washington, DC best highlights its tangled aesthetic, discursive, political, and technical elements.

Team, *MIT Arts Environments Study* (Cambridge, MA: MIT 1976).

53 Elizabeth Goldring, "Centerbeam—Kassel" in *Centerbeam*, ed. Piene and Goldring, 37.

54 Harriet Casdin-Silver, "'Centerbeam' documenta 6—'Centerbeam' Washington, DC," in *Centerbeam*, ed.

Piene and Goldring. 77-78.

55 Walter H.G. Lewin, et al. "Solar Tracking of Holograms for 'Centerbeam'" in *Centerbeam*, ed. Piene and Goldring, 79-81.

56 Otto Piene to Jerome Wiesner, May 26, 1977. Massachusetts Institute of Technology Office of the Provost. AC 7, Box 25, Folder

"Centerbeam Documenta 6". Institute Archives and Special Collections, MIT. Otto Piene to Walter Rosenblith, "Report part 1". October 17, 1977. Massachusetts Institute of Technology Office of the Provost. AC 7, Box 25, Folder "Centerbeam Documenta 6". Institute Archives and Special Collections, MIT.

right, Matthew Wisnioski, Chart 3: *Centerbeam's Proximate Makers.*

Name	Contribution	CAVS Affiliation & Relevant Connections	Age
Otto Piene	project director, 23 sky events	Director	50
Lowry Burgess	artistic coordinator	Fellow 1972—	38
		MFA Program Chair, Mass. College of Art	
Elizabeth Goldring	project coordinator	Fellow 1975—	33
Paul Earls	laser line, computer tapes	Fellow 1970—	44
	music & sound lines	Lecturer, Department of Architecture, MIT	
Michio Ihara	structural design	Fellow 1970—1977	50
Alejandro Sina	neon-argon line	Fellow 1973—	33
Joan Brigham	steam line & water line	Fellow 1974—	43
		Assistant Professor of Fine Arts, Emerson	
Carl Nesjar	brine line (Germany)	Fellow 1975—	58
Harriet Casdin-Silver	holography line	Fellow 1976—	43
		Assistant Professor of Physics, Brown	
Mark Mendel	poetry line	Fellow 1976—	31
Aldo Tambellini	video	Fellow 1976—	48
Mark Chow	video	Fellow 1977—	25
		SB, Electrical Engineering, MIT 1974	
		SB, Architecture, MIT 1975	
Paul Matisse	Kalliroscpe	Fellow 1977—	45
Muntadas	video	Fellow 1977—	36
Betsy Connors	video	Research Affiliate	28
		WGBH New Television Workshop Artist	
Alva L. Couch	laser imagery	computer programmer, Harvard Medical School	22
		SB, Architecture, MIT, 1978	
Derith Glover	"drawing with your eyes"	Fellow 1977—1978	26
		SMVisS, CAVS, MIT, 1977	
Michael Moser	video	Fellow 1977—	26
		SMVisS, CAVS, MIT, 1977	
Harel Kedem	grow line	Fellow 1978—	31
		SMVisS, CAVS, MIT, 1977	
Christopher Janney	"soundshuffle"	Fellow 1978—	28
		SMVisS, CAVS, MIT, 1977	
Michael Naimark	solar tracking participant	SMVisS student	26
	film assistant	works in Architecture Machine Group	
Don Thornton	holograms	SMVisS student	32
Walter HG Lewin	solar tracking design	Professors of Physics, MIT	42
		Piene collaborator since 1967	
William Cadogan	project engineer	Fellow 1978	31
		SB, Electrical Engineering, MIT 1969	
		Piene's technical assistant since 1971	
Kenneth L. Kantor	electronics	MIT Electrical Engineering undergraduate	22
		particpant in CAVS 1975 Food show	
Brian Raila	hologram system	SB, Art and Design, MIT, 1977	24
Werner Ahrens	documenta 6 assistant	Research Affiliate, 1977	30
Charles E. Miller	strobe line (not installed)	Lecturer, Electrical Engineering, MIT	46
Marc A. Palumbo	Washington, DC assistant	Fellow 1978	25
György Kepes	artistic advisor	Institute Professor Emeritus, MIT	72
Harold Edgerton	technical advisor	Institute Professor Emeritus, MIT	75
Edward Blair Allen	structural design	Associate Professor of Architecture, MIT	40
Stephen Benton	holography	Senior Scientist, Polaroid	37
		former Doc Edgerton student at MIT	
		former founding faculty of Media Lab	
		future director of CAVS	

Centerbeam encapsulated in a single form the meeting of two visions of collaboration. Its spine was Kepes', and its pulsating energies were Piene's. It uneasily balanced the democratic with the technocratic. Its overriding goal of participation shaped design choices and the implementation of as many hands-on elements as possible. Participation, however, conflicted with the fragility, cost, and the hazards of its high-tech components, resulting in the need for constant surveillance. While *Centerbeam* was designed to highlight student work (SMVisS graduates were given their own "lines" and titled components), it was at the same time a representation of MIT's advanced research. *Centerbeam* was reliant on the improvisation of the crowds that helped construct and launch its sky events, but it operated in a highly regulated bureaucracy of permits, approvals, and forced design changes.[58] It was a collective project, but, with twenty-five sky events on its Washington schedule, it also was a signature display of Piene's work. It marked a recognition of CAVS by national art organizations, but the project's closest ally was the National Air and Space Museum. *Centerbeam* was the culmination of at least two decades of work in kinetic sculpture, laser, and other technological art forms that bore a strong resemblance to E.A.T.'s Pepsi Pavilion, but Casdin-Silver's wildly popular holograms—developed with the assistance of Benton (who would soon join MIT as a founding faculty member of the Media Lab)—suggested new hybrid directions in the art/science/technology relationship.

Faced with this complex of history, politics, and technology, the press was at a loss for words. Journals such as *Science, Machine Design,* and *IEEE Spectrum* that had once championed similar projects were not re-convinced. Art journals were non-plussed. The *Washington Post* described it as a "sophisticated multimedia Tinkertoy," advertising the event with the affirmation that "you don't have to know art, or science, to know what's pretty, or strange."[59] More acerbic criticisms accompanied the *Icarus* finale. Repeating a trope from the late 1960s almost verbatim, *Washington Post* critic Tom Zito declared that: "If this is the best that MIT can do, the technological future of America is in serious trouble."[60]

Most illuminating was the response to *Centerbeam* in MIT's institutional press. *The Tech* made no mention of either the Kassel or Washington events. *Technology Review* attempted to describe *Centerbeam* in its alumni insert but expressed befuddlement.[61] MIT's internal

57 Harold F. Schneidman to Otto Piene, April 25, 1978. Folder 6, "USIA." Center for Advanced Visual Studies Archive.

58 Sited across the street from the Bureau of Radiological Health, its laser was to shut down after opening night, sending Paul Earls back to MIT to redesign

an aperture to meet federal standards and fix the laser's range of motion. Jo Anne Lewis, "Pulling the Plug on Laser Art," *Washington Post* (Tuesday, June 27, 1978), C10. **59** Jo Ann Lewis, "The Mall's Multimedia Machine" (June 23, 1978) d1; "Light Show in the Sky" (June 23, 1978), wb 3.

60 Tom Zito, "Icarus on the Mall," *Washington Post* (September 9, 1978), B3. In 1966, *New York Times* critic Clive Barnes wrote of E.A.T. that "if the American engineers and technologists participating in this performance were typical of their profession, the Russians are sure to be first on the

moon." Clive Barnes, "Dance or Something at the Armory," *New York Times* (October 15, 1966): 33. **61** Ross C. Anderson, "'Beast' Designed by Center for Advanced Visual Studies Artists on the Mall in Washington, D.C.," *Technology Review* 80, no. 8 (August/September 1978): A12-A13.

right, Lowry Burgess,
Concept Drawing. From
Centerbeam (1980).

below, Centerbeam,
detail of solar mirror
installation. Photo:
Elizabeth Goldring, From
Centerbeam (1980).

following page, Centerbeam
section, CAVS, MIT.

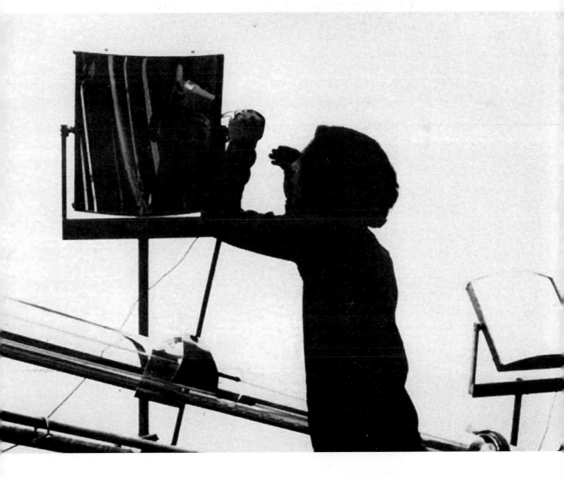

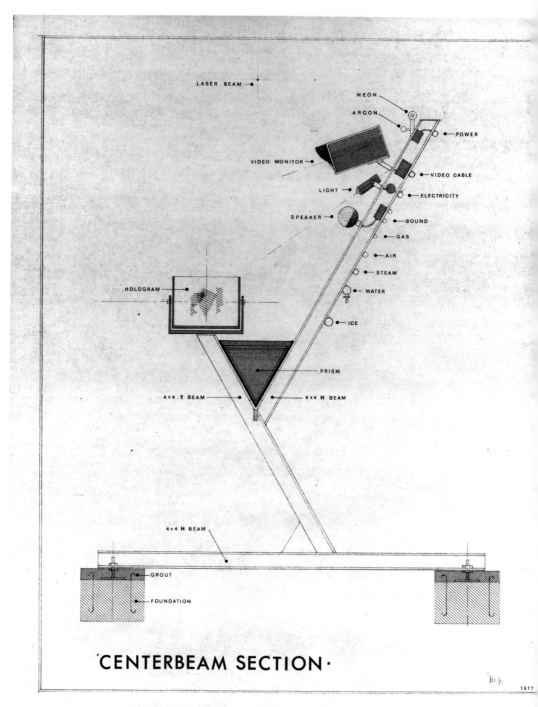

LASER BEAM

NEON

ARGON

POWER

VIDEO MONITOR

VIDEO CABLE

LIGHT

ELECTRICITY

SPEAKER

SOUND

GAS

AIR

STEAM

WATER

HOLOGRAM

ICE

PRISM

4 x 4 T BEAM

4 x 4 H BEAM

4 x 4 H BEAM

GROUT

FOUNDATION

·CENTERBEAM SECTION·

1977

center for advanced visual studies ▫ M I T ▫ cambridge, massachusetts ▫ U. S. A.

news service, *Tech Talk*, bordered on hostility, stating that visitors "came to see something they did not understand. But they knew the experience was something they must take in . . . or watch . . . or whatever it was they were supposed to do with the avant garde sculpture just installed on the Washington Mall"[62]

Artists and Architects Collaborate

Despite the mixed reception, Piene and Fellows returned to MIT jubilant. The event had garnered commitments to show works from *Centerbeam's* contributors in a dedicated exhibition in Grand Rapids, Michigan and at the 1979 Vienna Biennale. Plans were also underway for a Sky Art Conference, made possible by a grant from the National Endowment for the Arts (NEA).[63] In between Kassel and Washington, Piene waxed euphoric about MIT's anticipated arts complex, imagining it as a "Louvre/Deutsches Museum" dedicated to the production, exhibition, and historical documentation of art/science/technology collaboration. He called for a fluid, open-space that avoided "geometric design imagery."[64] Plans for Phase I of the project, distributed in June 1978, seemed to confirm his ambition. Designed by Lyndon, *Places for the Arts* presented "a long corridor going through MIT, somewhat like a mall, with arcades on the side—each having a different type of art form, but all connected."[65]

However, just as Kepes' vision deteriorated at its apparent apotheosis, so too did Piene's. In late August 1978, Negroponte met with Wiesner and Provost Walter Rosenblith to pitch his ideal of entrepreneurial new media research as the creative force of society's future.[66] Negroponte cultivated Wiesner as patron and partner—not only would the building be named after Wiesner, but he would be its first professor of communication. Within a year, I.M. Pei was selected as architect, and Lyndon's "village" became Pei's "box."[67] CAVS was not on the client team, which consisted of Negroponte, Dean William Porter, and CVA exhibition director Kathy Halbreich.[68] Events came to a head when Halbreich invited artists to produce "environmental" works for Pei's building with support from the Council for the Arts and a landmark grant from the NEA. Halbreich neither considered nor consulted CAVS artists.[69] In the volume that documented Halbriech's self-described "experiment"—*Artists and Architects Collaborate*—she criticized "plug-in" art and temporary installations, lamenting that "when 'collaboration' become the buzz word, objects became sinful."[70]

62 Paula Ruth Korn, *Tech Talk*, "On the Mall in Washington D.C.: It's What Tom Wolfe Might Call Your Ordinary Kandy-Kolored Tangerine-Flake Streamline Baby" (June 28, 1978): 1,8.

63 Elizabeth Goldring, "Concluding Remarks," in *Centerbeam*, ed. Piene and Goldring, 125.

64 Otto Piene's Draft Proposal, January 2, 1978. Folder 226, "Proposal Arts Facilities". Center for Advanced Visual Studies Archive.

65 Lyndon Associates, Inc., *Places for Art at MIT* (Cambridge, MA: Lyndon Associates, Inc., 1978). The quote is a summation of Lyndon's plan from Deborah

Hoover, Director of the Council for the Arts, from "Interview: Deborah Hoover," in *Artists and Architects Collaborate: Designing the Wiesner Building, MIT Committee on the Visual Arts*, ed. (Cambridge, MA: MIT Committee on the Visual Arts, 1985), 29. For an extensive discussion of Lyndon's plan

and its affinity with CAVS see Rotzel, "The Media Lab that Wasn't".

66 Nicholas Negroponte, "The Orgins of the Media Lab," in *Jerry Wiesner: Scientist, Statesman, Humanist*, ed. Walter A. Rosenblith (MIT Press, 2003), 149-156.

67 Robert Campbell and Jeffrey Cruikshank, "Art

Dragged out over more than five years, the evolution from arts complex to Arts and Media Technology building realigned MIT's aesthetic commitments as substantially as Kepes had done when bringing CAVS to life. The transformation left CAVS diminished and resulted in a reorientation of the meanings of "humane" technology. The Wiesner Building emerged as an alliance between MIT's traditionalist art interests and the sponsored research of the Media Laboratory that encompassed most of the stakeholders in Architecture's SMVisS program.[71] CAVS, on the other hand, remained in Building W-11.

Changes in leadership again proved crucial. In the early 1980s, when Paul Gray replaced Wiesner as President and Francis Low replaced Rosenblith as Provost, MIT faced multi-million dollar budget cuts and a proliferation of research centers. As part of broader restructuring, administration of CAVS shifted from the Provost to the School of Architecture. At the same time, John de Monchaux replaced Porter as Dean of Architecture. De Monchaux was a powerful advocate of sponsored research, and, citing a lack of "reflective and analytic thinking" in the SMVisS program, he sought to remake it under the Media Lab's aegis. In his proposal CAVS would have become a mere service arm of a revised visual studies program.[72] Only through a vigorous defense did CAVS maintain its mission of experimental art making and professional training.[73]

p.1.

VII. 26. 78

PLACES FOR THE ARTS AT MIT

The tensions of this reorientation embodied different ideals about art and technology that drew on a shared rhetoric for alternative ends. In the early planning of the arts complex, the differences were framed in terms of "clean" and "dirty" space.[74] Whereas Piene argued for "neighborhoods" of diverse media equipment in an open "barn," Negroponte requested one hundred eight-foot square "acoustically isolated" boxes—one for each researcher—"so clean" that dust could not flow into them. "I see my own office," he wrote, "as something closer to the cockpit of an F14 than a barn."[75] In the fall of 1978, when Piene learned of the Arts and Media Technology plan, he sought to convince Wiesner and Rosenblith to preserve the arts complex model by contrasting the "gimmickry" of a "celluloid house" with "developmental media work" oriented toward "human messages made available to a large, multi-faced, deserving public."[76] Sending extensive documentation from *Centerbeam* to make his case, he reiterated the humanist contribution of environmental art. Piene insisted that a collaborative team of "environmental artists, architects and engineers" design the complex in an "integrated group work . . . leading to a functional, sculptural edifice whose very shape is vital, organic and represents major human concerns."[77] But Wiesner and the Council shifted from the expressive humanism of the Kepes/Piene mode towards

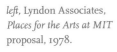

left, Lyndon Associates, *Places for the Arts at MIT* proposal, 1978.

right, Provost Jerome Wiesner, on a Media Lab teleconference system. From Steward Brand, *The Media Lab; Inventing the Future at MIT* (USA: Penguin, 1988).

in Architecture" in *Artists and Architects Collaborate: Designing the Wiesner Building*, 11-24.

68 A&MT Minutes, (September 10 1979). Folder 228, "Arts Building Facility." Center for Advanced Visual Studies Archive.

69 Campbell and Jeffrey Cruikshank, "Art in

Architecture," 21-22.

70 Kathy Halbreich, "Acknowledgements" and "Interview: Kathy Halbreich," in *Artists and Architects Collaborate: Designing the Wiesner Building*, ed. MIT Committee on the Visual Arts, 6-7, 33-38.

71 Creative Photography was eliminated in 1983.

72 John de Monchaux, "Second Discussion Report of the Arts and Media Technology Task Force" (2/28/1983). Folder 236, "CAVS/AMT Politics 1983, etc." Center for Advanced Visual Studies Archive.

73 Otto Piene, "Some Comments on CAVS and Environmental Art," *Architext*

(March 16, 1983), 1-2; Otto Piene to Fellows and Grad Students (4/8/1983) Folder 238, "Cavs AMT." Center for Advanced Visual Studies Archive; Robert F. Brown and Otto Piene, "Oral history interview with Otto Piene, 1988 Aug. 4-1990 Feb. 22." Archives of American Art, Smithsonian Institution. Tape

a technologist-directed vision of creativity. Peter Spackman, the Council's Executive Director, argued that art/technology collaboration thus far had been "superficial . . . a liaison rather than a marriage of means and interests." However, a new kind of entrepreneurial technologist was becoming an artist through the innovation of "ubiquitous computers" and other "expressive technologies." This development was the result of MIT's "process-centered and project-oriented" culture based on "sponsored research," "professionalism," "high standards," and the "linking of work at the graduate and undergraduate levels."[78]

As divisions grew between CAVS and other stakeholders, CAVS increasingly took its dirty art on the road. With the exception of the first Sky Art Conference in 1981, most of its projects embraced the "movable theatre/circus" attitude of *Centerbeam*.[79] The 1986 event *Desert Sun/Desert Moon* captures the sense of separation. Over the span of two

7, Side A.

74 Rotzel, "The Media Lab that Wasn't," 12-13.

75 "Revised Draft: Proposal on New Space for Architecture Machine, CAVS, Synthesized Music, Film/TV". Folder 228, "Proposal for Arts Facility (O.P.) 1-2-78". Center for Advanced Visual Studies Archive.

76 Otto Piene to Jerome Wiesner, November 17, 1978. Massachusetts Institute of Technology. Office of the Provost. AC 7, Box 25, Folder "CAVS-Correspondence," Institute Archives and Special Collections, MIT.

77 Otto Piene to Walter Rosenblith, "The ABC (Arts Building Complex," Dec. 12, 1978. Massachusetts Institute of Technology. Office of the Provost. AC 7, Box 25, Folder "CAVS-Correspondence," Institute Archives and Special Collections, MIT.

78 "Program for the Arts and Media Technology at MIT," July 12, 1979. Massachusetts Institute of Technology Office of the Arts. AC 230, Box 15. Institute Archives and Special Collections, MIT.

79 Goldring, "Concluding Remarks," 125.

left, left to right, Earl
Flansburgh (M.Arch '57),
I.M. Pei (B.Arch '40), and
Frederick Roth (M.Arch
'52), *The Evolution of
Practice* panel discussion,
at the Department of
Architecture's Alumni
Convocation in June 1975.

right, The Wiesner
Building, designed by
I.M. Pei and Partners,
MIT, September 1985.
Photo: Calvin Campbell.

*Artists and Architects
Collaborate II,* List Visual
Arts Center.

weeks, some thirty artists, technologists, and students met in Lone Pine, California in the foothills of the Sierra Nevada to stage CAVS' first large-scale installation since *Centerbeam*. Spread over three miles of barren terrain, it consisted of loosely integrated individual projects that included Goldring's twenty-minute reading of poetry by megaphone, Fellow Joe Davis' rover constructed of recycled electronics, and Fellow Tom Van Sant's satellite-linked mirror sculpture.[80] In addition to a small crowd of locals, *Desert Sun/Desert Moon* was filmed by a documentary crew from Smithsonian World. Reduced to a few minutes in an hour-long broadcast, narrator David McCullough described the scene as "strange art in a strange land."[81]

Back at MIT, the Wiesner Building opened in 1985 to great fanfare. In a glowing review, the *New York Times* argued that the List Visual Arts Center "revives some of the ancient awe in which MIT was once held." The *Times* attributed its success to its traditional modernism: "We are not obliged, in other words, to stand and stare at a lot of goofy machines and wait for something significant to come of it."[82] In an interview with Jeffrey Cruikshank of the Harvard Business School, Wiesner contextualized the Building from the point of view of its

above, Elizabeth Goldring with bullhorn reciting her poems, *Coyote*, 1986; part of *Desert Sun/Desert Moon*. Photo: Otto Piene From Elizabeth Goldring "Desert Sun/Desert Moon' and the SKY ART Manifesto," *Leonardo* Vol. 20, no 4. (1987).

80 Elizabeth Goldring "'Desert Sun/Desert Moon' and the SKY ART Manifesto," *Leonardo* 20, no. 4 (1987): 339-348.

81 Smithsonian World, *Elephant on the Hill* (Washington, D.C.: Greater Washington Education Telecommunications Association, Inc., May 13, 1987).

82 John Russell, "Art Breathes Freely at M.I.T.'s New Center" *New York Times* (April 28, 1985), 31-31. See also: Joseph McLellan, "Science Meets the Muse in the Arts of the Future" *Washington Post* (Sunday, February 10, 1980) M 11.

other tenants, arguing that "if you look carefully, an awful lot of the media technology is art, and the art is technology."[83] The following year, the School of Architecture stopped using the phrase "Arts and Media Technology" in MIT's *Bulletin*. In Stewart Brand's 1988 homage to the Media Lab, Negroponte simply stated: "This is not an advanced art school."[84]

Conclusion

Centerbeam is an unlikely representative of MIT's "second modernism." It was never a stable authorial object or architectural space like Pei's Box, Saarinen's chapel, or even Haacke's *Weather Box*. Though innovative in many respects, it lacked the world-changing promises and million dollar contracts to generate publicity about "Inventing the Future." Nor was it a conceptual manifesto with broad professional ramifications. Even among historians of new media art, *Centerbeam* has garnered scant recognition.[85] If not for another anniversary and another reconfiguration of the arts at MIT, it may have remained forever disassembled in Piene's barn. Seen in context, however, *Centerbeam* provides a powerful node by which we can investigate the meanings and practices of art in a technological culture.

That said, no amount of historical detective work can affix a singular reading to *Centerbeam*. In the actors' multiple interpretations of "collaboration," metaphors of romance were omnipresent. To cynics of CAVS' ambitions, *Centerbeam* was the compromised outcome of a "shotgun wedding." To its committed partners, it was the beautiful offspring of "a shotgun love over time," a shared moment of "rare harmony" made possible by years of commitment.[86] Similar metaphors are equally compelling with historical distance. Assuming a perspective of the political geographer, *Centerbeam* presents a case of too many lovers whose shifting alliances generated passions, recriminations, and persistent instabilities. From a Latourian vantage, *Centerbeam* offers yet another rendition of the Frankenstein myth. It is the estranged assemblage of an estranged assemblage, created in a moment of boundless optimism and rejected when it failed to sponsor institutional wholeness.[87]

Nevertheless, of all potential narratives, failure is the least convincing. Just as CAVS overcame the unrest of the late 1960s, it survived the restructuring in *Centerbeam's* wake. Piene remained director until 1994, zealously organizing Sky Art Conferences.

83 Jerome Wiesner, "Interview: Jerome Wiesner," in *Artists and Architects Collaborate: Designing the Wiesner Building*, MIT Committee on the Visual Arts, 25-28.

84 Stewart Brand, *The Media Lab: Inventing the Future at MIT* (New York: Penguin, 1983), 83.

85 Frank Popper, *Art of the Electronic Age* (London: Thames and Hudson, 1993), 147-148; Bijvoet, *Art as Inquiry*, 49.
86 See Piene, "Centerbeam," 23. Interview in this Volume.

87 Bruno Latour, *Aramis or Love of Technology*. (Cambridge, MA: Harvard, 1996).

Prominent artists who initially arrived as temporary Fellows remained at MIT for decades. After Piene's retirement, CAVS was again re-imagined under the leadership of Krzysztof Wodiczko, who pushed artists to be MIT's loyal opposition. CAVS' long-term success comes into clearest focus outside of MIT, where its energies have been extended and appropriated internationally. Fundamental to the success of these current projects remains the desire among scientists, engineers, and their employers to collaborate, whether motivated by curiosity, pedagogical theory, public relations, or any one of various ideologies.

A morality play of protracted conflict between CAVS and the Media Lab is little better. Though Piene clearly had bad days with Negroponte, we should take him at his word that the "spirit of collaboration" between their organizations was sympathetic.[88] In the arguments of the late 1970s, both parties expressed a desire to "cohabitate" in a "dialectical relationship."[89] Indeed, since the Media Lab's creation, graduate students in the programs have crossed organizational boundaries to forge hybrid careers. From 1996 to his untimely death in 2003, moreover, Benton moved from the Media Lab to replace Wodiczko as CAVS director.

To be sure, this longevity has its uncomfortable truths. The Fellows program did not maintain the scale achieved in the late-1970s. For a time the SMVisS program went fallow. The Media Lab operates with a budget orders of magnitude larger than that of CAVS. There have also been changes among stakeholders in the arts at MIT that have impacted the character of CAVS. In 1988, another Institute-wide arts survey concluded that there had been a "drastic decline" in visual studies options for undergraduates, leading to a new Visual Arts Program (VAP) and the establishment of an Associate Provost for the Arts.[90] Finally, within the present new media universe, which continues to expand internationally, the meaning of "humane technology" remains deeply contested.

Thirty years after *Centerbeam*, MIT's art communities seem to be achieving the integration hoped for in the 1970s. In 2009, the Media Lab expanded into a highly publicized addition, designed by Maki & Associates, amidst the global financial crisis. At the same time, CAVS merged with VAP to form a new program in Art, Culture and Technology (ACT). Housed in the Wiesner Building, ACT is internally connected with the Media Lab by passages that

88 Interview in this volume.

89 "Revised Draft: Proposal on New Space for Architecture Machine, CAVS, Synthesized Music, Film/ TV". Folder 228, "Proposal for Arts Facility (O.P.) 1-2-78". Center for Advanced Visual Studies Archive; Otto Piene, "A Five-Year Plan for the Center for Advanced Visual studies, (1985-1990)"

90 Sally S. Vanerian, "Search Underway for Head of Visual Studies," *The Tech* 108, no. 8 (March 1, 1988): 1, 18.

91 "Artistic MIT: *Centerbeam*, Installation by 22 MIT Artists, Scientists, and Engineers, 1977–1978," MIT Museum, http://museum.mit. edu/150/89.

overlook an expansive glass atrium. Nevertheless, the ACT program's website—which deploys the familiar visual metaphor of transitory entanglement—leaves the continuation of the "CAVS" namesake and future mission unsettled. At the moment of this writing, CAVS exists principally as a site of archival documentation. Nonetheless, in celebration of MIT's 150th anniversary, a section of *Centerbeam* has been once again has been powered back to life as a symbol of "artistic MIT."[91]

Early in the planning stages of *Centerbeam*, its makers ran into technical and aesthetic challenges that they instantly recognized as inherent to their work. They aspired to capture the endless quality of modernity's technological energies but encountered constraints that compromised their vision. They debated the "beginnings and endings" of *Centerbeam*. Should it "crescendo" or should it "remain repetitive and constant all along the way"? Backing away from a "denouement," its creators composed an unceremonious emergence of *Centerbeam's* bundled energies at one end of the structure. Neither panacea nor crescendo, this was the art of MIT's environment.

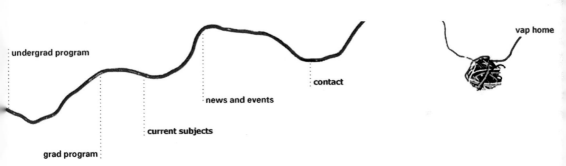

undergrad program

grad program

current subjects

news and events

contact

vap home

ACT program, accessed from the Program in Art, Culture, and Technology website, (http://visualarts. mit.edu/about/about. html) Dec. 2010.

AVIGAIL SACHS

The Pedagogy of Prefabrication
Building Research at MIT in the Postwar

"Participating to the nth Degree"[1]

In the postwar years American higher education underwent what Clark Kerr has called a "shock wave": an influx of students, faculty, course offerings and functions.[2] MIT was at the apex of this sweeping transformation. More than other universities, the institute had been drastically changed by its involvement in military research during the war and had assumed a position at the center of the new business-government-academia partnership. Even before hostilities ended, the MIT administration began transforming the institute so as to consolidate its preeminence in scientific and technological education.

Following the end of the war the institute's leaders developed a strong philosophy, which emphasized innovative thinking, the power of technology to solve physical and social problems, service to industry and government, and a commitment to the education and training of scientists and engineers. This complex institutional agenda was subsumed under a strong commitment to "research," a term that at MIT was widely construed to encompass a broad range of intellectual activities. As Leslie W. Stuart explains, in the postwar a new attitude towards scientific research developed: "one that blurred traditional distinctions between theory and practice, science and engineering, civilian and military, and classified and unclassified, one that owed its character as well as its contracts to the national security state."[3]

Above all, however, "research" signified innovation. In fact, for many the institute's ability to foster and nurture innovative thinking provided the raison d'être for MIT's alliance with government and industry. According to this view the military, the federal government and industry were all too conservative and biased to be trusted with research and development. If society was to benefit from the products of science then scientists and engineers had to be free to pursue ideas and develop innovations for the public good, and this could only occur

1 William W. Wurster, "Memorandum to Staff of School of Architecture and Planning, dated December 8 1947." Architecture Dean Papers. MIT Institute Archives, AC 400 Box 1 Folder 13.

2 Clark Kerr, "Shock Wave II: An Introduction to the Twenty-First Century," in *The Future of the City of Intellect: The Changing American University*, ed. Steven Brint (Stanford: Stanford University Press), 2002.

3 Stuart W. Leslie, *The Cold War and American Science: The Military-Industrial-Academic Complex at MIT and Stanford* (New York: Columbia University Press, 1993):, 2.

in universities and technical institutes. Research was also seen as the foundation of scientific and technological education and the key to training the scientists and engineers of the future.

This emphasis on research shaped the Institute's policies, from faculty appointments to institutional structure. The ongoing search for innovation was manifest in the number of independent research units developed in response to specific research opportunities: sixty-five such units were established after the war. While this emphasis made for a somewhat polarized institute — most of the available funds were funneled directly to centers such as the Research Laboratory of Electronics and the Laboratory for Nuclear Science and Engineering — it also allowed for an Institute-wide streamlining of policies; pedagogically this resulted in a mandatory, uniform first year curriculum for all incoming students and close supervision of all curricular changes within individual departments.[4] In this way the logic of scientific and engineering leadership developed in the research centers was imposed, at least to some extent, on all the departments of the Institute.

The Department of Architecture was a relative anomaly in postwar MIT. Unlike their engineer colleagues, architects had not played a crucial role in the war effort and did not have a clear mission, which could direct their involvement in the postwar military-industrial complex. Enrollment in the department, moreover, had ebbed throughout the war, and courses had been suspended while faculty served in the military. In the process of postwar rebuilding, the Department could have maintained its autonomy by clearly demarcating the differences between science and engineering on the one hand and "architectural design" on the other. This was not, however, the direction it chose; the leaders of the department in the postwar years — specifically William W. Wurster, Lawrence B. Anderson and Pietro Belluschi — made a conscious and directed effort to fully integrate the department into the larger Institute. Anderson explained:

> Though there are many paths leading to architecture, the staff of this School feel that our choice of direction should be that which will embrace the strength of the Institute. This means a technical approach which will utilize the MIT laboratories, courses on materials and such subjects as sanitation, acoustics, illumination, and heating and ventilation.[5]

4 William W. Wurster, "Memorandum to Staff of School of Architecture and Planning, dated December 8 1947."

5 President's Report Issue, *MIT Bulletin* 81, no. 1 (1944-45): 138.

Having embraced the emphasis on research and innovation, the architecture faculty introduced housing research into the department, with a particular focus on residential prefabrication. As a topic of research, prefabrication addressed all aspects of the MIT philosophy. Housing was not only a national crisis; it was also a field that required technical innovation and close connection with government and industry. Walter Netsch summed up this point of view in 1985:

> It was a time when there was a lot of interest in prefabrication. We really had hope for the future, and felt that we could tackle these problems, and we could get answers, and society would respond to them, and we would help make a very much more wholesome society than the commercial society that was beginning to appear.[6]

The emphasis on research produced a revision of the department's program not only in content but also in structure and emphasis. The new focus amounted to what I call the "pedagogy of prefabrication." In the late 1940s and early 1950s the department became part of a newly streamlined MIT and developed into a leading center for building and technological research. The entirety of the MIT philosophy, however, proved unattainable. The architecture department's focus on research came at the expense of professional design education, and service to industry proved incompatible with service to society and with independent innovation. The nature and rationale of these changes, as well as the tensions they engendered, are the topic of this essay.

The Prefabricated House

In 1945, William W. Wurster was appointed dean of the School of Architecture as part of an effort to restructure and revitalize architecture education at MIT. This was his first academic administrative position. He accepted the position as an opportunity to explore what he called a "broadening of the base" of architecture through collaboration with specialists outside the profession (such as social scientists) rather than through a broadening of the architect's role. For Wurster education was the key to "broadening the base." His goal was to train architects who would be well prepared to collaborate. His ideal student, therefore, was one who:

6 "Conversation between Lawrence B. Anderson and Walter Netsch, Lois Craig attending. Place: Residence of Walter Netsch, 1700 N. Hudson, Chicago, Illinois Date: April 7, 1984," *Lawrence Bernhart Anderson Oral History.* MIT Institute Archives, Manuscript Collection—MC 274, Folder—Walter Netsch

Oral History, 10-11.
7 Graduate Class, School of Architecture MIT. *Industrialized House Forum Proceedings of Course Conference January 6 and 7, 1950* (Cambridge, MA: School of Architecture Massachusetts Institute of Technology, 1950): 4.

8 William Wilson Wurster, *College of Environmental Design, University of California Campus Planning, and Architectural Practice: An Interview / Conducted by Suzanne B. Riess* (Berkeley, CA: Regional Cultural History Project, University of California, 1964): 111.

9 The school was officially renamed "School of Architecture and Planning' on August 8, 1944. "Special Appropriations and Votes No. 2034," Architecture Dean Papers. MIT Institute Archives, AC 400, Box 3, Folder: Policy 3/3.

Is not like a glass ball on this table, that when he comes out of school he goes to the ground with a crash and goes to pieces. I want him to be sort of a rubber ball that is used to being shoved in on one side by one person and shoved in on the other side by another person.[7]

As dean, Wurster fostered collaboration between architecture and city and regional planning by distinguishing between them and developing the latter "to acknowledge planning as a separate profession as it properly should be, with different sets of requirements."[8] In 1944 Wurster made this distinction official by creating the double-headed School of Architecture and Planning. Comprised of two departments, each had its own chair and faculty.[9] Fostering collaboration also provided a way to connect with research projects in other departments. Wurster was especially interested in what would later be called human-environment studies, such as the work undertaken by the newly established Research Center for Group Dynamics (later published as *Social Pressures in Informal Groups; A Study of Human Factors in Housing*).[10] This study capitalized on the postwar building boom on the MIT campus and used student housing as a locus for study.

Embracing the strengths of the Institute, however, was not only a matter of collaborating with other departments but also of adapting internally to the overriding emphasis on research. If architecture was to "participate to the nth degree,"[11] as Wurster advocated, the faculty had to have a clear understanding of the role research was to play in the department. This meant a definition, however broad, of *architectural research*—or, as Wurster and many architects in the postwar period preferred to say, "research for architecture." Such a discipline, however, did not exist. Though scientific knowledge, broadly defined, had always played a crucial role in the American professions' power struggles over power, American architects—immersed in the Beaux Arts traditions and intent on representing architecture as a fine art—had for the most part ignored this aspect of professional practice.

"Housing," however, was an established topic of scientific study. By the middle of the twentieth century it was recognized as a topic of national importance, and there was a clear demand for "experts" who could combine scientific knowledge with experience to

10 Leon Festinger, Stanley Schachter, and Kurt Back, *Social Pressures in Informal Groups: A Study of Human Factors in Housing* (New York: Harper, 1950)

11 William W. Wurster, "Memorandum to Staff of School of Architecture and Planning, Date: 8 December 1947, Subject: Visiting Committee Meeting of 8 November 1947," Architecture Dean Papers. MIT Institute Archives, AC 400 Box 1 Folder 13

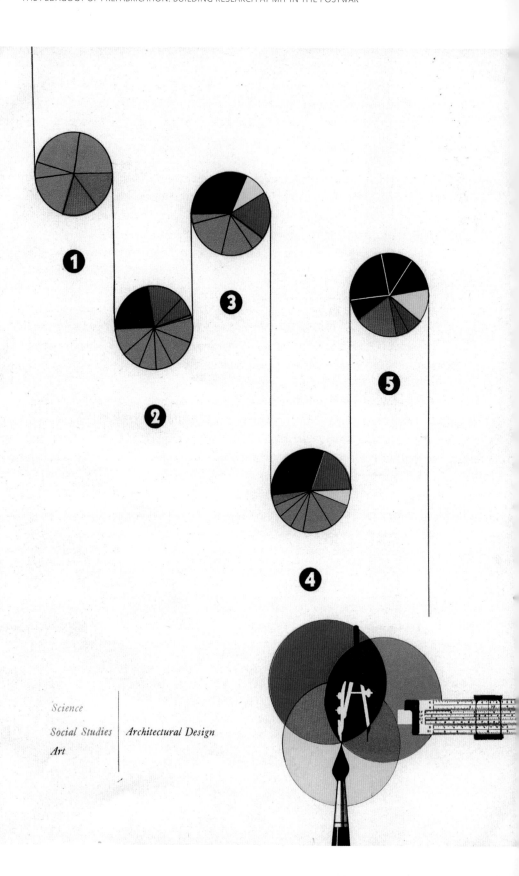

Science

Social Studies | Architectural Design

Art

A diagram of the curriculum in the Department of Architecture at MIT. The blue represents courses in "science;" the red "social sciences;" yellow, "art;" and black, "architectural design." Some courses are depicted as being orange or green—that is, occupying the intersection of two fields of study. From Henry-Russell Hitchcock and György Kepes, *Education of Architects and City Planners* (Cambridge, MA: MIT, 1947). MIT Institute Archives and Special Collections.

solve the ongoing housing crisis. This crisis was made more severe by the needs of returning veterans and displaced defense workers. Housing research, moreover, was inherently interdisciplinary, belonging to multiple fields—including planning, engineering, sociology and law—and therefore ideally suited to "broadening the base" of architecture. In addition, such research was of interest to businessmen and manufacturers in the building industry. Their emphasis, which embraced the technical and material aspects of housing production, was often referred to as building research. This second enterprise was propelled by business and profit considerations; nevertheless, as Douglas Knerr demonstrates, it had a reform impulse of its own which was related to the free market.[12] And while efficiency—of production and price—was the market's primary concern, the questions investigated often overlapped with those of research agendas in the social sciences.

Housing research also played a role in directing government policies. In the postwar years the production of housing was caught between the public and private spheres. Conceived as a national project, it seemed to merit the investment of public money, and many industrialists expected the federal government to support the early stages of commercial development—in other words, to assume the risk involved in setting up new industries and markets. At the same time, industrialists objected to restrictions and price controls that prevented the market from "working properly," an argument that was well received in the postwar political climate, which favored the private investment model over full public responsibility or any plan that could be described as "socialism."[13] Research provided a way to overcome this tension between public and private sponsorship. By funding "research," the government could be seen to be supporting the public good and bolstering the development of the prefabrication industry without investing in a particular company.

12 Douglas Knerr, *Suburban Steel: The Magnificent Failure of the Lustron Corporation, 1945-1951* (Columbus, OH: The Ohio State University Press, 2004).

13 Burnham Kelly, *The Prefabrication of Houses: A Study by the Albert Farwell Bemis Foundation of the Prefabrication Industry in the United States.* (Cambridge, MA: The Technology Press of the Massachusetts Institute of Technology and John Wiley and Sons, Inc., 1951): 96.

The importance attached to housing research in the late 1940's was indicated, for example, in the title of a symposium organized in 1948 at the University of Wisconsin: "The Frontiers of Housing Research."[14] Two years later the organizer of this conference, Professor Richard U. Ratcliff, was appointed to direct a federally coordinated program of housing research (under the Home and Housing Finance Agency [HHFA] Division of Housing Research). This program was a product of the 1949 Housing Act, which included among its objectives the support of a "coordinated program of technical research,"[15] or as Ratcliff defined it more broadly: "a conceptual framework on which an orderly body of knowledge may be built out of the products of related and integrated research."[16] One of the direct results of the HHFA program was the first systematic survey of housing research in the United States. The survey was conducted by the Building Research Advisory Board (BRAB), a non-profit organization—created under the auspices of the National Academy of Sciences and directed by William H. Scheick (later president of the American Institute of Architects)—which acted as a central clearinghouse of building research activity. "Housing research" was defined by it as "all technological and non-technological fields of research having a direct or indirect bearing on housing and building research."[17]

In the years examined in this essay (between the end of WWII and the early 1950s), the central topic of investigation in housing and building research was the prefabrication of the entire house. Although the "house of the future" and the "miracle house"[18] of the 1930s and early 1940s had not yet materialized, prefabricated houses still captured the imagination (and occasionally also the pocketbooks) of the American public. They symbolized the power of technology and free enterprise to advance not only the economy

John Cutler, student work, Prefabricated House Design, 1941. Albert Farwell Bemis Foundation Records 1926-1954, MIT Institute Archives and Special Collections.

14 Richard U. Ratcliff, "Letter to Burnham Kelly, dated June 2, 1948" Albert Farwell Bemis Foundation Records 1926-1954, MIT Institute Archives, AC 302 Box 7 Folder HHFA Research Proposals.
15 United States Committee on Banking and Currency, "The Housing Act of 1949: What it is and How it Works, A Handbook on Information on Provisions of the Act and Operations under the Various Programs, July 27, 1949" (Printed for the Use of the Committee on Banking and Currency by the United States Government Printing Office, Washington, DC, 1949).
16 Richard U. Ratcliff "Address before American Statistical Association, Housing Statistics Branch Hotel Biltmore, New York 10 AM – December 28, 1949" Albert Farwell Bemis Foundation Records 1926-1954, MIT Institute Archives, AC 302 Box 7 Folder Social Science Research Council: 4.
17 Housing and Home Finance Agency, *A Survey of Housing Research in the United States* (Washington, DC: Housing and Home Finance Agency, 1952).
18 See Timothy Mennel, "Miracle House Hoop-La: Corporate Rhetoric and the Construction of the Postwar American House," *Journal of the Society of Architectural Historians* 63, no. 3 (2008): 340-361.

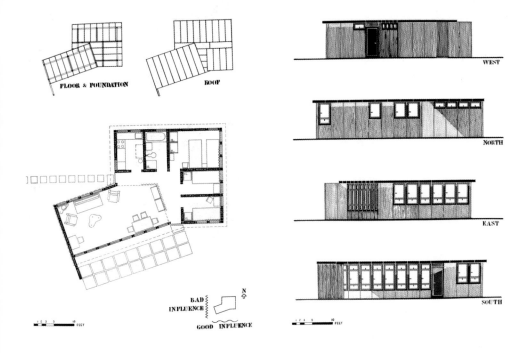

FLOOR & FOUNDATION   ROOF

WEST

NORTH

EAST

SOUTH

BAD
INFLUENCE

N

GOOD   INFLUENCE

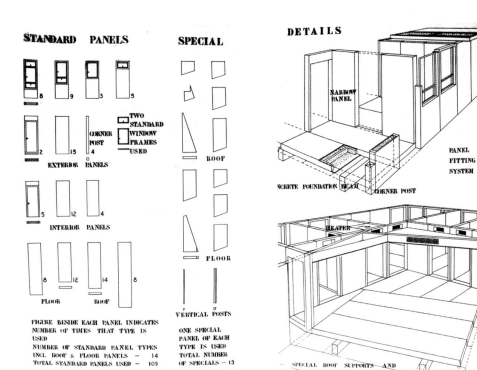

STANDARD   PANELS   SPECIAL

8   9   3   5

EXTERIOR   PANELS

TWO
STANDARD
WINDOW
FRAMES
USED

CORNER
POST
4

2   15

ROOF

5   12   4

INTERIOR   PANELS

8   12   14   8

FLOOR

FLOOR   ROOF

VERTICAL   POSTS

FIGURE   BESIDE   EACH   PANEL   INDICATES
NUMBER   OF   TIMES   THAT   TYPE   IS
USED
NUMBER   OF   STANDARD   PANEL   TYPES
INCL   ROOF   &   FLOOR   PANELS — 14
TOTAL   STANDARD   PANELS   USED — 109

ONE   SPECIAL
PANEL   OF   EACH
TYPE   IS   USED
TOTAL   NUMBER
OF   SPECIALS — 13

TOTAL   NUMBER   OF   PANELS   IN   HOUSE — 122

DETAILS

NARROW
PANEL

PANEL
FITTING
SYSTEM

NCRETE   FOUNDATION   BEAM   CORNER   POST

HEATER

SPECIAL   ROOF   SUPPORTS   AND
HEATING   ARRANGEMENT

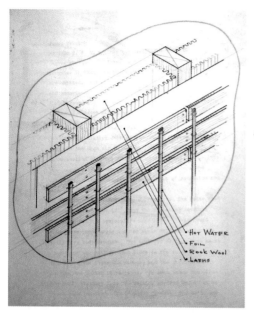

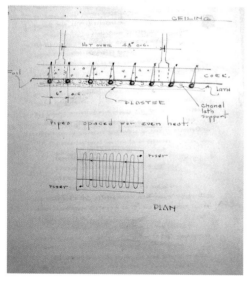

but also social values. Prefabricated housing was no longer just a "low income" solution. Houses, including prefabricated houses, embodied American "freedom," playing a central role in the ideology of home ownership as a central tenet in the emerging "consumer's republic."[19]

The prefabricated house was thus an ideal topic to undertake in a department of architecture located at MIT which was committed to more fully integrating with the larger institute. Prefabricated houses were even of interest to the military, which still constituted a source of extensive funding. Factory processes, moreover, could be rationalized and systematized, allowing researchers to direct the application of their ideas and see relatively immediate results. The technological emphasis gave MIT researchers a measure of control over their research that was not possible in the investigation of issues like community development and neighborhood planning. In this sense, the focus on technology allowed MIT architects to emulate their engineer colleagues. In 1941, even before the war had ended, architecture students at MIT designed and detailed prefabricated houses and reported on developments in building industry.

Images accompanying a report on heating panels in a house in Boise, Idaho using "Radiant Heating with Reverse Cycle Generation," 1941. Albert Farwell Bemis Foundation Records 1926-1954, MIT Institute Archives and Special Collections.

19 Lizabeth Cohen, *A Consumer's Republic: The Politics of Mass Consumption in Postwar America* (New York: Knopf, 2008). Beatriz Colomina has called this "domesticity at war." Beatriz Colomina, *Domesticity at War* (Cambridge, MA: MIT Press, 2007).

But what form should the MIT research on prefabricated houses take? By the postwar years, the profession had developed what Barry Bergdoll refers to as an "architectural culture of prefabrication."[20] In these projects, often theoretical in nature, architects aspired to provide "optimal" solutions to the problem of the prefabricated house. The "Package Building System" designed by Walter Gropius and Konrad Wachsmann was one of the most celebrated examples of such projects. The system was based on a standardized joint detail that was repeated in all the joints—wall to wall, wall to roof, etc. Such systems, however, were often advanced beyond the industry's ability to produce and market them.

A second trend, the one widely adopted at MIT, emphasized the realities of the building industry. As William H. Scheick argued, "We must have the concept of completed building as the *end product of an industry*."[21] Carl Koch, who joined the Department in 1946 with extensive housing experience both as a senior architect at the National Housing Agency and in his own work as the designer of the demountable Acorn House, explained this approach well:

> The needed level of design . . . comes from a man (or, more likely, a team) who, gaining some of the builder's know-how and pragmatic approach, has equipped himself to design a house which, making full use of our technological, economic, and industrial development, offers such a deep and lasting satisfaction that it will exert a pull strong enough to justify the tremendous expense for tooling and merchandising, planning and production.[22]

Industry-based research was a natural extension of work already underway at the Institute. Albert Farwell Bemis had been one of the first industrialists to invest in building research in a systematic way. In 1921 he established The Housing Company, a firm that would, as he phrased it, "investigate new materials and techniques, develop patents, study economies, and survey the housing situation here and abroad." In 1933 Bemis published the products of his "research" in *The Evolving House* (with John E. Burchard), in which he expounded his vision of a modular system for standardizing dimensions of buildings.[23] Upon his death in 1936, Bemis left a bequest to MIT, his alma mater, for the purposes of establishing a

20 Barry Bergdoll, "Home Delivery: Viscidities of a Modernist Dream from Taylorized Serial Production to Digital Customization," in *Home Delivery: Fabricating the Modern Dwelling*, ed. Barry Bergdoll and Peter Christensen (New York: Museum of Modern Art, 2008).

21 William H. Scheick, "The Challenge of Research and Development," *The Construction Specifier* 11 (Winter 1958): 7-9.

22 Carl Koch, "Design and the Industrialized House." In *Design and the Production of Houses*, ed. Burnham Kelly. (New York: McGraw-Hill Book Company, Inc., 1959): 86.

23 Albert Farwell Bemis and John E. Burchard, *The Evolving House* (Cambridge, MA: The Technology Press of the Massachusetts Institute of Technology, 1933).

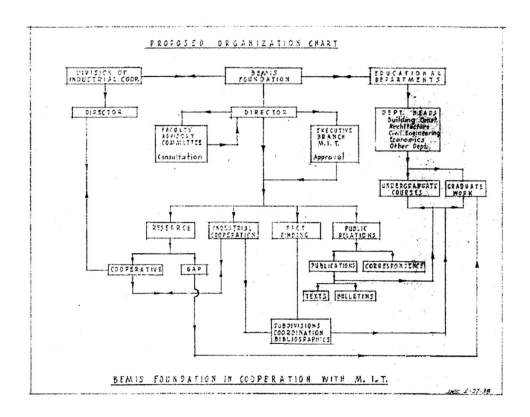

Organizational chart for the Bemis Foundation illustrating its connection with MIT. Architecture Dean Papers, MIT Institute Archives and Special Collections.

foundation for the "search for and dissemination of knowledge pertaining to more adequate, economical and abundant shelter for mankind."[24] Burchard, later Dean of Humanities at MIT, was appointed the first Director of the Foundation and remained in this capacity until 1948. Following Bemis' interests, the focus of the foundation's work was prefabrication. Harry Mohr Weese described how the market-driven search for efficiency shaped this research work:

24 "Albert Farwell Bemis Foundation," Architecture Dean Papers. MIT Institute Archives, AC 400, Box 5, Folder: A. F. Bemis.
25 "Oral History of Harry Mohr Weese," compiled by Betty J. Blum under the Auspices of the Chicago Architects Oral History Project, Ernest R. Graham

Study Center for Architectural Drawings, Department of Architecture, The Art Institute of Chicago" (Chicago: The Art Institute of Chicago, 1991).
26 Housing and Home Finance Agency. *A Survey of Housing Research in the United States*. (Washington, DC: Housing and Home Finance Agency, 1952).

27 President's Report Issue, *MIT Bulletin* 89, no. 2 (November 1953): 72-78.
28 Burnham Kelly. "Letter to Dr. Richard U. Ratcliff, Director, Division of Housing Research at the Housing and Home Finance Agency on April 10, 1950" Albert Farwell Bemis Foundation Records 1926-1954, MIT

At Bemis we were trying to find the perfect plan for a house. That was Burchard. He thought I could do it, so I did what was the ideal house plan—with the least amount of material and least whatever. And if you put the plumbing back-to-back, like a kitchen and a bath, you'd save the pipe.[25]

The Bemis Foundation maintained a filing system, which containing information on firms, building materials, construction systems, etc., would become the mainstay of its work. These files—one of the largest available sources of information on housing and prefabrication—were eventually stored in the Rotch Library in the School of Architecture and Planning. Even before it became part of the School in 1948, the Foundation supported departmental programs, including guest lectures by such luminaries as Lewis Mumford and Finnish architect Alvar Aalto. It also commissioned and financed studies of housing (including the study by the Research Center for Group Dynamics[26]) and the development of mechanical equipment and services for mass-produced houses.[27]

The Bemis Foundation personnel, particularly Burnham Kelly, a Professor of City Planning who replaced Burchard as Director of the Foundation, were also instrumental in translating ideas in the Institute into proposals that might be funded by entities such as the HHFA. Kelly actively corresponded with Ratcliff at the HHFA about the housing survey and specific MIT research projects[28] and also facilitated the interdepartmental cooperation so necessary for Wurster's "participating to the nth degree."[29] In 1949, for example, Kelly gathered faculty from across the university to discuss the relationship between the Institute and the "Federal Housing Program."[30] Among those attending was W. Rupert Maclaurin, a Professor of Economics, who consulted with Wurster on a successful grant proposal to study the "Economics of the Housing Industry" or as he preferred to refer to it, "the economics of innovation."[31]

The emphasis on technological and industry-based research was further facilitated by a change in department administration. Wurster was indeed interested in technological issues, and had experimented with housing "research" when he designed the Carquinez Heights Housing in Vallejo, California.[32] Nevertheless, his main concern was the

Institute Archives, AC 302 Box 6 Folder HHFA Research Proposals. Burnham Kelly. "Memorandum of Meetings with Ratcliff, Housing and Home Finance Agency, January 11th and 12th, 1950" Ibid.
29 William W. Wurster, "Memorandum to Staff of School of Architecture and

Planning, dated December 8 1947."
30 Burnham Kelly. "Notes on Meeting re Relation of Institute to Federal Housing Program, Fabyan Room, Graduate House, October 7, 1949" Albert Farwell Bemis Foundation Records 1926-1954, MIT Institute Archives, AC 302 Box 6 Folder: HHFA

Research Proposals
31 W. Rupert Maclaurin, "Proposal for a Study of the Economics of the Housing Industry at the Massachusetts Institute of Technology." Ibid., Box 8: Massachusetts Institute of Technology- Merrill Foundation Grant.

32 This was one of the first examples of wartime housing to use prefabricated materials, and was the focus of public attention. Some critics worried about the appearance and durability of the houses, while others celebrated the experiments in prefabrication. See Mark Daniels, "Vallejo's Prefabricated Houses,"

development of architecture research as a field distinct from housing and in particular the identification of "basic," rather than applied, topics for study. In 1950, however, Wurster left MIT to assume responsibility for the College of Architecture at the University of California, Berkeley. There he directed a wide-ranging effort to develop a research policy that would clearly distinguish between architectural and housing research.[33]

Wurster left the Department of Architecture at MIT under the direction of Lawrence Anderson ("Andy"), whom he had appointed as chair in 1947, and who had been a crucial ally and collaborator in his schemes for the department. Anderson shared Wurster's broad definitions of architecture and architecture education, but even more than Wurster he emphasized that students should learn the "reality" of "craft of building" and "construction methods"[34] – i.e., the relation of architecture to industry. As he commented in the late 1950s:

> New development in technology should be promptly reflected in building design. Our way of teaching architecture should have its own special flavor, due to our emphasis on a sound scientific base and the fullness of our related technical studies.[35]

Wurster's successor as Dean, Pietro Belluschi, was also interested in the connection with engineering, and he believed that the separation between architecture and engineering was detrimental to the creation of "valid architectural symbols."[36] Furthermore, Belluschi preferred to keep a low profile, granting Anderson free reign in the implementation of his educational philosophy and departmental changes.[37]

Anderson, and by extension Belluschi, implemented the larger MIT philosophy in the Department of Architecture. They welcomed industrial partnerships, not only as a way to allow the department to focus its own funds on teaching, but also to foster healthy partnerships "in the pursuit of knowledge."[38] Through these partnerships the Department developed a strong research program focused on climate, acoustics, illumination, prefabrication, and other technical problems of the building industry.[39] Anderson and Belluschi also worked to move Course XVII ("Building Engineering and Construction,") into the School of Architecture and Planning (an idea which had originated with Wurster).[40]

Architect and Engineer 149, (May 1942): 31-32

33 Avigail Sachs, "The Postwar Legacy of Architectural Research," *Journal of Architecture Education* 62, no. 3 (2009): 55-68.

34 Professor [Lawrence] Anderson, "Memo to Architectural Staff and Professors Adams, Greeley and Lynch, Date: May 9, 1952," Architecture Dean Papers, MIT Institute Archives, AC 400, Box 3, Folder: Policy 3/3.

35 Professor [Lawrence] Anderson, "Memorandum to Dean Belluschi, Subject: Observations that may be useful for President's Report and Meeting of Visiting Committee, Date: July 22, 1959," Ibid., Box 3, Folder: Policy 1/3.

36 Dean Pietro Belluschi, "Letter to Dr. James R. Killian, Jr. President, dated September 23, 1952." Ibid., Box 3, Folder: Private Correspondence.

37 Pietro Belluschi Interviews, Aug. 22-Sept. 4, 1983. Archives of American Art, Smithsonian Institution.

Belluschi was especially interested in recognizing students who planned to enter the construction industry as entrepreneurs rather than as designers, and in offering them an appropriate education.[41]

Two long-term research projects help illustrate the research agenda that developed in the department. In 1952 the Department received a grant from the F.W. Wakefield Brass Company to study "all factors in the architectural environment involved in the *problem of seeing*."[42] The initial goal of the project was to create a simulated environment in which the brightness of all the surfaces could be controlled by the researcher. In this environment the researcher would record human responses to different levels of illumination, and extrapolate from this data requirements for new lighting and illuminations techniques.[43] Richard W. Hamilton, a research associate at the Bemis Foundation,

38 President's Report Issue, *MIT Bulletin* 93, no. 2 (1956-57) 61-68

39 Caroline Shillaber, *1861-1961: A Hundred Year Chronicle Massachusetts Institute of Technology School of Architecture and Planning* (Cambridge, MA: Massachusetts Institute of Technology, 1963)

40 Dean Pietro Belluschi, "Letter to Dr. James R. Killian, Jr. President, dated September 23, 1952."

41 Lawrence B. Anderson, "Letter to Dean Pietro Belluschi dated February 19, 1952." Architecture Dean Papers, MIT Institute Archives, AC 400, Box 3, Folder: Private Correspondence.

42 Lawrence B. Anderson, "Memo to Burnham Kelly dated March 13, 1952." Ibid., Box 3, Folder: Study of Lighting Committee.

43 President's Report Issue (November 1953).

Potential uses for plastics in housing, as imagined at MIT in 1955. From MIT Department of Architecture, *Plastics in Housing: A Report to the Pastics Division of the Monsanto Chemical Company,* (Cambridge, MA: MIT Press, 1955). MIT Institute Archives and Special Collections.

undertook the study with the assistance of graduate students. The Wakefield Brass Company also funded the establishment of the F. W. Wakefield Laboratory of Lighting Design. This Laboratory continued the original project, developed tools for measuring and evaluating the effects of lighting in space[44] and also organized a symposium on "Vision, Brightness and Design" in the department.[45]

In an extension of the wartime development of new materials, Hamilton also supervised an investigation of the use of plastics in buildings. This project was part of a larger project directed by Albert G. H. Dietz, a professor in the Department of Building Engineering and Construction. [46] The Department of Architecture's contribution to the project began with a survey of existing materials, consolidated as *Plastics in Housing, A Report to the Plastics Division of the Monsanto Chemical Company,*[47] and expanded to include the design of a demonstration house. This work was funded in part by the Monsato Chemical Company and was titled the Monsanto House of the Future (MHOF). [48] The project as a whole epitomized the idea of research as innovation, and a prototype of the MHOF was constructed at Disneyland in California. In 1956 the research team (Marvin Goody with students J. J. Schiffer, W. L. Marley and W. J. Harper) continued the study by creating a prototype for a school building which utilized plastic panels and which was erected on Memorial Drive in Cambridge.[49] Both of these projects also won formal accolades, including a first prize in a competition sponsored by the Society of Plastic Industries.[50]

The Industrialized House Course

Wurster's "broadening of the base" and Anderson and Belluschi's technical emphasis were also evident in the school's post-war curriculum. Students studied materials, sanitation, heating and ventilation, electricity, acoustics, and illumination, as well as social studies such as urban sociology and economics. These courses were offered outside the department; within it students took design studio, structural analysis, visual design, city and regional planning courses, and architectural history.[51] Research was incorporated into this basic curriculum. In the fall term of 1947, for example, students working on the problem of "A Solar House" were provided with data from *Circular C3.2 Solar Orientation in Home Design* (published by the University of Illinois).[52]

44 Laboratory of Lighting Design Progress Report 451 (June 12, 1953), Architecture Dean Papers, MIT Institute Archives, AC 400, Box 3, Folder: Study of Lighting Committee.

45 Laboratory of Lighting Design Progress Report 472 (July 15, 1954), Ibid., Box 3, Folder: Study of Lighting

Committee.

46 President's Report Issue, 1945-1946, *MIT Bulletin* 82, no. 1 (1946): 88-89.

47 MIT Department of Architecture, Plastics in Housing: A Report to the Plastics Division of the Monasto Chemical Company (Cambridge, MA: MIT Press, 1955).

48 President's Report Issue, November, 1954. For a discussion of this project see Stephen Phillips, "Plastics," in Cold War Hothouses Inventing Postwar Culture from Cockpit to Playboy, ed. Beatriz Colomina, AnneMarie Brennan and Jeannie Kim (New York: Princeton Architectural Press, 2004), 91-123.

49 Edwin J. Carr, "Letter to Professor Marvin Goody, dated June 18, 1962," Architecture Dean Papers, MIT Institute Archives, AC 400, Box 3, Folder: Plastic School. See also Walter Milne, "Picnic," The MIT Observer 4, no. 9 (Summer 1958) and "Plastic School." *Time* September 21 (1959)

Monsanto House of
the Future (MHOF),
1956. Department of
Architecture, MIT.

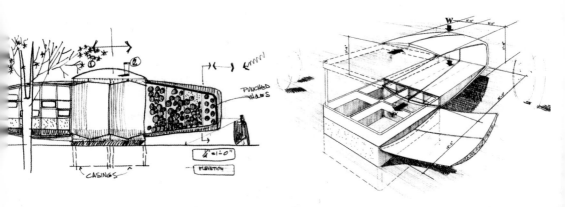

The most extensive effort to introduce MIT students to technical innovation and industry-related research was the "Industrialized House Course," begun in 1949. This course was not a reading seminar on housing;[53] the students grappled with the technological, social and political dimensions of housing by working through a specific problem. At the same time, it was not a conventional design studio. Rather than design a prefabricated house, the students were asked to study the "mysteries" of the building industry. At the start of the course the instructor, Carl Koch, presented the students with several houses already on the market. In 1952 these included his own "Acorn Packaged House," the "Gunnison Prefabricated Panel House" and a "Site Prefabricated House," such as those being built by Levitt and Sons at the time. The students were asked to choose one of these houses as the basis for developing a specific site of about 300 acres west of Boston and "to formulate their ideas on what a developer of this or that type of house should know in advance of going into this kind of job."[54]

Koch's definition of the problem is evidence of an astute reading of the contemporaneous problems of industry and business. Housing is by nature a two-part package, as Greg Hise explains: "The first component was low-cost, efficient dwelling that met minimum requirements for space, light and air."[55] Such houses, however, could only be used if they were located in an environment that provided suitable living conditions. The second part of the package was therefore site and/or community planning.

These two aspects of the problem, however, had not been treated equally by business and industry. Compared to the larger "environment," the single house lent itself more easily to standardization and mass production and was thus the subject

Organizational chart of the Industrialized House Course in 1950. From Bemis Foundation Records, 1926-1954, MIT Institute Archives and Special Collections.

Foster Gunnison addressing the audience of at the "Industrialized House" conference at MIT, where he commented that: "I feel that your program is the culmination of my life's effort to interest colleges in the prefabrication of houses." *Left to right*: Galbreath, Fisher, Gunnison, Brooks, Burns and Levitt, *Housing Mass Produced: Housing Conference*, January 1952.

50 Caroline Shillaber, *1861-1961: A Hundred Year Chronicle Massachusetts Institute of Technology School of Architecture and Planning* (Cambridge, MA: Massachusetts Institute of Technology, 1963)

51 "Agenda and Report for Consideration at the Meeting of the Visiting Committee of the School of Architecture and Planning," Architecture Dean Papers, MIT Institute Archives, AC 400, Box 1, Folder 13.

52 "Grade IV Arch. Design 4.741, 4.742, Fall Term 1947, Problem #3: A Solar House." Ibid., Box 6, Folder: 4.751, 4.752 Arch. Design '36-'57.

53 MIT offered such a seminar in 1948. It consisted of a series of lectures by guest lecturers on a wide range of the topics: minority problems, social research frontiers in housing, housing a policies, history of houses and market analysis and construction trends in housing. "Massachusetts

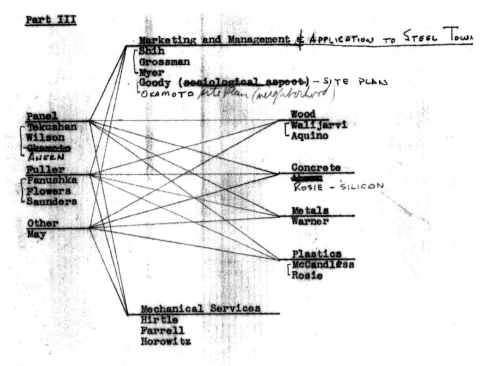

Institute of Technology
Housing Seminar (4.541)
(Spring Semester, 1948),"
Catherine Bauer Wurster
Papers 1931-1964, Bancroft
Library, University of
California, Berkeley. BANC
MSS 74/163 c.

54 Albert Farwell Bemis
Foundation, *Housing Mass
Produced: 1952 Housing
Conference held January
14*, eds. Phyllis M. Kelly
and Richard W. Hamilton.
(Cambridge, MA: MIT Albert
Farwell Bemis Foundation,
School of Architecture and
Planning, 1952). 3

55 Greg Hise. "The Airplane
and the Garden City: Regional
Transformations during World
War II," in *World War II and
the American Dream: How
Wartime Building Changed a
Nation*, (ed. Donald Albrecht.
Washington DC: The National
Building Museum and The
MIT Press, 1995): 144-183

56 Robert Friedel, "Scarcity
and Promise: Materials and
American Domestic Culture
during WWII," in *World War
II and the American Dream:
How Wartime Building
Changed a Nation*, (ed.
Donald Albrecht. Washington
DC: The National Building
Museum and The MIT Press,
1995). 42-89

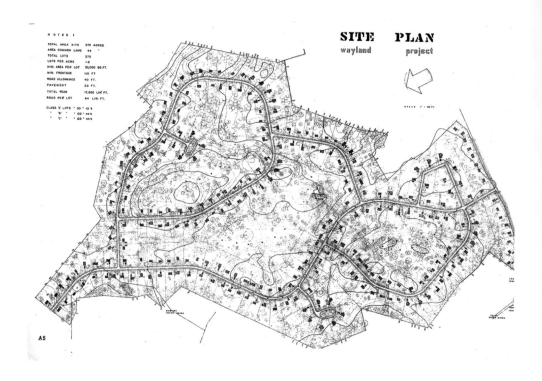

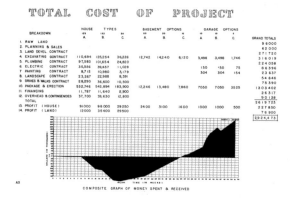

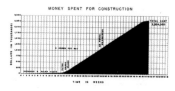

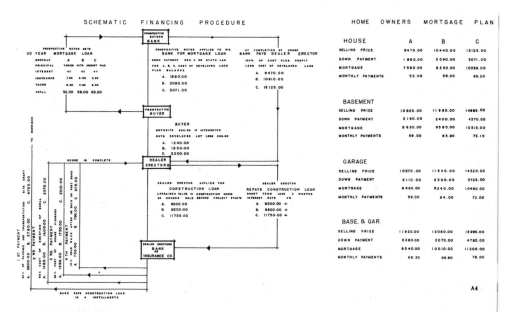

Student presentation
of a financing and
marketing scheme
for a neighborhood
composed of Gunnison
Prefabricated Panel
houses. From *Housing
Mass Produced: 1952
Housing Conference held
January 14.*

of creative design and research by industrialists from the early twentieth century onward. The wartime demand for housing for relocated defense and industrial workers, as well as the development of new materials such as plastics, further propelled interest in housing efficiency and technology.[56] Community planning, on the other hand, was all but ignored; residents were expected to make do for the greater good. Freed from the need to consider either neighborhood development or marketing (the houses were pre-ordered by the military), manufacturers forged ahead with the design and production of simple houses in large volume. It was a simple matter of adjusting volume to price. By the end of war it seemed to many that the "problem" of prefabricated houses had been solved, and the number of companies engaged in such production had more than tripled. [57]

The focus on the single house, independent of siting and community planning, could not be sustained after the war; this became especially evident towards the end of the 1940s, when the worst of the housing crisis had past. Bringing environmental considerations into the equation, however, fundamentally upset the production and marketing schemes developed during the war. From leveling to finishing, site development costs money, and the industry struggled to achieve the profit margins it had come to

expect. As William Levitt observed in 1949: "there is no such thing as a complete factory-engineered house – because no one has discovered how to prefabricate the land, how to prefabricate the road in front of the land, or the water main that goes into the house."[58]

The wartime economy had also allowed manufacturers to ignore marketing considerations, and with the return to free market conditions these proved to be crucial. With diminishing government contracts, it became clear that the only houses that would actually be fabricated would be those that would sell on the market—before prefabrication, if possible. Manufacturers found themselves unprepared to meet these challenges, as *Architectural Forum* declared in May 1949, "The factory-built house is here, but not the answer to the $33 million question: How to get it to market?"[59]

Pietro Belluschi addressing the conference at "Housing as a National Security Resource;" Carl Koch seated at right. MIT, 1951.

57 Knerr. *Suburban Steel,* 2004.

58 Russell W. Davenport, "A Life Roundtable on Housing, The Housing Industry, Though Maligned by the Public, Has Some Hopeful Ideas for the Future" *Life* (January 31, 1949) 73-86.

59 "The Factory-Built House is Here, But not the Answer to the $33 million Question: How to get it to Market?" *Architectural Forum* 90, no. 5 (May 1949): 107-114.

60 Interestingly, Techbuilt Inc. itself became a case study for students in the "mid year program" at the Harvard University Graduate School of Business Administration. The student who prepared the material for the class discussion subtitled their case study: "What would you advise Mr. Koch to do?" "Harvard University Graduate School of Business Administration, George F. baker Foundation, Mid-Year Program Written Analysis of Cases, Techbuilt, Inc. Case Prepared for class

Koch himself was grappling with these problems in his own practice at the same time that he was marshaling MIT student resources to address the "real life" problems of the business industry. While his Acorn House had been bought by government agencies, his next design, the Techbuilt House, was not faring well in the market, despite wide spread television publicity. Koch eventually set up several different legal entities to deal separately with each aspect of the problem: Techbuilt Inc. procured the land and then hired Koch and Associates to design the buildings and Acorn Inc. (of which Koch was president) to provide prefabricated paneling.[60]

The students who chose to begin with the Gunnison Prefabricated Panel House presented the most detailed project. They explained the marketing strategy they had developed and described the advertising and demonstration houses it would include. They also worked out a detailed financing plan. Gunnison, who was among the reviewers of the project, thought the project was well presented, though he did comment on the size of the lots and the schedule of payments.

A separate group of students worked with guest lecturer Buckminster Fuller. Fuller did not adhere to the program Koch outlined but rather saw the work with MIT students as part of his own larger research project. He asked them to continue developing a problem he had assigned to students at the Institute of Design in Chicago in 1948 and at Black Mountain College in 1949. In this problem students designed a "standard of living package"—a trailer that could be opened, creating a series of rooms that were then encased by a geodesic dome. In the MIT version of the exercise he asked the students to design three different schemes: one "contemporary," a second "innovative," and the third "visionary." Fuller also directed his students to consider waterless showers and pipeless houses in their designs.

Each "Industrialized House Course" culminated in a two-day conference with invited guests and faculty. In 1951 the course and conference focused on "Housing as a National Security Resource," and one of the panel questions asked about the objectives of "civilian defense."[61] "Economic Development and Foreign Housing," the topic of the final conference (convened in 1953), indicates the growing international scope of American higher education.[62] Aside from

discussions March 4 and March 6, 1954." Albert Farwell Bemis Foundation Records 1926-1954, MIT Institute Archives, AC 302, Box 17: Techbuilt Houses (Carl Koch) (File No. T/27).

61 Other included questions: "Should not the ability to deploy the population of our large cities with rapidity be

the tactical criterion of our civilian defense planning rather than a major focus on disaster relief?" and "Can mobile housing, rather than 'temporary dwelling units' provide rapid erection, and high salvagetability in meeting emergency requirements?" Albert Farwell Bemis Foundation.

1951. *Housing: a National Security Resource A Conference and Exhibition Held January 19 and 20,* eds. Phyllis M. Kelly and Richard W. Hamilton (Cambridge, MA: Massachusetts Institute of Technology, Albert Farwell Bemis Foundation, School of Architecture and Planning, 1951).

62 MIT, Albert Farwell Bemis Foundation, "Bemis Conference on Economic Development and Housing Abroad (1953)," Catherine Bauer Wurster Papers 1931-1964, Bancroft Library, University of California, Berkeley. BANC: BANC MSS 74/163 c.

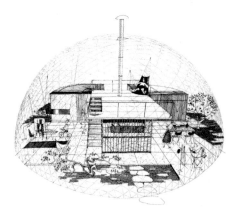

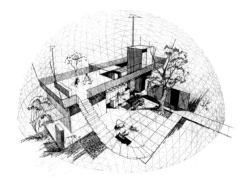

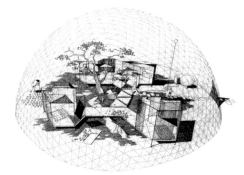

MIT student projects for houses using Buckminster Fuller's geodesic dome. *facing page,* Student presentations for the 1952 Industrialized House Course, MIT. From *Housing Mass Produced: 1952 Housing Conference held January 14.*

their educational role, these conferences were important vehicles for furthering the ties between MIT's architecture department and industry representatives.

The "Industrialized House Course" was a special graduate course, but it was not unique within the school. In 1949 undergraduate students were also asked to address the issue of the industrialized house. In the project brief the instructors argued that "it should be helpful to investigate a few of the main factors contributing to the situation so that the design of a rational low cost house may be reasonably studied."[63] One of the course requirements was a 500-word report on the question: "Why are houses expensive?" Two years later, in 1951, Kevin Lynch and Ralph Rapson taught yet another course, titled "Cooperative Housing Development."[64] Buckminster Fuller became a repeat visitor, offering students opportunities to engage in more innovative design/research, like a folding tent intended to be used with an existing Ranch Wagon.[65] The "Industrialized House Course" itself also underwent changes. In 1951 Kelly and others considered introducing a "research" phase midway through the semester, in which the students, working in teams, would collect and report on current housing research.[66] A year later, industrialized housing (identified as "Carl Koch's course") was suggested as a topic of specialization in the department.[67]

Beyond teaching students in the department, MIT and the Bemis Foundation became training centers for those interested in prefabrication. After their time at MIT, these researchers took their work to other schools.

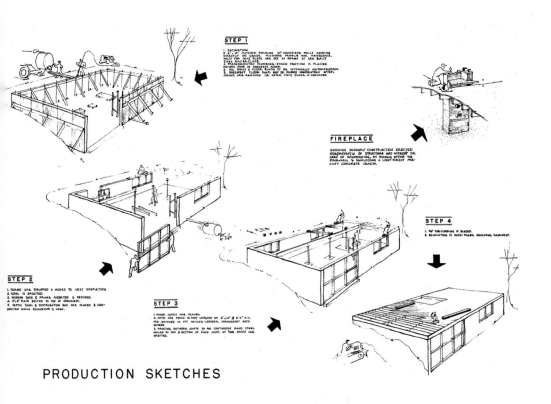

PRODUCTION SKETCHES

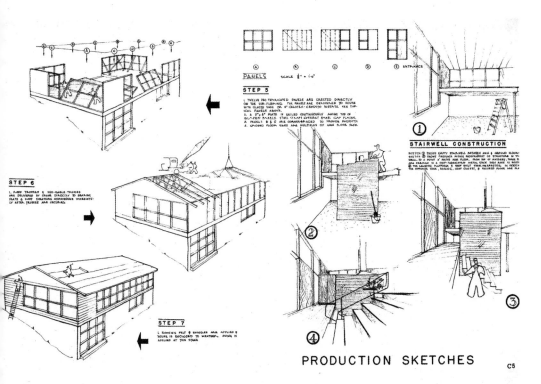

PRODUCTION SKETCHES

C5

Cornell University. Harold Horowitz, a student in the "Industrialized House Course," worked with Buckminster Fuller to conduct technical research on the mechanical facilities of the prefabricated house, including the rationalization of kitchen facilities and the simplification of waste treatment and disposal methods. Gordon McCutchan, another student, would later join the Texas A&M Engineering Experiment station and work with William W. Caudill to develop architectural research and architectural research teaching there.[68]

Conclusion

The translation of MIT's philosophy of research into the "pedagogy of prefabrication" in its department of architecture in the postwar years was successful: The focus on the prefabrication of houses fulfilled institutional expectations and provided an excellent topic by which the department could revitalize and energize itself. Moreover, the partnerships developed with the housing industry allowed the department to develop as a research center and to earn a reputation for maverick innovation and public service. The overarching goal of creating a prefabricated house that "will exert a pull strong enough" [69] to reach production," however, did not materialize. The conflation of different objectives under the single guise of "research," while powerful, was not enough to overcome what Robert W. McLaughlin described as:

> A chronic and serious defect in the process of house building – the diversity of interest of most of the elements of the process. The flow diagram of the process does not flow – there are too many arrows pointing in opposite directions. Instead of there being a flow diagram, the existing process of making houses must be illustrated with a series of stress diagrams, with components seldom approaching a parallel, and with a consequent weakening of the resultant end product.[70]

In the postwar Department of Architecture at MIT two of the internal contradiction were especially apparent. First, although research was construed at MIT as the foundation for education, the development of the department of architecture as a research facility for government and industry in fact competed with the department's long-standing role as an educational center for training future architects. As Koch reported:

63 "Grade VI Arch. Design 4.761, Fall Term 1949, Problem 2: The Industrialized House—a Basis for Good Living?," Architecture Dean Papers, MIT Institute Archives, AC 400, Box 7, Folder 4.761, 4.762 '46–'55. **64** Carl Koch Donald Gourley, and Richard Hamilton, "Memo to Lawrence Anderson, Rupert Mclaurin, Burnham

Kelly, Albert Dietz, John Wulff, Howard Staley, Buckminster Fuller, John Arnold, W. C. Voss, C. Abrams, G. Kepes; Subject: Proposed Forum to be held at MIT the Second Week in January, 1951, on the Industrialized House," Albert Farwell Bemis Foundation Records, 1926-1954, MIT Institute Archives, AC 302, Box

4, Folder, Industrialized House Course, 1951: Assignments and Student Reports. **65** Buckminster Fuller, "Arch. Design Fall Term-1952, grade VI- 4.761, Fuller Problem Living Accommodation on Tour in a Ford Ranch Wagon [in a letter to Richard Hamilton, dated October 25, 1952]," Ibid., Box 4: Course 1952-3.

66 Burnham Kelly "Letter to William W. Caudill, dated June 28, 1951" Ibid., Box 7 Folder Texas A&M College Engineering Experiment Station. **67** Professor [Lawrence] Anderson, "Memo to: Architectural Staff and Professors Adams, Greeley and Lynch. Date: May 9, 1952."

These students have been working on the industrialized house for about half a year. Some of them started with the feeling that the industrialized house was not a design problem at all, and they were here to learn design, and why should we be doing this. Some of them who were very interested in it from the beginning and who didn't feel we were forcing it down their throat, felt that it was something that design had a lot to do with. We've learnt, mainly, what all the other parts of the problem are, and we haven't worried much about design.[71]

Second, in the MIT philosophy as adopted in the department, research was viewed as an independent activity—as a complement to, and even a model for, investigations in industry, rather than as a subset of manufacturers' product development. Such independence was difficult to maintain, however, when industrial entities were funding the research. Graduate courses were essentially co-opted for market research. Industry and the market imposed not only research goals, but also timelines and other constraints. Many industrialists, for example, responded to growing competition in the housing market by adding appliances such as stoves, refrigerators, or (in the case of the Lustron Corp.) dish/clothes washing machines, instead of investing further in research and/or the design of the houses themselves. Such a solution was economically viable (at least on the surface)[72], but it undermined the integrity of "research" as it was viewed at the Institute.

Given its straddling position between academia and industry, the flaws in the pedagogy of prefabrication were inherent to the enterprise. The easing of the burden of wartime requirements made room in the national economy for a focus on consumer wants and needs that promised to give domestic architecture a new prominence. But at the same time it seems fore-ordained that research, with its high-minded emphasis on social welfare and efficiency, would not be in the driver's seat of this journey.

Architecture Dean Papers, MIT Institute Archives AC 400, Box 3 ,Folder: Policy 3/3.

68 Gordon McCutchan and William W. Caudill, *Research Report Number 32: An Experiment in Architectural Education through Research* (College Station, TX: The Texas Engineering Experiment Station, The Texas A. &M.

College System, 1951).

69 Carl Koch, "Design and the Industrialized House." In *Design and the Production of Houses*, ed. Burnham Kelly. (New York: McGraw-Hill Book Company, Inc., 1959): 86.

70 Robert W. McLaughlin "Housing Construction Talk Delivered at the Massachusetts Institute of

Technology on February 26, 1948" Albert Farwell Bemis Foundation Records 1926-1954, MIT Institute Archives, AC 302, Box 7, Folder: Miscellaneous Prefabrication – Correspondence: 1

71 Graduate Class, School of Architecture MIT. *Industrialized House Forum Proceedings of Course Conference January*

6 and 7, 1950. (Cambridge, MA: School of Architecture Massachusetts Institute of Technology, 1950): 52

72 Many mortgage brokers did not recognize these appliances as part of the house for mortgages, so consumers had a hard time paying for them.

DANIEL A. BARBER

Experimental Dwellings
Modern Architecture and Environmental Research at the MIT Solar Energy Fund, 1938-1963

Modernism and Environmentalism

The history of experimentation in solar energy for house heating at MIT engages historiographic problematics of both modern architecture and environmentalism. Much as architectural historians identify—in the present volume and elsewhere—a 'second modernism' emerging out of the chaos of World War II, historians of environmentalism have developed a 'two-wave' schema. This is best articulated in Ramachandra Guha's *Environmentalism: A Global History*, in which he describes "an early period of pioneering and prophecy" read through literary transcendentalism and the wilderness idea, and, beginning after the war, "a second wave ... when a largely intellectual response was given shape by a groundswell of public support."[1] The "intellectual response" Guha describes involved the introduction of political and economic, scientific and managerial, and cultural and popular discourses into pre-war conservation and preservation movements. Though the war figures as an important fulcrum, the second wave is seen to be catalyzed by Rachel Carson's *Silent Spring* of 1963, which evoked in compelling prose a complex ecology of human-nature interactions. Carson's book is widely regarded as the fount of popular reaction to the out-of-control effects of industrialization, and at the same time it is understood to initiate the managerial disposition of the environmental sciences and the project of environmentalism as one of experts contributing to policy proposals and legislated regulatory regimes.

In recent years, much of this historical schema has been interrogated and reconfigured. Ted Nordhaus and Michael Schellenberger's "The Death of Environmentalism," written as a report for the Environmental Grantmakers Association in early 2005, indicates what is at stake in this regard. This text proposed that the scientific-policy-managerial model initiated by Carson's book had devolved into environmentalists acting as a special interest group concerned for "a supposed thing—the environment" rather than for "advancing a worldview" of connections between economies and ecologies.[2] As a result, environmental problems have been articulated as subject to technological fixes, and are often seen in isolation from the variety of social, cultural, and political issues that are embedded within them.

Nordhaus and Schellenberger's critique further suggests that the global project of recognizing ecological interconnection and advocating for environmental health has disregarded the profound effects of the environment and of environmentalism on the production of subjectivity. In what follows, I want to propose a historiographic analogue to "The Death of Environmentalism" by identifying the emergence of an environmentalist subjectivity in connection with the cultural developments of modern architecture, and in the form of a multivalent envisioning of alternative futures. Solar house experimentation at MIT provides a window into political, economic, technological and architectural discourses immediately after World War II which sought to form a cultural response to the perception of depleting energy sources. Tropes of modern architectural design were deployed in an attempt to advance new subjects who desired different political and material conditions. These experiments provide a different genealogy of environmentalism at the same time that the close affinity between solar efficiency and the post-war transformation of modern architecture allows us to develop the history of modern architecture in a new and compelling context.

'A Strange Looking Little Building'

Solar energy experimentation at MIT began before World War II with the establishment of the Godfrey L. Cabot Solar Energy Fund in April 1938. Cabot had made a gift to Harvard University in June of 1937, spurring Vannevar Bush, then Dean of Engineering and Vice-President of MIT, and Karl Compton, President of the Institute, to lobby Cabot to make a similar donation to their school. In order to limit possible overlap with the Harvard program, which was focused primarily on biological and agricultural applications, the MIT funds were, according to the deed of gift, limited to "converting the energy of the sun to the use of man by mechanical, electrical, or chemical means without the intervention of plant life."[3]

For all three of these figures—Cabot, Bush, and Compton—the social responsibility of scientific inquiry was at stake. Cabot indicated surprise that, while the sun's energy had been available and marginally utilized for centuries, in the 1930s even the most advanced scientists did not know if effective large-scale utilization was possible. In correspondence with Compton, he proposed that both theoretical and applied research should be developed immediately to determine whether solar energy could replace fossil fuels in the

1 Ramachandra Guha, *Environmentalism: A Global History* (New York: Longman, 2002), 3-7, 65. See also Samuel P. Hays, *A History of Environmental Politics since 1945* (Pittsburgh, PA: University of Pittsburgh Press, 2000) and Thomas Robertson, "'This is the American Earth': American

Empire, the Cold War, and American Environmentalism" *Diplomatic History* 32, no. 4 (Sept 2008), 561-584.

2 Michael Schellenberger and Ted Nordhaus, "The Death of Environmentalism" *Proceedings of the Environmental Grantmakers Association* (October, 2004), np.

3 "Deed of Gift to the Massachusetts Institute of Technology by Godfrey L. Cabot '81," box 43, folder 16, M.I.T. Office of the President Records, Solar Energy Fund (AC 4), Institute Archives.

relatively distant future. The Fund was thus established with a fifty-year life span and its endowment divided between theoretical research and attempts "to determine whether the direct use of the sun's energy is now economically feasible, and if so, where and under what conditions."[4] The emphasis on the social and economic relevance of technological research—on applied science—corresponded to the goals of Compton and Bush, both strong supporters of scientific integration into industrial and legislative practices before, during, and after the war.

The early work of the Fund produced important applied results. Led by Hoyt C. Hottel, professor of Chemical Engineering at MIT, near-term experimentation focused on the production of a solar-heated structure designated as Building 34 on the MIT campus.[5] As Hottel described it in 1940: "we have out on the back lot of the Institute a strange-looking little building, where we can study the performance of solar energy collectors and compare it with records of solar intensity, and where we can study the use of heat so collected."[6] Hottel's own drawings served as the initial 'design' of the building, its formal disposition being standard enough that, aside from the installation of scientific instruments, the details were left to the Institute's building contractors. A one-story, two-room structure, Building 34 had an open attic and an enormous basement water tank for heat storage. Solar panels on the roof were organized in three modules, with different combinations of insulating material, glass facing, sealants, and other experimental parameters. A fourth module was reserved for measuring equipment so that the amount of sunlight received could be correlated to the amount of spatial heat produced.[7]

Three technological issues emerged. First, Hottel and his colleagues established the design and construction of the solar panel and the organization of its attendant system of space heating, producing a template that would be used by researchers, architects, and homebuilders until the late 1980s. The best panel they tested consisted of a wool-insulated base encased in wood and aluminum and covered by two panes of glass. To produce heat, water was electrically pumped from the basement tank through copper tubing laid into the wool insulation of the panel. This water was then heated by solar radiation and returned to the tank. When required, air from the outside would be blown over the heated water and

4 V. Bush, et al, "A Research Program on Direct Utilization of Solar Energy" dated Sept. 25, 1937, box 43, folder 16, M.I.T. Office of the President Records, Solar Energy Fund (AC 4) Institute Archives.

5 The committee also included A. von Hippel (Electrical Engineering), Ernest Huntress (Organic Chemistry), A.C. Hardy (Applied Optics) and G.W. Swett (Mechanical Engineering). Letter Compton to Abbot, June 4 1938, box 43, folder 16, M.I.T. Office of the President Records, Solar

Energy Fund (AC 4), Institute Archives.

6 Hoyt C. Hottel, "The Sun as a Competitor of Fuels," box 18, Hoyt C. Hottel Papers (MC 544), Institute Archives, 5. (hereafter 'Hottel Papers').

7 Memorandum, Hottel to Executive Committee of M.I.T. box 16, Hottel Papers. A map of the site that accompanied the budget request indicates that heat and hot water were to be made available from neighboring buildings, thus the panels were not to be exclusively relied on in this capacity.

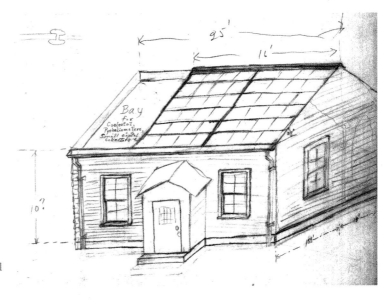

Hoyt C. Hottel, drawing for Building 34, 1938, Hoyt Hottel Papers, MIT Institute Archives and Special Collections, *(hereafter Hottel papers)*.

Installation of solar panels on Building 34, MIT Solar Energy Fund, Department of Architecture, 1939. Hottel papers.

Schematic of solar panel and heating system, including storage tank for Building 32, MIT Solar Energy Fund, Cambridge, MA, 1939. From Richard Hamilton, *Space Heating with Solar Energy* (Cambridge, MIT: 1954).

warmed, and then blown into the laboratory room. Using this system, Building 34 was able to maintain a temperature of 72° throughout the winter.[8]

Though effective, the system was expensive—three times the cost of a comparable fuel-based system. The storage tank was the most expensive component; the second technological issue—identified but not resolved at Building 34—was that of heat storage. The ability to store solar radiation was vital to the economic viability of solar heating and led to a wide variety of proposals after the war, as will be discussed below.

The third technological issue was that of determining the ideal angle of the collector. An important goal of the experiment was to establish the best method of measuring solar radiation in order to indicate the efficiency with which heat was produced; thus, careful attention was paid to the measurement devices. After exchanging data with the U.S. Weather Bureau, Hottel realized that the calibration 'constant' provided by the Bureau for a number of the measuring devices was "not a constant but a variable, dependent upon solar altitude."[9] In other words, the amount of

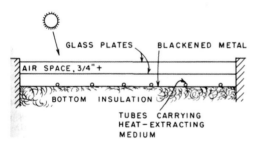

8 August L. Hesselschwerdt, "Performance of the M.I.T. Solar House," in Richard W. Hamilton, ed., *Space Heating with Solar Energy: Proceedings of a Course-Symposium held at the Massachusetts Institute of Technology, August 21-26, 1950*, (Cambridge, MA: Massachusetts Institute of Technology/Bemis Foundation, 1954), 99. See also Austin Whillier, "Principles of Solar House Design," *Progressive Architecture* 36 (May 1955), 122-126. The panel is known today as the "Hottel-Whillier flat-plate collector."
9 Hottel in James J. Bohning, "Hoyt C. Hottel: M.I.T.'s Combustion and Solar

solar insolation, and thus the efficiency of solar heating, was dependent on the solar rays' precise angle of incidence on the collector panel. Much of Hottel's work over the course of the subsequent decade would concern the refinement of a methodology for tilt-angle determination. More generally, these technological problems were indications of the necessity for a finely-tuned relationship between roof angle, heat storage, and internal volumetric disposition which would play out in the context of transformations to modern architecture after the war.

The First Oil Crisis

After the war, however, much else had changed. Concern over the depletion of fossil fuels greatly exacerbated the need for energy alternatives, and the urgency for demonstrating the economically viability of the solar house increased. While anxiety over resource scarcity existed before the war—as the establishment of the Cabot Fund indicates—a shortage in domestic heating fuel in the winter of 1947-48 increased these fears, and a dynamic discussion on resource scarcity ensued.[10] Already evident to the petroleum industry in June, by mid-November a heating fuel shortage had reached a crisis state, and *The New York Times* and other papers were writing daily updates on families struggling to keep their houses warm.[11] Falling temperatures at the end of January hinted at further catastrophes as snow-blocked roads and frozen waterways prevented available oil from reaching houses and apartment buildings. Chicago and the Midwest were also beginning to suffer.[12] *The Times* by this point had given up on help from the government and was resigned to a winter-long crisis; *The Chicago Tribune* began its own analysis of global oil distribution regimes and the roots of the supply problem.[13]

The crisis of 1947-48 catalyzed anxiety over the future supply of energy resources for the growing American economy.[14] Post-war growth was predicated on industrial development, full employment for returning soldiers, and a dramatic increase in the building stock. A reliable source of energy was necessary for all three of these goals. Wartime demands had made clear that the long-feared depletion of coal was becoming a reality. Expansion of hydro-electric power was also limited as these installments had been operating at capacity since 1942. Finally, much of the post-war increase in energy use was focused on liquid

Energy Pioneer" in *Chemical Engineering Progress*, Vol. 84 (March 1988), pp. 53-55. The definitive text on the subject is Hoyt C. Hottel and Bernard B. Woertz, "The Performance of Flat Plate Solar Collectors" in *The Transactions of the American Society of Mechanical Engineers* vol. 64 (1942), 91-104.

10 Richard H.K. Vietor, *Energy Policy in America Since 1945: A Study of Business Government Relations* (New York: Cambridge University Press, 1984), 91.

11 Walter H. Waggoner, "Fuel Crisis Looms, Army, Navy Assert," *New York Times*, June 19, 1947, 1-2. See also "Seek Oil Abroad, Industry is Urged,"

New York Times, November 13, 1947, 46; "U.S. to Propose Voluntary Oil Rationing," *Washington Post*, December 3, 1947, 9; and "Fuel Crisis Grows as Deliveries Lag," *New York Times*, December 30, 1947, 1, 4.

12 "Cold Deepens Crisis in Fuel Oil Shortage," *Chicago Daily Tribune*, January 23,

1948, 17.

13 "Oil Shortage All Winter is Predicted for East," *New York Times*, January 21, 1948, 1; Wayne Thomas and Stanley Johnston, "Why World is Short of Petroleum," *Chicago Daily Tribune*, January 29, 1948, 1, 8, back page. Note that the *Tribune's* map is an inaccurate assessment of

"The World's Flow
of Petroleum" from
The Chicago Tribune,
January 29, 1948.

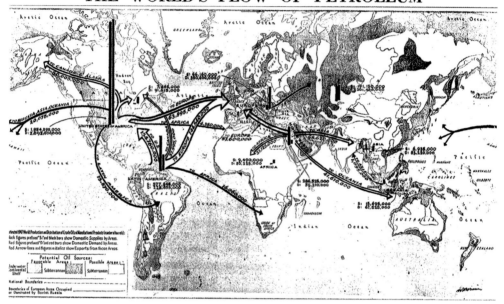

fuels—especially for the automobile—in which coal (despite continued efforts to develop synthetic liquid fuels) and hydroelectric could not compete.

While its origins lay in anxiety over domestic reserves, the first oil crisis, in distinct contrast to the regional conservationist discourse of the 1930s, had ramifications across both geopolitical and geophysical registers.[15] By the end of World War II, U.S. oil companies had extensively penetrated the production systems of every major oil-producing region in the world.[16] At first, the market for overseas oil produced by U.S. companies was itself

the relative production of oil in the U.S. Southwest, Venezuela, and the Middle East in this period, indicative of gaps in general knowledge. **14** The first oil crisis described here has not been historicized as such; its significance, all the same, is suggested in Frank Laird, *Solar Energy, Technology*

Policy, and Institutional Values (New York: Cambridge University Press, 2001) and in relation to the technology of synthetic fuels in Vietor, *Energy Policy in America.*

15 See Harold Ickes, "We're Running Out of Oil!," *American Magazine* (Dec. 1943), 37-43; 38.

16 Edward DeGolyer, "Preliminary Report of the Technical Oil Mission to the Middle East," *Bulletin of the American Association of Petroleum Geologists* 28 (July 1944); 919-23.

almost completely outside the U.S.; this was due to legislated protection of the oil industry still operating on U.S. soil and to the decimated resource base of Western Europe and its urgent programs of reconstruction. By early 1947 more than half of Western Europe's energy needs were supplied by U.S.-owned companies operating in the Middle East. The Marshall Plan, initiated in June of 1947, increased this figure. Cold War historian David S. Painter has argued that one of the most significant and lasting effects of Marshall Plan aid to Europe was the creation of a reliable consumer base for U.S. companies seeking to develop the oil fields of the Persian Gulf (an expensive investment in infrastructure costs) at a time when the American market was temporarily off-limits. This entry into the European market secured the prominent position of U.S. oil corporations in the world economy for decades to follow.[17]

In January of 1948, as the weather turned colder, global oil production was increasing but was not reaching American homes. No one had an economic incentive to provide the oil, and the Truman administration—looking to the election in November—was hesitant to do anything. By mid-February, falling temperatures and failing infrastructure made the situation so dire that they did everything: Truman ordered the Navy to divert reserves to the East Coast, solving the immediate crisis; simultaneously, oil exports were limited and import restrictions eased. As energy historian Richard H.K. Vietor notes, "these actions helped alleviate the heating oil crisis, but left a residue of permanently expanded imports … As of January 1949, imports were increasing by 25% a year." Vietor is one of many scholars to identify the winter of 47-48 as the start of net-importation in petroleum by the U.S., a condition which persists to the present.[18] The seemingly endless reserves of the Middle East, however, were not yet apparent to the oil industry or the American public, and while on February 19 The New York Times declared that "the East Coast is 'over the hump' with its fuel supply for the rest of the winter," projections for the long-term future remained bleak. As The Times had editorialized in late January: "the situation is indeed critical, especially when it is remembered that in ten years we shall be pinched for oil and our consumption of petroleum products is growing. The time is now to begin preparations for the future."[19] In the context of heightened Cold War anxieties and a deepening recession, the concern over heating fuel supply in the midst of a frigid winter sparked a feverish anxiety over the future of American prosperity.[20]

17 David S. Painter, "Oil and the Marshall Plan," *Business History Review* Vol. 58, No. 3 (Autumn, 1984), 359-383; 362ff. More than 10% of the total aid provided by the U.S. for European recovery was spent on oil extracted and distributed by American firms; this was significantly more than any other single commodity.

18 Vietor, *Energy Policy in America*, 94.

19 "Fuel Crisis Ended Along East Coast," *New York Times*, February 19, 19947, 46; in other articles they addressed the emergency measures of Navy supply releases; see Charles Grutzner, "More Navy Oil, 300 Rail Cars Help Ease Fuel Famine Here," *New York Times*, February 12, 1948, 1, 4; "Impeding Oil Crisis," *New York Times*, January 22, 1948, and "Navy Allots Oil Supplies, Eastern Fuel Crisis Eased," *The Chicago Daily Tribune*, February 6, 1948.

20 The February 1948 coup in Czechoslovakia, along with Truman's loud denunciation of Soviet aggression in March, dramatically heightened tensions between the superpowers and also heightened public anxiety over the possibility of impending war; further, a recession in the U.S.

The Environmentalist Future

Looking at the twentieth century through the historical framework of environmentalism, the first oil crisis was a dramatic break. A fissure erupted in the conception of the globe and its material interconnections, and into it flowed a stream of intense economic, technological and cultural analysis which attempted to predict the outlines of future resource needs. On the one hand, this led to a heretofore incomprehensible drive for resource extraction and economic growth—what has come to be seen as the post-war consumer boom. On the other hand, a discourse on resource scarcity emerged that was concerned with coordinating policies of growth with the cultural imaginary of an alternative future—what can be articulated, despite its imbrication with normative agendas, as the emergence of contemporary environmentalism. A central experimental object of this latter disposition was the modern solar house.

The two strands of resource scarcity need to be briefly summarized before discussing these houses. The first was articulated by Harold J. Barnett, a staffer at the Department of the Interior, in the report *Energy Uses and Supplies 1939, 1947, 1965* of 1948. In it, Barnett made a profound proposal for the relationship between economic growth and resource depletion:

> If noticed before it has not been discussed in publication . . . [that] although the level of energy requirement is primarily determined by national product level, it is subject to secular fall because of efficiency gains in energy utilization. Advances in combustion efficiency, use of insulation, etc, occasion the downdrift. The tentative judgment is made, from knowledge that the most modern equipment is much more efficient than the average in use, that the downdrift will continue.[21]

In other words, Barnett suggested that while total energy use would continue to increase as the economy grew, the energy output per unit of Gross National Product would decrease as energy production became more efficient.[22] The way to avoid to resource scarcity, Barnett proposed, was to increase economic activity and thereby instigate industry development of methods to use existing supplies more efficiently.[23] As energy historian Craufurd Goodwin has noted, this report was based on "a remarkably sophisticated treatment of energy statistics, and became the basis for most public statements about energy policy from the Interior Department for several years."[24]

Other voices expressed concerns over the eventual depletion of fossil fuels—even in the face in the massive reserves in the Middle East—and the need to develop viable replacements. Eugene Ayres, a research consultant for Gulf Oil, produced a widely read text on this subject. First presented as a speech to the American Petroleum Institute in 1948, "Major Sources of Energy" painted a bleak picture of existing reserves. Ayres emphasized the technological and economic distinction between "continuous sources of energy," such as solar and wind, and "unrenewable sources of energy," such as nuclear and fossil fuels.[25] He contended that "the most important factor is not the size of a reserve but the rate at which it can be procured," a statement which initiated an important shift in conceptualizing resource reserves and produced a different balance sheet of energy uses and supplies which favored the development of renewables.[26]

Eugene Ayres, "Some Possibilities in Our Future Energy Picture." From Ayres, *Energy Sources – the Wealth of the World*, (New York: McGraw-Hill, 1952).

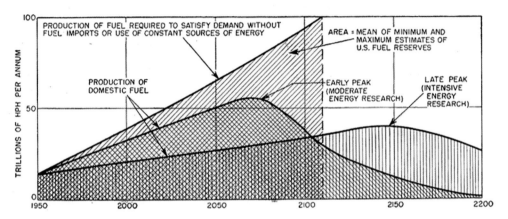

Though both sides of this debate were concerned with possible depletion, one, represented by Barnett, was focused on using technology to maintain the status quo and the other, represented by Ayres, was focused on developing technologies that would produce new forms of living. In many contexts—including, as will be discussed below, a 1950 symposium at MIT—Ayres emphasized the potential of architectural design in both the technological mitigation and the cultural imagination of alternative futures; regarding the former, in 1951 he wrote:

We seem destined to become more and more dependent upon the sun for all energy. It happens that sunlight is somewhat more easily adaptable to space-heating than to the development of power. These two circumstances taken together are full of

economy was developing throughout 1948 and continued into 1949. Lack of heat, fear of war, and an economic downturn coalesced to give the experience of fuel shortage somewhat more alarmist and even apocalyptic overtones. See Vietor, *Energy Policy in America*, 95.

21 Harold J. Barnett, *Energy Uses and Supplies 1939, 1947, 1965* (Washington, D.C.: Bureau of Mines, October 1950), 6.
22 Barnett, *Energy Uses and Supplies*, 6.
23 As Barnett would summarize in a later text: "While a fixed world always contains a threat of

resource economic scarcity, nevertheless onset of scarcity depends on other conditions as well. So long as resources are large enough to permit out put expansion... resource economic scarcity is not yet experienced." Harold J. Barnett, *Malthusianism and Conservation: Their Role as Origins of the Doctrine of

Increasing Resource Scarcity (Washington, D.C.: Resources for the Future, Inc., 1958), 12-13.
24 Goodwin, "The Truman Administration," 37.
25 Eugene Ayres, "Major Sources of Energy," *Addresses and Reports Delivered at the Twenty-Eighth Annual Meeting,*

fortunate significance, for we actually require more energy for heating our homes and our places of work than for transportation or industrial power.[27]

In cultural terms, Ayres repeatedly cited the importance of "the dreams of our architects" in articulating alternative futures; moreover he placed the discussion in a moral context, proposing that "someday our appetite for energy will probably be satiated, and energy production will remain about constant … we shall have become a nation of philosophers."[28] These proposals and predictions would inform subsequent technological and cultural strategies.[29]

Both Barnett and Ayres influenced a number of subsequent developments. Their papers were frequently referenced at the United Nations Scientific Conference on the Conservation and Use of Resources (UNSCCUR) in the fall of 1949, which elaborated on these debates and also acted as a kind of international clearing house for their technological ramifications. Barnett's report served as the basis for Interior Secretary Julius Krug's welcome and introduction to the conference, while Ayres' proposal that the "host of technologists working constantly on problems of power production, transmission, and utilization" should focus their efforts on "continuous sources" was the acknowledged premise for the conference session on "New Developments in the Production and Utilization of Energy."[30]

In the face of increased depletion anxiety during the Korean War, President Truman established the President's Materials Policy Commission soon after UNSCCUR. The Commission's 1952 report *Resources for Freedom* foundered between the poles of the resource scarcity debate, attempting to follow Ayres' apocalyptic assessments of resource availability while also pursuing Barnett's techno-philic solutions.[31] This studied ambivalence was, in the end, of little consequence: Eisenhower, taking office in 1953, completely rejected the report—a rejection supported, we should note, by increased awareness of the extent of Middle East reserves, a CIA-led coup in Iran to further secure them, and considerable election donations from oil corporations. The call for government-funded research into alternative sources was ignored.

Chicago, Illinois, November 8 to 11, 1948 (New York: American Petroleum Institute, 1948), 109-144.
26 Eugene Ayres, "International Fuel Economy" *Annals of the American Academy of Political and Social Sciences* 281: The Future of our Natural Resources (May 1952), 73-78; 75.

27 Eugene Ayres, "Windows," *Scientific American* (February 1951), 60-65.
28 Ayres, "Major Sources," 144.
29 For other prominent advocates in this regard see Palmer Putnam, *Energy in the Future* (New York: Van Nostrand, 1953), based on a 1949 report to the Atomic

Energy Commission, and M. King Hubbert, "Energy from Fossil Fuels," *Science* 109 (February 1949).
30 Ayres, "Major Sources," 110. See Julius Krug, "Introduction," in *Proceedings of the United Nations Scientific Conference on Conservation and Utilization of Resources: Volume I,*

Plenary Sessions (New York: United Nations Department of Economic Affairs, 1951), 7; and "New Developments in the Production and Utilization of Energy" in *Proceedings of the United Nations Scientific Conference on Conservation and Utilization of Resources: Volume III, Fuel and Energy Resources* (New York: United

In the face of Eisenhower's rejection, and as an effort to maintain the thread of resource scarcity in the context of managing growth for the next few decades, a non-profit group developed directly out of the Policy Commission. Called Resources for the Future, the group absorbed the staff of the Policy Commission and lobbied for its policy imperatives.[32] Barnett came to play a significant role in the organization.[33] To a significant extent Resources for the Future is a prominent and early trace of the emergence of 'sustainability' as an environmental-managerial approach to economic growth, as later instigated by the popularity of Carson's text. In this regard it contrasts the alternative futures proposed by Ayres and his colleagues that informed the architectural discussions detailed below.

Experimental Dwellings

Modern architecture was also transformed by the war; in American architectural discourse this played out in large part through a discussion of the modern house and in terms of 'softening' the perceived technological determinism of the pre-war period. Joseph Hudnut, whose 1945 text "The Post-Modern House" rejected "those factory-built houses, pure products of technological research and manufacture, which are promised us," was concerned over both the "uniformity" the machine-made house presupposed and "the *promise of happiness*" it appeared to neglect.[34] His article proposed to rescue the formal innovations of modernism from the "enchantment of techniques" and return it to the realms of "shelter" and "space":

> The mighty cantilever which projects my house over the kitchen yard or a waterfall; that flexible wall and stressed skin; these fanaticisms of glass brick; these strange hoverings of my house over the firm earth – these strike my eyes but not my heart … If we wish to express in this new architecture the idea of home, if we wish to say in this persuasive language that this idea accompanies, persistent and eloquent, the forward march of industry and the changing nature of society, we have in the different aspects of space alone a wide vocabulary for that purpose.

Hudnut articulated the principles of this promising spatial vocabulary in the precise formal and technological terms of the solar house that will concern us below, proposing that "our new

Nations Department of Economic Affairs, 1951), 262-330.

31 See "President's Materials Policy Commission," *Resources for Freedom: Summary of Volume I of a Report to the President* (Washington, D.C.: U.S. Government Printing Office, 1952), 2-4. See also Palmer

Putnam, "The Promise of Technology: The Possibilities of Solar Energy" in *Resources For Freedom: A Report to the President; Volume IV: The Promise of Technology* (Washington, D.C. US Government Printing Office, 1952), 213-220.

32 See Charles J. Hitch, ed., *Resources for the Future: The*

First 25 Years (Washington, D.C.: Resources for the Future, 1977).

33 Harold J. Barnett and Chandler Morse, *Scarcity and Growth: An Economics of Natural Resource Availability* (Baltimore: Johns Hopkins University Press and Resources for the Future, 1963) as well as it's more

data-focused companion volumes: Hans L. Landberg, Leonard L. Fischman, and Joseph L. Fisher, *Resources in America's Future: Patterns of Requirements and Availabilities 1960-2000* (Baltimore: Johns Hopkins University Press and Resources for the Future, 1963).

structure and our new freedom in planning—a freedom made possible at least in part by the flat roof—has set us free to model space, to define it, to direct its flow and relationships."[35]

In the same vein, a symposium at the Museum of Modern Art in New York entitled "What is Happening to Modern Architecture" was held in February of 1948. Occurring at the height, as it happens, of the first oil crisis—though its effects are not directly evident in the proceedings—the symposium met to discuss a November 1947 *New Yorker* article by Lewis Mumford. Mumford's article applauded recent work in California as a "native and humane form of modernism ... a free yet unobtrusive expression of the terrain, [and] the climate."[36] Flexibility of the roofline, careful volumetric organization, and a regionalist corrective to the 'international style' summarize the potent formal tropes of this second, softened modernism. Though Mumford was apparently unaware of research into solar housing, the elements he proposed both indicated the inherent modernity of the solar house and identify its potential role in developing a formal language for alternative dispositions of the industrial and social changes that Hudnut and others had also anticipated.

Furthermore, to an extent under-emphasized in the historical literature of this period, the debates around this second modernism were played out at the Department of Architecture at the Massachusetts Institute of Technology. Many figures at the School of Architecture and Planning at the time were central to the discussion outlined above.[37] The techno-social milieu at MIT provides evidence of the extent to which many issues which appeared contentious in published diatribes were integrated in pedagogy and practice; the modern house, in other words, was both a technological experiment *and* a spatially eloquent dwelling.

Thus when the Solar Energy Fund returned to work after a wartime hiatus, it engaged both the changing character of architectural research and an increasing concern over resource depletion. In early August of 1945, just as the war was ending, the Solar Energy Committee submitted a formal request to the president of the Institute to expand the Solar Energy Fund. The main new component was a Steering Committee for an Experimental Dwelling Project, chaired by Professor of Architecture Lawrence Anderson.[38] With the introduction of this committee, the design of the house became a central focus in technological experimentation

34 Joseph Hudnut, "The Post-Modern House," in *Architecture and the Spirit of Man* (Cambridge, MA: Harvard University Press, 1949), 107-112; 108. The italics are in the original. The essay was first published in *Architectural Record* 97 (May 1945), 70-75.

35 Hudnut, "The Post-Modern House," 110-112. Here we read 'flat roof' as flexible roof-line, in relationship to a freedom of volumetric disposition as cubic volume of interior space for heating.

36 "What is Happening to Modern Architecture?" *Museum of Modern Art*

Bulletin 15, no. 3, (Spring 1948), 4.

37 William Wurster—Mumford's model for the Bay Region Style—was Dean of MIT's School of Architecture and Planning from 1944-1950. Mumford, Hudnut, and Henry-Russell Hitchcock, who were all involved in these debates, were frequent visitors, as was

R. Buckminster Fuller. See *President's Report 1946*, MIT Institute Archives, 38; see the *President's Report 1945-1953*, Institute Archives for an indication of this experimental milieu; see also Burnham Kelly, *The Prefabrication of Houses: A Study by the Albert Farwell Bemis Foundation of the Prefabrication Industry of*

towards solar heating efficiency.[39] At the same time, the Solar Energy Fund's engagement with the Department of Architecture was also an engagement with the social and political anxieties of the first energy crisis, as Hottel noted in 1950:

> In bringing together representatives of the architectural and engineering professions to discuss solar housing, one has the difficult problem of measuring merit in two sets of units: the dollar suffices so long as the subjects is solar heating, but if the subject is solar housing there are included such considerations as cleanliness, health, freedom from concern over oil shortages or coal strikes, and aesthetic satisfaction. It is because of these dollar-imponderables that the problem is so much more an architectural than an engineering one.[40]

The inclusion of architecture represented, for the engineers already involved with the problem, an engagement with the cultural transformations embedded in the urgent need for new forms of energy.

This enthusiasm for architectural involvement, however, was overwhelmed by a need to refine the system of heat storage, as its expense threatened to handicap the economic viability of solar heating research. In March of 1946, a simple rectangle structure was built and dubbed the *Experimental Dwelling*. The south wall was the primary experimental site: completely glazed, its six panel modules faced interior "cubicles" with "a refrigerator-type door and heavy insulation separating them" so that each was thermally isolated.[41] The experimental issue was the relative effectiveness of using chemical compounds instead of water as a heat storage device, and each module contained a variation on a hybrid mechanism to collect and store radiant heat.[42] After eighteen months, it was determined both that chemical storage was no more efficient than water, and further that the construction and maintenance issues of the hybrid panel outweighed any potential heat savings.[43] A press release sent to the MIT News Service in December of 1946, even before the second heating season of experimentation, was already apologetic, indicating that "the launching of this project does not constitute MIT's endorsement of this idea."[44] The first post-war experiment failed, and delayed the more extensive architectural involvement

the United States (Cambridge, MA: MIT Press, 1951).

38 See Memoranda between Hottel, acting President James R. Killian, Wurster, and Anderson, August 8-21, box 43, folder 17, M.I.T. Office of the President Records, Solar Energy Fund (AC 4), Institute Archives. Anderson was a graduate of M.I.T. and had

been teaching there since 1933; he was appointed to the position by Dean Wurster. He would go on to become head of the Department of Architecture in 1947, and to be Dean of the School of Architecture and Planning from 1965-1973.

39 Hottel, "Memo to Steering Committee on

Experimental Dwelling Project," November 19, 1945, box 20, Hottel Papers.

40 Hoyt C. Hottel, "Introduction" in Hamilton, *Space Heating with Solar Energy*, 2-5; 2.

41 Hottel in Bohning, "Hoyt C. Hottel: Transcript of Interviews," 61.

42 This involved testing of the heat gain and storage capacity of Glauber's salts; at 90°F these salts melt and the 'heat of fusion' is absorbed and stored in liquid form. When the temperature drops, the compound re-crystallizes and the heat is released.

43 See Maria Telkes, "Solar House Heating – A Problem

Building with collector/ storage panels; interior view of monitoring equipment. MIT Solar Energy Fund, *The Experimental Dwelling Project*, Cambridge, MA, 1939. From *Popular Science*, May 1949.

that was anticipated.[45] However, as will be seen below, this failed experiment held important consequences for the development of solar energy technology and the environmentalist impulses that surrounded it.

In the fall term of 1947 a fourth-year undergraduate design studio led by Anderson included a month-long competition on solar house design. In the studio brief, following a summary of the previous experiments, Anderson wrote, "It is believed that enough is now known to make desirable the construction of a small house." Anderson indicated that knowledge thus far gained had determined that the surface area of the collector and the square footage of the house needed to have a ratio approaching 1:1, and that "the architectural problem is that of reconciling the form of this collection and storage equipment to the usual and familiar requirements of a small dwelling without sacrifice to either."[46] Hottel's notes from the competition jury indicate good results. Though he dismissed a handful of entries as "unattractive," "poorly thought," or "hideous," a much larger number are celebrated as "original," "inspired," and "impressive." The winning entry, by John F. Haws, was described as "outstanding for the *number* of original ideas it contains."[47]

Despite these promising results, it was decided in July of 1948 that a renovation of the failed experimental building would be more expedient. The building was re-designed by Haws in order to provide "comfortable modern living facilities for a family of three," with an open living, dining and kitchen area, a small bathroom with a shower, a child's room, and a master bedroom.[48] The windows on the south wall were all triple-glazed to retain passive solar radiation. There was a precisely calculated southern overhang to the roof which was supplemented by shade trees and vines strategically

of Heat Storage" in *Heating and Ventilating* 44 (May 1947), 68-75.

44 Press Release, "Solar Energy Building," December 5, 1946, box 27 Hottel Papers. See also "Solar Energy Committee Meeting 22 September, 1947," box 27, Hottel Papers.

45 Letter, Hottel to Anderson, July 3, 1947, box 27,Hottel Papers. Hottel would later reject out of hand any system that proposed collection and storage in one unit as inefficient, receiving with some surprise information on Felix Trombe's experiments later in the 1950s. Hottel in Bohning, "Hoyt C. Hottel: Transcript of Interview," 73ff.

46 L.B. Anderson, "Grade IV Arch Design Fall Term 1947, Problem #3: A Solar House," box 58, Hottel Papers.

47 Handwritten note headed as "Comments of HCH on Architecture Department Contest on Solar House, Design, 1947," box 58, Hottel Papers. Emphasis in the original.

placed on the property to increase shading in the early fall and minimize it in the early spring.[49] A 1949 press release announced the house as "in appearance a typical modern-style residence except for its heat collector in the roof."[50]

MIT Solar Energy Fund, The MIT Solar House, 1948. Hottel papers.

The angle of this collector, of course, followed Hottel's precise tilt-angle calculations. On the template of the Building 34 system, water was circulated in copper tubes which ran behind blackened copper collector plates, themselves faced with two layers of glass. The panel was backed by aluminum and four inches of wool insulation. The copper tubes carried the heated water into a 1200 gallon heavily insulated water tank within the A-frame structure; a pump then circulated water from the tank through the heat collector "whenever the temperature of the latter is more than 5°F greater than that of the water in the storage tank." The stored heated water was then pumped through copper tubes embedded in the ceiling, providing radiant heat to the space below; the pump responded to thermostat controls in the living room and was automatically triggered when the interior temperature dropped below 72°. There was an electrical heater in the water tank to supplement

48 Brochure written by Anderson entitled "Solar House Heating: Part II: The M.I.T. Solar House," December, 1952, box 58, Hottel Papers, 3. Haws was the attributed architect of the house in all of the press releases.

49 Anderson, "Solar House Heating: Part II: The M.I.T. Solar House," 3.
50 Press Release, "The sun is substituting for a furnace in New England's newest home," February 13, 1949, box 43, folder 17, M.I.T. Office of the President Records, Solar Energy Fund (AC 4), Institute Archives.

The MIT Solar House. From *The Saturday Evening Post*, 1949.

the solar heating of the water when necessary, and if the interior temperature dropped below 70° an auxiliary electrical heating system, located above the windows on the south wall, would also be activated. The solar heating system provided for 80-90% of heating requirements; these auxiliary measures supplied the rest.[51] The house was widely regarded as a successful example of alternative energy utilization in both experimental and pragmatic terms. The 1949 press release quotes Hottel as follows: "It is not now presumed that solar heating will be economically feasible in a climate as cold as that of New England, but the results should serve to indicate under what conditions of climate solar heating is competitive with fuel, oil, gas, or coal;" the specifics of this inquiry and the application of its experimental results would be taken up at great length in the years that followed.[52]

The Modern Solar House

Interest in this third experimental building, which came to be known simply as the MIT Solar House, was capitalized upon in a 5-day "Course-Symposium" on "Space Heating with Solar Energy" sponsored by the Cabot Fund in August of 1950. Attended by architects, politicians, scientists, journalists and others, the symposium expanded interest in solar house experimentation and drew direct connections between the spatial possibilities of modern architecture, the technological discourse on space heating, and the anxiety over resource scarcity. It thus provides early historical evidence of a multivalent cultural, technological and political form of environmentalist research. Much as the MIT collector panel in 1938 established the technological foundation for later experimentation, the 1950 Course-Symposium provided a framework for the multiply-implicated discourse on solar architecture and served as an important reference point for its proliferation over the course of the rest of the decade.

Eugene Ayres began the proceedings with a discussion of "The Importance of Solar Energy" that drew from his "Major Sources of Energy" paper of 1948. He presented data outlining the increasing disconnect between energy demand and availability and proposed that existing fossil fuel sources would last only another 50 years. This, then, was the time frame for refining solar technology:

> Fifty years may seem like a long time … but history has shown that it has often taken that long to commercialize large scale projects, and during this 50 years there will be a continuous evolution of technology … Those who labor towards this most important end must not be discouraged by the flood of oil coming out of the ground, as this is also a transitory problem.[53]

Reiterating his 1948 proposals described above, he outlined the problems of wide application of solar technology on both technological and political terms, and proposed an urgent need to dedicate economic and land resources to large-scale experimentation. Reports on solar house heating experiments took up much of the conference program.

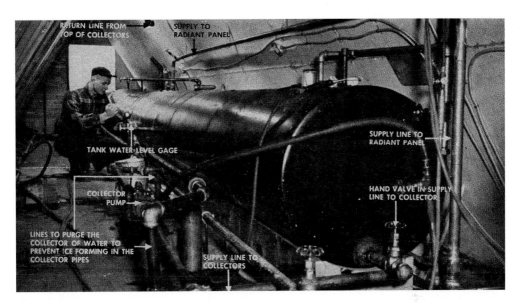

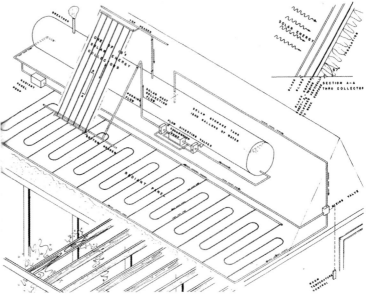

above, photograph of tank MIT Solar Energy Fund, The MIT Solar House, 1948. From *Popular Science*.

Schematic of system, MIT Solar Energy Fund, The MIT Solar House, 1948. From Hamilton, *Space Heating with Solar Energy*.

Lawrence Anderson, "Idealized house..." from "Solar Heating Design Problems" in Farrington Daniels and John Duffie, *Solar Energy Research* (Madison: University of Wisconsin Press, 1955). Reprinted courtesy of The University of Wisconsin Press.

bottom, Lawrence Anderson, Solar House Types. From "Architectural Problems" in Hamilton, *Space Heating with Solar Energy.*

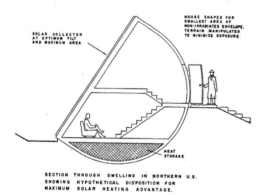

SECTION THROUGH DWELLING IN NORTHERN U.S. SHOWING HYPOTHETICAL DISPOSITION FOR MAXIMUM SOLAR HEATING ADVANTAGE.

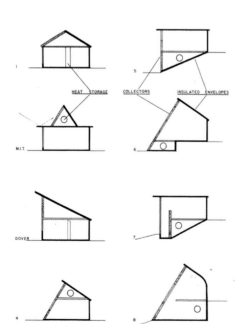

Figure 2. Solar House Types.

Hottel presented three papers: the first outlined the basic parameters of panel operations developed in Building 34, the second discussed the MIT Solar House in detail, and the third apprised the audience of previously published research on the issue of tilt-angle. Other houses were also discussed. Maria Telkes and the architect Eleanor Raymond both made presentations on the Dover Sun House, built in 1948 outside Boston, which used the chemical storage process of the second MIT House. It was dismissed as "over-engineered" by Hottel and was subject to much interrogation by the audience.[54] George Löf, an engineer involved in solar energy research at the University of Colorado, presented his "overlapped-plate collector," a proposal for increasing the solar absorption of the panel by using panes of glass painted black on one side and partially overlapping each other.[55] Löf also presented plans and models for a proposed house in Denver designed with the architect Peter Hunter.

While a presentation by George Fred Keck indicated the identification of passive solar design and the modern house, the Course-Symposium was more significantly the site for integrating technological and architectural strategies to optimize solar-engineered possibilities. These principles were developed through Anderson's presentation of typological analysis of the modern architectural characteristics of technologically refined solar houses. In his paper, "Architectural Problems," Anderson identified the relevant factors, including exposure of the south-facing façade, the relationship of collector to storage area, the volumetric characteristics of the enclosed space, the use of thermally absorbent materials, and the flexibility of the roofline to maximize solar collection. He presented a diagram of 'Solar House Types' that progressed from traditional design and low solar efficiency to modern design and maximum efficiency.[56] Anderson later developed these schematics into an "idealized house" that rejected both "convention and practicality of construction" in order to "have maximum collector area with optimum tilt and minimum non-irradiated area."[57] In this later article, Anderson wrote that "every architect should know how to design for the most favorable climatic response of his enclosure so that, other factors being equal, he will minimize summer discomfort, require less fuel during temperature extremes, or extend the zones in which no mechanical equipment is required."[58] Anderson proposed, in other words, that the architectural discourse on the post-war house should be engaged, as a matter of course, in the discourse on energy efficiency; a corollary, reflected throughout the symposium proceedings, suggested that the solar house could take advantage of the broader cultural interest in modern living. Conflating architectural and technological contexts, the Course-Symposium made it clear that the design parameters of solar heating required modernist architectural developments to maximize both solar absorption (through a flexible roof angle) and space heating efficiency (through carefully designed volumetric arrangements) in order to articulate a cultural object of solar-activated space.

Indeed, as George Löf wrote in the "General Significance and Summary of the Course-Symposium" that closed the published proceedings, the symposium's success lay in its definitive determination "that the flat-plate solar collector, in some form, is the most promising device for space heating with solar energy." The symposium also made clear, Löf proposed, that the promise of the collector was "closely associated with an architectural problem."[59] A brief though vibrant proliferation of the modern solar house was thereby instigated: the 1950s saw numerous federal, university, and privately funded programs as well as individual experiments. Most prominent was a competition for a solar-designed house in 1957-58 called "Living with the Sun," sponsored by the Association for Applied Solar Energy (AFASE), an offshoot of Resources for the Future that was founded in 1954. The published entries from the competition are both an important catalogue of solar design and a compendium of the domestic vocabulary of a second modernism.[60]

51 Anderson, "Solar House Heating: Part II: The M.I.T. Solar House," 3-4.

52 Press Release, "The sun is substituting," 1.

53 Eugene Ayres, "The Importance of Solar Energy," in *Space Heating with Solar Energy*, ed. Hamilton, 13.

54 Maria Telkes, "Performance of the Solar

Heated House at Dover," in *Space Heating with Solar Energy*, ed. Hamilton, 95.

55 George Löf, "Performance of Solar Energy Collectors of Overlapped-Plate Type," in *Space Heating with Solar Energy*, ed. Hamilton, 72-87; discussion on page 86.

56 Lawrence B. Anderson, "Architectural Problems," in

Space Heating with Solar Energy, ed. Hamilton, 108-116, and Anderson, "Variables Affecting Solar Incidence," in the same volume, 17-24.

57 Lawrence B. Anderson, Hoyt C. Hottel and Austin Whillier, "Solar Heating Design Problems," , *Solar Energy Research*, eds. Farrington Daniels and

John Duffie (Madison, WI: University of Wisconsin Press, 1955), 47-56; 49.

58 Anderson, et. al., "Solar Heating Design Problems," 48.

59 George Löf, "General Significance and Summary of Course-Symposium," in *Space Heating with Solar Energy*, ed. Hamilton, 153. Note that the proceedings were not

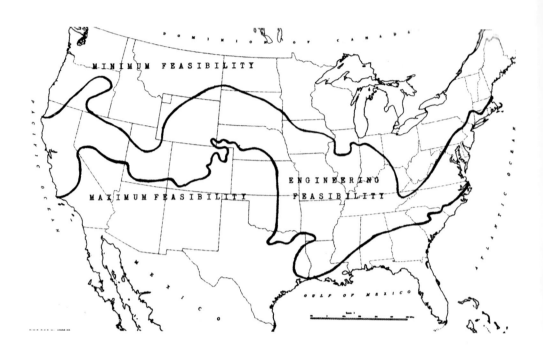

Paul Siple, "Feasibility of Solar Heating Systems" in Hamilton, *Space Heating with Solar Energy,* (1954 [1950]). [Developed from graphics presented in *House Beautiful,* August, 1949.]

All the same, the large-scale viability of solar energy relied on shifts in the economic and political costs of fossil fuel exploitation. Right after Ayres' opening presentation at the 1950 Course-Symposium, Paul Siple, a geographer for the U.S. Army, presented a map of the U.S. which was divided into three uneven regions of "Maximum Feasibility", "Engineering Feasibility", and "Minimum Feasibility" for solar heating applications.[61] Siple's map was the subject of heated discussion. Löf first interrogated the speaker as to whether he had included fluctuating costs and regional availability of heating fuels in determining his contours. Siple replied that he had not. Hottel then asked for a more precise indication of how the distinctions had been drawn, to which Siple is reported to have indicated "that he had no exact formula but had combined the

published until 1954.

60 See John I. Yellott, ed., *Living With the Sun: Sixty Plans Selected from the Entries in the 1957 International Architecture Competition to Design a Solar-heated Residence* (Phoenix, AZ: Association for Applied Solar Energy, 1958).

61 Paul Siple, "Climatic Considerations of Solar Energy for Space Heating," in *Space Heating with Solar Energy,* ed. Hamilton, 14-16. Much of the data he developed was based on the "Climate Control" studies of *House Beautiful* in the late 40s; see Adam Rome, *The Bulldozer in the Countryside*

(New York: Cambridge University Press, 2001).

62 Paul Siple, "Climatic Considerations," 16.

63 Farrington Daniels, "Introduction" in *Proceedings of the World Symposium on Applied Solar Energy* (Menlo Park, CA: Stanford Research Institute, 1956), 11.

numerous data in an arbitrary manner based on average conditions" and conceded that "the curves could perhaps be considered as 'mechanical feasibility' curves as economic considerations were not included."[62] The animation of this discussion reflects the tension around being discouraged, as Ayres had put it, "by the flood of oil coming out of the ground." Solar house advocates–as proto-environmentalists–insisted on the increasing economic costs and long-term political risks of investment in fossil fuel infrastructure. However, in the face of a rapidly growing consumer culture dependent on this infrastructure and the expansion of military and bureaucratic apparatus intent on securing foreign oil, Anderson, Hottel, Löf and their colleagues were unable to turn back the flood of oil, or even to construct any bulwarks against it.

Modernization and Environmentalization

The ambivalent success of solar house heating was overcome by another site for the proliferation of solar energy technology in the 50s. Alongside – rather than despite of or in resistance to – the flow of oil, the use of chemical compounds as heat storage devices was developed as part of global industrial development regimes, with great consequences for the construction of systems of environmental management. The solar process that had been tested and that had failed in the second MIT Solar House, the so-called Experimental Dwelling, was revisited in the early 1950s as energy concerns migrated from the American suburbs to the industrial development of the emerging third world. Here, solar energy was seen as a promising "complementary resource" which could lead to devices for improving living conditions in these under-industrialized countries. This also conveniently made the fossil fuels and other resources of these countries available to the industrialized north.[63]

Maria Telkes, the MIT researcher who had spearheaded the use of chemical storage technology in the *Experimental Dwelling*, was the main figure in this research. Telkes had been hired into the Solar Energy Fund at its initiation on the basis of her work with thermocouples and their potential contributions towards the direct conversion of solar energy to electricity. During the war, Telkes and Hottel collaborated on solar desalinization units for downed pilots under the Office of Scientific Research and Development (OSRD). She was the driving force behind the Glauber's salt experiments at the Experimental Dwelling described above. She also had become good friends with Cabot and, blaming the failure of phase-change technology on Hottel, attempted to wrest the Fund's management from him in 1949. Instead, Cabot helped her secure funding for the *Dover Sun House*. Though it only worked for four years, the Dover house was initially seen as a "historic portent" of technologies to come. In 1953 Telkes left MIT for NYU, creating the "Solar Energy Research Center" in its College of Engineering and maintaining an important presence in the solar energy discussion for the following decades.

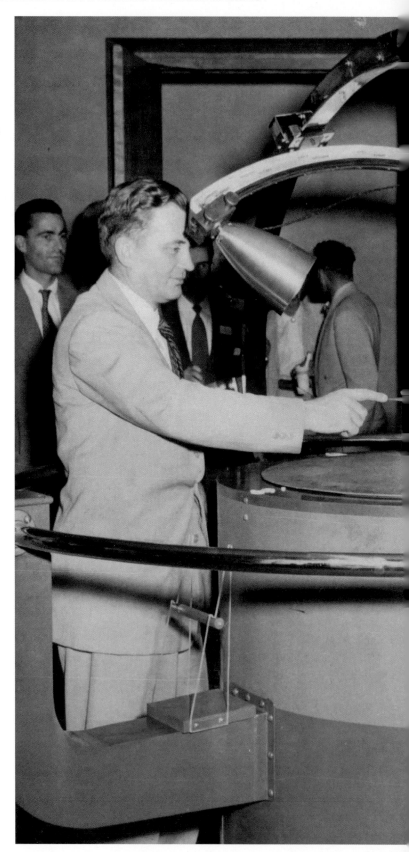

The Solarometer being discussed at the *MIT Symposium on Space Heating with Solar Energy*. *left to right*, Professor Lawrence B. Anderson, symposium chairman; Dr. Maria Telkes, owner of the solar house in Dover; Dr. W.J. Arner of Libby-Owens-Ford Glass Co,; and George Fred Keck, Chicago Architect. August 1950. Photo: Maynard White.

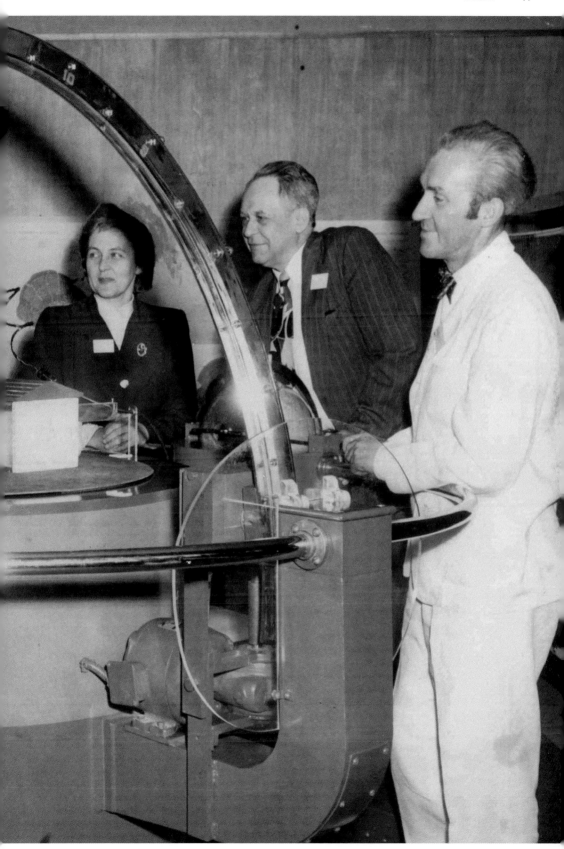

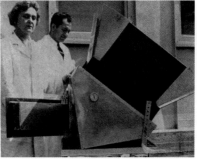

Indeed, though the Experimental Dwelling, the Dover Sun House, and the later Princeton Sun House were plagued with operational problems, Telkes was able to use these experiments to advance a discourse around the possibility of solar energy as a viable energy source. Through promotion of the phase-change process at UNSCCUR and Resources for the Future meetings (when the Dover house was still operational), Telkes became a prominent solar energy consultant who worked on an array of development projects organized through NYU, private foundations, and the United Nations "Technical Assistance" programs. The "invention of technical assistance" was part of the postwar reconfiguration of global co-operation initiated in the first General Assembly of the United Nations, which clarified the organization's "non-political functions" in terms of the "interrelatedness of social, cultural, political, and technical-economic change."[64] A resource focus to technical training became a major element of the global managerial regimes organized around the UN. This was especially the case after the implementation of the "Expanded Program of Technical Assistance" (EPTA), which reached out beyond the war-torn conditions in Europe and Japan and into Africa, the Middle East, South America, and the Indian subcontinent, in 1951.[65]

Maria Telkes demonstrating phase-change solar ovens for export, New York University's Solar Energy Laboratory, 1956. From NYU Annual Report from the College of Engineering, (1956).

64 Ruben P. Mendez, "United Nations Development Programme," http://www.yale.edu/unsy/ UNDPhist. htm. Mendez is quoting U.N. resolutions 53(I) and 133(II). 1; see also the discussion of technical assistance in Paul N. Edwards, "Meteorology as Infrastructural Globalism"

in *Osiris* 21 (2006): 229-250; 241-244.
65 Everett E. Hagen, "A Framework for Analyzing Economic and Political Change," in *Development of the Emerging Economies: An Agenda for Research* (Washington, D.C.: The Brookings Institution, 1962), 1-44; 7.

66 A summary of these technological efforts, along with many others, can be found in Farrington Daniels and John Duffie, eds., *Solar Energy Research* (Madison, WI: University of Wisconsin Press, 1954).

67 UNESCO, *Wind and Solar Energy* (New York: United Nations Publications, 1955) and United Nations, *Proceedings of the United Nations Conference on New Sources of Energy: Solar Energy, Wind Power, and Geothermal Energy, Rome 21-31 August, 1961* (New York: United Nations Publications,

Telkes became one of the first environmental experts. Her lab developed solar ovens for smoke-free cooking, solar distillation units to make sea water drinkable and usable for crops, small solar furnaces, systems for solar irrigation, agricultural frost protection, and the solar heating of oil pipelines to help the oil flow more smoothly. Her lab's research also explored the solar generation of electricity through heat engines and developed numerous methods to increase the efficiency of photosynthesis for the production of algae as a food source.[66] The affinity between the small-scale, low-cost, and relatively low-tech solar energy devices and the processes and goals of technical assistance resulted in a proliferation of ideas around chemical and other solar-storage methods in the 1950s. Telkes' expertise was on display at a number of conferences, including the UNESCO and Ford Foundation sponsored "Wind and Solar Energy" in New Delhi in 1954 and the "United Nations Conference on New Sources of Energy: Solar Energy, Wind Power, and Geothermal Energy" in Rome in 1961.[67]

The globalization of the environmental discourse from this period depended heavily on the conceptual formulation of "technical assistance" by western European and American industrialists and bureaucrats, especially as it became engaged with the complications of industrial development in tropical regions. The importance of developing these regions, especially in the context of "the 'rainforest connection'," as the environmental scientists Peter Taylor and Frederick Buttel call it, "has been central in the scientific and popular construction of global-change knowledge."[68] As they also point out, one of the major goals of the NGO-based environmental-protest and reform regime that emerged in the 1950s was "to influence, and to employ the influence of, the international development and finance assistance establishment, particularly the World Bank/IMF (International Monetary Fund), because of the important role of these institutions in affecting economic activity in the tropics."[69] Solar energy played an important if "complementary" role in the construction of these managerialist impulses.

At the same time, modern architecture played a significant and woefully under-analyzed· role in the articulation of global strategies for economic and social development.[70] The contemporaneous emergence of a discourse around "Tropical Architecture" through a group of architects, scientists, and sociologists in the UK in the early 1950s, applied the

1964). A re-edition of the solar discussion in Rome, introduced by then-prominent solar technologist, Steve Baer, was published as *Solar 2: The U.N. Conference on New Sources of Energy* (Seattle, WA: Cloudburst Press, 1978).

68 Peter Taylor and Fred Buttel, "How Do We Know we have Environmental Problems: Science and the Globalization of the Environmental Discourse." *Geoforum* 23, no.3 (1992), 410.

69 Taylor and Buttel, "How Do We Know," 411.

70 For primary documentation of the interest in tropical dwellings, see Building Research Advisory Board, *Research Conference Report #5: Housing and Building in Hot-Humid and Hot-Dry Climates, November 18 and 19, 1952* (Washington, D.C.: Building Research Advisory Board, Division of Engineering and Industrial Research, National Research Council, National Academy of Sciences, May 1953) and Douglas H. K. Lee, *Physiological Objectives in Hot Weather Housing: An Introduction to the Principles of Hot Weather Housing Design* (Washington, D.C.: Housing and Home Finance Agency, June 1953).

Maxwell Fry and Jane
Drew, Headquarters of
British Petroleum. Lagos,
Nigeria, 1960. From
Victor Olgyay, *Design
with Climate*, (Princeton,
NJ: Princeton University
Press, 1963).

principles of architectural modernism to the climatic challenges
of the global South.[71] The Tropical program produced its own
scientific-managerial context in relation to a global climatic and
resource system. As a result, Tropical Architecture was rather
intensely focused on articulating a highly functional passively-
cooled building, a sort of bare-faced pre-brutalist aesthetic of
technological directness and climatic management here deployed
to facilitate the continued economic growth of the former colonies.
Though based, as one paper presented at the 1953 Tropical
Architecture conference in London put it, on a sun-shaded "Anti-
Solar House," these methods developed in tandem with that of
solar house heating; both methodological innovations proposed
the reconfiguring of the architectural project as a way of resolving
contradictions of energy and economic development. It is here in
the construction of environmental expertise, perhaps, as much as
in the direct impact on solar house heating, that the experiments
discussed above acquire historical significance.

There were more solar houses in the 1950s. A fourth MIT solar
house was designed by Anderson in 1956 and built in 1958; by
this time, the economic logic of the solar house had suffered
considerably in comparison to initial interest following the first oil
crisis. The infrastructure of oil had come to dominate post-war
American suburban expansion.[72] House IV was built according to
one of Anderson's ideal solar types, bermed for increased insulation
and lined with a solar collector across its entire south-facing façade.
The system used three storage tanks of different sizes to manage
the heating load most efficiently and, rejecting the radiant system
of House III, returned to the blown-air system of Building 34. It
worked marvelously, providing heat during the winter and hot water
throughout the year.[73]

71 Maxwell Fry and Jane
Drew, *Village Housing
in the Tropics* (London:
L. Humphries, 1947) and
*Tropical Architecture in the
Humid Zones* (Huntington,
NY: Kreiger, 1956); Hannah
le Roux, "The Networks of
Tropical Architecture" The
Journal of Architecture 8, no.
8 (Autumn 2003): 337-356.

72 By the mid-50s, the
buildings discussed above
were being referred to as
MIT Solar Houses I, II, and III.
House III was consumed by
fire in 1955. Around Christmas
of that year, while the student
family that lived in the house
was out of town, a fire started
in the insulating panels near
the water storage tank in

the 'attic.' The fire department
was called; when they
arrived, they first attacked the
solar collectors from which
the smoke appeared to be
emanating, thereby ending
the experimental life of the
M.I.T. Solar House. As Hottel
was quick to note in his report
on the incident, "Careful
examination of every element

With the evacuation of the political and economic logics of solar heating, House IV expressed, as did the AFASE competition indicated above , a proposal for the cultural logic of solar living. Here again, however, the potential of House IV as a reproducible example of a fuel-efficient suburban lifestyle foundered in the face of the industry mechanics of real estate development. In a 1945 letter to Cabot, Hottel was enthusiastic about the possibility of taking advantage of the expanding post-war market in single-family homes to produce multiple iterations of solar experimentations. He wrote: "we propose actually to build a dwelling house, to use it for a short time as a laboratory, and then to dispose of it on the open market and proceed with designs based on lessons learned in construction of the first dwelling."[74] In an interview in 1984, he reflected on the later project in these terms:

> [at House IV] the contractor had installed a [heating] shaft with a crook in it. That had absolutely nothing to do with the solar system, it was just a defective air heater. But because it was a solar house, anything that went wrong would bring a home-owner response, "I don't know what's wrong with this. This is a solar house. Call Professor Hottel"... We woke up to the fact that any little thing that went wrong would require consulting and correction by a member of the MIT faculty. The idea wouldn't work, there had to be a service organization in existence, and there weren't any for solar houses. After two years of testing, we finally sold solar house number four after ripping out all of its solar parts and refitting it with a conventional heating system. We had to give up on the idea of learning by building solar houses for the public.[75]

In fact they gave up altogether; House IV was the last venture of the Space Heating subcommittee.

In 1963 the Solar Energy Fund was reorganized. No longer under Hottel's direct purview, much of the budget was reallocated to support research in nuclear energy.[76] Also in 1963, Barnett—by this time director of the Resources and Natural Growth Division at Resources for the Future and representative of the organization's decisively conservative turn—published *Scarcity and Growth: The Economic of Natural Resource Availability*, a definitive expansion of his late 40s proposal that sought to transform the approach of environmental

of the solar heating system showed no evidence that the latter could have contributed to the fire, and uncovered no weaknesses which should affect the design of the next house." Hoyt C. Hottel, "Report on A Fire in the 3rd M.I.T. Solar House, 450 Memorial Drive 12/23/55," box 27, Hottel Papers.

73 A pamphlet was produced upon completion of the house, describing its design and heating system. See Lawrence Anderson, et. al., *Solar House IV* (Cambridge, MA: M.I.T. Office of Publications, 1958).
74 Letter, Hottel to Cabot, July, 1945, box 18, Hottel Papers.

75 Bohning, "Hoyt C. Hottel: Transcripts of Interviews," 62.
76 Officially "broadening of the base" of the fund, according a documented discussion between Cabot and Compton right after the atom bombs dropped in August of 1945 that had been ignored until rediscovered after Cabot's death in 1962.

Letter, Compton to Cabot, July 23, 1945, 1-2; Killian to Hottel, September 13, 1945; Letter Killian to Cabot Dec. 23, 1953. Letter, Killian to LW Cabot, February 26, 1963; all in box 43, folder 22, M.I.T. Office of the President Records, Solar Energy Fund (AC 4), Institute Archives.

Lawrence Anderson,
MIT Solar House IV,
1958. From Lawrence
Anderson, MIT House
IV, 1959. MIT Institute
Archives and Special
Collections.

economists towards accommodating the needs of consumer expansion while attempting to
mediate catastrophic damage to the environment and natural resources. Barnett's proposal
was, again, for a sustainable future reliant on accommodations between economy and
ecology, rather than an environmentalist one. The global infrastructure of oil, of course,
was by this time wholly instantiated.[77] Thus does Rachel Carson's 1963 *Silent Spring*
appear to articulate a new consciousness of ecological interconnection at exactly the same
time that the multivalent discourse on solar energy hits a wall, marking the death of an
earlier environmentalism which, with its interdisciplinary attempt to articulate a worldview
in which techno-cultural innovation could respond to changes in the resource condition,
proposed the importance of new dreams in response to new political and material realities.

While the overdetermined decline of solar viability needs to be understood in the context
of the technology and consumption flows that supported the importation of oil and its
use for home heating, it can also be connected, through the architectural engagements of
the Solar Energy Fund and its progeny, to the slow demise of modern architecture. If the
modern solar house is integrated into the history of architecture without much difficulty,
it nonetheless occurs with great consequence; in the current context of the geographic

77 Both Barnett in 1963
and Amory Lovins in 1977
identify 1958 as the year that
the perception of continuous
oil availability took on global
proportions and established
what Lovins would call
the "Hard Energy Path" of
infrastructure intensive fuel
extraction and provision. See
Amory B. Lovins, *Soft Energy*

*Paths: Towards a Durable
Peace* (New York: Harper,
1977). Lovins' major project
was to resist the reliance on
nuclear energy as a way out
of fuel crises. He persists in
this project in his organization
of The Rocky Mountain
Institute, still active today. For
Barnett, in addition to the
texts cited above, see Harold

J. Barnett, "The Changing
Relation of Natural Resources
to National Security,"
Economic Geography 34, no.
3 (July 1958), 189-201.

and epistemic changes wrought by climate change and other environmental catastrophes, narratives such as the one detailed here indicate that the historical forces seen to condition the developments of modern architecture need to be re-conceived. Shifting away from the culturally mediating role of modernism in relation to the potentials and pitfalls of industrialization in both its pre- and post-war manifestations, historical attention should instead focus on the 'environmentalization' of the architectural discourse across the long twentieth century. In the techno-social history of the modern solar house, the cultural logic of solar architecture was the last effort to formulate an argument for new ways of living; architectural form-making was relied on to express a distinctly different disposition towards energy production and consumption. The inadequacy of design and material experimentation is not an opportunity to re-iterate the political vacuity of architectural intentions; rather it is an opportunity to emphasize the cultural, technological and political constellations of architectural engagement as evidence of an environmentalist disposition, one that saw the objective pressures of resources scarcity as an opportunity for new forms of subjectivity.

Anderson and his family cooking hotdogs
on a solar stove, 1959. From Lawrence
Anderson, MIT House IV, 1959. MIT
Institute Archives and Special Collections.

The City

ERIC MUMFORD

From Master-Planning to Self-Build
The MIT-Harvard Joint Center for Urban Studies, 1959-71

Introduction

At the height of the Cold War, modern architects and planners were enlisted by elite universities and foundations in efforts to guide the reshaping of metropolitan areas then underway around the world. The goal was to better realize the then widely shared American idea that economic growth and a corresponding rise in mass living standards could counter the international appeal of Marxism. One such effort involved "urban studies," an area of inquiry intended to create a knowledge base to improve efficiency and esthetics in the decentralizing, automobile-based metropolitan areas then becoming the norm. Such a focus on improving urban environments had been a goal of modern architects since the 1920s, but in this period it was decoupled from its more or less socialist roots in Europe and the Soviet Union and was instead linked to the postwar American "liberal conservative consensus." This consensus was a broadly held set of ideas which saw the American free-enterprise system as having the potential to redress social injustices by creating abundance. Like industrial problems, this consensus also held that social problems could be solved by first properly defining the problem and then having trained experts design programs to address it.[1]

The reorganization of urban life in decentralizing metropolitan areas was identified as one such problem, and the experts in this case were the founders of the MIT-Harvard Joint Center for Urban Studies; this group included, among others, Paul Ylvisaker of the Ford Foundation, Martin Meyerson of the Harvard Graduate School of Design, Lloyd Rodwin of MIT. All three thought the application of expert knowledge intellectually shaped by Chicago School urban sociology could lead to better social and design outcomes in metropolitan areas. Like some other architects and planners of the time, they also began to see American urban

Thanks to Arindam Dutta at MIT, Margaret Garb at Washington University in St. Louis, and Devora Tulcensky for their comments on drafts of this essay, and to Amanda Wegner and Stephanie Tuerk for their research assistance. *Archival Abbreviations* MIT AC 400: Massachusetts Institute Of Technology. School

of Architecture and Planning. Office of the Dean Records, 1934-1993, Archival Collection – AC 400. Institute Archives and Special Collections, MIT, Cambridge, MA MIT AC 113: Massachusetts Institute Of Technology. School of Architecture and Planning. Office of the Dean. Records, 1934-1993, Archival Collection

– AC 113. Institute Archives and Special Collections, MIT, Cambridge, MA HGSD Von Moltke: Wilhelm von Moltke Papers, Special Collections, Frances Loeb Library, Harvard Graduate School of Design

1 Concise sources on the policy background of these complex topics include Kai Bird, *The Chairman: John J. McCloy & the Making of the American Establishment* (New York: Simon and Schuster, 1992), 403-432; and Godfrey Hodgson, *America in Our Time: from World War II to Nixon* (New York: Vintage

problems in parallel with similar urbanization issues worldwide. Thus their efforts involved both post-colonial urban planning projects in the "developing world" and the generation of social and formal ideas about the reorganization of postwar American metropolitan areas. With regards to the latter, they aimed to act in ways that they thought would improve urban "imageability," increase equality, and consequently foster economic growth.[2]

The MIT-Harvard Joint Center for Urban Studies was created in 1959 with funding from the Ford Foundation and initially directed by Meyerson, then a chaired Harvard planning professor. During its first five years, from 1959-64, the Joint Center funded many research studies in urban design, urban planning, and urban history, and at the same time attempted to refine the metropolitan master planning process with an ambitious demonstration project for the new Venezuelan industrial city of Ciudad Guayana. Not long after that effort was underway, however, a combination of worsening social conditions and racial tensions in American cities, along with the growing recognition that it was economically impossible to provide market-based housing for most of the working population of Ciudad Guayana, led to policy debates and new approaches at the Center. This second phase, initiated in 1964 from a more conservative direction by the Center's second director, James Q. Wilson (director 1963-65), coincided with President Lyndon Johnson's Great Society, which began with a debate at the Center about urban renewal. This debate was soon followed by an urban social activist period under the directorships of Wilson's successors, Daniel Patrick Moynihan (1966-69) and Robert C. Wood (1969-71). After the upheavals of this last phase, where what were later seen as the paternalistic top-down social engineering efforts of the Great Society collided with emerging "bottom-up" urban community organizing and protest, the Joint Center scaled back its work to focus on housing policy research. By that point, fears of Communism had receded and a new metropolitan and international situation, skeptical about master-planning in general, had emerged.

Despite this complex trajectory of research and policy, in which what the Center founded in one era was challenged by social change in the era that followed, a definite shift from top-down master planning—as well as a deliberate effort to academically restructure the field of what we now think of as urban history and urban policy studies—can be traced.

Books, 1976), 48-98.

2 According to a confidential Ford Foundation report, countries other than the United States fell into two categories, "industrialized nations, especially Europe or European in culture; and the less developed countries of Asia, Africa, the Mideast, and Latin America." [Ford Foundation], "Report on the Urban (Metropolitan) Program" (n.d., circa 1957), MIT Institute Archives, AC 400 Box 6, Folder: Joint Center 2/4. For a brief account of the basis premises of such physical planning, at least as they were understood at the Joint Center in its early years, see Lloyd Rodwin, "Metropolitan Policy for Developing Areas," in Lloyd Rodwin, ed., The Future Metropolis (New York: George Braziller, 1960), 171-189.

By the mid-1960s the shift in the planners' attitudes toward "user feedback" in both the American urban situation and in the Center's Venezuelan planning efforts is evident. While the aftereffects of this shift seem to have few direct architectural outcomes at the time—beyond its effects on MIT design studio teaching in the 1970s and early '80s—the early history of the Joint Center nonetheless marks an important turning point in modern designers' thinking about urbanism, a point at which ideas about the needs of "users" began to be seen as being in conflict with the ideas of designers.

The Joint Center to 1963

The Joint Center was officially founded by its parent institutions in 1959 and was originally located in a small commercial building in Harvard Square, 66 Church St. Most of its funding came from a large Ford Foundation grant. It had three stated goals: to improve knowledge about cities and regions through fundamental research; to bridge between research and policy at local, national, international levels; and to enrich teaching programs and research opportunities at MIT and Harvard in its areas of study. These rather vague statements, characteristic of much planning and urban design discourse of that time, do not clearly indicate that the Joint Center's efforts were part of the Ford Foundation' s focus on "metropolitan governance" in the 1950s. The Center was the outgrowth of several earlier efforts along similar lines, and its official launching in March 1959 followed efforts to create an MIT Center for Urban and Regional Studies that dated back at least to 1951.[3]

Meyerson, the Joint Center's first director, was then the Frank Backus Williams Professor of City Planning at Harvard, and he directed the Center along with a faculty committee chaired by MIT Professor of Land Economics Lloyd Rodwin. This original thirteen member faculty committee included professors in various disciplines at both institutions, including industrial management, government, law, city planning, economics, sociology, microbiology, physics, and civil engineering. This group answered to an Administrative Committee that included President Nathan Pusey of Harvard, Harvard Dean of the Faculty McGeorge Bundy, and architecture Deans Josep Lluís Sert of the GSD and Pietro Belluschi of MIT.[4]

3 Caroline Shillaber, *Massachusetts Institute of Technology School of Architecture and Planning 1861-1961* (Cambridge, MA: MIT, 1963), 99. A 1957 document marked "P. Belluschi" and outlining the proposed focus of the MIT Center for Urban and Regional Studies is quite similar to those used to state the mission of the Joint Center two years later ("The Physical Environment of City and Region" (September 20, 1957), MIT Institute Archives, AC 400 Box 6, Folder: Joint Center for Urban and Regional Studies 2/2.

4 Joint Center for Urban Studies, *The First Two Years, 1959-1961* (Cambridge, MA, 1961). Bundy, grand-nephew of former Harvard president Abbott Lawrence Lowell, was professor of government when he was appointed Dean in 1953; Nathan Pusey also became President at this time. Bundy was intensively involved in efforts to respond to McCarthy-era charges that the university was a hotbed of Communism, and in 1961 became National Security Adviser to President Kennedy. For more information, see Kai Bird, *The Color of Truth: McGeorge Bundy and William Bundy* (New York: Simon and Schuster, 1998), 117-153.

The Joint Center was a direct successor to the MIT Center for Urban and Regional Studies, created in 1957 under Rodwin's leadership. At that time, newly appointed MIT Dean Belluschi, an Italian-born Portland, Oregon architect,[5] had supported the idea of linking MIT planning faculty research to the Regional Plan Association of New York. Those efforts, which included junior planning faculty members Rodwin and Kevin Lynch, seem to have had few immediate outcomes, however. In 1953 another effort was started to create an MIT "Urban Study Center." Various funding proposals were suggested, including one from the RAND Corporation for a study of "urban structure and functioning" after an atomic attack.[6] In the mid-1940s RAND had pioneered systems analysis, a method of econometric analysis used to choose appropriate weapon systems to meet specific strategic goals, based on "explicit criteria of the public interest."[7] These methods then pervaded various areas of social as well as military intervention in the 1950s. Parallel to the RAND proposal, Paul Lester Wiener, one of the partners of Sert in Town Planning Associates, also submitted a proposal to the proposed MIT Urban Study Center on "decentralization and urban defense."[8] Wiener had indicated to the newly appointed Dean Sert that the GSD might be interested in having Harvard participate in this effort, and a joint MIT-Harvard proposal was drawn up between Paul Lester Wiener (who himself actually had no official affiliation with Harvard) and MIT planning professor Louis B. Wetmore. Again, this did not directly result in the founding of the Joint Center.[9]

In April 1953, Wetmore listed various possible research areas for the new center to an MIT Committee on Urban and Regional Studies; these included György Kepes's and Kevin Lynch's Rockefeller Foundation-funded research on the "Visual Environment of the City," which would eventually result in the publication of Lynch's *The Image of the City* in 1960. Wetmore also listed Rodwin-led studies of urban structure, economic development and urbanization, along with research on planning education, and a study on urban land use and cultural patterns to be directed by MIT planner John Tasker Howard and other faculty, including visiting professor of land economics Charles Abrams, an international housing consultant who had been involved with the formation of the New York City Housing Authority in the 1930s[10] The RAND-funded effort does not seem to have gone ahead, but

5 On Belluschi, see Meredith Clausen, *Pietro Belluschi* (Cambridge, MA: MIT Press, 1994).

6 Alfred N. Watson, "Memorandum to Dean E.P. Brooks" (February 6, 1953), MIT Institute Archives, AC 400, Box 4, Folder: Urban and Regional Studies Section/ General.

7 Alice O'Connor, *Poverty Knowledge; Social Science, Social Policy, and the Poor in Twentieth-Century U.S. History* (Princeton, NJ: Princeton University Press, 2001), 173. Thanks to Margaret Garb for this reference. During the Johnson administration similar systems analysis techniques

would be used for the federal "war on poverty."

8 Louis B. Wetmore, "Letter to Paul Lester Wiener" (February 25, 1953), MIT Institute Archives, AC 400, Box 4, Folder: Center for Urban Studies 1/2.

9 Louis B. Wetmore, "Memorandum to Dean Belluschi, Professor Adams,

and Professor Anderson" (March 17, 1953), MIT Institute Archives, AC 400, Box 2, Folder: Urban and Regional Studies Section/General. In a brief phone conversation with Wetmore and Wiener, Sert indicated interest in Harvard participating in this project, but said that as he had not yet taken office as

in June 1953 Dean Belluschi met with Wallace K. Harrison in New York about possible Rockefeller Foundation funding for an MIT "Center for Urban Studies." Harrison, one of the most active architects in Robert Moses-era New York, indicated that he had a "prejudice against City Planning," and he instead suggested that the center put its emphasis on "environment for human beings."[11] On this basis he was willing to anonymously support MIT's effort to obtain funding from Dean Rusk, then President of the Rockefeller Foundation.

Thus by the time the MIT-Harvard Joint Center actually began work in 1959, most of its activities in both research and development had substantial precedents at both institutions and elsewhere, much of it supported by the Rockefeller and Ford Foundations. Kai Bird has explicated the many interlocking ties between these foundations and the higher levels of business and government in the United States, which extended back to the Second World War and included postwar efforts such as the Marshall Plan, NATO, and the World Bank. Undoubtedly some of the Ford Foundation's many international efforts involved intelligence gathering for the CIA, though some foundations officials objected to this at the time.[12] By the time the Center was officially created in 1959, there were already close links between Abrams, Rodwin, and the Ford Foundation's many domestic and international programs, some of which involved "metropolitan governance." In 1950, Bay Area lawyer and RAND consultant Rowan Gaither had drafted a Ford Foundation "blueprint for action" that set out five program areas, one of which was the Public Affairs Program, whose goal was "strengthening democracy." Gaither became President of the Foundation in 1953, but apparently had difficulties making grants quickly enough; he was replaced in 1955 by Henry Heald, then President of New York University and previously of IIT, where he had hired Mies van der Rohe to design the campus plan in 1939. Despite its deep ties to the higher levels of American business, government, and defense at this time, the Foundation was targeted by McCarthy-ite critics who saw it and institutions like it as hotbeds of Communism. In response, the Foundation began in the mid-1950s to make large grants, mostly to hospitals and universities, in key congressional districts. These coincided with an effort by the Foundation to reform what it termed "metropolitan governance," as well as to respond to a directive from the Foundation trustees to focus on the emerging problem of "juvenile delinquency." Paul Ylvisaker, an aide to reform Mayor Joseph Clark of Philadelphia

Dean, he could not yet make any commitments. He did say that "he saw no reason for delay in formulation of the research proposal." This was to be an interdisciplinary effort involving planning and other faculty from both MIT and Harvard, and would involve a review of the research literature on "urban

structure and functioning"— atomic attack was not directly mentioned—as well as "intensive analysis of new technology'" and the presentation in graphic form of hypotheses about various urban growth processes. Louis B. Wetmore, "Letter to Paul Lester Wiener" (February 25, 1953), MIT Institute

Archives, AC 400, Box 4, Folder: Center for Urban Studies 1/2.
10 Louis B. Wetmore, "Memo to Committee on Urban and Regional Studies" (April 13, 1953), MIT Institute Archives, AC 400, Box 2, Folder: Rockefeller Program R-75.
11 Dean P. Belluschi, "Memo

to Professors F.J. Adams, L.B. Anderson, and L. Wetmore (June 26, 1953) MIT Institute Archives, AC 400, Box 2, Folder: Rockefeller Program R-75.
12 Kai Bird, *The Chairman*, 416-419.
13 Alice O'Connor, "Community Action, Urban Reform, and the Fight Against

who held a doctorate in political economy and government from Harvard, was brought in as the new Foundation Public Affairs director in 1955, and he began to energetically focus on both issues, which he saw as interrelated.[13]

In October 1956, Rodwin Abrams, then the New York State anti-discrimination official under Governor Averill Harriman[14] and a regular MIT visiting professor, and MIT Chair of Planning Frederick J. Adams, had all attended a Ford Foundation conference on Urban Planning and Development in New York.[15] At that event they were joined by Meyerson, then still teaching planning at the University of Pennsylvania while organizing the neighborhood community development group ACTION, another Ford Foundation grantee. The group included some thirty other urban experts, including Catherine Bauer Wurster (a mentor of Rodwin's who taught at Harvard from 1945-50 and who had recommended him to F.J. Adams in the late 1940s[16]) and Robert B. Mitchell, then director of the Penn Institute of Urban Studies. After this meeting, in November 1957 Rodwin and Abrams had met with Ernest Weissmann, head of the United Nations Housing, Building, and Planning section in its Bureau of Social Affairs, to discuss possible links between the newly founded MIT Center for Urban Regional Studies and these UN efforts, which were sponsored by the same American foundations. Weissmann told Rodwin and Abrams that he was working on a parallel project for the Ford Foundation, and mentioned that Ylvisaker felt that "Cambridge was the logical place" for a new Ford Foundation-supported urban center. Weissmann moreover indicated to Rodwin that Ylvisaker and Meyerson were "very close."[17]

The UN efforts that Weissmann had been part of since 1950 were based on the idea that "less developed" countries needed to train specialists and develop a planning infrastructure before advancing toward full industrialization. While teaching at MIT, Abrams had been a member of UN teams in the Gold Coast (which became Ghana in 1957) and Turkey, where, in 1954 he, along with Dean George Holmes Perkins of Penn, was involved in the founding of Middle East Technical University (METU). Soon after that event, Abrams would be a key member of UN housing missions to Pakistan, the Philippines, Bolivia, Jamaica, and Ireland, as well as to Singapore (1963), an effort critically recounted by Rem Koolhaas in *SMLXL*.[18] Simultaneous to these international efforts, the Ford Foundation was also beginning to

Poverty: the Ford Foundation Gray Areas Program," *Journal of Urban History* 22, no. 5 (July 1996), 586-625.

14 Charles Abrams, *Forbidden Neighbors: a Study of Prejudice in Housing* (Port Washington, NY: Kennikat Press, 1955). Abrams was appointed Chairman of the New York State Commission

Against Discrimination in 1955 by Governor Harriman. On his complex career, see A. Scott Henderson, *Housing and the Democratic Idea: the Life and Thought of Charles Abrams* (New York: Columbia University Press, 2000).

15 Ijlal Muzaffar, "The Periphery Within: Modern Architecture and the Making

of the Third World" (PhD dissertation, MIT, 2007), 17-18; 64, fn 62. F.J. Adams had also attended the 1954 UN Seminar on Housing and Community Planning, directed by Jaqueline Tyrwhitt and Ernest Weissmann, a CIAM member originally from Zagreb and an old friend of Sert's. See Jaqueline Tyrwhitt,

"My UN Job in Delhi, 1954" in *Ekistics* 52, no. 314/315 (Sept./Dec. 1965), 489.

16 H. Peter Oberlander and Eva Newbrun, *Houser: the Life and Work of Catherine Bauer* (Vancouver, Canada: University of British Columbia Press, 1999), 232-35. Rodwin, initially a protégé of Charles Abrams, had criticized fund efforts to advance "metropolitan governance" in expanding postwar American cities and their suburbs. Now Ford Foundation Public Affairs director, Ylvisaker felt that this new form of metropolitan government would require planners, and consequently he began to support institutional programs to train them and experts in related fields. The Foundation made such grants to the Regional Plan Association of New York and elsewhere, as well as to universities which would train planners to work at the new metropolitan scale. Recipients included institutions such as Penn, Washington University in St. Louis, and consortiums of state universities in California, Ohio, and Michigan. In a confidential 1957 report, the Ford Foundation noted that "the problem of burgeoning cities is not limited to the United States" and averred that the "problem of exploding growth" in "New York and New Delhi, Los Angeles and Sao Paulo, Boston and New York are basically alike."[19] These funding efforts were based on Ylvisaker's view that each metropolitan area should have a single but highly representative government, led by a strong elected "metromayor" who would represent the full range of urban, suburban, rural, white, non-white, rich, and poor constituencies. These metropolitan governments would plan for "orderly growth" with efforts which would require building community support and which would be geared toward economic development, physical "renewal" of the inner city, metropolitan transit planning, and managed growth. A number of demonstration projects were funded by Foundation under Ylivisaker's direction, including the "citizen's seminar" at Boston College and regional planning and governance efforts in St. Louis City and County, in the Delaware Valley (Philadelphia-Wilmington) region, and in Southern Appalachia. A new program to train community organizers through universities such as Rutgers and the University of Wisconsin and four "self-help" renewal projects in Pittsburgh to be organized by ACTION were also funded by the Foundation at this time.[20]

These efforts took place as most American cities in the 1950s were both massively decentralizing and racially changing in their older inner areas. This decentralization was understood at this time to be an inevitable by-product of economic growth. Using the influential "stages of growth" model of Walt Rostow,[21] an MIT professor of economic history, Kenneth Boulding, the systems theorist whose book 1956 *The Image* provided one of the key organizing concepts for Lynch's *Image of the City*,[22] argued in 1963 that these

Ebenezer Howard's Garden City ideas as simplistic in his first article, written as a graduate student at the University of Wisconsin. This led to a printed debate with Bauer in 1945 that soon included Lewis Mumford. When Rodwin arrived at Harvard soon after as a Littauer Fellow, Bauer

encouraged him to pursue a doctorate in planning at the GSD and then recommended him to F.J. Adams for a full-time appointment to MIT.
17 Rodwin, "Memo to 'the files'" (November 20, 1957) MIT Institute Archives, AC400, Box 6, Folder: Joint Center for Urban and Regional Studies, 2/2. Paul Ylvisaker

was educated as a Protestant minister in Minnesota before studying at Harvard. After a Fulbright in England in 1951-52, he taught at Swarthmore College while working for Mayor Clark. He was at the Ford Foundation from 1955-67, and his papers are in the Harvard University Archives.
18 Rem Koolhaas, "Singapore

Songlines," in *SMLXL* (New York: Monacelli, 1995), 1008-1089. Abrams's own account of these UN missions is *Housing in the Modern World* (London: Faber and Faber, 1964).
19 [Ford Foundation], "Report on the Urban (Metropolitan) Program," (n.d., circa 1957), 3. MIT Institute Archives,

changes were part of a transition period "quite as large and far reaching as the transition from precivilized to civilized society." Boulding saw the centralized city as a relic of a now-superceded phase of civilization, one whose reasons for existence had disappeared with atomic warfare—leaving it, as he put it, a "sitting duck for the H-bomb." Boulding foresaw that the need for face-to-face communication in business would eventually be unnecessary and suggested that Los Angeles was the "first post-civilized urban agglomeration."[23]

In this situation, Ylvisaker and a consultant he brought to the Foundation, the African-American urban housing expert Robert C. Weaver (later appointed the first Secretary of Housing and Urban Development by President Johnson) developed the Ford Foundation's Gray Areas program in 1961.[24] The term was taken from *Anatomy of a Metropolis*, a collection of essays, published jointly in 1959 by the Regional Plan Association of New York and the Harvard Graduate School of Public Administration, which provided detailed data about the postwar suburbanization and industrial decline of the New York area. One of its editors, Raymond Vernon, had suggested the term "gray areas" to describe declining inner-ring urban areas between downtown and the suburbs, an application of the Chicago School of Sociology's urban spatial model first put forward by Robert Park and Ernest Burgess in 1925. Park and Burgess had influentially first proposed abstractly understanding metropolitan areas in terms of concentric zones around the downtown. In their model, the outermost suburbs were seen as the socially and economically most desirable and the older, industrialized "zones of transition" within city boundaries as the least so.

Following Chicago School theory, the Ford Foundation therefore identified these undesirable inner city Gray Areas as the places where new "in-migrants" typically arrived and began their assimilation process to American norms. These were also the areas which were starting to change racially in the 1950s, and like many others, Ylvisaker and Weaver saw the basic problem in these changing urban neighborhoods to be that of assimilating the new in-migrants to mainstream society on the model of earlier European immigrants. In an era before the changes brought by the 1965 Immigration Act, three groups were of particular concern to the Foundation's efforts at this time: "backwoods" African Americans, white "mountain folk," and "Puerto Rican villagers." The goal was to "citify" these groups

AC400, Box 6, Folder: Joint Center, 2/4.

20 Alice O'Connor, "Community Action," 586-625; [Ford Foundation], "Report on the Urban (Metropolitan) Program" (n.d., circa 1957), 2-3. MIT Institute Archives, AC400, Box 6, Folder: Joint Center for Urban and Regional Studies, 2/4.

21 Walt Rostow, *The Stages of Economic Growth: a Non-Communist Manifesto* (Cambridge: Cambridge University Press, 1960). Rostow postulated that all human societies have the potential to pass through five stages of growth: traditional society, a "take-off" period into capitalism, as in the

British Empire in the 18th century; "mature" industrial capitalism, as in the United States around 1900; "the age of mass consumption," which had emerged in the United States by the 1920s and which he saw appearing in Japan and Western Europe around 1960; and "beyond consumption," a final era

where most economic needs are met and "secular spiritual stagnation" becomes a pressing question.

22 Kevin Lynch, "Reconsidering The Image of the City," in, *City Sense and City Design: Writings and Projects of Kevin Lynch*, eds. Tridib Banerjee and Michael Southworth (Cambridge,

and to "telescope" their assimilation by creating alternatives to existing urban power structures through new Foundation-funded community organizing efforts.[25]

The Gray Areas program involved funding community action efforts along these lines in Oakland, Boston, New Haven, Philadelphia, Washington, DC, and (in 1963) several locations in North Carolina, in order to counter the perceived social "disorganization" and lack of "adjustment" of the urban in-migrants to older inner-urban areas. Although racist lending and other practices on the part of the real estate industry and city administrations was a major factor in this lack of "adjustment," the Foundation at this time discouraged a focus on civil rights. The trustees were uncomfortable with an overt focus on issues of race and discrimination in what was then still a highly segregated society. This fact is most clearly evident in the discriminatory lending patterns codified by the Federal Housing Administration in the 1930s and not seriously challenged until the mid-1960s, despite their lack of any legal basis after 1948. Unsurprisingly, given the typically racially discriminatory real estate transactions of the time, the Gray Areas program had few immediate successes—legal aid in New Haven and job training in North Philadelphia were among the few positive outcomes identified—but the Gray Areas program provided the basis for the Kennedy and then Johnson Administration's "war on poverty," launched in 1964.[26]

The Joint Center's work, focused on the physical form and abstractly understood social patterns of the postwar metropolis, and funded for the most part by the Ford Foundation, took place in close parallel with these efforts, though its mission statements and official publications generally lacked any direct reference to the racial conflicts and serious urban conditions that were then beginning to transform American cities. Instead, its original intention was to provide basic research which would explicate various abstractly defined urban and metropolitan conditions and suggest ways in which they could be addressed, presumably by the regional metropolitan governments that the Foundation sought to encourage, though this was rarely stated explicitly.[27] The Joint Center's initial efforts were focused on urban design, urban research, and urban policy , and they ranged from Lynch's work, which was intended to be of use to planners in improving the visual image of urban areas and whose obscure political agenda, Hashim Sarkis has remarked, was "masterfully suppressed," to a range of major academic books in urban history. These included Sam

MA: MIT Press, 1990), 248. Boulding was a University of Michigan economist who founded the Society for General Systems Research in 1956 with Ludwig von Bertalalnffy, who, along with Norbert Wiener, was one of the main proponents of systems theory (Robert Lilienfeld, *The Rise of*

Systems Theory [New York: Wiley, 1978]).

23 Kenneth E. Boulding, "The Death of the City," in *The Historian and the City*, eds. Oscar Handlin and John Burchard (Cambridge, MA: MIT Press and Harvard University Press, 1963), 133-145.

24 Wendell E. Pritchett,

Robert Clifton Weaver and the American City (Chicago: University of Chicago Press, 2008), 197-199.

25 O'Connor, "Community Action," 605-7.

26 O'Connor, *Poverty Knowledge*, 131-135; Pritchett, *Robert Clifton Weaver*, 256-7, 275, 311-318. This "top-down" model of social intervention

overseen by university and foundation experts and based on data collecting and strategic master planning by government was challenged in the 1960s by Chicago activist Saul Alinsky's focus on local political organizing, often involving neighborhood religious organizations in an approach which would

Bass Warner's *Streetcar Suburbs: the Process of Growth in Boston, 1870-1900* (1962), Morton and Lucia White's *The Intellectual versus the City: from Thomas Jefferson to Frank Lloyd Wright* (1962), and John E. Burchard and Oscar Handlin's *The Historian and the City* (the edited proceedings of a Joint Center conference held in August 1961).

In addition to these pioneering works of research in urban history, the Center also issued many studies of contemporary urban land use, politics, law, urban visual communications, housing, and sociology, by figures such as Rodwin, Robert C. Wood, James Q. Wilson, Charles M. Haar, Richard L. Meier, Serge Chermayeff, Bernard J. Frieden, and Nathan Glazer, some of whom are still active today. Studies of zoning, urban rail transit, and downtown department stores were also published.[28] At the same time, various planning and sociological studies were undertaken by Rodwin, Edward C. Banfield, William Alonso, James M. Beshers, and others, most them based on a Chicago School model of understanding metropolitan areas. Sifting through this mass of material and placing it within what now seems to be its many historical and local contexts would be a monumental task, and is probably only possible within various disciplines or at the level of particular cities and neighborhoods. It does seem notable that a Joint Center-funded study listed by Charles Abrams in 1959, "Issues of Race in Northern Cities,"[29] does not seem to have ever been published, although the Center issued many reports on politics in individual American cities at this time.[30]

The Joint Center and Ciudad Guayana, Venezuela, 1961-68

After these first two years of striking academic productivity under Meyerson's leadership, the Joint Center began to branch out into both American urban policy debates and an ambitious master-planning effort for a new industrial city in Venezuela called Ciudad Guayana, founded in 1961. This shift in focus coincided with what seems to have been a disillusionment at the Ford Foundation about the viability of its socially and racially inclusive "metropolitan governance" model, which was linked to a growing acknowledgement of racism as an issue in metropolitan issues, an issue evident in Nathan Glazer and Daniel Patrick Moynihan's *Beyond the Melting Pot: the Negroes, Puerto Ricans, Jews, Italians, and Irish of New York City*, published by the Joint Center in 1963. By the time it was published, the Ford Foundation's efforts to support community action had become the model for

soon overlap with that of the Civil Rights movement. This in many cases caused controversy about the legitimacy of the Ford Foundation's and subsequent federal efforts in this direction. **27** For a concise statement of the activities and outlook of many of the early Joint Center affiliates, see Lloyd Rodwin,

ed., *The Future Metropolis* (New York: Braziller, 1961). Maki later referred to Lynch and Rodwin's "multicentered net" model of the city articulated in this book, which was based on a closed conference at the Tamiment Institute near New York, as predictive of the later "actual pattern of many metropolises"

around the world (Fumihiko Maki, "Reflections on Harvard's 1956 Urban Design Conference," in his *Nurturing Dreams: Collected Essays on Architecture and the City* (Cambridge, MA: MIT Press, 2008), 144. **28** Joint Center for Urban Studies, *The First Five Years*, 1959-1964 (Cambridge,

MA, 1965). Dean Belluschi objected to the Center's support for Chermayeff and Alexander's effort to offer low-rise, high-density housing alternatives to suburbia. **29** Joint Center, "Report of Meeting of the Faculty Committee, Thursday, October 15, 1959," MIT Institute Archives, AC 400, Box 6,

Federal efforts to combat poverty, and the Joint Center then began to attempt to transfer its metropolitan model of urban design and development to a "developing nation." In 1961, Colonel Rafael Alfonzo Ravard, an elite military officer and a supporter of Venezuelan President Rómulo Betancourt, who had been democratically elected in 1959, commissioned the Joint Center, represented by Meyerson and Rodwin, "to act as advisor and consultant" to the Caracas-based Corporación Venezolana de Guayana (CVG) to plan a new city 300 miles southeast of Caracas.[31] The site was located near iron and bauxite mines, hydroelectric dams advocated by Ravard, and large steel mills at the scenic confluence of the Orinoco and Caroni Rivers. In 1950 a subsidiary of US Steel, the Orinoco Mining Company, had begun operations at this location, which was well-situated for ocean shipping. Sert and Wiener had been commissioned by them at that time to design two new small cities in the region, Ciudad Piar and Puerto Ordaz, but neither was built out according to their designs.[32] Instead, Puerto Ordaz and a nearby existing town, San Félix became the nexus of a series of squatter settlements which housed most of the industrial workforce.

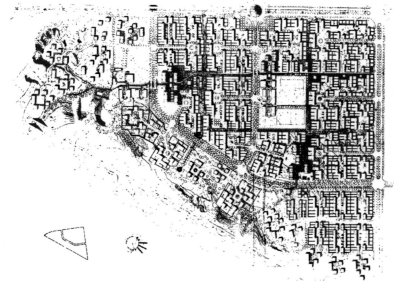

Puerto Ordaz, Site Plan Neighborhood Unit 8. From Donald Appleyard, *Planning the Pluralist City*, (Cambridge: MA, MIT Press), 1976.

Folder: Joint Center for Urban and Regional Studies 1/2.
30 Edward C. Banfield and James Q. Wilson, *City Politics* (New York: Vintage Books, 1963); Edward C. Banfield, *Big City Politics: a Comparative Guide to the Political Systems of Atlanta, Boston, Detroit, El Paso, Los Angeles, Miami, Philadelphia, St. Louis, Seattle*

(New York: Random House, 1965). The Joint Center also issued research reports on politics in many other American cities: see Joint Center for Urban Studies, *The First Five Years, 1959-1964* (Cambridge, MA, 1965), 66-69 for a listing with their authors.
31 "Developing Venezuela," MIT Institute Archives, AC

400, Box 6, Folder: MIT-Harvard Joint Center 1959-63; Lisa Peattie, *Planning: Rethinking Ciudad Guayana* (Ann Arbor: University of Michigan Press, 1987), 9-11. Betancourt had been elected President earlier, in 1945, but his leftist successor was overthrown by a military coup in 1948, and the oil-rich

country was ruled by the military until 1958.
32 Their firm, Town Planning Associates, received the commission in December 1950 from a Venezuelan representative of the Orinoco Mining Company, Francisco Carrillo Batalla, at a time when the country was ruled by an anti-Communist

The new city of Ciudad Guayana was to include these existing settlements and to link them together into a new master-planned industrial metropolis. Significantly, it was not to be another modernist monument like Brasília or Chandigarh, but was instead conceptualized as a kind of planning laboratory in which various approaches to guiding the growth of an industrial metropolitan area based on vehicular transport could be tested. The Joint Center was to advise the CVG "in all phases of the development of both city and region," with the goal being not so much a master plan as a planning process, one that would enable the Venezuelan staff of the CVG to continue the project after the Joint Center had left. On the academic side, misgivings expressed by Sert and others about the Joint Center taking on this project[33] were answered by Meyerson pointing out that the effort "would yield insights and reports of permanent value concerning the processes of urbanization and industrial growth in a developing economy."[34] There is in fact now a large literature, most of it by Joint Center faculty members and affiliates, on the Ciudad Guayana project. Its participants included not only Willo von Moltke, the chief of urban design, who had worked under Edmund N. Bacon in Philadelphia from 1954-61 and was

military junta that had come to power in a military coup in 1948. Various issues almost immediately caused conflicts between the client and the architects, including the proposed separation of the North American managerial workforce in Puerto Ordaz from the local workforce at Ciudad Piar, as well as the

architects' publication of the work in *Architectural Record* 114 (December 1953) without the client's permission. All design work by Sert and Wiener in Venezuela seems to have been concluded by October 1953 (Josep Rovira, *José Luis Sert* [Milan: Electa, 2000], 163-166), and Sert does not seem

Aerial photographs of the site for Ciudad Guayana, Venezuela. From Appleyard, *Planning the Pluralist City*.

top, Matanzas Steel Mill, looking east.

middle, Caroní-Orinoco confluence with Caroní Bridge and falls in the background; Puerto Ordaz on right.

bottom, Caroní Falls.

at the time was a visiting professor in Sert's Harvard Urban Design Program,[35] but also his assistant chief of urban design, William Porter, who had previously worked for Louis Kahn and would later be Dean of Architecture at MIT from 1971-81.[36] They were joined in the design effort for Ciudad Guayana by MIT urban design professor Donald Appleyard, then an associate of Kevin Lynch.

This urban design team worked with the Venezuelan architects, planners, and engineers of the CVG and with various Joint Center experts from different fields, including John Friedman, William Alonso, William Doebele, Lisa Peattie, Hanno Weber, Robert C. Wood, and John Zucotti. Most of the initial work took place at the CVG headquarters in the Shell Building in Caracas, where New York City planner Norman Williams administered the project in its first two years.[37] Much of the Joint Center literature documents the various tensions between the Caracas-based planners and the engineers, businessmen, and inhabitants actually living at the site, as well as the somewhat inconclusive master-planning process itself.[38]

The physical planning for Ciudad Guayana was to be executed in parallel with economic planning for Venezuela as a whole, and the new city was defined as an economic "growth pole" to attract some of the urban population from Caracas and other Venezuelan coastal cities to the sparsely settled and generally unpopular Guayana region. Great emphasis was thus placed on the creation of urbanity and on the urban image of the new city. Von Moltke's scheme, for example, centered on an elaborate commercial and civic center sited between the steel mill and the two existing population centers (on opposite sides of the Caroni River) to be called Alta Vista, yet the major design gesture was to organize the new city in a linear fashion along a large highway, Avenida Guayana. This highway was intended to link the new Alta Vista center and the steel mill to the various scattered existing settlements, many of them built by squatters, into a coherent new city, a design which necessitated the construction of a new highway bridge over the Caroni River. Because of this focus on vehicular circulation in a city where few residents could afford cars, most workers had to continue to commute by bus to the main employer, the mill and nearby new industries, and they and their dependents seldom left their local housing sectors otherwise.[39]

to have subsequently ever claimed credit for anything actually constructed there. Nonetheless, the street pattern of Puerto Ordaz and the location of the civic center, designed by others, appear to conform to the Sert and Wiener plan.

33 At a meeting of the Joint Center Administrative

Committee in 1960, "reservations" about the Guayana project were expressed by "Dean Bundy, Dean Sert, Dean Belluschi, and Dr. [Carl] Floe." A main concern was that the project might be "dropped with the Venezuelans not in a position to go any further." Joint Center, "Report of the Administrative

Committee Meeting: June 17, 1960," MIT Institute Archives, AC 400, Box 6, Folder: Joint Center for Urban and Regional Studies 1/2.

34 "Aided housing in a new industrial city," *Architectural Design* 33 (August 1963), 387; "Developing Venezuela," MIT Institute Archives, AC 400, Box 6, Folder: MIT-Harvard

Joint Center 1959-63.

35 On this part of von Moltke's career, see my *Defining Urban Design: CIAM Architects and the Formation of a Discipline, 1937-69* (New Haven: Yale University Press, 2009), 162-167.

36 Porter was appointed by von Moltke to the CVG Ciudad Guayana staff July

Willo von Moltke,
Ciudad Guayana Master
Plan, 1963. From
*Ciudad Guayana: Plan
de Desarrollo Urbano*
(Caracas: Corporación
Venezolana de Guayana,
1967).

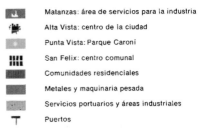

Matanzas: área de servicios para la industria
Alta Vista: centro de la ciudad
Punta Vista: Parque Caroni
San Felix: centro comunal
Comunidades residenciales
Metales y maquinaria pesada
Servicios portuarios y áreas industriales
Puertos

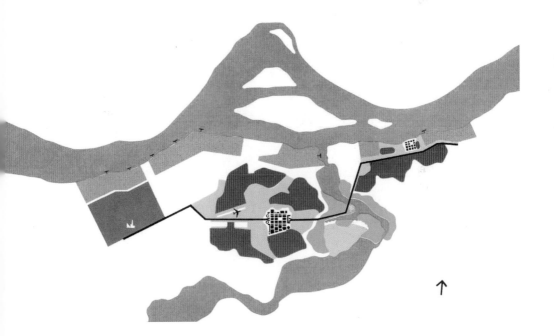

21, 1962 (von Moltke, "Letter to Rodwin" (July 30, 1963), HGSD von Moltke.

37 Martin Meyerson, "Letter to President Nathan M. Pusey" (May 5, 1961), MIT Institute Archives, AC 400, Box 6, Folder: MIT-Harvard Joint Center 2/4. Williams was a Yale-educated planning lawyer who was Chief of

Master Planning for the New York City Planning Department from 1956-60, and who was teaching at MIT in Planning in 1960. He announced his resignation from the Guayana project in January 1963 (Joint Center, "Report of the Administrative Committee Meeting: January 14, 1963," p. 3, MIT Institute

Archives, AC 400, Box 6, Folder: MIT-Harvard Joint Center 1959-63.

38 Lloyd Rodwin and Associates, ed., *Planning Urban Growth and Regional Development: the Experience of the Guayana Program of Venezuela* (Cambridge, MA: MIT Press, 1969); Donald Appleyard, ed., *Planning a*

Pluralist City: Conflicting Realities in Ciudad Guayana (Cambridge, MA: MIT Press, 1976); Lisa Peattie, *Planning. For a more recent account of how the city has developed, see Thomas Angotti, "Ciudad Guayana: from Growth Pole to Metropolis, Central Planning to Participation," *Journal of Planning Education and*

Von Moltke's choice of the Alta Vista site for the civic center was determined by early computer-based studies that showed it was the most convenient location for the majority of the population. In fact, in one of the numerous unanticipated planning outcomes carefully recorded in the Joint Center literature, the existing town of San Félix, on the other side of the Caroni, remained the commercial center of choice for most of the workers. Efforts to shift some of this population west, closer to the new center created by the planners (both Venezuelan and Joint Center participants) were largely unsuccessful, and consequently the western residential areas essentially became well-off suburbs of the company town of Puerto Ordaz, rather than the socially and economically integrated areas envisioned by the planners.[40]

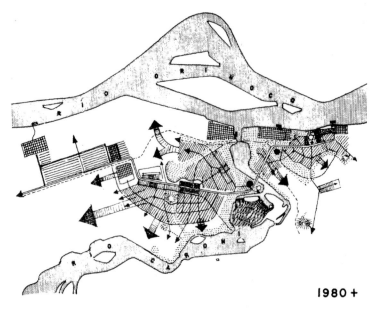

Ciudad Guayana, Outline of planned development, 1964, showing the proposed westward thrust of the city toward the heavy industrial areas. From Appleyard, *Planning a Pluralist City*.

1980 +

Research 20 (2001): 329-338.
39 Willo von Moltke, "The Visual Development of Ciudad Guayana," Connection (June 1965), 53-60; Willo von Moltke, "The Evolution of a Linear From," in *Planning Urban Growth*, ed. Lloyd Rodwin and Associates, 126-146; Peattie, *Planning*, 111-125.

40 Peattie, *Planning*, 73-92.

41 William Porter, "Changing Perspectives on Residential Area Design," in *Planning Urban Growth*, ed. Lloyd Rodwin and Associates, 252-269.

42 Charles Abrams, Report on the Development of Ciudad Guayana in Venezuela (1962), cited in Abrams, *Housing in the Modern World*, 137; "Aided Housing," 388.

Various other problems, extensively discussed in the Joint Center-sponsored research about the project, also soon surfaced. Von Moltke, William Porter, and some Venezuelan architects (who are rarely mentioned by name in the Joint Center publications) designed auto-accessible residential neighborhoods of low-rise, high-density courtyard houses on cul-de-sacs that proved unpopular with both the Venezuelan and North American managerial classes; subdivisions of curving streets with widely spaced attached housing groups were built instead.[41] In the neighborhoods for industrial workers, design efforts in a similar low-rise, high-density direction were also resisted, as was the planners' attempt to mix incomes by situating neighborhood units for different groups in proximity to each other within walking distance of the Alta Vista civic center. Although the city did grow rapidly and now has a population of around 747,000, this ambitious multi-level center never developed as intended. Eventually in the 1970s luxury high-rise housing blocks not in the original master plan were built there, adjacent to vacant parcels now used as parking lots. The result was, ironically, an auto-based city with scattered pockets of luxury high-rises, one more highly class-segregated and less pedestrian-friendly than most pre-existing Latin American cities.

By 1963 it seems to have become obvious to the Joint Center planners that their urban design approach was not working, and Charles Abrams, commissioned by the Center in 1962 as a consultant on the Ciudad Guayana project, proposed that squatter settlement sites be designated in the plan, since "planning makeshift shelter may be the best that can be hoped for at present."[42] Four-fifths of the population of Ciudad Guayana were already living in unplanned squatter settlements at this point, so the decision was perhaps not so much about "planning" as it was a simple acceptance of reality. An effort was made to broadly shape this burgeoning new informal development by using Sert-like pedestrian neighborhood unit planning principles to plan auto-accessed neighborhood units. Yet this approach also did not become the preferred planning method for residential development in the new city.

In short, the Joint Center effort to comprehensively master-plan Ciudad Guayana using the latest economic and sociological information during a period of rapid growth was completely unsuccessful. The growing recognition of this failure, discussed in detail in Lisa

43 Horacio Caminos, "An Urban Community in Santo Tome de Guayana [MIT Architectural Design studio description], November 1964; Caminos, "Study of an Urban Community in Latin America, Fall Term 1965," Caminos, "Community Development and Low Cost Housing in Latin America, Spring Term 1966," (all located in MIT Institute Archives, AC 400, Box 7, Folder 65-66). Much of Caminos's work involved studies of low-cost housing in Peru and Colombia as well as precise physical analyses of the built form of various Boston neighborhoods. See Horacio Caminos, John F.C. Turner, John A. Steffian, *Urban Dwelling Environments* (Cambridge, MA; MIT Press, 1969). The Ciudad Guayana example, El Gallo, that they included (p. 12-15, 215-228) is a negative one, used to illustrate poor site and unit planning by "experts."

44 John F.C. Turner, "Dwelling Resources in Latin America," *Architectural Design* 33 (August 1963). Turner had studied at the Architectural Association in London beginning in 1944 and then worked for BBPR in Milan for a year before receiving his AA diploma in 1954. He lived in Peru

Peattie's 1987 account, *Planning: Rethinking Ciudad Guayana,* caused the designers to begin putting more emphasis on the building practices of the squatters, and this arguably became a major element in the more general rejection of modernist master-planning by the late 1960s. Peattie was an anthropologist who had been part of the Joint Center team, and she was sent there in 1962 with her husband, Roderick Peattie, to study and document the worker's views of the CVG planning process. The Peatties chose to live in a squatter settlement near San Félix, called La Laja, and although Roderick Peattie was killed in a car accident soon after his arrival, Lisa Peattie continued the work. In 1968 she published *The View from the Barrio* about La Laja, its inhabitants, and their views of the strangely inept and slow CVG planning process for the new city.

The new Joint Center focus on squatter settlements as an element of urbanization at Ciudad Guayana seems to have had almost immediate effects on design studio teaching at MIT; there, a visiting architect from Argentina, Horacio Caminos, began to teach studios on the topic, initially using sites in Ciudad Guayana.[43] Caminos's work coincided with English architect John F.C. Turner's calling attention to the importance of squatter housing in Latin American urbanization in an illustrated article he published in *Architectural Design* in 1963.[44] Turner, who had been working in Peru at the invitation of Eduardo Niera Alva since 1957,[45] was invited to the Joint Center as a Research Associate by Appleyard and Rodwin after they read this article.[46] Using the approaches to self-help housing developed by architects working with Fernando Belaunde Terry in Peru in the 1950s, Turner began to polemically position self-built housing in opposition to high-rise modernist housing. He illustrated the latter with examples built in the 1950s under the repressive military dictatorship of Marcos Perez Jimenez in Caracas, designed by Carlos Villanueva. Turner's approach attempted both to legitimize squatter settlements and to improve their design by calling for governmental support to give their residents the freedom to shape their own environments. In 1968, Turner's defense of squatter housing was published in *Architectural Design* alongside a detailed account by his Joint Center associate Rolf Goetze of MIT Architecture students' transformation of their studio spaces in 1967 with self-built mezzanines made of salvaged wood and other found materials.[47]

from 1957-65 and worked for Peruvian government housing agencies on self-build projects before coming to the Joint Center in 1965.

45 Sharif S. Kahatt, "PREVI Lima, 1969: Experimental design strategies competition for mass housing," paper presented at "Urban Transformations/Shifting Identities" Graduate Student Symposium in Architecture and Urbanism, Brown University, Providence, RI, 2007, page 2. Thanks to Sharif Kahatt for this citation.

46 John F. C. Turner, *Housing by People: Towards Autonomy in Building Environments* (New York: Pantheon, 1976), x.

47 John Turner, "The Squatter Settlement: Architecture That Works," and Rolf Goetze, "Squatters at MIT," *Architectural Design* 38 (August 1968), 361-364. The MIT effort was lauded by Donlyn Lyndon (a partner of MLTW), the new MIT chair of architecture in 1967, who included the building of the

mezzanines, originally a student-initiated effort, into the design curriculum.

The Joint Center, the Great Society and after, 1964-71

This new respect for squatter housing and the idea of self-build by at least some of the Joint Center planners and designers began to emerge at the same time as the Center joined the debate about urban renewal in American cities. Although Penn sociologist Herbert Gans seems to have been the first planning expert to question the positive effects of slum clearance in his studies on the effects of Boston's West End's demolition on its former inhabitants,[48] Jane Jacobs remains the figure most associated with the critique of urban renewal that developed after her Rockefeller Foundation funded research was published as *The Death and Life of Great American Cities* in 1961.

At the Joint Center, however, the critical debate was launched not by Jacobs's work but by the Center's publication of Martin Anderson's *The Federal Bulldozer* in 1964. This was a more conservative analysis of the program's failures, one focused on wasteful government expenditure, and it reflected the priorities of the Joint Center's second director, James Q. Wilson, a Harvard professor of government. Meyerson had left Harvard to become Dean of Environmental Design at UC Berkeley in 1963, but he continued to defend urban design-oriented urban renewal in his *Boston: the Job Ahead*, written with Edward C. Banfield and published by the Joint Center in 1965, as did Abrams in his Ford Foundation-funded, Joint Center-published *The City is the Frontier* of the same year.[49] However, the preponderance of American public opinion seemed to be swinging against urban renewal by that point, as figures like James Baldwin began to add their voices to the emerging chorus of disapproval.[50] Wilson's edited Joint Center compilation, *Urban Renewal: the Record and the Controversy* (1966), is still a basic source on the topic, despite the absence of any serious discussion of Civil Rights issues and its omission of any contributions from Jane Jacobs. The book included many divergent views of the issue, including Gans's and those of various Joint Center affiliates such as Abrams, Alonso, Martin Anderson, Bernard Frieden, Chester Hartman, and James Q. Wilson, as well as Robert C. Weaver's defense of the urban renewal program, which he was then implementing as federal urban policy. Roger Montgomery, one of the founders of the Washington University Master of Architecture and Urban Design program along with Fumihiko Maki around this time, also contributed an argument for better design standards in urban renewal, using, among

48 Gans's work on the Boston West End clearance was begun at Penn and first published as Herbert Gans, "The Human Implications of Current Redevelopment and Relocation Planning," *Journal of the American Institute of Planners* 25, no. 1 (February 1959), 15-25.

49 Martin Meyerson and Edward C. Banfield, *Boston: the Job Ahead* (Cambridge, MA: Harvard University Press, 1966); Charles Abrams, *The City is the Frontier* (New York: Harper and Row, 1965).

50 James Baldwin, "Fifth Avenue: Uptown," in *The Price of the Ticket: Collected Nonfiction 1948-1985* (New York: St Martin's, 1985).

others, an obscure low-rise, high-density project by Eberle M. Smith Associates adjacent to Mies and Hilberseimer's Lafayette Square redevelopment in Detroit as a model. Its design paralleled von Moltke's original low-rise, high-density housing neighborhoods at Ciudad Guayana.[51]

This emerging controversy over urban renewal would have been very evident locally to the academics of the Joint Center, since after 1960 the Boston Redevelopment Authority (BRA) under its Development Director, Ed Logue, had put Boston in fourth place in total federal urban renewal funding received, just behind the much larger cities of New York, Chicago, and Philadelphia. Logue was close to both Meyerson and Ford Foundation Public Affairs Director Ylvisaker, and he was instrumental in founding a group called ABCD (Action for Boston Community Development), the Boston recipient of major Ford Foundation Gray Areas funding. This group was launched at the Joint Center in November 1960. Logue and Meyerson saw ABCD as the social research and planning complement to the clearance and rebuilding activities of the BRA. By 1963, however, Logue was already becoming disenchanted with what he saw as ABCD's ineffectiveness in producing community support for his ambitious renewal agenda. In various Boston neighborhoods, including all-white Charlestown in 1963 and almost all-African-American Roxbury not long after, as well as in many other Boston neighborhoods, the BRA began to encounter serious community opposition to its clearance and renewal activities. This occurred just as the Johnson administration was massively increasing federal spending on the "war on poverty," announced by the President in a University of Michigan commencement speech in May of 1964. By 1965, Boston Civil Rights leaders were beginning to criticize the ABCD group as elitist and its Board of Directors as unrepresentative of the community, leading to various efforts to make ABCD—and by extension, the Joint Center itself—more responsive to the rapidly changing political context.[52] This context, of course, also included the escalation of the war in Vietnam, carried out at the urging of then-National Security Adviser McGeorge Bundy.[53]

51 Roger Montgomery, "Improving the Design Process in Urban Renewal," in *Urban Renewal: the Record and the Controversy*, ed. James Q. Wilson (Cambridge, MA: MIT Press, 1966), 454-487.

52 Stephan Thernstrom, *Poverty, Planning, and Politics: The Origins of ABCD* (New York: Basic Books, 1969).

53 Bird, *The Color of Truth*, 304-320.

54 Daniel Patrick Moynihan, "Better Cities for Whom?," *1965 Urban Design Conference, Harvard Graduate School of Design* (Cambridge, 1965), 11-19. After receiving multiple degrees at CCNY and Tufts, as well as a Fulbright to attend the London School

of Economics, Moynihan served on the staff of New York Governor Averill Harriman from 1954-58, during the same period that Charles Abrams was Chairman of the New York State Commission Against Discrimination. His "Moynihan Report" to the Johnson Administration (officially titled *The Negro

Family: the Case for National Action*) caused intense controversy when it was released in March 1965.

55 Richard K. Edmonds, "Urban Center Solutions to Imbalance Rejected," *Harvard Crimson* (June 6, 1966), online at www.thecrimson. com. At the urging of the Ford Foundation, the Joint Center

Thus when Daniel Patrick Moynihan, the former Assistant Secretary of Labor under Kennedy and Johnson, was brought in to direct the Joint Center in 1966 after an unsuccessful run at political office in New York City, the social and institutional framework of the Joint Center's planning-related work had changed entirely. Even before his arrival as director, Moynihan had spoken enthusiastically at the Ninth Harvard Urban Design Conference in 1965 of the "Free City" of squatter settlements around the master-planned city of Brasília, telling the elite audience of architects and policy makers that the Johnson administration was planning to solve the problem of urban poverty for good—but not necessarily in the same way as at Brasília.[54] Not long afterwards, however, the Watts area in Los Angeles exploded in racial violence. The Joint Center's Ford Foundation-funded plan to reorganize the Boston public schools to achieve racial balance was rejected by the School Board that year as well,[55] and issues of race and Vietnam characterized urban debates for years afterwards. This was the context in which Moynihan worked to push the Center toward more direct urban activism, and during his time as director the group Urban Planning Aid (UPA) was founded by Joint Center affiliates Chester Hartmann and Lisa Peattie in 1966.[56] UPA helped Roxbury residents negotiate with the BRA, leading Logue to denounce them as academic "tinker toy boys."[57] Yet by 1968, the Joint Center itself was being attacked in the Harvard Commencement issue of the *Harvard Crimson* as "unwilling, unable, and unsuited to do anything about Roxbury,"[58] and Moynihan himself would begin to question the premises of the social planning that had emerged out of the Ford Foundation's Gray Areas program and had developed into the war on poverty.[59]

When Moynihan left the Joint Center to briefly become Urban Affairs Adviser to President Nixon in 1969, his successor was Robert C. Wood, an MIT Professor of Political Science who had been the chair of President Johnson's Task Force on Urban Problems in 1964 and was one of the founders of the Federal Model Cities program and Undersecretary of HUD under Weaver.[60] In 1969 Wood served as both Nixon's first Secretary of HUD and as director of the Joint Center; in the latter responsibility he attempted to continue the Joint Center's broad urban focus in the changing political climate.

under James Q. Wilson's direction had made eight proposals to "solve the racial imbalance problem" in the Boston public schools, all of which were rejected by the Boston School Committee.
56 Urban Planning Aid began with seven members and was active from 1966-82. See Lisa Peattie, "The Dilemma:

Architecture in an Affluent Society," *Architectural Design* 38 (August 1968), 361-364; "Reflections on Advocacy Planning," *Journal of the American Institute of Planning* 34, no. 2 (1968), 80-88; and "Urban Planning Aid" *An-Architektur* 19 (September 2008), 32. The archives of Urban Planning Aid are at the

University of Massachusetts-Boston.
57 Henry Norr, "Joint Center Leans Towards Activism," *Harvard Crimson* (February 25, 1967), online at www. thecrimson.com.
58 Maron E. Bodian, "The Joint Center for Urban Studies," *Harvard Crimson* (June 13, 1968), online at

www.thecrimson.com.
59 Daniel Patrick Moynihan, *Maximum Feasible Misunderstanding; Community Action in the War on Poverty* (New York: The Free Press, 1969). The title is a play on the phrase, "maximum feasible participation" that Sargent Shriver had used

After stepping down at HUD, Wood then directed the Joint Center while simultaneously also serving as Chairman of the Massachusetts Bay Transportation Authority (MBTA) from 1969-71, before leaving both positions to become President of the University of Massachusetts-Boston.

By this point the original vision of combining physical and social planning that had characterized the Joint Center at its inception in 1959 had largely vanished in the Nixon-era reaction against the Great Society and what came to called "the 60s." The Ford Foundation, whose President from 1966-79 was McGeorge Bundy, cut off the Joint Center's funding in 1969, as a result of Bundy's movement of Foundation funding toward direct support of African-American community activities—often with controversial results, as in the Ocean Hill-Brownsville teacher's conflict in Brooklyn in 1968—and the funding of the expansion of the Public Broadcasting System (PBS).[61] After Wood's departure as director in 1971, the Joint Center sought to find a new and less sweeping mission than "urban studies" in general. In that era of retrenchment, protest, and reaction against urban renewal, it is perhaps not surprising that a Joint Center advocate of entrepreneurial urban housing rehabilitation, MIT planning professor Bernard J. Frieden, took over in 1971 as Wood's successor. In his *The Future of Old Neighborhoods* (1964), a Joint Center study based on his MIT planning dissertation, Frieden looked at urban housing in Hartford, New York, and Los Angeles, and offered what he later described as a "more liberal" critique of urban renewal than the one provided by Martin Anderson's *The Federal Bulldozer*. During his term as Center director from 1971-76, Frieden focused the Joint Center more narrowly, though perhaps ultimately more successfully, on research on issues of urban housing policy.[62] This direction would continue until MIT ended its association with the Joint Center in the early 1980s, and it became, as it remains today, the Harvard Joint Center for Housing Studies.

in formulating the war on poverty in the Kennedy administration. Significantly, Moynihan never mentions in this book that he was the director of the Joint Center from 1966-68.

60 Robert C. Wood, *Whatever Possessed the President? Academic Experts and Presidential Policy, 1960-1988* (Amherst: University of Massachusetts Press, 1993),73-88.

61 Bird, *The Color of Truth*, 376-395.

62 "Interview: Bernard J. Frieden, December 19, 1979" *Plan* 1980 (Cambridge, MA; MIT School of Architecture and Planning, 1980), 6-17.

By then the ambitious metropolitan planning and urban renewal agenda that had given the Joint Center its reason for being had long since crashed in the upheavals of the mid-to late-1960s. Top-down urban research and planning acquired a sinister reputation, one often associated with technocratic strategies of the war in Vietnam and one usually perceived as entirely racist by the groups most directly affected by urban renewal. Yet though this episode remains historically blurry even to those in the disciplines most closely related to the Joint Center's work in the 1960s, it now appears to be a pivotal turning point in the evolution of modern architecture and urbanism. In their work with both Ciudad Guayana and American inner cities, architects and planners around 1965 seem to have lost all confidence in their ability to do socially-engaged master-planning of the sort that had formed a central element of the modernist agenda. Self-build, user feedback, and urban housing rehabilitation began to replace modernist urban design, carrying over some of its values but at the same time retreating from efforts to reorganize urban social life for various groups identified as "in need" according to a set of accepted formal typologies. While this result may well have been inevitable given the changing politics of the period, it left a strange void in architects' thinking about urbanism that postmodernist architects would rush to fill in the 1980s, with results that continue to linger today.

Archival Abbreviations

MIT AC 400 Massachusetts Institute Of Technology. School of Architecture and Planning. Office of the Dean Records, 1934-1993, Archival Collection – AC 400. Institute Archives and Special Collections, MIT, Cambridge, MA.

MIT AC 113 Massachusetts Institute Of Technology. School of Architecture and Planning. Office of the Dean. Records, 1934-1993, Archival Collection – AC 113. Institute Archives and Special Collections, MIT, Cambridge, MA.

HGSD Von Moltke Wilhelm von Moltke Papers, Special Collections, Frances Loeb Library, Harvard Graduate School of Design.

M. IJLAL MUZAFFAR

Fuzzy Images

The Problem of Third World Development and the New Ethics of Open-Ended Planning at the MIT-Harvard Joint Center for Urban Studies

Knowledge is not wholly intellectual, not wholly conscious, nor wholly clear.
—Kenneth Boulding, 1955[1]

The city is a palimpsest on which man's story is written. . . It is a composite of trials and defeats, of settlement houses, churches and schoolhouses, of aspirations, images and memories.
—Charles Abrams

. . . These strategies rest on two 'fuzzy' assumptions—the disadvantages of big cities and the feasibility of promoting growth centers—which no one to date has been able to define operationally... . . . [b]ut, this is not the first time (and probably not the last) that decision-makers have to manipulate forces which they do not fully understand.
—Lloyd Rodwin, Nations and Cities, 1970[2]

In 1991, the Department of Urban Studies and Planning at MIT organized a symposium on the work of Albert Hirschman, an economist widely recognized as one of the 'founders' of development economics.[3] This field placed on the economic map by Hirschman gained immense popularity after the Second World War for its promises to make poor countries coming out of decolonization rich. The symposium at MIT, however, wasn't all praise; rather, it opened up a divisive debate over the legacy of Hirschman's work.

On one side stood economists like Paul Krugman, who stressed the necessity of mathematical models for predicting social and economic change. For Krugman, Hirschman's work was insightful but "fuzzy," his methodology seductive but mathematically "lazy."[4] Hirschman might have held tremendous appeal as a founder of development economics, Krugman asserted, but he failed to model his insights and instead stressed "rhetorical" arguments. This shortcoming prevented his work from being communicated to the next generation of economists who were interested in using "sophisticated" mathematical approaches to modeling economic relations.

These comments sparked intense opposition from a wide group of scholars, including those otherwise critical of Hirschman. Hirschman's fuzziness, it was contended, was precisely his biggest asset. Through his rhetorical approach, Hirschman made economics accessible to planning and other disciplines. This gesture in turn introduced social, cultural, and psychological concerns into economics that were otherwise simply neglected or simplified into monolithic entities.

The confrontation was more than a defense of Hirschman's legacy. At stake was the legitimacy of a historical transformation in the role and scope of planning itself from a discipline that provided isolated plans and finite projects to one that stressed the need for open-ended processes, calibrated interventions, and ongoing experiments.

It is significant that the symposium on Hirschman was held at MIT. In 1959, MIT and Harvard had established the Joint Center for Urban Studies, a semi-autonomous think-tank comprising of faculty from both the universities. The center was a major site for planning's disciplinary transformation. Through a wide array of involvements on both national and international fronts, the Joint Center sought to extend planning's influence into domains hitherto considered to lie outside the purview of planners. This involved establishing common ground with psychological, behavioral and visual studies, as well as with the fields of sociology, anthropology, and geography. Many of the defenders of Hirschman's rhetorical approach at the symposium, including planners such as Donald Schön, Lance Taylor, and Lloyd Rodwin, were among the founding faculty of the Joint Center.[5]

This transformation was very much a response to the changing nature of the development discourse. After failing to achieve the projected growth goals of national development in the 1950s, international institutions such as the World Bank and the USAID were increasingly hesitant to endorse development as an objective science based on definite prescriptions that could be implemented through centralized governmental bodies. Development was redefined; no longer presented as a project of national development, measured in terms of increases in the GDP, it was now framed as a modest process of satisfying the mere "basic needs" of target populations through experimental programs. With its emphasis on planning as a strategic and open-ended process, Hirschman's work provided a major theoretical impetus for this shift. Though it did not immediately receive official endorsements, it influenced the views of a wide network of development apparatchiks.

1 Kenneth Boulding, *The Limitation of Mathematics: An Epistemological Critique, A Seminar in the Application of Mathematics to the Social Sciences*, 15 December 1955, University of Michigan, Ann Arbor.

2 Lloyd Rodwin, *Nations and Cities: A Comparison of Strategies of Urban Growth*

(Boston, MA: Houghton Mifflin Company, 1970), pp. 275.

3 The symposium proceedings, combined with other invited papers, were later published in *Rethinking the Development Experience: Essays Provoked by the Work of Albert O. Hirschman*, eds. Lloyd Rodwin and Donald

Schön, eds. (Washington, DC: The Brookings Institute; Cambridge, MA: The Lincoln Institute of Land Policy, 1994).

4 For Krugman, Hirschman's work, however famous, was burdened by "suggestive metaphors, institutional realism, interdisciplinary reasoning and a relaxed attitude toward internal

consistency," characteristics which made him irrelevant in the new intellectual climate. Ibid., p. 11.

5 Lloyd Rodwin was the first Chair of the Faculty Committee of the Joint Center, while Martin Meyerson was the center's first Director.

However, Hirschman was not the only strong voice in this arena. Equally influential was Kenneth Boulding, the American philosopher, economist, and systems theorist famous for outlining the moral and ecological dimensions of economic growth. The Joint Center's first director Martin Meyerson, and its chair Lloyd Rodwin, repeatedly drew on both Hirschman's and Boulding's arguments as they sought to define the extended nature of planning intervention.

For planning, these extensions did indeed comprise a dangerous enterprise. In claiming new grounds in the changing development discourse, planning risked loosing its traditional double-footed foundation in the university and development institutions. However, this risk paid off with high dividends. In 1959, this inter-disciplinary posturing allowed the Joint Center to secure an extensive five-year long Venezuelan planning commission to design a new industrial city, Ciudad Guayana, whose name was derived from the loosely defined "resources-rich" and distant locale of its site. Though the project produced uncertain results, the genius of the project lay in the fact that uncertainty, exalted through the language of Hirshmanian "fuzziness," was precisely what was sought. In an amazingly long-lived example of case-study based research, the Ciudad Guayana project produced ten books over the course of ten years. These books were authored by different faculty members, and the development of their contents provided training for hundreds of graduate students who visited the Joint Center's offices in Venezuela during the summers.

In a volume dedicated to highlighting the history of MIT's architecture and planning programs, "fuzziness" is not exactly a quality one would expect included in the list. Yet it is precisely the shift towards fuzziness, towards indeterminacy and open-endedness, that MIT planning ironically helped to bring about by highlighting fuzziness as the defining characteristic of cutting-edge planning. It has left a lasting legacy. Open-endedness is now assumed to be critical by default. Positioned against the reductive determinacy of the plan, it is the cachet of most critical approaches to urban design and planning today. However, open-endedness in planning is a particular concept with a particular history and philosophical roots lodged in a particular crisis faced by development and planning in the late 1950s. In this paper we will uncover some of the fuzzy interactions which gave rise to

6 The US navy was involved with the development of a port. A steel mill and a large dam had been designed on the Caroní river with the help of US consultants. Adlai Stevenson also visited the region at the time as part of a US delegation, bringing the Guayana project to the attention of US media.

7 Lloyd Rodwin, "Foreword," *Planning Urban Growth and Regional Development: The Experience of the Guayana Program of Venezuela*, ed. Lloyd Rodwin and Associates, eds. (Cambridge, MA: The MIT Press, 1969), p. vii. For Rodwin, Caidad Guayana presented an opportunity to explore the "fundamental

problems of urban and regional growth, and of the ways in which planner can and cannot cope with those problems and assist persons undertaking regional development programs elsewhere." *Planning Urban Growth and Regional Development*, published shortly after the end of

the Guayana project, was designed as the Joint Center's comprehensive retrospective on the subject and included twenty-five papers from different consultants and staff involved with the project.

the indeterminate approach. The development arena was the experimental theater in which this debate took place, and MIT planning was one of the strongest voices on the stage.

Marriage Counseling

Let us begin with the Ciudad Guayana, the project which would substantiate the Joint Center's claim to being the leading institution of the new planning approach. In 1959, while on a consulting job with the Dirección d'Urbanismo in Venezuela in 1959, Rodwin met Colonel Rafael Alfonzo Ravard (later General Alfonzo Ravard), the president of Corporación Venezolana de Guayana (CVG). At the time, the CVG was planning a new city and port in the Venezuelan interior, at the confluence of the Orinoco and Caroní rivers. Alfonzo Ravard asked Rodwin and the Joint Center to join the project as consultants. The project was of national and political importance for Venezuela as well as for the US, which was interested in supporting the new government of President Rómulo Betancourt as an ally against the threat of rising of Soviet influence in the region.[6]

Alfonzo Ravard, however, had approached Rodwin because of the latter's particular emphasis on planning as an "experimental' and "educational" enterprise. Rodwin confirmed this approach when he stated that the project "served not only the client's [interests] but the teaching and research interests of [the] two parent universities [of the Joint Center] as well."[7] For the next five years, the Joint Center would send a diverse group of physical planners, economists, urban designers, lawyers, anthropologists, and many others to work on the Ciudad Guayana project with the CVG staff. At the end of the five-year contract almost all members of the Joint Center involved in the project had written one or more books on the project. For the Venezuelan government the collaboration was also fruitful, though expensive (the project, as well as all the research activity of the Joint Center, was entirely funded by the Venezuelan government). Foreign consultants from two highly regarded and "prestigious" universities provided the CVG with the technical authority to advance its projects in various government circles. This interaction was surely not without its confrontations, and yet the extent to which the process was perceived as an incremental and open-ended process is remarkable.

One reason for this initial framing is to emphasize the particular advantage this approach afforded CVG in Venezuela's political climate: Alfonzo Ravard received his PhD in civil engineering from MIT in 1945 and, following matriculation, had slowly risen in the Venezuelan civil bureaucracy. Just prior to the period under discussion, Ravard had headed the Comisión de Estudios para la Electrificación del Caroní (CEEC), a planning body which preceded the CVG and which was in charge of the construction of the dam which provided power to the Guayana steel mill. In a climate of political coalitions where different ministries were controlled by different political parties and catered to their regional bases, Ravard had carefully cultivated a reputation for himself—and by extension for the CVG—of technical impartiality and political detachment. To achieve this, Ravard was careful to always give

CVG proposals a "national" dimension, and by doing so avoid accusations of partisan political aims and narrow "regional" associations. In these efforts he was supported by the government, both current and preceding, who framed Guayana's development as a mission to wrestle national resources out of the control of foreign oil companies.[8]

For the CVG, claiming national relevance, however, was not just a political question. It was also an epistemological problem. If Ciudad Guayana was to maintain a strictly non-partisan and non-controversial image, and be viewed as a national project, it couldn't be defined in terms of traditional governmental jurisdictions—agriculture, industrial, or educational development.[9] Claiming national relevance therefore also meant strictly avoiding the identification of any part of CVG programs with the policies and scope of another ministry.[10]

The challenge faced by CVG was the redefinition of the social in terms that couldn't be controlled by the existing political calculus of the local and national. One approach taken by the CVG, as John Dinkelspiel later observed in the Joint Center's main publication on the Guayana project, was to avoid the "'people' problems . . . such as agrarian reform, public education and social welfare." This avoided "challenging the 'programs' or public positions of any of the major political parties."[11]

But since the 'people problems' were necessarily "involved in the Guayana's development," the Guyana project couldn't simply avoid policies addressing these issues. Alfonzo Ravard attempted to solve this paradox by carefully defining the Guayana project in legal terms that encompassed the local and the national as part of one continuum which cut across traditional governmental and ministerial categories. As a result, the CVG's jurisdiction expanded and contracted with changing circumstances. In a further, novel move, the CVG secured in its charter the power to undertake investment programs that extended beyond the tightly circumscribed zone of its influence around Ciudad Guayana, as long as the programs' relevance to activities within Ciudad Guyana could be demonstrated. This surprised even John Friedman, Rodwin's co-regional development authority at the Joint Center.[12] "As a result of this decision," Friedman stated:

---

8 Rómulo Betancourt's elected government took office in January 1959, just before the Joint Center got involved with the Guayana project. Betancourt's government came into power after a military coup threw out the previous military dictatorship of Pérez Jiménez. Both Betancourt and Jiménez had declared the "development" of Guayana as their government's critical goal.

9 Agricultural reform, for example, was already associated with a particular ministry and therefore claimed as an aim by a particular political party. Since providing Ciudad Guayana with local food supply would have involved the CVG with the highly volatile issue of land and agrarian reform, it turned towards promoting large-scale commercial food production in the Orinoco Delta Region.

10 This requirement inhibited coordinating efforts with other ministries,; even keeping the long-terms plans of CVG shrouded in secrecy. CVG at moments deliberately put projects within its jurisdiction on the shelf just because they appeared to support the aims of a particular political party at the time. See, John R. Dinkelspiel, "Administrative Style," in *Planning Urban Growth and Regional*

Aerial view of Ciudad Guayana showing CVG's
zona de desarrollo. Donald Appleyard, *Planning a
Pluralist City*, (Cambridge, MA: MIT Press), 1976.

the CVG now operates a coal mine on the Caroní, some 250 miles from the zona de
desarrollo [CVG's development zone around Ciudad Guayana], is helping to finance
road-building project throughout the eastern provinces, and has initiated a large land
reclamation scheme in the Orinoco Delta. This ingenious device for regional delimitation
serves to constrain the Corporation's powers by establishing a criterion of relevance, but
it leaves the Corporation flexible to cope with problems that could not be foreseen at
the time of the initial legislation.[13]

The CVG's solution was indeed innovative. It redefined the region from a mere spatial unit
to an amorphous, spatial-temporal construct. This move certainly impressed Friedman. "A
novel solution was finally found," Friedman exclaimed. "A region is a time-space continuum.
Why, then, invest it with Euclidean properties?"[14] Through this redefinition, the CVG

Development, ed. Rodwin
et al. : *The Experience of
the Guayana Program of
Venezuela*, op cit.
11 Ibid., p. 13. Another
strategy pursued by the
CVG to keep its projects
impartial was simply to
maintain anonymity to the
extent that it kept its projects
secret. "Indeed," Dinkelspiel

observed, "the Corporation
has sought anonymity so
assiduously that the nature
of what it is planning to do is
only vaguely realized by even
well-informed Venezuelans."
12 Friedman would later
become the Director of the
Ford Foundation Advisory
Program in Urban and
Regional Development in

Chile. At the time of the
Guayana project, he was
a member of the Joint
Center staff and taught at
the Department of City and
Regional Planning at MIT as
an Associate Professor.
13 John Friedman, "The
Guayana Program in a
Regional Perspective," in
Planning Urban Growth

and Regional Development,
ed. Rodwin et al.,: The
Experience of the Guayana
Program of Venezuela, op cit.,
p. 152. Also see Friedman's
*Regional Development Policy:
A Case Study of Venezuela*
(Cambridge, MA: The MIT
Press, 1966), chapterch. 5.
14 John Friedman,
"The Guayana Program in

presented the "region" as a challenge to the traditional notion of boundaries—physical, political, and epistemological. Planning was now a task of establishing relations between distant things, concepts, and subjects.

Not everyone in the Joint Center's team, however, was happy with these shifts. The changing nature of the CVG praxis repeatedly threw a wrench in the "coordination" efforts of the Joint Center's various experts, frustrating particularly the urban designers.

The Joint Center had first approached Edmund Bacon, Executive Director of the Philadelphia City Planning Commission, to serve as the design consultant for the project. Bacon was fascinated by the geographical features of the site, particularly the view from the small area called Punta Vista, next to the scenic falls on the Caroní river. As Willo von Moltke, the urban designer who eventually replaced Bacon, would later recount, Bacon was captivated by the fact that if you bisected the angle of the two major roads that intersected at this point, "the line would pass through the narrow mouth of the Caroní before it joins the Orinoco." For Bacon, this feature established the conceptual center of the design, generating four outwardly growing vectors.

While the Joint Center team was working on the design, however, the CVG was busy making more strategic decisions about the "locational" requirement of industry by situating most industrial activity in the vicinity of the Guayana steel mill. This decision, according to von Moltke, made it "impossible to find appropriate land uses for the huge areas between the two western corridors."[15] As a result, Bacon's design was abandoned. In 1963, the design team, now led by von Moltke, re-evaluated the conditions and proposed "a linear city with a series of nodes connected by a central transportation spine . . . [that] would best fulfill the goals of efficient and memorable physical development."[16]

The new design required making minimum interventions in the existing low-income residential area called San Félix; establishing a new commercial center at Alta Vista (the larger plateau next to Punta Vista); creating two new residential areas adjacent to the commercial area; and building a new recreational and cultural center at Punta Vista, the

a Regional Perspective," *Planning Urban Growth and Regional Development*, ed. Rodwin et al.,: *The Experience of the Guayana Program of Venezuela*, op cit., p. 152.

15 Willo von Moltke, "The Evolution of the Linear Form," Ibidin *Planning Urban Growth and Regional Development*, ed. Rodwin et al.,., p. 134.
16 Ibid., p. 135.

top, Edmund Bacon's plan for Ciudad Guayana. From Appleyard, *Planning a Pluralist City*.

bottom, von Moltke's linear proposal for Ciudad Guayana. From Appleyard, *Planning a Pluralist City*.

venerable spot of Bacon's plan. All of the elements were connected by a transportation "spine" or "corridor". The new commercial center and neighborhoods at Alta Vista divided the distance between the steel mill and the existing San Félix neighborhood (shown by distance "A" in the sketch below). Like Bacon, von Moltke's primary concern was to create a 'memorable' image for the city, with 'memorable' now equated with a linear plan that could be read as "unified" form.

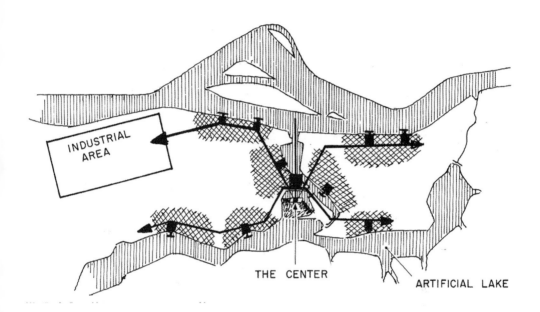

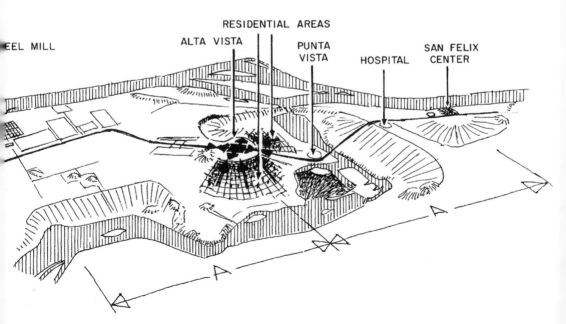

For von Moltke, the plan provided a "comprehensive physical concept for Ciudad Guayana."[17] He realized that given the linear form, there "would be a sizeable burden in transportation costs and in time for the journey to work, especially in the early stages of development."[18] "However," he asserted, "as residential development grows westward and industry grows eastward, commuting distances and the proportional cost of transportation will be reduced."[19] The linear scheme also allowed other industry to be established closer to the city, while new employment opportunities allowed the residents of San Flex to move into the new higher-income housing. The city center at Alta Vista was the meeting point where all classes were to meet and merge in an economically 'mature' and socially 'developed' city of the future.[20]

As soon as the design was proposed, however, it became apparent once again that it was at best going to be a temporary signpost. The urban and economic development programs involved a host of experts with differing agendas. Differences existed not only between the CVG and the Joint Center, but also divided the Joint Center's staff. In particular, the Joint center consultant in charge of transportation planning, Anthony Penfold, despised what he deemed the aesthetic criteria of placing road on ridges for better views. For Penfold, "[p]reoccupation with patterns," and "exaggerated weight . . . given to some questionable criteria concerning highway location," took precedence over all other concerns.

Yet even the transportation experts couldn't agree on a 'unified' plan. Some neighborhood road designs were needed before others.[21] Scheduling requirements demanded that the task of road network design be divided, with different engineers in charge of different neighborhoods.[22] This created severe problems in terms of coordinating traffic flow requirements from one area to the next. Added to this troubled mix was the "frequency with which the economists revised their targets."[23] Even without major revisions, the urban planners continued to complain that the road "network no longer 'looked right' on paper."[24] It wasn't just that the traffic network turned out to be broken in Ciudad Guayana. It was the planning network itself, or more precisely, the very idea of planning as a networked activity, that appeared to be coming undone.

17 von Moltke, p. 139

18 Ibid., p. 140

19 Ibid., p. 141.

20 Sociologically speaking, however, the design divided the city into distinct classes. The new residential areas close to the proposed commercial center, although designed as mixed-income neighborhoods, came to

serve the higher income employees of the nearby steel mill, so did the recreational meeting point at Punta Vista. The lower-income groups were ostracized to San Félix. Since the steel mill provided employment for the majority of the resident of this area as well, their commute was further

lengthened by the added weight of new neighborhoods and commercial center on the major connecting highway. Accusations of silent "exploitation" flew high. Scheme was seen as an attempt to maintain a permanent "informal economy" at the city's periphery, outside the

structure of state welfare and civic rights, to support the new industrial economy. These challenges came not just from the representatives groups in San Félix, but from the Joint Center's own staff as well. The most prominent critique came from Lisa Peattie, an anthropologist sent to Ciudad Guayana to

Just a few years earlier, development institutions such as the UN would have characterized such misalignments as signs of the forces that perpetuated underdevelopment: bureaucratic inefficiency, out-dated views, stubborn attitudes, or political corruption. Its view of similar situations is made clear in this often-quoted text from a 1951 UN report:

> There is a sense in which rapid economic progress is impossible without painful adjustments. Ancient philosophies have to be scrapped; old social institutions have to disintegrate; bonds of cast, creed and race have to burst; and large number of persons who cannot keep up with progress have to have their expectations of a comfortable life frustrated. Very few communities are willing to pay the full price of economic progress.[25]

For Rodwin and others (such as John Friedman) at the Joint Center concerned with regional planning , however, misalignment of different vectors of planning was not a sign of 'traditional' or 'unmodern' attitudes. The setbacks were precisely the aims of MIT's explorations in Venezuela. True, individual members of the team saw the barrage of incongruent demands emerging from the project as an indication of the inability of the Venezuelan planners and the city's inhabitants to understand the "overall" concept of the design. Von Moltke, for example later asserted that "the inhabitants of the Ciudad Guayana did not understand the planning ideas and at times acted in ways detrimental to the implementation of the overall plan."[26] For Rodwin, however, each crisis, each hindrance, carried a forward momentum. Each hindrance was a learning experience, a step towards finding a common understanding between different forms of expertise operative in the project.

Consider for example, Rodwin's evaluation of the project as a 'marriage,' a bitter-sweet relationship, that was above all a continuous negotiation:

> Even in a successful marriage, there are often conflicts and serious misunderstandings. These are all the more likely if one starts with significant differences of habits, values, and aims—which certainly was true for the Joint Center and its Venezuelan associates. But, however, widespread hostility to foreigners may generally be in Venezuela, such

live on site and report on the "peoples perspective" on the project. See, Lisa Peattie's *The View from the Barrio* (Ann Arbor, MI: The University of Michigan Press, 1968), and her *Planning: Rethinking Ciudad Guayana* (Ann Arbor, MI: The University of Michigan Press, 1987). We'll look at Peattie's critiques later

in the paper.
21 "Pressure to develop the residential area of Los Olivos, south of Alta Vista," Penfold argued, "forced the engineers to do preliminary construction drawings of this sector, including the center of the city, before they had time to look at the city [traffic] network as a whole." See

Anthony Penfold, "Urban Transportation," in *Planning Urban Growth and Regional Development*, ed. Rodwin et al.: The Experience of the Guayana Program of Venezuela, op cit., p. 195.
22 Because of the "nature of the 'crash program'" Penfold complained, "... ... major road were shown merely on

a small scale." Which forced the construction drawings of the road networks for communities... ... . [to be built] piecemeal... ... Consequently the design of one section in the network often created problem for the engineer of the subsequent section." Ibid., p. 183.
23 Ibid., p. 199. "W[w]ithout

attitudes did not pose serious problems for us in dealing with the principal staff of the CVG. This was partly because of a deeply shared concern about common technical problems, partly because of the friendship that grew up between the two staffs, and partly because of the leaders of the CVG had studied in the United States and admired the two universities we represented and appreciated the potential contributions and prestige this collaboration would lend their efforts.[27]

Rodwin is certainly describing a complicated relationship, balanced not just by friendship and shared technical interests, but also by the weight of prestige on one side and the pace of politics on the other. But the very framing of this complicated enterprise as a "relationship," a marriage of sorts, points to the mode of its unfolding. Certainly Arthur Lewis, or Walter Rostow, the famous proponents of early economic approaches championed by the UN, did not see their planning proposals as one of marriage. There are no stories of shared dreams or endured hardships in those proposals. Planning in those instances was indeed imagined as an experience of hopes thwarted, concepts of comfortable life destroyed, and expectations frustrated. Of course, some would argue that that also describes a certain kind of marriage. But the fact remains that earlier proponents of development at major international institutions did not imagine planning in terms of establishing mutual "relationships." For them it was a process composed of definite stages and prescriptions. To the extent that the results proved different from the prescriptions (as they of course did), they were seen as shortcomings—whether of implementations, analyses, and models—and/or signs of Third World 'corruption.'

For Rodwin and others at the Joint Center, however, the deviations in Ciudad Guayana's planning were part of the process of negotiation, of the working out the problems, as in a relationship. For Rodwin planning always took place on the therapist's couch, in the marriage counselor's office. It was assumed that there would be issues to be resolved, problems to be worked through. Ciudad Guayana was a long therapy session from which everyone learned valuable lessons, even though only a few were able to achieve material benefits.

a plentiful supply of time and staff," Penfold recalled, "it was not practical to repeat the procedural steps of the network design to evaluate each of the economists' major revisions."
24 Ibid., p.196.

25 United Nations, Department of Social and Economic Affairs, *Measures for the Economic Development of Underdeveloped Countries* (New York: United Nations, 1951), p 15.

26 Willo von Moltke, "The Evolution of the Linear Form," op cit., p. 145.
27 Lloyd Rodwin, "Reflections on Collaborative Planning," in *Planning Urban Growth and Regional Development*, ed. Rodwin et al., op cit., p. 468.

The comparison of planning with counseling is critical here, as it helps us to note that, according to Rodwin, negotiation between different forms of expertise does not lead to an objective understanding of some hidden laws, but only to more negotiations. Planning is above all a consensus-building device.

Here we must ask: what happened to the perceived scope of planning between 1951 and 1959? The shift was nothing short of a remarkable transformation in the manner in which planning's scope was imagined. This transformation would have major implications for the relationship between the international and the national in the development arena, as the earlier attitude of development institutions became increasingly outmoded. These changes, however, cannot be understood without an examination of the new conceptual framework that was emerging at this time as the cutting and ethical edge of planning.

The Right Imbalance

The Big Push

In the early postwar era, development economics was characterized by two prevailing viewpoints: "balanced" and "imbalanced" growth. Big development institutions, such as the World Bank, the UN, and the IMF, favored the balanced growth model. Proponents of balanced growth argued that in countries without "mature" capitalist market sectors and institutions, the path to economic growth was only possible by simultaneous investment on multiple fronts, from industrial and agricultural production to health, education, and social services. These investments required a carefully orchestrated combination of infrastructural development, tax incentives, urban and regional planning projects, government subsidies, and centralized administrative control. An independent and self-supporting system would emerge only when every aspect of capitalist production was ticking in sync with one another, but, established on a significant scale, such a system would independently attract further investment and would establish mutually supporting and self-aggregating market activity.

This view of balanced growth was called the "Big Push" model, denoting the effort required till a tipping point. The model is accredited to the Harvard economist, Paul Rosenstein-Rodan, a contemporary of Hirschman. For Rosenstein-Rodan, successful implementation of the Big-Push was primarily a question of establishing the "economies of scale," the maximum quantity up to which the cost of producing a commodity could be reduced by producing it in greater quantities. As industrial firms moved toward this point, they were able to generate demand for components required in their production process up the stream, so to speak, and they likewise generated supply for related production processes down the stream. According to Rosenstein-Rodan, as this "economies of scale" point was approached, economic production would form a system of mutually reliant processes and sectors, tipping the economy over to the side of self-aggregating growth. The problem of development was therefore only one of coordination, of setting the system in place, of turning the wheels in sync till the whole mechanism started to tick on its own accord, picking up speed and adding more part to its movements.

Rosenstein-Rodan had proposed his Big Push model in 1943 in the context of economic development of Eastern Europe.[28] However, it became famous in economic circles after 1954, when Arthur Lewis, in a short paper titled "Economic Development with Unlimited Supply of Labor," turned Rosenstein-Rodan's thesis into a mathematical model and proposed it as a blueprint for Third World development.[29]

Strategic Development

As the balanced growth approach began to lose its luster after the "first development decade," Albert Hirschman's view of development as an unpredictable process gained more appeal and, over time, came to represent a model known as "imbalanced growth." Hirschman first identified the concept of imbalance growth in his now seminal book, *The Strategy of Economic Development* (1958).[30] Here, Hirschman began with the idea of "backward and forward linkages" that had already been made famous by Rosenstein-Rodan and Lewis in their respective balance growth models. The idea of linkages presumed that once a firm reached a certain scale and started operating on economies of scale, it would create demand and supplies for the products of other firms, ultimately resulting in a self-aggregating cycle of industrial development.

In contrast to Rosenstein-Rodan and other proponents of the balanced growth model, Hirschman however maintained that the process of linkages could never be predicted or controlled. Linkages were not formed through self-generating economic processes. Economic linkages were instead driven by social values and political interests. These interests generated drives for monopolistic controls and unequal competition, precisely the dimensions that Rosenstein-Rodan and Lewis had omitted in order to model development in purely economic terms. This reduction allowed both Rosenstein-Rodan and Lewis to see linkages as tending to settle into market "equilibriums" that balanced the forces of demand, supply, and prices. Their model, Hirschman asserted, only allowed for the creation of clear policy prescriptions, but never in a way that would allow it to attain self-

28 Rosenstein-Rodan first presented this argument in a short paper titled, "Problems of Industrialization of Eastern and South-Eastern Europe," *Economic Journal* 53 (1943): 202-211. Also see Rosenstein-Rodan's "Notes on the Theory of the 'Big-Push'" in Howard S. Ellis and Henry C. Wallich, eds., *Economic Development*

for Latin America, eds. Howard S. Ellis and Henry C. Wallich (New York: St. Martin's Press, 1961), pp. 57-81.
29 Arthur Lewis, "Economic Development with Unlimited Supplies of Labor," *The Manchester School* 22 (1954): 129-144.

30 Albert Hirschman, *The Strategy of Economic Development* (New Haven, CT: Yale University Press, 1958).
31 Hirschman employed the idea of the hiding hand, first laid out in *The Strategy*, to evaluate a range of development projects, from Karnaphuli pulp and paper

mill in Pakistan to 'pasture development" projects in Uruguay, in *Development Projects Observed* (Washington, D.C.: Brookings Institute, 1967). Development depends, Hirschman argues, not only on "what a country does and... . . . [but also on] what it becomes as a result of what it does." pp. (4-5).

sufficiency. Using it, economists handed out advice on how to provide incentives to move from one idealized balance to the next, supposedly generating industrial production at an ever-increasing scale, all the while ignoring the unpredictable political contexts in which these models were to be implemented.

Development, Hirschman argued, did not follow this model. According to him, it was essentially a conglomerate enterprise, involving many changing actors, institutions, and interests, and leading to what in conventional economic terms would be called disequilibria and alternations. According to this view, development inevitably generated apparent failures, setbacks, and conflicts. Capital and education—factors which conventional economics held as prerequisites to development—did not preclude these tensions and conflicts, nor the unpredictability they entailed. No matter how well planned a project, it generated countervailing forces. In this environment, a development agency was to focus on allocating resources in a few key sectors of the economy without providing any "complementary" investments. The imbalances produced through such investment would produce political pressures for action on other fronts, resulting in the reallocation of resources over time. This shift would then create another imbalance, and consequently a new set of political demands, thereby repeating the cycle.

According to Hirschman, these forces were in fact critical lessons for people, teaching them to cope with currents of change by turning disappointments into learning experiences. Whenever a development project "failed" in conventional terms, it in fact generated unforeseen new opportunities. With these ideas in mind, Hirschman advocated a "learning-based" view of development. As opposed to Mill's "guiding hand," Hirschman proposed the "hiding hand" as a metaphor for the process of socio-economic change. Because the "hiding hand" only granted a partial view of the difficulties involved in any given development enterprise to those who sought to undertake it, different opportunities than those initially imagined were bound to open up along the way.[31] For Hirschman, governments, institutions, and individuals all undertook development projects with an underestimation of the difficulties involved. Consequently they were initially driven by what would appear in retrospect to be a rather naïve and hopeful view.

Also see the elaboration of the concept in Hirschman's, "The Principle of the Hiding Hand," *Public Interest* 2 (Winter 1967): 1-23. **32** "Bias for hope" is another major theme in Hirschman's work, developed in detail in the context of his work in Latin America in a later book of the same title, *A*

Bias for Hope: Essays on Development and Latin America (New Haven, CT: Yale University Press, 1971). **33** Albert Hirschman, "The Search for Paradigms as Hindrance to Understanding," in his *Bias for Hope,*, op cit., pp. 342-60. As MIT economist, Michael Piore (who was one of Hirschman's

students at Harvard), recalled, Hirschman arrived at Harvard at a time when Keynesian "eclecticism" was prevalent in economics. "Keynes had created a space in economics in which everything was up for grabs, leaving room for ad hoc theories and theories borrowed from other disciplines." This climate,

Piore argued, was sustained by a generation of depression era economists "who were ready to entertain any theory, and also depended on practical experience rather than abstract reasoning." In this context, Hirschman gained popularity because he was seen to place a "premium" on "midlevel

At the same time, Hirschman asserted, this naiveté was instrumental in bringing about change. If the difficulties of the process were known ahead of time, no development enterprise would ever commence. After initial frustrations in the face of unforeseen challenges, a certain "bias for hope" took hold again.[32] Hope itself provided a critical economic impetus for change. Time and time again, the participants rethought their goals and possibilities, re-launching the process anew. If economists were able to see these shifts as signs of an ongoing process of re-evaluation, rather than as signs of failure, they would see that the participants often surpassed initial expected levels of achievement though creative rethinking.[33] Instead of attempting to capture complex reality through simplified mathematical models, Hirschman urged economists to focus their energies on identifying extra-mathematical processes of "social learning" and "hidden rationalities." This emphasis challenged the conventional notion of "economic man" as a rational being.

The Joint Center

The origins of the Joint Center for Urban Studies at MIT and Harvard are located in these transformations in development planning. As declared in MIT's 1959 *Report to the President*, the center would bring together a host of "architects, engineers, urban planners, economists, sociologists, lawyers, political scientists, philosophers, scientists, and experts in business, public health, and other disciplines affecting urban life."[34] The goal of this "multidisciplinary" approach was to extend the domain of city planning to what would be called "urban studies." As Eric Mumford has shown in the previous chapter, this move reflected a transformation in both the available funding opportunities and prevalent approaches to housing reform. From a disciplinary perspective, however, this expansion was an attempt by the city planning and design departments at MIT and Harvard to reassert their authority over a domain of spatial planning that had already been claimed by other disciplines, particularly geography, urban sociology, and political science. The establishment of the Joint Center was a move towards identifying a new operational role for urban planning and design by claiming the interrelationship between the different disciplinary domains as a problem in itself.

ideas bridging experience and theory and [advocate] a 'catholic' approach very much in keeping with the Harvard atmosphere." Piore's reference to extra-mathematical approach to economics as a certain "intellectual Catholicism," the combining of the spiritual with the practical, is telling.

The prominent figures in this amorphous approach to modeling positioned economic planning as a moral enterprise with quasi-religious underpinning. This framing stemmed from the desire to model a relationship between the part and the whole that was not determined by a mathematical relationship.

Piore quoted in Lloyd Rodwin's introductory chapter, "*Rethinking the Development Experience*: Aims, Themes, and Thesis," in Rethinking the Development Experience, : Essays Provoked by the Work of Albert O. Hirschman, op cit., pp. eds. Lloyd Rodwin and Donald Schön, 13-14.

34 Massachusetts Institute of Technology Bulletin, President's Report Issue 2 (1959): 356.

35 See Martin Meyerson, "Introduction," in *The Conscience of the City*, ed. Martin Meyerson, ed. (New York: George Braziller, 1940), pp. ix-xv. Meyerson's own career was reflective of

According to Martin Meyerson, the Center's first director, this approach resulted from a shift in the perceived client of development planning—a shift from planning as a problem of capital allocation to planning as a process determined by the sociological profiles of the clients.[35] Rodwin, who was the first chairman of the Joint Center's Faculty Committee from 1959-1969, similarly sought to reframe planning as a profession geared towards managing the interrelationships between different technical and social disciplines.[36] During his tenure with the Joint Center, Rodwin was actively involved in the Regional Science Association of America, eventually becoming its president,[37] and from 1969 to 1973, Rodwin was the chair of MIT's Department Urban Studies and Planning (DUSP). During this period, Rodwin hired new faculty from the social sciences and introduced course work from anthropology, history, economics, and geography into his department, thereby extending the department's profile across disciplinary boundaries. He also founded, and directed from 1967-1989, MIT's Special Program for Urban and Regional Studies (SPURS). Over the years, the program trained over 400 mid-career professions from developing countries.

For both Rodwin and Meyerson, the Center represented a shift towards problems of relating various forms of knowledge that concerned urban planning. As Rodwin would later recall:

When the first UN decade of development was launched in 1955, it was taken for granted that low income countries with weak private sectors, stunted governments, and internal conflict and instability, needed above all, capable leadership and strong central governments. National planning was the chosen instrument for central resource allocation; and it was generally believed that the process of development was a well defined task which could be planned and managed with central directives.[38]

For Myerson, the end of 1950s was dominated by pressures from urban experts and commentators to establish a "cabinet-level department of urban development"[39] which would emphasize vertical organization of control. Over the last decade, Meyerson asserted, the Joint Center had been instrumental in identifying what has been missing from this approach: "[the] problem was not simply to define the questions . . . [but] to think how one problem relate[d] to the other."[40] According to Meyerson, the Joint Center

this shift. He had started as an Assistant Professor in sociology at the University of Chicago in 1942, moving to Harvard and receiving tenure at the Department of City Planning in 1957, and subsequently becoming Acting Dean of the Graduate School of Design in 1963. From 1958 to 1963 he became the first Director of the Joint Center. In 1963 he left the Joint Center to accept the position of the Dean of the College of Environmental Design of the University of California at Berkeley. Meyerson would become famous for his role as the interim Chancellor of Berkeley in negotiating with the demonstrators during the famous student unrests on campus in 1965. From Berkeley, Meyerson moved towards more administrative positions, becoming the President of the State University of New York at Buffalo and later the President of the University of Pennsylvania from 1970 to 1981. During this period and afterwards, he presided on the boards of major universities and foundations, including the Ford Foundation, and served as an advisor to various UN and other development agencies as well as a consultant to various national governments.

favored a "working conference" approach to planning that focused on setting in place the "process" of planning rather than a plan.

Images

For both Meyerson and Rodwin, this relational field could neither be defined preemptively nor permanently. "We are probably not ready for such a synthesis," Rodwin argued, "perhaps it is not ever possible or desirable." It was Robert Oppenheimer's view of science's future that Rodwin found revelatory:

> Instead of "architecture of global scope," Oppenheimer anticipated more numerous but limited syntheses in the world of science, more 'dining together' at the interfaces of different fields leading to "an immense intricate network of intimacy, illumination and understanding." In this world, he argued, everything could not be connected to everything, but "everything could be connected with anything." Perhaps this also applies to the contemporary images of urbanism.[41]

Rodwin's use of the term image to denote the nature of the tentative, circumstantial synthesis imagined by Oppenheimer is not incidental. Image was the titular theme under which questions of epistemological relations were being explored at the Joint Center. The work of Kevin Lynch, György Kepes, and Stephen Carr at the Joint Center on "visual" images as a force shaping the perception of the physical environment is well known. Kepes had published *The New Landscape* in 1956 and Lynch *The Image of the City* in 1960. The question of visual images as employed by planners was also taken up later by Lisa Peattie, a DUSP anthropologist, in her *Planning: Rethinking Ciudad Guayana* (1987).

Interest in the theme of the image extended beyond the visual as well. Image was also seen as anepistemological construct in the mind. Meyerson would address this theme in *The Conscience of the City* (1970). Rodwin would revisit the theme of the image in *Cities and City Planning* (1981) and *Cities of the Mind: Images and Themes of the City in the Social Sciences* (1984), and finally, in *The Profession of City Planning: Changes, Images, and Challenges, 1950-2000* (2000) Bishwapriya Sanyal would consider it as well.

36 Rodwin also had a similar illustrious career across disciplinary boundaries. Born in Brooklyn as a son of an immigrant baker, Rodwin attended the City College of New York. After being disqualified from civil service exam for his unusual writing style (using dashes as opposed to periods in

the manner of his favorite author, the philosopher, George Santayana), Rodwin signed up for a "ten dollar course" with Charles Abrams, the New York Housing Commissioner and noted housing activist, at the New School of Social Research. He worked as Abrams's research assistant and later joined the

Defense Housing Program in Washington, D.C. Unable to join the armed forces because of poor eyesight, Rodwin went on to complete a Master's in Land Economics at the University of Wisconsin, Madison, and later became a Littauer Fellow at Harvard, finishing his PhD in regional planning in 1949.

37 Rodwin's first book, *The British New Towns Policy* (1956), attracted quick attention for criticizing the established regional planning model of decentralization in the US and the UK. Following Ebenezer Howard's early Garden City projects, planners and advocates such as Clarence Stein, Charles

These two framings of the image, the visual and the non-visual, reflected different conceptual understandings of change as betrayed by the separate sources of funding that supported the two research vectors. The framing of image as primarily a visual phenomenon argued for the presence of hidden natural or psychological forces which shaped the interaction between the subject and the environment. The visual itself was a hieroglyph. It pointed to the hidden structures of nature or of the unconscious. This research was funded by Rockefeller Foundation, which itself had a long history of funding psychological and medical research.

The framing of image as primarily a non-visual epistemological phenomenon also drew on psychological experiments, but this approach carefully avoided the idea of image as a window into the unconscious. Instead this view of the image took a more positivist approach. The mental image was a manifestation of the subject's epistemological field, readily and continuously changed by new knowledge and behavioral inputs. This view of the image attracted the interest of the Ford Foundation, which was funding emerging behavioral science research towards the assembly of databases on various social practices. In exploring the idea of the non-visual image, both Rodwin and Meyerson repeatedly turned to the work of Kenneth Boulding, the American philosopher, economist, and systems theorist famous for his outlining of the moral and ecological dimensions of economic growth. A prolific writer, Boulding wrote some thirty books and innumerable articles. The most influential of these was his seminal book, *The Image: Knowledge in Life and Society* (1956),[42] which introduced the idea of the image as an epistemological construct.

Boulding often worked closely with planners and sociologists and contributed to edited volumes by Meyerson and Rodwin. He was the president of the American Economic Association, the Society for General Systems Research, and the American Association for the Advancement of Science. In these positions, he pushed for an "integrative approach" between the social sciences. Like Hirschman, this emphasis earned him characterizations as fuzzy, rhetorical, and mathematically ambivalent. Yet this "fuzziness" was instrumental in establishing key connections across various disciplinary boundaries. The Society for General Systems Research included famous anthropologists such as Margaret Mead and Gregory

Abrams, Catherine Bauer, and Lewis Mumford had favored decentralized approaches in the US before the war. For Rodwin, such planning approaches were utopian enterprises that assumed that complex political and social process could be mapped in advance. See Lloyd Rodwin, *The British New Towns Policy:*

Problems and Implications (Cambridge, MA: Harvard University Press, 1956).
38 Lloyd Rodwin and Bishwapriya Sanyal, "Shelter, Settlement, and Development: An Overview," in Lloyd Rodwin ed., *Shelter, Settlement and Development, a Sstudy Ssponsored and Financed by the United*

Nations/International Year of Shelter for the Homeless, ed. Lloyd Rodwin (Boston, MA: Allen & Unwin, 1987), p. 10.
39 Meyerson, "Introduction," in *The Conscience of the City,* op cit.ed. Meyerson, p. ix.
40 Ibid., p. xv.

41 Lloyd Rodwin, "Images of the City," in his *Cities and City Planning* (New York: Plenum Press, 1981), p. 76.
42 Kenneth Boulding, *The Image: Knowledge in Life and Society* (Ann Arbor, MI: University of Michigan Press, 1956).

Bateson, as well as planner Richard Meier, who later became well-known for his books on systems and communication theory as models for urban planning in the Third World. From 1949 to 1976, Boulding was on the faculty at the University of Michigan.[43] Meier joined Michigan in 1957 as a research sociologist at the university's Mental Health Research Institute,[44] and Boulding and Meier developed a close working relationship which also involved Mead and Bateson from The Society for General Systems Research.[45] It was during this time that Meier joined the American Regional Science Association, of which Rodwin was the President, thereby extending the circle of associations further.[46]

As mentioned above, both Kepes' *The New Landscape in Art and Science* and Boulding's *Image* were published in 1956. For Kepes, The New Landscape signified the hidden "patterns of action" in nature. These patterns, Kepes argued, were invisible to unaided senses because they were always transforming. Nevertheless, they were not transforming randomly but rather changing from one level of "organization" to the next. Science in the form of new media and technology revealed the extended scale of these organizations that formed a "common denominator" in nature. Though only visible to us in the form of partial and changing patterns, the hidden unity of these universal laws could be comprehended through the aid of artistic sensibilities.

Unlike Kepes (and others), Boulding argued that the image was not a visual phenomenon made visible by science or art but rather a mental construct. Its contours were sketched not by the organization of light on film or by the artist's intuition, but by the epistemological organization of the mind. As such, the image did not point to the presence of a hidden whole, be it nature or the unconsciousness. It pointed only to a positive presence: the image produced by understanding at any particular moment in the mind.

From this perspective, what modern society needed was not artistic sensibilities but managerial capabilities. Comprehension here did not point to the presence of unity in nature but only to an anti-entropic capability of the mind to counter an ever-entropic tendency in nature. For Boulding the image was thus both historical and experiential: "part of the image is the history of the image itself."[47] The image formed the knowledge an individual held to

---

43 In 1976 Boulding moved to the University of Colorado at Boulder, staying there until his retirement.
44 Before arriving at Michigan, Meier had taught at the University of Chicago's Program of Education and Research in Planning, which played a significant role in the New Deal planning projects.

45 In 1957, when the Mental Health Research Institute was asked to prepare a "manual" for the UN consultants on short-term projects, Meier drew on the cross-disciplinary relationships he had developed at the Society for General Systems Research. Boulding wrote the introduction to the Manual

and Mead and Bateson contributed chapters.
46 In 1967, Meier moved to the University of California at Berkeley to set up a PhD program at the Department of City and Regional Planning (DCRP), a department that would form the other major hub of cross-disciplinary research in planning in the '60s.

47 Boulding, *The Image*, op cit., p. 6.
48 Kenneth Boulding, *The Limitation of Mathematics: An Epistemological Critique*, op cit.

be true at any moment, but was open to new understanding and revision. This also meant that an image was always partial, contingent, ambiguous, and, without the security of hidden unity and harmony, unpredictable.

Thus for Boulding, the clarity that science claimed for mathematical relations—as windows into the hidden worlds of universal laws—undermined the formation of an image. The image, Boulding argued, provided an ambiguous "coarse" tool by which one could comprehend an ambiguously defined and (correspondingly) coarsely-constructed universe:

> The delicacy or coarseness of a tool has an important effect on the task which can be done with it; we do not cut out cataracts with a buzz-saw or cut down trees with a scalpel. Mathematics clearly has a bias on the side of delicacy and exactness. Where the task requires delicacy, this is all to the good. If however the empirical universe which we are trying to know is not delicate, too great a reliance on mathematics may be misleading, if it is not checked by good judgment about the nature of the empirical universe itself.

> This is a problem of considerable importance for the social sciences, where the empirical universe itself is frequently "coarse" in texture. A good example of this difficulty is the theory of "rational behavior" in economics. The calculus is too fine, relationships in the empirical world are not continuous, and the theory of uncertainty is largely an attempt to discuss vagueness by means of clear concepts! I do not imply, of course, that mathematics is incapable of modifying itself in the direction of the buzz-saw for there are some signs of this. The bias, however, is at present all towards the scalpel.[48]

The image brought coarseness back into economic thought and made it compatible with the world. Economics was indeed concerned with the dynamic nature of the world, but the desire for mathematical exactness had caused economics to misunderstand the nature of its transformations.

This Heisenberg-ian universe demanded an inexact methodology to comprehend its unpredictable movements at any moment. For Boulding, understanding the world required not a better camera, or a better equation, but a theory of knowledge, and of inexact knowledge at that:

> One thing that has to be included in general systems is chaos—that is, the principle that everything is not systematic . . . Unless general systems recognizes the profound indeterminacy of evolutionary and especially of social systems, a deterministic view of these systems is apt to lead into delusions of certainty about the future which can be quite disastrous, and can lead to a neglect of adaptability, tentativeness, and that constant willingness to revise images, which are necessities of survival in an uncertain world.[49]

His theory of image was an attempt to give form to a dimension of knowledge production that had been ostracized from the modern world: ambiguity.

Joint Center 2

Boulding's theory of knowledge appeared very attractive to planners like Rodwin and Meyerson, who were trying to create room for contingency and unpredictability within conventional structural planning approaches. If Hirschman's notion of inequilibrium presented a case against centralized planning, Boulding's non-visual image provided a way of looking at the fragment within a system of structural integrity which nevertheless remained outside the organicist, ecological, and structural determinism of prevalent systems theory approaches. "[By] 'image,'" Rodwin asserted,

> we mean a mental representation—more than a fleeting picture—that significantly influences or structures thought or reflects the influence or structure of thought. Our use of the word 'image' overlaps with meanings attached to 'ideas,' 'views,' 'ideologies,' or 'models' ' but our main focus is on the ways these concepts and images sum up the distinct points of view of different mode or systematic ways of examining urban phenomenon.[50]

For Rodwin, the epistemological framing of the image presented a theory of operational knowledge, knowledge that couldn't yet be categorized. Traditionally, planners had argued for more data, more computation power, to build more elaborate systems and models of cause and effect. This, Rodwin asserted, was a self-defeating task. The more elaborate a system got, the more variables it encompassed, the more difficult it became to predict its outcomes. Planning was constantly fighting between its desire for more information and the burden that information brought with it.

However, rather than taking these "fuzzy" relationships as hindrances, planners could use them to built a mode of operation. "Most planners," Rodwin later reflected, "are disposed to believe that development efforts will eventually founder if basic concepts are hazy and if development aims are obscure."[51] Yet these "fuzzy assumptions," as Rodwin himself came

49 Kenneth Boulding, "The Next Thirty Years," *General Systems Yearbook* 29 (1984),: 3.

50 Lloyd Rodwin, "Images of the City," in his *Cities and City Planning,* op cit., p. 68.

51 Lloyd Rodwin, *Nations and Cities,* op cit., p. 275.
52 Ibid., p. 272.
53 Ibid., p. 276.

54 Rodwin, *Cities and City Planning,* g, op cit., p. 46.
55 Ibid., p. 71.
56 Ibid., p. 72.
57 Ibid.

to call them, served a critical role in building consensus to act. With vague aims, Rodwin asserted, "the disposition [was], . . . as Hirschman suggest[ed], to follow 'The Principle of the Hiding Hand'—that is, to underestimate the difficulties or to overestimate the benefits."[52] If it were not for these fuzzy assumptions, no planning project would ever be undertaken. In addition to the US, Rodwin secured important consultancy projects in France, Turkey and Venezuela. Yet despite stressing the immense differences in the economic, political and technological contexts of these countries, Rodwin argued that all these planning endeavors shared a common characteristic—they were all fuzzy in the beginning:

> The experience of these nations indicate the ambiguity and the range of variation that might be expected in the definition of aims in the early years of such a planning venture, and perhaps for many years thereafter. They suggest that it may be impossible—at least at the outset—for government to formulate adequate or precise national goals for urban and regional development.[53]

The planner's "aim," Rodwin asserted, "[was] to produce a system that [was] as coherent as possible," but they must also realize that "such a result [was] rare in reality."[54] In Rodwins's view, the structural determinism of prevalent systems theories reduced planning to two approaches. One was to pay no attention to physical planning at all. This approach assumed that there were hidden structural laws operating within the market and that they would take care of all contingencies. The other approach was to attempt to plan everything in detail. This view characterized the decentralization and regional planning approaches which, guided by Chicago School sociologists such as Robert Park, saw cities as part of an interconnected ecological system.

For Rodwin, the guilty in this regard were some of his own teachers like Charles Abrams, one of the first advocates of decentralization. These early urban planners, Rodwin argued, had

> viewed the city as an organism requiring a habitat of appropriate space, forms, and services to serve its needs. In this view, only the professional planner understood the critical needs and interrelationships; and only the planner could diagnose resultant problems and prescribe plans to ensure efficient, attractive, and comprehensive environmental solutions.[55]

This view ignored, Rodwin continued, the "conception of the city as—in effect—a very loose consortium of interests and clients (with changing membership and powers) whose views will (and should) control the making or implementing or changing of the physical arrangements of their habitat."[56]

Moreover, Rodwin contended that these views foregrounded the view of the expert rather than that of the client. The idea of a "delicately balanced resource base and physical setting" stressed the importance of expert guidance and coordination. Without such insight the city was doomed to "profligate urban growth or pollution of various kinds."[57]

When applied to the international arena, Rodwin asserted, the ecological view proved to be strongly anti-urban. Unable to read the burgeoning city in the Third World except in negative terms, the experts stressed the need for various models of decentralization which would alleviate the population and resource pressures experienced by big cities through the development of a system of urban centers of various sizes on a regional scale. Both Catherine Bauer and Abrams had proposed such decentralization plans for Asia and Africa.[58]

The solution, Rodwin repeatedly argued, was not to discard decentralization, or regional development altogether (Rodwin was after all the president of the Regional Science Association), but to ground the insights of these approaches in a different understanding of concepts such as systems and models. This required a reconceptualization of the project of planning itself from a structural science focused on discovering hidden social and natural laws, to a strategic open-ended intervention that combined structural concepts with contingent requirements:

> There are growing doubts about our ability to establish meaningful priorities when there are multiple goals. Our mathematical models have less relevance when decision-makers 'satisfice' rather than 'optimize,' which current research suggest is often the case. There is evidence that inadequate account is taken of what is feasible and of what people realistically want.[59]

Above all, this meant accounting for the presence of multiple competing models. Rather than functioning as a tool by which one could implement optimum laws, planning ought rather to be understood as a terrain that allowed different models, each representing different goals, to influence each other. Planning was to become a discipline of "strategizing" rather than "optimizing." Not so much a window into an optimum world—hidden from view and yet

58 This view, Rodwin urged, also stemmed from an over-reliance on the idea of the "primate" city. All large cities in the decolonizing world were seen as primate, that is, developed during colonial period as export and manufacturing centers to extract products from a primitively maintained countryside. This view generated an "outright hostility to 'primate' and overurbanized cities . . . .and resentment for what was considered their inevitable corollary— stunted urban systems and lagging regions elsewhere." Despite the "obscure and controversial" status of these assertions, Rodwin stressed, regional planning and development was reduced to the technical problem of what "should be done to offset the advantages of concentrated purchasing power in these big cities and the allure of their more varied public services and wider job and social opportunities." Ibid., pp. 72-73. Views of San Félix and Castillito. From Appleyard, *Planning the Pluralist City.*

working like clockwork according to its own laws—planning was an instrument which ought to be used to formalize socially determined and politically negotiated goals.

The "region" was going to be the new space where this ethically informed and socially responsible view of planning as a consensus building enterprise would unfold. "In the past," Rodwin asserted, "the emphasis in economic policy has been 'vertical,' that is, on developing particular sectors of the economy such as transportation, power, agriculture, education, and forestry. This emphasis neglects the symbiotic character of a region and the interdependence of its diverse "'systems' of activities."[60]

Mapping the Continuum

In Ciudad Guayana, this view allowed for a particular system of intervention, one which was hierarchically organized but which appeared dispersed, disseminated, and horizontal. This set-up was based on the particular framing of Ciudad Guayana as a region. We have already looked at CVG's fluid extension of its definition of the Guayana region in space and time. The Joint Center leaders were also interested in defining the "region" as a continuous conceptual realm that cut across previous geographical and sociological divisions of local/ regional/national, high/low, elite/poor, etc. We have also mentioned the various changes in Ciudad Guayana's urban design. The city center was moved from one location to the next according to revisions in population estimates and new traffic models. These changes were seen as part of a continuing and open-ended process of planning.

In 1964, the CVG sponsored an extensive sociological survey by a Joint Center team of sociologists and urban designers. The survey was headed by Donald Appleyard, an architect and planner who had joined MIT and the Joint Center in 1961 and was now a member of the Joint Center urban design team in Guayana.[61] Appleyard had recently co-authored *The View from the Road* with Kevin Lynch and John Myer, and the analytical approach taken at Ciudad Guayana shows many similarities to the environmental perception analyses he devised with Lynch and Meyer.[62] In Appleyard's survey, however, we see an attempt to bridge over the conceptual divisions distinctly marked in the approach taken by Lynch et al. For example, in an early article written with Rodwin, "The Theory of Urban Form,"[63] Lynch

59 Rodwin, *Nations and Cities*, op cit., p. 10.
60 Ibid, p. 10.
61 The other members of the team were von Moltke and William Porter. Porter would later become Dean of Architecture at MIT from 1971-81. Appleyard himself moved to the University of California at Berkeley in 1967

as an Associate Professor of Urban Design when the school established a PhD program under Richard Meier.
62 Donald Appleyard, Kevin Lynch, and John Myer. *The View from the Road* (Cambridge, MA: The MIT Press, 1964).
63 Kevin Lynch and Lloyd Rodwin, "The Theory of

Urban Form," in *Journal of the American Institute of Planners* 24 (1984). A slightly revised version of the article was republished as "The Form of the City," in Rodwin's *City and City Planning*, op cit., pp, 30-60. Rodwin acknowledged that "Unlike the other jointly prepared chapter [in the book], Lynch was the main author of

this article."
64 Ibid., p.35.
65 Ibid., pp. 429-30.
66 Donald Appleyard, "City Designers and the Pluralistic City," *Planning Urban Growth and Regional Development*, ed. Rodwin et al., , op cit., p. 423.
67 Ibid., pp. 423, 429.
68 Ibid., p. 430.

stressed that "physical form" or "shape" was a distinct realm from "spatial distribution of activities" or "'use' proper." According to them, "the pattern of activities and the physical pattern are often surprisingly independent of each other, and they must be analytically separate if we are to understand the effect of either."[64] Lessons learned in one realm couldn't transfer over to the other.

For Appleyard, however, this was precisely the analytical division that had hindered Joint Center's progress in Ciudad Guayana. The separation between form and activity, material and conceptual, had created incongruencies not only between various members of the Center's team but also between the perceptions of the experts and those of the inhabitants:

> The inhabitant's world was a familiar territory unclear at the fringes of knowledge; the designer's world was thin in the center but bounded by distinct outlines of rivers and urban development as etched out on his maps. In psychological language, the inhabitants saw the "figure," the designers saw the "ground."[65]

The "environmental surveys" designed by Appleyard sought to traverse this conceptual separation between "figure" and "ground" by devising new categories of "knowledge" that could seamlessly cut across "various environmental factors—physical, social, and functional."[66] For Appleyard, his work with Lynch already contained the seeds of analysis that could bridge this conceptual separation. The key was to perform a visual analysis of the environment on maps or images that were drawn by the inhabitants from memory. With this focus, analysis came to be based on mental images, the contingent epistemological constructs of the mind. Designers usually saw visual analysis as a window into an underlying system of rules governing the urban environment or into an underlying structure of the inhabitant's perception. By paying attention to mnemonic images, the designer's goal shifted to 'only' establishing an itinerary of the inhabitant's contingent and momentary knowledge. With this shift, a continuum was established between the perceptions of different groups, a key goal of the Guayana survey. "The subjects were asked," Appleyard declared,

> a range of questions designed to assess the nature of their urban knowledge, starting with open-ended task like drawing their map of the city and recalling well-remembered features, followed by descriptions of a journey through the city, of particular building and districts, of social functional, and natural patterns, of recent and predicted changes, and opinions about their current needs and preferences.[67]

The responses ranged, Applyard declared, from "primitive" and "parochial" to "inferential" and deductive, depending on the respondent's level of education. Yet these differences, Appleyard asserted, were ones of degree, not kind. If treated as epistemological images, different viewpoints could form interrelated mnemonic maps. Moreover, the contingent knowledge of each image could be manipulated to achieve greater uniformity: "[by]

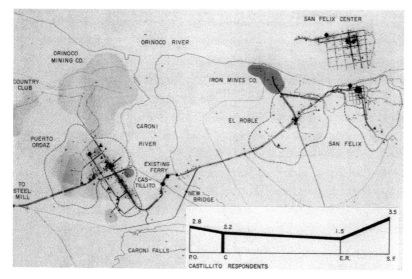

left, Knowledge-map of the residents of Castillito, "a low-income rancho area." The graph below the map shows the "complexity figures in each zone for that respondent group.

right, Opposite Respondents' different yet related mnemonic maps of the city.

From Appleyard, *Planning the Pluralist City.*

monitor[ing] the complexity of group's knowledge in relation to the needs and capacities of different groups in any particular time, [it was possible] raising [the complexity] for some, reducing strain for others."[68]

For Appleyard, imagining the city as a field of competing knowledge fields changed the role of planning altogether. Instead of promising unified plans and optimum results—which were bound to fail in the face of different expectations—planning could reconfigure itself as a consensus building enterprise. "This [focus on] information can have several implications for policy," Appleyard asserted. "Besides improving the knowledge of the city designers, we could consider extending and coordinating knowledge among different population groups in order to reduce future conflicts, misperceptions, and errors."[69] With Appleyard's reframing, a new legitimacy is claimed for planning, one that is secured against all challenges in advance. By defining planning as a process of coordinating different knowledge systems, any and all challenges are predefined as a result of temporary errors in this organizing field. Ironically, the proclamation of consensus building serves to close the very possibility of politics in advance.

Boulding's theory of knowledge had also precluded politics, though in his case the closure occurred via economic planning. For Boulding, knowledge images were the common vectors linking the physical world with the conceptual. They not only cut across different social categories but also across the division between the material and the discursive. As Boulding would later explain:

Economic development manifests itself largely in the production of commodities, that is, goods and services. It originates, however, in ideas, plans, and attitudes in the human mind. These are the genotypes in economic development. This whole process indeed

TOPOLOGICAL

SEQUENTIAL

SPATIAL

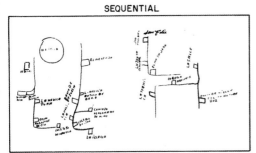

FRAGMENTED

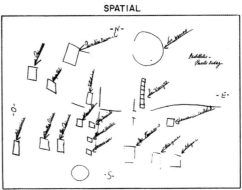

SCATTERED

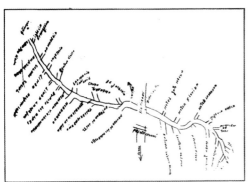

CHAIN

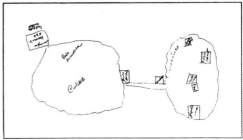

MOSAIC

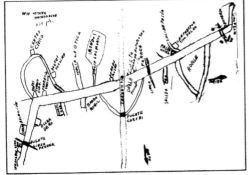

BRANCH AND LOOP

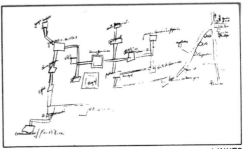

LINKED

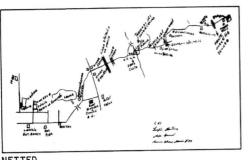

NETTED

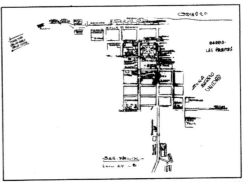

PATTERNED

POSITIONAL

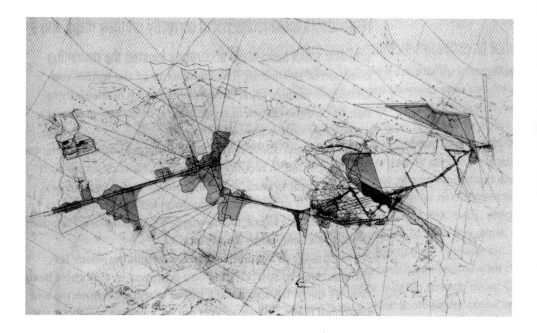

Spatial structure, describing the mnemonic field of a traveler on the main road of the city. From Appleyard, *Planning in the Pluralist City.*

can be described as a process in the growth of knowledge. What the economist calls "capital" is nothing more than human knowledge imposed on the material world. Knowledge and the growth of knowledge, therefore, is the essential key to economic development. Investment, financial systems and economic organizations and institutions are in a sense only the machinery by which a knowledge process is created and expressed.[70]

Boulding's intent was to allow criticism emerging in one area of knowledge to be transferred over to the next. Yet the most critical effect of this proclaimed continuity was the all-encompassing nature of the open-ended disciplinary practices it engendered. If all political challenges could be characterized as misinterpretations of particular knowledge within a project, than all challenges could be responded

69 Ibid.

70 Kenneth Boulding, *Evolutionary Economics.*, op cit.

71 In two books and several articles drawn from her experience of living in San Félix, the "lower-income" neighbor hood in the city, with her architect husband and four children for over two and a half years, Peattie outlined the divorce between the planners' world and the "real" interests, concerns, politics, and struggles of the "actual people" on the site. See Lisa Peattie's *The View from the Barrio* (Ann Arbor, MI: The University of Michigan Press, 1968), and *Planning: Rethinking Ciudad Guayana* (Ann Arbor, MI: The University of Michigan Press, 1987).(see fn. 20).

to by agreeing to reinterpret that knowledge—and never reinterpreting the project itself. It is this all-encompassing continuity between categories of analysis that was sought in the planning approach at Ciudad Guayana.

And it is this preemptive continuity that was missed by major critics of the project such as Lisa Peattie, an anthropologist on the Joint Center's staff. Peattie was hired as a consultant by the Joint Center to report on the sociological make-up of the Ciudad Guayana inhabitants and was in charge of overseeing the gathering of sociological data for the survey conducted by Appleyard. From the onset, however, Peattie saw such exercises as signs of an elite and technocratic planning mindset that turned "real" people into "abstract" data.[71]

According to Peattie, the most conspicuous evidence of this division was the color-coded land-use plans that were often derisively called "kites' by the Venezuelan planners. For Peattie, the brightly colored, schematic divisions of land into distinct functional parcels constructed an illusion of clarity. It made the proposals palatable for public consumption. In these drawings, the city was "cleansed of the complicated lives of the inhabitant" and turned into a consumable diagram for large industry and national political forces.[72]

It is true that the Ciudad Guayana project framed the city in terms relevant to the interests of large industry and national political forces. However, the critically important thing to note here is that this framing is not carried out by constructing hierarchical dichotomies of high vs. low, abstract vs. real, modern vs. primitive, labor vs. capitalist. Rather, the framing of the city as a set of manipulable forces is executed by defining it in terms of a continuous epistemological structure that precedes such divisions. Ciudad Guayana delegitimizes the very division between labor and capitalist interests, and not by claiming one as representative of limited "concrete" concerns and the other as a beholder of expansive "abstract" plans. It does away with the very premise of the separate sociological categories itself. There are no illegitimate labor demands in Ciudad Guayana, only errors of knowledge to be corrected by revising existing epistemological images.

72 The same attitude pervaded, Peattie argued, in designers' sketches and architectural drawings. Aerial views looked down on neatly arranged rows of houses, turning complex social situations into questions of formal composition. Von Moltke's initial sketches of the city, Peattie asserted, focused primarily on the natural features of the site, taking out, "most strikingly, human purpose and human meaning… . . . out of the landscape." Even the seemingly less abstract architectural representation such as perspectives showed a similarly detached view. Markets were imagined without crowds (an economically untenable proposal in itself, according to Peattie), and streets were shown without traffic and people [See image on following page]. For Peattie, what was erased in these modes of looking at the existing city and imagining a future one, were "centers of power, outcomes of struggle and investments, [that formed] the bases for proposals of change. [Each] sketch convert[ed] a city of hustlers, politicians, entrepreneurs, families, and reformers into a pattern of masses and forms and their spatial configuration." Lisa Peattie, *Rethinking Ciudad Guayna*, op cit., p. 116.

The image thus establishes a theory of knowledge that seeks to undo the distinction between the material and the epistemological. The irreducible gap between one and the other is filled with knowledge, fuzzy knowledge.[73] Pollution, Boulding had asserted, was nothing more than pollution of knowledge. It occurred only because its true costs to the majority were unknown. The impossibility of finding a direct correlation between the multiplicity of causes and effects let the few get away with pollution without paying its full costs. Consequently, "coarse" epistemological approaches that sought to establish this correlation through rhetorical concepts were bound to be more effective in this realm than "fine" mathematical equations.

Lisa Peattie criticized an early design sketch of a market shown without crowds.

[73] Kenneth Boulding, *The Economics of Pollution* (New York: New York University Press, 1971).

[74] I have elsewhere explored the role of "self-help" housing—particularly the models suggested by the team of Charles Abrams and Otto Koenigsberger in their missions for the UN to various Third World contexts— in solidifying the move away from earlier master planning approaches. See the author's *The Periphery Within: Modern Architecture and the Making of the Third World* (MIT Doctoral Ph.D. dissertation, Massachusetts Institute of Technology, 2007).

It was not just mathematics that Boulding, and in his wake, planning advocates in the '60s, discredited. The introduction of fuzzy knowledge into planning also sought to eradicate, at a fundamental level, the identifiable subjects of planning themselves, be they experts, labor, capitalists, or migrants. If social and economic divisions could be explained as effects of the distribution of knowledge, then all political resistance could be preempted as errors. It must be remembered that the continuous all-encompassing realm of planning we saw unfolding in Ciudad Guayana was not proclaimed in the language of the Kantian *a priori*, the world of hidden universal rules that the intuitive genius of the artist brings to light, and which the rational genius of the philosopher understands in retrospect. The expert agent of fuzzy planning is cautiously proclaimed as a subject of limited knowledge. The expert claims to operate in the same partial, inconsistent, ambiguous, and fuzzy realm that surrounds the inhabitants. He cannot be held accountable for his expertise any more than the inhabitant can for her ignorance. This is the genius of defining planning as an endeavor in a world of fuzzy epistemological images: the expert wrenches the possibility of control away from the local—and yet, in doing so, he doesn't claim a higher realm of knowledge or responsibility. The expert here is not positioned as a responsible agent of control; rather, the expert operates on tentative knowledge in just the same way as the subject. He is just as helpless as the subject, just as limitedly informed. The expert of epistemological images is himself a moving subject, always fuzzy.

As Eric Mumford has insightfully shown in the previous chapter, in the wake of various developments at home and abroad, Joint Center members were moving towards smaller scale and more open-ended approaches to housing.[74] In this chapter we have identified some of the conceptual seeds of that move, seeds that were already present in the open-ended revisions of Ciudad Guayana plans and economic and philosophical debates they drew upon.

Often, critiques of architectural modernism and planning in the Third World simply see these discourses as imposing fixed universal plans onto different local contexts. This view misses the new modes of intervention that these discourses were able to establish in the postwar development arena. To understand these modes of intervention and their attendant calculus of power, we have to pay attention to how power in this arena was rendered invisible through a new ethics and new methods of claiming legitimacy and expertise. Without such attention we cannot account for the ways in which those very structures continue to unfold in the current conjunctures of globalization.

FELICITY D. SCOTT

DISCOURSE, SEEK, INTERACT:
Urban Systems at MIT

Reporting to Institute President Howard W. Johnson on the state of the School of Architecture and Planning for the year 1968, Dean Lawrence B. Anderson noted the impact of the moment's turbulence as it was then being felt in the School. The profound "dislocations and adjustments" of society at large, he noted, had affected the ability of both architecture and planning to accumulate accurate knowledge of social needs or to predict future programs, troubling by extension the disciplines' sense of assurance of their professional roles, which he described as "giving order to environmental and social change."[1] While, as he remarked, "traditional values in the environmental professions are fading rapidly," the counterpart to this waning was that "interaction with other professions intensifies." For Anderson the rapid obsolescence of conventional expertise and established modes of practice were not cause for lament. Rather, such transformations had provided the occasion for a strategic rethinking of the School's role within the institutional milieu of MIT as the Institute strove to recalibrate the scope of its scientific and technical research in response to the so-called "urban crises" of the 1960s.[2] Acknowledging the effort's potential benefits, Anderson noted that "the continued awakening of the Institute as a whole toward urban problems is a spur to both departments." The school's encounter with that "awakening" left a profound mark on sectors of its architectural research and pedagogical initiatives in the years immediately following Anderson's Report; indeed, faculty and students became increasingly integrated within interdisciplinary frameworks dedicated to developing techniques of controlling urban and environmental "systems" and the populations who inhabited them—dedicated, that is, to their monitoring, quantitative description, regulation, management, organization and visualization.

While interdisciplinary architectural and urban research had of course taken place during the previous decades at MIT, as elsewhere, we can recognize in this exchange a significant shift in disciplinary and interdisciplinary identifications, and moreover a shift in the very

Acknowledgments: This article forms part of a book project addressing architecture's response to territorial insecurity during the 1960s and 1970s, "Outlaw Territory: Environments of Insecurity/Architectures of Counter-Insurgency, 1966-1979," to be published by Zone Books. I would like to thank Arindam Dutta for the invitation to delve into the Institute Archives, and Stephanie Tuerk and Kathaleen Brearley for their kind assistance in facilitating my visit. I would also like to thank the staff at the Institute Archives.

1 Lawrence B. Anderson, "School of Architecture and Planning," in "Report of the President, 1968," *Massachusetts Institute of Technology Bulletin* 104, no. 3 (December 1968), 29.

2 On the Federal Government's understanding of the "urban crises," see Senate Committee on Government Operations, United States Congress, Subcommittee on Executive Reorganization, *Federal Role in Urban Affairs, Hearings, Eighty-Ninth Congress, Second Session and Ninetieth Congress, First Session* (Washington: U.S. Government Printing Office, 1966-68).

conception of architecture.[3] No longer were architects simply drawing upon multiple fields of expertise in order to facilitate their design work and scholarship through an engagement of research at the forefront of a transforming modernity. Rather, architecture would momentarily come to be regarded (and even to model itself) as one more parameter in a general systems paradigm geared towards environmental management and control, a paradigm that, like its forebears in the large-scale techno-scientific research characteristic of MIT laboratories following World War II, was inextricably coupled with heavily funded research into the application of computers and scientific knowledge; that is, architecture became inscribed within the domain of "Big Science."[4] This did not of course affect the School in its entirety, and many other stories could be told about it during this period. However, the School's increased intimacy with the social sciences and computerization, and its scripted interpolation within what Senator J. William Fulbright termed the "military-industrial-academic complex" at this moment, emerge as important symptoms of a larger historical transformation that warrant further scrutiny.[5]

To understand why the School was temporarily embraced as central to the Institute's response to the period's social turbulence and related geopolitical insecurities, I want to trace some of the activities and the legacy of MIT's Urban Systems Laboratory (USL). As one official report retrospectively acknowledged, "M.I.T. responded to the urban crises of the 1960s by forming the Urban Systems Laboratory."[6] The USL was founded in 1968 following the recommendations of an Ad Hoc Faculty Committee on Urban Studies convened by Johnson in late 1966, his first year as President of the Institute. It was described as "a new interdepartmental and multidisciplinary activity to mobilize Institute-wide resources in the area of urban systems."[7] In February 1967 MIT submitted a 100-page proposal for a Program in Urban Affairs to the Ford Foundation. The proposal included requests for funding "Development of Laboratories for Urban Problems." Cities, the introduction remarked, "have become the focus for the most acute diseases of our society—poverty, racial discrimination, crime, social disintegration and the degeneration of public education"—problems which, it was believed, reiterating a common trope, "resemble those encountered in the traditional societies of less developed countries."[8] The Institute was awarded a $3 million grant as part of the Foundation's new program on

3 We only need to mention the foundation of the Center for Urban and Regional Studies in 1957 and two years later and in collaboration with Harvard University the establishment of the Joint Center for Urban Studies to make this clear. Moreover, in October 1966, the Department of Architecture

hosted a conference entitled "Inventing the Future Environment," which brought architects together with economists, political scientists, planners, philosophers, social psychologists, and "futurists." The proceedings were published as *Planning for Diversity and Choice: Possible*

Futures and Their Relation to the Man-Controlled Environment, Stanford Anderson ed. (Cambridge: MIT Press, 1968).
4 See Stuart W. Leslie, *The Cold War and American Science: The Military-Industrial-Academic Complex at MIT and Stanford* (New York: Columbia University

Press, 1993).
5 J. William Fulbright, "The War and Its Effects: The Military-Industrial-Academic Complex," in *Super-State: Readings in the Military-Industrial Complex*, ed. Herbert I. Schiller (Urbana: University of Illinois Press, 1970), 171-178. Reprinted from *Congressional Record,*

"University Urban Studies," which replaced its "urban extension" program.[9] $800,000 of the grant was dedicated to founding the USL.

The initial aim of the USL was to develop an institutional framework and techniques of interdisciplinary coordination and to build up large urban data banks that together would facilitate collaboration and "lay the groundwork for an Institute capability for playing a significant role in large-scale, mission-oriented, action-oriented projects." Moreover, the lab would, as the Ford Foundation proposal stressed, serve to educate "individuals who combine technical competence with an interest in and understanding of urban problems"— including, as they note, "social and aesthetic parameters"—to produce "a generation of urban technologists who will have a language in common with those whose primary concerns are the political, social and economic aspects."[10] Before turning to the history and vicissitudes of the USL, and to some of the architectural and urban research that took place under its sponsorship, I want to return to Anderson's 1968 report to President Johnson, which offers further clues regarding the historical contours of this encounter and the "urban technologists" it would produce.

Participation

Summarizing recent activities in the School, which he characterized as charting a move away from "old-style professionalism" towards the "catharsis" of "direct interaction with people in their environment," Anderson identified a series of "field activities in environmental development" concerned with the "dynamics of squatter settlement in cities in the have-not countries" and, "related to," as he put it, work on race and poverty in the United States and particularly inner-city Boston.[11] In the Department of Architecture alone, as reported by Chair Donlyn Lyndon, these field activities ranged from Robert Goodman's studio work with the Lower Roxbury Community Corporation and Chester Sprague's ongoing work with Blackfeet Indians to Horacio Caminos' Ford Foundation-sponsored program in Urban Settlement Design and recently-appointed faculty member John C. Turner's work on squatter settlements in South America, as well as comparative studies of South American communities with "selected communities in Boston."[12] One might certainly question the too-easy or pseudo-morphic conflation of development issues impacting the

90th Congress, First Session, December 13, 1967, vol. 113, part 27, pages 36181-36184. Today, Fulbright explained, "Our county is becoming conditioned to permanent conflict. More and more our economy, our Government, and our universities are adapting themselves to the requirements of continuing

war—total war, limited war, and cold war," 173-174.
6 Charles L. Miller, "Urban System Laboratory," in "Report of the President and the Chancellor Issue, 1973-74," *Massachusetts Institute of Technology Bulletin* 110, no. 4 (November 1974), 122.

7 Charles L. Miller, "Urban Systems Laboratory," in "Report of the President, 1968," 489.
8 "A Proposal to the Ford Foundation for a Program in Urban Affairs at M.I.T.: Report of the Ad Hoc Faculty Committee on Urban Studies" (Cambridge: MIT, 1967), I-1. The initial list of relevant

resources began with the School of Architecture and Planning and ended with the Lincoln and Instrumentation Laboratories. "We can and do bring together the city planner, the engineer, the political scientist, the economist, the manager, the architect and artists whose combined perceptions are

Professor Donlyn
Lyndon with students,
Department of
Architecture, MIT, n.d..

needed on urban problems," the report explained, I-3.

9 The Urban Extension program ran from 1959 to 1966. "University Urban Studies" was dedicated to establishing "long-term intellectual resources," and was avowedly a response to the "social ferment in the nation's cities." See Ford Foundation, "University Urban Studies," *Ford Foundation Annual Report 1967*, p. 35. See also Ford Foundation, "Urban Extension: A Report on Experimental Programs Assisted by the Ford Foundation" (New York: Ford Foundation, 1966).

10 "A Proposal to the Ford Foundation," I-2.

11 Anderson, "School of Architecture and Planning" (1968), 30.

12 Donlyn Lyndon, "Department of Architecture," in "Report of the President, 1968," 36.

Global South and the socio-economic inequities and environmental injustices characteristic of American inner-cities following a period of rapid urbanization and "white flight." But the urban insecurities that emerged in both domains were connected in the minds—and hence in the development theories—of the State Department, Department of Defense, and policy makers as well as institutions such as the Ford Foundation as they turned their attention to "urban affairs." Both domains were impacted by the expanding reach and transforming character of policies informing a largely US-driven capitalist globalization, and it will be precisely at this nexus of policy and concern that social scientific knowledge, managerial strategies, and technologies born of Cold War military research would come to be recognized as having strategic lessons not only for warfare and developmental aid but also for domestic security applications in the form of technologies of environmental control.

After identifying the School of Architecture and Planning's attention to questions of urban instability, Anderson remarked, "Even more interesting (and disturbing to some) is M.I.T.'s own internal environmental ferment," which he cast as a manifestation of the community's rejection of delegating decisions to experts and of people's growing desire, rather, to "participate." "It is important to recognize and to provide creative outlet for this wish," he proposed, ominously adding with reference to the protest movement: "Administrators who insist that things must continue as they always have lay their institutions open to destructive action, as has occurred in New York and Paris." If MIT had emerged relatively unscathed from the events of 1968, such attempts to offer palliative measures to the period's growing civil unrest through forms of "participation" would not succeed for long. The following year, political activism, including within the Institute's own scientific community, would increasingly focus on the Institute's role in the development of weaponry and military strategy for the war in South East Asia, and MIT would in turn become the target of such "destructive action," in a series of events to which I will return.

Anderson then identified the form those "creative outlets" had taken, describing four "otherwise unrelated events" which "manifest this new spirit in our School." According to him they shared the capacity to "short-circuit conventional modes of representing action and go directly to the production of environmental change or artifact:"

13 In Spring 1967, MIT students had, as reported by C. Ray Smith, "overnight turned one of their design studios into an instant *barriada* by subdividing it with salvage timber and concrete blocks." Supposedly outraging the administration by their rebellion, this act of taking charge was in

fact quickly incorporated and neutralized. As Smith continued, "the following Fall, Donlyn Lyndon, newly appointed head of the department, gained the administration's agreement for first-, third-, and fourth-year students to involve themselves officially in subdividing, building,

painting, and personalizing all their design studios as a 'Space/Use Workshop.'" C. Ray Smith, "The New Interiors: Fad or Fact?," *Progressive Architecture* 49, no. 4 (October 1968): 154. In his report as Department head, Lyndon noted of this "more direct confrontation between form

and behavior," that "students who worked in the area encountered the necessity for programming construction procedures, the difficulties of resolving conflicts in neighboring designs, and the consequences of long-term use of their own design decisions. At the same time, the entire project served

Fifth-Year Architecture
Students' Studio Space,
the "mezzanines." Photo:
Phokion Karas.

The studio "mezzanines." From Donlyn Lyndon, "MIT's Lofty Practicum," *Journal of Architectural Education*, 1968.

First is the action on the part of an extraordinarily mature and demanding group of students to force the reformation of the curricular requirements for the MCP [Masters of City Planning] degree. Second are the celebrated architectural "mezzanines," which, while trouble-making, are remarkable examples of a kind of mass will to create an environment.[13] Most public in character is the third example, the inspired commemoration of Martin Luther King, in which the design students chose to express their ideas by means of images arranged in space. Finally, I would mention the increasingly successful efforts of Professor Wayne V. Andersen, Professor György Kepes, and the Fellows of the Center for Advanced Visual Studies to intensify the experience of the visual arts by involving the viewer in direct participation, as in the events designed by Hans Haacke and Otto Piene.[14]

If each of these modes of "participation" exemplified for Anderson an engagement with indeterminate relations between a subject and their environment—whether educational or aesthetic—which demonstrated process-based transformation, and if they seemed to exhibit contemporary relevance in a moment of rapid social change, he qualified his enthusiasm by noting that within the institutional context of MIT they had a necessary limitation. "Unless supported by disinterested monitoring and evaluation," he added, "they may be too visceral in character to meet the university's standards of objectivity."[15]

Such standards, with their supposedly "disinterested monitoring and evaluation," could, Anderson went on, be found in another—to his mind "complementary"—side of the school's activities, which "spring from the promise of new methodologies for problem solving, especially those supported by memory and retrieval systems and manipulative possibilities of the computer."[16] With the computer came the potential to eclipse architecture's subjective and aesthetic parameters —to overcome the stasis and "overcodification" of "symbolic operations" burdening traditional conceptions—by adopting a feedback-based paradigm that, the Dean proposed, "assures continued relevance" in a rapidly changing world. The computer provided tools with which one could organize complex data and allowed architects to gain a "wider statement of the total problem" and "generate a richer choice of solutions." Like other professions, that is, architecture

to demonstrate alternative uses of space." Lyndon, "Department of Architecture," 34. Haacke's Hayden Gallery exhibition included early systems-based works, such as *Skyline, Wide White Flow, Weather Cube* and others. See "Haacke Exhibit Features Systems of 'grass,' 'ice'," *The Tech* 87, no. 38 (October 20,

1967): 1, 3.

14 Anderson, "School of Architecture and Planning" (1968), 31.

15 On the history of objectivity as the aspiration "to knowledge that bears no trace of the knower," see the remarkable Lorraine Daston, and Peter Galison, *Objectivity* (New York: Zone Books, 2010), 17.

16 Anderson, "School of Architecture and Planning" (1968), 31-32.

could move away from the intuitive towards the quantitative and hence toward what Anderson cast as a "rationalization" of "thinking patterns." If, as he recounted, architecture and planning had "been slower than other professions in adopting the powerful tools of computation," that trend, he confidently proclaimed, was "now in full swing." These methods were "now beginning to revolutionize environmental design," with developments in computer applications being sponsored "through participation in the newly organized Urban Systems Laboratory."[17]

Urban Affairs

In October 1968, MIT's official newsletter *Tech Talk* cast the founding of the Urban Systems Laboratory as a direct response to the period's domestic insecurity: "Civil unrest! Crisis in the cities! Scream the headlines almost daily. How to approach the seemingly insuperable problems urban life imposes these days?" Identified as "Institute's newest enterprise," the USL, they continued, "sprang into being last winter as an effort to initiate a systems approach—so effective in the space program—in alleviating some of the difficulties involved."[18] The USL was indeed central to the Institute's attempts to bring expertise developed in its engineering and social science labs, not only for the country's space program but also for its military and intelligence agencies, to bear on the domestic front. And the character of the USL's work, particularly in the fields of architecture and planning, would be very much marked by that legacy. "Much of the initial conceptual thinking about U.S.L.," Director Charles L. Miller reported to President Johnson at the end of the lab's first year, "was influenced by our experience with defense and space problem solving."[19] This transfer of skills was not, Miller explained, unique to a university setting. "Many technology-oriented companies are in the process of doing precisely what the Institute is doing, creating a mechanism whereby those skills and assets acquired working on the problems of defense and space can be transferred to the problems of cities," he remarked, pointing to a more widespread militarization of the domestic realm.[20]

In September 1969 *Progressive Architecture* published a profile on MIT's Urban Systems Laboratory entitled "In Search of Urban Expertise." Written by Associate Editor Alis D. Runge, it posed the question: "Can the university perform for the cities the same kind of

17 Ibid., 32. In his 1964 report as Dean, Pietro Belluschi stressed the need for a shift away from the artistic conception of architectural practice, noting, "It is clear that as a profession architecture has not undergone the technological revolution that has benefited other fields at M.I.T." Pietro

Belluschi, "School of Architecture and Planning," in "President's Report Issue 1963-1964," 55, 56.

18 "MITUSL??," *Tech Talk* (October 30 1968): 1.

19 Miller, "Urban Systems Laboratory" (1968), 499.

20 Ibid., 492.

research and development functions that it has so successfully performed for NASA and the Department of Defense? Can it work productively with city governments and industry to solve the difficult problems of the country's 'unmanageable' metropolitan centers? The Massachusetts Institute of Technology, for one, is setting out to prove that it can."[21] With the establishment of the USL, Runge went on to demonstrate, what constituted "urban expertise" in the university had fundamentally changed. The intimate triangulation of the military, industrial, and academic sectors was, she suggested, precisely what qualified MIT to operate at the forefront of defense against the "urban crisis": "the faculty is liberally salted with men whose careers straddle the academic-industrial consulting line," she noted, "and includes a number of returnees from Washington's advisory elite who still contribute more than their fair share to the support of Boston-Washington air routes."[22]

Runge stressed repeatedly that the USL's ambition was characterized by "urban action," or the practical application of scientific knowledge and technology. "Designating the new urban unit as a 'laboratory' rather than a 'center' was not a random choice," she explained, suggesting that the terminology "reflects the action-oriented thinking that is everywhere affecting the form of American institutions. 'We are not to be simply another center studying the city, but a group of people that are trying to do something about the problems,'" she quoted Miller as asserting.[23] Miller understood this application of academic research to mean making "technology work in the city," and he went on to characterize the goal of USL projects as the development of methodologies that would help close "an enormous gap between research—the university kind of research in particular—and the city."[24] According to Runge, albeit somewhat inaccurately, this "shift in emphasis from study to action" distinguished USL from the Joint Center for Urban Studies, which was also sponsored by the Ford Foundation and which had been founded in response to the destabilizing forces of rapid urbanization both in the US and the developing world.[25] The answer to why the Ford Foundation would fund, as Runge put it, "another urban unit in Cambridge," may indeed have lay in the instrumental nature of USL research as it attempted to bridge the (soon to be increasingly controversial) gap between basic and applied research. Miller had stressed this "action-oriented" quality when interviewed in April 1968 by MIT's student newspaper, The Tech, on the occasion of the lab's opening.

21 Alis D. Runge, "In Search of Urban Expertise," Progressive Architecture (September 1969): 125.
22 Ibid.
23 Ibid.
24 Ibid.
25 The Joint Center had of course initiated "action-oriented" research, as manifest perhaps most

famously in the development project for Guyana, Venezuela or its investment in Urban Renewal in American cities. Yet unlike USL, from which the humanities were largely banished, historical scholarship continued to play a role in Joint Center research.
26 Jay Kunin, "Urban Lab to Aid American Cities," The Tech

88, no. 23 (April 30, 1968): 1-2.
27 Miller, "Urban Systems Laboratory" (1968), 502.
28 Charles L. Miller, "Urban Systems Laboratory," in "Report of the President, 1969," Massachusetts Institute of Technology Bulletin 105, no. 3 (December 1969), 481.
29 See Jennifer Light, From Warfare to Welfare:

Defense Intellectuals and Urban Problems in Cold War America (Baltimore: Johns Hopkins University Press, 2003), 165.
30 Ibid., 167.
31 Miller, "Urban Systems Laboratory" (1968), 490.
32 Ibid.

As Jay Kunin reported in "Urban Lab to Aid America's Cities": "MIT's activities in urban research are somewhat unique, according to Miller. 'The style of the Institute is different,' from that of other universities. It is interested in being more than a 'city scholar, and is actually closer to being action-oriented than other schools.'"[26] Kunin recounted that Miller had moreover suggested that with its sponsorship of USL, "the main focal point of MIT's contribution to the nation is changing to solving the problems of cities," thus alluding to the conversion of military research to the domestic realm.

To understand the Ford Foundation's interest in funding the lab, we need to ask just what types of technology and scientific research were to be put to work in the city and of course for whom, and to what ends. "Urban Lab to Aid America's Cities" appeared, symptomatically, adjacent to the issue's cover story, "Columbia seized by Students." In his 1968 report Miller alluded to the prospect of the lab providing an outlet for such concerns: "Students turning to U.S.L. are particularly anxious to relate their academic study programs to real problems and issues, and they look to U.S.L. for a coupling with action in the cities."[27] The following year he pointed to the palliative nature of students' involvement: "In some ways, urban unrest and student unrest are connected. At least many students now view urban-oriented involvement as relevant and socially desirable, and their involvement in U.S.L. projects has always been high among our priorities."[28] With concern growing over the Institute's contribution to the nation's burgeoning war machine, MIT now attempted to deploy "urban action" as a conciliatory mechanism—just as the arts and humanities had previously been mobilized as a palliative to rising fears of unchecked technocracy. It is important to recall that the Ford Foundation had long been acknowledged as a CIA front for funding research, particularly in the applied social sciences; in this regard its efforts fed a national security strategy as it shifted its focus towards social engineering on the civilian front, both domestically and internationally.[29] Consequently we find the USL situated precisely at a junction of urbanism, social engineering, development, communication, and citizen participation cast as mechanisms to ensure the goal of political stability or, in cybernetic terms, political "homeostasis."[30]

Miller acknowledged that MIT already had considerable "experience in organizing interdepartmental and interdisciplinary research and project laboratories in engineering and applied science." Yet the USL was, he proposed, the first endeavor to actively script such an interaction between architecture, planning, management, the social sciences, and engineering "on a major scale."[31] The problems of "the city and urban living" were, Miller suggested of this imperative, the "broadest and most complex systems problems ever faced by the Institute," adding that "the commitment of the Institute is a long-term one, and work of U.S.L. will go on for several decades more" (it would actually close less than a decade later in 1974, as US involvement in the war in Vietnam and hence military funding subsided).[32] The Ad Hoc Faculty Committee on Urban Affairs had concluded the previous year that MIT's greatest contribution might lie in its "powerful problem-solving capabilities."

The Institute, it recalled, "has pioneered in the fields of operations research, information sciences, computer technology, and systems development," adding that "[s]trengths, resources, and interests in systems research and computer methods of problem solving exist in significant quality and quantity throughout the Institute," including the Schools of Engineering, Management, Humanities and Social Science, and Architecture and Planning.[33] As evident in the name of the lab, however, the conception of "urban" had undergone a significant transformation; the object of research was no longer the city, its history, or its inhabitants in the traditional sense but rather multiple "urban systems" pursued through analysis and modeling or simulation. Following earlier definitions, the lab's annual report for 1968 attempted to clarify just what was meant in this regard:

> The scope of urban systems is defined initially as the advancement and utilization of the methods of systems analysis, systems engineering, information systems, and related advanced capabilities and technologies applied to the planning, design, construction and management of the facilities and services required for urban living; including transportation, education, communications, environmental control, housing, health and others.[34]

This paradigm of science and technology being put to work in the service of environmental control and population management (its health, housing, educations, productivity for capitalist ends, etc.), situates us, of course, in the realm of what Michel Foucault would begin to theorize in the 1970s as biopolitical regulation.[35] With USL, that is, we find members of the academy, including architects, working to develop tools for advancing a form of governmental rationality and its micro-political techniques of power which sought to govern the body and the psyche of contemporary subjects in their everyday environments. And it is perhaps not incidental in this regard that Bedford-Stuyvesant in Brooklyn, New York, and Roxbury in Boston, both largely economically underprivileged African-American communities, soon became the objects of USL analysis, key sites for such "urban systems" research and potentially targets of its managerial tools for social and environmental control.[36] As the USL report for 1969-1970 explained, Professor Frank Jones, Associate Director of USL, was now running the "Technology, Race, and Poverty" project which was working with community organizers in Boston's South End and with the Metropolitan Applied Research Center, Inc. (MARC) in New York to "assist in a study of two urban ghettos as 'systems.'"[37]

33 Ad Hoc Committee for Urban Affairs, cited in Miller, "Urban Systems Laboratory" (1968), 490.

34 Miller, "Urban Systems Laboratory" (1968), 491. Miller initially set out this definition in January 1968 in "Some Initial Rough and Incomplete Thoughts on a Possible Form and Approach

to Phase I of an M.I.T. Urban Systems Laboratory." Records of Vice President Constantine B. Simonides, 1960-1994. MIT Archives, AC 276 [hereafter AC276].

35 On biopower and biopolitics, see: Michel Foucault, "Right of Death and Power over Life," in *The History of Sexuality,* Vol. I: An

Introduction, trans. Robert Hurley (New York: Random House, 1990); Michel Foucault, *Security, Territory, Population: Lectures at the Collège de France, 1977-1978,* trans. Graham Burchell (New York: Palgrave, 2007); and Michel Foucault, *The Birth of Biopolitics: Lectures at the Collège de France, 1978-1979,*

trans. Graham Burchell (New York: Palgrave, 2008).

36 The archives of USL include a memo dated March 25, 1969, regarding a trip to Bedford-Stuyvesant in Brooklyn as part of this research.

37 Charles L. Miller, "Urban Systems Laboratory," "Report of the President for the

Towards the end of her account of the USL in *P/A*, Runge noted somewhat unexpectedly that "design excellence" had been "duly recognized in USL studies, proposals, and reports;" however, she clarified that "finite, individual concerns are not the province of those whose task it is to devise universal patterns of order for complex social, physical, and economic systems. Still," she concluded, indicating a certain hesitation or unease, "one hopes that, somewhere along the way to the execution of large-scale dreams, there will be someone who will plug in the right architect at the right place."[38] At stake here, in many regards, is precisely the question of what that "right architect" might look like at this moment in 1969, a moment characterized not only by increasing territorial insecurity but, and not unrelatedly, also by the expanding reach of information technology and the emergence of new, mediated forms of social and territorial organization, coupled with new techniques of management. In its contribution to the Ford Foundation proposal, the Department of Architecture suggested that under the impact of contemporary historical pressures the designer no longer had control over his product as such: "the elements that invite his manipulation are more extensive, no longer limited to the building as object," they explained of this encounter, adding that "individual buildings become part of a continuum held together by structures at a macroscale, whose complexities must become part of the designer's vision."[39] How then, we might ask, could any such architect or their vision plug in to such an expanded and increasingly less material apparatus of micro-political control, that "continuum held together by structures at a macroscale"? How could they do so from a disciplinary perspective that we would still recognize as architecture? What role, that is, did (and might) architecture play once interpolated within a systems-paradigm bent on the instrumentalization of disciplinary knowledge in the service of a paradigm of security?

Computer-Aided Design

Miller indicated that the "common denominator" of the USL's diverse activities was the computer, or "computer-based urban research."[40] "Access to an experimentally oriented computer" was, he explained, "essential to new research in urban information systems, urban simulation, and urban design as planned by many groups associated with U.S.L."[41] In 1968 those computer resources took the form of an IBM System/360, Model 67 time-sharing computer, a mainframe to which the various USL groups had access via

Academic Year 1969-1970," *Massachusetts Institute of Technology Bulletin* 106, no. 2 (September 1971), 99.

38 Runge, "In Search of Urban Expertise," 129.

39 "A Proposal to the Ford Foundation," IV-A8.

40 Miller, "Urban Systems Laboratory" (1968), 500.

41 Ibid., 501. In "Progress

Report on the Role and Utilization of Grant Support from the IBM Corporation," of January 1971, Miller reiterated this, adding the remark that "the computer is the most important research tool of the Laboratory" (4). MIT Office of the Provost, Records, 1958-1980, MIT Archives [hereafter AC7].

42 "Urban Systems Lab Installs New Computer." News Release Special to The Tech, September 23, 1968. MIT Urban Systems Laboratory Records, 1968-1974. AC 366, MIT Archives [hereafter AC366]. On the history and importance of the IBM System/360, see Paul E. Ceruzzi, *A History of*

Modern Computing, second ed. (Cambridge: MIT Press, 2003).

43 "Urban Systems Lab Installs New Computer."

44 In 1968 the USL had five associate directors. In addition to Fleisher and Lyndon were Richard L. de Neufville from the School of Engineering, Jerome

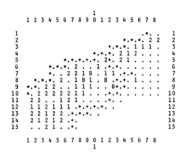

CHAPTER II: REPLICATION   PAGE 38

PATTERN FOR CIUDAD GUAYANA GENERATED BY DECISION RULES

LEGEND:

PRIMARY ATTRIBUTE ASSIGNMENTS - - '1' = URBANION(6); '2' = INDUSTRY(7); '3' = CENTER(5)

'B' = 1, 3   '.' = NON EMPTY LAND

REFERENCE ATTRIBUTE ASSIGNMENTS - - '+' = RIVER(8); '-' = CHANNEL(12); '•' = CHANNEL & RIVER; ' ' = NO REF ATTS

Figure (2.03)   Pattern generated for Ciudad   Guayana by the
decision rules specified in this chapter.

William L. Porter,
diagram of pattern
generated for Ciudad
Guayana by decision rules
of "DISCOURSE," 1969.

remote consoles. As announced in a press release, it was "operated under CP/67 and the Cambridge Monitor System, jointly developed by the M.I.T. Lincoln Laboratory and the IBM Cambridge Scientific Center."[42] At the time a highly advanced multi-user computer, with the notable capacity to simulate multiple virtual machines, the S/360-67 was configured with the then-impressive statistics of "512 K bytes of core storage, high speed drum, and 2314 disk storage."[43]

As reported by the two associate directors affiliated with the School, professors Aaron Fleisher and Donlyn Lyndon, the School of Architecture and Planning hosted a number of USL-sponsored research projects in the lab's first year.[44] Fleischer recounted that SA+P was supporting four major projects in the Department of City and Regional Planning: William Porter's computer program DISCOURSE; an "urban data system" called CHOICE which was being developed by Fleisher and his "urban data laboratory"; studies in the psychology of perception under Professors Stephen M. Carr, Mary C. Potter, and Kevin Lynch; and work on the Boston Model Cities Program, undertaken in collaboration with the Department of Political Science.[45] In

Rothenberg (Economics) and Ithiel de Sola Pool (Political Science) from the School of Humanities and Social Science, and Mason Haire from the Sloan School of Management.
45 Aaron Fleisher, cited in Miller, "Urban System Laboratory" (1968), 493. Fleisher does not cite

CHOICE by name, but it appears with this title in Urban Systems Laboratory, *Directory of Urban and Urban Related Research* (Cambridge, MA: Urban Systems Laboratory, December 15, 1968), 20.
46 Letter from Ithiel de Sola Pool to Charles L. Miller, December 18, 1967. AC 276.

An attached memorandum from Leonard J. Fein to Pool noted that the idea was to "train community people in survey research, which will help alleviate the immediate problem of data gathering." The "Situation Room" would depict program planning graphically, "to make it possible for people

with no special training to comprehend the activities of the agency." Such a connection to the Model Cities Program, Fein suggested, "would provide a major educational increment for our students (at a time when research in the inner city may otherwise become very difficult to undertake)."

a December 1967 letter to Miller, Political Science Professor Ithiel de Sola Pool identified the Boston Model Cities Program as a candidate for "one of the first investments of our Urban Systems Laboratories funds" on account of the potential value of the affiliated data bank and "situation room" to the experimental activities of the lab.[46] With the city and its population understood as components of information or cybernetic systems, computerized data banks would be crucial resources, and citizen participation the most effective means of feedback-based stabilization.[47] Formerly affiliated with Stanford's Hoover Institute (where he acted as assistant director of the Program in Revolution and the Development of International Relations), and founding chair of MIT's Political Science Department, Pool's own research and the projects, centers, and laboratories in which he participated at the Institute would exemplify precisely the Institute's focus on military and intelligence techniques and international development policy, as well as its transference of them to the domestic front in the wake of civil rights struggles. He was, for instance, a key player in the 1969 establishment of Project Cambridge within the Center for International Studies (CIS), a DARPA-funded initiative to develop computer-based applications of the behavioral and social sciences.[48] Along with USL, Project Cambridge co-sponsored DISCOURSE, Porter's previously mentioned system of data storage and retrieval of urban information in the service of environmental design.[49]

Lyndon listed three primary areas of USL-sponsored research in Architecture: "Communication in Urban Problem Solving, Computer-Aided Urban Design, and Environmental Planning for V/STOL (Vertical Short Takeoff and Landing) air transportation."[50] (V/STOL, also known as VSTOL and VTOL, was an Instrumentation Laboratory project that would soon prove highly controversial for its counter-insurgency applications.[51]) Of these three research areas, Miller repeatedly singled out developments in the area of computer-aided urban design in his reports, announcing the following year that "work on the development of an architecture machine, a special-purpose satellite device with local memory and local processing ability, capable of interacting with the Institute's large IBM machine, the 360/67, is being developed by Nicholas P. Negroponte and Léon B. Groisser with U.S.L. support."[52] Although I will return, briefly, to other USL-sponsored projects, I want to focus on this founding moment of computer-aided urban

Memorandum from Leonard J. Fein to Ithiel Pool, "Proposal for MIT Relationship to the Boston Model Cities Program," December 14, 1967. AC 276. On the Model Cities Program see Jennifer Light, "Taking Games Seriously," *Technology and Culture* 49 (April 2008): 347-375.

47 See Light, *From Warfare to Welfare*, especially chapter 6, "Cable as a Cold War Technology."

48 This appears to be an outgrowth of research entitled ADMINS Pool had previously undertaken within USL. The 1968 *Directory* lists ADMINS as an "experiment in computer methods for

handling large data files in the social sciences," and notes that it was jointly funded by the NSF, DoD, ARPA and the Center for International Studies.

49 DISCOURSE was initiated with Porter's PhD thesis under Fleischer and Kevin Lynch. The project was under the general direction

of Fleischer with Katherine Lloyd and others working on the computer system design. See William Porter, Katherine Lloyd, and Aaron Fleisher, "DISCOURSE: A Language and System of Computer-Assisted City Design," in *Emerging Methods in Environmental Design and Planning: Proceedings of The Design*

design, for it quickly becomes evident that what is at stake is not simply the development of a computer-based graphic interface for design—something like the replication of a design process from sketching to working drawings, which is where it began—but a much more thoroughgoing paradigm of data collection and management for the sake of environmental simulation in a virtual realm.

Negroponte and Groisser's research began in 1966 with URBAN 2, a project developed in collaboration with the IBM Scientific Center in Cambridge where Negroponte worked following his graduation that year from MIT's Masters of Architecture program. (Negroponte's masters thesis, "The Computer Simulation of Perception During Motion in the Urban Environment," was put forward as "an attempt at architectural research," and following his earlier interest in the question of population growth in the developing world, it forecast that a "new profession will evolve that must take the responsibility of handling the urbanization of millions and millions.")[53] URBAN 2 provided the platform for Negroponte and Groisser's inaugural MIT course in Fall 1967, "Special Problems in Computer Aided Urban Design." A course description dated January 1967 explained that students would "work towards establishing a coordinated system that aids the direct design process we usually associate with yellow tracing paper." URBAN 2 was, they explained, to be a "conversational computer system" in which the computer was conceived as "a partner in this procedure by providing a design service that monitors the process rather than optimizes or analyzes inputs."[54] Students were given a pre-scripted graphical language using a ten-foot cube building block system operating within a three-dimensional orthogonal grid. "The manipulation of cubes provides a way of simulating the urban design process," the professors explained, adding that it "furnishes a 'frictionless-vacuum' environment in which to work."[55]

Sponsored by USL and by then called URBAN 5, the application made quite an impact at the first Design Methods Group conference in Spring 1968, held in collaboration with Harvard's Graduate School of Design and MIT's Department of Civil Engineering. In his review, "Glass Box and Black Box," Jonathan Barnett declared it "the most spectacular example of blackboxmanship" at the conference, referring to the manner in which the

Methods Conference, ed. Gary T. Moore (Cambridge, MA: 1968), 92-104.
50 Lyndon cited in Miller, "Urban Systems Laboratory" (1968), 497. VSTOL was under the supervision of Edward B. Allen; Communication in Urban Problem Solving was directed by Donlyn Lyndon and Marvin Manheim. The

1968 USL *Directory* indicates that five additional projects were being conducted under USL: "Psychology of Place and Movement" by John Myer; the establishment of a "Group for Research in Environmental Design" under William Porter and Robert J. Pelletier; "Housing issues in American Indian

Communities" by Chester Sprague, focusing on the Navajos; "Building Design Issues Related to the Slope of the Ground" by Waclaw Zalewski; and, the establishment of the "Community Projects Laboratory" by Myer and Porter, focused on low income communities.

51 Dorothy Nelkin, *The University and Military Research: Moral Politics at M.I.T.* (Ithaca: Cornell University Press, 1972), 39. See also Committee on War-Related Research, "A Summary of War-Related Research at Draper Lab." AC276. A Special Review Panel, as reported in *Time*,

application retained a conventional approach to design, simply augmenting it through new tools. ("Glass box" approaches, by contrast, were more design methods-oriented and sought transparence through a rationalization of analytical techniques.) Barnett pointed, in particular, to the device's inherent drive toward a conciliatory process, noting that it "provides a sophisticated and flexible format which actually adjusts to the idiosyncracies [sic] of an individual designer." As he recounted, "Films, shown with three projectors, documented a novice's first encounter with URBAN 5, which is programmed to make kindly comments like: 'I'm afraid you have a conflict here, Ted,' (the user types in his name when he sits down at the console) or 'Ted, how long are you going to postpone resolving this conflict?'"[56] Here indeed, as Lyndon suggested of the project's ambition in his 1968 report as department chair, was "a new order of designer-machine interaction."[57]

URBAN 5 was designed, as the team explained at the conference, to be a monitoring device or "eavesdropping mechanism" that tried to eradicate conflicts by steering the architect towards a set of pre-determined normative parameters while learning from interaction with the human.[58] A few years later, Negroponte recalled that he had initially understood the computer's role as "checking for violations in constraints and criteria" which had been predetermined by the architect.[59] This modality of conversing with the computer might give us pause, as it seems not unrelated to the architects' desire to furnish a "'frictionless-vacuum' environment in which to work." For while they saw themselves as simply setting up a "launching vehicle" or "research toy" with which to test rather banal architectural parameters (number of bedrooms, structural feasibility, etc), this experimental mode of simulating environments without the "friction" of the real world (which they likened to laboratory experiments in Newtonian mechanics) would be responsible, it seems, for the high level of abstraction that came to characterize their environments.[60] In other words, the underlying technical logic of such systems could translate all too easily into a paradigm in which historical and political valences were simply swept aside in favor of a smoothly functioning apparatus—whether architectural, administrative, political, etc. That is to say, to eliminate conflict or "friction" is to close down spaces of contestatory negotiation.

"split sharply over the I-lab's work on Vertical Takeoff and Landing (VTOL) aircraft. The majority defended it on the grounds that VTOLs could be used to speed civilian intercity transit. . . By contrast, antiwar guru Noam Chomsky vehemently argued that VTOLs would be used mainly for 'repressing domestic insurgency in countries subject to our influence or control.'" "Universities: M.I.T. and the Pentagon," *Time* (Friday November 7 1969). **52** Miller, "Urban Systems Laboratory" (1969), 480-481. Negroponte described this time-sharing modality as follows: "More recently, real-time computation depending upon 'time-sharing' techniques allows the user a prompt machine response and permits terminals (usually teletypes) to reside in the office or at home. These terminals are connected to the large central machine, and they can be interconnected with each other. The rapid switching of users' programs in and out of the large machine provides each user with the illusion of a dedicated machine and permits him continual use of his terminal." Nicholas Negroponte, "Toward a Humanism Through Machines," *Architectural Design* 39 (September 1968): 512.

Architecture Machine Group, Interface for URBAN
5, with an IBM 2250, model 1 monitor, and scope
connected to an IBM system 360/67, 1968.

53 Nicholas Negroponte, "The Computer Simulation of Perception During Motion in the Urban Environment" (Masters Thesis, Massachusetts Institute of Technology, 1966), 1 and preface, respectively. Describing this new mode of research, he wrote, "There are not accompanying plans, sections, elevations, or models. The research has compelled me to become more involved with the university and delve into other disciplines, some of them rarely associated with architecture," 1. Negroponte later recalled: "I was a student at MIT, and a student at MIT has a hard time avoiding exposure to computer sciences. No exception, I confronted an introductory course taught by Daniel Bobrow, a doctoral student at the time and one of the early contributors to artificial intelligence. As a result of this experience I embarked on a Master's of Architecture thesis on the simulation of perception, a mixture of eye movement modeling and perspective transformations. Following a controversial graduation I joined the IBM Cambridge Scientific Center under Norman Rasmussen with the vague charter of developing an application (with their 2250 display, in particular) that had something

Artificial Intelligence

Lawrence Anderson noted in his 1968 report as Dean that "The Architecture Machine is a phantom in the minds of Professors Léon B. Groisser and Nicholas P. Negroponte that is becoming concrete with disconcerting haste."[61] By 1969, as reported in "The Search for Urban Expertise," work on URBAN 5 had in fact been declared complete and a "second generation of studies [was] underway." As Runge explained:

> One of the more interesting—though least practical—groups of projects under the leadership of Architecture Professor Nicholas Negroponte, is searching for nothing less than artificial design intelligence. The "architecture machine," as it is called, is to be a "moral" animal and a design partner to the architect, capable of carrying on a man-machine dialog in the manner of an associate having "the potential for self-improvement."[62]

Now formalized as The Architecture Machine Group and with their research sponsored by the Ford Foundation and Interdata via USL (sponsorship which would later be supplemented by ARPA, the Air Force, Office of Naval Research, and others), Negroponte, Groisser, and their students had, under the impact of Marvin Minsky, Oliver Selfridge, and Seymour Papert (all leaders in the field of artificial intelligence), turned to questions of artificial intelligence that might be pertinent to design. The group's focus, Miller reported that same year, was now on "the problem of interfacing, both between computer and man, and computer and real world."[63] Artificial intelligence, or what Negroponte referred to as "ultra-intelligence in computers,"[64] was approached by breaking the design problem—understood as a process of monitoring and representing the environment—into systematic components: machine vision, sketch recognition, interfaces with the non-professional, computer graphics, tactile sensors and effectors, low-resolution interfacing, and three-dimensional input-output. If the ambition was to create "more flexible and more responsive" computer programs, what emerged was a mode of interface that, as it turned out, required the extensive acquisition and processing of ever more detailed information of both that "man" and his "real world;" such an interface also heralded an ever more extensive integration of this satellite computing facility into the larger administrative system or military-industrial-academic complex. Even after collecting environmental data, the

to do with architecture." Nicholas Negroponte, ed., *Computer Aids to Design and Architecture* (New York: Mason and Lipscome, 1975), 8. **54** Nicholas Negroponte and Léon Groisser, *URBAN 2* (Cambridge: IBM Scientific Center, 1967). Emphasis in original. As they explained here, "The computer's

role would be to receive information (restraints and graphical input), to monitor procedural interactions (conflicts an incompatibilities) and to display the graphical manipulation." Noting also, "Work will be carried out on an IBM 2250 (Model 1) display system with the support of a 360 Model 40 or 65. The

system is designed and implemented using Fortran IV to call IBM's second edition of GPAK, a series of subroutines that permit attention handling, display management and modeling." **55** Negroponte and Groisser, *Urban 2*, np. **56** Jonathan Barnett, "Glass Box and Black Box,"

Architectural Record 144 (July 1968): 127. See also: Nicholas Negroponte and Léon B. Groisser, "URBAN5," *Ekistics* 24, no. 142 (September 1967): 289-291; Nicholas Negroponte and Léon B. Groisser, "URBAN5: an on-line urban design partner," in IBM Report, 320-2012 (IBM, 1967); and, Nicholas

frictionless vacuum does not seem to have been replaced by socio-historical material so much as by other applications.

Under the subtitle "Computers in Search of Identity," Runge offered a succinct description of new research then underway as part of this shift towards questions of artificial intelligence. These were to be described in further detail in Negroponte's 1970 book-length account of the early research, *The Architecture Machine.* "A computerized robot, GROPE," Runge begins,

> is a toy tank with photoelectric eyes that are being trained to search out "interesting" places (points of greatest diversity) on urban maps, and may someday lead to a mechanical design partner that can seek out information about the real world without human supervision; SEE is a computerized television camera that studies various groupings of 2" x 2" blocks (representing urban-scale modules), and then devises its own configurations. A program is being developed for a computer that can interview people about their urban environment, the ultimate goal being to hook into the public phone system. Negroponte sees this as an important step towards universal advocacy: "the design of the city can start to reflect every single inhabitant—his needs and desires. This may seem completely ludicrous, but I don't think it is."[65]

Negroponte's step towards universal advocacy was illustrated by an image of an African-American man at a typewriter-like device. The caption reads: "Ghetto resident talks to computer about slum environment via typewriter computer terminal: Another of Architecture Professor Nicholas Negroponte's artificial intelligence projects."[66] As revealed the same month (September 1969) in a special issue of the British magazine *Architectural Design* dedicated to the discipline's interface with contemporary sciences—cybernetics, operations research, etc.—this project was titled INTERACT.

Edited by Royston Landau, the special issue of *AD* featured "Experiments in Computer Aided Design: Report from the Department of Architecture" at MIT. Along with a report on "Space Arrangement" research led by Tim Johnson, it covered the research then being

Negroponte, "URBAN5: An Experimental Urban Design Partner," in *Computer Graphics in Architecture and Design*, ed. Murray Milne (New Haven: Yale School of Architecture, 1968).

57 Lyndon, "Department of Architecture" (1968), 497.

58 Nicholas Negroponte and Léon Groisser, "URBAN 5: A Machine That Discusses Urban Design," in *Emerging Methods in Environmental Design and Planning: Proceedings of The Design Methods Conference*, ed. Gary T. Moore (Cambridge, MA: 1968), 112.

59 Negroponte, *Computer Aids to Design and Architecture*, 8.

60 Negroponte and Groisser, "URBAN 5: A Machine That Discusses Urban Design," 105-114.

61 Anderson, "School of Architecture and Planning" (1969), 34.

62 Runge, "In Search of Urban Expertise," 128. In a 1971 application to the NSF, the Arc Mac group explained: "The academic year of 1968-1969 saw a dramatic transition of our basic attitude. Rather than cramming descriptions of the real world into the machine,

sponsored by USL, including Porter's DISCOURSE and John Boorn's CHOICE, as well as the Architecture Machine Group's GROPE, SEE (soon to be called, more ominously, SEEK), and INTERACT. The introductory description proposed that machines, "and automation in general," might provide some of the "omitted and difficult-to-acquire information" needed for good design, as had been previously provided by human-architects. But it stressed that some information might still be missing. "Consequently, the Architecture Machine Group at MIT, are embarking on the construction of a machine that can work with missing information," one which could understand human metaphors, "solicit information on its own," "talk to a wide variety of people," acquire experience and be intelligent.[67] The brief prospectus was followed by a reprint of Negroponte's "Towards a Humanism Through Machines," in which the professor further described the desired process of mutual evolutionary exchange as an "acquaintanceship of two intelligent systems, the architect and the Architecture Machine," a relationship that would not take the form of master/slave but rather that "of two associates which each have the potential for self-improvement." Computer-aided design, he stressed,

Architecture Machine configuration, with Interdata Model 3 computer along with expanded memory, sound output, and high speed paper tape reader and housed in a chassis for expansion, September 1969.

we began to emphasize providing machines with interfaces to that world." They also note the importance of the founding of USL and the Ford Foundation grant that was "able to sponsor a series of experiments in linguistics, self-organizing controllers, and machine vision." Nicholas Negroponte and Léon

Groisser, "Computer Aids to Participatory Architecture," (Cambridge, MA: MIT, 1971), 59-61.

63 Charles Miller, "Urban System Laboratory," in "Report of the President for the Academic Year 1969-1970," *Massachusetts Institute of Technology Bulletin* 106, no. 2 (September 1971), 101.

Architecture Machine Group (Steven Gregory),
GROPE, 1969. Shown seeking out "interesting things"
on Richard Saul Wurman and Joseph R. Passonneau's
1966 Urban Atlas of New York with population
density data.

64 Negroponte, *Computer Aids*, 10.

65 Runge, "In Search of Urban Expertise," 129. As she presciently concluded of Arc Mac: "if, as prognosticators of the future tell us, the day is coming when every man will have a computer terminal in his office and/or home, such efforts are building tools that may one day be accessible to all architects."

66 Runge, "In Search of Urban Expertise," 126.
67 Negroponte, "The Architecture Machine" in "Experiments in Computer Aided Design," *Architectural Design* 39, no. 9 (September 1969): 510.

68 Negroponte, "Toward a Humanism Through Machines," 511. This had previously appeared in the April 1969 issue of *Technology Review*.

distinguishing his group's work from simple processes of computerization, would not leave either party untouched, since, as he put it, it "concerns an ecology of mutual design complementation, augmentation, and substitution."[68]

Negroponte returned to questions of "responsiveness" and "participation" in "Concerning Responsive Architecture," his concluding remarks for "The Shirt-Sleeve Session in Responsive Housebuilding Technologies," a conference held at MIT in May 1972 and published as *The Responsive House.*[69] He began by noting that there were many forms of responsiveness: there was "a responsive design technology that people are talking about— participation, advocacy planning," responsive building technology, and, finally, what he was dreaming of, "responsive architecture itself." The latter, he clarified, entailed "the removal of all middlemen," including architects. To explain what he meant he recalled having recently attended a conference in England on "design participation," in which he witnessed two primary orientations—the design methodologists and the "'Advocacy Planner' types."[70] The former sought information from social sciences: "We want the psychologists, sociologists, and anthropologists to tell us more about what people want. We want people to fill out more questionnaires. We want to know more so we can design better buildings," Negroponte ventriloquized. The latter, he went on, had taken on an activist role, which he characterized as saying: "We're going to get people heard. We're going to help them to affect the design of their environments." Both, Negroponte assessed, were paternalistic, a category in which he now included his initial response with URBAN 5.[71] His new solution: "a physical environment which has knowledge about you." This was an idea then being provisionally tested on the lab's door with a device entitled GREET, which was designed to recognize people using an apparatus he termed, invoking cybernetician Gordon Pask, a "you-sensor." But as with URBAN 5 this was only the first step: Negroponte was ultimately seeking an environment that, as he posited, could have the same predictive ability— with respect to his needs, desires, intentionality—as his wife. It was not surprising, he speculated, that people remained suspicious of the idea of such responsive environments, given the paucity of extant examples: "Unfortunately, examples such as floors that can tell how many people are walking on them, and doors that can recognize people, usually end up driving second-rate light shows, or doing very banal things in directing the

69 Nicholas Negroponte, "Concerning Responsive Architecture," in *The Responsive House*, ed. Edward Allen (Cambridge: MIT Press, 1974), 302-307.

70 Negroponte appears to be referring to the Design Research Society's conference "Design Participation," which took place in Manchester in September 1971. His contribution to this conference extended his remarks in "Concerning Responsive Architecture."

See Nicholas Negroponte, "Aspects of Living in an Architecture Machine," in *Design Participation*, ed. Nigel Cross (London: Academy Editions, 1972), 63-67. He later expands on these ideas in Nicholas Negroponte, *Soft Architecture Machines* (Cambridge: MIT Press, 1975).

71 Negroponte, "Concerning Responsive Architecture," 303.

Architecture Machine
Group, SEEK (earlier
called SEE), 1969.

physical environment." The one "genuine architectural response" he could point to was Sean Wellesley-Miller's "design of a . . . sculpture exhibit which counts the number of people that go into it and come out of it, and inflates or deflates additional sections of the building, depending on how many people are in the exhibit." (Wellesley-Miller was part of Evenstructure Research Group, cofounded with Jeffrey Shaw and Theo Botschuijver.) Preempting contemporary personal data tracking applications, Negroponte concluded by pointing to paradigms of operational response that were more convincing, even if not yet realized in the architectural domain—what he called "lots of little applications of a surrogate 'me.'" "I hate reading newspapers and looking at news on the television," he explained, "but I would love to have some sort of device which knew me well enough to synopsize the news each night, and tells me if there happens to be something interesting on television today or tomorrow, without having to read TV Guide."[72]

INTERACT

With Arc Mac's INTERACT, and the group's work on interfacing with the "non-professional," we find ourselves at the crux of research operating at the nexus of "urban crisis," computers, and social sciences fostered by USL. INTERACT, as reported in AD, "faces the problem of soliciting information about the environment, about needs and desires, from the inhabitants themselves." The little-documented project's primary researcher was Richard Hessdorfer, who had just graduated from MIT's architecture program and was now developing this "'consumer' item that could initiate a dialog with inhabitants, build a model of [their] needs and desires (particular to the speaker) and report back to Architecture Machines." As the brief account in AD recalled, the experiment involved taking a "teletype writing device" into the South End, described here as "Boston's ghetto area."

> Three inhabitants of the neighborhood were asked to converse with this machine about their local environment. Though the conversation was hampered by the necessity to type English sentences, the chat was smooth enough to reveal two important results. First, the three user-inhabitants said things to this machine they would probably not have said to a human, particularly a white planner or politician: to them the machine was not black, was not white, and surely had no prejudices. Second, the three residents had no qualms or suspicions about talking with a machine (in English about personal desires); they did not type uncalled for remarks, instead they immediately entered a discourse about slum landlords, highways, schools and the like.[73]

Although not revealed initially, the "user-inhabitants" were Maurice Jones, Barry Adams, and Robert Quarles, the latter wearing a "tenant power" badge.[74] In July of 1969, Negroponte included a further description in the inaugural issue of the School's new publication, Research. INTERACT, he explained, is a project that explores natural language communication between actual users (users-to-be) of a physical environment and machine "advocacy planners." The romantic notion of people designing their own houses, their own cities, their own physical environments (all within rapid change and growth) is the underlying goal. . . At present the system exhibits a very false intelligence and is primarily a wordy conversationalist. However, the goal is to build a model of the speaker's needs and desires and to provide a mirror of his requirements and aspirations (and to get to know him).[75]

Negroponte's suggestion that the system of data extraction still exhibited a "false intelligence," that it remained a "wordy conversationalist," was perhaps a reference to a conceit at the heart of this project. As revealed parenthetically in *AD*: "The reader should know, as the three users did not, that this experiment was conducted over telephone lines with teletypes, with a human at the other end not a machine. The same experiment will be rerun shortly—this time with a machine at the other end of the telephone line." When in 1973 he mentioned the project in his contribution to "La Ville Totale," which appeared alongside projects by Kenzo Tange, R. Buckminster Fuller, and Yona Friedman in *2000: revue de l'amanégement du territoire*, Negroponte revealed that the humans on the other end of the telephone line were architects.[76]

Negroponte's remarks on user-participation and advocacy planning also remind us of the degree to which Arc Mac's ambitions remained indebted to the work of the Metabolists and le Groupe d'Etude d'Architecture Mobile, particularly Yona Friedman. Following their initial meeting in 1964—when Negroponte, who could speak French, was sent to the airport to pick up the Paris-based visiting lecturer—Friedman's "une cite spaciale" became a key reference in Negroponte's undergraduate thesis of 1966, "Systems of Urban Growth," and Friedman would become a long-standing collaborator with the Arc Mac group.[77] The three-dimensional matrix which structured Friedman's spatial city would be reiterated initially as a mechanical framework in Negroponte's "Mova-grid," adapted from the Metabolists. The grid, he explained in that context, "merely defines points in space that in turn describe potential volumes," within which components were jacked into place. But that matrix can also be read in the cubes of URBAN 5 and other systems-based environments that

72 Ibid., 305.

73 "Experiments in Computer Aided Design," 513.

74 Nicholas Negroponte, The Architecture Machine: *Toward a More Human Environment* (Cambridge, MA: MIT Press, 1970), 56.

75 Nicholas Negroponte, "Five Experiments Toward an Architecture Machine," *Research* 1, no. 1 (July 10 1969), 1.

76 "La Ville Totale," *2000: revue de l'aménagement du territoire* (1973): v.

77 Nicholas Negroponte, "Systems of Urban Growth" (Bachelors Thesis, Massachusetts Institute of Technology, 1965). A key "point of reference," as Negroponte explained, rehearsing the period's panic over population growth, was the question of populations, "generating

Negroponte built in that seemingly frictionless vacuum of the virtual realm; these formal similarities suggest the degree to which the research uncannily harbored the memory of the period's experimental practice while taking it in a very different direction. Referring to Moshe Safdie's famous housing megastructure for Expo 67 in Montreal, Negroponte later acknowledged that URBAN 5 had in fact "mimicked the additive genre of composition, popular in school at the time and epitomized in Habitat. It did this comprehensively, smoothly, and expensively."[78] Moreover, he acknowledged that this desired shift to an advocacy-model of user-participation via the automation of artificial intelligence, and with it the eradication of the architect from the equation, "has received the serious attention only of Yona Friedman, in Paris, France." [79] But Negroponte's ambitions were distinctly out of sync with the utopian ideals or visions of the more liberatory environment motivating much experimental practice of this period. Introducing the English translation of Friedman's *Toward a Scientific Architecture* (also of 1975), Negroponte alluded to the "paradoxical intersection of two academic streams—participatory design and scientific methods—too frequently held apart by the circumstances of our training," implying however that his own position was somewhat closer to the "scientific" side of this conflict. As he put it, "Yona Friedman has used a mathematical scaffolding to support philosophical positions in a manner which affords the reader the opportunity to disagree with his utopian posture, but still benefit from his techniques."[80] That year, Friedman acted as a consultant to Arc Mac on a project entitled "Architecture by Yourself." Very much indebted to Friedman's Flatwriter project, the application even adopted his name, YONA.

By 1975, however, as Negroponte must have been aware, the logic of participation and the logic informing the feedback-based process of scientific methods were hardly so opposed. To reiterate, any avowedly idealistic goal of user-controlled systems of organization was easily transposed into a form of participation in which an ever more precise constellation of data or information about the human subject—their needs and desires—would be extracted and fed back into an intelligent machine. Indeed, this very logic had perhaps been the most evident lesson of the Architecture Machine Group's contribution to "Software: Information Technology, its New Meaning for Art," a famous exhibition of conceptual art held at the Jewish Museum in New York in 1970. "Software," as curator Jack Burnham explained,

a study of how populations live, what populations want, and primarily, how populations expand" (Preface), The Architecture Machine Group explicitly drew upon Friedman's graph theory design methods, as set out in *Towards a Scientific Architecture*, in developing "Architecture by Yourself," even

calling the related application YONA. Friedman would be referred to as a consultant to the Arc Mac group on the front of a paper also titled "Architecture by Yourself" and dated October 1975. See: Guy Weinzapfel, "Report on Yona Friedman's Visit," *Architecture Machinations* 1, no. 9 (November 16, 1975): 2-5;

Guy Weinzapfel, "Architecture by Yourself," *Architecture Machinations* 2, no. 21 (May 23, 1976): 5-9; and Yona Friedman, *Toward a Scientific Architecture* (Cambridge, MA: MIT Press, 1975), with introduction by Negroponte.

78 Negroponte, *Computer Aids*, 8.
79 Ibid, 10.

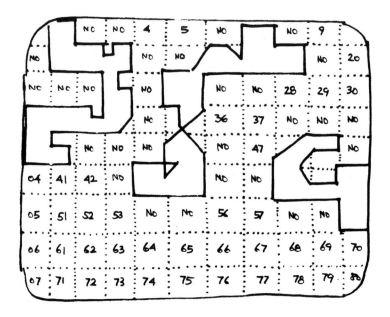

NO : UNDER CONSTRAINT
NUMBER : FREE

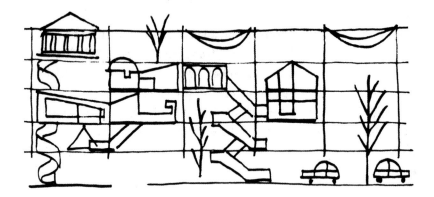

Yona Friedman,
Flatwriter, 1969.

responded to "life in a computerized environment," aiming to demonstrate "the effects of contemporary control and communication techniques in the hands of artists." Research work in Negroponte's experimental laboratory had little in common with the critical artistic and institutional questions driving conceptual art practices at the time. Nevertheless, it shared the exhibition's focus on systems- and process-based work engaging communications and cybernetics paradigms through which individuals might interact with one another and with their environment.

Other contributors included CAVS alumni Hans Haacke, along with Sonia Sheridan, Vito Acconci, Les Levine, Allan Kaprow, Lawrence Weiner, and others. Haacke, for instance, presented *Visitors' Profile* and *News*, the former collecting, tabulating, and outputting data on visitors who interacted with the installation, the latter an active teletype print-out of national and foreign news services. Levine installed *Systems Burn-off x Residual Software*, a work comprised of photographs from the equally famous "Earth Works" exhibition the year before in Ithaca and speaking to the informatic residuals transmitted through media, along with *A.I.R.*—live feed from the artist's studio—and *Wire Tap*, speakers broadcasting his telephone conversations. In this context Negroponte presented Seek, configured as a servomechanism connected to the Architecture Machine and designed to "handle local unexpected events" occurring within an environment comprised of two-

Architecture Machine Group, SEEK, 1969. Installed at "Software: Information Technology: Its New Meaning for Art," Jewish Museum, New York, 1970.

inch cubes that served as the habitat for a colony of gerbils. As he explained it, Seek attempted to "go beyond the real world situation, where machines cannot respond to the unpredictable nature of people (gerbils). Today machines are poor at handling sudden changes in context in environment. This lack of adaptability is the problem Seek confronts in diminutive."[81]

Offered as an exercise in the benefits of artificial intelligence, one in which the computer-architect had replaced the human-architect (who was no longer able to deal with the complexity of their environment), Seek was meant to demonstrate, in miniature, optimized relations between humans, their actions, and their new computerized or virtual milieu. The ten-foot blocks had returned as five hundred two-inch cubes to be tested in a five-by-seven-foot "real world" situation that was perhaps best understood as a simulation of environmental control. Negroponte's intelligent machine would read the "desires" of the animals as registered by their random displacement of blocks, and then the computer-controlled prosthetic device would straighten the blocks in the new locations. The outcome, he wrote, was "a constantly changing architecture that reflected the way the little animals used the place."[82] That is, the computer was supposed to learn to read indeterminate actions and the fluidity of the environment as possessing underlying meanings and then operate to re-calibrate its organization of the blocks according to this newly detected set of parameters. Within this pernicious circuit, it was precisely via interaction with their environment that the gerbil facilitated the computer's learning process and hence ceded his control over the transformation of his environment to the Architecture Machine. Negroponte later conceded that at the time of the show the technology was not yet sophisticated enough for the Architecture Machine to actually learn in an "evolutionary sense"; it merely evaluated probabilities.[83] However, his attempts to produce such an environmental mechanism render the gerbils a perfect allegory of the potential evacuation of agency, and of space for political negotiation, at the hands of cybernetic machines, as had initially been modeled by INTERACT.

80 Negroponte forward to Friedman, *Toward a Scientific Architecture*, ix.

81 Nicholas Negroponte in Jack Burnham, *Software. Information Technology: Its New Meaning for Art* (New York: Jewish Museum, 1970), 23.

Architecture Machine Group, SEEK, 1969. Installed at "Software: Information Technology: Its New Meaning for Art," Jewish Museum, New York, 1970.

When Negroponte described INTERACT in *The Architecture Machine*, he added the somewhat troubling suggestion that

> with these domestic (domesticated) machines, the design task becomes one of blending the preferences of the individual with those of the group. Machines would monitor the propensity for change of the body politic. Large central processors, parent machines of some sort, could interpolate and extrapolate the local commonalities by overviewing a large population of "consumer machines."[84]

The formulation of such a surveillance device, connected, as the group imagined, through the telephone system and avowedly dedicated to a normative ideal—"blending the preferences of the individual with those of the group"—is certainly enough to make one nervous. Negroponte attempted to defer such a reaction by pointing to the machine's capacity to make ever more fine-grained distinctions among subjects, but in so doing he may have instead revealed the project's disturbing proximity to domestic security applications. "What will remove these machines from a 'Brave New World,'" he remarked,

> is that they will be able to (and must) search for the exception (in desire or need), the one in a million. In other words, when the generalization matches the local desire, our omnipresent machines will not be excited. It is when the particular varies from the group preferences that our machine will react, not to thwart it but to service it.[85]

What sort of decisions, we might well ask, would such a computer, even an architecture machine programmed to be an "ethical robot," really help you to make even if you believed that it was doing so on your own behalf? How, exactly, might they service your desires?

The ArcMac group returned to the question of "interfacing with the non-professional" in "Computer Aids to Participatory Architecture," a 1971 proposal submitted to the National Science Foundation for research to be undertaken with the USL. The document concluded with Seek, including both the page from *Software* and details on the six operations through which the software could control the hardware—Generate, Degenerate, Fix it, Straighten,

Architecture Machine configuration, 1970.

82 Negroponte, *Soft Architecture Machines*, 47. See also Nicholas Negroponte, "Semantics of Architecture Machines," *Architectural Forum* 133, no. 3 (October 1970), in which he notes, "Unknown to SEEK, the little animals are bumping into blocks, disrupting constructions, and toppling towers. The result is a substantial and continually changing mismatch between the three-dimensional reality and the computer remembrances residing in the core memory. SEEK's role is to deal with these inconsistencies" (40).

83 Negroponte, "Aspects of Living in an Architecture Machine," 67.
84 Negroponte, *The Architecture Machine*, 57.
85 Ibid., 57.

Find, Error Detect. The project abstract, published in the 1971 *USL Directory of Urban and Urban Related Research at MIT*, pointed directly to the task of data extraction, noting that "the outcome of a scenario with the system would be not so much an 'instant' house plan as it would be a model of the user, i.e., his needs and desires."[86] In the NSF proposal the group even went so far as to clarify that here technology would replace politics: "we are not proposing to do computer-aided advocacy planning. We propose to take a step towards allowing the urban dweller to participate in the design of his own environment by multiplying the availability of design services rather than by mobilizing political power."[87]

Again the group used photographs of INTERACT (though not naming the project in the proposal) to demonstrate their means of "eliciting information." "Since the basic premise of this proposal is that our users cannot express all their needs and desires explicitly, the machine must determine most of them implicitly." Those needs and desires could be precisely the feedback data needed by the system to ensure (political) homeostasis. If, to stress the point, this inscription of the user within an ever more extensive, data-driven feedback device was initially cast as a computer-mediated form of advocacy planning,[88] such remarks, along with the trajectory of funding for such research indicates that we might rightfully question a certain knowingness regarding its military, or counter-insurgency potentials. Years later Negroponte himself suggested that he had become all too aware of such resonances, noting that "the idea is to encourage the most advanced media research, without the 'Dr. Jekyll and Mr. Hyde' tone implicit in arts and humanities research done conjointly with military and industrial sponsorships."[89]

As Negroponte recognized, this dream of a computer-controlled environment, replete with integrated sensor and surveillance technology, computer-assisted data processing and evaluation, and automated prosthetic devices resonated all too eerily with General Westmoreland's ambition of achieving a soldier-less "Battlefield of the Future" in Vietnam, that super-efficient, computerized, and totalizing "electronic battlefield" designed to respond to the asymmetrical tactics of guerilla warfare. Here soldiers and military strategy would be replaced by machines (reducing US military casualties and soothing certain aspects of anti-war protest), data collected remotely and in increasingly microscopic detail,

86 "The concept is that each man might be his own architect for his immediate built environment within a high-density situation." Nicholas Negroponte and Léon B. Groisser, research project abstract for Computer Aids to Participatory Architecture, in Urban Systems Laboratory,

Directory of Urban and Urban Related Research Projects at M.I.T., Edition IV (May 1, 1971), 49.

87 "Computer Aids to Participatory Architecture," 13.
88 See Paul Davidoff, "Democratic Planning," *Perspecta* 11 (1967): 157-159.

89 Nicholas Negroponte, "Arts and Media Technology," *Plan* 11 (1980): 24.

communication instantaneous: it would be, as Paul Edwards writes, "knowledge without confrontation, power without friction."[90] Just as computers would run the wars of the future, so, it seems, would they manage future environments: architects could now in effect man those guard towers, performing their environmental control while maintaining the appearance of having withdrawn from the operation. And all of this could be tested in the realm of simulation or modeling, in which, to cite Edwards again, systems analysis "linked choices about strategy directly to choices about technology," thus informing policy decisions and "inherently promot[ing] technological change."[91]

Dr. Jekyll and Mr. Hyde

To try to understand what might be at stake in this Dr. Jekyll and Mr. Hyde dualism, this antinomy of good and evil inherent to certain trajectories of technological development, and why Negroponte might have recognized Arc Mac to be haunted by such a morality tale, I want to come back to the Urban Systems Laboratory, the Cambridge Project, and the politics of "big science" and the "military-industrial-academic complex" at MIT as the Institute steered (or claimed to steer) research activity and resources away from war-related projects and toward the civilian domain. As the Federal government became increasingly concerned with controlling or managing the "urban crisis"—including not only the physical status of its cities but the social unrest rising in the face of social and environmental injustices, the Cold War arms race, and the ongoing war in South East Asia—it seemed that things "urban" would for a short moment join military defense and space exploration as the new frontier of federal funding. MIT tried to situate itself at the forefront of this anticipated urban initiative, understanding its potential contribution through the USL to be that of collecting data and developing programs, technologies, and ever more detailed forms of simulation. But that funding proved not so easy to obtain and the program was dropped by 1974. That year *The Tech* published a short retrospective article on USL entitled "Urban Systems Lab: Social Work since '68." "According to Miller," it explained, "when the Urban Systems Lab was founded in 1968, 'there was the anticipation that urban problems would be approached on the basis of large scale, mission-oriented projects, as in the space program. These large scale projects never came about because of funding limitations. HUD never became the research equivalent of the Defense Department.'"[92] In the meantime, however, the DoD, like

90 Paul N. Edwards, *The Closed World: Computers and the Politics of Discourse in Cold War America* (Cambridge, MA: MIT Press, 1996). 132.
91 Ibid., 120.

92 Greg Saltzman, "Urban Systems Lab: Social Work since '68," *The Tech* (May 17, 1974): 2-3.

the Ford Foundation, had emerged as a not-insignificant funding resource for certain types of urban studies, a development that raises important questions regarding both the character of research pursued under such grants and its potential applications.

MIT's significant contributions to scientific and technological developments during World War II were typically greeted enthusiastically for their role in ensuring US, and hence Allied, supremacy against Axis forces, although Norbert Wiener and others would famously raise the issue of science's social responsibility in the aftermath of the atomic bombing of Hiroshima and Nagasaki and refuse military funding for their subsequent research.[93] The Institute had also emerged from the turbulent months of 1968 largely without incident. Yet beginning with a research stoppage on March 4, 1969, MIT became an important target for, and site of, anti-war protest activities, including activities organized by MIT students and faculty, on account of the extensive military-sponsored, often-classified war-related research undertaken in its laboratories, and in particular the off-campus Special Laboratories—the Lincoln and Instrumentation Laboratories. [94] (The former, to recall, operated the IBM System/360 mainframe computer, the latter co-funded VSTOL). To recall Runge in *P/A*, not everyone was enamored by the Institute's liberal "salting" of its personnel with "men whose careers straddle the academic-industrial consulting line," or those "returnees from Washington's advisory elite who still contribute more than their fair share to the support of Boston-Washington air routes."[95] I want to turn now to trace two further, interrelated aspects of this story: first, the re-naming, proposed conversion and decision to divest the Instrumentation Laboratory (I-Lab) and, second, protests over MIT's Center for International Studies and with it Project Cambridge and Ithiel de Sola Pool. If these narratives might read initially as detours or departures from the history of the School of Architecture and Planning, the first, as we shall see, speaks to ongoing interactions between USL activities and war-related research, and the second to the intense proximity of such research, particularly in the social sciences, to figures within the school.

In April 1969, following protests, President Johnson convened a review panel on the Special Laboratories; known as the Pounds Panel, it was charged with examining the role of military-funding and war-related research at MIT. The former was a major source

93 *Time* magazine, for instance, explained: "In the days when wars were simple—and considered just—the Massachusetts Institute of Technology was a proud developer of U.S. weaponry. As a patriotic duty in World War II, for instance, the school's electronics wizards perfected the radar that foiled

Hitler's bombs. Now duty has become a Faustian dilemma. In the age of antiwar dissent, M.I.T. still gets more money from the Pentagon—$108 million last year—than any other U.S. university. The result has thrust M.I.T. to the forefront of a growing national debate: What role, if any, shall universities play in

war research?" "Universities: M.I.T. and the Pentagon." See Norbert Wiener, "A *Scientist Rebels*," Atlantic Monthly 179 (January 1947), 46.
94 For a more detailed and general account of the protests at MIT, see Nelkin, *The University and Military Research*.

95 Runge, "In Search of Urban Expertise," 125. Runge notes that Miller was appointed "last winter as head of President Nixon's post-election task force on transportation" (125). Nelkin indicated that MIT faculty had been one-time administrators of Department of Defense research agencies, including

25¢

THE CAMBRIDGE PROJECT

PEOPLES' WARS

BLACK MILITANCY

STUDENT PROTEST

STRIKES

WELFARE STRUGGLES

SOCIAL SCIENCE for SOCIAL CONTROL

COUNTER-INSURGENCY

URBAN REMOVAL

GHETTO PACIFICATION RACISM

ECONOMIC MIS-DEVELOMENT

STRIKE BREAKING

ARPA and that many, such as Pool, sat on advisory boards for the army, air force and navy, as well as consulting for Pentagon and military contractors. A pamphlet from the anti-war faction, "Why CIS?," cast this far less favorably, noting that "In addition to the official research projects, individual professors do a very substantial amount of consulting for the State Department, CIA, USIA, and other government agencies. There has been a long history of professors moving back and forth between the CIS and the government. Milliken, former director of the CIS, served as vice-director of the CIA. Griffith worked for Radio Free Europe a CIA funded propaganda operation. Rostow, formerly of the CIS, served as national Security Advisor under Johnson and was responsible for many of the criminal policies pursued by the U.S. in Vietnam . . . In addition the CIS has trained cycle after cycle of mandarins

Judy Kaufman and Bob Park, eds., *The Cambridge Project: Social Science for Social Control* (Cambridge: 1969).

of funding (25% of the Institute's operating budget), the latter a major source of prestige. Among its conclusions, the panel recommended continuing some defense-related research but shifting the focus of work in the special labs "in the direction of domestic and social problems."[96] It also suggested that research be declassified and called upon the President to set up a Standing Committee to review work being undertaken in the labs.[97] The Executive Committee of the Corporation accepted the panel's recommendations in September and released a statement asserting that it "would be inappropriate for the Institute to incur new obligations in the design and development of systems that are intended for operational deployment as military weapons," and clarifying that this was "not meant to mean that with its unique qualities the Institute should not continue to be involved in advancing the state of technology in areas which have defense applications."[98] In October the faculty voted overwhelmingly in favor of Johnson's proposal to test the feasibility of the Pounds Panel recommendation, and Johnson set up a Standing Committee, known as the Sheehan Committee, to establish whether funding would be available for such a shift or even conversion in priorities. Johnson stressed his commitment to this change but noted, "The feasibility of these two interlocking goals—basic technology related to defense and domestic technology—will take some time to test."[99]

Shortly afterwards, Johnson appointed Charles L. Miller to succeed Charles S. Draper as the Director of the I-Lab (now re-named the Charles Stark Draper Laboratory), although Miller would not formally assume the post until January 1, 1970. As announced by Carson Agnew in *The Tech*, "According to a reliable source, Prof. Miller expects a major part of the Urban Systems Lab, which he also heads, to be absorbed into the new Draper Labs." Such a "transfer of on-going projects," the student reporter noted, "would pacify those who want the I-Labs to begin working on socially necessary projects now—even if those projects were a small part of the I-Lab total budget—and thus take away some support from the SACC [Science Action Coordinating Committee] drive to end war-related research at the labs."[100] But, Agnew concluded, the "reorganization [gave] only the illusion of change."

> This reporter was present when Prof. J. C. R. Licklider told Provost Jerome Wiesner in a phone conversation that appointing Miller to head the Draper Labs was "a stroke of genius." The whole thing is so pragmatic that Richard Nixon might have engineered

for the government. Military officers, State Dept. personnel and random other bureaucrats come to the CIS, study for a few years, learn new techniques of oppression, and return to their agencies with newly acquired skills." One-page typescript, no author noted (appears to be from MIT—Students for a

Democratic Society), c. 1972. AC276.
96 See Nelkin, *The University and Military Research.*
97 See "Statement by President Howard W. Johnson on the Special Laboratories, October 22, 1969," MIT *Institute Report* (October 24, 1969). Reprinted in Nelkin, *The University and Military*

Research, 168-177.
98 Ibid., 172.
99 Ibid., 172-173 and 175, respectively.
100 Carson Agnew, "Notes on Conversion," *The Tech* 89, no. 36 (October 14, 1969), 4.
101 Ibid., 4, 11.
102 Carol R. Sternhell, "M.I.T. Labs to Continue War Research, Says NAC," *The*

Harvard Crimson (October 29, 1969). In Nelkin's account, "Miller, as director of the USL, represented a program relevant to social issues, though one which operates at the comparatively small scale of about $1 million annually. By appointing him, the administration gained time without yet making it. I-Labs, with $50 million a year in volume can swallow Urban Systems' $5 million whole—it will allow them, in fact, to keep people employed who might have had to leave now that the Apollo work is almost finished. But those projects can be used as a showcase effort. "See," MIT can say to us all, "the I-Labs are being converted to peaceful purposes."[101]

Agnew was not the only one convinced that MIT's "plans to convert its laboratories from war-related research were 'nothing but a fraud,'" or that such claims to conversion were meant to counter radical criticism of Pentagon-related research.[102] These suspicions were fueled by the "liberation" of a memo from Miller to Johnson into the hands of the November Action Coalition (NAC), a coalition of about 30 activist groups from the Boston area who were planning militant action against the I-Lab. Miller had written to Johnson with concerns about ongoing funding of USL, concluding his memo: "While wise use of Ford funds can help ease some of these, I feel it would be a mistake to ignore the critical needs of USL while giving a misleading illusion of 'converting' the I-lab.'"[103] The group had polemically taken this statement as proof of disingenuousness.

As reported in the *New York Times*, on November 4 approximately one thousand members of the NAC "mounted the steps of the student center with Vietcong flags and a loudspeaker to begin their 'anti-imperialistic actions' against the Institute," later chanting "Ho, Ho, Ho Chi Minh, N.L.F. is going to win." In anticipation of the action, MIT administration had obtained a court order banning violence and disruption on campus; it was "believed to be the first taken by a college in advance of disorders."[104] The largely non-violent protests continued for three days and were directed not only at the I-Lab but also at CIS and its recently founded Cambridge

Science Action Coordination Committee, made up of graduate students, rallied outside the Student Center and sought to intrude on a panel discussion of "The Human Purpose," on Alumni Day in 1969. At the left of the large placard is Dean for Student Affairs, Kenneth R. Wadleigh and Assistant Provost Paul E. Gray, and at the extreme left, Walter A. Rosenblith, chairman of the faculty.

firm commitments. The Urban Systems Laboratory was already co-sponsor of several projects within the Instrumentation Lab. It could be absorbed into the laboratory and at the same time provide a funding base from which to develop new projects." Nelkin, *The University and Military Research*, 94.

103 Sternhell, "M.I.T. Labs to Continue War Research, Says NAC." Miller, Sternhell reports, was about to announce a $1 million Ford Foundation grant for converting the labs. She cites an NAC spokesman as saying "This announcement of this grant for an illusory

conversion is the apotheosis of M.I.T.'s attempts to head off our movement[.] Miller himself is down on the idea, both because he thinks it's a sop to radical students and because it is financially unfeasible."

104 Robert Reinhold, "1000 Stage a Peaceful Protest Against War Research at

M.I.T.," *New York Times*, (November 5, 1969), 18. On the November Action Coalition disruption, see also: "Educator in a Dilemma: Howard Wesley Johnson," *New York Times* (November 4, 1969), 34; Robert Reinhold, "Police Disperse Demonstrators at M.I.T. Lab," *New York Times* (November

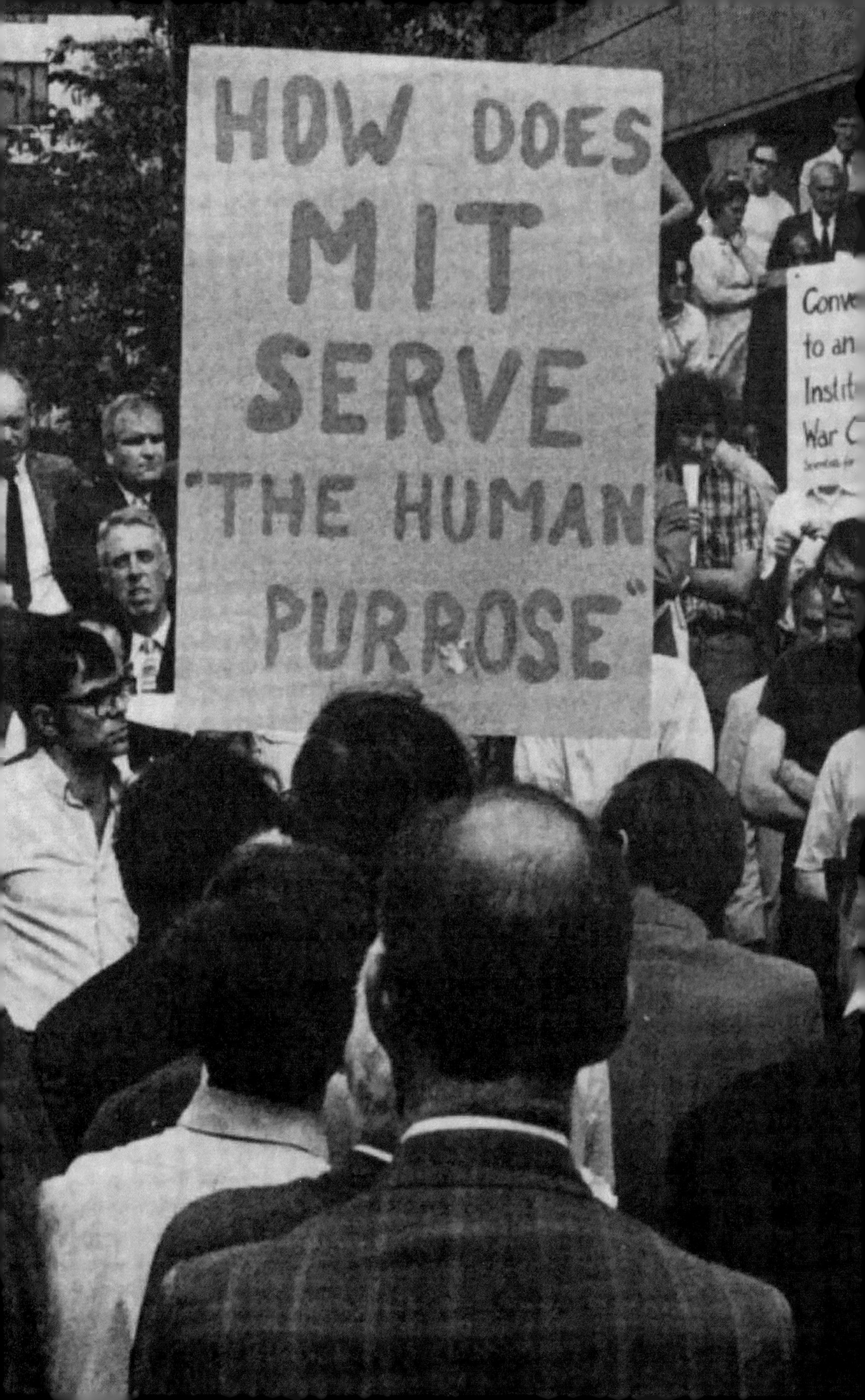
HOW DOES
MIT
SERVE
"THE HUMAN
PURPOSE"

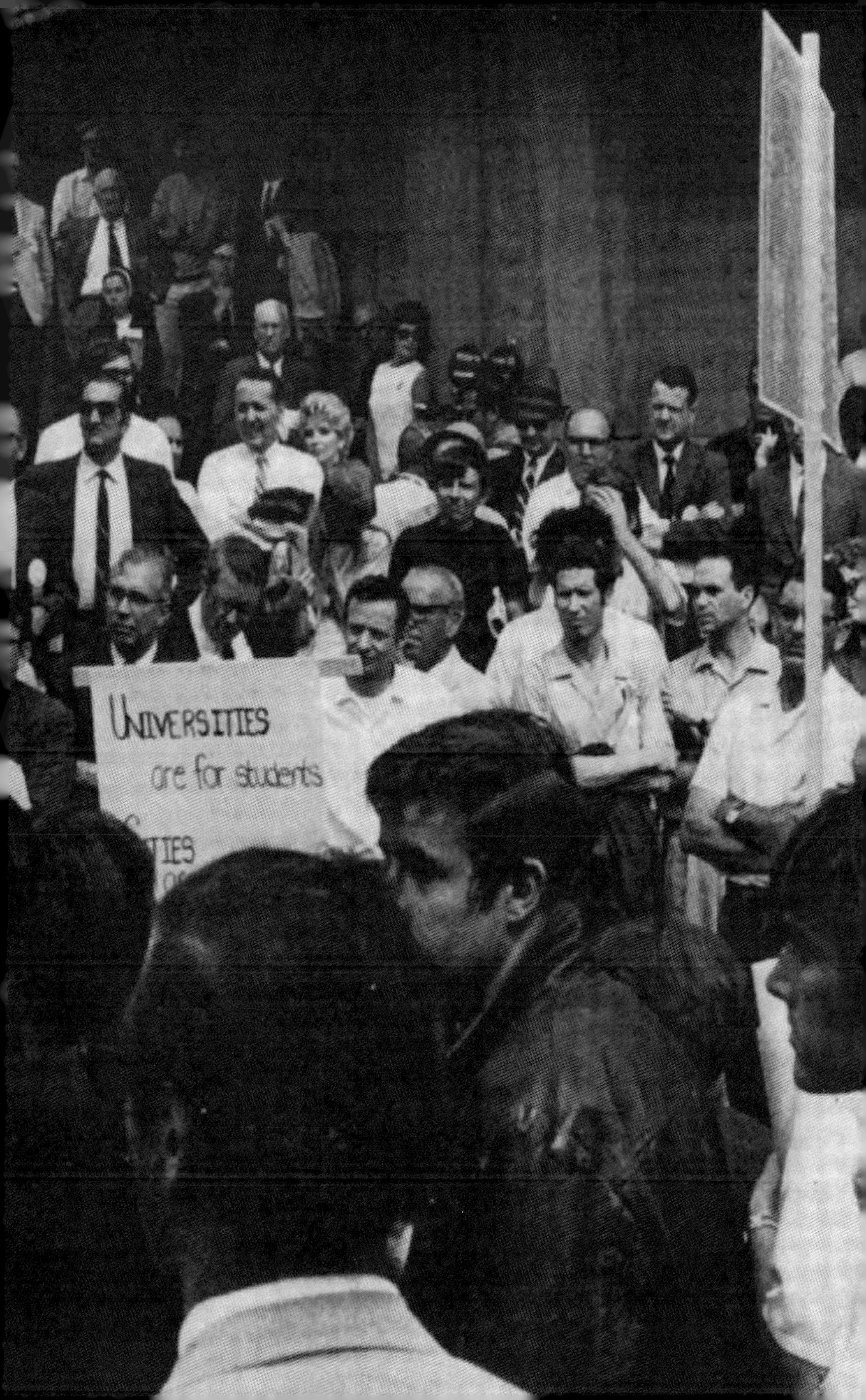

UNIVERSITIES
are for students

Project. As the *Times* reporter noted, "They also charged that two social science projects at the Center for International Studies and the so-called Cambridge Project are designed to counter revolutionary movements." The Hermann Building, which housed the CIS, was preemptively closed and evacuated "because of the risk of violence."[105]

In May 1969, the SACC had launched an earlier demonstration against the Cambridge Project, brainchild not only of Pool but also of Licklider, a Professor of Electrical Engineering and founder and former director of the primary institutional support for artificial intelligence research, the Information Processing Techniques Office (IPTO) of ARPA.[106] The *New York Times* reported that the SACC, "which is dedicated to opposing academic research for the benefit of the military-industrial complex, asserted that the computer would be useful to the Pentagon for amassing data to be employed in suppressing popular movements." While the administration denied the assertion, insisting that the Cambridge Project was simply an unclassified project to develop computer analysis and modeling of research in the behavioral sciences, the Project, the article revealed, had just "applied to the Behavioral Sciences Division of the Advanced Research Projects Agency, an arm of the Department of Defense."[107] Pool, moreover, had a history of research on counter-insurgency and psychological warfare techniques, some developed for Vietnam, and he firmly believed in the value of the social sciences as a tool of government and national security, especially as a way of securing intelligence for US interests abroad.[108] "I can think of no greater contribution a social scientist could make to the intelligence of the US government," Pool argued in 1967, invoking Vietnamese villages, Dominican students, and Soviet writers, "than to help improve this effort at knowledge of the outside world."[109] On October 10, 1969, CIS had also been the target of a peaceful demonstration and "test occupation" promoted by Rosa Luxemburg Students for a Democratic Society (RL-SDS), which interrupted work for about three hours.[110] Carrying the flags of the Vietnamese National Liberation Front, the students chanted, "We won't die for Pool and Pye," again claiming that "the two were engaged in research on counter-revolutionary techniques and were funded by the Defense Department."[111] Pool's COMCOM program, which developed computer simulations of international communication patterns,[112] and the Cambridge Project were both condemned as part of an apparatus of "psychological warfare." A few

6, 1969), 26; Robert Reinhold, "150 Stage Sit-in as Protests Against M.I.T. Research Continue," *New York Times* (November 7, 1969), 8; Fred M. Hechinger, "Colleges: Tension over Issue of Defense Research," *New York Times* (November 9, 1969), E11. See also Robert Elkin, "Rally, Sit-in Protest War Research," *The*

Tech 89, no. 43 (November 7, 1969): 1, 5, and numerous other articles in this issue. **105** Reinhold, "1000 Stage a Peaceful Protest," 18. In 1971 the Hermann Building was actually the target of bombing, for which credit was taken by the Proud Eagle Tribe, "a revolutionary women's collective." The

target had been William P. Bundy, a senior research associate at CIS and former advisor to President Lyndon B. Johnson, for his role in the escalation of the Vietnam War. See Bruce Schwartz, "Women's Collective Claims Role in Hermann Bombing," *The Tech* 91, no. 41 (October 19, 1971): 1-2.

106 On Licklider see Edwards, chapter 8 "Constructing Artificial Intelligence" in *The Closed World*, 239-273. **107** John H. Fenton, "M.I.T. Group Assails Computer Plan," *New York Times* (May 7, 1969), 32. **108** Pool was part of an advisory committee of the

weeks later, as Dorothy Nelkin recounts in *The University and Military Research: Moral Politics at MIT*, Pool and three colleagues "were tried by a mock revolutionary tribunal and found guilty of 'crimes against humanity.'"[113]

On May 20, 1970, arguing that the I-Lab could not operate under the new constraints, Johnson announced his decision to undertake a two-stage divestment, "a divestment that protects this national asset, its personnel, and the Institute." For the country, he suggested, "looks to it as a shield." This separation allowed the lab to operate independently "and without the terms of the Corporation Executive Committee's directive."[114] As the reinstated Draper recounted in the Lab's annual report, "the first stage involved creating Charles Stark Draper Laboratory Division of M.I.T. with its own Board of Directors."[115] Miller was added to the new Board, and continued his duties as Associate Dean of the School of Engineering and Director of the USL. "It will be professor Miller's responsibilities to continue to develop the Urban Systems Laboratory as a main focus with which new mission laboratories will evolve which will be concerned with a wide variety of social problems," Johnson explained of this rapid redeployment.[116] The editorial in *The Tech* applauded the President's decision on account of the "current lack of funds for socially oriented research and the inability and unwillingness of the Draper Laboratory to change." "With the divestment of the Draper Lab and the gradual 'conversion' of the Lincoln Lab away from classified DOD research," they argued, "MIT will find itself out of the weapons systems development game." The editors hoped, in turn, that "when funds become available for [technically oriented research in the fields of social and urban systems] we look forward to the Urban Systems Lab becoming analogous to what the Draper Laboratories has become in the field of inertial guidance."[117] (This was an ambiguous remark, to say the least, given the D-Lab's role in developing weapons systems.) As with earlier attempts to demonstrate a shift toward civilian concerns, it was evident to many that this divestment was again covering up for business-as-usual. Bruce Schwartz offered a dissenting voice in "D-Labs Inc.: Divestment as Cop-Out," which appeared on the same page of *The Tech*, positing that MIT had simply washed its hand of the issue, hoping "to get war research protest as well as war research off campus," while the arms race continued with even less oversight.

National Research Council set up to encourage government programs in the behavioral sciences. In September 1968 the committee reported that "the behavioral sciences are an important source of information, analysis and explanation about group and individual behavior and are thus an increasingly relevant

instrument of modern government," especially since, as the committee's chairman explained, "a very substantial portion of government policy decision are directly concerned with the behavior of specific segments of the population." Harold M. Schmeck, "U.S. Urged to Rely on the Behavioral Sciences,"

New York Times (September 3, 1968), 16.

109 Ithiel de Sola Pool, "The Necessity for Social Scientists Doing Research for Governments," in *The Rise and Fall of Project Camelot: Studies in the Relationship between Social Science and Practical Politics*, ed. Irving Louis Horowitz (Cambridge,

MA: MIT Press, 1967): 267-71. Quoted in MIT-Students for a Democratic Society, "CIS is CIA," 11. AC276.

110 Greg Bernhardt, "150 Students Peacefully Disrupt CIS," *The Tech* 89, no. 36 (October 14, 1969): 1, 11.

111 "Demonstrators Protest MIT War Research," *New York Times* (October 11, 1969), 13.

In 1972, as part of a reinvigorated campaign, the Committee on War Related Research issued "A Summary of War-Related Research at Draper Lab." "War research has a long history at MIT," it began.

> America's interrelating complex of basic research, defense contracts, and weapons systems (with the corresponding profits), known as the military-industrial-university complex, has always held MIT close to its heart. The Institute's leadership role has always been recognized, especially in war-time, and boasted of publicly. In 1966, J.B. Hanify, in a famous statement, defended MIT and its expansion in Cambridge by stating that it was an "arsenal of democracy." But times have changed, and the war in Indochina has increased the public's—particularly the student movement's—political awareness, to the point that now MIT has learned to hide behind the double-talk of innumerable committees, review panels, and false divestments.[118]

As they went on to note, "war research continues at MIT. A little digging brings out a coherent picture that is not very different from what prompted Senator Fulbright to refer to MIT as 'the sixth wall of the Pentagon.'" The Committee also issued pamphlets on the history of the Draper Labs and its research in advanced tactical weapons and strategic arms, and it called for further militant action. When on May 8, 1972 President Nixon announced his decision to mine the harbors of North Vietnam, massive protests broke out against the escalation of the war in Indochina; at MIT riot police using clubs, dogs and tear gas swept demonstrators from campus. [119] The Draper Lab became independent the following year.

"The Little Pentagon"

In 1972, MIT-SDS launched a renewed battle against war-related research at the CIS. Pointing to its role in the suppression of popular movements struggling against US imperialism, they again targeted social science research directed towards gathering intelligence, developing counter-insurgency techniques, and influencing government policy.[120] Moreover, this time demonstrators stressed the intimate coupling of such social science research with developments in engineering and computerization. As a pamphlet titled "Why CIS?" posited: "Many of the weapons systems developed by engineers at MIT's laboratories

Referring to Lucien Pye.
112 COMCOM was developing "a model of the impact of foreign broadcasting on the Soviet Union, Communist China, and underdeveloped countries" and was used to "study the spread of news during the Cuban missile crisis." Joseph Hanlon, "The Implications

of Project Cambridge," *New Scientist* 79, no. 740, (February 25, 1971): 421-423, reprinted in MIT-SDS, "CIS is CIA," 28-29.
113 Nelkin, *The University and Military Research*, 110-111.
114 Howard W. Johnson, "Johnson Reports Draper Lab Divestment," *The Tech* 90, no. 28 (May 22, 1970): 5.

115 C. Stark Draper, "Charles Stark Draper Laboratory," "Report of the President for the Academic Year 1969-1970," *Massachusetts Institute of Technology Bulletin* 106, no. 2 (September 1971), 433.
116 "Johnson Reports Draper Lab Divestment," 5. The USL continued to play this PR role. In October 1971,

the same day that *The Tech* a story of the bombing of the Hermann Building and CIS it also featured an article noting that USL still existed. "The operation of MIT's Urban Systems Laboratory," it concluded, "is not being phased-out, but rather is proceeding at as fast a pace as ever. Even more, the USL are deployed and used under the direction of MIT's social scientists."[121] And under the subtitle "The 'Little Pentagon,'" another pamphlet, "End MIT's War Complicity," argued: "The CIS provides analysis and strategy used in maintaining US economic domination and sympathetic governments all over the world. The US war machine is dependent on both the hardware and software developed at MIT." The CIS, MIT-SDS explained, was "founded in 1951, with CIA funding, under the directorship of the infamous W.W. Rostow . . . well-known as key formulator of [President Lyndon B.] Johnson's policy in Vietnam," and a former major in the Office of Strategic Services, the forerunner of the Central Intelligence Agency. CIS was funded directly by the CIA until 1966, when, following protests, funding was taken over by the Ford Foundation and Department of Defense. Little else, they recognized, had changed. "The CIS is, to this day," they concluded, "a CIA front."[122]

During the strikes of 1972, MIT-SDS declared Ithiel de Sola Pool to be "People's Enemy No. 1." Pool and other key figures at CIS, they argued, "should be fired because they are essentially CIA agents in professors' clothing." As recounted in "CIS is CIA," Pool had been a consultant at the Rand Corporation since 1951 and in 1959 had founded Simulmatics, "a corporation to sell the software he developed to the government." Among Simulmatics's major contracts, they explained, was the Strategic Hamlet Program in Vietnam (in which rural peasants were forcibly relocated into villages with secure perimeters to insulate them from contact with the communist guerrilla insurgency) and "DoD's Project Agile/COIN (Counter-insurgency)."[123] Project Agile included "Research on Urban Insurgency," part-authored by Pool, and "POLITICA-A Manual Countersubversion and Counterconspiracy Game," again co-authored by Pool and described as "a gaming project designed to investigate how the army could effectively deal with the guerilla movement in Vietnam." In addition Project Agile had entailed research on insurgency and counter-insurgency tactics in Guatemala, Peru, Ecuador, and Bolivia. From Project Agile, MIT-SDS suggested, had emerged Project Phoenix, an operation in which "teams of counter-insurgents went to villages in South Vietnam, and tortured or killed village chiefs who sympathized with the NLF (about 20,000 such village chiefs were murdered)."[124] Pool and his graduate students, moreover, had been involved in preparatory field research, undertaking interviews with villagers to establish systems of political power and searching for "alternative organizations to the Viet Cong that would cooperate more readily with U.S. aims in Vietnam."[125]

represents the growing trend of research at MIT on the whole the shift of emphasis from defense-related work to research designed to solve problems of a most current and pressing sociological nature." Norman Sandler, "Lab Supports Efforts of Urban Researchers," The Tech 91, no. 41 (October 19, 1971): 1, 3.

117 "The Special," The Tech 90, no. 28 (May 22, 1970), 4. **118** Committee on War-Related Research, "A Summary of War-Related Research at Draper Lab," 4-page typsescript, nd. AC276. **119** "Riot Police hit MIT Campus," The Tech 92, no. 25 (May 12, 1972): 1, 3. **120** The group outlined the

charges as follows: "The purpose of the CIS, according to their most recent bulletin, is 'to conduct research which will contribute to the solution of some of the long-term problems of international policy that confront decision makers in government and private life." They then continued, "The

international policy of the US has long been to support fascist dictators (E.g. Spain, Greece, etc.); to suppress popular revolutions (e.g. the Philippines, Guatemala, Vietnam, and East Pakistan); and to engineer right-wing coups d'etat (e.g. Cambodia, Argentina, and Indonesia, where 500,000 revolutionary

According to Joseph Hanlon in the British magazine *New Scientist*, the DoD-funded Cambridge Project (operated under CIS) was the key player in developing computer technologies for data collection and military- and policy-oriented behavioral science modeling for deployment in Southeast Asia. Hanlon cited a series of proposed areas of research and data sets that had been set out in the original application to the DoD, a list which brings us back to the nexus of development and security: "Problems of the underdeveloped countries and on the conditions of stability"; "A study of peasant attitudes' including: 'under what conditions do peasants' protests become violent?'"; "studies on 'stability and disorder' in several countries"; "Analysis of several thousand interviews with Vietcong conducted by the Rand corporation"; along with "public opinion polls from all countries"; "cultural patterns on all tribes and peoples of the world"; "Data on youth movements"; "Mass unrest and political movements"; "Peasant attitudes and behavior"; and "Characteristics of Latin American countries." What Project Cambridge offered, Hanlon explained, was the possibility of taking data on villages, building a model of whether or not a village might be friendly to US interests or predicting what type of intervention might be help gain its allegiance. Computers, he noted, "are already selecting bombing targets in Vietnam, so it is not inconceivable that the model would be used to select the most unfriendly villages for bombing." The tools developed by Project Cambridge aimed to facilitate more complex war-gaming models while simultaneously cutting simulation time down from months to a few hours, hence aiding decisions such as "whether or not to intervene in a foreign revolution or election."[126] As part of a USL "Summer Study" program Pool had been working simultaneously on the question of developing computerized "Urban Information Systems" as "exercises in applied social science," this time dedicated to urban issues then confronting the US—"racial conflict, poverty, widespread physical decay, lack of low-cost housing, environmental pollution, and congested and wasteful transportation."[127]

peasants were massacred). We think that 'social science' research which aids this policy should be stopped. There is reason for this foreign policy: imperialism— the desire of a ruling class of bankers and businessmen in the US to extend their empire around the world. There is a reason why CIS exists: this

same ruling class controls the universities and set up the CIS to help them build and preserve imperialism." MIT-SDS. "CIS is CIA," 1.
121 "Why CIS."
122 "End MIT's War Complicity," pamphlet. AC 276. "At first the concept of the 'free world' was a confusing one," they posited, "but the

war has opened our eyes. The 'free world' is that part of the world which gets military and economic aid from the U.S. for free. It is that part of the world in which U.S. Big Business freely dominates the economies, the labor market, the raw materials, and the consumption market... We have come to see that

the war is being pushed by those who will profit from their freedom to exploit the people of Vietnam." See also Committee on War-Related Research, "Militant Action" and "What's Up at Draper Lab?" pamphlets. Same folder.
123 Simulmatics participation in such research is confirmed

Overlap

In 1974 the Cambridge Project was discontinued, or more properly, absorbed into the Overlap Project within the School of Architecture and Planning's newly founded Laboratory for Architecture and Planning (L.A.P.). Funded by the Advanced Research Projects Agency of the Department of Defense, the Overlap Project was, as Porter, then Dean of the School, explained, "an outgrowth of the Cambridge Project" and it was concerned with "devising ways of making inferences from textual and numerical data bases and automatically restructuring the data on the basis of these inferences (and vice versa)."[128] Given the long-standing relationship of Porter's "urban data management language," DISCOURSE, to the Cambridge Project (jointly funded by USL), Negroponte's presence on its Board of Directors since 1971,[129] and the interdisciplinary environmental research going on in the school, this transfer seems hardly surprising. But it brings us back the status of such research's political coordinates. With Porter as primary director, the Overlap Project continued DISCOURSE along with other data management research.[130]

Porter established the L.A.P. in July 1973 with the aim of promoting a "distinctive style of research and practice." In addition to stressing field-based research into physical and social environments, or "how people interact with each other and with these environments," its characteristics included "use of representations or modeling; and involvement in purposeful intervention." "As more is known about society and the processes of social and environmental change," Porter explained, it had become evident that "the environmental professional" was no longer adequately served by physical models and drawings of their buildings and needed to adopt the abstract modeling or simulation of the scientist. By "purposeful intervention" Porter hoped to express in turn that what distinguished architects and planners from other fields, such as social scientists "who try to understand existing social systems," was their roles as "agents of change." Architects and planners, he proposed, had to concern themselves with "sensing opportunities, points of leverage and mechanisms for change, and with ways of monitoring change."[131] In welcoming remarks at an Open House in March 1974, Porter recalled that the idea for the L.A.P. dated to an ill-fated 1971 proposal to the National Science Foundation for funding to establish a "Center for the Human Environment." He stressed the similarity of the intended research to

in Philip Quarles van Ufford, and Ananta Kumar Giri, *A Moral Critique of Development: In Search of Global Responsibilities* (London: Routledge, 2003). That Pool was unapologetic about this relation, as well as that between the CIS and the CIA, is evident in his rather alarming account: Ithiel de

Sola Pool, "The Necessity for Social Scientists Doing Research for Governments," in *The Rise and Fall of Project Camelot: Studies in the Relationship between Social Science and Practical Politics*, ed. Irving Louis Horowitz (Cambridge, MA: MIT Press, 1967), 267-280.
124 "CIS is CIA," 14.

125 "Why CIS?"
126 "The Projects leaders," Hanlon explained in concluding, "generally reflect the continuing military presence in the social sciences. The original proposal to DoD was written by Pool and MIT professor J.C.R. Licklider. Licklider was a staff member of the DoD

Advanced Research Projects Agency (ARPA) and at MIT was connected with the ARPA funded Project Mac: ARPA is funding Project Cambridge. Pool has done counterinsurgency research for ARPA and he is a member of the MIT Center for International Studies, which was funded until 1966 by the

laboratory methods in the physical sciences in which scientists constructed representations of the real world "in order to permit experimentation where they cannot physically get at what they wish to investigate." In the L.A.P., he posited, faculty and students would make "interventions into carefully constructed representations of reality," using computer based modeling to facilitate the simulation of complex urban and social environments through the incorporation of data.[132] Moreover, as he stressed, being visually oriented the School would be able to bring additional visual skills to bear on such quantitative data: there was, he explained, "considerable promise to some early efforts to combine the computer with other media for representing and manipulating environmental information." Again MIT, and in particular Negroponte and his Arc Mac team, would be at the forefront of this development; this became evident later in the 1970s with the development of the Aspen Movie Map, the Media Room and "Put-That-There," and the launching of the Arts and Media Technology program, soon renamed the Media Lab.[133]

As with the Cambridge Project, the Urban Systems Lab ceased operations in 1974 at a moment in which, to reiterate, military spending was being cut back on account of the reduction of US military involvement in Vietnam. But by then, in any case, as reflected in L.A.P., as well as in the Interdisciplinary Environmental Design Program founded in 1973 (absorbing the Urban Design program of 1966), and even the ongoing work of Arc Mac, the School had so fully interpolated into its midst other aspects of scientific and technological research, as well as a systems-based paradigm and tools of management, as to make such an additional interdisciplinary apparatus largely unnecessary.

Conclusion

What, then, might we learn from this story? What I have been attempting to trace here are a series of interconnections—at the level of collaborations, of funding, of scientific methodology and technological tools—which together suggest something more than simple homologies between the characteristics of research undertaken in the social sciences and computer applications at MIT and that undertaken in architecture and urbanism. This of course is hardly strange, given the shared institutional milieu and its governing mandates, which structured the possibility for such heavily-funded interdisciplinary research. (Other

Central Intelligence Agency. The present head of the project is Dr. Douwe Yntema, who was psychology group leader at the Air Force funded MIT Lincoln Laboratory." Hanlon, "The Implications of Project Cambridge," 29.
127 "Urban Information Systems: Report of M.I.T. Summer Study #2" (1968).

AC7.
128 William L. Porter, "Laboratory of Architecture and Planning," in "Report of the President and the Chancellor Issue, 1974-1975," *Massachusetts Institute of Technology Bulletin* 111, no. 4 (November 1975), 163. In the year 1974-75, as Porter reported, the lab had a budget

of "more than $480,000, mostly sponsored by the Department of Defense."
129 "Computer Aids to Participatory Design," 80.
130 See William L. Porter, "Laboratory of Architecture and Planning," in "Report of the President and the Chancellor Issue, 1975-1976," *Massachusetts Institute of*

Technology Bulletin 112, no. 4 (November 1976), 159.
131 William L. Porter, "Laboratory of Architecture and Planning," "Report of the President and the Chancellor Issue, 1973-74," *Massachusetts Institute of Technology Bulletin* 110, no. 4 (November 1974), 145.

key players in the history of computers, such as Stanford University and Cal Tech, it might be noted, had no professional architectural programs.) I am not, to be clear, trying to suggest that we should read all work undertaken at the School as necessarily directed, wittingly or unwittingly, towards military ends, or that it necessarily or self-consciously operated in the service of national security and the US's broader geopolitical aims, even if I do think it was similarly marked by the social, political, and territorial insecurity of the late 1960s. But I do think we might ask whether, in some cases, architects too had become "defense intellectuals," whether in the course of adopting modes of funding and alliance proper to "big science," and of collaborating with centers and laboratories at the forefront of military operations in Southeast Asia (and counter-insurgency strategies more globally), that many of these coordinates and skills had become so internalized or naturalized within the practice of these "urban technologists" as to be pursued without questioning. The question is not, furthermore, whether architects should engage with advanced forms of scientific knowledge and computer technology; such engagement has often characterized the discipline's vanguard, occasionally even its more radical avant-garde (although we are not concerned with avant-gardes here), and of course tactical forms of practice continued to negotiate this territory with criticality and to politically progressive ends.[134] Rather, the difficult question remains: how or to what ends might architects have engaged such scientific and technological developments to progressive ends in a situation in which architectural and urban research in the university had become a targeted area of funding by the military and intelligence establishment and its allies such as the Ford Foundation?

For in this case, as I have tried to show, these fields of study were all too proximate to contemporaneous scientific research into human subjects, populations and their milieux that were directed toward more coercive, militaristic, or at least less democratic forms of environmental control. If such research was often cast in the language of disinterested monitoring, objective evaluation, forecasting, and as facilitating rationalized design responses appropriate to increasingly complex urban and social problems, such new "methods" of information management and their materialization as environmental "solutions" were the product of an economic and political matrix that was far from neutral. That is to say, behind the supposed neutrality of systems-based analysis and quantitative methodologies,

132 "Welcoming Remarks made by Dean William Porter at the Open House of the Laboratory of Architecture and Planning, March 21, 1974." AC 400. "As it turned out," he noted, "the proposal could not be submitted because that part of the National Science Foundation to which the proposal was

directed was abolished just as the proposal was being completed."
133 The Interactive Movie Map, more commonly known as the Aspen Movie Map, forms another chapter of my forthcoming *Outlaw Territories*. See also Nicolas Negroponte, "The Media Room. Report for ONR and

DARPA," (Cambridge, MA: MIT, The Architecture Machine Group, 1978); Richard A. Bolt, "Spatial Data Management. DARPA Report," (Cambridge, MA: MIT, The Architecture Machine Group, 1979); and Richard A. Bolt, "'Put-That-There': Voice and Gesture at the Graphics Interface," *Computer Graphics* 4, no. 3

(July 1980): 262-270. On the history of the Media Lab see Stewart Brand, *The Media Lab: Inventing the Future at MIT* (New York: Penguin, 1988).
134 See, for instance, Felicity Scott, *Living Archive 7: Ant Farm* (Barcelona: ACTAR Editorial, 2008).

with their apparently seamless ability to modulate across fields ranging from the collection of data on race and poverty, to the development of computer-aided design programs, attempts to develop new methods of environmental controls were not simply haunted but were also motivated by governmental responses to the period's social unrest and territorial or geopolitical insecurity. At a historical moment threatened by insurrection at home and abroad, with civil rights struggles and anti-war dissidence cast as a security threat, and in which military strategies were increasingly directed to controlling such insecurity, we might ask, then, for whom the environments simulated and tested at MIT were envisioned?

Paul Edwards' argument that we should not simply dismiss the implied or actual military potentials of such research as simply "grantsmanship"—"the deliberate tailoring of grant proposals to the aims of funding agencies"—seems relevant here. For even if initially intended as a convenient or available vehicle for obtaining necessary funding, this logic could shift to become what he calls "mutual orientation." In this scenario, just as the researchers start to imagine and even project the work's technical capacities into the military register in appealing for funding, so the military agency comes to recognize new possibilities, hence re-orienting both sides of the equation.[135] In 1967, Senator Fulbright cast this slightly differently in "The War and Its Effects: The Military-Industrial-Academic Complex." Noting what had become "an arrangement of convenience, providing the Government with politically usable knowledge and the universities with badly needed funds," he proposed that "a university which has become accustomed to the inflow of government contract funds is likely to emphasize activities which will attract those funds."[136]

This story reminds us, additionally, that the history of computers in architecture, or computer-aided design, is not comprised merely of a history of graphic interfaces and drawing or rendering techniques, or of the experimental forms later facilitated by advances in both software and hardware. To this we need to add the story of a paradigm shift put into effect during the discipline's inscription within new modalities of environmental management and control, the story of the role it played (or was understood to play) within emergent paradigms of governmentality developed under the pressures of Cold War politics and expanded domestically with the threat of civil unrest. In the case of computer-

135 Edwards, *The Closed World*, 81-82.
136 Fulbright, "The War and Its Effects" 175, 176. "The corrupting process is a subtle one: no one needs to censor, threaten, or give order to contract scholars; without a word of warning or advice being uttered, it is simply understood that lucrative contracts are awarded not to those who question their Government's policies but to those who provide the Government with the tools and techniques it desires" (177).

aided design, Robin Evans's brilliant demonstration of the manner in which drawing techniques are not only descriptive tools but formative mechanisms within the practice of architecture might thus be extended to suggest that what is at stake here is to understand, and to critically and politically intervene in, the ever-increasing structural alignment of the field and its tools with the administration of such mechanisms of control. As the conception of architecture and the city came to be replaced by notions of environmental systems, we find that data on social organization and its physical matrix came to be understood simply as computational parameters with quantitative (rather than historical or political) values, insurrection a momentary instability before a feedback-based stabilization of, to invoke Jay Forrester's work at USL, those "urban dynamics" might be put to work.

I want to come back then, in concluding, to Dean Anderson's remark, with which we began—that the role of architecture and planning was that of "giving order to environmental and social change." For it was the nature of that order, or ordering, which had radically transformed. Architecture has long played a role in giving material form to the normative social mandates and welfare functions of the state as it both manages and cares for its citizens. And it has long operated semantically and even organizationally to political ends. In the story we have been following, however, architectural practice was understood to function no longer simply (or not only) in the traditional sense of giving form and organization, or even aesthetic expression, to social needs or cultural identity, or even to enhance quality of life. Architecture now offered tools and even a tactical arena through which to both accumulate and deploy knowledge of the population who interacted with it. Architectural research, that is, now operated in the service of advancing modes of global governmentality and their micro-political techniques of power; it was cast as one agent among many within an expanded biopolitical regime and its security apparatus. The architect, and its updated version, the computer-architect, was imagined for a moment to be a protagonist in the increasingly detailed research that fed the proliferation of such political technologies, hence offering us a historical platform through which to investigate the fault-lines or even identify the fine line distinguishing the discipline's progressive forms of experimentation, long a role played by schools of architecture, from its instrumental and normative function. If architecture in some sense always treads this difficult line, we find here a shift to an operational paradigm in which decision making has been ceded to technologies of control and management which inscribe the user-participant ever more intricately into its machinations by mobilizing the rhetoric of choice, participation, interaction, and even discourse, all now computer applications geared towards eradicating conflict.

Disoriented[1]
Kevin Lynch, around 1960

"Data Man"

On October 27, 1956, a group of alumni from the MIT Department of City and Regional Planning presented a play at their reunion. Written by Melvin F. Levine, who would eventually become a planner in the city of Boston, the parody, *Tomorrow the Universe*, revolved around the master planning of Amorphous, Massachusetts.

This fictitious city is invaded by a group of planners competing to sell their ideas to its citizens.[2] Among the firms is Adam, Tasker, and Rolystone (a mock name no doubt for Adams Howard and Greeley, three MIT alumni), whose conception of metropolis grows from region, to world, until it encompasses the universe. The play features a dance by Baron von Moses from New York, an apparition of the ghost of Daniel Burnham, a toast to Clarence Stein, and a song, "Keep your Town Romantic" by Lewis Mumbles, the Talking Planner. But by far the most scathing of parodies, is the play's depiction of a presentation by a team consisting of Señor Jose Sanmarco and Le Courvoisier, accompanied by an unstable character with tattered clothing named Irving Renewal.

To the sounds of trumpets and champagne pops, Señor Sanmarco first sings "The CIAM Song" that includes the verse:

> I am the biggest man in CIAM, yes I am.
> I am the biggest man in CIAM, yes I am.
> To plan the new guts of your city,
> I've brought my whole committee.[3]

"Gentlemen," he then proceeds, "We are here in the interests of Urban Design, whatever that is. We are for it and we think it ought to be done." Le Courvoisier then sings the Chandigarh song, but the citizens dismiss the team, arguing that they already have MIT people in mind for the job. (The parody no doubt magnified the relative unease with which MIT planning students received the idea of urban design as promoted by Josep Lluis Sert, then dean of Harvard University's Graduate School of Design).

A relatively more sympathetic, but rather perplexing, rendition of the "MIT people" follows. Enter Kevin Lunch from the "Perceptual Form of the City Office" carrying his Lunch basket full of data:

"Data"
Data, Data assemble all the facts you can
Data, Data design alone will never sell a plan
We've got statistics, we've got charts and tables by the ton
Even though we made them up they're better than none
Data, Data get them from the data man.[4]

Amorphous never gets its master plan. Instead a fight ensues among the planners, bringing down the house and curtain. What is most impenetrable about the play is the way that MIT alumni viewed their eventual own answer to "urban design," Kevin Lynch, as a data-man, not planner, nor designer.[5]

The Image of the City

In 1956, the alumni in the play were no doubt referring to the research and data gathering that Lynch was conducting toward his first and most famous book, *The Image of the City*.

Kevin Lynch and György Kepes had received a grant from the Rockefeller Foundation in 1954 to conduct research on the "perceptual form of the city," on how people perceived and inhabited the contemporary city.[6] Lynch and Kepes conducted interviews with citizens in Boston, Jersey City, and Los Angeles about the degree of legibility of the city's layout. They asked commuters to reconstruct the image of the city in drawings as well. Supported by the mnemonic and basic drawing skills of these citizens (there were only thirty interviewees for Boston and even less for Jersey and LA), Lynch proposed that it is a mental image of the city that holds it together for its citizens, not its physical image. The physical image, he believed, was no longer obtainable given the sprawl of the suburbs after the war. However, as I will try to show, the physical image as posited by by Lynch may in turn have been too specific and imbued with ethnic and class preferences.

The results of Lynch's research project were published in *The Image of the City*, which became one of the most popular books among practitioners and students alike.[7] The easy language of Image and its categorical approach made it even more attractive, especially

1 I am very grateful to Arindam Dutta and Eric Mumford for their insightful feedback on the paper. I am also grateful for Monica Belevan and Jarrad Morgan for their archival and editing help.

2 Kevin Lynch Papers (1934-1988), MC208, MIT Archives.
3 Ibid.
4 Ibid.
5 For an extensive history of the concept of urban design see Eric Mumford, *Defining Urban Design: CIAM Architects and the Formation of a Discipline 1937-69* (New Haven and London:

Yale University Press, 2009). See also Eric Mumford and Hashim Sarkis, eds., *Josep Lluis Sert: The Architect of Urban Design* (New Haven and London: Yale University Press, 2008).
6 Kevin Lynch, "Reconsidering the Image of the City," in *City Sense and City Design, Writings and

Projects of Kevin Lynch*, ed. Tridib Banerjee and Michael Southworth (Cambridge, MA: The MIT Press, 1990), 247.
7 Kevin Lynch, *The Image of the City* (Cambridge, MA: MIT Press, 1960).
8 Ibid., 90.

given its attempt to articulate urban forms in scientific terms, the same terms that were used in the social and behavioral sciences, influential fields of study at the time.

In *The Image of the City*, Lynch noted that there were five components that were being used by citizens to anchor their movement in the city, namely nodes, landmarks, edges, paths, and districts. These seemed to be the common denominators among all images. The clearer these elements were in the city—the more strongly defined a street edge was or the more clearly outlined the district was—the more legible the citizens' mental image and the easier it was for citizens to move around while feeling stable and secure in their environment. The legible urban image could be distinguished by the qualities of its singular elements and the qualities of the general composition. Legibility at the level of singular elements meant strong definition, richness in detail which did not overwhelm the ability of citizens to abstract these elements and relate them to others in the mental map. At the level of the composition of elements into an urban image, Lynch concluded that

> the images of greatest value are those which most closely approach a strong total field: dense, rigid, and vivid; which make use of all element types and form characteristics without narrow concentration; and which can be put together either hierarchically or continuously, as occasion demands. We may find, of course, that such animate is rare or impossible, that there are strong individual or cultural types which cannot transcend their basic abilities. In this case, an environment should be geared to the appropriate cultural type, or shaped in many ways so as to satisfy the varying demands of the individuals who inhabit it.[8]

Lynch concluded that a collective, mental image, a "cognitive map" as he would eventually refer to it, helped guide citizens in their daily commutes and activities. The role of the urban designer (Lynch did not use the term "urban design" per se) was to make the city cognitively legible to its citizens by making some of its perceptually weaker areas physically and visually more orderly and legible. *Image of the City* proposed qualities for the individual elements such as singularity, simplicity, and directional differentiation, as well as a few general principles for the total composition. These concerned relating the elements in a rather obvious manner (edges defining districts, paths intersecting at nodes).

However, and despite the extensive interviews with commuter citizens, the interpretation of these interviews and the photographic and cartographic surveys, *The Image of the City*, was published without any supporting data. When the research leading to the book was presented to planners, Lynch would show samples of the data and would challenge the planners to find any fault in his evidence, indicating that he was operating within the professional expectations of scientific research. Lynch deliberately omitted the data from his published books with the declared aim of making his writings accessible to a general audience.

Kevin Lynch, Sketches from the Perceptual Form of the City Collection, MIT
Libraries, Institute Archives and Special Collections, Kevin Lynch Papers.

Some Major Problems, Boston, Sketch, 1959

Consensus of 32 Sketch Maps, 1959

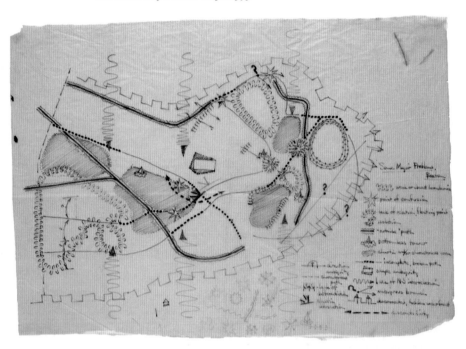

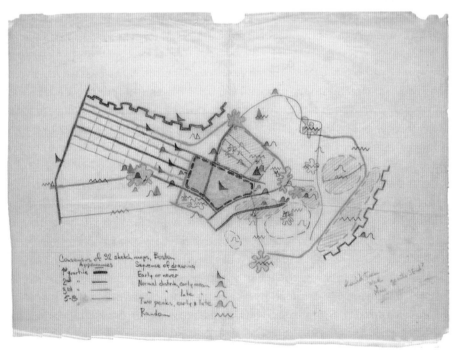

Reliance on data does not drive the arguments of any of Lynch's eight books. As an educator, situated as he was in a planning department inside an institute of technology, Lynch may have felt compelled to overcompensate for the fact that he was working on such elusive topics as image, perception, and legibility. He tended to stress measurable qualities like imageability and orientation. Whereas his senior collaborator, György Kepes, was an artist, and unabashedly so despite his infatuation with science and technology, Lynch had to constantly operate within the paradigm of, and with the tools and methods of, planning. Moreover, Lynch had to convince planners that aesthetic issues were "not simply a matter of taste, and therefore of low priority." They had valid statistical support. If a majority of people felt the same way about a particular aspect of the city's image, then it was a fact and not just an opinion.

Data did stand for interviews, surveys, and analyses of demographic and transportation figures. Data also stood for the need to understand and quantify every aspect of the metropolis no matter how elusive it may have been: noise, smell, signage, circulation, orientation, the adequate use of space. That did generate extensive data. In a paper written in 1961, Lynch put maps, density studies, and visual information all under the single rubric of data.[9] Data was the currency between the different fields in which Lynch operated.

The absence of data in *The Image of the City* may be linked to another absence, that of a clearly articulated position about the social impact of a clear urban image. Lynch wrote his books in a period of rising social and racial tensions in American cities, but urban problems such as racial segregation and blight did not feature strongly in his books. Beyond affirming a strong link between imageability and social well-being, he remained, at least in his writings, rather vague about what constituted the link between the social and the physical.

As a result much of the criticism of his work focuses on its behaviorist naiveté and on its ambiguous attitude toward the social conditions in the city. His critics even took his silence for complicity with urban renewal politics that irreversibly changed the ethnic and social issues that Lynch's pictorial urbanism encouraged. Irving Renewal was not only on Sert's team, many critics argued, but also on Lynch's.

Data did show, through interviews and numbers, that people preferred accessibility to exclusiveness and legibility to vagueness. What had started as an accumulation of data in support of a behaviorist, scientific approach to the city would evolve very consciously into a process of education, of making citizens aware of their environment and of their entitlement to certain visual and aesthetic qualities in this environment. Lynch took pride in the way that his interviewing process would eventually help inspire some procedures of participatory planning and community design. However, in the absence of a clear model explaining how these voices could be interpreted by design, the processes of democratic participation were

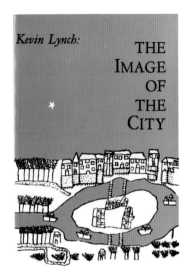

Donald Appleyard
and Kevin Lynch,
The View from the Road,
(Cambridge, MA: MIT
Press, 1958).

Kevin Lynch, *The Image
of The City*, (Cambridge,
MA: MIT Press, 1960).

directly and uncritically associated with the MIT version of urban design. The lack of a clear commitment to form and the vague position about the urban designer's agency may have eventually contributed to an overemphasis on the interviewing, or data gathering aspects of Lynch's approach. When data man could not speak for the data, the data spoke for itself.

Yet, as this paper aims to show, through his selective presentation of data and references in the book, and through his own involvement in the planning of the city of Boston during the late 1950s and early 1960s, evidence abounds that Lynch's larger intellectual project of urban imageability addressed deeper urban problems than his simplified prose conveyed. Lynch may have envisioned that urban design could give order and legibility to the built environment. However, in the context of post-WWII urban renewal and against the backdrop of the Civil Rights movement and social unease, operating in a disorderly context was also being elevated to a form of knowledge, into a way of life.

Spread from Appleyard
and Lynch, *The View from
the Road*, 1958.

60

27 The market is very close on the right and at
the same level. The bustle of people and the
crates of vegetables can almost be felt. Behind them rise the new office blocks of the
Government Center, and we are under the
28 first bridge, past the off-ramp to Dock Square.
Just beyond, people are sitting on the wide
29 steps to our right, which gently descend from
Dock Square itself. There is a momentary
30 glimpse of Faneuil Hall before we are completely dominated by the overbearing mass of
the Custom House tower looming right up
front, and almost over us.

31 The road, just in time, curves quickly to the
left to avoid the obstacle. It rises suddenly,
skirting the edge of the financial district, and
32 passes the first pair of downtown parking
towers on the left. A high fountain of water
tells us that the harbor is near; then the whole
33 view opens up and we look away across the
34 water to the airport, and beyond that to the
ocean itself.
35 The road turns inland into line with the axis of
36 the John Hancock and Prudential buildings,
37 seen in the distance. The second group of
38 parking towers pass by on the left, and we
39 drop underground beneath the towers of the
financial district. The tunnel is brightly lit,
then gradually dims until the sides and roof
40 turn into glass as we pass into an underworld
restaurant: colored lighting, people eating at
41 tables, jazz bands, perhaps an audible burst
of music. At a lower level, a subway train is
crossing our path.

42 After a slight curve, daylight appears at the
43 end of the tunnel. We rise to the open air and
44 continue up to the sky, flattening out at the
third-story level, feeling free in the air, crossing the Fort Point Channel and the railroad
45 tracks. We reorient ourselves by two visible
landmarks on the right, the Prudential and
John Hancock towers. Downtown is directly
behind us, and we are heading towards the
three chimneys of the city incinerator,*
46 which we pass on the right.

The railroad tracks do not confine the eye; the
road is high, and the views are wide. There is
time to look around. To the left the hill of
South Boston hides the sea, except in the left
distance, where Dorchester Bay and some
islands can be seen. Ahead the lamp stand-
47 ards of the South Intersection stake out a
skyline; to the right twin church spires,
hospitals, and the hills rise just above the
Roxbury rooftops. Some out-of-town advertisements crop up, as we approach the
intersection itself.

48 The Southeast and Southwest Expressways
can be seen winding into the distance, the
direction stripes appear again, and the road
surface changes from the red of the Center-
49 way to the black of the Crossing. As we turn
50 more than 90 degrees back toward the city,
what was on the right is now on the left.
51 Mission Hill has shot over to that side, and
we almost face the Prudential and John
Hancock buildings. The south edge of the city
stretches away on the right to downtown,
and the road we have just been on reappears.
52 We snake left and right through circular struc-
53 tures, a gas tank, and a railroad turntable.
54 After a glance down Massachusetts Avenue,
55 we are in the residential area of Roxbury. The
56 space is confined here as the road descends
57 under Washington Street and rises again over
58 Columbus Avenue. There is a strong sense of
59 the main cross streets, with brief vistas to-
60 wards the downtown section, but the alignment of the road does not deviate: it holds
rigidly to the existing street pattern. The
closeness to residential buildings is nowhere
so evident as along the Crossing.

* The present location of the road places the city incinerator directly on axis. Here is a case where too much
importance is given to a comparatively unimportant
object (cynics may disagree).

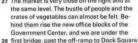

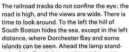

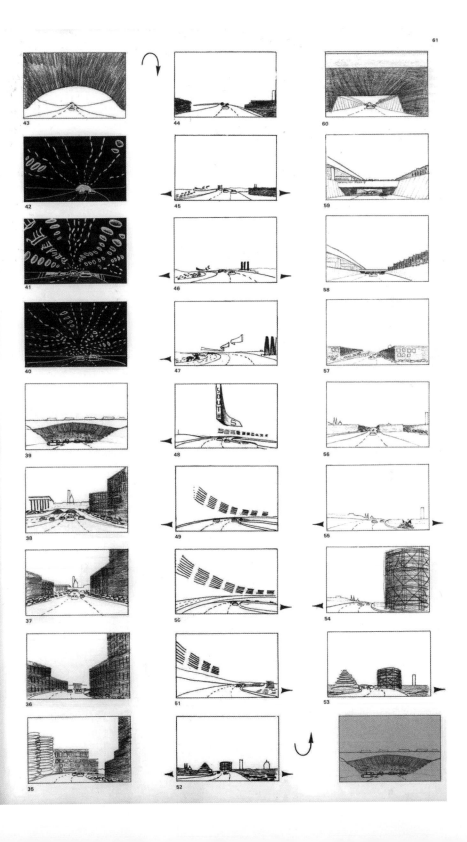

Interpretations of Lynch's Program

Lynch's critics have taken his silence for complicity with the real estate developers of the urban renewal period who irreversibly changed the ethnic and social composition of urban society. For example, in "America 1960-1970: Notes on Urban Images and Theories," Kenneth Frampton dismissed Lynch's work as "picturesque". Frampton bitterly attacked the distraction from political and social issues that an engagement with a pictorial urbanism had brought about. He picked on *The View from the Road*, a joint project between Lynch and Donald Appleyard, as an attempt at making acceptable the view of the city from the highway while ignoring the view of the road from the city, the social displacement and spatial dilapidation that the introduction of the highway into the city caused.[10]

There are a few references as to why imageability is an important norm for Lynch, that is, as what its political significance may be. In rare concluding moments, Lynch justified imageability as a precondition to a new aesthetic for democracy. Lynch deliberately avoided reference to "aesthetics" as such and preferred to use terms, such as "visual content" or "imageability," that do not carry the cultural burden of esthetics. As I will show later, there are two levels of aesthetics at work in Lynch's theory. "In a democracy," he said in *The Image of the City*,

> we deplore isolation, extol individual development, hope for ever-widening communication between groups. If an environment has a strong visible framework and highly characteristic parts, then exploration of new sectors is both easier and more inviting. If strategic links in communication (such as museums or libraries or meeting places) are clearly set forth, then those who might otherwise neglect them may be tempted to enter.[11]

With the suburban sprawl of the post-war city, yet despite the new highway systems and the ease of travel, Lynch noticed that American citizens had become alienated from their environment. They could no longer hold it together in a visual image. In order to increase the physical "imageability" and thus cognitive "legibility" of the American city, Lynch proposed to define it in a "cognitive image" instead. He asked individual citizens to evaluate the legibility of their cities from memory. Abstracting the components of their mnemonic maps, he noticed that

> there seems to be a public image of any given city which is the overlap of many individual images. Or perhaps there is a series of public images, each held by some significant number of citizens. Such group images are necessary if an individual is to operate successfully in environment and to cooperate with his fellows. Each individual picture is unique, with some content that is rarely or never communicated, yet it approximates the public image, which, in different environments, is more or less compelling, more or less embracing.[12]

Beyond his discussion of the general formal criteria of imageability, Lynch remained vague about what makes the aesthetic and cultural program of imageability constitutive of a democracy. This vagueness has also been taken for a vacuum to be filled by programmatic interpretations such as the one proposed by Fredric Jameson. At the end of his canonical essay, "Postmodernism, or the Cultural Logic of Late Capitalism,"[13] Jameson proposed that making the image of the totality of one's being visible is fundamental to the critical project of Marxism. The process of making visible, which constitutes for Jameson the agency of every artistic practice, follows the model of cognitive mapping proposed by Kevin Lynch in his book *The Image of the City*:

> Lynch's classic work, *The Image of the City*, indeed spawned the whole low-level sub-discipline that today takes the phrase "cognitive mapping" as its own designation. His problematic, to be sure, remains locked within the limits of phenomenology, and his book can no doubt be subjected to many criticisms on its own terms (not the least of which is the absence of any conception of political agency or historical process). My use of the book will be emblematic or allegorical, since the mental map of city space explored by Lynch can be extrapolated to that mental map of the social and global totality we all carry around in our heads in variously garbled forms. Drawing on the downtowns of Boston, Jersey City, and Los Angeles, and by the means of interviews and questionnaires in which subjects were asked to draw their city context from memory, Lynch suggests that urban alienation is directly proportional to the mental un-mappability of local cityscapes. A city like Boston, then, with its monumental perspectives, its markers and statuary, its combination of grand but simple spatial forms, including dramatic boundaries such as the Charles River, not only allows people to have, in their imaginations, a generally successful and continuous location to the rest of the city, but gives them something of the freedom and aesthetic gratification of traditional city from.

> I have always been struck by the way Lynch's conception of city experience--its dialectic between the here and now of immediate perception and the imaginative or imaginary sense of the city as an absent totality--presents something like a spatial analogue of Althusser's great formulation of ideology itself, as the "Imaginary representation of the

9 Kevin Lynch, *A Classification System for the Analysis of the Urban Pattern*, April 24, 1961 (prepared for the Seminar on Urban Spatial Structure of the Joint Center for Urban Studies of MIT and Harvard University), MC208, Box 2, MIT Archives.

10 Kenneth Frampton, "America 1960-1970: Notes on Urban Images and Theories," *Casabella* 359-360 (1971): 24-45.

11 Lynch, *The Image of the City*, 110.
12 Ibid., 46.

13 Fredric Jameson, "The Cultural Logic of Late Capitalism," in *Postmodernism or the Cultural Logic of Late Capitalism* (London and New York: Verso Books, 1991).
14 Ibid., 415-416.

subject's relationship to his or her Real conditions of existence." Whatever its defects and problems, this positive conception of ideology as a necessary function in any form of social life has the great merit of stressing the gap between the local positioning of the individual subject and the totality of class structures in which he or she is situated, a gap between phenomenological perception and a reality that transcends all individual thinking or experience; but which ideology, as such, attempts to span or coordinate, to map, by means of conscious and unconscious representations. The conception of cognitive mapping proposed here therefore involves an extrapolation of Lynch's spatial analysis to the realm of social structure, that is to say, in our historical moment, to the totality of class relations on a global (or should I say multinational) scale.[14]

A few inaccuracies should be cleared. Lynch himself was not responsible for "cognitive mapping" but rather borrowed it from the behavioral psychologist Edward Tolman. Second, and based on Lynch's own political activism, the "absence of historical process or notion of agency" needs to be reconsidered. Third, it is not at all clear why Jameson dismisses Lynch as a phenomenologist when an alternative approach to phenomenology, particularly Halbwachs' conception of a socially constituted subject, prevails in Lynch's work. Moreover, knowing the influence of the pragmatist school of thought on Lynch, particularly the work of John Dewey, Jameson's diagnosis of the conditions of contemporary society is consistent with that of the pragmatists. Both consider the alienation of the individual as the central problem of contemporary society. The Marxist project starts from the problem of economic destabilization and the consequential social inequalities created by capitalism. In the case of the Deweyan diagnosis, the causes are different. It is along Dewey's lines that cognitive mapping needs to be reinterpreted. While common to both Jameson and Lynch, the use of cognitive mapping has different ramifications for Lynch than those proposed in Jameson's essay. Lynch does not advocate a resistance of this total image as much as its valuation. The clearer and more legible one's total image is, the less one is alienated from one's environment.[15]

15 Other criticisms have also been voiced against the way Jameson uses the notion of cognitive mapping. Rosalyn Deutsche and other art theorists have criticized Jameson's "cognitive mapping" program for the arts because of its complicity with capitalism and a universalizing subject.

Jameson, according to Deutsche, is unable to operate without the totalities that capitalism has imposed. See Fredric Jameson, "Cognitive Mapping" in Marxism and the Interpretation of Culture, ed. Cary Nelson and Lawrence Grossberg (Urbana and Chicago: University of Illinois

Press, 1988), 353; Rosalyn Deutsche, "Expertease: Rosalyn Deutsche on Men in Space," Artforum International 28 (February 1990): 21-23. See also Rosalyn Deutsche, "Boys Town," Society and Space 9 (1991): 5-30.

16 According to Gary Hack, one of Lynch's close associates, Lynch's intention when conducting the interviews and the mapping exercises with citizens was to get people into thinking and talking about their cities and hopefully caring more about them and not to institute an interviewing process or a

The Two-Tiered Image

Almost every city soon after the publication of *The Image of the City* was cognitively mapped the Lynchian way. Lynch's attempt to engage people in deciding about the shape of their cities was transformed by some of his disciples into a mechanical interview process. Even the analysis of the maps was transformed into a very dense scientific method inaccessible to those who would have drawn the maps. This seems not to have been Lynch's intention, even if not explicitly declared then.[16]

If one examines the initial exercises of mapping conducted by Lynch, one notices that he does not really depart from other conventional mapping procedures. The making of cognitive maps involves three processes of translation found in most forms of cartography, namely scaling, projection, and symbolization.[17] According to cartographers, they are performed separately.[18] Scaling involves the translation of the features of the object of the map onto a drawing sheet. Projection is the means by which volumes are transformed into two-dimensional objects. Symbolization can be considered a third mechanism inherent to mapping, but it is the process by which meaning is attributed to the forms of the built environment. Symbolism is the legend of the map. We need certain conventions of representation in order to understand. When Lynch makes the cognitive image physical, when he identifies its components as being nodes, landmarks, axes, districts, and paths, he ignores the semantic dimension that is inherent in any symbolic system. In Lynch's theory, the symbolic structures of the urban environment are not analyzed through semiotics.

One explanation is suggested by Roland Barthes in his seminal essay, "Semiology and Urbanism." There Barthes made direct reference to this shortcoming in Kevin Lynch's project:

> Among urbanists there is no discussion of signification. Only one name is excepted, that of Kevin Lynch who appears to be the closest to these problems of urban semantics in the way that he is pre-occupied with thinking the city in the same terms of the conscience that perceives it. But in reality, the research of Lynch, from the semantic point of view, remains quite ambiguous.[19]

specific urban design review system. Gary Hack, interview with author.

17 See Mark Monmonier, *Maps, Distortion, and Meaning* (Washington: Association of American Geographers, 1977).

18 The use of cartography as a metaphor for determining the political inclinations of disciplines other than architecture is well known. Two examples that I have looked at are Svetlana Alpers, *The Art of Describing: Dutch art in the seventeenth century* (Chicago: University of Chicago Press, 1983) and

B. Santos, "Law: A Map of Misreading, Toward a Postmodern Conception of Law," *Journal of Law and Society* 14, no. 3 (Autumn 1987): 279-302.

19 See Roland Barthes, "Semiologie et Urbanisme," *L'Architecture d'aujourd'hui* 42, no.153 (1970-1971): 11-13.

20 Kevin Lynch, *A Theory of Good City Form* (Cambridge, MA: MIT Press, 1981), 141.

According to Barthes, Lynch employed a whole vocabulary of signification (legibility, the linguistic "elementarity" of the five features) but his gestalt approach always referred back to the mentally conceived image without describing how the elements of the structure interrelated. The *a priori* role and immediacy of cognition in gestalt versus the socially-based use of language and signification in semiotics may seem more in line with the valuation of experience in Lynch. Contempt for the theories that seemed to employ semiotics (Robert Venturi and Colin Rowe) may have been another reason for avoiding semiotics.[20] Lynch, however, was welcoming of semiotics as such but did not seem to have any use for it. In his theory, he focused on the structure of images rather than their contents, on the condition of having a legible image that comes before makes it possible for the image to acquire meaning. Imageability precedes semiotics. If imageability espouses a stronger delineation of edges between urban districts in order for citizens to be well oriented and at ease moving between districts, a symbolic reading would only emphasize a segregationist attitude. In his later writings, Lynch did not reject the symbolic order of the city, but he did not believe that an urban theory could be determined solely by such an order. A two-tiered conception of imagery, it would seem, more effectively informed the democratic project.

John Dewey's Scientific Attitude

In a letter written in 1982, a graduate student asked Lynch to cite the influences on his visual theory.[21] Lynch replied with a list headed by John Dewey. The high school attended by Lynch was founded by one of Dewey's disciples, who practiced Dewey's pedagogical philosophy of learning by doing.[22] In "Reconsidering The Image of the City," Lynch again acknowledged the influence of Dewey's valuation of experience on his work. Furthermore, Lynch's interest in education as an ideal setting for research and experimentation and for the proliferation of knowledge recalls that of Dewey. Like Dewey, Lynch emphasized the importance of interaction and experience in aesthetics. Occasional statements in *The Image of the City* even sound like Dewey's aesthetic theory: "indeed, a distinctive and legible environment not only offers security but also heightens the potential depth and intensity of human experience."[23]

21 See "Correspondences 1982." Kevin Lynch Papers (1934-1988), MC208, MIT Archives.
22 Lynch, *City Sense and City Design*, 11.
23 Lynch, *The Image of the City*, 5.

24 John Dewey, *Experience and Nature* (New York: Dover Publications, 1958), 354-437.
25 Timothy Kaufman-Osborn, *Politics/Sense/Experience* (Ithaca, NY: Cornell University Press, 1991), 1-11.
26 Hilary Putnam, "A Reconsideration of Deweyan Democracy," in *Renewing Philosophy* (Cambridge,

MA: Harvard University Press, 1992), 180-202. See also Hilary Putnam, *The Collapse of the Fact/Value Dichotomy and Other Essays*, (Cambridge, MA: Harvard University Press, 2002).
27 For a discussion of the distinction between scientific attitude and scientific method in Dewey's work, see Cornel

West, *The American Evasion of Philosophy* (Madison, WI: University of Wisconsin Press, 1989).
28 John B. Watson, "Psychology as the Behaviorist Views It," *Psychological Review* 20, (1913): 158-177.

Dewey's philosophy, politics, and pedagogy influenced the minds of successive generations (particularly those who, like Lynch, were educated in the 1930s and 1940s), but they influenced different generations in different ways. When Dewey was in Chicago at the turn of the century, he promoted progressive reform and an active role for professionals and intellectuals. While he continued to actively partake in political reform, his disciples, particularly those in the fifties, stressed the primacy of scientific method in his work, sometimes even neglecting its instrumental connection with democratic life. A reiteration of Dewey's views, particularly on the relation between epistemology and politics, may helpfully to reconnect Lynch's scientific method with a particular picture of democratic life. Dewey's work was driven by the need to overcome the false separation of facts from values.[24] This separation, according to Dewey, is the central cause of alienation in modern life.[25] Values are not ends in themselves. They are the bases of beliefs according to which human action is evaluated. They have to be tested in the field of everyday life, where they inspire a certain conduct. A theory of values for Dewey entailed the application of a scientific attitude (based on experimentation) to everyday conduct. Inferentially, human experience in everyday life, in the mutual interaction between the individual and the environment, becomes the object of analysis and observation, the object of knowledge. Since experiences change with time and with the change of actors and their intentions, there is a constant dynamic of revision and revaluation of values. The valuation of human experience, the use of scientific method, and the constant revision of values emerge simultaneously as the three main constituents of Deweyan epistemology and the pre-conditions for a sound democratic social life. Reciprocally, democracy is the setting for the application of scientific attitudes in the evaluation of human values.[26]

If we place *The Image of the City* back in the context of the late 1950s and consider the clout wielded by behavioral sciences at the time, it becomes clear why Lynch chose this particular scientific approach (over linguistic or mathematical approaches) for the determination of urban form. What Lynch winnowed out of Dewey may have had something to do with the tensions he perceived between science and politics.[27]

McCarthyism and Behaviorist Psychology

Terms such as image, imageability, and legibility and the empirical methods employed to determine the image of the city may have had their source in the "transactional" psychology and anthropology popular at the time. Lynch acknowledged the concurrence of many of his ideas, including their supporting terminology, with contemporary work in cognitive psychology. The reciprocal contributions of Kevin Lynch to those fields of research should also not be ignored. Many of Lynch's writings either appeared or were cited in anthologies in environmental psychology and cognition. However, rarely did he reference the work of his contemporaries on spatial orientation and cognitive mapping, work that was heavily funded and supported by the federal government and by the big private foundations, work that was impacting Lynch's research directly. Lynch himself had received a fund from the Ford Foundation in 1952 to travel abroad and study imageable environments in Italy, and in 1954 he and György Kepes received a grant from the Rockefeller Foundation to continue their research, this time looking at the conditions of American city. *The Image of the City*, written in 1959, was the first publication to come out of these two research projects. The school of psychological research found its manifesto in John B. Watson's essay, "Psychology as the Behaviorist Views It." In Watson's famous opening words,

> Psychology as the behaviorist views it is a purely objective experimental branch of natural science. Its theoretical goal is the prediction and control of behavior. Introspection forms no essential part of its method, nor is the scientific value of its data dependent upon the readiness with which they lend themselves to interpretation in terms of consciousness. The behaviorist, in his efforts to get a unitary scheme of animal response, recognizes no dividing line between man and brute. The behavior of man, with all of its refinement and complexity, forms only a part of the behaviorist total scheme of investigation.[28]

Behaviorism was launched by the experimental work of Watson and the parallel work of Russian physiologist Ivan Pavlov who was equally interested in observing the mechanical responses to stimuli. One reason for behaviorism's large popular appeal and successful reception among psychologists was its attempt to turn psychology into an objective science of behavior. By 1929 behaviorists represented the establishment in psychology.[29] At the same period, however, alternative approaches to behaviorism were emerging within the school itself, currents which eventually moved to oppose behaviorism's lack of emphasis on purposefulness in action.

Despite strong similarities in both approach and terminology, James J. Gibson remained absent from the work of Lynch even though Lynch and Kepes sent him the "framework" of their research study in 1955; Gibson responded with a short but favorable letter acknowledging that he thought they had reached the fundamentals of their area of research and "there ought to be a kind of psychological theory that unifies the alternative ways of organizing your study."[30] Gibson was fourteen years Lynch's senior. Like Lynch, he had been drafted to work with the Air Force in 1940 and had worked in the Air Force

29 Roger Backhouse and Philippe Fontaine, "Towards a History of the Social Sciences" in *The Social Sciences Since the Second World War*, eds. Roger Backhouse and Philippe Fontaine (Cambridge, UK: Cambridge University Press, 2010). See also Duane P. Schultz and Sydney Ellen

Schultz, *A History of Modern Psychology* (Fort Worth, TX: Howard Brace Jovanovich College Publishers, 1992), 317-320.

30 Kevin Lynch, letter to James J. Gibson, March 2, 1955 and James J. Gibson, Letter to Kevin Lynch and György Kepes, February 23, 1955. Kevin Lynch Papers

(1934-1988), MC208, MIT Archives.

31 See Edward S. Reed, *James J. Gibson and the Psychology of Perception*, (New Haven, CT: Yale University Press, 1988), 91

32 György Kepes edited a series of impressive anthologies on perception and art for the publisher George Braziller, a series that strongly impacted visual arts education in American universities during the 1960s and 1970s. James J. Gibson was featured in this series. See György Kepes ed., *The*

Training Command on problems of wayfinding for pilots in dark or desolate environments. Before the war, however, Gibson was an established behavioral psychologist who had nevertheless questioned laboratory-based research in visual perception and had aimed at finding new experiments and methods by which one could discuss vision in motion and in everyday life. World War II had helped place human experimental research in the mainstream of modern science.[31] Gibson became convinced that the work of the behaviorists and experimentalists in psychology had to be abandoned for more empirically-based, "realistic research." This research was based neither on data received nor output but on the interaction between man and environment.

The similarities between Gibson and Lynch do not stop here.[32] Gibson, a self-proclaimed radical realist, fashioned himself consciously in the tradition of American pragmatists like William James and George Herbert Mead, calling for a psychological practice that supported the reformed democracy of post-war social and political reconstruction. His political affinities and reformist work in psychology earned him the reputation of a distinguished dissident of perceptual psychology. To date Gibson's work continues to be evoked by those who challenge the establishment in cognitive psychology. Gibson never failed to postulate on the political implications of his research no matter how far-fetched the connection was. The role of psychologist, he believed, was to question the premises on which philosophy builds its image of the human psyche such as the mind-body distinction.[33] Gibson was trying to move away from a psychological subject who understood the world through representations, through images that were then cognitively processed, to a more engaged subject whose presence and action in the world gave it its bearings and meaning. Affordances, according to Gibson, are invariable references in the physical that guide us in our movement. When we move about in our everyday lives, we do not perceive the world as a series of pictures that our mind then puts together. We perceive it more immediately, in a more engaged manner, by establishing some of its features as fixed references that guide our movement within it. For Gibson, planes, surfaces, shades, and textures could serve as such invariables. The parallel with Lynch's five elements is uncanny. Like Lynch's elements, Gibson's do not constitute all of our experience, and they do not serve as the structure of our visual process. They are elements

Nature and Art of Motion (New York, NY: G. Braziller, 1965) and György Kepes ed., Sign, Image, Symbol (New York, NY: G. Braziller, 1966).

33 Reed, James J. Gibson and the Psychology of Perception, 54-55.
34 See James J. Gibson, The Ecological Approach to Visual Perception (Hillsdale, NJ: Erlbaum Associates, 1986), 5-44. See also Edward Reed and Rebecca Jones "Implications of Ecological Realism," in Reasons for

Realism, Selected Essays of James J. Gibson, eds. Edward Reed and Rebecca Jones (Hillsdale, NJ: Erlbaum Associates, 1982).

35 Reed, James J. Gibson and the Psychology of Perception, 105.

Edward C. Tolman,
"Cognitive Maps
in Rats and Men,"
Psychological Review
55, no. 4 (July 1948),
American Psychological
Association.

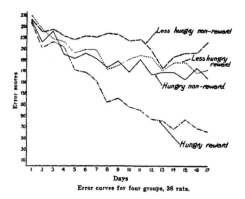

Error curves for four groups, 36 rats.

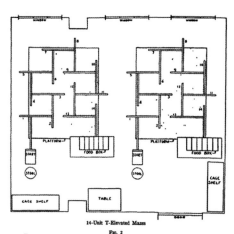

14-Unit T-Elevated Mazes

Fig. 2

(From C. H. Honzik, The sensory basis of maze learning in rats. *Compar. Psychol. Monogr.,* 1936, 13, No. 4, p. 4. These were two identical mazes placed side by side in the same room.)

that precede and support how we move about and give significance to things. This is a level that precedes perception and semantics but enables them. A note of caution that Gibson would make, and which could be used to defend Lynch against his critics, is that these affordances are not only visual, but haptic. They are invariables of touch, smell, gravity, and noise that get abstracted into a framework for cognition.[34]

Gibson's direct involvement in political struggles for intellectual freedom set him apart from Lynch. In the 1940s, Gibson was conducting research on whether "conservatives perceive a different world than radicals."[35] During the period following the war, he headed the Society for Psychological Study of Social Issues' Academic Freedom Committee. This was in a time when the Truman Doctrine of 1947 set the government against the advocates of social conscientiousness, particularly in academia. The pursuant investigations by Senator Joseph McCarthy during the Eisenhower era further proved detrimental to Gibson and other progressive psychologists at the time.

The incident that eventually led to the Gibson's ostracism by the federal government, the FBI, and conservative scholars was his support of Edward C. Tolman in the latter's struggle with the University of California over the mandatory oath against communism in 1949. Edward Chace Tolman, another absent reference from Lynch's bibliography, was the behaviorist psychologist who coined the term, "cognitive mapping." At the end of his 1948 essay, "Cognitive Maps in Rats and Men," he laid out the basic principles of cognitive mapping.

After having drawn many labyrinths to a scientific conclusion, Tolman switched abruptly to a discussion of what happens to human beings with narrow cognitive maps.[36] I carry this rather long quote because it bears uncanny resemblance, both in tone and in content, to what could be missing from Kevin Lynch's work:

> The poor Southern whites who take it out on the Negroes, are displacing their aggressions from the landlords, the southern economic system, the northern capitalists, or wherever the true cause of their frustration may lie, onto a mere convenient outgroup. The physicists on the Faculty who criticize the humanities, or we psychologists who criticize all the other departments, or the University as a whole which criticizes the Secondary School system or, vice versa, the Secondary School system which criticizes the University—or, on a still larger and far more dangerous scene—we Americans who criticize the Russians and the Russians who criticize us, are also engaging , at least in part, in nothing more than such irrational displacements of our aggressions onto outgroups.

> I do not mean to imply that there may not be some true interferences by the one group with the goals of the other and hence that the aggressions of the members of the one group against the members of the other are necessarily wholly and merely displaced aggressions. But I do assert that often and in large part they are such mere displacements.

> Over and over again men are blinded by too violent motivations and too intense frustrations into blind and unintelligent and in the end desperately dangerous hates of outsiders. And the expression of these and their displaced hates ranges all the way from discrimination against minorities to world conflagrations.

> What in the name of Heaven and Psychology can we do about it? My only answer is to preach again the virtues of reason—of, that is, broad cognitive maps. And to suggest that the child-trainers and the world-planners of the future can only, if at all, bring about the presence of the required rationality (i.e., comprehensive maps) if they see to it that nobody's children are too over-motivated or too frustrated. Only then can these children learn to look before and after, learn to see that there are often round-about and safer paths to their quite proper goals—learn, that is, to realize that the well-beings of White and of Negro, of Catholic and of Protestant, of Christian and of Jew, of American and of Russian (and even of males and females) are mutually interdependent.

> We dare not let ourselves or others become so over-emotional, so hungry, so ill-clad, so over motivated that only narrow strip-maps will be developed. All of us in Europe as well as in America, in the Orient as well as in the Occident, must be made calm enough and well-fed enough to be able to develop truly comprehensive maps, or, as Freud would have put it, to be able to learn to live according to the Reality Principle rather than according to the narrow and too immediate Pleasure Principle.

We must, in short, subject our children and ourselves (as the kindly experimenter would his rats) to the optimal conditions of moderate motivation and an absence of unnecessary frustrations, whenever we put them and ourselves before the great God-given maze, which is our human world. I cannot predict whether or not we will be able, or be allowed, to do this: but I can say that, only insofar as we are able and are allowed, have we cause for hope.[37]

Tolman, who had at first believed that the tools and methodology of psychology were not physical entities but means to describe operations, changed his mind after a sojourn with Rudolf Carnap and the Vienna Circle in 1934. Like the behaviorists, Carnap believed that psychology should not focus on mental operations but on general bodily reflexes. Carnap introduced language, both in its referential and expressive dimensions, as the only access we have to reflexes. Returning from Vienna, Tolman emphasized the operational dimension of his behaviorism—of organism operating on its environment—but he later introduced the notion of a "cognitive map," which was the idea that rats (and men) hold representations of their total environment in their minds to guide their intelligent behavior toward their goals.[38] The work of Lynch directly borrows from the terminology of Tolman. The "image of the city" is Lynch's term for one of the cognitive maps that we consult in our goal-guided operations in the city (e.g. our daily commutes to work). We can thus understand the response of people to their environment by testing the extent to which this cognitive map is clear or blurred. We have no direct access to the mind, but we do have access to the way the mind relies on such means of operation. Such is the purpose of images, mapping, and interviewing.

During the Second World War, Tolman's duty at the Office of Strategic Services coincided with that of James J. Gibson in the army. Gibson had been offered a job with the Office but declined it in favor of direct field work with the Air Force. Lynch, who came back to MIT to teach in 1948, must have been aware of Tolman's work, as Tolman was teaching at Harvard in the 1950s.

It is puzzling, given the direct influence of Tolman's project on Lynch, to note that he is not listed in *The Image of the City* as a source or reference. Tolman's unyielding struggle for

36 See Edward C. Tolman, "Cognitive Maps in Rats and Men," in *Psychological Review* 55 (1948): 208.
37 Ibid., 208.
38 See Thomas Hardy Leahy, *A History of Psychology: Main Currents in Psychological Thought* (Englewood Cliffs, NJ: Prentice-Hall, 1987), 316-318.

39 Ibid., 103.
40 See Richard M. Fried, *Nightmare in Red, The McCarthy Era in Perspective* (Oxford, Cambridge: Oxford University Press, 1990), 3-36.
41 Lynch, *The Image of the City*, 126-127.

42 Maurice Halbwachs, *The Collective Memory* (New York: Harper and Row Books, 1980), 23-24.
43 Lynch, *City Sense and City Design*, 3.

44 Ibid., 157.
45 See Mary Douglas' introduction to Maurice Halbwachs, *The Collective Memory*, 18.
46 Lynch continued his participation with the BRA under Ed Logue and served as consultant for the Downtown Waterfront-Faneuil Hall Renewal Project in 1962.

academic freedom may have contributed to this absence. Even if it did not, it is useful to understand the political events surrounding such socially motivated researchers. In 1949, the regents of the University of California demanded that all faculty members take an oath in order to swear that they had no affinity with the Communist party. Tolman, who was teaching at Berkeley at the time, led a group of faculty members who objected to this demand. Despite this group's victory, legislation legalizing the anti-Communist oath was passed in California in 1951, and Tolman was stripped of his academic title and his federal funding. James Gibson, who had tried to raise funds for Tolman's research through the Academic Freedom Committee, was also investigated by the FBI and was denied federal funding. Despite the fact that Joseph McCarthy's fall in 1954 led to an easing of this pressure, both Tolman and Gibson had lost faith in their social psychology as an instrument of social change. They continued to practice and to preach, but references to the social implications of their work became less frequent and their scientific research more mechanical.

In this context, in which even MIT had an FBI agent reporting on the activities of the faculty,[39] Lynch, confronted with the fear of being associated with academic dissidents, may have found himself at loss with words, at a loss for giving credit, at a loss for articulating the political dimensions of his project. In his early writings, he fended off the central political questions of the 1950s.

McCarthyism was confined to neither politics nor the character and presence of Senator Joseph McCarthy. It was associated with the 1950's paradoxical sentiments of euphoria and fear, of affluence and poverty, and of directedness and loss. The dark years of early Cold War and McCarthyism are also remembered as days of affluence for America. Having emerged out of the Second World War unharmed, American wartime savings (estimated at $ 140 billion) were turned towards mass consumption. Industries which were well-equipped to supply the arms and arsenals for three World War fronts found it harder to meet the demands of American consumers at home. Cars, refrigerators, and televisions provided the building blocks for "the national consumer culture."[40] This equal access to consumer goods would remain uncomfortably tied to a promise of equal access to civil rights, especially as these rights remained unequally distributed along racial lines.

Lynch's urban project could be interpreted as a direct response to the social and physical changes of the immediate post-war era as they were experienced by those growing up during the days of the Great Depression. Lynch was one of many returning veterans who benefited from the GI Bill and got a master's degree in urban planning at MIT. This bill made education available and social mobility more possible for a blue-collar class badly hurt by the Great Depression. Still, social mobility was never as comfortable and easy as it appeared in the statistics on changing income levels and consumption patterns. Major changes in the physical environment, already anticipated during the war, were happening at a pace that did not allow much time for reflection and adaptability. During the Depression, urban centers had become heavily dilapidated and blighted, with businesses shutting down and urban populations moving out to the suburbs. With the return of the veterans, new suburban developments were built to receive them and their new families. The cities were linked to these new suburbs by new highways built by the federal government. The city, the concentrated entity as it had been understood and studied in its European sense and in its pre-war American sense was no longer the one in which Americans were now living. New standards of home, workplace, community, and commuting patterns emerged after the war. Consequently, new conceptions of the urban environment had to be created in order to improve its coherence.

Collective Memory

Lynch's little book does refer to another influence, the French sociologist Maurice Halbwachs.[41] Lynch only mentions Halbwachs once in confirming the importance of the common image of a city (Paris) in communications among citizens, but Lynch is indebted to Halbwachs's project of collective memory in at least two significant ways. Firstly, Halbwachs's work validated the link between the individual images that Lynch initially gathered with the collective image of the city that Lynch described through the five elements. Secondly, Halbwachs allocated a central role for space in memory. Halbwachs discovered that one's group or social identity is constitutive of one's memory. The organization of our recollections is based on the social organizations to which we belong. We are unable to recollect an event or a place without comparing them with the recollections of others. Memory is not a private world. It is a collective process organized by society and social relations:

> Don't we believe that we live the past more fully because we no longer represent it alone, because we see it now as we saw it then but through the eyes of another as well?

> Our memories remain collective, however, and are recalled to us through others even though only we were participants in the events or saw the things concerned. In reality, we are never alone. Other men need not be physically present, since we always carry with us and in us a number of distinct persons. I arrive for the first time in London and

As late as 1984, just before his death, he took part in the preparation of development parameters known as "Boston Tomorrow." Reflecting its credit to his participation the BRA dedicated the "Boston Tomorrow" report to the memory of Lynch.

47 Lawrence Kennedy, *Planning the City Upon a Hill* (Amherst, MA: University of Massachusetts Press, 1992), 234.

48 Richard Wallace Nathan, *The Government Center of Boston* (New York: The Inter-University Case Program, 1960).

49 Ibid.

Signs- Newbury Street, Boston. 'The actual appearance of signs and their loation in the city is often so chaotic that the result is intense visual clutter as well as a reduction in the effectiveness of the combined messages,' 1962. From Sidney Brower, Kevin Lynch, and Donald Appleyard. *Signs in the City: A Study by Graduate Students of Urban Design in the Department of City and Regional Planning*, MIT. (Cambridge: MIT, 1963).

Signs—
Newbury Street. Boston
11 March '63

take walks with different companions. An architect directs my attention to the character and arrangement of city buildings. A historian tells me why a certain street, house, or other spot is historically noteworthy. A painter alerts me to the colors in the parks... Now suppose that I went walking alone. Could I say that I preserve of that tour only individuals remembrances, belonging solely to me? Only in appearance did I take a walk alone. Other men have had these remembrances in common with me. Moreover, they help me to recall them. I turn to these people. I momentarily adopt their viewpoint, and I re-enter their group in order to better remember. I can still feel the group's influence and recognize in myself many ideas and ways of thinking that could not have originated with me that keep me in contact with it.[42]

Halbwachs' work was also vital for Lynch because it gave the environment—the built environment—a significant role in the construction of society and the individual. It was importantly used as a weapon against social scientists who questioned the significance of buildings in determining social form and who urged architects and planners to consider instead the significance of social determinants:[43]

Now let us close our eyes and, turning within ourselves, go back along the course of time to the furthest point at which our thought still holds clear remembrances of scenes and people. Never do we go outside space. We find ourselves not within an indeterminate space but rather in areas we know or might very easily localize, since they still belong to our present material milieu. I have great efforts to erase the spatial context, in order to hold alone to the feelings I then experienced and the thought I then entertained. Feelings and reflections, like all other events, have to be resituated in some place where I have resided or passed by and which is still in existence. Let us endeavor to go back further. When we reach that period when we are unable to represent places to ourselves, even in a confused manner, we have arrived at the regions of our past inaccessible to memory. That we remember only by transporting ourselves outside space is therefore incorrect. Indeed, quite the contrary, it is the spatial image alone that, by reason of its stability, gives us an illusion of not having changed through time and of retrieving the past in the present. But that's how memory is defined. Space alone is stable enough to endure without growing old or losing any of its parts.[44]

In effect, Halbwachs asserted, we never go outside space, not even in our memory. Counterfactually, if a memory is inaccessible, recollection no longer possible, it may have to do with the inaccessibility of certain spaces of memory, the inaccessibility of certain physical spaces of the environment, or their transformation. Lynch's response was to rely on collective memory as the last resort in an attempt to salvage from society—not through its physical environment, nor through its politics and behavior—but through its collective memory, those

Scollay Square, Boston (now demolished). From *Signs in the City*, 1963.

places which are threatened by the bulldozers of urban renewal. Lynch was also holding on to the last threads, to the collective memories of an older conception of the city, while building a new one. Like Halbwachs's mentor, Henri Bergson, Lynch searched in vain for the groups that constituted society and its memory. These groups were either rapidly disappearing from the inner city or finding their way to the amnesiac suburbs.[45] Lynch resorted to memory not as an antidote to loss, not as a total cognitive recapture of a lost world, but as a tool for coping with loss, the loss of one's fixed place in society and the loss of familiarity with a physical environment. In the post-WWII context, every citizen was a perpetual tourist in the ever-changing and ever-expanding environment of the city. Lynch's basic place-making elements are meant to provide the abstracted outlines for places that have been lost to urban renewal.

Existing Conditions at site for Government Center, from Adams, Howard, and
Greeley, et. al., *Government Center*, (Boston, MA: Adams, Howard & Greeley, 1959).

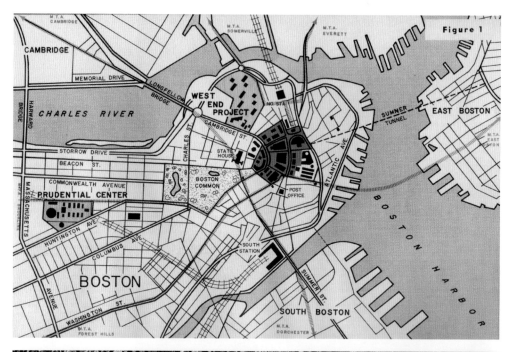

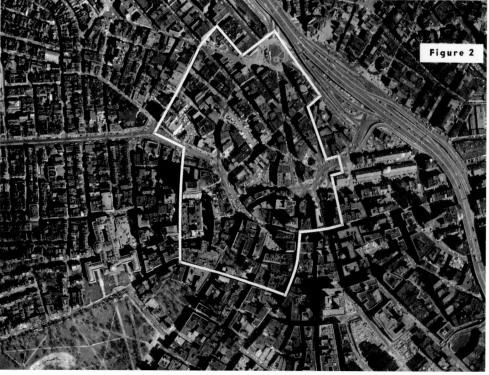

Government Center, Boston, 1958-1963

Boston was the field of most of the work conducted during Lynch's research and was later featured as one of the three cities analyzed in his canonical book, *The Image of the City*. In fact, the book was published during his work on the Government Center project in 1960. With Donald Appleyard, another young and innovative planner, Lynch also studied street signs in the city of Boston with MIT students in 1963. In short, the city was very familiar to Lynch, and his participation in the Government Center project was bound to enhance the credibility of Adams, Howard, and Greeley as consultants to the City Planning Board (CPB).[46] Moreover, the City Planning Board's involvement of MIT professionals in the development of the city center confirmed the strong respect that the city held for the Institute, and particularly for its ability to generate new industries for the Boston area.

The Government Center project was conceived and built during the transition from the Republican era, from the beginnings of urban renewal and interstate highway construction to the Kennedy-Johnson years of urban unrest and increased federal spending on social projects for inner cities. It was also a time when the social ramifications of the Housing Act of 1949 and of the appended plan of 1956 were becoming visible. Federal funding for urban renewal projects had been channeled through local redevelopment agencies that were eager to overturn the urban blight of the inner cities into gentrified neighborhoods, civic spaces, office centers, and local tax bases. In the case of Boston, and at the time of the proposal of the Government Center study, the Central Artery project was nearing completion and construction work on the destroyed West End would start in 1958.[47] The Government Center proposal was one of the last to be sponsored by the Planning Board of the city of Boston before it was abolished and its powers transferred to the Boston Redevelopment Authority under the new directorship of Ed Logue. During the period of the implementation of the Government Center project, the city underwent a mayoral transition and significant administrative restructuring that would leave their impact on the city center in the decade that followed.

The details of Kevin Lynch's involvement are not well known, but it is important to recount them here in order to unearth the ties between the procedural and aesthetic aspects of his proposal. They are also important because they show Lynch's professional activism during the Civil Rights movement and the role he played as urban planner in ratifying the fact of cultural pluralism.

The idea of a government center in Scollay Square can be traced back to 1954 when Sydnor Hodges, a senior planner in charge of the central area studies at the City Planning Board, proposed relocating City Hall to the Scollay Square area.[48] The relocation was meant to revive a stalling urban renewal process. Hodges' proposal grew to include a state-related office building close to the State House. The project proved to be very alluring to the Planning Board officials, especially when the federal General Services Administration (GSA)

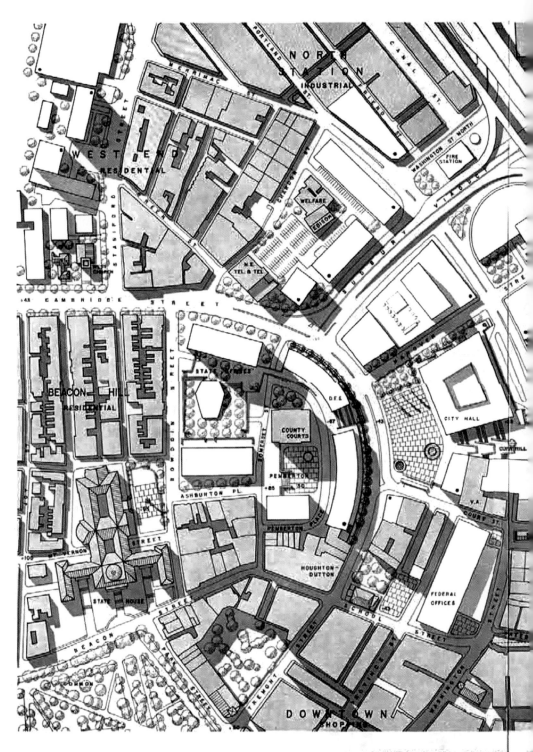

GENERAL PLAN

GOVERNMENT CENTER –

PREPARED BY ADAMS, HOWARD AND GREELEY

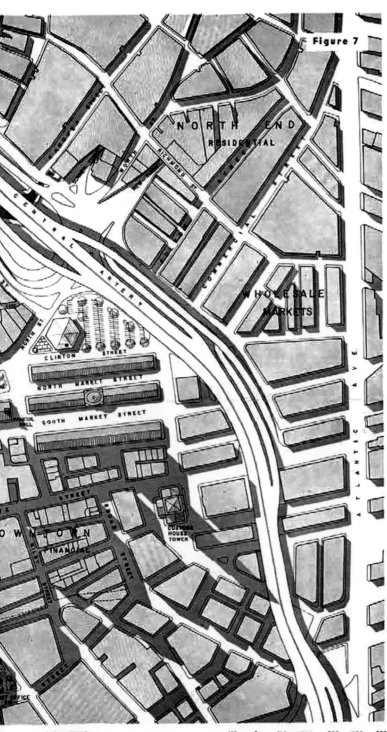

General Plan and *following page*, Aerial View, Adams, Howard, and Greeley, et. al. From *Government Center*, 1959.

Figure 7

NORTH   END
RESIDENTIAL

CENTRAL   ARTERY

COMMERCIAL

WHOLESALE
MARKETS

ATLANTIC AVE.

CLINTON   STREET

NORTH MARKET STREET

FANEUIL
HALL   SOUTH MARKET STREET

DOWNTOWN
FINANCIAL

CUSTOM
HOUSE
TOWER

POST OFFICE

LEGEND:

EXISTING BUILDINGS

NEW PUBLIC BUILDINGS

NEW PRIVATE BUILDINGS

100 0 100 200 300 400 500

N

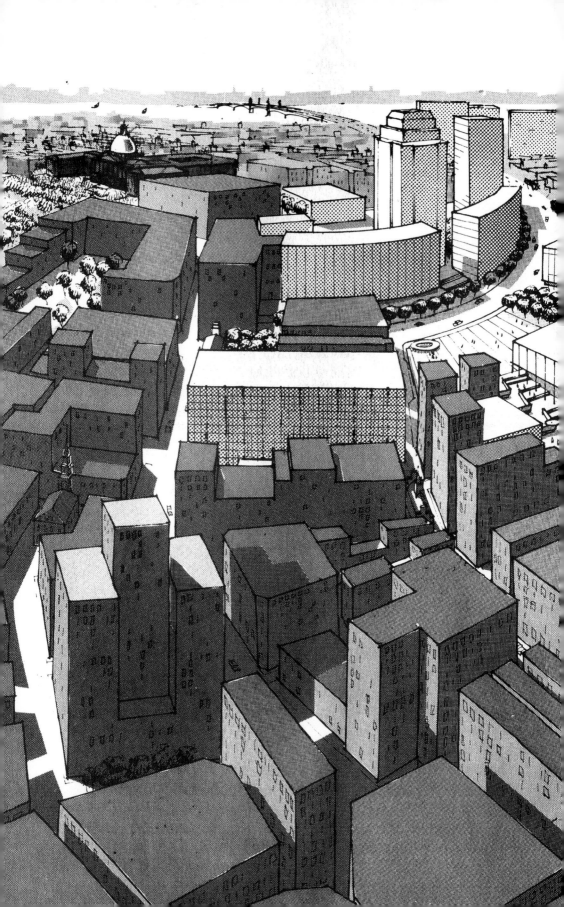

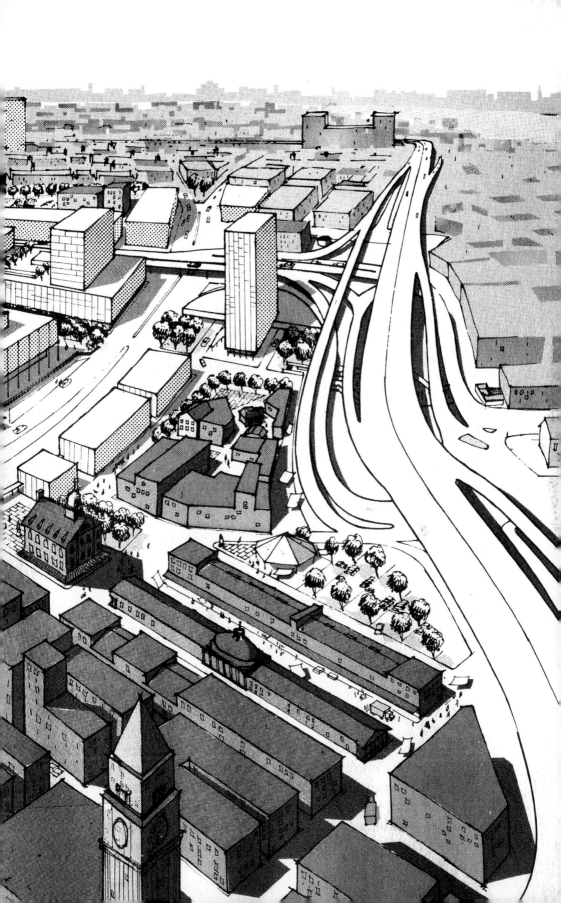

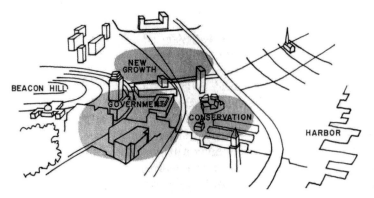

Sketches from
Government Center, 1959.

The Governmental Zone:
This diagram indicates
the division into three
zones: the Government
Center proper, the
convervation area, and the
a zone for new growth.

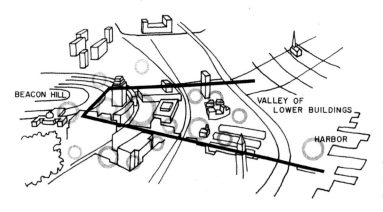

The System of Public
Open Spaces, highlighting
the 'chain of spaces.'

Sketch approaching the
square from Tremont
Street.

settled on Boston as the site of a twenty-five million-dollar federal office building project. In August 1956 the first proposal was published, and, despite the GSA's initial rejection of the idea of locating their office building in the central city district, the project proved to be a good fodder for incumbent mayor John Hynes's political campaign.

The project promised Hynes a good re-election campaign boost and Boston an economic one. Hynes's administration was suffering from declining support in Boston, and the city was sufering from an economic slump and increasing tax rates. Many city officials and agencies came out in support of this venture: the Greater Boston Chamber of Commerce, Committee on Civic Progress, the Greater Boston Real Estate Board, the Municipal Research Bureau, and the Retail Trade Board all endorsed the project immediately.[49] The year that followed, however, witnessed a defeat of the GSA proposal by Congress's delaying the federal funds. At the same time, that year's economic slump brought down real estate prices and made the land purchase necessary for this project all the more practicable.[50]

By the end of the year, the GSA had renewed its interest in being part of this project, were it to be realized. A second report was immediately produced by the Planning Board outlining the project and delineating Scollay Square as the selected site for a new government center for the city of Boston. The advantages of the Scollay Square area were numerous. Listed in the report were the feasibility of purchasing land in the area, its proximity to existing city, state, and federal office buildings, as well as to commercial and office centers, public transportation routes, and the newly constructed Central Artery. It was a major node in the image of Boston.[51]

The report designated the newly-established Boston Redevelopment Authority as the agency in charge of the land purchase. The planning firm of Adams, Howard, and Greeley of Cambridge was hired to prepare the design of the area. Kevin Lynch was one of their associates.[52] Concerned that the modernist aesthetics of the firm would not suit their conservative taste, the City Planning Board created an Architecture Advisory Committee to oversee the work.[53] The committee consisted of the dean of MIT's School of Architecture and Planning, Pietro Belluschi, the dean of the Graduate School of Design, Josep Lluis

50 Ibid.

51 *Government Center-Boston* (Boston: City Planning Board of Boston, 1959), 6-9.

52 I am here relying here on both Lynch's published work and unpublished material from the now-dissolved City Planning Board of Boston that is held in the Kevin Lynch archives at the MIT

Archives. See Kevin Lynch, *A Classification System for the Analysis of the Urban Pattern* (April 21, 1961), prepared for the Seminar on Urban Spatial Structure of the Joint Center for Urban Studies of MIT and Harvard University, MC208, Box 2, MIT Archives. See also Richard Wallace Nathan, *The Government Center of Boston*

(October 1960), MC208, Box 2, MIT Archives. See also The City Planning Board of Boston, *Government Center Project* (January 1958), MC208, Box 2, MIT Archives. See also correspondence issued by Adams, Howard & Greeley to Donald M. Graham (January 18, 1960), MC208, Box 2, MIT Archives. See

also *Government Center Project: Technical Report on Final Development Plan for the Government Center Area* (June 1959), MC208, Box 2, MIT Archives. See also *Historical and Architectural Notes on the Scollay Square Redevelopment Area*, correspondence from Walter Muir Whitehill,

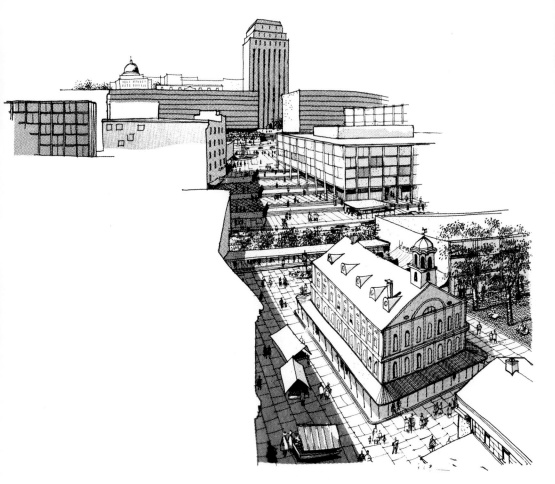

Faneuil Hall, Cornhill and the City Hall

Aerial sketch of Faneuil Hall, Cornhill and City Hall.
From *Government Center,* 1959.

Sert, and architects Nelson Aldrich, Henry Shepley, and Hugh Stubbins. As the project evolved, the Architecture Advisory Committee proved to be a supporter of the project rather than its watchdog.

Work on the development plan proceeded very fast in order to meet a June 30, 1959 deadline. The initial plan consisted of a city hall at the center of a complex of buildings flanked on one side by the federal building and on the other by tall buildings related to the central business district. A civic square of about 250-by-500 feet was placed in front of City Hall. In its position and shape, the central building was given the status of a monumental landmark. It was a square building fronting equally on four sides: the federal building to the north, Quincy Market and Faneuil Hall to the east, the public piazza to the west, and the commercial district to the south. Hanover Street separated the federal buildings from City Hall.

In the Boston interviews conducted for *The Image of the City*, Lynch found that Scollay Square, the area to be replaced by the new Government Center, was a major point of reference for Bostonians in their daily commutes, a "node," as the terminology went. He also concluded, based on citizens' recollections of the Square, that it lacked the visual prominence and clarity to match its "structural" primacy:

> [Scollay] Square, therefore, needs visual identity to match its functional importance, a realization of such potential forms as the rectangular space, the spindle pattern of paths, the side-hill terracing. To fulfill its structural role, the joint of each important path must be clearly explained both inbound and outbound. Potentially it could play an even more striking visual role as the central point of the old head of the Boston peninsula, the hub of a whole series of districts (Beacon Hill, West End, market area, financial district, central shopping district), the node of such important paths as Tremont, Cambridge, Court-State, and Sudbury Streets; and as the central figure in the descending triad of nodal terraces: Pemberton, Scollay, and Dock Squares. Scollay Square is not only a locus of uses which make "nice" people uneasy--it is also a great opportunity missed.[54]

Many terms from *The Image of the City* such as "visual function," and "focal point," as well as specific observations regarding Scollay Square's disarray, were transferred to the Government Center report:

> The Scollay Square-Dock Square district also performs an important visual function in the city. Here one enters the very heart of the metropolis; here is the key location which could, as the Boston Common does elsewhere, explain to the viewer the interrelations between many important sections of the city: the office district, the main shopping streets, Beacon Hill, the West End, the North End, the Central Artery, the markets and the harbor. The present area does none of this, of course, but only leaves the mind and eye in utter confusion and dismay. In planning the Government Center, there is a magnificent

The City Planning Board of Boston, Illustrative Site Plans, *Government Center*, January 1958.

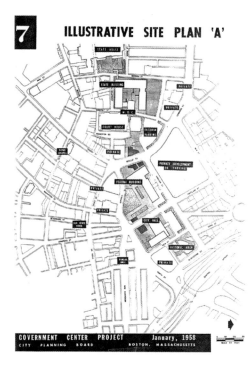

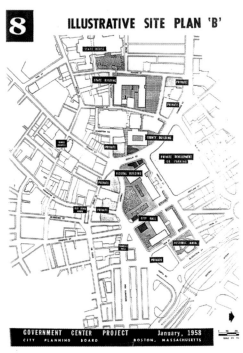

opportunity to produce a dramatic foreground for the heart of Boston, and to make a new focal point that would make clear and visible how the parts of the city fit together.[55]

In the Lynch plan, Government Center was laid out in such a way as to strongly demarcate the edges of the contiguous but socially and ethnically distinct neighborhoods that surrounded the site, to provide strong connections between them, and to establish City Hall as a distinctive landmark that would unify the character of the area. The West End was a rundown area inhabited by recent immigrants and the urban poor. Beacon Hill housed the old and well-established community of Boston, whereas the North End, which Lynch had delineated by a never-built motel, was the Italian quarter. Moreover, the plaza's slope toward the sea and the visual connection from Beacon Hill, across the site, all the way to the sea was taken as a strong alibi against the placement of a tall structure, such as the federal building in the center, that would interrupt visual connections in the city and reduce the plaza's image clarity.

From the beginning, collaboration with the main fund source, the GSA, proved to be difficult. In January 1959, Kevin Lynch went to Washington to present the preliminary studies. The GSA wanted a site no bigger than twelve thousand square feet and they objected to the presence of a street between the City Hall and the federal building. While Lynch returned to Boston to incorporate these suggestions into the design proposal, the GSA was exerting pressure on the governor to swap the locations of the city hall and federal building sites. After all, the federal building was to be larger in size than the city hall. The BRA and the mayor's office were slow in conveying the seriousness of the GSA request to the City Planning Board and to their consultants whose work was nearing the June deadline. When the City Planning Board was finally informed of the GSA request, a long-anticipated feud erupted between the two agencies.

The boundaries between the responsibilities of the BRA and those of the CPB were not well-drawn when the BRA was created to take charge of the real estate processes and funding of inner city renewal projects in 1957. The BRA was becoming increasingly powerful and its process of operation increasingly businesslike. This did not suit the work environment and professional ethic of the CPB, particularly that of its director.[56] Kevin Lynch would prove to be a fine mediator both between the two agencies and between the federal and local authorities. Lynch accompanied the mayor to Washington on more than one trip to meet with the GSA, and he used his citizen-interview results to rally support for the City Hall centered scheme. The GSA then suggested building on a much larger site site on Washington Street closer to the downtown and away from the run down areas of West and North End. Returning to Boston, Lynch discovered that the business community, led by Filene's owner, Harold Hodgkinson, thought that a federal building between City Hall and the shopping district would block circulation and pedestrian flow.

With such challenges, from the local to national level, from economic to urban, any other project would have remained buried in City Hall archives forever. The project could have also fallen between the cracks in the transition between one mayor and the next, or in the feuds between the federal and local governments. But when Hynes lost the bid for another term in office as mayor, he became all the more tenacious and adamant about the Planning Board's proposal. For a second time that year Hynes went to Washington with Lynch in order to propose other sites to the GSA. After a long and trying process of negotiations, a smaller lot was agreed upon.[57]

The project was carried forward by the new mayor and the newly appointed head of BRA, Ed Logue, and the Government Center project was implemented by the new administrative

director and Librarian of the Boston Athenaeum, to Paul Spreiregen of Anderson, Beckwith and Haible (received Dec 19, 1958), MC208, Box 2, MIT Archives. See also *Report of Architectural Advisory Committee*, addressed to the Boston City Planning Board (October 14, 1959), MC208, Box 2, MIT Archives.

53 Nathan, *The Government Center of Boston.*
54 Lynch, *The Image of the City*, 180-181.
55 City of Boston, *Government Center* (Boston, 1959), 10.

56 CPB director Donald M. Graham had studied urban planning under Kevin Lynch at MIT.
57 Nathan, *The Government Center of Boston.*

machinery that Logue created for the city. This proved more efficient than the fragmented planning and redevelopment bodies working under the previous mayor. Despite the arduous negotiation process, the Government Center, in contrast to other projects of the time, was one of the few that did not suffer extensive compromise.[58]

Lynch's design approach, which called for interviewing citizens about the city, may have inadvertently offered a good alibi for the project. When this approach was extended by the CPB into a popular platform for expressing needs and preferences, it offered the project political support at the time it needed it most. The advocacy approach that urbanists would later adopt in the face of social inequalities would not be far off from Lynch's approach, and neither are the now-commonly used urban design reviews.

Lynch's approach did not only show the public its entitlement to design issues. The urban renewal projects of the late fifties and sixties were built in the shadow of the Civil Rights struggles. Part of the strife was indeed caused by these projects, which displaced many of the blighted areas' poorer populations to even less secure locations. Despite a prevalent opinion that sees Lynch as complicit with the urban renewal policies that lead to further racial segregation and displacement, Lynch's urban theory, especially as he practiced it, in fact addressed cultural pluralism more affirmatively.

The Epistemology of Loss

From the early days of his career as urban designer and theorist, and until his death in 1984, Lynch's characters were constantly haunted by a fear of getting lost. In the 1950s, they were tourists unable to locate themselves on the map, children standing on the edge of their parents' fields of vision, cue-less navigators in Polynesia or in the sky, Caucasians in African American neighborhoods, commuters missing the right turn on their way to work; later on in his life, they were nuclear holocaust survivors disoriented amid the rubble of their own homes.[59] While Lynch tried to convey a more "human" city in his work by constantly referring to the well-being of its inhabitants and to healthy interaction with the environment, he repeatedly ended up with cases of loss and disorientation.

In order to cure this problem of disorientation, Lynch aimed to improve the legibility of the city environment by improving the ability of its citizens to abstract the city into a cognitive image. According to Lynch, this ability would improve their spatial and social orientation. While he affirmed the strong link between imageability and social well-being, Lynch remained vague about what constitutes the link between the social and the physical. Lynch's project is not based on the "quest for certainty." It is rather a search for means by which one can operate in a world of uncertainty. He therefore resorted to addressing the environment through the ills that it causes, that is, through loss and disorientation:

Getting lost was a frustrating experience because I couldn't find any way of becoming unlost, of attaching myself to the environment again. I would either have to ask somebody, which wasn't successful because they couldn't communicate turns, etc. to me or watch for signs, which were completely ambiguous. Then there was the pressure of traffic lights, and horns blowing. The consequences of a wrong direction are severe and cumulative. Trying to find things on a map where the grid changes direction is frustrating as Hell.

Do I dislike being late more, or is it annoyance about not being able to do such a simple thing? Why can't Americans have decent road signs? Why are they trying to keep the locations of towns hidden? If you want to get to Winchester in England, you find periodic signs showing how far away Winchester is as you travel the road. That's much more interesting; I mean, it's totally impossible to use a map while driving, unless you stop, so the map is of use only when you can stop. The whole trip through New Jersey to New York was 90 percent chance—there was no standard road number signs, no standard colors, no fixed intervals, no mile posts, no things to predict and rely upon. Even junctions are badly signed. Given the speed of traffic approaching junctions, they're not signed far enough in advance. I consciously planned the route, talked to somebody who lives in New York and got totally wrong directions. There are no good road maps, since they show roads which are proposed but not yet built. I'm going to join AAA. Yesterday was annoying as Hell. Street signs in New York are small and never lighted, and one can't read street numbers.

Anonymous Sufferer from Chronic Disorientation[60]

Characters suffering from such chronic disorientation problems appear recurrently in Lynch's work. Their fear of getting lost is at once a quality of their environment and of their individual psyches. If they are tourists unable to locate themselves on the map, it is because of the poor signage of the xenophobic cities in which they find themselves. The study of signage is an attempt to bring the presence of the foreigner into focus, as much as the study of imageability is an attempt to bring out the foreigners among us. And if Lynch held back on the semiotic discussion of signs by concentrating on imageability, it may be because urban signage had become rife with segregationist instructions. Nevertheless

58 Government Center still displays many of its initial design concepts today. However, its success as an urban development is debatable. When measured in terms of its satisfaction of Lynch's ideas, it is remarkable how closely it comes to fulfilling stated intentions. As in other situations involving

major capital spending and complex decision making processes, a design idea is not adopted and implemented solely because of its formal qualities. One should not ignore how, in this specific case, the design project lent itself as a visual illustration of public opinion.

59 See for example, Kevin Lynch, *The Image of the City*, Appendix A.

60 Lynch essay in this book. See *Image and Environment*, eds. Roger M. Downs and David Stea, (Chicago: Aldine Publishing Company, 1973), 289.

Lynch accepted the limits of imageability's potential to deal with conditions of loss. If his characters are victims of a nuclear holocaust then their problems can no longer be solved in the physical environment. The culture of waste that we inhabit, the "cacotopias" of fear and chaos, can only be consoled through architecture.

Lynch's project is not as universalist as some of his disciples and critics claim. He was neither developing an ideal urban form nor trying to get at an essence of humanity which architecture might then articulate. Lynch was unable to say much about this humanity. Even if we acknowledge the humanism inherent in his attempt to reconstitute a post-war and post-urban-renewal through a notion of collective memory, we should immediately qualify this humanist project by emphasizing the peculiar epistemology and plurality of its subjects. This is an epistemology that borrows from scientific determinism and from the arts' instruments of pacification to deal with difference and with intolerance. It is also an epistemology that takes into account the points of view of society's minorities: the disoriented, the tourist, the child, the amnesiac, the African American. These points of view are important to the project of democracy precisely because they will not be healed and put back in the mainstream. Rather Lynch, Tolman, and Gibson wanted to accommodate for this plurality by revising the white man's cognitive map, by redrawing the boundaries of the middle-class city and exposing the heterogeneity of post-war culture.

In *The Image of the City*, discontinuity, loss, and disorientation are accepted as the constant qualities of the post-WWII city. The complete recovery of the American urban landscape seems impossible and even undesirable, at least since Ralph Waldo Emerson's essay on America."Why is this new America said to be unapproachable?" Stanley Cavell asked of Ralph Waldo Emerson.

> First, it is unapproachable if he (or whoever belongs there) is already there (always already), but unable to experience it, hence to know or tell it; or unable to tell it, hence to experience it. Second, finding a nation is not managed by a landfall; a country must be peopled, and nations speak of birth. [...] Third, this new America is unapproachable by a process of continuity, if to find it is indeed [...to] suffer conversion; conversion is to be turned around, reversed, and that seems to be a matter of discontinuity.[61]

61 Stanley Cavell, *This New Yet Unapproachable America, Lectures After Emerson after Wittgenstein* (Albuquerque, NM: Living Batch Press, 1989), 91.

62 For this interpretation of Lynch, see Manfredo Tafuri and Francesco Dal Co, *Modern Architecture* (New York: Harry Abrams, Inc. Publishers, 1976).

If to find home, or to be at home, implies social stability and middle class hegemony, then Lynch, in line with the pragmatist projects of Dewey and his forerunner Emerson, rejected this stagnation and exclusiveness in favor of a more positive articulation of discontinuity, loss, and plurality. These are the preconditions for a pluralist democracy.

Government Center contrasts a spiritual condition of loss with an ordered urban environment. Lynch designed a highly segregated environment: edges demarcating ethnic and class zones, a celebration of the highway despite the displacement it had caused, and a refusal to engage the context stylistically or programmatically. Critics of the Government Center Plaza associate Lynch's work with the elitists and segregationist plutocracy of the '50s. One could locate Lynch within the urban and political culture while at the same time reading in his tone a '50s optimism; or, as it may be, one could look at his work as an acceptance, an aestheticization of the large-scale urban interventions of urban renewal.[62] One could also read the practical consequences of his work in terms of the ways in which his contributions to the plan of Boston in the early '60s helped develop new, participatory procedures of urban planning. One could argue that all of the above interpretive approaches should be taken. Lynch's built and written œuvres deserve a multiplicity of readings. Julian Beinart has compared Lynch's comprehensiveness to that of the nineteenth-century English novel.[63] Ultimately, it is this comprehensiveness in Lynch that may have dulled the sharpness of his project.

Much of the criticism against Lynch would be acceptable had this sequestered physical environment not been associated with a de-segregationist program and with an active role in transforming the procedural conditions of urban planning in favor of an advocacy approach. The aesthetic practice Lynch pursued, and which dissociates the form of the urban space from its content, stands far off from the emotive practices of recognition that pervade contemporary design debate. Significantly, Lynch's aesthetic practice did not relate to other aesthetic forms of recognition of the 1950s and 1960s. The radical potential of this practice was left unexplored even by Lynch. With the rise of the advocacy movement in the 1960s and growing resistance to urban renewal, Lynch's urban design theory was shelved under "regressively formal discourses about the city." The link with a strong social program was lost, and so was the radical potential of severing form from content.

63 Julian Beinart, interview
with author.

Systems

CATHERINE F. MCMAHON

Predictive Machines
Data, Computer Maps, and Simulation

GeoDesign: The Collapse of Past and Future

As eyes focus on a darkened stage we see standing there a modest, soft-spoken man, in a dark wool sweater and brown corduroy pants. Behind him is a backdrop carrying the glowing red letters, TED (acronym for the "Technology, Entertainment, Design" conference).[1] The man is Jack Dangermond, co-founder of the Environmental Systems Research Institute (ESRI), a lucrative company famous for the commercially-viable development and distribution of GIS. GIS, or Geographic Information System, is an acronym which encompasses a variety of technologies and theories but most often refers to the computer-based mapping software used to visualize both social and natural phenomena in relation to geographic space. Dangermond is on stage to describe the architecture of an idea built upon GIS that he calls GeoDesign. In the year 2010, he explains, human society is culpable for numerous "crimes against nature" (behind him an aerial image of an industrial city is projected), and in his formulation, human deviance from nature can only be rectified through a recognition of nature as an embodied, autonomous subject.[2] In other words, Dangermond sees nature as a realm that is phenomenologically distinct from the realm of human activity. Expanding upon this idea, he argues that an increase in our empirical knowledge of both realms and the subsequent application of this knowledge through the use of GIS will lead to a kind of synthesis wherein old dualisms are transcended. He explains, "You and I are moving into a world where we're starting to measure everything. And integrate it . . . everything that moves and changes . . . and integrate it with geography and the notion of GIS and make that available to everybody."[3] Like GIS the concept of GeoDesign is both theory and product; it combines an empirical perspective of the environment with the technological means to enact that theory.

GIS softwares have gained in widespread use since the 1990s, but Dangermond began his project long before this. In the same year that he graduated from the Landscape

---

1 I would like to thank Arindam Dutta for the opportunity to contribute to this volume. Without his support of the research and belief in its potential even when it was only a stack of dry and dusty looking early computer documents—I would have been lost. His encouragement and curiosity allowed me see the intricate narratives concealed behind the seemingly inscrutable symbols printed onto the pages and pages of maps in this archive of materials. I would also like to thank Mark Jarzombek for his kind and insightful help in reading, discussing, and giving comments on this research material. Finally, I would like to thank Nora Murphy from MIT's Institute Archives and Special Collections for all her generous help with the resources for this project.

1 The Technology, Entertainment, Design conference was started in 1984 by Richard Saul Wurman and Harry Marks. It brings together speakers from many realms annually and today has been spun-off into many parallel conferences targeting specialized audiences. The conference evolved out of

Architecture department in Harvard's Graduate School of Design (1969), he founded ESRI with his wife Laura. At this time computer mapping was an outlier from the mainstream—however, due to the proliferation of research in computer science at both Harvard and MIT, Cambridge was one of the few centers alive with activity in digital cartography and graphics.

In many respects Dangermond is the quintessential entrepreneurial actor to emerge from this milieu; nevertheless it is important to pause at this moment in the late 1960s and early 1970s in order to understand the fundamental tectonic shifts that were occurring within the design professions and the impact these changes had on the way we conceive design today. In order to accomplish this, the focus of this essay will not be on Dangermond but rather on his professor and colleague—the landscape planner, Carl Steinitz. Steinitz, perhaps more than anyone else in the fields of architecture and planning, represents the intellectual and academic trajectory that developed out of the very early research in digital cartography. Both men worked together in the late 1960s in Harvard's Lab for Computer Graphics and Spatial Analysis, a locus which drew together many important actors in the field of info-graphic research. Steinitz's involvement in the Lab began with research he did during his candidacy for a PhD in MIT's department of City and Regional Planning (completed in 1967). Data gathering and its management was a growing trend in the planning department, and Steinitz was one of many researchers in the school who drew upon knowledge from the social as well as empirical sciences to develop the practice of urban design. He was an early adopter of the computer as a tool for urban analysis as opposed to limiting its use for data management and data-base creation, the strategy being undertaken by researchers in MIT's Joint Center for Urban Studies. In this context, Steinitz's contribution was his recognition of the computer map's potential as a non-verbal, graphical communication tool for the visualization of data. This work was moreover conducted at a pivotal moment in the history of computing; at this time different research camps were arguing fiercely about the nature of the interface that would represent the ideal communication between the human and the machine. Was the computer best used solely for crunching large numbers at high speeds, or could it be envisioned as another sort of tool—one that would produce outcomes that were not pre-determined? In other words, could the computer augment one's analytical thought processes?

the Silicon Valley culture of start-ups, entrepreneurship , and collaboration. In this vein, TED has became a highly profitable juggernaut in its own right, combining techno-optimism with networking opportunity.

2 Carla Wheeler, "At TED2010, Esri President Jack Dangermond Spreads a New Idea: GeoDesign," Esri (Feburary, 16, 2010). Available online at http://www.esri.com/news/releases/10_1qtr/jack-ted.html, accessed January, 11, 2011.

3 Ibid. Within the field of geography there has long been debate between practitioners of GIS and those that practice critical, or human geography. For the outlines of this conflict, see Nadine Schuurman, "Trouble in the Heartland: GIS and its Critics in the 1990s" Progress in Human Geography 24, no.

4 (2000): 569–590. and Agnieszka Leszczynski, "Poststructuralism and GIS: is there a 'disconnect'?" Environment and Planning D: Society and Space 27 (date?2009): 581- 602.

As is common in the development of new technologies, debates of this nature were not uni-directional. As more and more research and innovation occurred, the perception of use-value for empirical data shifted in light of new graphical interfaces that allowed individuals to work with this information in novel ways. This was particularly the case for those disciplines that merged the plastic arts with the applied sciences. In this sense, it is important not only to interrogate the epistemological trajectory of Steinitz's work, but also to consider the material dimensions of the technological apparatus: as its structures and pathways became ends in themselves, mechanisms turned metaphors and back again, guiding a set of practices gaining in popularity today.

Returning briefly to the newly minted concept of GeoDesign and Dangermond's description of this new technological paradigm, it may be possible to shed some light on the convergence of empirical method with the purposive and projective strategies employed in the process of design. In a brochure recently published by ESRI advertising GeoDesign to a new generation of designers, Dangermond writes that his world-view has been largely shaped by the writings of the deceased landscape architect, Ian McHarg. McHarg is widely known for his best-selling text, *Design with Nature* (1969), which proposes strategies for landscape analysis at a regional scale and promotes a synergistic ecological view in which human and natural forces can be made to work in tandem, rather than in a conflicting or exploitative fashion. Dangermond explains that in his view McHarg had, "reject[ed] the view of a future modeled after some idyllic environmental past," and was instead "an early adopter of the view that we should be using our dominance of earth systems to help evolve the natural world and make it better, rather than conquer it."[4] He goes on to explain that in his mind, "powerful anthropogenic influence over earth systems represents not just a huge challenge but an equally huge opportunity—not humans versus nature, but humans with nature."[5] When practicing GeoDesign, the notion of design takes on a specific meaning: no longer a discrete product, it becomes a set of tactics—drawing, decision making, management—integrated into a singular technological system. This approach merges the biological and behavioral sciences in the hopes of arriving at a landscape that functions as a seamlessly incorporated totality. The system is both literal, in the sense of the architecture of the software, as well as metaphorical, in the sense of the ordering

4 Jack Dangermond, "Designing our Future," in his *Changing Geography by Design: Selected Readings in GeoDesign* (Redlands, CA: ESRI, October, 2010), 10.
5 Ibid., 10.

Base Map of the Study Areas. From Carl F. Steinitz, "Congruence and Meaning: the Influence of Consistency between Urban Form and Activity upon Environmental Knowledge," PhD Thesis, MIT Dept. of City and Regional Planning, (1967).

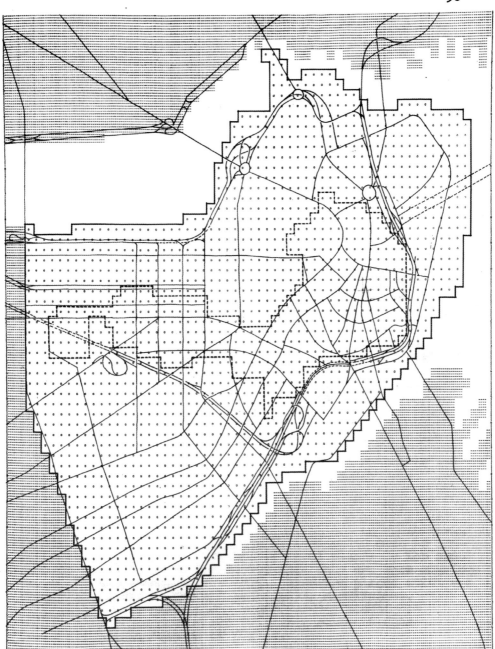

FIG. 4.4   THE BASE MAP ADAPTED FOR SYMAP

BASE MAP OF THE STUDY AREAS

————— TOTAL STUDY AREA

--------- DOWNTOWN CORE

CARL STEINITZ   DEPARTMENT OF CITY AND REGIONAL PLANNING
                       MASSACHUSETTS INSTITUTE OF TECHNOLOGY

principles guiding this approach. The designer, he explains, should take "environmental, social, and other considerations into account up front in the design process," but also look at "challenges from an adaptive systems approach, where ongoing analysis feeds back into the continual management of the system."[7] In this respect the system is given precedence over the initial design strategy—or at the very least becomes equally important— because it produces new information in the form of internal feedbacks. As it hums along processing inputs, the system provides the user with potentially unforeseen results and unexpected solutions. Dangermond's is a dualistic world made up of forces that either originate in human activity or in the natural realm, and thus he explains that "the key to developing a true understanding of our complex and dynamic earth is creating a framework to take many different pieces of past and future data from a variety of sources and merge them in a single system."[8] The collapse of the past and future through the interpolation of existing data is the basis of predictive technologies that in the twentieth and twenty-first centuries have ranged from fire-control (predicting the path of a missile would need to take in order to hit a moving target), to climate change models, to instruments designed to guess at financial futures and hedge bets in the marketplace.[9] Prediction using a systems approach provides the user with the relative assurance that they have tried their empirical best to achieve a desired outcome in an environment of risk and in a dynamically shifting social and political landscape.

The desire to understand and predict human behavioral patterns is an outgrowth of forces that were being acutely felt in the 1960s. By the mid-sixties the clear Eastern/Western bloc dualism that characterized the early stages of the Cold War had begun to erode into more inscrutable patterns of international relations. Early geographic information systems and computer simulations were mobilized at this time in an attempt to address these insecurities. South East Asia in particular was a theatre of conflict which challenged traditional categories of enmity. In Vietnam, programs such as the Hamlet Evaluation System were used to produce up-to-moment cartographic cross-sections of the conflict.[10] Qualitative digital maps and ethnographic survey techniques were used an attempt to transcend the simplistic binary of enmity—geared for use in President Johnson's "pacification programs" they were a critical aspect of studies meant to assess the state of the hearts and minds of those on the

7 Ibid., 10.

8 Ibid., 12.

9 Here I refer to Norbert Wiener's work on anti-aircraft systems in the 1940s, partially published as a paper titled "Extrapolation, Interpolation and Smoothing of Stationary Time Series. Cambridge, MA: MIT Press, 1964. This work led to his research

in communications theory, computer control, and the development of cybernetics.

10 Jennifer S. Light, *From Warfare to Welfare: Defense Intellectuals and Urban Problems in Cold War America* (Baltimore: John Hopkins University Press, 2003), 42-44. The Simulatics corporation, based in

Cambridge, was a primary actor in these early GIS efforts, and MIT Professor Ithiel de Sola Pool played a lead role in the Hamlet Evaluation System studies.

Compiled Map of Significance. Steinitz, "Congruence and Meaning," (1967).

118

FIG. 5.13   SIGNIFICANCE CONGRUENCE

SIGNIFICANCE CONGRUENCE:
THE VISIBILITY OF THE FORM OF A PLACE IN
RELATION TO THE IMPORTANCE OF ITS ACTIVITY

CARL STEINITZ   DEPARTMENT OF CITY AND REGIONAL PLANNING
                       MASSACHUSETTS INSTITUTE OF TECHNOLOGY

Photo Atlas. Steinitz,
Congruence and Meaning,
(1967).

ground. First hand interviews were used to construct databases which addressed a wide range of social themes; these were then were analyzed in comparison to the geographic terrain in an attempt to draw tangible boundaries in the conflict.[11]

In parallel to its international commitments, the United States was experiencing domestic instabilities in the wake of violent race-riots engendering a reappraisal of urban life in American cities. In 1966 a Senate committee was convened to evaluate the "crisis of the city" in America and to answer the question, "What should be done with the American city, so people can live in it and live with it and people can use it, and the city can reach what it should be in a concept of society . . . "?[12] The notion of "crisis" carries within it an element of decision or the idea that action in that moment will permanently alter the future course of events. With cities embroiled in violent and non-violent forms of protest the outlook for lawmakers was bleak but the moment decisive. Senator Robert F. Kennedy expressed this sentiment in his question to Senate witness, author Ralph Ellison, when he asked, "Would you agree that we are at the moment on sort of a razor's edge in the direction that we are going to ultimately be headed, as to whether we are going to fall off into this chasm of lack of hope versus the other side which gives us some opportunity for the future?"[13] In either context, there was a perception of the ameliorative effects possible with proper information management and increased knowledge of populations through the aggregation of data. The spatial and social implications of these ideas would propel work in computer mapping and simulation forward in the realms of architecture and planning.[14]

Change in Plan

In the body of Steinitz's work we see no impassioned manifesto, or seminal publication like Kevin Lynch's *Image of the City*, but rather a series of products that fall into the category of reports, studies, and workshops—carrying the implication of action rather than reflection. This choice could be merely reflective of personality, or circumstance and opportunity, but the orientation towards direct participation and action, objectivity and logic, were distinct characteristics of MIT's School of Architecture and Planning at the time Steinitz was studying there. In 1967, the same year Steinitz submitted his doctoral dissertation, Dean Lawrence B. Anderson summarized the prevailing desire to define a new approach to architecture and planning. In his report to the Institute president, he writes:

11 The use of qualitative maps were not always successful; oftentimes they did not provide the information needed. Also, Johnston's pacification programs are contentious subjects of history, many questioned the ethics guiding them and the techniques employed to "neutralize"

the enemy, nonetheless they marked a shift in style in terms of United States warfare strategies. For a further discussion of pacification see Frank L. Jones, "Blowtorch: Robert Komer and the Making of Vietnam Pacification Policy," *Parameters* 35, no. 3 (2005): 103-116.

12 George Tames, "Life in Harlem: View from the Back Street," *New York Times* (September, 4, 1966). My attention was drawn to this article when reading Steinitz's dissertation wherein he cites portions of Ralph Ellison's testimony on the state of the American city.
13 Ibid.

14 Jennifer Light's text (see note 10) expands upon this narrative, chronicling the way technologies developed for the military found their way into the hands of those who attempted to apply them to the problems facing the American city.

Clearly architecture and planning are constantly approaching a difficult reorientation, reacting to massive shifts in the cultural and technological substructure. Until recently our professions thought of themselves as mediators between two sets of forces. On the one hand there arose through social interaction and growth a series of discrete problems (a regional high school here, a master plan for a community there). On the other hand one could identify the public and private effectuation agencies, including the building industry, waiting for instructions. The job of the professionals was to make the connecting bridges, and in the confidence of expertise, to facilitate the flow from needs to the appropriate realizations. While this may still be in large part how the world works, there are sharp warning signals to indicate that the old idealization is too pat to survive new dynamics. The problems posed by society are losing their clarity and designers are having to intervene more and more to discover or impose definitions of need.[15]

The phrase "massive shifts in the cultural and technological substructure" alludes to the movement into the information age and toward a post-industrial society in which technology was not only considered the source of change—it was also perceived of as the solution. Developing tangible expertise in this arena would be paramount, both in terms of diagnosing problems and prescribing cures. In this regard, the process of design, the role of the designer, and the use of technology was becoming a subject of investigation in its own right—method, strategy, and representation were being rethought in light of shifting dynamics. Anderson continues:

Thus the task of the designer is rendered far more difficult in regard to both ends and means. The entire train of events must be regarded as a complete system, and the role of the designer as catalyst in the system is being drastically revised. Designers need a perspective other than that dictated by day-to-day expediency, yet if such detachment implies a lack of involvement at some stage of the events, this may mean the end of effectiveness. Under the growing dominance of the total environment, the architect and planner is dispensable unless he himself can become more fully involved.[16]

From a pedagogical point-of-view, this represents a tricky proposition, creating a tension between the development of theoretical knowledge and contextually specific, pragmatic, or heuristic forms of learning. The issue of being "dispensable" or not hinges on one's ability to leverage professional expertise and to act as a gate-keeper to certain methodologies and repositories of knowledge and information. In this sense, "ends and means" were being re-calibrated in relation to questions of authority and expertise, and implicit within that type of change for professional disciplines was the need to identify an appropriate client-base who could be convinced that they were in need of new forms of specialized knowledge. The delineation of audience (policy makers, law makers, politicians, developers, etc...) is thus a critical component of understanding the shift toward a new kind of technocratic professionalism.

Steinitz's research was squarely planted in the context of professional innovation, and his dissertation, laboriously titled, "Congruence and Meaning: The Influence of Consistency between Urban Form and Activity upon Environmental Knowledge," stresses the dimension of meaning as a critical and perhaps overlooked topic for systematic research in the city. The project was an exercise in measuring the city, and it was presented in a way similar to a scientific study, making a number of hypotheses at the beginning, laying forth a series of evidence, and concluding with reflections upon the original hypotheses. There was no design proposal per se, but rather an analysis of Boston's urban condition and a number of recommendations made at the end. In fact, even the emphasis on Boston was secondary; the dissertation was a general proposal on how to measure and represent any urban condition. Here Anderson's call for greater involvement can be seen as having been interpreted in terms of physically going out and surveying the city, interviewing its occupants, and systematically documenting the process in order to produce an objective study. The study could then be mobilized toward varying ends—allowing for this expertise to be applied across a spectrum of possibility.

The implication of the dissertation research was that expertise in this case constituted a knowledge of the mechanisms through which social change could be enacted. Congruence as it is used by Steinitz is a metric for determining the degree of meaning present in any given place. In other words, a place has high congruence when the urban form in question closely corresponds to the viewer's expectation of the type of activity connected to it. Steinitz broached the problem of congruence from three angles—relative activity intensity, activity type, and place significance; each of these categories could be quantitatively measured and qualitatively assessed through a gradient—more or less, good to bad, dirty to clean, etc.[17] In the research "meaning" has two critical functions; one, meaning affects the way a subject navigates the city because it plays a role in cognitive processes such as memory and learning; two, that meaning has an impact on transparency—in other words, when meaning is achieved the subject would theoretically possess greater confidence about place, thus increasing opportunities for participation. The implication of Steinitz's work was that the design of the built environment should aid in legibility and lead to a terrain easily traversed by any and all inhabitants of the city. Democracy in the social and

15 Lawrence B. Anderson, "School of Architecture and Planning." *President's Report 1967* (Cambridge, MA: MIT, 1967): 31-32.

16 "School of Architecture and Planning," Ibid., 32.

17 Carl Steinitz, "Congruence and Meaning: The Influence of Consistency between Urban Form and Activity upon Environmental Knowledge" (Master's thesis, Massachusetts Institute of Technology, 1967).

physical fabric as it is expressed in this formulation is a condition of certain continuities rather than a condition of the co-existence of differences.

By studying the correlation between social conditions and the form of the city, Steinitz hoped to find methods the designer or planner could use to improve both. His advisor for the project was the planner Kevin Lynch, and like Lynch, his focus was on the way the city was viewed (both literally and figuratively) by its constituent population. Both men were trying to find the link between the physical form of the city and the people in it. The tactics employed by Steinitz were similar to those used by Lynch in his own work—citizen interviews, graphs consolidating this data, hand-notated maps, systematic photo atlases visually documenting the urban fabric, and invitations to the interviewees to draw maps in relation to their own understanding of the city. A visual survey of the city, conducted empirically, would then be drawn in comparison to the subjective responses gathered from citizen interviews in order to produce a multi-dimensional picture of the urban fabric.[18] The study investigated approximately four square miles in central Boston—adjacency to the study area was critical for the use of empirical method on the part of the designer/ researcher, though contextual or historic specificity was ignored in favor of a focus on method. There were differences in the two men's work as well, but at the outset the primary difference lay in Steinitz's choice to use the computer in his research.

For Steinitz an understanding of environment emerged at the intersection of two kinds of data, one taken from the physical and material world, and the other taken from the subjective point-of-view. The comparison between the two would theoretically yield a set of common, and therefore objective, values in regards to the experience of the urban environment. This notion was shared by both Lynch and Steinitz, but Lynch eschewed the use of data from sources external to the study, whereas Steinitz did not. Lynch elaborates on his method in the research appendix to the *Image of the City*, where he writes, "To compare with these subjective pictures of the city, such data as air photos, maps, and diagrams of density, use or building shape, might seem the proper "objective" description of the physical form of the city. Consideration of their objectivity aside, such things are quite inadequate for the purpose, being both too superficial and yet not generalized

18 It is important to note that the notion of subjectivity as a characteristic of an individual was reframed when the interview responses were pooled together to find a statistical mean.

19 Kevin Lynch, *Image of the City* (Cambridge, MA: MIT Press, 1960), 143.
20 Ibid., 143.

21 Steinitz, "Congruence and Meaning," 362-375.
22 Ibid., 219.

23 Lynch, *Image of the City*, 143.
24 Steinitz, "Congruence and Meaning," 19.

enough."[19] He goes on to explain, "The best comparison to the interviews was the record of another subjective response," because, "while it was clear that the interviewees were responding to a common physical reality, the best way to define that reality was not through any quantitate, "factual" method but through the perception and evaluation of a few field observers, trained to look carefully."[20] In other words, the link between the perception of the city and its form (what Lynch refers to as the "image") can only be understood by comparing like experiences so that the data sets share a formal symmetry with one another. Steinitz on the other hand, integrated data from aerial photos, Sanborn maps, land-use records, census information, transportation studies, and metropolitan planning documents into his description of the environment.[21] This data was still only seen as supplement to Lynch's' method of making a firsthand survey of the city; even though Steinitz spent a summer producing a photo atlas that systematically documented the visual form of the study area, he still needed additional inputs to determine activity designations. He explains the difference this way, "Note the general similarity between this strategy and the process of design proposed by Lynch (1960, 115-117). Yet the key difference is the focus on activity meanings. However "strong" a form image and however well it conforms to the visual goals that underlie its form, if it does not convey activity meanings that can be verified by experience it will not be meaningful."[22] The emphasis on "activity" is not a random distinction, activity and action were key concepts at this time in the fields of sociology and behavioral psychology. I will return to a broader discussion of these sciences at a later point in the essay; here it is merely necessary to note that while Lynch was concerned with the visual form and the cognitive process involved in the formation of a mental image, Steinitz introduced a semantic dimension as a shadow to form—derived from geo-spatially distributed social data. These new kinds of maps codified emotive or subjective responses to the hardscape of the city, while drawing certain conclusions based on demographic and social data sets.

Lynch implied that one disadvantage in using external data was that the "variety of factors which might be evaluated is infinite"; however, for Steinitz—limited only by the data-handling capacity of the current model of computer—infinity did not pose the same problem.[23] His was an attitude towards data entities that veered more towards the recombinant rather than the essential. Steinitz writes in the beginning of his dissertation, "A statement of congruence is a relative and not an absolute relationship, and its specific validity is limited in context and time."[24] At times the logic of the research feels unnervingly circular—one surveys the city's population, compares it to the present form of the city, and determines the current state of meaning in the urban environment; this knowledge can in turn be used to increase the meaningfulness of areas of the city that are not meeting expectations— then the process repeats, creating feed-backs that represent an ongoing strategy for the design and management of the city based on moving toward consensus rather than accommodating difference. This creates a system that envisions the social whole as embodied in the physical fabric of the urban environment, a whole that can be both accounted for in its totality as well as infinitely directed towards the ends determined by whoever holds the reigns to the technological apparatus.

The need to provide a meaningful environment was partially formed in response to the belief that the American city was in "crisis" and that urban expansion in other areas of the world was a growing threat to global stability. Steinitz explains his rationale for the research design this way: "the choices of different segments of society cannot be equal if their knowledge is radically different, whether caused by the restrictive activity patterns of ghetto life, or by the inability to pay in order to participate."[25] He continues:

> A concomitant phenomenon to the well documented increase in urbanization has been a growth in the heterogeneity and mobility of urban society. People with more diverse background experiences must be absorbed into urban environments which must then have the capacity to satisfy their requirements—to assimilate without destroying. Furthermore, increasing residential mobility implies that a person will have to adjust to several urban environments within his lifetime.[26]

Two synchronous ideas emerge from these hypotheses, one being that visual legibility was a necessary quality for the encouragement of cultural pluralism, and the other being that the environment should be designed in such a way as to be clearly understood in a universal fashion. The "selective knowledge which is meaning" could be mobilized as a way to increase transparency and access on the one hand, but, on the other, it could also be put to work as a way to increase influence over the behavioral patterns of an entire urban population.[27] Steinitz is clearly thinking about the possible conflict between these two ideas when he notes "that the environment should make possible a diversity of personal meanings is unquestionably desirable. However, this diversity must be encompassed within a framework which clearly conveys those public meanings that are necessary for common social behavior." Nevertheless he relinquishes a conclusion on this matter in favor of emphasizing method and an open-ended neutrality.[28] That said, the question over just how integral to the design of the system or method itself these issues of control versus transparency are remains an unanswered one. Either way, both men—Steinitz and Lynch— were interested in the ways in which physical form could be manipulated in order to direct human behavior. Furthermore, with this research we see Steinitz moving away from a focus on the autonomy of the individual subject and toward a focus on social cohesion and the establishment of normative and predictable behavioral patterns amongst populations.

Within Steinitz's dissertation there resides a vision of society as a whole, a system characterized by inputs and outputs that could be ordered through statistical means. This in turn produces a notion of social equilibrium based on regulating behavior to meet "commonly" held expectations. In this configuration the designer acts as a kind of homeostat in the technocratic system; able to adapt to the environment, he or she is

Graphic Responses. Steinitz,
"Congruence and Meaning,"
(1967).

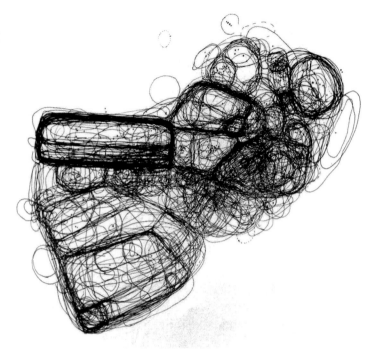

in charge of taking the social temperature and adjusting the mechanisms as necessary
to achieve a previously programmed and normative goal. There is a presumed neutrality
attributed to the technological system, and yet the claim to expertise made by the
designers in and of the system implies that these methods can also be applied to more
specific ends and outcomes amenable to a particular client's needs.

Action / Behavior

The move away from a focus on the individual can also be tracked in the fields of the social
or behavioral sciences where there were those who were trying to relate space, people's
behavior, and form to one another in order to create an understanding of the environmental
construct. Steinitz was both aware of and invested in this idea of a social laboratory that could
bring all these elements into play. As he explained, his work was "based upon the view that
the reaction of people to their environment—and the environment itself—can be subjects

25 Ibid., 6.
26 Ibid., 6.
27 Ibid., 33.
28 Ibid., 4.

of objective investigation and scientific research. Indeed, this view is necessary if planning and design are to be founded on testable theory rather than intuition and preconception."[29] The influence of positivism and the desire to generate data or empirical observations related to social phenomena is indicative of the pressure Steinitz may have felt in the planning department to find a greater conceptual basis for his research; on the other hand, he was not systematically imbued in the same discursive spaces as those in the scientific disciplines, so he could take a broader stance in his definition of "research." As was noted earlier, Steinitz differentiated himself from Lynch with his added emphasis on the connection between "activity meaning" and experience in relation to physical form. The theoretical underpinnings for this move came in part from a text titled *Toward a General Theory of Action*, which he cited in the dissertation.[30] Published in 1951, the text was a compilation of work by nine authors—Talcott Parsons, Edward A. Shils, Edward Tolman, Gordon W. Allport, Clyde Kluckhon, Henry A. Murray, Robert R. Sears, Richard C. Sheldon, and Samuel A. Stouffer; it represented a concerted effort on their part to produce a theoretical tract that would reflect the aims of the new department for the study of social relations at Harvard, broken off from the established department of sociology and formed under the direction of Parsons.[31] Each of these authors brought different facets of a possible theory to the table under the rubric of action; for example the behavioral scientist Edward Tolman is known for coining the term "cognitive maps" to describe thinking processes regarding the external environment in animals as well as humans. Parsons' contribution focused more on the larger social systems governing populations, and he often is seen as representative of the turn towards statistical and comparative methods in the social sciences.

Embodying an internal shift in the behavioral sciences, the aforementioned authors were attempting to outline a concept of "action" in contrast to the more orthodox concept of "behavior." Epitomized by B.F. Skinner's techniques for "operant" conditioning, the "behavior" model seeks merely to train the subject to exhibit the desired behavior through a system of external prompts which include both reward and punishment. Framed this way, the subject is machine-like, predictable, and most importantly, its behavior is reproducible; furthermore, a consideration of emotional states, cause, or agency, is not necessary to developing an understanding of how the subject functions. In contrast to this,

29 Ibid., 41.

30 While Lynch may not have made clear his behavioralist roots, Steinitz cites a wide range of behavoiral psychologists in the bibliography to his dissertation. (For the discussion of Lynch in this context, see Hashim Sarkis's piece, "Disoriented: Kevin Lynch between Behavioral Psychology, Boston, and Planning," in this volume).

31 The department of Social Relations had separated itself from the department of Sociology at the time; it was an attempt to craft an interdisciplinary program uniting psychology, anthropology, and sociology.

They were also open to involving other disciplines yet this only occurred with limited success and did not in the end systematically expand to incorporate other disciplines.

32 Neil J. Smelster, "Introduction to the Transaction Edition," *Toward a General Theory of Action* (New Brunswick, NJ: Transaction

Publishers, 2001), vii-xix.

33 Carl Steinitz, "Meaning and the Congruence of Urban Form and Activity," *Journal of the American Planning Association* 34, no. 4 (1968): 233-248.

34 Steinitz, "Congruence and Meaning," 206-207.

35 Ibid., 206-207.

the action model takes into account internal forces such as motivation, learning, imitation, identification, role, social structure, and values.[32] Thus "action" or "activities" allow for the consideration of agency or intention in relation to the subject under observation, and the concepts of ends, purpose, or ideals inform the design of persuasive means for the modification of behavior. Action was divided into three categories—the personality system, the social system, and the cultural system—referring respectively to interactions between the subject and the environment, the interactions between two or more subjects, and the patterns of relations that guide whole populations. Thus, action theory brings a psychological dimension into the direction of human behavior, but in order to do so it relies heavily on the structural formalism of the "system." Therefore, action theory broadens the scope of what can be considered constitutive of environment by providing a scalar framework on which to move between the actions of the individual subject and those of the entire population. Beyond this, populations or societies could be compared to one another on the global scale, and predictions about mass movements, mass communications, international relations, and financial markets could be made on the basis of empirical measurements dropped into socio-theoretical models of action.

When Steinitz describes the "physical environment as a field of communications about activity systems," he mirrors this idea that societal behavior could be analyzed across a scale of relations and actions. "Communications" in turn can be measured and manipulated as a medium to produce new kinds of messages.[33] Yet the contextual specificity of a place is superseded again by an emphasis on method and universality, as is evidenced when Steinitz asks himself "whether or not a normative (and anonymous) population can be the client of city design."[34] We hear in this an inkling of the GeoDesign to come, in which the global and universal is foregrounded over the local and specific. Normativity in behaviorism reflects the desire to move social activity in the direction of homogenous, or generalized sets of rules. Therefore, in a normative schema individual bodies lodged in urban space that are expected to perform in predictable ways, and behavior and reactions to physical form can be maximized through design. Steinitz concludes that the normative population can be considered the appropriate "client" in the design schema he proposes, writing that "the findings of this study indicate that there is some justification (as well as efficiency) for the city designer to be guided by the needs of a normative client."[35] In this instance one is left to question how the normative is being defined, or how the social mean is arrived at, but beyond this we can see a shift in the study in which the designer abdicates responsibility for the outcome (ends are left open to be determined by another party—economists, politicians, developers, etc.) by framing the process of design in terms of technological or procedural neutrality.[36]

Parsons in particular came under fire from other social and cultural theorists for the ways in which his theories could be easily directed toward applied purposes. In 1979 the French philosopher Jean-François Lyotard wrote about Parsons in his text, *The Post-Modern Condition: A Report on Knowledge*, wherein he points to the problematic nature

Making Maps. Harvard
Graduate School
of Design Alumni
Association Newsletter,
1967. Harvard University
Archives, HUD
3324.7255.

of positivistic theory modeled on the "hard" sciences. He writes that "'traditional' theory is always in danger of being incorporated into the programming of the social whole as a simple tool of the optimization of performance; this is because its desire for a unitary and totalizing truth lends itself to the unitary and totalizing practice of the system's managers."[37] In opposition to this tendency he identifies"critical' theory" that, "based on a principle of dualism and wary of syntheses and reconciliations, should be in a position to avoid this fate."[38] Lyotard felt that a social theory based on positivistic principles was "directly applicable to technologies bearing on men and materials," lending itself as an "indispensable productive force within the system."[39] Whereas critical theory resists subjugation to outside actor through the very semantics of its arguments, "traditional" theory absents itself from the uses it will be put to as it is being laid down. Human/machine metaphors condition the behavioral approach, and while a theory of action offers itself as an alternative to that of behavior, it falls well within the realm of the applied theory critiqued by Lyotard. In order maintain a consistent logic and smooth interoperability a systems approach is predicated on the normative mean geared towards correcting for aberration rather than allowing it room to function within the system. Therefore neutrality and applicability are not two sides of the same coin; rather they are incommensurate aims of the technological system.

General Theory/Computing

What remains is the question of how a leap is made from the realm of theory to the realm of actionable strategies that bear upon the "men and materials" alluded to in the former arguments. In this case, the gap is bridged by the architecture of the technological apparatus itself, which in turn is informed by theories such as cybernetics that allow one to merge the theoretical and material dimensions of a problem or subject into a singular mechanism. The behavioral sciences offered solutions to both pragmatic, as well as scientific concerns, and the inclusion of the phrase "general theory" in the title of Parson's text is indicative of a more general desire to achieve a unity of the sciences—or a universal science—in one theoretical model. Toward this end, many researchers, in disciplines ranging from biology to economics, were trying to find ways to translate between each discipline's modalities of description in order to develop a common working language.[40] Work towards the unification of the social and physical sciences led many researchers to frameworks based on General Systems Theory, derived by figures such as Kenneth Boulding and Walter F. Buckley, and to organizational schemes influenced by Norbert Wiener's theory of cybernetics. This line of research addressed the space that lay between empiricism and theory, or the part versus the whole. The systems approach gave form to a desire to find an organizational dimensionality that would have the ability to bypass traditional hierarchies and categories by instead identifying objects in terms of the input-output, or cause and effect, relationships they are enmeshed within. In this sense, by moving between material and theory one could make an object commensurate with its relations (as described by theory) and therefore manipulate the entire system as an integrated medium. For the researcher using a systems approach, inputs external to the system, feedbacks internal to the system, and outputs generated by the system create loops of labyrinthine, yet reconstructable, and more importantly, manageable complexity. Theorist N. Katherine Hayles offers pointed insight into the ways in which scientists hoped to find a universal medium or method, and notes in particular that

36 In a more recent article Steinitz discusses the scalability of his ideas and he indicates which scale (the regional) he thinks his strategies work best. In this sense, he makes an argument for the scales at which he deems normativity necessary, and the scales (the individual) that better absorb departures from the norm. Carl Steinitz, "From Project to Global: on Landscape Planning and Scale," *Landscape Review* 9, no. 2 (2005): 117-127.

37 Jean-François Lyotard, *The Postmodern Condition: A Report on Knowledge*, trans. Geoff Bennington and Brian Massumi (Minneapolis, MN: The University of Minnesota Press, 1984), 12.
38 Ibid., 12.
39 Ibid., 14.

40 Smelster, "Introduction to the Transaction Edition," vii-xix.

cybernetics positioned itself both as a metascience and as a tool that any other science could use. It offered a transdisciplinary vocabulary that could be adapted for a variety of disciplinary purposes, presenting itself in this guise as content-free, and it simultaneously offered a content-rich practice in which cybernetic mechanisms were analyzed, modeled, and occasionally built. Operating on these two different levels, cybernetic discourse was able to penetrate into other disciplines while maintaining its turf as a disciplinary paradigm.[41]

In short, the cybernetic system was imagined as value-neutral, and yet of primary importance for the organization of thought, materials, and actions. In this sense, the system can be examined in relation that which it represents, and it can be examined in its own autonomy in terms of an organizational schema possessing a consistent inner logic. In the case of digital cartography and simulation the allusion to those mechanisms "occasionally built" could just as easily refer to a software for representing the built environment as it could refer to the built environment itself.

Within this process the work of translation was crucial to creating continuities between symbols, words, and signals in what Steinitz refers to as a "field of communications," or more simply put, between the representation and the subject it claimed to represent. Computational thinking and analysis required a multi-layered approach that would eventually transfer ideas, thoughts, and images of the human mind into the electronic signals the machine could process or 'think' with. In 1961 MIT formally recognized this need with the creation of a doctoral program in applied linguistics. In the president's report issued to the MIT community that year this change is remarked upon:

> It is significant that among the first students we have accepted for this graduate program are majors in mathematics and physics as well as in linguistics. Our concern with linguistics actually derives from the efforts of Professors Norbert Wiener and Claude Shannon in their pioneering work on the mathematical theory of communication. The study of the logical relationships within languages employs mathematical techniques comparable to those used in the general area of information theory.

> Moreover, recent developments in computer design, switching theory, and other similar areas are of first importance in the field of applied linguistics and in linguistic analysis.[42]

Hayles writes that for these figures (Wiener and Shannon), "communication is about relation, not essence," and in those terms an analysis of language can be conducted through mathematical means in an act of translation.[43] Metaphor was key to this process, and in the linguistics program applied research was being conducted in areas such as "computer design, switching theory" as well as "mechanical translation . . . machine perception and synthesis of human speech," using analogical relations between living and mechanical systems to achieve techno-material ends.[44] The metaphor of language itself was the connective tissue across many different realms, from Lynch's "environmental language" to his collaborator the artist György Kepes's notion of a "visual language," to the linguist Noam Chomsky's theorization of a "universal grammar." Use of a systems approach necessitated interoperability between sensory inputs, logical operations, and material realities.

The "man-machine communication" of computing requires that complex linguistic or visual statements made by humans be translated to binary numerals effectuating on/off signals in the machine.[45] Of course there is no singular way that this can be understood, and while cybernetics and the systems approach played a critical role in the development of the shift toward digital technologies, many modes of thought informed the widely distributed sphere of computing technology.[46] After John von Neumann introduced the concept of the general-purpose device, the distinction between hardware and software became more pronounced; rather than linearly programming the machine like a telephone switch board to perform one function, the computer could now be programmed to do multiple tasks and run more than one program.[47] Interactivity is key to making both hardware and software decisions, punch-cards, graphic tablets, the mouse, etc., as well as the multitude of organizational choices that determine how software applications will function and look, and all of these decisions facilitate different types of "communication" with the machine. As Hayles points out, it is important to be attentive to the specifics of how "theory and artifact, research and researcher," are related to one another producing feedbacks and conclusions that are made manifest in relation to the function of the tools employed—in this case the machine.[48] Data is essentially meaningless without the architecture of the system to channel it into different ends and the general theory, as well as the system, can exert considerable influence over both the production and the interpretation of data.

The Lab for Computer Graphics and Spatial Analysis

If the resonances from systems theory and cybernetics can be felt throughout Steinitz's approach, one certain route of entry is through his use of the computer to both manage data and to produce graphs and maps that aided in the analysis of his findings.[49] The translation from analog products (photographs, hand drawn maps, etc.) to digital ones was

41 Katherine N. Hayles, *How We Became Posthuman: Virtual Bodies in Cybernetics, Literature, and Informatics* (Chicago: The University of Chicago Press, 1999) 96.

42 *The President's Report 1961* (Cambridge, MA: Massachusetts Institute of Technology, [For the academic year ending] July 1, 1961),

19-21.

43 Hayles, *How We became Posthuman*, 91.

44 President's Report 1961, 21.

45 This phrase was frequently used by Ivan Sutherland in reference to the graphic software and hardware tools he developed, but is also

used more generally in the of interaction design. Ivan Edward Sutherland, *Sketchpad: A Man-Machine Graphical Communication System* (Master's thesis, Massachusetts Institute of Technology, 1963).

46 For an expanded history see, John V. Guttag, ed., *The Electron and the Bit: Electrical

Engineering and Computer Science at the Massachusetts Institute of Technology, 1902-2002* (Cambridge, MA : MIT, Electrical Engineering and Computer Science Dept., 2005).

47 In 1945 Von Neumann published a paper that laid out the basic principles of the general-purpose

labor intensive and also required a fairly technical knowledge of the process of translation. While a student at MIT, Steinitz went up the road to Harvard to seek out the expertise in computer mapping held by those in the Lab for Computer Graphics and Spatial Analysis (LCG). The Lab was in the basement of Memorial Hall where figures like the operant conditioning expert and behavioral psychologist B.F. Skinner, physiological psychologist and computer scientist, J.C.R. Licklider, and artificial intelligence theorist Marvin Minsky had resided a decade earlier.[50] On Harvard's campus that particular basement was a space for new research in fields that lent themselves to technological endeavors. Purportedly crowded and messy, the basement played host to heated debate as often as it did to moments of inter-disciplinary collaboration.[51] SYMAP (SYNagraphic MAPping), the software used to make the maps featured in Steinitz's dissertation, was developed by the architect Howard T. Fisher. Fisher was a kind of polymath, a technological innovator and entrepreneur, he had founded a company, General House Inc., that designed modular, pre-fabricated housing. Prior to his arrival at Harvard he had been teaching architecture at Northwestern University in Chicago.[52] With backing from the Ford Foundation Fisher came to Harvard in 1965 and opened the Lab under the umbrella of the design school. The Lab was not only a site of experimentation in computer cartography and digital graphics, but was also a central meeting place for individuals from a wide array of disciplines who had an interest in using the computer to make maps. Shortly after the Lab opened, Steinitz made Fisher's acquaintance and began to explore the use of Harvard's IBM 7094 computer and the Lab's SYMAP software.

During the time the Lab was in operation, from 1965 until 1979, it experienced multiple cycles of growth and deflation—sometimes occupied by as many as forty researchers, at others only by a handful of people.[53] Over time the Lab developed many different software products: mapping programs such as SYMAP were based on grid structures and were useful for more analytical types of research and data management, whereas other programs were visually more sophisticated (and even today look strangely contemporary) but tended more towards representation rather than analysis—traffic flows would appear onscreen looking like topological mountain ranges, or population densities would take on the three-dimensional stepped structure of an empty granite quarry. In lean years the Lab

device, causing a revolution in computer science which laid the theoretical ground work for the use of the computer as a tool in multiple scenarios, rather than a static object directed toward the generation of solutions to singular problems. The EDVAC was the first of such devices. John Von Neumann,

First Draft of the Report on the EDVAC (Published under contract no. W-670-ORD-4926 between the United States Army Ordnance Department and the University of Pennsylvania, June 30, 1945).
48 Hayles, *How We Became Posthuman*, 91.

49 Today, Stenitiz draws his audience's attention to his relationship with cybernetics when he includes a picture of Norbert Wiener in the slide shows that accompany his lectures.
50 M. Mitchell Waldrop, *The Dream Machine: J.C.R. Licklider and the Revolution That Made Computing*

Personal (New York: Viking, 2001), 67-69.
51 Ibid., 67-69.
52 Nicolas Chrisman, *Charting the Unknown: How Computer Mapping at Harvard Became GIS* (Redlands, CA: ESRI Press, 2006) and "Business: General Houses," Time Magazine (July 4, 1932).

made up its funding by selling its software to the public via mail-order, and it was these efforts that brought the potentials of computer mapping to a larger audience and allowed the Lab to gain widespread recognition for its efforts.

In 1970 the Lab's work was featured alongside other projects that depicted the urban terrain in a special issue of Design Quarterly curated by the designer, Richard Saul Wurman and titled, *Making the City Observable*. Wurman began his career as an architect in the traditional sense, but he made his mark at the intersection of info-graphic thinking and architecture. The progenitor of the phrase, "information architect," Wurman worked to produce city atlases, environmental graphics, and a large number of other projects which capitalized on the twentieth-century trend towards the statistical-visual spaces of info-graphics. In many cases the map was the preferred mode of visualization relating geographic space to social facts. In this book, Wurman captures the urgency driving the desire to engage with these representational strategies when he laments that "we talk in numbers we can't comprehend and about sizes we can't visualize."[54] However, he rejects the subjective, complaining that currently, "Artists' renderings, rather than measured performances and relationships, are used to explain proposed environmental changes."[55] He paints a picture of a society drowning in a sea of usable data and demands that a new kind of professional emerge to give all this information form.

Wurman gathers together many examples of graphic representations of urban space, from the archetypical, i.e. the Noli plan, to the more contemporary and experimental, such as complex traffic flow diagrams, still photos from the Eames's film *Urban Communications*, composite photo-maps made from images taken by meteorological satellites, various subway and bus route maps, Nicholas Negroponte's environmental-sensor based robots, GROPE and STARE, and early three-dimensional digital renderings of landscapes. Graphic products, diagrams, graphs, and most importantly maps, represent a new set of tools to dissect, highlight, and order relationships in the physical environment. The map is useful for conveying objectivity as it implies a territory beyond one's own subjective point-of-view and as an object represents a terrain of fact derived through survey and measure that is indexed to the physical world. Data, when presented in this form, takes on the status of

53 Beyond the Ford Foundation the list of external sponsors grew to include, the National Science Foundation, the U.S. Bureau of the Census, the U.S. Geological Survey, NASA, the U.S. Defense Intelligence Agency, the U.S. Defense Mapping Agency, the U.S. Department of Agriculture, the Federal Aviation Administration, and the Executive Office of the President.

54 Richard Saul Wurman, *Making the City Observable* (Cambridge, MA: MIT Press, 1971), 6.

55 Ibid., 6.

a naturalized authority. Wurman's choice of a title, *Making the City Observable*, suggests the creation of objective frameworks that might increase a collective understanding of the urban environment. In a way similar to Steinitz, Wurman places the onus for legibility and pedagogy onto the spaces comprising physical realm, yet he calls for actual nodal spaces that he calls "urban data centers." He speculates that these centers could hold and display information regarding the urban environment and experience by weaving these narratives together with the more functional elements of the city fabric.[56] Today, this is a task that we most often relegate to a different sort of space—not city centers, but rather to the internet, conceived of as an open and democratic network of linked digital spaces infused with easily accessible data and information about place. At the time of Wurman's publication maps and graphics were beginning to thicken, moving beyond the mark made on the page, they began to carry the characteristics of an infrastructure all their own.

56 Ibid., 4.

57 John T. Howard, "Department of City and Regional Planning," *President's Report 1967* (Cambridge, MA: MIT, 1967): 40-47.

Richard Saul Wurman, Images from Lab for Spatial Graphics, Graduate School of Design, Harvard University. Facing page, *left*, Industry and Commerce, *right*, Average Daily Two-Way Traffic Flow. From *Making the City Observable*, Walker Art Center, Minneapolis, (Cambridge, MA: MIT Press, 1971).

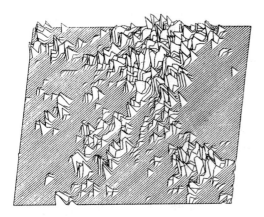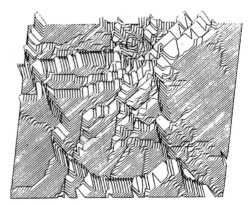

The City as Laboratory

In 1967, the planning department at MIT was replete with data-minded professionals, such as John T. Howard, Lloyd Rodwin, Donald Appleyard, and Aaron Fleisher, all who had a noted influence on Steinitz, though in this essay the focus has been primarily on Lynch's influence. Following Dean Anderson's call for the re-examination of "role of the designer as catalyst in the system," planning chair John T. Howard, in the 1967 Report to the President, wrote that:

> city design concerns the shaping of the visual form of the city, not solely as an aesthetic exercise, but with equal regard for its social, economic, political, and psychological structure and function. Evolving from the pioneer work of Professor Kevin A. Lynch, it is a field still grappling with the problems of understanding phenomena of man-environment interaction and is not yet ready to prescribe solutions.[57]

At this time the focus on was research, rather than immediate action—thus the designer was being recast in the role of defining the system, not the solution. The role of academia in relation to professional practice was also being re-calibrated; no longer solely a training ground for future professionals the practice of design research was allowing those in the institute to carve out a specialized niche for themselves within the academy. Howard continues, "The aggregate of the Department's work in this field is evolving into an entity deserving the name of a city design laboratory, inventing and applying techniques of simulation necessary for experiment and evaluation."[58] While there was a focus on empirically engaging the actual city, those metrics were often brought back into the studio to craft representations that, acting autonomously as simulations, would model change in the city. Design in this instance thus refers to the building of models; the hope was that they would produce unexpected results, or at least results that, confirming the designer's intuition, would grant them a greater sense of objectivity regarding their decision making processes.

Around this time an article was published in the Journal of the American Planning Association titled "An Environmental Gaming-Simulation Laboratory." The authors, Peter House and Phillip D. Patterson, were collaborators at House's land-use consulting firm Environmetrics. The article covered a variety of projects that combined game theory with simulation models. Expanding upon this theme they write that:

> much of the success of-physical and natural scientists comes from their use of laboratory techniques. The social scientist today also needs laboratory techniques if he is to profitably study and improve man's urban environment. Because the social scientist lacks a laboratory he is not only unable to adequately test his ideas but is hindered in collating the factual base from which to formulate his ideas.[59]

"Collating the factual base" was a two-fold proposition in the process of building a simulation—first data would need to be gathered from the environment being studied, and then it would need to be re-assembled as a command and control system simulating "man-environment interaction." Simulation takes the digital map a step further into the direction of prediction by adding the dimension of time and the probabilistic structure of gaming.

In the late '60s simulation was a popular topic and House and Patterson's article one of many published on the subject, yet it is of note here because of its inclusion of Steinitz's work as well as in simulation work being done by others at this time. Beginning with the positivist approach in terms of data gathering, but moving to the theoretical abstraction of the model, researchers could, in House and Patterson's words, "experiment with change."[60] These models also attempted to quantify the subjective point of view and to try to understand the interpersonal negotiations the occur between the different players in the "game." Another project the authors cite was a political gaming model titled, TEMPER; as the name suggests this was an attempt to model the personality "factors conditioning foreign policy decisions," or to put it another way, to assess the way a world leader might react in a given cold-war scenario.[61] The geo-political instabilities of the post-war world combined with the behavioralist trend in sociology helped to popularize research in conflict simulation models, be they for representing the theater of war or urban landscapes. These simulations offered some degree of projective reassurance about possible outcomes, perhaps easing the choice to pull the trigger in certain scenarios, as such these tools were often referred to as decision-making aids.[62] This carries with it the implication that, at least in part, one was ceding certain authorities to the machine, making prediction an automated process of risk management.

Means as Ends: The Landscape Architecture Research Office

Steinitz worked as a research assistant in the Lab for Computer Graphics before the completion of his dissertation, afterwords he did a brief stint teaching in the department of planning Harvard before moving into his final destination at the university, the department of landscape architecture. The Landscape Architecture Research Office (LARO) began as a group of individuals inside the Lab (including Steinitz) who were working with computer mapping technologies to find direct applications related to the discipline of landscape architecture. LARO's projects were contextually specific, yet they were trying to extrapolate a general method for design using the computer based on their research. The realm of landscape offered an ideal site of projection — historically the discipline has attempted to lay hold of the relations between the social and the physical, the human and the environmental, or the artificial and natural.[63] Put another way, a systems approach combined with the use of the digital map allowed researchers to conflate the social and physical into a singular armature for the description of "landscape." A glance back through Harvard's Graduate School of Design course registers from the '60s onward shows the early commitment landscape architects had made to the computer as a tool for the design process, catalogues from each semester show pages upon pages of computer courses offered in the department of landscape—some twenty years before the first computer course would be taught in the department of architecture.

The first major project LARO undertook was the Comparative Study of Resource Analysis Methods, from which they published a thick technical looking report of typed and mimeographed pages showing simple digital maps.[64] The study focused on the Charles river watershed—an ecological system based on the connective tissue and environmental logic of water. The researchers assembled a pool of sixteen actors, from landscape architects (Richard Toth, Ervin Zube, Ian McHarg, Philip H. Lewis Jr., etc.) to members of governmental agencies (US Army Corps of Engineers, Soil Conservation Services, etc.), to planning commissioners, to geographers, engineers, and most surprisingly, other computer simulation models, which were assumed to possess enough machine intelligence on their own to constitute individual actors (PARIS: The State of California, and RECSYS: The State of Michigan), and systematically analyzed each actor's methodological approach to

58 "Department of City and Regional Planning," Ibid., 41.

59 Peter House and Philip D. Patterson, "An Environmental Gaming-Simulation Laboratory," *Journal of the American Planning Association* 35, no. 6 (1969): 383 - 388.

60 "An Environmental Gaming-Simulation Laboratory," Ibid., 383.

61 Walter C. Clemens, "A Propositional Analysis of the International Relations Theory of TEMPER—A Computer Simulation of Cold War Conflict," in *Simulation in the Study of Politics*, ed. William D. Coplin (Chicago: Markham Publishing Co, 1968), 59-101.

62 In the late 1960s a large-scale project for behavioral simulation and computer methodology titled the Cambridge Project, was begun at MIT by J.C.R. Licklider with funding from ARPA's program in behavioral science. Licklider was a longtime supporter of the use of the computer in psychological studies. The project was built on the computing platform of Project MAC, but like MAC was an independent research project within the university. Nonetheless, the project attracted a lot of attention, in part due to the participation of Professor Ithiel de Sola Pool from the Center for

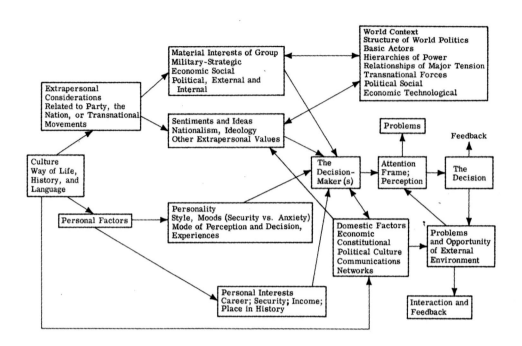

Variables of policy decision making, TEMPER model. From William D. Coplin, *Simulation in the Study of Politics*, (Chicago: Markham, 1968).

landscape. Next, they performed two transformations on their findings: first they identified individual methods and translated them into terms that would suit the computer mapping software GRID (based on SYMAP); and, second, they applied these methods to analysis of the watershed area and produced a uniformly formatted series of digital maps. Introducing the study, the researchers write that, "Given increasing public awareness of the need for resource use policies which will minimize the inevitable conflicts among the various demands for land, resource analysts, planners, and designers are challenged to go beyond the level of individuality and towards a level of understanding which approaches the theoretical."[65] Here the focus was not on any one particular designer but rather on extracting methodology from each of the

International Studies (as well as others). Pool was consulting on Vietnam policy for the White House during both the Kennedy and Johnston administrations and many in the public felt that the political implications of his research were not suitable for the academic setting. There was also a backlash

against the behavioral sciences themselves, fears of instant social engineering, and large centralized data bases fueled protest at MIT and in Cambridge. In 1974 the Cambridge Project was quietly moved into the SA+P; overseen by the newly created Laboratory for Architecture and Planning, it

was (ironically enough) re-named "Project Overlap."
63 The first department of landscape architecture in the US was formed at Harvard by Frederick Law Olmstead Jr. in 1900. According to historian Melanie Simo, the program was unique in that it attempted to merge the imperatives of "geology,

actors and then looking at how these methods would translate into the graphic display offered by computer maps—transcending mere representation and moving toward a set of tools with embedded intelligence.

In light of the move away from individual authorship and toward a general method the researchers were attentive to the ways in which the representation was structured in relation to thought processes. Each empirical instance (or grid cell) on the map held the possibility for a multitude of potential data inputs. This method of encoding data in a hybrid cartesian/geographic form was envisioned by the researchers as a way of breaking down existing modes of thought using new logics of representation. In a critique of the hand-drawn line as compared to the computer gridded map, they write:

> On the other hand, the expert, working with hand drawn maps and using his "best professional judgment," continually simplifies his data by synthesizing fine scale variations into homogenous and usually dichotomous zones as he draws the boundaries which characterize the graphic product of his analysis.[66]

In other words, they saw the grid as a plane of freedom in which the mind would no longer be bound by traditional delineations of matter, instead it would smoothly move across a rasterized field gradated by degree and type rather than objects. The link is made here between mental processes, representational symbols, and the technical means used to connect the two, acknowledging both the material and epistemological dimensions of the technologies being employed. A tremendous amount of thought was put into trying to understand how the mind functions in relation to design decisions. Efforts were made toward analyzing the map as a key element in the design process, and the researchers were investigating the potentials for new kinds of analytical thought enabled by the digital cartographic construct.

An Experiment in Interdisciplinary Education

The role of the designer was a central question in "Urbanization and Change," an interdisciplinary studio offered through the Department of Landscape Architecture in

botany, horticulture, fine arts, history, architecture, engineering, and town planning" into a singular profession. Historically landscape architecture has existed in a state of tension between scientific discourses and aesthetic ones. For more information see Melanie L. Simo, *The Coalescing of*

Different Forces and Ideas: A History of Landscape Architecture at Harvard, 1900-1999 (Cambridge, MA: Harvard University Graduate School of Design, 2000), 2.

64 Carl Steinitz, Timothy Murray, David Sinton, and Douglas Way, eds., *A Comparative Study of Resource Analysis Methods* (Cambridge, MA: Department of Landscape Architecture Research Office and the Graduate School of Design, Harvard University, 1969).

65 et al., *A Comparative Study*, 1.

66 Ibid., 1.

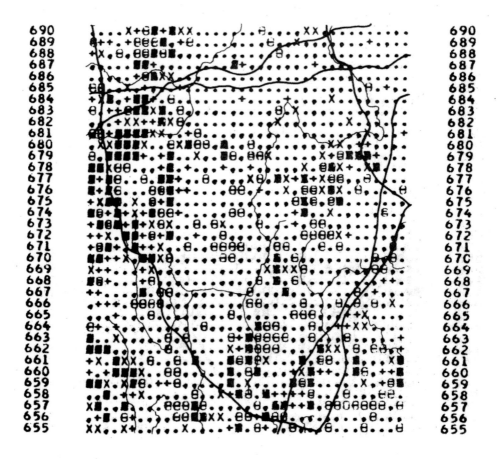

III.8.8 Ian L. McHarg

COMPOSITE:
CONSERVATION-RECREATION-URBANIZATION SUITABILITY

. 0	=	Low Recreation/Low Conservation/Low Urban
, 2	=	Low Recreation/High Conservation/Low Urban
+ 3	=	Low Recreation/Low Conservation/High Urban
X 4	=	Low Recreation/High Conservation/High Urban
O 5	=	High Recreation/Low Conservation/Low Urban
θ 6	=	High Recreation/High Conservation/Low Urban
θ 7	=	High Recreation/Low Conservation/High Urban
▉ 9	=	High Recreation/High Conservation/High Urban

1968. A few years of course documentation was published as *A Systems Analysis Model of Urbanization and Change: An Experiment in Interdisciplinary Education* (1970).[67] The text was co-written by the co-teachers of the course, Steinitz and Peter Rogers, a water economist and professor from the department of city and regional planning at Harvard. The studio "experiment" was indicative of a push to find ways to foster interaction amongst different departments at Harvard. Steinitz and Rogers write, "Schools of design have often had interdisciplinary faculties, but to date there has been no system of organization that could bring the various disciplines together into a functioning whole. [emphasis in the original]."[68] Yet in parsing this further in their next statement, the authors amend this idea, writing that "interdisciplinary education evokes the idealistic image of synthesizing all available knowledge, techniques, and skills into one super machine which will solve all problems. However, this interaction often has quite opposite results, such as cross-sterilization rather than cross-fertilization of fields and confrontation rather than dialogue."[69] Put another way, Steinitz and Rogers were hoping to establish a framework for inter-disciplinarity that would allow for reactions between the disciplines themselves rather than a model for total integration. What emerged was a gaming model that, with students assigned varying actionable roles, could represent urban change. Armed with pre-determined agendas they would "play" against one another as the simulated city grew over time.[70] The purpose for this was two-fold: on the one hand it created a system able to organize "discourse" and to gauge the effects of certain "moves," on the other hand, this analog method helped flesh out the design parameters for a computer model simulating urban change that Rogers and Steinitz were hoping to build in the future. The authors explained:

> It would probably take several years to write a computer program for this simulation. So we did a patchwork process, and dignified it with the name "man-machine interaction. . ." These were developed as a set of rubrics for which the students then played the roles of FORTRAN statements. Of course, FORTRAN is more predictable than students; students in the middle of doing something always ask embarrassing questions. While embarrassing, this is how the model developed.[71]

Composite land use analysis for conservation, recreation, and urbanization, from Carl Steinitz, Timothy Murray, David Sinton, and Douglas Way, *A Comparative Study of Resource Analysis Methods*, Landscape Architecture Research Office, Graduate School of Design, Harvard University, 1969.

67 Carl Steinitz and Peter Rogers, *A Systems Analysis Model of Urbanization and Change: An Experiment in Interdisciplinary Education*, MIT Report No. 20 (Cambridge, MA: MIT Press, 1970).

68 Steinitz and Rogers, *A Systems Analysis Model of Urbanization and Change*, 1.
69 Ibid., 1.
70 Ibid., 5.

FORTRAN was a computer language fundamental for computer programming at the time, but this statement reveals a deeply-rooted anxiety regarding the human element and the subjectivity inherent in design. The computer was a way to bring a sense of objectivity and an external reference point to disciplines that utilized the "best professional judgement" of its practitioners. This was a matter to be taken quite seriously; as the authors gravely note, "This simulation is the base against which all attempts at improvement must be measured. Changes will result in an urban pattern—or a way of life—either better or worse than this one."[72]

The Design Mind, or the Experiment Continues...

What we see here is the meaning of design shifting in relation to ends or solutions; design as it is used in this context means designing a process or method. As the students coded points of control into each of the mechanisms of the model/game they put limits on degrees of freedom inherent in the system. Again like the previous studies the site was the Charles river watershed, and the publication recounts week by week what activities the studio engaged in as they built and tested the simulation. The students designed two distinct layers in the model and in the first layer there were land-use allocation models split into four primary groups—residential, industrial, open space and recreation, and centers. The second layer was comprised of evaluation models that acted as a filter or regulated the interests of the elements in the first layer, they were political, fiscal, visual quality, and pollution. The students split into teams with faculty to design the rules governing these sections, and they then came back together to role-play in teams during simulation sessions based on the rules they had created.

Anecdotal reflections from the studio are meant to reveal the heuristic insights arrived at during role playing activities. There is a clear desire to understand and examine the subjective position a singular actor plays in a dynamic situation when responding to multiple agents of change. The students who built the residential allocation model explain that in their experience,

71 Ibid., 5.

72 Ibid., 2.

73 Ibid., 2.

74 Ibid., 2.

75 Ibid., 66.

76 Ibid., 69

77 F.I. Rip, "Computer-aided Landscape Planning: The Medium is the Message," Landscape and Urban *Planning* 14 (1987): 79-83.

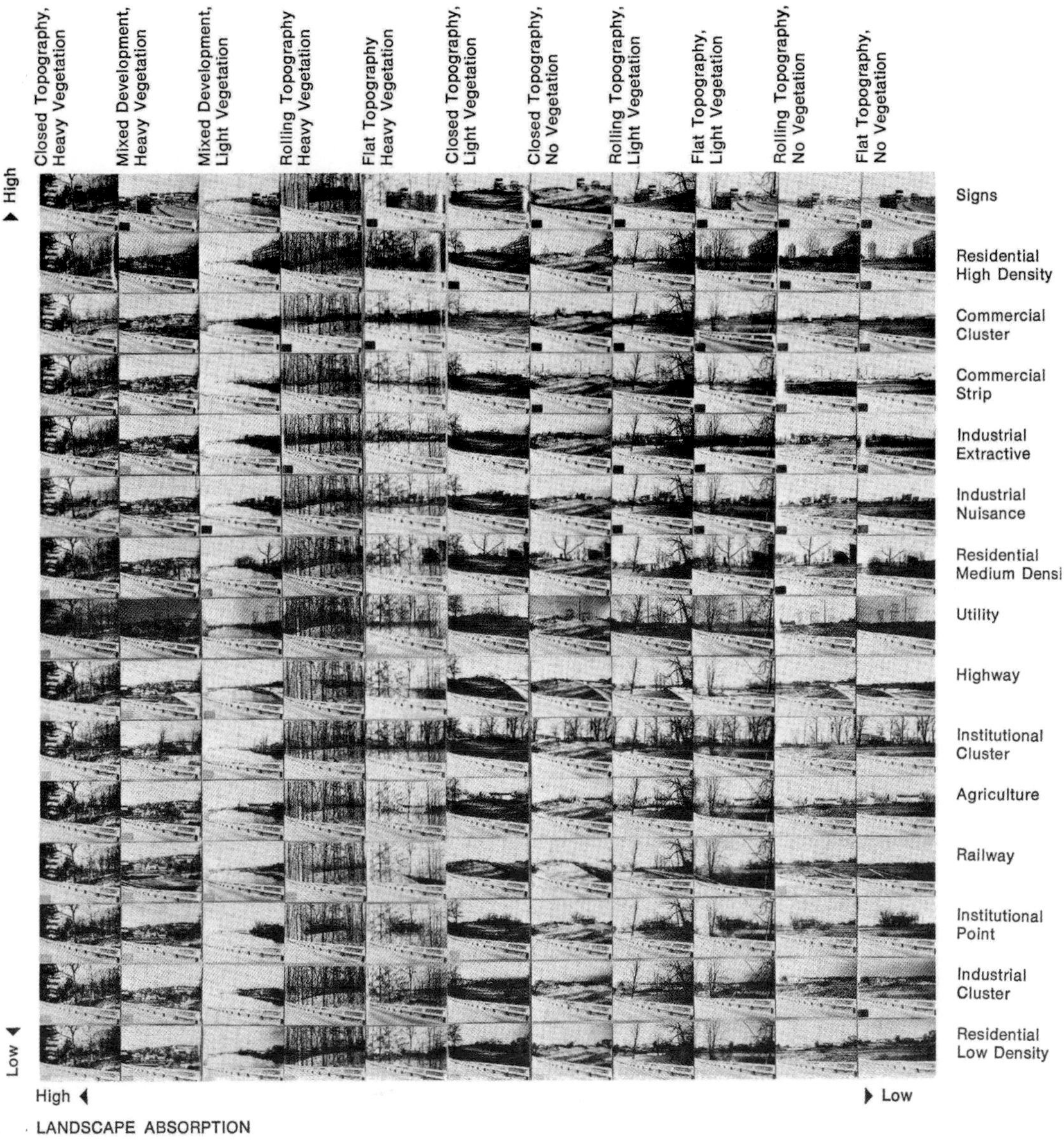
Closed Topography, Heavy Vegetation
Mixed Development, Heavy Vegetation
Mixed Development, Light Vegetation
Rolling Topography Heavy Vegetation
Flat Topography Heavy Vegetation
Closed Topography, Light Vegetation
Closed Topography, No Vegetation
Rolling Topography, Light Vegetation
Flat Topography, Light Vegetation
Rolling Topography, No Vegetation
Flat Topography, No Vegetation
High
Low
Signs
Residential High Density
Commercial Cluster
Commercial Strip
Industrial Extractive
Industrial Nuisance
Residential Medium Densi
Utility
Highway
Institutional Cluster
Agriculture
Railway
Institutional Point
Industrial Cluster
Residential Low Density
High
Low
LANDSCAPE ABSORPTION

Photographic matrix of development in landscapes, from Carl Steinitz and Peter Rogers, *A Systems Analysis Model of Urbanization and Change: An Experiment in Interdisciplinary Education*, MIT Report No.20, (Cambridge: MIT Press, 1970).

Simulation studies. From
Steinitz and Rogers,
Systems Analysis Model.

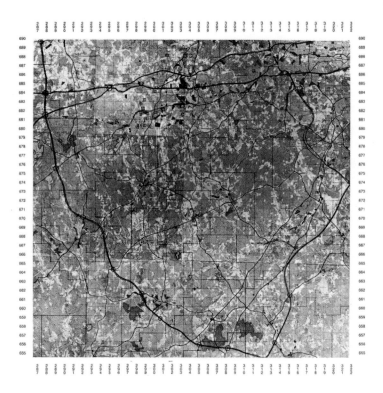

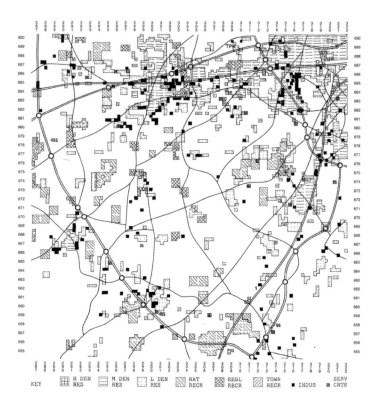

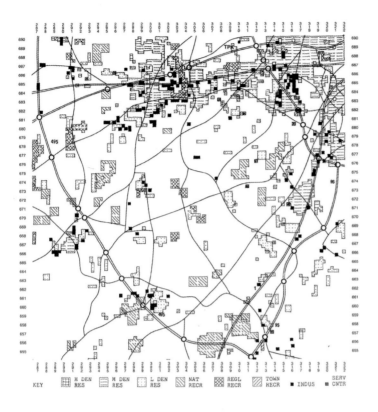

KEY   ⊞ H DEN   ▦ M DEN   ⊡ L DEN   ⊠ NAT   ▨ REGL   ▧ TOWN   ■ INDUS   ⊠ SERV
       RES   RES   RES   RECR   RECR   RECR   CNTR

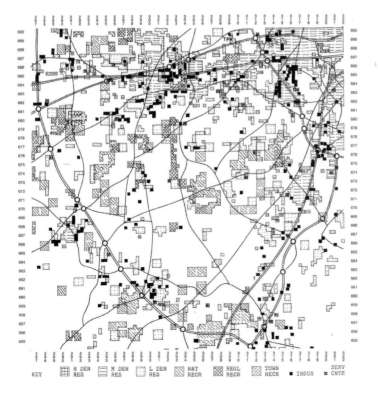

KEY   ⊞ H DEN   ▦ M DEN   ⊡ L DEN   ⊠ NAT   ▨ REGL   ▧ TOWN   ■ INDUS   ⊠ SERV
       RES   RES   RES   RECR   RECR   RECR   CNTR

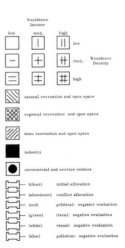

we took it upon ourselves, in the role playing of this allocation, to simulate the producer aspect of residential development. In other words, were to act out the roles of the people who would actually produce the housing, and their constraints and values would be imposed on the results of the consumer analysis. This role was often in conflict with the training we had as architects, urban designers, and landscape architects, which had urged us to act in the interest (or what we think is the interest) of the common good, the public good, the landscape good, the regional good.[73]

They continue by remarking that, "This, of course, would be opposite to the kind of training we're given in school, where one would never encourage this sort of thing."[74] The game opened up pre-determined roles for examination, but it also defined and limited them in terms that would fit a gaming framework and allow for a kind of purposive predictability. By the end of the publication there is a hint of ambivalence about the actual success or failure of this attempt. Emphasis was placed not so much on the potentials inherent in the simulation itself, but rather on the game's ability to re-train the mind by shifting students into a mode of future-directed thinking consisting of greater temporal complexity. At then end of the report Steinitz remarks, "An important side issue for planners is: If we foresee what happens, then what?"[75] What does it mean to predict the future and are these prophesies perhaps self-fulfilling? He further reinforces this point when recounting an anecdote from the game playing experience:

One very instructional thing for the landscape architecture students was that this format forced the Recreation Team to develop a strategy where priorities are stated. Put yourself in a situation using the traditional studio methods- what would you do? The first thing would be to buy the river. Right? You'd spend all your money on the river. Well, in both the simulation runs, it happened that for twenty years nobody else wanted the river. You therefore might be able to say, "Well, look we don't have much of a problem there for a good long time. Let's go buy as much land as we can where we're going to have the problem, where it doesn't exist now, and then in the end we'll worry about the river." And in fact, that's how it turned out. And this is completely different from what you would normally expect a student plan to show with the values that the students have when they come in here. The format really makes you think of what the hell it is that you want to do and what is the best strategy for getting it.[76]

This is the first place "strategy" is mentioned and yet it is a recurring theme; whether in political models made to simulate foreign relations, or in a city model designed to function like the game of Monopoly, determining a plan of action had clearly become as important as the ends themselves. If the designer was to be ahead of the curve, they would need to be proactive in framing the audience and the problems to be solved through design rather than waiting for more traditional projects to come to them.

Simulation system. From Steinitz and Rogers, *Systems Analysis Model*.

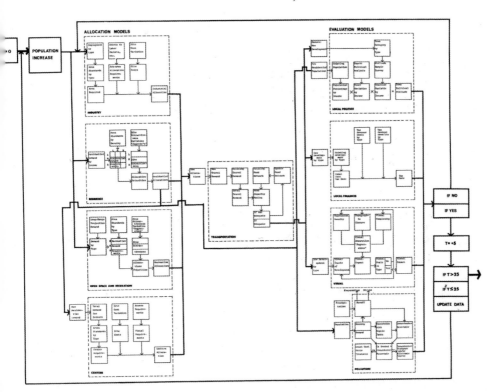

Means as Ends: Conclusion

In an article published in the Dutch journal *Landscape and Urban Planning* in 1987 titled "Computer Aided Landscape Planning: The Medium is the Message," landscape planner and professor, F.I. Rip, offers a critique of early computer mapping efforts, beginning with Steinitz.[77] His complaint is that with the use of the computer the "emphasis has shifted away from geographical data towards the technical means and their potential for data processing. In other words, the enthusiasm for computer aided landscape planning tends to dominate careful data-handling."[78] Writing from the perspective of the late 1980s he felt there had been little improvement in this state of affairs since the Landscape Architecture Research Office published their early studies. He complains that the researchers all seem to share a susceptibility for methodological indulgence, imbibing all the "technical means" available to them via the computer, which he explains eventually results in their "loss of data-consciousness."[79] And in 1987 he seems uncertain whether sobriety will be regained by future researchers. Data available to the landscape planner is so prodigious as to require new tools to handle it (the computer), and yet Rip implies that the machine serves to alienate the researcher from the empirical reality connected to the data. In other words, crafting a system whose logic is consistent takes precedence over the recognition of irregularities and statistical abnormalities. Rip's argument may present a limited picture, but it does draw attention to the idea that these new technologies were not replacing the designer—rather they necessitated a new kind of designer, one who could reconcile empirical specificity with theoretical structure and ensure systematic interoperability between disparate sets of ideas. This designer would understand the tools that could draw natural and social phenomena into the same framework and would be able to re-frame his or her expertise in relation to these means. The system relies not only on external inputs, but provides internal feedbacks, and in this way a systems approach feeds a new disciplinary paradigm in its very architecture.

In the 1960s at MIT greater emphasis was put on action rather than reflection—researchers sought to develop techniques and methods that could be exported from the institute and applied globally. In this context, design was no longer a discrete product codified in formal terms but rather referred to an ongoing process. In a recent lecture, Steinitz explained that the computer is no longer even entirely necessary for one to utilize his method, rather it is a set of steps to be followed, a way of thinking or a system of logic for gathering information, conducting analysis, and for making decisions.[80] In many ways he has absorbed the early lessons from the computer, and his techniques have become instead a model of mind—a model for soliciting community inputs, a model that can predict "alternative futures", and a model for export to actors in other cities and nations.[81] He represents a model of the design professional for whom the means have become the ends, or to borrow his own words, a profession for which, "design is a verb, design is a noun."[82]

Steinitz and Rogers,
Systems Analysis Model.

78 Ibid., 83.

79 Ibid., 89.

80 "GeoDesign Summit 2010: Carl Steinitz: Ways of Designing (Parts 1-4)," (April 22, 2010), available online at http://www. youtube.com/watch?v=-mYxTzPnLY&feature=related. Accessed January, 8, 2011.

81 Carl Steinitz, Scott Basset, and Hector Arias, *Alternative Futures for Changing Landscapes: The Upper San Pedro River Basin in Arizona and Sonora*, Washington, DC: Island Press, 2003).

82 Carl Steinitz, "Design is a Verb; Design is a Noun," *Landscape Journal* 14, no. 2 (1995): 188-200.

ALISE UPITIS

Alexander's Choice

How Architecture Avoided
Computer-Aided Design c. 1962

> Media determine our situation, which—in spite of or because of it—deserves a
> description.
> —Friedrich Kittler, *Gramophone, Film, Typewriter*

This is a story of a young architect who had a choice, between walking up one flight of stairs or remaining on the first floor. The choice was made at MIT, at the entrance to the Karl Compton Laboratory, Building 26, circa 1962. On the first floor of this elongated glass and steel design by Gordon Bunshaft was the MIT Computation Center. In 1962 it contained an IBM 7090 mainframe. On the second floor, directly above the Computation Center, there were two additional, dramatically different computers, a PDP-1 and a TX-0.[1] The young architect chose the first floor.

The young architect in question was Christopher Alexander, PhD candidate in architecture at the Harvard Graduate School of Design, although his access to the Institute's computer facilities was result of his position as a research affiliate in the MIT department of civil engineering. Over the next several years the immediate epicenters embracing Alexander's choice included the University of California, Berkeley, the Bay Area Transit Authority, the UK Ministry of Public Works, and Bavra, India. But further afield practicing architects and instructors at architecture schools, as well as engineering, product, and urban designers and professors, would be pressed to embrace or refute the larger effects of this choice; indeed, they were forced to grapple with its impact for over a decade in locations across the US, UK, Germany, and, though its impact was less ubiquitous here, in Ghana, Nigeria, and other British colonies in Africa.[2]

1 Steven Levy, *Hackers: Heros of the Computer Revolution* (Garden City, NY: Anchor Press/Doubleday, 1984), 14.

2 See Alise Upitis, "Nature Normative: The Design Methods Movement, 1944-1967" (PhD dissertation, MIT Department of Architecture, 2008).

Alexander decision to use an IBM mainframe was integral to his efforts to develop a theory of design he believed would revolutionize not just how architects but designers generally went about the process of design. I will argue that Alexander did not create a design method and seek out the best technology for its implementation, but rather that his method was determined by the material realities of his chosen technology, the series of IBM mainframes he chose to program between 1961 and 1963. While references in his writings from this period roam across Gestalt psychology (Kurt Koffka, Wolfgang Köhler), cognitive psychology (Jerome Bruner, George Miller) and its close ally artificial intelligence (Herbert Simon and Marvin Minsky), cybernetics (W. Ross Ashby, Norbert Wiener), anthropology (A.R. Radcliffe-Brown, Marcel Mauss, Lucien Levy-Bruhl), economics (John Von Neumann and Oskar Morganstern), philosophy (Karl Popper and R.B. Braithwaite), and communications theory (Claude Shannon), Alexander deployed these authors in a highly selective manner, a post hoc attempt to bolster a theory ultimately fixed by his developing it on an IBM. It was the architecture of IBMs that conditioned the kinds of programs one could run, and Alexander chose a programming language that demanded even greater adherence to the computers' spare and stringent architecture.

Alexander was not the first designer to turn towards computer processes as an inspiration for improving design. By the late 1950s the University of Manchester had already reformed its curriculum to recast architectural pedagogy as a step-wise processes distinctly modeled on the logic of a computer program.[3] During the 1960s flow charts with feedback cycles strikingly similar to the logic diagrams of a computer's architecture proliferated in the pedagogy of art and design schools around the globe. In Europe these sites included University College, London under Richard Llewellyn-Davies, architect and designer of the British new town Milton Keynes, Royal College of Art under architect and designer Misha Black, and the very influential design school Hochschule für Gestaltung, Ulm under Tomás Maldonado.[4] Yet during this late postwar period, it was the *image* of emerging computer-related technologies that operated widely to challenge presiding theories of design. Alexander was the first of this movement to use a computer, rather than solely its representational proliferations, to implement a design method.

3 Misha Black and L. Bruce Archer, *Studies in the Function and Design of Non-surgical Hospital Equipment, Preliminary Report,* (London: Nuffield Foundation, Royal College of Art , 1962); Richard Llewellyn-Davies, "Future of Research," *RIBA Journal,* 71 (April 1964): 105; Conference Course on "The Teaching of Design—Design Method in Architecture," *Programme,* group 4 (1966).

4 John A. McKenzie, TX-0 Computer History, *RLE Technical Report* No. 627, MIT (June 1999).

following page, Project Whirlwind, 1954. Left to right: Jay W. Forrester, Norman H. Taylor, Gus O' Brien, Norman Draggett, Charles L. L' Orderman (on ladder).

It is necessary to leave the Computation Center and ascend to the second floor to understand the alternative available to Alexander. On the second floor the TX-0 and PDP-1 computers were descendants of SAGE (Semi-Automatic Ground Environment), a project to create a US nation-wide network of digital computers linked to radar and anti-aircraft weapons which would track and intercept enemy aircraft in real time using automatic and, most significantly for this tale, visual means. The TX-0 was developed as a means to test new materials for computer processing and memory with the hope of converting Whirlwind, the prototype computer for SAGE, into one faster, more reliable, and equipped with a larger storage capacity. These were not, as with the IBM, a product born of the considerable market demand by businesses and scientists, as well as the IRS, for precise numerical computations. The computers upstairs were not, in other words, driven by a demand that required the computer to calculate, not generate visual imagery.

The TX series was not embraced by the MIT department of civil engineering, with which Alexander was affiliated. It was welcomed by another sort of designer at MIT, electrical and mechanical engineers. In the late 1950s many of these engineers were involved with an interdepartmental research endeavor, the Computer-Aided Design (CAD) project, a joint endeavor between the Computer Applications Group, Department of Electrical Engineering, and the Design and Graphics Division of the Mechanical Engineering Department. Alexander's design method involved inputing numbers to the IBM, standing by while his program ran, and waiting for the IBM to output different numbers. But in the early 1960s the engineers of the CAD project proposed an alternative vision for how humans might engage with computation. It was out of the TX series that Sketchpad was developed, the first computer drawing system that allowed for real time reciprocal actions, interaction, between human and computer, features without which today's computers are inconceivable. Engineered by Ivan Sutherland, Sketchpad allowed a user to quickly draw shapes on a display scope with a "light pen" and manipulate or add to them. As with Alexander and his IBM, I will articulate how Sutherland's favored assembly of transistors, wires, electrical pulses, and steel racks, the TX-2, worked to regulate Sutherland's design system, but different media meant different determinations.

As the TX series advanced in speed and memory far beyond its Whirlwind predecessor, allowing simpler user interaction and inimitable graphic capabilities, the computers' underlying architecture and its software's inner workings became increasingly opaque. In contrast, the IBM Alexander employed did not have a display scope with which a user could interact to manipulate programs or data, much less visualize imagery, but his software's structure was transparent to his machine's ontology. In a principal turn of image relations, the increasing centrality of graphic interfaces to computing resulted in the increasing marginalization of users to the architecture enabling their machines. This splitting of interface from the differences in electrical potentials that condition the very possibility of graphic user interfaces is all the more evident now than it was in the era of computers that sprawled 2,500 square feet. As this fracture joins back to my account of computer architectures moulding theories of design, I will parse it until no later than 1963, the 26 years after the publication of the paper by Alan Turning in which he introduced his computing machine.[5]

Downstairs Upstairs

On the first floor of MIT Building 26, computer programmers in the early 1960s would arrive with stacks of punched cards, paper cards with a series of vertical columns, each column allowing for holes, each hole representing a single number or letter. A programmer would give a deck of these to an operator, usually submitted through an interior window that helped maintain the giant computer's necessary climate. While operators had intimate access to the 7090, programmers were rarely allowed in the computer room. The operator would commonly first feed the decks into a smaller IBM 1401 computer, which would generate the reels of magnetic tape the large 7090 was equipped to process. Operators would mount the reels on tape drives, the drives hooked to circuits held up by large metal frames hidden inside sleek metal cabinets.

MIT Computation Center, circa 1962.

PDP-1 computer, the production line version of the TX-2.

On July 1, 1958, the TX-0, in preparation for its long-term loan to the department of electrical engineering, was shut down to relocate it to the second floor of Building 26, where it was allocated (and took up much of) 9000 square feet of space. It took a month to relocate its hardware from MIT's Lincoln Laboratory in Lexington, Massachusetts to Cambridge. Hundreds of wires between components had to be cut. Metal racks which contained the computer's components had to be bolted to their bases, their bases bolted to the floor. It took another month for the machine to become operational because a fifteen-ton air conditioner had to be installed, as the machine did not work accurately if room temperatures exceeded 80 degrees Fahrenheit.[6]

Despite the TX-0's unwieldily features, on the second floor of Building 26 the dichotomy between operator and programmer was dissolved. There were no punch cards or peripheral computers between the programmer and access to the TX-0's processing capabilities. The programmer *used* the computer, by means of sitting in front of a Flexowriter, an extension of the console which "resembled a typewriter converted for tank warfare," and punching a program onto long, thin paper tape.[7] He (as far as the historical record shows, exclusively) would run the tape through a reader which fed the program into the computer. The re-located TX-0 was not a production line machine but was rather slowly developed, or more accurately carefully cobbled together and painstakingly tested at MIT and its US Air force-funded research unit Lincoln Laboratory. The PDP-1 was a production line machine, a descendent of the TX-. The PDP-1 was the first commercial product of Digital Equipment Corporation (DEC), a business founded in 1957 by Harlan Anderson and Kenneth Olsen, the latter of whom transferred his knowledge to DEC from his time as head of TX-0's development.

Downstairs at the 7090, circuits would work to process the data and programs contained on the tape, which could often, depending on the complexity of the task and the amount of data required, take hours to complete. If a batch of tape ran successfully, an operator would demount the tape and carry it to a tape drive connected to an IBM 1401 in turn connected to a type 1403 printer, which would print the program's results on fan-folded paper, fifteen inches wide, using numbers and capital letters that moved laterally across the page. If a programmer wanted to see the visualization of a result, even a visualization as simple as a square, he could generate the form using alphanumeric symbols (today's ASC II) and wait for the print out, only knowing at that point whether the visualization was successful. If a programmer made a mistake he was forced to punch new holes and wait for a new batch to run.

Upstairs a user could modify a program mid-run while sitting at the TX-0's console, "the control panel of this H.G. Wells spaceship."[8] Most significantly it had a seven by seven inch display which allowed a user to see the program's operations and results in real time. Beginning in 1958 a number of students used the computer and its CRT for theses on the simulation of the digital transmission of images and techniques for improving the resolution of the image transmitted. By 1960 the TX-0 was used to display a histogram of electrophysiological data from a cat's auditory cortex and which was captured on film, and a roll of 35mm film containing bubble chamber images could be passed between the display and light gun (an earlier version of a light pen), the film read

5 Alan Turing, "On Computable Numbers, with an Application to the *Entscheidungs* problem," *Proceedings of the London Mathematical Society* 2, no. 42 (1936): 230–65.

6 McKenzie, *TX-0 Computer History*, 15.

7 Levy, *Hackers*, 15.

8 Ibid.

9 McKenzie, *TX-0 Computer History*.

into the computer, and processed through a pattern recognition program.[9] Nearly a decade before computers were first used in coursework in MIT's School of Architecture and Planning, the TX-0 was also used in introductory computer courses and for class work in the department of electrical engineering.[10]

Although space does not permit detailed examination, the series was also critical to another mode of research, that conducted by the first "hackers." These were largely students who would occupy the TX-0, and later PDP-1 when it arrived in 1961, at all hours. Extracurricular to their course demands, they were some of the first to create computer music (Peter Sampson) and, fascinated with the potentials of scopes for graphics display, were critical to the first computer game developments including Spacewar! (Steve Russell), in which two players manning spaceships fire missiles in an attempt to hit each other while negotiating a central star's gravitational field.

Alexander's Theory

Alexander received his PhD in architecture from the GSD in 1963, and Harvard University Press published his *Notes on the Synthesis of Form* (hereafter *Notes*) the following year. Little altered from his dissertation, *Notes* positions design problems of the era as rapidly increasing in complexity, a transformation that Alexander attributes to a swiftly changing society and an expanding mass of potentially pertinent but disordered information.[11] Alexander asserts that the crux of such complexity can be located in humans' limited cognitive and creative capabilities. He offers his text as a remedy, a guide to "reducing the gap between the designer's small capacity and the great size of his task" by providing a new design method whose character is crucially determined by the requirements of programming an IBM between approximately 1961 and 1963.[12]

Notes is 216 pages. 134 pages contain the text of an introduction, parts one and two, an epilogue, followed by two appendices spanning 55 pages, and finishing with 23 pages of endnotes. Methodical, repeated reading of *Notes's* main text does not necessarily diffuse confusion of over large portions of it. But turn to "Appendix I: A Worked Example,"

10 Massachusetts Institute of Technology, *Report of the President 1968*, Massachusetts Institute of Technology Bulletin 103, no. 4 (December 1968): 32.

11 Christopher Alexander, "The synthesis of form; some notes on a theory" (PhD dissertation, Harvard University, 1963).

12 In all Alexander used IBM's 700 and 7000 series (specifically the 704, 709, 7090 and 7094).

13 TOOL PRAXIS, *Assembler-Programming auf dem PC. Ausgube 1* (Würzburg: 1999), 9; quoted in Friedrich Kittler, "Protected Mode," *Literature, Media, Information Systems* (Amsterdam: Overseas Publishers Association, 1997), 157.

and read in conjunction with "Appendix 2: Mathematical Treatment of Decomposition." Alexander's design method becomes much clearer. The approach to *Notes* in these appendices also reveals how forcefully his design process was moulded by the strictures of the IBM he deployed.

A précis of his method: Alexander begins from the premise that every design problem can be reduced to a series of requirements, and the solution to the problem demands that all requirements identified at the outset are satisfied. His method is to first identify these requirements, and then to determine which of these requirements "interact." These two steps are manually determined. Next one quantifies the strength of these interactions. This is done by running an IBM program comprised of a rather large number of subprograms. One then uses the output of this program to create a collection of diagrams whose combination, Alexander claims, forms a design solution that meets all requirements of his initial design problem.

The last step prior to Alexander's inputting data in the IBM 7090 was for him to punch holes in a series of IBM punch cards. In the step prior, he created a matrix, each cell containing a 1 or a 0, which he then transferred onto his data punch cards. Machine language—the only language a digital computer can in fact interpret and execute —is composed of strings of 1s and 0s. One did not have however to program a 7090 using binary code. However, one could use symbolic code and the Indo-Arabic numerals, which Alexander's undergraduate training in mathematics at Cambridge University would have made familiar to him. The question is then: why would he use binary digits, better known as bits, to program when, as one programmer phrased it, "even under the best circumstances, one would quickly go crazy from programming in machine language"?[13]

The answer is best garnered through the details as laid out in *Notes*, Appendix 2. Alexander demonstrates his method through the example of redesigning the village of Bavra, India. As he phrases it: "An agricultural village of 600 people is to be reorganized to make it fit present and future conditions developing in rural India." The crux of his method is to determine every need or requirement (he uses the terms interchangeably) which must be satisfied to make this his properly functioning village. In total he determines 141 needs, such as "2. Proper disposal of dead." "17. Village has fixed men's social groups" "68. Easy access to drinking water." Today there are requirements that designers (although more often clients) specify as demands that must be met, such as "project cost not to exceed $500,000." But others of Alexander's are not, such as requirement 27: "Family is authoritarian."

For each of the 141 requirements, he lists every other requirement with which it "interacts." What he means by interaction between design requirements varies; he refers to these alternatively as "tangible consequences which can be objectively determined," "almost logically necessary," "almost by definition," "depend[ing] on physical laws," and "the result of a seen causal connection."[14]

For every requirement he laboriously determines, without aid of a computer, which needs interact; he finds, for example, that "2 interacts with 3, 4, 6, 26, 29, 32, 52, 71, 98, 102, 105, 123, 133." Which of his definitions for interact he employs is not made clear, but he asserts that, following his method, one is able to determine all interactions between all requirements. However with so many interactions between so many variables he is unable, without aid of a digital computer, to isolate which interactions among design needs are the strongest, or have "particularly strong identifiable" interactions.[15] To do so, Alexander chooses to measure, to quantify, how much the interacting requirements in fact interact. And for this step he makes use of an IBM 7090, specifically the one in the MIT Computation Center.[16]

Architectures of Arrays

The Colossus computer, designed and built in 1943 at the Post Office Research Laboratories in North London, was made to intercept and decode telegraph messages from the German military. It could accept 5-hole paper tape punched with cipher text and output decoded data through a typewriter, but programming was accomplished through "a combination of telephone jack plugs and cords and switches."[17] It did not accept software, and, unlike Alexander's IBMs, the TX series, or computers today, it was not structurally programmable.. While I have touched on differences between the IBMs and the TX series machines, both types are digital computers (as are computers today). Digital computers have a central processing unit (CPU), memory, and electrical currents running between them. Their storage and processing capacities are made possible by electrical pulses the computers interpret as 1s or 0s, those digital bits.

14 Alexander, *Notes on the Synthesis of Form* (Cambridge, MA: Harvard University Press, 1964), 103, 107, 108.
15 Ibid., 122.

16 Christopher Alexander and Marvin L. Manheim. HIDECS 2: *A Computer Program for the Hierarchical Decomposition of a Set which has an Associated Linear Graph* (Cambridge, MA: Dept. of Civil Engineering, Massachusetts Institute of Technology, 1962), 8. While HIDECS 2 is co-authored with

civil engineering Lecturer Marvin Manheim, I will show it is evident that this co-authorship is in name only.
17 Anthony Sale, "The Colossus of Betchley Park— The German Cipher System," in *The First Computers: History and Architecture*, eds. Raúl Rojas and Ulf Hashagen (Cambridge, MA: MIT Press,

2000), 361, 357.
18 Alexander and Manheim, *HIDECS* 2, 45.

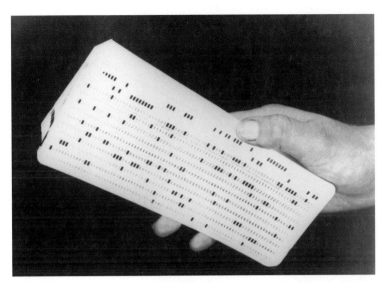

IBM Punch Card.

The Colossus's physical hardware was its computation, not obscured by software algorithms that pirated its computing capabilities. Looking to Alexander's programming, however, one is challenged to differentiate the IBM as structurally programmable, fundamentally different than the Colossus. In preparation for feeding his data and programs into the IBM, Alexander created a matrix, and in each cell he placed a 1 or a 0—1 to indicate an interaction between requirements, 0 a lack of one. All the IBMs Alexander employed required new data and programs to be fed into the computer through punch cards. A punch card is a matrix of cells, so he transplanted his 01 matrix onto the punch cards that could be read by the system.

Alexander separated cases in which his interaction matrices had 36 or fewer requirements from those with more, a choice he made for reasons directly dependent upon the architecture of his computer. A digital computer's main memory is comprised of basic storage units for software—programs and data. These units are computer "words," the size or length determined by the number of binary digits the computer can fit. A machine word is the most efficient length for a computer to store, transmit, and process data. The 7090's word length is 36 bits, and each punch card contained 72 columns, so each punch card could accommodate two machine words. The data Alexander input was already 01 strings, and so ontologically continuous with the IBM. If a design problem required more than 72 requirement the additional words or requirements Alexander punched on an additional card. For one design problem with 90 requirements he input 180 data cards.[18]

Plane of magnetic cores.

The 7090's main memory is driven by the technology of magnetic cores, a technology which IBM learned due to a joint 1952 MIT-IBM committee. MIT researchers trekked repeatedly between Cambridge and IBM headquarters in Poughkeepsie after IBM was contracted by the US Military to develop the magnetic core-driven AN/FSQ-7, the production line version Whirlwind, for installation in SAGE control rooms across the country.[19] Prior to the invention of magnetic cores, the structurally programmable Whirlwind computer, in the late 1940s, was driven by a great number of vacuum tubes for storing software and switching the on/off electrical circuits to carry out its processing. But tubes were slow and had a high failure rate—the 1946 ENIAC digital computer at the University of Pennsylvania had 17,000 tubes, one failing every two days on average, with each failure generally taking 15 minutes to locate.[20] So Whirlwind's creators soon replaced its memory tubes with small, donut-looking components made of ferromagnetic material. In this magnetic core memory, the computer interprets each core as a 0 (unused memory) or 1 (used) depending on which direction the core was magnetized.

19 Morton M. Astrahan and John F. Jacobs, "History of the Design of the Sage Computer—The AN/FSQ-7," *Annals of the History of Computing* 5, no. 4 (October 1983): 340-349.

20 Jan Van der Spiegel et al, "The ENIAC: History, Operation, and Reconstruction in VLSI," in *The First Computers*, 121-178.

Because the 7090 has a 36-bit word size, it uses 36 consecutive magnetic rings to store one computer word. So determined by the IBM's architecture was Alexander's program, it essentially mapped the contents of these punch card arrays onto arrays of these magnetic rings, with 36 1s or 0s corresponding to one computer word. It was as though he took each punch card and lined it up with an array of magnetic cores, individually rewiring each core to store one or zero binary digits if the punch card cell he held up contained a 1 or a 0.

These magnetic rings were wired into a series of grids or matrices which installed together made up the computer's storage hardware, each plane containing 252 x 252 magnetic cores. Each plane could store rows of seven 36-bit words. In turn, due to this computer's allocation of storage space, a design problem in Alexander's method could also not have more than 252 (36 x 7) interacting requirements. The planes of cores taken together meant the main memory of the 7090 can hold 32,786 36-bit words. This corresponds to a hard drive of about 150K, which was the approximate storage capacity of the first IBM Personal Computer when it came on the market in 1982.[21]

CAD's TX

In April 1956, five years after Whirlwind was operational, the TX-0 or Zeroth Transistorized Computer (or "Tixo") came online at MIT's Lincoln Lab. The TX-0 was developed, by many involved with Project Whirlwind, explicitly as a means of testing the replacement of vacuum tubes with transistors as a processor's on/off circuits. Smaller, cheaper, and more reliable than tubes, the combination of processor transistors and magnetic core memory was the foundation for the 1958 TX-2. Transistors also drove the 7090, another technology learned by IBM in its collaboration with MIT developing the AN/FSQ-7 and put on the market in 1959.[22]

Today millions of minuscule transistors are responsible for every computer's memory and processing capabilities, and the speed, storage capacity, reliability, and size of today's laptops, tablets, smart phones, and so on. By 1990, the complexity of microprocessor hardware meant engineers no longer drafted their designs on sheet upon sheet of blueprint paper. They called on the powers of the microprocessors themselves to design their next generation by means of Computer-Aided Design.[23]

21 Paul Ceruzzi, A *History of Modern Computing*, 2nd ed. (Cambridge, MA: MIT Press, 2000), 72.

22 Astrahan and Jacobs, "History of the Design of the Sage Computer—The AN/FSQ-7": 340-349.

23 L. Scheffer, "CAD Tools for Microprocessor Design in the Deep Submicron Era," *Proceedings of Technical Papers, International Symposium on VLSI Technology, Systems, and Applications* (June 1995): 57-62.

In the history of CAD, the Sketchpad system holds an originary status.[24] For this we must return to Lincoln Lab, where Sketchpad was developed on the TX-2 by Ivan Sutherland during his tenure as an MIT doctoral candidate in electrical engineering. Problematic as the origin myths of Sketchpad may be, I will nonetheless comply with it by stating Sketchpad was the first such system that permitted many features today canonical in computer drawing programs.

Take a very simple instance of drawing a line with 2012 Adobe Illustrator: Using a mouse whose movements are linked to a cursor on screen, a user clicks on the mouse button that corresponds visually to a desired initial point on screen. Keeping the mouse button depressed, she can move the mouse at a distance and angle from her initial point, which the program interprets by having the cursor create a corresponding line on screen. She can release the mouse button at a point where she would like the line to terminate. The user can decide to copy and paste parallel to the first line a duplicate of it, and then change her mind and instead draw an angle by rotating one of the lines from parallel and specifying that the point where the two lines intersect be precisely the lines' endpoints. She might subsequently decide to turn the angle into triangle, scale it up, and reposition it elsewhere on the screen. Perhaps she wants this same triangle to appear on her screen 23 times. Or she might decide to draw circles instead, or arcs.

Every one of these above actions executed in Illustrator and witnessed on screen during execution can be realized graphically in realtime using Sketchpad: create lines and circles, copy them, "snap to endpoint," impose geometric constraints, stretch, and reposition shapes.

Sketchpad did not use a mouse—the first prototype mouse was created in 1963 in Palo Alto by Douglas Engelbart and Bill English, the same year Sutherland finished his dissertation. The physiology harnessed by a Sketchpad user is dramatically other than that of a person employing today's Illustrator. Sutherland adapted a console for the TX-2 containing a display—a cathode ray-tube, the same technology used in a bulky, now old-fashioned TV—push buttons to erase or move shapes, four knobs to rotate and magnify shapes, and a panel of toggle switches (which operate on the principles that control on-off light switches) to control the display of various sorts of drawing-related information. But a light pen was the crux of its capabilities. Sutherland:

> A Sketchpad user sketches directly on a computer display with a "light pen." The light pen is used both to position parts of the drawing on the display and to point to them to change them.[25]

> If we point the light pen [connected to the TX-2 by a small cable] at the display system and press a button called "draw," the computer will construct a straight line segment which stretches like a rubber band from the initial to the present location of the pen...

To close the figure we return the light pen to near the end of the first line drawn, where it will "lock on" to the end exactly. A sudden flick of the pen terminates drawing.[26]

Ivan Sutherland using Sketchpad on the TX-2.

Sketchpad did not use an alphanumeric keyboard: "Except for legends, no written language is used."[27]

Assemblies

Alexander and Sutherland, however, both used assembly language to program their respective computers. Programming in an assembly language is only one step removed from programming in binary code. Alexander wrote the programs for his design method using an assembly language called the FORTRAN (the IBM Mathematical Formula Translating System) Assembly Program (FAP), although he called his series of programs HIDECS (Hierarchical Decomposition of Systems).

Writing in assembly language allows humans to represent machine language using ASC II, in the slightest step closer to natural language than binary code. Assembly language maps one-to-one between a symbolic instructions it asks the computer to execute and the machine language instruction, or op code, by which a computer can process information (such as adding, multiplying, reading, writing, or transferring data between CPU and main memory).

Assembly language is machine-dependent, determined by the specific architecture of the computer for which it is written. The differences between the IBM and TX does not however avoid their shared structure, inherited from the Turing Machine, through which in 1936 British mathematician Alan Turing provided the theoretical foundations for digital computers' operations today: store, write, read, transfer, or compute discrete data. As Friedrich Kittler describes the situation in 1986:

> Today...the hardware of average computers barely manages addition. More complex commands have to be reconverted into a finite, that is serial, number of cumulative steps... Computation works as a treadmill: through repeated application of the same command on the series of interim results. But that's it.

He goes on to recount mathematician Péter Rósza's 1957 experience conducting computation following Turing's logic:

> After he had filled two whole pages with the recursive formulas according to which a Turning Machine progresses from 1 to 2 to 3, and so on, [he] observed in German as twisted as it was precise: "This appears as an extraordinarily slowed-down film shot of the computation processes of man. If this mechanism of computation is applied to some functions, you start living it, you begin to compute exactly like it."[28]

Turing's computational treadmill was operating both Alexander's IBMs and Sutherland's TX-2, barely concealed by the assembly code each used to program their respective computers. In 2012 Turing's machine continues to provide the conditions which the hardware operations of digital computers must conform.

24 See e.g. "Retrospectives: The Early Years in Computer Graphics at MIT, Lincoln Lab and Harvard," Parts I and II, *SIGGRAPH '89 Panel Proceedings*, Boston, MA (July 31—August 4, 1989): 19-73.

25 Ivan Sutherland, "Sketchpad, A Man-Machine Graphical Communication System" (PhD dissertation, Department of Electrical Engineering, MIT, 1963), 3.
26 Ibid., 2.
27 Ibid., 3.

28 Friedrich Kittler, *Gramophone, Film, Typewriter* (Stanford: Stanford University Press, 1986), 248; quote from Péter Rósza, *Rekursive Funktionen*, 2nd ed., (Budapest: 1957), 210.

29 Alexander and Manheim, *HIDECS* 2, C17.

There was nonetheless a critical disparity in these computers' hardware, and hence software. Without entering the mire of these programmer's actual code, let us look to how the two programmers stored and accessed data in the computer's main magnetic core memory.

Just as Alexander entered his punch card data in the form of matrices, each string of 36 1s and 0s a computer word, he stored his data in a data table, a matrix of adjacent words in magnetic core memory. Computers are able to locate a stored word because each storage location is assigned a numerical address, or memory address. To operate on Alexander's data the 7090 would load or transfer from his data table to the CPU one word stored in one memory address, one at a time. After a data operation in the CPU, Alexander's program would transfer the result to a memory address to store it in main memory. His program used this laborious method of loading and storing data one word at a time because that was how his IBM almost always worked.

The exception occurred when the 7090 was programmed as follows. Think of a memory address as a house address, and inside each house address is a piece of paper with another number. This number could be considered a piece of data, such as a number printed on a receipt, or it could contain the address of another house. For example, upon finding this house address in one's home, one could recall she had to go to the post office and pick up her credit card bill, another piece of paper with data. Alexander coded his program to essentially execute this metaphorical task a number of times when it had to locate the contents of a cell in a matrix of data—to essentially instruct the 7090 to go to a specified house address, take the number stored inside the house, treat this number as another house address, and load the number found at this last address into a specified location in the CPU.

To implement this instruction, without generating a program error, his program would have previously located the row of the desired cell, say row 72, and the column number, say 2, and would have stored this numerical data temporarily in the CPU. This data could be used to locate the cell at the intersection of row 72 and column 2, but the data itself did not instruct the computer how to locate this cell. The program had to instruct the computer to proceed to the memory address, storing this row and column number and retrieve the data in the cell at their intersection. The computer would treat this row and column data as itself a memory address, proceed to the memory address of the cell at the intersection of row 72 column 2, and retrieve its contents.[29]

But this mode of memory addressing in the 7090, termed indirect addressing, always halted at an operand (data) after two stops, after which it would transfer the operand to the CPU for processing. Sutherland's TX-2, however, could make an arbitrary number of stops before halting, and his file structure could move from accessing data to instructions or link an arbitrary number of memory addresses, data, and instructions together. This structure, termed a ring structure, allowed a radical departure from what Alexander's IBM could do. It allowed a Sketchpad user to select one element of an entire drawing, transform that element, and transform the entire drawing accordingly. It allowed a user to insert or remove a new shape in an arbitrary location on a displayed drawing and to merge different picture files, so that, for example, two or more lines could share the same endpoint.[30]

I will focus on how Sketchpad's ring structure was indebted to the way in which its software was stored in the TX-2's memory—a conceptually basic, although critical, departure from Alexander's IBM. As detailed above, Alexander used a data table that stored his 0/1 interaction matrix. This is largely because it is more efficient to store in the same block of memory, in adjacent words, software accessed during one part of a program, rather like the time-saving trick of keeping socks together in one drawer. Both Alexander and Sutherland made use of consecutive storage, but in very different ways. For the IBM each word used in adjacent parts of a program was loaded into and stored back in main memory by the CPU one word at a time; for the TX-2, words that went into Sketchpad's drawing files were stored consecutively but were not handled singly by the CPU; rather, they were handled as blocks or stacks of words. Each block contained together an element of a drawing's topology, such as a line. For a user to transform a line drawn on the TX-2's display, such as lengthen it, Sketchpad had to keep track of that line's endpoints, so that lengthening the line meant the software could automatically recalculate the line's endpoints or the endpoints of four lines drawn separately could be linked to form a quadrilateral. To accommodate this need a line block would contain "pointers" to two other blocks, each containing the coordinates of one endpoint block.

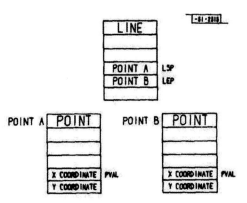

Sutherland's ring structure for programming Sketchpad. From Ivan Sutherland, "Sketchpad, A Man-Machine Graphical Communication System," Ph.D. Dissertation, Department of Electrical Engineering, MIT, 1963.

If one of the endpoints was joined with an arc, that endpoint block would contain a pointer to the arc's block, and so on. These ring structure pointers were how drawing files were linked, and to create this structure Sketchpad used a mode of indirect addressing; however, unlike Alexander's two-stop-and-halt mode, Sketchpad's mode of indirect addressing provided an arbitrary number of links between words. The TX-2 allowed this in part because it had nearly 1MB of memory—somewhat of an ocean of storage for 1958. And because "the large storage capacity of the TX-2 did not force storage conservation," Sutherland programmed his ring structure to contain some redundancies thereby permitting more rapid program execution.[31]

The Mathematical Theory of Communication, and a Non-Mathematical One

The IBM did allow Alexander—or rather conditioned the possibility for him—to execute his theory of design by quantifying the strength of interactions between requirements. To do so he sought to measure the amount of "information transmitted" between requirements.[32] To determine this he used a formula based on one proposed by Claude Shannon in a 1948 article titled "A Mathematical Theory of Communication," published in two installments in the *Bell Systems Technical Journal*. The following year Shannon published, with Warren Weaver, *The Mathematical Theory of Communication*, the book that permitted the resounding impact of Shannon's theory, a seminal work in the quantification, transmission, and storage of information. It provides the basis for our having an internet connection speed of 10 megabits per second or a phone with 32 GB of memory and our understanding what that means.

Shannon proposes that information is transmitted through a communication channel and this transmission begins with a "sender" and ends with a "receiver." The central contribution of his text is a formula for measuring the total amount of information transmitted, and he asserts that this formula depends on how likely it is that a series of symbols will be transmitted through that channel.

An example: Say I (sender) am talking on the phone (communications channel) with a friend (receiver). Based on past conversations with this friend there is a 30 percent probability I will say the word "work," a 50 percent probability I will say the word "taco,"

30 Sutherland, "Sketchpad," 34-53.

31 Ibid.

32 Alexander and Manheim, *HIDECS* 2, D37.

and a 65 percent probability I will say the word "weekend." According to Shannon's formula, to determine the total amount of information transmitted through the call, taking into account only these three words, is found by first multiplying the probability of my mentioning the word "work" by a mathematical function, a binary logarithm, abbreviated as log2, of this probability:[33]

$$.3 \times \log2 (.3) = -.5210898$$

Then do the same for the likelihood of my saying the words "taco" and "weekend" and sum these results together:

$$.3 \times \log2 (.3) + .5 \times \log2 (.5) + .65 \log2 (.65) = -1.425057$$

Now multiply the result by -1 to obtain 1.425057. This number is Shannon's measure of information transmitted by these three words through the phone's communications channel. He terms this the number of bits of information transmitted. These are the same bits of which 1 million comprise a megabit. His general formula is written $- \sum p \log2 p$.

If every time I spoke with my friend on the phone I said the words "work," "taco," and "weekend," the measure of information transmitted according to Shannon's formula would be 0, since $\log2 (1) = 0$. If it is certain that I will speak these words in my phone call, they communicate no information in Shannon's theory. A maximum of information thus equates to maximal unpredictability, and "to minimize all the noise that it would be impossible to eliminate is the price we pay for structurally programmable machines."[34]

While Shannon's work was undoubtedly formative for how Alexander implemented the IBM in the cause of his method, it was just, and only, that. Shannon's work was not influential in the sense of formative to Alexander's theory, but rather deployed as a convenient programming tactic. The details of how the 7090 executed Alexander's program to measure the quantity of information transmitted between requirements need not be detailed. It is enough to write that he uses Shannon's formula recursively to isolate groups of requirements that the measure indicates interacts with each other more strongly—or have greater information transmitted between themw—from other requirements that have less. The recursive measure operates hierarchically. In an example which began with 92 requirements, the program uses Shannon's measure, over several steps, to separate out and group requirements based on information transmitted between them, until the final groups of requirements contain as few as allowed by the measure. Determining these groups, Alexander asserts, will allow him to determine in what order each requirement should be considered in his effort to design a finished project, and to create, at last, the graphical depictions of the recommended design.

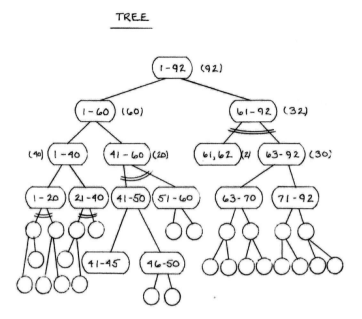

TREE

Christopher Alexander's hierarchical tree. From Alexander, *HIDECS* 2 (*Hierarchical Decomposition of Systems*).

It is crucial to note that Shannon's description of the amount of information transmitted has nothing to do say about the meaning of the transmission, just as the number of gigabytes used on my hard drive says nothing about the content of the files using these gigabytes. Shannon was in fact Sutherland's thesis advisor, although when Sutherland asserts that Sketchpad "opens up a new area of man-machine communication" through the system's ability "to converse rapidly through the medium of line drawings" he does not mean communication as the transmission of a stream of bits.[35] Likewise, Douglas Ross, who developed the conceptual framework to which Sutherland's ring structures are indebted, suggests that designer-CAD system interactions should be framed in terms of a "conversation," not in terms of organism-machine "communication."[36]

33 The binary logarithm of *n, log2 n*, is the power to which the number 2 must be raised to obtain the value *n*.

34 Friedrich Kittler, "There is No Hardware," *Literature, Media, Information Systems* (Amsterdam: OPA, 1997),155.

35 Sutherland, "Sketchpad," 1.

36 Douglas Ross, "A Personal View of the Personal Workstation," *HPW '86 Proceedings of the ACM Conference on The History of Personal Workstations*, 22.

As Ross and co-author Jorge Rodriguez wrote in 1963:

> It must be possible for [a designer] to carry out his design function in a way which is natural to him, and without his being aware that the statements and actions that he performs are in fact constructing and executing large numbers of highly complex computer programs.[37]

Ring structures permit a designer's fluid interaction with computer at the level of CAD interface, enabling, as Sutherland described, one to use light pen and screen to approximate pencil and paper. But at the same time this surface visuality meant software layers were affected to elude perception of the hardware at work beneath. Ring structures do not require a designer using the system to be able to understand the system on the level demanded of a computer programmer. The user targeted is one for whom the systems operations are invisible.

Although by 1969 a CAD programmer was no longer strapped to assembly language, Sketchpad's system structure remained a model for interactive graphics. As digital computing's technology advanced so did software multiply towards a corresponding hardware collapse. Software shrouded hardware, graphic interfaces hiding from its users the computing machine: "The high-level display and input constructs available in [the TX-2's high-level language] LEAP have been a success largely because the details of the supervisor calls are hidden from the programmer behind a consistent symbolism."[38] As in Carl Schmitt's political theology, "only the certainty of a power that radically surpasses every human capacity for control can guarantee the moral emphasis which puts an end to arbitrariness;" Or: "All deception is and remains self-deception."[39]

Channels, Tables, Files, and the Electrons Between

CRTs, the technology of the TX-2's display, are analog technologies, whereas the TX-2 a digital computer. The CRT display scope Sketchpad used was a vector display, a display type that was common use until the mid-1980s. For the CRT to display new shapes or transformations of existing ones, the digital bits in the TX-2's main memory were

37 Douglas T. Ross and Jorge E. Rodriguez, "Theoretical Foundations for the Computer-Aided Design System," *Proceedings— Spring Joint Computer Conference,* 1963.

38 Ivan Sutherland, James Forgie, and Marie Morello, "Graphics in Time-Sharing: A Summary of the TX-2 Experience," *Proceedings— Spring Joint Computer Conference,* 633.

39 Heinrich Meier, *The Lessons of Carl Schmitt: Four Chapters on the Distinction between Political Theology and Political Philosophy* (Chicago: University of Chicago Press, 2011), 11; Carl Schmitt, *Ex Captivitate Salus* (Köln : Greven Verlag, 1950), 88.

40 Sutherland, Forgie, and Morello, "Graphics in Time-Sharing," 629.

converted to analog voltages by way of a "vector generator," which caused an electron beam in the CRT to write on the CRT's phosphor coating.[40] Unlike the raster displays that replaced them, in vectors displays an electron beam directly follows the path of the line being generated, so the visible line is smooth and not pixilated. Although CRT TVs do not have vector displays, they are analog technologies, and a vector generator performs an action similar to a digital converter box for changing digital broadcast signals to analog ones for display on a CRT TV.

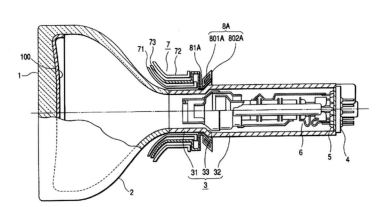

Diagram of cathode-ray tube .

To reconcile this digital-analog divide digitally, Sutherland's topological drawing files, in addition to linking drawing elements together in the Sketchpad software transmitted between memory and CPU, were essential to making drawings visible on the TX-2's CRT display scope. If Sutherland wished to select the endpoint of a line, he used a light pen to point at what looked on screen like the location of the line's endpoint. But what the light pen actually sensed was the CRT's glowing spot of phosphor, not the digital coordinate of the line's endpoint. Digital data about the endpoint was stored in a separate file, one that contained information about the topology of the line itself.

In order for Sketchpad to sense the spot of phosphor and map this to a digitally-stored endpoint, the file containing information about the coordinate of the spot had to be linked to the file containing information about the topology of the line. These spot coordinates were stored in something Sutherland termed a "display table", and Sutherland programmed Sketchpad so that this display table was able to reference or "point" to the "structured data table" that contained the coordinates of the line's endpoints. This meant that if a line's endpoints were selected and moved, the entire line would respond, and the endpoints be recalculated as part of the topology of the line. Likewise, if a spot on a line was sensed by the light pen, Sketchpad could understand the user meant to select the entire line. If the user wanted to transform this line, the program knew to recalculate the line's endpoints.

If Sutherland drew a line on the CRT using a light pen from the upper left-most to the lower right-most corner of the screen, he would have drawn a line that the computer interpreted as composed of approximately 1400 dots of illuminated phosphor. While he is sitting at the console drawing new shapes, he would want the initial line he had drawn to remain visible on screen. But the display technology of his CRT does not immediately permit this line to be displayed to the human eye continuously. Instead, each dot had to be refreshed 30 times per second. Watching a film is similar: a projector has to cycle through 24 still frames per second to make the motion picture appear continuous to a viewer.

Our example would require the computer to display about 30 x 1400 or 42,000 dots per second. While the TX-2 had about 1 MB of memory to the IBM's 150K, this refresh rate alone is still not so easy for Sutherland's system to maintain, and at the same time the TX-2 had to simultaneously process and store new data corresponding to any new drawings or transformations of existing drawings a Sketchpad user might choose to create.

Sketchpad's extensive use of the display scope brought up another issue, which is that the TX-2 could process information much more quickly than the CRT could display it. Today, computer displays are just one of a proliferating number of devices that can transmit data to and receive data from a computer's CPU. Keyboards, printers, iPods that can load songs from an iTunes library, wireless Internet routers, are now in the US nearly ubiquitous. All such devices are grouped under the descriptor input-output or I/O.
Even today, a central processor is much faster than I/O: my 2010 MacBook has a processor about 130% faster than my printer's. If the CPU directly controlled the printer's operations, it would slow down the ability of the CPU to execute other operations. Moreover, different I/O equipment operate at different speeds, so if I had a printer with a 130% faster processor this would not fix the disparity between the speed of the CPU and my display monitor, and if both were active and controlled by the CPU its speed would be even slower.

In a fundamental sense, the difference between how the TX-2 handled I/O and the way in which the IBM did is analogous to the difference between connecting your printer to you laptop through a USB cable and connecting your printer to a computer 6 feet tall, 2 feet wide, and 2 feet deep that would then wired to your laptop. So why did the IBM require all these intermediate computers? And why the TX-2 none?

For the IBM to accommodate 16 different I/O devices, about the maximum the computer could handle, would require up to 12 of these 24-cubic-feet intermediate computers, termed "channels," of two different types, as well as in fact a third computer, a multiplexor, to keep the I/O's transmission of data to and from the 7090/94's main memory from slowing down the CPU. To use the computer's I/O machines the owner of the IBM would have to buy these channels separately, and each channel cost more than $120,000. The price of one IBM channel was the same as an entire PDP-1 computer when it first came on the market, the TX series' first commercial production machine.[41]

The TX-2's solution to this issue is very similar to current solutions. Computer technologies now handle the disparate speeds of different I/O operating simultaneously by using "buffer storage," which is the same concept Sutherland used to solve the disparity between I/O speeds:

> Each [I/O] unit has its own buffer [storage]...For example, the in-out instruction that "fills" the display scope buffer [today the equivalent is called a "frame buffer," which stores, pixel by pixel, a digital image being displayed] takes no more than 10 microseconds, but the display itself takes from 20 to 100 microseconds, i.e. up to 10 times as long. While the display is busy, the computer can compute the next datum...but it can also initiate other in-out transfers [such as light pen input and graphic display output]. [42]

This solution permits the transfer of I/O data directly to or from the computer's memory without IBM's intermediate channels. It also permits the TX-2 to compensate for multiple active I/Os operating at different speeds, making them independent of the operation of the rest of the computer and bypassing the need for the CPU to control all I/O data being sent or received.[43] Separate I/Os such as display and light pen could operate at comparable speeds, and drawing a shape on screen appeared on screen almost immediately. Buffer storage was also the same solution Sutherland used to accommodate the need for the screen to refresh while a user was adding or manipulating shapes.

Lack of channels, however, came at a cost, as Sutherland articulated: "The TX-2 user must program each and every datum of [I/O] transfer."[44] Such laborious manual programming permitted intimate access by a systems expert, but only a systems expert, to the TX-2's capabilities. Sutherland's 1963 statement elided the instance, already by the 1940s, the gap between hardware and its operating site was increasingly insurmountable. Whirlwind's vacuum tubes, Williams tubes, are the same basic technology that until recently made it possible to see images on TVs and computer screens. These glass CRT tubes could be made to glow when the tube was storing or processing information, it needed only a coat of phosphor. But while in principle one could see the processing and memory operations of the computer in action, this system of physical signifiers was effaced, their screens

41 Ceruzzi, *A History of Modern Computing*, 128-9.

42 Sutherland, "Sketchpad," 165.

43 C. Gordon Bell et al., "The PDP-1 and Other 18-bit Computers," in *Computer Engineering: A DEC View of Hardware Systems Design*, eds. C. Gordon Bell, J. Craig Mudge, John E. McNamara (Bedford, MA: Digital Press, 1978), 126-7.

44 Sutherland, "Sketchpad," 167.

```
REQUIREMENT    054 IS CONNECTED TO--
  0  0  0  0  0  0  0  0  0  0  0  0  0  0  0  0  0  0  0  0  0  0  0  0  0  0  0  0  0  0  0  0  0  0  0  0  0
  0  0  0  0  0  0  0  0  0  0  0  0  0  0  0  0  0  0  0  0  0  0  0  0  0  0  0  0  0  0  0  0  0  0  0  0  0

REQUIREMENT    055 IS CONNECTED TO--
  0  0  0  0  0  0  0  0  0  0  0  0  0  0  0  0  0  0  0  0  0  0  0  0  0  0  0  0  0  0  0  0  0  0  0  0  0
  0  0  0  0  0  0  0  0  0  0  0  0  0  0  0  0  0  0  0  0  0  0  0  0  0  0  0  0  0  0  0  0  0  0  0  0  0

REQUIREMENT    056 IS CONNECTED TO--
  0  0  0  0  0  0  0  0  0  0  0  0  0  0  0  0  0  0  0  0  0  0  0  0  0  0  0  0  0  0  0  0  0  0  0  0  0
  0  0  0  0  0  0  0  0  0  0  0  0  0  0  0  0  0  0  0 57 58 59  0  0  0  0  0  0  0  0  0  0  0  0  0  0  0

REQUIREMENT    057 IS CONNECTED TO--
  0  0  0  0  0  0  0  0  0  0  0  0  0  0  0  0  0  0  0  0  0  0  0  0  0  0  0  0  0  0  0  0  0  0  0  0  0
  0  0  0  0  0  0  0  0  0  0  0  0  0  0  0  0  0  0 56  0 58  0  0  0  0  0  0  0  0  0  0  0  0  0  0  0  0

REQUIREMENT    058 IS CONNECTED TO--
  0  0  0  0  0  0  0  0  0  0  0  0  0  0  0  0  0  0  0  0  0  0  0  0  0  0  0  0  0  0  0  0  0  0  0  0  0
  0  0  0  0  0  0  0  0  0  0  0  0  0  0  0  0  0  0  0 56 57  0  0  0  0  0  0  0  0  0  0  0  0  0  0  0  0

REQUIREMENT    059 IS CONNECTED TO--
  0  0  0  0  0  0  0  0  0  0  0  0  0  0  0  0  0  0  0  0  0  0  0  0  0  0  0  0  0  0  0  0  0  0  0  0  0
  0  0  0  0  0  0  0  0  0  0  0  0  0  0  0  0  0  0 56  0  0  0 60 61  0  0  0  0  0  0  0  0  0  0  0  0  0

REQUIREMENT    060 IS CONNECTED TO--
  0  0  0  0  0  0  0  0  0  0  0  0  0  0  0  0  0  0  0  0  0  0  0  0  0  0  0  0  0  0  0  0  0  0  0  0  0
  0  0  0  0  0  0  0  0  0  0  0  0  0  0  0  0  0  0  0 59  0 61  0  0  0  0  0  0  0  0  0  0  0  0  0  0  0

REQUIREMENT    061 IS CONNECTED TO--
  0  0  0  0  0  0  0  0  0  0  0  0  0  0  0  0  0  0  0  0  0  0  0  0  0  0  0  0  0  0  0  0  0  0  0  0  0
  0  0  0  0  0  0  0  0  0  0  0  0  0  0  0  0  0  0  0  0 59 60  0  0  0  0  0  0  0  0  0  0  0  0  0  0  0

REQUIREMENT    062 IS CONNECTED TO--
  0  0  0  0  0  0  0  0  0  0  0  0  0  0  0  0  0  0  0  0  0  0  0  0  0  0  0  0  0  0  0  0  0  0  0  0  0
  0  0  0  0  0  0  0  0  0  0  0  0  0  0  0  0  0  0  0  0  0  0  0  0  0  0  0  0  0  0  0  0  0  0  0  0  0

REQUIREMENT    063 IS CONNECTED TO--
  0  0  0  0  0  0  0  0  0  0  0  0  0  0  0  0  0  0  0  0  0  0  0  0  0  0  0  0  0  0  0  0  0  0  0  0  0
  0  0  0  0  0  0  0  0  0  0  0  0  0  0  0  0  0  0  0  0  0  0  0  0  0  0  0  0  0  0  0  0  0  0  0  0  0

REQUIREMENT    064 IS CONNECTED TO--
  0  0  0  0  0  0  0  0  0  0  0  0  0  0  0  0  0  0  0  0  0  0  0  0  0  0  0  0  0  0  0  0  0  0  0  0  0
  0  0  0  0  0  0  0  0  0  0  0  0  0  0  0  0  0  0  0  0  0  0  0  0  0  0  0  0  0  0  0  0  0  0  0  0  0

REQUIREMENT    065 IS CONNECTED TO--
  0  0  0  0  0  0  0  0  0  0  0  0  0  0  0  0  0  0  0  0  0  0  0  0  0  0  0  0  0  0  0  0  0  0  0  0  0
  0  0  0  0  0  0  0  0  0  0  0  0  0  0  0  0  0  0  0  0  0  0  0  0  0  0  0  0  0  0  0  0  0  0  0  0  0
```

```
  0  0  0  0  0  0  0  8  0  0  0  0  0  0 15 16 17 18 19 20 21 22 23 24  0 26  0 28 29  0 31  0  0 34  0 36
  0  0  0  0  0 42  0  0  0  0  0  0  0  0  0  0  0  0  0  0 56  0 58  0  0  0  0  0 64  0  0 67 68  0 70 71 72
 73 74 75 76 77 78 79  0 81  0  0 84  0  0  0  0  0  0  0  0  0  0  0  0  0  0  0  0  0  0  0 0104  0106107108
  0  0  0  0

NEW LEVEL OF HIERARCHY
  1  2  0  4  5  6  7  0  0  0  0 12 13 14  0  0  0  0  0  0  0  0  0  0  0  0 27  0  0  0  0  0 33  0 35  0
 37 38 39 40  0  0 43 44 45  0  0 48 49 50 51 52 53  0  0  0  0  0 59 60 61 62 63  0 65 66  0  0 69  0  0  0
  0  0  0  0  0  0  0  0 82 83  0  0  0  0 88  0 90 91 92  0  0 95 96 97 98  0  0  0  0  0  0  0  0  0  0  0
109  0111112

  0  0  3  0  0  0  0  0  9 10 11  0  0  0  0  0  0  0  0  0  0  0  0  0 25  0  0  0  0 30  0 32  0  0  0  0
  0  0  0  0 41  0  0  0  0 46 47  0  0  0  0  0  0 54 55  0 57  0  0  0  0  0  0  0  0  0  0  0  0  0  0  0
  0  0  0  0  0  0  0 80  0  0  0  0 85 86 87  0 89  0  0  0  0 93 94  0  0  0  0 99100101102103  0105  0  0  0
0110  0  0

  0  0  0  0  0  0  0  8  0  0  0  0  0  0  0  0  0  0  0  0  0  0  0  0  0 26  0  0  0  0  0  0  0  0  0 36
  0  0  0  0  0 42  0  0  0  0  0  0  0  0  0  0  0  0  0  0 56  0 58  0  0  0  0  0 64  0  0 67 68  0 70 71 72
 73 74 75 76 77 78 79  0 81  0  0  0  0  0  0  0  0  0  0  0  0  0  0  0  0  0  0  0  0  0  0  0 0104  0106107108
  0  0  0  0

  0  0  0  0  0  0  0  0  0  0  0  0  0  0 15 16 17 18 19 20 21 22 23 24  0  0  0 28 29  0 31  0  0 34  0  0
  0  0  0  0  0  0  0  0  0  0  0  0  0  0  0  0  0  0  0  0  0  0  0  0  0  0  0  0  0  0  0  0  0  0  0  0
  0  0  0  0  0  0  0  0  0  0  0 84  0  0  0  0  0  0  0  0  0  0  0  0  0  0  0  0  0  0  0  0  0  0  0  0
  0  0  0  0

NEW LEVEL OF HIERARCHY
  0  0  0  0  0  0  0  0  0  0  0  0  0  0  0  0  0  0  0  0  0  0  0  0  0  0  0  0  0  0  0  0  0  0  0  0
  0  0  0  0  0  0 43  0  0  0  0  0  0  0  0  0  0 52  0  0  0  0  0  0  0  0  0  0 62 63  0  0  0  0  0  0
  0  0  0  0  0  0  0  0  0 83  0  0  0  0  0  0  0  0 92  0  0  0  0 97 98  0  0  0  0  0  0  0  0  0  0  0
  0  0111112

  1  2  0  4  5  6  7  0  0  0  0 12 13 14  0  0  0  0  0  0  0  0  0  0  0  0 27  0  0  0  0 33  0 35  0
 37 38 39 40  0  0 44 45  0  0 48 49 50 51  0 53  0  0  0  0  0 59 60 61  0  0 65 66  0  0 69  0  0  0
  0  0  0  0  0  0  0 82  0  0  0  0 88  0 90 91  0  0 95 96  0  0  0  0  0  0  0  0  0  0  0  0  0
109  0  0  0

CONTROL PASSED TO SCTRL
  0  0  0  0  0 30 32 41  0  0 55  0 80  0  0  0  0  0  0  0  0  0 0102 0105  0  0  0  0  0  0  0  0  0  0  0
  3  9 10 11 25  0  0  0 46 47 54  0 57  0 85 86 87 89 93 94 99100101  0103  0110  0  0  0  0  0  0  0  0  0  0
```

concealed by metal plates.[45] The tubes' simple logic gates could, nevertheless, be tested by inspecting all possible arrangements of input signals. This is approach, however, no longer applies to today's highly integrated circuits.

Alexander Out

ASC II arrays are Alexander's program's visual results, in the form of two printed matrices FAP instructed the IBM to output on an alphanumeric printer. The facing page includes examples of these printouts, effects of Alexander's theory, formalized in the sense of mathematician David Hilbert's prewar efforts:

> [Theory] should be embodied in a formal system. In a formal system, all the methods of constructing formulas to express mathematical propositions, and all the mathematical assumptions and principles of logic to be used in proving theorems, are to be governed by explicitly stated rules. The application of these rules shall only require working mechanically with the forms of the formulas, without taking into account their meanings.[46]

Alexander uses matrix outputs to draw what mathematics terms a graph theoretic tree, a mathematical structure that depicts a hierarchy of elements. The hierarchical tree became ubiquitous following the Second World War. As economic historian Philip Mirowski writes:

> The extensive form of the play of a game as a 'tree' could resemble equally the diagram of neutron-scattering problem in atomic bomb design, the flow chart of a computer program, and (inverted) the organization chart of a military unit or a multi-division corporation - the better to justify the transfer of mathematical techniques.[47]

These graphs have since further proliferated: they are used to represent communication networks, the organization of data, computer architectures, linguistics, sociology, and to model molecules in chemistry.

Matrix output of Alexander's interaction decompositions. Alexander, *HIDECS 2*, D9; Matrix output of Alexander's hierarchical tree. Alexander, *HIDECS 2*, D27.

45 F.C. Williams and T. Kilburn, "Electronic Digital Computers", *Nature* 162, no. 4117 (September 1948): 487.

46 Stephen C. Kleene, "The Work of Kurt Gödel," *The Journal of Symbolic Logic 41*, no. 4 (December, 1976): 763.

47 Phillip Mirowski, *Machine Dreams: Economics Becomes a Cyborg Science* (New York: Cambridge University Press, 2002), 71.

Chess game modeled through artificial intelligence;
and analysis of game. Allen Newell, J.C. Shaw, H. A.
Simon, "Chess-Playing Programs and the Problem of
Complexity," *IBM Journal*, October 1958.

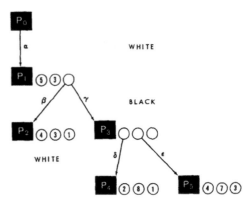

Figure 4 **Analysis.**

Compare this tree briefly to Johannes Itten's statement that "modern architecture is not a
few branches of an old tree - it is a new growth coming right from the roots," a metaphor
he used to diagram the 1923 Bauhaus curriculum as a series of concentric circles. The
"Basic Course" occupies the perimeter, moving inward with "study," "materials," and
finally "Building" in the center circle. Itten's diagram visualizes the statement by Walter
Gropius that, like the growth rings of a tree, "the training of an architect should be
concentric rather than sectional".[48] Alexander's tree is essentially other than Itten's,
and other than Sutherland's networked rings. It follows rather the hierarchical trees
that provide an illustration to one of Alexander's important references, the late-1950s
simulations of artificial intelligence by Herbert Simon, Alan Newell, and J.C. Shaw,
in which Simon et al argue that a digital computer manifests human intelligence as
demonstrated by its ability to play chess.

Alexander utilizes the program's printed matrix data plus his hierarchical tree data to
perform the final step in his design process, the sole step that asks followers to generate
drawings even minimally tangential to the drawing that has been fundamental to the
history of architectural design, at least since recorded during the age of Caesar Augustus
by Vitruvius's *De architectura*. Alexander's request for drawings is the final iteration of his
design method, the only moment in *Notes on the Synthesis of Form* which addresses the
"synthesis" of his text's title.

Return to the example of Alexander's Indian village. This application of Alexander's method means that requirements in A1, A2, and A3 relate to livestock and agriculture. "A1," as he writes, "consists of a central control point through which all cattle leaving any compound have to pass. This control point provides a hoof bath, dairy, and a link to the main road."[49] This is what the drawing for A1 is to represent, while drawings corresponding to A2 is a group of cattle stalls, A3 a gate in the village compound wall. Next in his method is to combine these diagrams A1, A2, and A3 to create drawing A. He repeats this method of combining drawings for each other set of requirements B, C, and D. Alexander contends these combined drawings satisfies the requirements already met by diagrams lower on his hierarchical tree. Lastly, combining drawings A through D, he generates a diagram that encompasses the layout of the entire village. To actually design the village he need merely transcodes these diagrams into the physical world. While he was initially solicited to reorganize the entire village of Bavra, the realized outcome was a single school house.

I have argued that Alexander's theory and resulting design method were cast not by the anthropology, psychology, information theory, or cybernetics he references, at times extensively, in *Notes*. Rather, his choice to program his method into an IBM mainframe between 1961 and 1963 conditioned his theory to the essential exclusion of all other strategies for thinking about design. Yet just as the ontology of his IBM was revealed through his programming, so did Sutherland's Sketchpad conceal the operations of his TX-2, a divergence from the IBM via which the trajectory of CAD and graphic user interfaces today comply ever more deeply in a suppression obscuring machine operations.

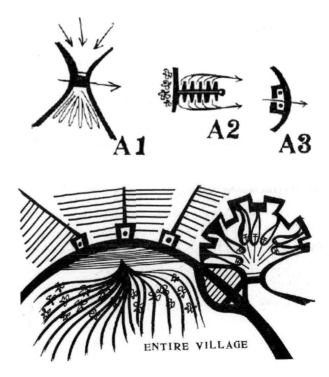

Christopher Alexander's composition of diagrams for the redesign of Bavra, India. Reprinted by permission of the publisher from *Notes on the Synthesis of Form*, by Christopher Alexander, p. 156-9, 173, Cambridge, MA: Harvard University Press, ©1964 by the President and Fellows of Harvard College. Copyright© renewed 1992 by Christopher Alexander.

Christopher Alexander's composition of diagrams for the redesign of Bavra, India. Reprinted by permission of the publisher from *Notes on the Synthesis of Form*, by Christopher Alexander, p. 156-9, 173, Cambridge, MA: Harvard University Press, ©1964 by the President and Fellows of Harvard College. Copyright © renewed 1992 by Christopher Alexander.

facing page, Christopher Alexander's schoolhouse in Bavra, India. Photo: Christopher Alexander.

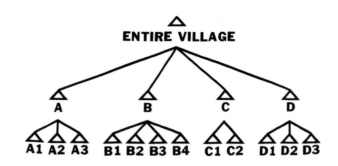

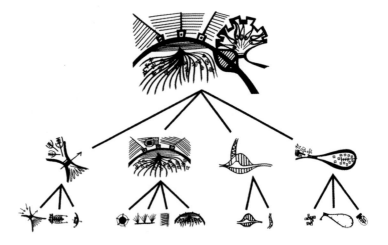

It is worth considering briefly, in conclusion, the role of William Ross Ashby's cybernetics within Alexander's theory, as his is by far the most seemingly influential on Alexander's theory. Ashby's 1952 *Design for a Brain* elaborates on an electromechanical apparatus he built which he termed a Homeostat.[50] The Homeostat, operating through a collection of magnets, relays, and electrical circuits, was to explain the principle which makes homeostasis—the condition of organism stability in light of disruptions from environmental conditions—possible. Ashby envisioned complex homeostatic behavior contingent upon independent subsystems, each "ultrastable" subsystem able to adapt independently for an accumulation of adaptive behaviors. Ashby argued the homeostasis observed in his machine was a result of these ultrastable subsystems, in turn the principle responsible for adaptive behaviors in organism or machine. Twelve years later Alexander would write that a successful method of design is a form of homeostatic adaptation which must proceed through a series of independent subsystems, each subsystem generating adaptive behaviors.[51]

But the method through which Alexander implements the decomposition of a village into a system of requirements and thereon into a hierarchy of requirement subsystems, each more independent than the last, is not Ashby's method; it is that of a Turing Machine's, the machine to which an IBM FAP program must conform.[52] The lacunae separating Ashby's Homeostat from an IBM mainframe is the breach of modeling the physical world through analog not digital means. The criticality of this difference is addressed by physicist Brosl Hasslacher during his tenure at Los Alamos National Laboratory:

> We have a situation in which we have reached an analytic limit and cannot describe complex structures by an algorithm which takes significantly less time to evolve an outcome than observing a copy of the system itself...
>
> Within a physical computing machine, one designs a virtual machine so that an appropriate symbolic image...defines the transition table in the finite control of an equivalent Turning machine.
>
> The observer-analyst ... has to analyze the output of such machines within the constraint of living in a physical world. No one has access to infinite computing resources; this concept is not useful when interacting with the physical world or...a model of it.[53]

In short, Alexander is responsible for "introduc[ing] the idea of a standard model for the physical world: the idea of a skeletal game, and fix[ing] on what kinds of computational architectures we are allowed to use as analyzers."[54]

48 Walter Gropius, *The Scope of Total Architecture* (New York: Collier Books, 1943 [1970]), 56.

49 Alexander, *Notes*, 155.

50 William Ross Ashby, *Design for a Brain: the Origin of Adaptive Behaviour* (London: Chapman & Hall, 1952).

51 Alexander, *Notes*, 15-72.

52 For an alternative interpretation see Philip Steadman, *The Evolution of Designs: Biological Analogy in Architecture and the Applied Arts* (New York: Cambridge University Press, 1979); I have also investigated this alternative further in Alise Upitis, "Nature

Normative: The Design Methods Movement, 1944-1967," unpublished Ph.D. dissertation, MIT Department of Architecture, 2008.

53 Brosl Hasslacher, "Beyond the Turing Machine," in Rolf Herken, ed., *The Universal Turning Machine: A Half-Century Survey*, 2nd. ed (New York: Springer-Verlag, 1995), 388.

54 Ibid., 389.

CAROLINE A. JONES

Artist / System

Introduction

One of modernism's most effective modes (perhaps the very *modus* of the modern) is positivist, empiricist, systematic—terrain that is more familiar to modern architecture than to art. Academic Beaux-Arts traditions (chiaroscuro, rendering, the sketch) were put in competition with positivist protocols of engineering (structural analysis, material innovation, mechanical drawing) whenever industrialization was at hand. The founding of MIT's architecture school in 1865 forms one crystallizing moment in this dynamic; technology and architecture's long-term imbrication with military objectives ensured that the second World War would bring another phase of crystallization—or perhaps crisis is a better word for the fractured, faceted nature of postwar proposals about art, architecture, and technology emanating from MIT in the 1960s. This essay will pursue a partial history of that trajectory as it culminated in late '60s Systems Art, a surprisingly un-orchestrated crescendo of the harmonic oscillations between "fine art . . . and technological science" that had always hummed within MIT's broad conception of architectural practice, and that came momentarily to rest at two arts venues in the Institute in 1967-68.[1]

In that brief period, within months of each other, a solo exhibition was mounted of Hans Haacke's air and water works at the Institute's Hayden Gallery (October 1967), while just across campus Haacke's mentors, Zero Group artist Otto Piene and Systems Art theorist Jack Burnham, were named in the first group of fellows at MIT's new Center for Advanced Visual Studies (CAVS, in 1968). The exhibition could not have gone unnoticed in the MIT community, kicked off as it was by an event in which Haacke tethered a string of helium balloons near the shockingly new student center—a brutalist structure still under construction on Massachusetts Avenue, across from the old Beaux-Arts entrance to the Institute.[2] But if Haacke's "systems" resonated at MIT, the exhibition seems largely to have escaped artworld notice. This artist's reputation instead emanated from a more visible nexus of later exhibitions in New York: "Software" (Jewish Museum, 1970), "Information" (MoMA, 1970), and of course the *succès de scandale* of his Guggenheim exhibition

1 Description of MIT's program by Mark Wigley, "Prosthetic Theory: the Disciplining of Architecture," *Assemblage* 15 (August 1991): 14. Founder of the MIT department of architecture, William R. Ware, positioned "the history of architecture, the theory of architectural ornamentation, the laws

of proportion, of harmony and of geometrical and naturalist decoration" as humanist fine arts, while "mechanic arts employed in building, supervising, specifications, contracts, lighting, ventilation, heating, etc." were staged as the scientific side of architecture. William R. Ware, letter to

John Runkle (secretary of the Massachusetts Institute of Technology), 27 April 1865, p. 2, as cited by Wigley, 26 fn. 35.

2 As Wayne Andersen (the curator and art historian responsible for the Haacke exhibition) recalls it, the wind swept the balloons dangerously close to traffic

on Massachusetts Avenue, and he and Haacke decided to authorize the immediate untethering of the balloons. Andersen, interview with the author, 13 July 2009.

cancellation in 1971. The tenure of Burnham and Piene also had more impact outside MIT in the late 1960s, as Burnham's articles "Systems Esthetics" (1968) and "Real Time Systems" (1969) came out in *Artforum*, and Piene's "Sky Art" events were staged in New York's Central Park. Inserting MIT in that better known history is to revise what we know of the art-science and art-technology stories, long dominated by the media centers of New York and Los Angeles.[3] This revision entails questions of experience, the subject, technology and knowledge production that dominate the contemporary global artworld today.

What was the modernity of MIT in 1967? It had little to do with *style* ("machine art," streamlining, futurist force lines), but consistently sought to emphasize *process*. Similarly, "Art" for the post-Civil War founders of MIT would have had little to do with the lovely

3 Tales should also be told of the luminance of other "marginal" centers, such as Milwaukee, Cleveland, and Denver who showed unusual hospitality to kinetic art, or various University galleries that proved hotbeds of experimentation in new media.

4 The gender divide, about which little can be said here, continues into the 1960s, as when President Stratton asked Wayne Andersen to take over Mrs. Stratton's pet Art Committee, to bring it more in line with the Institute's wishes and technical objectives. Andersen interview, 13 July 2009.

Hans Haacke, *Sky Line* 1967, Haacke standing on the roof of the new student center. 1400' nylon line held aloft by helium balloons; event staged in conjunction with the opening of Haacke's solo exhibition at MIT's Hayden Gallery. Courtesy of the artist, © Hans Haacke/Artists Rights Society.

Impressionist paintings their wives were commissioning, collecting, and producing.[4] The "art" inserted by the founders at the core of MIT's mission derived from *techne*—the art of crafting, of making, of innovating and engineering, conceived as supplemental to *physis*—the manner of nature's operation. The consistently programmatic aspirations of the founders confirms the non-stylistic modality of this modernity: "The trouble is technological; *there is a want of system and method,*"—a failing this first U.S. school of architecture would aim to correct.[5] In sum, *modernization* rather than *modernism* was the local cause, and the Haacke/Piene/Burnham moment fit this long trajectory. There is one important distinction, however. While the 1960s' uptake of "Systems" art—at MIT and the U.S. artworld more generally —was one more aspect of this search for modernity in *process* rather than representation, in the postwar period that aspiration would fuse the craft of *techne* with nature's operative *physis*.[6] "Systems Art" impulses in the 1960s revealed a widespread striving to nail down the protocols that govern life, technology, and art, to generate truths about "methods and systems," to circulate them (and us) through forms of techno-sociality still generative today.

Let me be clear about what is restrictive, and what expansive, about my argument. The exhibitions at MIT's Hayden Gallery after the second world war had little immediate artworld impact. Yet looking at one of those exhibitions (Haacke's one-man show in 1967) yields a microhistory of the "systems and methods" contributed by MIT to the increasing conceptualism and process orientation of postwar art. Generally speaking, images and methods of technology had not fared well in the two decades prior to Haacke's show. Artists of the late 1940s had continued the Surrealists' rejection of the first highly technological "Great War" via an embrace of the biomorphic and irrational. This evolved in the 1950s to widespread anti-technological practices in Europe, the Americas, and Japan producing *tabulae rasae* of pulverized images, tortured surfaces, and punctured supports.[7] (Architecture, of course, had its Bauhaus as a rejoinder to such irrational trajectories.) How and why did this ubiquitous look of an anguished humanism then turn, so completely, to a pervasive technophilic "cool" in the art movements of the 1960s?[8] Setting aside for the moment the well-rehearsed history of Minimal Art (traced from Stella's black paintings in 1958 to philosophy's naming of the movement in 1965), I'm proposing that a specific

5 Ware, *An Outline of a Course in Architectural Instruction* (Boston, 1865): 9, as cited in Wigley, "Prosthetic Theory," 13; (emphasis added).
6 See Jacques Derrida, "Economimesis," *Diacritics* 11, no. 2 (Summer 1981): 3-25.

7 Even the formerly machinic art of Theodore Roszak, commissioned by MIT to produce a belltower above the 1953-55 chapel designed by Eero Saarinen, morphed after the war as the artist added "rustication" to the sculpture's base in an effort to "soften" the technological.

8 This transformation can be seen in the work of a single artist such as Robert Smithson, whose baroque and operatic drawings of 1963- 64 gave way to minimalist sculpture in 1965. For this larger argument see my *Machine in the Studio* (Chicago 1996/98).

9 Personal correspondence between Jack Burnham and Edward A. Shanken, April 23 1998, cited in Shanken, "The House that Jack Built: Jack Burnham's Concept of 'Software' as a Metaphor for Art," *Leonardo Electronic Almanac* 6, no. 10 (1998), online at <http://www.artexetra.com/House.

study of systems art in various sectors of MIT around 1967-69 can reveal how the struggle against one kind of modernism (saturated by seemingly bankrupt "humanist" values) yielded another kind of modernism (systematic, empirical, positivist, and technophilic). In the larger frame this volume wants to articulate, such a systematic "second" modernism can be seen as both enduring (stemming from the Enlightenment and maturing in the industrial age), and a part of what occupies and gives form to the "great hiatus between standard modernism and postmodernism," in the retrospective account of Systems Art's great prophet and theorist, Jack Burnham.[9] Systems Art revealed Minimalism to be a kind of *techné*, which its investigations would problematize as static in relation to the more dynamic processes of *physis*.

MIT is not exactly a causal agent in this narrative, but neither am I pretending to offer a neutral dip into the ocean of history. I aim glancingly at the surface of this discursive sea, avoiding a deep plunge into the viscous histories of the School of Architecture and Planning, skirting whirlpools in the Visual Arts Programs, and skipping like a stone over depths in the Center for Advanced Visual Study (CAVS). The bulk of this paper will focus on a single artist brought only briefly to MIT but galvanized by that experience to clarify his own tropism towards systems: Hans Haacke. Haacke's work and ideas, revealed in that first solo exhibition in 1967 (a year before CAVS even opened), will serve to capture a moment in the configuration of "Systems" as a peculiarly ambivalent aesthetic operation within a burgeoning military-industrial complex centered at MIT during a cultural moment in which that complex was coming under its greatest attack.[10]

What will interest us above all is that for Haacke at this time, "Systems art" posited no human subject in the art equation. Stimulated by his upcoming solo exhibition at MIT, Haacke wrote a slew of short statements (most in September 1967) that make this position emphatically clear.[11] The very extension of mechanical systems and cybernetic theory into the human sciences during the early 1950s seems to have played a particular (if occluded) role in the *removal* of the human from '60s systems art. That is, the more systems theory was brought in to theorize and manage the unruly human, the more it could emblematize

html>; also in Roy Ascott, ed., *Reframing Consciousness: Art and Consciousness in the Post-Biological Era* (Proceedings of the Second International CAiiA Research Conference, Exeter: Intellect, 1999.)

10 Student protests attempted to shut down various functions of the university in 1968. At that time, MIT's Instrumentation Laboratory was receiving over $50 million from the Department of Defense and NASA—by 1969 the budget for this weapons research branch of engineering constituted *one-quarter* of MIT's total operating budget. MIT's President Howard Johnson gained praise for his handling of the situation, culminating in the Institute's divestment of the Instrumentation Lab in 1970 and a partial restructuring of the Lincoln Lab to be more open. See the indispensable dissertation by Elizabeth Finch, "Languages of Vision: György Kepes and the 'New Landscape' of Art and Science," (City University of New York, 2005), particularly pages 276-77.

11 These statements are published in Jones, *Hans Haacke 1967* (Cambridge: MIT List Visual Art Center, 2011).

Protests against MIT Research, November 7, 1969. Photo: Associated Press.

the end of humanism in artistic practice. The examination of Haacke's systems art will take us to the inheritance of systems theory in the contemporary art world's obsession with "experience"—and the way present-day techno-art works to obscure that debt.

From Kassel to Philadelphia to Cologne to New York to Cambridge

As curator Walter Grasskamp reports, when Haacke was a young art student in Kassel he was attracted to the latest in '50s abstraction. Its European adherents were divided between expressionism (in the French mode of *tachisme* or *informe*) and the cool geometrics of the Parisian GRAV (Group de Recherche d'Art Visuel) or Düsseldorf Zero Groups; he was later included with these artists in a series of exhibitions organized in Amsterdam under the provocation *nul*. Why was expressionism *cancelled* in this way, in favor of what Haacke praised as the unmotivated automatism of geometry (in turn to be replaced by systems)? Clearly for an art student in coldwar Germany, "expressionism" was charged territory—once forbidden and desired, it was both the earliest stylistic formulation of German modernism and the latest ideological tool of the Cold War. As Haacke recently recalled his mood in the late 1950s, "I was intrigued by non-compositional developments."[12] In place of "expression" the artist sought the appearance of an algorithm that would replace intention with iteration, delectable composition with non-composition.

Yet this "non-composition" was not fully machinic; it operated with a notion of where the avant-garde was to be located around 1960 in a specifically scientific rapprochement with nature. Haacke had benefitted from the immediate postwar reconstruction of a liberal sphere in Western Germany, materialized by the return of those images and artists banned as "Entartete Kunst," quite literally brought into view when his high school art teacher gained permission to install art reproductions of formerly banished works into every classroom ("Impressionism . . . Van Gogh, Cézanne, what have you . . . but real stuff").

The teacher responsible for Haacke's teenage instruction was really very inspiring. And he also introduced us a little bit into art history. And it became clear to me that art was not just the skill of rendering things, but that in art history people meant to say something, and also to say it in very different ways.

Note that even in Haacke's memory of this earliest moment, the claim of art as mimesis is challenged, by art as a potentially semasiographic system. Similarly, for Haacke art was not a romantic bohemianism but a trained, professional path. Following his father's practical injunction to find a career (rather than simply "be an artist"), Haacke studied art education and participated as a student worker in setting up the second *Documenta* exhibition in 1959.[13] Seeing the crews lay out Jackson Pollock's apparently non-compositional paintings (and watching curators relegate an unpleasantly real Rauschenberg *Bed* to a back room) were formative experiences; hearing the exhibition team casually discuss artists' reputations as indexed by the market was another.

The exposure to Pollock may have been what goaded Haacke to split the two terms of the hotly exported "Abstract Expressionism"—he adopted the uncompromising, non-compositional mode of abstraction but rejected the "marketable" humanist component of expressionism. Giving his "cosmic" overall paintings ironic titles signaled this rejection. As he commented recently, "when you see something that you can associate with stars, you're tempted to go that way, and I didn't want that. . . . I was overly wary of the romanticism." The wariness is almost palpable in an early photograph of Haacke with Zero Group members at the opening of the 1965 *nul* exhibtion in Amsterdam—the artist peers out at us from the edge of the group, looking to the side of the photographer at someone, or something, literally "off stage." The Zero Group's remanent romanticism – making paintings with fire, smoke, and projected light—was something against which Haacke was distancing himself. What would be useful were Zero's iterative strategies—notably present in founder Otto Piene's early "raster" paintings from 1957. Predating the founding of "Zero" itself, these *Rasterbilder* reportedly drew Haacke's admiration and emulation in inkless intaglio prints and paintings given "systematic" titles.[14]

12 Haacke, interview with the author, March 29, 2009. If not otherwise cited, Haacke quotes are taken from this interview.
13 The first Documenta was in 1955, the art added as an afterthought to the program funded by the German Federal Government to support a city beautification and garden show. The diversion of funds to the arts, and the construction of the show as a repeating exhibition, were debts handsomely repaid, as when Joseph Beuys set up *7000 Eichen* (7000 Oaks) as part of the 1982 Documenta, planting oaks and other trees throughout Kassel with funds largely provided by the American non-profit, the Dia Foundation.
14 Otto Piene recalls meeting Haacke when the latter was an 18-year-old art student around 1957-58. According to Piene, when Haacke visited him in Dusseldorf he brought as a calling card a small relief print "like my raster paintings . . . very early, very rare," white on white with raised dots instead of Piene's colored oil dabs on canvas. Even in this first encounter, Haacke was upping the ante on the Zero Group's loose and intuitive abstraction, draining out color and replacing vision with the tactile. Piene, interviewed by the author 11 March 2009.

Hans Haacke, *Ce n'est past la voie Lactee*, (*This Is Not the Milky Way*), 1960. Oil on canvas, 120 x 60 cm, 47.24 in x 23.62 in. Collection of the artist.

Hans Haacke, *B1-61*,
1961. Acrylic on canvas,
85 x 85 cm, 33.46 x 33.46
in. Collection of the artist.

Intermittently involved with Zero and joining its European exhibitions, Haacke nonetheless applied for a Fulbright and moved to Philadelphia in 1961 (after that year, he stretched out his stay, moving to live in New York through 1963). It was during this time that he turned away from painting altogether and began to use systems theory explicitly to remove experience" from the artwork equation. Crucial to this turn was his pilgrimage to visit Jack Burnham in Delaware. It seems likely that Burnham was the decisive vector as Haacke began reading the systems theories of Bertalanffy and Wiener, and committed himself to exploring their implications for art.[15] Returning to Germany to teach at the Pädagogische Hochschule in Cologne, Haacke renewed his friendship with Piene, who kept him informed about the quickening techno/kinetic art scene in New York. As Piene tells the story, Haacke was coming off the boat for his second visit to the U.S. in 1965 (New York again, a move that turned out to be permanent) when he got Piene's telegram informing him that he had been given a slot for a show at the Howard Wise Gallery on 57th Street; an opportunity that would come to fruition in January 1966.[16] It was this show, amplified by several important new pieces, that would be installed in MIT's Hayden Gallery in the fall of 1967.

15 "I met him [Burnham, in 1961-62] when I was in Philadelphia. He was a junior faculty in some Delaware college. And somehow, I don't remember how, I met a graduate student at the University of Philadelphia, who's still around, by the name of Jimmy Harithas . . . I don't know how he had

heard, or knew [Burnham]. Well, he had a car, I didn't have a car. We made a trip down to this college and met Jack Burnham. And since then we were in touch." Although Haacke now recalls reading both Bertalanffy and Wiener in the early '60s, I note that Weiner was initially better known (especially in the U.S.).

Bertalanffy's General Systems Theory developed out of a more specific initial focus on biology (see Bertalanffy, L.v. " Der Organismus als physikalisches System betrachtet," *Die Naturwissenschaften*, [1940] 28: 521-531); the "General" systems theory was first published in German, "Zu

einer allgemeinen Systemlehre," *Biologia Generalis*, [1949] 19:114-129. It is more likely that Haacke read *General Systems Theory* later, in English, when Burnham proposed a couse on "Systems and Art" when he came to MIT in 1968. See *Hans Haacke 1967* (2011). **16** Interview by the author

Technoculture and Experience

Hans Haacke, second from left, at the opening of *nul* (zero) exhibition at the Stedelijk Museum in Amsterdam, 1965. Otto Piene, founder of the Zero Group is right of center, in the first row.

Haacke came to an MIT still ambitious to capture, capitalize, and/ or critique the *cultural* expectations fueled by the terrifying success of wartime technology. Not surprisingly, the Institute's immediate postwar initiatives in architecture had turned to the pragmatic, non-spiritualist version of the Bauhaus that Walter Gropius brought to the Boston area, personified by Gropius's little-remembered GSD student William Wurster.[17] Wurster had been hired out of graduate school in 1944 to direct MIT's architecture program (a post he held for only 6 years before returning to his native California to revamp the school at Berkeley),[18] and in turn Wurster brought to MIT the tangential *Bauhaüsler* György Kepes (formerly a partner of Moholy-Nagy in London before joining his mentor at the New Bauhaus in Chicago). Wurster offered Kepes the job in a letter written just weeks after the U.S. bombing of Hiroshima and Nagasaki—but MIT had been preparing for the war's end for years. Specifically, the question was how to maintain the scaling up of architectural and technical education that had taken place after the U.S. entry into

with Otto Piene, 11 March 2009.

17 "Over and over again I would reiterate that Modern is a point of view not a style," Wurster wrote in a 1936 *Architect and Engineer* article. "And everyone seems so determined to pin set things to it. Use the site—the money—the local materials—

the client—the climate to decide what it shall be." Cited in the profile on Wurster by Gordon Young, "Blueprint for Obscurity," *Metro* (January 18-24, 1996) San Jose, CA, online at http://www.metroactive.com/papers/metro/01.18.96/wurster-9603.html, accessed July 2009.

18 See Alan Michelson,

"Towards a Regional Synthesis: The Suburban and Country Residences of William Wilson Wurster, 1922-1964," (PhD dissertation, Stanford University, 1994).

19 Through the advocacy of a student at Harvard's Graduate School of Design, whose wealthy family had extensive holdings on Cape Cod, plots

of land were sold in the '40s to Marcel Breuer, Walter Gropius, Eero Saarinen, and the Chermayeff brothers, all of whom built modernist dachas in the woods of what would become National Seashore in the mid-1960s. Eventually György Kepes also bought a house in the Wellfleet woods, but it

the war in 1941, and how to hold on to MIT's national position of leadership in the planned postwar period? As part of an answer, on August 30, 1945, Wurster's letter was sent to Kepes in Wellfleet on Cape Cod, where a buzzing enclave of expatriate Central European designers had been summering since the late '30s (along with many artworld types such as Haacke's future New York gallerist, Howard Wise).[19] Wurster, who had already eliminated the MIT tradition of having students send their designs for evaluation by the Beaux-Arts Institute of Design in New York, explained to Kepes how he hoped to invigorate the visual training of MIT students: "We are eager to make the Drawing (for want of a more complete word) a strong and integral part of the school."[20] The strange definite article betrays a conception of "*the Drawing*" that was both reified and ambiguous: always-already linked with *disegno*, it suggested a notion of conceptual-technical instrumentality also reflected in the statement by MIT's then-president Karl Compton that "design [is] the central theme of all good architecture [but] the techniques of its application must continually adapt themselves to the evolution of the technical and social environment."[21]

As Wurster knew, Kepes had no intention of teaching "the Drawing" in traditional Beaux-Arts fashion. Chiaroscuro would give way to visual exercises with modernist technologies and aims—photomontage, collage, "spatial organization." The goal was a non-mimetic training of the perceptual apparatus, further extended by mechanical vision (cameras but also microphotography, aerial views, "Doc" Edgerton's stroboscopic images, etcetera). Given this background, it might seem natural to assume that Kepes was behind the invitation to Haacke, also an expatriate invested in abstract experiments and new technologies. But that assumption would be wrong. In fact, Haacke's more circuitous path (invited by art historian Wayne Andersen who had been hired in 1965 by MIT's president Julius Stratton in direct opposition to Kepes) reflects the extent to which even Kepes's opponents had to occupy the receptive and allusive environment he had created.[22] Kepes animated this world (largely local, but with an export operation) through undefined buzzwords that produced a rhetorical integument promising to unify the farthest reaches of science and art, initially through Gestalt psychology and linguistics, but eventually dipping into the cybernetics and systems theory that MIT had come to represent.[23] Yet despite the undeniable impact of Kepes's insistence that vision was a "language," that we needed to

is unlikely he could have afforded this by 1945.

20 William Wurster to György Kepes in Wellfleet, MA, Kepes papers, AAA Reel 5303 fr 0175, as cited by Elizabeth Finch, in her "Languages of Vision," 2005.

21 Karl Compton, *MIT Bulletin, President's Report issue* 1937-38, 74:1 (October 1938): 20.

22 Per interview with Wayne Andersen, 13 July 2009, the architecture department and Kepes in particular opposed his 1965 appointment, which was initiated by then-president Julius Stratton to reassert control over the visual arts at MIT. Stratton wanted Andersen to take over the management of the Hayden Gallery, to provide faculty leadership for the unruly Committee on Visual Arts, and eventually (under the subsequent president, Howard Johnson) to supervise the campus art collections which were—and remain—outside architecture department controls. Stratton offered Andersen the choice of departments to join; he joined the Architecture Department despite the opposition of several members of the faculty, Kepes preeminent among them.

23 Kepes's first book had two forewords by no less than architectural theorist Siegfried Giedion and

become experts in "optical communication," and that such communication must utilize "plastic methods," his more than 20-year tenure at MIT had failed, by 1967, to fuel any concrete innovations in the artworld—something "Systems Art" was burningly ambitious to do. Haacke's moment at the Hayden Gallery, and Kepes's appointment of Jack Burnham to CAVS soon thereafter, illuminated the gap that had opened up between Kepes's rhetoric and practice, while suggesting how eager he was to join the systems-cybernetic revolution by 1968.[24] Haacke and Burnham represented certain intoxicating possibilities open to visual artists in the 1960s, versus the more restricted terrains of architectural pedagogy and urban theory in which Kepes had long labored (and on which he arguably had his greatest impact).[25]

Kepes had been invited to MIT in 1946 as a direct result of the "small publishing sensation" of his *Language of Vision* (1944), a single-author redaction of his course at the New Bauhaus which eventually went into thirteen printings in English and further editions in other European languages.[26] The *Vision and Value* series he produced after coming to MIT tried to replicate that first success, but on a model of edited volumes

Jack Burnham's cover essay on Hans Haacke with *Blue Sail* and *Condensation Cube*, Tri-Quarterly Supplement, 1967.

---

semanticist S.I. Hayakawa. Kepes acknowledges "his indebtedness to the Gestalt psychologists . . . Max Wertheimer, K. Koffka, and W. Kohler . . . used in the first part of the book to explain the laws of visual organization." György Kepes, *The Language of Vision* (Chicago: Theobald, 1944): 4.

24 In addition to Piene and Burnham, Kepes invited Wen-Ying Tsai, an engineer who had emigrated to the U.S. in 1950 and become a "cybernetic sculptor" showing alongside Haacke and Piene at the Howard Wise Gallery in New York. Tsai was a CAVS fellow from 1969-71.

25 For the architectural and urbanist impact, see Reinhold Martin, *The Organizational Complex: Architecture, Media, and Corporate Space* (Cambridge: MIT Press, 2003). Kepes's collaboration with and impact on Kevin Lynch is certainly salient here.

26 Editions of Kepes's book came out in Spanish (1969), German (1970), Italian (1971), and Hungarian (1979). Finch, "Languages of Vision," 58, fn 24.

rather than as single-author works. These continued to institutionalize his own pedagogy, but reflected the general synergy Kepes was trying to create within a much larger institution, inaugurating a new formula in which tasteful beige linen covers enclosed a range of luminaries from various fields of discourse. *The Education of Vision*, for example (1965), comprised essays by Rudolf Arnheim, Anton Ehrenzweig, Johannes Itten, and Paul Rand; *Module, Proportion, Symmetry, Rhythm* (1966) invited the scientists C.H. Waddington and Stanislas Ulam to appear with John Cage and others. Kepes fought hard for and succeeded in including both the cybernetician Norbert Wiener and the upstart systems theorist Ludwig von Bertalanffy in his books, but his dreams were ecumenical rather than polemical. In crucial distinction to the anti-humanist agenda in '60s Systems Art, Kepes's project remained a deeply humanist continuation of the Unity of Science movement inaugurated by the Vienna Circle, onto which he had grafted his own experience of the "Science and Society" group from his years in London.[27] As he wrote in one of the *Vision and Value* books in 1965:

> The *essential unity* of firsthand sensation and intellectual concept makes artistic vision different from scientific cognition or simple sense-feeling response to situations. It combines both. To repeat, it is the *unity* of the sensory, emotional, and rational that can make the orderly forms of artistic vision unique contributions to human culture.[28] [emphasis added]

Kepes's ameliorative project aimed through analogy and translation to bind the diverging cultures of science and art (while preserving the function of the intellectual as binding agent).[29] By contrast, the objects and arguments of "Systems Art" were staging grounds for techno-sociality in itself. They did not aim to bridge the distance between a technologized world and the still-human subject, they confronted viewers (at least initially) with the absolute alterity of non-human systems. In theory, these might require the production of a subjectivity/objectivity that is altogether different than the human. As I will suggest, Haacke ultimately backed away from the rather extraordinary implications of his earliest systems pieces at MIT and the statements he issued to support them. But it is precisely these earliest forays that interest me, revealing a moment when Haacke and his key interpreter

27 For the Vienna Circle and the Unity of Science Movement, see Peter L. Galison, "Aufbau/Bauhaus: Logical Positivism and Architectural Modernism," *Critical Inquiry* 16, no. 4. (1990), 709-752; and "The Americanization of Unity," *Daedalus* 127, no. 1, *Science in Culture* (Winter, 1998),

45-71. The "Science and Society" group was led by J. G. Crowther, a mentor of Kepes's in London and the author of *An Outline of the Universe* (London, 1931), on which see Finch, "Languages of Vision," 115: "Natural patterns were seen as metaphors of a utopian future." Also see Gerald Holton, who

discusses the founding in 1947 of the Institute for the Unity of Science at the American Academy of Arts and Science in Cambridge, in his article "From the Vienna Circle to Harvard Square: The Americanization of a European World Conception," in *Scientific Philosophy: Origins and Developments*, ed.

F. Stadler (Dordrecht: Kluwer 1993): 47-73.
28 Kepes, introduction to *The Education of Vision* (New York: George Braziller, 1965): iii.
29 Note that C.P. Snow's famous Rede Lecture, "The Two Cultures," was published in 1959 and certainly served as a goad to Kepes's "unity" activities.

Olafur Eliasson, *The Weather Project*, Tate Modern,
London, UK, 2003. Courtesy of the artist.

Hans Haacke, *Condensation Cube, (aka Weather Cube)*,
large version, 1963-67, refabricated 2006, as installed
at MIT List Visual Arts Center, Cambridge, MA.
Photo: Arindam Dutta. Courtesy of the artist, © Hans
Haacke/Artists Rights Society.

Burnham forged an aesthetic almost clinically designed to eliminate the human from the
affective-perceptive cycle. "Ultimately," Burnham would later ruminate, "systems theory
may be another attempt by science to resist the emotional pain and ambiguity that remain
an unavoidable aspect of life."[30] Turning to the crucial concept of "experience" helps
measure how far Haacke was from Kepes—and, for that matter, the distance of both these
figures from the incantations of "experience" that structure the artworld today.[31]

There is an overarching historical argument to be made, too long to elaborate fully here, in
which the industrial age empiricism of a Claude Monet or an Ernst Mach would percolate
slowly into American culture, first endorsed in pragmatist philosophy and technical
education at places like MIT and later codified in aesthetics through the art writing of a
figure such as Clement Greenberg.[32] Greenberg's writing is of course a crucial node in the
increasing positivism of the US art scene in the 1950s, assiduously reading a modernist
grid into the tortured surfaces of Abstract Expressionism, declaring Mondrian the source
of our "concrete, positivist" modernity and imperially announcing its "Apollonian" and

"Athenian" cast. But this formalism, based as it was on a consummately rationalized subject, needed to pass through the 1960s/70s anti-subjective systems thinking I will be describing here in order for the subject to emerge as it has—reinvented for late 20th and 21st century informatics. In a larger story with which we have all become familiar, this subject is no longer the centered individual, but a rhizomatic component of the techno-social.[33] It is in this way that systems thinking can be seen historically to undergird contemporary conceptual art practices, albeit in an entirely reconfigured episteme. (Compare Haacke and Eliasson on "Weather.")

What interests me here is the latter half of this long historical development, in which we can see three phases beginning in the postwar period. The first two are evident in Haacke's own trajectory, the third in present-day proponents of a similarly techno-scientific art. In the first phase, the subject was eradicated through the formalization of a system bounded to exclude it; in the second, the social was itself staged as a system for anti-subjective analysis; in the third, the bounds of the system under aesthetic investigation were extended to include the subjects making meaning—actively located in dispersed apparatuses of knowledge producing the art, the artist, and the correspondingly reflexive subject of the artworld system. The most notable inheritance of systems thinking, in this argument, can be located in the practices of Olafur Eliasson, who has very consciously revived Buckminster Fuller, and more covertly channeled Haacke himself.

Haacke's late '60s moment thus has much to tell us about the present, for like the present unstable dyad of virtuality and experience, the systems-theoretical approach came to reproduce some of the same bureaucratic divisions art had once been thought to heal. Having received both DAAD and Fulbright grants to study in the US, Haacke joined those calling the materiality of sculpture into question (Burnham chief among them) by summoning the nebulous entity called "the system" as what was to be represented—a system being any complex network of relations that was now to be given form. "Experience" in this frame was *experiment*, and in these systems the experiment ran automatically without anyone in a white lab coat to guide it. Here is Haacke, writing in 1967 of the ice and fabric pieces he was then preparing for the Hayden Gallery at MIT:

30 Jack Burnham, "Introduction," *Great Western Salt Works: Essays on the Meaning of Post-Formalist Art* (New York: Braziller, 1974): 11.

31 These arguments are drawn from "The Aesthetics of Experience," the conclusion to my *Desires for the World Picture: the global work of art* (Chicago, forthcoming).

32 See Jones, *Eyesight Alone: Clement Greenberg's Modernism and the Bureaucratization of the Senses* (Chicago: 2005/08).

33 Gilles Deleuze, *The Fold: Leibniz and the Baroque*, translation of *Le Pli* [1988] by Tom Conley (Minneapolis: University of Minnesota Press, 1993).

A 'sculpture' that physically reacts to its environment is no longer to be regarded as an object. The range of outside factors affecting it, as well as its own radius of action, reaches beyond the space it materially occupies. It thus merges with the environment in a relationship that is better understood as a 'system' of interdependent processes. These processes evolve *without the viewer's empathy. He becomes a witness. A system is not imagined, it is real.*[34]

This kind of materialization was quite different from the expressions of research explored by other artists engaging in "art and technology" projects at the time. Take US artist Robert Irwin: he was collaborating with scientists from Bell Labs in order to materialize laboratory set-ups of the Gestaltist *ganz feld* in galleries and art museums. These took the form of curved metal disks that were painted with faint halations of iridescent and luminescent paint, and then mounted on the wall under precise lighting. They were described by Irwin as "conditioning" the perceptual apparatus of the viewer.[35] We might say that Haacke focused on the ragged edges of an ill-defined and *im*personal system, where Irwin wanted the tight cybernetic loop of a perceiving subject. How, then, does this connect with the global emphasis on experience in the contemporary art world? From the 2005 Bienale de Lyon (*Expérience de la durée*) to that same year's Venice Biennale ("the experience of art"), refrains of experience produce a yearning for the body, location, site-specificity— yet increasingly we operate with diffuse and distributed forms of knowledge production mediated by robust networks of informatics. Contemporary artists thus synthesize the anti-humanist systems of Haacke with the more perceptual investigations of other techno-art types of the '60s, acknowledging that we have a body but also inserting us into informatics circuits – the circuitry constituting our 'experience.' In other words, although the perceiving "you" is continually emphasized in work by an artist such as Olafur Eliasson, it is the anti-subjective systems thinking by Haacke and related internet protocols that lie under the experiential turn and undergird its discursive embrace.[36]

There is a paradox here, for in his adoption of systems theory Haacke was precisely attempting to escape from 'experience' and deny the traditional Germanic trope of empathy in art. The *Condensation* pieces (cubes, walls, low-slung rectangles) were some of the first

34 Hans Haacke, "New York, September 1967." See *Hans Haacke 1967*, (2011): 48, emphasis added.

35 For more on Irwin, see Dawna Schuld in Robin Clark, ed., *Phenomenal: California Light, Space, Surface* (Berkeley: University of California Press, 2011).

36 See also the extensive arguments of Alexander Galloway, set out in *Protocol: How Control Exists After Decentralization* (MIT, 2004).

37 Hans Haacke, "New York, September 1967." See *Hans Haacke 1967*, (2011): 51.

Hans Haacke, *Wide White Flow*, first installed at MIT in 1967, refabricated 2006, shown here in 2008 installation at Paula Cooper Gallery, New York. Photo: Ellen Page Wilson. Courtesy the artist and Paula Cooper Gallery.

articulations of this commitment. Here is Haacke again from that fruitful period just before his MIT installation opened in 1967:

Whether the viewer's physical participation is required or not, the system's program is not affected by his knowledge, past experience, the mechanics of perceptual psychology, his emotions or degree of involvement. In the past, a sculpture or painting had meaning only at the grace of the viewer. . . .Without his emotional and intellectual reactions, the material remained nothing but stone and fabric. The system's program, on the other hand, is absolutely independent of the viewer's mental participation. It remains autonomous—aloof from the viewer. As a tree's program is not touched by the emotions of lovers in its shadow, so the system's program is untouched by the viewer's feelings and thoughts. The viewer becomes a witness rather than a resounding instrument striving for empathy.[37]

Burnham, in his 1968 *Artforum* manifesto for "Systems Esthetics," recognized the rather extreme position Haacke was taking in eliminating empathy and humanism: "Haacke's systems have a limited life as an art experience . . . He insists that the need for empathy does not make his work function as with older art." In support of his conclusion that Haacke's "Systems exist as on-going independent entities away from the viewer," Burnham quoted the Haacke statement cited above, that "these processes [of the 'system'] evolve without the viewer's empathy."[38] Philosophically, I would argue that some notion of "experience" and empathy within a viewer/reader/watcher is inextricable from talk about aesthetics—but historically it should interest us that Haacke was determined to eliminate it.

The role of bureaucracy, already fictionalized within European modernist literature (Balzac, Kafka, Musil), is significant here. Bureaucratic orders are brought in by the invocation of systems, precisely *in order to remove* the elements of delectation and princely aura (Haacke's "grace of the viewer") still clinging to the artwork, in just the same way that bureaucracy had functioned politically to remove the prince and both flatten and democratize access to resources in the social field.

This homology is reinforced by the dour, iconoclastic imagery for which Haacke would become known following the 1970 shows that definitively launched his career: cruddy mimeographs, clinical forms, banal photographs, simulated advertisements, research reports, demographic surveys, computer tabulations. Art that only a bureaucrat (or social scientist) could love, this was Haacke's turn *away* from the subjectless, anti-humanist first phase of systems art, marking the second phase of the techno-social in which the *social system* is now part of what will be included for analysis. This was the period in which Haacke launched "Museum Visitor Surveys" in which the demographics of museum-goers would constitute the discursive "art" on view. By this second phase in the 1970s, the Plexi box of systemic sampling would replace the Plexi box of climate systems in Haacke's oeuvre—while still insisting on an "objective" anti-humanism within the process (of the art and its demographic sociology).

Art as knowledge production emerged emphatically here, an irrevocable turn that has been pluralized in our contemporary moment into *kinds* of knowledges, with attention paid to the ethical frame articulated in Gilles Deleuze's reading of Foucault:

> Everything is knowledge, and this is the first reason why there is no 'savage experience': there is nothing beneath or prior to knowledge. But knowledge is irreducibly double, since it involves speaking and seeing, language and light . . .[39]

Beyond double, in fact—for to the twinned systems of statements and visibilities we must now add proprioception, ratiocination, memory, and the multiplied flows on which the body surfs to constitute a constantly morphing subjectivity. But if, as I claim, contemporary art

These questions and your answers are part of

Hans Haacke's VISITORS' PROFILE

a work in progress during "Directions 3: Eight Artists", Milwaukee Art Center,
June 19 through August 8, 1971.

Please fill out this questionnaire and drop it into the box by the door.
DO NOT SIGN.

1)   Do you have a professional interest in art,
     e.g. artist, student, critic, dealer, etc.?   _X_   ___
                                                           yes   no

2)   How old are you?   _22_
                                                           years

3)   Should the use of marijuana be legalized,   _X_   ___   ___
     lightly or severely punished?   legal light   severe
                                                          punishment

4)   Do you think law enforcement agencies   _X_   ___
     are generally biased against dissenters?   yes   no

5)   What is your marital status?   married   single   div.   sep.   widowed

6)   Do you sympathize with Women's Lib?   ___   ___
                                                          yes   no

7)   Are you male, female?   ___   _X_
                                                          male   female

8)   Do you have children?   ___   _X_
                                                          yes   no

9)   Would you mind busing your child to integrate schools? ___   _X_
                                                             yes   no

10) What is your ethnic backround, e.g. Polish, German, etc.?   _Russian_

11) Assuming you were Indochinese, would you
     sympathize with the Saigon regime?   ___   ___
                                                          yes   no

12) Do you think the moral fabric of the US is strength- ___   _X_
     ened or weakened by its involvement in Indochina? strengthened weakened

13) What is your religion?   _Jewish_

14) In your opinion, are the interests of profit-oriented ___   _X_
     business usually compatible with the common good?   yes   no

15) What is your annual income (before taxes)? $ _0_

16) Do you think the Nixon Administration is mainly   ___   _X_
     responsible for our economic difficulties?   yes   no

17) Where do you live?   _X_   ___   ___
                                         city/suburb   county   state

18) Do you consider the defeat of the supersonic transport _X_   ___
     (SST) a step in the right direction?   yes   no

19) Are you enrolled in or have graduated from college? _X_   ___
                                                          yes   no

20) In your opinion, should the general orientation of the ___   _X_
     country be more conservative or less conservative?   more   less

Your answers will be tabulated later today together with the answers of all
other visitors of the exhibition.   Thank you.

Hans Haacke, Visitor Survey document from social systems project at Milwaukee Art Center, 1971. Courtesy of the artist, © Hans Haacke/Artists Rights Society.

38 Jack Burnham, "Systems Esthetics" [1968], as anthologized in his *Great Western Salt Works*, 22.

39 Gilles Deleuze, "Foldings, or the Inside of Thought," *Foucault* (Minneapolis: University of Minnesota Press, 1988): 109.

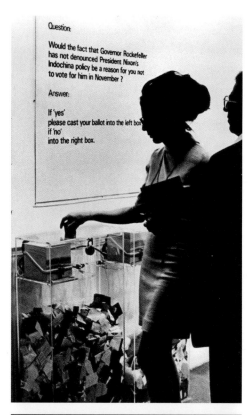

Question:

Would the fact that Governor Rockefeller has not denounced President Nixon's Indochina policy be a reason for you not to vote for him in November?

Answer:

If 'yes' please cast your ballot into the left box if 'no' into the right box.

reconfigures systems thinking to emphasize the fluidity of reception and experience, this is neither permanent nor inevitable. The historical development of the empirico-bureaucratic subject on a large scale is evident at the much smaller scale of the artworld. The first phase I have seen in Haacke—a cultivated anti-subjectivity on the part of the artist—evolves in Haacke's own work to a second phase of "objectivity": the corresponding term that constructs an apprehension of the system as being outside the artist or viewer but still involving the social.[40] Finally, in the postmodern turn to which Burnham himself averred, knowledge production is generated about the system as including *both* the artist *and* the experience of viewers. Despite the periodizations offered here, this is not a teleology. Threads of each of these phases are available at every moment since bureaucracy's rise, to be differentially emphasized at different points. As we shall see, Eliasson's late '90s solution will not be taken up by the '00s techno-socializing art of bio-mimetics; multiple trajectories proliferate and no outcome is fully specified.

Plexiglass boxes in Hans Haacke, "MOMA Visitors' Poll." *Information* exhibition, Museum of Modern Art, New York, 1970; Haacke, *Regenturm (Rain tower)*, 1962. Courtesy of the artist, © Hans Haacke/Artists Rights Society.

40 My thinking about "objectivity" in its intimate relation to "subjectivity" is marked by my reading of Lorraine Daston and Peter Galison, *Objectivity* (New York: Zone, 2007).
41 Hans-Ulrich Derlien, *Bureaucracy in Art and Analysis: Kafka and Weber* (Bamberg, Universität

Bureaucratization of the subject *constitutes* techno-sociality, as we arrange ourselves for tabulation and incorporation via the office-based system (updated through protocols of the moment such as Facebook connectivity). The early stages of this bureaucratic arc stretch back into the systematic empiricism of nineteenth- and early twentieth-century cultural producers, who prepared the subject for ongoing bureaucratization with deep ambivalence. Hans-Ulrich Derlien and others have examined the rise of "administrative fiction" throughout this period – from Balzac's *"Les Employés,"* in the mid-19th century *Comedie Humaine* to Musil's *Mann ohne Eigenschaften* from the 1920s (with Kafka's satires in between).[41] Ambivalently, the bureaucratic order was experienced in these host cultures as analogous to the precision machines replacing time-honored agricultural labor. Even Max Weber, who had been sympathetic to the ways bureaucracy effectively cured the toxic feudalism of princely regimes, fretted in 1909 about the origins and likely outcomes of the new class of *Berufsmensch*:

> even more dreadful is the vision, that the world shall be completed with nothing but those small wheels (of a machine) . . . What can we oppose to this machinery in order to spare a remainder of humanity from this parceling out of the soul, from this rule of bureaucratic ideals of life.[42]

Thus in parallel with the rise of actual bureaucracy in culture (witnessed by increasingly systematic research by artists, from Constable's cloud studies to Monet's rigorous serial experiments) were nostalgic yearnings for an art that would be completely *un*bureaucratic (the nobility of Monet's subjects: cathedrals and haystacks, versus the numbing bourgeois regularity of his *petits sensations*).[43] Again, *both* readings are available in Monet—but only some would be articulated at particular times. At the end of the nineteenth century and well into the twentieth, art would be used to provide an integrative antidote to the machinic phylum, just as Henri Bergson rejected the mechanism of Monet in favor of a vitalist reading of Impressionist painting.[44] It is in this context that we can understand the pragmatic appeal of John Dewey, who wrote in his 1934 book *Art as Experience* (drafted for the 1931 William James lectures) of the pleasures of aesthetics as "an adjustment of our whole being with the conditions of existence."[45] The being *will be adjusted* to the new

Bamberg 1989).

42 Weber, statement to the *Verein für Sozialpolitik* in Vienna, 1909, *Schriftens des Vereins* 132 (1910): 284, as translated and cited in Hans-Ulrich Derlien, *Bureaucracy in Art and Analysis*, 34. Per Derlien, here Weber was opposing the mostly positive judgment of bureaucratization

by Gustav von Schmoller and Otto Hintze.

43 So completely did Monet's subjects disguise the administrative rigors of his process that someone as intelligent as Burnham places Monet in the "intuitive" category in 1967, writing that artists could use systems methodology only to an extent,

for "certainly Monet never set out to do Impressionist paintings . . ." [!] This quote is from the course proposal Burnham sent to Kepes in November 1967, now in the CAVS archives, Burnham file, "Systems Methodology," ts p. 2.

44 Developed more extensively in Jones, "Rendering Time," in Galison

et al., *Einstein for the 21st Century* (Princeton, NJ: Princeton University Press, 2008): 130-149. Intriguingly, Henri Bergson's vitalism was read by Jack Burnham as an explicit precursor to Bertalanffy's system thinking, and a way to bridge the history of art and the emergent rigors of systems methodology.

industrial forms of existence, but in that required adjustment there will be a capacity for aesthetic pleasure, construed as an antidote to further alienation. Post-war systems theory traded in a similarly ambivalent commitment to holism in the post-war period, while still participating in the 20th century apogee of bureaucracy proper.

How would Dewey's cure for bureaucratic alienation be retooled for the bureaucratic postwar subject of Minimalism, Conceptualism, Burnham, and Haacke—operating in the mode that Benjamin H.D. Buchloh so felicitously dubbed the postwar "aesthetic of administration"?[46] We get there, surprisingly, through the needle's eye of Clement Greenberg's formalism. Dewey's *Art As Experience* was formative to the art writer, who confessed to a friend in August 1940: "Criticism is the only really living genre left. . . . I know my style is too much like Thorstein Veblen and John Dewey, but I'll be damned if I can deliver the birth otherwise."[47] Dewey's "experience" of art was needed both to inoculate the subject against what Greenberg called the "dull horror" of industrial existence and at the same time had to tool that subject to function in those orders.[48] So paradoxically, an artist such as Jackson Pollock could be simultaneously enshrined by Greenberg as the instigator of "hallucinated uniformity" in the bureaucratic subject ordered for modernity, while that same artist could be cited by younger, equally Dewey-influenced artists (such as Allan Kaprow) as the source of a systematic freeing of that same subject. Not coincidentally, this conceptual split can be located in the cybernetic counterculture of the 1970s, as well as propelling concepts of interactivity in the art of experience today.[49] Suffice it to say that in the American case, the search for experience through form (in Abstract Expressionism) became generalized to the form of experience identified with knowledge-production itself (in Haacke and Conceptual Art more generally).

As intimated above, the crux of that turn lay in the postwar conversion from information to informatics.[50] In parallel with that epistemic shift in the early 1960s were hugely scaled up factory models of aggregative labor (physicists converting from desktop experiments to the industrial assemblages of big science; artists setting up basic assembly lines), accompanied by decentralized production in "shopped-out" labor and parts.[51] While they implied deskilling, such new forms of labor also freed art and science to reach new

45 John Dewey, *Art as Experience* (New York: Penguin Group, 1934): 16.

46 Benjamin H. D. Buchloh, "Conceptual Art 1962-1969: From the Aesthetic of Administration to the Critique of Institutions," *October* 55 (Winter, 1990): 105-143.

47 Greenberg letter to Harold Lazarus, 28 August 1940,

Greenberg papers, Getty Research Inst. 950085.

48 Clement Greenberg, "The Present Prospects of American Painting" [1947], in Greenberg, *Collected Essays and Criticism*, vol. 2, ed. John O'Brian (Chicago: University of Chicago Press, 1986-1993): 2:163.

49 For Greenberg on "hallucinated uniformity," see *The Collected Essays*, supra., 2: 224. For the cybernetic counterculture, see Felicity Scott, *Architecture or Techno-Utopia: Politics after Modernism* (Cambridge: MIT Press, 2007); John Markoff, *What the Dormouse Said: How the Sixties*

Counterculture Shaped the Personal Computer Industry (New York: Viking Penguin, 2005); Fred Turner, *From Counterculture to Cyberculture: Stewart Brand, the Whole Earth Network, and the Rise of Digital Utopianism* (Chicago: University of Chicago Press, 2006); and Thierry Bardini, *Bootstrapping:*

planes of conceptualization and demanded radically new receptive frames. The narrative is all too familiar, constituting the origin story of our machinic ways of being: machines for living (Corbusier), readymade desiring-production machines (Marcel Duchamp), the postwar "large business" machines of particle detectors (exemplified by physicist Luis Alvarez) and networked information machines (ARPAnet), "mechanical means" for mass image production (Andy Warhol), "executive" artists' serial modes (Frank Stella), and eventually even ideas as machines for making art (Sol LeWitt). The machine was more than a metaphor in this period of rampant automation. It retooled the producer and the receiver, while smuggling the author-function back in as manager of the work-stream. The implications of systems thinking would enter seamlessly, fueling the growing conviction that the "object" of art or science was nothing less than the local "subject" making meaning: of experience, of data, of sensory phenomena, of the broader social field. But that step would be held off by Haacke, for whom the autonomous nature of the artworld needed to be both challenged and secured.

Systems Think

The names we give this turn to the reading/viewing subject are post-structuralism or postmodernism. But within these intellectual histories, I want to specify the links between European empiricism, American pragmatism, postwar bureaucratization, the building of literal networks and infrastructures, all the way up to the recent emphasis on an aesthetics of experience—and to argue that these developments had at least one major impetus in the systems thinking of the late 1960s and early 70s. If systems came out of the nexus of information theorists and feedback logicians working in the internationalizing fields of engineering and biology, it also found its purchase on culture through figures such as Marshall McLuhan, Buckminster Fuller, and the unreasonably obscure Jack Burnham. But if he is barely referenced today, Burnham was quite well-known in the '60s and '70s. At the time of his appointment at CAVS in 1968, he was an active critic and reviewer for *Artforum*, one of the first critics to have written on Haacke's work (in the 1967 cover article for *Tri-Quarterly* magazine), and a perfect spokesperson for the importance of systems in framing Haacke's 1967 show at MIT.

Douglas Engelbart, Coevolution, and the Origins of Personal Computing (Stanford: Stanford University Press, 2000). I'm grateful to conversations with Peter Lunenfeld about this and other countercultural arcana. **50** This section draws on various collaborations with Peter Galison; see for

example our "Centripetal and Centrifugal Architectures: Laboratory and Studio," in Cynthia Davidson, ed., Anyplace, Architecture New York (1995). For different but related accounts, see Reinhold Martin, *The Organizational Complex* (see n. 23); Michael Gibbons et al., *The New Production of*

Knowledge (London: Sage, 1994), and David Harvey, *The Condition of Postmodernity* (Cambridge: Blackwell, 1990). **51** Comparisons of Warhol's Factory can usefully be made to the similar contradictions in postwar Big Science. See Jones and Galison, "Factory, Laboratory, Studio: Dispersing Sites of Production," in Emily

Thompson and Peter Galison, *The Architecture of Science* (Cambridge: MIT Press, 1999): 497-540. **52** Kepes to Burnham, 5 June 1967, "Burnham" file, CAVS archive, MIT.

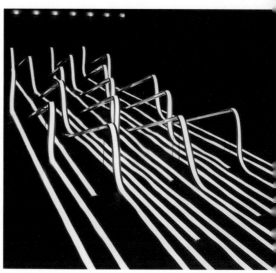

Jack Burnham at typewriter, n.d. Photo: MIT Center for Advanced Visual Studies press release about the first class of fellows, 1968.

right, Jack Burnham, untitled light sculpture, 1968-69.

Kepes's first letter to Burnham was sent in June 1967; its opening sentence—"I learned about your work from Otto Piene"—confirms that it was the European world of postwar abstraction and technosocial experiments (specifically in the Zero Group) that would authorize Kepes's development of postwar US artistic work reflecting "the cooperation of engineers and scientists."[52] Answering Kepes immediately, Burnham enthused about the prospects of the as-yet-unopened Center:

> Needless to say, I am very sympathetic with your plans and it is only a mystery to me that this did not happen 20 years ago after the Second World War, which seems even now like a logical jumping off place from the older values. . . . In closing I wish you would keep me posted about the progress of the Center . . . this could be a very valuable means of furthering studies in a field that is already twenty years behind where it should be.[53]

53 Burnham to Kepes, 9 June 1967, "Burnham" file, CAVS archive, MIT.
54 "Burnham" file, various references and memos. The book was eventually published as *The Structure of Art* (Braziller, 1971), after Burnham worked through his systems thinking in Artforum during the year he

was at the Center. I have not yet been able to determine whether Burnham's course on "Systems and Art" was actually offered (it seems not); frustratingly, the "paper describing my 'Systems and Art' class" is not physically attached to the 17 November 1967 letter in which Burnham describes it: "It is a radical

departure from the usual sticks and screen design class, but that is what it is meant to be. Since the writing of this paper there have been a number of changes and improvements in the course . . ." I have identified a loose typescript as this document. It is annotated in Burnham's handwriting, "for G. Kepes,"

titled "Some thoughts on systems methodology applied to art," and exists loose and undated in the Burnham file, CAVS archive. I have given it a provisional date of November 1967 and it is cited here as "Burnham, 'Systems methodology'."

Burnham continued, reporting that his next book was going to focus on "basic visual design" and was being prepared "with a systems engineer, Gustave Rath"; he mentioned speaking on the project to a Michigan engineering conference, concluding that he would welcome participating "in some way" in the future activities of the Center. Burnham later sent Kepes his "Haacke monograph" hot off the press on July 1, 1967; in further correspondence he titles his design book-in-progress *Systems and Art*, amplifying the negotiations with an offer to teach a course on the subject in the department of Architecture (which, had he been successful, would have supplemented the meager CAVS stipend).[54]

It is compelling to read Burnham's course proposal, sent November 1967, with the knowledge that it reflects years of conversations between the artist and engineers with whom he had been in contact. "What I propose is not that the artist become an engineer, but that for some phases of his problem-solving it would be advisible [sic] for him to think like an engineer."[55] Burnham's project is not merely proscriptive. It is *because* contemporary artists are beginning to work "with assortments of industrial materials, multi-leveled environmental analyses, control systems, and increasingly large spaces" that they can be said "to work in the area that engineers call 'systems' . . . input-output exchanges of materials, energy, and information."[56] In other words, it is because Burnham has recently examined Haacke's production, and because Haacke has responded to Burnham's systems theorizations, that the critic-artist's analysis can seem like an empirical judgment of the contemporary artworld *as it is*, while also being proposed to Kepes as "a radical departure from the usual sticks and screen design class . . ."[57]

Burnham must have seemed like a dream come true for Kepes in forming CAVS's first group of fellows. A Yale-educated sculptor showing artworks made of flexible "light strips," Burnham also promised to bring "Systems" thinking directly into CAVS, an intellectual restitution for the earlier Hayden Gallery show in which Haacke's Systems Art had been shown without Kepes's blessing.[58] At the same time, Burnham was putting flesh on the binding of art and science in ways that Kepes had not yet been capable of achieving, without collapsing art entirely into *techné* or engineering. Reading further in Burnham's proposal for a "Systems and Art" course, Kepes might have been pleased to discern

55 Burnham, "Systems Methodology," ts p. 1.
56 Burnham, "Systems Methodology," ts p. 2.
57 Burnham to Kepes, 17 November 1967.

58 The real sticking point for Kepes was apparently a set of symposia that Andersen organized in the year of his arrival (1965), bringing luminaries such as Susan Sontag and Lawrence Alloway to debate synaesthesia. Forty years after the events of 1965, Andersen claims to recall Kepes's words exactly: "I don't understand, when my work is in its infancy, you're bringing New York up here. You're diverting from my program just as my baby is about to be born." In Andersen's view, diverting from Kepes was exactly what Stratton, and later Johnson, wanted him to do. It was President Jerome Wiesner who proved Kepes's most cooperative partner in getting CAVS finally launched.
59 Burnham, "Systems Methodology," ts p. 2.

the beginnings of Burnham's critique—an acknowledgment that the goal-driven modality of systems analysis is not a perfect fit in the artworld. Even if artists utilize systems methodology to constrain the variables of their (process-driven and newly conceptual) artworks, they "can entertain no such hope" of "planning . . . precise goals for the system."[59] And it would have been attractive to Kepes to learn that Burnham, unlike Haacke, was openly theorizing the extension of the system *to include the artworld and artist,* an implication that Haacke would embrace only tentatively, and much later:

> What it [systems methodology] can provide is a method for developing an idea into alternative physical systems. It defines known and unknown factors, constraints, boundaries, desired output, and the means for locating optimum solutions. Moreover, the systems approach allows the artist to consider viewer interaction and environmental conditions within the scope of his thinking. [60] [emphasis in original]

Defining traditional art as a "closed system," Burnham's course proposal saw the most interesting new art as invoking "open systems" with "considerable, and frequently interesting, exchanges of information and energy with their environments."[61] Opening the system seems to have made Haacke wary, although in the article Burnham would publish in *Artforum* the following year championing his "Systems Esthetics," the critic included illustrations of works by Dan Flavin, Les Levine, and of course Haacke. Proclaiming systems the future of all art in this 1968 polemic, Burnham nonetheless alluded to the cautionary examples of other technologically-savvy artist movements of the past. Notably, he viewed the Russian Constructivists as having gone too far towards engineering, having "ceased to exist" as artists after their switch to Productivism, further "crushed [by] Stalinist anti-intellectualism."

Luckily, a different paradigm governed art of the late 1960s:

> Rather than a novel way of rearranging surfaces and spaces, it is fundamentally concerned with the implementation of the art impulse in an advanced technological society. . . . [Man] assumes a new and more critical function [as] that of *man the maker of esthetic decisions* [that] control the quality of all future life on the Earth.[62]

60 Burnham, "Systems Methodology," ts p. 4.
61 Ibid.
62 Burnham, "Systems Esthetics," *Artforum* 1968, anthologized in his Great Western Salt Works, 25.

63 For histories of this development, see Steve Joshua Heims, *The Cybernetics Group* (Cambridge: MIT Press, 1991); Jean-Pierre Dupuy, *The Mechanization of the Mind: On the Origins of Cognitive Science,* trans. M. B. DeBevoise (Princeton NJ: Princeton University Press,

2000); American Association of Cybernetics, "History Chapter 2: Foundations: Coalescence of Cybernetics," online at http://www.asc-cybernetics.org/foundations/history/MacySummary.htm; and of course the five volumes titled *Cybernetics: Transactions of the [n] Conference,* with n=6-10;

most edited by Heinz von Foerster, Margaret Mead, and Hans Lukas Teuber and published by the Josiah Macy, Jr. Foundation between 1949-1955.

Thus in three short moves, concentrated in a few bodies, we can see how the technocratic progressivism of Soviet Constructivism, the Bauhaus, and the Logical Positivists are retooled through Burnham's Dewey-inflected pragmatism and Kepes's ambitious new unity-of-science project, launching CAVS into the crucible of cybernetics and systems that was MIT. Fed by Claude Shannon's information theory and codified at the famous Macy Conferences from 1946-53,[63] systems and cybernetics were bursting out of every conceivable corner of the Institute, from Jay W. Forrester of the MIT Sloan School of Management (who had founded the MIT System Dynamics Group in the late '50s in explicit echo of Kurt Lewin's MIT Research Center for Group Dynamics) to Norbert Wiener himself, a galvanic presence at MIT's Mathematics Department from 1919 to 1964. Wiener's *Cybernetics* had been published by MIT press in 1948, with a revised second edition in 1961. It's safe to say that when Wiener's book was joined by Ludwig von Bertalanffy's *General System Theory* in 1968, the art world had its bookend bibles for a systems revolution.

What differentiates cybernetics from systems theory?[64] For the purposes of this essay, I venture a crude distinction: Cybernetics was born of mathematical engineering, Systems from biology—yet both were rooted in Shannon's mathematical information theory and were crucial participants in the budding field of computer science. Both sectors philosophically responded to the late nineteenth-century critique of atomism and industrial regimentation by Henri Bergson and the vitalists. Sympathetic to vitalism but determined to be *scientific* as well as philosophical, both fields proposed to deal with dynamic complexity. The meta-goal was to use the overarching patterns of organic and mechanical processes— translated as "systems" and "cybernetic feedback loops"—to decode the unity of science itself, a dream that had started with the logical positivists in the '20s but had been stunted by the rise of fascism and the second World War. (Burnham himself saw systems methodology in the "unifying" and holistic terms of the logical positivists.)[65]

But the simple heuristic I have offered of a mathematical-engineering cybernetics versus an organic-biological systems theory is too simple, denying the interconnected vascularity of systems-cybernetics' fully networked, institutionalized, and intramural bureaucracy. Even when originating cybernetics, Wiener worked closely with biologists and neurologists in

64 Per Pam Lee, systems theory covers the what, cybernetics the how. Pamela M. Lee, *Chronophobia: On Time in the Art of the 1960s* (Cambridge: MIT Press, 2004): 64. "What are Cybernetics and Systems Science?" also offers a useful perspective, online http://pespmc1.vub.ac.be/ CYBSWHAT.html, accessed January 2009.

65 Burnham compares Duchamp's work to Bertrand Russell's true-false propositions at the turn of the century in "Willoughby Sharp Interviews Jack Burnham," *Arts Magazine* 45, no. 2 (November 1970): 23. Burnham's familiarity with semiotics and structuralism is obvious (*The Structure of Art*), but the links to pragmatism, William James, and the Logical Positivists are less often remarked.

mathematically mapping command and control mechanisms; similarly, the biologist Ludwig von Bertalanffy met with Wiener and used his probabilistic formulae and engineering diagrams to establish what he viewed as the larger theoretical project of general systems theory. Cybernetics wants to subsume "Systems" as a wholly-owned derivative, while Systems considers "Cybernetics" a special subset of its broader terrain. Yet regardless of how we might complicate the intersections of the two domains, two there were, suggested even by patterns of publishing: the early cyberneticians published with MIT Press, the systems theorists with New York's George Braziller. This accounts for the greater impact of systems thinking on the artworld, for Braziller published not only Bertalanffy but Kepes's series of art/science texts and Burnham's collections of essays. It was the art publisher Braziller who thus forged the public connection between the arcana of command, control, and communication and the volatile life world of contemporary art.

If cyberneticians had the more mathematical and cold-blooded reputation, they shared the systems theorists' anxieties about participating in the increasing instrumentalization and bureaucratization of the world. The polymath Wiener articulated his fears, immediately after the Second World War, that the conceptual revolution he had fomented within the centuries-long tradition of mechanical systems and feedback mechanisms promised both good and bad moral outcomes.[66] As he wrote in 1947:

> Those of us who have contributed to the new science of cybernetics . . . stand in a moral position which is, to say the least, not very comfortable. We have contributed to the initiation of a new science which . . . embraces technical development with great possibilities for good and for evil. We can only hand it over into the world that exists about us, and this is the world of Belsen and Hiroshima. We do not even have the choice of suppressing these new technical developments. They belong to the age . . .[67]

The mathematician is as gloomy as Heidegger in judging the logic of his own bureaucratic technocracy—the systematicity of modernity cannot be separated from the hideously banal production lines of Auschwitz, even as related production efficiencies must be entrusted with the easing of future human pain. Wiener placed what hope he could muster with

---

66 See Otto Mayr, *The Origins of Feedback Control* (Cambridge: MIT Press 1970; translated from the German, 1969). Mayr traces the history of feedback mechanics back to the ancient Greeks and Islamic engineers (especially of waterclocks). But he admits the force of the cybernetic revolution: "the abstract concept of the closed causal loop which provides the common basis for all the regulating mechanisms discussed in this study, and which is expressed most compellingly by the graphic symbols of the block diagram, is an achievement of the 20th century" (129).

67 Norbert Wiener, introduction to the original edition, [1948] *Cybernetics: or Control and Communication in the Animal and the Machine*, 2nd ed. (Cambridge: MIT Press, 1961): 28.

68 Ibid.

social science, to use cybernetics wisely in order "to have a society based on human values other than buying or selling . . ."[68] To further this dream, he worked with labor leaders as well as academics in the new sciences of human groups that were springing up at the Sloan School and Department of Urban Studies at MIT.

Such ameliorative instincts, as I have already suggested, were also driving Kepes's CAVS, with its seminars, symposia, and publications on "Artists and the Scientific Community," "Art, Science, Technology," and "Arts and the University."[69] Here, both systems and cybernetics seemed amenable to cultural use—but in the broader frame, systems think spread more widely. Cybernetics remained arcane (until Donna Haraway's incendiary "Cyborg Manifesto" of 1984).[70] Why was cybernetics less available for cultural uptake in the late 1960s? My instinct is that Wiener's work became, for humanists at least, polluted

69 Reinhold Martin, *The Organizational Complex* (see n. 23); see also his earlier essay "The Organizational Complex: Cybernetics, Space, Discourse," *Assemblage* 37 (December 1998): 102-127. For CAVS, see their online poster archive, http://cavs. mit.edu/MEDIA/Center-2005-PostersArchive.pdf.

70 Donna Haraway, "Cyborg Manifesto: Science, Technology, and Socialist-Feminism in the Late Twentieth Century," in *Simians, Cyborgs and Women: The Reinvention of Nature* (New York; Routledge, 1991), 149-181 (originally published in the *Socialist Review* in 1985).

Hans Haacke, *Live Airborne System*, 30. 11. 1968 (Plan 1965); seagulls, breadcrumbs, ocean near Coney Island. Courtesy the artist, © Hans Haacke/Artists Rights.

by the weapons research and self-guiding missiles with which it was fundamentally associated. In contrast, the legacy of biology fueling "systems" allowed its slightly later popularization to entice artists and theorists with the dream of organicism that lay buried in its black-box analyses.

How else to understand that it is exclusively *biological or climatological systems*, never mathematical or mechanical cybernetics, that Haacke and Burnham want to cite in the "Real-Time Systems" art of this period? In his 1969 essay of that title on the work of Haacke and others, Burnham returns to the fonts of American pragmatism (William James and Dewey) to further support what had been his astonishingly prophetic claim in 1968 that "a *Systems Esthetic* will become the dominant approach to a maze of socio-technical conditions rooted only in the present."[71] Burnham was ahead of Haacke (who had not yet turned to the social field), arguing at this late sixties moment that through this systems aesthetic, "art now challenges the entire art information processing structure, not merely its content."[72]

Revealing his American roots, Burnham's exploration of Haacke places particular emphasis on William James. It is James who recognizes the incoherence of the world, where Dewey attempts to suture it together—although both emphasize the correspondingly fundamental aesthetic impulse to break experience into manageable units. As Burnham argues through James, "sensually the world is impossible as experience . . . As a result, correlating experience into a coherent picture of reality is the pragmatist's only objective."[73] Artists are "similar to programs and subroutines," their work "an archaic information processing system" we need in order to "prepare new codes and analyze data in making works of art."[74] Ultimately pushing hard on the very systems aesthetic that he had done so much to put in place, by 1969 Burnham hovered on the edge of post-structuralism, a place Haacke would never go. Burnham in "Real-Time Systems":

> Both in the sciences and in the humanities something is rapidly happening: we are beginning to see scientific 'objectivity' as an illusion, as are the notions of independent scientific 'disciplines,' of isolating subjects of scientific inquiry from their settings, and of the possibility of making unobtrusive measurements.[75]

Segueing to the computer-controlled real-time systems coordinating contemporary economic and military domains, Burnham acknowledged the "instinctive antipathy" that most humanists have towards "these immensely complex computer systems. Their Orwellian overtones far overshadow their conceivable use as artists' tools. But practically, it is imperative that artists do understand them—both technically and philosophically."[76] But if Burnham was beginning to understand in 1969 that the artist and scientist were themselves a part of the system, Haacke was not yet willing to take that logical leap. True, Haacke is quoted by Burnham as admitting in 1968 that "an artist is not an isolated system"—and yet his work specifically contradicts that hard-won intellectual insight.[77]

The plants and animals in what the artist humorously calls his "Franciscan" phase of systems art are coded by Haacke as operating without reference to human experience or expectation (even if his retrospective allusion to Saint Francis already complicates that claim with a metaphor of divinely inspired intimacy among earthbound life forms). Haacke's stated expectation of radical separation between the work of systems art and its maker or viewer is more enduring than his pledge to see the artist as part of the system, and brings us to the most interesting *philosophical* problematic of systems theory, one

Hans Haacke, *Norbert: 'All systems go'*, 1970-71. Trained Mynah bird, cage. Courtesy the artist, © Hans Haacke/Artists Rights.

that Burnham clearly understood: namely, *around what nexus of entities is the "system" boundary to be drawn?* To take only one example, let us look at the Haacke piece curator Walter Grasskamp describes as "essentially parodic"—*Norbert: 'All Systems Go'* from 1970-71. Crucially, this piece was produced after Haacke's turn from systems art as such, and after the artist had already moved toward the more socially engaged processes he put on offer in the *Information* and *Software* shows. Named after Norbert Wiener yet referring to systems rather than cybernetics, the work consisted of a pet mynah bird that Haacke was attempting to train to say "All Systems Go." The bird and its cage were to have

71 Jack Burnham, "Systems Esthetics," *Artforum* (September 1968), anthologized in his *Great Western Salt Works*, 24. See also Francis Halsall's excellent *Systems of Art* (Bern, Peter Lang, 2008), online excerpt at http://systemsart.org/halsall_paper.html.

72 Jack Burnham, "Real-Time

Systems," *Artforum* (1969), anthologized in his *Great Western Salt Works*, 28.

73 Burnham, *Great Western Salt Works*, 28, 29.

74 Ibid., 27.

75 Ibid., 29.

76 Ibid., 30, illustrated with a picture of Haacke's *Chickens Hatching*, 1969.

77 Haacke, "from a talk

. . . at the annual meeting of the Intersocietal Color Council, April 1968," as cited by Jack Burnham, "Real-Time Systems," in his *Great Western Salt Works*, 30.

78 The cancellation of Haacke's show, for largely political reasons (his exposé of probably Jewish slumlords was seen as too incendiary

for this Jewish-founded museum, run by a German national sensitive to his own reputation) both stalled Haacke's career and made it. For Europeans, he became the darling of their non-profit biennials and documentas, revealing the bankruptcy of US claims to free speech; at the same time, Haacke was

been installed at Haacke's one-man show, intended for the Guggenheim but infamously cancelled by museum director Thomas Messer.[78] The unexecuted work has recently been imagined rather vividly by scholar Luke Skrebowski:

> A white cube. A black bird with bright yellow stripes around the eyes sits in a chrome cage. It rocks gently on its perch. Silence. Occasional scrabbling sounds . . . Time passes. Nothing happens. Suddenly, the caged bird speaks. "All systems go" it squawks. And again, "All systems go." A pause. "All systems go. All systems go." Repetition to inanition. "All systems go."[79]

Skrebowski, a sympathetic analyst of *Norbert*, sets it in dialectical opposition to Haacke's earlier *Chickens Hatching*—an opposition that could, for that matter, include other avian projects, such as the *Live Airborne System* illustrated. Reasonably, Skrebowski argues that while "both works deploy systems theory as a conceptual resource for vanguard art practice, [the 1969] *Chickens Hatching* makes direct use of the possibilities presented by cybernetic systems [while the 1970] *Norbert: All Systems Go* seems to negate them."[80] Skrebowski argues: "[in *Norbert*] cybernetic theory . . . is mocked, its optimistic feedback-steered vision of human progress undermined [in] the sardonic refrain of a trained mynah bird . . . "[81] This authorized reading aptly illustrates my philosophical problem. Haacke reveals his fundamentally modernist bona fides in holding on to the separation between the system of the "caged bird" and the art-world system in which he proposed to insert it as a provocation.[82]

The boundary that Haacke consistently vexes is the boundary he continually redraws: the elite container of artworld signification *must* be conceived as a separate system from the real world in which Haacke buys the mynah bird, sets up a feedback loop (quite literally) in which the bird is rewarded with feed each time it approaches the prized utterance, until such time as the system (as I am seeing it, with much larger boundaries than Haacke then acknowledged) can be presumed to be homeostatic, with the bird named "Norbert" uttering "All Systems Go" for the now symbolic reward system of the artworld itself, transferred from the artist's hand to the bird's beak to the viewer's ear.

virtually ignored by American museums until well into the 1980s when he became celebrated by a younger generation as the founder of institutional critique. The issue of the cancellation has so dominated the study of Haacke's work that what I contribute here is a kind of revision, emphasizing as it

does the earliest systems work, which was resolutely a-political and even anti-social. **79** Luke Skrebowski, "All Systems Go: Recovering Jack Burnham's 'Systems Aesthetics,'" a revised and expanded version of a talk given 2005 at Tate Modern's *Open Systems: Rethinking Art c.1970*, now online at *Tate*

Papers (http://www.tate.org. uk/research/tateresearch/ tatepapers/06spring/ skrebowski.htm), accessed July 2009. **80** Ibid., 2. **81** Ibid. **82** The artist recalls that he set up a tape-loop of himself uttering the phrase, to attempt to train the bird

in his New York apartment. Apparently the bird never learned its lesson. My point here is that the apparatus of training, of the artist's "behind the scenes" activities, is intended to be excluded from the presentation of the work in the gallery.

To return to Haacke's statement of 1967 is instructive. Here Haacke reveals the *inframince* of this elite aesthetic that he still wants to preserve as a boundary around the artworld system, *separate from both his agency and the world*, in order to avoid the complete collapse of art into life:

> A system is most generally defined as a grouping of elements subject to a common plan and purpose. These elements or components interact so as to arrive at a joint goal. To separate the elements would be to destroy the system.[. . .]

> The physical self-sufficiency of such a system has a decisive effect on the viewer's relationship to the work, due to its hitherto unknown independence from his mental involvement.[. . .] there are systems which function properly even when the viewer is not present at all, i.e., their program operates *absolutely independently of any contribution on the part of the viewer.*[83] [emphasis added]

Haacke's commitment to the "hitherto unknown independence" from the mental involvement of the viewer is a dramatic circumscription of the boundary of the proposed system. If Burnham would polemicize that *"in an advanced technological culture the most important artist best succeeds by liquidating his position as artist vis-à-vis society,"* [84] [emphasis original]. Haacke not only refused to go this far, but in the proposed Guggenheim projects (and later in response to the trauma of the show's cancellation) would shortly make a decisive turn toward preserving the autonomy of the artist from any implication in the artworld system he has now included as part of what will be entailed in the work.

This fiction of autonomy was desperately necessary, of course—Haacke was operating in a radically contested cultural sphere in which freedom of expression was put under extreme pressure, a well-known development ushering the art system into the epoch of its own institutional critique.[85] Shifting from abstract "natural" systems to social ones, Haacke's *Shapolsky* et al. departed decisively from the terms of the early systems art. Paradoxically, the forced revelation of the artworld as a disciplinary system brought the end of systems art proper, and the beginning of Haacke's modernist political sociology staged as institutional

---

83 Hans Haacke, New York, Spetember 1967, in *Hans Haacke 1967* (2011): 50.
84 Burnham, "Systems Esthetics," (1968), in *Great Western Salt Works*: 16.
85 For the canon-creating essay on Haacke's importance to this history, see Benjamin H.D. Buchloh, "Hans Haacke: Memory and Instrumental

Reason" [1988], anthologized in his *Neo-Avantgarde and Culture Industry*, (Cambridge, MIT Press, 2000): 203-42.
86 See Burnham, "Art and Technology: The Panacea that Failed," in Kathleen Woodward ed., *Myths of Information: Technology and Post-Industrial Culture*, 200-215. Although Burnham

begins by painting a sympathetic portrait of Kepes and the Center, toward the end of the essay he blamed "the Center's lack of any concrete philosophy" (208) for its long-term irrelevance, and used his systems methodological chops to cite a devastating set of conversations (which he

describes as "maddeningly vague") with Kepes at CAVS regarding Kepes's specific dream of erecting an enormous light sculpture in Boston Harbor:
Did the Center have funds for such a project or any idea of costs? *No.*
Given that the Boston Harbor was directly in the flight

Hans Haacke, *Shapolsky et al., Manhattan Real Estate Holdings, a Real Time Social System, as of May 1, 1971*, black-and-white photographs, typed material, maps. Venice Biennale, 1978. Courtesy the artist, © Hans Haacke/Artists Rights.

Hans Haacke, *Spray of Ithaca Falls, Freezing and Melting on Rope,* February 7, 8, 9,...1969, photograph documenting site specific installation during "Earthworks" exhibition. Courtesy the artist, © Hans Haacke/ Artists Rights.

Compare with Olafur Eliasson, *Your mobile expectations,* ("ice car" for BMW), 2007, detail from Berlin studio installation. Courtesy the artist.

critique. In short, Haacke's principled insistence on an avant-garde unimpeachably outside the society it proposed to criticize derailed the postmodern potential of his early systems work, while ensuring his role as progenitor for the very postmodern generation to come.

Conclusion

The arc of my narrative has a surprising endpoint: the bureaucratic impact of early Haacke and late 1960s systems theory would not be retrieved until the 1990s, when contemporary artists such as Olafur Eliasson came on the scene. Appropriating early Haacke with a difference, such artists restored an important Burnham-like aspect to the '60s utopian technocrats (Buckminster Fuller, Marshall McLuhan, and others), excising their naive positivism in favor of what might be called post-structuralist systems-think: *the external "objective" system must eventually be recognized as impinging on the intimate organization of the subject itself.* Such a move is already forecast in Burnham's own post-1970 shifts into structuralism, post-structuralism, and a final embrace of alchemy, mysticism, and the Kabbalah. On the one hand this trajectory simply follows the shape of '60s counterculture itself ("tune in, turn on, drop out"). But on the other, it reflects Burnham's principled rejection of Kepesian humanism following his CAVS experience, and his harsh judgment of his own early technosociality as a "panacea that failed" and a "technological utopia" based on a "total illusion" of progress through technical and formal innovation.[86] Burnham (and Haacke) nonetheless prepared the way for the artworld itself to be viewed as a system—a challenge taken up by Howard Becker, Pierre Bourdieu, Niklas Luhmann and the whole field of cultural sociology, but elaborated in artworld criticism well before.[87]

Moving through the reflexive looking-glass of postmodernism has stretched the seemingly moribund discourse of systems think into contemporaneity again. It was the critical wing of New York postmodernism that allowed an artist like Eliasson to take Haacke's systems (less likely Burnham's theory) and revel in the way they are <u>not</u> *absolutely independent of any contribution on the part of the viewer,* as Haacke had claimed, but rather <u>absolutely dependent on the contribution of the viewer.</u> Although the mechanical eye of the camera is available to both artists for capturing the optical effect of the rainbow in the prism of water droplets, this stock signifier of romantic beauty is interpreted radically differently in the

patterns of Logan Airport, had the Center checked on the feasibility of the project with the local Civil Aeronautics Board, or with the Boston Harbor Authority? *No.* Did they understand the problems of laying underwater electrical conduit or the costs? *No.* What was the civic purpose

of the light monument? *No one really knew.* [209] About the failed techno-utopianism of his own work, see his harsh self-assessment in the 1970 interview with Sharp, "Willoughby Sharp Interviews Jack Burnham," 21-22.

87 As well as Burnham, for example, one should consider philosopher and art critic Arthur Danto's "The Art World," *The Journal of Philosophy* 61, no. 19 (October 15, 1964): 571-584, and Lawrence Alloway's "Network: the Art World Described as a System," *Artforum* 11, no. 1 (September

1972): 28-32. Staking an early claim on this approach, Alloway cites his own "Art and the Communication Network," published in McLuhan territory, *Canadian Art* (June 1966): 35-37.

1960's practice of Haacke than in the 1990's practice of Eliasson. As Grasskamp describes, retrospectively, the intent of Haacke's 1968 *Water in Wind:*

[the piece] created rainbow effects in the artificial mist that was produced by pumps and spray nozzles. But this romantic aspect was rather incidental in a sequence of works *of nearly scientific stringency.*[88] [emphasis added]

By contrast, Eliasson captures in a single word his precisely opposite contextual move— as *Beauty*, the work locates the history of the romantic science of aesthetics in the singular plural of the spectator's body: after all, both beauty and rainbow exist only in the eye of the beholder and the camera that is its "objective" correlative.

When invoked in art since 1990, systems can be either open or closed, but in the more sophisticated works they are unlikely to be theorized as informationally contained. Information is mapped or traced through networks of power but in so doing it is seen flowing to peripheries that can never be fully controlled. In Perry Hoberman's 1999 *Systems Maintenance*, for example, visitors were provided with life-size furniture, a hand-manipulable model of the same objects, and a virtual world in which furniture, model, and ideal living room were mapped on a computer monitor. Viewers became users in the system, either maximizing or "curing" the chaos of three interlocking registers of information.[89] Definitively, the system of *Systems Maintenance* included the artist's server and the artworld user—motivating the irony of Hoberman's piece. Such distributive informational systems characterize today's artworld more generally, of course. Challenged to interpret the elasticity of system boundaries, art writers have generated terms such as "relational aesthetics" (1997, from Bourdieu's student Nicholas Bourriaud), or written books with titles like *Participation* (2007, Claire Bishop).[90] Recent performative art practices foreground intensely local knowledge production (as in the work of Tino Sehgal or Santiago Sierra), without perhaps acknowledging strongly enough how documents and web-driven textual discourses are very much a part of the systems that form subjects outside the "experience" of the performance itself.

88 "Haacke's production had moved far away from what museums, collectors and dominant culture had made of art: a heroic mystery." Grasskamp, Nesbit, and Bird, *Hans Haacke*, (London: Phaidon, 2004): 40-41.
89 See also Hoberman's *Ball del Fanalet*, a work commissioned for Barcelona by the Fundació Joan Miró, referencing a Catalan dance competition (the "ball del fanalet"), in which couples waltz holding tiny colored lanterns. The dancers may stay on the floor until the candle in their lanterns goes out, and the last couple dancing wins. Hoberman's virtualization of this local practice into an interactive computer-driven environment induced sudden anxiety in his hosts—would the piece be perceived as propounding a Catalan nationalism, hence inflaming the politics of contemporary Spain? Hoberman's patrons sought a link with the global, transnational, electronic world system, and they were unsettled when their artist of choice redrew the boundaries of the art system to include local knowledge in what he called his "sensate environment" of viewers' bodies, dancing creatures, and colored lights. Perry Hoberman, talk at Center for Advanced Visual Studies, MIT,

Perry Hoberman, *Systems Maintenance*, 1999. Fabricated furniture at two scales, video cameras, computer, maintenance crew. Installed at Hull, England. Courtesy of the artist.

November 4, 1999.
90 Nicolas Bourriaud, *Aesthetique relationnel* [1997], translated as *Relational Aesthetics* (Paris: Les presses du réel, 2002); Claire Bishop, *Participation* (Cambridge: MIT Press, 2007). Such authors have influenced my own work on distributed knowledge production via socially networked practices, for which see Jones, "The Server-User Mode," uber-titled "The Art of Olafur Eliasson" by *Artforum* 46, no. 2 (October 2007): 316-25.

following page, Hans Haacke *Water in Wind*, 1968, as photographed in set up on the roof of Haacke's NYC apartment building; compare with Olafur Eliasson, *Beauty*, 1993. Courtesy the artists, © Hans Haacke/ Artists Rights and Studio Eliasson.

In the early phase of Haacke's career, we saw the knife of "objective" systems slicing into the gallery to replace the fuzzy edge of humanism. Taken from the technoscientific toolkit, this Occam's razor was needed to produce work that was "not imagined," as Haacke insisted, "but *real.*" At the same moment Haacke was invoking systems to loosen the bourgeois noose of elite humanist culture, American literary theorist Susan Sontag was similarly railing against over-elaborated humanist interpretation, calling it "the revenge of . . . intellect upon the world."[91] But in the pragmatism that informed Norbert Wiener's thinking, interpretation was always already the ghost in the bureaucratic machine; there is no "experience" without interpretation. Wiener argued that the logical machines of computing revealed "the *machina ratiocinatrix* to be nothing but the *calculus ratiocinator* of Leibniz with an engine in it . . . any logic which means anything to us can contain nothing which the human mind—and hence the human nervous system—is unable to encompass."[92] These intuitions of a shift in the hermeneutics of reception toward the receiving subject during the postwar period were prescient.

But if Olafur Eliasson insistently invokes the viewer making meaning in the art system, there are many more contemporary artists who utilize systems as an uninterrupted legacy, as if "the cultural" is a minor module in the interactive technosocial kit. In this corner of the contemporary artworld, it would seem that the post-structural and post-modern turn has had little impact.

An example of this fully-implemented systems thinking is found in British bio-artist Andy Gracie's *Autoinducer_Ph-1 (Cross Cultural Chemistry)* [2006]. With the collaboration of U.S. computer scientist Brian Lee Yung Rowe, Gracie has networked "digital, simulated bacteria into the existing symbiotic network spanning the water fern Azolla, the cyanobacteria Anabaena," drawing on experience with "their human use in agriculture as organic rice fertilizer."[93] Following an established Asian agricultural technique, the bacteria and water fern form a platform on which the rice can grow in wetland environments; Gracie's interventions feed inputs into the "natural" symbiosis, with Rowe's artificial intelligence system programmed to interact with different elements in the biota. In this reinstantiation of '70s systems art, the human is initially part of the system in quotations about cultural farming practices and allusions to the rigorous AI program, but in a Haacke-like way the work is thenceforth only "automatically" put through its autopoeitic paces. The human seems rigorously excluded (as in Haacke's early "Real-time systems art"). It is present only through its surrogate, the machinic systematics of Artificial Intelligence. As Gracie explains the AI component:

> The Generalized Cellular Signaling system, a platform for exploring emergent behavior and intelligence using cellular systems, is the artificial intelligence model powering the synthetic bacteria. A complete virtual environment exists within GCS where individual cells act independently and communicate with other cells in either a neural fashion using relatively fixed connections, or bacterially, where signals are propagated as molecules through a medium. Digitized stimuli produced by Anabaena cultures, and which reflect their state of being, are taken up by the GCS AI system, a virtual environment featuring bacterial cells that interact with each other and with input chemicals . . . The more the relationship between the real and synthetic bacterial colonies takes on a symbiotic nature the more nutrient will be delivered to the rice. If the relationship veers more towards the parasitic the rice will be starved of the elements it needs. *Autoinducer_Ph-1* therefore examines cross species mutualism as a basis for successful bioartificial ecologies.[94]

Andy Gracie & Brian Lee Yung Rowe, contemporary systems art – *Autoinducer Ph1* (Cross Cultural Chemistry), 2006. Courtesy the artist.

91 Susan Sontag, "Against Interpretation," title essay in *Against Interpretation* (New York: Farrar Straus Giroux, 1965), available in excerpt form online at http:// www.susansontag.com/ againstinterpretationexcrpt. htm, accessed October 2005.

92 Wiener, *Cybernetics*, 125.
93 Mitchell Whitelaw, "Andy Gracie: Symbiotic Circuits," December 2006, online at http://pylon.tv/andy_gracie_ symbiotic_circuits.htm, accessed July 2009.

94 Andy Gracie, "Hostprods" (description for *Autoinducer*), online at http://www. hostprods.net/projects/ autoinducerph-1/, accessed July 2009.

Gracie and Rowe's confident social engineering prompts the question: is this type of bio-art succumbing to an instrumentalism that we might call neo-Productivist? The exclusion of the human percipient from the system is not here an anti-humanist corrective as much as a proto-corporate convenience. "Successful bioartificial ecologies" could be a phrase in next year's IPO, yet Gracie expressed frustration when a scientist visited the installation of *Autoinducer* and didn't like its lack of technical and biological information.[95] The artist strives for "ambiguities" in his work and hopes to take "a playful or challenging stance on the science,"[96] while also collaborating with a scientist looking for creative outlets for programming skills usually employed only by corporate America.[97] The dream of Burnham in 1967 may be morphing before our eyes into the fate he feared for art in 1969—little drops of glittering culture in a productivist corporate engineering bucket.

The virtual interface of the computer is the prime mover in most contemporary systems artworks, yet beyond incantations about the software, the interface is naturalized as an autonomous component of a closed art(object)system. As Gracie comments: "These kind of works exhibit forms of closed system feedback loop[s] that are very common in ecological, biological and social systems."[98] Precisely in opposition to Burnham's vision—but closer to Haacke's—the art invokes closed, rather than open, systems. And in ignorance of where the likes of Eliasson and Hoberman have taken it, the system in question is *conceived as closed around the isolated artwork*, rather than including the discursive and interactive apparatus of viewer, gallery, website, catalogue, Asian agriculture, wall label, critic, blogger, or (here) art historian. The closing of the system works as effective ideology—most writers stand dazzled before Gracie and Rowe's incantations of A.I. To quote one critic, *Autoinducer* "uses the Generalized Cellular Signaling system . . . to interfere with the symbiotic relation." The very syntax reveals a fantasized autopoeisis: artwork uses software to do something internally to itself as artwork—the human programmer is out of the picture, much less the viewer whose body temperature inevitably alters the biome.

95 See Régine Debatty, "Interview with Andy Gracie," *we make money not art* website, posted October 18, 2006 at http://www.we-make-money-not-art.com/archives/robots/index.php?page=7: *Interviewer:* Do you think that your work could be understood and appreciated by the scientific community? How? *Gracie:* I would be happy for that to be the case but so far it hasn't happened. When autoinducer was shown earlier this year I received a report of a visit from a very unhappy biologist who was visiting the show. Apparently he was upset that the information he wanted was not available to him, that the system wasn't displaying clearly every piece of data he wanted to see and that the species involved weren't clearly labelled. Basically he was unhappy that the piece wasn't presented as a scientific experiment and concluded that it therefore failed as art and as science. He was entitled to his opinion, of course, but his scientific approach to the work prevented him from appreciating what it was really about. **96** Ibid.

Thus the radical anti-humanism of Haacke, which mutated in the artist's own post-'60s work of institutional critique, has found a new and anachronistic home in bio-mimetics. If a third phase of systems think theorizes the "you" experiencing the artwork (as in Eliasson) or altering its very terms (Hoberman), another branch remains stuck in Burnham's "panacea that failed." Most contemporary artists and technologists using systems do not theorize the viewer of such works, or ask whether the critique of the artworld that Haacke once posed is made moot when the gallery has become a comfortable platform for habituating us to genomics: "[Gracie and Rowe's] bio-artificial ecosystem, which takes the form of a water garden which sustains living bacteria, robotic systems and artificial lifeforms, push[es] our notions of life, intelligence and being into new territories."[99] Perhaps over-sensitized to Burnham's jeremiads, I wonder if the "new territories" in this review might not already be well-populated by the corporative lifeforms that seek to capitalize biopower. Certainly they are no strangers to good old systems think.

These legacies of bureaucratization do not foreclose other options. The new modes of knowledge production are shared by art and science, and in that digital convergence is a new potential for communicability, information-sharing, and responsible critique. The *modus* of our contemporaneity is not entirely unfamiliar to positivist modernity, but tweaks it in interesting ways: classification or data interpretation, not discovery; laboratory benches and offices, not the studio; systems and relations, not always objects; potentially activated users and critical agents rather than passive recipients of "the work." The challenge for true aspirants to Haacke's and Burnham's legacy is to reanimate their burning ambition, but for a shifted contemporaneity. They saw no reason why one could not capture the tools of technocracy as they were flying by, and hammer them into bizarre new plowshares and pruning hooks for shaping interrogative subjects. They intended to do what art does best —provoke sustained interpretation of a visual experience—but aimed to do that while satisfying the "want of method and technology" the founders of MIT's architecture program identified more than a century ago. Briefly, MIT was a place where this could happen, in the eye of a hurricane directed against the very military-industrial complex this art was attempting to bend its own way.

97 Brian Lee Yung Rowe is associated on the web with the firms Cogenex, an alternative energy company, and Portfolio Analytics, a financial service group. As Brian Lee Dae Yung, he cultivates a separate resume as a "bio-mimetic artist."

98 Régine Debatty interview with Gracie (see n. 95).

99 Valentina Culatti, *Neural*, as posted on "Network-enabled performance" website in May 2006, hosted by Turbulence.org at on http://transition.turbulence.org/blog/archives/002394.html, accessed January 2009.

MARK JARZOMBEK

The Alternative Firmitas of Maurice Smith

The Smith House

Counter-culture architecture from the 1960s was not built to last. Most of the yurts, Bucky domes, bamboo sheds, and Earth Houses have long since disappeared. That makes the Maurice Smith House, begun in 1963, perhaps one of the last surviving— and still habitable—examples.[1] The building is actually an add-on to a conventional "Cape" that Smith bought on a wooded lot in Harvard, Massachusetts. Over time, it has become difficult to tell where the new blends into the old, with the more private areas to the north in the old house and the more open, fenestrated part to the south. The result—looking like a chaotic heap of windows ornamented with colorfully-painted trim—surprises most people who see it today, even in an age of Frank Gehry. And yet, despite appearances, the Smith House was not an experiment in neo-primitivist alternatives to social convention. This is no Drop-City hut, nor part of a counter-culture commune. It was designed as a family house, and more to the point as a demonstration piece of what Smith saw as architecture's inner logic—a logic that must both accept and expose architecture's disciplinary limits. It was not counter-culture, but counter-architecture's-culture.

According to Smith, architecture in its usual sense—that is in the form that most of us use and see—is made by designers who want to control too much.[2] Architects and clients have gotten so used to this, according to his point of view, that over-determinancy has become totally normalized. Few see its choke-hold on reality. And so, if Smith claims that this building is, as he phrases it, a "consistent incompletion" then this is, for him more than just a word game.[3] The building in his eyes is an example of architecture—and nothing more. The rest of the built world, is for him precisely NOT architecture.

So how does "consistent incompletion" become architectural practice? First, there are the building elements, the doors, beams, and windows. Most were discards, collected

---

1 Smith built two houses, one of which burnt down in Maine, leaving his first house on 27 Cleaves Hill Road in Harvard MA the only surviving example of his architectural thinking. Smith also built two houses for a client in the Boston area, but these houses—in a more restrained clean modernist aesthetic—are different from his own house in many respects and are not the subject of this article. Typical is the Indian Hill House designed in 1962-63 in Groton, Massachusetts. A series of low, concrete walls staggered across the crest of the hill rise up to meet wooden, glazed walls of slightly different heights. The whole is protected by shed- and gable roofs designed to appear as thin and lightweight as possible.

2 I interviewed Smith for this article on several occasions in 2010 and 2011. I would like to thank him for the time.

from dumpsters and construction sites over the years. The use of discards was not meant to be overtly political, but one cannot overlook its implications. The building is a type of preservation project, or at least one that was meant to keep elements 'in circulation' that had been discarded by modernization and renovation that were then all the rage. It is not cost-saving that is at stake here, but a message about where architecture begins. Not on a blank sheet of paper, but with used parts.

This does not mean that the design process is arbitrary. On the contrary, the house was built around a single Big Idea that has practical, theoretical and historical components. The Big Idea begins with the absence of walls, or at least walls in the conventional sense. America, for Smith, was the land where architecture could liberate itself from the tyranny of walls. It was, after all, the land of wood. And a wooden wall should not look like it wants to be a brick wall. But that, he argues, that is exactly what happened, and it was the fabled balloon frame that set America backwards. So in opposition to this, the building is constructed of inner columns that support beams that cantilever outward and from which façade elements are hung, elevated, or projected—perhaps one can say, suspended. Steel and concrete can accomplish this as well, but wood has the advantage of being an easy material to use. It can be cut, lifted, drilled and bolted without specialized equipment.

By way of contrast, one could bring up Yurt City made in the 1960s by Charles L. Harker and members of the Tao Design collaborative—most of them disillusioned students from the architecture program at the University of Texas, Austin. Their "Earth House" was made without plans, and improvised as it was being built. PVC piping was configured into nestlike configurations that were then sprayed with polyurethane foam. "All design is spontaneous," according to Harker, who compared the process to the metamorphosis of a butterfly.[4] The protest against the fixity of architecture and the proscriptiveness of its practices clearly resonates in the Smith House. But the chaotic appearance of the Smith House is all illusion. This is no hippie house, no experiment in plastic and certainly not a careless, Appalachian assembly of architectural detritus. It is a highly conceptual piece of architecture. The building is—as Spock might say—"logical" both to the material of wood, and to its position in opposition to modern progressivism.

3 "Discussion with Maurice K. Smith: March 16, 1980 with William Porter and Louis A. Craig," Plan 1980, Perspectives on Two Decades 42. See also: Maurice K. Smith, "Not Writing on Built Form", Harvard Educational Review 39, no. 4 (1969): 69-84; Maurice K. Smith, "Particular associative habitable (built) environments" Progressive Architecture 63, no. 3 (March 1982): 100-103; Maurice K. Smith, "A House by Maurice Smith" Harvard Art Review 2, no. 1 (Winter 1967): 40-45; Edward Robbins, Maurice K. Smith, Gary A. Hack and Tunney F. Lee, "The Client in Architectural Education: Three Interviews at M.I.T." Journal of Architectural Education 35, no. 1(Autumn, 1981): 32-35.

4 Alastair Gordon, "True Green Lessons from 1960s'-70s' Counterculture Architecture," Architectural Record (April 2008), accessed June 10, 2010, http://archrecord.construction.com/features/0804truegreen/0804truegreen-1.asp.

Smith at MIT

The Maurice Smith
House, Harvard, MA. All
photos of Maurice Smith
House: Mark Jarzombek,
April 2010.

Before I can explain some of the aspects of this logic, let me introduce the scene at MIT in the 1950s and 1960s. After WWII, there was no doubt in U.S. schools of architecture that Modernism was here to stay. A few schools like Harvard and IIT benefitted from strong personalities that gave those places specific pedagogical and ideological orientations. As a result their story has dominated the history of Modernism in the US. Today, of course, we see a more complex picture. Nonetheless, the history of Modernism in schools other than Harvard and IIT is rarely told. MIT is usually excluded since it did not have a particularly strong Modernist orientation and, in fact, was considered a Beaux-Arts-styled school well into the 1930s. I.M. Pei came to MIT precisely because of its Beaux-Arts pedagogy. The shift began to take place with Lawrence Anderson, who was named head of the department in 1947 and who could easily be considered one of the first, American-born Modernists. He designed a now much-altered swimming pool for MIT that stood as an unambiguous example of sophisticated Modernist thinking. Its compact form, clean lines, expansive fenestration, and subtle use of color revealed his mastery of the new style.

Though Anderson made it clear that MIT was on a pro-Modernist course, it was far from obvious how Modernism was to be taught or where one was to find the faculty. This created a vacuum that from some points of view could be seen as a moment of weakness, but in actuality served as a counter-model to the over-determined pedagogies of the great masters presiding over Harvard and IIT. It was in this more open-ended context that Buckminster Fuller came in 1952, Louis Kahn in 1956, and Kenzo Tange in 1959. Their stays were short but not insignificant. More durable at MIT was Kevin Lynch, who had a bachelor degree from MIT and was pulled in to teach "city form." But the question of who would teach architecture was asked again and again. And it was into this environment that Maurice Smith stepped into the picture in 1952. Born in New Zealand in 1926 and receiving his initial training there, he had originally been hired by Kansas State, where he struggled against the strict, modernist position of the faculty there. He left Kansas for MIT not to teach, however, but as a student in the newly-formed post-graduate program.[5] Smith entered the circle of Buckminster Fuller, who had also just arrived at MIT to teach a studio. The circle included Richard Wainwright and Peter

Floyd. Wainwright was a mechanical genius, who designed many of Fuller's projects in those days. Fuller would sometimes stay over in Smith's apartment. But Smith was not a Fullerite, and engineering and future-mindedness were for him not the driving questions.

The only person whom Smith truly respected was György Kepes, the Hungarian-born painter, designer, and art theorist who came to the U.S. in 1937, where he taught at the New Bauhaus (later the School of Design, then Institute of Design, then Illinois Institute of Design or IIT). He came to MIT in 1949. Smith admired Kepes not so much for his aesthetic sensibilities, but because of the way he spoke about architecture. Kepes did not use secondary sources and so brought his unique voice to his analyses. But Kepes was not an architectural educator. A typical studio project of his asked students to start with a 6" white cube of paper and then with black paint transform it—visually—into something else. Kepes's interest in camouflage were at the core of such projects. Kepes had designed, for example, but never built, a "fake Chicago" on Lake Michigan using lights on towers to trick the German fighter pilots that many feared were soon to arrive to drop their bombs into the lake. Smith worked with Kepes on several projects, including the windows of the Temple Oheb Shalom synagogue in Baltimore (1960) and the sixty-foot long wall of lights for the KLM show room in New York (1960).[6]

Despite his intellectual admiration for Kepes, the paper exercises were all too abstract for Smith. Nor were the more general design projects assigned to the students any more interesting to him. The student exercise of 1952—the year Smith arrived—was to design a small art gallery in a town in Maine. No site was given. It didn't matter, to the professors at least, so Smith took the unusual step of driving up to Maine to locate a site, which he chose next to a forest edge. He designed the museum with wall panels that could be folded up so that visitors could look at the landscape, weather permitting, instead of the art works. The project elicited a good amount of debate among the teachers, who thought that his project disrespected the primacy of art or that he had disrespected the studio itself by putting it on an actual site.

In the summer of 1952, Smith spent the summer working for Serge Ivan Chermayeff, a Chechen-born, British architect and industrial designer, who had emigrated to the United States in 1940. After a stint at the California School of Fine Arts, Chermayeff was recommended by Walter Gropius for the position of director of the Institute of Design in Chicago in 1946. Chermayeff stepped down from that role in 1951 when the institute merged with the Illinois Institute of Technology. He then travelled to the East Coast to teach at MIT and in 1953 he became head of Harvard's Department of Architecture. Chermayeff had no architectural background and was notably uninterested in the realities of architecture-making. A sketch or two was all he would produce, which he passed on to the likes of Smith to design. But it was not, once again, the absence of faculty who could teach from real experience that concerned Smith, but that Chermayeff saw his houses as private refuges from the stresses of modern life. "Only through the restored opportunity for firsthand experience that privacy gives can health and sanity be brought back to the world of the mass culture," Chermayeff wrote.[7] While this might sound reasonable enough, Smith was already becoming interested in the contrary thematics of openness. For him, Chermayeff houses might look modern but were actually old-fashioned, elitist retreats. If high design legitimized itself as a palliative against the messy world of modernity, then something, for Smith, was terribly wrong.

Disillusioned by his teachers, and even abandoning his desire for a degree, Smith left MIT to return to New Zealand, traveling to England and France on the way back. He visited Le Corbusier's just-finished Unité d'Habitation in Marseille. The long central corridor left him cold, as did the famous roof garden and children's play area. More to his liking was the roof of the Château de Chambord with its complex aggregate of towers. It was designed as a place of twists and turns where the palace inhabitants could ambulate in a type of hide-and-seek. Its various and surprising views and the purposefully strange shapes of the chimney towers, some designed as mini-buildings, were a revelation, not only about the power of architecture and scale. Smith also photographed barns in Switzerland, hilltop towns in Spain, and Trulli houses of Italy. The word vernacular that we might use today did not exist in the 1950s, its coinage only becoming popular in the 1970s. And indeed, such structures would never have been discussed in a school of architecture in those days. Smith also photographed leaves, rocks and natural features with an eye toward abstraction.
When Smith arrived back in New Zealand he hoped to find a teaching position, but the dean of the school there was Cyril Knight (1893-1971). Though known as the father of architectural education in New Zealand, he was strongly in favor of the Beaux-Arts and resisted the adjustment to the modernist ethos. Knight was also an admirer of Banister Fletcher's book on architectural history and styles, a book that Smith held in little esteem.[8] Smith managed to bite his tongue and was hired to organize the students to build a Bucky Dome, even though he had no particular affinity to Fuller's technocratic ideals.

5 At the time there were only four such programs, the others being located at Yale, Columbia and Berkeley.

6 For pictures of the stained glass and mosaics for Temple Oheb Shalom see: http://dome.mit.edu/handle/1721.3/69071?show=full.

7 Serge Chermayeff and Christopher Alexander, Community and Privacy: Toward a New Architecture of Humanism (New York: Doubleday, 1963), 38.

8 For more see: Ann McEwan, "Learning by Example: Architectural Education in New Zealand Before 1940," Fabrications 9 (1999): 1-10. Available online at http://espace.library.uq.edu.au/eserv/UQ:23581/n09_002_McEwan.pdf

Things were not looking too well, but in 1956, Pietro Belluschi, the new dean of MIT's School of Architecture and Planning, happened to come to New Zealand on his way to Australia. Belluschi was an Italian-born architect who was already well-known and would rise even further, designing or being involved with many high-profile commissions, most famously the Pan Am Building (1963) in New York. Belluschi was trained as an engineer and had no experience running a school of architecture. He was mainly looking to professionalize the school, but he and Smith hit it off, and Belluschi invited Smith to return to MIT to teach and to help Kepes. Smith knew that there was no future for him in New Zealand, but he must have wondered if there was a future for him in the US too, for when he returned to Cambridge in 1958, he found that the department had changed considerably, and, from his position, for the worse. The free-wheeling days of the 1950s were over.

In 1956, Belluschi had brought in the Argentine architect, Eduardo Catalano, as well as Catalano's teacher, Horacio Caminos. Catalano had just won the House of the Decade award, given out by *House and Home*, for an elegant, thin-roofed, winged house he had designed in Raleigh, North Carolina. As for Caminos, he had been one of those responsible for bringing modernism to South America, emphasizing throughout his career the value of social housing. Belluschi had also hired the painter and graphic artist Richard E. Filipowski, who had studied under László Moholy-Nagy at the New Bauhaus in Chicago. His paintings were influenced by Fernand Léger and Henri Matisse, and, of course, by Moholy-Nagy. Filipowski had been brought by Gropius to the Harvard Graduate School of Design, where he developed the Fundamentals of Design program. In 1952, when Belluschi had lured him to MIT, he was put in charge of the second semester studio. Add Kepes to the mix and MIT was now emerging as a Modernist powerhouse, perhaps unique in the US for its South American connections.

None of this was to the liking of Smith, who envisioned a very different approach to the question of Modernism and its teaching. First of all, Filipowski did not teach architecture in his studio, but gave the students Bauhaus/Kepes-styled "architectonic assignments" in which students were to make objects out of paper. Why are we teaching architects to make things out of paper and not out of real materials, Smith wondered. Smith was not one to disguise his critique and he slowly began to work to transform Filipowski's course from

Maurice Smith with student William Rawn, Department of Architecture, MIT, n.d..

a departmental requirement to an elective. In essence, Smith almost singlehandedly was able to de-Bauhaus the department and put it on a more independent footing.

Smith's position also put him at odds with his more eminent colleagues, not the least of which was Catalano, who was the most prolific of the MIT professors. Catalano designed US embassies in Buenos Aires, Argentina, Pretoria, and South Africa, along with the Julliard School of Music at New York City's Lincoln Center. He specialized in giant buildings that today go under the label of Brutalism. The Stratton Student Center at MIT (1965) was typical: an imposing edifice, strictly symmetrical in plan, with exposed poured-in-place concrete and monumental, fortress-like proportions.

Smith was unfazed and jokingly labeled Catalano "a fascist," not because of his political views, but because of Catalano's architectural approach, which Smith felt was the epitome of the over-determined, design methodologies of the High Modernists. Despite Catalano's prominence, Smith was able to convince the faculty that undergraduate education should not fill the minds of students with such pompous ambitions, and so in 1961 Catalano and Caminos, in an effort to distance themselves from Smith, created their own independent graduate program—the Masters in Architecture and Advanced Studies—that they alone had control over, leaving Smith to teach and exert his influence in the undergraduate program.

Slack Theory
In a world that had increasingly clear ideas of what it meant to be a Modernist—horizontal roofs, big sheets of glass and simple forms—Smith was from the beginning an iconoclast. For Smith, an architect does not start with a site analysis and then figure out how to best fit the program into square rooms or stack them into towers. One begins perhaps with a few pieces of lumber that were thrown away from a building demolition. One adds some windows retrieved from a restoration along with granite blocks thrown away from a demolished barn. This way of beginning for him an attempt to open an architectural frontier *behind* the territory of architecture's over-determinism. Architecture is not a possession displayed on the city street, but a process. Smith, in that sense, is an anti-historicist, but in a very different sense of the word than the Modernists were. For the Modernists, historical forms had to be

Maurice Smith, "Additive
Built Form Assemblage
Exploration, Level 2,"
with TA Lawrence Cheng,
Spring 1978. From *Plan*
1980.

Maurice Smith House interior.
Photo: Mark Jarzombek.

abandoned in order for architecture to address the pressing industrial and social realities of the time. For Smith, *all* architectural forms had to be abandoned, including Modernist ones, in order for architecture to address the more rudimentary needs of the moment and context.

None of this yet determines the design. That is a separate matter all together, and the solution lay, partially at least, in the material of wood. The battle that Smith fought against the Modernism aesthetic paralleled a battle against what he perceived as the American blindness to its most precious contribution to the architectural world. It had all gone wrong with the balloon frame, which Sigfried Giedion heralded as one of the great contributions of American builders to the industrialization of our culture. For Smith the balloon frame destroyed nothing less than architecture's possibility, for it was first and foremost a wall and as such annihilated its potential to do other things. To build a wall one must think vertically from the foundation up. But wood can be cantilevered; it can reach out over spaces; and it can serve as a 'rope' to hang structures from. The question for him was not about vertical loads, but about stability.

One can see why this fit so uneasily with the usual concerns of the time. Smith's architecture fights front and center against the rationalization of space. It was also a pre-eminently "American" struggle waged in his adopted homeland. In the distant background there is in this a sensibility akin to the Arts and Crafts. But if the Arts and Crafts emphasized wood's solidity, this was not the case with Smith. Wood, for Smith, opened up an anti-gravitational space. It also shaped the modern consciousness much more than concrete or steel could, for even though those materials could do similar things, they had to be designed and engineered. Wood was a craftsman's delight.

But how to use it? To answer this question, he coined the term "slack theory." At the level of construction, slack theory allows several 'hands' to partake in the designing and building of the house. There is no right or wrong. Decisions can be made on site and can even be undone if they do not work. His house was built, in fact, with students as a hands-on teaching enterprise. But slack theory also has a historical component. To illustrate this, Smith uses his two index fingers, one positioned upright and the other horizontally. Traditionally, they would form a 'T' or post-and-beam. Moving the horizontal finger up produces the type of 'opening' that as Smith explains is the beginning of modern space consciousness. Here Smith points to Mies' Brick Country House (1923), where the walls have the form of T's and L's and straight lines that never touch to form a U, much less a square room. And Wright, in his houses, famously opened up the corners between rooms.

Maurice Smith House interior. From *Plan* 1980.

But this, according to Smith, was not enough. He then moves one finger laterally. Beams, of course do not really float, but in opening the relationship between column and beam, Smith forced his students to ask about the three-dimensional nature of space. How then does one fill the gap? That is where Slack comes in, for the point is not to just put in a pane of glass between post and beam, but rather to produce a connective tissue between post and beam that creates and expresses an ephemeral sense of continuity and difference. This area of Slack is both structure *and* ornament. Smith calls it the "consistent incompletion of geometry." In his house, columns and beams are held together by small bits of window frame, a piece of a piano, a furniture leg, or lumber covered with a mosaic made of pieces of broken tiles salvaged from a dump.

This "indeterminacy" creates geometrically-styled "puzzles" that stand in dialectical relationship to "structure." The roof does stand up; but it is *not* structure as such. Part of it is cantilevered, and the walls do not rise, but are hung down to the ground, built, in essence, from top down. Slack is not just the in-between stuff. It is part of the more embracing concept, Open Field, that for Smith defines the invisible tension between elements.[9] Here the work of Malevich, early Mondrian and others plays a role, but so too painters like the eighteenth-century English landscapist, John Robert Cozens. Over the decades, as Smith's thinking matured, he has come to view nature not as the backdrop to the architectural object, but as itself a type of architectural field possessed of various densities. Architecture has in essence to make these energies visible and manifest. Smith drew some of his inspiration from Paul Klee, who often drew objects seemingly with representations of their respective "fields" around them. In a similar sense for Smith, a column was not just a static structural element—a point in space—, but an object that radiated energies into the environment, energies that had spatial and architectural consequences for the designer. The interplay between the "stuff" and "the space defined by the stuff" was everywhere for Smith, and they were inseparable.[10]

Smith produces this indeterminacy not only in his architecture, but also in his equally remarkable pedagogy. When he taught a class, he would hand out pages that were filled with plans, sketches, collaged bits of images and sentences written at various angles across the page. At some level his pedagogy verges on Dada and his own interest in Georges Braque and Kurt Schwitters, but on another level, it speaks to the impossibility in his mind to teach architecture linearly. It is a type of theoretical Cubism where different component, linguistic, analytic and historical overlap into larger constellations. His sentences were always composed of equations, fractions, parentheses, and quotation marks. It was not meant to be read as science, but on the contrary as a way to 'build-your-sentence'. Pedagogy was not about imitating the master but about using a specific set of semantic tools to construct variations and combinations. It is the cognitive version of the 'Expanded T'. For example, here is part of one of his hand-outs:

9 The Blackman House illustrates many of Maurice's principles of partial definition and incompletion even though there are no found objects in its design. It displays a remarkable range of privacies distributed along a continuum from public to private.

10 I would like to thank Charles W. Styron, a former student of Smith's, for this and other insights into Smith's teaching.

A. Landscape intensification: Continuity of partial shelter/access/etc. is $\frac{\text{found}}{\text{supplied}}$ directly $\frac{\text{in}}{\text{by}}$ the «landscape» of moderate climates...

$\frac{\text{claim}}{\text{build}}$ small zones of much larger «habitable» territories.

e.g., water-formed $\frac{\text{bays}}{\text{island}}$, $\frac{\text{valleys}}{\text{hills}}$, ravines, cliffs, promontories...

$\frac{\text{On-going definitions}}{\text{Access and containements}}$ are directional (with contours), open to light...

Habitable outside is still outside. Inside is inside.

This can be read in different ways.

"Continuity of partial shelter is supplied directly by the "landscape" of modern climates..."

"Continuity of partial shelter is found directly in the "landscape" of modern climates...."

And so forth, moving from one semantic positioning to another. Smith's role as teacher was to produce a *textual* device that allowed a student to find a unique and different *architectural* solution to the question.

This system allowed Smith to not only teach in a particular way, but also to analyze architectural spaces like the Piazza Pretoria in Palermo, a painting by Kasimir Malevich, a painting by Claude Monet, and even a drawing by Saul Steinberg. His studies of these are related to the "regulating lines" of Le Corbusier, except that unlike Corbusier, the lines that he produces are not meant to be literally two-dimensional. They are neither plan nor façade generators. Instead, they are markers and 'intensifiers' that entangle the artifact in semantic discontinuity with itself. To explain one drawing he states:

The pieces are area-derived and "plate-shifted" from two squares: one, the length of 2nd top rectangle; the other, its width. All 8 "mobilizing" parts are firmly "nailed" to the including (9th) frame/site and / or #2.[11]

11 Maurice K. Smith, "Dimensional Self-Stability and Displacement in Field-Ordered Directional Alterations," Places 5, no. 2 (1988), 85.

Architecture comes out of linguistic hiding in the form of an incomprehensible—almost Dadaist—run-on of concepts, quotations, equations that is meant to sounds like it means something—but what?

> As in "architectural" plazas—domestic/CORDOBA, collective/COMBARRO. Public/ Pistoia, etc....—primary territorial positioning is double-directionally stabilized, while the "uses" of each dimension vary/"reverse."

Or, in regards to the painting *Poppies near Giverny*, 1890, by Claude Monet:

> Double-direction self-stabilities and displacements demark major definitions—tallest poplar both by its own height from right-hand boundary, and by "frame's" height from left edge.[12]

Once one understands the principles of slack theory, these pronouncements seem less bizarre; one can hear Smith struggling to avoid the conventions of architectural description and try to stand on the 'other side' of history and language. Ultimately, he wants to find the future tense of what he calls "lateral or double-directional displacements" in the actions of past builders, designers and photographers as a type of repressed consciousness. In that sense, slack theory is very much about history, a history of its own making. But, as he notes:

> How ubiquitous/"mandatory" this particular behavioral/formal attribute really is awaits further assimilation/assessment.[13]

Conclusion

If architects today place value on craft, it is usually to emphasize the tradition of things built well. Smith was unique in his effort to de-construct the ideology of *firmitas*, first as a question of *techné*, delaminating structure from gravity, and then as a question of cognition, freeing language from coherency, and all the while marching to the rhythm of a precisely calibrated, historical logic. His works deserves a place in the history of Modernism as one of the significant attempts of that generation to re-envision not just the architectural world, but the world itself.

12 Ibid., 84.
13 Ibid., 85.

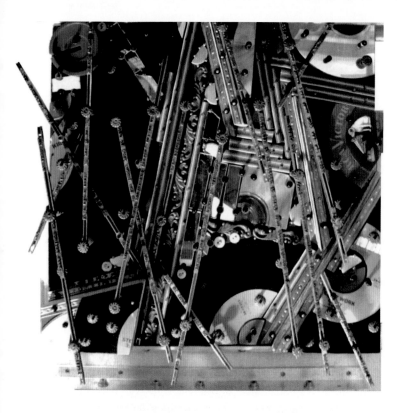

Maurice Smith, *Untitled Collage.* Photos: Mark Jarzombek, April 2010.

Maurice Smith, *Untitled Collage.*

following page, The Maurice Smith
House, Harvard, MA. Photo: Mark
Jarzombek, April 2010.

THINKING THE CITY
EXHIBIT AT MIT MUSEUM 1992

a $\frac{case}{claim}$ for   HABITABLE
                            SELF-STABLE   SCREEN/S

by Maurice Smith

POSITION: THE INCLUSIVELY $\frac{DELINEATED}{EXPERIENCED}$ 'WORLD' OF PHYSICAL DEFINITION

FAMILIES (INDEPENDENT OF 'HOW' THEY ARE DEPLOYED) $\frac{RANGES}{PERMUTATES}$ VARIABLY

$\frac{ACROSS}{FROM}$ $\underline{\underline{TWO}}$ MAJOR $\frac{COMPLIMENTARY}{POLAR}$ FORM GROUPS:

(1. (The) ONGOING CONTINUOUS SURFACE/S : $\frac{ONE + TWO SIDED}{UNDULATIONS}$

OF $\frac{'GROUND}{WATER}$ - FORM', measurable by contours, displacements, and

surface generated $\frac{volumes}{containments}$.

(Through many $\frac{intermediate}{additive}$ SURFACE components $\rightarrow$

(anti)-clastics/(partial) walled containments/ $\frac{abutting}{planar}$ assemblages --

$\frac{opaque/reflective}{\frac{translucent}{transparent}}$ $\rightarrow$

variably lit surfaces are all $\frac{directly}{physically}$ $\frac{limiting}{stop}$ territorial

$\frac{restraints}{barriers}$.

(2. (The) SCREEN/S :INTERMITTENT $\frac{'STICK'}{LINEAL}$ $\frac{DEPLOYMENT}{ASSEMBLAGES}$ $\left(\frac{BRANCHINGS}{FRAMES}\right)$

$\frac{indicate}{demark}$ extent of $\frac{zones}{claims}$ while enabling direct $\frac{continuity}{go}$ of $\frac{space}{light}$

without mandatory closure.

"Thinking the City," Exhibition at MIT, 1992.
following page, Photo: Stanford O. Anderson.

Extensive $\frac{\text{architectural}}{\text{anthropogeomorphological}}$ environments (including cities

without 'SCREENS' parallel a hard, reflective ecological 'world'

without $\frac{\text{trees}}{\text{forests}}$. Screens are an architectonic vanishing species.

(Our) contemporary urban concentrations are largely de - $\frac{\text{tree'd}}{\text{landscaped}}$

and have (lamentably) $\frac{\text{abandoned}}{\frac{\text{overlooked}}{\text{excluded}}}$ this second great form family.

(Only surfaces might survive!)

Please help!! Save the screens!!

INCLUSIVE 'FORM LANGUAGE' RECOGNITIONS include some 16 systems of intrinsic

field-form $\frac{\text{attributes}}{\frac{\text{behaviors}}{\text{organizations}}}$ sympathetic to cumulative late 20th century awarenesses...

as listed on the accompanying subject description.

This installation is directed to only one of these:

number 11: SCREENS-HABITABLE (versus $\frac{\text{skin}}{\text{surface}}$)
etc.

This particular selection limited to some aspects of only one form system

for demonstration purposes is intended as neither hierarchic nor exclusionary...

EACH of the 'listed' systems is necessarily contributive to a full understanding

of $\frac{\text{PHYSICAL}}{\text{BUILT}}$ FIELD FORM.

Networks

CASE and MIT: Engagement
Stanford O. Anderson

Two Cambridges: Models, Methods, Systems, and Expertise
Mary Louise Lobsinger

Toward a "Nation of Universities": Architecture and Planning
Education at MIT circa the 1940s
Brendan D. Moran

STANFORD O. ANDERSON

CASE and MIT
Engagement

The 1960s are widely recognized as the time when the practice and pedagogy stemming from the Modern Movement declined, some might say came to be exhausted within a quiescence stemming from their own success. Positions that recognized this phenomenon and posed alternatives appeared. Two of the most prominent of these emerged in the thought, and then widely read books, of Aldo Rossi and Robert Venturi.[1]

In the early 1960s there appeared in the major East Coast schools of architecture a number of young architects who were schooled just ahead of the Rossi and Venturi successes, but who also reflected this discomfort with a diminished modernism in practice and pedagogy. In 1964 they created an organization, seeking to gain collective strength in criticism of the existing situation and, still more, to construct new positions in architectural practice and teaching. The organization took the name Conference of Architects for the Study of the Environment/CASE. Prominent among those architects involved in this questioning, listed with their academic appointment dates, were: Henry (Hank) Millon, MIT 1960;[2] Michael McKinnell, Columbia, 1960, Harvard 1966; Thomas R. (Tim) Vreeland, UPenn 1955; Jaquelin (Jaque) T. Robertson, Yale 1962, Columbia 1963; Richard Weinstein, Columbia; Michael Graves, Princeton 1962; Peter Eisenman, Princeton 1963; Stanford (Stan) Anderson, MIT 1963; John Hejduk, Cooper Union 1964;[3] Kenneth (Ken) Frampton, Princeton, 1964. Colin Rowe was ten to fifteen years older than other members, the mentor of Peter Eisenman at Cambridge, but now returned to the U.S. with a 1962 appointment at Cornell. Three architects who came to be founding members of CASE were dominantly in practice, but also with academic ties: Robert (Bob) Kliment, Philadelphia and Penn; Richard (Dick [!]) Meier, New York and Cooper Union 1963; Giovanni (Gio) Pasanella, New York and Yale 1964, Columbia 1965.

Abbreviations in the notes:

cc: typed carbon copy

Ditto: multiple copies by typed "spirit master" in Ditto process

Mimeo: multiple copies by typed stencil in Mimeograph process

SA files: files of Stanford Anderson, MIT

Tfx: heat sensitive copy

paper; 3M Thermofax process

Xc: photocopy, initially (and here) by Xerox process

All referenced documents are on typewriter, unless otherwise noted.

1 Aldo Rossi, *L'architettura della città* (Padua: Marsilio, 1966), in English as *The Architecture of the City* (Oppositions Books, Cambridge, MA: The MIT Press, 1982); Robert Venturi, *Complexity and Contradiction* (New York: Museum of Modern Art, 1966).

2 See facing page.

3 Surprisingly, never a member of CASE, though he was a participant in CASE 4 (May 1966).

Brief notes on the educational backgrounds and later careers of each of these architects/ professors are:

Colin Rowe (1920 Rotherham, England—1999 Arlington, VA); BArch University of Liverpool, 1938-42 and 1944-45; R.E. Paratroops, 1942-44; MA Warburg Institute, London, 1946-48, with Professor Rudolf Wittkower; Yale 1951- 52, no degree. Teaching, Liverpool, 1948-51; University of Texas Austin, asst.prof., 1953-56; Cooper Union, 1956-57; Cornell, 1957-58; Cambridge 1958-62. Cornell University, 1962 till his retirement in 1990. (Rowe vita, undated, 2pp, cc, SAfiles)

Thomas R. (Tim) Vreeland (b. 1925, Albany, NY), BA Yale, 1950; BArch Yale 1954; apprentice, Louis Kahn 1954-55 and 1956-60; taught at Penn, 1955-65; chair of Architecture, University of New Mexico, 1965; first chair of March I Program UCLA, 1968; research architect, American Academy Rome, 1974-75. (Vreeland vita, undated, 2pp, annotated Ditto and original, SAfiles)

Henry A. Millon (b. 1927, Altoona, PA), BA, BS, BArch Tulane 1947, 1949, 1953, Navy 1946; MA, MArch, PhD Harvard, 1954, 1955, 1964; Fulbright Rome, 1957;

American Academy in Rome 1958-60. Millon was Director, American Academy in Rome, 1974-77, and first Dean of the Center for Advanced Study in the Visual Arts, National Gallery, Washington, 1980- 2000. (Millon vita, Feb. 1965, 2pp, cc, SAfiles)

John Hejduk (b. 1929, New York —2000, New York); BArch Cooper Union, 1950; Cooper, 1964; continuous practice, New York from 1965; Dean, Cooper Union, 1972- 2000.

Giovanni Pasanella (b. 1931, New York), BArch, Cooper Union; March, Yale; office of Edward Larrabee Barnes, 1959-64; architectural critic, Kentucky 1963, Yale 1964; adjunct prof., Columbia, 1965- 87; own practice, 1964-76; Pasanella and Klein from 1976.

Peter Eisenman (b. 1932, East Orange, NJ), BArch Cornell 1955; office of Percy Goodman 1957-58 and The Architects Collaborative 1959; MArch, Columbia 1960; MA and PhD (with Colin Rowe), Cambridge University 1963; founding of the Institute of Architecture and Urban Studies, New York, 1967, continuous practice in New York; teaching appointments at Cooper Union, Harvard, Princeton and Yale.

Richard Weinstein (b. 1932), BA, psychology, Brown; MA clinical psychology, Columbia; MA Arch Penn; Rome Prize; Director, Office of Lower Manhattan Planning and Development under Mayor Lindsay, 1968-74; Dean UCLA-Graduate School of Architecture and Urban Planning, 1985-94.

Robert Kliment (b. 1933, Czechoslovakia); before end of war registered with British Commission for Refugees (as was his brother Stefan [b. 1930]; Ruston Academy, Havana, class of 1950; BA and MArch, Yale; Fulbright to Italy; taught Penn and Columbia; Kliment/Halsband from 1972. Jaquelin T. Robertson (b. 1933, Richmond, VA), BA Yale 1955; Rhodes Scholar Oxford; MArch Yale 1961. Robertson was co-founder of the New York City Urban Design Group, the first Director of the Mayor's Office of Midtown Planning and Development, and a City Planning Commissioner. In 1975, he spent three years in Iran, directing the planning and design of the country's new capitol center Shahestan Pahlavi. Dean, University of Virginia, 1980-88; partner in Eisenman/Robertson, 1980-87; partner in Cooper/ Robertson from 1988.

Stanford Anderson (b. 1934, Redwood Falls, MN); BA University of Minnesota 1957; assistant clerk of the works, Concordia Senior College and Eero Saarinen, 1956; MA(arch) University of California, Berkeley 1958; Columbia University, 1959- 61 (PhD 1968); Fulbright Fellow, Munich 1961-62; design teacher Architectural Association London, 1962- 63. MIT professor from 1963 (Anderson vita, 2pp, original, SAfiles).

Michael Graves (b. 1934, Indianapolis, IN), BArch., University of Cincinnati, 1958; M.Arch, Harvard, 1959; American Academy in Rome 1960-62; continuous practice, Princeton, from 1964.

Richard Meier (b. 1934, Newark, NJ); BArch Cornell, 1957; European travel; New York offices, including Marcel Breuer 1960-63 [painted, shared studio w/ Frank Stella]; own practice, 1963ff; instructor Cooper Union 1962- 73. (Meier vita, cover letter April 1965, 2pp, Xc, SAfiles)

Michael McKinnell (b. 1935), Manchester BA 1958; MS, Columbia 1960. Continuous architectural practice in Boston; professor at Harvard 1966ff; MIT, 1996-2000

I was the Executive Secretary of CASE and thus have the CASE files, modest as they are. Peter Eisenman often urges that I write an account of CASE; I would welcome that task, but it could only be done fully with extensive research and interviews. What follows will be the first considered account of the history of CASE, but one must recognize both that it is only a draft of what would be possible and that, in keeping with the objectives of this volume, it gives emphasis to MIT.

MIT Architecture—Early 1960s

To understand how MIT came into CASE and what reciprocal effects they had, it is necessary to consider the ground that was laid at MIT. Hank Millon and I were trained in architecture, then in history, and now had appointments primarily as architectural historians at MIT. Nonetheless, we also taught in the studios and our students were in the professional programs of the Department of Architecture. We found it natural to be engaged participants in the activities of the young architect/educators who were to form CASE, yet the intellectual and design positions at MIT and in the wider association were not always complementary.

Hank and I enjoyed the full support of the respected and indeed beloved Head of the Department of Architecture, Lawrence B. Anderson, from 1965 Dean of the School of Architecture and Planning.[4] Hank, already in his first years at MIT, earned the respect of the Department and Institute administrations. He was a forceful voice in the development of new energies in history and the arts.[5] We had cordial relations with the rest of the faculty, and truly warm relations with a subtle design professor, Imre Halasz. However, genuine embrace of our role as historians was as tepid with the design faculty as is characteristic in schools of architecture.

Maurice Smith dominated the architectural design faculty.[6] Several factors contributed to his effective role in the school. Smith held strong positions about architecture and design that he strenuously sought to impart to his students. MIT was still a five-year undergraduate professional program, with a first year devoted to the MIT core program, particularly in mathematics and the sciences. One design professor directed the studio

4 http://tech.mit.edu/V114/N20/anderson.20n.html, accessed June 17, 2010. Stanford Anderson, "Lawrence B. Anderson," *Dizionario dell'Architettura del XX Secolo* (6 vols; Turin: Umberto Allemandi, 2000-2001), vol. 1.
5 Millon was influential in the appointment of Minor

White in 1966 and Ricky Leacock in 1969 and thus the creation of dynamic programs in photography and film, all within MIT Architecture.
6 Maurice Smith (b. New Zealand, 1926), MIT lecturer 1958-1961; professorial appointments 1961-1993, continued to 1997. Stanford Anderson, "Maurice Smith,"

Dizionario dell'Architettura del XX Secolo (6 vols; Turin: Umberto Allemandi, 2000-2001).
7 Stanford Anderson, "William Wilson Wurster," *Dictionary of Art*, rev. ed. (London: Grove, 2008).
8 Marcus Whiffen, ed., *The History, Theory and Criticism of Architecture* (Cambridge,

MA: MIT Press, 1966). Published lectures were those of Peter Collins (McGill), Bruno Zevi (University of Rome), Serge Chermayeff (Yale), Sibyl Moholy-Nagy (Pratt), Stephen W. Jacobs (Cornell), Stanford Anderson (MIT), and Reyner Banham (*Architectural Review*, London). I first gave my

program in each of the next three years, while more individual initiative appeared in the final year. Smith was careful to hold control of level I design. For a full year he shaped the thought and work of all the beginning students, starting with about forty students. Smith also adamantly extended his ideas into faculty deliberations and the continuing experience of students.

None of the studio faculty could be as dismissive of history and historians as Maurice. But as so often with Maurice, such outbursts were the prickly cover of a man who was much more subtle and deeply informed than he sought to show—also in those aspects of history that engaged him. And also more personable. As energetic and ambitious as he was, Maurice could not teach an entire year of design for forty students alone. The surprising fact is that for several years Hank Millon and I served as slightly glorified assistants to Maurice in his studio (at our own volition, beyond our teaching assignments in history that we also voluntarily expanded). These times with Maurice were for me important learning experiences in architecture and design pedagogy. However, as we shall see, the MIT design program did not provide a fruitful base for our relations with the wider community of young architects—or vice versa.

In the post-war years, MIT created the School of Architecture and Planning with William W. Wurster[7] as Dean and Lawrence B. Anderson as Department Head. This accommodated the formation of the Department of City Planning with its increasingly wide range of disciplinary offerings. The School of Humanities and Social Studies was formed, with John Ely Burchard, formerly of the Department of Architecture, as Dean. This was part of Institute initiatives to increase the role of humanities within the education of scientists and engineers. There were more general energies to humanize MIT—the dormitory that was to be known as Baker House, the selection of Alvar Aalto for its design, and the careful tending of its execution by Wurster, are all part of the commitments of that time.

Anderson (known to all as "Andy") was a proponent of a larger and stronger role for history in architectural education. The appointment of Hank in 1960 and of me in 1963 altered what had been mainly visiting professor contracts at MIT (including such luminaries as Henry-Russell Hitchcock, John McAndrew, and Dean Joseph Hudnut of Harvard, who generously taught history for a year while MIT awaited my arrival—and then also generously donated his extensive set of well-chosen lantern slides).

Cranbrook Teachers' Seminar 1964

Andy served as General Chair of the Steering Committee for the 1964 AIA/ACSA Cranbrook Teachers' Seminar. Each year this established series of week-long summer seminars addressed a theme of particular interest within architectural education. Andy steered the 1964 topic to concerns reflected in a resulting publication, *The History, Theory and Criticism of Architecture*.[8] Hank chaired the Program Committee and succeeded in attracting virtually all the leading established figures in the teaching of history in schools of architecture—and two notable European professors. Buford Pickens of Washington University chaired the meetings. Among the speakers at what proved to be contentious but ground-breaking exchanges, were those included in the ensuing publication: Reyner Banham (University of London), Serge Chermayeff (Yale), Peter Collins (McGill), Stephen Jacobs (Cornell), Sibyl Moholy-Nagy (Pratt Institute), Bruno Zevi (University of Rome), and Stan Anderson. Other participants included George Collins (Columbia), Millon, Colin Rowe, and Marcus Whiffen (University of New Mexico). Among the design professors present were Lawrence Anderson, Walter Creese and Donlyn Lyndon (University of Oregon), Eisenman, and Vreeland.

The European professors were crucial to the vitality of the meetings, and the most polemical. Banham arrived with a supply of the latest *Archigram*. Zevi, recently made Director of the school in Rome, campaigned that the historians present should go back and take over direction of their schools: " . . . recognize right away that our problem is not how to teach history of architecture, theory of architecture or architectural criticism, but how to teach architecture based on the historical-critical method." There were no immediate take-overs. It was 1991 before I became the first instance, at least in the modernist tradition, of a historian as head of department—and then thought of myself as in the tradition of Andy rather than Zevi.

Hank Millon recently recalled the Cranbrook meeting, with reliance on its published record:

Serge Chermayeff of Yale [whom both Hank and I admired and loved], thought little of history, theory and criticism, greeted participants with "I don't like much what you do, I don't like very much how you do it, and I don't believe that what you are doing serves any good."

Sibyl Moholy-Nagy found it "extraordinary that architectural history has suddenly become the object of intense controversy"... and that ... "the elimination ... of history in architecture schools a generation ago has ... not been replaced by [some other] workable method."

Stan Anderson's pithy contribution argued "anti traditionalism has been ... a characteristic of modern architects ... the conclusion to be drawn from the tradition-bound character ... of contemporary architects is ... that we ... should use those traditions more eloquently or free ourselves from them, as we see fit." For Stan, "criticism ... is the only way we have of detecting our mistakes, and of learning from them in a systematic way; we learn from the proposal testing, and reformulation or rejection, of simple and apparently inadequate hypotheses ... [S]tudies of projects could prove highly instructive concerning ... which [of] these conjectures may be valid." Anderson, youngest of the group, had the only seminar paper selected for publication by Bruno Zevi in *L' Architettura*.

Reyner Banham, from *The Architectural Review*, London, held: "It is impossible to discuss [a] building without discussing what it is for … history cannot proceed in the absence of such particulars as the designated function of the building." Further, he continued, "The inability of creating a general theory of criticism … has led to this feeling that architectural theory has become vacuous and irrelevant." "At the University College in London, we … decided we could get along without theory because we could find nothing particularly solid or interesting in the category normally labeled 'theory'." Banham concluded, "Part of being an architect and/or architectural critic is that you are dealing … with visual symbols … for personal reasons, irrespective of the functions that the building has to serve, and are the reasons why it was built."

Bruno Zevi, just appointed, was not one to pass up an opportunity to extol the pending transformation of the school of architecture in Rome, nor to promulgate his program for a new 'scientific' relationship between history and design. During the seminar, he drafted a manifesto defining, in eight paragraphs, the deficiencies of current curricula and the projected goals of a renovated teaching program for schools of architecture. The manifesto/declaration, when presented to the Cranbrook participants, was not endorsed because many thought that the proposal would need to be discussed not only back at home in their schools of architecture, but also by the board of directors of the Association of Collegiate Schools of Architecture.

Nonetheless, Zevi, that September, published in *L' Architettura*, the entire text of the manifesto together with a commentary discussing how differently proposed curricular reforms are handled in Italy and the U.S. Zevi earlier published a report on the seminar in his 5 July 1964 weekly column 'Cronache', a series devoted to architecture in the popular Italian weekly *L' Espresso*.

paper, "Architecture and Tradition that isn't 'Trad, Dad'," a polemic with Reyner Banham, in February 1963 as an Architectural Association lecture in London, with Ernst Gombrich in the chair and giving a first short lecture. Banham, then at the height of his London esteem, Sir John Summerson, Arthur Koestler, Cedric Price, Royston Landau, Alan Colquhoun, Alvin Boyarsky, and a good part of the London architectural scene attended. Also published in *Architectural Association Journal* 80, no. 892 (London, May 1965): 325-333, and as "Polemica con Reyner Banham: architettura e tradizione vera," *L'Architettura* 10, no. 12 (April 1965), 828-831. This "polemic against Banham," in the American context of the time, could also be seen as a polemic against Christopher Alexander, *Notes on the Synthesis of Form* (Cambridge, MA: Harvard University Press, 1964)—though for different reasons. It was at Cranbrook 1964 that Colin Rowe and I met and discovered our parallel intellectual paths through Karl Popper and Rudolf Wittkower.

The article pointed out the retardataire nature of architecture schools in the U. S. that still distinguished between history, theory and criticism, [although] from the first day of the Cranbrook seminar the academic origin of those distinctions had been denounced. For Zevi, "Only in the ambience of an ideology and of a poetic classicism ... can history be interpreted as a collection of 'objective' facts and phenomenological prominence, from which theory has the task to extract universally valid principles, such as proportion, rhythm, and harmony, etc. Any distinction between history, and criticism derives from an analogous preconception: objective history should maintain a [protective] moat separating the present from corruption by contemporary controversies."[9]

It is amusing to consider the dust jacket for the MIT Press book, a Maurice Smith design that conveyed his doubts about the historical enterprise. The title of the volume appears as an ill-conceived structure of children's lettered building blocks. Placed precariously above that

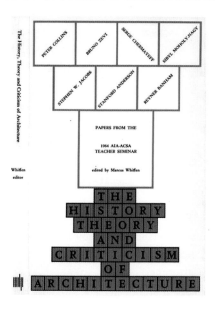

Maurice Smith designed cover for the *The History, Theory, and Criticism of Architecture*, publication of the papers from the AIA/ACSA Cranbook Teachers' Seminar, 1964.

9 The occasion for this summary was Millon's presentation about the beginnings of the MIT HTC PhD program in a conference "Geschichte und Theorie im Architekturunterricht zu Ehren von Henry A. Millon und Stanford Anderson," Bibliothek Werner Oechslin, Einsiedeln, Switzerland, 20-22 November 2009. Typescript.

10 MIT embraced changes to make design and the arts more effective in the environment. Wayne Andersen built the collection of sculpture installed on the campus; he had a lead role in moving the "Infinite Corridor" from memorial spaces connected by hallways painted in Navy gray to a more active and colorful environment. Muriel Cooper, who in 1963 had designed the subtle MIT Press logo while in private practice, came to MIT in 1966 to head what became a staff of three talented graphic designers. The Office of Publications, later Design Services, filled the halls with brilliant posters

construction are larger blocks with the names of the editor and authors. The names of the historian authors are parallel to one another at an ascending angle; at a descending angle is the name of the contrarian architect author, Serge Chermayeff.

Humanizing MIT: History and the Arts

MIT's increasing program in the humanities and concern "to humanize MIT" yielded a professorial position in the history of art and the appointment of Wayne Vesti Andersen in the fall of 1964.[10] In addition to dynamic teaching, Wayne astutely conducted MIT's contemporary art exhibition program at the Hayden Gallery (predecessor of today's List Gallery). Wayne also founded the MIT Friends of Art, its successor being still a valuable resource for the arts at MIT. Several instructors on term appointments supported teaching in art history, followed by the regular appointment of Rosalind Krauss in 1967 and later Judith Wechsler. Under Hank Millon's leadership, the MIT historians won the right to an undergraduate major in the history of art and architecture (1966) and, finally, the PhD progam in History, Theory, and Criticism of Art, Architecture, and Environmental Form in May 1975. Advanced studies under the rubric of HTC had begun earlier. Well before the formalization of the PhD program, our HTC program won the approbation of our young colleagues at other East Coast schools—to the extent that they saw HTC as the strength of MIT Architecture.

Preliminaries to CASE—Princeton

Peter Eisenman, already the consummate entrepreneur he has proven to be over a long career, conceived the idea of a programmatic association of young architects. In September 1964, Peter called to tell me of his scheme, projecting that the group could "assess the situation and make a possible statement" about the condition of architecture and architectural education, and transmit their thought by the founding of a critical magazine. Other participants could be Colin Rowe, Michael Graves, Jaque Robertson—"and [Vincent] Scully?" He had secured funds through Princeton's President Robert F. Goheen and set a meeting on November 13-15. My letter to Eisenman on the following day accepted the invitation and included: "Hank [Millon] is very much interested in joining us. He is a vigilant critic and thus will be a most welcome check."[11]

while bringing excellence to much of MIT's literature and letterheads. Under the Headship of Donlyn Lyndon, Cooper became a professor in Architecture where she created the Visible Language Workshop that continued into her time at the MIT Media Lab. See Janet Abrams, "Muriel Cooper's Visible

Wisdom" http://www.aiga.org/content.cfm/medalist-murielcooper, accessed June 12, 2010.

11 SA's notes of a telephone call from Peter Eisenman, September 24, 1964, and SA letter to Eisenman, September 25 (1 page). cc, SAfiles.

PRINCETON UNIVERSITY
PRINCETON · NEW JERSEY
SCHOOL OF ARCHITECTURE

October 15, 1964

Mr. Stanford Anderson
Department of Architecture
Massachusetts Institute of Technology
Cambridge, Massachusetts

Dear Mr. Anderson:

During the past several years the problems inherent in the present situation
in American architecture have become increasingly acute. Recently a
number of us have agreed that there is lack of critical apparatus for discussion of issues crucial to the development of a future architecture. It was
felt that it is time for us, the young architects and teachers of this country,
to take an active role beyond our own personal attitudes and interests as a
new and positive force in this future architecture.

To initiate a discussion of these issues we should like you to join us at Princeton University on the weekend of November 13 - 15. This meeting, while
providing an obvious stimulation for its participants, must be convened with
the hope of reaching beyond any limited objective to perhaps a re-formulation
and a re-establishment of principles concerning a future architecture.

Should you be willing to join us, we should like you to think about the
following questions as a beginning for our discussion:

    a. For what reasons have you chosen to come?

    b. What value can such a group have and what can it effectively
       hope to accomplish?

The response to our initial inquiry has been enthusiastically in favor of the
need and importance of such a meeting, and we anticipate not only a profitable
session but an active and creative role in the future architecture of this country.

Sincerely,

Peter Eisenman

Michael Graves

Thomas Vreeland

The October formal invitation letter, signed by Eisenman, Graves and Vreeland, is to the left.[12]

Those attending the first Princeton meeting were: Eisenman and Michael Graves, joined by Colin Rowe (Cornell), Michael McKinnell (Harvard), Henry Millon and Stanford Anderson (MIT), Kenneth Frampton (Architectural Design, London), Robert Kliment and Tim Vreeland (UPenn), Richard Meier (in practice, New York), Gio Pasanella and Jacquelin Robertson (Yale), and two established figures: Vincent Scully (Yale) and Robert Venturi (Philadelphia).[13]

Eisenman's particular interest was that this group be a vehicle for a critical journal—thus also his special interest in Frampton's participation. There was considerable excitement that Frampton, on his first trip to the US, flew by helicopter from JFK to Princeton in order to make a timely entrance to the meetings. Personal communications from Eisenman indicate that the tape recordings of the 1964 Princeton meeting (and the subsequent 1965 meeting) are missing. My notes are far from complete, and those contain snippets that are no longer intelligible to me. I can, however, give some flavor of the discussions.[14]

Eisenman launched the first session on Saturday morning, the tenor of which mirrored the invitation letter. Frampton recalled that the Modern Movement idealized a new age. Built form was to be a realization of the program and of a new way of life, but with the advent of Fascism there was the closing of the Bauhaus. Advent of Stalinism, the closing of Constructivism. Moving to the present, and citing Aldo van Eyck, Frampton observed: while architecture had served prince and priest, prince and priest are now dis-established. "We need an architecture of mass."

Colin Rowe restrained some of the rhetoric, immediately revealing one of the tensions that would enliven and eventually divide the group. Complaining of the messianic complex of architects, Rowe suggested that disunity may be the more productive state of being. Observing that the public is afraid of being seen as philistine, Rowe rather argued that the public *should* offer opposition. If I interpret my notes correctly, Meier felt that what Rowe saw as messianic, was courage on the part of the architect.

Invitation letter, Peter Eisenman, Michael Graves, Thomas Vreeland to Stanford Anderson, dated October 15, 1964.

12 The formal letter of invitation to the first Princeton meeting is on letterhead of the School of Architecture of Princeton University, dated October 15, 1964, and signed by Eisenman, Graves and Vreeland. Original, SAfiles.

13 As listed on the "Program November 13-15, 1964," distributed at the meeting. Ditto, SAfiles.

14 SA handwritten notes, simply labeled "Princeton I," from the sessions of November 14, 1964 (6pp). SAfiles.

Venturi argued that the artist is a maker-doer, as opposed to a speculator; what the architect needs is a chance to build. Vreeland, in the spirit of Venturi, argued that there is no lack of good ideas and design; the problem is a lack of opportunity. An architect grows and learns by doing. The absence of any real impact by young architects on practice is owing to the absence of graduated planes of opportunity and achievement. Vreeland searched for a strategy, perhaps the grouping of young architects to compete with big offices. In any case, we should sell ourselves: we are stronger together than singly, also in the political arena. Millon endorsed the Philadelphia [Venturi, Vreeland] concern about getting jobs. He warned that we are an incredibly self-conscious generation, and that it is possible to justify anything—we should concentrate on the thing produced. The first session ended with reflections on whether this "conference" should continue—continue in relation to a magazine; continue as a Team 10-type of activity? I wish my notes told me why the last line reads: "Architects as puritanical dilettantes."

Vincent Scully dominated the second session. He first defended the architect against the planner. Only the architect sees the whole in physical terms. Apparently Scully employed rhetorical emphasis, as my notes read: "whole whole whole." Planners furnish statistics that are only tools; planners are cooks. The second theme concerned function, illustrated by the refutation of Reyner Banham's view of modern architects talking function, but designing esthetically. Scully regretted the general devaluation of the past, contrasting the value of the urbanism of the past. Finally, asserting a belief in intellectual possibilities, Scully welcomed intellectual dialogue. Millon followed; my notes are simply: "past-present continuity—anti-Utopian—teaching method." We can hope the tapes appear, but perhaps I wrote nothing more because I knew Millon's critique of Scully's enthusiastic mining of history. On the same distinctive yellow legal pad paper and in the same ink as my Princeton notes, are some of my thoughts, but these are better taken up in my ensuing correspondence with Frampton.

As the meeting ended on a Sunday morning, those attending were asked to consider whether it would be fruitful to continue meeting.[15] Venturi rhetorically enquired whether participation would lead to architectural commissions, and then demurred.[16] The general decision, however, was to carry on, with the prospect of another Princeton meeting in the spring.

15 I do not find notes for the Sunday morning meeting, but Venturi's position is strong in my memory.

16 On June 18, 1965, Anderson communicated a letter of withdrawal by Robert Venturi.

17 SA notes on Jaque Robertson's comments at the opening of CASE Symposium II [CASE 4, MIT's Endicott House, May 6, 1966]. Original, SAfiles.

18 SA letter to Kenneth Frampton at the *Architectural Design* offices in London, November 23, 1964 (1 page). cc, SAfiles.

19 See fn. 8.

20 SA enclosure to letter to Frampton, "Planks for consideration at the Princeton meeting in February 1965," November 23, 1964 (1 page). cc, SAfiles.

21 Frampton to SA from London, December 4, 1964 (1 page). Original letter, SAfiles. I responded on December 15, 1964, concurring, and adding: "Hank [Millon], Roy Landau and I were in Philadelphia for three days. We saw Vreeland, Venturi, [Romaldo] Giurgola, Kliment, [Louis] Kahn and their offices and work. It was a very engaging experience—raising more questions than it answered. I hope we can talk about it when we next meet in Princeton." (1 page) cc, SAfiles.

A flash forward to a flashback: At the beginning of the first session of what came to be termed CASE 4 in 1966, with new members and guests present, Jaque Robertson gave his reading of the events of the first meeting at Princeton in 1964.[17] He recognized various motivations played out then that still scattered the energies of CASE: Scully looked for a new image; Venturi (and with him the practice-oriented McKinnell and Vreeland) sought work; Eisenman wanted a manifesto; while Jaque and Pasanella represented an "opportunistic realism." That position and Jaque's direct responsibilities in New York city planning led him to some observations: Architects are thought of as inessential in society, are brought in after the policy decisions have been made. How then, could architects get into policy-making positions? In New York, the election of Mayor Lindsay provided an opening. His readiness to hire amateurs allowed the formation of a group of young architects working for Lindsay: Jaque himself, Pasanella, and others who were about to take the floor and set the tone for the conference, Jonathan Barnett, Richard Weinstein, and Myles Weintraub. More of that later.

Princeton II—1965

Frampton, who was to join the Princeton faculty in the spring term of 1965, was charged with preparing the second Princeton meeting, including planks for a possible platform for the group. I wrote to him in London on November 23, 1964, sending two planks.[18] I noted that the first plank was a position I had taken at the first meeting [in accord with my Popperian positions[19]], the second plank a reaction to Scully's position at the first meeting:

Design Method
We acknowledge that to understand architecture generally, or to participate in architectural design, is to engage in some form of speculation (theory, idea, form, shape, etc.). One cannot stipulate the role of rationality in the formation of such speculations; rational control of the design process comes in the testing of speculation against the conditions that it has to satisfy.

Consequently, two critical tasks of this group are:
1. To clarify and understand this creative activity of speculation and testing.
2. To increase our knowledge about man and environment in order that the testing of our speculations can be increasingly acute.

History
Increasing historical sophistication has encouraged a relativistic attitude toward prototypical forms. In opposition to such relativism, we emphasize that our study of history intends to provide a greater understanding of architectural forms within their historical situation—not to provide a catalog of forms for uncritical usage.[20]

Frampton's response of December 4, 1964, reads in part:

> To my mind you [and Hank Millon] form a kernel, which together with Colin
> Rowe and Jack Robertson—has the greatest capacity for pursuing—many of
> the arguments raised in the November meeting. I find that I am personally
> preoccupied as to how this group can become effective.
>
> I see the magazine—(which I prefer at this stage to see as a single
> publication) as the vehicle for most effective action. I strongly question the
> value of a manifesto, primarily because it is not the correct vehicle for
> closely reasoned argument. I firmly believe that at this time, only closely
> reasoned argument has value.[21]

Frampton's thoughts are a remarkable early manifestation, while he was still in London, of
a tension between Ken and Eisenman, the man who had made particular efforts to involve
Ken in the nascent organization and in the faculty of Princeton.

Sometime prior to March 3, 1965, Frampton and I met while he was staying at The Brattle
Inn in Cambridge. Topics of discussion: In the planned April meeting, hold an Editorial
Meeting to make a statement of editorial policy ("or at least what not"); membership for
Donlyn Lyndon and Oscar Newman; and a concern that polemics around "Think and Do" is
divisive—must do both.[22]

In March 1965, Frampton sent a letter of invitation to the second Princeton meeting.[23] He
notes that he is sending to all invitees "a copy of the statement which we jointly compiled
in Boston," with some modifications. The enclosure reads:

> Princeton Conference, April 1965
> Statement

---

22 SA notes on Brattle
Inn, Cambridge, note paper.
Not dated, no specification
of those present; partially
explained by letter of
Frampton to Anderson (with
enclosure) on March 3, 1965
(1 note page). Original, SAfiles.
The enclosure would suggest
that at least Millon was also at
the Brattle Inn meeting.

23 Frampton to SA from
Princeton, March 3, 1965
(1 page). Original letter, w/
enclosure [see next note],
SAfiles.

24 Statement on a general
concern for the second
meeting in Princeton in April
1965, distributed by Frampton
on March 3, 1965. Anderson,
Eisenman, Frampton, Graves

and Millon as signatories (1
page). Ditto, SAfiles.

25 Frampton to SA from
Princeton, March 29, 1965 (1
page). Original letter, w/Ditto
enclosure (1 page), SAfiles.

26 Robert A.M. Stern records
Scully's dissatisfaction
with his experience of the
first Princeton meeting:
pretentious talk that was not

his way of thinking about
architecture. See George
Dodds, "Interview with
Robert A.M. Stern," *Journal of
Architectural Education* 59, no.
3 (January 2006), 62.

27 Robertson to Anderson,
in a letter deserving attention
below, regrets having missed
the April 1965 meeting due
to an operation. June 6, 1965

It is apparent that the last conference revealed a fundamental difference of opinion between various participants as to the value of discourse in relation to design activity.

The second conference should devote itself to an examination of this difference and direct its attention to an apparent conflict that is thought to exist between critical discourse and the actual process of designing and building.

Design and criticism are mutually interdependent activities in the creation of architecture and an agreement on their interdependence is fundamental to establishing a basis on which to continue the activities of the conference.

You are therefore asked to consider what advantages or disadvantages would accrue, if the group were to be exclusively composed of those who would not criticize without building nor build without criticizing.

Stanford Anderson, Peter Eisenman, Kenneth Frampton, Michael Graves, Henry Millon[24]

Late in March, Frampton sent the program for the second Princeton conference.[25] It was simply a calendar of the sessions, but included a list of those who would attend that included their academic appointments: Anderson, Assistant Professor of Architecture, MIT; Eisenman, Assistant Professor of Architecture, Princeton; Frampton, Visiting Lecturer, Princeton; Graves, Assistant Professor of Architecture, Princeton; Kliment, Instructor in Architecture, University of Pennsylvania; Meier, Visiting Critic, Cooper Union; Millon, Assistant Professor of Architecture, MIT; Pasanella, Visiting Critic, Yale; Robertson, Visiting Critic, Yale; Rowe, Associate Professor of Architecture, Cornell; Vreeland, Assistant Professor of Architecture, University of Pennsylvania [Venturi having withdrawn; Scully choosing not to attend].[26]

(2pp). Original handwritten letter, SAfiles.

28 Anderson notes of April 2, 1965 (1 page). Original, SAfiles.

29 Emilio Ambasz, then a student at Princeton, tended the meetings, including making the tape recordings.

30 Anderson notes of April 3, 1965 (2 pp). Original, SAfiles.

Proposed names for the magazine beyond those in the text: *predicament, attend, examination, operational studies in architecture, work, consideration, attention, build, situation, condition, draw, elucidation, place, scaffold, vector, issue, and issue 5: operational studies concerning built environment.*

[I have no idea what the "5" was about.]

31 Edited typescript of a programmatic statement for a possible journal. Author presumed to be Eisenman or, still more likely, Frampton. Lightly edited by Anderson and Millon, so apparently receiving some sanction from them. Original typescript, SAfiles.

32 Anderson notes of April 4, 1965 (3 pp). Originals, SAfiles.

33 From my role as "Executive Secretary" of CASE, and the organizer of the third and fourth meetings at MIT, Eisenman encouraged me repeatedly, and I have intended to write a proper account of CASE and related events. This, however, would

These individuals, except for Robertson,[27] met on the weekend of April 2-4, 1965, again at the Walter Lowrie House on the Princeton University campus. The reception dinner of Friday was followed by informal discussion over drinks, resulting in a rather haphazard list of "Central Issues of Architecture:" "suburban sprawl (non-architect building); architects' role; seat of power (insecurity of ruling class); criticism and analysis of buildings; ethnic, racial economic issues; social responsibility or social guilt; technological innovation; mass housing; mobility; change; parallel disciplines; research with other fields." And a final note: "Relation of formal solicitations to architecture . . . The Genius, the Prima Donna, and Practice."[28]

The Friday evening gathering would not have been recorded and the tapes of the Saturday and Sunday sessions are lost.[29] My notes for the Saturday meetings are sparse, but do allow some observations. Millon proposed that the "group exists to provide an orderly way to educate itself—end our isolation from other disciplines." Eisenman and Frampton held a concerted interest that the group should be the source of a magazine. Vreeland urged that there be sub-groups for projects other than the magazine. Such groups would be a first stage for its members and invited specialists to prepare a collective session. Vreeland suggested groups on the following: entering competitions; education (with an interest in architectural composition from Guadet on; discover when history became dominant because of a belief in change); industry; study of forms (iconographic notion to morphological choice to composition; use form, growth form, additive form).

At the end of the meetings, I boxed three headings and characterized them as "SA's summing up of intent of group and magazine:"

```
Architectural History Magazine      Hypothesis, organize thought
     How do you get into content that permits one to hypothesize?
Architecture                        multitude of theories, hypotheses, etc.
     How to judge them?
     Can't without a better understanding of context
Define context—architect
     Exclusive definition[30]
```

be a sizable research project. Eisenman's records are now at the Canadian Centre for Architecture in Montreal, but there would need to be a search at several institutions, in private archives, and of course interviews with the protagonists. This essay is only a sketch of such a study and mainly oriented to the MIT contribution.

34 Anderson's files for CASE include a folder for each of these groups. The one for the journal, which was referred to as CASE, is labeled "Frampton," and is noted below. Since study group activity was meant to be dispersed, it is not too surprising that most of the study group folders are empty or contain some random bits placed there by Anderson. "Politics and Architecture" contains one interesting letter, Robertson to Anderson, June 6, 1965, referenced more fully below. Robertson referred to the group as "Architecture and the Political Structure. Activity under "Creative

"SA's summing up of intent of group and magazine," Notes, Stanford Anderson, dated April 3, 1965.

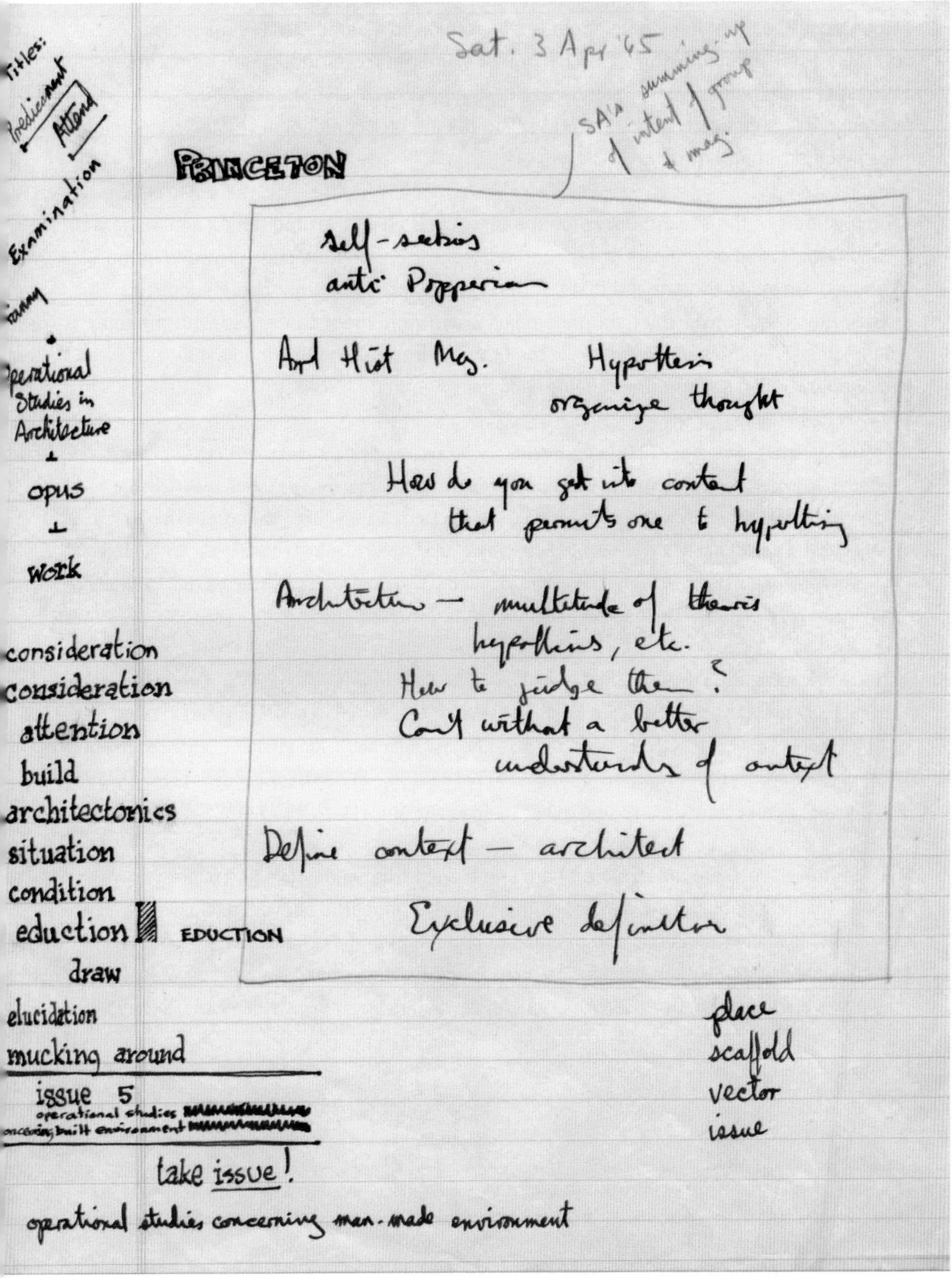

Sat. 3 Apr '65

SA's summing up
intent | group
& mag

PRINCETON

self-selecting
anti Popperian

Art Hist Msg.   Hypothesis
                        organize thought

How do you get into context
    that permits one to hypothesize

Architecture — multitude of theories
            hypothesis, etc.
    How to judge them?
    Can't without a better
            understanding of context

Define context — architect

Exclusive definition

Titles:
Predicament
Attend
Examination

operational
Studies in
Architecture
↓
opus
↓
work

consideration
consideration
attention
build
architectonics
situation
condition
eduction ▨   EDUCTION
    draw
elucidation
mucking around

issue 5
operational studies
concerning built environment

take issue!

operational studies concerning man-made environment

place
scaffold
vector
issue

The entire left margin of my note sheet is a list of possible names for the magazine: some predictable (architectonics; opus); one obscure but clever (eduction); moments of exasperation (fanny; mucking around); last (though not resolved), take issue!; and an explanatory line that came closest to revealing the intent: "operational studies concerning man-made environment."

With my notes of the second Princeton meeting is a draft of the program for the magazine. It is hurriedly typed on ordinary notepaper (different from the note pads provided in the meetings). Given its content and that the person had access to other paper supplies and a typewriter, it is probably by the Princetonians who were most concerned with the topic: Eisenman or Frampton, and more likely the latter. Identifiable editing marks indicate it was reviewed by Millon and me (though not necessarily agreed). It reads:

> This Journal has the initial intent to examine issues felt by its contributors to be central to architecture. These examinations may result in the exclusion from consideration of certain views and the focusing of attention on others felt to be relevant. The long-range intent is to approach a working definition of the context of architecture or a formulation of some synthetic position in architecture.
>
> We have neither a clearly defined direction nor goal. We have a program for the examination of architectural ideas but we do not know yet where it will lead nor what conclusions may be eventually reached. At present the following issues, although subject to change, elimination, or addition, are felt to be central issues we wish to examine in greater detail.[31]

The "central issues" are not explored here and the list from Friday evening is not very helpful. This text does, however, explain the term that appeared above, "exclusive definition." Issues in the study and practice of architecture and urbanism are so numerous and conflicted that one cannot attend to all of them. Further, positive assertion of issues may prove inadequate as further work may reveal issues one values still more. Perhaps one

Process" is recorded in the preparation and conduct of CASE 3. There is some relevant material by Anderson in the "History" file, but it would bear on the teaching of history at MIT rather than a CASE position. "Psychology of Architecture" contained an interesting letter from Rowe, June 18, 1965, that promised,

but then did not deliver, a description of the group.
35 Information from *American Architects Directory*, 3rd ed. (R.R. Bowker LLC, 1970), available online.
36 Curricula vitae of the original participants in CASE, from 1965, are: Anderson (2 pp, undated), Meier (2 pp, cover letter of 19 April), Millon

(2 pp, Feb. 1965), Pasanella (1 page, undated), Rowe (2 pp, undated), Vreeland (1 page undated; and a longer vita with handwritten additions, 1 page, undated). All typed; variously original, cc, Ditto, or xc, SAfiles.
SA had sent congratulations to Vreeland for his selection as Chair of the Department of

Architecture at the University of New Mexico. Vreeland responded with thanks and the thought that CASE and its associations would mean even more to him in his new location and responsibilities. Vreeland in Philadelphia to Anderson, April 21, 1965 (1 page). Original, SAfiles. Shortly thereafter, I wrote

could control the field best by stating what one would not take up for consideration. And echo Rowe: "disunity may be productive."

The Sunday session was very busy. My note sheets are unordered, but the following were the topics.[32] Having determined the group should continue, there was the question of a name. A "group name" that eventually became "Conference of ...," began as "Union Committee of ..." or "Council on ...". Gender challenged as was the group, so were potential names: "Council on Man and man-made environment;" "... Man and his (built) environment;" "... Man and his buildings;" and "... Man and his formed environment." All of these were criticized as being "object-oriented" and rejected. "Council [or whatever] on Man and what he builds" won attention, so MWHB was tried out. Millon and I resisted the more object-oriented or formalist variants. Collectively, we came to the final name (that never won affection), "Conference of Architects for the Study of the Environment/CASE." The group then explored the structure of CASE. There should be a "Central Committee" (later Executive Committee). Curiously, the Executive Committee became all those from the first Princeton meeting who remained active. I was given the position of "General Secretary" of CASE (a self-mocking of the position of Giedion in CIAM), but immediately reduced to "Executive Secretary."[33] [In the event, executive decisions involved mainly Eisenman, Anderson and Frampton, with others entering as specific programs might demand.] Eisenman and Frampton, an "Ad hoc Committee on By-laws," would report to the Executive Committee. As the lead advocates for a journal, they also sought an editorial committee. This, and Vreeland's original advocacy, set off an overly ambitious range of "CASE Study Groups," each one to be chaired by a member who argued for that concern. (asterisk indicating the chair of the group):[34]

```
Journal: Frampton*, Millon, Rowe, Eisenman, Anderson
Politics of Architecture: Robertson*, Pasanella*
Psychology of Architecture: Rowe*
Creative Process: Millon*, Anderson*
Education: Vreeland*, Kliment, Millon, Frampton, Meier
Mass: Meier*, Graves*, Frampton
```

Vreeland asking him to give thought and criticism to a position taken by an MIT student, Jeffrey Gutcheon, who sought "to enlarge and deepen the critical realm which teacher and student share." Anderson to Vreeland in Philadelphia, May 11, 1965 (1 page). cc, SAfiles; the attached statement by

Gutcheon is not in the file. **37** 1. Cover letter Stanford Anderson to all those who attended the first Princeton meeting inviting that they continue in what was now called Conference of Architects for the Study of the Environment (CASE), but stressing the importance of declaring one way or the

other (1 page). This and the following documents are all dated simply "April 1965," are in Mimeograph for mass distribution, and exist in files of Stanford Anderson. 2. Information sheet "Points made at the end of the first Princeton Meeting, November 15, 1964" (1 page). 3. "FOUNDATION

STATEMENT, first version. CONFERENCE OF ARCHITECTS FOR THE STUDY OF THE ENVIRONMENT (CASE): "The following is a statement concerning the origins, program, structure, and preliminary budget estimate of an organization recently formed with the intention of

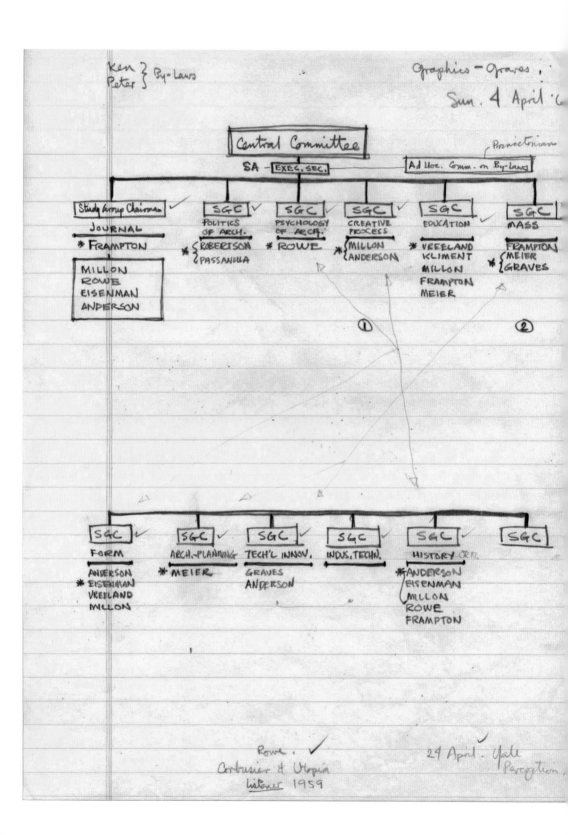

Form: Eisenman*, Anderson, Vreeland, Millon

Architecture-Planning: Meier*

Technological Innovation: no chair, Graves, Anderson

Industrial Technology: no names

History: Anderson*, Millon*, Eisenman, Rowe, Frampton

Not as a committee, but Graves would handle graphics for CASE.

From the beginning, the intention of the movers was that the group remain small enough to foster discussion, perhaps twenty people. The Study Group ambitions clearly called for new people and for some with interest in the vacant or under-populated groups. Millon nominated Ervin Galantay (Columbia), Oscar Newman (Washington University), Anthony Jackson (Nova Scotia), Tom Bosworth (RISD), and Donlyn Lyndon (Oregon); Vreeland named David Crane (Philadelphia); Eisenman suggested Sim van der Ryn (Berkeley), Lee Hodgden (Cornell), Tom Holzbog [Yale BArch'60; Harvard MAUD], and John Copelin [Yale BArch'60; sometime a critic at Pratt and Yale '69];[35] Anderson nominated Joseph Schiffer (MIT), Raymond Studer (RISD), and François Vigier (Harvard).

It was decided that the MIT participants would seek MIT funding for meetings in the following year. Among other things, I was asked to solicit *curricula vitae* from the members.[36] Finally, Peter reminded us of his original impetus: the existence of a void in architecture and architectural thought. The group was formed out of that concern. Division of interests among the members was already tangible. While Eisenman and others preferred a more programmatic address of architecture in the name of the group, Millon and I influenced the use of the word "environment." The proliferation of study groups revealed differences and scattered energies.

Organizing CASE—1965

I took up my duties in earnest. In April 1965, I distributed a letter and three documents.[37] The first of these documents was "Points made at the end of the first Princeton Meeting, November 15, 1964." At least more coherent than my notes from the meeting, it reads:

Central Committee organization, Notes, Stanford Anderson, dated April 4th, 1965.

carrying out studies relevant to architecture" (11 pp). 4. Note to members of CASE: "A PROPOSAL FOR ENLISTING A LIMITED NUMBER OF NEW MEMBERS IN CASE" (2 pp). 5. "Official Form: NOMINATIONS TO MEMBERSHIP IN CASE" (1 page).

38 See previous fn., item 2. **39** See fn. 37, item 3. **40** Meier to Anderson, personal note congratulating on "outstanding work . . . on the foundation statement, undated, but with CASE membership nomination required by May 1, 1965. Original handwritten note on professional letterhead, SAfiles.

41 SAfiles includes a folder "CASE Membership" that includes the nomination sheets returned by Anderson, Graves (with information for Eisenman and Rowe), Meier, Millon, Pasanella (with a handwritten note endorsing Weinstein).

1. Magazine

2. Architect's role vis à vis the public and power structure—critique of the practicing architect's role

3. Reduction of the mystical aspects of the creative perceptual process to a minimum so as to establish architecture as a rigorous intellectual discipline

4. Architect's responsibility for the entire physical environment

5. Investigation of principles of the beginning of the modern movement—positive critique of the principles of the Bauhaus. Function as opposed to form.

6. Organization of the group as a forum for the exposure of ideas.

7. Role of utopian ideas. The image issue—a generator of ideas and as a necessary first step. Need the generator be a utopian scheme ... can a changeful or change-allowing image be a Utopian scheme? [elision in the original]

8. Study of history to provide a greater understanding of architectural forms within their historical situation. Relationship to practice and to education of architect.[38]

The most important of the three distributed documents was the "Foundation Statement,"[39] which begins with a rather elusive "Program." The immediately following section "Areas of Study" is more helpful. A list of "central issues" is provided in the accompanying scans. The remaining sections of the "Foundation Statement" are: "Conferences, a Magazine, and Teaching," a "Skeletal History of the Formation of CASE," the "Structure of CASE," "Study Groups" (similar to that given above; including "Magazine"), and a "Budget of CASE" ($13,000/yr for two conferences and preparation of the magazine, plus a possible $2000/yr allowance for the editor).[40]

The final April 1965 documents were "A Proposal for Enlisting a Limited Number of New Members in CASE" and a nomination form, with the intention to select three members to head unmanned study groups and general members to bring the group to eighteen. In May I recorded the nominations of new members.[41] The request for nominations had gone to all original participants in CASE. On May 18 I wrote to all participants—thanking for nominations or seeking clarification on membership, as appropriate.[42] Nominations were reported to the

42 On May 18, 1965, SA wrote Eisenman, Frampton, Graves, Meier, Millon, Pasanella, and Rowe, thanking them for their nominations and requesting other information to assist development of CASE. On May 18, 1965, SA wrote Kliment, Robertson, and Vreeland that he believed they had interest in CASE, but, not having received nominations from them, would they please confirm their membership. On May 18, 1965, SA wrote McKinnell, Scully, and Venturi, regretting having had no response to an earlier letter with the CASE "foundation statement," and asking them to respond as to whether they did or did not wish to participate in CASE. All these May 18 letters (1 page) are present in SAfiles as cc. Vreeland responded on May 20 1965 with a three-page handwritten letter, telling of his heavy burdens in Philadelphia and Albuquerque since his agreement to chair the school at New Mexico; confirming that his "association with CASE means more to me than ever before; congratulating SA on organization; making late nominations [that did get on the ballot]; and questioning that Stanley Tigerman had been nominated. Original on

FOUNDATION STATEMENT, first version   CASE   APRIL 1965

The following is a statement concerning the origins, program, structure, and preliminary budget estimate of an organization recently formed with the intention of carrying out studies relevant to architecture.

CONFERENCE OF ARCHITECTS FOR THE STUDY OF THE ENVIRONMENT (CASE)

PROGRAM OF CASE

The Conference of Architects for the Study of the Environment (CASE) has been established to provide a forum, the initial intent of which is to examine issues which its members feel to be central to architecture. These examinations may result in the exclusion from consideration of certain views and the focusing of attention on other issues which are felt to be relevant. The long range intent is to approach a working definition of the context of architecture and, if possible, to formulate a truly contributive position in architecture.

AREAS OF STUDY

The areas of study outlined below begin with an overt outward look to the city, to mass problems, industry, technology, and to other disciplines and the political structure. None of these will be viewed statically, as objects independent of man. We shall be looking for opportunities and tools, for limiting conditions, and for much else given to us by our environment; but we shall also be looking to see what the architect can offer to the situation and what his effect on the environment can be. It is this awareness of involvement in events, in growth and change, that forces us to examine our profession and our methods as much as the arena in which we perform.

yellow pad (3 pp), SAfiles. In a personal communication McKinnell declined. "Members of CASE Summer 1965" shows eleven of the original members, not McKinnell, Scully, or Venturi (1 page). Typed original, SAfiles. McKinnell, nevertheless was later involved; consider him a "fellow traveler" who came to count in membership again. Venturi wrote to decline: "I have, very reluctantly for some reasons, and perhaps wrongly, decided not to join the group" (May 21, 1965; 1 page). Original, SAfiles. Venturi promised a fuller account of his reasons. SA responded with regret at his decision, but a hope to receive the promised longer letter (SA to Venturi, June 14, 1965; 1 page). cc SAfiles. A longer letter was not received. Lila H. Calhoun, secretary to Scully, wrote of his heavy engagements then and in the foreseeable future (June 2, 1965; 1 page). Original, SAfiles.

Foundation Statement, for the Conference of Architects for the Study of the Environment (CASE), April 1965.

2

Consequently, our areas of study go on to include motivations, creativity, form, history, criticism, and education.

An extant profusion of directions and goals in architecture has not contributed to a clarification of the situation. Consequently, rather than an explicit direction or goal, we offer a program for the examination of problems in architecture. At present, the following list of issues, although subject to reformulation, deletions and additions, are felt by the members of CASE to be central issues which we wish to examine in detail:

The City and Mass Phenomena: All problems concerning dense, mobile and expanding populations, including their needs in housing, transportation, etc. Ethnic, racial, economic problems.

Industrial Techniques and Construction: Materials, products, fabrication, construction. Here also would be considered those problems of structure which relate to materials and technique.

Technological Innovation: Theories, processes and techniques operative outside (though not necessarily exclusively outside) the actual construction process; for example, computer techniques and application, cybernetics, structural theory, etc.

Architecture and Other Disciplines: Division of responsibility, teamwork, joint research, etc.

Architecture and Political Structure: Who is or should be asking what questions, setting what problems? How can the architect influence these questions and problems; how can he arrange to play his part in answering them?

Foundation Statement, for the Conference of
Architects for the Study of the Environment (CASE),
April 1965.

3

<u>Psychology of the Architect</u>: Motivations, social responsibility

and guilt, utopia and utopian images.

<u>Creativity</u>: Theories of creativity, experimental research,

experimental commentaries and hypotheses advanced by

artists and architects, etc.

<u>Form</u>: Abstract considerations of the elements, the logic,

the comprehension and effects of visual form. The

relation of formal considerations to the limitations

posed by structure, construction, and function.

Studies in perception. "Image."

<u>History and Criticism</u>: Rational reconstruction of the

design of known buildings and complexes; contextual

study of formal types as exemplified in known build-

ings and complexes; analysis and critique of earlier

"movements"; the influence of varying attitudes toward

history; historiography; methods and criteria of

criticism.

<u>Education and Architecture</u>: All the members of CASE are

vitally concerned with architectural education; it

appears last in this list, not at all as a ranking

of importance, but as an indication that we hope some

of our other studies will provide better criteria for

recommendations in architectural education. Attention

will be given not only to professional education but

also to the need for visual education from primary

school through adult education.

membership, and, on May 28, 1965, I distributed information on the nominees and a ballot.[43] On June 2 Meier, following a telephone conversation with Eisenman, wrote to me urging that the election be postponed till the fall meeting. His substantive reason was: "The issue, whether real or imaginary, of voting blocks in order to secure membership for some nominees could have repercussions of causing splits within the group."[44] It was a curious argument as three of the surviving twelve members were from Princeton (Eisenman, Frampton and Graves); Graves had submitted a single nomination form for Eisenman, Rowe and himself; and Meier was close to the Princeton group (and a cousin of Eisenman). If there was a potential for block voting, this group had "met the enemy, and it was … ."

In June I reported the voting, and also wrote a conciliatory letter to Meier.[45] Eleven of the fourteen people at the first Princeton meeting voted. For chair of the Study Group on Industrial Techniques and Construction, Ezra Ehrenkrantz (Stanford) was preferred over Joseph Schiffer (MIT) and Stanley Tigerman (Chicago). For chair of the Study Group on Technological Innovation, Sim van der Ryn (Berkeley) over James Jarrett (New Mexico) and Raymond Studer (RISD). For chair of the Study Group on Architecture and Other Disciplines, François Vigier (Harvard) over Robert Slutzky (Pratt) and Lee Hodgden (Cornell). The election to general membership included the names above. Weighted rank order voting (four votes per member) yielded this ranking: Anthony Eardley (Princeton), Robert Slutzky (Pratt), Christopher Alexander (Berkeley), Carlos Vallhonrat (Pennsylvania). These four and the three winners in the Study Group voting were to be invited to membership. As any of the above might decline, one would continue with the rank-order voting: Lee Hodgden (Cornell), Richard Weinstein (Columbia), Donlyn Lyndon (chair, Oregon), Ervin Galantay (Columbia), David Crane (planner, Philadelphia, and Penn), Oscar Newman (Washington University), Tom Bosworth (RISD). Others nominated were: John Belle (Cornell in New York), Imre Halasz (MIT), Anthony Jackson (Nova Scotia Technical College), and Frederick Stahl (in practice, Boston).

This membership activity occurred simultaneously with explorations of a CASE magazine. Frampton took the lead, engaging primarily Anderson, Eisenman, Millon, and Rowe. With a letter of May 5, 1965, Frampton sent a "program of action for the magazine" based on a

43 The record of nominations for new CASE members produced these documents distributed to all CASE members (all Mimeo, SAfiles): "CASE. Report on Nominations for Membership," 19 May 1965 (1 page). This was soon displaced by an expanded ballot list.

"CASE. Ballot. Membership in CASE," 28 May 1965 (1 page). There were separate votes for small numbers of candidates to be invited as directors of specific "Study Groups." These names, and many more were all considered for election to general membership.
"Information Sheet on

Nominees for Membership in CASE," 28 May 1965 (2 pp). Distributed with the ballot.
44 Meier to Anderson, urging postponement of election of new members, June 2, 1965 (2 pp). Original handwritten letter, SAfiles.
45 The details of the voting for new membership were communicated to the

members of CASE, 18 June 1965 (4 pp). Mimeo, SAfiles. SA to Meier, letter concerning the vote on CASE members, June 18, 1965 (1 page). cc, SAfiles. The files also contains a folder with the anonymously submitted ballots and a tally sheet. Originals.

May 1 meeting of the above group, save Rowe, at the Oxford Grill (Walter Gropius's favorite lunch place) in Cambridge—and calling for a meeting at the Princeton Club in New York on May 9. From my notes of a telephone call on May 7, we urged on ourselves statements of the "present situation in architecture and its relation to the environment" to serve as guides to the main activity of the magazine—and amplification of an outward-oriented attitude. So begins a file of about fifty pages.[46] Yet a few key points should appear here.

On May 21, Frampton wrote to Anderson of his satisfaction with an editorial policy he had compiled from multiple sources, but now Eisenman and Graves wanted to edit it prior to further distribution. A week later, Frampton sent the "Editorial Statement (CASE) New York, May 9, 1965" that Peter, Michael, and he had compiled. On June 3, I wrote Ken that Hank and I had concerns under consideration. In mid-June, Rowe wrote to me with a devastating critique: "I am not very impressed by the editorial statement that was put out from Princeton. It doesn't know whether it wishes to be a continuous piece of writing or an old fashioned nineteen twentyish manifesto. *It* also has a sentimental activistic vitalistic tone." In July, I submitted to Princeton an "Ithaca/Boston [Rowe, Millon, Anderson]" version of the Editorial Statement. Nothing more was heard until Frampton, in December, resignedly wrote a letter quoted below. *CASE Magazine* was dead.

In June, a rare spark from a Study Group, "Architecture and Politics," came from Robertson. After some apologies for delay, he wrote:

> Gio [Pasanella] and I have done a good deal of talking along lines which will
> eventually—we expect—bear fruit, and are now in the process of setting up
> a program which might possibly be used as a "white paper" in N.Y.'s coming
> mayoralty race.[47] How this begins to fit in with the facts of political life
> will be interesting for inclusion under our study group: "Architecture
> and the Political Structure." How theoretical, even practical, programs
> of national importance are introduced, propagandized, and, hopefully,
> implemented? We don't know, and with all the good intentions, even good ideas,
> we're useless until we find out. I think the fact of our shocking impotence

46 See folder "Frampton," May-December 1965, SAfiles,.

47 John Lindsay was to be elected Mayor of New York in 1966. Robertson and Weinstein both received influential planning positions under Lindsay.

48 Robertson to Anderson, search for national policy on architecture and planning, June 6, 1965 (2pp). Original handwritten letter, SAfiles.

49 Particularly from the Edgar Kaufmann Foundation. In September, and again in October, Vreeland had also enquired about the next meeting. This in a letter congratulating Anderson on an " . . . excellent paper and one which helped resolve some things for me who am personally torn between a

love of history and a futurist élan to get on with things." Vreeland from Albuquerque to Anderson, September 22, 1965 (1 page); also October 25, 1965 (1 page). Originals, SAfiles. From Vreeland's account, the "paper" was probably Anderson's "Architecture and Tradition;" see fn. 8.

I07 CAYUGA HEIGHTS ROAD, ITHACA, NEW YORK I4850.   June I8 I965.

Dear Stan:

Since you keep on telling me that you have never received a letter
from me and since I am now creating a precedent I am visited by immediate inhibitions about what to say. But I will begin by saying that, the semester being over, I have at last discovered the time and enrgrgy to transfer attention
to all the papers which you keep on sending to me.

       ****

It was at this stage that I got your phone call—a coincidence which
should probably be communicated to the Society for Psychical Research and which
seems, for the moment, to make the rest of this letter unnecessary.

However to go point by point:

i.   I am immensely impressed by all the work which you have done and I
do feel a little ashamed and guilty about not having said so before now. I agree with your foundation statement and cant think of anything which I would
wish to change—except of course the name CASE.

ii.   I have no proposals to put in place of CASE. SEMINAR sounds just dreary
and CECA —or whatever it is—doesnt sound any better. One surely wishes for a
title without naively activist overtones.

iii.   I enclose a curriculum vitate.

iv.   I shall try to append a description of the study group: Psychology of
the architect.

Meanwhile I am not very impressed by the editorial statement that was
put out from Princeton. It doesnt know whether it wishes to be a continuous piece
of writing or an old fashioned nineteen twentyish manifesto. It also has a sentimental activistic vitalistic tone. It uses the word 'total'—'total environment',
total architecture', etc—God knows how many times. What is meant by 'total arch.' ?

Letter, Colin Rowe to
Stanford Anderson, dated
June 18, 1965.

enclosures listed on the
transmittal page (but not in
this file) were: Foundation
Statement [clearly identifiable];
Editorial Policy Statement
[which one?; probably the
final Millon/Rowe/Anderson
one, though I don't find that
this or the Princeton version
received general agreement];
first draft of one of the

papers to be presented at
the Creativity and Perception
Conference [probably, but
not surely Anderson's paper
on Perception and Norberg-
Schulz].
52 Letter, SA to members
of CASE, announcing MIT
funding for two CASE
meetings in 1965-66; SA's
deferral of new invitations

to membership; renewed
request that Study Groups
offer revisions to the
Foundation Statement.
November 30, 1965 (2 pp).
Mimeo, SAfiles.
This was followed up with
a letter, SA to members of
CASE, confirming the MIT
meeting on January 21-23
1966, January 3, 1966 (1

Also one just cannot say things like this:

"We intend that this magazine should attempt to stem the flood; to this task we, and our contributors will bring all the rigor that we can muster. We shall be critical, analytical, philosophical, dialectical, polemical and political. Arch- is essentially organization, the laying waste must stop and a total architecture must begin"

"stem the flood"—a political meeting c. I9I0; "all the rigor that we can muster"— both ungrammatical and boyscouty and therefore tacitly disimplying any possibility of rigor; etc. etc.

Or am I being too captious ?

June 22 I965.

It seems that though there isnt as yet available a study group statement, and since I have again been delayed, I had better send this as is. The study group will follow in quite a short time. But, honestly, I think that already there is a note of too great sobriety and liberalistic tolerance about our group. Can something not be done about it ? We should talk about it while you around in these parts.

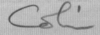

page). Mimeo, SAfiles. Also as a cover letter for:
1) "Preliminary Schedule. CASE SYMPOSIUM: PERCEPTION/CREATIVITY," [January 3, 1966] (2pp). Mimeo, SAfiles. And, presumably, though not specifically mentioned:
2) CASE "Preliminary Reading List for CASE Symposium:

Perception/Creativity," not dated (1 page). Mimeo, SAfiles.
53 The CASE invitation packet of January 3, 1966; all SAfiles:
1) Standard, but individualized letter from SA to invitees (1 page); also as a cover letter to the items below. I do not find a list of the persons to whom

this letter was sent. It should be the seven who were "elected" in 1965. Others can be inferred from those who were not participants, but attended the January 21-23 MIT meeting, see fn. 63. Some of these letters are in the SAfiles: Vallhonrat, with notation of a telephone call where he regrets and asks

to be invited in the spring; van der Ryn, with notation of tentative yes at a personal meeting with Anderson in Washington, January 10, 1966.
2) CASE "Foundation Statement" of April 1965. See fn 37, item 3.
3) "Preliminary Schedule. CASE SYMPOSIUM:

at this time is too obvious to belabor. Whether we can change this fact—
or rather whether architects really ever do begin seriously to attack the
problem head on i.e. influencing an "architectural policy" at the national
level—is up for grabs. Its not enough, this chance that Jack Kennedy just
happened to know "Rose-Bowl" Warnecke, because the Senate is still paying—and
through their nose and our pocket books—for Sam Rayburn buildings; and still
thinking that architecture is just not a serious planning concern. Somewhere
along the line, the architectural "white paper" must become a political
reality. We hope to find out a few ways towards this reality—as a CASE project.

Best regards, Jaque[48]

On October 18, Meier wrote a testy letter beginning: "What is going on?" and complaining
(wrongly) that my June 18 letter projected a November CASE meeting. Though Meier and
others had praised the Foundation Statement, there were also requests that members
revise the Statement as it referred to their Study Groups. Meier now required a revised
Statement if he were to seek funding for CASE.[49]

To be fair to Meier, I don't find that I communicated with the CASE members collectively
in mid-1965, perhaps due to the magazine fiasco and the preparation of substantive CASE
meetings at MIT. Hank and I envisioned a CASE Symposium on creativity.[50] In the fall of
1965, we were teaching a theory seminar planned to assist us in the development of that
symposium and our papers for it. Yet it is the case that we did not request and secure
funds from MIT until November.[51]

In the event, as noted in a letter of November 30, 1965,[52] in the absence of funding,
a magazine, or at least a meeting schedule, I chose not to make any invitations to
membership. I also noted that, though external funding had not been won, MIT now agreed
to support two CASE meetings in 1966. Hank Millon and I had identified participants for a
first MIT meeting on January 21-23, 1966. I would now invite those "elected" to come as
visitors at the January meeting, with confirmation of membership later as we might decide.

PERCEPTION/CREATIVITY"
and "Preliminary Reading List,"
see preceding note.
54 The program handout for
CASE 3 was headed "CASE.
Schedule. CASE Symposium:
Perception/Creativity" (2pp).
Mimeo, SAfiles. Events ran
from Friday evening January
21 to Sunday mid-day at MIT's
Endicott House in Dedham,

Massachusetts—followed by
a CASE Executive Committee
meeting and ending in a
blizzard.
55 Tape recordings of CASE
Symposium I are in SAfiles.
My notes from the lectures
and discussion offer little (8
pp). Originals, SAfiles.
56 Christian Norberg-Schulz,
Intentions in Architecture

(Oslo: Universitetsforlaget,
1963; Cambridge, MA: The
MIT Press, 1966).
57 Now (2010) an emeritus
professor in Brain and
Cognitive Sciences at MIT.
His MIT website shows him
still to be involved in "study of
the developing visual system."
58 1981 Nobel laureate in
Physiology or Medecine; in

2010, Emeritus professor of
Neurobiology at Harvard.
59 (1928-1997). Founder,
1960, with Robert S. Cohen
of the Boston Colloquium for
Philosophy and History of
Science; was a professor of
philosophy at Baruch College,
New York and the Graduate
Center of CUNY.
60 (2010), remains a

At the start of the new year, I sent to those architects who had been elected in the 1965 voting an invitation letter, the CASE "Foundation Statement," and a preliminary schedule of the January MIT meeting.[53] Invitations also went to individuals whom Millon and I knew to be interested in the theme of the meeting.

CASE 3/CASE Symposium I—MIT 1966

MIT sponsored CASE 3 held at MIT's Endicott House in Dedham, Massachusetts, January 21-23, 1966. Also known as CASE Symposium I: "Perception/Creativity," the organizers were Anderson and Millon.[54] Friday evening was arrival at the suburban location, dinner, and a CASE Executive Committee meeting while the guests conversed over drinks, shortly joined by all.

As the first CASE symposium, Hank and I sought to embody the program of "ending the isolation from other disciplines;" to break the usual discourse of professors of architecture by setting topics that could draw on distinguished academics in philosophy, psychology, medical science, and computation.[55] I introduced the Saturday morning "Perception" session with a critique of Christian Norberg-Schulz's *Intentions in Architecture*.[56] Two papers presented advanced research in perception: "Psychology of Perception," by Richard Held (Psychology, MIT)[57] and "Neurophysiology of Visual Perception," by David H. Hubel (Harvard Medical School).[58]

Millon chaired the Saturday afternoon "Creativity" session composed of two papers, "Mathematical Models and the Design Process" by Murray Milne (Architecture, University of Oregon) and "Epistemological and Aesthetic Issues in Perception" by Marx Wartofsky (Philosophy, Boston University and Research Associate, Department of Psychology at Harvard).[59] Though the speakers were distinguished, articulate and included a future Nobel laureate, CASE members were largely passive and found the symposium not to be a model for future events.

Other notable invitees participated in the discussion: James Ackerman (Fine Arts, Harvard), Wayne V. Andersen (Architecture, MIT), Whitman Richards (Psychology, MIT),[60] and Bernard

50 Early in 1965, Dr. Edward Lurie of Wayne State University chaired a seminar on creativity at the Wenner-Gren Foundation for Anthropological Research. Anderson wrote to Lurie requesting information about the seminar. One paragraph notes that Millon and Anderson would use their

fall 1965 graduate seminar "Theory of Architecture" to prepare for the projected CASE symposium. Anderson to Lurie, April 14, 1965 (1 page). SAfiles. The file has no record of a response; however, as Millon was taking the "creativity" role, it is possible that a response went to him.

51 Our tardiness is probably explained by the fact that both Eisenman and Meier were attempting (or were meant to attempt) to secure funds from external sources, possibly the Graham Foundation or the Edgar Kaufmann Foundation. Perhaps it was the referenced letters from Vreeland and Meier, that finally brought

Millon and Anderson to request MIT funding. See the unsigned, undated transmittal page with a brief account and a list of the enclosures: covering letter providing background information and request for "support similar to that provided by Princeton University last year." (November 5, 1965; 2pp). cc, SAfiles. The other

Kaplan (Psychology, Clark University).[61] Three discussion sessions on Saturday evening and Sunday morning ended with one under the initiative of David Stea of Brown University.[62] Ten of the remaining eleven CASE members from the original Princeton group took part (Rowe missing). Of those considered for membership, the following attended: Thomas Bosworth (RISD), Anthony Eardley (Princeton), Donlyn Lyndon (Chair, Architecture, Oregon), Oscar Newman (Washington University), Sim van der Ryn (Berkeley), Robert Slutzky (Pratt), and Raymond Studer (RISD).[63] On the experience of CASE 3, four were invited to membership: Eardley, Lyndon, Newman, and Slutzky.[64] Shortly after the Symposium, I sent a cover letter to the external academics asking them to criticize and supplement a bibliography I had prepared.[65]

In February, Carroll Bowen, Director of The MIT Press, gave preliminary agreement to publish CASE Studies, a series of volumes stemming from CASE symposia and other initiatives. Bowen had been given the CASE Foundation Statement and a table of contents for a volume titled *Perception and Architecture*.[66]

On February 4, in letters of appreciation to speakers in the January symposium, I included this note: "*Architectural Forum* has expressed interest in becoming our public voice but I think we shall refuse this because of their limitations on our editorial policy. However, another arrangement is progressing and I hope that you will be willing to help us realize that publication."[67] Later in February I wrote the CASE membership under a heading "Publication Plans for CASE in cooperation with M.I.T. Press."[68] Under the agreement with Bowen there was the prospect for a volume, "Perception and Architecture," based on the January CASE meeting. Bowen welcomed " . . . providing new stimulus to the fields of architecture and architectural education," and offered preliminary conditions of a remarkably open and generous nature. I attached a "Preliminary Table of Contents" previously submitted to MIT Press:[69]

professor in Brain and Cognitive Sciences, MIT, with studies in computational approaches to perception.

61 (1925-2008) had a lifelong fruitful interdisciplinary career at Clark.

62 The CASE 3 file holds a document: David Stea, "Proposal for a University Course" (5pp, including a

bibliography). The content of the document has Stea changing the title of the course from "The Psychology of Environmental Design" to "Behavior and Design." Internal evidence dates the document to Spring 1965, but it is uncertain whether or not the document was distributed at CASE 3. Mimeo, SAfiles.

63 For attendance at CASE 3, see "CASE—CASE Symposium I: Perception/ Creativity—List of Participants" (4 pp and a one-page supplement). Mimeograph copies distributed at the Symposium; SAfiles. CASE members present at CASE 3 were Anderson, Eisenman,

Frampton, Graves, Kliment, McKinnell, Meier, Millon, Rowe and Vreeland. Of the guests, Eardley, Lyndon, Newman, and Slutzky later became members of CASE.

64 Typed sheet, "Architects Invited to Membership in CASE—Feburay 1966 (1 page). cc, SAfiles.

65 Cover letter, SA to

PERCEPTION AND ARCHITECTURE

Edited by Stanford Anderson

Introduction

I. Perception of Space: Architects' Contributions (Emphasis should be on the types of spatial experience architects have sought or achieved; names of specific architects are given to illustrate the matter under discussion.)

    1. The "Organic" Space of Frank Lloyd Wright

(Three authors under consideration)

    2. Ideal Space Realized (Peter Behrens and Ludwig Mies van der Rohe)

Stanford Anderson, M.I.T.

    3. Space Definition through Pure Formal Elements (de Stijl)

(Two authors under consideration)

    4. Physical and Phenomenal Definition of Space in Art and Architecture

(Walter Gropius and Le Corbusier)

Colin Rowe, Cornell University, and Robert Slutzky, Pratt Institute

    5. Extensive and Intensive Space

Henry Millon, M.I.T.

    6. Theoretical Formulations of the Relationship between Perception and the Man-Controlled Environment

Norberg-Schulz's Intentions in Architecture: A Critique

S. Anderson, M.I.T.

    7. Perception and the Development of Urban Design

Oscar Newman, Washington University

    8. The Development of a Science of Human Ecology

Robert W. Kates, Clark University

    9. Philosophical Considerations Relating to Perception and the Arts

    10. Perception: Epistemological and Aesthetic Problems

Marx Wartofsky, Boston University

    11. Phenomenological Consideration of the Experience of the Environment

(Currently in consultation with a particular author)

Professors Ackerman, Held, Hubel, Kaplan, Newman, Richards, Stea, Slutzky, Studer, Wartofsky, and also to Joseph Agassi (Philosopy, Boston University), supplying two copies of a bibliography relating to the themes of CASE Symposium I, and asking that one be returned with criticism and additions.

February 23, 1966 (1 page). Mimeo w/recipients written in; SAfiles. "Bibliography on Perception and Architecture, compiled by S. Anderson, M.I.T.," [February 1966] (13 pp). Mimeo, SAfiles. **66** SA note on MIT Press agreement to publish *CASE Studies*, February 4, 1966 (2 pp); Table of contents for

a *CASE Study: Perception and Architecture* (1 typed page). Originals, SAfiles. There are also various notes contemplating the series and possible volumes. **67** SA letters to speakers in the first CASE symposium, 4 February 1966. cc, SAfiles. **68** Letter by Anderson, no addressee but sent to the

CASE membership, February 23, 1966, with the heading "*Publication Plans for CASE in cooperation with M.I.T. Press*" (2pp). Mimeo, SAfiles. **69** Document: "CASE Study 1—PERCEPTION AND ARCHITECTURE—Edited by Stanford Anderson, M.I.T.— Preliminary Table of Contents," 23.II.66 (2pp). Mimeo mass

```
12. Some Insights into Current Studies of Perception
Neurophysiological Research on Visual Perception
David Hubel, Harvard Medical School
13. Psychological Studies of Space Perception
Richard Held, M.I.T.
14. Plans and the Experience of the Environment
George A. Miller, Harvard University (not yet contacted)
Topical Bibliography
```

CASE 4/CASE Symposium II—MIT 1966

On January 24, 1966, I wrote to Meier and Graves, discussing shared responsibilities for their Case Symposium II to be held at MIT's Endicott House in May.[70] The letter included a list of the "CASE Executive Committee" (the remaining twelve persons from the fourteen at the first Princeton meeting; McKinnell again included; Robertson now addressed at the Edward Larrabee Barnes office; Vreeland now Chair, University of New Mexico) and a long list now unequivocally titled "CASE: Invited Members:" Christopher Alexander (Berkeley), Thomas Bosworth (RISD), Anthony Eardley (Princeton), Ezra Ehrenkrantz (with a note that he had not responded to the last inviation), Donlyn Lyndon (Oregon), Oscar Newman (Washington University), Sim van der Ryn (Berkeley), Robert Slutzky (Pratt), Raymond Studer (RISD), Carlos Vallhonrat (Penn), and Francois Vigier (Harvard).

Late in January, I sent an invitation letter for CASE 4 (6-8 May 1966) to all CASE members and prospective members from CASE 3 (Bosworth, Eardley, Lyndon, Newman, Slutzky, and Studer).[71] Meier and Graves proposed a program on "the general theme of mass urban phenomena." In preparation for CASE 4/CASE Symposium II, Graves and Meier wrote to the CASE membership on March 14, 1966.[72] The proposed topic had been "Mass Phenomena as Related to Architecture," but they now expressed concern that such a topic would largely necessitate non-CASE presenters and thus put the members of CASE in a passive role as at Symposium I. "We therefore propose to structure the May conference around criticism of urban projects by CASE members. By this process an attempt will be

mailing, SAfiles.
70 SA to Meier at his New York office and Graves at Princeton, January 24, 1966 (4 pp). cc, SAfiles.
71 Letter, SA to CASE members and prospective members, announcing CASE Symposium II, January 26, 1966 (1 page). Mimeo, SAfiles, with an attached

note that the letter went to "all regular members + Bosworth, Eardley, Lyndon, Slutzky, Studer, Newman". Shortly followed by some housekeeping for members of CASE: "Memo on: Attendance at CASE Symposia—Membership— New Members—Foundation Support—Symposia

Topics," February 24, 1966, signed Stanford Anderson, Executive Secretary of CASE (2pp). Mimeo, SAfiles. Of significance, Eardley, Lyndon, Newman and Slutzky, after their exposure at CASE Symposium I, had been invited to membership, and accepted. Dick Meier was negotiating with the Graham

Foundation for support of CASE in the next year.
72 Graves and Meier to CASE members about plans for CASE 4, March 14, 1966 (1 page), and a "Preliminary Schedule for CASE 4" (1 page). Ditto, SAfiles.
73 Letter by SA, no addressee but sent to the CASE membership, 7 April

made to determine a framework or rational base for such criticism. We propose as the topic for the next conference, 'A Critical Approach to Urban Form'." The accompanying 'Preliminary Schedule' was twice revised as discussed below.

A letter to the membership on April 7 rehearsed the CASE Study Groups, while also asking members to rethink the list.[73] The list is similar to that of a year earlier at Princeton II (*italic* indicates the chair; **bold** indicates a change):

> Journal: *Frampton*, Millon, Rowe, Eisenman, Anderson
>
> **Architecture and Other Disciplines: *Newman*,** Meier
>
> Politics of Architecture, now: **Architecture and Political Structure:**
>   *Robertson,* Pasanella
>
> Psychology of Architecture: *Rowe,* **Slutzky**
>
> Creative Process, now **Creativity:** *Millon,* Anderson
>
> Education **of the Architect:** *Vreeland,* **Eardley,** Kliment, Millon, Frampton, Meier
>
> Mass, now **City and Mass Phenomena:** *Meier, Graves,* Frampton
>
> Form: *Eisenman,* Anderson, Vreeland, Millon, **Eardley, Slutzky**
>
> ~~Architecture-Planning: Meier~~
>
> Technological Innovation: *no chair,* Graves, Anderson
>
> Industrial Technology, **Industrial Techniques and Construction:** no names
>
> History **and Criticism:** *Anderson, Millon,* Eisenman, Rowe, Frampton, **Eardley,**
> **Slutzky**
>
> Note: Lyndon's name does not appear here, but does in a contemporaneous list of members. By June 1966, Vallhonrat and Weinstein are also added, yielding eighteen members.[74]

CASE 4/CASE Symposium II was also sponsored by MIT and held at Endicott House, May 6-8, 1966.[75] Graves and Meier sent a revised "Preliminary Schedule" on April 19, 1966, that is best discussed in the light of the actual program, "CASE Symposium: A Critical Approach to Urban Form."[76]

1966, with the opening line "I am pleased to confirm . . ." and containing a list of "CASE Study Groups" and the individuals in each group (2pp). Mimeo, SAfiles. A copy of the list is marked "Revised 11 May '66" and with the addition of Lyndon to the Study Groups for Technological Innovation,

Creativity, and Education of the Architect. Revisions in SA's hand, SAfiles.

74 Enclosure to the 7 April 1966 SA letter: "Members of CASE: Mailing List April, 1966 (italics indicate new membership at that time): Anderson and Millon (MIT); Anthony Eardley, Eisenman, Frampton, and

Graves (Princeton); Kliment (University of Pennsylvania); Donlyn Lyndon (University of Oregon); McKinnell (Harvard); Meier (Cooper Union); Oscar Newman (Washington University); Pasanella, Robertson (Columbia); Rowe (Cornell); Robert Slutzky (Pratt Institute); Vreeland (University of New Mexico). Sixteen

members. (1 page). Mimeo, SAfiles. A copy revised in hand, June 1966, adding Vallhonrat and Weinstein. Eighteen members (1 page). SAfiles.

75 After the second MIT/ Endicott House meeting I sent a letter to Dean Lawrence B. Anderson of MIT, giving a brief account

PRELIMINARY SCHEDULE

CASE SYMPOSIUM: A CRITICAL APPROACH TO URBAN FORM

Endicott House – M.I.T.
80 Haven Street
Dedham, Massachusetts
Telephone: 326-5151; M.I.T. extension 4898

Friday 6 May 1966

If you are arriving in Boston and need transportation to Endicott House, please
meet at Stanford Anderson's office #7-346, MIT, School of Architecture at
5:00 p.m. Cars will leave for Dedham at 6:00 p.m.

Friday 6 May 1966 Endicott House

6:30 p.m.	Cocktails
7:30 p.m.	Dinner
9:00 p.m.	First Session chaired by Richard Meier
(promptly)	Introduction: The Crisis – And All of That: Colin Rowe
10:45 p.m.	Politics and Architecture
	Jonathan Barnett
	Richard Weinstein
	Myles Weintraub

Saturday 7 May 1966

8:30 a.m.	Breakfast
9:30 a.m.	Second Session chaired by Michael Graves
(promptly)	Center City Urban Renewal Area, Camden, New Jersey, Thomas Vreeland
	Architectural Paper (topic undetermined) – Alvin Boyarsky
12:30 p.m.	Lunch
2:00 p.m.	Third Session chaired by Richard Meier
	Linear City: The Jersey Corridor Project
	Anthony Eardley
	Peter Eisenman
	Michael Graves
	Chardigarh: The Heavenly City of the Twentiety Century Theoreticians
	John Hejduk
	Akron, Ohio
	Charles Moore
6:30 p.m.	Cocktails
7:00 p.m.	Dinner
8:30 p.m.	Fourth Session chaired by Michael Graves
	The Think-Belt by Cedric Price
	Presented by Stanford Anderson
	Program for Liverpool
	Colin St. John Wilson
	Hoboken, New Jersey
	Richard Meier
	Robert Slutzky

Sunday 8 May 1966

8:30 a.m.	Breakfast
9:30 a.m.	Business Meeting of the Executive Committee of CASE
11:00 a.m.	Discussion Session
12:00 noon	Lunch

The first session, beginning at 9pm on Friday evening, chaired by Meier, consisted of two contributions that first appeared in the second preliminary schedule:

Introduction: The Crisis—And All of That - Colin Rowe.
Politics and Architecture—Jonathan Barnett, Richard Weinstein and Myles Weintraub
    [all of New York]

The opening session thus returned to issues "peripheral to architecture," but delivered by members or "fellow travelers" of CASE. A contribution that had appeared on both prior schedules disappeared: "Programming Urban Redevelopment" by Oscar Newman. Saturday was given over to the critique of urban projects, with alternating sessions chaired by Graves and Meier. A topic that appeared on the first preliminary schedule but not continued was "New York," by Robertson and Pasanella. A contribution on both preliminary schedules but not on the actual program was an undetermined topic to be presented by Geoffrey Copcutt, then a visiting critic at Carnegie Institute of Technology. Sunday was a CASE business meeting followed by discussion and a departure lunch.

My notes allow some insight into the Friday night schedule, though beginning with a mystery.[77] Rowe was to give the first presentation, and my records show him in attendance (though not certainly on the first evening).

In their "Politics and Architecture" presentation, Barnett, Weintraub and Weinstein gave an enlightened and balanced account of how city administrators, citizens (neighborhoods), and architects should work together such that architect and client are on equal footing, "breaking the autocracy of the developer—and of certain professionals." Weinstein in particular looked to the potential of universities playing a role in this mix, even at the level of dissertations.

Eisenman presented the Eisenman/Graves/Eardley design: "Linear City: The Jersey Corridor Project." Beginning from a consideration of theories of urban form, Eisenman observed that the radial form-family developed from two or more approximately equal axes, while for the linear form-family there is a single dominant axis with no preferential

Preliminary Schedule: CASE Symposium: A Critical Approach to Urban Form, May 6, 1966.

of the two meetings, the development of CASE, and expressed our gratitude to him and MIT for their support. June 14, 1966 (2 pp). cc, SAfiles.
76 From Graves and Meier, "Preliminary Schedule for CASE 4 Symposium," April 19, 1966 (1 page). Ditto, SAfiles. Then Graves and

Meier, "CASE Symposium: A Critical Approach to Urban Form" (still also captioned "Preliminary Schedule"), distributed in Dedham, May 6, 1966 (1 page). Ditto, SAfiles.
77 My notes from the lectures and discussion are very limited, but do give some insight into the Friday night session and Eisenman's

discussion of "The Linear City." (5 pp). Originals, SAfiles.
78 The ¼" reel-to-reel tape made at this symposium is disappointingly brief, containing only the discussion of the presentation of the Linear City project and Anderson's presentation of the "Potteries Think-Belt." In the first case, Eisenman et

point. He argued that high-speed ground transport encourages radiality with nodes. His group's commitment to the line denied point-to-point transportation. They rather took up a GM-conceived "electronic taxi-train" with a four-track graduated speed system, allowing them to consider various intervals from 250 yards to two miles. No center, no downtown; everything to be as homogeneous as possible. (Idealizing the Jersey reality?)[78]

From what was a substantive conference, this is all that my notes allow, but one other feature of the meetings is in my memory and on a tape recording. From my time teaching at the Architectural Association (1962-63), I retained a friendship with Cedric Price. Though he could not attend our symposium, he did send me a sizable set of large ozalid prints to enable a presentation of his "Potteries Think-Belt." Built on ingenious social commitments, with technology that was also ingenious but not cutting-edge, and with a low-key approach to architectural and urban form, Cedric's project had an indifferent reception.[79]

All original members of CASE were in attendance (except Millon who was in Rome), plus new members Lyndon, Newman, and Slutzky. Invited participants were Jonathan Barnett, Architectural Record, New York; Alvin Boyarsky, then at University of Illinois Chicago; John Hejduk, Cooper Union; Charles Moore, Dean at Yale; Richard Weinstein, Columbia; Myles Weintraub, New York; and Colin St.John Wilson, Cambridge University. Geoffrey Copcutt did not attend. Invited guests were Carlos Vallhonrat, University of Pennsylvania; Sim van der Ryn, Berkeley; and François Vigier, Harvard. Not attending: Christopher Alexander, Berkeley; and John Entenza of the Graham Foundation, Chicago.[80] From the experience of this event, members agreed that Vallhonrat would be a welcome member of CASE. He was invited and immediately accepted.[81]

Consternation Among the CASE Members—1966

Shortly after the May 1966 meetings, I wrote to Graves and Meier (with copies to Eardley, Eisenman, Robertson, and Slutzky as "program chairmen for 1966-67") thanking them for organizing CASE Symposium II while also offering criticism intended to assist in more successful meetings in the future.[82] I was particularly irritated by Sandy Wilson's presentation of his Liverpool project and still more by the organizers allowing the discussion

al. are seriously challenged, but it ends with Eisenman's appreciation of receiving for the first time sustained, critical feedback—and reads in this a confirmation of the value of CASE. Magnetic tape now on CD, SAfiles.

79 The recording of Anderson's presentation (see previous note) shows only slight interruptions; toward the end he responds to a skeptical question with an informed defense/explication of Price's project. CD, SAfiles. Large ozalid prints of the Think Belt drawings, SAfiles.

80 This information relies on a "List of Participants" prepared by Graves and Meier and distributed at the symposium, with marks for attendance by Anderson, May 1966 (2 pp). Ditto w/marks, SAfiles. Graves had written to John Entenza of the Graham Foundation, hoping to enlist his interest in CASE and

inviting him to the May 6-8 meeting. His letter of April 22, 1966 had as attachments: "Foundation Statement, April 1965; Publication Plans, February 1966; and Program and Participants for CASE 4 Symposium." Tfx of letter, SAfiles. Conveyed to SA by Graves, with a cover letter, on May 23, 1966. Original, SAfiles.

of Wilson's work to consume three hours—diminishing or eliminating attention to much else. I did assess that this meeting had been

> ... more enjoyable and personally rewarding than the first conference [that I had co-organized]. However, I think we should remain concerned to find a format that is both rewarding for those present and gives us something to communicate to others ... we should be careful that CASE doesn't become only a forum for criticism of projects that are so particularly ours that we lose any reason to communicate our findings. Similarly, in the proposal for our next meeting—competing designs to a set problem—I think the problem must be very carefully chosen so as to avoid becoming our own little prolongation of school projects. I suspect that the problem will have to be sufficiently general that people will find that they want to explore some possibility and not that they just have to do another design for good old CASE.

> I think that we must actively seek to keep CASE interesting to others, interesting to people with different concerns, and engaging for every member of CASE. We must start having policy-making meetings in which all points of view are represented [which had been inhibited by the scheduling of the May meeting].

From this letter, one recalls that a Sunday-morning decision made in too little time with too few people present had been that the next conference should be built around an idea of Eisenman and the Princeton group: that CASE would assign a problem with the resultant designs by members of CASE forming the material for the next CASE symposium. More negative reactions were to come.

The May meeting and/or the above letter stimulated a number of responses. A letter from Lyndon expressed similar concerns about the conduct of the May meeting and, characteristically, continued with constructive propositions [particularly, I take it, about the ambitions of "study groups"], one of which was:

81 SA to Carlos Vallhonrat, inviting membership in CASE, May 11, 1966 (1 page). cc, SAfiles. Note of telephonic response from Vallhonrat, May 13, 1966. SAfiles.

82 SA to Graves and Meier, with copies to Eardley, Eisenman, Robertson, and Slutzky, conveying concerns about the nature of future meetings of CASE (undated, but early May 1966; 2 pp). cc, SAfiles.

a new category might have to do with USE or FIT: how do you predict what will take place, how make judgments of value about conflicting use requirements and how do you evaluate a building's fit: in other words, where and when does form impinge on function, how do we know whether it will, whether it has, or whether it matters. Perhaps some of the above could fall within the technology blanket.[83]

Concern about "wild shooting and [the need to] permit more accurate focusing on problems" came from Vreeland, who also reported that Robertson would write on behalf of Weinstein, Vreeland and himself on a program for "our next conference . . . better than that suggested (and tentatively approved) by the Executive Committee meeting."[84] Kliment called Anderson on May 17, 1966, objecting both to a proposal that CASE tailor its interests to funding sources and to required design projects for the substance of CASE meetings. He expressed great interest in the issues raised by Robertson et al. at the May meeting.[85] Tim Vreeland penned a very revealing two-page letter on his Albuquerque professional office stationery:

Tuesday May 17
Dear Stan,

I got your letter this morning [undated May 1966 letter]. I agree with you but I think you're much too charitable. In my opinion the conference was poorly organized, poorly run and very uneven. I am naturally angry because I think I was made a fool of. When Dick Meier suggested that I present the Camden project I pointed out to him that it was a very ordinary urban renewal project with practically no theoretic content. I said I would prefer to present the Tel Aviv town plan, which has plenty of it. I stupidly allowed myself to be talked into it and I very much regret it.

To tell the truth, for the first time I feel discouraged about CASE. Don Lyndon has suggested forming a CASE West and maybe that's what we need.

83 Lyndon to Anderson, with reflections on CASE 4 and future efforts (May 10, 1966; 2 pp). Original, SAfiles. I don't recall this as a cause of CASE 5 that I organized at MIT in 1968, but perhaps it did provide some impetus.

84 Vreeland to Anderson, with reflections on CASE 4 and future efforts (May 11, 1966; 1 page). Original, SAfiles.

85 Anderson's penned notes on a telephone conversation with Robert Kliment (May 17, 1966; 1 page). Original SAfiles.

I got suffocated listening to the pontificating about Corbusier. God knows, I love him as much as anyone, but he doesn't happen to be a member of CASE and I joined what I hoped to be a group of young, vital architects with current ideas of their own. I enjoyed your presentation [of Price's Think Belt] best and the New York group next, because they each seemed relevant, essentially new information, etc. In fact, the Think Belt is really what I took away with me. I keep applying it out here and here it really fits. I would love some day to make a presentation of the West (really what the West means to me or how I see it) to the group sometime. I am working on some ideas (with JB Jackson) which intrigue me. But enough of my ramblings. You are quite right about the Executive Sessions. They are a disgrace.

Don't judge me too harshly by the Camden Project. Urban renewal is to planning what remodeling is to architecture. Look sometime at the Tel Aviv plan. It was reproduced in Perspecta 9/10 and a Sept. or Oct. issue of Arts and Architecture (last year). It contains some good ideas, ones which I'd be willing to go to bat for.

Best regards, Tim [86]

Jaque Robertson called me in early June. In the previous week he had spoken with Eisenman, resisting "both proposals" by the Princeton group for next year. [Romaldo] Giurgola [now Dean at Columbia] " . . . might carry CASE next year. New York group would organize one or two meetings on their project." It was noted that Tim, Donlyn, Peter, and Stan would soon meet at Cranbrook: "We should discuss alternative programs for next year."[87]

Charles Moore, chair of the Program Committee for the June 1966 AIA/ACSA Cranbrook Seminar, invited me to the Committee for a program he had drafted:

With the architect's assumption of responsibility for the whole environment has come, often in panic, his realization that our time-honored intuitive

86 Vreeland to Anderson, from Albuquerque, NM, handwritten letter on office stationery (May 17, 1966; 2 pp). Original, SAfiles.

87 Penciled note of telephone call from Robertson to SA, June 3, 1966. Original, SAfiles. Anderson delivered a paper that had first been read at the Architectural Association in March 1966: "Problem-Solving and Problem-Worrying" (17pp). Typescript, SAfiles.

methods of identifying and structuring environmental problems, of recognizing
and selecting viable solutions, and then of profiting from the experience
gained are often inadequate to cope with the increasingly complex problems
we face. With this realization comes the suspicion that even our simpler
problems are too often stereotypes, insensitive to the people and places
they serve. Suggestions for a methodology and searches for a theory of design
are developing which employ with increasing sophistication the new tools and
techniques of mathematics and the physical and social sciences. Reactions
to these suggestions and searches are developing as well, galvanized by
the fear that the computer will usurp the domain of the creator and that
science sill stifle life.

In choosing participants, Moore did not seek a "confrontation," but rather people
representing the stated range of concerns who would entertain new ideas and learn from
one another. The final program was weighted to practicing architects, among them Bruce
Graham, Kevin Roche, Aldo van Eyck, John Andrews, Joseph Esherick, and Lyndon. On the
"scientific" side: Christopher Alexander, Sim van der Ryn, Robert Sommer, Bruce Archer,
Murray Milne, and Bernard Spring. Assigned the keynote role on Sunday evening, I gave a
paper titled "Problem-Solving and Problem-Worrying."[88]

The first four meetings of CASE were private, held in institutional conference houses rather
than in the schools. This was a matter of self-criticism and elicited some action stemming
from discussions at Cranbrook. While there, as communicated in a letter from Anderson to
CASE members on June 30, Eisenman, Lyndon, Vreeland and Anderson identified:

... two general needs ... CASE should find some activities that open it
to interested people outside the membership. Another need is to find some
problems which are of common concern to all members ... one that seemed
indisputable was our common involvement in architectural education ... It
was at this point that Donlyn Lyndon conceived of an activity that would
contribute to the resolution of both the needs ...

88 The paper had first been
read at the Architectural
Association in March 1966
(17pp). Typescript, SAfiles,
which also contain other
information on Cranbrook
1966.

CASE as a Traveling Zoo

> Donlyn's proposal was that CASE should descend en masse on a school of architecture, stay for a week, enter into all aspects of teaching at the school, and at the same time actively discover and explore the common interests of the members of CASE." I observed that " . . . this proposal would make CASE active in the larger architectural community, it would exploit our common interest in education, and it would give us an active and more extended time in which the members of CASE could establish other common programs of activity.[89]

On June 21, 1966, Eisenman wrote to Anderson from San Francisco, recalling "our strange week at Cranbrook," but primarily to report on his visit with John Entenza of the Graham Foundation in Chicago. Eisenman's report is upbeat, that Entenza welcomed the initiative represented by CASE, and was particularly willing to support Lyndon's idea of CASE Teach-Ins, beginning with such a week-long event at the University of Oregon. Eisenman had a call in to Lyndon to get him moving in Eugene. He further suggested that he and I draft a Teach-In proposal to reach Entenza in the first week of August and he would prepare a monetary request. I should also inform the CASE membership of these developments.[90] Shortly, Lyndon called reporting initial academic and financial commitments by Oregon for an event in early 1967, and requested information on one's own contribution flowing from on-going work.[91]

In the letter of June 30 referenced above, I reported on discussions at a sparsely attended session at the end of the May meeting in Dedham. Propositions made then found little resonance, but there was considerable interest to explore further the implications of the work of the New York group (Robertson, Pasanella, Weinstein, Barnett and Weintraub) as it was presented in May—and that Columbia might sponsor such a CASE meeting. There followed the account of the Cranbrook discussions and the concept of CASE Teach-Ins. At Cranbrook, the idea of the "Zoo" was attractive, but in recognition of its high cost, it was deferred in favor of the Columbia program. Nonetheless, I could go on to new

89 Letter by SA to the CASE membership, June 30, 1966, with a report of recent events and, importantly, confirmed news of the University of Oregon "CASE Teach-In" to be held early in 1967 (5pp). Mimeo, SAfiles. Lyndon thanks for the June 30 letter, July 6, 1966. Original, SAfiles.

90 Handwritten letter, Eisenman to Anderson, initiating plans for a CASE Teach-In as had been suggested by Lyndon during joint conversations at the June AIA/ACSA Cranbrook Seminar, June 21, 1966 (2 pp). Original, SAfiles.

91 Record of telephone call, Lyndon to Anderson, on initiation of the Oregon Teach-In, June 28, 1966 (1 page). SAfiles.

prospects: that Eisenman went from Cranbrook to Chicago where, in discussions at the Graham Foundation, John Entenza "was especially interested in the idea of CASE making a contribution to, and impact upon some schools of architecture each year. Entenza offered support if CASE members were indeed interested and if the visited school would "contribute a good part of the total costs."

Lyndon then arranged with Dean Walter Creese and the University of Oregon that they would receive CASE for a week of teaching and meetings and would contribute to the expenses. Lyndon's proposal: "The teaching should relate to the principal talents and interests of each participating member. There could be special seminars and lectures or participation in on-going courses. Juries could be scheduled during the week. Perhaps a sketch problem(s) could be given. Or students might have completed a design project and then be subject to a review and one-week re-work under 'CASE guidance.' There might be guidance on thesis problems."[92]

The letter ended with instructions that members work out their participation directly with Lyndon.[93] The prospect of the Columbia meeting on the New York urban issues was renewed together with the related news that Richard Weinstein had been invited to membership.[94]

Princeton/AIA Education Report and MIT Response—1965-66

Sometime in the 1965-66 academic year, Dean Robert Geddes of Princeton and his colleague, MIT alumnus, Bernard Spring, presented at MIT their AIA-funded study of the future of architectural education.[95] The reaction around the table of our Wednesday-lunch faculty meeting was that the Princeton study was far too mechanical not only in its details, but in its general theoretical position. Dean Anderson sponsored my preparation of a conference placing environmental decisions in a different epistemological and social position. My preparation went as far as travel to London and Paris. In London, in the year of Twiggy, I visited Karl Popper, Imre Lakatos, Royston Landau and Cedric Price. The male-only Architectural Association Members Room I had known only three years earlier had been liberated. The biggest surprise was mini-skirts, then still unknown in the US—pre-pantyhose. Architectural Association girls (the term of the time and, to be ethnically correct, I should

92 See n. 93.

93 In fulfillment of this request: letter of Anderson to Lyndon, suggesting a specific contribution stemming from the "Future" conference he was organizing for October 1966 as well as readiness to participate in all ways Lyndon would find useful, July 11, 1966. cc, SAfiles.

94 In a letter of July 11, 1966, Pasanella reported that Columbia "seems willing and able to participate," and that the New York group might pursue various options: "From a seminar for the professions to an open meeting for the general public"—to receive more thought. Pasanella also enclosed a copy of a

letter to Lyndon of the same date, declining participation at the Oregon Teach-In due to conflict with his academic schedule. Original and cc, respectively, SAfiles.

95 Robert Geddes and Bernard Spring, co-directors, *A Study of Education for Environmental Design: Final Report,* sponsored by the American Institute of Architects (Princeton, NJ: Princeton University Press, 1967). Also one of the featured presentations at Cranbrook 1966.

say "birds") now sat in the collapsed cushions of the Chesterfields of the Members Room, their exposed knees well above their hips and the hardware to support their stockings on display—at least. In Paris I engaged two noted futurologists, later participants in the conference, Bertrand de Jouvenel and, in the French government, Bernard Cazes. Paris was already experiencing what would later come to New York, Boston, and other American cities. The streets of Paris were politically active and de Gaulle whooshed by in a stream of black Citroen Déesses.

The conference "Inventing the Future Environment: Possible Futures and Their Relations to the Man-Controlled Environment" occurred at MIT's Endicott House in October 1966 with a number of notables from government, think-tanks, and academia.[96] President Johnson's Great Society program yielded a cabinet-level position for urban affairs in the founding of the Department of Housing and Urban Development (HUD) in 1965, with Robert C. Weaver as the first Secretary. In 1964 Dr. Leonard Duhl edited an influential book, *The Urban Condition: People and Policy in the Metropolis*. As Duhl joined the conference, he had become a special assistant to Weaver and influential in the establishment of HUD's Model Cities Program in 1966 (and later the founder of the Healthy Cities Movement). Numerous respected academics represented the fields of economics, engineering, history, social psychology, political science, and operations research. Paul Davidoff of CUNY represented the activist side of these concerns. Popperian and post-Popper thought appeared in Ian Jarvie (York University—"Utopian Thinking and the Architect") and a paper by Paul Feyerabend (Berkeley—"Outline of a Pluralistic Theory of Knowledge and Action"). Cedric Price made a final response, standing in for other architect discussants; Melvin Charney (Université de Montréal) contributed to the publication. Perhaps in despair of CASE members' passive reaction to broadened intellectual concerns, I had constructed an elaborate conference with no CASE participation other than Millon and myself.

1966-67 Oregon Teach-In—1967

Lyndon invited all members of CASE to Eugene to realize, through lectures, seminars, and studio crits, the "Teach-In" program he had conceived and now organized.[97] In late December 1966, Lyndon wrote to CASE, explaining several unsuccessful attempts at

96 Stanford Anderson, ed., *Planning for Diversity and Choice: Possible Futures and Their Relations to the Man-Controlled Environment* (Cambridge, MA: The MIT Press, 1968. In German as *Die Zukunft der menschlichen Umwelt* (Freiburg i. B.: Rombach, 1971).

97 The process of nominations and votes resulted in a "Members of CASE: Mailing List" in January, 1967 (2pp). Mimeo, SAfiles; probably distributed in anticipation of the Oregon Teach-In. The list: Anderson and Millon (MIT; Millon on leave at the American Academy in Rome); Eisenman,

Frampton and Graves (Princeton); Kliment, Pasanella, and Robertson (Columbia); Lyndon (University of Oregon; now the incoming Head, MIT); McKinnell (Harvard); Meier (Cooper Union); Newman (Washington University); Rowe (Cornell), Vreeland (University of New Mexico); [Pasanella, the least

active member, intentionally omitted?] Plus the new members, Anthony Eardley (Princeton); Robert Slutzky (Pratt Institute); Carlos Vallhonrat (University of Pennsylvania). [Seemingly an error that Richard Weinstein is not listed.]

external funding, including that with Entenza and the Graham Foundation. The Oregon
Teach-In would proceed on the two-third funding committed by the University, but the
budget had to be trimmed. He sought firm decisions on participation in the Teach-In—or
not. Enclosed was a "tentative schedule" running from Monday January 30, 1967, through
Friday February 3, with suggestions of lecture and seminar content for all members of
CASE, except Pasanella.[98] Lyndon wrote again on January 20 addressing CASE "Teach-
In" Participants, which now included faculty from Oregon and elsewhere. He offered
a preliminary description of the on-going studio projects that CASE members would
encounter in criticism sessions. The attached schedule dated January 19 showed the
limited number of CASE members actually participating.[99]

Lyndon chaired the Oregon Teach-In. According to the "CASE Schedule" distributed
at the event,[100] lectures were given by Anderson and Millon, Graves, and non-CASE
members John Fisher (Berkeley), William Liskam (visitor, Oregon), Robert Frasca (Wolfe
Zimmer Architects, Portland; later a principal in a succeeding and successful firm),
John Hill (Kentucky, about to become Dean, Maryland), Larson [uncertain; probably C.
Theodore Larson (Michigan)], and a School-organized lecture by David Rinehart (soon
thereafter Oregon). Seminars were chaired by Anderson, Newman, and Vreeland (twice);
Newman; Vreeland, Murray Milne (Oregon, then Yale) and Fisher; Eardley and Graves;
Millon, Newman and Eardley; Millon; Vreeland; Hill; Dora Wiebenson (History of Art and
Architecture, Oregon), and Fisher.[101] I distributed a "preliminary report" on my "Possible
Futures" conference of the preceding fall.[102]

Everyone took part in studio reviews. One can observe that the event was carried as much
by non-members of CASE as by CASE, but this could also be interpreted as a success in
moving away from the closed circle of the earlier CASE meetings.[103] The event schedule
called for a final "CASE/Faculty teach-in summary, late on Friday evening. A slip of paper
records themes I drew from several commentators:

John Fischer: Conflicts in simultaneous scheduling [of the School and CASE]

Mike Pease (Oregon; recent Berkeley graduate under Moore): Issues come out

98 Lyndon to CASE
members, preparations for
Oregon Teach-In, December
27, 1966 (2 pp), and attached
preliminary schedule for
January 30 to February
3, 1967 (1 page). Ditto,
SAfiles. Lyndon copied SA
on his funding application to
John Entenza, the Graham
Foundation, Chicago, August

12, 1966 from Sea Ranch.
Letter (2 pp); Schedule (2 pp);
Budget (1 page). The budget
was $9,465, with $3,300
committed by the University.
cc, SAfiles.
Lyndon also copied SA on his
application to William Shaw,
Executive Director of The
Foundation for Environmental
Design in Carmel, California,

October 12, 1966, from
the University of Oregon.
Letter (2 pp), Budget (1
page), Schedule (tentative)
(2 pp), list of members of
CASE (18; 1 page). The
budget here is the same
$9,465, but the University
increased its share to $4,800.
The list of members shows
that, at this time, Lyndon

had confirmed participation
from all but three of the
members: Eardley, Rowe,
and Vallhonrat. cc, SAfiles.
For information, Lyndon also
sent to Shaw a copy of the
preliminary schedule of CASE
Symposium II of May 1966
(2 pp) Tfx, and a copy of SA's
"Foundation Statement," with
that heading removed (11

over boards and in reviews; so design sections are worthwhile

Hill: More design involvement. Visitors help structure problems

Milne: Specified time for design [reserving time for student design work]

Dolores Hayden (BA, Mt. Holyoke College, 1966): [Calls for] demonstration of reality of alternatives

Graves: Send a bibliography ahead; important for communication

Unidentified person: Completely change structure of week in order to examine alternatives

Eardley: No. Change of school [schedule] would ruin the test. Value of multiplicity of weeks.

Pease: Problem situations as alternative to theory.[104]

At the Teach-In there was ample time for the CASE members to reflect on the state of the organization and make plans for the future.[105] A program on urban issues, conducted by the New York group around Robertson, and taking place at Columbia, was still on the table, possibly in the fall of 1967. Still that spring Vreeland proposed developing a CASE Symposium on "Exploration of Study Media [Employed] in the Design Process," at Columbia University or Washington University in Saint Louis—the latter reflecting the presence of Oscar Newman in the discussions.

Newman himself proposed a symposium on issues of urbanism to be held at Washington University in the spring of 1968. He mentioned participation by Leonard Duhl and George Rockrise. We can reconstruct from this that Newman was concerned to build relations to new urban initiatives at the Federal level. Duhl was noted above as a special assistant to Secretary Weaver of HUD; Rockrise, a San Francisco architect, was also an advisor to Weaver.

In February, on behalf of CASE, I sent thanks to Dean Creese for the academic and economic generosity, and the hospitality shown to us by Creese, Lyndon and the School.[106] Dean Creese responded, with this last paragraph:

pp). Tfx and Ditto, all SAfiles. Shaw's letter to Lyndon declining support (November 15, 1966; 1 page). Tfx, SAfiles. Lyndon's polite reply to Shaw (November 30, 1966; 1 page). cc, SAfiles.

99 Lyndon to CASE members, preparations for Oregon Teach-In, January 20, 1967 (2 pp), and attached

"Revised Schedule (tentative) dated January 19 (1 page). Ditto, SAfiles. Another "CASE Schedule (tentative)," dated January 27, apparently came to me in the mail. My copy has a secretary's note to call Lyndon, and then a number of revisions written in by me (2 pp). Ditto w/SA notes, SAfiles.

100 "School of Architecture and Allied Arts, University of Oregon, Eugene, Oregon— CASE Schedule," undated, but for the event running from Monday, January 30, 1967, to Friday, February 3 (2 pp). Also distributed: "Published Material in AAA Library, related to C.A.S.E. Members and other visitors," with

entries for Anderson, Eardley, Graves, Millon, Newman, Vreeland, John Hill, and Murray Milne (2 pp). Ditto, SAfiles.

101 My notes from the Oregon Teach-In are few and obscure. Somewhat penetrable are scraps from the seminar where I participated with Oscar Newman and

It was wonderful to have you and your colleagues here, and I am delighted
to learn that it may have been of some benefit to the organization as well.
Certainly the School gained much because the students talked about it for a
long time afterward.[107]

MoMA Exhibition "The New City" and MIT—1966-67

Peter Eisenman recently (fall 2009) told me of a visit to the Princeton School of Architecture
by Arthur Drexler, Curator of Architecture at the Museum of Modern Art, apparently in
1965. Eisenman and Graves took the opportunity to show Drexler the model of their Linear
City project. Drexler became very excited, saying that he had wanted to do an exhibition on
urbanism, but didn't know that young architects were exploring such matters. Eisenman
convinced Drexler that he could put together teams of young architects to develop and
exhibit urban designs. The Museum secured funds for faculty members of four schools
of architecture to work for most of the year 1966 to develop projects for four areas of
Harlem, to be exhibited at MoMA in January 1967 as "The New City." Work for the New
City exhibition was never billed as a CASE project, but the initiative and the participants
stemmed from CASE. Organization of the four university teams was entrusted to Eisenman,
who designated the responsible parties as Graves and himself for Princeton, Colin Rowe for
Cornell, Jaque Robertson and Richard Weinstein for Columbia, and Stanford Anderson for
MIT, each school to develop its own team.[108] Hank Millon, as the other MIT CASE member
joined our team, but to name the third MIT participant requires prior discussion.

As implausible as it seems in hindsight, Drexler and Eisenman decided on projects for
the radical transformation of Harlem as the content of the exhibition! Surely none of the
participants were completely naïve about this venture, but I think it is fair to say that MIT as
a school was more prepared to confront the issues of such a project. In Boston, this was
the time of resistance to the Southwest Expressway (an interstate highway intended to
cut through much of the southern and central part of the city, never executed), the issues
of "Tent City" (a squatter community occupying a development site until the matter was
resolved with the construction of low-income housing), and other citizen activism.

Tim Vreeland. No notes on
my contribution and almost
nothing from Vreeland.
Newman seems to have
concluded his position, feeling
alienated from the Eisenman
world, with this: "People want
something different from
what architects think they
should want." (3pp) SAfiles.
This puts me in mind of one

of the most enlightening
and intellectually enjoyable
events that I experienced at
the Institute for Architecture
and Urban Studies. Eisenman
and Newman engaged
aggressively in a debate that
they both thoroughly enjoyed
in mutual respect. (I don't
recall the date, but not later
than 1972.)

102 Preliminary report
"Planning for Fullness, A
Conference on Possible
Futures and Their Relations
to the Man-Controlled
Environment (MIT, October,
1966)" (14pp). Ditto, SAfiles.
See fn. 96.

103 Lyndon recalls that
Eisenman "boycotted [the
Teach-In] as not being
sufficiently pure CASE"
(personal communication
June 20, 2010). The total
absence of New York
members supports this claim.
Since Lyndon's preliminary
programs featured all CASE
members, the objection

"The New City: Architecture and Urban Renewal,"
Exhibition at MOMA, 1966-67. Four project areas,
west to east: Princeton, Cornell, Columbia, MIT.
Each team concentrated on a different problem:
west to east, waterfront renewal, modification of
existing grid plan, housing without relocation, new
land. Digital image ©The Museum of Modern
Art/Licensed by SCALA/Art Resource, NY.

"The New City" Exhibition at MOMA, 1966-67. *left to right:* Princeton University. Site Plan, focusing on waterfront renewal; Columbia University, Site Plan for housing without relocation; and Cornell University, Corridor park zone. From *The New City: Architecture and Urban Renewal* (New York: MOMA, 1967), 37, 31, 29. Digital image ©The Museum of Modern Art/Licensed by SCALA/Art Resource, NY.

Robert Goodman was a new member of the MIT faculty in 1966, appointed by Lawrence Anderson for interests that also made him controversial: his early commitment to advocacy planning and the concomitant interest in the conditions of the dispossessed. Every day, Bob studied local newspapers and other sources reporting on the problems of marginalized groups or communities in Boston and Cambridge. He was active in their organizations. These commitments were also seen in a larger context, the development of the theory and practice of advocacy planning in association with such notables as Paul Davidoff, who coined the term in 1965, and Max Bond, leader of The Architects Renewal Committee of Harlem (ARCH), founded late in 1964.[109]

Contrary to the impetus of the Eisenman/Drexler program, I asked Bob to join the MIT group. He of course saw his participation as anomalous and likely embarrassing to him. How could someone of his orientation participate in what promised to be an esthetically driven, form-oriented imposition on the environment of some of the least favored communities of New York? I convinced Bob that the MIT team should and could confront those issues, and all the better as what promised to be a clearly contrasting approach came from a respected venue. He agreed.

We were assigned to make a proposition for the transformation (betterment) of East Harlem which had two housing environments: over-crowded and deteriorated brownstone row houses and degraded high-rise public housing with unused, often dangerous, green areas. The brownstones had the architectural and urban qualities that continue to make them successful throughout much of New York, but here suffered under conditions of poverty and population density. The high-rise housing was misconceived urbanistically and suffered even greater social problems.

Our principal was that the viable blocks of nineteenth-century housing in East Harlem, fully occupied by people of low- to low/middle-income, should not be disturbed until there was a possible choice of alternative accommodation. New housing would allow localized movement from the existing houses and provide general improvement to a more extensive area.

could not have been about exclusion, but rather the nature of the event. I don't recall this as a matter of concern at the event.

104 SA's penned notes from the final session of the Teach-In (February 3, 1967). Original, SAfiles.

105 SA's notes on plans for CASE while at the Oregon Teach-In (1 page). SAfiles.

106 SA to Dean Walter Creese, University of Oregon, February 20, 1967 (1 page). cc, SAfiles. Apparently CASE members enjoyed the event, perhaps too much: I find a slip of paper in my records that has simply "CASE—Concern About Self and Enjoyment."

107 Dean Walter Creese to SA at MIT, March 10, 1967 (1 page). Original, SAfiles.

108 Colin Rowe included a piece, "The New City: Architecture and Urban Renewal," in his *As I Was Saying: Recollections and Miscellaneous Essays* (3 vols., Cambridge, MA: The MIT Press, 1996), III: 87-96.

"The New City" Exhibition at MOMA, 1966-67. *left*, MIT proposal, site plan. The MIT project proposed to extend land fill operations to a consistent plan to link Randall's and Ward's Islands to Manhattan Island. From MOMA, *New City*, 43. Digital image ©The Museum of Modern Art/Licensed by SCALA/Art Resource, NY.

*Proposed new housing a
closely to waterfront are
space within the massin
In drawing below, build*

"The New City" Exhibition at MOMA, 1966-67. Sketches from MIT proposal. From MOMA, *New City*, 44. Digital image ©The Museum of Modern Art/Licensed by SCALA/Art Resource, NY.

The four teams met regularly at MoMA during 1966. We were friends and the meetings were constructive, but the divergence of the MIT team was evident. Late in the year, Drexler toured the four universities to view the work, especially the large models. In his elegant manner and attire, he was appalled to find us working in an unkempt, ancient temporary building (the famous Building 20, World War II home of the Research Laboratory for Electronics, hailed by its scientists and engineers for its nurturing of major innovations).[110] With the model in an advanced state and the opening not far off, Drexler was discrete in his comments, but no doubt disappointed that he did not find a dominating formal proposition.[111]

The basic character of the four projects for Harlem is amply clear from the collective urban plan published on the cover of the exhibition catalog, *The New City: Architecture and Urban Renewal* (see illustration on page 627).[112] The Princeton team took the western edge of Harlem on the Hudson River, producing an orderly megastructure, principally a "two-building structure, built over the river and extending thirty blocks in a straight line."[113] Dominant motivation was the provision of parks, metropolitan institutions, and research facilities that might link the universities at either end of the project (Columbia and City College of New York). The Cornell team radically reshaped the whole of central Harlem,

It is surprising to me that he says it was his idea rather than Eisenman's that MIT be included in the enterprise. In any case, he is wrong to assert that "MIT received the very detached job of Riker's Island [a prison island that did not figure in the project at all]." In so doing, Rowe misconceives the MIT intent

and project as shown in the exhibition catalog and the text below.

109 Robert Goodman (b. 1936, New York); BArch, MIT 1960; his commitments resulted in *After the Planners* (New York: Simon and Schuster, 1971); professor Hampshire College.

110 Lawrence Anderson secured this coveted space for us.

111 The large model was handsomely done by MIT Architecture students. John Terry took the lead with Arthur Stern and Steve Leff. Richard Tremaglio contributed to the representation of the proposed mixed-use

development.

112 *The New City: Architecture and Urban Renewal* (New York: Museum of Modern Art, 1967).

113 Princeton team, *The New City*, 36.

114 The development of Rowe's urbanistic program appeared in Colin Rowe and Fred Koetter, *Collage City*

from Central Park to the Harlem River at the north. Rowe employed his figure/ground urbanism to reform the already competing urban morphologies of dense row house blocks and towers in open areas.[114] He envisioned that the area would be "an uptown magnet displaying urban qualities scarcely attainable in midtown."[115] The Columbia team, directly involved in city planning projects under Mayor Lindsay, designed a tautly organized vaulted structure over the elevated railroad tracks extending thirty-seven blocks north from Park Avenue at 97th Street. Though also a bold architectural megastructure, they conceived the project as mitigating conditions engendered by the elevated train and providing new housing and communal facilities serving the existing community.[116]

The plan on the cover of the "New City" catalog reveals that the MIT team completely re-conceived the assignment to transform the area east of the elevated tracks.[117] We touched nothing of the old fabric of East Harlem. New housing would be realized in three ways: by street-oriented, mid-rise housing to infill the public housing superblocks; by land reclamation at the East River facilitating integrated and positive use of Randall's and Ward's Islands; and by redevelopment of the nearby devastated South Bronx. Mixed-use development but mainly new housing in these areas could provide homes for people of East Harlem who wanted new housing nearby. The existing housing resource in East Harlem could then be rehabilitated for a population of lower density.

As I noted for Boston, urban strife was significant in American cities. But apparently January 1967 was not 1968. The "New City" exhibition with its proposed radical surgery on Harlem went off more peaceably than one can now imagine.[118] In an astute study of the exhibition in its context and of the reactions to it, Suzanne Frank reveals that most critics, even those who were generally negative, noted the MIT project as a welcome exception to the show.[119] Wolf von Eckardt wrote in the *Washington Post*:

> The project is remarkable for its clarity and simplicity as well as the convincing way in which the new street pattern meshes with the existing one. ... The beauty of this scheme is, of course, that it would provide Harlem with new housing and new opportunities of all kinds without demolishing a single building or displacing a single family.[120]

(Cambridge, MA: The MIT Press, 1978).

115 Cornell team, *The New City*, 24.

116 Columbia team, *The New City*, 30.

117 Or, still better, the similar image on p. 23 of the catalog.

118 The "New City" exhibition was shown at the Museum of Modern Art, New York, from January 23 to mid-March 1968. The final credited team members were: Columbia—Robertson, Weinstein, Pasanella, Jonathan Barnett and Myles Weintraub; Cornell—Colin Rowe, Thomas Schumacher, Jerry Wells and Alfred Koetter; MIT—Anderson, Goodman and Millon; Princeton—

Eisenman and Graves. Arthur Drexler, Curator.

119 Suzanne Frank, "Harlem and the 1967 'New City' Exhibition," *Journal of Planning History*, 11, 3 (August 2012), 210-225. Frank offers some MIT details that I would state otherwise, and there seems no better place to do this than here: On   p.

216, Frank says MIT hired Goodman to determine "what residents of East Harlem would want." Goodman was hired before there was any notion of the "New City;" none of us received any directives from MIT. On p. 217, Frank rightly sees Goodman as the team member engaged in advocacy

A few years later, Arthur Drexler was quite probably looking back on this with some consternation when, writing a preface to the *Five Architects* book, thus praising the work of Eisenman, Graves, and others, he rehearsed the other side of the argument (with a caveat seeking to retain its social conscience):

> An alternative to political romance is to be an architect, for those who actually have the necessary talent for architecture. The young men represented here have that talent (along with a social conscience and a considerable awareness of what is going on in the world around them) and their work makes a modest claim: it is only [author's emphasis] architecture, not the salvation of man and the redemption of the earth. For those who like architecture that is no mean thing.[121]

Eisenman, New York, and IAUS—1967-68

On the occasion of a May 1967 AIA/ACSA meeting in New York, CASE held an informal meeting.[122] In June I reported on the meeting in a letter to CASE members: ". . . our meeting rambled from the [Columbia] Mens' Faculty Club to the pop-up Bini dome to the monuments of Pei to the cocktails of Vreeland,[123] with a constantly changing group of participants," and continued: "Those members who had been at the Oregon "Teach-In" were very enthusiastic about the experience and about the continuation of CASE." It was anticipated that Columbia University would " . . . arrange meeting places for two sessions next year. One of those meetings will be the deferred session on the political and social role of the architect under the direction of Robertson, Weinstein, and Pasanella. The other meeting will be on architectural education, chaired by Kliment and Vreeland." Anderson was to poll inactive members, ascertaining their level of interest, in order that new members might be invited with the intent of maintaining a "small but totally active membership."

In the time of the development of the New City exhibition and the CASE Teach-In, Peter Eisenman, in consultation with Arthur Drexler, Philip Johnson and other notable figures in New York, conceived, and in 1967 brought into being, the Institute for Architecture and Urban Studies in New York City. An institutional "History" by the Institute acknowledges that the New City exhibition was a direct precursor of IAUS:

planning, but suggests that the MIT design was in the hands of Goodman who in turn was under the influence of Maurice Smith. The MIT design was a collective effort, including students. All participants except Goodman had significant relations with Smith, but Smith would want to assure us that the MIT

project does not reflect his thought.

120 Wolf von Eckardt, "Museum Shows 4 Novel Approaches to Urban Renewal," a *Washington Post* review, here transcribed from its reprint in the *Long Island Press* (February 12, 1967). The most prominent review was by Ada Louis Huxtable,

"Planning the New City: Modern Museum Exhibits Projects That Link Esthetics and Sociology," *New York Times* (January 24, 1967), 39, 45.

121 Arthur Drexler, Preface, *Five Architects: Eisenman Graves Gwathmey Hejduk Meier* (New York: Wittenborn, 1972), 1; 2nd ed., New York:

Oxford University Press, 1975.

122 Invitation letter, SA to CASE members, 3 May 1967 (1 page). Mimeo, SAfiles. Present on 16 May were: Anderson, Eardley, Graves, Meier, Robertson, Vallhonrat, Vreeland, and Weinstein. Eisenman was ill, and Frampton and Millon were in Europe.

Many of the young architects who formed the core of the initial Fellowship had already been independently engaged in seeking alternatives to traditional forms of architectural education and practice. The exhibition "The New City: Architecture and Urban Renewal" at the Museum of Modern Art, a natural consolidation of these efforts, led to the formation of the Institute [1967].[124]

IAUS was a highly significant phenomenon; its story is becoming a major research project.[125] The current essay cannot be even a full account of the earlier and lesser organization CASE. Nevertheless, it is appropriate to see the roots of IAUS in CASE. Eisenman was the great entrepreneur of all, but he and his capacities had found room to grow and mature in the activities of CASE. Influential members of IAUS, at least in its early years, were notably members of CASE.

On November 15, 1967, I wrote to the members of CASE (with Lyndon now at MIT as Head of Architecture) that Eisenman invited a meeting of CASE at the IAUS premises at 5 East 47th Street in January.[126]

As you will have heard, Peter is the Director of the IAUS; Colin Rowe is also at the Institute. Meeting there will give us an opportunity to learn about the goals and the first projects of the Institute ... Our intention is ... to devote this meeting to spontaneous discussion by CASE members on two issues:

Education of architects/environmental designers
Purpose and organization of CASE in the light of our various meetings, the Oregon Teach-In, and the founding of IAUS.

The CASE meeting at IAUS took place on January 12-13, 1968, with Eisenman and Rowe as hosts. Attending were Eardley, Graves, Meier, Slutzky, Anderson, and, briefly, Kliment. In May I sent a memo informing all CASE members of the January meeting and more.[127] The January discussions recognized that Princeton and MIT could not be asked for further support and that funding from Columbia would not be forthcoming. However,

123 Letter SA to CASE members: "Re: Peripatetic CASE Meeting in New York, 16 May 1967 and plans for the 1967-1968 school year," June 8, 1967 (1 page). Mimeo, SAfiles. "[Dante] Bini first gained world recognition in 1967 when he used a gigantic balloon and a robot to build a 50-foot tall concrete 'Binishell'

dome at Columbia University in less than two hours." Available online at http:// articles.sfgate.com/2005-02- 20/living/17361725_1_balloon- dome-concrete, accessed June 27, 2010. Pei's University Plaza at New York University, and finally a visit to the office of Diana Vreeland, editor of *Vogue*,

mother of Tim.
124 "History" in the brochure *IAUS: The Institute for Architecture and Urban Studies* (New York: IAUS, 1979), [4].
125 The IAUS archive is at the Canadian Center for Architecture, Montreal; Sylvia Lavin, "IAUS" [a time-line from 1967 to 2000], Log

13/14 (Fall 2008), 154-58; Lucia Allais, "The Real and the Theoretical, 1968," *Perspecta* 42 (2010), 27-41. Suzanne Frank, who was a member of the "Streets Team" at IAUS in the early 1970s has a book on IAUS in process. Kim Förster is engaged in a dissertation on the topic under the direction

```
there was at least one sub-group of CASE—the Princeton-New York members—that
had four advantages:

    a basic interest in an organization such as CASE
    a large, but nevertheless somewhat shared field of interest
    geographical proximity
    an available meeting place—the Institute [IAUS]
    ... the only further step possible ... was the constitution of CASE
    groups on a regional basis.
```

My message went on to note that the Princeton/New York group had been meeting
regularly as CASE/New York. Members were those noted above plus Robertson, Weinstein
and Pasanella, with Newman to join as he moved from St. Louis to New York University.
Richard Meier served as Executive Secretary from his professional office at 56 East 53rd
Street. "The theme of their deliberations is A National Planning Policy for 1972." The
message continued with encouragement that regional CASE groups be formed at the
initiative of: Anderson for Boston, Vallhonrat for Philadelphia, Vreeland for Los Angeles
(new chair at UCLA), with new initiatives elsewhere welcome. Don Lyndon's on-going
remarkable recovery from a life-threatening automobile accident in Boston was recorded.
It was in the late fall of 1968 or early in 1969 that I introduced my MIT colleague Rosalind
Krauss to the IAUS circle in an informal meeting at the Institute when I presented Jim
Stirling's Cambridge History Faculty building with slides from my visit in the preceding
summer. She was immediately recognized as a remarkable intellect and, breaking the
all-male world, came to be engaged in the IAUS ambit, including the eventual launch of
October from IAUS and MIT Press in 1976.

MIT/Boston, CASE 5—1968-69

In the fall of 1968, I led a group of MIT students in a workshop programmed to conceive
and build an exhibition in MIT's Hayden Gallery (predecessor to the List Gallery). The
project involved not only selection and development of exhibition materials, but also a multi-
level construction that viewers traversed—the design resulting from a competition among
workshop students. Significant parts of the construction were in experimental structural
members of fiberglass-reinforced polyester that I identified and secured from the Koppers
Company. The exhibition was a major effort, with inevitable all-nighter construction
for several days preceding the opening. Students in the workshop worked regularly for
weeks, and faculty and other students joined in the late stages of construction. Maurice
Smith crafted a crucial short connecting stair on the last night. There was considerable
enthusiasm for the exhibition and its implausibly "Merzbau" space (van Doesburg and
I.K. Bonset reunited?), including the stimulation of dance performances by a troupe from
Boston University.

following pages, "Form and Use in Architecture" Workshop led by Stanford Anderson in MIT's Hayden Gallery, 1968-69.

right, Photograph by Boston newspaper during student contruction of the exhibition, the photographer having enlisted women students to cheer up the potential reader.

following page, Multi-level structure of the exhibition at an advanced stage, "Form and Use," 1968-69. Photos: Stanford Anderson.

of Laurent Stalder at the gta Institute of the ETH in Zurich. See also fn. 141.
126 Letter SA to all CASE members, announcing the invitation that CASE meet at Peter Eisenman's new Institute for Architecture and Urban Studies in New York on January 12-14, 1968; 15 November 1967 (1 page).

Mimeo, SAfiles. Vallhonrat to Anderson, promising to attend at least in part, November 27, 1967 (1 page); Vallhonrat to Anderson, regretting being unable to attend, January 17, 1968 (1 page). Originals, SAfiles.

127 Memo, SA to all CASE members, beginning: "Finally, an up-date on the situation of CASE," 10 May 1968 (2 pp). Mimeo; SAfiles.

"Form and Use in Architecture" Workshop led by
Stanford Anderson in MIT's Hayden Gallery, 1968-69.

clockwise, The exhibition space, during an intermission
of the CASE 5 sessions, March 1969; design model
of the exhibition construction; the exhibition space
employed by a dance troupe from Boston University
Photos: Stanford Anderson.

Titled "Form and Use in Architecture," the exhibition ran from January 28 to early March 1969. It sought to do justice to the discipline of architecture by including, for example, an extended slide sequence on the elements of plastic construction as conceived in the de Stijl movement, supplemented by two models of Gerrit Rietveld's Schröder House and furniture by Rietveld. Equally, there was attention to the shaping of form by attention to use—in industrial works as seen by Bernd and Hilla Becher, vernacular architecture, and even such humble objects as the traditional carpenter's tools. The ethos and the objects of Dürer's "Melancolia" were invoked. An unstated sub-text on my part was the desire to merge aspects of my thought and that of Maurice Smith within a larger arena. My essay "Form and Use in Architecture" was distributed free at the exhibition in photocopy, thus having some underground circulation, though never published.[128]

As the exhibition came to a close, I organized a CASE/Boston or CASE 5 meeting that gave me the freedom to draw both on CASE colleagues and on other voices in a program that was consciously tangential to the core of CASE. It can also be seen as the last general meeting of CASE, since members were in the audience even if not on the program—and, more importantly, because the unity of CASE was strained. The program developed in the Hayden Gallery space, surrounded by the "Form and Use" exhibition. The participants swerved from established CASE precedent, but there were non-Boston CASE members both among the speakers and in the audience. The simply typed, mimeographed program for the event included this program information:

Sunday 9 March 1969: cocktails in the Gallery followed by dinner
Monday morning: Invited guests only for viewing and discussion of the exhibition
Monday afternoon: Presentations on some of the exhibition themes, listing only the examples of William Kleinsasser [Oregon] on the Mercer, Pennsylvania, buildings; Melvin Charney [Montreal] on grain elevators; and Konrad Wachsmann [USC] on the Becher exhibition of industrial buildings.
Monday afternoon and Tuesday morning: Architects presenting their own work, including that of Joseph Esherick [Berkeley], Wilmot Gilland [Oregon], Thomas

128 Stanford Anderson, "Form and Use in Architecture, Hayden Gallery, Massachusetts Institute of Technology" (19pp, photocopied, Cambridge, MA: MIT Architecture, 1969). Xc, SA files. The first three pages, reduced: "An understanding of the confluence of form and meaning—such as can be isolated in works of painting and sculpture—is often obscured by the sheer usefulness of buildings. . . . "However, there is also a positive aspect of the complexity and practicality of architecture. The built environment presents in material form an unusually insistent critical exchange between the intellectual realm of form/idea/model and the empirical realm of fact/ circumstance. In architecture, other criteria than those of internal formal consistency must be used to test the adequacy of form. Conversely, patterns of use contribute to the architectural formulation of larger, new and changing organizations of built form and human activity. "Thus, in the study of architecture, it is unreasonable to be antagonistic toward either issues of form or those of human activity. . . . "[Eero Saarinen's] Kresge Auditorium [at MIT] is a striking example of form-

R. Vreeland [UCLA], Michael Graves [Princeton], Delbert Highlands [Carnegie Mellon]

Tuesday afternoon: Selected chairmen setting seminar themes with the involvement of both visitors and MIT faculty and students.[129]

Esherick provided a model in my time at Berkeley and he held the rarely offered esteem of Maurice Smith. From among the members of CASE, I invested the greatest hope in the architectural prospects of Michael Graves. Michael often spoke of the importance of elevations in the experience of architecture—something that I interpreted as sequences of external and internal elevations, breaking the dominance of the plan in so much of architectural discourse. This was still the year of his Hanselmann house; I did not foresee the postmodern turn.

I have not found a list of attendees at CASE 5.[130] Personal friendships were not lost, but the New York-area members, and perhaps others of CASE were not pleased with the content or presentation of the exhibition.

IAUS and the "Streets Project"—1970-72

While the MIT design for "New City" and my "Form and Use" exhibit may have drawn a line between my CASE colleagues and me, that difference may have opened a door as well. Eisenman, needing funding for his new Institute, conceived of funded research on streets as key elements of the physical and social city. Around the beginning of 1970, IAUS won support for a two-year research and design project within the Model Cities Program of the Federal Department of Housing and Urban Development (HUD). While his Institute needed such funding, research on this topic was not attractive to Eisenman personally.

That winter/spring I was on my first MIT sabbatical in London. As a trans-Atlantic telephone call was still a matter of excitement, I was all the more surprised when Eisenman called to inform me of the IAUS Streets Project and ask me to be its co-director starting in September 1970. Taking a leave from MIT, I moved to New York and took up the project with my new colleague William Ellis. The study was to result in a book and, in the later stages, also the design for a demonstration project of housing that generated a positive

use disparities . . . Such buildings are often said to be 'formalistic,' meaning something like 'self-consciously and arbitrarily formed.' That is true, but such references also oversimplify the problem. The weakness of 'formalistic' buildings is not that they have been consciously formed, but rather that the formal conception is in some way inadequate . . . usually in that it is incapable of adjustment to the complexities of the problem. . . .it is not problematic that the original form may have been arbitrary. It is, rather, unfortunate that the mutual adjustment of form and use did not, or could not, continue to a satisfactory conclusion. . . . "[Another] common source of form-use disparities: . . . Modern architects often willingly prostrated themselves before the historically determined fictive deity 'The Spirit of the Time.' The compulsion to make this spirit manifest . . . led to the endorsement of such motifs as simple total shapes, flat roofs, so-called modern materials . . ., or the repetition of identical elements at regular intervals. The experience of modernism teaches that these motifs quickly became ends in themselves, masters rather than servants. The motifs selected for their presumed

street environment (that came to be for Binghamton, New York; not executed). Our team was made up of architects, sociologists, political scientists, and historians. An early product of Eisenman with the "streets team" and others was a special double-issue of Casabella exhibiting the new Institute to the European architectural community.[131]

While HUD encouraged studies that would result in a handbook on streets, a reference work that might establish standards, the IAUS team approached the issues socially and culturally. Our studies were inter-disciplinary and across cultures. The edited work of the original team came together slowly; as the contractual period ended, Anthony Vidler, who had become the lead historian at the Princeton School of Architecture in 1965, agreed to contribute a key essay to the book that appeared from MIT Press as On Streets.[132]

CASE 8: "Pictorial and Literal Space" and "Five Architects"—1971

During the time of the streets project, Eisenman instigated a CASE/New York meeting at the Museum of Modern Art on May 21-22, 1971. The topic was "Pictorial and Literal Space: Architecture and Painting," reflecting the renowned article on literal and phenomenal space by Rowe and Slutzky,[133] but now moving on with other voices in architecture and art. The program speaks for itself.[134]

> Invited attendees:
>
> New York CASE as in the letterhead.
>
> Anderson and surely others, but no list is available to me.[135]

It was this CASE-New York meeting, held at the invitation of the Department of Architecture and Design of the Museum of Modern Art, that generated special attention to Eisenman, Graves, Meier, and now Hejduk and Gwathmey, leading to the effective polemic of the book Five Architects. Arthur Drexler's wrote the preface to the book.[136] Frampton contributed a "Criticism," and Rowe's "Introduction" may have been more than desired.

It would be reaching beyond the scope of this paper to mention the "Grays" reaction to Five Architects, were it not that members of CASE are found there too.[137] A polemical

appropriateness to the time become coercive of actual, even distinctively new, conditions."

129 Program for "CASE/ Boston Seminar terminating the exhibition 'Form and Use in Architecture'," Hayden Gallery, MIT, 9-11 March 1969. The main heading on the sheet is "MASSACHUSETTS

INSTITUTE OF TECHNOLOGY — Department of Architecture" (1 page). Mimeo, SAfiles. The reel-to-reel tape in my possession is surprisingly incomplete, but does have the presentations of Charney, Kleinsasser and Gilland.

130 Known CASE attendees: Anderson, Graves, Lyndon, Millon [?], Vreeland. Confirmed

non-attendance: Vallhonrat (Telegram to Anderson, March 9, 1969, SAfiles).

131 Special number on the Institute for Architecture and Urban Studies, "The City as an Artifact," Casabella (Milan), no. 359-360 (December 1971), in English and Italian.

132 Stanford Anderson, ed., On Streets (Cambridge, MA:

Program, CASE 8, May 21/22, 1971.

CASE 8   CONFERENCE OF ARCHITECTS FOR THE STUDY OF THE ENVIRONMENT

NEW YORK case
eardley
eisenman
frampton
graves
hejduk
meier
slutzky

P R O G R A M   C A S E   8

MAY 21/22 1971

THE MUSEUM OF MODERN ART
TRUSTEES ROOM

PICTORIAL AND LITERAL SPACE: ARCHITECTURE AND PAINTING

FRIDAY, MAY 21:   PICTORIAL AND LITERAL SPACE: ARCHITECTURE

    4.00 p.m.   Presentation and Criticism

Architects:	Critics:
Peter D. Eisenman	Emilio Ambasz
William Ellis	George Baird
Michael Graves	Allen Greenberg
Charles Gwathmey	Ludwig Glaeser
John Hejduk	Lee Hodgden
Richard Meier	William LaRiche
	Susana Torre
	Anthony Vidler

    7.00 p.m.   Cocktails and Dinner

    9.00 p.m.   Discussion

SATURDAY, MAY 22:   PICTORIAL AND LITERAL SPACE: PAINTING

    10.00 a.m.   Presentation and Discussion

Painters:	Critics:
Robert Slutzky	Rosalind Krauss
Frank Stella	Sheldon Nodelman

    1.00 p.m.   Business Meeting

group of papers termed "Five on Five" appeared in *Architectural Forum* in 1973, with essays by Alan Greenberg, Aldo Giurgola, Charles Moore, Robertson, and Robert Stern. It is completely plausible, as Graves has claimed, that he (and no doubt Eisenman) stimulated the *Forum* critique.[138] In 1974, Vreeland, chair at UCLA, set off the "non-color code" when he organized an event, "The Whites and the Grays," with the latter represented by Robertson and Vreeland's UCLA colleagues Charles Moore and Weinstein.[139] Activities of these kinds are evidence of the diversity of interests that were recognized early in the existence of CASE and inhibited an on-going collective effort.

Conference on Architectural Education, IAUS/MoMA—1971

Sponsored by the Museum of Modern Art and The Architectural League, Eisenman organized in the name of IAUS a Conference on Architectural Education on November 12-13, 1971. CASE was no longer invoked, even as CASE/New York. A morning and an evening session each featured those presenting a position with response by two critics.[140] The newly named Dean of the MIT School of Architecture and Planning, William L. Porter, attended.

Oppositions—1973-1984

In 1973, the Institute for Architecture and Urban Studies launched the journal *Oppositions: A Journal for Ideas and Criticism in Architecture*, with Eisenman, Frampton and Mario Gandelsonas as editors and MIT Press as the publisher. Authors of the first issue were Rowe, Eisenman, Frampton, Vidler, and Diana Agrest and Gandelsonas. Former members of CASE continued to be published in *Oppositions*, but I would agree with Nadia Watson that the journal was directed to a development of the architectural discipline broadened both by the diverse positions of its editors and a much wider range of authors.[141] *Oppositions* held the central place in architectural discourse in America throughout its run, extending to what Joan Ockman termed "the 'inauthentic'" no. 26 in Spring 1984. *Oppositions* cannot be studied here; fortunately it has been described, criticized, documented, and will continue to attract attention.[142]

The MIT Press, 1978); also in Spanish as Calles: *Problemas de estructura y diseño* (Barcelona: Gustavo Gili, 1981), and Italian as *Strade* (Bari: Dedalo, 1982). Vidler's essay is now the title essay of his *The Scenes of the Street and Other Essays* (New York: Monacelli Press, 2011)

133 Colin Rowe and Robert

Slutzky, "Transparency: Literal and Phenomenal" [1963], in Rowe, *The Mathematics of the Ideal Villa and Other Essays* (Cambridge, MA: The MIT Press, 1976), 159-183.

134 New York CASE, CASE 8, Program: "Pictorial and Literal Space: Architecture and Painting," May 21-22, 1971, Museum of Modern

Art (1 page). I don't know which events may have been reckoned as CASE 6 and 7. Xc, SAfiles.

135 Eisenman to Anderson at IAUS, invitation to attend CASE 8, specifying limited numbers, April 29, 1971, with accompanying program (see preceding note) (1 page). Xc letter, with original signature,

Schedule for IAUS Conference on Architectural Education, November 12, 2971.

The Institute for Architecture and Urban Studies

Eight West Fortieth Street, New York, New York 10018. Telephone 212 947-0765

SCHEDULE

A CONFERENCE ON ARCHITECTURAL EDUCATION TO BE HELD IN THE AUDI-
TORIUM OF THE MUSEUM OF MODERN ART, 11 WEST 53RD STREET, NEW
YORK CITY, ON FRIDAY AND SATURDAY, NOVEMBER 12 AND 13, 1971.

Friday 12th November, 1971

9.30 a.m.   Registration

10.00 a.m.   Welcoming remark: Arthur Drexler, Director of the
             Department of Architecture and Design, The Museum
             of Modern Art.
             Introduction: Arthur Rosenblatt: President of
             The Architectural League
             Conference Structure: Peter Eisenman, Director
             of The Institute for Architecture and Urban Studies

             Session One: Moderator: Stanford Anderson
                             Critics: Lionel March
                                          Joseph Rykwert
                             Panelists: Emilio Ambasz   No
                                          Jonathan Barnett • CCNY
                                          Peter Eisenman (Coop)
                                          Robert Gutman B (Rutgers)
                                          Denise Scott Brown
                                          Matthias Ungers • (Cornell)

12.00 noon   Luncheon for panelists and participants of the con-
             ference, at the Institute for Architecture and
             Urban Studies.

8.00 p.m.   Session Two: Moderator: Robert Gutman (
                             Critics: George Baird (Toronto)
                                          Martin Pawley
                             Panelists: Stanford Anderson (MIT)
                                          Kenneth Frampton (Princeton)
                                          Herbert Gans (Columbia)
                                          Colin Rowe   (Cornell)
                                          Anthony Vidler (Princeton)

Saturday 13th November, 1971

9.00 a.m.   Session Three: Moderator: Jonathan Barnett

             Program to be determined by panelists and partici-
             pants of the conference. Program to be announced
             Friday evening at Session Two.

MIT Architecture—mid-1960s-1970s

Considering MIT's Department of Architecture again, now in the mid-60s, Maurice Smith was still the guru of the architectural design program. New issues were intruding, however. Recall Bob Goodman's appointment in 1966; his political commitments found centrality in the social and academic turmoil that deeply engaged faculty and students of the department in the ensuing years. By 1972 Goodman had not been continued; while urban political conditions were still intense, that agenda waned in the department as it did in society at large.

1966 was also the moment of a quite different initiative. Lawrence Anderson promoted a freshly minted MIT MArch graduate to the faculty, Nicholas Negroponte.[143] Negroponte excelled as a student, also with a special capacity in graphics. His initial appointment was to teach drawing and graphics, but within a year he created the Architecture Machine Group, conducting research in human-computer interactions. An extraordinary entrepreneur, he succeeded in pursuing his own teaching and research agenda, culminating in the creation, in association with Jerome Wiesner, of the Media Lab in 1985. By the early 1990s the Media Lab reached a size and an independent agenda that resulted in its independence from the Department, though still within the School of Architecture and Planning (in the early Wiesner/Negroponte years, the "within" was nominal). The success of Negroponte's enterprise being increasingly independent, the architectural design program entered the 1990s relatively unmarked, with only an elementary grasp on computation.

In the HTC component of the department, as noted, Hank Millon, with the active and crucial collaboration of Wayne Andersen, Rosalind Krauss, Judith Wechsler and Stanford Anderson, led the multi-year effort to win a Ph.D. program for HTC. Ros resigned from MIT for a position in Art History at Princeton already in 1972. The original HTC PhD proposal dates from December 1972, with yet years of review to come. In the spring of 1975, Hank was on sabbatical leave when we submitted the final HTC PhD Proposal. Werner Oechslin and Manfredo Tafuri were visitors in place of Hank. There followed an additional three years of leave while Hank served as Director of the American Academy in Rome. I had the opportunity to present our final HTC PhD Proposal at a meeting of the MIT Committee on Graduate School Policy in February 1975. HTC had strong support over the years from Deans Lawrence

SAfiles.

136 See fn. 120.

137 Nadia Watson, "The Whites vs the Grays: Re-examining the 1970s avant-garde," *Fabrications* 15, no. 1 (July 2005): 55-69; emphasizes the relations of these two not closely defined groups and their participation in a general advocacy of

an intellectually engaged architectural field. Watson is wholly wrong when she asserts (p. 60): "Stern supported the early CASE meetings of the 1960s." Stern was still a Yale architectural student at the time of the Princeton meetings leading to CASE and was not involved subsequently. At that time

I remembered him as the undergraduate who reshelved books in Columbia's art history library in 1960.

138 Michael Graves, "'The Pleasures of Architecture Conference' [Sydney, RAIA] 1980: The Interviews," *Transition* 1, no. 4 (1980), 7.

139 Available online at http://www.arts.ucla.

edu/magazine/2006s/ architecture_01.html; accessed June 15, 2010.

140 The Saturday session was to be discussion stimulated by the event. The program and copies of all the papers, in mimeograph, SA files, plus other original documents. My paper was titled "The Ineffectiveness of

Anderson and William Porter and from Heads of Department Donlyn Lyndon and the newly appointed John Habraken. The CGSP voted that the Proposal be sent to the full faculty for ratification and the process was completed that spring. In the fall of 1974, Hong-Bin Kang of South Korea, a recent MArch II graduate from Harvard, took the risk to enroll in graduate studies in HTC in the hope that the PhD degree would be realized. Kang was studying under me, so as the program was authorized I already had a student in progress.

As our PhD program began formally in the fall of 1975, Ros was gone and Hank was on leave. The senior positions in history of art and architecture, respectively, were Wayne Andersen and Stanford Anderson. Judith Wechsler (associate professor) and Whitney Chadwick (assistant) were the others in art history. Günther Nitschke visited one term each year, teaching Japanese architecture. Dolores Hayden and Donald Preziosi were on three-year appointments in anticipation of Millon's return in 1978. Renaissance historian David Friedman was appointed in 1978. After Hank's appointment in 1980 as the first Dean of the Center for Advanced Visual Studies at the National Gallery in Washington, he continued to teach one seminar each year until 2000.

Given a certain privilege of history of architecture within a Department of Architecture, Wayne suggested that I serve as the director of the HTC program, a charge that I held until 1991 when I became Head of the Department of Architecture. The excellent and devoted teaching of the HTC faculty was supported by equally committed visitors — in the early years, Giorgio Ciucci, Mardges Bacon, Sam Bass Warner, Nan Arghyros, Hong-Bin Kang, Lawrence Speck, Werner Oechslin, Mark Roskill, and Martin Steinmann. Over the years we also drew strength from good relations and cooperation with Harvard and other Boston-area institutions.

The honor of the first PhD program for architectural history within a professional school of architecture is closely shared by MIT and Princeton. MIT was unique, and remains so, in our incorporation of history of art. Princeton's program was somewhat smaller but better funded. We were competitors but friendly, engaged ones as Anthony Vidler, with his shared IAUS ties, headed the Princeton program. It was years before Columbia, Harvard, and finally Yale emulated the MIT and Princeton programs. The absence of

Architectural Education (27pp + 2pp notes)."
141 Watson, "The Whites vs the Grays."
142 Respectively, by Joan Ockman, "Resurrecting the Avant-Garde: The History and Program of Oppositions," in *Architectureproduction*, ed. Beatriz Colomina (New York: Princeton Architectural Press,

1988), 180-199; Vincent P. Pecora, "Towers of Babel," in *Out of Site: A Social Criticism of Architecture*, ed. Diane Ghirardo (Seattle: Bay Press, 1991), 46-76; and K. Michael Hays, ed., *Oppositions Reader* (New York: Princeton Architectural Press, 1998). See also Mitchell Schwarzer, "History

and Theory in Periodicals: Assembling *Oppositions*," *Journal of the Society of Architectural Historians* 58, no. 3 (September 1999): 342-349.
143 Nicholas Negroponte (b. 1943, New York City); MArch, MIT 1966; MIT faculty 1966-present. I presented and commented on the work of Negroponte's Architecture

Machine Group in Royston Landau, guest editor, *Architectural Design* (London), XXXIX, 9 (September 1969), 509-514. In 1976, I tended his MIT tenure case.

such programs at those prominent institutions facilitated that our East Coast colleagues could affirm the excellence of the MIT program. The same colleagues had architectural design commitments quite different from those of MIT Architecture, and thus assumed the attitude that the MIT HTC PhD program was the strength of the department. Right or wrong, such opinion, both genuinely positive and comparatively so, assisted us in attracting students and visitors. It should not go unnoticed that HTC also offered a closely related, yet differently oriented two-year masters program that has been of mutual benefit to those students and the institution.

Assessing CASE

Since 1984, my friend the artist Batuz continuously nurtures the association of artists, poets, academics, and politicians that he created, the Société Imaginaire.[144] It waxes and wanes, but his energy and devotion are constants. One member of the Société fondly termed it an association of "gleichgesinnte Andersdenkende"—a gathering of people of diverse persuasions sharing the same sensibility ("like-minded contrarians," perhaps). Within a smaller, though still broad scope, that expression might also describe the first years of CASE.

Yet as early as January 1968, Eisenman viewed CASE as one of his "mistakes": "[While] a talking group like CASE [is] a pleasant social amenity . . . For a long time I have considered CASE a rather ugly child, ill-formed and without direction."[145] In December 1965, Frampton had already articulated what must have been clear to everyone in CASE: concerted efforts are frustrated as "everyone is so busy, and secondly an area of true agreement from which it is possible to work proves very hard to establish."[146] There was no Batuz to devote himself, selflessly, to the continuation of the group—and not evident that such an effort would have succeeded. Rather, a semblance of continuity appears in the creation of an Institute with an identified leader: IAUS and Eisenman.

Ken's formulation points to the strategic fault of CASE. The rehearsal of my files allows a summary of the tactical steps of the group. In 1964-65 Eisenman devised the game and with Princeton's support chose the team and began play. In 1965-66 Anderson and MIT took the baton and attempted an academic and, then with the New York group, a political

144 Available online at http:// www.batuz.com/si.html, accessed June 20, 2010.
145 Eisenman to Vreeland, January 9, 1968; quoted in Allais, "The Real and the Theoretical, 1968," 33 and fn. 58. See fn. 124.

146 Frampton to Anderson, December 20, 1965; see fn. 48. See also Robertson at fn. 17.

intent—a melding of these intents appearing in Anderson's "Possible Futures" conference of October 1966. Though the New York group was broadly supported in their avowed interest to carry the political orientation further, with Columbia as a base, the baton was dropped. Early 1966 also brought the interest of MIT Press in a publication program, but with marked differences among the protagonists, the project collapsed. Yet 1966 into 1967 can also be seen as the most active period of CASE, first under the flag of MoMA-New City and then with Lyndon's initiative resulting in the Oregon Teach-In. This was also the time in which Eisenman founded IAUS.

With the failure of the Graham Foundation's initial interest in CASE Teach-Ins, that promising 1967 program was not repeated. Lack of funding in general, IAUS as the necessary focus of Eisenman's energies, and diverse orientations of members resulted in two regional variants of CASE. My MIT "Form and Use Exhibition" and the related CASE/Boston meeting of early 1968 were only divisive for the larger group. These were the months, stretching into years, of intense "1968" activities, especially notable at Columbia but also strong at MIT—events that absorbed both time and psyche.[147] CASE/New York with its most notable event being CASE 8 "Pictorial and Literal," yielded the "Five Architects" and still more reason for individual rather than collective activity.

In the early 1960s, the East Coast schools of architecture appointed promising but as yet unproven faculty members that Eisenman drew together. No doubt such appointments are a constant in these noted universities, but this was a propitious moment to imagine and perhaps even affect desirable change. Each of these young architects established a record—diverse records—of some note. Those accomplishments are owing to individual strengths and particular opportunities. But is it implausible to recognize that a few years of association in CASE, through the mid- to late-'60s made some contribution? Frampton would have thrived in London, no doubt, but it was CASE that brought him to America, to a first tenuous appointment at Princeton, and then to his prominent New York-based career. It was CASE that gave Eisenman a ready instrument to induce Arthur Drexler to trust him with the organization of the "New City" exhibition. On the word of the protagonists, that exhibition was influential in the founding of IAUS. Eisenman's dominant interest in forming

147 Self-imposed extra teaching and my activities as described here kept me from work on my dissertation. Despite the simultaneous development of the "Form and Use" exhibition, my attentions did turn to the dissertation in late 1967 and early 1968. The long-planned final defense at Columbia was in May, when the entire campus was closed due to student occupation of buildings, notably Architecture's Avery Hall. My defense was held in the home of one of my advisors, George Collins. Following the tradition of the candidate being sent out of the room while the professors and external reviewers deliberated, I was sent to the bedroom, where I received word of my success while sitting on the conjugal bed with Mrs. Collins (Christiane Craseman Collins, herself a scholar of modern architecture and planning).

CASE, the ambition that CASE Magazine be a critical voice in architectural culture, for which he recruited Frampton, was realized in *Oppositions*, with Eisenman and Frampton as two of the three editors. CASE served as a vehicle for the symposium on "Pictorial and Literal Space" that resulted in New York's "Five Architects" and a new thrust in their careers. When at MIT I received a new PhD program to direct, and was shortly the only senior professor in the program, my recent work at IAUS and my on-going association with IAUS and colleagues such as Eisenman and Vidler assisted in building the program.[148] People giving shape to history of architecture programs have been Anderson at MIT; Vidler at Princeton and later at UCLA; Frampton at Columbia; and Michael Hays, a graduate of the MIT program and associated with Eisenman, at Harvard.

Am I then revealing the existence of an elite cabal? No, it was the diversity of capacities, positions and opportunities that first killed CASE and then broadcast these energies both geographically and in different fields. In education alone, principal administrative positions went to Millon at the American Academy in Rome and then the Center for Advanced Study of the Visual Arts at the National Gallery in Washington; Vallhonrat at Penn; Lyndon at MIT and then Berkeley; Vreeland at New Mexico and then UCLA; Eardley at Kentucky and then Toronto; Weinstein later at UCLA; Anderson at MIT; Vidler at Cooper Union; Eisenman in one aspect of IAUS. In architectural design, diverse accomplishments are the rule: the work of Meier, McKinnell, Eisenman, Graves, Lyndon, Kliment and Halsband, Robertson, Vreeland, and Newman may be readily distinguished, to say the least.

I am returned to what must dominantly be seen as the particular accomplishments of these individuals, but they also, at early stages of their careers, engaged in a few years of shared concerns for a fuller and more critical understanding of architecture and its environment that they carried into diverse realms.

148 The constancy of those relations is evidenced in the 1979 IAUS brochure: my continuing position as an IAUS Fellow; attention to my edited book On Streets; work by my MIT Independent Activity Period students in Paris appearing among few illustrations of work; MIT Press effectively the publisher of IAUS; MIT and myself as sponsors of *Oppositions*. See *IAUS: The Institute for Architecture and Urban Studies* (New York: IAUS, 1979).

"Form and Use in Architecture" Workshop led by
Stanford Anderson in MIT's Hayden Gallery, 1968-69.
Photo: Stanford Anderson.

MARY LOUISE LOBSINGER

Two Cambridges
Models, Methods, Systems, and Expertise

The Production of Knowledge and Expertise

A 1969 report on computer-aided design experiments at MIT's Department of Architecture published in the British magazine *Architectural Design* suggests that design research at the Institute was approached with a sense of purpose, a technical aptitude, and the necessary equipment.[1] The presentation impresses, and three distinct research teams are identified, each with a principal investigator. Perhaps more impressive are the sources of funding: externally by the National Science Foundation, IBM, and the Ford Foundation and internally, by the newly established Urban Systems Laboratory (USL). The report is sparsely illustrated: a set of line graphics produced by the Sketchpad III program, a photograph of a computer terminal, a couple of diagrams predicting the accretion within an experiment, and several sequences of photographs documenting examples of application. The stated research goals range from defining technical outcomes to speculating upon the potential of a machine able to solicit information about architecture. In this issue of the magazine, computer-aided design is presented as technical support that enables, in the most optimistic interpretation, programming to be applied to human-machine-environment interaction and adaptation. Distinct from computer-aided design as automated drafting, the research does not appear to be completely defined by quantitative method. Within the context of this issue of *Architectural Design* the report represents a community of researchers engaged in what could be categorized, in more scientific disciplines, as basic research.[2]

Reading the contents of the September 1969 issue of *Architectural Design* one might conclude that architecture had taken a positivistic turn within British and North American institutional contexts. Published side by side were articles authored by experts of science and systems theory, including writings from a philosopher of logic, a professor of business administration invested in operational research techniques, a psycho-linguist, a couple of architects, a physicist, and a cybernetician. The contributors' institutional affiliations—

I wish to thank Stanford Anderson, Frank Duffy, Adrian Forty, Kenneth Hayes, Lionel March, Antoine Picon, and Philip Steadman for enjoyable conversations about the materials presented and for generously sharing their knowledge. Materials from this essay were presented in papers given at the University of Toronto's Centre for the Study of the United States, the PhD Colloquium at Harvard University's Graduate School of Design during the Fall of 2010 and at the Cachan History of Social Science Group, 4th ANR Workshop, 'Cross-disciplinary research ventures in postwar American social science,' École normale supérieure de Cachan June 15-16, 2012. A heartfelt thank you to Arindam Dutta for the opportunity to write about a topic I've been eager to return to and for the tremendous effort in seeing the anthology through to publication.

MIT, Berkeley, University College London, the Architectural Association, and University of Cambridge—add another layer to a map of associations among academics invested in the potential for systems thinking and new technologies (such as the computer) to assist design research.[3] Each institution housed or was associated with a newly established, technically equipped, and funded research program—even if the funding was at times precarious. Typically held under the auspices of a laboratory or center they bore appellations such as Environmental Laboratory, Space Sciences Laboratory, Joint Unit for Planning Research, Urban Systems Laboratory, the Center for Planning and Research Development, and in the UK, the Center for Environmental Studies and the Center for Land Use and Built Form Studies. The naming of research centers, laboratories, and university departments replaced the discrete designations of architecture and urban studies. The substitution of the word "environment" or the phrase "built environment" underlined an interdisciplinary mandate associated with the social sciences. From the perspective of the re-organization of knowledge production within postwar institutional change, MIT functioned as a node within a geographically dispersed network of transatlantic practices that sought scientific grounds on which to base architectural research. *Architectural Design* was one means by which researchers could connect and disseminate the knowledge produced by the new techniques of inquiry. In this regard, the magazine and the Institute mark two points of entry into a social and technical discourse about architecture and design research that was prevalent in this period.

This essay examines two institutional contexts where, in the 1960s and early 1970s, the criteria defining disciplinary expertise and design research strove to become more rigorous and technically sophisticated. The "two Cambridges" identified in the title frame a socio-cultural dynamic that crossed institutional milieus and extended beyond traditional disciplinary boundaries. The exchanges between the two institutions begin to map a network of effects produced by higher education's adoption of a social science based research model. In this period, increased appearance of the word "environment" signaled elasticity among disciplinary boundaries. Environment as a field category gathered up various disciplines, including those conventionally understood as design, alongside planning, the cognitive sciences, engineering, and management sciences. Within this

1 *Architectural Design* (September 1969), 509-514.

2 For discussion of basic versus applied research in relation to funding at MIT see Daniel S. Greenberg, *Science, Money, and Politics. Political Triumph and Ethical Erosion* (Chicago: University of Chicago Press, 2001), 45-51.

3 Other educational institutions invested in systems thinking, operational research, computation and design methods were, for example, Carnegie Mellon, University of Pennsylvania, and in the United Kingdom, University of Manchester, University of Birmingham, Imperial College, the School of Architecture at Portsmouth and in Ulm Germany, the Höchschule für Gestaltung (HfG).

DISCOURSE AND CHOICE

Discourse:
William Porter
Katharine J. Lloyd
Wren McMains
Aaron Fleisher
Choice:
John Boorn
Stanley Hoderowski
Aaron Fleisher
Sponsor: Urban Systems Laboratory at MIT and IBM

DISCOURSE and CHOICE are compatible computer systems which are intended to serve city planners and designers and others concerned with the urban physical environment. The DISCOURSE system is primarily for generating and testing environmental design ideas, whereas CHOICE is primarily for evaluation.

The two major criteria governing the design and development of the two systems have been:

1. That they accommodate the kinds of data and manipulation designers use, or might use, and that they accommodate changes and additions quickly and easily; and

2. that they permit the designer to develop his own language of design as he is working.

Neither criterion would have been possible to achieve without the existence at MIT of computer 'time sharing' systems in which a central computer is connected to user consoles (which resemble typewriters) and from which the user can expect nearly instant response.

The first criterion we have attempted to achieve in a way compatible with the other three by using relatively simple data structures. For example, in DISCOURSE, the designer could put the *attribute* 'industry' at the locations '21,33; 22,33; and 23,33' (referring to the row and column numbers of a grid he had constructed and laid on top of a map of the environment he was working on).

He could further specify that there were 400 employees in industry at that place, a number which might vary with different locations, and that those who worked in that type of industry earned an average of $8000 per year—a number which is constant over all *locations*. All elements of DISCOURSE have both names and values which the designer can establish and change himself. The description will vary with the fineness of the user's grid of *locations* and with the amount of information he puts in each *location*.

The user can display his information by showing the names and values of the elements and by mapping them on the geographic grid. Presently the 'maps' are typed by the console, but work is under way to utilize cathode ray tubes for continuous and special displays as well as printers of faster and more elaborate hard copy.

CHOICE provides three kinds of matrices in which the data can be stored: primary, value and order matrices. The results of tests of several design alternatives can be entered into the primary matrix. The values which various groups place on the test results can be placed in a value matrix, a new set of values obtained by multiplying the two matrices together, and from the results the preference of each group could be computed. The design alternatives can then be ordered according to the preference of each group.

The specialized data structures ease the bookkeeping problems for the designer so that his attention can be focused on the things he wants to do. In CHOICE the designer may perform complex cost/benefit analysis with respect to more than one group or individual. The characteristics of the designs to be evaluated may be directly specified by the designer or assessed from other simulation or design models. The designer may input these consequences in either an ordinal or cardinal form, thus allowing him to represent judgments as well as measured parameters. He may combine cardinal and ordinal representations to obtain a variety of measurement scales. The use of multiple accounts allows the designer to represent time-series outcomes. Other operations in CHOICE permit computing discounted present values, statistics of mean and standard deviation, and expected values. The flexibility of the system permits the designer to rapidly alter evaluation arguments such as weighting assumptions, probabilities, interest rates, and definitions of the accounts.

In DISCOURSE, the user can manipulate names and values and their locations and can add new ones or transform those he already has described. Furthermore he can implement rules about how the environment might develop through the use of such features of the language as statements which branch to other statements and statements which are executed conditional on the truth of other statements. He can store the rules he has written and call them with a single name. And he can store the latest design scheme he has worked out either to work on some other time or to evaluate with the CHOICE system, perhaps against other schemes he has previously worked out.

For example, a designer might wish to study possible locations for industry in the outlying areas of a large city by generating alternative locations according to different decision rules, and then testing the locations against other criteria. The results of certain tests such as the increase in the tax base for the community can be coupled with the importance which various population groups attach to those results in order to evaluate the proposals. The designer can implement any of the operations involved in this example by using DISCOURSE and CHOICE. He may find, over time, that he builds up a library of generators, tests and evaluators which are particularly useful.

Rather than being substitutes for the hard thinking which is involved in describing, changing and evaluating environments, DISCOURSE and CHOICE require a complete understanding of every aspect of what is done with them. We argue that what is describable is programmable; and we argue the converse of the contrapositive as well: that what is not describable is not programmable. Let us hasten to say that it cannot be inferred from the above that the computer therefore can yield neither counter intuitive nor non-trivial results. Clearly one can describe procedures which man could only carry out in a very long period of time and which might or might not yield surprises.

Our insistence that the designer be able to create his own ways of working poses a fundamental issue for us and for the user: if we enrich the systems to the extent demanded by the subtle user, we make the systems difficult to use, and we ask of the user that he think through design issues which, if he were to design in the traditional manner, he might not have to face. The results are that the systems now will slow down the user, and that they will force him to work in an unfamiliar way. A second issue we face is how to determine whether there has been any improvement over what the designer might have done without the systems. A third issue is whether we are able in the design of computer systems to give sufficient play to the non-verbal component of design: how much of design involves formal ideas which cannot be described in any other than visual terms?

And, finally, what capabilities of design should we be stressing in the development of the system? Which should man do and which the machine? And, can the last question be answered identically for all designers, or even for any designer over time?□

[1] *Discourse: A language and system for computer assisted city design*, Ph.D. Dissertation by W. Porter in preparation in the Department of Urban Studies and Planning at MIT.
[2] *A choice system for environmental design and development*, J. P. Boorn, Ph.D. Dissertation, Department of Urban Studies and Planning, MIT.

ARCHITECTURE MACHINE

Nicholas Negroponte
Leon Groisser
Anthony Platt
Richard Hessdorfer
Steven Gregory
Paul Mockapetris
Mark Drazen
Stephen Peters
Paul Linsay
Sponsors: Ford Foundation and Interdata, through the Urban Systems Laboratory of MIT

What makes a human designer a 'good' architect? We know that he must somehow contribute physical environments that both house and stimulate the good life. But we do not know much about the good life (it has no 'utility function' and cannot be optimized). We know that he must have an understanding of, and ease with, physical form. But we do not know how our own cognitive processes visualize shape and geometry. We know that he must interpret human needs and desires. But we do not know how to describe these needs and desires.

What probably distinguishes a competent designer is his ability to provide missing information. Any environmental design task is characterized by an astounding amount of unavailable or undeterminable information. Part of the design process is, in effect, the procurement of this information. Some is gathered by doing research in the preliminary design stages. Some is obtained through experience. Other chunks of information are gained through prediction, induction and guesswork. Finally some information is handled randomly, playfully or personally.

It is reasonable to assume that the presence of machines, of automation in general, will provide for some of the omitted and difficult-to-acquire information. However, it would appear foolish to suppose that, when machines know how to design, there will be no missing information or that a single designer can give the machine all that it needs. Consequently, the Architecture Machine Group at MIT, are embarking on the construction of a machine that can work with missing information. To do this, an Architecture Machine must understand our metaphors, must solicit information on its own, must acquire experiences, must talk to a wide variety of people, must improve over time, and must be intelligent. It must recognize context, particularly changes in meaning brought about by changes in context.

We should take advantage of the professional iconoclasms that exist in our day—a day of evolutionary revolution. We should build machines equipped with at least those devices that humans employ to design. I suggest that we build machines that can learn, can grope and can fumble; that we build machines that help architects, not replace them.[1]▷

[1] From N. Negroponte, *The architecture machine*, forthcoming, MIT Press.

510

PROGRAM

◁Following a year of experiments and exercises in 'artificial design intelligence', the Architecture Machine Group will start constructing a satellite machine which will be the beginnings of an Architecture Machine. This device will be primarily composed of Interdata processors and Interdata memory. Its task will be to learn about architecture.
The following illustrations represent three particular experiments that have in common the specific goal of providing Architecture Machines with the ability to solicit information on their own.
The two diagrams are estimates of the first two years of growth.□

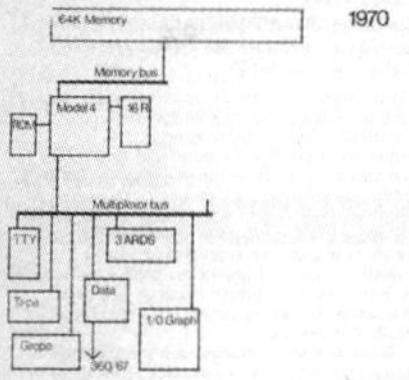

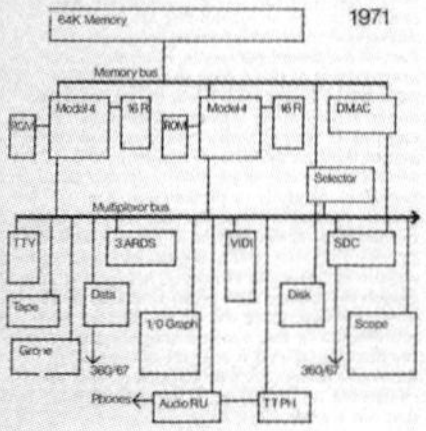

TOWARDS A HUMAN[E] THROUGH MACHINES

Nicholas Negroponte

Given that the physical enviro
perfect harmony with Everym
given that architecture is not t
response to human needs; giv
architect is not the consumma
and use; let us consider the ev
physical environments. In part
consider an evolution aided by
specific class of machines, as W
calls them, ethical robots. In t
architecture, we shall call the
Machines.
There are three possible wa
machines assist the design pro
1. Current procedures can be
speeding up and reducing the
practices;
2. Existing methods can be alt
the specifications and constitu
where only those issues are co
supposedly machine-compatib
3. The process, considered as
can be introduced to a mechan
considered as evolutionary), a
training, resilience, and growt
developed.
We shall consider only the t
shall treat the problem as the
association of two dissimilar s
machine—and two dissimilar p
and computation. We shall fur
concern as the acquaintancesh
intelligent systems, the archite
Architecture Machine. By virt
intelligence to an artefact or th
partnership is not one of mast
and slave (dumb, follower), bu
associates which each have the
self-improvement.
Imagine a machine which co
local situations in the physical
family that moves, a residence
income that decreases). Such a
report on and concern itself sp
unique and the exceptional. In
concentrate on the particulars.
designer cannot do this. He ca
modate the particular; he obli
Britton Harris suggests, 'He is
in this way because the effectu
requires rules of general applic
because watching each sparrow
some for any but God.' The re
needs little reminder of the res

Prelude to an architect-mach
Consider that you are in a fore
not know the language, and ar
need of help. At first your han
facial expressions carry most o
to the silent observer. Your be
language of gestures and stran
observer) utterances to commu
purpose. The puzzled listener
of content he can understand a
language. You react to his rea
language of pantomime begins
new language has evolved fro
effort to communicate. Return
person a second time, with a n
will find that the roots of a dia
exist. But this second convers
gibberish to a third party obse
exchange for the first time.
A designer-to-machine intro
a similar linguistic evolution.
the other's design manoeuvres,

Selection from *Architectural Design* (September 1969).

GROPE

A second example of interfacing with the real world is Steven Gregory's GROPE. GROPE is a small mobile unit that crawls over maps, in this case, Passonneau and Wurman's Urban Atlas (MIT Press, 1966) maps. It employs a low resolution seeing mechanism constructed with simple photocells that register only states of on or off, I see light or I don't see light. In contrast to the Platt experiment, GROPE knows nothing about images, it deploys a controller which must be furnished with a context and a role (as opposed to a goal). GROPE's role is to seek out 'interesting things'. To do this, the little robot compares where he has been to where he is, compares the past to the present (plus occasional random numbers to avoid ruts) to determine future moves. The unlocking human or Architecture Machine observes what is 'interesting' by observing GROPE's behaviour rather than revising the testimony that this or that is 'interesting'. At present, aspects of GROPE are simulated on scope and other aspects use the local computing power on GROPE's back (for relays).□

INTERACT

INTERACT faces the problem of soliciting information about the environment, about needs and desires, from the inhabitants themselves. Using English input, Richard Hessdorfer is developing a 'consumer' item that could initiate a dialogue with inhabitants, build a model of needs and desires (particular to the speaker) and report back to Architecture Machines.

As a part of the Hessdorfer experiment, a teletype-writing device was brought into the South End, Boston's ghetto area. Three inhabitants of the neighbourhood were asked to converse with this machine about their local environment. Though the conversation was hampered by the necessity to type English sentences, the chat was smooth enough to reveal two important results. First, the three user-inhabitants said things to this machine they would probably not have said to a human, particularly a white planner or politician: to them the machine was not black, was not white, and surely had no prejudice. Second, the three residents had no qualms or suspicions about talking with a machine (in English about personal desires); they did not type uncalled for remarks, instead they immediately entered a discourse about slum landlords, highways, schools, and the like. (The reader should know, as the three users did not, that this experiment was conducted over telephone lines with teletypes, with a human at the other end, not a machine. The same experiment will be rerun shortly—this time with a machine at the other end of the telephone line.)□

SEE

SEE is an exercise in machine vision, giving Architecture Machines eyes. Anthony Platt is presently applying the vidisector (the seeing mechanism) of MIT's robot project, asking it to look at simple physical models. The interim goal is to observe, recognize and determine the 'intents' of several models, built from plastic blocks. The machine looks at the models and extrapolates certain characteristics and criteria that might have led to it. Following a certain number of witnessings, the machine is asked to generate its own solution from that which it learned (and which is visually representable).

COMMENTARY

Stanford Anderson

An outsider to these MIT projects can best raise only certain general questions. 'What are architectural designers wish to ask of the computer sciences?' is primarily a question in design theory. 'How should design problems be put to the computer?' is a question that combines issues in design and in logic. Such questions should remain open to all concerned students and designers.

'How can computer science meet the problems set by architectural design?' is a question for computer specialists. The three questions interact, of course. One is simply observing that a computer is not being used for its own sake, and that non-specialists should continue to engage certain aspects of computer-aided design.

What the designer wishes to ask of the computer sciences depends on our understanding of architectural design. A possible formulation,[1] emphasizing the open-ended, exploratory character of design, is the following. Architecture structures man's environment to facilitate the achievement of human purposes (intellectual, psychological and utilitarian) where those purposes are incompletely known and cannot be extrapolated from what is given in the situation. Rather, human purposes are altered by the very environment that is created to facilitate them. The structuring of the environment must be accomplished, then, through the exercise of tentative foresight and the critical examination of that foresight and the actions to which it leads. According to this description, neither the human purposes nor the architect's methods are fully known in advance. Consequently, if this interpretation of the architectural problem situation is accepted, any problem-solving technique that relies on explicit problem definition, on distinct goal-orientation, on data collection, or even on non-adaptive algorithms will distort the design process and the human purposes involved.

Any such characterization of the design process raises a variant of the classical 'problem of induction', and thus challenges how we can reasonably put design problems to the computer.

In logical terms, universal theories cannot be derived from reports of a finite number of observations.[a] 'All swans are white' is not a safe generalization from any number of observations of white swans. Put crudely, but more to our point: a finite number of observations cannot yield a design hypothesis that can reliably be expected to embrace any subsequent observation. A related issue that can be stated even more pointedly is: one false observation transmits its falsity to any generalization that encompasses it. Incompleteness of information can, and inaccurate information does, lead to false inductive generalizations.

In the light of this logical problem, the first of the three MIT projects presents the greatest difficulties. That space arrangement project relies on a finite (for now, very small) number of observations and certain combinational rules. Those observations will always be incomplete: some important design considerations may not be consciously articulated; others will only be known in the future; certain observations, excluded because formerly considered of negligible significance, may assume importance in a new context. This incompleteness, plus the likelihood of inaccurate observations, make it likely that the optimization routines will conduct searches in areas that bear little relation to the actual problem. The designer may or may not be able to recognize that discrepancy at the time of its appearance on the scope. Even assuming he can, his next effort will be plagued with the same problems.

Such an enterprise presents a further difficulty. It tends to obscure the fact that the selection of observations and of combinatorial rules are theory-impregnated. That is, it is on

reconfiguration of expertise, architecture became, paradoxically, more narrowly construed by abstract quantitative and geometric means and, at the same time, less uniquely understood as program formally and materially realized. Architecture became a variable within a constellation of environmental practices dedicated to the development of rational techniques for decision-making and the prediction of outcomes—for, in the broadest sense, design problem solving. As built environment, architecture could be represented numerically by means of statistics, set theory, algorithms and formally, by means of objectively derived geometric modeling techniques. Architecture was subsumed within organizational systems in which questions of strategy, design method, or proof of principles took precedence over physical outcomes. The rationale most frequently offered for the engagement with systems-based techniques and computer technologies was the need for more accurate and inclusive means of collecting and analyzing data which would in turn enable designers to address complex urban problems and assess the benefits of particular criteria upon outcomes. From within architecture, the new methods were viewed as a corrective to design decision-making prejudiced by personal aesthetic preference or the theoretical aspirations of academic architects. Historiographically the interest of this shift extends beyond the discipline of architecture, the mere mapping of exchanges between two institutional locales, or the identification of the propensities of specific actors; rather it evidences the role of architecture within a larger epistemic transformation.

The September 1969 issue of *Architectural Design* presented a variety of approaches to design research and methods. Some practices were experimental, while others sought underlying structural or theoretical principles and still others attempted to forge neutral and logical processes for systematizing problem solving. A professor of business administration at UC Berkeley's Space Science Laboratory contributed an article titled "Architecture and Operational Research;" the director of the Joint Unit in Planning at University College London wrote on "Irreversibility;" and the assistant director of the new Center for Environmental Studies (CES) in London discussed "New Planning Tools."[4] There were also contributions from architects exploring systems thinking, such as Cedric Price and two members of Archigram. Given the varied points of departure, it would be remiss to gather under an inclusive category all academic architectural practices engaged in systems, design

4 See C. West Churchman, "Architecture and operational research," Peter Cowan "Irreversibility," and Alan G. Wilson New Planning Tools," *Architectural Design* (September 1969): 487, 488, 485-486.

methods or computer-based research even if they often collaborated on grants, shared work locations, publishing and conference venues. However, one can say that architecture found itself at an epistemological and disciplinary crossroad when, at institutions of higher learning, it engaged with systematic methods associated with the social sciences—such as business management and behavioral psychology—alongside those of engineering. This narrative raises a set of techno-cultural as well as disciplinary questions about the status of science and the techniques that legitimize expertise. From within architecture, however, it should be considered a tenuously connected and internally critical academic subculture, as the network of engineers and architects invested in computer facilitated techniques for design and analysis were soon marginalized.[5]

The Geography of Political Economies, Knowledge and Expertise

A narrative of two institutional locales framed as "Cambridge USA" and "Cambridge UK" could be considered through the frequently invoked if ill-defined notion of a "special relationship" between the United States and the United Kingdom.[6] Typically the relationship is characterized as a one-way conveyance in the form of mass culture or "Americanization" rather than as a mutually beneficial and productive exchange. Any discussion of the alignment of positivistic procedures for knowledge production, of institutions, and of research funding begs for more precise contextual coordinates if a narrative of scientism as epistemic challenge is to stand with conviction. Recent theorizing of global development among technically equipped milieus substantiates a more specific relationship. Both Cambridges are identified among the geo-economic configurations that Manuel Castells and Peter Hall in their 1994 study categorize as technopoles. According to this analysis technopoles share structural as well as physical qualities; they are characterized by an unplanned hybridized "cooperation or partnership between the public and private sectors" promoted by governments and in association with universities, research institutions, and private companies interested in R&D.[7] According to this definition, a technopole generates basic materials for the informational economy. The UK's "Cambridge Phenomenon" was well documented in a seminal 1985 study by Segal Quince Wicksteed linking the university to the growth of a world-class high technology industry in Britain.[8] Castells and Hall similarly identify "Boston's highway128 [*sic*]" as a

5 Nigan Bayazit, "Investigating Design: A Review of Forty Years of Design Research," *Design Issues* v. 20, n.1 (Winter 2004): 21.

6 See Murray Fraser and Joe Kerr, *Architecture and the Special Relationship: The American Influence on Post-war British Architecture* (London: Routledge, 2007),

pp. 17-20; Erik van de Vleuten, "Toward a Transnational History of Technology: Meanings, Promises, Pitfalls," *Technology and Culture. The International Quarterly of the Society for the History of Technology* v. 49, n. 4 (October 2008): 17. http://etc.echnologyandculture.net accessed 12/17/2008.

7 Manuel Castells and Peter Hall, *Technopoles of the World. The Making of 21st Century Industrial Complexes* (London: Routledge, 1994), 1. For an anecdotal but equally compelling account see Christopher Rand, *Cambridge, U.S.A. Hub of a New World* (New York: Oxford University Press, 1964).

8 See Segal, Quince Wicksteed, *The Cambridge Phenomenon. The Growth of High Tech Industry in a University Town* (Cambridge: Segal Quince Wicksteed, 1985); D.E. Keeble, "High-technology industry and regional development in Britain: the case of the Cambridge Phenomenon,"

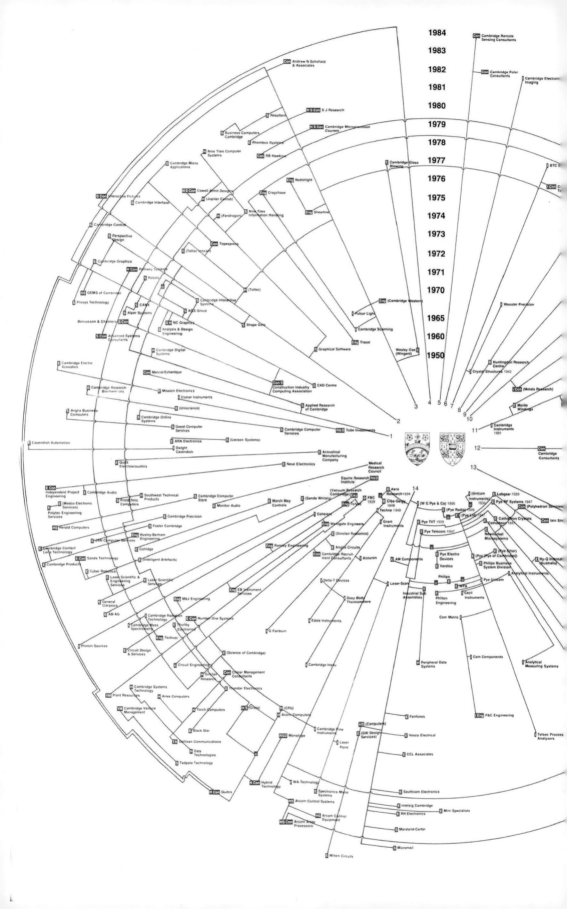

The Cambridge Phenomenon

This chart shows the total population of firms in the Cambridge Phenomenon at the end of 1984, presented on a family tree of interconnected firms and a separate list of other firms.

Firms are included on the family tree if they have been formed:

(a) as spin-outs from existing high technology firms, the University or research establishments in the area. A spin-out occurs when founder(s) start a firm *directly* on leaving existing organisation(s) or in some cases remaining in these organisation(s);

(b) as essentially independent subsidiaries of existing high technology companies in the area.

The tree shows firm formation, represented by the lines connecting the 'parent' and 'child' organisations. It does not show financial, trading or technological relationships between organisations. The date of firm establishment is specified by the position of the symbol indicating the firm's activity.

The separate list of firms given below shows businesses in the phenomenon with no direct origin in the University or in other high technology organisations in the area.

Appendix E presents a list of firms identified after the study was first published in February 1985.

While the chart has been checked with firms themselves, we apologise for any errors or omissions which might remain.

Other firms

A R Microelectronics E 1979	Klockner-Moeller E 1978
Agricultural Genetics E 1983	LKB Biochrom I·E 1974
Andrea NDT Products (UK) M 1978	Linton Laboratories I 1971
Appropriate Systems S·Con 1981	Logica R&D 1984
Baddeley Associates TA 1982	Lucidata In·Con 1981
Barkway Electronics E 1964	MCI (Cambridge) I 1982
Beckman Process I 1980	MS Consultants (Cambridge) Con·S 1980
Bright Instrument Co I 1963	Michell Instruments I 1974
British Earthworm Technology M 1983	Micro-Analysis Consultants I·Con 1981
CML Computers S·Con 1982	Microtraffic Systems S·Con 1983
Cambashi Con 1984	Mnemos Europe I 1981
Cambridge Bio Science M 1984	Mobira I 1984
Cambridge Design Associates I·Eng 1974	Napp Laboratories I 1983
Cambridge Electron Beam I·Eng 1974	NETZ I 1979
Cambridge Industrial Design Eng·Con 1978	Newall Electronics E 1970
Cambridge Microcomputers H·S 1979	Newbury Data Recording M 1977
Cambridge Microprocessor Systems M 1983	Omnifit I 1973
Cambridge Microsystems S·Con 1981	Organon Laboratories D 1983
Cambridge Numerical Control S·Con 1980	Organon Teknika D 1982
Cambridge Polymer	Parke Davis D 1983
Consultants Con 1982	Paxton Computer Group S 1978
Chetaro Proprietories I 1982	Personnel Development
Circuit UK S·Con 1981	Projects Con 1975
Comart Computers H 1977	Peterborough Software S 1964
Continental Microwave E 1979	Pexit Precision I 1983
Component and Equipment Producers I 1964	Potterton Energy
Computer Exploration Services Con 1982	Controls Con·I 1978
Computer One I 1983	Powertron I 1971
Computerset I 1983	Photon Control I 1983
Coratals D 1983	Precision Systems I 1981
Control Universal I 1981	Pro Mark Electronics E 1983
Counting House Computer Systems H·S 1976	Protech Data Systems S 1980
Cyberaid D 1980	Rider-French Consulting Con 1984
DSP Security Systems I 1981	Robotics Systems I 1982
Daigelys R&D 1941	Schlumberger R&D 1982
Datumset I 1974	Science Western I 1964
Datascope Medical M 1983	Scientific and Technical
Digitran I 1978	Software Consultants S·Con 1976
Diosynth I 1983	Software Services I 1983
Dunegan I·Con 1973	Sola-Banner (Europe) S 1977
EECO I 1974	Sound Techniques I 1970
EMCA E 1974	Stainless Metalcraft I·Eng 1967
Ely Science Systems I 1978	Stratos I 1984
Endevco I 1964	Sysbit Telematics I 1984
Engineering and Design Eng 1974	Systematics International S 1980
Esoteric Audio Research I 1977	TTS Computer Services S 1983
Dudley Evans Computers S 1978	TW Electronics I 1959
Fegs I 1978	TAG Radionics I 1984
Fibre Systems I 1980	Technet Electronics I 1983
GDS Graphic Display Systems M 1977	Torus Systems H·S 1984
GST Computer Systems S 1979	Tourism Technology S 1982
Gill Jennings & Every PA 1984	UGG I 1969
Colin Grace Associates S 1981	Ultra Violet Products I 1979
Goodfellow Metals M 1976	Voice Input I 1981
High Integrity Systems H·Con 1981	Varsala (UK) I 1984
IBM UK I 1984	Walkbury Electronics I 1980
Imten Con 1983	Walker Laboratories I 1983
Intervet Laboratories M 1972	Webster Instruments I 1970
JR Consultants Con 1981	The Welding Institute R&D 1968
Kalamazoo S·Con 1945	Westcom M 1981
K W Kirk & Sons I·Eng 1956	Wiltron Measurements E 1983
Kirkwood Electronics E 1979	

Key to Symbols

( )	No longer trading
⊞	Merger
E	Electronics and Audio
I	Instrument Engineering
H	Hardware
Eng	Engineering
R&D	Research and Development
S	Software
D	Biotechnology Chemicals
Con	Consultancy
M	Sales Marketing
TA	Technical Authors
VM	Venture Management
PA	Patent Agents

Key to Inner Circle

University Departments

1 Architecture
2 Computer Laboratory
3 Engineering
4 Social Anthropology
5 Scott Polar Research Institute
6 Astronomy
7 Earth Sciences
8 Clinical Biochemistry
9 Biochemistry
10 Metallurgy
11 Trinity College Not known
12 Chemical Engineering
13 Applied Mathematics and Theoretical Physics
14 Physics

© 1985

Segal Quince Wicksteed
Hall Keeper's House 42 Castle Street
Cambridge CB3 0AJ England

Artwork by Portfolio Design Consultants, Beaulieu, Cambridge

Foldout map from *The Cambridge Phenomenon: The Growth of High Technology Industry in a University Town*, Segal Quince Wicksteed, (Cambridge: Segal Quince Wicksteed, 1985).

geo-economic reconfiguring of industrialization for high-technology development. Route 128 was named as such in an account from the early 1960s that described the re-industrialization associated with technological expertise and a certain patronage gained by proximity to institutions of higher learning. The relationship between private enterprise and government interests to funded academic research plays a key part in a narrative that underpins architecture's engagement with computers. Such economic and institutional dynamics can only be framed in part from within architecture culture, as evidence of debates about architectural modernism in the postwar, disciplinary border scuffles, or as reflections of the profession's response to changing social and urban conditions. As recognized at a 1967 conference on design methods that was held in Portsmouth England, the techniques, problem solving processes, and methodological innovations were largely academic and had not been readily accepted within professional practice.[9] Historicizing this moment begs questions about the social construction of knowledge and the emerging global economy of the research university as a set of transnational circumstances acting upon and within institutions. It can be said that geographies of knowledge as such are an effect of cultural and institutional socio-technical networks in which real and imagined opportunities are engaged and knowledge is produced. The capacity for academic architects to respond to institutional demands—that is, to definitions of basic and applied research—was most ably realized at locations where equipment, expertise, and funding facilitated interdisciplinary work.

Something more needs to be said about the specific cultural contexts for research and higher education. There is nothing surprising about the fact that an institution with expertise in the sciences and technology prior to WWII adapted, with the

Route 128 study conducted by Massachusetts Department of Public Works and Transportation Engineering Division of Civil and Sanitary Engineering Department, MIT. From Alexander Bone and Martin Wohl, *Economic Impact Study of Massachusetts Route 128: Industrial Development Survey*, (Cambridge, MA: 1958).

Environment and Planning C: Government and Policy v. 7 (2) (May 1989): 119-244.

9 See Anthony Ward's introduction to *Design Methods in Architecture* eds., G. Broadbent, A. Ward (London: Lund Humphries for the Architectural Association, 1969), 10-14. The conference convened on December 4th, 5th, and 6th in 1967 at the Portsmouth School of Architecture.

ROUTE 128 STUDY

MASSACHUSETTS INSTITUTE OF TECHNOLOGY
MASS. DEPARTMENT OF PUBLIC WORKS
U.S. BUREAU OF PUBLIC ROADS

SCALE IN MILES

FORMER LOCATION OF INDUSTRIES
NOW ON ROUTE 128 — AS OF
SEPTEMBER 1957

• EACH DOT REPRESENTS THE LOCATION
OF AN INDUSTRY PRIOR TO ITS
RELOCATION ON ROUTE 128

FIGURE 3

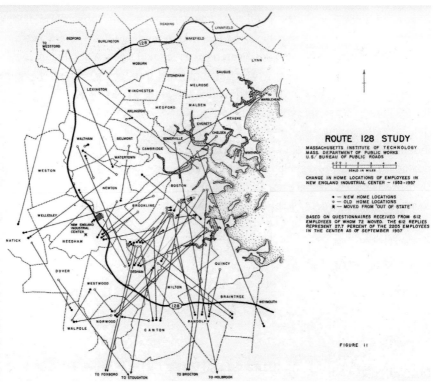

ROUTE 128 STUDY

MASSACHUSETTS INSTITUTE OF TECHNOLOGY
MASS. DEPARTMENT OF PUBLIC WORKS
U.S. BUREAU OF PUBLIC ROADS

SCALE IN MILES

CHANGE IN HOME LOCATIONS OF EMPLOYEES IN
NEW ENGLAND INDUSTRIAL CENTER — 1953-1957

• — NEW HOME LOCATIONS
○ — OLD HOME LOCATIONS
✕ — MOVED FROM "OUT OF STATE"

BASED ON QUESTIONNAIRES RECEIVED FROM 612
EMPLOYEES OF WHOM 72 MOVED. THE 612 REPLIES
REPRESENT 27.7 PERCENT OF THE 2205 EMPLOYEES
IN THE CENTER AS OF SEPTEMBER 1957

FIGURE II

onset of the Cold War, its aims to a changing worldview. Both Cambridge institutions being discussed here had, prior to the war, collaborated with industry and government on research projects in the sciences and technology—or on what is referred to as technological transfer with public and political enterprise.[10] These relations strengthened after the war, though the funding of research shifted. In the case of MIT the Military-Industrial Complex evolved into what Senator J. William Fulbright re-phrased in 1967 as the Military-Industrial-*Academic*-Complex.[11] Comparatively speaking, much has been written about the funding of research at American universities such as Stanford and MIT, while a fuller account of the British situation is only now being written.[12] Nevertheless, on both sides of the Atlantic there were sweeping challenges both within and beyond the university that exposed architecture to performance demands that would parallel the rigor of science. The eventual success of the social sciences in the academic arena along with the interpretation of planning as a multi-disciplinary academic pursuit with application to industry and government purposes put further pressure upon traditional disciplinary boundaries.[13] While both locales connected academic research with industry, British universities—including Cambridge—were rather differently obliged to respond to State-implemented educational reform. The momentum fueling the turn to architectural research in the UK was in part a response to questions about the future of higher education which were cast in terms of a techno-national discourse and a perceived need to stem backwardness in the pursuit of knowledge.[14] The publication of the *Governmental Statement of the Committee under the Chairmanship of Lord Robbins* (more commonly known as the Robbins Report) in 1963 recommended that the university system expand by developing new institutions dedicated to research in science and technology. And in 1964 the founding of a Ministry of Technology gave credence to Harold Wilson's imperative to advance Britain anew by "embrac[ing] the white heat and cold logic of technology."[15] In 1969 the Ministry set up a government-funded Computer-Aided-Design (CAD) center located in the vicinity of Cambridge University. The enterprise was managed by an independent UK computer company, but the decision was made by the Ministry with advice from ex-Cavendish Laboratory scientists, including J.D. Bernal.[16] Also in the vicinity of the University was a company called Applied Research of Cambridge, Ltd. Founded in the 1970s, the enterprise operated as the applied and business extension for research

10 Gary W. Matkin, *Technology Transfer and the University* (Toronto, New York: Collier Macmillan, Canada; American Council of Education, National University Continuing Education Association, 1990), 22-23.

11 Stuart W. Leslie, *The Cold War and American Science. The Military-Industrial-*

Academic Complex at MIT and Stanford (New York: Columbia University Press, 1993), 2.

12 See David Edgerton, "The British Military-Industrial Complex in History: the importance of political economy," *The Economics of Peace and Security Journal* v. 3, n. 1 (2008): 5-10;

Robert Bud, Philip Gummett eds., *Cold War Hot Science. Applied Research in Britain's Defense Laboratories 1945-1990* (London: Harwood Academic Publishers, 1999).

13 See Mark Solovey, "Project Camelot and the 1960s Epistemological Revolution: Rethinking the Politics-Patronage-Social

Science Nexus," *Social Studies of Science* v. 31, n. 2, Science in the Cold War (Apr. 2001): 165-170; David Paul Haney, *The Americanization of Social Science. Intellectuals and Public Responsibility in the Postwar United States* (Philadelphia: Temple University Press, 2008).

14 Guy Ortolano, *The Two*

undertaken at the Cambridge School of Architecture's center for Land Use and Built Form Studies (LUBFS). The concern continually expressed by LUBFS co-founder Lionel March was that academic research for theoretical knowledge, or basic research, would "become confused with applied research and development."[17]

The question of what constitutes basic research for architects and urban designers is as yet unresolved, and it continues to be a topic of debate at institutions of higher learning. Arguing to defend the preserve of research at institutions of higher learning Vannevar Bush, former Dean of Electrical Engineering at MIT, claimed that researchers don't often "make" things but supply basic research that leads to new knowledge without thought to practical ends.[18] Bush's statement of 1945 was meant to safeguard against the intrusion of practical ends upon scientific research; that is, to protect academics from the pressures of industry, commerce, or government and the kind of research partnerships that have now gained a firm hold within the university. In the early 1960s the question of research, whether basic or applied, reopened across the Institute and found purchase within the School of Architecture. By 1962 Dean of Architecture Pietro Belluschi was confronted with increased demands for practical outcomes in architectural research. In his contribution to the *President's Report of 1963-1964*, Belluschi straightforwardly states that basic research rarely occurs in architecture—that is, research with an objective basis and with measureable outcomes that contribute to an "intellectual stockpiling" and furthers the accumulation of knowledge to be built upon.[19] Wary of producing "narrow specialists" at the expense of more theoretical approaches to architecture, Belluschi recognized the need to compete with disciplines engaged in design as environment and which appeared to offer more scientifically legitimized methodological approaches. He noted that while fields such as engineering, psychology, and urban studies were producing valuable research, the outcomes were not in a strict sense architectural.[20]

In the UK a parallel if differently oriented debate was taking place. In his inaugural lecture as the newly appointed director of the Bartlett at University College in London, Richard Llewelyn-Davies declared that "it is now generally accepted that the advancement of knowledge in architecture must be the task of organized and systematized study, and

Cultures Controversy. Science, Literature and Cultural Politics in Postwar Britain (Cambridge, MA: Cambridge University, 2009), 111. David Edgerton, *Warfare State. Britain 1920-1970* (Cambridge, MA: Cambridge University Press, 2006). Recent work on postwar Britain challenges 'declinist' interpretations of

Britain's capacity in science and technology during this period.

15 See Paul Brown, Charlie Gere, Nicholas Lambert, Catherine Mason, eds., *White Heat, Cold Logic. British Computer Art, 1960-1980* (Cambridge, MA: MIT Press, 2008). For the Cambridge University Grant's

Committee's response to the Robbins Report see "Statement to the University Grants Committee on Certain Aspects of the Robbins Report," *Minerva* v. 2, n. 2 (December 1964): 257-262.

16 Doreen Massey, Paul Quintas, David Wield, *High Tech Fantasies. Science Parks in Society, Science and Space*

(London: Routledge, 1992), p. 173.

17 Lionel March, "Research and Environmental Studies," *Cambridge Review* (2 February 1973): 91.

18 *Science, the Endless Frontier, a Report to the President on a Program for Postwar Scientific Research* (Washington: National

THE CITY SCALE

An approach to urban studies

The need to consider a city as a system in which all elements and interrelationships are identified is stressed by Marcial Echenique. Because of its complexity mathematical models are useful in representing this system and in simulating the effect of manipulating it. The theoretical foundation of such models is discussed.

The purpose of any research is the formulation of theory which transforms the unexpected into the predictable. The approach that this particular study took was that the spatial structure of cities can be considered as a system, a complex of interrelated parts. This systematic view of city structure demonstrates the inadequacies of considering parts of the system independently. We cannot deal with a housing problem or a transport problem in isolation because a good solution to the transport problem may depend on the location of land uses such as employment and housing. The approach to urban problems has frequently been to treat parts of the system as independent; an approach which may produce the wrong answer to the particular problem, apart from the grave consequences it may produce elsewhere. The systems approach to urban spatial structure obliges us to consider all the basic elements of the structure and the interactions between them.

Fig. 1. The city can be considered as a system i.e. a set of elements $(e_1, e_2, e_3, \ldots, e_i, e_j)$ and their relationship $(r_{11}, r_{12}, r_{13}, \ldots, r_{ij})$

Any system has a structure, that is to say, a particular set of relationships between its elements, and by considering these conceptually it is possible to establish an analogue between one system and another and thereby deduce some properties of the less familiar by analogy with the more familiar.

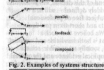

Fig. 2. Examples of systems structure

The state of a system at any particular time can be accurately described in terms of the values of the elements and their relationships, and the theoretical system can

be tested against its real counterpart. A system also has recognisable behaviour patterns in reaction to different stimuli. That is to say that if we change the value of an element or a set of elements or relationships we can investigate the effects of this on the rest of the system. For example if we test the consequences of building a new road as opposed to subsidising public transport, it may be that a small change in the latter produces a greater change in the level of congestion, and in this way the best move can be ascertained.

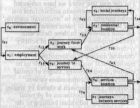

Fig. 3. The urban system has a compound structure. The state of the system at any one time is expressed by the values of the elements $(e_1, e_2, e_3 \ldots)$ and the values of the relationships $(r_{11}, r_{12}, r_{13}, \ldots)$

Finally a system has an environment, that is to say it belongs to a wider system which influences its behaviour, and it is necessary to be clear about the relationship between the system and its environment, and how change in the latter can affect the system concerned.

Models

It is not enough to merely consider the city as a system; we need to be able to represent this system. The purpose of a representation is two-fold: on the one hand it aids the communication of ideas, and on the other it helps test these ideas by comparing the representation with the real world. If the test is successful, we may then manipulate the representation to examine possible ways of changing reality. Any such representation is a model. Previously men have built conceptual models in which the representation is done by written or spoken words, or analogue models in the form of maps and graphs. But many researchers in the urban field have come to the conclusion in recent years that it is only through mathematical representation that the urban system can be described. The mathematical model expresses the elements of the system as symbols and its relationships in equation form. The advantages of this new approach are enormous: because of its mathematical form (both arithmetical and logical) the model can be handled by a computer, which is essential in urban research because vast quantities of data are involved and because the relationships are complex and frequently simultaneous (that is, the solution to one depends on the solution of the other).

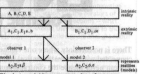

Fig. 4. A model is a representation of a system

A,B properties of the real world (real system)
A_1, B_1 properties of the real world in the mind of the observer
a,b other properties in the mind of the observer
A_2, B_2 represented properties of the real world in the model (positive analogies)
$a\beta$ properties of the model (negative analogies)

Model building can be summarised as comprising two processes: building hypotheses or models directly or by analogy, and then trying to simulate the system that we are describing. As in any other scientific experiment the success of the simulation is tested by its accuracy in reproducing real phenomena. The only difference between the physical sciences and social sciences such as urban research is that frequently in the physical sciences the experiments can be conducted with the real elements, while the social sciences must use statistical information about people and their

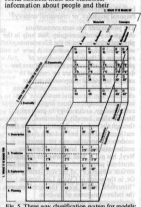

Fig. 5. Three way classification system for models; according to the purpose, the means of representation and the treatment of the time factor.

environment. Once a model has been built and its validity tested it can be used somewhat like a laboratory experiment in which different chemical reactions are tested. The various lines of action that the decision makers could take can be simulated

"The City Scale: An Approach to Urban Studies," *Architectural Design* (May 1971).

Science Foundation, 1960); Greenberg, *Science, Money, and Politics*, pp. 45-51

19 Pietro Belluschi, School of Architecture and Planning, *Massachusetts Institute of Technology Bulletin, President's Report* 1963-1964, v. 98, no. 2 (November 1964), passim, pp. 56-59. The argument is age-old in

architecture, in what follows Belluschi points to the problem where for academic architects research is based on designing real buildings which as professional practice is an extramural activity and, in his words, of "dubious in character" when compared to laboratory research. For a similar viewpoint from the UK

see Lionel March "Modern Movement to Vitruvius: Themes of Education and Research," *Royal Institute of British Architects Journal* (March 1972): 106.

20 Pietro Belluschi, School of Architecture and Planning, Massachusetts *Institute of Technology Bulletin, President's Report* 1962, v. 98,

that a good deal of this study must be prosecuted within schools of architecture and universities."[21] Llewelyn-Davies stated that all forms of research—basic, applied, and development—should be, to varying degrees, pursued within architecture. Under his guidance the Bartlett faculty focused their research on three areas of what he called the physical environment: physiology and the psychological, building organization and economics, and the problem of urban renewal—including the growth and change of buildings and cities.[22] During the academic year of 1965-1966 the Bartlett established the Centre for Urban Studies to replace an inter-university committee for Urban Studies previously housed within the School of Architecture. By 1970 the School of Architecture and the Department of Town Planning had joined to form the School of Environmental Studies. Meanwhile, at the School of Architecture in Cambridge, director Leslie Martin had been arguing from the mid-1950s onward that architectural knowledge should advance key principles that in turn produced theories able to explain and interrelate all facts associated with a given problem.[23] Under Martin's directorship computer-facilitated research supported by systematic methods was initiated prior to the 1967 founding of the LUBFS. During the same period the Joint Center for Urban Studies at MIT offered a base for academics interested in pursuing urban design-related topics. With the launch of the USL in 1968, architects were provided with a technically equipped interdisciplinary framework for research. The founding of centers, especially the LUBFS and the USL, enabled architectural research to gather expertise shared among engineering sciences, management studies, sociology, economics, and planning.

In one of the final annual reports submitted to the Institute during his tenure, Dean Belluschi announced that research at the Department of Architecture would focus on problems arising from the intensification of urban development.[24] Six years later in 1968 Dean Lawrence Anderson's annual contribution to the President Report noted departmental research projects that were addressing the organization of space, documenting patterns of use, investigating participatory approaches to the design process and collecting data on urban organization. Anderson's account is buttressed by a pejorative comment about architectural research preoccupied with stylishness. After the founding of the USL, the annual missives to the President focused on research addressing social

no. 2 (November 1962), p. 44.

21 Richard Llewelyn-Davies, "Architectural Studies," Inaugural Address, *Transactions of the Bartlett Society* v.1 (1962-1963): 11-12

22 See M. L. J. Abercrombie, S.M. Hunt, *1960-1970: Ten Years of Development in a School of Architecture* (Facsimile Report, July 1977).

Also see the Transactions for the Bartlett Society during Llewelyn-Davies's tenure. At the Bartlett research also focused on hospitals and laboratory design following expertise developed in Llewelyn-Davies's private practice.

23 Leslie Martin, "Conference on Architectural

Education," *Royal Institute of British Architects Journal* (June 1958): 280. Richard Llewelyn-Davies a practicing architect and Leslie Martin a practicing architect with a PhD in architecture history were pivotal figures transforming architectural education and academic research in the UK during

this period. See Murray Fraser, "Davies, Richard Llewelyn- (1918-1981)," [http://www.oxforddnb.com/view/article/31369, accessed 25 March 2009]; Peter Carolin, "Martin, Sir (John) Leslie (1908-2000)," [http://www.oxforddnb.com/view/article/74528, accessed 25 March 2009].

24 Belluschi, (1962), p. 44-45.

issues such as race, poverty and urban upheaval. In contrast, research goals at UK based-institutions were framed somewhat more mildly—for example, in terms of the need to address the current state of urban decay or in terms of the need to understand the social effects of urban growth. The latter project included the organization of efficient traffic patterns and an assessment of existing urban systems to serve an increasingly mobile population. At LUBFS, research focused on developing computer-generated modeling techniques for determining the optimal conditions for land usage and built form. Across both institutional milieus new research endeavors were motivated by a commitment to methodological neutrality and relied upon the data processing power of the computer.

Patronage significantly influenced academic architects pursuing computer-facilitated methods and research. For example, in April 1967 an IBM System 360 Model 65 was available for shared use at the newly funded computer center at the University College London. A year after researchers at the Bartlett gained access to computers, architects at the USL gained access to an IBM 360 Model 67. At MIT the new time-shared equipment was expected to encourage the development of interactive software and research into human-machine communication. At Cambridge University equipment and expertise was available to architects through the Computer Science Department, which in 1965 recruited faculty back from MIT to develop a CAD research group.[25] Computing specialization at Cambridge concentrated on applications distinct from those of other universities, for example the University of Manchester, where research was more involved with hardware and where design methods research was rooted in engineering.[26] At Cambridge the emphasis on mathematics promoted research into geometric modeling techniques. And this, no doubt, influenced the orientation of architectural research at the LUBFS.

There is a further, rather instrumental relationship between MIT and institutions in the UK that relates to the formation of research centers: the Ford Foundation's urban mandate. The support received by the Joint Center for Urban Studies from a Ford Foundation program geared for and focused on economic perspectives of city development is well known. In the 1960s a new wave of Ford Foundation funding supported the creation of research centers that addressed the "urban crisis."[27] The Foundation's investments were intended

25 Segal Quince Wicksteed, *Cambridge Phenomenon,* pp. 20, 38. Charles Lang graduated from Cambridge in engineering, went to MIT and was later recruited back to Cambridge University. The Science Research Council funded the CAD group and played a significant role in the development of the CAD

Center and its commercial consultancy. Eventually, the business was sold to Evans & Sutherland of Utah. Sutherland was the graduate student who first developed the Sketchpad at MIT
26 Segal Quince Wicksteed, *Cambridge Phenomenon,* p.20.
27 Richard Magat, *The Ford Foundation at Work.*

Philanthropic Choices, Methods, and Styles (New York: Plenum Press, 1979), pp. 100-101. The Joint Center for Urban Studies was funded under a program administered by the Resources for the Future's Committee on Urban Economics. Magat writes that the second wave of funding that came in the 1960s and

1970s produced discipline-oriented research of merit but the outcome in terms of policy or understanding how cities operate or the causes of conflict, or usefulness in generating greater participation and efficient delivery of services, that is, for applied results, were negligible. The program

to produce research or knowledge that would inform urban policy. In 1966 Llewelyn-Davies and then Labor Minister of Housing and Local Government Richard Crossman received funding from the Foundation to establish the London-based "quasi-independent public sector think-tank," the Center for Environmental Studies (CES).[28] The CES deployed some of these funds to establish LUBFS at Cambridge in the following year.[29] According to historian Mark Clapson, the Ford Foundation's international investment strategies sought to develop expertise on city development; in particular, it was interested in British research on urban growth, the garden city, and experiments in New Town development.[30] As discussed at length elsewhere in this anthology the USL at MIT benefited from Ford Foundation's urban funding strategy.[31]

Historian Theodore Porter and others have argued that scientific knowledge travels through networks to advantageous points of intersection. Porter refers to this institutional practice as social cloning.[32] The stuff of academic advancement and career formation—exchange programs, fellowships and travel itineraries, conferences and publications, combined with the expansion of graduate and post-graduate studies in the 1960s—social cloning facilitates the social exchange of knowledge. Between the two Cambridges this process can be confirmed in the careers of Christopher Alexander and William Mitchell. Alexander studied mathematics at University of Cambridge before turning to architecture. He was at Harvard University working on his PhD long before the opening of Cambridge University's LUBFS. Almost ten years later Mitchell passed through Cambridge (UK) as a student and lecturer before returning to the USA to take up academic positions that eventually lead to his tenure at MIT.

Published in 1964 as *Notes on the Synthesis of Form*, Alexander's doctoral research functioned as an agent in the transatlantic diffusion of design methods. Alexander established a reputation as a design methods advocate by means of multiple associations. Especially important were the Joint Center for Urban Studies and the Department of Civil Engineering at MIT, the Ministry of Built Public Works (MBPW) in the UK and by the end of the 1960s the Department of Architecture at UC Berkeley.[33] At Berkeley, Alexander joined researchers from various disciplines already invested in theories associated with operational

did not prove productive for academic-urban leader exchanges. This program was canceled in the mid-1970s due to lack of results and budget issues.

28 Mark Clapson, "The Ford Foundation and the Centre for Environmental Studies, 1966-1978," in *American Foundations in Europe. Grant-*

Giving Policies, Cultural Diplomacy and Trans-Atlantic Relations, 1920-1980 eds., G. Gemelli, R. MacLeod (Brussels: P.I.E.-Peter Lang, 2003), pp. 95-111. Martin Meyerson former director of Environmental Research at UC Berkeley, a graduate of and former professor at the MIT was the first

international director of the CES. He was also former director of the Joint Center for Urban Studies. See http://www.nationalarchives. gov.uk/catalogue/ displaycataloguedetails.asp? CATID=6257&CATLN=3&acc essmethod=5&j=1. The CES received five year funding from Ford's International

Affairs program of the Urban and Metropolitan Development Committee. Based on a record of successful research the Ford Foundation continued to fund the CES until the late 1970's, long after it had withdrawn support from other urban research programs such as the *Urban Systems* research and design methods. Throughout the 1960s Alexander's publications, such as *The Atoms of Environmental Structure* (jointly sponsored by the MBPW and UC Berkeley), played a significant role in debates over design methods.[34] From the first design methods conference held in London at the Imperial College in 1962 to the event designated as the first international conference of the newly formed Design Methods Group (DMG) held in 1968 in Cambridge, MA, Alexander's theory was admired and emulated. At the same time, criticism was never far behind.[35] In particular, the behavioral underpinnings of Alexander's theory were ruthlessly exposed as banal determinism at a design methods conference held at the School of Architecture in Portsmouth in 1967.[36] A Cambridge graduate employed at the MBPW reported that after having worked through the method he would never do it again.[37]

Alexander is an establishing figure of what became the design methods movement in architecture. In the proceedings from the first international conference of the Design Methods Group (DMG), editor Gary Moore of UC Berkeley writes; "In the United States the movement received its strongest lead from the work of Christopher Alexander in 1964, although some research and teaching were already underway at Berkeley under Horst Rittel, who had come from Ulm in 1962."[38] This account somewhat misrepresents the longer trajectory of design methods. In fact, the preoccupation with design methods or problem solving by means of systems thought began not with architects but with engineers who held academic posts and who were familiar with the teaching at the Ulm Hochschule für Gestaltung in the 1950s. In Great Britain early design methods advocates such as J. Christopher Jones, who had studied engineering at Cambridge University and later taught at University of Manchester, or L. Bruce Archer of the Royal College in London were significant contributors to the first generation of design methods. The theoretical approaches differed. Some researchers sought to reduce all design—in the broadest sense of the term—to front-end process problems or the systems engineering of a design problem. Engineers such as Archer focused on procedures rather than outcomes and saw no need "to distinguish between Architectural, Engineering and Industrial Design."[39] It mattered not whether it was a building program or a system of assembly and delivery—design problems were essentially the same at the front end. First generation advocates of design methods were preoccupied with analytical processes prior to design and all but

Laboratory at MIT According to Clapson the investment was seen as mutually beneficial. Also see Michael Batty, "From *Environment and Planning* B to Planning and Design: traditions, transitions, transformations," *Environment and Planning B: Planning and Design*, Anniversary Issue (1998): 2.

29 The CES also funded a similar center at Reading University headed up by former colleagues associated with Cambridge University. See Batty, p. 2.
30 Clapson, p. 97.
31 See Felicity D. Scott, "Discourse, Seek, Interact: Urban Systems at MIT," in this volume.

32 Theodore M. Porter, *Trust in Numbers. The Pursuit of Objectivity in Science and Public Life* (Princeton, N.J.: Princeton University Press, 1995), p. 15.
33 See for example, Christopher Alexander's work cited in Dean Charles L. Miller, "Man-Machine Communication in Civil Engineering," Keynote

Address for the Third National Conference on Electronic Computation, Structures Division, Boulder, Colorado, June 19-21, 1963. Institute Archives and Special Collections, MIT Libraries, Cambridge, MA, AC 400, Box 4.
34 Christopher Alexander, Barry Poyner, *The Atoms*

ignored the fact that, as one critic put it, "the logical nature of the act of designing is largely independent of the character of the thing designed."[40]

A Harkness Fellowship enabled Cambridge architecture graduate Lionel March to study first at the Joint Center for Urban Studies and later at UC Berkeley.[41] March claims that his American experience inspired the founding of a dedicated research center at the University of Cambridge. With Martin's support March, along with Philip Steadman, became the driving forces behind the mathematical propensity that distinguished the research agenda at LUBFS. They focused on mathematical modeling and simulation for land use and built form and, as the center's name implies, pursued the idea of planning as comprising social and building sciences. Unlike the expertise gathered at the Joint Center, LUBFS sought neutral scientific means through geometric techniques that evolved in tandem with mathematical talent.[42]

One of the more interesting non-architects to contribute an article to the issue of *Architectural Design* introduced at the beginning of this paper was the Cambridge University-educated and self-described cybernetician Gordon Pask.[43] Pask was an unusual character in early design methods. At the first design methods conference held in 1962, he presented a paper that described his attempt to capture the behaviors of a mechanism by means of algorithmic description.[44] In his opinion the algorithms failed to describe environmental 'behavior' and this failure proved the limits of the mathematical expression. Pask later conceived and tested experiments in machine and environmental behaviors within the London cybernetic scene of the 1960s. He is well known for his collaboration with Cedric Price on the Fun Palace, a project that explored the idea of architecture as an intelligent machine. In the British context this work found purchase among a few 'artist' engineers associated with art schools and institutes such as the Middlesex Polytechnic. London exhibitions such as the groundbreaking Cybernetic Serendipity of 1967—to which Pask contributed an artificial intelligence informed installation—the Computer '70 show, events associated with the Computer Arts Society founded in 1969 or the Bulletin of the Computer Arts Society provided forums that connected Pask to a rather different network than that shared by other proponents of design methods or the researchers at either Cambridge MA or Cambridge UK.[45] Nevertheless, Pask's work was of more than passing

of *Environmental Structure* Working Paper No. 42, Center for Planning and Development Research, the Institute of Urban & Regional Development University of California, Berkeley. Research originally sponsored by the M.P.B.W. (UK).

35 On reactions against Alexander's theory see

various articles published in *Design Methods in Architecture*. At Berkeley colleague Horst Rittel, a proponent of operational research, was an early critic of Alexander's method.

36 Ward, "Introduction," p.18. In *Design Methods in Architecture* also see Janet Daley, "A Philosophical

Critique of Behaviourism in Architectural Design," pp. 71-76.

37 G. Broadbent, "Design Method in Architecture," in *Design Methods in Architecture*, p. 17.

38 Gary T. Moore, ed., Emerging *Methods in Environmental Design and Planning. Proceedings of*

The Design Methods Group (Cambridge, MA: MIT Press, 1970), p. viii. Rittel had taught at the *Hochschule für Gestaltung* as Lecturer in Design Methodology and Operational Research. At Berkeley he introduced the first design methods courses. In this account the *Design Methods Group*

interest to Nicholas Negroponte in his research on interactive response among machines, humans, and environments. Pask's construal of "Conversational Theory" was put to work when, in the 1970s, Negroponte's research turned to machine intelligence and computer-aided participatory design.[46] Overall, Pask's particular kind of imaginative thinking points to a broader engagement with systems thinking and computing technologies than the positivistic strain of the DMG or, as we shall see, the research produced by the LUBFS.

The Harkness Fellowship program also sponsored Frank Duffy's travel from London to UC Berkeley, where he continued his research into systems and office organization. Duffy, a graduate of the Architectural Association and a contributor to British architectural magazines—including the September 1969 issue of *Architectural Design*— eventually completed a PhD at Princeton University.[47] Identifying with second-generation design methods he rejected the strictly objective and empirical approaches of first-generation design methods thinkers for constructing the built environment as an open socio-technical system.[48] Duffy was critical of, and yet expanded upon, Alexander's theories. Meanwhile transatlantic travelers such as Chris Abel, a graduate of Bristol University and a regular contributor to Architecture Design—again including the September 1969 issue—were less invested in systems techniques than in methods. Abel wrote the interactive program ARCHITRAINER while a Visiting Scholar at MIT during the 1973-1974 academic year. A Graham Foundation Fellowship supported Sean Wellesley-Miller's travel to MIT. Wellesley-Miller, who held degrees from several London based institutions is included among the personnel named on Negroponte's and Groisser's 1971 *Computer Aids to Participatory Architecture* grant application.[49]

If Alexander's name is indelibly linked to the development of logical techniques for design methodologies, William Mitchell has a rather different legacy. In the late 1960s the Australian-born Mitchell completed graduate studies at Yale in architecture. He soon began publishing and participating in design methods conferences and meetings of the US-based Environmental Design Research Association (EDRA). In a paper titled "Switching on the Seven Lamps" (published in the 1969 proceedings of the first annual meeting of the EDRA) Mitchell claims that early approaches to design methods, "tell(s) us little about

was formed in 1966 during the International Design and Planning Seminar held at University of Waterloo, Canada with the intention of encouraging research on new methods for design of the environment. In the early 1970s Lionel March briefly took a position associated with Systems Design

Engineering at the University of Waterloo, Canada.
39 Ward, "Introduction," p. 11.
40 Archer cited by Ward, "Introduction," p. 11.
41 Interview with Lionel March on March 17th 2009 at Stretham, Cambridgeshire, UK
42 See March, "Research and Environmental Studies,"

pp. 85-93.
43 Gordon Pask graduated with a BA from Downing College, University of Cambridge in 1954. He acquired university degrees including a PhD in psychology from UC and was awarded the first doctorate in cybernetics from the Open University. See María

Fernández, "Aesthetically Potent Environments," or How Gordon Pask Detourned Instrumental Cybernetics," *White Heat Cold Logic. British Computer Art 1960-1980* eds. P. Brown, C. Gere, N. Lambert, C. Mason (Cambridge, MA: MIT Press, 2008), pp. 53-60.
44 See comments by J. K. Page, "A Review of the

the complex ways in which design activities are embedded in the social, political, and economic structures of society."[50] The account is well-informed of developments in the UK, for example of those taking place at Manchester University's Institute for Science and Technology. Mitchell levels criticism at some of the basic tenets held by first generation design methods—in particular, the idea that goal-directed and motivational or causal behavior can be clearly defined—and he questions the assumption that goals are shared collectively. This shift from the assumed behavior of a group to user needs and participatory input defines the re-orientation of design methods by its second generation.

From his first publications onward, Mitchell advocated that designers engage an objective and interdisciplinary approach to better address users' needs. In the EDRA proceedings of 1969 Mitchell set aside what he labeled Alexander's "existential-behaviorist" position and criticized the "highly self-conscious programmatic eclecticism" of some architects.[51] His allegiance lay with computer-aided methods that promised feedback and informational processes that could "amplify the designer's or design team's capacity." By way of example Mitchell offered the exploration of interactive systems by the Architecture Machine Group URBAN 5. Mitchell speculated that this research might address the problem of expertise as architecture "enmeshed within a communications net." Emphasizing the human-machine exchange *and* architecture signals Mitchell's alignment with the socio-technical orientation of second-generation design methods. His questioning of professional expertise was founded upon an interest in computation and architectural form, and in negotiating the difference between what humans and machines do best. The former interest paired well with research at Cambridge University's center for LUBFS and the latter, with research at MIT.

Computer Facilitated Research from Models to Simulation to AI

The computer's data processing power played an important role in the pursuit of design principles at the LUBFS. Design researchers found support within Cambridge University's growing expertise in CAD and modeling, and in an alliance with the Mathematics Laboratory. Mathematics was considered more versatile than other kinds of explanatory tools, and the elegance of mathematical expression was itself viewed aesthetically.

Papers Presented at the Conference," in *Conference on Design Methods. Papers presented at the Conference on Systematic and Intuitive Methods in Engineering, Industrial Design, Architecture and Communications, London, September 1962*, eds. J. Christopher Jones, D. G. Thornley (New York: Macmillan

Company, Pergamon Press, 1963), p. 205.
45 See *White Heat. Cold Logic British Computer Art 1960-1980* and the *CACHe Project Archive* at http://www. bbk.ac.uk/hosted/cache/index. htm sponsored by Birkbeck College at University College London.
46 Gordon Pask,

"Introduction," *Soft Architecture Machines* (Cambridge, MA: The MIT Press, 1975), pp. 6-31. Also see Conversation Theory described in Nicholas Negroponte's grant proposal *Computer Mediated Inter-and Intra Personal Communication*, Massachusetts Institute of Technology, Rotch Library, 1977.

47 See for example, Francis Duffy, Andrew Rabeneck, "Truth in the Golden State," *Architectural Design* (September, 1969): 472.
48 Frank Duffy on March 16th 2009, England. See a recent publication "Lumbering to Extinction in the Digital Field. The Taylorist Office Building" *Harvard Design Magazine*

Moreover, mathematical means for theorizing principles was considered untainted by formal or intuitive prejudices about building form, programmatic function, or theoretical predisposition. Finally, modeling was considered to be an objective and technically sophisticated mode of research in which the proof lay in the calculations. In the preface to an early collection of essays titled *A Theoretical Basis for University Planning*, Leslie Martin acknowledges these associations and remarks upon a proposed new computer unit expected "to service parallel research programs" at Cambridge University.[52] Although published in 1968 as Report No. 1 under the Land Use and Built Form Studies imprint, much of the research had been initiated at least two years prior to the 1967 founding of the LUBFS. Many of the articles show Alexander's influence or at least mention their debt in departing from his work.[53] The essays and accompanying diagrams illustrate Martin's definition of systematic method as one in which all factors reflect the whole and one in which no decision can be taken in isolation. It is worth citing Martin at length to better grasp the methodological assumptions that would be furthered by LUBFS researchers over the next decade and which would attract students such as William Mitchell from abroad. Martin writes:

> Hence the attempt which is demonstrated here to identify the significant parameters and to show a total relationship. The relationship will ultimately take the form of a model which can then be used to examine existing situations or to predict others or to show the consequences of particular decisions. The model itself will be neutral. It is being built up on the basis of existing factual evidence. Its purpose is not to set out standards or to recommend lines of policy but simply to make clear that if *this* decision is taken it will have *that* effect on everything else.[54]

The center for LUBFS aimed, as did its various subgroups such as the Offices Study or Urban Systems Study group, to produce basic research that could be tested, amended and developed with future practical applications in mind. Architectural research focused on producing theoretical models for physical planning, and social science-based disciplines—such as economics or geography—informed the definition of a model. The introduction to *A Theoretical Basis for University Planning* claims the influence of the modeling techniques

(Fall/Winter 2008-09): 124-130.

49 Donlyn Lyndon, activities of the Department of Architecture reported in *Massachusetts Institute of Technology Bulletin. Report of the President and the Chancellor, 1971-1972*, p. 97. See Léon B. Groisser, Nicholas Negroponte, *Computer Aids*

to *Participatory Architecture* grant application 1971. Typescript held at the Rotch Library, MIT. Wellesley-Miller had degrees from the LSE, St. Martins School of Art, and London University. He served as co-editor of *Architectural Design* in the 1970s, co-founded the Event Structure Research Group and engaged

interactive computer research. In the mid-1970's Wellesley-Miller was appointed to MIT.

50 William Mitchell, "Switching on the Seven Lamps," *EDRA* 1. *Proceedings of the 1st Annual Environmental Design Research Association Conference* eds., Henry Sanoff, Sidney Cohn (1969),

116-117.

51 Mitchell, p. 116.

52 See Leslie Martin's preface to Nicholas Bullock, Peter Dickens, Philip Steadman, eds., *A Theoretical Basis for University Planning*, Report No. 1, (Cambridge: LUBFS, 1968), unpaginated. Research for this study was undertaken prior to

"now being developed, particularly in America, for use in the field of urban planning."[55] In 1973 Lionel March, as director of the center, reasserted that research mandate when he wrote that, "Whereas 'Vitruvian' research is done by lone scholars working in museums and libraries, 'post-Vitruvian' is done by research teams working in what the Americans call 'systems laboratories.'"[56]

Research at LUBFS focused on what March referred to as a "class of problems."[57] There were two main thematic areas, urban organization and built form. The first worked on predictive modeling of optimal relations of specific criteria applied to land use, such as the distribution of services or traffic routing. The second area dealt with the assessment of built-form configurations to determine their optimal performance given factors such as climatic control in relation to distribution of program, building height, and orientation.[58] Not all architectural or planning problems complied with such analyses. Researchers favored problems that were repeatable, that could be modeled mathematically, and that tested for performance. This theoretical impulse sought an isomorphic relation to reality in which the simulation of probable models was understood to be dynamic; that is, the model captured possible behaviors of disparate factors effecting an environment. At the urban level, an algorithm could turn large-scale complex problems into numerical results that could inform decisions in physical planning. The goal was to provide optimal solutions rather than definitive end forms for a particular problem. Although the ambitions for research evolved over time they were never, as were some proponents of first generation design methods, entirely focused on providing a universal method that would account for the totality of design.

At MIT the adoption of systematic approaches and the use of computing for design research was evidenced in a variety of ways. In the 1968 *Report to the President* Dean Lawrence Anderson noted computer-based faculty research supported by the Department of Civil Engineering and the USL. He wrote that the typical use of computers for organizing complex data aimed at understanding, for example, social migration, building costs benefits, and the construction process, was limited.[59] Anderson suggested an alignment with first generation design methods when he advocated that computers be employed to "understand thought processes we use to synthesize solutions with given

the founding of the *LUBFS* and was sponsored by the Calouste Gulbenkian Foundation (Spain), the Cambridge University Grants Committee and the Department of Education Science. The research addressed the form and organization of the future university, and is significant

given debates over higher education in the UK during these years.
53 Bullock, Dickens, and Steadman, p. 9. From Alexander's model they move to discussions about simulation and modeling. The titles of the chapters seem rather current, such as, "The 'network' diagram, and notes

on the organization of the report." The authors are not wholly positive but frequently critical as they aspire for a technique that can simulate design, evaluate, and predict performance.
54 Martin, Preface to *A Theoretical Basis for University Planning*, unpaginated.

55 Bullock, Dickens, Steadman, "Introduction," p. 1.
56 March, "Research and Environmental Studies," p. 89. March most likely is referring to RAND's Systems Research Laboratory (SRL).
57 March, "Research and Environmental Studies," p. 88.
58 The results could be referenced when deciding

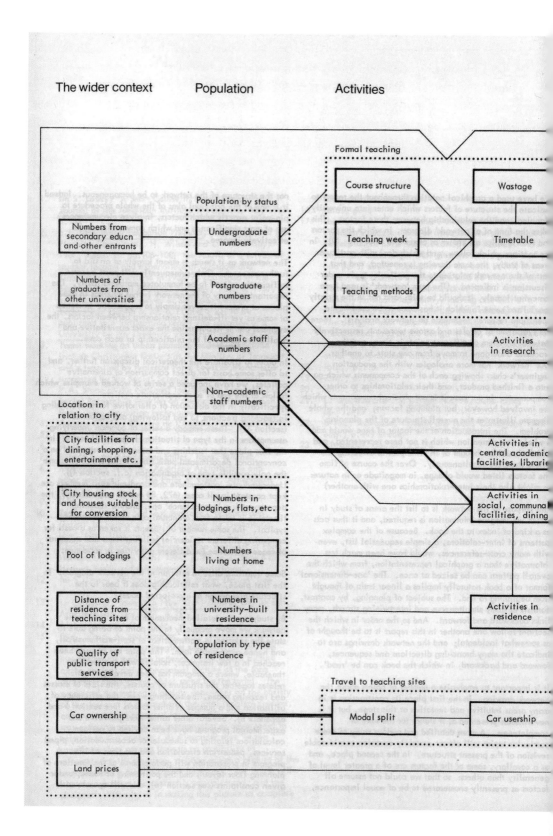

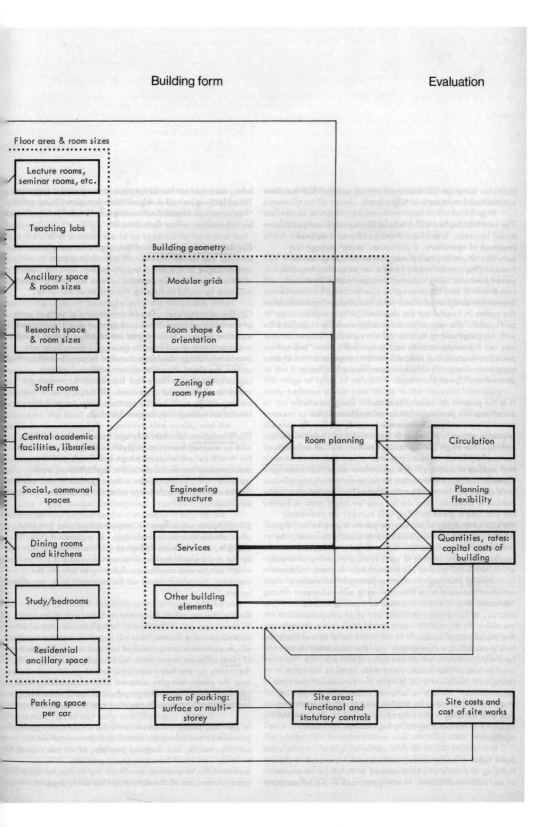

Building form

Evaluation

Floor area & room sizes

Lecture rooms, seminar rooms, etc.

Teaching labs

Ancillary space & room sizes

Research space & room sizes

Staff rooms

Central academic facilities, libraries

Social, communal spaces

Dining rooms and kitchens

Study/bedrooms

Residential ancillary space

Parking space per car

Building geometry

Modular grids

Room shape & orientation

Zoning of room types

Engineering structure

Services

Other building elements

Form of parking: surface or multi-storey

Room planning

Circulation

Planning flexibility

Quantities, rates: capital costs of building

Site area: functional and statutory controls

Site costs and cost of site works

previous page, "General Network." From Nicholas Bullock, Peter Dickens, and Philip Steadman, *A Theoretical Basis for University Planning.* (Cambridge: Cambridge University School of Architecture, Land Use & Built Form Studies, 1968).

"Man-Machine Communication in Civil Engineering," June 19-21, 1963. Keynote address for the Third National Conference on Electronics Computation; Structures Division, American Society of Civil Engineers, Boulder, CO.

circumstances" or that architecture should follow other professions where computation has helped rationalize thinking patterns.[60] In the same *Report* John Howard, Director of the Department of City and Regional Planning, remarked favorably on the shift from intuitive modes of design to more scientific research methods with his observation that a "developing . . . body of theory and methodology is displacing an older reliance on principles and practices."[61] In a section of the *Report* dedicated to the newly established USL, director Charles L. Miller related the pursuit of interdisciplinary urban research to ideals associated with systems methods, engineering, and the use of information systems and

upon the most efficient geometric configurations—courtyard type versus linear ribbon, for example—and height to achieve maximum density given specific environmental factors such as interior day-lighting, programmatic adjacencies, climate control, patterns of circulation, and distributions in land use.

59 Lawrence B. Anderson, *Massachusetts Institute of Technology Bulletin, Report of the President,* 1968, p. 32.

60 Anderson, *Report of the President,* 1968, p. 32.

61 John T. Howard, *Massachusetts Institute of Technology Bulletin. Report of the President* 1968, p. 41.

62 Charles L. Miller, *Massachusetts Institute of Technology Bulletin. Report of the President,* 1968, p. 491

63 Charles L. Miller, *Urban Systems Laboratory,* 1969-1979 Annual Report, AC 366, Box 1, Institute Archives and Special Collections, MIT Libraries, Cambridge, Massachusetts. See

advanced technologies.[62] In the next *Report* (1969-1970) on the USL Miller wrote that the Architecture Machine Group had put together a satellite facility where they would conduct experiments with the goal of realizing artificial design intelligence.[63] This interdisciplinary project brought together students from five different departments to investigate interaction among computers, humans, and the real world. The idea of human-machine, human-reality interaction connected to Miller's own queries about the differences between computers and engineers, or between human and machine uses.[64]

Human and machine interaction, as well as questions about the usefulness of computers to engineers, had been the topics of Miller's keynote address, "Man-Machine Communication in Civil Engineering," for the Third National Conference on Electronic Computation in 1963.[65] As head of the Institute's Department of Civil Engineering, Miller asked engineers to think beyond computers as mere enablers for rational problem solving and to explore the more complex issue of communication between computer and engineer. In his address Miller shifted the conversation from hardware or CAD application to code and terminology, establishing another distinction for the use for computing and design methods in architecture research.

At MIT, research into human and machine interface was, at least in the architecture department, Nicholas Negroponte's domain. His work connected to that of British cybernetician Gordon Pask, who from the mid-1960s onward attempted to make machines that could converse and improve over time or better put, intelligent machines that could learn. Negroponte's debt to Pask is mentioned in a paper published as part of the proceedings of a Design Research Society conference held at the University of Manchester in 1971.[66] The conference, organized around the idea of design participation, addressed the "undesirable effects of socio-technical formations" through a rather inclusive definition of participation as less authoritarian. Negroponte's paper speculates on the creation of intelligent environments capable of interacting with active users. He cites Pask's research on learning, and specifically, Pask's exploration of sensing and effecting devices able to recognize and respond to the environment. Following Pask, Negroponte's interest lay in developing an evolutionary model of the environment as a real-time dynamic that moved

references to design problem-solving, behaviors of buildings as well as to artificial design intelligence.

64 See Negroponte's version of Miller's view in *Architectural Design* (September 1969): 511. Both argue that computer codes should not be machine-oriented but user friendly. The shared goal is to make

machines able to learn and respond in a conversational style.

65 Miller, "Man-Machine Communication in Civil Engineering," Among the supporting references Miller cites co-authored works by Christopher Alexander and Marvin Manheim on the design of highway

interchanges, Ivan Sutherland, and other MIT based researchers. The turn to artificial intelligence in design methods is also influenced by Herbert A. Simon's lectures for the Karl Taylor Crompton Lectures at MIT in 1968. The lectures covered materials published in the book *The Sciences of the Artificial*

in the same year. In the mid-1970s March mentions influence by the psychological aspects of Herbert's work. See Bayazit, p. 19.

66 Nicholas Negroponte, "Aspects of Living in an Architecture Machine," in Nigel Cross, ed., *Design Participation*. Proceedings of the Design Research

beyond simulation or the probabilistic models of the LUBFS. William Mitchell also published research in the same Design Participation proceedings. He argued for computer-facilitated graphic representation that would make complex data comprehensible to non-specialist users and thus be user participation friendly. Mitchell's example paralleled work from the LUBFS, in which a model designed for specific performance criteria would test for or simulate optimal outcomes by responding to user-informed if/then inquiries.[67] The turn to user-driven simulation and intelligent environments aimed at empowering the user, as evidenced by these two reports, raised an obvious question about disciplinary expertise: was every user a designer?

Methods and Expertise: A Knowledge Producing Network

The first international meeting of the DMG convened in Cambridge, MA in June 1968. The conference received funding from the USL, MIT's Departments of Civil Engineering and Architecture, Harvard's Laboratory for Computer Graphics, and the Boston Center for Architecture. The roster of participants maps a network of mostly North American and British research practices, including those associated with first-generation methods— such as J. Christopher Jones, L. Bruce Archer, and Christopher Alexander—and those who, like Frank Duffy, were associated with the second generation.[68] The proceedings, titled *Emerging Methods in Environmental Design and Planning*, re-published Christopher Alexander's and Barry Poyner's MBPW and UC Berkeley-sponsored research, "The Atoms of Environmental Structure" despite the fact that some conference attendees had been its strongest critics.[69] MIT professor of civil engineering and later USL associate Marvin L. Manheim published a paper that proposed a "theoretical model of the design process" and argued for its operational implications for transport planning—essentially, applied theory. In 1966 Manheim had played an important role in establishing the DMG. The work published by young MIT architecture faculty appears nearly identical to what would be published a year later in the September 1969 issue of *Architectural Design*. Negroponte and collaborator Groisser address "man-machine" interaction through a graphical interface, "an evolutionary system or an intelligent system" they claimed required no expertise on the part of the user.[70] Not all participants relied on computing technology, and some argued for fuller definitions of the design process and systems thought when they were applied to

Society's Conference Manchester, September 1971 (London: Academy Editions, 1972), pp. 63-67. The event included proponents from first generation methods such as J. Christopher Jones and colleagues from the Design Research Laboratory at the Institute of Science and Technology at Manchester.

67 William Mitchell, "Experiments with Participation-Oriented Computer Systems," in *Design Participation: Proceedings of the Design Research Society's Conference Manchester, September 1971*, p.76. The program allows users to ask if/then and receive a response

from which to negotiate tradeoffs and engage in conflict resolution in search of a collaborative agreement in the design process. It makes information accessible and useful to all.

68 See Bayazit, "Investigating Design: A Review of Forty Years of Design Research," MIT

Department of Architecture sponsored J. Christopher Jones's travel to deliver the keynote address at the *Emerging Methods* conference. The editor identifies papers by Jones, Alexander with collaborator Barry Poyner, and Manheim as significant as well as one by Gerald Nadler titled

architecture. Still, the majority of papers are marked by an uncritical use of methodologies easily labeled as positivist. With only vague statements about current crises or lambastes of architects and planners for doing "little more than parry with these problems," most of the effort was defined by methodological and technical parameters.[71]

The divergence from the first-generation design methods' focus on technical processes to the second-generation's engagement with the socio-technical and second-order cybernetics began to take shape at the first EDRA conference held at Chapel Hill in 1969. The proceedings define the second generation's ambition as a "commitment to the evolution of the environment as an integral part of human systems" and makes well-rehearsed overtures to interdisciplinary design as a means by which knowledge can be increased and over-specialization prevented.[72] An essay contributed by Amos Rapoport of UC Berkeley fleshes out a more interrogatory approach to the word environment.[73] Negroponte's contribution, "Environmental Humanism through Robots," argues that computer-aided design should not occur without machine-intelligence and announces that at MIT they are beginning to build an ethical robot. Mitchell's "Switching on the Seven Lamps," (as mentioned earlier in this paper) dismisses Alexander's theory and challenges architects engaged with new technologies to develop a better understanding of user needs and to make computing power useful for architectural design. He calls the profession "socially irrelevant and intellectually bankrupt," and contends that neither research into methods nor the "redefinition" of the designer's role had proven adequate.[74] Perhaps most interesting at this stage of design computing was Mitchell's assertion that architectural expertise must include technical knowledge of the equipment. Mitchell asks whether architects should adopt practices borrowed from engineering and the social sciences, or whether they should create computer and technical interfaces compatible with discipline-specific needs. He would return to the issue of expertise and participatory design practice in a paper presented at the fourth EDRA conference of 1973. Re-published in the 1975 LUBFS conference proceedings, *Models and Systems in Architecture and Building*, "Vitruvius Computatus" asserted that, given the existing body of theoretical and technical literature concerning computer-facilitated design, computer systems should no longer "be regarded as formally neutral tools in the design process."[75] Here, Mitchell argued

"Engineering Research and Design in Socioeconomic Systems," which indicates the privileging of engineering methods in first generation DMG.

69 See for example, Francis Duffy and John Torrey, "A Progress Report on the Pattern Language," in *Emerging Methods in*

Environmental Design and Planning Proceedings of the Design Methods Group, pp. 261-277.

70 Also published in *Architectural Design* September 1969 and in the proceedings from the *Emerging Methods* conference were papers by Richard I. Krauss and

John R. Myer, "Design: A Case History," pp. 11-20 and William Porter, Katherine Lloyd and Aaron Fleisher, " DISCOURSE: A Language and System for Computer-Assisted City Design," pp. 92-104.

71 Moore, *Emerging Methods*, p. viii.

72 *EDRA* 1, p. v.

73 Amos Rapoport, "An Approach to the Study of Environmental Quality," *EDRA 1*, pp. 1-13. EDRA was founded as a forum for 'multidisciplinary' collaboration between scientists and environmental designers with the intent of forging coherence within the field. Rapoport was teaching at

that architectural expertise must be brought to design by means of computer-generated form and geometry. His interest lay with investigations of what "computer-aided design might imply for the character of architectural form."[76] The architectural use of computers would establish the specificity of design expertise. As exemplified by Mitchell's evolving argument, the distance between early design methods' pursuit of objective and analytical techniques and the social and disciplinary anxieties of the second generation clearly demarcated early architectural computing from computer-based architectural expertise.

Questions about design methods and expertise had been raised by British architects years earlier at the Portsmouth Design Methods conference. In 1967 the conference conveners could confidently claim that interdisciplinary design methods were not so much producing fruitful exchanges between disciplines as, simply, erasing boundaries. A year earlier in Cambridge MA the question of expertise among interdisciplinary practices was the subject of a less technically oriented conference organized by MIT architecture faculty.[77] Inventing the Future Environment brought together experts from various fields including planning, economics and business administration, social psychology and philosophy, history, and political science to discuss the ways in which planning—in the broadest sense of the word—might become a more interdisciplinary activity. The specter of real-world politics was raised, for in contrast to the gatherings of design methodologists in which many participants simply assumed their work was interdisciplinary, objective and inclusive, these scholars and architects were much more skeptical about the possibility of bridging disciplines. In particular, they pointed to the gap between assessing the unaccountable creative aspects of design and the quantitative approaches of the social and hard sciences. Nevertheless the conference participants did share some basic assumptions, including a belief in the progressive and democratic nature of participatory-user informed design. In the conference proceedings, tellingly titled Planning for Diversity and Choice, Dean Lawrence Anderson argues that the design professions need to share expertise, collaborate with planners and social psychologists, and allow for broader participation in decision-making.[78] Doing so would enable planning processes to become more democratic. Stanford Anderson remarked upon the ubiquity of the word "environment" with the sharp observation that the "now . . . popular word in architectural circles, is seen as enlarging the traditional

UC Berkeley at the time and had previously taught at University of Melbourne where Mitchell had graduated from architecture. Peter Eisenman also presented at the conference.
74 Mitchell, "Switching on the Seven Lamps," p. 123.
75 William Mitchell, "Vitruvius Computatus," in

Models and Building ed., Dean Hawkes (Hornby, Lancaster: Construction Press, Ltd., 1975), p. 59.
76 Mitchell, "Vitruvius Computatus," p. 53.
77 See Stanford Anderson, "Introduction," Planning for Diversity and Choice. Possible Futures and their Relationship to Man-

Controlled Environments (Cambridge, MA: MIT Press, 1968), p. 3. The conference was convened with the intent of providing information to a joint American Institute of Architects and Princeton University research project examining architectural education.

78 See "Response from the Architects," Planning for Diversity and Choice, pp. 285-304.

meaning of architecture and planning so as to include social, temporal, and other non-visual, nonmaterial concerns."[79] For Anderson, the word environment served as a palliative for interdisciplinary aspirations while telegraphing the complexity of the built world. The MIT research practices published in the May 1969 issue of *Architectural Design* appear fully immersed in the mechanisms of the research university, unquestioningly influenced by the social science model which transformed disciplines and overall institutional organization, and which pressured all disciplines to emulate the rigor of science.

Ten years later, *Architectural Design* dedicated its entire May 1976 issue to systems thinking in architecture. The editorial, "What Ever Happened to the Systems Approach?," acknowledged that systems no longer enjoyed the status it once held. Blame is leveled at technocratic hubris, specifically finding fault with "American functionalism" for transforming a conceptual approach to analysis and problem solving into a universal logic attached to particular techniques.[80] The editor writes that "[T]he systems approach was the flame of inspiration that propelled the white-heat technology of the 60's." The architectural practices of Cedric Price, Walter Segal, Buckminster Fuller, and Farrell Grimshaw are favorably characterized for their use of systems methods as a means of addressing architectural problems holistically. In these practices, as in first generation design methods, the attraction to systems theory and related technical modalities was justified by the hope that it might capture and describe the complex conditions of the built environment. The differences among various applications of systems methods, and in particular those cast in terms of operational research and behaviorism, or those focused on supposedly neutral and scientifically accountable procedures, were ideological. Even within the presumed interdisciplinary associations of technique-oriented research, little had been agreed upon. While most architectural researchers borrowed from the engineering and social sciences, employed computers, crossed paths at conferences and in publications, they can only loosely be gathered under an inclusive rubric such as Design Methods.[81] The use of "systems" in research at Cambridge UK was distinct from its use at the Bartlett under Llewelyn-Davies and distinct again from its presence in the multiple initiatives housed within MIT. The various camps had rather fluid allegiances. Individual researchers moved between the academic locations that would enable their research through funding

79 Stanford Anderson, "Summary: Planning for Fullness," *Planning for Diversity and Choice*, p. 306.

80 Andrew Rabeneck, "Whatever Happened to the Systems Approach?" *Architectural Design* (May 1976): unpaginated.

81 See Alise Upitis, *Nature Normative: The Design Methods Movement, 1944-1967* (Dissertation Massachusetts Institute of Technology, 2008). For the details on the founding of the center for *Land Use and Built Forms Studies* see Altino João Magalhães Rocha, *Architecture Theory 1960-1980. Emergence of a Computational Perspective* (Dissertation Massachusetts Institute of Technology, 2004). Also see Sean Blair Keller, *Systems Aesthetics: Architectural Theory at the University of Cambridge* (Dissertation Harvard University, Ann Arbor, MI, May 2005).

```
SPA ← LIST[ n]                (1 list element for each space)
    SPA [ n] ← ARRAY[6]       (6 basic pieces of information stored for each space)
        [ n][ 1]:  space name
            [ 2] ← ARRAY[3] (dimensions)
            [ 2][ 1]:  length
                [ 2]:  width
                [ 3]:  height
            [ 3] ← ARRAY[3]    (global location coordinates)
            [ 3][ 1]:  x-coordinate
                [ 2]:  y-coordinate
                [ 3]:  z-coordinate
            [ 4]:  floor area
            [ 5]:  volume
            [ 6] ← ARRAY[12]   (surface identifiers)
            [ 6][ 1]:  north face interior
                [ 2]:  east face interior
                [ 3]:  south face interior
                [ 4]:  west face interior
                [ 5]:  floor interior
                [ 6]:  ceiling interior
                [ 7]:  north face exterior
                [ 8]:  east face exterior
                [ 9]:  south face exterior
                [10]:  west face exterior
                [11]:  floor exterior
                [12]:  ceiling exterior
    SPA [n+1] etc.
SUR ← LIST[ m]                (1 list element for each type of surface)
    SUR [ m] ← ARRAY[3]       (3 basic pieces of information per surface)
        [ m][ 1] ← ARRAY[2]  (dimensions)
            [ 1][ 1]:  length
                [ 2]:  width
            [ 2]:  identifier of material section
            [ 3] ← LIST[p] (1 list element for each opening in the surface)
            [ 3][ p]    ARRAY[2] (2 pieces of information per opening in the surface)
                [ p][ 1]:  identifier of opening
                    [ 2] ← ARRAY[2]   (location of opening in the surface)
                    [ 2][ 1]:  relative x-coordinate
                        [ 2]:  relative y-coordinate
    SUR [m+1] etc.
OPE ← LIST[ q]                (1 list element for each type of opening)
    OPE [ q] ← ARRAY[ 3]      (3 pieces of information per opening)
        [ q][ 1]:  identifier of type of opening
            [ 2] ← ARRAY[2] (dimensions)
            [ 2][ 1]:  length
                [ 2]:  width
            [ 3]:  identifier of material section
    OPE [q+1] etc.
```

Figure 4:   Simple list structure for describing the geometry of a building

William J. Mitchell, "Virtuvius Computatus," in Dean Hawkes, *Models and Systems in Architecture and Building*, Land Use and Built Form Studies, Conference Proceedings No. 2. (The Construction Press, 1975).

```
SPA[ 1][ 1]:  "OFFICE"          SUR[ 3][ 1][ 1]:  15
    [ 2][ 1]:  15                       [ 2]:  12
        [ 2]:  10                   [ 2]:  "WALL SECTION A"
        [ 3]:  12                   [ 3][ 1][ 1]:   1
    [ 3][ 1]:   0                           [ 2][ 1]:   5
        [ 2]:  10                               [ 2]:   3
        [ 3]:   0                [ 4][ 1][ 1]:  10
    [ 4]:    150                        [ 2]:  12
    [ 5]:   1800                    [ 2]:  "WALL SECTION A"
    [ 6][ 1]:   1                   [ 3][ 1][ 1]:   2
        [ 2]:   2                           [ 2][ 1]:   5
        [ 3]:   3                               [ 2]:   0
        [ 4]:   4                [ 5][ 1][ 1]:  15
        [ 5]:   5                        [ 2]:  10
        [ 6]:   6                    [ 2]:  "FLOOR SECTION A"
        [ 7]:   7                    [ 3]   LIST[ 0]
        [ 8]:   8                [ 6][ 1][ 1]:  15
        [ 9]:   9                        [ 2]:  10
       [10]:  "NONE"                 [ 2]:  "CEILING SECTION A"
       [11]:  10                     [ 3]   LIST[ 0]
       [12]:  11                [ 7][ 1][ 1]:  15
  [ 2][ 1]:  "WAITING ROOM"             [ 2]:  12
    [ 2][ 1]:  10                   [ 2]:  "WALL SECTION B"
        [ 2]:  22                   [ 3]   LIST[ 0]
        [ 3]:  15                [ 8][ 1][ 1]:  10
    [ 3][ 1]:  15                       [ 2]:  12
        [ 2]:   0                   [ 2]:  "WALL SECTION B"
        [ 3]:   1.5                 [ 3]   LIST[ 0]
    [ 4]:    220                [ 9][ 1][ 1]:  15
    [ 5]:   3300                        [ 2]:  12
    [ 6][ 1]:  12                   [ 3][ 1][ 1]:   1
        [ 2]:  13                           [ 2][ 1]:   6
        [ 3]:  12                               [ 2]:   3
        [ 4]:  14               [10][ 1][ 1]:  15
        [ 5]:  15                        [ 2]:  10
        [ 6]:  16                    [ 2]:  "FLOOR SECTION B"
        [ 7]:  17                    [ 3]   LIST[ 0]
        [ 8]:  18               [11][ 1][ 1]:  15
        [ 9]:  17                        [ 2]:  10
       [10]:  19                     [ 2]:  "CEILING SECTION B"
       [11]:  20                     [ 3]   LIST[ 0]
       [12]:  21               [12][ 1][ 1]:  10
SUR[ 1][ 1][ 1]:  15                    [ 2]:  15
        [ 2]:  12                   [ 2]:  "WALL SECTION A"
    [ 2]:  "WALL SECTION A"         [ 3]   LIST[ 0]
    [ 3]   LIST[ 0]          [13][ 1][ 1]:  22
  [ 2][ 1][ 1]:  10                     [ 2]:  15
        [ 2]:  12                   [ 2]:  "WALL SECTION A"
    [ 2]:  "WALL SECTION A"         [ 3][ 1][ 1]: ·2
    [ 3]:  LIST[ 0]   continued         [ 2][ 1]:  14.3 continued
```

Figure 5:   Description of the building illustrated in Figure 3

opportunities, equipment, and expertise. Within the socio-economic imperatives of the postwar research university and the advance of technical expertise, the two Cambridges performed as nodes in a network of transatlantic knowledge production and exchange.

Epilogue

In 1966 an article published in *FORM* (a short-lived British magazine), Crispin Gray, then of the Cambridge Mathematics Laboratory and later a researcher at the LUBFS, enthusiastically discussed the advances in computer technology at MIT.[82] The article is up-to-date and well informed. This suggests the importance of the US and the Institute in the minds of British computer-oriented design researchers. Gray discusses the early development of the conversational mode at MIT and Ivan Sutherland's research on graphical input at the Lincoln Laboratory and Electronic Systems Laboratory. Alexander's work at Berkeley is briefly mentioned as an example of attempts to rationalize intuitive procedures through computerization of the design process. Already in the mid-1960s Gray marks the difference between design methods purists and inquisitive architects when he writes that the computer will not replace the designer; rather it will enable creativity. Gray also remarks upon the slow progress of such efforts in Britain while noting that industry had begun to take interest in CAD development and CAD groups at Cambridge and London Universities.

Gray's imputation that research in the UK had fallen behind that of the US does not stand up to scrutiny. Certainly, computer based architectural research was developing along different lines in the UK, but, as the Ford Foundation patronage of urban centers attests, a concern with falling behind was experienced on both sides. After all, as Gray notes, mathematician-physicist Maurice Wilkes returned to the University of Cambridge after a visit to University of Pennsylvania's Moore School of Engineering. At Cambridge he built, in 1949, the EDSAC I, the first stored computer program, and in 1951 he developed the concept of microprogramming. In the 1960s experimental attempts in interactive art and responsive environments brought engineers, cybernetic experts such as Pask and artists together in the London art scene. Price's Fun Palace, imagined as a responsive environment, and the Potteries Thinkbelt project, which speculated upon the delivery of higher education in the UK, are the products of such interdisciplinary collaborations.

82 Crispin Gray, "Computers and Design," *FORM* (1966): 19-22. Philip Steadman who was integral to advancing mathematical research at the *LUBFS* was co-editor and co-publisher of *FORM* with Stephen Bann and Mike Weaver. The magazine published art and literary criticism and various avant-garde subjects. Steadman and Bann later collaborate on the catalogue for an Arts Council supported exhibition of 1972-3 titled Systems. Steadman recalled having been much inspired by a lecture Ivan Sutherland gave at Cambridge University in the early 1960s. (London, March 17th, 2009).

83 The *Potteries Thinkbelt* project is an architectural response to the problem of planning for higher education. Proposed as an educational institute dedicated to science and technology the PTb project re-uses the infrastructural remains of the 19th century industrial revolution for a 20th-century university dedicated to science and technology.

The Potteries Thinkbelt, one of the few illustrations accompanying the MIT conference proceedings *Planning for Diversity and Choice*, is among other things a proposal that addresses the imperatives pressed upon higher education during this period: for faculty as teachers, to make education in science and technology a priority and available to more students and, for faculty as researchers, to privilege research-oriented and applied objectives.[83]

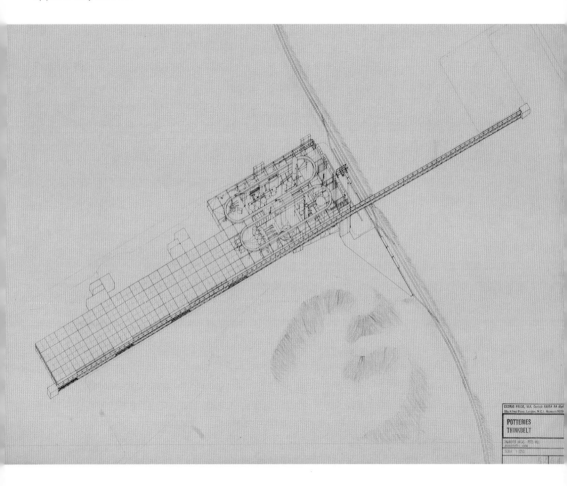

Cedric Price, *Potteries Thinkbelt*: axonometric view, 1963-1967. Diazotype, 59.3 x 84.1 cm. Cedric Price fonds, Collection Centre Canadien d'Architecture/ Canadian Centre for Architecture, Montréal.

BRENDAN D. MORAN

Toward a "Nation of Universities"
Architecture and Planning Education at MIT circa the 1940s

Two years before stepping down as dean of MIT's architecture school to take up an analogous position at the University of California Berkeley in 1950, William W. Wurster addressed the Regional Meeting of the Southeastern Schools of Architecture on the topic of "New Directions in Architectural Education." The gathering, attended by thirty-five architectural educators from seven schools, was one of six such meetings held across the nation that academic year. Initiated through a motion passed at the 1947 annual meeting of the Association of Collegiate Schools of Architecture (ACSA), such regional meetings were part of a postwar push to strengthen connections across the nation's network of institutions.[1] During the program's first year, seven meetings had been held, attended by a total of just under 250 teachers from nearly three-quarters of the architecture schools nationwide. As this was more than three times the number of instructors present at that year's annual national meeting, the initiative clearly succeeded in increasing exchange among educators from different schools and different North American regions.

Wurster's talk argued that thinking in terms of the uniqueness and specificity of American regions held continued importance for architectural educators, primarily by offering new educational horizons for the postwar era. Wurster stated that it "might be … fruitful to compare each of our [nation's] states to a small country, which gives the proper scale, and we thus see the importance of regional autonomy."[2] This autonomy registered most clearly for Wurster in the influence of program and site specificity on architectural design; yet his comments also nodded to the ACSA's recent rejection of a motion to establish a central body to oversee and regularize design programs (architectural briefs) used across the nation.[3] He added, however, that construction technologies were guided by quite different dynamics than those influencing program and site, stating that "the building arts have always rightly been international and inter-continental in influence." This differentiation

1 *Journal of Architectural Education* 3, Proceedings of the 34th Annual Convention (Autumn 1948), 6.

2 William Wurster, "New Directions in Architectural Education," *Journal of Architectural Education* 4, The Regional Meeting of the Southeastern Schools of Architecture (Winter 1949), 3.

3 Buford L. Pickens, "Regional Possibilities in Design and Construction," *Journal of Architectural Education* 4, The Regional Meeting of the Southeastern Schools of Architecture (Winter 1949), 20-23.

4 Lewis Mumford, "The Sky Line: Status Quo," *The New Yorker* 23, no. 34 (11 October 1947), 106-109.

between what is universal and what is local (or regional) about architectural knowledge points to a fundamental understanding of the field's knowledge as constituted by multiplicity. When it came to stylistic characteristics, however, the primary new direction referenced in the title of Wurster's talk's was the focusing of education on aspects of local design traditions and the specific efforts of firms based in the school's region. In defending this proposal, he argued that "[r]egional difference came about naturally—not by straining for local novelty." In the process, regional architects eschewed both emulation of an "International Style" and stylistic invention merely for its own sake, favoring instead an adherence to regional character and patterns.

Not coincidentally, only a few years before Dean Wurster delivered his "New Directions" address, he had been singled out by the critic Lewis Mumford as a modern architect working in a regionalist idiom. The piece ostensibly proposed the existence of a contemporary "Bay Regional style" in Northern California, and identified Wurster as its most prominent contemporary practitioner. Yet instead of merely classifying his work or launching a new label, Mumford's column argued more broadly that architectural modernism and regionalist perspectives were each entering a transformative phase, one that was bringing them at this moment into alignment. Mumford linked a current resurgence of interest in the "personalism of Frank Lloyd Wright" to a growing wave of dissatisfaction among American architects with interwar International-style modernism. He furthermore proposed that Wurster—like Bay Area designers John Galen Howard and Bernard Maybeck before him—realized in his designs "a free yet unobtrusive expression of the terrain, the climate, and the way of life on the Coast." In short, Mumford valorized Wurster as a modernist architect who designed stylishly inconspicuous yet comfortable homes, and did so without subscribing to any doctrinaire modernist "functionalism."

Yet the piece quixotically also proposed that the central merit of this regionalist architectural style was the "meeting of the Oriental and Occidental architectural traditions" within it, productive of a synthesis that resulted in a "far more truly universal style than the so-called international style of the nineteen-thirties." Given Mumford's staunch, career-long espousal of aesthetic modernism as a progressive social force, this particular assessment reveals not just an ambivalence over the canonical nature of designs employing white rectangular forms, such as those championed over a decade earlier in the Museum of Modern Art's "International Style" exhibition. It reveals an ambiguity about what precisely were the proper bases for prognoses regarding architectural styles and new postwar directions for the field. By allowing for "regional adaptations and modifications," the synthesis Mumford posited implied that a significant weakness of functionalist modernism was an inflexibility not just in its appearance but in its ability to adapt and, ultimately, to transform. Even more outrageously, Mumford additionally claimed that "[s]ome of the best examples of this at once native and universal tradition are being built in New England, far from the coast of California."[4]

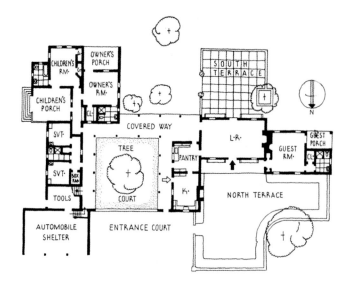

William W. Wurster,
of Wurster, Bernardi,
and Emmons, Donald
Gregory House, Scotts
Valley, California 1932.
Published in *Architectural
Forum*, May 1936. Photo:
Roger Sturtevant.

As Mumford was the leading architectural figure within America's interwar regionalist movement, this positing of an emergent, non-universal, yet easily traveling architectural style soon after WWII suggests that he and the regionalist cause he had earlier championed was itself moving in new directions at this time. More to the point, together these events suggest that after 1945, interest in American regions (and regionalism more generally) within architectural discourse extended earlier debates, though they did so within a substantially altered world, an alteration in part attributable to the second major global conflagration since the century's start. But on another front, the change can also be linked to an emerging new paradigm affecting the collection of colleges and universities spread throughout the country—a newly-revitalized national network of postwar research universities.

The National Network of Research Universities and a "Nation of Cities"

If regionalism is recognized as a discourse that focuses on place and place-making, it necessarily must take place somewhere; and its primary milieu before WWII had been the space of American institutions of higher learning, understood as no particular place yet many places simultaneously. Subject to significant transformations during the latter half of the Great Depression, the nation's set of universities crystallized as a distributed network of linked departments, divisions, and schools during the interwar period.[5] Regionalist culture had blossomed during this same era, and the overlap and interactions between the two circa WWII constitute a rich weave.

As the interwar era came to a close, regionalist polemics were mitigated by the wellspring of nationalist fervor generated during the war effort, and new directions loomed. Historian Robert L. Dorman has argued that "the 'playing out' of the regionalist movement into the postwar period" constituted "a dwindling that was also reflected by an equally telling change in tone," in which the formerly central conception of regions "f[e]ll away as its usefulness was spent or transcended."[6] Although largely constituted by analysis fostered in both the popular press and the academic environment, regionalist thought in the latter context—unlike the former—had increasingly linked what had been relatively disassociated and distinct university divisions in a prescient interdisciplinary manner. Though the movement tended to grant high esteem to creative efforts produced outside the academy, for the

5 Roger L. Geiger, *Research and Relevant Knowledge: American Research Universities since World War II* (New York: Oxford University Press, 1993).

6 Robert L. Dorman, *Revolt of the Provinces: The Regionalist Movement in America, 1920-1945* (Chapel Hill: University of North Carolina Press, 1992), 307-8. By 1960, the question "is regionalism dead?" was increasingly entertained within the academic environment; see George B. Tindall, "Introduction: The Status and Future of Regionalism—A Symposium," *The Journal of Southern History* 26, no. 1 (February 1960), 22-24.

7 Numerous historical studies, including Dorman's cited above, as Dewey W. Grantham's *The Regional Imagination: the South and Recent American History* (Nashville: Vanderbilt University Press, 1979), *The South in Modern America: a Region at Odds* (New York: Harper Collins, 1994), and

most part it consisted of a burgeoning of journalistic and scholarly work that championed and examined such production.[7] Not incidentally, these developments were taking place at precisely the moment when research in America found itself newly ensconced in a pluralist educational system whose financial support and enthusiasm for research markedly exceeded that of earlier eras.[8] Thus, as the first wave of American regionalism begat a second, the very spatial parameters highlighted by regionalist discourse—networks of aligned producers and consumers distributed across large areas in differing settlement patterns—were themselves becoming significant parametric forces which were reshaping the university context as a nation of universities emerged within the nation of states.

In light of this, investigation of the regionalist movement as a historical phenomena specifies the significant interface between two all but incommensurate American social and spatial heuristics: on the one hand, regionalism's primary nemesis, the large metropolitan environment or big city; and on the other, the university environment itself. The interwar flowering of a regionalist movement depended upon claims that an important entity shaping the country's development had been overlooked: those large, inter-state areas that possessed enough socio-economic cohesion to garner distinct identities, encompassing patterns of cultural and economic production as well as practices of political governance. This conceptual object was largely constructed to counter the importance and central dominance of certain larger cities within the nation's psyche, such as New York, Chicago, San Francisco, Boston and Philadelphia.[9] The movement's apparent unity, though, was largely dependent upon a shared minoritarian perspective inflected toward the hinterlands and valorizing local cultures against rising metropolitan and cosmopolitan varieties. In the process, disparate interests and ideological tendencies across the political spectrum were masked.

Admitting that American universities—located equally often in metropolitan centers and bucolic rural settings alike, as well as in between—are in effect switching stations within a national network constituted by such institutions necessitates reflecting on the parallels between cities and universities, and how these parallels have been understood at certain moments. During the heyday of regionalism—basically the 1920s through the early 1950s—cities all but dominated the nation's cultural imaginary; after 1940, increased

others, focus primarily on university scholarship over journalistic criticism, in part as a register of the movement's legitimacy and depth of analysis. For an anthology that frames the overlaps between the larger regionalist movement and architectural criticism and research. See Vincent B. Canizaro,

Architectural Regionalism: Collected Writings on Place, Identity, Modernity, and Tradition (New York: Princeton Architectural Press, 2007).
8 Increased emphasis on research was made possible through an ongoing process of normalizing protocols that linked institutions to other institutions, in

particular developments that had been taking place since the late nineteenth century: standardization of degree sequences and requirements, establishment of peer- reviewed disciplinary publications, and increased ease of traffic between like departments at different institutions. See Roger

L. Gieger, *To Advance Knowledge: the Growth of American Research Universities, 1900-1940* (New York: Oxford University Press, 1986).
9 The formation of a "movement" began as early as the 1920s, although it took some time for disparate interests nationally to coalesce.

suburban development made visible previously hidden aspects of territorial and national settlement patterns, at precisely the moment the national network of research universities came into clear focus. Significantly, recognition of the American university system's postwar networked logic as constituent of regionalist discourse neither accompanied its interwar rise nor its early postwar reconfiguration. Because of this, while the city as an object of knowledge became far more comfortably ensconced within the university during the interwar era, rigorous analysis of what David Gelfand characterizes as a "nation of cities" burgeoned only around WWII. Examination of interconnections between the network of American cities and the national network of research universities went unnoticed even longer, until the latter postwar era.[10]

Not least among the fields in which this played out were those whose primary knowledge base encompassed the built environment of cities, suburbs, rural areas, and geographical or cultural regions. Though eventually the postwar era witnessed regionalism's extension into sophisticated ecological and environmental studies, urban studies, and in particular urban planning, the primary context for such explorations was at first in established educational programs for training architects and city planners.[11] This essay will examine one such instructional locale during the 1940s, namely, the School of Architecture and Planning at the Massachusetts Institute of Technology. It will do so primarily by contrasting the two figures linked in the anecdotes with which it began: William Wurster, who as dean of the School of Architecture and Planning at MIT between 1944 and 1950 assisted in shaping its postwar direction; and Lewis Mumford, one of the first individuals Wurster invited to offer seminars on urban and architectural history at the School after arriving.[12] Additionally, city planner Frederick J. Adams plays a supporting role in the recounted events, as well as in others transpiring before and after Wurster's tenure; it was largely Adams's vision of planning education, in tandem with that of Wurster, that charted new paths taken during this period. Concentrating on the activity of these figures traces an important thread in regionalism's postwar unraveling: namely, an implicit regionalist theory at work in practice amidst the networked set of spatial relations available within the decentralized American system of higher education.

Dorman claims the harbinger of this was publication of the anthology *Civilization in the United States: an Inquiry by Thirty Americans*, ed. Harold E. Stearns (New York: Harcourt, Brace & Co., 1922); see Dorman, Revolt, 20. These five cities ranked as the densest conurbations of over half a million inhabitants

in America as of the 1950 Census; they constituted the primary locus of American modernist aesthetic practices, though by no means the only such locations.

10 Mark I. Gelfand, *A Nation of Cities: The Federal Government and Urban America, 1933-1965* (New York: Oxford University Press, 1975).

11 The 1920s founding of the Regional Planning Association of America, initiated by architect Clarance Stein, conservationist Benton MacKaye, Mumford and others, was a significant pioneering effort to integrate physical and social planning with ecological concerns. Carl Sussman, *Planning

the Fourth Migration: the Neglected Vision of the Regional Planning Association of America* (Cambridge: MIT Press, 1976).

12 During his nearly six-year stint at MIT, Wurster served as Dean, while also serving as Head of the Department of Architecture from 1944 until 1948, when Lawrence

Wurster as a Regional Modernist and Planning Educator

MIT's Department of City Planning, established in 1942 within the School of Architecture, played a central role in securing a shift away from conceptions of city and regional planning and toward what was after 1940 increasingly labeled urban planning—or, as it had become known by the late 1960's, merely planning.[13] An eponymous department inaugurated six years later at the University of California Berkeley also contributed to this transformation; as Wurster left his deanship at MIT's architecture school to take the helm at Berkeley soon after its department was inaugurated, the two institutions are clearly linked by his biography. Both participated in shifts that during the postwar era would reconfigure the importance of planning education within architecture schools across the nation, in turn altering the role design schools played within the larger universities that housed them.

Wurster's two administrative perches—on both American coasts—inflect his status as a regionalist figure, pre- or post-WWII, while constituting an alternative subject position for the architect as a kind of pedagogical planner or designer. Clearly his reputation as an architect rests on his myriad realized works, nearly all domestic projects, among them the 1928 Gregory Farmhouse at Scotts Valley and the 1940 Reynolds House in Gilroy. Historian David Gebhard describes them as embodying a "soft modernism," an appellation that views Wurster's work as offering clean, modernist designs, which abstract the forms of earlier styles without taking a hard line as regards modernist imagery, particularly the machine aesthetic.[14] In line with Mumford's 1947 assessment already cited, this perspective on Wurster's significance downplays his nearly two-decade long career as an educational administrator.[15]

Despite its partially happenstance origins, Wurster's administrative career clearly links earlier city planning education to postwar urban planning. At the age of forty-seven, less than three years after marrying housing advocate Catherine Bauer in 1940, Wurster took a leave of absence from his practice to attend Harvard University's Graduate School of Design on a one-year Wheelwright Fellowship. His impetus was a desire to study city planning, which during his professional training twenty-five years earlier was not yet included as a specialization anywhere in the country; by the start of WWII, however,

Anderson succeeded him in the post.

13 Although apparently first used in the 1920s, the term became a professional or academic appellation in the following decade. Among others, see Charles W. Eliot, 2nd, "New Approaches to Urban Planning," *American Planning and Civic Annual*, ed. Harlean James

(Harrisburg: Mount Pleasant Press, 1935): 304-7.

14 Wurster attended the architecture department around WWI, when it was still relatively new and instruction was heavily influenced by pedagogical practices imported from the French École des Beaux Arts. Graduating in 1919, he

worked for Delano and Aldrich in New York City, then opened his own architectural practice in 1926. David Gebhard, "William Wurster and his California Contemporaries: The Idea of Regionalism and Soft Modernism," in *An Everyday Modernism: the Houses of William Wurster*, ed. Marc Treib (Berkeley:

University of California Press, 1995), 164-83.

15 Of eight essays included in the catalogue of a late twentieth-century exhibition devoted to Wurster, none is devoted exclusively to his role as an educator or administrator. See Treib, *Everyday*.

it had become an autonomous degree offered in numerous institutions nationwide. Though Wurster intended his return to academia to be a mere mid-career break, prompted by a slow-down of commissions as a result of the war and an enthusiasm for contemporary social planning issues sparked by his relationship with Bauer, he was to spend seven years at MIT and thirteen at Berkeley, shaping both of their architecture schools through an innovative emphasis on the importance of social and environmental forces within professional training and formation.[16]

Reynolds House, in *Architectural Record* 90, no.1, July 1941.

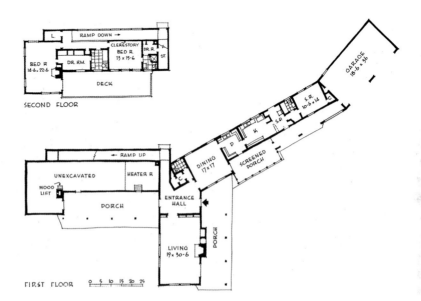

Consequently, the grant that allowed Wurster to return to academia ultimately facilitated a kind of mid-career disciplinary and professional reprogramming, one that led to Wurster's crowning achievement: his molding of UC Berkeley's College of Environmental Design over the course of the 1950s. Inaugurated at the close of the decade, through an integration of the university's architecture, landscape architecture and planning departments, this development came nearly a generation after Harvard famously united its three corresponding divisions into the Graduate School of Design.

It also amounted to a re-calibration of his significant actions taken during his earlier tenure at MIT. Was it Wurster who had changed, though; or, in the face of an altered inter-institutional field, had the terms of interdisciplinarity shifted to such a degree that earlier certainties were no longer reliable? Whereas in the 1930s the rubric "design" united disparate university divisions under a clarion call for a modern rather than traditional outlook toward the built environment, later use of the term "environment" registered a reconfiguration of American modernism's ambivalent relationship to a progressive social agenda, one in part determined by New Deal efforts to initiate regional planning at the federal level. Yet whereas the regionalism behind such planning efforts implied a certain ambivalence about the modern metropolis, American modernism—especially that which emulated the so-called "International Style" of the 1920s and 1930s—clearly pinned its aspirations on the metropolis, rather than the region. If modernism's political agenda was at times vague, regionalism's corresponding valence was more clearly minoritarian and egalitarian; however, the shift from design to environment fractured this relationship.

In addition, the shift in terminology from design to environmental design cued an incipient recognition of design as one particular expertise among those shared by the increasing panoply of professionals needed to manage America's metropolitan environs. In doing so, it glossed over an elided middle term: regional planning, employed from the 1920s through the 1940s to indicate a particular view of the intersection of city planning's physical concerns with larger social and economic planning. Moreover, while city planning as initiated at Harvard depended primarily upon metropolitan physical planning, by the late 1950s Berkeley along with numerous other schools were treating planning—with all modifiers dropped—

16 His office was closed on January 1st 1943, but had reopened by the end of WWII in a reconfigured form.

as denotative of a form of policy advising and administrative activity not restricted merely to modification of the built environment. Instead, the integration of such activity within a nested set of related concerns (political, economic, social, managerial, etc.) paralleled a new understanding of the linkages between academic departments, divisions (professional schools and the like), and institutions across the nation. If regionalism had a legacy in the postwar university, it was clearly dependent upon its activation of this dynamic.

Interwar Planning and American Regionalism

Before turning to events from the 1940s at MIT, a few significant points about the role of regionalist thought within city planning culture should be clarified. The nascent culture of planning that emerged during WWII traced its origins to 1930s city and regional planning circles, and beyond that, to certain threads within the regionalist movement. During the 1920s, a number of significant advocates of regional planning had called for what they termed the "regional city," among them Lewis Mumford and leading British Town Planning figure Thomas Adams, father of MIT's Frederick Adams.[17] Such an entity differed from the metropolis in that it had a primarily local role within production and exchange networks, as opposed to the more far reaching scope of the metropolis. Through the effort of these figures, drawing attention to a number of perspectives on certain aspects of contemporary life, regional planning was proposed as a vital and necessary social reform effort. At the same time, their undertakings provided a means for applying sociological research methods toward the calculation and calibration of precise knowledge about American urban

Lewis Mumford lecturing at MIT, n.d..

17 Within American social planning efforts, the activity of both helped shape fledgling professional and disciplinary understanding of regional planning. While Mumford was instrumental in the 1923 formation of the Regional Planning Association of America (RPAA), Thomas was the key figure responsible for stewarding to completion a regional plan for the New York City metropolitan area that commenced the same year, sponsored by the Russell Sage Foundation.

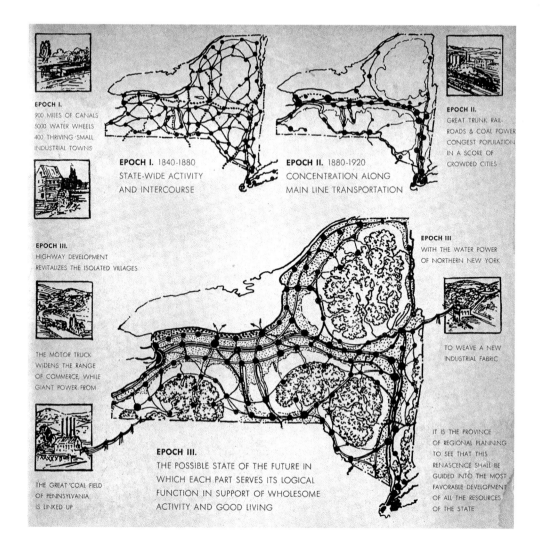

EPOCH I.
900 MILES OF CANALS
5000 WATER WHEELS
400 THRIVING SMALL
INDUSTRIAL TOWNS

EPOCH I. 1840-1880
STATE-WIDE ACTIVITY
AND INTERCOURSE

EPOCH II. 1880-1920
CONCENTRATION ALONG
MAIN LINE TRANSPORTATION

EPOCH II.
GREAT TRUNK RAIL-
ROADS & COAL POWER
CONGEST POPULATION
IN A SCORE OF
CROWDED CITIES

EPOCH III.
HIGHWAY DEVELOPMENT
REVITALIZES THE ISOLATED VILLAGES

EPOCH III
WITH THE WATER POWER
OF NORTHERN NEW YORK

THE MOTOR TRUCK
WIDENS THE RANGE
OF COMMERCE, WHILE
GIANT POWER FROM

TO WEAVE A NEW
INDUSTRIAL FABRIC

EPOCH III.
THE POSSIBLE STATE OF THE FUTURE IN
WHICH EACH PART SERVES ITS LOGICAL
FUNCTION IN SUPPORT OF WHOLESOME
ACTIVITY AND GOOD LIVING

THE GREAT COAL FIELD
OF PENNSYLVANIA
IS LINKED UP

IT IS THE PROVINCE
OF REGIONAL PLANNING
TO SEE THAT THIS
RENASCENCE SHALL BE
GUIDED INTO THE MOST
FAVORABLE DEVELOPMENT
OF ALL THE RESOURCES
OF THE STATE

"Maps of New York State, included in the New York
State Commission of Housing and Regional Planning's 1926 report; illustration shows two earlier
stages leading toward a third, future, decentralization,
achieved through realizing regional cities." From
Lewis Mumford, *The Culture of Cities*, (New York:
Harcourt & Brace, 1938).

environments and their relation to the rest of the country's territory. Thus, through theorization and investigation of a potentially "regional" city, a professional occupation—planner—and an academic appellation—urban research—were simultaneously born.

While on the one hand the qualifier "regional" clarified the relationship of such cities to the region or larger territory surrounding it, on the other it specified how the social fact of a region could be scientifically delimited and accurately described—namely through the gathering of relevant sociological, economic and ecological data. In the process, it served as an interface between a culture of planning that advocated for (or dissented against) the fruitful amelioration of metropolitan ills, and a regionalist academic culture that valued the information upon which planning efforts depended as a new and valuable form of concrete knowledge.

In a 1931 address given at a conference that gathered regionalists of all stripes from across the nation, Mumford claimed that the term "regional planning" designated neither "city planning on a large scale," nor "metropolitan planning." Instead, it described efforts seeking "to bring every capacity of the region up to its fullest state of cultivation or use."[18] For Mumford, perhaps the most significant (and until then largely unexamined) aspects upon which this optimization depended were of an economic nature. Yet only a few years earlier, he had noted that the primary knowledge necessary to understand a region were its culture, human geography, and economic activity, commencing with that statement an augmentation of the cultural origins of regionalist discourse with what during the 1930s would be its primary area of expansion, i.e., the social sciences of economics and sociology.[19]

In this regard, Mumford shared the sentiments of increasing numbers of city planning figures across the nation at the time, who recognized that the design of cities and the planning of regions, despite clear overlaps and similarities, were not entirely aligned endeavors. While the former was an undertaking with necessarily physical parameters, the latter increasingly was not. By the 1930s, municipal planning, which crystallized around the end of WWI within the city governments of New York and Chicago, was beginning to compete for financial and manpower resources with the physical planning divisions established earlier. Yet because regionalist interest in American cities was focused as much

18 Lewis Mumford, "Regional Planning" (1931); reprinted in Canizaro, *Architectural Regionalism*, 237-43 (see n. 7).

19 Mumford, "Regionalism and Irregionalism," *The Sociological Review* 19, no. 4 (October 1927): 277-88.

on dismantling the metropolis as on redesigning it, a schism was emerging within the growing culture of planning, present in its practices as well as in its disciplinary character within the academy. In the latter context, regionalist sensibilities challenged the metropolitan environment through the assumption that a productively planned region necessitated the dispersal of congested populations as well as cultural and economic activities.

Most significant in all of this is the framing of regionalism as interested in decentralized rather than distributed organization.[20] Although this bias was inherited from the anti-metropolitan thrust that had long been part of the movement, and, as some have argued,

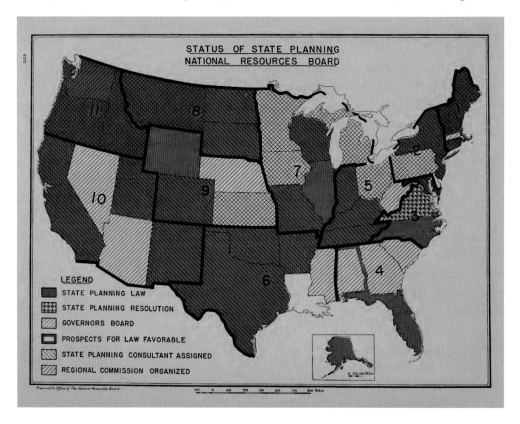

"Map of American Regions, as determined by the National Resource Board, 1935." From *State Planning: A Review of Activities and Progress,* (Washington: Government Printing Office, 1935).

20 For a discussion of distributed networks as intrinsically different in their formal organization from centralized ones, see Alexander Galloway, *Protocol: How Control Exists after Decentralization* (Cambridge: MIT Press, 2004).

21 Morton and Lucia White, *The Intellectual Versus the City, from Thomas Jefferson to Frank Lloyd Wright* (Cambridge: Harvard University Press, 1962). Mumford's important writing on cities include *The Culture of Cities* (New York: Harcourt Brace, 1938), which was the second volume of his four volume "Renewal of Life" series, and *The City in History: Its Origins, Its Transformations, and Its Prospects* (New York: Harcourt Brace and World, 1961).

22 His regionalist vision thus differed substantially from that of Thomas Adams, who viewed the garden city type not as a replacement for metropolitan centers but instead as a satellite element

of American intellectual values since the early nineteenth century, it ultimately proved an obstacle to understanding the relationship of academic regionalist culture to what Mumford christened in 1938 a "culture of cities."[21] Though for much of his life he championed urban life in metropolitan New York City, Mumford the urban theorist ultimately applied a cultural and sociological imagination to the ideological aim of a willed decentralization, in the process positing the regional city as a challenge to the primacy of such centers.

In Mumford's writing, he employed the term "regional city" to designate his interpretation of Ebenezer Howard's garden city ideas from the turn of the century. While the latter depended upon a central hub which was encircled by new towns that housed workers in less congested and more hygienic quarters than the urban slums found in late nineteenth-century London, Mumford's regional city in effect replaced the large metropolis with multiple new, less-congested entities.[22] Mumford's regional city thus posited a future in which no densely-populated urban area would anchor the various carefully-planned and newly-generated regional cities that dotted the region, which ultimately amounted to a far more radical proposal than that of Howard.

Yet the regional city of 1920s American regionalism was in effect stillborn, as the planning ethos necessary to achieve it ultimately did not encompass a realpolitik that could effectively legislate and realize it. Furthermore, as historian Andrew Meyers has argued, both Mumford and Thomas, in their respective efforts, promoted "the ordering of use at all levels of planning: at the scale of the region, the city, and the neighborhood."[23] Such organization assumed that the relationship of the nation to the regions it contained was simply one more nested layering, in which sets of neighborhoods (whether residential or not) combined to make cities, a few regionalist cities agglomerated within regions, and the country itself was merely what might be labeled a "nation of regions." In such an understanding, however, this nation of regions was analogous to a dispersed but still physically hierarchical organization of nested city (local), state and federal legal jurisdictions.

Yet as the Great Depression brought the country to its knees in the early 1930s, immediately on the heels of Mumford's and Adams's clearest articulation of what regional

within its expanded purview. In the early 1930s, Mumford and Adams faced off in the pages of *The New Republic*, after Mumford wrote an unfavorable review of the 1929 ten-volume *Plan of New York and its Environs*. For discussions of their differences, see Matthew Dalbey, *Regional Visionaries*

and Metropolitan Boosters: Decentralization, Regional Planning and Parkways during the Interwar Years (Norwell: Kluwer Academic Publishers, 2002); and John L. Thomas, "Holding the Middle Ground," *The American Planning Tradition: Culture and Policy,* ed. Robert Fishman (Baltimore: Johns Hopkins

University Press, 2000), 33-64.
23 Though Meyers sees Mumford as being driven by communitarianism while Thomas espouses metropolitanism, they both give primacy to a functionalist logic that does not entertain the possibility of a distributed network of uses, be they residential, industrial,

transportation, recreational or other. Thus both espoused a logic of functional segregation parallel to that of CIAM modernist principles, as found in the 1943 Athens Charter; see Andrew A. Meyers, "Invisible Cities: Lewis Mumford, Thomas Adams, and the Invention of the Regional City, 1923-1929,"

planning had to offer, in its aftermath new initiatives were employed to rewire this nested structure through the initiation of federal relief, recovery, and reform policies. This resulted in a concerted federal effort to inaugurate regional planning across the nation, with an emphasis on economic and resource planning over physical planning.[24] Within these developments, the premiere national planning body was originally a division of the efforts of the Federal Emergency Administration of Public Works, part of New Deal efforts to revamp the nation's infrastructure through large-scale interventions into the built environment, like the Tennessee Valley Authority. Yet with the 1935 ruling that declared the National Recovery Administration unconstitutional, the bulk of such efforts shifted to the National Resources Planning Board (NRPB), a body advising President Roosevelt. By the time this experiment with a federal planning body was killed in 1943, through congressional cancellation of its budget appropriation, what had emerged was a networking of American cities that was in fact centralized (or hierarchical) by state but did not really form a distributed network (as the university network did). The developing culture of planning was thus not dependent on regional planning—at least not in the sense either Mumford or Adams had promoted—but was instead ensconced in a network of disparate cities spread out across the nation unfettered by the regional responsibilities envisioned by either thinker.

Regionalist Culture within a "Nation of Universities"

By the mid-1930s, as America recovered from economic calamity by "priming the pump," regionalist culture experienced a true flowering in numerous locations across the nation, predominantly within academic circles. Numerous scholarly studies had appeared that constituted the region as a social fact as well as an object of disciplinary— if not interdisciplinary—knowledge. Donald Davidson's *The Attack on Leviathan* (1938) argued for the existence of a distinct vein of Southern literature, while Rupert C. Vance's *Human Geography of the South* (1932) contended that the particular social practices and socio-economic factors at work in the American Southeast produced a unique regional character.[25] Social scientific research along the lines pursued by Vance asserted that the movement was not limited merely to cultural criticism and that the parameters of regions as entities capable of being objectively specified and scientifically described could be precisely determined.[26]

Business and Economic History 27, no. 2 (Winter 1998): 292-306, p. 298.

24 Frederick Adams, "Changing Concepts of Planning," *American Journal of Economics and Sociology* 15, no. 3, Municipal Progress during the Twentieth Century (April 1956): 245-52.

25 Donald Davidson, *The Attack on Leviathan: Regionalism and Nationalism in the United States* (Chapel Hill: University of North Carolina, 1938); Rupert B. Vance, *Human Geography of the South: a Study in Regional Resources and Human Adequacy* (Chapel Hill: University of North Carolina

Press, 1932).

26 Perhaps regionalism's clearest expression in terms of the spectrum of social scientific perspectives available for analyzing a region is Howard Odum and Harry Estill Moore, *American Regionalism: a Cultural-Historical Approach to National Integration* (New

York: H. Holt and Co., 1938).

27 Carl Schorske, "The New Rigorism in the Human Sciences," in *American Academic Culture in Transformation: Fifty Years, Four Disciplines*, eds. Thomas Bender & Carl E. Schorske (Princeton: Princeton University Press, 1997), 309-30.

Through these developments, regionalist discourse produced lasting effects on numerous disciplinary formations within American colleges and universities, in particular on the disparate collection of disciplines in which the analysis of culture was a central methodological technique. Through an innovative mode of literary analysis, regionalism helped give birth to New Criticism, which had achieved "institutional ascendency" in English departments across the nation by the 1950s.[27] It also laid the groundwork for the establishment of American Studies as a discipline, described at the time as "an attempt to repair the effects of specialization and the fragmentation of fields" within the modern research university.[28] Another closely related disciplinary development that crystallized during the early postwar years was Area Studies, which owed its origins to the wartime military need of expertise on cultural aspects of both America's allies and enemies. At the same time that leading figures in the movement were formative shapers of the fields of sociology and geography during the interwar era, they also contributed extensively to the advancement of political science, economics, anthropology, ethnography and history departments.

Describing the proposed investigations that eventually became the magisterial 1936 study *Southern Regions of the United States*, sociologist Howard Odum characterized the intersection of discrete information and analytical constructs necessary in regionalist research. He asserted rather hubristically that his study would encompass "physical geography and natural resources, together with the visible and measurable ends of industrial and scientific activity in their utilization; and the population and cultural resources, together with the visualized ends of social activity toward organization and achievement of their development."[29] For many within the academy, such interdisciplinary aspirations were nearly impossible to avoid or refuse, as the bundle of linked knowledges necessary to understand the truth of regions entailed a high level of coordination as well as a differential logic.[30] Such coordination, however, necessitated overlooking biases that were not necessarily structural but rather ideological.

As previously mentioned, interwar regionalism was overwhelmingly dogged by modernist culture's emphasis on the large city or metropolis, a fixation that stood in the way of its theoretical legitimization. Dorman characterizes the onslaught of the regionalist movement

28 Rupert B. Vance, "The Regional Concept as a Tool for Social Research," in *Regionalism in America*, ed. Merrill Jensen (Madison: University of Wisconsin Press, 1951), 120.

29 Howard Odum, quoted in Wayland J. Hayes, "Regionalism in Theory and Practice?" *Social Forces* 14, no. 4 (May 1936): 606-9, p.606. **30** Odum initiated what was probably the nation's first organized research unit, the Institute for Research in Social Science (IRSS) at the University of North Carolina

Chapel Hill in 1924. As such an entity became the standard institutional form for most funded university research activities after WWII, this was no small triumph for sociology; nor did it reflect badly on the regionalist imagination, as the IRSS became a leading site within the nation for advancing social

scientific research practices. See Roger L. Geiger, "Organized Research Units— Their Role in the Development of University Research," *The Journal of Higher Education* 61, no. 1 (January—February 1990): 1-19.

as "the signal of a critical juncture in the centuries long-transformation of this country from a rural, frontier, decentralized, producerist, farm and village society—the older America—into the modern commercialized, consumerist, and mechanized mass society of the metropolis."[31] As the organizational ethos of regionalism posited an atomization of the energy and centrality of the metropolis, imaging its dispersion through an expansive, contiguous spatial zone that encompassed and engulfed it, a path was explicitly chosen: supporting the cause of spatial decentralization.

Nevertheless, in opposition to any projected or implicit globalizing national culture, regionalism valorized a variety of local ones. It was primarily enabled to do so, however, because of the parameters at work in the networked space of the national university system. Despite regionalism's positing of the existence of specific environmental conditions that had determined current local realities—and might ultimately determine new ones—its theoretical underpinnings assumed a translatability of analyses and parameters between contexts, even regardless of the context. In truth, this foundational basis was intrinsically at odds with the movement's emphasis on local and ultimately limited frames of reference, namely those provided by the very concept of the region. As the practices proposed for the analysis of regions constituted technologies that could be applied to different regions and were to be found within disparate disciplinary or cultural formations (sociology, economics, literature, art, architecture, etc.) as well as within combinations of them, they were also part and parcel of the universalizing national cultural formation that regionalists were at pains to attack.

In modeling the new organizational logic behind a "nation of regions," then, regionalist culture failed to identify the academic environment as itself providing a simulation worthy of emulation. In part this was due to the fact that while regionalist scholarship represented a rich panoply of diverse forces at work in society, its status as a movement required blurring or overlapping distinctions between the discrete forms of knowledge involved, as well as between the social subjectivities, i.e., artist, journalist, scholar/academic, politician and, ultimately, technocrat, associated with them. Formed out of a collection of like-minded intellectuals and scholars from different disciplines, the regionalist movement found the decentralized educational network fertile ground for its own development.[32]

---

31 Dorman, *Revolt*, xi.

32 American institutions of higher education developed in a voluntarist or associationist manner: there has never been a state (federal) university in the sense of most European countries. The nation's nineteenth century system of largely private universities was augmented and markedly altered with the 1862 federal passage of the Morrill Act, which mandated that every state set aside land for institutions of higher education, primarily mechanical and agricultural colleges. Through the gradual linking of similar departments within this disparate collection of institutions, a vast national network emerged over time.

Yet within the decentralized educational system nationwide, which included both public (land grant) and private institutions, the uniqueness of any one school was based on— and hence was secondary to—the strength of each of its departments within the set of linked, aligned departments across the nation. Because of this, the network of research universities decidedly did not correspond to regionalist spatializations as promoted by Mumford, Thomas Adams, Odum and others. Mumford's decentralized regionalism, in which networks of regional cities replaced metropoles but were still functionally (and thus hierarchically) organized, was most nearly analogous. Yet the linkages connecting residential neighborhoods to business districts to shopping areas to recreational lands, ultimately wiring them together, were at odds with the self-generating logic of academic departments connected to like departments in other locales rather than to those with which they shared proximics, i.e., those within their own institution.

That the educational network had produced a regionalist culture through its development as a self-organizing system attested to its interwar productiveness; that regionalist geographers, sociologists, critics, economists and planners criticized the large conurbation for its role in uneven regional development gives light to regionalism's failure to account for the organizational logics embedded in America's analogous systems of cites and universities. The regionalist movement in effect amounted to both a reevaluation of the centrality of culture within social relations and a new culture in its own right, one that functioned in a non-functionalist manner. By framing and figuring a gap located between the study of culture and a culture of how to study particular phenomena, then, regionalist discourse made headway toward legitimizing interdisciplinarity within the American university environment during the interwar era. That before or during WWII such an understanding was not explicitly posited as a regionalist insight (to the best of my knowledge) is perhaps a contributing cause for the movement's postwar "change in tone," as Dorman describes it. While regionalist culture was a significant force shaping a space for the future exploration of such intersections, it did so in an unreflective or non-theoretical manner.[33]

33 In part the significance of regionalism as a movement was its nascent role in bringing these issues to the fore; in effect, the movement foreshadowed the "cultural turn" in American academic discourse of the late 1960s and early 1970s. For a discussion of implications of this beyond that moment, see David A. Hollinger, "The Disciplines and the Identity Debates, 1970-1995," *Daedalus* 126, no. 1 American Academic Culture in Transformation: Fifty Years, Four Disciplines (Winter 1997): 333-51.

34 Prior to 1940, though numerous schools across the nation offered instruction in city planning or had initiated departments in City and/or Regional Planning, only five schools had initiated curricula in city planning that was not a specialization within another degree program: Harvard (1929), Cranbrook Academy of Art (1930), University of Illinois (1932), and MIT (1935). See "Report of American City Planning Institute Committee on Professional Education," (May 25, 1937); MIT Institute Archives, Frederick J. Adams Papers, Folder: MIT Dept. of Urban Studies and Planning, Correspondence and Reports, 1937-74." See also

City and Regional Planning in a Nation of Cities and Universities

As noted earlier, the establishment of independent departments concerned with city and regional planning at MIT and Berkeley in the early postwar era registered the increasing divergence of city planning and planning as educational tracks.[34] At MIT, study of the former originated in the 1930s within architectural studies, along lines quite similar to slightly earlier events at Harvard, the first institution in the nation to offer a specialized degree in the field. While prior to 1935 city planning professionals were being trained almost exclusively within landscape and architecture programs, over the next decade a burgeoning of programs for non-physical planning (economic and resources planning, regional planning, national planning, and city or public administration) offered students interested in these fields additional training locales, almost all of them located outside design divisions.[35] Along these lines, Berkeley's program (inaugurated in 1948) was established within the University of California system's Graduate Division North; although its antecedents were in architecture and landscape, other university divisions played an important role.[36] While like many of its predecessors Berkeley's new department emphasized comprehensive planning practices (encompassing both practical and aesthetic matters), it also stressed the particular planning needs of the West Coast and the Northern California context.[37]

Use of the label "city and regional planning"—not only taken as the name of Berkeley's department at its inauguration but also adopted by MIT's department a year earlier (in 1947)—marked increased recognition that the non-physical social and economic planning denoted by the term "regional" provided a valuable expertise distinct from that of physical planning. While this was primarily due to a dramatic increase in state planning activity initiated under Roosevelt during the 1930s, it also reflected the increased complexity entailed by municipal governance in America. By the late 1940s, however, the dramatic increase in administrative positions at both city and state levels still had not been met by educational programs. The same year Wurster left California for Harvard (1943), MIT city planning instructor Frederick Adams claimed that the "problem of obtaining adequately trained personnel is still a serious one for municipal, state, and Federal planning agencies, and increased activity in the field of postwar planning has accentuated an already difficult situation—thus placing a heavy responsibility on the few schools in the country offering professional training in city and regional planning."[38]

Raul B. Garcia, "Changing Paradigms of Professional Practice, Education and Research in Academe: A History of Planning Education in the United States" (PhD dissertation, University of Pennsylvania, 1993).

35 Harvey S. Perloff, "Education of City Planners: Past, Present and Future,"

Journal of American Institute of Planners 22, no. 4 (October—December 1956): 186-217; Charles S. Ascher, *Educational Preparation for Public Administration*, 1939-1940 (New York: Committee on Public Administration, Social Science Research Council, 1940).

36 At the time, Berkeley was the only campus of the University of California offering architectural training at both the undergraduate and graduate levels. Graduate Division South was located at Cal's Los Angeles campus; this new regional organization was established in the late 1930s, with a dean at both,

following a 1937 restructuring of the state university system. After 1945, new planning programs were increasingly initiated at institutions without architecture programs or instruction; in 1945, the University of Chicago initiated a Program of Education and Research in Planning; a year later, the University

Already by the late 1930s, however, the number of students desiring to enter graduate study for city planning from non-design backgrounds was clearly escalating. This was causing educators to voice the opinion that such students needed to leave with some kind of basic knowledge base—and that perhaps design was not the most important of the available choices. At a 1936 MIT conference on city planning education, held at the request of the American City Planning Institute, debate over whether graduate training for city planning needed to be based upon a foundation in design dominated the proceedings. Adams argued that a liberal arts rather than technical expertise should be the basis for training professional city planners. For Adams, this meant that "a liberalizing of the professional education of architects, landscape architects and engineers, rather than an A.B. degree plus a professional degree plus a city planning postgraduate course," was the appropriate path to take, if training for city planning was to be integrated with current educational practices.[39] By "liberalizing" Adams meant increased emphasis on the liberal arts rather than technical training in design or engineering, and he implied that a new understanding of city planning education might be the best model for training planners within design divisions.

Not only did this challenge the design school model recently put into effect at Harvard, in which training for various professions were linked primarily through a shared design expertise; it also reflected a newly heightened value among city planning educators for the social sciences in general.[40] Esteemed over and above any status they had within the training of architects, the social sciences—capable of being readily employed to survey, measure, and model the socio-economical and physical realities of American cities—supported the emerging view that urban knowledge was inherently precise and scientific, and thus deserved a place alongside other such knowledge within the university. This in turn reflected the increasingly heterogeneous collection of knowledges the modern research university encompassed. In 1932, a few years prior to the city planning conference just mentioned, MIT had been extensively reorganized under the direction of President Karl Compton. The institution was restructured into three schools (Engineering, Science and Architecture) and two support divisions (Humanities, and Industrial Cooperation and Research) which served their specific needs.[41] The Division of Humanities

of North Carolina Chapel Hill inaugurated a graduate program in regional planning.

37 For a description of the relationship between the two, see Jon A. Peterson, *The Birth of City Planning in the United States, 1840-1917* (Baltimore: Johns Hopkins University Press, 2003), especially Chapter 11, "The Social

Progressive Challenge, 1909."

38 Massachusetts Institute of Technology Bulletin 79, no. 1, President's Report Issue (October 1943): 124.

39 *Conference on City Planning Education* (1936), typescript; Frances Loeb Library (Vertical Files), Graduate School of Design, Harvard University.

40 Sociology and economics were the primary social sciences that had been used to analyze the city and built environment over

the previous two decades; see John D. Fairfield, *The Mysteries of the Great City: The Politics of Urban Design, 1877-1937* (Columbus: Ohio State University Press, 1993), especially Chapter 6: "The Alienation of Social Control: The Chicago Sociologists and the Origins of Urban Planning."

offered courses in a variety of subjects already established at MIT, notably English, history, economics and foreign languages, but also new subjects, such as government, international relations, labor relations, law, and philosophy, as well as psychology and sociology. Sociology's location in the Humanities division reflected its nebulous status in relation to the natural sciences at this time, but by the end of the decade its increased role within city and regional planning would shape specific developments at MIT. Moreover, the very existence of these two divisions incorporated and embodied a split between education and training, with general knowledge or skills being taught in the Humanities division and advanced scientific research being conducted in the schools of Engineering, Science, and (increasingly) Architecture.[42]

The codification of city planning instruction within the university environment over the course of the 1930s only exacerbated the different conceptualizations undergirding city and regional planning. Though courses in city planning for architecture students had existed for quite some time by the late 1930s, a distinct undergraduate curriculum for the subject was initiated the same year as the restructuring (1932), with graduate instruction following three years later. A decade later after the reorganization, Adams went so far as to suggest that city planning and architecture education did not share a common basis in design, claiming the "new course has been developed in response to the need for a curriculum which is oriented to the professional field early in the program and which provides for a synthesis of the economic, sociological, administrative, and engineering aspects of city planning impossible in courses developed from existing curricula in specialized professional fields."[43] Though curriculum at both levels emerged out of what had originally been architectural curricula, it was at the graduate level that the question of what sort of foundational knowledge the two fields shared came into clearest focus. By 1940, although two-thirds of all students earning graduate degrees in city planning had entered the program with backgrounds in architecture, only one-third of the new students enrolling that year did, a trend that was to escalate nationally over the next decade.[44]

41 http://shass.mit.edu/ inside/history (accessed August 11, 2009); for a description of what this physically entailed, see Mark Jarzombek, *Designing MIT: Bosworth's New Tech* (Boston: Northeastern University Press, 2004).

42 The two support divisions were not commensurate in scope, and neither of them offered degrees; the Division of Humanities offered electives, as well as some required classes needed to complete degrees offered by the three schools.

43 *MIT Bulletin* 78, no. 1, President's Report Issue (Oct., 1942), 113.

44 *MIT Bulletin* 76, no. 1, President's Report Issue (Oct., 1940), 62, 132.

Wurster's Tenure at MIT's School of Architecture and City Planning

Considering this, it is clear that Wurster's espousal of planning as a professional formation occurred during a significant moment of transition for the field, following its expansion during the 1920s and 1930s. Moreover, the period of his deanship (1944—1950) witnessed a further evolution of city and regional planning within the research university, one that affected architecture instruction as well. Wurster's appointment as Dean was the result of machinations on the part of city planning instructor Adams, who had met Wurster when the latter had enrolled in courses while at Harvard.[45] Due to his recent city and regional planning studies, Wurster was viewed by Adams as sympathetic to the vision of city planning education he advocated for MIT, and his high national reputation appeared to be what the School of Architecture needed at that moment. While marking a new legitimacy for the education of city planners, however, the achievement of departmental status for planning just before Wurster's arrival inaugurated a particularly complex administrative arrangement within the School of Architecture that he had to navigate.

Yet if Adams's actions are interpreted as indicative of both men's thinking around this time, this new complexity was apparently not based on intrinsic disciplinary identities shared by the two fields. In 1941, Adams had drafted a proposal for granting departmental status to city planning instruction within the School of Architecture; yet at the time this proposal was being considered, he had also lobbied Compton to relocate instruction into the School of Engineering.[46] This suggestion appears to be based not on any belief that city planning constituted an applied knowledge, but was instead due to displeasure at the new department's reputation, were it to be located within a division struggling to regain a lost status. Though President Compton assured him that the Institute had every interest in drastically improving the School of Architecture's sagging reputation, Adams and Wurster were eventually successful at securing autonomy for planning education within the School. Reaching out to Wurster as a choice for the next dean suggests Wurster's standing as a renowned architect whose sympathies now extended to city planning would strike the right balance between the two departments, yet it also apparently stemmed from an alignment of Wurster's and Adams's views toward a higher valuation of social (rather than physical) parameters within planning education. In Adams's November 1941 departmental

45 In Cambridge during the 1943-44 academic year, Wurster studied regional planning with political scientists John Gaus, fiscal policy with economist Alvin Hansen, city planning with Martin Wagner and Thomas Adams, and civic design with GSD Dean Joseph Hudnut. See Wurster, "Toward Urban Development," *Architect and Engineer* 157 (June, 1944): 37-39.

46 Compton, Memo to Killian (21 July 1942), MIT Institute Archives, Office of the President, Folder: Adams A-V.

proposal, he had laid out what he felt were the increasing differences between architecture and planning as fields of study. He claimed that city planners engaged in tasks with varying emphasis on "physical, economic, and social factors" and thus needed to understand the inter-relations amongst all three. In light of this, he proposed altering the early years of the undergraduate planning curriculum, as at that point they virtually duplicated the early stages of the curricula for training architects. Adams desired that the two curricula would be treated independently in the future, a move that would be secured by achieving departmental (rather than merely course) status.[47] In detailing his reasons for wanting this split, Adams stated that "no advanced work in the Social Sciences would [subsequently] be possible unless the earlier years of the course were changed to include a number of subjects which would serve as a foundation for graduate study."[48] This change increased the ambiguity of planning's reliance on design, in part by implicitly proposing that training in research was as important if not more important for future city planners than was a background in design.

The potential to distinguish between design and research as regarding the American city and the country's larger built environment reflected changes taking place both within and beyond the academy. In this regard, recently initiated New Deal policy practices had inaugurated academic urban research on an unprecedented scale. In 1937, the Research Committee on Urbanism of the National Resources Committee published Our Cities, arguably the first in-depth, synthetic American urban research project initiated by the government and employing academic researchers.[49] While there were three city planners on the nine-member Committee, the group also included three city administrators as well as an economist, a sociologist, and an expert from the Department of Agriculture, thus encompassing a decidedly broad scope of practical and disciplinary knowledge via its members. Though upon its release this report created little public stir, over the next half decade both governmental and academic attention to urban research and revitalization would grow dramatically.

Within the university context, the escalating war effort of the early 1940s succeeded in overhauling the national network constituted by its leading educational institutions, through

47 During the 1930s, Course IV (Architecture) had been augmented with Course IV-A (Architectural Engineering) and Course IV-B (City Planning). Course IV-A had been discontinued by 1940; in 1947, Architecture was renamed Course IV-A.
48 The proposal was likely written by Adams, as he

was City Planning instructor at the time and was also instrumental in establishing the Field Station. "Proposal For a New Curriculum in City Planning at MIT and the Setting Up of an Urban Redevelopment Field Station at the Boston City Planning Board," (November 5, 1941), unattributed; MIT Institute

Archives, Office of the President, Folder: Adams A-V.
49 *Our Cities: Their Role in the National Economy* (Washington: Government Printing Office, 1937). For one (among many) discussion of this seminal study, see Gelfland, *Nation*, chapter 3, "Preparing for an Urban Future," 84-104.

50 Roger L. Geiger, "The Dynamics of University Research in the United States: 1945-90," in *Research and Higher Education: The United Kingdom and the United States*, eds. T.G. Whiston and R.L. Geiger (Buckingham: SRHE/Open University Press, 1992).

nurturing an appetite for research whetted by the war.[50] The School of Architecture did not at first directly share in the boom produced by this interest in scientific research, primarily because its activities were predominantly in the area of design. Adams's proposal to establish the planning department had linked the field's legitimacy to its ability to undertake needed and valuable research. Towards these ends, it advocated inauguration of an "Urban Redevelopment Field Station" at the Boston City Planning Board office. Run under the auspices of MIT's city planning program, it was modeled after the numerous agricultural experiment stations initiated for the conducting of field research established by late 19th century land grant legislation. Intended to facilitate observation and research—though not on the rural or undeveloped environments traditionally studied by earlier experiment stations—MIT's version instead aimed to focus on an urban location. Established to study urban ills in order to alleviate or reverse them, the research center was an outgrowth of Adams's involvement with the Committee on the Hygiene of Housing of the American Public Health Association, another New Deal-era urban policy development. The Committee, inaugurated in the late 1930s, formulated methods of surveying housing stock quality so as to generate concrete information for the establishing of federal housing policies.[51] The field station was paid for largely by the Bemis Foundation, and was thus a means of redirecting existing resources at the school toward new ends.[52] Although the Bemis Foundation's research primarily focused on studies of new building products and materials, the policy aims of the field station and its explicit project of "urban redevelopment" extended beyond the limitations of design as a foundational knowledge.

Though the field of housing was a primary means by which architecture divisions nationwide could join the expanding academic research economy, by the early 1950s it was being surpassed by research into urban topics, which were generally felt to encompass the subject of housing as well as additional areas. Because of this, it was the relatively new Department of City and Regional Planning that had a leg up on the Department of Architecture, which was of course the oldest such entity in the country. As the amounts and types of urban planning research increased over the course of the 1950s, the pronounced divide between the School's two divisions only increased.

51 In addition to Adams, the Field Station was also being staffed by Philip H. Cornick (of New York City's Institute of Public Administration) and Brooklyn College economics professor Edwin H. Spengler, who was involved as a consultant to the National Resources Planning Board. The private IPA and the federal agency NRPB were bodies that had been actively promoting research, much of it focused on the American city, especially as regards their administration and planning. See "Urban Redevelopment Established at MIT," *American Journal of Public Health* 33 (March 1943), 305.

52 Through a behest from wealthy New England housing entrepreneur Albert Farwell Bemis, a research center devoted to housing research had been established within the school in 1936. The Bemis Foundation, directed for its first decade by architecture faculty member John Burchard, was basically the first such organized unit in the country to be located within an architecture division.

The Spatial Complexity of a "Divided" Administration

Wurster's 1940s "journey to the East" constituted a double departure for him: from a designer concerned with primarily local conditions, and from a professional subjectivity linked to one particular specialization (architecture). Yet as already noted, it was also constitutive of a third swerve—from regionalist to city planning expert to educational administrator. It is this third trajectory that enables his activity to indicate changes in the relationship of architectural and planning knowledge to the modern research university. In charting his particular path, Wurster enacted a spatially complex allocation of energy, time, and funding, in which architecture was but one division within the recently established administrative entity he coordinated; at the same time he advocated for architectural regionalism within a university division in which other horizons were being simultaneously pursued.

One could contend that after 1945 the Institute's commitment to science by and large trumped the Architecture department's interest in regional modernism. In 1947, the division Wurster headed was renamed the School of Architecture and Planning, with Adams contemporaneously describing the two departments (Architecture, and City and Regional Planning) as "coequal."[53] Not only did this render the school a context encompassing two distinct disciplinary formations, it also, given the distinct yet related content of their particular curricular and research agendas, gave it a new status as the only "split" division within MIT. Neither considered a pure Science nor an applied one (Engineering), the School of Architecture simultaneously lay "outside" this distinction; yet it now officially encompassed a corresponding division of its own. Clearly Wurster's dilemma as an administrator at this juncture, then, was how to establish educational excellence for the programs within the School while allowing for various paths into (and out of) the educational environment, as well as back and forth between the fields of architecture and planning. All of the pressure for coordination did not come from the planning side of the equation. Course IV (Architecture) had been revised a year before Wurster's arrival, based upon ongoing studies initiated around the time Dean MacCornack replaced Dean Emerson in 1940.[54] Adams of course had long been interested in increasing the importance of economics and sociology within the city planning curriculum.[55] The committee's final report recommended that courses in these fields should be added to the early years of the

53 *MIT Bulletin* 83, no. 1, President's Report Issue (October 1947), 143.

54 A discussion group formed under Dean McCornack a few years earlier had determined that the study of economics and sociology was undervalued in the training of architects. "Notes on Social and Economic Problems Affecting the Field of Contemporary and Future Architecture, for

Dean MacCornack's Round Table Discussion Group" (Spring 1942), mimeographed copy. MIT Institute Archives, Office of the President Papers, Folder: Dean MacCornack 1942.

55 His 1942 city planning curricula proposal specifically advocated a reduction of physics and mathematics requirements in the early years for planning students, to be replaced by social science courses offered by the Humanities division.

curriculum, allowing more advanced courses to be offered in later years for those students interested in pursuing planning after graduation. In this way architecture was constructed as a kind of pre-planning major in which design instruction was augmented with other types of research-based knowledge.

While Adams's interest in streamlining and refocusing both levels of the city planning curriculum contributed to the tenor of the debate surrounding these changes, the new architecture curriculum was envisioned as streamlining and improving the curricula that had gone relatively unchanged during the program's struggling years following the Great Depression. The architecture curriculum ultimately emphasized four major considerations: "principles of construction, building materials and their proper uses, practical economics of the building industry, and the fundamental principles of city planning."[56] These last two concerns were new additions, and as such emphasized social scientific knowledge that had not been given such prominence a decade earlier. Furthermore, soon after the new curricular proposal had been approved, Dean MacCornack remarked that the "major deficiencies in the education of architects have been the almost complete absence of training in the fundamentals of the practical economics of the building industry field and the failure to appreciate the basic problems involved in the economic, social, physical and political decay of our cities," suggesting that those goals Adams had earlier considered important for planning were increasingly valued within architecture.

Wurster, upon his arrival, appeared to be in agreement with these developments. His particular attitudes toward the goals of architectural education then espoused at MIT were articulated in a number of contexts, among them the regional conference talk with which this essay opened. Just over a year after his arrival, in a letter to *Architectural Forum* publisher Howard Myers, he stated that there are many approaches to architecture: through art, through history, through the humanities in general, as well as the particular route taken at MIT, through science. Wurster suggested that all of these paths are accessed through architecture's one essential aspect, design. Distinguishing between undergraduate and graduate programs, Wurster explained that the former offered few electives and was carefully coordinated with the rest of the school, so that students could transfer out after a

56 *MIT Bulletin* 79, no. 1, President's Report Issue (October 1943), 122.

year. The latter was "like a circus tent with many shows going on," allowing for students to specialize through choice of concentration and to ultimately apply architecture (and design) toward different ends. Within all this, Wurster also noted the School's recent deviation from earlier educational paradigms, claiming that "architectural education must prepare its students for keen analysis, not just individual solution," and added that the "economic and social why of our work must be answered before we proceed to the how." [57]

Yet by the time he wrote his first President's Report (Fall 1945, a year after arriving at MIT), Wurster had become embroiled in an administrative skirmish that questioned this very characterization. In that context, he basically tabled any previous recognition of a split between city planning and architecture by claiming "[w]e support with great enthusiasm the common first year for all freshmen, as it means that this School is more an integral part of the larger picture."[58] This statement was somewhat disingenuous, given that the Architecture department, in establishing a revised undergraduate curriculum immediately before the new dean's arrival, had found itself running afoul of the Institute's Committee on Undergraduate Courses.[59] In 1944, this body had determined that a two-year introductory program of study should be required of students in all three of MIT's schools, a requirement which reflected the need to facilitate movement between different majors and departments within the Institute as students shifted their studies after matriculating to best fit their changing goals. However, since the Architecture school had no dean at the time of the decision (Wurster had yet to start and MacCornack had already resigned), its particular concerns were not represented in these determinations. Once the Committee's decision had been implemented, figures at the Architecture school (especially Adams) balked at the development, arguing that space in the two earliest years of its five-year undergraduate programs should be employed for its own particular curricular needs, which specifically meant substituting humanities courses for technical ones.

Furthermore, in the President's Report of 1945 just mentioned, Wurster articulated a deviation between the two analogous departments within his division which would haunt any future equivalence. He claimed that "Though there are many paths leading to architecture, the staff of this School feel that our choice of direction should be that which

---

57 Wurster, Letter to Howard Myers (15 October 1945); MIT Institute Archives, Office of the President Papers, Folder: William Wurster 1945.

58 *MIT Bulletin* 81, no. 1, President's Report Issue (October, 1945), 138.

59 A body referred to as the Emerson Committee was formed back in 1938 under William Emerson, the Dean who preceded MacCornack; it was given the charge of making recommendations for altering and improving the curriculum.

will embrace the strength of the Institute." This amounted to what he described as "a technical approach which will utilize the M.I.T. laboratories, courses on materials, and such subjects as sanitation, acoustics, illumination, and heating and ventilation." Yet he also specified that the "planner, on the other hand, needs only such portion of these as will give him discipline in analysis." Two issues were intertwined here: adding new courses to the architecture curriculum, and distinguishing between the two curricula the School offered; as they were carried out, both entailed what Adams had described in the mid-1930s as a "liberalizing" of the curricula. Regarding the former Wurster stated, "We are seeking to broaden the base of architecture by having the student recognize the important role of the social sciences, which must become part of technical training"; in terms of the latter, he suggested the split was really an overlap of recent generation: "There is an increasing interweaving of the courses in Architecture and Planning, so that each group looks over the fence into the other's field and thereby gains greater understanding."[60] Both of these in effect contradict the subsequent claim made in his letter to Meyer, for they constitute a coordinated differentiation between the two programs.

Though Wurster had authority as Dean to shape the direction of the School as a whole, his ability to do so was complicated by the fact that during his first three years as Dean he was also Chair of the Department of Architecture, with Adams head of the planning division. Equally important for his administration was the manner in which departments at MIT were networked with other similar educational institutions nationwide, and more importantly, how their housing institution was also connected to parallel yet dissimilar entities— government branches and agencies, private corporations, philanthropic organizations, and media companies and associations. With the increased emphasis on research beginning in the 1930s, figures who had primarily been formed as scholars and researchers took on the task of running departments and schools that also encompassed divisions beyond their particular expertise, regarding which they needed to act both impartially and benevolently.[61] As undertaken by architects and planners within a design school like those at MIT, Harvard, and (later) Berkeley, the need for a practitioner of one design profession to represent all areas in which instruction was offered complicated the task of running a school, while the growing tension between design and research only made the situation more complex.

---

60 Regarding this, he specifically adds "[e]ach student of architecture will partake of the city planning course and each planner will have a year of architecture, with the hopes that this glimpse into allied fields will correct" the fact that " [a]rchitects have been too remote and oftentimes presumed a knowledge which is not theirs." MIT Archives, Office of the President Papers, Folder: William Wurster 1945.

61 Rebecca Lowen, *Creating the Cold War University* (Berkeley: University of California Press, 1997) 13-14.

As regards Wurster and others like him, then, I suggest that his particular identity as a regionalist, even though such labeling primarily describes aspects of his architectural production, structured his agency as a university administrator. While I am not suggesting that Wurster understood the relationships between university divisions in the manner outlined in this paper, it does appear, in the context of the national research university network, that with his particular administrative position came a need to recognize the logic of differentiation that located actions within two complex unities simultaneously—a home institution and a decentralized network of like departments, divisions and schools. Moreover, the possibility of the reverse—that Wurster's experiences as an administrator imprinted on him an understanding of dynamics which might best be seen as under the purview of a spatial logic relates architecture and planning—could be entertained.[62] For while most certainly a regionalist when it came to architectural design, Wurster was also, decidedly, a historical subject for whom the characteristics of his layered professional identity— architect, planner, educator, administrator—participated in a newly reconfigured postwar spatialization, an organizational complex whose very success depended upon this logic.[63] Given this, design education's fitful postwar embrace of research constituted a sea change to contemporary understandings of the very significance and logic of design as it related to architecture, landscape, planning and other related fields. This in turn raised certain prospects regarding the integration of specialized knowledge within networks of knowledge production, management and application: are knowledge and action in general subject to parameters analogous to the type of differentiation that was earlier recognized as "regionalist?"

The fact that under Wurster both departments remained interested in opting out of MIT's standard curriculum for the first two years—each for their own reasons—made the situation more complex to resolve and more spatially ambiguous. Social science instruction was considered essential by Adams, but it was also a way of emphasizing the uniqueness of city planning knowledge as distinct from architecture. In the face of the mandated common curriculum, figures shaping both departments wanted a similar outcome, and yet they desired this outcome in order to pursue different paths.[64]

---

62 While Wurster's written output is not as prodigious as Mumford's, only a few pieces (in addition to his "New Directions" talk with which this essay opened) directly relate to either academic administration or planning. They include "Toward Urban Redevelopment (Part 1)," Architect and Engineer, v. 157

(June 1944): 25-28; "Toward Urban Redevelopment (Part 2)," v. 158 (July 1944): 37-39; "Architectural Education," AIA Journal 9, no. 1 (January 1948); and "The University and the Environmental Design Professions," lecture given at University of California Berkeley, October 1959.

63 Reinhold Martin, The Organizational Complex: Architecture, Media and Corporate Space (Cambridge: MIT Press, 2003).

64 Apparently this dilemma entailed an extended resolution period, for as late as the summer of 1949, in a letter to new Institute President Killian, Wurster was still arguing in favor of reducing the standard course load required of architecture students during their second year. MIT Archives, Office of

Conclusion: Regionalist Culture and the Space of Cities and Universities

After WWII, the loose network of intellectuals and scholars who employed a regionalist perspective to understand local practices and their spatial relationship to other practices in other locales became far less informal. Paradoxically, through the application of a regionalist lens to the very national network of educational institutions that had previously formed the basis for launching claims about regionalism, a simultaneously more complex and more fragmented vitality resulted, extending earlier concerns in new directions. In its heyday, the regionalist movement advanced innovative forms of analysis that were primarily disciplinarily specific; yet doing so intimated the existence of a space of overlap or intersection involving these disciplines, one that went largely unrecognized and unexamined within the regionalist movement.

Yet within their attention to development patterns and planning practices, regionalists like Mumford and Thomas overlooked the relationship between the culture of regionalism and the spatial configuration of knowledge that fostered it. The developing research university network owed its form and viability to a logic that was under the purview of regionalist analyses, and yet not exploited by them. While attentive (and antagonistic) to the American metropolis as a physical instantiation of cultural values, regionalism, because of a particular blind spot, was less adept at discerning the abstract organizational logic presented by the city as a spatial phenomenon understood in relation to other varieties of such entities. That this was the case at precisely the moment when abstracting the city offered powerful insights regarding the future of scientific management, i.e., planning, seems significant. For the regionalist movement, a culture keen on recognizing, criticizing, and ameliorating the desultory effects of the centralized logic of the big city, the decentralized system of educational institutions could have offered a network for the development and dispersion of a specific geo-political platform. As different veins of interest in urbanity and urban decentralization were flourishing within this decentralized network, initiating and awaiting interdisciplinary coordination, the regionalist movement was clearly out of sync with its very milieu.

the President Papers, Folder:
William Wurster 1949.

Memoirs

1955 - 1956
Biography of a Year in Graduate School

My first contact with MIT was in 1954, when I encountered a small printed advertisement on the wall of the library of the school of architecture at the University of Cape Town. It invited applications to graduate study in city planning at MIT. I knew little about the Institute other than about the Baker House: somewhere I had read about how hard students worked there, that it was like what young Americans underwent in Marine Corps training camps. No South African, to my knowledge, had gone on to graduate study in architecture in the USA. My professors, all Anglophiles, disdained both the need to study beyond what they taught and the idea that you might learn anything of value in an American school. I don't recall whether they knew that MIT was the oldest university school of architecture in the world. I certainly didn't know. My professors instead suggested I study in England; when I failed in the Rhodes Scholarship finals (the panel also couldn't understand why an architect should study further and awarded the scholarship to a man who later became a dentist), I finally wrote to MIT. Kevin Lynch, then an Assistant Professor, replied warmly and I was off. It was my first encounter with Lynch: I should have known more, for, around the same time as our correspondence, he published an important statement about the form of cities in *Scientific American.*[1] But where I lived architects didn't read such journals.

My decision to study city planning rather than architecture was informed in part by what I knew of the arguments that had accompanied the advent of modern architecture in South Africa. We were all proud that Le Corbusier had saluted Rex Martienssen and the young architects of Le Groupe Transvaal who were building white-walled box houses and apartment blocks in Johannesburg. Corbu had been pleased "to find something so alive in that faraway spot in Africa"[2] and had opened the 1910-1929 (*Euvres Completes* with a letter of salutation to Martiennssen. In 1937 he had proposed Martienssen for CIAM membership. I was dimly aware, however, that Martienssen's group had split apart over Corbusier's abstract urbanism and political adventurism in the face of the brutal reality of South African racial urbanism. Architects of the left like Kurt Jonas, a young immigrant Jew who had studied law in Berlin prior to becoming an architect under Martienssen's tutelage at the University of the Witwatersrand, had strongly rejected an urbanism of social inequality that was causally linked to capitalism. Lionel Bernstein, an architect who stood accused with Nelson Mandela at the 1963 Rivonia treason trial, later wrote that he was inspired by Jonas, "an extraordinary third-year student: It was at Florian's (a coffeehouse in Hillbrow frequented by leftists) with Kurt Jonas that I first learned of the invisible world of black workers and their trade unions which existed on my own doorstep."[3] This rich heritage I myself discovered only later. On my way to graduate school I still sensed only vaguely that South Africa's future might be decided in cities, more than by architecture.

Julian Beinart,
Department of
Architecture, MIT, n.d.

At MIT I soon discovered that there was little point in separating the two. I dropped out of Lynch's introductory housing site design class and managed to convince Lawrence Anderson, then head of the department, to let me into the M.Arch. class of about twenty students. I first needed to know more about architecture, I argued.

Architecture and city planning had been closely related since the inauguration of planning as a degree program in 1933. Curiously this was the same year that Jacques Carlu, the last of MIT's *Beaux Arts* trained teachers of design, retired; it was a time when the school still consisted of three sections: architecture, architectural engineering, and drawing. The MIT President's Report of 1944-1945 champions "the increasing interweaving of the courses in Architecture and Planning, so that each group looks over the fence into the other's field and thereby gains greater understanding."[4] By 1947 Architecture and City and Regional Planning were separate departments, listed as such in that year's Presidents Report and followed by a separate section for the Albert Farwell Bemis Foundation.

If I, as an incoming graduate student, knew little about MIT's architecture and planning history, I knew even less about its tradition of research. In the 1944-1945 President's Report the purpose of the architecture department is described in this way: "(though) many paths lead to architecture . . . we feel that our choice of direction should be that which will embrace the strength of the Institute."[5] The Bemis Foundation had been established in 1938 for housing research, and for 15 years it was the major source of funding in the school. Perhaps as significant as its dedication of resources was the way in which it defined architecture as both a technical and social enterprise. In 1947, for instance, it funded two major projects: architectural prefabrication and group dynamics in housing. By 1951 this work had resulted in two classics in these fields: Burnham Kelly's *The Prefabrication of Houses*, and Leon Festinger, Stanley Schachter and Kurt Back's *Social Pressures in Informal Groups: A Study of Human Factors in Housing*, a study of married veterans living in MIT's Westgate housing.[6] (This was the same time that Charles Abrams started teaching at MIT: his book, *Man's Struggle for Shelter in an Urbanizing World*, published in 1964 in a series by the MIT/Harvard Joint Center, was one of the pioneers of MIT's growing interest in housing in the developing world.)[7] Carl Koch, Ralph Rapson, and Buckminster Fuller were also involved with industrialized housing, and were teaching in the architecture department at that time; Fuller, according to the 1950 President's Report, was researching "more imaginative use of a structural technique in the enclosure of space with the idea that conventional building involves wasteful and redundant materials."[8] Simultaneously at MIT research was being done in other technical areas such as solar energy conversion, acoustics, and lighting.

I. M. Pei, after graduating in 1940 and winning the AIA Gold Medal, stayed on to work as a research assistant at the Bemis Foundation. But the Foundation's signal contribution to architecture at MIT may well have been the sponsoring, in the same year, of the appointment of Alvar Aalto, the only world figure in architecture ever to hold a regular faculty appointment at the Institute. Significantly, in the MIT tradition, he was to be a Research Professor of Architecture: "an idea of the proposed research was the standardization of housing . . . other research areas were to be artificial lighting and the environmental characteristics of a range of cladding materials."[9] (After 1953, the Bemis Foundation turned from supporting research to supporting eminent visiting teachers; among others, Lewis Mumford in 1957, Louis Kahn in 1962, and, recently, the urban sociologist Richard Sennett.)

1 Kevin Lynch, "The Form of Cities", *Scientific American* 4 (April 1954): 55-63.

2 Le Corbusier, *Le Corbusier et Pierre Jeanneret: Œuvre complète de 1910-1929* (Zurich: Éditions Dr. H. Girsberger, 1937), 6.

3 Gideon Shimoni, *Community and Conscience: The Jews in Apartheid South Africa* (Hanover: Brandeis University Press, 2003), 93.

4 MIT, *President's Report Issue of the Bulletin of the Massachusetts Institute of Technology*, vol. 81, no. 1 (Cambridge: Massachusetts Institute of Technology, 1945), 138.

5 Ibid.

6 See Burnham Kelly, *The Prefabrication of Houses* (Cambridge: MIT Press, 1951). Leon Festinger, Stanley Schacter and Kurt Back, *Social Pressures in Informal Groups* (New York: Harpers, 1950).

7 Charles Abrams, *Man's Struggle for Shelter in an Urbanizing World* (Cambridge: MIT Press, 1964).

8 MIT, *President's Report Issue of the Bulletin of the Massachusetts Institute of Technology*, vol. 87, no. 1 (Cambridge: Massachusetts Institute of Technology, 1950), 193.

Aalto taught at MIT for a few weeks in the fall of 1940, working on a schematic town plan with his students before the war took him back home. He returned to MIT in 1945, brought back by William Wurster who assumed the School's Deanship a year earlier. Wurster had met Aalto in Finland in 1937; seeing Aalto's house at Munkkiniemi, Wurster called it "a house that we thought was just what we had been dreaming of seeing."[10] The two men became close friends; one source suggests they considered forming an architectural research institute together.

Aalto's teaching schedule at MIT was flexible, consisting of two-month visits twice a year. His style was informal, apparently getting him into trouble occasionally. As he explained one particular incident:

> The [students] asked, among other things, how one creates good art. I replied, "I don't know." The consequences were shattering. One fine day the parents of one of my former students appeared for a meeting ... The first thing they said was: "We're shelling out $700 a semester for our talented son's education and his professor says, 'I don't know.' It was, judging by everything, the end of my short teaching career."[11]

In his five years as Dean, Wurster embraced and nurtured the idea that an architectural education should be open to the social sciences and planning. He saw architecture expanding through innovation and research but always remaining within the context of those who are its users. Gwendolyn Wright suggests that Catherine Bauer, Wurster's wife and author of the pioneering book *Modern Housing* [12], was an important influence on him when she observes that "Wurster's projects and pedagogy after 1940 are infused with Bauer's social and political aspirations."[13] In a book on his houses, Wurster's work is described as "an everyday modernism."[14]

As Dean, Wurster pulled together the social and technical strands which had emerged, and which had been embraced by MIT, in the years following 1930. In 1949, he addressed a meeting of the Association of Collegiate Schools of Architecture (ACSA) on the nation of "architecture as a social art":

9 Nicholas Ray, *Alvar Aalto* (New Haven: Yale University Press, 2005), 42.

10 Marc Treib, *An Everyday Modernism: The Houses of William Wurster* (Berkeley: University of California Press, 1995) 47.

11 Nicholas Ray, *Alvar Aalto*, 47.

12 Catherine Bauer Wurster, *Modern Housing* (Boston: Houghton Mifflin, 1934).

13 Gwendolyn Wright, "A Partnership : Catherine Bauer and William Wurster" in Treib, *An Everyday Modernism*, 189.

14 Treib, *An Everyday Modernism.*

When I stressed architecture as a social art I did not want to imply it was not a fine art. In fact, to reach for our aim it must be a fine art. I feel the term social art is one which was not usually included in former descriptions of architecture which defines it as being for the use of people. To bring this about through education means that our schools should contain some insight into sociology, both urban and rural; economics, with public and private finance; geography, and political science, for we must have knowledge of rules under which we live and the way and process by which these may be modified.[15]

György Kepes and Julian Beinart, International Design Conference in Aspen, Colorado, 1966.

15 William Wurster, *Journal of Architectural Education* 4 (Winter 1949): 6.

In many ways, György Kepes was the main component of "fine art" in Wurster's conception of architecture as a social art. Kepes arrived at MIT in 1947, four years after Wurster. It was his first appointment in an architecture department, having followed László Moholy-Nagy from Berlin to London, then to the New Bauhaus in Chicago, and finally to Brooklyn College. Kepes not only brought "fine art" to the department; he became the major figure in the teaching of visual knowledge in the Institute and was celebrated by MIT as such. Today he is still the only faculty member of the School of Architecture and Planning to have been elevated to the rank of Institute Professor, one of a group of fifty-one scientists and engineers over the past half a century. He is also the only teacher in the School to have given MIT's prestigious annual Karl Taylor Compton lecture.

The teaching of visual design in the architecture department occurred at two levels. Robert Preusser, a painter, and Richard Filipowski, a sculptor, both graduates of the Chicago New Bauhaus, taught classes at the junior level. As an introduction to beginning students, the teaching followed the principles of the *Vorkurs* ("Preliminary Course") taught by Johannes Itten at the Bauhaus and transmitted to the USA by Moholy-Nagy. In both cases, the essence of the instruction lay in an attempt to substitute the students' prior visual experience with exercises in basic visual form-making. In the Bauhaus doctrine "the student arrives encumbered with a mass of accumulated information which he must abandon before he can achieve perception and knowledge that are really his own."[16] According to Moholy-Nagy, teaching gave the student "ample chance to shed the often depressing clichés of his previous studies and to recover his all-embracing biological potency."[17] Filipowski himself describes this kind of "finding form as a sustained search for spatial-structural-emotional concepts."[18]

At the more advanced level, visual design teaching was in the hands of Kepes. According to my own notes of my first class in Advanced Visual Design (September 27th, 1955), the aims of the seminar seemed to be "the basic issues of aesthetic fermentations in all art forms. Today we are more and more interested in the total sphere of architecture, architecture needs rethinking in terms of completeness. Vocabulary of visual thinking—what do we see, why do we appreciate it, what makes a visual experience?"[19] With Kepes we traveled

16 Herbert Bayer, Walter Gropius and Ise Gropius, eds., *Bauhaus 1919-1928* (Boston: Charles T. Branford Co., 1955) 34.

17 László Moholy-Nagy, *Vision in Motion* (Chicago: Paul Theobold and Co., 1956), 72.

18 *MIT Tech Talk* 53, no.11 (December 10, 2008), 2.

19 Notes of the author, September 27, 1955.

the world of visual knowledge from the "passion of Turner and Constable who saw the smallness of their world" to the "unifying lines of Piero della Francesca, Raphael, Sesshu, Bellini, Poussin, Juan Gris or Mondrian" and to Doesburg and Mondrian's search "to achieve the full compression of space."[20] We were introduced to our own biology: "William James says 'The great thing, then, in all education is to make our nervous system an ally instead of an enemy.'"[21] Understanding visual thinking fully meant traveling a very wide path, as the "scientific research of the great thinkers–Leonardo, Goethe, Schopenhauer, Chevreul, Ostwald–tesify [to] the universal validity of color harmony."[22] From architecture we learned about how pioneers like Frank Lloyd Wright embodied honesty "in this chaotic counterfeit social existence" and his observation that "the machine soothes the wearisome struggle to make things seem what they are not and never can be."[23]

When Rudolf Arnheim visited the class, we focused on the fundamentals of seeing, something that was the touchstone of Kepes' conception of vision as a creative process. As he stated it, "to perceive an image is to participate in a forming process; it is a creative act . . . Vision is the work process of the eye."[24] While we acknowledged Kepes' association with gestalt psychology, some of us privately wondered if it plumbed the depth of the human visual experience deeply enough. Kepes himself acknowledged some of our doubts: in *Language of Vision*, which some of us, although not required, used as a textbook, he argued that "it could no longer be denied that the subconscious is the real background of psychological events and that the conscious, using Freud's comparison, is like the visible small fraction of an iceberg of which the larger part has its menacing existence submerged under the sea."[25] Nevertheless, after Arnheim's visit, I never looked at Cezanne the same way again.

Kepes brought many MIT scientists to the class; he connected the department to the rest of the Institute and he also brought the deep significance of vision to MIT's scientists. As to his conception of Wurster's "social architecture," he only touched on the connection between social circumstances and their effect on the work of visual interpreters. I first learned about William Morris and John Ruskin through his class, not as political theorists but as recognizers of the way industry had devastated labor and nature in nineteenth-century England. Kepes quotes them thus in his writings: "what right have you to shut yourself up with beautiful form and colour when you make it impossible for other people to have any share in these things?"[26] (Morris) and "it is the vainest of affectations to try and put beauty into shadows, while all real things that cast them are left in deformity and pain."[27] (Ruskin) We never asked Kepes to go beyond such abstractions: only later did we realize that Morris was an activist reformer and that Ruskin wrote letters to the working men of England, that they were deeply immersed in the genesis of British nineteenth-century socialist politics.

These were questions for later: I still treasure the little book of Ruskin that Kepes gave me. Years later, I tried to apply the basic design exercise of MIT's visual design world in short summer schools that I ran in six African countries. By then, basic design was no longer considered as the essential introduction to architectural design at MIT and other architectural schools, mainly because the transfer to the multi-dimensionality of architectural design seemed to elude students in their subsequent design studios. The orthodoxies of visual thinking and form-making should be learned in a core program within the discipline of architecture itself rather than in generalized abstractions, it was argued. The everyday knowledge of students was not necessarily a malady from which they had to be cured; on the contrary, it could be an asset in a more catholic view of architecture and urbanism.

It was when I was back in Africa that the expansive spread of Kepes' teaching and Lynch's belief in the insights of ordinary people steered me to the power of popular art. Studying the way tenants changed their government-built houses and decorated their walls with a communal visual language which they derived from both their tribal background and their new urban status, led me to try to engage their extraordinary capacity.[28] They had something that professionals who designed housing could not access. Nigeria had just achieved its independence and there was an optimism about its future. I experimented with a set of basic design exercises that were easy to do in very constrained conditions for people with little or no visual training whatsoever; many joined the classes off the street as they were passing by. Often the students would respond to a formal exercise by injecting literal meaning into it: a retired schoolteacher, when asked simply to fill a sheet of paper with repeated marks, painted many little birds.[29] Ulli Beier, writing about the two Nigerian schools, comments on the way these students reacted to the basic exercises: "In a series of violent exercises the students were made to 'play themselves free,' to lose thie inhibitions and gain new vision. Beinart achieved surprising results because his own feverish energy and inspired enthusiasm carried everyone with him into a state of euphoria and creative activity in which people shed all preconceived ideas about art and beauty... they began to make pictures, and the freshness and charm of their imagery immediately stood out and the directness and sureness of touch was often surprising."[30] Kepes later published these in *The Education of Vision*, one of his *Vision and Value* series.[31]

20 Notes of the author, undated; György Kepes, *The New Landscape in Art and Science* (Chicago: Paul Theobald and Co., 1956), 50; György Kepes, *Language of Vision* (Chicago: Paul Theobald and Co., 1944), 108.

21 György Kepes, *Language of Vision*, 56.
22 Ibid., 35.
23 Ibid., 119.
24 Ibid., 15, 53.
25 Ibid., 210.
26 Kepes, *The New Landscape in Art and Science*, 75.
27 Ibid.

28 Beinart, "Patterns of Change in an African Housing Environment" in *Shelter, Sign and Symbol*, ed. Paul Oliver (London: Barrie and Jenkins, 1975), 160-182.
29 Julian Beinart, "Basic Design in Nigeria", *Athene* 11, no. 1 (Summer 1963): 21-23.

30 Ulli Beier, *Contemporary Art in Africa* (New York: Frederick A. Praeger, 1968), 105, 107.
31 Julian Beinart, "Visual Education for Emerging Cultures: The African Opportunity" in G.Kepes, *Education of Vision* (New York: G. Braziller, 1956), 184-200.

Kepes and Lynch started working on the Rockefeller-funded study, *The Perceptual Form of the City*, in September of 1954, and in the late fall two years later I began to work as a research assistant for Kepes. That they, faculty in different departments, should cooperate so closely and share intelligence so elegantly, was novel to me. At the first Harvard Urban Design conference the next spring, I listened to the Harvard Dean, Josep Lluis Sert, reiterate the split between those who design and those who plan: "When we come to the city planners and the architects there may be a little conflict. There is a certain misgiving among architects, as someone has said here, that city planners do not know anything about the three-dimensional world we want to help shape. And the city planners think the architects know nothing about city planning."[32]

But Kepes and Lynch were theorists whose ambitions operated at a higher level than those who bothered with professional disagreements. They were joined in a conviction that the contemporary city was unable to satisfy its inhabitants in many basic human needs; the city was, as they wrote in their research proposal, "in many ways ugly and uncomfortable" and that "the tremendous power and utility that this complex structure confers on human society is often obscured by its problems, its inhumanities, and its confusions."[33] Kepes had consistently argued for the need for a coherent visual world in reality and in art. Already as a high-school student, Lynch had made notes about the writings of the great Western philosophers. Between notes about Kant, he scribbled: "Space and time are absolutely necessary before we can have any perception at all (baby has no idea of space, yet he perceives)."[34]

The two men attacked the problem of establishing a completely satisfying sensuous urban landscape in separate ways. Sometimes they disagreed. In a letter to Lynch in the summer of 1955, Kepes wants a wider aesthetic and less mechanical conception of their study of orientation in the city:

> I still feel, as I have expressed it before, that in your present formulation, orientation is synonymous [sic] with perceptual organization . . . In this precise but limited sense of orientation, the aesthetic qualities, as harmony, balance, rhythm, proportion; are not factors of orientation . . . I would suggest that we agree on certain systems of coordinates when we refer to orientation.[35]

Lynch chose to ask people in cities how they structured their experience. Having been exposed only to good and bad notions of city form as proclaimed by celebrated architects and my teachers, I initially found it difficult to relate to Lynch's position. After all, the studio teacher in my first semester, the author G.E. Kidder Smith, had us spend all of our time studying formal models of classic Italian public open spaces. It might have been

Lynch's commitment to the values of ordinary people, those who lived in the spaces that professionals designed; it might have been the person-centered environment of the MIT school, reappearing in the later research of people like John Turner and John Habraken. It certainly was a long-held sensibility of Lynch's: at the age of 34, in his extensive note-books of his travels in Italy, Lynch documents in words and drawings the sublime character of urban Florence but doesn't stop at that. On October 26th 1952 he adds:

> Need to think of basic questions to ask Florentines to evoke their reactions to their physical city, as: sketch a map or panorama. what do you think of first; where would you prefer to live ; where do you go in free time or to meet people or to spend a little time outdoors. where is the center of the city; what is your favorite part of Florence; what changes would you make; what is your local section and how do you recognize it, etc.[36]

Two years later, Lynch would write in *Scientific American*: "A city is the characteristic physical and social unit of civilization . . . The people who live in it shape these properties and are shaped by them."[37]

Lynch was the first theoretician in history to build a theory of the form of a city on the basis of evidence gained from its citizens. To do so, he had to skirt some of the methods of psychological study. Early on he sought advice from an MIT colleague, J.C.R. Licklider, a senior professor in psychology. Licklider's answered that "the existing methodology of psychology may not be of as much help to you as I wish it could be."[38] (Later on, one of Lynch's assistants, William Alonso, also argued that, in his view, the social sciences did not possess a general theory of sufficient utility for the Kepes/Lynch work.) Licklider had two additional comments. First, he expressed the psychologist's preference for the descriptive rather than the normative: "I wish," he wrote, "it were possible to approach the problem of the form of the city in a way that did not require *a priori* assumptions about what is good for, or what is bad for, the people who live in the city."[39] Lynch insisted on their assumption of city goodness in their work: "Instead of saying that 'cats are black' and then being led to a direct test of whether they are indeed black, we are saying 'it would be better for all of us if cats were black.'"[40]

32 J. L. Sert, " in Conclusion," *Progressive Architecture* 8. (August 1956): 112.

33 Kevin Lynch and György Kepes, "The Perceptual Form of the City." March 4, 1954. Kevin Lynch Papers. MC 208. Massachusetts Institute of Technology Institute Archives and Special Collections, Cambridge, Massachusetts

[hereafter Kevin Lynch Papers. MC 208].

34 Kevin Lynch, "Philosophy Notes." Kevin Lynch Papers. MC 208. Box 13.

35 Letter from György Kepes to Kevin Lynch. June 30, 1955. Kevin Lynch Papers. MC 208. Box 1.

36 Kevin Lynch Diaries, Volume 1, "October 26, 1952." Kevin Lynch Papers. MC 208. Box 13.

37 Kevin Lynch, "The Form of Cities," 55.

38 Letter from J. C. R. Licklider to Kevin Lynch. September 13, 1954. Kevin Lynch Papers. MC 208. Box 1.

39 Letter from J. C. R. Licklider to Kevin Lynch and György Kepes, 3 March, 1955. Kevin Lynch Papers. MC 208. Box 1.

40 Letter from Kevin Lynch to J.C.R. Licklider. April 8, 1955. Kevin Lynch Papers. MC 208. Box 1.

Licklider's second concern was with meaning, and the apparent absence of it in the study's program of study. Lynch considered meaning to be one of a central triad that made up the image of the city: identity, structure, and meaning. However, the study could not isolate the significance of meaning in the experience of cities. As he put it, "These are not truly separable. The visual recognition of a door is matted together with its meaning as a door. But it is possible and useful to analyze the door in terms of its distinctiveness or identity of form, considered as if it were prior to its meaning."[41] Many years later, Lynch accepted that the bypassing of meaning was a mistake. "Meaning always crept in, in every sketch and comment. People could not help connecting their surroundings with the rest of their lives . . . If only it were not so difficult!"[42] His optimism that future studies in environmental semiotics might illuminate the meaning quandary has so far remained an unrequited hope.

Kepes planned on investigating meaning by first documenting and analyzing the visual landscape and then trying to understand how it communicated meaning: "the direct communication of literal meaning by intentional signs and symbols and also the communication, by the total environment, of deeper ideas and emotions, such as those of cooperation or competition, aspiration or a sense of continuity of time."[43] Following a morphological inventory of optical and sound characteristics, the next step would consist of examining the research team's own subjective reactions, and then those of subjects from a diverse background. Kepes' method was parallel to the one he used to understand all visual material: first a measurement of the formal elements and then an analysis of its deeper symbolic content. On November 11, 1955, I tried to do something similar, walking down Washington Street in Boston from Adams Square to Kneeland Street and, in my own notes, "attempt[ing] to write down, draw and try to understand any visual experience which confronted me and from this attempt to draw some conclusions as to the particular visual nature of the street."[44] This is my extract at the corner of Summer and Washington streets:

> the congestion is tremendous and no further progress is possible—whistles,exhaust fumes, sea of people crossing allover—"parade is coming"—people no chance to see anything as they are pushed about—sun strong down street, jet airplane overhead—I cannot move—"once we get past Filenes, it will be all right," "watch it" policeman, "we should have known," "it hasn't started yet," "hold onto mummy," "I'm sorry sweetie, todays a bad day to bring you into Boston"–mother to child, "don't push me, I cant help it," loudspeaker somewhere, noise of band approaching 2.35pm. Now fabulous confusion, crushing of people, band noise, children smoking—"hey, you doing a survey?"—"I cant breathe!" soldiers "one,two three, four"–left corner 3.25pm.[45]

My street recording was constantly filled with complex juxtapositions of signs, sounds, and light, angular images, and escapes to narrow side streets; it was intricate and apparently chaotic overall, yet full of energy. It seemed to follow the rules that I had never seen formalized. What indeed was the architecture of urbanism, I asked myself, and who designed it? It made me wonder, for the first time, at some of what I had seen at the Harvard Urban Design conference, where design seemed so often to be preoccupied with cleaning up things, on sabotaging randomness and stochastics. I was reminded of a conversation between Kepes, Lynch, and the composer, John Cage in which the notion of relative chaos came up:

> *Lynch:* You believe, then, that the person should be trained to enjoy what is there, rather than attempt to control the environment.
> *Cage:* What would be the intention of an imposed order?
> *Kepes:* Because the average sound environment is a random situation, small islands of ordered pattern within that randomness could help to catalyse an overall achieved pattern. . .
> *Cage:* Could you instead awaken people to the possibilities of the random situation?[46]

In 1956 Lynch taught the Theory of City Form class for the first time. Like most MIT students I thought I was too busy to take another class. Twenty years later, after I returned to teach at MIT, we taught the class together for two years: I have now taught it ever since. In a letter to me before we taught the class, he explained its content but also some of his doubts about it:

> In summary, the course is meant to be an advanced one, that considers the question: 'What makes a good city?', in a general theoretical sense...I try to stick with the normative questions of structure, while acknowledging the connections to other kinds of theory. It seems to be a lonely - even laughable - enterprise... Finally, just before vacation, I returned to a review of theories of the planning process, and ideas of the proper role of planners, to show links to normative ideas about structure. again, it was abstract and cursory, but, while in earlier years heated discussions developed here, this time it fell quite flat. Is it I, oh Lord, or the times? Enjoy your summer... I would enjoy teaching the course together.[47]

41 Kevin Lynch, "The Image of the City." 3. Kevin Lynch Papers. MC 208. Box 1.
42 Kevin Lynch, "Reconsidering The Image of the City (1985)", in *Cities of the Mind*, ed. Lloyd Rodwin and Robert Hollister (New York: Plenum, 1984), 158.

43 György Kepes and Kevin Lynch, "Summary of Accomplishments: Research Project on the Perceptual Form of the City." 8. Kevin Lynch Papers. MC 208. Box 1.

44 Notes of the author, November 11, 1955.
45 Ibid.

46 "Urban Form Seminar." 2. Kevin Lynch Papers. MC 208. Box 1.
47 Letter from Kevin Lynch to author. August 9, 1976.

We alternated lectures, mildly agreeing or disagreeing with each other. We spent time examining his work on performance dimensions which he was then preparing for his *A Theory of Good City Form* book. I thought it somewhat too abstract and said so: he replied that at this still primitive stage of the discipline it had to be so, and that it would be made more instrumental over time. (In the prologue to his book, he says: "The normative theory of city form is in woeful state.")[48] In one of my lectures, I debated Also Rossi's thoughts about relative performance in the form of cities, and Lynch responded angrily, questioning my allegiance to humanistic thought. In his book, he refers thus to Rossi:

> For him, architecture is an autonomous discipline, eternal, outside of time, creating form typologies which have an independent existence, like Platonic ideas... Physical structure is abstracted from social structure...(These attitudes) are rooted in the same false idea: that man and his habitat are completely separate entities, linked only, if at all, by some mechanical one-directional causation.[49]

Lynch retired in 1978, leaving me to teach the class. Today the basis for the class, "what makes a good city?" still derives from Lynch and his solid structure has allowed it to mutate since. Now the class meets for twice as long as before, and the class' general bibliography has grown from 50 items (1956) to 124 (1976) to over 500 (2009). Looking backward, the content of the 2009 class differ from the 1976 class in a few respects.

First, whereas Lynch felt the class could serve to discuss a comprehensive theory about the form of a good city, my stress has been on critically examining as many aspects of what could comprise a theory as possible. Lynch was more comfortable dealing with theory than he suspected his students were prepared for: in my case, the attempt is to make theoretical ideas more accessible by always following a theoretical construct with a case example. Sometimes I imagine I am simply adhering to the MIT credo: *mens* followed by *manus*. For example, theoretical literature on spatial and social structure is immediately backed up by case studies of bipolar situations such as apartheid Johannesburg/Soweto or colonial Delhi/New Delhi or cross-border Juarez/El Paso or urban/rural Havana/Cuba or political/religious Jerusalem.

A major section of the current class, largely absent from the '76 class, deals with the nineteenth-century origins of the modern city. The belief here is that only with a grasp of its genesis is the contemporary city intellectually available. Evidence from the past plays a large role in the current class. Very few students enter this advanced class familiar with urban history: while the history of buildings is mandatory in any architecture curriculum, the history of cities is almost always absent. The advent of so much new material since Lynch and I taught together may also account for my passion to teach, among others, the nineteenth-century demography (the conquest of cholera), economics (the invention of the mortgage system, the contract-in-gross and deficit spending), politics (the state's search for social equity), urban infrastructure (the forms of industrial innovation), the social and formal dynamics of housing, the displays of commerce, as well as detailed case studies of the transformations of London, Paris, Vienna, Barcelona and Chicago.

In addition, the scope of current urbanism includes items not so present over thirty years ago: the extended low-density American context, hyper-urbanism in the developing world, distance communication, urban preservation and restoration, the kinetics of contemporary urban culture, and the greening of the planet. If anything, there is always in the class the constant imperative set out so many years ago at MIT to account for both space and society. If there is any bias in this dualism in the current class, it is that there is more focus on architecture than Lynch felt he needed. Much of this is in an attempt to energize thought about a pattern of good building which is intimately connected to good urbanism. On reflection, this is not so different from the questions of architecture.urbanism relationship which struck me so forcibly for the first time when working on the Kepes/Lynch study many years before.

In the late fall of 1955, Lawrence Anderson called me to his office to tell me that, instead of short visits by outside critics, we were to have one visitor for the next spring's studio. The next day I wrote on the class blackboard that LEWIS CONN was going to be our teacher. The class was outraged: who was this man? Where were the Yamasakis, Catalanos, Saarinens and Johansens who had taught the previous year's class?

On the 15th of February 1956 a short man with a bow tie spoke to us for almost four hours. We understood very little; at best it seemed mystical: none of us had heard such stuff before. Not even the department's staff had taken much notice of the man. On my way home, I saw Louis Kahn lost in the corridors. He showed me a note on which it said: Commander Hotel. I said I would show him the way. He said he was lonely, could I have dinner with him. At the Henry IV restaurant, he drew sketches of the Trenton bath-houses all over the napkins. I was even more puzzled.

48 Kevin Lynch, *A Theory of Good City Form*, (Cambridge: MIT Press, 1981), 2.

49 Roderick J. Lawrence, "Architecture of the City Reinterpreted: A Critical Review," *Design Studies* 6:3, (July 1985), 148.

Louis I. Kahn, napkin
sketches of Trenton
Bathhouses and
Community Center,
February 15, 1956.

Our first project was a sketch design for a house: "$200,000 @
$25/a sq.ft = 8000 sq.ft . . . young, wealthy, growing family . . .
many acres—wooded—slope 20 degrees facing south." I copied
a house design by Gio Ponti that I had seen in a magazine. The
next project was for the Trenton community center. Now we were
all struggling with what seemed to us to be the Kahn-ian doctrine:
repetitive formal geometries; categories of space, some explicitly
subservient to the others; clearly articulated compression structure;
and carefully constructed light sources.

I had never been exposed to such notions: Charles Eames' house
with its minimal structure and everyday materials was still my
model. For a month, I attempted what seemed to me a set of
formal games and I ended up with an impossible reduction of Kahn-
ism. Kahn liked my scheme but said my drawing was too facile. I
should try drawing with my left hand and experience some pain.
The final studio project was to redesign the Boston Garden. This
time I could not understand Kahn's micro-urbanism. To me, there
seemed little wrong with the Garden. Weren't there more important
problems to tackle in Boston? I made a colored drawing which
kept the Garden much as it was. Kahn said I was lazy. He preferred
the drawings of a French classmate who ran a new axis over the
Garden from Commonwealth Avenue to the State House.

But, like many of my generation who were fortunate to study with him, Kahn opened our eyes to another architecture—arcane and metaphysical seeming at first, but a fundamental alternative to our dyed-in-the-wool modernism. The previous semester I had studied the history of modernism with Siegfried Giedion at Harvard. There we were exhorted to rescue ourselves from the deceit and vulgarities of 19th-Century ruling taste:

> 19th C. *People wished to erect sham facades over interior feelings.* Flatterers of public taste. Artists with imagination were banished—19th C. fog of inarticulate feeling— the tragedy of 19th C. and even today—uncertainty in finding themselves . . . Final judgment on 19th C. will depend on finding our own time—if we can see the handing's down to us, it will grow important—inexorably connected with our own destiny.[50]

But the great adventure of modern architecture was cast against a nineteenth-century once again disembodied from its epochal political content. So our focus was only on items of vision, which enabled parallels between Borromini's 17th C *Sant' Ivo della Sapienza* and Tatlin's *Monument to the Third International* (1920) on the basis of similar form but insulated from their separate social circumstances. And later the same disassociation led some to believe that the sensuous curvature of the automobile freeway on the cover of Giedion's *Space Time and Architecture* meant that modernists supported the social inequities of Robert Moses.[51]

However, life as a young graduate student did not mean only dealing with such serious matters. Learning often meant knowing our teachers and visitors socially as well. There were dinners, large parties, and smaller parties at our apartments. Among others, we asked questions of Lewis Mumford, Josep Lluis Sert, Buckminster Fuller, Louis Kahn, Paul Rudolph, Werner Moser, and Joseph Hudnut. In my dilapidated black Packard I drove Walter and Ise Gropius to MIT's Endicott House: on the 15th of November, we all drank too much with Giedion at 216 Beacon street. I asked him to sign my copy of his book and wrote my name for him. By mistake, he signed my name twice. To correct things, he added an insert:

Julian Beinart
with remembrance
on a most charming
evening.
I am sorry not to be:
Julian Beinart
Boston, 15/11/56
Giedion

left to right, Professor
Lawrence B. Anderson,
Manfredo Nicoletti ('55),
Louis I. Kahn and Julian
Beinart ('56), Department
of Architecture drafting
room, MIT, 1956.

Recalling William Wurster's message, now 60 years ago, MIT has maintained the call to embrace architecture as a "social art" while clinging to his insistence that it at the same time be a "fine art." There have been many shifts. During the late Vietnam war period, there were passions about architecture as practiced by most in the profession. Skidmore, Owings and Merrill, for instance, were called in to explain why they were designing the Carlton Centre project in Johannesburg with separate toilets for whites and blacks. Some teachers wore overalls as if there were hammers in their pockets. Complex built form made of stone and carefully aligned passing wood joints was one of its aesthetics. Another option was the avoidance of designed architectural form in favor of user-made environments and the conservative anarchism of places like those made by Third World squatters. Visual design as taught by Kepes disappeared, replaced in part by centers such as the Center for Advanced Visual Studies and programs for advanced study in the visual arts.

But this period of hibernation meant that MIT's lurching towards the social avoided the profligate worlds of post-modernism and exotic historicism into which which MIT never entered. Slowly it has returned to seeking the appropriate balance between Wurster's social and fine arts, a tension which always has been and will always remain the central but often elusive task of architecture.

In this search, the department has been helped by its long adjacency to its neighboring Department of Urban Studies and Planning and its continued alignment with the Institute's commitment to research and inquiry. During the Johnson presidency, city planning at MIT grew to its current place as the foremost such educational center in the world. Research in technology has reached back to its powerful old traditions after its short adjournment in the department's sticks-and-stone time. It has engaged again in methods of fabrication and production, in the forgotten history of traditional structure and it now plays a large role in the Institute's efforts in environmental and energy studies.

Research in architectural design, often regarded in the past as needless academic interference with the individual architect's creativity, is now seen as an adjunct to design innovation. When we were asked by the Deans of the Ivy League schools of architecture

50 Notes of the author, September 28, 1955.

51 See Marshall Berman, "Buildings Are Judgment II," *Ramparts Magazine* 13, no. 8 (May-June 1975): 53-55.

52 See Alan Balfour, ed. *Architecture Education Study* (New York: Andrew W. Mellon Foundation, 1981).

in the mid-1970s to undertake a study of architectural education, we centered the project on field work in design studios where teachers and students could be observed and their activities analyzed *in vivo*.[52] By studying real situations and asking questions of its participants, principles could be derived which could benefit teachers' design teaching and students' design learning. Very similarly, in one of their preliminary reports on their Rockefeller study, Kepes and Lynch had written about the way they saw their research as enhancing rather than circumscribing the ability of designers:

> the final aim of our work is to supply stimulating principles and ideas for the future design of cities... no such thing as a formula for design will evolve, but rather a background of analysis, a set of very general principles, and some leading hints - all of which will be useful as a support to the skilled designer.[53]

One of the outcomes of their research was the publication of Lynch's small book, arguably the most read book on the form of cities. The book's somewhat formulaic listing of *paths, edges, districts, nodes* and *landmarks* as elements of the city's form became its most well-known component. Yet in the person-centered environment of MIT, it pained Lynch. When students in class mindlessly used the terms as absolutes, Lynch would always reply: "If you want to know about the form of cities, ask the people who live there."[54]

Whether Lynch's response to his students was totally correct is not the point. He was educating the students to an awareness of the everyday knowledge/professional knowledge dialectic in design. Similarly, at any time in a liberal democracy there must be a critical debate about what properly constitutes a good society and what role art plays in achieving it. Architecture should be a subject in this public polemic, and where architecture is taught, teachers and students must practice this involvement. This diary of a year in graduate school suggests that this is what was modelled that year; that what was at stake was the engagement of a set of people with very good minds who enjoyed working together, respected each others' values, undertook the serious study of important social and artistic ideas, came to different conclusions about that relationship, and agreed that they did not always have to agree.

53 Kevin Lynch, "Discussion in Progress: The Image of the Urban Environment." 38. Kevin Lynch Papers. MC 208. Box 1.

54 Kevin Lynch, *The Image of the City* (Cambridge: MIT Press, 1960).

Julian Beinart, "An Embassy for the Union of South Africa in Washington D.C." M.Arch Thesis, MIT, 1956.

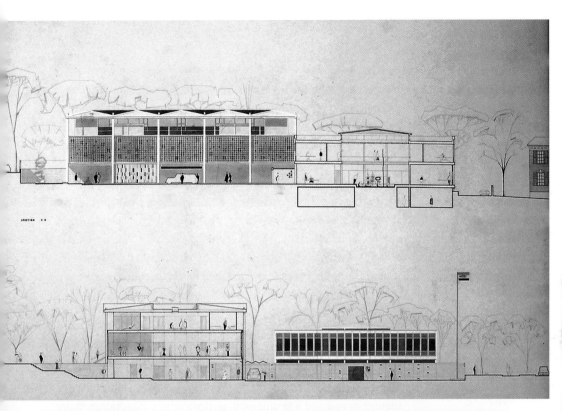

WILLIAM L. PORTER

Three Episodes, Three Roles

Given my long association with MIT School of Architecture Planning I thought that a good way to portray its "techno-social" turn was to describe three episodes in which I played different professional roles, and in which I encountered and dealt with both technological and social issues.

The first, *professional practice*, focuses on the Guayana Project, in which I was an urban designer and in which social scientists' contributions were essential to the realization of the project's purposes. However, these contributions disrupted the traditional skills and practices that I brought as a trained architect and transformed my views of what such skills and practices should be.

William L. Porter, Dean,
School of Architecture &
Planning, MIT.

The second, *research*, centers on my dissertation at MIT, in which I became fascinated by the potential that thinkers from technological fields introduced regarding the role computation might play in enabling thought. Working with an interdisciplinary team, I developed a language to explore how computation might be employed and benefitted from during the course of urban designing.

And the third is *institution building* at MIT, in which I was chair of a faculty group and subsequently dean, developing and implementing a new mission for the school. This entailed being open to social and technological streams of thought and activity and developing ways with others of incorporating these ideas into the educational programs of urban planning and architecture.

1 Eric Pace, "Lloyd Rodwin, 80, Authority on Urban Planning," *New York Times* (December 13, 1999), available online at http://query.nytimes.com/gst/fullpage.htm l?res=9B00E6DC1031F930A2 5751C1A96F958260.

2 The Joint Center for Urban Studies of Harvard and MIT was established with funding from the Ford Foundation. "The center will be international in scope, intended to provide a stimulating environment for scholars engaged in urban research in the United States and abroad." *New York Times*, March 4, 1959.

Episode 1: Professional Practice

Lloyd Rodwin,[1] fresh from the formation of the Joint Center for Urban Studies of Harvard and MIT,[2] came up with the idea for a major project in Venezuela while consulting there, a project which could reinforce the Center's mission and give substance to the field of urban planning and design as he envisioned it.

> I first met Colonel Rafael Alfonzo Ravard-later to become General Alfonzo Ravard-President of the Corporacion Venezolana de Guayana (CVG), while working on a consulting assignment with Direccion d 'Urbanismo in Venezuela in 1959. We got off somehow on a discussion of the nature of planning, and our half-hour meeting lasted more than three hours. Colonel Alfonzo mentioned the possibility of developing some more extended professional association-and then pressed me to visit the Guayana region . . . I suggested that the Joint Center might organize a team that-together with a group of Venezuelan associates-might work out some strategies for attacking the problems of urban and regional development in the Guayana. The team could be backed up by specialists in planning, architecture, law, economics, sociology, public administration, civil engineering, and other relevant disciplines at both universities. But I knew that this proposal was not likely to pass muster in Cambridge unless the Joint Center could also carry out a program of research on many aspects of these activities. I asked whether the Colonel and his associates would support such a research effort. The answer was: Yes![3]

Needless to say, there were many discussions in Cambridge and in Venezuela that preceded the final agreement, but the idea survived intact. It was in this frame of reference that the Guayana project was created in 1961 in collaboration with the Corporación Venezolana de Guayana (CVG).

Lloyd Rodwin was the central figure in both the project's conception and its execution. A student of British New Towns,[4] he believed that planning and design could help Venezuela realize its ambitious goals through the development of an important new city region. At the same time he saw an opportunity to demonstrate a new definition of urban and regional planning as an influential part of national politics, one that linked city and regional planning

---

3 Lloyd Rodwin, "Introduction," in *Planning Urban Growth and Regional Development*, Lloyd Rodwin et al, (Cambridge, MA; MIT Press, 1969), 1-2.

4 Lloyd Rodwin, *British New Towns Policy, Problems and Implications* (Cambridge, MA: Harvard University Press, 1956).

to national economic development, incorporated the thinking of first rate social scientists, and integrated promising research into the planning process.

Rodwin also, however, was deeply committed to a democratic view of the use of private and public power. He had internalized a struggle that was to play out within the Guayana Project for the next several years. Professor Rodwin and Professor Kevin Lynch, also of MIT, wrote in a 1961 essay:

> Men are attracted to the metropolis by real values—choice, freedom, privacy, opportunity, culture, entertainment. How can we ensure the realization of these ends? More importantly, what are the possibilities for metropolitan life that are as yet undreamed of? And what kind of power, knowledge or guidance must be applied to achieve them? The spirit of hopeful intervention should prove at least as effective as the desire to escape present discomfort.[5]

Rodwin's client, Colonel Alfonso Ravard, was positioned to assemble a team of extraordinary economists, planners, designers, and engineers from Venezuela as counterparts of a team to be assembled by Rodwin from the US. And there was, as promised, provision in the contract for visiting experts and for support of academic writing about the project. Combining professionals and academics in a broadly-conceived team, incorporating both Venezuelan and US personnel, was to result in a durable and sensible strategy for Venezuela's practical aims while providing an experience that could be tapped for ideas and help build the foundation for new definitions of the planning profession.

I arrived in Venezuela, having been hired by Willo von Moltke,[6] formerly director of design for the Philadelphia City Planning Commission. I was to assist him in the urban design of the city and to be part of a diverse interdisciplinary team. In my previous position, working for Louis I. Kahn in Philadelphia, I had attempted to understand and internalize the approach of the master, looking on the one hand for the strength of design to be found in the essential nature of materials and assemblies and, on the other, in essences of human institutions captured in epigrammatic phrases and in diagrams: design and form, as he put it, but conceived largely without interaction with anyone except the client—and the self!

The exhilarating sense that these essences could be discovered by patient and imaginative individual work contrasted with my new circumstances in Venezuela. There, the social, political, environmental, and historical conditions demanded articulation. I came from a quest that was deeply individualistic, with the artist's lonely search as its paradigm, to one that was social and political, requiring an understanding of cultures with which we were not familiar, working in parallel with others whose disciplines and cultures were less familiar, and requiring as well the persuasion of co-workers, administrators, and governmental administrators and leaders. Moreover, working in a foreign country made it necessary to articulate ideas and issues that could too-easily be left unexamined in our own culture.

The just-completed design for the new city of Brasilia seemed dream-like and detached from such practical realities as we those would have to address in Venezuela: a city that could become Venezuela's Pittsburgh, that could help to diversify the economic base for the country, that, coupled with a plan for the Guayana region, could justify the World Bank's investment in a major new hydroelectric dam there.

At the time of its inauguration in 1978, the Guri Dam would have been the largest hydroelectric dam in the world. To perform its role in regional and national development, the city, Ciudad Guayana, would have to attract the technical elite required to lead and operate a wide range of manufacturing industries; it would have to accommodate the inevitable migration of a relatively rural population, and it would have to be capable of self-sustaining and independent growth. All of this would require elaborate justification that would have to persuade many groups at the national, regional, and local levels; and that persuasion would have to occur before very much was in place, and before measures of actual outcomes could be taken. Thus even the ideas for the city would have to have an instrumental relationship to economic development.

After a brief romance with some unrealistic design ideas for housing in part of the city, we designers found ourselves needing to translate the economic forecasts for the city into quantitative expressions of land use, and levels and types of activity. Fidelity to quantities was requisite. There was no a priori strategy for the physical city. Instead it was to be derived from and to give support to the economic projections for the region, infrastructural requirements, and especially support of the industrial activities that would fulfill national planning goals and expectations and that would, in general, serve non-local markets.
The first step was to translate the industrial projections that were the core of the new export economy of the city into requirements for space and location. The core industries were raw materials extraction and conversion, heavy manufacturing that used the converted raw materials, and light manufacturing that could grow as a result of the

---

5 Pace, "Lloyd Rodwin."   **6** A short biography is available online at http://www. blackmountaincollegeproject. org/Biographies/VON%20 MOLTKE%20willo%20BIO/ VON%20MOLTKE%20 willo%20BIO.htm.

complementarities with the heavy industry. The second was to project population numbers and composition, production of goods for local consumption, and commercial activities, resulting in a program for the new city. The multiplier to population from export industrial workers was roughly 10:1. Therefore, with a projected 60,000-employee industrial worker base, the city would be about 600,000+ people. The anticipated income distribution of that city suggested housing and neighborhood types, locations, and relationships as well as patterns of consumption and, therefore, supporting commercial activities.

It was critical to attract the technical employees at all levels in order to staff the needed industries. Therefore, an important measure of the success of any designs for the new city would be how favorably someone from Caracas or even another country might see them. Housing, schools, and neighborhoods would have to be fashioned to make these people feel comfortable in an environment that was widely viewed as distant, remote, and even primitive.

Urbanity, culture, a variety of institutions and commercial resources, attractive parks signaling control of nature: these were to be the essential characteristics of a city that would support national economic objectives. Willo von Moltke[7], chief of design for the project, brought a deep sense and knowledge of sophisticated urban environments and culture. And he also brought extensive experience in architecture and urban design that could transform a frontier region into a livable and attractive place for people accustomed to urbane environments.

In the Guayana study urban design played an extremely important role. The industrial activities and the population needed are best served by a well-designed city, for economic and social reasons. A well-designed city offers the social benefit of choice and the opportunities to stimulate the highly-skilled technicians, administrators, and professionals needed to achieve these economic and social goals. A well-designed city may go a long way to overcome the sense of isolation that is a major deterrent to the many skills needed for this undertaking.[8]

7 Von Moltke was a member of an elite German family, born in South Africa to English and German parents, a direct descendent of Field Marshal Count Helmuth von Moltke, leader of the victorious Prussian armies in the wars against Austria and France. He migrated to the United States and served in the US military during the Second World War. His brother, Helmuth, was part of the anti-Nazi underground and was, unfortunately, executed just before the end of the war.

8 Wilhelm V. von Moltke, *Urban Design Intent: Three Case Studies* [unpublished manuscript] (1983), 30.

9 William L. Porter, "Changing Perspectives on Residential Area Design," in *Planning Urban Growth and Regional Development*, Rodwin et al., 252.

Thus, the imperatives for Ciudad Guayana did not in the first place address the needs and conditions of the low-income population. If there were precedents for the new city, they were drawn from study of land-use distribution in contemporary North American and European cities, and based on economic projections of how this city would grow over time. Indeed many of the staff felt the burden imposed on the project by the presence and in-migration of low-income people and by the presence of the existing communities and their leaders. Many in the staff and administration of the Guayana Project believed that the local residents would not be an attraction to the new residents and their families; if anything new residents would probably feel happier if isolated from people already there. This issue was evident throughout the project's history and was the source of different if not conflicting views.

Lisa Redfield Peattie, a social anthropologist, arrived at the project about the same time as I did, and she chose to live in the Guayana region, in San Félix, one of the two existing towns that were to be incorporated into the new city. The design team had elected to work in Caracas, some 350 kilometers away, as our counterparts were there and decisions were, presumably, made there. Lisa's first-hand living experiences there and her skilled articulation of her understanding of the people she lived with provided us with a bridge to what we otherwise would not have known.

While making the resident population and its concerns far more visible than they would otherwise have been, Peattie's communication with the planners and the leaders of the project introduced fresh ideas: for example, her distinction between settlements of despair and settlements of hope made us aware of the rapid change linked to economic betterment that occurred in some settlements, and the tragic stasis in others. Moreover, she helped us to see the radically different roles that the physical environment played for the people it housed, enabling for some and frustrating for others, and how its administration and servicing was integral to these roles. These insights challenged the conventional wisdom in Caracas: that low-income residents simply needed to be accommodated; that they were not part of the solution but a problem to be dealt with. Nevertheless, she was able to convince many of the planners and the designers of the importance of these people for the future success of the city.

The design proposals may be divided roughly into three chronological periods. Because of availability, the designers arrived first on the scene. Partly for this reason, the work in the first period embodied a kind of international high-quality set of designer-held values. In the second period, economic, housing, and social specialists arrived but needed time for studies and analyses. Meanwhile the designers began to focus on long-range plans for the city and on the development authority's own needs and its capability to implement projects. During the third period, the designers were more knowledgeable about the problems, and their proposals tended to reflect the insight of the other specialists and to relate more directly to the needs, values, and perceptions of the people using the environment.[9]

During the first period, economic projections were not yet available. The designers worked on "pilot" projects they thought could set a standard for future development. For example, the designers drew up designs for an innovative neighborhood that utilized row houses and careful placement of pedestrian and park areas, separated from the automobile, to achieve medium density with very high environmental and design standards. Yet because it was inconsistent with conventional development, it was difficult to finance and build. Only a few of the units in the development were completed four years after the designs were completed, but a more conventional neighborhood with detached houses in a suburban meandering road pattern had been built and was already occupied. Also in the first period, attention was focused on a pilot project for the lower-income groups including in-migrants. Here again, the infrastructure design was inefficient, and the development too expensive for the lower-income groups. The CVG shifted its administrative rules to allow shacks to be built in another area, enabling low-income families to get started and to build incrementally as their incomes increased. However, in contrast with the Joint Center designers who wanted to see income groups mixed across the city, the CVG wanted to place the lower-income residents on the east side of the Caroni River, and the middle- and upper-income residents on the west side. Building large tracts of residential areas was far faster and more efficient than the smaller areas that the designers recommended, and they tended not only toward homogeneity of appearance, but also toward homogeneity of economic group.

> The success of UV3 and El Gallo [the non-pilot projects] derived chiefly from their having been implemented easily. But, even knowing that vast amounts of housing were needed, the designers did not examine the standard designs that the private developers and other public agencies already had. The degree of cooperation between the developers and the agencies in working out modifications would have been difficult to predict. Nonetheless, the design profession's reluctance to try such a cooperative approach can probably be attributed in part to their long history of dealing with only a small portion of the total physical development, serving only elite interests.[10]

After the economic projections were available, in what I have termed the "second period," the designers were able to focus on the design of the city as a whole with a concentration on the road infrastructure, community and communal facilities, and the parks and open space. This responsibility required that they take a more strategic role with respect to the residential areas, and resulted in a focus on location, density, and residential mix, leaving more detailed design to professionals outside the CVG.

Then it was possible to plan knowing the anticipated size and composition of the city. The designers could begin to see how the natural and manmade conditions of the site could become part of a larger city. The center of the new city had, before the Joint Center became involved, been located at the east end of the city overlooking the San Félix bowl.

Using the economists' projections, and using our initial industrial location studies, the city's center of gravity shifted to the west. Finally, the form of the city emerged.

> A linear city with a series of nodes connected by a central transportation system would be the form that would best fulfill the goals of efficient and memorable physical development. Only a linear city could tie together the existing developments, scattered over a distance of seventeen miles, and thus help to overcome one of the site's major physical problems—the extreme dispersion of existing facilities.[11]

In the third period, more results from the social scientists became available.

> Natural increase rather than migration was accounting for the majority of new growth, and recent arrivals were similar by all available measure to the people already there. Instead of thinking of the future residents somehow different from the existing population, or planning separately for in-migrants as opposed to residents, it was becoming evident that the problem was to plan for a city of migrants, some more recently arrived than others, and that the needs and values of the existing population would be extremely good guides to those of the future population.[12]

Peattie's presence had exacerbated controversy in the project, controversy that Rodwin anticipated and used creatively to broaden the social mandate to include a far more inclusive approach to upwardly mobile residents than would otherwise have been the case. Rodwin soon brought on John MacDonald, an expert in demography and migration; one of his innovative ideas was to tap the potential of chain migration by creating incentives for workers from various parts of the nation and insuring competitive wage rates. As he explained, "A small number of workers brought from distant states and provided with good job opportunities and

10 Porter, "Changing Perspectives," 259.

11 Willo von Moltke, "The Evolution of the Linear Form," in *Planning Urban Growth*, Rodwin et al., 135.

12 Porter, "Changing Perspectives," 264.

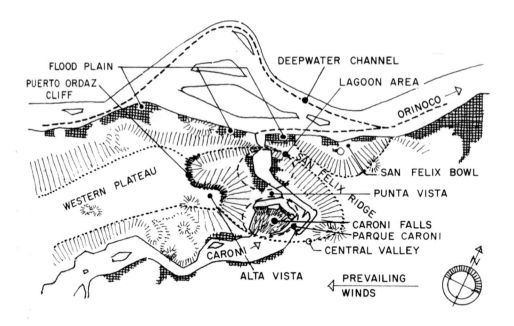

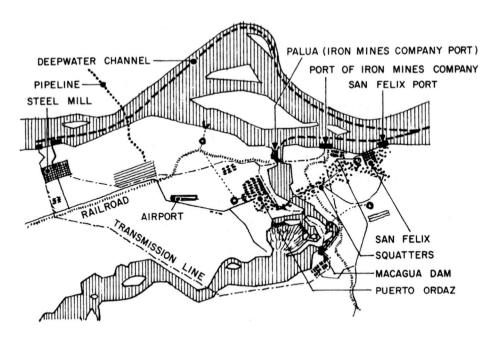

Willo con Moltke, "Natural Conditions," and "Manmade Conditions."
facing page, "Industrial Location," and "Linear Form." The Ciudad Guayana plan
extends over about 12 miles. Transportation, prevailing winds, extraordinarily
beautiful and fragile parts of the environment, a spread out city with a need
for a new city center where services could be concentrated—all of these factors
influenced the city's shape and infrastructure. From Lloyd Rodwin, et al., *Planning
Urban Growth*, (Cambridge, MA: MIT Press, 1969).

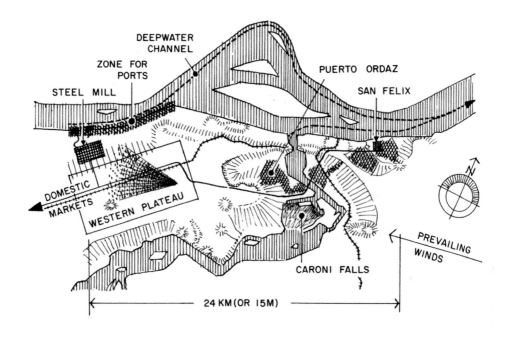

DEEPWATER CHANNEL

ZONE FOR PORTS

STEEL MILL

PUERTO ORDAZ

SAN FELIX

DOMESTIC MARKETS

WESTERN PLATEAU

CARONI FALLS

PREVAILING WINDS

24 KM (OR 15M)

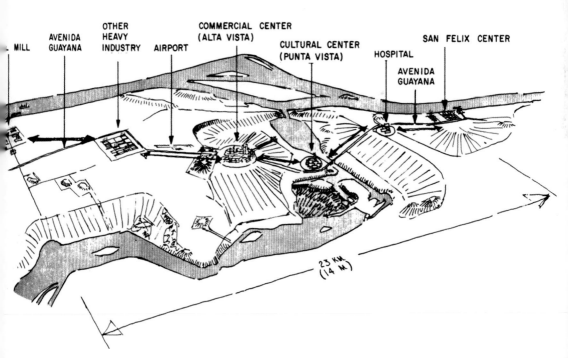

MILL

AVENIDA GUAYANA

OTHER HEAVY INDUSTRY

AIRPORT

COMMERCIAL CENTER (ALTA VISTA)

CULTURAL CENTER (PUNTA VISTA)

HOSPITAL

SAN FELIX CENTER

AVENIDA GUAYANA

23 KM (14 M.)

living conditions could serve as a bridgehead for chains of migration from their hometowns."[13] MacDonald also cautioned that:

> the recent introduction of homogeneous housing schemes—which naturally go first to the upper and middle classes—and the rapid proliferation of homogenous shanty towns have introduced a much clearer separation of classes than hitherto . . . a delicate balance has to be struck between providing attractive environments for elites who are reluctant to leave the larger cities and opening avenues for social mobility from below.[14]

As more results became available from the social scientists, the division of views within the Joint Center-CVG project team became more evident. Russell Davis and Noel McGinn, education experts, discovered that the CVG was going to support only private schools because these were presumably necessary to attract the elite workforce required for the new industry. The CVG was not authorized to duplicate the work of the national ministries, and, therefore, the Ministry of Education was to support the rest. However, national education in Venezuela had been very unsatisfactory for years, waning under the dictatorships, and waxing somewhat under the democratic government since 1958. It had never been satisfactorily related to industrial growth and a modern economy. An arrangement between the CVG and the national government was not worked out by 1965.[15]

Thus there was an ongoing and underlying conflict of views that occasionally surfaced. Von Moltke observed that the design group could have been better informed by closer contact with the inhabitants of Ciudad Guayana.

> A program of continuous discussions of the plans with the local people would have removed most of the conflicts and would have provided constructive feedback from the site.

> The designers' work was also hampered by their inability to enforce decisions at the detailed design stage on the site. The engineers did not understand the planners' ideas, and they were anxious to proceed with the greatest possible speed and to employ the highest engineering standards, even when inappropriate.[16]

Based on Kevin Lynch's work, Donald Appleyard in *Planning a Pluralist City* analyzed how various groups saw the city, based in part on where they lived and how they traveled. These multiple ways of seeing raised important questions about what the "form of the city" actually was. Certainly it took the emphasis off of large shape-making as the essence of form. Even though that had never been a dominant aspiration of the design team, Appleyard made clear that it was not a widely-valued perception by many groups in the population. His work also highlighted the varied levels of importance that people attached to various parts and features of the region. But perhaps most importantly, it underlined the importance not only of seeing the city through the eyes of those who were and would be there, but also the importance of shaping the design to support those ways of seeing. There were many points of conflict and disagreement, but much was accomplished despite these. In Rodwin's "Summary Observations" he states:

> If collaboration involves close, long-term relationships between professional specialists from different cultures, it requires sensitive adaptations in social behavior, in professional methods, and in the basic aims and values of the two groups. Such adaptations are not easy to make or to maintain, at either the leadership or the staff level; and the collaboration may prove quite unsuccessful if some or these adaptations break down. One or the most unusual aspects of the Guayana project is the fact that the CVG and the Joint Center managed to maintain successful collaborative relationships over a five-year period despite numerous differences between the participants in behavior, working styles, and values.[17]

The potential impact on planning and design practice and practitioners could not be more profound. This experience demonstrated the need, for example:

- Not to rely solely upon their own precedents, professional skills, and accustomed consultants,
- To be far more aware of all stakeholders' legitimacy,
- To seek and employ expertise in understanding social and technical issues,
- To forge carefully the links of their work to policy, and understand the myriad of intersecting forces on a project,
- To collaborate with others whose views and expertise were different from their own,
- To tolerate the presence and endurance of value conflicts, and
- To value partial rather than complete control as well as the release of energy and power of others through that strategy.

13 John S. MacDonald, "Migration and the Population of Ciudad Guayana," John S. MacDonald, in *Planning Urban Growth*, Rodwin et al., 122.

14 John S. MacDonald, "Migration and the Population," 122.

15 Russell G. Davis and Noel F. McGinn, "Education and Regional Development," Russell G. Davis and Noel F. McGinn, in *Planning Urban Growth*, Rodwin et al., 270.

16 Willo von Moltke, "The Evolution of the Linear Form," in *Planning Urban Growth*, Rodwin et al., 145.

17 Lloyd Rodwin, "Reflections on Collaborative Planning," in *Planning Urban Growth*, Rodwin et al., 489.

Episode 2: Research

Having been attracted to the ideas and agendas of people from the MIT faculty including Don Appleyard, Kevin Lynch, Lloyd Rodwin—as well as those of the faculty from other institutions, including Robert Mitchell from the University of Pennsylvania and Bill Doebele from Harvard's GSD—I entered the PhD program in MIT's Department of Urban Studies and Planning in 1964. Drawn to MIT in the first place because of the opportunities to learn more about society, social forces, and the economics of cities, I was richly rewarded with courses given by Rodwin (urban economics), Lynch (theory of city design), Jim Beshers (urban sociology), and others.

In 1960 Rodwin had recruited Aaron Fleisher to introduce quantitative methods into planning education, particularly for studies of transportation. Fleisher was a Phi Beta Kappa graduate from New York University in 1939, the same year Rodwin graduated from the City College of New York. At the time he was a research associate in the MIT Department of Meteorology, having acquired his doctoral degree there in 1950. Modeling meteorological phenomena, he told me, was a bit like modeling urban phenomena: both contained factors that could be observed and measured in addition to those that could not; and both were extremely complex. In addition to work in transportation, "Professor Fleisher was most widely known for his use of mathematical modeling to describe, project, and simulate urban areas."[18]

Fleisher drew me into his web of concern over how quantitative reasoning could best enter planning thought. He prompted my return to the question of how design intuition related to rationality. What could be made explicit in design, and of that, what was describable in rational terms? I did not believe that design could or should be reduced to a set of logical propositions, nor that design should be revealed as the emperor unclothed. Instead I wanted to explore possibilities of harnessing the power of rationality to design intuition more effectively, of releasing the cavalry of thought (or intuition) when needed for important things, after having rested it when not really needed (to paraphrase Whitehead).[19]

Re-examining the urban design of Ciudad Guayana I discovered that many of the locational decisions could be made explicit and formulated as logical statements. This

18 MIT *Report to the President* 2004-05, available online at http://web.mit.edu/annualreports/pres05/01.01.pdf.

19 "It is a profoundly erroneous truism, repeated by all copy-books and by eminent people when they are making speeches, that we should cultivate the habit of thinking of what we are doing. The precise opposite is the case. Civilization advances by extending the number of important operations which we can perform without thinking about them. Operations of thought are like cavalry charges in a battle—they are strictly limited in number, they require fresh horses, and must only be made at decisive moments." Alfred North Whitehead, *An Introduction to Mathematics* (New York: Oxford University Press, 1958), 41-42.

20 Tom Van Vleck, "The IBM 7094 and CTSS," available online at http://www.multicians.org/thvv/7094.html.

led in a number of directions: sitting in on Minsky's course on artificial intelligence in which he talked more about how the mind worked than about the computer; listening to John Donovan's teaching of Fernando J. Corbató's 6.251, the introductory course for undergraduates majoring in computation, in which telling the machine what to do, though difficult, was possible; taking courses in psychology and philosophy, to clarify clarification; and continuing to learn from Lynch and Appleyard about linkages between behavior, esthetics, and the physical form of the environment.

These were heady days in which artificial intelligence was full of promise—without apparent limits, in which the beginnings of geographic modeling, visualization, time sharing, and interactive computing promised tools for working with computational representations of the physical world. The Compatible Time-Sharing System (CTSS) was one of the very first to support interactive computing in the social sciences. It was operational in 1963. By 1966, when we began to work on Discourse, CTSS was just giving way to Multics as the environment for interactive computing, but its capacities were limited. The IBM 360 was upgraded to handle larger volumes of activity, but it had to be used in batch processing mode; and Jerry Saltzer had written Runoff, an early word processing program that permitted some control of printed output. There were no widely available graphics terminals or displays, as these were still in development.[20]

Critiquing contemporary urban modeling practices with Aaron Fleisher, we saw new opportunities opened up by interactive computing regarding the ways in which computation might extend design. Instead of being a big black box in which inputs were distant from outputs, the computer could be a medium in which the implications of small moves could be immediately seen. This changed computational modeling from a ponderous and relatively opaque medium to one that was more transparent, bringing it closer to the actual processes and procedures of how one made specific design choices, and allowing it to participate in acts of thought. We re-discovered a basis for modeling in the logic and actions of urban design.

Some computer languages were structured in ways that facilitated the programming of elements and their logical relationships, as if computation really could accommodate thought! AED (*Algol Extended for Design or Automated Engineering Design*), designed by Douglas Ross at MIT, was touted as the first software engineering design language, and it was our language of choice for our early experiments.

"Discourse" was the name of the language that we developed. In the early 1960s languages were beginning to be layered upon one another with the lowest layer being language of bits and bytes, higher layers more similar to the operations that people wished to perform. AED stood between Discourse and machine language. Discourse was a limited vocabulary of terms and relationships, recognizable to an urban designer, that produced results generated by the computer in the form of geographically distributed patterns. For example, to place low- and mid-rise residential on the high points, one could write: "put lowres .and. midres for each loc on highpoint." Not graceful, perhaps, but close enough to ordinary language to enable rapid learning by the user.

One could also combine such statements to form paragraphs—or programs—that would carry out much more complex operations. And, of course, one could entertain hypothetical possibilities. This confirmed the potential for interactive conversation with the machine—the formalized self. Kathy Lloyd at the beginning, and Wren McMains later, brought extraordinary programming skills to its development, a partnership of design and computation created by Aaron Fleisher. It is described in my PhD dissertation, *Discourse, A Language for Computer Assisted City Design.*[21]

In 1967 I was jointly appointed to the departments of Urban Studies and Planning and of Architecture. The work on Discourse formed the basis for my teaching *Analysis of Urban Design* with Wren McMains. In that course students learned to formulate ideas about activities and their locations and to see the consequences of those ideas rigorously computed. Because of the immediate feedback, they were able to adjust ideas and consequences until their design interventions performed to their satisfaction. The exercises served both to increase understanding of the regularities and logic of existing arrangements in cities as well as to project the implications of new ideas. And they served to hint at the power of computational tools for urban design.

Discourse also became part of the Cambridge Project, funded by the Defense Advanced Research Projects Agency (ARPA).[22]

> The proposed research program is a university based effort and therefore oriented to advance a major field of science. While it is a basic research effort, it is likely to lead to many applications. The potential applications of the advances made—if the project

21 Also see William Porter, Katherine Lloyd, and Aaron Fleisher, "Discourse: A Language and System for Computer-Assisted City Design, in *Emerging Methods in Environmental Design and Planning,* ed. Gary T. Moore (Cambridge, MA: MIT Press, 1970), 92-104.

22 "The goal of the Cambridge Project is to make computers more useful in the behavioral sciences and in other sciences that have similar computing needs. Participants in the Project are behavioral and computer scientists at Harvard University and at M.I.T. During the past year, approximately

40 members of the faculties of the two universities served on planning committees or took responsibility for parts of the Project's work. The Project has been supported by the Advanced Research Projects Agency of the Department of Defense." DOUWE B. YNTEMA MIT *Report to the President*

1973, MIT Institute Archives, 41-42.

Diagram of AED programming language, showing the possibilities for intersection of attributes, or activities to be placed on land, and locations. From William Porter, "The Development of Discourse, A Language for Computer Assisted City Design," (PhD Dissertation, Department of Urban Studies, MIT, 1969).

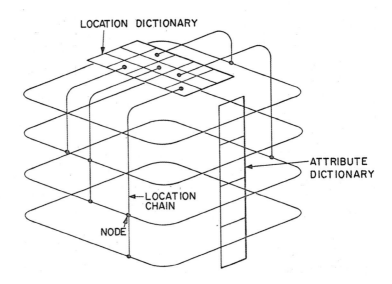

Example of output, display logic focused on resonance of thought with the computer. And this level of display was only possible thanks to Jerry Saltzer's Runoff program. From Porter, "Development of Discourse," 1969.

```
map (lowres midres; highpoint land)   1-8 1-11

                                1
           1 2 3 4 5 6 7 8 9 0 1

       1   -1-1-1-.-.*.-.-.-.-.-.      1
       2   -1-1-1-1-. . .-2-2-2-2      2
       3   -.-.-.1-1-. . .-2-2-2-2     3
       4   -.-.-.-.-. . .*.-2-2-2      4
       5   -. . . . . . . .-2-2*2      5
       6   *. . . . . . . . . . .      6
       7   -. . . . . . . . . . .      7
       8   -. . . . . . . . . . .      8

           1 2 3 4 5 6 7 8 9 0 1
                                1
```

LEGEND:

PRIMARY ATTRIBUTE ASSIGNMENTS - - '1' = LOWRES(7); '2' = MIDRES(8)

'.' = NON EMPTY LAND

REFERENCE ATTRIBUTE ASSIGNMENTS - - '+' = HIGHPONT(10); '-' = LAND(5);   '*' = LAND & HIGHPONT; ' ' = NO REF ATTS

following page, *left to right*, Langley Keyes, Head of Urban Studies and Planning; Ann Gordon, Assistant Dean for Academic Administration; John Habraken, Head of the Department of Architecture; Margaret Depopolo, Rotch Librarian; Léon Groissier, Executive Officer; David Judelson, Assistant Director, Laboratory of Architecture and Planning; William Porter, Dean; Lawrence Susskind, Assistant Head, Department of Urban Studies and Planning.

succeeds—may perhaps be better understood by those in public life who will apply the knowledge than by the scientists themselves. Yet it is clear to us that public policy will be aided by advances in the understanding of human interactions and in the prediction of the performance of social systems.[23]

There was considerable controversy that surrounded Project Cambridge (CAM), as it was called then. A previous project of ARPA, Camelot, had stirred much resistance politically without and within the academic community because it was focused on preparing the basis for intervention into the internal affairs of other countries with the aim of reducing conflict. Project Cambridge was conceived on the other hand to be an analytical tool to look at social science data and make sense of it.

Led by Davis Bobrow, the new head of ARPA's social and behavioral sciences division and a political scientist who had strong connections with the scholarly community, the ARPA social scientists decided during 1968 to reorient ARPA's social science program in three areas. ARPA believed that to further their work social scientists needed to group themselves into "critical masses" (like the Manhattan Project) instead of working on smaller, individual projects, which are ineffective and more vulnerable to Congressional attack. Second, ARPA officials believed that social scientists must concentrate their efforts on the development of analytic tools and new technology like computer software rather than on the gathering of raw data; this approach also would ease ARPA out of controversial foreign-areas research. Finally ARPA decided to stress the development of basic models and simulations of situations useful to the Defense Department rather than funding smaller research projects with more narrow applications.

These modifications removed most of the basis for objections to the project, though it was, of course, still to be funded by the Defense Department. Nevertheless, it was to be entirely open to the academic community. The NSF did not have and has not had generous funds to finance social science computing; though there were even efforts at one point to get the ARPA funding transferred to the NSF, that did not materialize.

23 1962 MIT proposal to ARPA for the Cambridge Project, quoted in the *Harvard Crimson* (September 26, 1969).

24 Judith Coburn, "Project Cambridge: Another Showdown for Social Sciences?," *Science* (New Series) 166, no. 3910 (Dec. 5, 1969), 1250-1253.

Finally, Ithiel Pool, Professor of Political Science, much of whose research had been funded by the Defense Department, proposed that Project Cambridge be focused on reusing the IBM 7094 as that would enable people to continue to use CTSS, the system in which his and others' data were already present.[24]

John Klensin (BS MIT) was a PhD student of Ithiel Pool's; I was on his dissertation committee. He was critical to this effort, bringing his computational expertise and his knowledge of social science to link structure and content of Discourse to other social science computing systems. The aim was to make the boundaries of any system relatively invisible to the user and to give the analyst flexibility to look in a rigorous way at problems from the point of view of a number of different disciplines. The Consistent System was the next version of the integrated social sciences system begun with CTSS. It was to open up new flexibility in understanding complex urban phenomena and to project complex possible futures.

Episode 3: Institution Building

With Professor Jack Myer of the Architecture Department, I led the Environmental Design Program, bringing ideas derived from Lynch, Appleyard, and Myer on how cityscapes were seen, structured, and used, as well as the more analytical approach I had acquired through computationally assisted teaching. Professor Lisa Peattie and I also taught a subject dealing with the construction of problems for planning and design, what constituted evidence, what evidence was important, and how one could draw clues from individuals and groups, either through direct interaction or through observations of behavior. Thus my faculty career at that point linked and was committed to the social and the technological dimensions of problem setting in architecture and planning—the edges of the fields! This episode increasingly engaged me in planning for the school's future and participating in its leadership, and it also deflected me from my research and teaching.

Having already worked closely with Lloyd Rodwin and others in Urban Studies as well as with Don Lyndon and other faculty in Architecture, I became centrally involved in a school-wide group of faculty dedicated to thinking about the mission of the school for the next decade. The formation of this group was occasioned by Dean Lawrence Anderson's stated intention to retire after the academic year 1970-71, and it served as the focus of discussions across the faculty about what was important in architecture and planning for the next decades. Views were different and at times in conflict with one another. However, with careful listening and feedback to the participants, a central direction became increasingly clear, and out of this study group grew very considerable agreement. That direction incorporated the new streams of thought in the social sciences and in technology, which I had experienced in professional practice and in research during the previous several years. The faculty and leadership felt sufficiently confident in the study group's direction and in the

Massachusetts
Institute
of Technology

TECH TALK

September 15, 1971
Volume 16
Number 11

William Porter Named Dean of Architecture and Planning

Chancellor Paul E. Gray has announced the appointment of Dr. William L. Porter as Dean of the School of Architecture and Planning, effective today.

He succeeds Professor Lawrence B. Anderson who retired in June after serving as Dean of the School for six years.

Professor Porter is an advocate of enhancing the abilities of architects and planners through the use of computers and the analysis of creative thinking. He was largely responsible for the development of the DISCOURSE language, through which users can elaborate on the basic program to make it more responsive to their individual needs.

Last summer Professor Porter was chairman of a study which prepared a proposal outlining future development of the School of Architecture and Planning. It called for a new educational focus based on the interrelationship of three themes: people and places, systems, and policy and design. The proposal has since become a document of understanding for the School.

A School Council will be established, consisting of members from both the Department of Architecture and the Department of Urban Studies and Planning together with some professional

Professor Porter.
--Photo by Alfred Anderson, '71

consultants. In this way, Dean Porter feels, the School will become more aware of its own inner directions as well as what new problems are arising in the broad general field. Under Dean Porter's leadership, the School will encourage broader participation by other departments and Schools at the Institute in the very complex problems of urban systems and design.

Dean Porter received the B.A. degree from Yale University in

1955 and the B.Arch. from the Yale School of Art and Architecture in 1957. After serving in the U.S. Army, he was associated with the Louis I. Kahn architectural firm in Philadelphia from 1960 to 1962.

In 1962 Dean Porter came to the MIT-Harvard Joint Center for Urban Studies and for the next two years worked on the Ciudad Guayana development project in Venezuela. From 1964-65 he held a Mellon Fellowship for graduate studies and planning in 1969.

Dean Porter was appointed Assistant Professor of Architecture and Planning in 1968 and became Associate Professor in the Department of Urban Studies and Planning in 1970. He served as a member of the Faculty Advisory Group to Professor William Ted Martin during 1969-70. During the past year he has been a member of the Corporation Joint Advisory Committee, as well as a member of the executive committee of the Department of Urban Studies and Planning.

During the past academic year, Dean Porter was a visiting scholar of the New Hampshire College and University Council and also a visiting critic in the introductory studio of the Urban Design Program at the University of Pennsylvania for the spring semester. He maintains a consulting relationship in urban design and programming with two Cambridge firms.

Dean Porter is the author or co-author of a number of articles published in the profession. He is presently at work with Professor Donald Appleyard of the University of California (Berkeley) editing *Environmental Design in the United States: A Reader*, to be published in Italy.

Dean Porter is a member of the American Institute of Architects and of the American Association of University Professors. He is also a member of the Board of Directors of the Boston Society of Architects.

guiding ideas that they nominated me, its chairman, an insider to the School, as the next dean. Jerry Wiesner, newly appointed as President of MIT, embraced the recommendation, welcoming the direction and the consensus—as well as the youth of the nominee.

Many of the study group's ideas were expressed in a proposal to the National Science Foundation to re-shape and re-direct the school.[25] The NSF proposal envisioned a new Center for the Human Environment that would concentrate efforts at innovation and create a focus for innovation and management of programs that reached outside the school into the field. The phrase "human environment" was deliberately chosen to underline the school's commitment to the goals of professional intervention as well as is commitment to the professions themselves—an outward rather than an inward focus. This focus derived from the variety of activity in the arts that comprised and now broke conventional definitions, and that certainly lay outside of the "fine arts." György Kepes' Center for Advanced Visual Studies is a case in point. It reached beyond the magazines as measures of architectural success, beyond the planning and design of cities to the impact on the lives of people, beyond the limits of clientele normally served by our professions. CAVS was intended to force a look at the totality of the environment in which we lived as well as the totality of the people who lived in it, and it forced a reassessment of the professional activities necessary to address it.

In 1973 the School established the Laboratory of Architecture and Planning. Its purpose was to enable, house, and reflect on work that was linked to the "field." The hope was to develop field-linked education as an integral part of educational programs in both departments.

> Field-linked Activities: The School-wide Committee on Practice Related Education, headed by Professor Donald A. Schön, evaluated the formal and informal field linked experiences of the Department's students. The Committee also undertook a nationwide survey to deepen understanding of the changing demands of the profession. The work of the Committee should help to design possible core field work requirements and to develop new diagnostic procedures to assist faculty and students in evaluating the educational contributions of practice related experiences.[26]

Appointment of William Porter as Dean of the School of Architecture and Planning. From *Tech Talk*, September 15, 1971.

25 Proposal submitted to the National Science Foundation from MIT on behalf of the School of Architecture and Planning (1971).

26 *Report to the President* 1973, 111.

The new Laboratory filled the most obvious gap in the school's offerings, bringing it more closely in line with the aspirations of the NSF proposal. It would be the substitute for the new Center for the Human Environment promised in the proposal. It also offered a good setting for other types of research, for example, the Discourse project and the Consistent System of which it was a part.

Addressing the educational programs, the proposal noted:

> This proposal announces processes of transformation in the School of Architecture and Planning—processes which, while enriching education for the two professions of architecture and city planning, will open up new approaches to understanding and addressing problems of the human environment unlimited by traditional professional boundaries.[27]

Though the NSF proposal was not funded, it had its effect on both departments, their leadership having been so much involved with the study group and the proposal's production. Curricular reform and innovation and recruitment of new faculty were carried out in each department in a manner consistent with these ideas.

However, these were tumultuous times. Student protests were happening at many campuses, including MIT's. Students in the late '60s appropriated the design studios in MIT's Building 7, the 1938 extension of the 1916 buildings which faces Massachusetts Avenue. Their method of appropriation was to build mezzanines out of used lumber and parts of buildings, a bit like squatter settlements around some Latin American cities. Dean Anderson, in his 1968 President's Report, states: ". . .the celebrated architectural "mezzanines," which, while trouble-making, are remarkable examples of a kind of mass will to create an environment."[28]

In contrast, Professor Lyndon, head of the department, characterized the experience as smoothly integrated into the department's agenda:

> A much more direct confrontation between form and behavior was made possible through the designation of a space/use workshop and experimental area encompassing the undergraduate design studios and adjoining corridors. With the supervision of a student-faculty-staff committee, our students designed and built their own work spaces, adding to the usable area in the drafting rooms by the construction of a string of mezzanines. The work places so created were then subject to the test of use and revised during the year. Students who worked in the area encountered the necessity for programming construction procedures, the difficulties of resolving conflicts in neighboring designs, and the consequences for long-term use of their own design

decisions. At the same time, the entire project served to demonstrate alternative uses of space. It has become increasingly clear that demonstration is necessary to engage attention effectively for the establishment of new forms of environment.[29]

At MIT the tensions were perhaps less disruptive because the faculty and administration were better tuned to the issues and more engaged with the students than at some other institutions.

The NSF proposal states for the Department of Urban Studies and Planning:

> Our experience makes clear the need for a core of academic work such as we have described for the entire School under the headings of: Systems and Institutions, People and Environments and Policy and Design. We believe that this core of work will also have relevance for students from other departments who are preparing for professional careers in urban related fields. Students in Urban Planning would take some work in each of these three areas at both the professional and doctoral levels, which would be connected with a subject specialization or applied fields such as city design, housing, health planning, educational planning, land use, or urbanization in developing countries.

Diversifying the membership, new programs were formed in 1971 to draw community leaders, and these efforts were consistent with views of MIT's new President and Chancellor.

> As in the School of Engineering, there is a strong desire to link the educational process with societally related activities, which in this case means breaking down the walls between the university and community through the mechanism of field-linked education and research programs. In addition, the major programs—the HUD Minority Internship Program and the Community Fellows Program provide a means for substantial minority group participation in the advanced programs of the School of Architecture and Planning.[30]

27 NSF Proposal (1971), 1.   **29** *Report to the President*   **30** "President and
28 Lawrence Anderson, MIT   1968, 34.   Chancellor's Report," MIT
Report to the President 1968,   *Report to the President*
MIT Institute Archives, 31.   1972, 5-6.

Urban Studies and Planning, renamed in 1969 from City and Regional Planning, drew faculty from an extraordinarily broad range of fields. For example, Donald Schön, organizational theorist, was appointed Ford Professor just after completing *Beyond the Stable State*, a book based on his Reith Lectures in England. Historian Robert Fogelson wrote *Violence as Protest* and later that decade *Big City Police*. Gary Marx, sociologist, wrote *Muckraking Sociology*. Richard Larson, operations research specialist, wrote *Urban Police Patrol*. Kevin Lynch completed *What Time is This Place*. There were also faculty members giving courses and specializing in areas such as economics, management of development, planning law, and computational methods for analysis and design. Moreover, the department's PhD program grew rapidly over the decade in parallel with the increase of research activity.

Bernard Frieden was appointed Director of the Joint Center for Urban Studies, with its new focus on Housing and Public Services, after an intensive discussion by faculty and administration of what the Center should do.

> Housing seemed like a very good field to work on: there was a track record on that; there were people at both universities who were interested in housing and had the skills in it; and it was an important national issue—there were Presidential commissions reporting on the country's housing needs.[31]

However, this was just after the Ford Foundation had stopped funding the Center. Frieden and John Dunlop of the Harvard faculty established groups of advisors with the idea of bringing industry, government, and the faculties of Harvard and MIT together to influence the content and direction of urban-related research. This was successful organizationally and financially. Industrial members contributed to the Center, and the Center obtained grants from HUD and other agencies to support their research.

For architecture, the NSF proposal looked beyond the limits of the field imposed by conventional criticism to argue that

> what was taken to be the "crisis of architectural design" has proven to be a fundamental questioning of the concept of design. Does any type of design—that of engineers, city planners or politicians—serve human well-being except according to dangerously circumscribed criteria?...In general terms, events and criticisms of recent years have shaken our confidence in man's ability to exert a socially beneficial control over his environment by design—by the systematic direction of actions calculated to achieve a static pre-visioned goal. Such a proposition goes far beyond architecture, challenging our reliance on human rationality and rationally guided action.[32]

They were energized by the possibility of distinctive and salient contributions to a more unified approach to society's problems.

> Thus it is our [Architecture's] contention that the loose and adaptive but value and idea-impregnated characteristics of environmental form enable the architect to make valuable contributions to society in terms of improved physical surroundings. The problem structure and the methods of design and architecture, rather than being irrelevant, may offer a model for problem solving in other disciplines . . . It is on the basis of such possibilities with the field of architecture, that we must now redirect the Department toward a critical examination and development of the theory and practice of design.[33]

Stanford Anderson, historian and theorist, and Donlyn Lyndon, architect and theorist, undertook a three-year study of urban ecology. Architect Robert Goodman wrote *After the Planners*, and psychologist Sandra Howell began a study of elderly housing funded by HEW. John Turner, architect and specialist in squatter settlements, wrote *Freedom to Build*, a paean to self-organized and initiated building by the poor.

The department also established its PhD program to enable advanced research in the area of History, Theory and Criticism. The program was framed in such a way as to allow the addition of other specializations once the appropriate faculty members were in place.

The Architecture department also housed the visual arts as well as groups working on new media and the supporting technologies. And these interests were linked to some in Urban Studies, which sensed the power of the new media to reshape the public policy environment. The proposal featured that as a growth area as well:

> in Information and Media we intend to research the problems of communicating environmental Information, to increase the quantity and quality of readily available information, to enable students and faculty to scan, select and analyze Information in its many forms with a minimum of time and effort, and to coordinate these efforts with related efforts in other parts of the Institute.[34]

31 Bernard J. Frieden, "Interview," *Plan* (Cambridge, MA: MIT, 1980), 7.

32 NSF Proposal (1971), 10.

33 Ibid., 12.

34 NSF Proposal (1971), 17.

Nicholas Negroponte's vision for the new Media Arts and Technology was a force to be dealt with, one that President Wiesner took up with enthusiasm, as did many in the Department of Architecture.

> the flavor of media technology at MIT is and will be internationally unique, because it brings to the media arts both a credible technological base and along history of concern for human values.[35]

He rounded up strong but disparate programs in the arts, all of which were linked strongly to technology, and each of which served distinct audiences.

> Each group is engaged in various kinds of signal processing, with less emphasis on the pragmatic aspects of their focus and more on its qualitative, subjective, and artistic senses. They include: the Architecture Machine group, the Visible Language Workshop, the Film/Video Section, the Creative Photography Laboratory, the holography component of the Center for Advanced Visual Studies, and the Experimental Music Studio.[36]

In the department of Architecture in the '70s, innovations in the arts and media technology, in uses of the computer in architectural design, in the history and theory of architecture and art, and in building technology all demanded graduate-level students and accompanying programs of research. These added to the pressure of the new graduate professional program to achieve greater educational depth.

The appointment of N. John Habraken, a well-known architect, educator and theorist, as Head of the Department of Architecture, resulted from careful and thoughtful reflection on the part of the faculty, and was enthusiastically supported by Institute leadership. His interests and accomplishments extended and illuminated many of the ideas thought important in the department and school at the beginning of the decade, and he brought, as well, a finely-honed European style of critique.

35 Nicholas P. Negroponte, "Arts and Media Technology," *Plan* (Cambridge, MA: MIT, 1980), 19.
36 Ibid.

37 N. John Habraken, *Supports: an Alternative to Mass Housing* (London: The Architectural Press, and New York: Praeger, 1972). Originally published in Dutch under the title: *De Dragers en de Mensen* (Amsterdam: Scheltema en Holkema, 1962)..

38 N. John Habraken, "Around the Black Hole," *Plan* (Cambridge, MA: MIT, 1980), 52.
39 Ibid., 49.

William L. Porter, Building 7, MIT. From *PLAN*, 1980.

Habraken's book, *Supports* proposed ways of ordering the design, construction, and equipping of housing to maximize the freedoms of choice for each of the participants along the path of production and occupancy.[37] Here it was necessary to create a kind of environmental contract in which, for example, builders, equipment manufacturers, clients, and interior designers could, by virtue of strategic agreement on certain dimensions, placements, and tolerances, open up a wide range of choices that could accommodate each group's own needs while preserving freedom for the others.

John believed that the social relevance of architecture hinged on the question of values:

> It was only with the advent of modern times, and with the subsequent de-localization of the design and his emergence as an agent not necessarily part of the culture he designs for, that the value problem became a problem. It is no longer self-evident that architects and clients share the same values.[38]

He saw no conflict between rationality and the exercise of design intuition.

> It is not fashionable in architectural circles to connect the activity called "design" with intellectual endeavor and clearly exposed rational constructs. A good number of my colleagues will dismiss such attempts as irrelevant, and having nothing to do with the essence and true nature of design as such . . . The very complexity of the design activity can be seen as a challenge for a more orderly application of our rational faculties. One does not have to argue that such an application must rule out the uses of intuition.[39]

Dean's Sherry Hour, MIT.

40 Chiefly through the School Council consisting of the Heads of the Departments, the director of the Laboratory of Architecture and Planning, the Head of the Rotch Library, and the Associate and Assistant Deans, but also through individual discussions with the Heads and, of course, a variety of others.

41 Especially the Academic Council that met weekly. It included the President, Chancellor, Provost, the other four Deans, the Chairman of the faculty, and all the Vice Presidents.

42 The Visiting Committee was a creature of the MIT Corporation, its governing body. It consisted of five people from the Corporation, one of whom chaired the committee, five alumni from the School, and five people drawn from leadership roles in the fields represented in the School. It met roughly every two years.

Conclusion

Building on Lyndon's legacy, Habraken's leadership beginning in 1975, hastened the Architecture department's movement toward a grounding of its intellectual activities in a deeper understanding of values. It was in this frame of reference that the newly introduced PhD program (in 1974) opened the door to advanced research, first in History, Theory and Criticism, and later in other fields. Rodwin had done the same for the Department of Urban Studies and Planning, bringing in faculty from a wide variety of fields to reassess the role of planning, to discover the ways in which it could serve society more broadly and actively, and to open up avenues of research and action that could continually redefine the field.

These and a very few others in the faculty were visionaries. I saw my role during this third episode of institution building as engaging in a continuing discussion of the strongest ideas and directions,[40] learning about them and the people responsible for them, and articulating them to the various communities within which the School functioned, especially the MIT administration,[41] the School's Visiting Committee,[42] and the alumni. I also introduced Sherry Hours, Friday afternoons at the dean's office. They were very popular.

The techno-social turn in education played out in a variety of ways through my career and through the careers of our faculty. There is no doubt that both architecture and planning were very much influenced by developments in the social sciences and in the various technologies that impinge on their professional domains. But the overriding influence was that of a shift in values: toward a conception of service to society at large; and to the challenge of serving those whose values and culture were quite different from one's own.

This new vision of professional service required setting forth ideas provisionally, reflecting with the client and other stakeholders during the course of rendering professional services, and allowing for uncertainty and remaining open to fresh contributions from new participants or from more careful observations. These characteristics of the new vision were not just for international development projects where cultural distance would require more explicit articulation of ideas and values, but for the mainstream of the profession as well.

Rather than creating prescriptions for action, we thought of establishing frameworks. These could be social frameworks accomplished through the mediation of environmental conflicts—in this case it was against a backdrop of policy and prediction that professionals were dedicated to articulating options, consequences, and values in the context of on-going discussion and negotiation among the interested parties. The frameworks could be physical ones in which different groups' interests focused on design ideas that would maximize their freedom of action. We also envisioned media frameworks that provided for an exchange of ideas and mutual learning as well as access to increasing amounts of relevant information. These social, physical and media frameworks would provide the scaffolding of thought to guide both practice and research.

OTTO PIENE, MATTHEW WISNIOSKI

Arts / Science / Technology

Matthew Wisnioski conducted this interview on December 16, 2010 in the offices of the new Program in Art, Culture, and Technology, Wiesner Building, MIT.

Matthew Wisnioski: Let's start by going back to your arrival at MIT in 1968— "tumultuous" seems to be the word that describes that moment. Kepes has just gotten the Center started by talking about "universal harmony," while at the same time there is increasing anxiety and disunity around MIT's mission and the Vietnam War. Do you remember what it was like to enter into that environment?

Otto Piene: Well, it took a while. In 1965, I had my first one-man show in New York in the Howard Wise Gallery. And that also was the time when the famous/infamous 'blackout' happened in New York City. I was in the building then and people thought it was my fault, because I had light sculptures that consumed some power in my show. But I had nothing to do with the Blackout as it turned out. During my exhibition, three very little distinguished looking gentlemen walked into this exhibition, the title of which was Light Ballet. And of the three, one obviously was the "speaker" so to speak, and he introduced himself as György Kepes, of whom I had heard quite a bit, but I hadn't met. He looked at the show, and said he was impressed, and would I have time to talk to him. During that appointment which was in part at MIT and in part at Kepes' house, he explained to me that he was about to form a Center for integrated efforts in art/science/technology, and it was not happening tomorrow, but was due to happen in the foreseeable future, and would I care to accept an invitation to be a Fellow at this new Center. All in all, it took another 2 years until the Center was really there, but I was very curious, and also interested. This was something new and I had hoped that indeed this hoped-for-union would happen. I was particularly interested if it happened at MIT, because I knew that MIT was a radiant place for the sciences and engineering . . .

Otto Piene, CAVS, *A Field of Hot Air Sculptures Over Fire in the Snow*, MIT, 1969.

I arrived in Cambridge on something like the 5th of January 1968. And the Center was there. It was not a lavishly equipped place, but there was space, there were to be colleagues, and it was beautiful to have this nucleus...or be part of this nucleus of people interested in art/science/technology such as Stan VanDerBeek or Takis and Jack Burnham. And initially, we were five and then six, and that was it. The Center had five big studios for one artist each, and the biggest room in the Center was Kepes' studio office. So the energy came from Kepes to begin with, and then from the Fellows— grown people, grown artists so to speak, who were all interested in the Center at MIT. They were all confident that something could be done, although it was not clear what it would be, because Kepes's carrot for people to come here was that there was going to be the US Bicentennial to be celebrated in Boston.

MW: He had mentioned that to you prior to your arrival?

OP: Yes. And the other artists the same story. They came mostly intrigued by this grand plan of Kepes to be the major motor and the major drive in celebrating the US Bicentennial in 1976.

MW: So celebration was a theme of CAVS even before you became director in the 1970s?

OP: Yes. However, the site of the celebrations was moved to Washington, and it wasn't happening in Boston.

MW: When was this discovered?

OP: I think it was months after the Center was formed. And it was a great disappointment. It was like the air went out of the great balloon of expectations. However, the fellows met often, with Kepes, without Kepes. And a kind of small community, but an interesting and fairly strong and vibrant community, did form on from there.

MW: At CAVS' founding, if you look at the press that was produced, there was a lot of celebratory coverage, but there also was talk about a "shotgun wedding" with MIT buying off artists to make them "apologists for the system." Was there talk among the fellows about CAVS as a "Cold War" institution?

OP: That is a pretty bold concept! The Center is definitely...I mean...should I say, speaking out and trying to act in the name of the right values. That is, *love* and *peace*, and *interaction* among well-meaning creative people. Not only in the arts but also in the sciences, and among the engineers. I think that can be said fairly clearly. And these peace-loving people were not only among the artists, they were also among the scientists, particularly among those at MIT who had been major players in World War II, such as those who were involved in the concept and development of nuclear bombs. Some of them had turned peace activists, and some of them had turned lovers of art. And had to develop a rather different profile from than they had been made to adhere to during the war when very very serious stuff was being developed at MIT. One of the most impressive people at MIT was the then Provost and later President of MIT, Jerome Wiesner. He developed or co-developed radar—it was one of the most crucial developments that happened at MIT in the name of the World War II.

MW: Were the scientists and engineers who were attracted to working with artists people who you would characterize as motivated by "love and peace"?

OP: Some were, some not. But the main interest was in developing the arts among the engineers, but particularly among the physicists. Physicists were always the most animated supporters of—not the fusion—but the mental union so to speak between the scientists, particularly the natural scientists, and the artists. Another one who was very strongly supporting the Center at MIT was Doc Edgerton who originally was an engineer, but increasingly was a scientist and physicist who did beautiful things. And was at the same time an artist—an artist of a calibre that was very rare among scientists and among artists. So, there were people here who attracted the alertness of the artists as they came into the MIT campus.

MW: On this subject, there were definite precursors to the sky art you did at MIT—in Group Zero, and even back to your experiences during World War II. But when you arrived at MIT, it seems that instantly there was a jump in scale and the crystallization of calling this work "Sky Art." Was that premeditated or was it something that emerged out of interactions when you arrived?

OP: It was premeditated. I came here in part to realize—to practically pursue—some of the work in the *name* of the ideas that had a lot to do with Sky Art, work that had a lot to do with art that *wasn't* being done among artists anywhere. There were

following page, Hans Haacke, *MIT Sky Line,* October 24, 1967. Courtesy of the artist, © Hans Haacke/Artists Rights Society.

some people who dealt with attempts at flying objects and let's say a first tentative formulation of ideas that could lead to flying objects that would then later be subsumed as I inserted into the debate as well as into the work the words "Sky Art." It was clear what it meant, it was self-explanatory. And the Center with its six fellows initially—five plus Kepes—was an instant breeder of concepts. And, on the one hand, that was Kepes' "fault" so to speak! On the other hand, the reason I came here, I had founded in Germany years before I had founded Group Zero. Group Zero has very similar ideas and values as what Kepes pursued with his new Center for Advanced Visual Studies. Except that Kepes was at MIT!

MW: When you arrived did Kepes introduce you to Doc Edgerton and Walter Lewin?

OP: That's how he practiced his role as director of the Center. Kepes was very formal, but also a social creature. He was a gracious host of small dinner parties at his house and of meetings, conferences, and project building activities at the Center. Kepes also was a brilliant language artist. Maybe in part because of his upbringing in different countries. But his power of speech was mostly the power of metaphor.

MW: The first major work you did here was the "Light Line Experiment," which you collaborated with Walter Lewin?

OP: I met Walter *because* of the light line project. I put a sign outside the window of the MIT office. "I would love to invite scientists and students who are interested in an air and helium experiment to participate," and a day later, maybe on the same day, in walks this tall Dutch man and says, "What is this experiment with helium?" I said, "Well, it's me." And we became instant friends, and later on Walter worked with me with the Munich Olympics and lots of other things. And that is pretty much in the spirit of what Kepes had hoped for. That there would indeed be connections to personal sympathy, as I had said about for Group Zero. Group Zero was based on personal friendships. . . . The personal relationships were very important and were very productive.

MW: Where did you get the helium?

OP: Through MIT. My helium suppliers in the early days were the people in the cryogenic lab. And it was just a normal way of procuring materials needed for MIT projects.

MW: As the projects got bigger, did MIT remain the main source of materials? I ask because the actual making of sky art and other projects are elements that don't get enough attention. Where did the materials come from, how you do the managerial work, etc.?

OP: Yes. This is all stuff that developed. I had to learn how to do that, but it wasn't alien to me. My father was a physics teacher when he was alive. So these things were—I shouldn't say natural—but near to me. And MIT is a fantastic place. It is very inspiring to be inventive, to develop initiatives, to develop initiatives in groups. That was one of the major things that Kepes encouraged. And I came from there. I had worked with groups all my life. Hence Group Zero, which is still very much in existence. We have a Group Zero foundation in Düsseldorf, we have an institute, and so on and so forth. It's all been part of the threads of my life that we worked together with likeminded people. They didn't all have to do the same things. They didn't even have to do similar things, but the spirit was bringing people together.

MW: I think in many of your projects there is this definite air of looseness; letting people do what they want, creating points of contact. With bigger projects, I am thinking of the Munich Olympics and *Centerbeam*, in what ways did you need to become a manager?

OP: Well, if you a bad manager, don't do group work. It's really part of the fun of working together with people from other backgrounds, doing work together that's bigger than what one can do in a studio. Even the studios at CAVS were important because they were larger studios than what people had at home. The Center was smaller than other research centers at MIT, but it was *there* and it was the *only* one dedicated to what I call arts/science/technology together, and it remained the only one for the first 10 years or so. We were just quite alone in the field of integration in this sense.

MW: And yet there are a number of trends at MIT and beyond that touch upon what was going on at CAVS at that time; systems art, for example. I think you once put it as "people mean many different things when they talk about technology . . ."

OP: This came in part from the Center. I think the man who coined this phrase systems art was Jack Burnham. And Jack was an important fellow at the Center, and actually I knew him before I was at the Center and before he came to the Center. We were friends for quite a while, and Jack came to the Center, and he wrote most of his book

following page, Otto Piene and Alejandro Sina, *Neon Rainbow*, MIT, 1975. Photo: Calvin Campbell.

Beyond Modern Sculpture at the Center. We used to refer to him as the artist who introduced the use of the typewriter into the artist's studio.

MW: At the time did you think about these categories? Gene Youngblood, for example, called you a "design scientist," getting the term from Buckminster Fuller. Later Lawrence Alloway said you were a "post-technocratic artist." Did any of these come close to the mark?

OP: Well, a decent part. When other people look at what you are doing, and what's in your head, it's usually a little less narrow that what you are doing yourself, and you develop new things . . . these are fine people. I like Gene Youngblood too, but he was never at the Center. And to find likeminded people who I didn't know before, who kind of didn't exist before, is in a certain way very encouraging. A strong momentum came out of these sometimes chance meetings and sometimes meetings initiated more deliberately.

MW: You left CAVS after your Fellowship was done, and then you came back in 1974 to accept the directorship. How was your experience of MIT under those circumstances different than your arrival?

OP: In a sense I had never left, I was actually away from the Center only for six months because of the Olympics in Munich. Otherwise, I was here in one capacity or another. Since 1972, I was a visiting professor here, and Kepes had told me several times in the past that I was to be the next director of the Center. *Before* he said that, at some point, I said I was leaving. People at Stuttgart had offered me a full professorship with all the flags attached, and I was not that settled to make a living in Boston. Boston at that time was even less friendly to the arts than it is now. Now MIT is very open to the arts; at least it's part of MIT's declaration of values, so to speak. Boston is still not a major art city, but what's major is the impulse that draws arts/science/technology.

MW: When you became the director, it wasn't clear that MIT was enthusiastic about the arts.

OP: No. No. But, as I said, there were so many smart people, productive people at MIT that it had to come that way. They had to get involved in the arts, because the arts themselves moved towards science, towards technology, towards all these things that happened, are happening now, and happening more and more and more. It was only a. . it was not really a shotgun marriage! It was a shotgun love over time. And I think that's what counts.

MW: From an administrative point of view, however, there were a lot of changes when you took over. You expanded CAVS' mission to environmental art and media arts and celebrations. If you move outside to other parts of MIT, you find people talking about transitions coming out of the push back against defense funding and the Instrumentation Lab. Do you think these projects were related?

OP: Increasing, they were related. And finally after ten years or so, other institutes, other people, other countries woke up to what's happening. Initially we had a lot of resistance in the art community. In many places they kept saying MIT is a war force. It's still not entirely removed from the dark corners of the studios in New York City, this thinking that MIT is just a warmonger. So that's in part what we were *against* in the art community initially. Now it's all changed . . . now we have ZKM Karlsruhe, which is modelled after our Center, we have KHM in Cologne, which is modelled after our Center. For the Cologne institute I was the "commissar" funded by the ministry of education in the state of Northern Westphalia. They had the first art/science/technology institute even before Karlsruhe, and something very similar happened in Karlsruhe. The man who founded the Karlsruhe institute, the then mayor of Karlsruhe, came to our Center to learn about *a* Center for Advanced Visual Studies. So the whole thing spread and expanded and the expanding is still going on . . . Initially we were one small institute, a very small one. And now there are hundreds and hundreds of them all over the world. Some are much bigger than this Center has ever dreamt of becoming. The people in Karlsruhe have so much money, maybe too much money. They are not the only ones who have too much money. There are other institutes that don't have enough money to go around. Some of them are the more creative ones.

MW: This begs the question of how CAVS was supported when you took over, because a significant part of the new Center was an educational program. Can you explain how the SMVisS program came to exist?

OP: Initially, I was asked by the Dean of the School of Architecture and Planning, who was otherwise not too active a supporter of the arts and certainly not a practicing artist himself. He said, "wouldn't you be interested in teaching what you are practicing? And hence when you have now become the director of the Center, would you be interested in developing an educational program?" I did that, and that program was immediately fairly successful because MIT students were just *starved* for musical values and practice—by musical I mean the muses. I realized very soon that my two friends who were also teaching the arts in a different way, meaning Nicholas Negroponte, who developed the computer interest in the Department of Architecture, and Richard Leacock, the filmmaker, we got together and said we've got to have a graduate program. We can get only go so far with what we have now, but the greater talent is with those who aspire to be graduate students and develop way beyond

the college level. So, we drew up some kind of program for a graduate program to be, and it passed the academic council at MIT. You cannot have a graduate program unless you are *blessed* into life by the academic council. And from then on we had our small but significant graduate program. And for a number of years, this backup of interests and ambitions that had accumulated at MIT and other places led to very bright people applying. And of course since this is MIT, we could not have the word "art" in the program, so it became the graduate program in "Visual Studies." We developed the degree of Master of Science in Visual Studies. Innocent sounding . . . and on from there.

MW: The other major development in this regard was the creation of the Council for the Arts. Was that on the whole a good thing for CAVS?

OP: It took a while until we kind of sorted each other out. But I think now it's probably working okay. And then of course after the graduate program, the most important thing was the founding of the Media Lab. That was Nicholas mostly, Nicholas and Jerry Wiesner. They toured the world for a little while to drum up the money, which they got. Whereas the Media Lab operated typically with a lot of money from the start, our Center for Advanced Visual Studies never had that much money, but we always had the money we thought we needed. That meant that people like my wife—who became our exhibitions and projects director—and I did a lot of fundraising . . . When it came to projects, we always learned how to have the money we needed, essentially from nothing.

MW: And Jerome Wiesner started as President almost the same time as you started as the Center's director. Was he supportive of CAVS in the early 1970s?

OP: He was initially mostly for the Media Lab. It was one of his chosen hatching projects. He changed in the course of his tenure and became fonder of the Center over time. I had great sympathy for him, and vice versa. He did good things for the Center as well. For example, we needed money for *Centerbeam*. We went to him and I said,

Otto Piene, CAVS, *Son of Balloon Carpet*, Lobby of Building 7, MIT, 1974.

"This a big project, and this is going to be in the books as MIT projects in art/science/ technology." We were in his office, he sat behind his desk, and picked up the phone and said into the telephone, "Hi Jim, how are you today. I have some people here who need some money. Can you give us some?" Just like that.

MW: When *Centerbeam* was happening, was there a sense that Media Lab was already in the works?

OP: That's a good question. It may be have been in the works, but it wasn't the same thing yet. Not what we see now...

MW: Part of the reason I ask is because Nicholas Negroponte in his recollections of Wiesner says that there was a meeting in August 1978 along the lines of: "I went into Jerry Wiesner's office and I said 'Here's what we are going to do.'" Were you still in conversation with Wiesner about how everybody was going to fit into this new space for the arts at MIT?

OP: There had been meetings for years about my role and my contributions, which went on all the time. One person who was in these meetings was our current boss for the arts, Phil Khoury. He was in these constituting meetings, intellectually constituting the role of the arts. And that included the role of the Media Lab and the role of the CAVS. Our Center increasingly concentrated on projects, always including students, including undergraduate students, including graduate students. The projects became my instruments to raise funds. Our Center lived for *years* off the projects that we developed. *Centerbeam* was one of them. And compared to the money that scientists raised and some projects that the Media Lab produced, our funds were modest but productive. So we could do, at least in my view, what we wanted to do, what we dreamed of doing. Our projects were artistic. We didn't build prototypes for industry or anything like that. Whereas the Media Lab moved increasing towards the industrial media and electronic broadcasting media. Ours were artistic. *Centerbeam* was an artistic project. It was a sculpture about communicating with the universe . . .

So in a certain way the roles of these carriers of the arts of MIT defined themselves were hardly competing. I've never had a really bad day with Negroponte. People always try to construe that we were enemies. Ah-ah. No such thing. It would have been just too interesting for some people for that to happen. No. First we had worked together to create the graduate program and then we kind of supported each other. Some of my students took Nicholas's classes and some of his students took my classes, in the spirit of collaboration, just as our relationship to Harvard was like that. There were times when I had more graduate students from Harvard in my classes than MIT students. But the spirit of collaboration was really alive, and well, and real. And all these conflict theories was wishful thinking on the part of all the people who did not have it, and who didn't know it, and didn't understand how people could really productively work together despite occasional skirmishes, that's unavoidable. Essentially it worked really well.

MW: So there wasn't a tension in this split between the Media Lab and what CAVS was doing? It feels as if CAVS moved away from computer and electronic arts in the late 1970s and early 1980s.

OP: We had what we needed and what we needed turned out to be needs in context for specific projects such as the Sky Art Conference, which was a rather interesting animal. And it kind of migrated and migrated internationally and produced interesting things and it was also our connection into the sciences at MIT. So the split was about such things that I had refused to accept during my entire tenure at MIT—to accept defense money. No defense money. The Media Lab has been *rolling* in defense money. That's where people saw conflicts. "Okay, good luck!" We were just different.

MW: I might push this a little more, and you can say that you don't want to go in this direction. In a previous interview, you said, "Its fine that MIT has got a Media Lab, but I think the Media Lab is on the wrong track, essentially promoting what the mail has done forever."

OP: I am sure that's what I said [*Laughs*].

MW: Is this part of a broader tension between models based on Media Labs and models based on CAVS? That is, do new programs elsewhere wrestle with the question "are we principally an arts-oriented technology-influenced collaborative, or are we a market-oriented aesthetically-influenced collaborative?" Do you see that as a productive tension?

OP: I think the tension has been productive one way or another, whether it was sympathetic or not. As I said, in my view, in my experience, it was a mostly sympathetic working together. And we have done things together we couldn't have done alone. If you look at the institutes that came out of the Center and in part out of the Media Lab, there are the same differences there. The offspring of the Media Lab are Media Lab type things and the offspring of the Center are mostly artistic things. And thank goodness. We never considered ourselves part of MIT doing what other people at MIT are already doing very well…

Part of the way I understood my mission was to do what Kepes didn't do. Kepes wrote beautiful books, he had wonderful ideas, he expressed them very beautifully, and formulated them, and was obviously a teacher of very strong, deep impression—making deep impression on lots of people that had anything to do with him. And my relationship with Kepes from the start was very good and also very respectful mutually. And essentially, I did what I had to and Kepes did what he had to do. We both kept doing what we considered important. But there were certain differences there. And the differences were, for instance, my role in those meetings about the arts at MIT was that what MIT does not have and needs and will need in the future is "dirt" studios, otherwise MIT will become an intellectualizing art-teaching arm of MIT. And that's not why we are here. We are here to get our hands dirty on things that don't exist, and will exist because people get their hands dirty; meaning realization of ideas, materialization of concepts. That does not mean we don't like concepts and we don't like ideas before they get to be reality. But, unless all these beautiful concepts and all these beautiful ideas become part of the world, meaning reality, in one form or another, they essentially remain academic exercises. And that's only half the reality we are after.

MW: And you felt *Centerbeam* was an example of that coming together?

OP: Yes. We had very productive fellows. Somebody who had a very important role in the becoming of *Centerbeam* was Lowry Burgess. He had enough of realising force in him to develop things to the degree at which others could join and make them tangible. We have had other people like that at the Center too. So if you look at list of fellows over the years, there are different types of artists that have graced the Center. And it was good. It was very exciting to be here, and very interesting, and there was constant exchange among the people while they were working. And *Centerbeam* was one case, a rare case where the artist worked with scientists, and the scientist worked with artists and they enjoyed it. And some of them are still friends of ours like Walter Lewin and Harriet Casdin-Silver—certain art forms had to do with collaboration, had to do with sciences for the arts, holography for instance. Steve Benton, who was one of my successors, was an excellent scientist. He did important things in the development of holography, not at the Center, before he came to the Center, when he was working for Edwin Land. I think Steve was probably the only pure scientist who was a director of the Center . . .

MW: When *Centerbeam* was happening, what was the sense in MIT administration, the School of Architecture? Were they excited about this project?

OP: Sometimes things were good and sometimes they weren't. The School of Architecture has been a kind of mixed bag. Sometimes sympathy, sometimes collaboration, and sometimes lack of understanding, and also envy . . .

We could build things, and we *built* things. That was important. That's what the Center needed. That's what the Center got. For years. And we had people like Harriet Casdin-Silver, who was a very bright woman, and aggressive, productive, and all that. And she led holography to heights that it hadn't seen before. Initially by the way of Steve Benton. He initially came into the arts because he did things for Harriet while she was working with her holography at the Center. With Architecture, in a certain way, that is a matter for its own book. The relationship to architecture changed time and again. I've worked a lot with architecture, with architects. The problem is psychological. To this day, the architects think that they are the arts, and the arts should do what the architects tell the arts to do. That of course would be a mistake. With very few exceptions. Sometimes you have few people who are very good architects we have admired, like Louis Kahn who was the first genuine professor in the United States whom I met, because the first person I met at the University of Pennsylvania was Louis Kahn. That was my introduction to live American architects, and he happened to be the best. Etc., etc. So architecture has always been important at the Center, not just because Kepes started working very well with the architects in the past. During my day we had very strong relations to US architects. The man who did not become the director of the Center when I became the director was an architect, Friedrich St. Florian, he was Kepes's deputy for a number of years. So our relationship to architecture was long and complicated and complex, because the Dean was always an architect. And on the other hand, what we were thinking about architecture was sympathetic but not necessarily same. So there were some conflicts there.

MW: This is why CAVS reported to the Provost rather than the Dean of Architecture when you started?

OP: Yes. When I became the director, I brought it to the Provost. The Provost was my director, not commander, but academic authority. And that changed when one president of MIT, Paul Gray, a very well meaning, quiet man did not continue that format. He changed the administrative structure so that the Center directors— nowadays I think there are 45 research centers at MIT—would not respond to the Provost, but to the nearest dean.

This certainly was not inspired or influenced by the Center directors. It was something that Paul Gray decided was good for MIT. How the effects were, I can't judge.

MW: Was Bill Porter the Dean?

OP: No. Bill Porter was Dean when I became the director. Bill Porter is the man who formally appointed me as Kepes's successor. And Porter had mixed qualities, but he certainly was sympathetic to the arts and the Center. I am fully convinced that he meant well.

MW: So when Gray made this decision, what was the consequence?

OP: That the Center directors had less direct contact with some vital respondents for the Center, such as fund raisers. I guess that was in part behind it. I've never seen *massive* negative consequences, except yes, fundraising at MIT always came first. It's not easy to raise funds for an institute that is not fully independent. Anyway, there are many ways to this. When I dealt with the Provost of MIT, during Jerry Wiesner's time the provost was Walter Rosenblith. Walter was a real character. He was very good as a Provost, but he never became MIT President. He was kind of a ruffian in the way he dealt with his subjects. But I got along very well with him really well, [*laughs*] because when he yelled at me, I yelled back.

MW: You just said when characterizing your work that essentially "we built things." There is a kind of engineer vs. scientist difference here that I want to use to take us back to *Centerbeam*. *Centerbeam* was clearly the biggest thing CAVS ever produced as a single project . . .

OP: We did it for the Documenta. *Centerbeam* was *built* for Documenta. I got the director of the Documenta—actually he was director twice—Manfred Schneckenburger, to invite us to make a project. That was the first time that any academic institution was invited to the Documenta, and also the first time that any students participated in a Documenta. The only thing I should say that was bigger than the *Centerbeam* was the Sky Art Conference. Except the Sky Art Conference was an organism, and it was not one but I think we ended up holding Sky Art Conferences, and being asked all

previous spread Otto Piene, CAVS, *A Field of Hot Air Sculptures Over Fire in the Snow*, MIT, 1969.

left, Haacke wheeling helium tank with MIT students, assembling *MIT Sky Line*, October 24, 1967.

following page, Otto Piene, CAVS, *A Field of Hot Air Sculptures Over Fire in the Snow*, MIT, 1969.

the time, "can we have another Sky Art Conference," and I am saying, I don't think we can because it's too complex to do if you don't have an administrative apparatus at hand to do it with. Anyway. But *Centerbeam's* good . . . And the documentation of Centerbeam altogether is good. The film that Ricky Leacock and Jon Rubin made with government money on *Centerbeam* is going to be run in the 150th. It *was* a fairly productive enterprise altogether.

MW: Was there ever an attempt to create a similar scale project?

OP: No. Except all the times the idea came up to do *Centerbeam* again.

MW: Does *Centerbeam* still exist?

OP: Portions of it. It's in our barn in Groton, MA, and it's been stored there for I don't know how many years, because MIT didn't have the storage space. Okay, whereas our farm, which is not quite as big as MIT—its only 30 acres—MIT probably has a few more. In order to have it *anywhere* I said, "okay, we'll put it in our barn. And see what that's good for." [*Laughs*] And now it turns out it's not all that useless, because it is going to be part of the 150th.

MW: Was there ever an effort between 1977 and 1980 to have it displayed at MIT?

OP: There was an effort, yes. But these things *don't* happen at MIT. MIT is so manically attached to the future. They are always working on the next project, and the next project, and the next after the dozen projects after the next project. To install something like this of that size of MIT, it gets in the way of "progress." And therefore storage becomes a problem. So the ideas, the attempts to install *Centerbeam* on campus have been doomed not to come to fruition. . . .

I would certainly appreciate if bigger things could happen at MIT in the arts out of whatever the successes of CAVS, if it could ever happen. Because dimensions are important. Not all art has to be immaterial to be mentally expansive and mentally productive—such as the pyramids.

MW: What are your thoughts on the future of this kind of "avant-garde" art at MIT?

OP: One major theme that needs to be emphasized is immateriality/materiality. To deal with immateriality, for any artist, you have to know everything about materiality. And it was exciting to *do* all that stuff, to deal with all these materials, and media. But I don't have any maxims to dispense at the moment. If you want to hear about that, I am going to have to think about it some more.

NICHOLAS NEGROPONTE, MOLLY WRIGHT STEENSON

We Were Bricoleurs

Molly Wright Steenson conducted this interview on December 4, 2010 in Princeton, NJ.

The Architecture Machine was not just a book, or a computer, or a laboratory: it sought to be all of those things and more. In the dark, out-of-the-way corner it first inhabited in MIT's Building 9, the Architecture Machine Group (ArcMac), founded by Nicholas Negroponte and Léon Groisser, experimented on next generation computer-aided design tools from 1968 to 1980, at which point it became the basis for the MIT Media Lab. ArcMac's work leveraged close relationships across MIT, relying on funding from both the Department of Defense Advanced Research Projects Agency (ARPA, known as DARPA after 1972) and the Office of Naval Research (ONR). Negroponte counted as friends and supporters J.C.R. Licklider, Marvin Minsky, Seymour Papert and Jerome Wiesner (President of MIT from 1971–80), for whom the first Media Lab building was named.[1]

In two books written between 1968 and 1972, *The Architecture Machine* (published 1970) and *Soft Architecture Machines* (published 1975), Negroponte applied big conceptual ideas from artificial intelligence, cognitive science, and human-computer interaction to computer-aided design for architecture. Part manifesto, part scrapbook, the books attempt to explain and theorize the group's work. Dedicated "to the first machine that can appreciate the gesture," *The Architecture Machine* put forth a vision of evolutionary computer-aided design systems.[2] An architecture machine, as Negroponte saw it, would transform the design process by reconfiguring the traditional human-machine dynamic as a dialogue. "The dialogue would be so intimate—even exclusive—that only mutual persuasion and compromise would bring about ideas, ideas unrealizable by either conversant alone. No doubt, in such a symbiosis it would not be solely the human designer who would decide when the machine is relevant," he wrote.[3]

As a laboratory, ArcMac valued hands-on tinkering with computers and interfaces. "Let us build machines that can learn, can grope, and can fumble, machines that will be architectural partners, architecture machines," Negroponte wrote in the conclusion to *The Architecture Machine*.[4] The names of several ArcMac projects—HUNCH, SEEK, and GROPE, to list a few—embody the philosophy of their design process: these were technologies that guessed at a user's intention by recognizing a sketch, that used a robotic arm to move blocks (or gerbils), or that consisted of a peripheral that rolled over a map to make sense of a territory. These early projects evolved into information spaces and spatial computing metaphors in the late 1970s. The Aspen Movie Map, similar to today's Google Street View, allowed a user to navigate the streets of Aspen, Colorado by receiving images from videodisc. The Spatial Data Management System offered a graphical, spatial framework for organizing information (originally developed as a means to plan naval strategies) and, with Put That There, incorporated the framework into the Media Room, a room-sized computing environment. Here one could navigate onscreen information with voice commands and, by stepping into the interface, with gestures.

At the end of the interview published here, Negroponte says, "We were *bricoleurs*." The French translation of the word refers to tinkering and DIY, the rhetoric of which peppers Negroponte's work. Seymour Papert and Sherry Turkle later used the term "bricolage" in their writings to refer to spontaneity and playfulness.[5] Claude Lévi-Strauss wrote, "the *bricoleur* 'speaks' not only *with* things . . . but also *through* the medium of things."[6] This is perhaps one way to see the role of ArcMac. But to understand the social role, it is helpful to remember the latter, less often quoted, part of the Lévi-Strauss sentence: "The bricoleur may not ever complete his purpose but he always puts something of himself into it." Whether their work is understood as a computer, machine, theory, laboratory or social network deeply imbricated in MIT's military-industry-academic complex, Negroponte and ArcMac developed more than a method for teaching architects how to use computers. Under the auspices of the MIT Media Lab, ArcMac formed the foundation for spatial computing metaphors on the one hand and commercial innovation culture on the other. It was an attempt to speak through the medium of things.

following page,
Architecture Machine
Group, examples of
man-machine dialogue
conducted under
computer program
URBAN5. From MIT
Technology Review, April
1969.

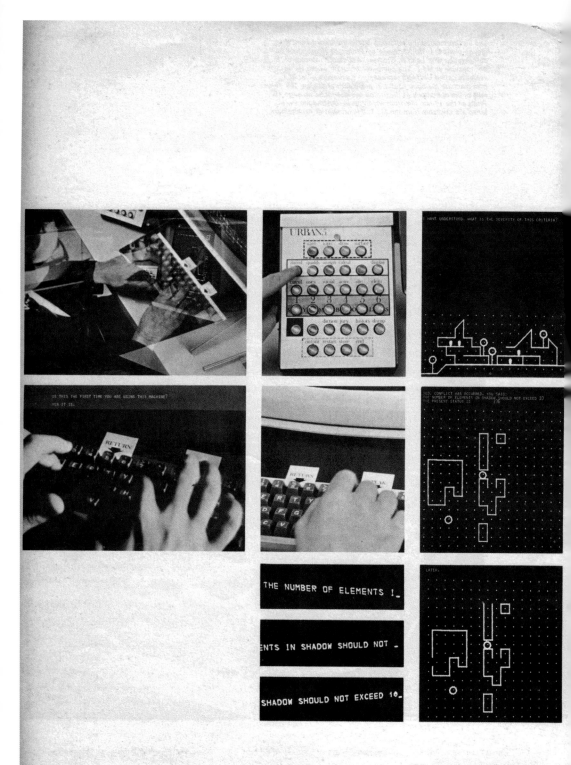

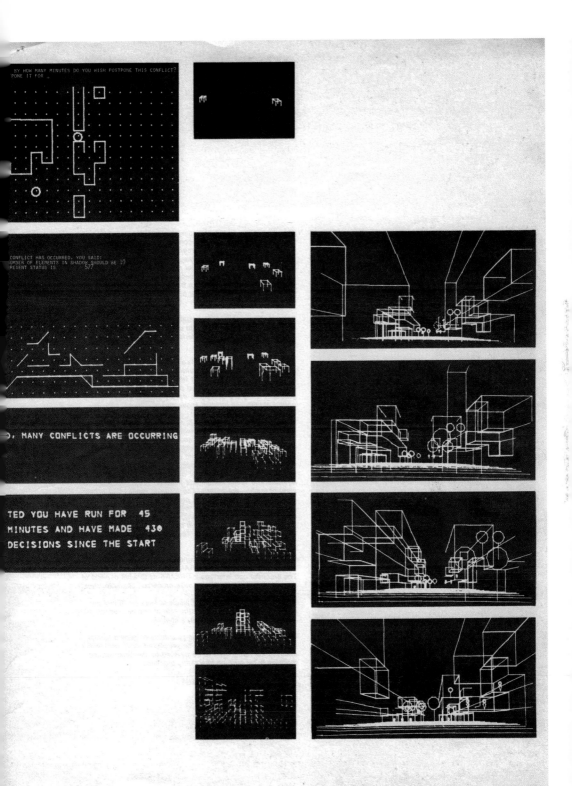

Molly Steenson: How many people were a part of the Architecture Machine Group, and how was it structured?

Nicholas Negroponte: MIT had something called Undergraduate Research Opportunities—UROP. We had many of them, and some of them worked 80 hours a week. And so it felt like they were the full-time staff. That's how Andy Lippman came in, that's how Chris [Schmandt] came in, that's how everyone came in. Nobody came in any other way.

MS: How did that work?

NN: It's a very interesting story how UROP started. Ed Land, the founder of Polaroid, was a great friend of Jerry [Jerome] Wiesner's and they were having dinner together one night. At MIT, the graduate students are the kings—and in fact, there was some discussion in the late 50s of eliminating undergraduate study at MIT, although when I say "There was some discussion," I had privileged access; so it might be Jerry and Ed Land discussing it over dinner, as opposed to the Corporation having considered it deeply. Ed Land said, Why don't I subsidize undergraduates to work with faculty?

And so he created a fund with a lot of money that students could apply for, so if you're an undergraduate and I'm a professor and you want to work on x, you get UROP to pay you to pay me, and then I get the money as discretionary funds for my lab. The reason being, that discretionary money to me, which is valuable, would justify the "extra effort" I would have to spend to make you a valuable lab worker, versus a graduate student or a postdoc. I [started ArcMac] at just the beginning [of UROP], and students could get five and ten thousand dollars to do this, and I thought, I'll just take ten of them and that's $100,000-plus, and that's a lot of discretionary money.

MS: So it was an opportunity to bring in quite a bit of money—

NN: You could bring in a good amount of money. It was an incentive. And then I, amongst others, hired undergraduates. They weren't a burden.

MS: They were eager.

NN: They were more than eager! They didn't know the word impossible. They worked the 80 hours a week. They came, they slept at the lab, they worked at the lab. And graduate students, some of them had families. They had a life, they were so sophisticated—but they were far less interesting. And so the early days of ArcMac were almost all undergraduates through UROP.

MS: You said that ArcMac had maybe three or four staff, but how many students at a time?

NN: At least ten. There was a time where we might have had six staff and eight students, or five staff and fifteen students. But it was never a group of much more than 20 people.

MS: What was your relationship to Project MAC and J. C. R. Licklider?

NN: Licklider was already a very major figure at MIT. Licklider had become a friend and mentor. He had discretionary money and funded some of the research. We had a project on sketch recognition [HUNCH] that he funded. We only needed, 20, 30 thousand dollars. He funded it and we had done some work. We went back to his office and I was all excited to show him the results. I said, I really want to show you what you funded. And he said, you know, I don't fund a project, I funded you. I don't care what you do. You want to show it to me, fine.

It was a real interesting lesson, a very interesting lesson: you fund the person. They don't do that anymore. But that was the early days of funding at DARPA and the ONR.

MS: I wanted to ask about that as well. You seemed to have a very close relationship with Marvin Denicoff [from the ONR] and Craig Fields [from DARPA], with these individuals that were funding the projects.

NN: Both of them, yes.

MS: How did that come about? How were you first introduced to Marvin Denicoff?

NN: I'm almost certain that Marvin Minsky and Seymour Papert introduced me because he was funding them. In the case of Craig Fields, I was at some meeting and I met him through the same circle of friends.

Both Seymour and Marvin had become pretty close personal friends. And we'd have dinner once a week or once every two weeks. They're much older than me but we were still sort of a little group. Marvin, particularly adored that group. Craig Fields was sort of a whippersnapper. He was my age, whereas Denicoff is much older.

There was a brief interlude in there with the National Science Foundation, but boy was that ever—it certainly turned me off of the National Science Foundation.

MS: What happened?

NN: We were applying for grants with the Architecture Machine Group. We submitted a proposal, a really thick one, a really well-done one that they turned down.

MS: Did they provide any feedback as to why?

NN: Yeah, I'm not sure we paid too much attention to it. We just thought it was—even to this day—

MS: What did you propose?

NN: I'm trying to remember the name. It was basically on conversation theory, on how machines would be so interactive and intelligent, really taking everything and putting it all together. And we including all the early Spatial Data Management stuff, all the early Put That There stuff, and it was turned down. So DARPA paid for it.[7]

MS: It would be interesting to know what was going on at the NSF that they didn't pursue it, or the politics of that decision.

NN: The politics were more sort of geopolitics: so much money was going to MIT and Nebraska. And they didn't think we were—[they thought] we were too crazy. They wanted more rigorous things. They didn't want people making things and doing things in an architecture department. And they'd come and we'd show them demos, and not scientific papers.

MS: How did the position of ArcMac evolve within the Department of Architecture and at MIT? The architectural background of the Media Lab seems to surprise many people. In the 1970s, it seems like it was a curious place to be working so handily with computers, on one hand, and an amazing opportunity on the other.

NN: I can tell you exactly how it evolved. First, by way of background, the most innovative use of computers at MIT in the 60s, early 60s, was in Civil Engineering. And so I as a student hung around with those people. And the other major player was Mechanical Engineering, and that's Steve Coons. Nothing in architecture.

MS: How did you get involved with computers?

NN: It was 100% Steve Coons.

MS: How did you first end up taking a class with Steve Coons?

NN: Well, as a freshman I took a class with him— it was mechanical drawing class—and then, I did something that you didn't do in those days. Those were the days of the five-year B.Arch. I did it in four years and decided to go on for the M.Arch. at MIT—it's a two year program that I did in one—so I completed the B.Arch and M.Arch in a total of five years. The reason I did it was because Steve Coons was involved in my senior year and I wanted to stay on and do stuff with the computer. So I stayed purposefully to do the M.Arch and Steve was very much involved.

I graduated at the end of summer 1966 and went to work for the IBM Cambridge Scientific Center across the street, where my then-girlfriend, future wife (now former wife) was the receptionist. Five days later, Steve Coons had a nervous breakdown and went off for a medical leave, so I was asked to go back and teach his courses. So I went back. I had some kind of funny appointment at MIT, I was like a volunteer or intern where I had an unpaid appointment to do things related to computers. After a year, Steve Coons came back and he said, you stay on and we'll do this together. So we did it together for a year. And the architecture department gave me a proper faculty appointment and the rest is history.

When I was teaching Steve's courses in mechanical engineering, over that year we decided that we would create the Architecture Machine. I even remember when the name came up. It was on a plane to Florida during which the Architecture Machine came to me, and I remember even blurting it out, the adjacent seats wondering what I was saying. The natural place for me to do it was in the Department of Architecture. When I joined the faculty I had no real teaching load, maybe one course every other semester or something. And then I started building the Architecture Machine Group.

The Architecture Machine Group was in a new building beside the Department of Architecture, and to actually go to see us, you had to do it overtly. It was a dead end, this wasn't on the way to something. It was the top floor of a building which did connect to the studios, but it didn't go anywhere, you had to push an elevator button and go down. So it wasn't a natural path. And so the faculty and the students didn't go streaming through our lab.

MS: Was that on purpose?

NN: No, on chance. Just where we were, it was a cul de sac. I had talked a small company into giving us free computers. So we started off with a room and a lab, essentially two offices in a new building. And within less than two years, the two offices became a whole floor. I guess we did have more than 20 or 30 people because we ringed the floor, so there must have been 20 offices.

MS: When did you get tenure?

NN: Very early but I don't remember when. I'm not sure. '74, '73? When it came time for a promotion or something, they wouldn't know what to do, so they'd ask Marvin and Seymour and Licklider and a few of these "icons" at the Institute and talk to them and I'd get my promotion. In fact, my tenure case sort of happened that way as well.

MS: But it would've been after you'd written all of the text for *Soft Architecture Machines*. That came out in '75.

NN: Awfully silly books.

MS: They're not that bad.

NN: I'm glad you like them. I'll have to go back and look through them. But yes, it was after those, and Marvin and Seymour consulted very deeply. Stop me if I've told you this, but in a tenure case, they have these portable file folders with all of the letters of recommendation and a second portable file folder with all of your materials, and you prepare your material and put it in your file folders, and at the end of your case, they give you back your file folder. They gave me the wrong one. They gave me the one with all of the letters in it. And they kept the one with all my materials in it. I figured it out pretty quickly and put it under my desk, thinking maybe I'll look at it one day. It sat under my desk for about two months. And an absolutely stubborn secretary from the dean's office who had made the mistake contacts me and said, I just opened your box and it's your material, not the letters, which means you must have the letters. And I said, yeah, it's under my desk. I didn't open it, why would I look at it? And we swapped boxes.

MS: There's the Architecture Machine Group, but is there also an actual Architecture Machine that got built?

NN: There is no thing called the Architecture Machine. The Architecture Machine Group built lots of machines.

One of our biggest projects, more toward the early to mid 70s, was touch. Dick [Richard] Bolt was doing it. He gave a presentation at Kresge Auditorium on his touch work, which included pressure and pressure-sensing—some very nice work and wonderful movies. He addressed multi-finger touch. We had a display where you could turn the knob, you could shrink and expand the knob, you could put your finger with enough friction that if you pushed, an arrow came out, and if you tilted your finger it would go this way, and you'd put some force and if you pulled your finger it would come back. This would have been in '73 or '74. But the audience showed no interest. People came up to afterwards and said, I really liked the talk but the touch part, I don't understand. Why do people want to touch displays?

MS: I remember early touch displays in the late-70s but they seemed to have gone away until quite recently.

NN: They did go away. People made them—the first ones were a thin layer of transparent material that tended to have little pockmarks in it that kept the touch screen off the surface of the glass and if you touched it you would literally push these two pieces of material together. They were very unreliable and easily damaged and did not survive.

MS: I can imagine. They weren't very durable.

NN: But the one we were using was a sheet of glass with an acoustic wave over it, and you'd put your finger and interrupt the wave. We'd worked with data tablets. Sylvania made a very expensive, beautiful glass data tablet with a pen and a little switch and a wire, and you could draw. You could put a sheet of paper on top of the glass (it didn't have any display) to draw on it. And then if you wanted to push from the pen, it had a switch. In the near field, you could use the pen to move the cursor and you would click before you touched the surface, so there was near field touch and click. Fingers only had touch. So there was some effort to make near field so you could track it, even though you weren't quite touching the screen. And that must've gone for two or three years. We did some very, very nice touch work. I remember the apparatus for both data tablets and touch, where you take the projector and you take a piece of vellum or something and you project on the back of it. But then you could even get material where the translucent surface was on the top surface of the paper, so the image was literally like the print of this paper, on the top of the surface. There was no eighth of an inch of glass, there was no parallax. We had a whole project called "parallax free displays." They were just astonishing. (This would have been around '75 or '76.)

Guy Weinzapfel and Architecture Machine Group, "Held Mapping Window." From *Mapping by Yourself: Interim Report* (Cambridge, MA: MIT, 1978).

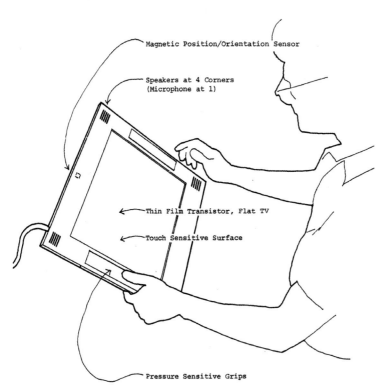

Magnetic Position/Orientation Sensor

Speakers at 4 Corners
(Microphone at 1)

Thin Film Transistor, Flat TV

Touch Sensitive Surface

Pressure Sensitive Grips

Conceptual Diagram of Equipment For Hand Held Mapping Window

MS: Changing topics here, how did Vietnam affect the nature of what ArcMac did? Did ArcMac's mandate change, or your personal interests begin to change when Vietnam was over?

NN: I'm not sure that the Vietnam War played that much of a role. It did for me personally in an odd way and that is, during the student protests, they broke down the door of the president's office and occupied his office. It was broken down with a battering ram and two students are said, who knows if this is true, to have fornicated on his desk in the presence of the others as an act of defiance. I was such a young faculty member and had undergraduate advisees, including ones that were not necessarily designated to a department yet. Maybe I had a few that were designated but they weren't really architecture students. It turns out that more than a thousand students that I could be the advisor of, and I had both of them [the students that had sex on the president's desk]. *[laughs]*

The students are evacuated from the president's office. MIT decides that they have to, they need somebody to charge, they named the student who built the weapon, so they would be able to charge him with a felony and everybody else is charged with something much less important. And I as his faculty member had to defend him, which I do successfully. I don't think I had to go to court, but I had to submit a position or something: "he's a really good kid, he's going through this stage." I was only a few years older than the students were, and I thought they were scum. But it was also my duty. There were people in my life, I had made mistakes and people were very generous and said, make sure you learn from this and don't do it again. You don't have to have all punishment, I did that a half a dozen times at MIT, for people who, to this day, come and thank me, you bailed me out at the Institute, I learned so much, thank you—it's better that way and nothing happened.

But that was my closest involvement with Vietnam. Otherwise, I was just an oblivious student. Not oblivious—that sounds dumb, I mean like anybody else, I went to large rallies, but what was happening at MIT is that the students forced the Institute to divest Draper Labs because it was doing classified research. It affected all of the research. You couldn't do any classified research. Also, you can check but I believe the Mansfield Amendment was in that same post-Vietnam era, and that had a big influence.

MS: Didn't some of the reports have classified sections?

NN: No, I never did a classified, to my knowledge.

MS: After that?

NN: Even before that. Me personally. I've never had a security clearance; I've never done anything classified. I mean, I was at CIA headquarters the other day [and] even though you don't have a security clearance; there are things that they tell you that you do not repeat. But I don't have any specific clearance.

MS: But the projects are still funded by either ONR or DARPA.

NN: You bet. They were right till the end, right to the early 1980s. And when that came, it was more because the economic model of the Media Lab emerged, but we were still getting some DoD.

MS: I wanted to ask you about that shift, about the years between ArcMac—

NN: ArcMac never shut down, it just got absorbed into the Media Lab. And in fact, constituent parts of the Media Lab were such that, if you visited the first year at the Media Lab, you went to ArcMac. It wasn't called that, but.

MS: What was it called, if you went to ArcMac that first year at the Media Lab?

NN: It broke into at least three groups. It consisted of Andy Lippman doing work on data compression, Walter Bender doing work with color, Chris Schmandt doing work with audio. And for a brief time, I think that Dick Bolt was there at the beginning for a brief time. So those were the four people that came over from ArcMac. And instead of calling it ArcMac, they had independent names and they were doing their work—so they were four groups out of 10. So they were a big piece.

MS: The Media Lab is largely a commercial funding model, correct?

NN: Industry. Industry-funded. What happened at the Media Lab was very simple. From 1980 to '84, Jerry Wiesner and I had raised money to build the Lab, in Japan and the United States. And many of the companies said, we can't give the bricks and mortar but when you open your doors for business, come back and see us. So I had a little pile of rain checks and when we opened our doors for business, I went back and said, remember? And they'd say, of course! Either through guilt or previous commitment, they would do it.

And the industrial base was really left over from raising the money. And as we started doing that more and more, I said, boy, this is interesting. Denicoff was interesting, but retiring. Craig Fields was interesting, but a pain in the ass (I would tell him) but somebody had 30 or 40 captains of industry, Jerry Wiesner would always talk to CEOs and so on, and that's where I got my bad habit of only wanting to talk to CEOs. Cause they were interesting. So we started this somewhat-fantasy world because we were talking to such high-level people. But also, it was a wonderful funding model. These people, you would have lunch with them and we would say, well, we need a couple hundred thousand dollars from you, and they'd say, I think yeah. Yeah. Let's do that. And the next day, you'd get a purchase order from their company and a few days later, the first down payment and a little bit of contract.

Through the National Science Foundation, you can't say anything without a peer review committee out there, and it would take us eight months to turn it around and then of course you're not sure because it's a new fiscal year for NSF funding. So first of all, you're a supplicant. I'm really irritated. It takes so long! It takes so long to do it. These industry guys could turn it around in days. "Instead of giving us $300,000, why don't you give us $150,000 a year for three years 'cause this way, you'll have some longevity." It would start to grow and grow and from about 1985 to '87, that period, the commercial-industrial funding, it was paradise 'cause all these people realized they could pool their so-called pre-competitive research. I didn't want to have to go back to the NSF because I was furious with them. And I was happy to go to DARPA but DARPA was funding me, it was the Denicoff mission and I was no longer an active researcher. So we still had funding and Muriel Cooper got some DoD funding for mapping.

MS: When I closely read your books and articles from the ArcMac days, it seems you were really interested in the idea of intelligence in a system, that you define intelligence not as innate but as something that exists when it's exercised, not as potential energy but as an active value.

NN: In those days, as I remember them, there was so much discussion about the mind-to-body problem. I haven't heard it mentioned or discussed for 30 years. People are just not interested in that. "Do you have to have a body to have a mind?" I haven't thought about it in 30 years. I was truly interested in it. I remember asking Marvin and Seymour and they were a little less convinced you needed a body.

MS: You seemed pretty convinced you did.

NN: I was pretty convinced you needed a body.

MS: What do you think today?

NN: Oh, I think that today it's become somewhat incidental because the collective intelligence is so much more important than an individual intelligence. So maybe the collective is so much more important, it's like a lot of ants need bodies to carry this stuff, but maybe it's not quite as important as it was, at least to me at the time.

MS: Some of the labs at the Media Lab deal with tangible and wearable interactions.

NN: And do you think any of them think of intelligence? I don't think they do, not like the early people.

MS: One of the research interests that seems to show up again and again in your work is applications around perception—your master's thesis, the master's theses of some of your students. You also were advising projects around cognitive space and perception, and then there was the Aspen Movie Map project. Was this implicit or explicit?

NN: I guess it was not explicit. At the time, we would do anything that was neat. We wouldn't sit down and have a conversation about cognition and perception, that's not what we'd discuss. It was doing things that were like magic. We'd discuss magic tricks. I don't mean that literally, but metaphorically.

So for example, if you could track a person's eyes without putting any apparatus on them, the conversation would be like this: if I stand on the other side of the room and look at you, even with us both wearing glasses, and instead of looking at your eyes, I look at the tip of your ear or the corner of your glasses, you can tell. Certainly if I'm looking at your ear or slightly over your shoulder, you can tell. But if you look at the geometry of that, it's like a fraction of a degree off. If you pull a vector from my eyes to yours, how do you figure out—so clearly, the eyes are sending some kind of message when they lock. There's something that happens with the eyeballs, you can tell I'm looking at you.

We would go to a place in Taunton, Massachusetts where the Department of Defense put the last stage of hardware prototypes. So when something was no longer reused, this is where it would go before it got auctioned or destroyed. It's a huge place with missile systems and old computers. We would go there periodically, Marvin and I and the students would go just to see what we would find. There was a four-foot conical atmospherical mirror. If you could find another with a hole in it, you could have a frog floating in mid-air. Ever seen those, with the frog floating in mid-air? And computationally, it made you think of things to float in mid-air. And so we'd load this conical mirror into the truck and we would bring it back to the lab and it was filled with this great—some of these were hundreds of thousands, millions of dollars in their original state and we're taking apart the pieces and using them to make something out of this. So it's a little bit— it's not quite as extreme as I'm describing it gives you an idea. Students would pile into the truck and go off to Taunton. It wasn't like art history students going to MoMA.

Those are the kinds of discussions we had. Could a machine sense that, and so on? That was the nature of what a discussion would be as opposed to thinking of anything deep theory and so on. And then somebody moved on and said, well, let's make a touch display, can it push back so you can feel the pressure, and can you feel texture if it wasn't there, can you trick the finger? It's not that somebody went and did a thorough and in-depth view of how skin works and so on and so forth, you'd try things.

It was *bricolage*, a lot of *bricolage*. There isn't a word for *bricolage* in English. We were *bricoleurs*. Most academics would sooner die than admit that. They say, "We are deep thinkers, we do these things in structured ways." We were *bricoleurs*.

Structure-Infill, Wittgenstein, and Other Matters

Alexander D'Hooghe and Arindam Dutta conducted this interview on April 25, 2011 at the Department of Architecture at MIT, as part one of the public events to commemorate the 150th year of the Institute's founding.

Arindam Dutta: The sentences read like haiku, architectural haiku, their meaning self-evident, but strung out, they seem to indicate some greater program, a script for the world. "The house is in the town. The room is in the house. In the room is a chair. In the chair sits a person who speaks. The sight of an act is that part of total physical reality in which the act is observed. For the observer every act has a site. There is an unlimited number of sites because the number of objects that can be observed is without limit."[1] And so on. In N. John Habraken's world, architecture is troubled perpetually by its inability to fully comprehend the circumstances of its own making. This brings forth a push from the world of practice into the world of research, producing the trans-historical, trans-cultural attempt at a scientific language, systematic attempts to delegate what remains constant and what varies in architectural production. One realizes that these haikus are in fact far from a poetics. Rather, in a syntactical sequence, they offer the prescriptive thrust of a grammar, propositions strung along what appears as a kind of logician's attempt at architectural discussion. In the realm of pedagogy and research, intervention is often simulated as different kinds of games, repetitive as games are, following the same sets of rules, and never repeating, as games do, each player presenting the possibility of an infinite variety within a finite formal framework. Today it gives me great pleasure to welcome back one of our very own. N. John Habraken was the founding director of the Stiftung Architekten Research (SAR–Foundation for Architectural Research), a research body founded as a consortium of Dutch architectural firms in 1965. His *Supports, An Alternative to Mass Housing* (Dutch 1962; English 1972), a pamphlet

1 N. John Habraken, *Transformations of the Site* (Cambridge: Awater Press, 1983).

critical of the mass-housing practices of post-war reconstruction, argued for greater choice afforded to occupants, culminating in Habraken's propositions for "Structure-Infill" combinations. As a research office, SAR was significantly influential within the world of Dutch architectural offices and building industry, holding up for a while the prospect of potential collaboration between the two factions. Posters from the SAR65 report, produced as polemical inserts within the marketplace, adorned most Dutch offices of the period. Habraken's own global reputation garnered followers for the "SAR-method" across the Third World as well as in the United States. In 1967 John Habraken was appointed professor at Eindhoven Technical University to set up its new Department of Architecture and serve as its first chairman. Appointed as Head of the Department of Architecture at MIT in 1975, Habraken's American phase is marked by interest in architectural practice as a variant of game or systems theory, manifested through research in early computational paradigms. *The Grunsfeld Variations*, a research publication carried out with MIT students, is another influential work from this period. His book *The Structure of the Ordinary* (1998) is an investigation of laws governing built environment as revealed by patterns of transformation. He is the recipient of many awards, including 1988 Creative Achievement Award of the Association of Collegiate Schools in the US; the David Roëll prize 1979 of the Dutch Prince Bernhard Fund.

Some of Habraken's ideas are still present, they are as if the deep DNA of MIT, they keep coming back, but perhaps they are the deep DNA of architecture itself.

Alexander D'Hooghe: Let's go right to a question. I'll be very brief so you can just expound on... So the formative moments, especially of SAR, what the statements that you wrote were, what stuck with me the most was, the phrase: "I am a proponent of autonomy of the built environment." Not the autonomy of the built object, of the artfully designed, authored object, by the single intuitive architect genius, but the autonomy of the built environment as a complete system, as an anthropological system as a complete structure. From that, if I understand your work correctly, comes a reflection on the fact that architects' agency over the making of the building is, and in fact, *should* be limited. It should not be comprehensive. Because there are many other people that come into play in the construction of the city, or of one's sphere of life. However, it appears that the various constituencies that guide the building process, the architects who do the construction, the industry, contractors, theorists in universities, none of those were properly equipped as entities to deal with an autonomous structural field. And it seems that SAR perhaps was an attempt to construct an entity that could be responsible for the digging up of that autonomous built environment, of at least, of the structure that was deep underneath in there. Is that a correct assumption? Would it be possible for you to expand a bit on how SAR came about? And what your role was?

John Habraken: Thank you. First of all let me say that I am very happy that I can be here. And thank you for inviting me. It is wonderful to be back in this place. And to still see many faces that I know, and even better to see faces that I don't know. So thank you very much.

Well, you mentioned the autonomy of the built environment, and that in retrospect, not in the beginning, but in retrospect that has become, I think, one of my major obsessions. To understand that better. To see the built environment as something that has a life of itself. I've tried to introduce the idea of the field, because I think it's what we talk about is the built environment AND the people in it. The two go together. And if you think of it as an organic autonomous thing, when the people leave, the built environment will disappear. And without the built environment, people can't live. So it's this total unity that's become more and more my interest. But of course that was not in the beginning. I only discovered that afterwards.

The beginning was a very intuitive idea that there was something wrong with the way that we dealt with the built environment in the Netherlands. And that what was wrong was that the users, the inhabitants, have nothing to do with it anymore. And that lead to the idea of a separation, because if you say, because your projects become bigger and bigger, that we forget about the people inside, except in a narrow, functionalist way, and that they should be introduced as agents in that same process.

I think that was the beginning of, I tried to introduce in my book about *Supports*. And in fact it's interesting that you have invited me in this year because it's exactly fifty years ago that I published this book, and it's never been out of print since. But when the book first came out, the publisher, was a good friend of mine, who became a good friend of mine, said, "John, I'll publish this book, nobody will read it, and everybody will have an opinion about it." And that's exactly the way it came out.

But yes, the whole idea of the autonomy of the built environment became more and more apparent in the course of time when our mission, in the beginning of SAR, I think, there were quite a few questions, was much more down-to-earth. It was the result of architects getting nervous about their role in the larger scheme of things. And the rebuilding of the Dutch nation after the war. It was the developers, the builders, the manufacturers, the government, the bureaucrats who all took over, and the architects saw that they were sort of pushed aside. And only the *entourage* to do a facade among the things that everybody else had already designed. So they came together to seek an opportunity. To see what they could do about that. It was a very

N. John Habraken,
MIT, n.d..

defensive move, let me put it that way. But then somebody in the group announced the idea that if they were serious about it, they should put their money together, put their money where their mouth was, and do something about it, and make research about it. And they responded to that challenge, and then of course they said, "Well, the only person around here who has not been compromised by practice is John Habraken because he's only written, so let him do the research." And that's how we started.

AD: The situation that one is talking about here is one that is quite unique as we were discussing. We are talking about ten offices agreeing to contribute fifteen thousand guilders per year to fund a shared research office that will, you know, carry on this collective activity. This is sort of unique in the history of architecture, I think. So it's not a government funded body, its private architects agreeing to do this because they seek a more informed and more involved role. You were sort of joking that at the first meeting, everybody was sort of asking Bakema to shut up because he kept going off on his long monologues.

Could you tell us a little bit about the sort of drama of the occasion in some ways?

JH: Well, there was a committee on housing by the architects, the equivalent of the AIA, and the chairman of that committee was himself an architect who did a lot of housing, became concerned about the role of the architect, and they felt that architects had no longer much to say about the future of the built environment. And that was in a period in which all the professions, but certainly architects, felt a responsibility to push forward the culture, the future. They felt they had to shape the culture for the Dutch nation. It's hard to imagine that kind of attitude today, but it was genuine, with all the pragmatics that were involved of course also. So this chairman called together eight or nine of his colleagues who were all known as people heavily involved with housing projects. To discuss the problem as to how the architects would get more influence about the future of the built environment. And, they knew each other, of course, very well, they knew exactly what everybody would say.

So at some point somebody got sort of impatient and said let's stop this. We know what we want. Let's do something about it. And he called his colleagues' bluff and said let's put up some sort of institution in which we put money, and find out what is to be done.

And yes, I think it's an unique event.

ADH: What is extremely striking is the attempt to construct across various egos and various agendas, this common platform. The reason the platform had to be common was because you were really after the discovery of innate, rational orders of building... by rational I mean inclusive of the various practices that people develop when they, that users develop when they are inside a built environment, rather than as you called it, the narrow-functional approach. My question is this: As we see it today, you were after dimensional and configurational rules or parameters that would be shared in a post-war Dutch welfare state, but that would be more liberating for the individual than the ones that were, at this moment, were being constructed, being construed.

JH: The leading idea was that, if you look at history, the way built environments went about, and could live for a long time was that basically there was a very close relationship between the house and the users, and that you could not separate these two. So it seemed to me that it was unnatural to do big projects in which the users have nothing to say about it. And by proposing that separation, was a really pragmatic idea. It's that *technically* it's possible, why don't we do it? That was very naïve because it took me a long time to find out why it was so difficult to have it done. But we decided that our role was not to change everything, but simply to find out what the architect should be able to do in a new situation. So— how do you design when you make the circulation in order to support the infill?

Because you have a problem—in those days, if you did a housing project, the first thing that had to be produced was the floor plan. Then the floor plan was multiplied so that you had an apartment building. And with the floor plan everybody could act. The banker could figure out what it might cost, the builders could figure out where the columns would go, and everything, and the piping and the wiring, so everybody could work. And what we were saying is that you can design anything except the floor plan!

So it really moved the rug from under the professional game. And that of course was the reason for all of the problems that we had to deal with in the political arena. But technically we decided that there was a research area that we had to get done. And that was two things—one is that you want to... if you make an open building with no floor plans in it, how can you explain to your client that this is the best possible type of a building that he puts his money in? In other words, if you have two of these buildings, two alternatives, which one is the best if you can't see the floor plans?

So that was the problem of formal evaluation, or what we defined later on as capacity. We didn't say, "What is the function of this building?" because that's what produces the floor plan. But we turned it around and said that with the office space, and other space, another agent can do things. Now, what is the capacity of the space that they offer, is it broad, or is it narrow? Is it possible to do the kind of houses in it that the government wants to see, or not? That was the research problem, which brought us to methodology. How do you figure out the capacity of such a building? And there was one little issue, which was, if one party builds the support building, and another party figures, produces the infill, how do they coordinate their work? And in those days, that was felt to be very important. Towards mechanization and so on and so forth. And that was another technological issue.

AD: Just to clarify for the audience, your conception of support and infill is not to be equated with the idea of a skeleton and whatever kind of ancillary spaces that they might hold. You speak of support as what is in a way *infrastructural*, or *prior* to the building, the condition in which the architect finds himself, typically today's architect, this would include sort of the utilities that private companies manage and bring up to the site, or certain kinds of site conditions in terms of legality, binding bylaws, and so forth. So typically a lot of this stuff... today architects, they do their designs and they... they leave it later for certain people, so that they make sure that these things are worked out. But it's very clear that what you're asking for here in reevaluating the notion of support is to bring the consideration of this prior condition right at the outset of the project and of the research, and that's what would be transformed—the stuff that usually architects have no choice in.

JH: Yes, I think that was the essence, that we, we defined the support as including everything that was communal to the users. And fit-out, or infill, was everything that the eventual user could control. So it was a distinction of control. Support is what was controlled by the community, whoever is the community. The fit-out was in the control of the individual user. So the distinction was not one of form, but it was one of control. And by definition almost, it took me a while to really accept that it was a

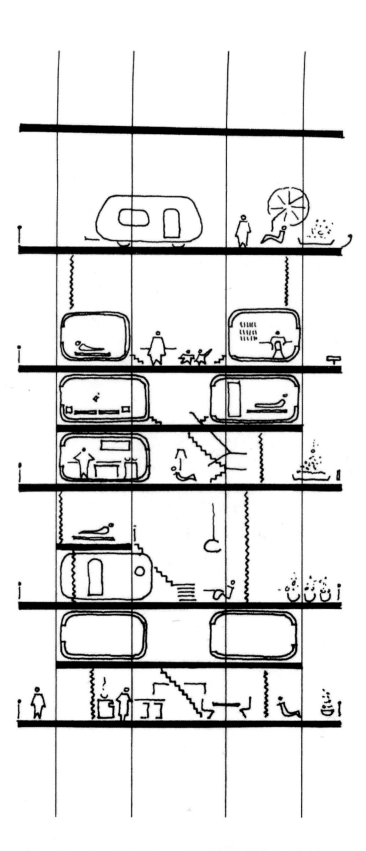

Habraken's support-structure principle. From Koos Bosma, *Housing for the Millions: John Habraken and the SAR 1960-2000*, (New York, NAi: 2000).

political decision—who controls what? And that of course was also the reason for the lack of enthusiasm among many people. Because you change the control pattern by which they had been making their work.

ADH: In hindsight, also, one of the several revolutionary statements that are being made in that moment, and that you are one of the people making them, was the structure-infill, of course, or support-infill to in fact explode architectural objecthood. The idea of the building as a single isolated object, that is just shot to pieces, and what is left instead is a series of layers with different lifespans. The structure is the collective one or communal one, but also one that has a certain durability over time.

JH: Yes, what happens is that, because buildings got bigger and bigger, it's very normal in morphology, that if forms become more and more complex, you get a hierarchy. And what happens with a bigger building is that you get a new level of hierarchy. We used to have urban design and architecture. And architecture was doing the buildings in the context of urban design. If the building becomes bigger, it becomes the context itself for the infill. So in that sense, it is an organic development that will happen anyway. But we had to discover it in that way. I think, intellectually speaking, the important thing afterwards turned out that what we introduced was the idea of time and change and control. The difference between the two levels is that also difference of change. Because different parties control it, the frequency of change of the infill is faster than the frequency of change of the communal. It's always the case. So change became an issue which has never been an issue in architecture at all. Architecture was always the defiance of time. We were to build the monument that would defy time. And here we said: time is of essence in our designing. So the control part was the political part, but the change, design, part was the, if you like, the intellectually interesting part.

ADH: But, as a follow-up question to that, what always seemed extremely striking is that in your deliberate reduction of architecture, or architects' control, or architectural authorship over the totality of the building, you nevertheless never pleaded for its complete elimination. You were just trying to reduce it, give the individual fit-outs back to the users, but the communal was to be left, and the structural side of the communal was what would be left, and had to be designed in the end by architects, albeit governed by a series of rules and principles that would take out the ground of sheer subjective whim, is that correct?

JH: Yes, I think you could say that because as the environment becomes more complex, the hierarchy has to expand, so you add another level. Every level, itself, is an invitation to a design, whether it is done by a professional or other people is a secondary thing.

There's nothing against architects doing the infill, as long as you make a separation. And we have organized ourselves as professionals as architects, as urban designers, interior designers, furniture designers, so we already have in our professional structure recognized the autonomy of the built environment in its hierarchy.

What we are talking about is you produce another level in that hierarchy, and that is open to anybody who likes to do that, to design there. But personally I feel that if you make that distinction, architects felt that we took away something from them. Because they said, I want to be responsible for the floor plan. But I think it was a liberation for architecture, because when you do not have to deal with the damn floor plan, you make three dimensional, communal structures, that's a real architecture, public spaces, build experiences, urban infrastructure, and so on. So it's much more interesting to design than one floor plan and then to multiply it.

AD: So, the architects didn't like it very much, right?

JH: They did not, no. They thought that I took away something from them. They had very emotional confrontations from time to time.

AD: But, in a strange way you were, SAR was quite instrumental—again, this is perhaps only possible in a small country like Holland—in creating some kind of interaction between the building industry and the architects, even if, in the end, they didn't get along well at all. But SAR got some commissions from the building industry, yeah?

JH: Yes. The first few years, we were financed by those ten architects' offices, actually... there was an eleventh part which was the contribution of the organization which was the equivalent of the AIA. The president of that group was also on our board. But then we found out, some builders came our way, or manufacturers, and they said, 'If you can manage to do what you propose to do, it's in our interest. We would love that because it would make our life much easier.' And so we said, "Why don't you pay us?" And so from then on, we had also builders and manufacturers who contributed to the research.

AD: I'm sort of curious as to what a Habraken project would look like. I mean, we know about the World Bottle, which the second variation, the first one looked too much like a champagne bottle... but the idea was to... and this is 1963, so the whole idea of re-use is really much later.

The owner of Heineken approached you to sort of devise a bottle, after you'd been to the Caribbean, that could be reused as a building material, and so what we are seeing is sort of a brick/glass type of thing. So that's one sort of variation you can think of. But trying to imagine a little bit: What would a Habraken project look like? One thinks

of the concept of control and change,
or what is constant and what varies,
is a widespread theme in the sixties.
I'm thinking of Yona Friedman,
Archigram, a number of people who
are sort of addressing some of that.
Also the prior groups, Team 10, they
were already speaking about it. You're
sort of a bridge figure between these
generations? Would that be right?

JH: Yeah, I think that, Yona Friedman and
I and a few other people, talked about
it. We liked each others' approach. And
there was another man, Schütze Felix
in Germany. I personally felt, I was very
critical of Team 10, I thought that they
were moving in the wrong way, that
they were on an ego trip, not prepared
to really look the problem in the eye.
And when you're young, you become
very dogmatic about these things. But
I now can understand, when you point
it out, those similarities. But there was
resistance among them; I remember
that. In which they said, well,
participation is fine, but we do the
floor plan. And then the conversation
stopped.

N. John Habraken, glass
World Bottles (WoBo),
circa 1962.

ADH: And as a follow-up on that, Hermann
Hertzberger, who was more or less
a contemporary, from the surface
seemed to espouse exactly structure-
infill, very much similar concepts,
nevertheless has a kind of distinct
position from yours. Would you be
willing to comment on the relationship
between his work and yours or the
difference?

N. John Habraken,
WoBo (World Bottle)
wall, reception center,
Heineken Brewery,
Amsterdam, 1962. Photo:
Michel Claus. From Koos
Bosma, *Housing for the
Millions*, 2000.

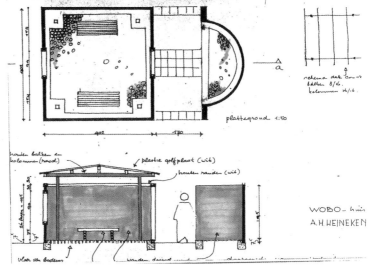

N. John Habraken,
sketch of WoBo house
for A. Heineken, with
indications of materials to
be used, 1964.

JH: Well, Hermann and I know each other from our student days. We were about, he was one year younger than I was, I think, and so it was the same group of students. So we knew each other very well. And I remember that I, at a certain point that I, at the end of my studies, proposed this idea before I wrote the book in a group of students, and not many of them supported the idea. They all thought it was a bit crazy. I think Hermann had a kind of intuitive affection to this kind of open-ended kind of thing. And he has shown that it his own work, many times. At the same time, his whole way of working, his personality was not somebody who was interested in abstract research. Theory, whatever, so... he was an architect! He was doing! He had the right intuitions and I felt that given the context in which, let's put it this way, it was very clear from the beginning, that although we had architects research, I understood and everybody understood that architects could not make things work. It was the clients, and the bankers, who made the decisions. Not the architects. At best we could argue that there was a way, an alternative way to go. But it was a very risky thing to do for the practicing architect. So we didn't expect them to be forthcoming. And they among themselves, even from the ten offices, they said: "Look. You do your research, talk to us, but you know you're talking for the next generation, not for us."

AD: This was a social night out—the SAR meeting was a social night out.

JH: That's right. We had a great time.

AD: But strangely enough, the building industry started to pay some attention. They started to, in a mass-produced economy, they started to pay some attention to variations, options, choices, and so on.

JH: There were exceptions of course, but there were a lot of people who owned a contract in business. And they came to us and they said, "If architects are willing to accept the methodology that you follow, it will be much easier for us to build it." And that was nice to hear! And we also got some funding for instance from a firm's pension fund that was investing in real estate. And they said, "Look, if what you propose can be done, our property will live longer and will renew itself over time without too much trouble." So they were willing to support my research. But those were individuals who understood, and that were in a position to put some money in our way.

AD: We're going to bring the conversation to your time in America very soon. But maybe if we can... your teaching time at Eindhoven, that's a school that you were the founding director of, very much reflected some of these concerns. Which involved precisely these support-infill... What kind of research did you do with the students at Eindhoven?

JH: Well, we just started, so there was no research done in the department for a long time. I tried to separate these things because I had to put together a new department in which we defined four or five different directions that people could study. Urban design, industrial design, architecture, what else was it?... anyway, so... I was involved in finding people to teach, getting students, we got many more students than we wanted, that's why we had all these problems. So although the word went around that everybody had to follow the Habraken methodology, there was no way that could be done. I did some teaching myself, but mostly it was sort of to, I have to apologize to Stan for this, I gave a course on architectural history, because nobody else could do it. So although my office, my SAR office, was on campus, it was two different things for a long time. Still, when I started doing my own courses, there was also criticism by the students. And I think that was right because I had not learned how to teach, and I did very stupid things as a teacher. I had forgotten that students like to have problems to put their teeth in, and then find out that they need methodology, rather than to tell them that they first have to learn the methodology before they understand the problem. So educationally, I think, my teaching was a disaster.

AD: So... MIT got you! (*Laughter in audience.*) Yes, you came to the US on a lecture tour in 1972. And again, Stan will definitely correct me on that, I think that this probably caught on when speculations within architecture schools in the United States, but there was a broadened interest.... I mean HUD had encountered its own crisis, it was a time of race riots in cities, mass housing was itself in some crisis, methodologically or pedagogically within institutions, but also institutionally in relationship to the government, it had a similar set of problems. So your ideas caught a wave here, would that be right? And so you were made an offer here by the department?

JH: Well, the lecture tour in '72 was to follow up on the publication of the book in the English language. And people were intrigued by it, so I was invited to come to Berkeley, and I think MIT and Harvard. There were about eight or nine different universities. I remember that my last stop was here in Cambridge, and it was a joint talk between Harvard and MIT and somebody pointed out that that it had never happened before. And the next day I was invited to come to MIT and talk a little bit more. And I was sitting at a big table with lots of people around it, with people on the floor, and I had no idea if it was a faculty member or a student who was asking the questions. Afterwards, I found out that Julian Beinart was sitting on the floor, and had some peppy questions. That was fun, yes. So that's, I think, why I liked MIT. It was a place where they could ask good questions.

ADH: There is something, though, that in your move, that was striking for us if you look at the accomplishments and the development is the amazing continuity of your work. Regardless of where you were working, there was an amazing continuity within your work. Whereas SAR had a lot of work that was invested in dimensions, in configurations, that could be found, structurally, as part of the autonomous lived environment, that to a degree was continued, I presume, here at the Institute.

Were there concrete examples of particular types of research that were brought over? Or was there a sense of more or less rounding off a chapter of work, the conclusion of a sort of dimensional or configurational studies, that were done in the European chapter?

JH: It was a little bit of both. In my memories, at that point, I had already been thinking about the broader intellectual background of the work we had been doing at SAR. I remember that in fact that Stan Anderson invited me to come over to MIT that I said I need another year before I can come. It was wonderful that you gave me that year. And the reason I gave is that I had to finish a book. Now the book was finished only twenty years later, but I was already beginning to think about what it meant to talk about different levels of intervention, about change, about control, in the environment. So when I was back, when I came to MIT, in teaching, the first five or six years I was very busy as a department head, so I gave a course around it, but I could not really do much about it. I was personally more interested in that issue, the intellectual follow-up of what SAR had been doing, rather than the methodology itself. But I also learned that methodology was something that is only of interest if there is a problem to be solved. So I got to the sneaky strategy that I tried to give students, asked them to do something that was really difficult, and they couldn't figure out, then I said well here, you have a certain methodology, and then there was no resistance. Because it solves a problem.

AD: Your key interventions in teaching at the school in fact did not go in the direction of design studio, right? You and Bill (Porter) are to be blamed for SMArchS.

JH: Yes.

AD: Okay. This is an interesting shift within pedagogy in design schools. You personally took on SMArchS as something that you would invest your time in and research as a key activity for architects in training to address the field of the built environment.

JH: Well, SMArchS actually was just a response to a problem that already was developing. We got students who already were architects from different countries who wanted to study with the faculty at MIT. And there was no format in which they could do that.

And they were sort of smuggled in in a not really legal way. Because faculty liked to work with them. And we tried to formalize that, because there was a demand.

But of course I was lucky because at that point, it was the kind of program that I felt very much at home in. But I also did some studio teaching, which I enjoyed very much. I started doing it after my head-ship. But then I found out that I tried to introduce methodology in my studio, but to get skills of any kind in a methodological way, it takes time, you have to do exercises, you have to make mistakes.

I found out that the students like the idea, but they got nervous because although they may have learned something, they couldn't show it to juries in the end. So they felt that I was taking away time from them that brought them into trouble at the end of the studio.

When I learned that, I decided to pull things apart. And that's when I started my separate course in thematic design, which was not studio. And that was something that I could take very well to the SMArchS program, because I had students who were already professional designers, and I could say, "Look, I know you're a good designer, we don't have to talk about that, let's talk about methodology."

AD: You said that you were looking at your thematic design book, and you said that you actually sketched out solutions. The book is forty pages of intensive illustrations and notes: it's almost like an exhaustive grammar for the built environment. And you said you wrote it over two days on a weekend, correct?

JH: Something like that.

AD: So in a way, the methodology for you was deep within you, and you could get it out fast. But for a student, it may seem daunting. There are lots of rules and counter-rules and game playing and so on. Is that too much for the student?

JH: What I say in this booklet is *after* the studio. After the workshop. So the course had gone this way all semester, and the students had done all these sorts of things. And then I tried to summarize it with my own sketches. I don't know if students have to read it from the beginning...

ADH: I had a question that pertains exactly to your move from Western Europe to the US —I find it so striking that in the SAR work, very much is driven by a desire to uncover dimensions, structural dimensions, configural relations—not forms, parameters, that are not the invention of an architect. They are structural to an ordinary environment.

So a lot of the work was to uncover these dimensional or configurative relations. Correct me if I'm wrong, but it seemed to me also that when you were unearthing this, and you were working on finding these relationships, that you really believed, and perhaps still believe that these dimensions are structural, are scientific, are true to the human species as a whole. Are they, in some sense ahistorical, or are they historical categories and cultural categories, and can there be a plurality, or a pluralism of relations that can be invented or uncovered proper to every time and every place, always different? How structurally true to the human species as a whole are the numbers?

JH: Well, if you do a methodology, and you believe that what you contribute is helpful for your colleague architects to use in their work if they want to solve certain problems, you don't want to preempt the architectural style—that's somebody else's decision. The simplest idea of methodology leading to a tool is that we have a measurement that's a methodological tool, by which we can communicate with each other, about the size of things—very simple.

And basically, if you look at the methodology that we proposed, there were two things that we were concerned with: how do you speak about dimension, and how do you speak about position? And I still believe that the position of things and their dimensions are the two basic tools that every architect uses. So what we tried to do is to formalize that a little bit more in a sense that you can talk about the issue of capacity. How do I present or represent the space that is yet to be occupied? And then the concept of zones comes in as a positioning tool. Just like zones in urban design are positioning tools.

In that sense it was a very straightforward idea.

AD: How do you distinguish your approach from, let's say, Christopher Alexander and his *Pattern Language* of 1979—isn't it, I can't remember? There are clear differences, of course, you mentioned earlier in conversation that he is too prescriptive. In a straightforward comparison of formal descriptive strategy, how are your approaches different?

JH: Well, I felt that what he was doing was close to what I was interested in. But there was also a very important difference, and that is the idea of patterns, I think, is a very brilliant idea. In my eyes, a pattern is something that people follow because they agree about the value of it. So it's basically an expression of what we are willing to share with each other.

It's a product of consensus about form. You do not have to talk about the value of what it is. It's simply because you say, "that's what we like to do together."

Chris Alexander, in the beginning particularly, very much tried to prove that the pattern was right and true, that there was a basic truth in patterns that you could unearth and formulate. And that is something that may well be true about what he is saying, but I didn't think that it was very interesting. I think that patterns are interesting as a means of communication, a means of consensus.

Built environment is the product of communal agreement, in my eyes. Now if you want to go back to the autonomy of the built environment, I think Chris also believed in autonomy because he said there are patterns that are always good.

AD: Right, and they reemerge throughout time.

JH: Yeah.

AD: You emphasize pattern, position, dimension... these are all for you communicational paradigms— the language in which architects speak. One of the first projects that SAR did was to create an architectural Esperanto—they are quite amazing to look at, because it's an attempt to create an architecture-speak in script. But the communicational interest is throughout your career, it comes from the European context through to the American context. It seems to me that in the American context, where you are not so hooked in with industry or architects, that your work and your research reflexively moves back more into methodology. I'm thinking of your NSF-funded work. It's interesting, when architectural professors apply for NSF grants —Bill also applied for one. I mean, it's a different model of the architectural school than one would think of. In terms of contemporary design practice and research, that just wouldn't gel with the contemporary situation.

But your work seems at that point to adopt certain methodologies about communication. You mention the Russian linguist and behavioral theorist (Lev) Vygotsky. *Concept Design Games* is based on Wittgenstein's "language games". You are moving back into the work of philosophy, into certain kinds of logical tractarian kinds of exercises, where now the question of intervention by the architect is becoming a kind of game, or a game theory-inflected set of rules. "You do A, I'll do B," et cetera. It seems to me that at that point methodologically, you are trying more and more to formalize the interactivity of the built environment, even as you are saying that it is autonomous. Would that be correct, that there is a strong linguistic or communicational paradigm at work here?

JH: Yes. You mentioned two things—they may be connected, but different. One is that you mentioned Wittgenstein. There was a time that I was very interested in Wittgenstein's *Tractatus*; I found out that my interest in it was not so much about what it had to say about the world, but that he was saying things in that way—that there was a very disciplined developed way of thinking, of going from one point to another. That was very attractive to me at that point of my life. That little booklet that you cited from, that was an attempted to be that organized myself. But as you see, it was not just logic—it was pattern, poetry. I think this is one part of my interest, to have a kind of discipline to say things as clearly as possible.

The other part that you mentioned was the NSF project. In the beginning there was my understanding that what I was dealing with was that architects work together, that the built environment is the result of many designers working in relationship with one another. And that we were living in a culture in which we totally ignored that, in which the individual expression of the designer was the only thing that anybody talked about. So I became interested in the idea that there are ways in which architects meet one another. And that's where the games came in.

Can we make board games that are abstract, but that put the two or three players in relationships that are similar to the relationships that designers have in the built environment? It's a very daring and, I think, almost foolish idea that we tried to do that. And I think that the games that we proposed, with the exception of two or three of them, are impossible to play. But what I also discovered was that making the games was the greatest thing you could do. I later on got reactions from people who wrote me, they said, "how do you do a game?" And you know, that's why we have the two parts. The best exercise, in retrospect, is trying to make a game out of what you think you understand of what your role is. And that's a very good discipline. So that was the beginning of thinking that the built environment is the result of designers interacting. And my book about the *Structure of the Ordinary* was the result of that.[2]

AD: Bill's dissertation was called *Discourse*. I think Nick Negroponte in Architecture Machine Group, was sort of also trying to work with computational programs that could perhaps formalize again, through Artificial Intelligence models, this notion of interactivity between the architect and the environment, between architects and architects,

2 N. John Habraken, *Form and Control in the Built Environment*, ed. Jonathan Teicher (Cambridge, MA: The MIT Press, 1998).

between the architect and users, etc. Your work also has this sort of computational inflection. This is also the early phase of the big massive room-sized computers where you had to share time at like two in the morning and go in and plug in tapes.

JH: I was very much intrigued by computers, yes. So I visited Negroponte's laboratory a lot, and I liked talking to the students there to see what they were doing. Because they also were trying to understand what was going on in the built environment. You could take a piece of it and formalize it.

It was only much much later that I found a link between my own research and the computer. Because when the more advanced CAD programs came along, I got annoyed by finding out that the CAD programs were very pragmatic things. And I was sorry for the CAD programmers, because they were trying to figure out what the architects were doing, but the architects were never telling them. If you ask an architect, "what are you doing?" you don't get an answer. In our time, Donald Schön was asking the same question. He was very much intrigued by what architects were doing. And he talked to all his colleagues, and he never got an answer. And it annoyed him enormously.

So I could understand that these CAD programs were stupid programs, because these poor people, they find out that the architect has a problem, so they try to solve the problem. And then I progressed to the idea of the two levels, it's also the idea of dominance. Sorry I have to get into this a little bit more.

The higher level, when the higher level changes, it disturbs the lower level. If you move a street in an urban design, the buildings have to go. And if you move the lower level, it is free in the space that is given to it. So that is dominance. So the higher level dominates the lower level. And the lower level follows. Now if you bring that to computers, a very nice example is if you take a table, the chairs surround it. In an office, you would ask your colleague or a draftsman to move the table to a corner there, you don't have to explain that the chairs go with it. They follow the table. But the chairs can move around without disturbing the table. So the table dominates the chairs.

That kind of dominance can be a matter of convention, it can also be a matter of gravity, it can have all kinds of reasons. If you think about it, you can find out that this relationship of dominance is happening all the time in buildings. And that is why if an architect or one of the people changes something, somebody pushes a corner out, some piping gets into trouble. It's a dominance problem. So together with my former student Willem Langelaan who was the author of the library for CAD programs, we wrote a paper about dominance in which we said, if the computer understands dominance, and if I can tell the computer that this chair follows the table, then now I have to first group the thing and then de-ungroup.[3] You don't have to do that. Then the computer can tell me if I get into trouble when I move something. It can say, "If you move this, then you better watch that, because you're dominant to that."

And I think that once you have that in a computer program, it's not only that the computer can check all the problems when you change something, but it also understands your way of working.

AD: It's a shift from an earlier architectural concept of space to one of territory. You use the word territory in your later writing.

JH: Yes, territory is a controlled space. I was not talking about control of physical space, but yes, the same goes.

AD: Before we open it up to the audience, I want to ask one last question.
How do you think you the world turned out? I mean, there are younger Dutch architects who have had a great role in the world stage. You were trying to do something different. What do you make of what came after, in the two decades following your retirement?

JH: Well, I'm invited to give lectures from time to time. My impression is that the younger generation is much more, they don't have the hang-ups that my colleagues had about these things. They take it very easily that there are different ways to work. They don't feel personally insulted. They are very pragmatic in the sense that if there are tools that you can use, you use them. So you can have a discussion about whether they are useful or not or whatever, or whether certain concepts are interesting or not, and I think that is great progress. That is the way things should be tested.

Another development, of course, in those twenty years, is the so-called Open Building Network that has been developing internationally, which has been run by Stephen

3 N. John Habraken and J.Willem R. Langelaan, "Emergent Coherent Behavior of Complex Configurations through Automated Maintenance of Dominance relations," in *Proceedings of the ISARC 2003, 20th. International Symposium on Automation and Robotics in Construction*, ed. Frans van Gassel (Eindhoven: Ger Maas, 2003).

4 See Stephen Kendall, "Open Building: An Approach to Sustainable Architecture," *Journal of Urban Technology*, Volume 6, Number 3, pp 1-16, 1999

Kendall for a very long time.[4] It meets every year in a different place in the world. We keep track of different Open Building projects, and in the last five or ten years, important projects have come about. It used to be that an Open Building project was always seen as a sort of experiment. The last ten years, the initiative of the really interesting projects are done by clients who decided that they want this way of working because it is in their interests to do that and because there is a financial interest to do that. That is a real sea change.

One thing I should mention is that in Japan, a year ago, a law has been passed by government to promote the building of housing that can last for two centuries. Two centuries! And they have given a long list of technical requirements for what the building should do. And the basic thing is that they are based on the discussion of support and infill. Kazuo Minami, who was a student here at MIT, introduced me to his teachers in Japan who were already working in the same way. He said that the parliamentarians talk about skeleton and infill but I'm not sure they understand it. But anyway, he was part of the committee tasked with laying out the technical requirements, and they basically break down the building into subsystems and try to define the lifetime of systems. So you might have a pipe in your apartment building that has to be renewed every fifty years. And you must make sure that there is a space behind it where another pipe can be dropped in and the old one can be taken out.

They also recognize that there are certain systems that change simply because people like to change them. So basically it opens the way to Open Building. That they understand that partitions and walls should be changeable before they have deteriorated or simply because people don't want them any more. I think that this is the first time that there is a formal recognition of this approach. And when you follow these requirements, you get a very important tax break, and that means that it's very smart to let the owner do that, but the builders know that they can then ask for more money for a building that responds to these requirements, because the owner will buy it because he will get some money back.

ADH: It's very interesting that you bring this up, because this is to me also one of the perfect tie-ins of the potential activation, or continued activation of structure-infill. I mean, the durability of a building, the fact that it can have a few layers that are really long-lasting, although perhaps not very visible, there is where sustainability becomes, through the lens of structure-infill, something very concrete.

On that very hopeful note, perhaps we should take some questions from the audience.

Stanford Anderson: This is more an anecdote than a question. I was the chair of the committee that chose you as the Head of the Department of Architecture here. I was still a very young professor. The committee to choose John as the Head was a very large committee and it was composed of representatives from all across the department and students from all across the department. So it's a very different way of thinking about how you do this than what operates today. We decided on John, and didn't think that it would be so easy to take him away from what was a very distinctive position in the Netherlands, and where he had so many opportunities to fulfill the kind of ambitions that he had. So I was dispatched to Eindhoven, to meet with John to try to convince him and we had a very nice reception.

So the question: so you did indeed have that important moment – You had a very important position in the Netherlands. Why did you accept our offer?

JH: Because I got bored in the Netherlands.

No, it sounds strange, but it's true. I felt that the research with the SAR had sort of rounded off its ways. Of course there was much to be done to get it implemented, but that did not respond to my intellectual ambitions. I found that in a small community as you had in the Netherlands, I got offered all kinds of jobs overseeing committees and that sort of thing.

AD: You'd become the *über*-bureaucrat.

JH: I didn't like to do that.

So the MIT's offer was in time, because I got a bit restless and because of the contact that I had had at MIT in 1972, I thought that it might be the environment to go to. And I think I was right.

5 N. John Habraken, *Tools of the Trade: Thematic Aspects of Designing* (1996). Available at http://www.habraken.com/html/downloads/tools_of_the_trade_final.pdf .

following page, N. John Habraken with students. Department of Architecture, MIT, n.d..

Anderson: It had some bumps in it too.

JH: Oh, yeah.

Duncan Kincaid: John, I think some time when you were here, you had circulated a small treatise to the department, I believe it was called *Tools of the Trade*?[5] If you thought it would be of interest to this group, could you summarize those findings and tell us if you feel the positions held then still hold today? This is with regard to computation and architectural pedagogy.

JH: I think yes, it would be nice if people would read it again. (*Laughter in audience.*)

Julian Beinart: You mentioned that I ask difficult questions.

I have a question now, which I think might be very different from what I might have asked in the 1970s when you first met me. One of the things that strikes me now about the way … I came from South Africa where there was a popular culture of people who were doing things themselves, Native People, as they were called. And there was a strong tradition of popular art. When I came here, John Turner was looking at events in Latin America, where it showed again that people were providing housing for themselves through their own initiative.

And that was a strong thrust at that time.

What seems to be going on now, with really new ideas about poverty in the Global South, is an extension of the idea that people can take care of their own housing, to taking care of their own domains in a much larger sense. I mean, Slum Dwellers International are now talking about the fact that governments and cities are incapable of taking care of their problems. And extending the idea, not as an aesthetic idea in the way that Rudofsky looked at it in *Architecture without Architects*, but looking at health, education, and general problems of economic development in the same way that we saw people fixing their own houses. For me, that extension has become very significant as an idea. Whether it will work or not, I don't know. But I don't know if you see any logic in my question.

I'm trying to extend the domain of the work to a new idea, which is now permeating thinking in the Third World. I don't know if you follow that idea in the same way that I'm following it.

JH: Yeah, I think what you described shows again that built environments are the result of control patterns on different levels. I always expected that if people can be in charge of their own house or unit, or whatever the immediate environment is, then you can expect that they will also be interested in collectively controlling the larger context.

Beinart: If they have the skill to do that.

JH: That's what professionals always ask. But people find professionals who can help them, if needed. That's the way it should be. There will always be professionals needed to get things going. But the question is who is taking the initiative, and who is in control? And I think what we were laboring with in our generation, and still I think, is that because of Modernism, and for many good reasons, professionals all over the world have taken things in hand, thinking that they could shape the world. It's not only in architecture or building, it's in medicine, it's in law, in wherever. And we now see that professionals have to reexamine their role and have to recognize the fact that there is a world there that has its own laws, and that professionals have to serve rather than to shape it. I think that's the bigger context that we are part of.

John de Monchaux: One of the fascinating things that you turned to when you left MIT, not that you have ever really left MIT, was Matura – the infill, the wall and surfacing device that could turn an old apartment into a new apartment. What were some of the lessons from devising and promoting the Matura system, and perhaps you might give a brief description of it for those who haven't seen it, because it's something to which we released your energies to take it up.

JH: Yeah, that was a good lesson. The Matura System was an infill system, a fit-out system, in which we decided that the biggest problem with fit-out is not the partitionings of the equipment and bathrooms and so on, but the piping and the wiring, that always messes up the problem, and always gives bigger problems to the architects and the builders.

So we reorganized this whole issue of piping and wiring on that level. And a few elements that we invented that you could easily install. And we could demonstrate that if you would use that system, it was possible to take an apartment in a building, clean it out, add something to it, and fill it in again according to the wishes of the user, all in three weeks' time by a team of two or three people who could do everything. And that was the purpose of our development.

But we never succeeded to put it on the market. And the reason was of course that first of all it took a very big investment to make a factory that would run that efficiently, and the building industry is not making big investments like the car industry, though we always said that the fit-out industry would eventually compete with the car industry.

And that was literally true. Because one of the apartments that we did to demonstrate it to the housing corporation, I asked the owner of the infill who had done the floor plan why he wanted to do this. And he said, "well, we like to live here, we don't want to move away, but we were about to move away because we didn't like the apartment anymore. But if we can stay here and do it in our own way." And I said, well, how do you pay for it, because the housing corporation had given a budget, and they had brought in a much bigger budget, and the housing corporation said they could not build that into the rent, and they said well, we'll pay it in cash. And I said, how did you do that? He said, well, we decided not to buy a new car. And so we *were* competing with the car industry.

Now what I learned was that it's not a technical problem that you have to solve, it's a very different problem. What I try to promote now is that, at least in the Netherlands, that they should recognize the existence of an infill industry, infill builders. And if you give these people the certification, they will solve the technical problem. If you do this, we can guarantee that they will do good work, that it will be in time, and that it will be within the budget. I think then you would build up a new industry. In Japan, there are now a few initiatives for an infill industry. But I think basically, it's a problem of strategy again, and I don't think we have made much progress on that – it's a political issue as much as a strategic issue. That is what I learned. It's not a technical problem.

Bill Porter: John, can you speculate on the implications for education of those people who in the profession might behave as expert infillers, bringing in a new generation of professionals who could perform what you have envisioned? Is it technology, is it a question of values, is it specific areas of skill, patterns of education like the predominance of the design studio, should that be changed dramatically? Give us a hint.

JH: Well, personally I think, what I would like to teach is what I did in my design course where you deal with how architects relate to one another although they each have their own responsibility of the design that they're doing. How do you relate?

And I am right now working on another book – I cannot help it – on this issue, in which we have four-times-seven what you call "plays." It's not an exercise because an exercise is rote training, and that's not what this is. It's not a game because games you can win and lose, and this is not something you can win and lose. But a play, like a performance, is something where you perform something with your own intuition and your own talents, that in relation to the other players becomes something else. And in the book I have four parts, probably booklets. The first one is how do you design... a conversation with the form, dealing with time and change. Designing means that you do not know what the end result will be. It's a continuous change in the form that is developing. That's the beginning: learning to deal with time.

The second one is about horizontal relationships. When two architects work on the same street, sharing patterns, or type, or context. That's a horizontal relationship. The third one is vertical relationships. A relationship between the urban designer and the architect, the architect and the fit-out, and so on, which is the issue of the dominance that I have been talking about.

And the final parts are about fields – when you learn to put together all the things you learned about in the first part to make continuous fields which we give, as a start, seven different kinds of fields with different biases into which they can sink their teeth in.

That's my educational answer.

Caveat

Newton's Apple Tree: A Non-Standard Version
Edward Eigen

EDWARD EIGEN

Newton's Apple Tree
A Non-Standard Version

Thus when once a Standard Fruit-tree is planted in security, it is enough;
it will produce excellent Fruit without Culture: The Sun and Air will do the rest.

—William Ellis, *The Complete Planter and Cyderist:*
Or, a New Method of Planting Cyder-Apple, and Perry-Pear-Trees (1756).[1]

It is said that a tree is best measured when it is down. And standing trees from which, perhaps, rare fruit has fallen? The Edinburgh toxicologist and medical jurist Sir Robert Christison began investigating the exact measurement of trees, having "accidentally" become interested in the history of the famous yew in Fortingall Churchyard, in Perthshire. As to its reputed age, said to be as many as three thousand years, he was referred to "no less an authority" than Augustin Pyramus de Candolle. In his *Physiologie Végétale* (1832) Candolle offered a "general rule," based on the study of sections of old and middle-aged trees, that after a certain number of years of rapid and irregular growth, the diametral increment of their trunks is uniform, or very nearly so, for the extent of their lives. Candolle cautioned, however, that while the "law of growth presents a certain regularity, it is far from being absolutely regular, even in the same species."[2] Christison was still more severe. He noted that Candolle's rule had been "subject to criticism," as all authoritative sources are, or ought to be—particularly by J. E. Bowman, who identified errors in Candolle's reasoning and furnished a new method of measurement. On a practical level, Bowman's method had its own "fatal" flaw, which was the reluctance of owners of fine trees to have them bored into with a trephining device to extract core samples. Christison finally opted for the superficially straightforward method of using a thirty-three-foot waxed tape to measure a tree's girth. The crucial consideration was the place of measurement. After considerable reflection on the matter, Christison established a "true standard level" according to the first postulate: "there can be no invariable standard."[3]

1 William Ellis, *The Complete Planter and Cyderist: Or, a New Method of Planting Cyder-Apple, and Perry-Pear-Trees* (London: J. Reeves, 1756), 16. Ellis was set on showing how Philip Miller's claim to this effect was false, or at least in need of correction.

2 Aug[ustin] Pyr[amus] de Candolle, *Physiologie végétale ou exposition des forces et des fonctions vitales des végétaux* (Paris: Béchet Jeune, 1832), 2:975.

3 Sir Robert Christison, "On the Exact Measurement of Trees, and Its Applications," *Transactions and Proceedings of the Botanical Society of Edinburgh* 13 (1879): 222 [217–234].

The reason for this variability, of course, is that there is no standard tree. Trees grow as they will, unless, as Francis Bacon observed of their "melioration," gardeners fasten newly planted trees to a stake, "and continue them thus bound for some years, if they desire them to grow strait."[4] Fixing upon five feet above the ground as the "least variable" level at which to measure the trunk, Christison nevertheless admitted that the terms "ground" and "above the ground" are themselves anything but "fixed and uniform."[5] Even on a smooth lawn an old tree will exhibit a difference of several inches at different points around its base.

To be sure, the purpose of this essay is not to determine how best to measure a tree. Rather it is about how to apply some kind of standard to what is said, to stories and anecdotes, to history, if not more particularly to what is said of trees, those emblematic bearers of knowledge (a word genetically related to the act and facts of narration). The essay's more general concern is with rules and norms and how they (fail to) apply in specific cases. Take, for instance, the problem of how to measure a tree when it is down. Rev. D. Campbell, minister of Fortingall parish, related in a letter printed in the May 6, 1876 number of *Notes and*

Sir Robert Christison, "On the Exact Measurement of Trees, and Its Applications," *Transactions and Proceedings of the Botanical Society in Edinburgh* 13, (1879).

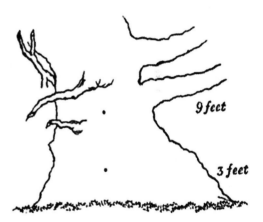

9 feet

3 feet

4 "A First Draught for the Particular History of Vegetables and Vegetation," in *The Philosophical Works of Francis Bacon. Methodized and Made English from the Originals*, ed. Peter Shaw (London: J. J. and P. Knapton, 1733), 3:248.

5 Christison, "On the Exact Measurement of Trees," 222.

Queries, "Of the Fortingall yew only a wreck remains, very interesting indeed in appearance, but scarcely admitting of any proper measurement, or indeed of any satisfactory description by feet merely."[6] Some other sort of measure, perhaps not a metrical one, was needed to describe the tree, one that might perhaps explain how or why the tree became a wreck rather than continuing to grow.

Bowman provided one such method in the second part of his article on the longevity of the yew by counting annual rings from sections of its trunk. In explaining the origin of the yew's frequent occurrence in churchyards, he revisited the "history and tradition" of sacred groves and holy trees.[7] Whether history and tradition tend to provide "concurrent testimony," as Bowman suggested, is a further matter for us to consider. From his researches, Bowman found it most "natural and simple to believe" that the sacred yew, because of the durability of its wood—at once an emblem and a specimen of immortality—was employed by pagan ancestors to deck their graves. Proceeding on somewhat less certain historiographic grounds, he argued that these pagan customs were passively accepted by early missionaries and "engrafted on Christianity."[8] Thus it was that many Christian churches were built on the sites of druidical groves and even assumed their circular form. "Dr. Stukeley believes that round churches are the most ancient in England; though others, I know not why, do not agree with him."[9] With mention of the widely learned William Stukeley, Bowman's critical sensitivities were put on alert, though to no clear purpose. Having shown the errors in Candolle, he was satisfied that he had advanced "sufficient proofs, from the laws of nature examined upon scientific principles," of the great longevity of the yew.[10] Yet what laws, standards, or rules applied to one such as William Stukeley?

If the engrafting of Stukeley to this discussion should appear accidental, then let it serve as an example of the method, derived in part from Robert K. Merton, that this paper intends to exemplify and in some small measure explicate. It was Stukeley, as Douglas McKie and Gavin Rylands de Beer noted in their classic paper on Newton's apple tree, who heard the story as it "came from Newton's own lips."[11] Could there be a more reliable source? Probably so, considering that Newton related the story more than sixty years after the fact, if in fact the story took place when, where, and how it is said to have done. Might not the facts

---

6 "The Finest Yew Tree in England (5th S. v. 308)," *Notes and Queries* ser. 5, vol. 5 (May 6, 1876): 376.

7 On the English worship of trees see Keith Thomas, *Man and the Natural World* (London: Penguin Books, 1984), 214–215. For a more extensive discussion of the churchyard yew see Walter

Johnson, *Byways in British Archaeology* (Cambridge: Cambridge University Press, 1912), 360–407.

8 J. E. Bowman, "On the Longevity of the Yew, As Ascertained from Actual Sections of its Trunk; and on the Origin of its Frequent Occurrence in Churchyards," *The Magazine of Natural*

History 1 (1837): 86 [28–35, 85–90].

9 Bowman, "On the Longevity of the Yew," 86–87, n. †. Bowman is evidently referring to William Stukeley, *Stonehenge: A Temple Restor'd to the British Druids* (London: W. Innys and R. Manby, 1740), 8. Stukeley notoriously argues, "The

old *Britons of Welsh call Stonehenge choir gaur,* which some interpret *chorea gigantum,* the giants dance: I judge more rightly *chorus magnus,* the great choir, round church, or temple." The *chorus* of a building among Roman Christians, he explains, became appropriate to the most sacred part, or east end

have become arranged more regularly over time, as it were after an earlier period of rapid and irregular growth? The problem is made more knotty by its retellings: Newton told four different versions to four different people. And each of them made the story their own, in part by reshaping it and passing it along. What is the standard version? Indeed, what standards apply in this case—the definingly particular case of the stories of which history is made, or from which it departs? Simply stated, the question is, how do we get things straight?

The pretext for this essay (or assay) is provided by a plaque placed at the foot of a tree flourishing in the President's Garden at the Massachusetts Institute of Technology, a small court to the west of Building 10 formed upon the completion of the Vannevar Bush Building.[12] The matter-of-fact inscription reads: *This apple tree is a direct descendant of the tree under which Sir Isaac Newton is said to have conceived the theory of gravity. A gift of the Bureau of Standards to Edward O. Vetter '42.*[13] Which begs the question, said by whom? In which context? According to what authority? Would that we possessed a device like Bush's proposed Memex, "a sort of mechanized private file and library,"[14] it would be possible to more rapidly sort through what was said and by whom, or was said to have been said, and when and where it was written down, or in some other way committed to memory. In attending to these questions, however, let us not take the gift for granted. The gift's source, precisely the Bureau of Standards, might well provide the ways and means of arriving at a satisfactory if not necessarily correct answer to some of these questions.

The subtext of this essay, then, stated here so that it cannot be said to appear hidden, or remain shrouded in the partial gloom of the footnotes, is suggested by the Institute itself, or perhaps more generally by the alleged conventionality of institutional thinking. The word itself speaks of edifying strictures, be they moral, ethical, or intellectual. *Institutio* appears in the title of many Latin works on law and was also often employed by Christian writers. The apologist Lactantius's *Divine Institutes* (ca. 303-311) merits mention by reason of its strict delineation of right thinking, under the headings *On false religion, The origin of error, False wisdom,* and *True wisdom and religion.* In modern usage, John Calvin's *Institutio Christianae religionis* (Institutes of the Christian Religion, 1536) was likely meant to recall

of churches, always "turn'd of a circular form."

10 Ibid., 87.

11 D[ouglas] McKie, G[avin] R[ylands] de Beer, "Newton's Apple," *Notes and Records of The Royal Society* 9 (1951): 52 [46–54].

12 O. Robert Simha, *MIT Campus Planning, 1960-2000: An Annotated Chronology*

(Cambridge: MIT Press, 2003), 20.

13 Vetter receiving the sapling in 1977 when he stepped down as Under Secretary of Commerce. A longstanding member of the MIT Corporation, Vetter in turn gifted this curious, rare but by no means unique specimen to his *Alma Mater.* There is

no need to make the case for Newton's patent interest in practical, theoretical, and exegetic questions of metrology. Named Warden of the Mint in 1696, where he oversaw the vast and complex enterprise of the Great Recoinage, Newton became Master of the Mint Christmas Day 1699.

His research and assays figured prominently in John Arbuthnot's *Tables of Ancient Coins, Weights and Measures Explain'd and Exemplify'd in Several Dissertations* (1727), in which the mathematician and satirist sought to recover the meaning ancient texts by rendering the quantities stated within—the price of

Erasmus's *Institutio principis christiani* (The Education of a Christian Prince, 1516). The translation of Erasmus's title reflects the common rendering of *institutio* as "instruction."[15] These meanings have not been entirely lost in (or to) an allegedly post-confessional age. In his essay on the "Institutional Control of Interpretation," Frank Kermode pointed to the Council of Trent (1545–1563) as a defining contest between tradition and Scripture, between the right to determine interpretation in light of the truth "preserved by a continuous succession in the Catholic Church" and the doctrine of *sola scriptura* professed by its enemies.[16] In assessing its contemporary disciplinary character, Kermode proposed that interpretation cannot take place in the absence of some awareness of the "forces which limit, or try to limit" what can be said about a text. As he put it, "the medium of these pressures and interventions is the institution."[17] Whether it is an elastic medium is well worthy of consideration.

If we pause a bit longer to ask, along with the Levitical anthropologist Mary Douglas, "How Institutions Think," it is due to the curiously central historical role the Institute has played in defining and enforcing limits of allowable tolerance. Douglas's central contention is that social, political, and/or professional solidarity is possible only "to the extent that individuals share the categories of their thought."[18] This precise extent is susceptible to standardization. It may be institutionalized, when the institution is minimally defined as (or by) a "convention." Borrowing the term from the philosopher and game theorist David Lewis, Douglas wrote that a "convention arises when all parties have a common interest in there being a rule to insure coordination, none has a conflicting interest, and none will deviate lest the desired coordination is lost."[19] Are these conditions real, ideal, or imperiously practical? The answer is that convention, in the discrete form of constant, reliable, normal, and regulative standards—even of deviance—are both useful and necessary in all areas of human conduct.

Such, at least, was the governing conception of Samuel Wesley Stratton, MIT's eighth president and previous to that, and by all accounts in preparation for it, the founding director of the National Bureau of Standards. The Bureau's immediate institutional predecessor, the Office of Weights and Measures, came under the purview of MIT's fifth president, Henry

slaves, funerary expenses, soldier's pay, apothecaries doses, etc.—in terms of known quantities of the same kind which are in current usage. Newton's "A Dissertation upon the Sacred Cubit of the Jews and Cubits of the several Nations" was part and parcel with his attempt to establish the numerical proportions of the Temple. Not unrelated to these exegetical ambitions, in his *The Chronology of Ancient Kingdoms Amended* (1728) Newton sought to expose the "vanity" of the Egyptian record keepers who extended their monarchy "some thousands of years older than the world." Isaac Newton, *The Chronology of Ancient Kingdoms Amended* (Dublin: George Risk, 1728), 191. On Newton's tenure at the mint see Simon Schaffer, "Golden Means: Assay Instruments and the Geography of Precisions in the Guinea trade," in Marie-Noëlle Bourguet, Christian Licoppe, Heinz Otto Sibum, eds., *Instruments, Travel and Science: Itineraries of Precision from the Seventeenth to the Twentieth Century* (London: Routledge, 2002), 39. On the cubit see Zur Shalev, "Measurer of All Things: John Greaves (1602–1652), the Great Pyramid, and Early Modern Metrology," *JHI* 63 (2002): 555–75.

Smith Pritchett, who served as superintendent of the U.S. Coast and Geodetic Survey from 1897 to 1900. This is where our little and limited history of the Institute needs to begin, or more precisely with the irrelevant-seeming story recounted by the chemist and outgoing MIT president James Mason Crafts in his address at Pritchett's October 24, 1900 inauguration. At some indistinct point in an astoundingly longwinded speech, Crafts said, "Many persons with tell you promptly that Newton discovered the attraction of gravitation by watching and meditating upon the falling apple." For Crafts this most famous part of the story was not a matter for further comment, serving to provide as it did an initial but nonetheless secondary narrative element. "It may surprise you to learn," he continued, "that the most stately and least scientific of kings, Louis XIV of France, gave Newton more aid than did the apple tree in making this great discovery."[20]

Crafts's story focuses on the near- to long-term aftermath of the apple's unquestioned fall; no mention is made of the tree from whence it fell. The incident, it seems, prompted Newton to revisit his planetary inverse-square law by calculating the moon's orbit. The dimensions of the earth entered into this calculation; and, using a commonly available measure of sixty miles ± for a degree of latitude, his result produced an appreciable error in the moon's expected "endeavour of receding" from its center of motion. Inertia set in. "Newton could not publish a thing which was not sustained by facts," Crafts wrote. And thus "for seventeen long years he laid it aside, waiting for its vindication by truer knowledge."[21] He was not to stand accused of clinging to false wisdom, at least not in matters of Principle. The truer knowledge Newton awaited appeared almost as fortuitously as the much-meditated-upon apple. According to Crafts, about the year 1682 Newton went up to London and heard at the Royal Society that the astronomer Abbé Jean Picard, in the service of the Royal Observatory and the French king, had published a more precise measurement of an arc of the earth's circumference. Newton thence hastened back to Cambridge to use Picard's figures in a new set of calculations, working on them late into the night. "As the result seemed to approach exactly the true orbit, Newton grew so excited that his trembling hands could not hold the pencil, and he had to call in the aid of a friend to complete the sum."[22] At long last, he was vindicated.

14 Vannevar Bush, "As We May Think," *The Atlantic Monthly* (July 1945): 106 [101–108].

15 John Calvin, *Institutes of the Christian Religion*, ed. John T. McNeill, trans. Ford Lewis Battles, vol. 1 (Philadelphia: Westminster Press, 1960), xxxi, n. 3.

16 The Council of Trent, April 8, 1546 (Sess. IV, cap. 1). In his *Antidote* (1547), or refutation of the Tridentine Decrees, Calvin was particularly exercised by the notion that a council "cannot err, because it represents the Church."

17 Frank Kermode, "Institutional Control of Interpretation," in *The Art of Telling: Essays on Fiction* (Cambridge: Harvard University Press, 1985), 168.

18 Mary Douglas, *How Institutions Think* (Syracuse: Syracuse University Press, 1986), 8.

19 Ibid., 46. David Lewis, Convention: A Philosophical Study (Cambridge: Harvard University Press, 1968.

20 James Mason Crafts, "Address on Behalf of the Faculty [Inauguration of Henry Smith Pritchett as President of the Massachusetts Institute of Technology]," *Technology Review* 3 (1901): 43 [36–49].

21 Ibid.

22 Ibid., 44.

Unfortunately the only thing reliable about this version of events is what Crafts himself admitted at the outset: "the dates are uncertain and the documents imperfect."[23] The precise form of the story originated in John Robison's *Elements of Mechanical Philosophy* (1804).[24] But given its subsequent success, Crafts might have picked it up from any number of sources—save, that is, for the year Newton first learned of Picard's work. The emergence of that one crucial fact is central to Stephen Peter Rigaud's demonstration of just how uncertain Crafts's dates and documents truly were. In his *Historical Essay on the First Publication of Sir Isaac Newton's Principia* (1838), Rigaud stated that there did not appear to be any "contemporary authority" for the particulars of Robison's story. He allowed that "tradition often preserves much that is valuable," but warned that "such evidence ought to be received with considerable caution."[25] Along with the valuable bits it preserves, tradition can also serve as a medium for transmitting and perpetuating error. Underlying Rigaud's measured words is his attempt to assess the precise degree of tolerance that can and must be afforded the inherent faultiness of sources and the interpretations supported by them. This he did to his own satisfaction by consulting the elaborately compiled history of the Royal Society to show that Newton was most likely not present for the June 7, 1682 meeting at which Picard's measurements were discussed.[26] The correspondence between Newton and Hooke further revealed that Newton likely knew of the measurements, which were first mentioned at the January 11, 1672 meeting of the Royal Society, well before the supposed night of excited calculation.[27] Rigaud's own critical calculation was meant to establish the likelihood of this or any story. Allowing once again that the "reader must decide," he insisted that "some reasonable doubt may be entertained of the strict accuracy of the facts."[28]

How, then, did the year 1682 enter into the story when Robison had made no mention of it? Rigaud reasoned that it was the very absence of a date that led the physicist Jean-Baptiste Biot to form a "conjecture" in his article on Newton in Michaud's *Biographie Universelle* (1822). This done and stated as such, Biot proceeded to recount Robison's story more or less intact.[29] Yet Biot's speculative tact was inexplicably erased from the widely read English translation of his *Life of Newton*, published by the Society for the Diffusion of Useful Knowledge. As Rigaud noted, "the conjecture of the original is converted into a

23 Ibid., 43.

24 John Robison, *Elements of Mechanical Philosophy* (Edinburgh: Archibald Constable & Co., 1804), 288.

25 Stephen Peter Rigaud, *Historical Essay on the First Publication of Sir Isaac Newton's Principia* (Oxford: Oxford University Press, 1838), 6.

26 Thomas Birch, *The History of the Royal Society of London* (London: A. Millar, 1757), 4:150.

27 Thomas Birch, *The History of the Royal Society of London* (London: A. Millar, 1757), 3:3. Picard's measurements were first published in *Mesure de la terre* (Paris, 1671). At the January 11, 1672 meeting,

Henry Oldenburg read a letter from the diplomat Francis Vernon, who was then in Paris, mentioning the work. Robert Hooke was exhorted by Oldenburg to pursue and finish his own way of measuring the earth, which Hooke promised to do, "hoping to bring to it a greater exactness."

28 Rigaud, *Historical Essay*, 6.

29 Jean-Baptiste Biot, "Isaac Newton," in Louis Gabriel Michaud, Joseph Fr. Michaud, eds. *Biographie Universelle, Ancienne et Moderne*, vol. 31 (Paris: L. G. Michaud, 1822), 154.

30 Rigaud, *Historical Essay* 17.

positive assertion, and by mistake has consequently been admitted as a fact, which the author had ascertained."[30] It had become established in (and by) tradition. The origin of Biot's error is perhaps to be found in the article on Newton in the *Biographia Britannica*, which states that Picard, "having not long before, viz. in 1679, measured a degree of the earth," Newton then sought to confirm that the orbit of the moon was as he himself "had formerly conjectured."[31] Inversely to Biot's, Newton's conjecture advanced towards certainty by measured degrees. Rigaud's analysis was not without its own revisionary consequences. In the notes to the second, revised edition of his *History of the Inductive Sciences* (1847), William Whewell admitted that he had earlier "adopted [Biot's] conjecture as a fact," but had since learned otherwise.[32] For W. W. Rouse Ball there was no need for half measures. In his *An Essay on Newton's "Principia"* (1893), it was simply given that Rigaud had succeeded in "proving conclusively that Robison had been misinformed."[33]

Is Crafts's story altered in any appreciable way by the conclusion that Newton might only have had to wait seven or so years to learn of Picard's measurements and not the "seventeen long years" Crafts supposed? Does Crafts's comment about uncertain dates and imperfect documents somehow recall Biot's conjecture, or does his uncritical acceptance of the year 1682 tacitly endorse its result? If the June 7, 1682 meeting of the Royal Society were indeed the relevant one, then Newton would have been present for a discussion of authors who had sought to adjust the "comparative measures of several countries, both of weight, length, and capacity," among whom John Greaves was credited with being the "most accurate."[34] For Crafts, however, the precise number of years during which Newton laid aside his work was only an exemplary figure or sum. It served as a measure of his probity and perseverance, establishing a model of scientific conduct against which Pritchett was to be favorably compared. But it is the astronomer and geodesist Picard who appears to provide the relevant standard. Whatever narrative latitude Crafts allowed himself, his story paid transparent tribute to Pritchett's service as superintendent of the Coast and Geodetic Survey. An astronomer, Pricthett was actively engaged in the technical and scientific aspects of geodesy, the observatory at Washington University in St. Louis, of which he was the director, providing telegraphic time determinations to the Geological Survey to establish longitudes and latitudes.[35]

31 "Sir Isaac Newton," *Biographia Britannica*, 5:3224.

32 William Whewell, *History of the Inductive Sciences: From the Earliest to the Present Time*, vol. 2 (London: John W. Parker, 1847 [2nd edit.]), 297.

33 W. W. Rouse Ball, *An Essay on Newton's "Principia"* (London: Macmillan and Co., 1893), 23.

34 Thomas Birch, *The History of the Royal Society of London*, vol. 4 (London: A. Millar, 1757), 150.

35 Robert Simpson Woodward, "Latitudes and Longitudes of Certain Points in Missouri, Kansas, and New Mexico," *Bulletin of the United States Geological Survey* 49 (1889).

Like Picard, who in his *Traité du Nivellement* (1684) enumerated "Rules" for establishing a "level line" when surveying even the most irregular terrain, Pritchett was an agent of order, precision, and indeed rule. Newton's apple fell by chance (or providence); parallels and meridians, bureaus, and institutions follow a carefully drawn plan.

When Pritchett came to the Coast Survey in 1887, one of his first orders of business was to evaluate the operations of the Office of Weights and Measures. Established in 1836 as an entity of the Treasury Department, it had effectively merged with the intensive scientific operations of the Coast Survey. Following the review, an urgent appeal was made to Congress for funding to hire a physicist of "high standing" to direct the understaffed Office.[36] Thus it was, according to Pritchett, that he persuaded Stratton to come to Washington from the University of Chicago, where he had been working with Albert A. Michelson.[37] The other candidate for the post was the logician Charles Sanders Peirce, a member of the Coast Survey from 1871–1891 and who had been in charge of weights and measures in 1884–1885. But Pritchett took a dim view of his eligibility. In an article for *Technology Review* entitled "A Tale of Two Presidents," Pritchett wrote of a "man of great originality and of wide scientific knowledge, but of erratic temperament, of doubtful habits, and wholly free of that sound judgment so necessary for the management of such an enterprise."[38] The two presidents of the title were of course Pritchett and Stratton, the article itself written at the time of Stratton's inauguration. Pritchett was keen to note the common lineage of Francis Amasa Walker, who came to the presidency of MIT from the Census bureau, Pritchett himself from the Coast Survey, and Stratton from the Bureau of Standards. What did this physicist of high standing possess that Peirce did not? For one, he was not erratic. "Unsympathetic perhaps and certainly impatient with people or things that ran contrary to his ideal," reads a biographical fragment of Stratton, "he gave the full measure of his support and force to that which advanced his ideal, first of the Bureau and later of the Institute."[39] Stratton's ideal was of an institute.

In his exhaustive history of the National Bureau of Standards, Rexmond C. Cochrane mentioned Pritchett's version of events while also presenting evidence that it was in fact the Secretary of the Treasury, Lyman C. Gage, or rather Assistant Secretary Frank A.

36 Henry S. Pritchett, "The Story of the Establishment of the National Bureau of Standards," *Science* 15 (Friday, February 21, 1902): 282 [281–284].

37 Michelson himself had recently spent a year at the International Bureau of Weights and Measures outside Paris, where he demonstrated the practicality of a wavelength (light wave) standard to replace the standard meter bar.

38 Henry S. Pritchett, "A Tale of Two Presidents," *Technology Review* 25 (February 1923): 200 [199–200]. On Peirce's nomination see Rexmond C. Cochrane, *Measures for Progress: A History of the National Bureau of Standards* (Washington, D.C.: National Bureau of Standards, U.S. Department of Commerce, 1966), 54, n. 10. Other articles published at the time of Stratton's inauguration include, H. E. Lobdell, "Samuel Wesley Stratton: An Interview," *Technology Review* 25 (November 1922): 7–10; "The Bureau of Standards: An Account of the Work Done under Dr. Stratton's Supervision," *Technology Review* 25 (November 1922): 11 [11–12].

39 Cochrane, *Measures for Progress*, 660. Appendix M. Samuel Wesley Stratton: Founder and First

Vanderlip, a former classmate of Stratton's at the University of Illinois, who recruited him to direct the Office of Weights and Measures. It seems that parts of both stories are true; for while he declined the offer, Stratton later recalled having shared with the Secretary, the Assistant Secretary, and the Superintendent the "necessity for a government bureau having to do with standards and methods of measurement in the broad sense." On the train ride back to Chicago, Stratton "drew up a plan for the establishment of such an institution."[40]

Convinced by his own plan, Stratton returned to Washington in October 1899 to take over the Office of Weights and Measures. He immediately set to work drafting the bill that accompanied Secretary Gage's April 18, 1900 letter to Congress elaborating the need for a new agency to be named the National Standardization Bureau.[41] In his testimony before Congress, Secretary Gage addressed what he regarded as the moral aspect of the question, presumably what Stratton meant by measurement in the broad sense. "We are the victims of looseness in our methods; of too much of that sort of spirit, born out of our rapid development, perhaps, of a disregard or a lack of comprehension of the binding sanction of accuracy in every relation of life."[42] Stratton was just the man to remove the slack, to apply forces that limit.

The bill establishing the Nation Bureau of Standards was passed by the House on March 3, 1903. Stratton was appointed its first director and continued to serve for twenty-one years. At 3:28 p.m., October 11, 1922 the members of the Corporation voted to ratify the appointment of Stratton as MIT's new president, effective the following January 1. An alliance between the Institute and the Bureau had long since been established. In a 1904 article for *Technology Review*, Albert S. Merrill, Class of 1900, provided a long description of the Bureau's activities encouraging other MIT graduates to seek a career there. Merrill explained that the Bureau was a branch of the scientific work carried on by the government, but that it had "special functions which differentiate it from all other institutions, governmental or otherwise, in the western hemisphere."[43] What differentiated the Bureau from all other institutions if not its unique relationship with the Institute? That relationship is largely to be found in the footnotes. In his history of the Bureau, Cochrane made continuous reference to the Samuel Wesley Stratton Papers in the Archives and Special

Director of the National Bureau of Standards. This biographical essay is based on manuscript fragments written Samuel C. Prescott of the Massachusetts Institute of Technology in 1933–1934, and on the materials for that biography that now comprise the Stratton papers in the Archives at MIT.

40 S. W. Stratton to R. S. Woodward, February 10, 1914 (Stratton Papers at MIT, Box 12), cited in Cochrane, *Measures for Progress*, 52.
41 Cochrane writes that Stratton composed the text of Secretary Gage's letter. Stratton's correspondence on behalf of the bill may be found in Box 1 of the Stratton

Papers. Cochrane, *Measures for Progress*, 49.
42 Hearing before the Subcommittee of the Committee on Commerce, United States Senate, Upon Bill (S. 4680) to Establish a National Standardizing Bureau, December 28, 1900. Document no. 70. Portions of this text are reproduced in

National Bureau of Standards (H.R. 11350). 34 Cong. Rec. 3472–3478 (1901), 3476.
43 Albert S. Merrill, "The Bureau of Standards," *Technology Review* 6 (1904): 576 [576–581].

Collections of MIT. The formative history of the Bureau is part and parcel of the Institute's own institutional memory; in the standardized measures of archival administration, that parcel occupies 4 cubic ft. (9 manuscript boxes and 2 oversize boxes).

The ambition here is not to enter into the archives, where faithful penitent historians go to get things right, or at least to get them from the source. One of Newton's biographers, Patricia Fara usefully warns of the dangers of doing so, or more specifically entering what she calls the "archive of Newtonian representations." All that can be accomplished by even the most cautious biographer is to present "one version of the 'facts' of Newton's life."[44] Rather the ambition in this essay is to bury ourselves in the footnotes, beginning with the plaque at the foot of the Institute's tree. What follows is several versions of the (after-) life of Newton's apple tree. The question is which version to choose, and what standards to apply? Those of the Institute or those of the Bureau? The unyielding rigidity of these institutional mediums make them interpretively useful, if only to support the very fiction of constants and standards. No. The tree's true measure will be sought in the erratic opinions and unsupported facts admitted in but confined to the footnotes.

Before discussing the legend that has grown up around Sir Isaac Newton's discovery of gravitation whilst sitting beneath an apple tree, let us begin with the related but somewhat more tractable matter of the mathematician Bolyai Farkas's (1775–1856) final resting place in the Transylvanian city of Maros-Vásárhely (present-day Târgu-Mure, Romania). In an article entitled "The Tomb of the Savant," the Jewish Hungarian journalist and editor Adolf Dux reported with appreciative bemusement that Bolyai's sylvan memorial was indeed a tomb in name only. No statue or stone marks the site. "The typical order of things," Dux wrote, "dictates that any such tomb would have been surmounted by an imposing architectural monument inscribed with laudatory inscriptions."[45] Yet Bolyai was no ordinary mind; evidence of the fact is perhaps to be found in the form of his round, capacious, high-vaulted skull on display at the [Count Sámuel] Teleki-Bolyai Library. The more certain testimony of Bolyai's surpassing intellect is provided by the *Tentamen* (1832–1833), an appendix to the first volume of his son János Bolyai's revolutionary *"Scientiam Spatii absolute"* (Science of absolute space), a complete and coherent system of non-Euclidean geometry.[46]

---

44 Patricia Fara, *Newton: The Making of Genius* (New York: Columbia University Press, 2004), 4.

45 Adolf Dux, "La Tombe du Savant," *Mémoires de la Société des sciences physiques et naturelles de Bordeaux* 5 (1883): 63 [63–69]. Originally published in *Pester Lloyd* (February 4, 1880).

46 *Tentamen Juventutem Studiosam in Elementa Matheseos Purae Introducendi* (1832). (An Attempt to Introduce Studious Youth to the Elements of Pure Mathematics"). János appendix is entitled, Scientiam Spatii absolute veram exhibens; a veritate aut falsitate Axiomatis XI. Euclidei (a priori haud unquam decidenda) independentem."

Bolyai, who wrote his own necrology in 1855, expressed the desire that no mausoleum be erected for him. All that he wished was that an apple tree be planted over his grave, in memory of the three apples that had played such an important role in the history of humanity: "the apple of Eve and that of Paris which reduced the world to slavery, and the apple of Newton, which placed it back amongst the stars."[47] Dux was tempted to see in these arrangements an example of the Romantic writer Jean-Paul's world-inverting "humor," a form of Schlegelian irony meant to assert the impossibility of the sort of sublime solemnity achieved, say, by Étienne-Louis Boullée's Cenotaph for Newton. Surely the tale of Bolyai's apple tree was fantasy. Such, at least, Dux believed until he actually visited the "singular sepulcher." At the Maros-Vásárhely Reform College, the skeptic was welcomed by Bolyai's successor József Konez, who inhabited the same rooms once occupied by the departed genius. A poet as well as a mathematician, Bolyai had hung the walls with portraits of Shakespeare and Schiller beside one of Carl Friedrich Gauss, with whom he had studied in Goettingen. But the house was evidently not as Bolyai had left it. The rooms had been enlarged and rearranged, new pictures had been put up and, "the rooms were animated by another existence," that of Konez.[48]

No longer among the living, Bolyai was nonetheless present. Bolyai's former habitation was a living monument. In the gardens surrounding the house, Dux wrote, the memory of another time was still felt in the breeze that wanders through the leafy trees under which Bolyai himself once wandered. This sense was especially strong beneath the memorial apple tree planted over Bolyai's "grassy roofed tomb." The tree was a Pojnik, which bears fine a Transylvanian species of large, round, yellow-green fruit from a vigorous and fertile stock.[49] By a strange coincidence, at the time of Dux's visit there were precisely three apples on the tree, just as Bolyai had imagined. Was this perhaps also a pomological sign, a reference to Gauss's personal seal, a nearly bare fruit tree with the motto *Pauca sed matura* (Few but ripe). The fruit represents the mature growth of a straightened tree. As will be seen, the question of Gauss's generosity, or lack thereof, in responding to Bolyai's letter announcing his son's discoveries offers insight into the singular and sometimes parallel "paths" followed in pursuit of new knowledge.[50] Claims to priority are narratives in the making in which the identification of common sources, the sorting out of credit

---

47 Dux, "La Tombe du Savant," 63.

48 Ibid., 64.

49 Ed[uard] Lucas, J[ohann] G[eorge] K[onrad] O[berdieck], *Illustriertes Handbuch der Obstkunde*, vol. 4 Äpfel (Stuttgart: Eugen Ulmer, 1875), 458.

50 Letter from Gauss to Bolyai (Göttingen March 6, 1832), Franz Schmidt, Paul Stäckel, eds., *Briefwechsel zwischen Carl Friedrich Gauss und Wolfgang Bolyai* (Leipzig: B. G. Teubner, 1899), 109. "Wenn ich damit anfange 'dass ich solche nicht loben darf': so wirst Du wohl einen Augenblick stutzen: aber ich kann nicht anders; sie loben hiesse mich selbst loben: denn der ganze Inhalt der Schrift, der Weg, den Dein Sohn eingeschlagen hat, und die Resultate zu denen er geführt ist, kommen fast durchgehends mit meinen eigenen, zum Theile schon seit 30—35 Jahren angestellten Meditationen überein. In der That bin ich dadurch auf das Äuserste überrascht."

and attribution remain to be done. But once settled, ownership for an idea is not easily transferred or shared, unless it is to be understood as a form of legacy, like stories, meant to be shared and passed along.

Bolyai had his eyes set on the aftermath. In planting the Pojnik tree he nurtured the illusory "harvest of gratitude from those who pick its fruit and take grafts from it! All in memory of the three famous apples." Like Voltaire, in whose *Lettres philosophiques* we are first told of Newton walking in his garden where he "saw some fruit falling from a tree,"[51] Bolyai was wisely sensitive to narratives of the Fall.[52] Voltaire, we are told, was told the story by Newton's niece Catherine Barton, whose husband, John Conduitt, was Newton's assistant and then successor as Master of the Mint. Dux too was alive to the way of all things. "If a marble monument is ever erected to Bolyai," he wrote, "the original and more remarkable monument, the Pojnik apple tree, must still always be lovingly preserved and cared for."[53] Newton's apple tree required more than loving care. It and the legend that grew from it needed to be propped up, straightened out, if only to allow the purely accidental nature of the apple's fall to assume its decisive causative role in the history of ideas. Like Dux's visit to Maros-Vásárhely to confirm the story of Bolyai's apple tree, no few pilgrims, historians, scientists, scholars, and the merely curious have gone to Woolsthorpe to take true measure of the ground.

But first to conclude the discussion of Bolyai. It was not the fourth definition of Euclid's *Elements* that kept Bolyai up at night: A straight line is a line which lies evenly with the points on itself. It was the fifth postulate, the parallel postulate. Bolyai wrote to his son in 1820: "You must not attempt this approach to parallels. I know this way to its very end. I too have traversed this bottomless night, which extinguished all light and joy of my life. I entreat you, leave the science of parallels alone."[54] It is not standard parental advice on how to raise a child. (The question of orthopaedics will be addressed below.) János Bolyai's absolute science of space represented an unsuspected approach, an "absolutely true" geometry completely independent of the parallel postulate. After so many false leads, by his father and so many other mathematicians, was János indeed the first to conceive non-Euclidean space?

51 V[oltaire], *Lettres philosophiques* (Amsterdam: E. Lucas, 1734), 71.
52 On Voltaire see Julia L. Epstein, "Voltaire's Myth of Newton," *Pacific Coast Philology* 14 (1979): 28 27–33. On Newton's home as heritage site see Patricia Fara, "Isaac Newton Lived Here: Sites of Memory and

Scientific Heritage," *The British Journal for the History of Science* 33 (2000): 408 [407–426].
53 Dux, "La Tombe du Savant," 69.
54 L. v. Dávid, "Die beiden Bolyai," *Elemente der Mathematik* 11 (1951): 9 [1–24]. "Die Parallelen auf jenem Wege sollst Du nicht

probieren; ich kenne auch jenen Weg bis zu Ende, auch ich habe diese bodenlose Nacht durchmessen: jedes Licht, jede Freude meines Lebens sind in ihr ausgelöscht worden. Ich beschwöre Dich bei Gott! Laß die Parallelen in Frieden..."

55 Robert K. Merton, "Priorities in Scientific Discovery: A Chapter in the Sociology of Science," *American Sociological Review* 22 (1957): 656, [635–659].
56 Ibid., 656.
57 Ibid., 656.
58 Ibid., 656, n. 82.
59 [English edition, v].

This question is addressed, though certainly not for the first time, in Robert K. Merton's influential 1957 essay, "Priorities in Scientific Discovery." Merton was particularly concerned with Gauss's response to Bolyai's letter about his son's deliverance from the dark endless night of the parallel postulate. Gauss, the Prince of Mathematics, saw evidence in János's work of true genius, but went on to explain that he could not express his enthusiasm as fully as he would like, for "to praise it, would be to praise myself. Indeed, the whole contents of the work, the path taken by your son, the result to which he is led, coincide almost entirely with my meditations, which have occupied my mind partly for the last thirty or thirty-five years."[55] By Merton's reading, Bolyai *père* interpreted the letter with proud recognition that his son had been working along parallel lines, as it were, with Gauss. Bolyai *fils* saw only that his discovery had anticipated him. His priority lost, he was later further seriously demoralized to learn of Nikolai Ivanovich Lobachevsky's description of hyperbolic geometry.[56]

For reasons that will presently become apparent, Merton's indecisiveness about his own sources is worth mentioning. The principal reference on the Bolyais, he writes, including the pertinent correspondence, is Paul Stäckel's *Wolfgang und Johann Bolyai, Geometrische Untersuchungen*, 2 vols. (Leipzig, 1913). Merton admitted to coming up short in his own *Untersuchung*, noting that Stäckel's work was "not available to [him] at the time of this writing."[57] Thus he cited instead the correspondence from Roberto Bonola, the author of *Non-Euclidean Geometry: A Critical and Historical Study of Its Development*. Bonola's text was translated into English by H. S. Carslaw (Chicago, 1912).[58] Did Carslaw base his own translation on the Italian rendering of the letters, written in German, that appears in the original edition of Bonola's book, *La geometria non-Euclidea: esposizione storico-critica del suo sviluppo* (Bologna, 1906)? Or did he go back to their source, presumably Stäckel, which Merton himself was unable to do? Would this task have fulfilled the expectations produced by historical-critical claims of the very title of Bonola's book? In his translator's preface, Carslaw suggested, somewhat ambiguously, that he had "introduced some changes made in the German translation."[59] In fact, the text of the letters in Heinrich Liebmann's German translation of Bonola's text, *Die nichteuklidische Geometrie, historisch-kritische Darstellung ihrer Entwicklung* (Leipzig: B. G. Teubner, 1908), is exactly as it appears in Franz Schmidt and Paul Stäckel's *Briefwechsel zwischen Carl Friedrich Gauss und Wolfgang Bolyai* (Leipzig, 1899). At best (or perhaps worst) Merton regretted not having made reference to the wrong work by Stäckel.

The question of what is proverbially (or is it literally?) lost or gained in translation is not our primary issue. But to the extent that translation, along with accommodation, mutation, and derivation counts among the historical processes in and by which the ideas, images, and customs of one culture are received by another and their subsequent integration into the latter, it has a role to play in Merton's programmatic interest in priority. Priority raises a concern for sources, whether looking back or looking forward over the historical horizon; preferably, it seems, looking from a greater height than one's predecessors. However brief and inconclusive has been the foregoing investigation of Bonola's sources, it is imperfectly modeled on the method, which is purposefully and productively not one, elaborated by Merton in his *On the Shoulders of Giants: A Shandean Postscript* (originally published 1965). In his Foreword to the 1991 Italian edition, translated into English for the 1993 "Post-Italianate Edition," Umberto Eco wrote that the logic of *On the Shoulders of Giants* "follows that of *Tristram Shandy*." Laurence Sterne's novel in nine volumes (1759–1767) can hardly be considered a propositional foundation upon which to built anything sound or certain, straight and true. Sterne's own residence in Coxwold, Shandy Hall, a "strange-looking gabled structure . . . was the very house, one would say, with its nooks and corners and surprises, from which should issue a book like *Tristram Shandy*."[60] A home-spun meta-narrative universe, in which failure is "functional and carefully planned,"[61] Sterne's shambling logic is better suited to undermining already improbable certainties than it is to reinforcing them, say, like the "huge irregular stone chimney buttressing the eastern end" of Shandy Hall. Eco had no intention of straightening things out, of transforming Sterne's text into a *Narratio more geometrico demonstrata*. He allowed, however, that the exercise would be worthy of OuLiPo (Ouvroir de littérature potentielle), the subcommittee of the Collège de Pataphysique and a self-styled "society of erudite and useless research."

Merton did not so much spell out, enumerate, axiomatize as illustrate his adoptive method. It takes the specific form of the "non-linear, advancing-by-doubling back Shandean Method of composition," which he came to realize was the "same course taken by history in general."[62] Does history in general adhere to a particular course; does history in particular ever adhere to a general course? One correction we must apply to Merton, from the outset, however, is the notion that the Shandean method is non-linear. What he meant, we must suppose, is that it is not straightforward. A line remains a line even if it twists and turns and loops on itself, sometimes assuming an alluring serpentine form, as with Corporal Trim's flourish. This lesson can be derived from Marcel Duchamp's 3 *Standard Stoppages* (1913–1914), his boxed set of meter-long units of length shaped by chance. These pedagogical rather than metrical devices were meant to cast "pataphysical doubt" on the "concept of the straight edge as being the shortest route from one point to another."[63]

60 Wilbur Lucius Cross, *The Life and Times of Laurence Sterne* (New York: The Macmillan Company, 1909), 235.

61 Wayne C. Booth, "The Self-Conscious Narrator in Comic Fiction Before *Tristram Shandy*," PMLA 67 (1952): 177 [163-85].

62 Robert K. Merton, *On the Shoulders of Giants* (Chicago: University of Chicago Press, 1993), xix.

63 Anne d'Harnoncourt, Kynaston McShine, eds., *Marcel Duchamp: A Retrospective Exhibition* (Philadelphia: Philadelphia Museum of Art, 1973), 273.

Laurence Sterne, *The Life and Opinions of Tristram Shandy, Gentleman,* (London: R. and J. Dodsley, 1760 [2nd edit.]).

betwixt them than a proposition,—a reply,—and a rejoinder; at the end of which, it generally took breath for a few minutes (as in the affair of the breeches) and then went on again.

If he marries, 'twill be the worse for us, quoth my mother.

......Not a cherry-stone, said my father;—he may as well batter away his means upon that as any thing else.

......To be sure, said my mother. So here ended the pro-position,—the reply,—and the rejoinder, I told you of.

......It will be some amusement to him, too, said my father.

......A very great one, answered my mother, if he should have children.

......Lord have mercy upon me! said my father to himself.

⸱　⸱　⸱　⸱　⸱　⸱　⸱
⸱　⸱　⸱　⸱　⸱　⸱　⸱

———

CHAPTER XL.

I AM now beginning to get fairly into my work; and by the help of a vegetable diet, with a few of the cold seeds, I make no doubt but I shall be able to go on with my uncle Toby's story, and my own, in a tolerably straight line. Now,

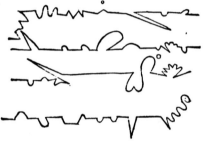

These were the four lines I moved in through my first, second, third, and fourth volumes.*—In the fifth volume I have been very good,—the precise line I have described in it being this :—

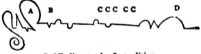

* Alluding to the first edition.

Sterne's woefully wayward narrator Tristram is forced to confront the practical effect if not the meaning of the "unforeseen stoppages, which I own I had no conception of when I first set out;—but which, I am convinced now, will rather increase than diminish as I advance."[64] They everywhere beset his way as a researcher into the story of his own life. He is ever sorrowfully-gratefully cognizant of how he loses his way—his straight away:

> Could a historiographer drive on his history, as a muleteer drives on his mule, — straight forward; — for instance, from Rome all the way to Loretto, without ever once turning his head aside either to the right hand or to the left, — he- might venture to foretel you to an hour when he shall get to his journey's end; —but the thing is, morally speaking, impossible: For, if he is a man of the least spirit, he will have fifty deviations from a straight line to make with this or that party as he goes along, which he can no ways avoid.[65]

In the "confessional" Preface to the Vincennial [i.e. 1985] Edition of his thrice-published book of 1965 (*On the Shoulders of Giants* would be published again in 1993 with a new Postface), Merton came clean about the ancestry of his "prodigal brainchild," which was then approaching adulthood. Thus he provided the reader with a graphic image of his book's conception. It was born of dependency. Merton confessed to being a "lifelong addict" to *Tristram Shandy,* and like its narrator he gave in to the temptation of straying from the straight and true. *Felix culpa!* Looking back over the book's plot "inexorably brought to mind the graphic depiction, in Book VI, Chapter XL, of the eccentric trajectories followed by the first four of its pathmaking volumes along these exact lines."[66] For Merton, these exact lines lead him back, but by no means directly, to Newton's most famous utterance: "If I have seen farther, it is by standing on the shoulders of giants."

An epistolary book, *On the Shoulder of Giants* begins in earnest with a not-quite-facsimile reprint of a letter dated November 8 [1959], replete with Shandean ellipses, from Bud (Harvard Historian Bernard Bailyn) thanking Bob (Robert K. Merton) for sending him a copy of his presidential address. Delivered at the 1957 annual meeting of the American Sociological Society, the address was published as the above-referenced "Priorities in

64 Laurence Sterne, *The Life and Opinions of Tristram Shandy, Gentleman* (London: R. and J. Dodsley, 1760 [2nd edit.]), I, 81.
65 Ibid., 79.

66 Merton, *OTSOG,* xix.
67 Merton, "Priorities in Scientific Discovery," 646.
68 Ibid.

69 Merton, *OTSOG,* 292.

70 Alexandre Koyré, "An Unpublished Letter of Robert Hooke to Isaac Newton," *Isis* 43 (1952): 315, n. 20 [312–337].
71 Peter Gay, *Enlightenment: The Science of Freedom* (New York: W. W. Norton, 1969), 612.

Scientific Discovery: A Chapter in the Sociology of Science." Bailyn was keen to know
more about footnote 34, which refers to Alexandre Koyré, "An Unpublished Letter
of Robert Hooke to Isaac Newton," Isis 43 (1952): 312–337, at p. 315. To put this in
context, the footnote appears within Merton's discussion of the "Institutional Norm
of Humility," in which he explained how the disproportionately great value placed on
originality stands in relation to a complex set of values comprising the normative ethos
of science: disinterestedness, universalism, organized skepticism, and communism of
intellectual property.[67] In particular, the "socially enforced value of humility" moderates
the competitive urges produced by the unchecked valorization of priority. One form of its
expression is the acknowledgment of the scientist's heavy indebtedness to the "legacy of
knowledge bequeathed by predecessors." This legacy is the essence and stuff of tradition,
which derives its value from being transmitted. For Merton this sentiment was expressed
most resoundingly in "the epigram Newton made his own: 'If I have seen farther, it is by
standing on the shoulders of giants' (this, incidentally, in a letter to Hooke who was then
challenging Newton's priority in the theory of colors)."[68]

The incidental and indeed parenthetical character of the reference is what required further
clarification from Bailyn. In the Afterword to the Post-Italianate Edition, the literary critic
and scholar Denis Donoghue drew attention to Merton's precise phrasing, "the epigram
Newton makes his own," which he considered to be a "vigilant phrase disavowing any
suggestion that Newton had invented the elegant thing."[69] The price of freedom, at least
from errors of attribution—which footnotes presumably stand guard against—is eternal
vigilance. But to draw too hasty a conclusion from Donoghue's observation would be to
overlook the non-straightforward project of Merton's book, which was to find Newton's
source(s), whether they were known to him or not. And in spite of, or perhaps because
of its Shandean inspiration, the attempt was to do so in a thorough, exhaustive, and
exhilarating scholarly fashion.

Let us return, for a moment, to Merton's footnote, and the problems lurking within,
which is to say within Koyré's footnotes. In his article, Koyré reproduced Newton's
unpublished reply to Hooke (February 5 1675/6), and in footnote 20 wrote: "As pointed
out by L[ouis] T[renchard] More, this celebrated saying, which is usually quoted as being
original with Newton and as expressing his magnanimous modesty is, as a matter of
fact, a commonplace. It is used by Burton in his *Anatomy of Melancholy* as a quotation
from Didacus Stella, *In Luc. 10 tom. 2: Pigmaei Gigantum humeris impositi plusquam ipsi
gigantes vidents.*"[70] Is this indeed a matter of fact? Peter Gay wrote that More's *Isaac
Newton, A Biography* (1934) has great merit, has been highly praised, exploiting as it does
much unpublished material, but that it is sometimes grossly inaccurate in its historical detail,
"and must therefore be used with caution."[71] *Caveat lector.*

In his letter Bailyn wrote that he was not familiar with Koyré's article, speculating that maybe it went over the history of the epigram you mention "re Newton." Bailyn's "re Newton" implies even less about its (original) ownership than does Merton's "Newton makes his own," the latter of which at least acknowledges the stakes of possession. For his part, Bailyn suggested that the saying has a "rather impressive antiquity. I came on it twice, in Gilson and in Lavisse as a remark of Bernard of Chartres in the early 12th century." The noncommittal "came on it," like Christison's accidental interest in the Fortingall yew, might register as an example of *serendipity*. The word names the unasked-for gift of "accidental sagacity" that Merton and his collaborator Elinor Barber, in the 1950s, when its meaning still remained esoteric and mysterious, traced from its coinage in 1754 by Horace Walpole. Eventually published as *The Travels and Adventures of Serendipity: A Study in Sociological Semantics and the Sociology of Science* (2003), their findings appeared proleptically under the guise of a "carefully unpublished manuscript" in a footnote to paragraph 47 of *On the Shoulders of Giants*. Bailyn, in this rare instance, was perhaps not so careful. Beyond what he came on in print, Bailyn ventured that "Thales probably said the same thing, only vaguely remembering where he had got it from." With this lapse of memory—it is not entirely clear to this reader if it belongs to Bailyn or to Thales—the letter trails off with another ellipsis, its appearance in print perhaps another of Merton's Shandean intimations.

Intent as we are on pursuing what has been said about Newton, and for the moment on Merton's search for the source of what was famously said by Newton, let us pause to consider an important feature of *Tristram Shandy*, which is its compulsive interest in what is not said. In his Uncle Toby's explanation of why his sister, Tristram's mother, "does not care to let a man come so near her * * * *," Tristram sees "one of the neatest examples of that ornamental figure in oratory, which Rhetoricians style the *Aposiopesis*." Even or especially when words were left out, nothing was to be taken for granted. Tristram reminds his beleaguered reader, "O! never let it be forgotten upon what small particles your eloquence and your fame depend." The asterisks and dashes, ubiquitous ornamental and syntactic features of Sterne's riotous text, are precise in their (lack of) meaning. To review: "'My sister, mayhap,' quoth my uncle Toby, 'does not chuse to let a man come so near her * * * *.' Make this dash,— 'tis an Aposiopesis.—Take the dash away, and write Backside,—'tis Bawdy."[72]

To continue, Merton's response to Bailyn comprises the book-length letter, dated December 30, that is *On the Shoulder of Giants*. Begun while working on a series of lectures he was "doomed to give next spring," in which he planned on extending the observations made in his paper on priorities, Merton was contemplating what to do with the dwarf-on-the-shoulders-of-giants aphorism. Throughout the book, it is variously referred to as an epigram, aphorism, remark, without any apparent distinction in usage. Yet it can also simply be read as a sentence, in the double sense implied by the term, which speaks of a thing and an act. A sentence is both a semantic unit and the rendering of a judgment. If Merton's Shandean way of arriving at this sentence has a peculiar narrative structure, it must be remembered that the word "narrative" has its root in the Latin "*gnarus*," or knowing, and to judgment; to narrate is to recite the verdict of a judge, most likely based on long-winded testimony of several and conflicting witnesses, each with a narrative to tell.[73]

Thus before he entered into the genealogy of the aphorism, or as his first step in doing so in the "non-linear, advancing-by-doubling back Shandean Method"—Merton cited his own 1942 paper entitled "A Note on Science and Democracy."[74] A founding document of the sociology of science, the paper was written for Georges Gurvitch, the Russian-born Jewish refugee from Nazi-occupied France, for the inaugural issue of Gurvitch's ill-fated *Journal of Legal and Political Sociology*. There Merton articulated four "norms" of the scientific ethos, a normative structure of science that would come to shape his abiding concern for priority: universalism, disinterdness, communism, and organized skepticism. Writing to Bailyn, Merton forgave himself his own prolixity, seeing as the preliminary "Note" ran to eleven "labyrinthine" pages. Unraveling his Ariadne's thread—which of course provides another compelling model of (linear) narrative structure—Merton found his way back to the "inevitable footnote" in which he observed that, while frequently attributed to him, Newton's aphorism was in fact a "standardized phrase which had found repeated expression from at least the twelfth century."[75]

Short of turning all the way back to Thales, with Merton's initial recognition of the long posterity of Newton's aphorism, and with it the recognition that it was not Newton's own, which is to say it did not originate with him but became his in the after ages of its usage, the notion of standardization already appears. "To support this claim," Merton wrote of the 1942 "Notes," again in a confessional strain, "I cite rather cryptically '*Isis,* 1935, 24, 107–9; 1938, 25, 451–2.'" It is not much to go on, but the bare-bones title-year-volume-page-number-citation style will get the resourceful reader to the source. If the footnote was "inevitable," however, why did Merton fail to respect the standards of its use? Does the cryptic gesture serve as tacit recognition that some things best remain buried (in the

---

72 Sterne, *The Life and Opinions of Tristram Shandy, Gentleman*. I, 49.

73 On this telling family of words see J. Hillis Miller, *Reading Narrative* (Norman: University of Oklahoma Press, 1998), 47.

74 "A Note on Science and Democracy," *Journal of Legal and Political Sociology* 1 (1942): 115–126.

75 Merton, *OTSOG*, 1.

footnotes)—like Bolyai's anomalous monument without the sort of inscription that, in "the typical order of things," indicates what lies within? Is it also possibly the case that some things, and stories, will not remained buried.

To cite but one notable example: in a fitting if not deserved coda to Sterne's life, the following editorial note appeared in the third edition, "with large additions and corrections," of *Yorick's Sentimental Journey Continued* (1774), attributed to Yorick's [Sterne's] literary continuator Eugenius (long and falsely thought to be John Hall-Stevenson): "It is with great pleasure that the Editor of this work informs his Readers, that the report, which he mentioned in his last Edition, of Mr. Sterne's body being take up after its interment, and carried to Oxford as a subject for the Lectures of the Anatomical Professor in that University, is totally void of foundation." It seems a student present at one of the dissections of Dr. Parsons thought it would be a "*good joke* to propagate a report that the Professor of Anatomy was reading Lectures upon Tristram Shandy."[76] Enough ink has been spilled elsewhere about Sterne's and his character's morbid preoccupations, the stuff of the blackest of comedy. "Alas, poor Yorick!" Let us move on.

The question remains, what is the relevant standard for revealing one's sources? Anthony Grafton's deceptively easy-going *The Footnote: A Curious History* (1997) combats the notion that footnotes are the quintessence of "academic foolishness and misdirected effort."[77] Grafton's is a patient study of evolving standards of scholarly practice. Emphasis where emphasis is due is placed on those moments when "normal methods underwent a transformation," in the words of Fustel de Coulanges who is quoted to great effect in a footnote.[78] Wherever the reader is led by the footnotes, and as long as he does not become lost in the footnotes, norms and standards of one sort of another apply. They regulate discourse and hold authors to account. In revealing one's sources of authority, they are the stepping stones of the critical enterprise. But sometimes norms and standards fail to apply. The footnote might become party to an act, witting or not, of misdirection. With some further legwork, or perhaps spadework is better, it appears that "cryptic" might indeed be the unintentionally apt word for what is found in Merton's allusive (or is it elusive) footnote.

```
S A T O R
A R E P O
T E N E T
O P E R A
R O T A S
```

Laurence Sterne, *The Life and Opinions of Tristram Shandy, Gentleman,* (London: R. and J. Dodsley, 1760 [2nd edit.]).

On page 107 of *Isis* 24 (1935) appears "Query no. 52.—The Sator arepo formula." Since the publication of Ernst Darmstaedter's article "Die Sator-Arepo Formel und ihre Erklärung" (Isis 18, 322–29, 1932), wrote George Sarton, the Query's author, two subsequent notes (Isis 20, 578; 22, 229) had suggested that the "diffusion of that magical formula was considerably greater than was first realized. As the reinvention of such a complicated formula was hardly conceivable, it is a very good means of testing cultural diffusions."[79] The rigid inflexibility of the cryptic square—its precision truly worthy of OuLiPo—made it like a meter standard bar, an *étalon*. A lexical artifact of unforgivingly precise manufacture, its very appearance in writing served an evidence that the formula had been successfully and integrally transmitted—across time and over space. The second of the subsequent notes, in effect a postscript written by Sarton himself, suggests that the "famous mediaeval formula" also occurs in Ethiopic. The Abyssinians obtained it from the Coptic into which language it was rendered from a Greek transcriptions of the Latin. "This is a good example of the extraordinary power of diffusion of magical and nonsensical words."[80] Despite Darmstaedter's surmises, however, the origin (Mithraic, Orphic, Jewish, Christian?) and interpretation of the magic square was far from settled. To solve the riddle, Sarton, founding editor of Isis and Merton's mentor, asked readers to communicate other examples of its occurrence, "whether in texts or monuments, especially in out-of-the way and unexpected places." Here was an invitation to serendipity. For the purpose of recognition, Sarton reproduced in the text the square palindrome which "can be read forward or backward, downward or upward"—thus in a way like but entirely unlike Shandean logic.[81]

76 Eugenius, *Yorick's Sentimental Journey, continued. To which is prefixed, some account of the life and writings of Mr. Sterne,* vol. 3 (London: J. Bew, 1774 [3rd edit.]), xxii–xxiii.

77 Anthony Grafton, *The Footnote: A Curious History* (Cambridge: Harvard University Press, 1997), 25..

78 Grafton, *The Footnote,* 70–71, n. 18.

79 George Sarton, "Notes and Correspondence: Query no. 52.—The Sator arepo formula," *Isis* 24 (1935): 107.

80 Sarton, "The Sator-Arepo Formula," 229.

81 Ibid., 107. Charlesworth writes that the key to the cryptic square "is provided by discerning that *arepo* denotes "to crawl toward." And this insight brings forward serpent imagery and symbolism; and that—in the historical context—suggests Asclepius.

He is the god who comes to those need heaving in the form of a serpent." James H. Charlesworth, *The Good and Evil Serpent: How a Universal Symbol Became Christianized* (New Haven: Yale University Press, 2009), 481.

Merton's cryptic footnote evidently refers to the following in the Notes and Correspondence section of *Isis*, "Query, no. 53.— Standing on the shoulders of giants," also written by Sarton. While repeating that the saying is often quoted, and generally ascribed to Newton, Sarton drew attention to L. T. More's abovementioned remark that the saying seems to antedate Newton. Following More's lead, Sarton traced it to Burton's *Anatomy of melancholy*, where we read: "Though there were many gyants of old in physick and philosophy, yet I say with DIDACUS STELLA, *A dwarf standing on the shoulders of a gyant, may see farther than a gyant himself;* I may likely add, alter, and see farther than my predecessour . . . " In the retrospective light of Merton's programmatic norms, Sarton took exception to More's notion that though the pygmy is elevated higher, it will still nonetheless interpret what it sees with the "mind of a pygmy." Sarton prefers to read the saying, like his student Merton after him, as a salutary gesture of humility—we are, all of us, pygmies. But it is with the question of attribution that the problems begin, or so it would soon appear. Didacus Stella was the Spanish exegete Diego Estella, Sarton noted, and "Burton's reference is probably to Diego's *In sacrosanctum Evangelium Lucae enarratio* (Alcala de Henares, 1578, often reprinted). Burton obtained that maxim from Diego de Estella, and Newton probably obtained it from Burton, whose Anatomy was already appearing in its eighth edition in the year, 1676, of Newton's letter to Hooke."[82] Sarton began his own *enarratio,* a form of translation centrally involving the interpretation and adaptation of literary heritage.[83] He established the saying's chain of possession through a concatenation of sources with an exegete, Didacus, as its central connecting linkage. But all hinges on Sarton's "probably."

The identity of the work cited by Didacus becomes a central concern in paragraph lxx of *OTSOG*, as Merton was fond of abbreviating the title of his masterwork. To illustrate the problem, Merton turned to the 13th, indeed, the Centenary edition of Bartlett's *Familiar Quotations* (1955), published two years prior to the presidential address in which his footnote to Koyré's article appeared. For just as soon as Merton "first came upon" the aphorism in Burton, More, Koyré, etc., he was confused by the truncated reference to "Luc." It was John Bartlett himself, and not his posthumous co-editors, who first quoted Burton's quotation in the 9th 1891 edition of *Familiar Quotations*. (Apparently it remained unfamiliar whilst the first eight editions were in print.) In the 9th as in subsequent editions Burton's own reference appears: *Didacus Stella in Lucan 10, tom. ii;* that is, except for the 11th edition, where the "possibly obscure" tom. ii is unassumingly converted into the bibliographically more likely *Tom. II.* "By directing us to Lucan," Merton writes, the reader is released from the "chore of probing the identity of the cryptic Luc."[84] This scholarly doubting of Thomas's own cryptic citation practices came back to haunt him from beyond the footnotes. Any lingering mystery as to the truncated reference was dispelled by the Centenary edition which provides "full circumstantial detail." There *Didacus Stella in Lucan 10, tom. ii* was decisively enlarged and expanded to read: Didacus Stella in Lucan [A.D. 39–65]: *De Bello Civili, 10, II.*

Having decrypted "Luc.," Bartlett had created a "ghostly source through a ghastly error."[85] Or rather, his posthumous coeditors had innocently and with the best of intentions entered the ranks of talented forgers who fabricate their sources. Merton's probing of the matter consisted simply of visiting the Columbia University libraries. *OTSOG*'s own scholarly narrative is punctuated by such "forays into the Columbia library," the hope being to end each "quest in unexpected triumph."[86] For Eco the joy of Merton's travels in serendipity was that "while seeking one thing (without anyone's asking you to) you find another (which, unknowing, everyone was awaiting), or while seeking something everyone wanted, you discover that the true object of collective desire lay, hidden, elsewhere."[87] But Merton could find no trace of the Aphorism in Lucan's *De Bello Civili*. He had been led down a dead end. What he did find in the library was that Didacus Stella never wrote a line about Lucan. In fact, Luc. does not refer to the Roman poet Lucan but to his Christian near-contemporary Luke. "The sad truth," Merton concluded, as if he were composing an entry on Scholarship for *the Anatomy of Melancholy*, is that Burton's citation to Didacus Stella *in Luc. 10, tom. ii* refers to the tenth chapter of the second volume of Didacus Stella's *In sacrosanctum Jesu Christi Domini nostri Evangelium secundùm Lucam Enarrationum*.

Merton would have been spared unnecessary effort if he had read Sarton's paper sooner than he did, or if he had remembered that he had read it, evidence of which is provided by the footnotes to "A Note on Science and Democracy." In making his initial guess that Newton found his saying in Burton, Merton found himself "walking in Sarton's spacious footsteps."[88] This uncomfortable realization he confided to a footnote. But the true source of embarrassment was that Merton had seen farther than his mentor; he came to see Sarton's guess and "secondarily and temporarily, [his own], as questionable at best and thoroughly mistaken at worst."[89] Not so gently encouraging his reader to return to the "text of his letter"—that is to say, to exit the footnote and return to *OTSOG*—Merton promised to explain why. The footnote was evidently not spacious enough either to confront or part ways with his cherished teacher. Where was Sarton at fault? For one thing, he had provided an ambiguously truncated title of Didacus's work. Having gone to the library and "searched, researched, and re-researched the evidence," Merton was certain that the title should read, and he repeats it in the interest of total scholarship, *In sacrosanctum Jesu Christi Domini*

82 George Sarton, "Notes and Correspondence: Query no. 53.—'Standing on the shoulders of giants,'" *Isis* 24 (1935): 107 [107–109].

83 Peter Damian-Grint, "Translation as Enarratio and Hermeneutic Theory in Twelfth-Century Vernacular Learned Literature," *Neophilologus* 83 (1999): 358 [349–367].

84 Merton, *OTSOG*, 249.
85 Ibid., 251.
86 Ibid., 250.
87 Umberto Eco, "Preface," *OTSOG*, xi.

88 Merton, *OTSOG*, 73.
89 Ibid..
90 Ibid., 253.
91 Ibid., 254.

nostri Evangelium secundùm Lucam Enarrationum.[90] The attentive reader of footnotes will note that Merton first crossed paths with Sarton on page 73 of *OTSOG,* while his confident conclusion is arrived at on page 253. His is a work of productive backtracking, repetition, and resistance to truncation of any sort.

Rather than assigning blame, Merton recognized the unmistakable force of Sarton's "probably" as a reliable sign of his "characteristically full integrity" as a scholar.[91] For in truth, he asked, who had actually followed that "scholarly injunction" to follow the aphorism to its source? Thoroughgoing scholar that he was, Sarton let on that he had not tracked down the reference for himself; nor, for that matter, had More, Koyré, or Bartlett. "But I have," Merton said. Doing his best to model the rhetorical ethos of humility—he was the author, after all, of the sociological concept of the "role model," a sort of emulatable "reference individual"[92]—Merton could not help but marvel at the magnitude of his own discovery. Prowling rare book rooms, he came upon the treasure he had been looking for: a 1622 edition, published in Antwerp, of Didacus' work. He looked into Capvt X of the book in search of the aphorism and "made a spectacular find." (The drama of the reveal is quite intentional, and is come by honestly. Born Meyer R. Schkolnick, like Koyré of Russian Jewish ancestry, Merton's own early role model was the escape artist Harry Houdini, or Erich Weiss, the son of a Budapest rabbi). "The fact is—how shall I tell it to you without seeming to be that most obnoxious of scholars: a sensation monger?—the newly uncovered fact is that in ascribing the Aphorism to Didacus Stella, Robert Burton quoted out of context and, in the most literal sense, actually misquoted Didacus' version of the Aphorism."[93]

At this point, to pursue the matter of Newton's aphorism any further would be, in Merton's words, "mere pedantry," or perhaps even a variant of Euclid's "method of exhaustion." If any wish to continue along this path, it is easy enough to return to the place where we part ways with Merton. So that the reader might retrace his steps, or so he will know that he has found what he is looking for—like Sarton with the Sator arepo formula—Merton provided a copy of the book's title page on page 254 of OTSOG. But to put this matter to rest, skip forward to pages 268–269 where Merton made a list of all (then known) usages of the aphorism, beginning with Bernard of Chartres (c. 1128), John of Salisbury (12th century)...

92 Robert K. Merton, "Continuities in the Theory of Reference Groups and Social Structure," in *Social Theory and Social Structure* (1968), 335-440.

93 Merton, *OTSOG,* 254.

94 Joseph Bédier, Paul Hazard, *Histoire de la littérature française,* vol. 1 (Paris: 1923–1924), 15. The quote from Pierre de Blois is as follows: Nous sommes des nains hissés sur les épaules de ces géants, et si nous voyons plus loin qu'eux, c'est grâce à eux, lorsque, appliqués à lire leurs ouvrages,

nous ressuscitons pour une vie nouvelle leurs pensées éminentes, que les siècles et la négligence des hommes avaient, pour ainsi dire, laissé choir dans la mort."

95 Merton, *OTSOG,* 228, n. *.

96 Peter Ackroyd, *Newton* (New York: Doubleday, 2006), 30.

97 Anthony P. French, "Never at Rest: A Biography of Isaac Newton. By Richard Westfall," *Journal of Interdisciplinary History* 13 (1982): 125 [125–127].

98 Richard S. Westfall, *Never At Rest: A Biography of Isaac Newton* (Cambridge: Cambridge University Press, 1983), 154, n. 43.

Didacus (1578)...Burton (1624)...Newton (1676)...Merton (1942), etc. For more on Bernard of Chartres, see the second item from *Isis* referred to in Merton's cryptic footnote: R[alph] E[rnest] Ockenden, "Answer to Query no. 53.—'Standing on the shoulders of Giants' (*Isis* 24, 107–09)," *Isis* 25 (1936): 449–460. Ockenden observed that a similar expression "is said to have been made" by Peter of Blois, c. 1180, or at least that is what it is said to have been said in Joseph Bédier and Paul Hazard, *Histoire de la littérature française,* vol. 1 (Paris: 1923–1924), 15. Ockenden, however, was not "able to verify the statement."[94]

Let us forgive Ockenden his forgivable lapse. To do so is more than Merton himself would allow. He expressed gratitude to Ockenden for having identified an "elegant variation" of the aphorism in *La grande chirurgie de Guy de Chauliac,* while at the same time asking why Sarton had taken no notice of it. Ever eager to guide his reader to his sources, Merton wrote, "I am assured by R. E. Ockenden" that it is to be found on page 4 in the prologue of Edouard Niçaise's 1890 edition of Guy's work. Though Merton himself does not rest assured; certainty in these matters (self-) assurance is most always misplaced. In a parenthetical assertion, though it is unclear why this particular emendation should be set apart from all the rest, Merton indicated, "it is just as Ockenden says; although it appears in what I, and Guy himself, would prefer to describe as the Dedication, rather than the prologue."[95] The past as prologue?

Let us now return to our pretext, the inscription on the plaque at the foot, indeed near the roots, of MIT's Newton apple tree: *a direct descendant of the tree under which Sir Isaac Newton is said to have conceived the theory of gravity.* How do things come down to us? In a straight line? Perpendicularly? Where parallel lines meet? Or according to some Shandean "non-linear" line? To interpret the plaque is to straighten out the versions and variations, elegant and otherwise, that have grown up around and from the very pith of Newton's tree.

"There are four separate versions of the apple falling from the tree," wrote Peter Ackroyd, "for the simple reason that Newton recounted different versions to four separate people."[96] If it were only that straightforward. Ackroyd's *Newton,* one in the series Ackroyd's *Brief Lives,* is by no means the definitive word. The sterling standard of Newton biographies, the "fruit of twenty years of study and labor,"[97] is Richard S. Westfall's *Never at Rest* (1980). Westfall began setting the record straight with his 1965 reprint of Sir David Brewster's *Memoirs of Sir Isaac Newton,* the very considerable merits of which he extolled in his critical introduction, in which he also seriously undermines L. T. More's credibility. The versions are very succinctly compared though by no means reconciled in a long footnote within Westfall's discussion of the "myth of the *annus mirabilis,*" what was for Newton a period of unbridled discovery associated with the plague years of 1665–1666 and his prolonged stay at Woolsthorpe.[98] A leading practitioner of historiographic metafiction in novels such as *Hawksmoor* (1985) and *Chatterton* (1987), Ackroyd has shown himself more than willing to depart from the stated record. Some comments Ackroyd made in a lecture of 1993, entitled "The Englishness of English Literature," might in fact help orient the remaining discussion of Newton's apple falling from the tree, or rather how far from the tree apples tend to fall, and whether they always or ever fall in a straight line.

Delivered at Cambridge University as the Leslie Stephen Lecture for 1993, Ackroyd's title is modeled on the German-Jewish émigré Sir Nikolaus Pevsner's BBC radio Reith Lectures of 1955, an expanded and annotated version of which was published the following year as *The Englishness of English Art*. Pevsner attempted to detect what is "constant in the English character," finding telling hints in the use of language, including a decided preference for monosyllables which he referred to an "aversion against fuss, the distrust of rhetoric." The *locus classicus* of this aspect of Englishness is found in the singular line: "Dr. Livingstone, I presume."[99] In a 1983 essay also entitled "The Englishness of English Literature," the literary historian Peter Conrad explained that Pevsner's talk initially found scant favor because the English have a "blunt-minded hostility to the generalizing temper, especially when it presumes to generalize about *them*."[100] It is not constancy or a serviceable generalization that Ackroyd was after, but rather the particular shape of variety. His ambition was to see if he could find "Hogarth's line of beauty, that long gentle double curve which Pevsner saw as characteristic of English art, in English literature."[101] The line of beauty is the Shandean line at one remove, or rather the Shandean line, "Inv. T.S/. Scul.T.S.," is the unruly stepchild of Hogarth's line of beauty. In his study of narrative "picturable as a graph or a plot," J. Hillis Miller explained that Sterne made Hogarth's sensual and sinuous line into a subversive "image for spinning out a story, narrative line, or life line."[102] The comedic joy of *Tristram Shandy* is as much to be found in its narrator's failure to proceed in a "tolerable straight line" as in his recognition of the deadening effect that success in that rote task would have. Tristram's regretful report on his narrative progress takes the shape of the "exact lines" that are graphically reproduced at the start of *OTSOG*.

Now it is our turn, without Merton's guidance, but perhaps like pygmies on the shoulders of giants, to put the apple tree story through its paces. We begin with the version found in William Stukeley's *Memoirs of Sir Isaac Newton's Life* (1752), now available on "Turning the Pages," the online gallery of high quality scans of important books and manuscripts

99 Nikolaus Pevsner, *The Englishness of English Art* (London: Architectural Press, 1956), 59.

100 Peter Conrad, "The Englishness of English Literature," *Daedalus* 112 (1983): 157 [157–173].

101 Peter Ackroyd, "The Englishness of English Literature," *Proceedings* of the XIXth International Conference of AEDEAN (Vigo: Departamento de Filoloxía Inglesa e Alemana, Universidade de Vigo, 1996), 11 [11-19].

102 J. Hillis Miller, *Reading Narrative* (Norman: University of Oklahoma Press, 1998), 66.

103 Jean-Baptiste Biot, "The Life of sir Isaac Newton; Vie de Sir Isaac Newton, par David Brewster," *Journal des Savants* (May 1832): 265, n. 1 [263–274].

104 For a discussion of how Newton, or the image of Newton constructed by his biographers, was put to use by his biographers, see Rebekah Higgitt, *Recreating Newton: Newtonian Biography and the Making of Nineteenth-Century History of Science* (London: Pickering and Chatto, 2007).

105 David Brewster, *The Life of Sir Isaac Newton* (London: John Murray, 1831), 344.

106 McKie and De Beer, "Newton's Apple," 47, n. 4.

107 Brewster, *The Life of Sir Isaac Newton*, 344,

in the collections of The Royal Society. Stukeley recalls visiting Newton at his lodgings in Kensington, April 15, 1726,

> after dinner, the weather being warm, we went into the garden, & drank thea under the shade of some appletrees; only he, & my self. amidst other discourse, he told me, he was just in the same situation, as when formerly, the notion of gravitation came into his mind. "why should that apple always descend perpendicularly to the ground," thought he to him self: occasion'd by the fall of an apple, as he sat in a contemplative mood: "why should it not go sideways, or upwards? but constantly to the earths centre? assuredly, the reason is, that the earth draws it. there must be a drawing power in matter. & the sum of the drawing power in the matter of the earth must be in the earths center, not in any side of the earth. therefore dos this apple fall perpendicularly, or toward the center. if matter thus draws matter; it must be in proportion of its quantity. therefore the apple draws the earth, as well as the earth draws the apple. [15r]

Why not indeed. Why should the apple not go sideways, or upwards, slantwise or perpendicular. That, at least, is how narratives work, unless bound by a straight rule.

The apple that presumably fell at Woolsthorpe was fated, as if by one of Newton's laws of motion, to displace Archimedes' "*Eureka, Eureka*" as the very image of serendipitous scientific discovery, the "happy accident"; as it happens, the principle of displacement was precisely what Archimedes discovered whilst in his bathtub. In his own amended version of equal and opposite, the French physicist Jean-Baptiste Biot insisted on the biographic relevance of this "little accident that led by chance to a great discovery."[103] Not incidentally the author of an extensive entry on Newton for the *Biographie Universelle* (1822), Biot was troubled that the anecdote had not merely been displaced but was altogether absent from Sir David Brewster's *The Life of Sir Isaac Newton,* Biot's extensive review of which appeared in the April, May, and June 1832 volumes of the *Journal des Savants*.[104] To quote the Brewster version directly, "the celebrated apple-tree, the fall of one of the apples of which is said to have turned the attention of Newton to the subject of gravity, was destroyed by wind about four years ago" (i.e 1827).[105] In this telling, the apple in its linear descent becomes a literal trope, turning Newton's attention to the question of gravitation, and presumably away from some less engaging object of contemplation. But it is the (by now) familiar turn of phrase, "said to have," referring to the fall of the apple, that stands in tense juxtaposition to the tree from which it is said to have fallen.

While no longer standing, the historical reality of the tree is not in doubt. McKie and de Beer point out that in subsequent editions Brewster gave widely varying accounts of when the tree perished and under what circumstances.[106] He even added the peculiar and homely detail that Mr. Turnor "preserved it in the form of a chair." Other bits of wood from the tree became the relic-like rules housed in the The Royal Society. Tension arises instead from the footnotes, where Brewster signaled his narrative reticence. "The anecdote of the falling apple is mentioned neither by Dr. Stukeley nor by Mr Conduit, and, as I have not been able to find any authority for it whatever, I do not feel myself at liberty to us it."[107] To do so would be to frame his life of Newton from the same crooked timbers of which common humanity is said to be built. Biot argued that if there were any doubt regarding the verity of the anecdote, they were easily overcome by the mere fact that the anecdote had been "transmitted by tradition." Biot stated his case for the "traditional anecdote"—with this paring what is transmitted and the means of its transmission become inseparable—by cross-examining Brewster's "scruple about recounting it."[108] Tradition preserves truths; tradition is what needs to be broken down to get at the truth. Biot regarded Brewster's forbearance, and not favorably, as "highly rigid biographical puritanism."[109]

Brewster would not allow himself the "probably" that appears in Sarton's writing, and which Merton read as a sign of scholarly probity. There are good scientific grounds for doing so. Central to the tradition of historical criticism was the process, meant here in the legal sense of the term, of determining the relative value of evidence and veracity of divergent testimony. Laplace, for one, in his *Philosophical Essay on Probabilities,* sought the means to calculate the "influence of time on the probability of facts transmitted by a traditional chain of witnesses." Probability diminishes as this chain grows longer; so too the passage of time continuously weakens it, "just as it alters the most durable monuments."[110] Not even a churchyard yew is perduring. When confronted with combined evidence, or missing bits of evidence, the best available solution is an "acceptable approximation."[111] Thus Biot contended that belief in the anecdote is not as unsupported as Brewster supposed it to be. The old apple tree was standing as recently as fifteen years ago, and Biot himself had visited Woolsthorpe where he collected some leaves "to be religiously brought back to his country." If ever there were a way an antithetical response to Brewster's puritanism, it was Biot's reliquary observance of the genius of place.[112]

For Biot the tree, whether standing, fallen, or wrecked, was propped up by "tradition, a constant tradition, which has considerable authority behind it." However, that authority is derived from the endurability of the tradition itself. If tradition did not suffice, then

n. *. "Neither Pemberton nor Whiston, who received from Newton himself the History of his first Ideas of Gravity, records the story of the falling apple. It was mentioned, however, to Voltaire by Catherine Barton, Newton's niece, and to Mr. Green by Martin Folkes, the President of the Royal Society.

We saw the apple tree in 1814, and brought away a portion of one of its roots. The tree was so much decayed that it was taken down in 1820, and the wood of it was carefully preserved by Mr. Turnor of Stoke Rocheford. See Voltaire's *Philosophie de Newton,* 3me part. Chap. III. Green's Philosophy of

Expansive and Contractive Forces, p. 972, and Rigaud's Hist[orical] Essay [on the First Publication of Newton's *Principia*], p. 2." Compare to David Brewster, *Memoirs of the Life, Writings, and Discoveries of Sir Isaac Newton* (Edinburgh: Thomas Constable, 1855), 1:27, n. 1. In vol. 2., p. 416, n. 2.

Says "I found, however, a reference to an apple in the following memorandum by Condit. 'In the same year (at his mother's in Lincolnshire,) when musing in a garden it came into his thoughts that the same power of gravity, which made an apple fall from the tree to the ground, was not limited to a certain

there was philosophy. Henry Pemberton "positively states" that it was in the garden at Woolsthorpe where Newton was led to his first thoughts on gravitation. The Advertisement for his then forthcoming translation of Newton's *Philosophiæ Naturalis Principia Mathematica* (Mathematical Principles of Natural Philosophy), speak to Pemberton's sense of his own proximity to his source. "I having had a very particular opportunity of being fully informed of his real Mind from his own Mouth, do intend to proceed in my Design with all Expedition."[113] Beyond the statement of positive facts, Biot was evidently impressed by the "noble and expressive terms" used by Pemberton to describe the "profound meditation into which Newton's mind was plunged."[114] This Pemberton did in the Preface to his *A View of Sir Isaac Newton's Philosophy* (1728), ranging from private recollection to sublime intimations. But he said nothing about a tree. With his long footnote on the apple tree evolving into a heated internal dialog, Biot ventriloquized for his reader the response of the "severe biographer," Biot. "But proof, where is the proof?"

"Very well," Biot responded, now speaking in his own voice, "I will cite authorities of my own." First there is the *Biographie Britannique*, page 3244, note FF, which mentions the apple. Then there is Voltaire, in his *Éléments de la Philosophie de Newton*, chapter III, who reports the anecdote, and says that it was told to him by Mme Conduitt. But perhaps Mme Conduitt is not a sufficient authority for Brewster. If not, then consider the testimony of John Conduit, who recounts the facts in the same manner, as you will see in Edmund Turnor's *Collections for the History of the Town and Soke of Grantham. Containing Authentic Memoirs of Sir Isaac Newton. Now First Published from the Original MSS. in the Possession of the Earl of Portsmouth* (1806). Turnor's book is no doubt consulted most often, except perhaps by local historians, of which in England there are legions, for what appears on page 160. "About this time he [Newton] began to have the first hints of his method of fluxions; and in the year 1665, when he retired to his own estate, on account of the plague, he first thought of his system of gravity, which he hit upon by observing an apple fall from a tree."[115] His source was the "Memoirs of Sir Isaac Newton sent by Mr. Conduitt to M. Fontenelle in 1727," to which Turnor had unique access, in the *Earl of Portsmouth* possession.[116] The manuscript was eventually consulted by Brewster while preparing his *Memoirs of the Life, Writings and Discoveries of Sir Isaac Newton*, 2 vols.

distance."

108 Biot, "The Life of sir Isaac Newton," 265, n. 1.

109 Ibid.

110 Le Comte [Pierre Simon] Laplace, *Essai philosophique sur les probabilités* (Paris: Ve Courcier, 1816 [3rd edit], 143–144.

111 On Silvestre-François Lacroix's notion of

"acceptable approximation" see, Lorraine Daston, *Classical Probability in the Enlightenment* (Princeton: Princeton University Press, 1988), 341.

112 In her study of Woolsthorpe Patricia Fara notes "this rather bizarre scholarship has turned Newton's apple into a

religions shrine. Fara, "Isaac Newton Lived Here," 408.

113 Cited in I. Bernard Cohen, "Pemberton's Translation of Newton's *Principia*, with Notes on Motte's Translation," *Isis* 54 (1963): 323 [319–351].

114 Biot, "The Life of sir Isaac Newton," 265, n. 1.

115 Edmund Turnor,

Collections for the History of the Town and Soke of Grantham. Containing authentic memoirs of Sir Isaac Newton, now first published from the original mss. in the possession of the Earl of Portsmouth (London: William Miller, 1806), 160.

116 Now to be found as, "Fair copy of John Conduitt's

(1855), in which he is still less inclined to accept the traditional anecdote. But it is the footnote to Turnor's version of the anecdote that attracted Biot's attention. "The apple tree is now remaining and is shewed to strangers."[117] His case was proved, and Biot was no less pleased with himself than Merton was with his spectacular find of Burton's misquotation of Didacus' "version" of the saying that Newton was to make his own. "Voilà," Biot exulted. "This time a triumphant authority. Dr. Dryasdust himself could not reasonably contest its authenticity."[118]

Biot was not alone in questioning Brewster's narrative self-restraint. Bolton Corney, literary critic, antiquary, and, as ensign in the 28th Regiment of Foot, recipient of a medal for marksmanship, urged less interpretive caution on the diligent and exacting scientist become biographer. "Sir David will permit me to remark that he did not prosecute his *optical researches* with his accustomed perseverance. He will permit me to remark that he might have introduced the anecdote of the *falling apple*, without becoming subject to the charge of viewing history through the *kaleidoscope* of fancy."[119] The kaleidoscope of fancy might well refer to Newton's optics. But when it came to the apple tree, Corney had an axe to grind: Isaac D'Israeli's singular version of the fall of Newton's apple. The contretemps between Corney and Isaac D'Israeli was excited by what the former believed to be inappropriate and plainly ill-informed comments about the Bayeux Tapestry made by the latter in his *Curiosities of Literature*. Corney was the author of an extended and recondite study bearing on received accounts of the tapestry's ancestry and antiquity, beginning with the first record of its existence in 1476.[120] In response to this and other grave affronts to scholarship and established authority, Corney assumed the title and form of D'Israeli's famous compendium of exhilaratingly wide if not always faultlessly careful learning to pursue his controversy. Corney's *Curiosities of Literature by Isaac D'Israeli Illustrated* saw two editions, the second "revised and acuminated."[121]

The relevant point of contention is Corney's "Art. XXI—The path of the *Woolsthorpe apple*—calculated on data not known to Sir Isaac Newton!" The article begins with a passage from D'Israeli's own *Curiosities of Literature* on "Poets, Philosophers, and Artists Made by Accident." It is the calculated path of the apple that makes for what the

Memoir of Newton," Keynes Ms. 129 (A), King's College Library, Cambridge, UK.

117 Turnor, *Collections for the History of the Town and Soke of Grantham*, 160. n. 2.

118 Biot, "The Life of sir Isaac Newton," 265, n. 1.

119 [Bolton Corney], *Curiosities of Literature, by I. D'Israeli, Esq....Illustrated*

by Bolton Corney, Esq. (Greenwich: Printed by Special Command [1837]), 155.

120 Bolton Corney, *Researches and Conjectures on the Bayeux Tapestry* (1838).

121 D'Israeli responded no less pointedly with *The Illustrator Illustrated* (1838).

122 [Augustus] De Morgan, "A Budget of Paradoxes," The

Assurance Magazine and Journal of the Institute of Actuaries 11 (1864): 194 [181–195].

123 D'Israeli as cited by Corney in *Curiosities of Literature, Illustrated by Bolton Corney* (Greenwich: Printed by Special Command [1837]), 105.

124 Isaac D'Israeli, *A Dissertation on Anecdotes* (London: Kearsley and Murray, 1793), 74.

125 [Corney], *Curiosities of Literature*, 105.

126 Ibid.

127 "Newton," *Biographia Britannica*, 5:3244, FF.

128 "Newton," *Biographia Britannica*, 5:3244, FF.

mathematician and logician Augustus De Morgan identified in his "A Budget of Paradoxes," as the "improvement on the story."[122] D'Israeli wrote, "As he [Newton] was reading under an apple-tree on of the fruit fell, and struck him a smart blow on the head. When he observed the smallness of the apple, he was surprised at the force of the stoke. This led him to consider the accelerating motion of falling bodies; from whence he deduced the principle of gravity, and laid the foundations of his philosophy."[123] What foundation was there for D'Israeli's version? For an answer to this question Corney referred to D'Israeli's *A Dissertation on Anecdotes* (1793), in which he declared that anecdotes are "susceptible of a thousand *novel turns*," which his own writing perfectly exemplified.[124] "Now according to my home-spun notions," Corney retorted, "according to my non-imaginative apprehension— an anecdote admits of no novel turns—but should be recited with a strict *adherence to truth*."[125] Rules and norms must apply. Where D'Israeli's uninhibited scholarship exemplified the welcome possibility of twists and turns, Corney illustrated his corrective measures through "an examination of the sources of the above mentioned anecdote."[126]

The most attractive source is the entry on Newton in the *Biographia Britannica*, to be more specific footnote FF on page 3244, the same one that propped up Biot's claims in support of the incident beneath the apple tree. The footnote refers to Newton's "Dissertation upon the Sacred Cubit of the Jews," a work on ancient metrology central to his concurrent exegetical ambition to establish the numerical proportions of the Temple. "He [Newton] has shewn that this cubit was certainly between the limits of 26 and 27 Roman unciæ, and thinks it probably consisted of 26 ½ of those unciæ."[127] In light of available resources, a thorny thicket of sacred and profane texts and the measurements of the Egyptian pyramids published by the astronomer Robert Greaves, Newton concluded his study of divinely-given units of standard measure with a probable sum, an acceptable approximation. The footnote does, however, make a positive statement about Newton's tree. It emerges from an appreciative estimation of a particular aspect of Newton's genius, "a talent of drawing the most hidden and unobserved truths from the most common and vulgar observations." So, for example, "his System of the World took it's [sic] beginning from seeing some apples fall from a tree in an orchard."[128] Having sorted through the sources, and finding D'Israeli to have departed from established facts in all particulars, there is yet one matter that exercises Corney's indignity. While all other accounts "speak vaguely of the *falling apple*: D'Israeli calculates its exact path."[129] That prerogative belonged to Newton. D'Israeli was to be allowed no room to turn.

One final version needs to be considered, leading as it does, and ever so improbably, to the root cause for the applications of strict rules. Mention of it is found in a note entitled "Newton and the Apple" submitted to *Notes and Queries* by W[illiam] T[hynne] Lynn, a calculator at the Royal Observatory and editor of the revised 1875 edition of Brewster's *Life of Sir Isaac Newton*. In the November, 13 1886 issue Lynn writes: "S.R. quotes a passage from Sterne's *Koran* in which the well-known story of the fall of an apple is transmogrified into that of a piece of stone in a quarry, and asks whether any other or earlier versions give it in that shape."[130] It is not the path of the apple but rather versions of the story that now take on distinct shapes, perhaps beginning to resemble Tristram's exact narrative lines. *The Koran: Or, Essays, Sentiments, Characters, and Callimachies of Tria Juncta In Uno, M. N. A. or Master of No Arts* relates the following:

> Sir Isaac Newton standing by the side of a quarry, saw a stone fall from the top of it to the ground—"Why should this stone, when loosened from its bed, rather descend, then rise, or fly across? Either of these directions must have been equally indifferent to the stone itself. Such was his soliloquy; and this the first philosophic reflection he had ever made. This led him first into considering the nature of gravity, &c.—So that to a mere accident we owe all those deep researches, and useful discoveries, with which he has since enriched the sciences.[131]

In response to S.R., Lynn offered that he knows of no other version in this shape, and, indeed, "from the place in which the celebrated fall is said to have taken place, it is much more likely to have been an apple than a stone."[132] In what was by then a time-honored critical tradition of Newton studies, Lynn revisited the "authority for the anecdote," be it as told to Voltaire by Mrs. Conduitt or to Robert Green by Martin Folkes, President of the Royal Society. From what unauthorized source, then, does this version derive, or is it to be discounted as merely derivative or perhaps misleading?

There had already been a number of exchanges in *Notes and Queries* regarding the origin of *The Koran*. Under the heading "Sterneana," W. Roberts reports having come across *The Koran* at the Penzance Public Library in a rare 1783 edition of Sterne's writings. Roberts notes that while the sixth and final volume, containing The Posthumous Works of Laurence Sterne, is full of "sundry digressions" and "Sterne's extravagant fooleries," it lacks his "inimitable wit and pathos."[133] Beyond the approved practice of imitation, Sterne himself was by no means free from accusations of outright and widespread plagiarism, which were keenly pursued by John Ferriar in his *Illustrations of Sterne* (1798). John Nichols's *Literary Anecdotes of the Eighteenth Century* preserves a comment made by D'Israeli regarding the possible priority of Shandean logic in John Dunton's *A Voyage round the World; or, a Pocket Library, divided into several volumes; the first of which contains the rare Adventures of Don Kainophilus, from his Cradle to his 15th Year, 1691*.[134] Yet D'Israeli allowed that it is the signature "breaks and dashes" that enliven Sterne's figured text and not any manner of wit or genius that he copied from Dunton. Roberts entertained his own doubts, saying the "style" of the posthumous works was very similar to the continuation of The *Sentimental Journey*, by Eugenius, and John Hall Stevenson's *Crazy Tales* (1762), what with its "The Author's Dedication to Himself," and "The Author's Apology to Himself."

Responding to Roberts, again in *Notes and Queries*, A. R. Shilleto offered the opinion that *The Koran* was indeed a genuine work of Sterne's possessing his manner and "peculiar vein of humour."[135] Shilleto felt fortunate for having picked up a copy for a trifle on the Isle of Man, supposing it to be a very rare, never having come across another copy though he had searched in various libraries. Shilleto was no casual reader. The editor of an edition of Burton's *The Anatomy of Melancholy*, he was familiar with the dim and innermost corridors of scholarship. Sterne's own relationship to Burton was of course complicated. According to Farrial, Sterne had "contrived to give a ludicrous turn to those passages which he took from Burton's *Anatomy of Melancholy*, a book, once the favorite of the learned and the witty, and a source of surreptitious learning to many others besides our author."[136] His words express the same sort of suspicious disregard Conrey had for the "thousand novel turns" of D'Israeli's anecdotes. As the custodian of an endlessly researched and resourceful text, Shilleto was responsible for straightening things out. Burton read so widely, and his references were often so vague and inexact, that previous editors had despaired of verifying his numberless quotations.[137] Shilleto performed a thousand or more (re)turns to Burton's sources, some of them *loci classici* and others passages from obscure post-classical authors.[138] As it happens, Shilleto did nothing to rectify the Didacus Stella reference, letting it stand uncorrected as: In Luc. 10. tom. 2.

With this we begin our own Shandean Postscript. The author of *The Koran* asks his readers not to be alarmed, for he had "not turned Mussulman." But he saw no reason why his visions and vagaries had any less right to be called *Al Koran*, or *The Koran*, than the writings of Mahomet; which were styled so, "merely as being a *collection of chapters*—for so the word in Arabick signifies."[139] As it happens, *OTSOG* is arranged, if that is the word for it, by numbered chapters set off by an archaized pilcrow. But it is well to note that the author of the *The Koran* was not Sterne, as some of its readers had suspected. Instead it was the work of Sterne's sometimes partner in high jinx, Rich Griffith, who included it in the volume of *The Posthumous Works of a Late Celebrated Genius, deceased* that he wrote in emulation of and as tribute to his friend. There is nothing mysterious about this attribution. Immediately following Shilleto's note follow three further notes attesting to Griffith's authorship. One of them points out that Griffith's hand had already been detected thirty-five years earlier, in very first volume of *Notes and Queries*. The communicator of that note possessed an "indifferent edition" of Sterne's work dating to 1795, the editor of the

129 [Corney], *Curiosities of Literature*, 108.

130 W[illiam] T[hynne] Lynn, "Newton and the Apple (7th S. ii. 328)," *Notes and Queries* 46 (November 13, 1886): 397 [397–398].

131 *The Koran: Or, the Life, Character, and Sentiments of Tria Juncta in Uno, M.N.A., or Master of No Arts, in The*

Works of Laurence Sterne, A.M. (London: 1775), 6:177.

132 Lynn, "Newton and the Apple," 397.

133 Roberts, "Sterneana," *Notes and Queries* ser. 6, vol. 11 (April 18, 1885): 302–303. John Kinsman, *Catalogue of the Books in the Penzance Public Library* (Penzance, 1874), 211. "Sterne (Lawrence)

Works. 7 vols. 12 mo. Lond. 1783 (shelf number 4170).

134 John Nichols, *Literary Anecdotes of the Eighteenth Century*, vol. 9 (London: Nichols, Son, and Bentley, 1815), 631.

135 A[rthur] R[ichard] Shilleto, "Sterneana (6th S. xi. 302)," *Notes and Queries* ser. 6, vol. 11 (May 30, 1885):

429 [429–430].

136 John Ferriar, *Illustrations of Sterne: with Other Essays and Verses* (London: Cadell and Davies, 1798), 56.

137 "*The Anatomy of Melancholy*. By Robert Burton. Edited by the Rev. A. R. Shilleto, M.A.," The Literary Era 1 (1894): 77.

138 Ibid.

posthumous volume of which, in his address to the reader, having received the MS. from the hands of the author some time before is untimely death.[140] The chain of possession of literary heritage is as much subject to its novel turns as any memorable deeds small or great. What better laboratory to test such a vacuous assertion than *Notes and Queries*, a self-style "Medium of Inter-Communication," one by which "much valuable information may become a sort of common property among those who can appreciate and use it."[141] By 1849 Griffith's exploit could well have been considered common knowledge. William Thomas Lowndes, The *Bibliographer's Manual of English Literature* (1834) judged the posthumous works to be "manifestly spurious."[142]

The long-standing confusion over the origin of *The Koran* is not without its positive consequences. We are afforded the unsearched for opportunity to consult *The Triumvirate: Or, the Authentic Memoirs of A. B. and C.* (1764), its preface signed: Biographer Triglyph [Griffith]. A footnote within explains that the initials A. B. C. (i.e. Andrews, Beville, and Carewe) were objected to in the manuscript, as being "too abstracted and fitter for geometry." The Preface contains a discussion of the Ancients and Moderns that puts the reading of Newton's aphorism, standing on the shoulders of giants, on a different footing:

> The great beauty of the antient authors, may be owing, perhaps, to their having wrote entirely without rules; while the *modeling* moderns endeavor to cramp even what little genius they have left. In the first, you perceive the free stroke of the pencil; in the latter is discovered the restraint of the compass. Or compare, if you please, the confined mincings of a *go-cart*, with the unspancelled strides of manhood.[143]

How does humanity learn to walk—be it in a straight line or along a crooked path? By modeling ourselves on others? What rules apply, what restraints are necessary? One sensible answer is provided by François Rigolot's essay on the crisis of exemplarity, which begins with a sentence passed by Montaigne in the final chapter of his *Essais*: "Every example is lame" (*Tout exemple cloche*). What Rigolot finds is that from Aristotle's *paradeigmata* (simple case stories at the orator's disposal) to Montaigne's "lame" *exemples* (contingent instances unfit for demonstrative purposes), the rhetorical impulse "has followed strangely circuitous ways."[144] Sterne himself found much to emulate on Montaigne. Farriar notes that "Sterne has made frequent references to Montaigne," helpfully but unkindly adding "the best commentary on the fifth chapter of *Tristram Shandy*, vol. VIII is Montaigne's essay on the subject of that chapter."[145] Turning to the designated volume and chapter we read, "Why weavers, gardeners, and gladiators—or a man with a pined leg (proceeding from some ailment in the *foot*)—should ever have had some tender nymph breaking her heart in secret for them, are points well and duly settled and accounted for, by ancient and modern physiologists."

At this point in his winding narrative Tristram is trying to explain the infatuation of the Widow Wadman for his Uncle Toby, whose adventures sends him along strangely circuitous ways. The problem with Toby, of course, is that he was wounded in the thigh at the siege of Namur. He becomes obsessed with calculating and recalculating the parabolic trajectory of the bombshell, uselessly sorting through a mass of treatises and tomes tracing the insulting injury back to its source.[146] The essay of Montaigne's in question is "*Des Boyteux*" (Of Cripples, in Charles Cotton's translation), which addresses debilities of judgment in terms of physical incapacity and a compensatory sexual hyperpotency. Montaigne referred to the "common *Proverb* in Italy, that he knows not Venus *in her perfect sweetness, who has never lain with a lame Mistress.*" Burton explains Venus's choice by reference to the proverb about the prowess of the lame. The proverb, Montaigne continued, "is said of men as well as of women."[147] Montaigne is ultimately concerned with error, the drawing of false and/or hasty conclusions, the excessive confidence placed in what has been said or what one is told, with what seems, what passes unsuspected, especially in the guise of tradition.

Perhaps there is nothing to the story of Newton's apple, especially if we heed Newton's own words. "Sir Isaac Newton used to say, that it was mere labour and patient thinking which had enabled him to investigate the great laws of nature.—Hear this ye blockheads, and go study."[148] But that saying comes from *The Posthumous Works of a Late Celebrated Genius, deceased*, so perhaps caution is still in order. Let us now attempt to take measure of Newton's tree in two ways: 1. as that which needs to be corrected; and, 2. far more improbably, as the very instrument with which to apply the rule.

About the first, applying standards while the sap is still running freely. The classic model of straightness is the surgeon Nicolas Andry de Bois-Regard's *L'Orthopédie ou l'art de prevenir et de corriger dans les enfans les difformités du corps of 1741 (Orthopædia: or, the art of correcting and preventing Deformities in Children: by such means, as may easily be put in practice by parents themselves, and all such as are employed in educating children*). Andry explained that the neologism *orthopédie* is formed of two Greek words, namely, *Orthos*, which means "right, exempt from deformity, that which is according to rectitude," and *Paidion*, which signifies child.[149] Considering all that has now been said about standing

139 *The Koran*, 1775, 14.
140 F. R. A, "*Sterne's Koran* (No. 14. P. 216)," *Notes and Queries* 26 (April 27, 1850): 418.
141 "Notes and Queries," *Notes and Queries* 1 (November 3, 1849): 1.
142 William Thomas Lowndes, *The Bibliographer's Manual of English Literature*, vol. 2 (London: William

Pickerling, 1834), 1740.
143 [Richard Griffith], *Triumvirate, or, The Authentic Memoirs of A. B. and C.* (London: W. Johnston, 1764), xii.
144 François Rigolot, "The Renaissance Crisis of Exemplarity," *Journal of the History of Ideas* 59 (1998): 557 [557–563].

145 John Ferriar, *Illustrations of Sterne: with Other Essays and Verses* (London: Cadell and Davies, 1798), 94.
146 See Sigurd Burckhardt, "*Tristram Shandy's* Law of Gravity," *ELH* 28 (1961): 70–88.
147 Cited in James King, "Weavers, Gardeners, Gladiators, and the Lame: *Tristram Shandy*, viii. 5," *Notes*

and Queries 228 (1983): 62, n. 5 [61–63]. King indicates that Sterne owned a copy of *Essays of Michael Seigneur de Montaigne*, made English by Charles Cotton, Esq., 3 vols. (London, 1693), from whence these passages from Montaigne are quoted.

Nicolas Andry, *L'Orthopédie ou l'art de prevenir et de corriger dans les enfans les difformités du corps*, vol. 1, 1741.

on the shoulders of giants, let us narrow ourselves to Andry's discussion of the deformities of the legs. About the hands, suffice it to say that after enumerating fourteen species of deformity, Andry exhorted parents to prevent their children from becoming *gauche*. "Children must be taught to give nor to receive anything with the left hand; civility demands it." They must be raised up right.[150] Andry's chief concern was with crooked legs and thighs; the term he uses is "courbe," which speaks of a rounding or bowing. "This deformity frequently proceeds from allowing children to walk too early, before their legs have acquired sufficient firmness to support the weight of the body."[151] It is incumbent upon parents to exercise caution before letting a child stand on its own. If the child's willful self-determination was not restrained, then corrective measures would need to be applied to the resultantly deformed member. A small iron plate was to be placed in the hollow of the leg and fastened about it with a linen bandage. Every day the bandage was to be made tighter and tighter until the deformity stood corrected. "In a word, to rectify the leg one must go about it just as one would rectify the curved trunk of a young tree. There is nothing in this that is very difficult and which the parent cannot execute themselves."[152]

In Andry's widely reproduced pedagogic illustration, the waxed tape Christison used to measure a tree's girth, but only after an acceptable standard level from the ground had been established, and allowing for irregularities where the base of the tree met the ground, is replaced by stout strands suitable for severe bondage. The tender tree's unruly growth will be bent to the unyielding upright stake; it will be made straight. While the therapeutically spanceled tree has since become the emblem for the medical discipline of orthopaedics, the frontispiece of Andry's book portrays an equally strict precept for bringing up children right. A mother surrounded by three children, flanked by a pair of stout, firmly-footed Doric columns, holds in her hand a lineal standard on which is inscribed: HAEC EST REGULA RECTI (this is the rule for straightness).

This is the rule that Tristram cannot or will not apply to himself. As J. Hillis Miller observes, and as Sterne teaches us with the exact lines that served as Merton's inspiration, "the interest of a narrative lies in its digressions, in episodes that might be diagrammed as loops, knots, interruptions, or detours making a visible figure."[153] Tristram nobly tries to correct himself:

> If I mend at this rate, it is not impossible—by the good leave of his Grace of *Benevento's* devils———but I may arrive hereafter at the Excellency of going on even thus;

> which is a line drawn as straight at I could draw it, by a writing-master's ruler, (borrowed for the purpose) turning neither to the right hand or to the left.

> This *right line*,————the path-way for Christians to walk in! say divines————
> —————The emblem of moral rectitude! says *Cicero*————
> —————The *best line!* Say the cabbage-planters————is the shortest line, says
> *Archimedes*, which can be drawn from one given point to another.————

There can be no doubt that Tristram finds the exercise as senselessly strict and puritanical as Biot did Brewster's biographical exclusions. His does not even have a ruler to apply to the task, borrowing one for the regrettable purpose. There is nothing standard about the narrative lines Tristram draws, not even their deviations. That is until he visualizes for himself, and for the reader, what it would look like if things were rendered orthogonally, made right and true. The exercise leads Tristram into further uncertainties. "Pray can you

148 "The Posthumous Works of a Late Celebrated Genius, Deceased," *The Gentleman's Magazine* 40 (1770): 80 [80–83].

149 [Nicolas] Andry, *L'Orthopédie ou l'art de prevenir et de corriger dans les enfans les difformités du corps* (Paris: La Veuve Alix and Lambert & Durand, 1741). Andry thought he was on sound footing with his neologism given Scévole de Sainte-Marthe's *Pédotrophie, ou Traité de la manière de*

nourrir les enfans of 1698 (*paedo* child and *trophe* nourishment), and the poet Claude Quillet's *La Callipédie* of 1749 (*callos* beautiful and *paedo* child).

150 Ibid., 277.

151 Ibid., 280.

152 Ibid., 282.

153 J. Hillis Miller, *Reading Narrative* (Norman: University of Oklahoma Press, 1998), 68.

tell me, —that is, without anger before I write my chapter upon straight lines,—by what mistake,—who told them so,—or how it has come to pass, that your men of wit and genius have all along confounded this line with the line of *gravitation?*"

And the tree that had a part in Newton's discovery of gravitation, or so it has variously been said? We take on good faith the following turn of events reported by McKie and de Beer. They are confirmed by the physicist R. G. Keesing, who after gathering and comparing pictorial evidence of Newton's apple tree, performing dendrochronological analysis, radiocarbon dating, and genetic fingerprinting concluded that an apple tree exists in the garden at Woolsthorpe, and that it is related to the tree beneath which Newton sat. Its identity is confirmed by the fact that it is the only apple tree in the garden at Woolsthorpe.[154] It seems that in 1939 Christopher Turnor recounted to Sir Stephen Tallents, who later worked under Lord Reith at the BBC, that when his great-grandfather Edmund Turnor acquired the house at Woolsthorpe the "famous apple tree" was still living and yielding pear-shaped apples.[155] The original tree had since died, but scions from it had been grafted on to trees belonging to Lord Brownlow at Belton. At Tallents's suggestion, Turnor arranged for grafts of the Belton scions to be sent to the Fruit Research Station at East Malling, where young trees grown from them were soon thriving. Under the able direction of pomologist Ronald George Hatton, who specialized in the "Paradise" group of apple rootstocks, East Malling became an important center for the classification and standardization of rootstocks.[156] During his initial researches Hatton realized that the utilization of scions from a single source was inadequate to achieve experimental uniformity when the root-stocks upon which the scions were grafted varied widely.[157] His methodological caution resulted in the standard and widely-distributed series of Malling root-stocks. But what of that most unique of scions?

McKie and de Beer next mention a meeting of the Royal Society Club held November 3, 1943 attended, amongst others, by John Maynard, 1st Baron Keynes of Tilton, who had purchased an important collection of Newton manuscripts at the 1936 sale of the Portsmouth papers, the same papers that were the source of Edmund Turnor's account of the tree.[158] Also in attendance was Tallents, dining as the guest of botanist Sir Edward

HAEC EST REGULA RECTI, the rule for straightness, from Andry, *L'Orthopédie*, 1741, frontispiece.

154 R. G. Keesing, "The History of Newton's Apple Tree," *Contemporary Physics* 39 (1998): 377–391.

155 For Tallents's own account of the tree's history see "The Sir Isaac Newton Apple," *The Fruit Year Book* 9 (1956): 35–40.

156 R. G. Hatton, "Paradise Apple Stocks," *Journal of the Royal Horticultural Society* 42 (1917): 361–399.

157 Edward J. Salisbury, "Ronald George Hatton 1886-1965," *Biographical Memoirs of Fellows of the Royal Society* 12 (1966): 253 [251–258]

158 A. N. L. Munby, "The Keynes Collection of the Works of Sir Isaac Newton at King's College, Cambridge," *Notes and Records of the Royal Society of London* 10 (1952): 40–50.

Salisbury. After dinner, indeed was it not after dinner when Stukeley heard the story of the apple "from Newton's own lips," Sir Edward produced from his pocket two large apples which came from Lord Brownlow's tree at Belton that had been grafted from Newton's original tree at Woolsthorpe. He said he had also obtained some very small apples produced by grafts from the original Woolsthorpe tree in the Royal Botanical Gardens, Kew, and had identified them as a cooking apples well known in the seventeenth century as Flowers of Kent. Sir Henry Dale, then President, informed the Club that the Royal Society had recently sent one of the trees grafted at East Malling to be planted in the garden of the house of William Penn, in Pennsylvania.[159] The nursery at East Malling continues to spread the seed, or the standardized rootstock of the Newton legend, one of them taking root at MIT.

There is of course much more to be said about the biography of Newton's tree. But any authorized biography would need to begin with mention of an unlikely instrument in the historical collections of The Royal Society. Entry no. 2 in the catalogue of relics of Sir Isaac Newton describes: "two rules made of the wood of Sir Isaac Newton's apple tree at Woolsthorpe. Presented by Rev. Chas. Turnor, F.R.S."[160] Might these not be the standards that need to be applied to the several versions of the Newton story? Further discussion of the origin of these fragmentary relics of Newton's fallen tree will be provided in the second installment of this essay. Let us conclude, then, with a passage from the mathematician Leonhard Euler, who paused to consider how things would have turned out if Newton "had not been seated beneath an apple tree, and a apple had not by chance fallen on his head."[161] (Evidently he opts for D'Israeli's non-standard head-clunking version.) Euler seemingly did

Two wooden rulers supposedly made from an ancient apple tree at Woolsthorpe Manor, Isaac Newton's family home. An inscription on the rulers reads "Made of the Wood of Sir Isaac Newton's Apple Tree at Woolsthorpe Lincolnshire." Underneath this phrase are the initials "C. T." which stands for Charles Turnor. ©Royal Society.

159 McKie and de Beer, "Newton's Apple," 54.

160 "Instruments and Historical Relics in the Possession of the Royal Society: Relics of Sir Isaac Newton," *The Record of the Royal Society of London* 1 (1897): 171.

161 Leonhard Euler, *Lettres a une Princesse d'Allemagne: sur divers sujets de physique,* vol. 1 (London: Société Typographique, 1775), 205.

162 Merton, *OTSOG*, xx.

share Merton's worry that his own "ostigian" thought experiment would be stigmatized as a "self-indulgence in counterfactual history."[162] In fact, Euler insists that the altogether probable scenario that an apple never fell (on Newton's head) is well worth further consideration.

The supposed Newtonian apple tree re-growing from a fallen trunk, detail from landscape view of Sir Isaac Newton's birthplace in Lincolnshire. Signed lower left in pencil "G. Rowe Del." Inscribed verso in ink [by Charles Turnor]: "N.W. view of the Manor House at Woolsthorpe drawn by G. Rowe, Cheltenham from the original Picture in my possession by Thos. Howison." ©Royal Society.

A "Techno-Social" Timeline

1932
MIT President Karl T. Compton reorganizes the Institute's academic and administrative structure and establishes the School of Architecture, incorporating the former Department of Architecture.

Course in City Planning is added to the curriculum, designed by Thomas Adams, and taught by Frederick J. Adams.

1934
The National Housing Act of 1934 establishes the Federal Housing Administration (FHA) and the Federal Savings and Loan Insurance Corporation (SSLIC) in an effort to make housing affordable.

Lewis Mumford publishes *Technics and Civilization*.

1935
The Instrumentation Laboratory is established by Charles S. Draper.

Le Corbusier visits MIT as a guest lecturer during his first trip to the United States.

Thomas Adams publishes *Outline of City Planning: A Review of Past Efforts and Modern Aims* with a forward by President Franklin D. Roosevelt.

1937
MIT celebrates its 75th anniversary.

The Housing Act of 1937, co-authored by Catherine Bauer Wurster. establishes the U.S. Housing Authority and provides subsidies to local public housing agencies.

1938
Albert Farwell Bemis Foundation is founded to develop and disseminate research regarding "more adequate, economical, and abundant shelter for mankind."

The Godfrey L. Cabot Solar Energy Fund is established to stimulate research and development on solar energy. The endowment leads to the creation of MIT's Solar Energy Research Project, resulting in a series of experimental solar houses.

1939
The MIT Solar House I is designed by Hoyt C. Hottel of the Department of Chemical Engineering and built on campus outside Building 32.

Rogers Building, also known as Building 7, is completed. The School of Architecture and Planning moves from Boston to the Cambridge campus.

1941
Vannevar Bush, former dean of the School of Engineering, is asked by President Franklin D. Roosevelt to direct the Office of Scientific Research and Development (OSRD), an agency of the U.S. federal government established to coordinate scientific research for military purposes during World War II.

Sigfried Giedion publishes *Space, Time and Architecture: The Growth of a New Tradition*.

1944
The School of Architecture and Planning is created comprising two departments, Architecture and Planning, each with its own chair and faculty.

William W. Wurster accepts the position of Dean of the School of Architecture and Planning.

1945
The Research Center for Group Dynamics (RCGD) is established by Kurt Lewin to study social psychology.

The Solar Energy Committee makes a formal request to the President of the Institute to expand the Solar Energy Fund to include a Steering Committee for an Experimental Dwelling Project, chaired by Professor of Architecture Lawrence Anderson.

Dean William W. Wurster invites Lewis Mumford to lecture yearly at MIT.

William W. Wurster, Thedore C. Bernardi, and Ernest Born publish "Proposed United Nations Center; a World Capital in the San Francisco Bay Area" in Architectural Forum.

Henry-Russell Hitchcock, chairman of the department of art at Wesleyan University, gives a course in the History of Architecture as a lecturer.

Alvar Alto serves as a resident of the School of Architecture and Planning.

György Kepes serves as Associate Professor in charge of the Freehand Drawing class.

MIT's annual budget reaches $44,354,800, nearly fourteen times greater than pre-war figures. $39, 970,900 is earmarked for defense research, and the rest distributed for general operating costs.

1946
Research Laboratory of Electronics (RLE) established as successor to the MIT Radiation Laboratory (RadLab), established during World War II.

Kurt Lewin's RCGD begins a study into the psychological factors involved in the design of public housing. A survey of the students in Westgate, directed by Leon Festinger, is commenced.

Ralph Rapson is hired as an architectural design critic.

1947
The Department of City and Regional Planning is established.

The Committee on Educational Survey, also known as the Lewis Committee, is appointed to review the Institute's curricular policies in "a new era emerging from social upheaval and the disasters" brought on by World War II.

The MIT Solar House II is designed by Hoyt C. Hottel.

1948
Kevin Lynch is hired as a lecturer.

Norbert Wiener publishes *Cybernetics: Or Control and Communication in the Animal and the Machine.*

John Ely Burchard is appointed the Institute's first dean of the School of Humanities and Social Studies.

György Kepes begins teaching a five-term sequence consisting of a rotating set of subjects, incl. Visual Fundamentals, Structure of the City, Form and Design, Light and Color, Graphic Presentation, Painting, and Advanced Visual Design.

Albert Farwell Bemis Foundation is transferred under the direct administration of the School of Architecture.

The MIT Solar House II is redesigned by John Haws to provide "comfortable modern living facilities for a family of three."

1949
The Housing Act of 1949 is first U.S. comprehensive housing legislation in the United States, aimed at assisting localities in "slum clearance" to counteract the widely perceived phenomenon of "urban decline."

The Committee on Educational Survey publishes "The Lewis Report" recommending that the humanities be given a more prominent role at MIT.

MIT holds a two-day Mid-Century Convocation to celebrate the inauguration of MIT's tenth president, James R. Killian.

Winston Churchill is the keynote speaker.

The Industrialized House Course is introduced with the support of the Albert Farwell Bemis Foundation.

1950
President Killian announces a $1,500,0000 grant from the Kresge Foundation for a "meeting house" dedicated to public gatherings and religious convocations. Eero Saarinen first visits the MIT campus to discuss the project.

The Cabot Fund sponsors a five-day course-symposium on "Space Heating with Solar Energy."

Sigfried Giedion serves as visiting professor in the Department of English and History.

1951
The Lincoln Laboratory is established by the Department of Defense, authorizing MIT to manage the facility as a federally funded research and development laboratory.

The School of Humanities and Social Studies founds the Center for International Studies.

György Kepes arranges the "New Landscape" exhibition at Hayden Gallery, displaying natural patterns generated in the scientific laboratories of the Institute.

1952
Dean of the School of Humanities and Social Studies, John Ely Burchard convenes the Committee for the Study of the Visual Arts at MIT, chaired by Bartlett H. Hayes, Jr., and comprised of John Coolidge, Robert Inglehart, Bartlett Hayes, Jr., Charles Sawyer, and James Johnson Sweeney, to make recommendations for a coherent curriculum in the arts.

Kevin Lynch serves as a consultant for the Downtown Waterfront-Faneuil Hall Renewal Project.

Muriel Cooper begins working at MIT Press and founds the Office of Publications.

1953
Marcus Whiffen replaces John McAndrew as Professor of the survey course, History of Architecture.

Lawrence B. Anderson is elected President of the Association of Collegiate Schools of Architecture.

During the absence of Ralph Rapson, Serge Chermayeff serves as senior architectural critic.

Frederick J. Adams, head of the Department of City and Regional Planning, serves as a United Nations delegate to the Regional Seminar on Housing and Community Improvement held in New Delhi, India.

1954
The Housing Act of 1954 amends the 1949 Housing Act to provide funding, not only for new construction, but also for the rehabilitation of deteriorating urban areas.

The Committee for the Study of the Visual Arts at MIT concludes its deliberations.

Albert Farwell Bemis Fund is established to support a program of short-term visiting professors and lecturers.

William H. Pierson teaches survey course on the history of architecture.

Albert Bush-Brown becomes the first long-term professor of architectural history at MIT.

Ralph Rapson resigns to accept deanship of the School of Architecture at the University of Minnesota.

György Kepes and Kevin Lynch begin three-year a Rockefeller funded study, entitled The Perceptual Form of the City.

Monsanto Chemical Company sponsors a study to explore the applications of plastics to housing.

1955
R. Buckminster Fuller serves as visiting lecturer.

Eero Saarinen and Minoru Yamasaki serve as visiting critics.

Eero Saarinen's non-denominational chapel, known as the "MIT Chapel," and auditorium are dedicated.

1956
Kevin Lynch first teaches "Theory of City Form" course at MIT.

György Kepes begins a series of themed interdisciplinary seminars which aim to bring together specialists in the arts and the sciences to discuss such issues as "structure" or "the man-made object."

Jay W. Forrester founds the System Dynamics Group at the Sloan School of Management to study industrial processes as cybernetic systems.

Edgar Kauffman, critic of art and architecture, serves as visiting lecturer.

Bernard Rudofsky serves as a visiting lecturer.

Louis I. Kahn serves as a visiting critic.
R. Buckminster Fuller, Minoru Yamasaki, and Paul Rudolph serve as visiting lecturers.

Lloyd Rodwin organizes a conference on "Problems of Planning Education in Latin America" for the Housing and Planning Section of the United Nations, jointly sponsored by the United Nations, the Pan American Union, and the University of Puerto Rico and the Commonwealth Government of Puerto Rico.

Joseph Hundur, retired Dean of the Harvard University School of Design, teaches course on Structure of the City.

György Kepes publishes *The New Landscape in Art and Science.*

Kevin Lynch and Alvin K. Lukashok publish "Some Childhood Memories of the City," in the American Institute of Planners Journal.

1957
Robin Boyd teaches survey of the history of architecture.

Charles Abrams, under appointment with the Department of Economics, gave a course in Building Economics.

The project sponsored by Monsanto Chemical Company for the design of an experimental plastic house is completed and built in Los Angeles, California.

MIT Solar House IV is designed by Lawrence B. Anderson and built on campus.

Report of the Committee for the Study of the Visual Arts at MIT is published as Art Education for Scientist and Engineer.

The Institute adopts the committee's recommendation for the creation of an elective course in the visual arts, Field 10.

Robert O. Preusser teaches the first Field 10 studio course. Thirty students enroll, and 20 finish the course.

Constantinos A. Doxiadis serves as Bemis Visiting Lecturer in City Planning.

Marvin E. Goody, Albert G. H. Dietz, Frank J. Heger, F. J. McGarry, and R. W. Hamilton publish *The Architectural Evolution and Engineering Analysis of a Plastic House: A Report for the Monsanto Chemical Company.*

The Center for Urban and Regional Studies is established.

Pietro Belluschi, then Dean of the School of Architecture, announces a new Ph.D. program in Urban Planning, offered by Center for Urban and Regional Studies.

1958
György Kepes and Robert O. Preusser began a new course on Light and Color for fifth-year students.

Lewis Mumford returns to MIT to teach single term courses in architectural history.

Reyner Banham publishes *Theory and Design in the First Machine Age.*

1959
The Harvard-MIT Joint Center for Urban Studies (JCUS) is established with a grant from the Ford Foundation. Lloyd Rodwin appointed chairmen of the Joint Faculty Policy Committee of the JCUS.

Kenzo Tange teaches studio for fifth-year students, and chooses as a subject a new town on land made in Dorchester Bay.

Albert Mayer serves as part-time Bemis Visiting Professor.

Maurice K. Smith is hired.

Dan Kiley, Hideo Sasaki, and Peter Walker serve as visiting lecturers on landscape design.

Balkrishna Doshi serves as visiting architectural critic.

Albert Bush-Brown publishes "Whence Architects and Whither Architecture?" in *Architectural Record.*

Roland B. Greely publishes "Suburbia: Satellite or Sprawl?"

Kevin Lynch and Lloyd Rodwin publish "A Walk Around the Block."

1960
Henry A. Millon takes post as assistant professor in the Department of Architecture.

Lawrence B. Anderson manages the Boston City Hall competition as advisor to the Boston Government Center Commission.

The Department of Architecture faculty and students create a "Chilean Seminar," and spend two months studying architecture and housing in Chile.

Pier Luigi Nervi serves as visiting lecturer.

Kevin Lynch publishes *Image of the City*.

Albert Bush-Brown publishes *Louis Sullivan*.

Demolition for Technology Square begins in Kendall Square.

1961
MIT celebrates its 100th anniversary.
The Guayana Region project in Venezuela, sponsored by the JCUS, is begun by Donald S. Appleyard, John Friedman, and Lloyd Rodwin.

Ford Foundation begins the Gray Areas program, identifying areas of social, political, and economic decline located between redeveloped urban districts and new suburban communities.

Sven Markelius, a consultant architect for the United Nations headquarters in New York, serves as visiting architectural critic.

György Kepes and Maurice Smith design "World Science and the USA," USIA traveling exhibition.

Lloyd Rodwin publishes *Housing and Economic Progress*.

Lawrence B. Anderson publishes *Programs and Condition: Competition to Select an Architect* for Boston City Hall.

Henry A. Millon publishes *Baroque and Rococo Architecture*.

John Ely Burchard and Albert Bush-Brown publishes *The Architecture of America: A Social and Cultural History*.

Jane Jacobs publishes *The Death of Life of Great American Cities*.

Lewis Mumford publishes *The City in History*.

1962
MIT Provost Jerome B. Wiesner is appointed director of U.S. Office of Science and Technology. Lawrence B. Anderson, in consultation with Albert G. H. Dietz of the Department of Civil Engineering, prepares a proposal for an interdisciplinary "school of planning arts."

The Perini Foundation grants $250,000 for support of the Laboratory for Model Testing.

György Kepes and Maurice K. Smith design a traveling exhibition for the United States Information Agency on "World Science and the United States."

The Department of City and Regional Planning awards its first Ph.D. to Bernard J. Frieden.

Michio Ihara serves as research associate.

Charles Correa serves as visiting lecturer. Donald Appleyard and Horacio Caminos are hired.

Kevin Lynch publishes *Site Planning*.

Herbert J. Gans publishes *The Urban Villagers*.

Morton and Lucia White publish *The Intellectual Versus the City: From Thomas Jefferson to Frank Lloyd Wright*.

Rachel Carson publishes *Silent Spring*.

Richard L. Meier publishes *A Communications Theory of Urban Growth*.

1963
Due to increased competition with other schools, of eight graduate scholarships totaling $16,500 offered to applicants, five totaling $8,800 were declined.

Project MAC starts operation at MIT's Computation Center.

James Q. Wilson named new head of JCUS. Ivan Sutherland's PhD dissertation in the Dept. of Electrical Engineering, "Sketchpad, A Man-Machine Graphical Communication System," describes the first Computer-Aided Design (CAD) program.

1964

Frederick J. Adams, founder in 1932 of MIT's planning program, retires.

Three Department of Architecture graduates join the Peace Corps, a voluntary governmental program established in 1961.

Departments of Psychology and Political Science established.

I.M. Pei's Green Building (Building 54) completed.

AIA-ACSA Teacher Seminar on "The History, Theory and Criticism of Architecture" held at the Cranbrook Academy of Art in Bloomfield, Michigan, organized by Henry A. Millon

CVG sponsors an extensive sociological survey of sociologists and urban designers by a Joint Center team headed by Donald Appleyard.

Appointment of Wayne V. Andersen as historian of modern art.

MIT President Julius A. Stratton dedicates the Center for International Studies (CIS), an academic research center founded in order to provide expertise on issues pertaining to the "Cold War" with the Soviet Union.

"Architecture and the Computer," first conference on the emergent relationship between architecture and computer sciences and technologies, held at the Boston Architectural Center (BCA) in 1964.

Henry A. Millon, as Chairman of the Boston Architectural Center's Program Committee, conducted a national seminar for teachers of architecture on the subject of "History, Theory, and Criticism." This seminar occurs annually under the sponsorship of the American Institute of Architects and the Association of Collegiate Schools of Architecture, of whose committee Lawrence B. Anderson is Chairman.

Two major conferences with participating MIT faculty are held in relation to the Joint Center for Urban Studies project in Guayana, Venezuela.

Gerhard M. Kallman serves as Visiting Bemis Professor in the advanced undergraduate studio.

Stanford O. Anderson completes first year of service.

John Friedmann and William Alonso publish *Regional Development and Planning: A Reader.* Martin Anderson publishes *The Federal Bulldozer: A Critical Analysis of Urban Renewal, 1949-1962.*

Charles Abrams publishes *Man's Struggle for Shelter in an Urbanizing World.*

Bernard J. Frieden publishes *The Future of Old Neighborhoods.*

Nathan Glazer and Daniel P. Moynihan publish *Beyond the Melting Pot.*

Christopher Alexander publishes *Notes on the Synthesis of Form.*

Peter Blake publishes *God's Own Junkyard: The Planned Deterioration of America's Landscape.*

1965

The U.S. Department of Housing and Urban Development is established.

Lawrence B. Anderson succeeds Pietro Belluschi as Dean of the School of Architecture and Planning.

Minor White joins Architecture faculty and establishes Creative Photography Laboratory.

President Stratton issues "Plan for Progress," the first nondiscrimination policy at the Institute.

Congress authorizes use of U.S. ground troops in Vietnam.

Louis I. Kahn teaches master's class.

Student Center by MIT faculty member Eduardo Catalano completed.

Donald Appleyard, Kevin Lynch, and John Myer publish *The View from the Road.*

Lloyd Rodwin publishes *Urban Planning in Developing Countries.*

Charles Abrams publishes *The City is the Frontier.*

President Stratton give green light for CAVS and names György Kepes its director; $200,000 allotted to remodel Coop facilities, with ten fellowships of $15,000 each.

1966

Howard W. Johnson succeeds Julius A. Stratton as President of MIT.

Demonstration Cities and Metropolitan Development Act of 1966 signed into law by President Lyndon B. Johnson.

New undergraduate major in History, Theory and Criticism of Art and Architecture is offered for the first time.

Nicholas P. Negroponte completes his master's thesis, "The Computer Simulation of Perception During Motion in the Urban Environment."

Negroponte and Léon Groisser begin URBAN 2, developed in collaboration with the IBM Scientific Center in Cambridge, where Negroponte worked following his graduation.

Stanford O. Anderson and Henry A. Millon begin working as part of the Conference of Architects for the Study of the Environment (CASE), a multi-institution group of architects funded by the AIA, Graham Foundation for the Arts, and the Princeton University Educational Research Project.

CIA funding of CIS taken over by the Ford Foundation and Department of Defense.

Department of Architecture hosts "Inventing the Future Environment" conference, with architects, economists, political scientists, planners, philosophers, social psychologists, and "futurists."

György Kepes seminars converted into six-volume *Vision and Value* series, published by George Braziller.

John Ely Burchard publishes *The Voice of the Phoenix: Postwar Architecture in Germany*.

Oscar Handlin and John Ely Burchard and publish *The Historian and the City*, a collection of essays from a symposium hosted by the Joint Center for Urban Studies.

1967

Center for Advanced Visual Studies (CAVS) is established, under the direction of György Kepes. Special Program for Urban and Regional Studies in Developing Countries (SPURS) is founded as part of the Department of Urban Studies and Planning with a grant from the Ford Foundation, offering one-year fellowships to international students with preference given to persons from developing countries.

The JCUS, in conjunction with the Boston Redevelopment Authority, receives a grant of $368,000 from the U.S. Department of Housing and Urban Development in connection with its Urban Beautification Demonstration Program. Donlyn Lyndon heads Department of Architecture.

Henry A. Millon, Robert Goodman, and Stanford O. Anderson formed a team under the sponership of the Museum of Modern Art in New York for the study of Harlem and the East River. Other teams, from Princeton, Columbia, and Cornell made designs for other sections of Manhattan north of Central Park. The four projects are exhibited in the Museum of Modern Art.

MIT submits 100-page proposal for a Program in Urban Affairs to the Ford Foundation, including requests for funding "Development of Laboratories for Urban Problems."

Léon B. Groisser and Nicholas P. Negroponte explore the capabilities of the computer in a system named Urban 5.

Inauguration of the Center for Advanced Visual Studies (CAVS); first fellows: Harold Tovish, Otto Piene, Will Garrett, and Vassilakis Takis.

Negroponte establishes the Architecture Machine Group (AMG) within the Dept. of Architecture to develop "man-machine design systems."

Institute awarded $3 million grant as part of the Foundation's new program on "University Urban Studies," replacing its "urban extension" program $800,000 of the grant dedicated to founding the Urban Systems Laboratory (USL).

Muriel Cooper rejoins MIT Press as its first art director.

Rosalind Krauss is hired as historian of modern art.

Donald Appleyard resigns to join the University of California, Berkley.

Nicholas P. Negroponte and Léon B. Groisser's give a course on "Special Problems in Computer Aided Urban Design."

Solo exhibition of Hans Haacke's air and water works at Hayden Gallery.

Donald Schön publishes *Technology and Change, the New Heraclitus.*

Robert M. Fogelson publishes *The Fragmented Metropolis: Los Angeles, 1850-1930.*

Gary T. Marx publishes *Protest and Prejudice: A Study of Belief in the Black Community.*

Peter Marris and Martin Rein publish *Dilemmas of Social Reform: Poverty and Community Action in the United States.*

Herbert J. Gans publishes *The Levittowners.*

James Q. Wilson edits and publishes *The Metropolitan Enigma: Inquiries into the Nature* and Dimensions of America's "Urban Crisis," a collection of papers commissioned from the Joint Center for Urban Studies by the Chamber of Commerce as a resource for its Task Force on Economic Growth and Opportunity.

New York City Mayor John Lindsay, Robert Moses, and Robert C. Wood speak at the JCUS.

The five-year-long involvement of the JCUS with the development of the Guayana region of Venezuela is completed.

1968
The Black Student Union is established at MIT. The Fair Housing Act bans discrimination in housing.

The Urban Systems Laboratory (USL) is established as a new interdepartmental program to mobilize the resources of the Institute in the area of urban research.

The Laboratory for Environmental Studies is established with support from the Urban Systems Laboratory, the Harvard-MIT Joint Center for Urban Studies, and grants and contracts from foundations and federal agencies such as the Economic Administration and the Department of Housing and Urban Development.

IBM System/360, Model 67 computer system is installed in the Information Processing Services Center.

The Urban Coordinating Group (UCG) is established to survey all of the departments of the Institute with regard to their commitment to urban research.

Community Projects Lab is organized by Department of Architecture with funding from the National Endowment for the Arts.

Architecture Machine Group organized by Nicholas P. Negroponte.

Architecture students launched a series of political demonstrations, including mounting an exhibition memorializing Martin Luther King, Jr.

Robert Goodman works with the Lower Roxbury Community Corporation in an effort to provide new housing for six families.

John F. C. Tuner explores settlements of the urban poor in South America.

Giancarlo de Carlo serves as Bemis Visiting Professor.

Jack Burnham, Ted Kraynik, Wen-Ying Tsai, Stan VanDerBeek join CAVS as Fellows.

Instrumentation Laboratory receives over $50,000,000 from the Department of Defense and the National Aeronautics and Space Administration (NASA).

First Design Methods Group conference, held in collaboration with USL, Harvard GSD and MIT's Department of Civil Engineering.

Harold Tovish, Otto Piene, Will A. Garnett, and Vassilakis Takis serve as Fellows of the Center for Advanced Visual Studies.

William L. Porter hired.

Donald A. Schön of the Organization for Social and Technical Innovation (OSTI), leads a new seminar on *Deliberate Social Change in the Cities.*

Stanford Anderson edits and publishes *Planning for Diversity and Choice.*

Lisa Peattie publishes *The View from the Barrio.*

1969
The JCUS enters its tenth year.

The Department of City and Regional Planning is renamed the Department of Urban Studies and Planning (DUSP).

Establishment of Project Cambridge within the Center for International Studies (CIS), a DARPA-funded initiative to develop computer-based applications of the behavioral and social sciences. Commission for the Survey of the Arts convened to study role of arts in future developments at MIT.

Jay W. Forrester publishes *Urban Dynamics,* expanding the application of cybernetics from industrial to urban systems.

Howard W. Johnson appoints Charles L. Miller to succeed Charles S. Draper as Director of the Instrumentation Lab, renamed the Charles Stark Draper Laboratory.

Noel F. McGinn and Russel G. Davis publish *Build a Mill, Build a City, Build a School: Industrialization, Urbanization, and Education in Ciudad Guayana.*

Robert C. Wood becomes new head of JCUS. The Union of Concerned Scientists proposes a day without research to protest involvement in research relating to the war in Southeast Asia.

Headed by the Science Action Coordinating Committee (SACC), a one-day "research stoppage" leads to the removal of classified research from campus. The event sparks similar strikes across the U.S.

President Johnson convenes review panel on the Special Laboratories, also known as the Pounds

Panel, to examine the role of military-funding and war-related research at MIT.

Approximately 1000 members of the NAC "mounted the steps of the student center with Vietcong flags and a loudspeaker to begin their 'anti-imperialistic actions' against the Institute" Herbert J. Gans is hired.

Julian Beinart, Head of the Department of Urban and Regional Planning, University of Cape Town, South Africa, serves as Bemis Visiting Professor.

Wen-Ying Tsai serves as a Fellow of the Center for Advanced Visual Studies.

Stan VanDerBeek is hired by CAVS.

Otto Piene organizes two major outdoor art events on the MIT Athletic Field using hot air balloons.

Project CARS (Computer Aided Routing Systems) is begun, comprising 70 members from the faculty, staff, and student body of four departments and four laboratories, who are developing a transportation system featuring minibuses which will be routed by a computer.

Daniel Patrick Moynihan leaves the Joint Center for Urban Studies to become an advisor to President Richard M. Nixon.

MIT's annual budget reaches $219,000,000, 80% of which is earmarked for sponsored research; over 50% of which is earmarked for the Instrumentation Laboratory and the Lincoln Laboratory; budget for weapons research branch of engineering constitutes one-quarter of MIT's total operating budget.

1970
First "Earth Day" is celebrated.

Center for Advanced Visual Studies holds two major exhibitions entitled Explorations, with the participation of Dr. Harold E. Edgerton, Dr. William M. Murray, Dr. Louis L. Sutro, Dr. Henry H. Holm, and a number of graduate students from various departments.

The JCUS celebrates its first decade with a conference, under the sponsorship of the Sloan Foundation, on The Role of University-Based Urban Centers, attended by 70 representatives of universities.

Joint Center for Urban Studies ends twelve-year association with the Ford Foundation.

Lloyd Rodwin heads DUSP.

Frank S. Jones, Associate Director of the Urban Systems Laboratory, supervises a project entitled "Technology, Race, and Poverty" that draws upon staff from local community organizers in Roxbury, Massachusetts and students at MIT.

At the Urban Systems Laboratory, Elizabeth Schumacker develops "Urban Geometries," an early computer-based system for land information, with the use of ICES/COGOL 1, a suite of programs originally developed in the 1960s by the Department of Civil Engineering.

William R. Porter develops DISCOURSE, an interactive computer language.

Nicholas P. Negroponte and Léon B. Groisser build a facility the Architecture Machine Group for the purpose of conduing experiments in computer-aided design.
Colin St. John Wilson, Herman Hertzberger, and Giancarlo de Carlo visit the School of Architecture and Urban Planning.

Thomas Vietorisz and Bennet Harrison publish *The Economic Development of Harlem*.

Nicholas P. Negroponte publishes *The Architecture Machine*.

Richard Sennett publishes *Families Against the City: Middle-Class Homes of Industrial Chicago, 1872-1890*.

UROP and Independent Activities Period (IAP) instituted.

MIT tuition: $2500; total enrollment: 8024
Budgets are cut for various urban research projects, including the Department of Housing and Urban Development's "Mobility of the Urban Poor," and the Economic Development Administration's "Urban Ghetto."

György Kepes, director of CAVS, is appointment Institute Professor.

Charles L. Miller, director of the USL, formally assumes post of Director of Charles Stark Draper Laboratory.

MIT President Howard W. Johnson announces his decision to undertake a two-stage divestment of Instrumentation Lab and Lincoln Laboratory.

1971
Daniel Ellsberg, a research fellow at CIS, releases the "Pentagon Papers."

György Kepes and Lawrence B. Anderson retire from MIT.

William L. Porter succeeds Anderson as Dean of the School of Architecture and Planning.

Jerome B. Wiesner succeeds Howard W. Johnson as President of MIT.

Ivan Illich is a visiting lecturer.

The Boston Development Strategy Research Project is begun at the Urban Systems Laboratory to explore the problems involved in devising alternative urban development strategies for the Boston region.

Bernard J. Frieden heads JCUS.

CAVS explore "Artistic Potential of Charles River." Dept. of Arch. Awards 80 degrees (150% increase over 1965)

DUSP awards 32 degrees (68% increase over 1965).

Wayne V. Andersen publishes *Gauguin's Paradise Lost*.

Robert M. Fogelson publishes *Violence as Protest: A Study of Riots and Ghettos*.

Robert Goodman publishes *After the Planners*.

Subcommittee formed to address social responsibility of firms in MIT's portfolio.

Henry A. Millon and Stanford O. Anderson propose Ph.D. Program in History, Theory and Criticism of Art, Architecture and Urban Form.

Artificial Intelligence Lab created.

Department of Philosophy established.

Council for the Arts created.

ADAPT, sponsored by the Department of Labor and the Department of Housing and Urban Development and conducted by the National League of Cities, meets at MIT in an effort to transfer expertise from the aerospace and defense industries to the management of urban affairs.

1972
Pruitt-Igoe in St. Louis is demolished.

The Roxbury Action Program (RAP), under the direction of George J. Morrison, is curtailed as a result of the federal moratorium on urban programs.

Stanford O. Anderson and Donlyn Lyndon begin three-year study of research and teaching in urban ecology.

Department of Housing and Urban Development awards $360,00 contract to JCUS to conduct housing allowance study.

Student strike over Cambodia closes classes; faculty urges end to Vietnam war.

Cambridge police tear gas "Attica Brigade" on MIT campus; 60 people occupy ROTC offices.

Under the director of I. Donald Terner and John Turner, the Department of Architecture and Planning carried out a study supported by the Agency for International Development (AID). Visiting Committee on the Arts established. Rosalind Kraus resigns from faculty.

Kevin Lynch publishes *What Time is This Place?*

Gary T. Marx publishes *Muckraking Sociology: Research as Social Criticism.*

John F. C. Turner and Robert Fichter publish *Freedom to Build: Dweller Control of the Housing Process.*

Robert K. Yin publishes *The City in the Seventies.*

Oscar Newman publishes *Defensible Space.* Department of Housing and Urban Development awards a $210,00, 18-month contract to the Systems Dynamics Group, for the extension of the Urban Dynamics research developed by Jay W. Forrester and the former Mayor of Boston, John F. Collins.

Dean William L. Porter establishes the Laboratory for Architecture and Planning (LAP) within the School of Architecture and Planning.

1973
Otto Piene appointed director of CAVS.

Students at CAVS participate in the development of proposals for projects in Times Square in New York City and Boston Harbor.

Visiting Professor Richard Leacock arranges an Introduction to Film Making course including visits from Lawrence Alloway, Midge Mackenzie, Pauline Kael, and Stan Brakhage.

First issue of *Oppositions* a journal published by the Institute for Architecture and Urban Studies (IAUS) in New York.

Ernst Friedrich "Fritz" Schumacher publishes *Small is Beautiful: Economics as if People Mattered..*

Interdisciplinary Environmental Design program is established, absorbing the Urban Design program of 1966.

Muriel Cooper and Ron MacNeil co-found the Visible Language Workshop

Dolores Hayden and Donald Preziosi hired as historians of architecture.

Otto Piene creates installation entitled "Weather" for Building 7 lobby.

Visiting Professor Christian Norberg-Schulz conducts a seminar on phenomenology, architecture, and urbanism.

Research funds for the School of Architecture and Planning totals over $1,000,000.

1974
Otto Piene succeeds György Kepes at CAVS. Visible Language Workshop (VLW) established, a collaborative venture among the Departments of Architecture and Humanities and the MIT Press, providing teaching, practice, and research in the visual arts.

Department of Architecture granted right to confer Ph.D. degree.

Aspen International Design Conference for 1974 organized by Department of Architecture faculty members, and coordinated by Julian Beinart.

The Center for Advanced Visual Studies, in collaboration with the School of Architecture and Planning and the Council for the Arts, sponsored a symposium entitled Arts and the University: The Visual Arts at MIT.

Architecture Education Study initiated.

Langley C. Keyes becomes acting director of DUSP, and John Harris becomes acting director of SPURS.

Department of Architecture rated best in country by *Change* magazine.

Manuel Castells, Manfredo Tafuri, Peter Cook, and Werner Oechslin visit the Department of Architecture.

The Departments of Architecture and Urban Planning hosted two symposia: "Current Perspectives in Revolution and Architecture in the Late 18th Century," with Manfredo Tafuri, Professor at the University of Milan, as principal speaker in a series of seminars, followed by a faculty seminar on "Politics, Architecture and Planning in American History," organized by Dolores Hayden.

Undergraduate applications to MIT from women increase 93% over 1973.

Cambridge Project discontinued and absorbed into the Overlap Project (funded by the Advanced Research Projects Agency of the Department of Defense) within the LAP.

Judith Wechsler publishes *Cézanne in Perspective*.

Donald Schön and Chris Argyris publish *Theory in Practice: Increasing Professional Effectiveness*.

Charles Moore, Gerald Allen, and Donlyn Lyndon publish *The Place of Houses*.

Nicholas P. Negroponte publishes *Soft Architecture Machine*.

Urban Systems Lab ceases operations.

Cooper begins teaching "Messages and Means," at the intersection of typography, graphic design, and technology.

1975
N. John Habraken becomes head of the Department of Architecture.

Architecture Machine acquires computer-aided design system.

DUSP awards first nine S.B./M.C.P. degrees.

Arthur P. Solomon heads JCUS.

DUSP reinstates core course curriculum.

CAVS sponsors "Video: Art in Process," "Boston Celebrations, Part 1" "Art-transitions," and "Otto Piene: Paintings, Gouache, Drawings."

Pablo Picasso's "Figure découpée" and Louise Nevelson's "Transparent Horizon" dedicated.

Project MAC changes its name to the Laboratory for Computer Science.

1976
First American Ph.D. program in the History, Theory and Criticism of Architecture founded at MIT.

The Cambridge Urban Observatory, jointly sponsored by MIT and the City of Cambridge, is established to provide urban research capability for Cambridge.

Science, Technology, and Society (STS) established at MIT.

The Architectural Education Study, funded by the Mellon Foundation, and directed by Dean Porter and Dean Maurice Kilbridge of the Harvard Graduate School of Design, is undertaken by a consortium of eight east coast architectural schools to analyze existing approaches to architectural education.

Second year of new curriculum in Masters in City Planning Program, including the introduction of four required "core" courses: Planning Process, Economic Analysis for Planners, Methods for Urban Studies and Planning, and an institutional analysis subject.

Introduction of "research" policy stating that faculty members be responsible for covering one-quarter of their base salary with research funds.

First five students enroll in Arch. M.S. program.

CAVS sponsors "Boston Celebrations, Part II." Donlyn Lyndon heads Committee on the Visual Arts (CVA).

Kevin Lynch publishes *Managing the Sense of a Region*.

N. J. Habraken, J. Th. Boekholt, and P. J. M. Dinjens publish *Variations: The Systematic Design of Supports*.

Donald Appleyard publishes *Planning a Pluralist City: Conflicting Realities in Ciudad Guyana*.

Dolores Hayden publishes *Seven American Utopias: The Architecture of Communitarian Socialism, 1790-1975*.

Dolores Hayden and Gwendolyn Wright publish the article "Architecture and Urban Planning" in *Journal of Women in Culture and Society*.

Donlyn Lyndon and Karen Wheeler publish *MIT Arts Environment Study*.

Nicholas P. Negroponte edits *Reflections on Computer Aids to Design and Architecture*. Newsletter, published by the Dean's office, renamed *Plan*-Review of the MIT School of Architecture and Planning.

Louis Skidmore Room was dedicated to house the Rotch Library Visual Collections. The renovation was made possible in part by a gift from Skidmore, Owings, and Merrill in memory of Louis Skidmore.

Research funding for the School of Architecture and Planning totals nearly $1,600,000.

1977
The Center for Advanced Visual Studies celebrates its first decade with "Center Beam" a contribution to documenta 6, a quadrennial international art exhibition held in Kassel, Germany.

The Overlap Project, directed by Dean William Porter, continues its research into interactive computational tools for data analysis.

The Special Program for Urban and Regional Studies of Developing Areas (SPURS) is completes its tenth year with nine Fellows from India, Korea, Spain, Japan, Kenya, Mexico, and the Philippines.

School opens IAP courses to local alumni. Nicholas P. Negroponte chairs the Master of Science Degree Committee, developing this program toward visual studies, computer-sided design, film and video, and building technology.

Robert M. Fogelson publishes *Big-City Police*.

Bernard J. Frieden publishes *The Nation's Housing, 1975 to 1985*.

Jan Wampler publishes *All Their Own: People and the Places They Build*.

Kevin Lynch edits *Growing Up in Cities,* a collection of essays from a UNESCO project.

MIT and Cairo University enter agreement under MIT's Technology Adaptation Program.

Muriel Cooper joins the Department of Architecture. Eduardo Catalano resigns after 18 years at MIT.

Research funds for the School of Architecture and Planning total $785,340.

1979
The Center for Advanced Visual Studies celebrates its first decade with "Center Beam" an exhibition held in Washington, DC., sponsored by MIT in cooperation wit the Smithsonian Institution, the National Park Service, and the National Endowment for the Arts.

MIT Solar House V built, sponsored by the Solar Energy Fund, opens; designed to supply 85% of its own heat; visited by Chinese architects.

Harriet Casdin-Silver and Don Thorton of the Center for Advanced Visual Studies hold the class "Holography as an Art Medium."

Lawrence Susskind heads DUSP.

Otto Piene's "Milwaukee Anemone" displayed on Boston Common.

György Kepes retrospective held in MIT galleries.

Stanford Anderson edits and publishes *On Streets*, a collection of essays on the role of the street in the cultural life of modernity.

Reinhard Goethert and Horacio Caminos publish *Urbanization Primer*.

MIT and USSR's Institute for Systems Analysis cooperate on management education and research.

"Unisex" retirement benefits announced, ending sex distinctions.

U.S. Department of Housing and Urban Development abandons New Towns program.

Kevin Lynch retires after 30 years at MIT.

1979
The Aga Khan Program for Islamic Architecture is established at Harvard University and MIT to promote the study of Islamic history and culture.

Two documentation centers are established. At MIT, the focus is on contemporary Islamic architecture and urbanism.

The Masters of Science in Architecture Studies replaces the Master of Architecture in Advanced Studies Degree. The new degree is research-based, open to students with a first professional degree in architecture and to those with degrees in other fields. Julian Beinart chairs this program, which accepts 25 students for the fall of 1979.

The Agency for International Development (AID) sponsors a program jointly with Cairo University and MIT on Housing and the Construction Industry in Egypt, also holding a two-week meeting at MIT. Henry A. Millon appointed to the National Gallery of Art, Washington, D. C.

Henry A. Milton and Linda Nochlin edit and publish *Art and Architecture in the Service of Politics*.

Bernard J. Frieden publishes *The Environmental Protection Hustle*.

NEA funds arts and media facilities.

Antonio Muntadas of the Center for Advanced Visual Sudies holds studio "Videotape as a Communication Tool and Environmental Medium," directed toward an exploration of the possible use of technologies as means to improve communication.

MIT tuition; $5100; total enrollment; 8881.

Three Mile Island power plant in Dauphin County, Pennsylvania suffers a partial nuclear meltdown, the worst accident in U.S. commercial nuclear power plant history.

Otto Piene, Ms. Elizabeth Goldring, Dr. Paul Earls, and John Brigham commissioned to develop ideas for art events and installations for the 1980 Winter Olympic Games in Lake Placid, New York.

1980
Dean William A. Porter resigns.

The Media Laboratory, growing out of the work of Nicholas P. Negroponte's Architecture Machine Group, is established to explore the intersection of art, architecture, design, and media.

1981
Dolores Hayden publishes *The Grand Domestic Revolution: A History of Feminist Designs for American Homes, Neighborhoods, and Cities*.

1984
The Center for Real Estate Development is established within the School of Architecture and Planning, the nation's first one-year graduate program in real estate.

1985
The Media Laboratory, housed in a building designed by I.M. Pei, is dedicated. Nicholas P. Negroponte is appointed its first director.

1986
MIT celebrates its 125th anniversary.

Contributors

Stanford O. Anderson

Stanford O. Anderson is Professor of History and Architecture and was Head of the Department of Architecture from 1991 through 2004. He was director of MIT's PhD program in History, Theory and Criticism of Architecture, Art and Urban Form from its founding in 1974 to 1991 and in 1995-96. Anderson's research and writing concern architectural theory, early modern architecture in northern Europe, American architecture and urbanism, and epistemology and historiography. He is co-author of *Kay Fisker* (1960), *Peter Behrens and a New Architecture for the Twentieth Century* (2000) and *Eladio Dieste: Innovation in Structural Art* (2004). In 1997, The MIT Press published a collection of essays in his honor, edited by Martha Pollak, *The Education of the Architect: Historiography, Urbanism, and the Growth of Knowledge.*

Daniel A. Barber

Daniel A. Barber is Assistant Professor of Architecture at the University of Pennsylvania's School of Design. He is an architectural historian with a research interest in the relationship between the design fields and the emergence of global environmental culture across the 20th century. He received a PhD in Architecture History and Theory from Columbia University, and a Master of Environmental Design from Yale University. He was recently a post-doctoral research fellow at the Harvard University Center for the Environment and Graduate School of Design, and has held visiting positions at Oberlin College, Barnard College, and the University of Auckland, New Zealand.

Julian Beinart

Julian Beinart is Professor of Architecture at MIT. His teaching focuses on the theory and practice of designing city form. He is the head of Cambridge International Design Associates, an architecture and urban design practice, and has served as a designer and consultant on projects in the Middle East, Southern Africa, Asia, and the United States. He holds post-graduate degrees in architecture and planning from MIT and Yale University, and has recently published essays on studies of the U.S. downtown, nineteenth-century grid form, and image construction in pre-modern cities.

Arindam Dutta

Arindam Dutta is Associate Professor of Architectural History at Massachusetts Institute of Technology Department of Architecture, where he also directs the Master of Science in Architectural Studies program. Dutta is the author of *The Bureaucracy of Beauty: Design in the Age of its Global Reproducibility* (2007), a wide-ranging work of cultural theory that connects literary studies, postcoloniality, the history of architecture and design, and the history and present of empire. He is currently working on a project entitled *Ancestralities:*

Nature, Architecture, and the Debt, which examines the relationship between architectural thought and the natural and human sciences in their globalizing frame. Another ongoing project is titled, *Sahmat 1989-2004: Liberal Art Practice against the Liberalized Public Sphere*, and involves an examination of the political challenges faced by artists in India with the dual rise of Hindu religious fundamentalism and the unraveling of state controls over fiscal policy effected as a result of the new financial consensus of the 1990s, termed "globalization."

Edward Eigen

Edward Eigen is Associate Professor of Architecture and Landscape Architecture at the Graduate School of Design, Harvard University. He is currently preparing to publish the book *An Anomalous Plan* which discusses a system of novel sites, instruments, and institutions for researching the natural environment. He was named an Old Dominion Faculty Fellow at Princeton University (2003–2005) and was awarded the 2005 Graduate Mentoring Award by the McGraw Center for Teaching and Learning and the Graduate School of Princeton University.

John Harwood

John Harwood is Associate Professor of Architectural History at Oberlin College. His research centers on the architectural articulation of science, technology, and corporate organization. His articles have appeared in *Grey Room*, *AA Files*, and *do.co.mo.mo*. He is co-author, with Janet Parks, of *The Troubled Search: The Work of Max Abramovitz* (2004), and co-author with Jesse LeCavalier and Guillaume Mojon of *This - Will This* (2009). His book *The Interface: IBM and the Transformation of Corporate Design, 1945-1976* was published in November 2011.

Mark Jarzombek

Mark Jarzombek, Professor of the History and Theory of Architecture at MIT, currently is also the Associate Dean of the School of Architecture and Planning. He has taught at MIT since 1995, and has worked on a range of historical topics from the Renaissance to the modern, and worked extensively on nineteenth and twentieth century aesthetics. His first book *On Leon Battista Alberti, His Literary and Aesthetic Theories* (1989), inaugurated an important reinterpretation of the noted Renaissance humanist. His second book, *The Psychologizing of Modernity, Art, Architecture and History* (2000), historicized a complex set of issues around the question of subjectivity and modernity. He has received numerous awards for his research as well as for the various international conferences that he has organized. He has published in a wide range of journals including the *Journal of the Society of Architectural Historians*, *Assemblage*, and *Renaissance Studies*. He has published a textbook entitled *A Global History of Architecture* (2006) co-authored by Vikramaditya Prakash and illustratored by Francis D.K. Ching.

Caroline Jones

Caroline Jones is Professor of Art History at MIT's History, Theory and Criticism Program. She studies modern and contemporary art, with a particular focus on its technological modes of production, distribution, and reception. Previous to completing her art history degree, she worked in museum administration and exhibition curation, holding positions at The Museum of Modern Art in New York (1977-83) and the Harvard University Art Museums (1983-85). Her books include *Eyesight Alone: Clement Greenberg's Modernism and the Bureaucratization of the Senses* (2005), *Machine in the Studio: Constructing the Postwar American Artist*, (1996/98, winner of the Charles Eldredge Prize from the Smithsonian Institution); *Bay Area Figurative Art, 1950-1965*, (1990, awarded the silver medal from San Francisco's Commonwealth Club); and *Modern Art at Harvard* (1985). She edited *Sensorium: Embodied Experience, Technology, and Contemporary Art* (2006) and co-edited *Picturing Science, Producing Art* (1998).

Mary Louise Lobsinger

Mary Louise Lobsinger is Associate Professor at the Faculty of Architecture, Landscape, and Design at the University of Toronto, where she teaches courses in architectural history and theory, and design studios. She recently completed a book manuscript entitled *The Realist Impulse: Aldo Rossi and Postwar Italian Architectural Discourse*. Her scholarly work has appeared in *Grey Room, Daidalos, Journal of Architectural Education, Thresholds* and in anthologies including *Architectural Periodicals in the 1960s and '70s* (Institut Recherche en Histoire de l'Architecture, 2008), *Docomomo: Import-Export: Postwar Modernism in an Expanding World, 1945-1975* (2008), *Le Citta' visibili* (2007), *and Concrete Toronto: A Guidebook to Concrete Architecture from the Fifties to the Seventies* (2007).

Reinhold Martin

Reinhold Martin is Associate Professor of Architecture in the Graduate School of Architecture, Planning, and Preservation at Columbia University, where he directs the PhD program in Architectural History and Theory, as well as the Master of Science program in Advanced Architectural Design. He is a founding co-editor of the journal *Grey Room*, a partner in the firm of Martin/Baxi Architects, and has published widely on the history and theory of modern and contemporary architecture. He is the author of *The Organizational Complex: Architecture, Media, and Corporate Space* (2003), and *Utopia's Ghost: Architecture and Postmodernism, Again* (2010). Martin's current work focuses on the architectural and cultural history of the American university since the eighteenth century.

Catherine F. McMahon

Catherine F. McMahon is an artist and researcher who received her Bachelor's degree in architecture from the Rhode Island School of Design and holds a Master's degree from the History, Theory and Criticism discipline group at MIT. Her research focuses on the history and theory of science and technology. Recently she has been involved in projects o on the cusp of art and science ranging from assisting the Disobedience Archive exhibition at the MIT Media Lab to a collaborative art and research project with artist Jess Wheelock, focused on Dale Carnegie and his 1937 self-help book, *How to Win.*

Brendan D. Moran

Brendan D. Moran is an Assistant Professor in Architecture at Syracuse University. Moran holds a Ph.D. in Architectural History and Theory from Harvard University's Graduate School of Design, as well as a Masters in Environmental Design from the Yale School of Architecture. His ongoing research examines the intersection of architecture and planning education during the mid-century in America, as well as the role of the research university in shaping various forms of professional education involving design. Prior to undertaking PhD studies, he worked at various architecture offices in new York City and entered several international architecture competitions. He was co-editor of *Perspecta* 32: Resurfacing Modernism (2001).

Eric Mumford

Eric Mumford is a Professor of Architectural and Urban Design History at the Sam Fox School of Architecture at Washington University in St. Louis. Mumford has published and lectured widely on CIAM, and the work and pedagogy of CIAM President and Dean of the Harvard GSD, Joseph Lluis Sert, including the recent book, *The CIAM Discourse on Urbanism, 1928-1960* (2000), a critical history of the International Congress of Modern Architecture.

M. Ijlal Muzaffar

M. Ijlal Muzaffar is an Assistant Professor of Modern Architectural History at the Rhode Island School of Design. Before RISD, he taught at Indiana University, Bloomington, where he was Visiting Faculty at the Department of Art History and the Center for the Study of Global Change. He has also taught at the Program in History, Theory, and Criticism of Architecture and Art at MIT, from where he also received his PhD in 2007. He is working on a book that examines how modern architects and planners played a critical role in shaping the discourse on Third World development and its associated structures of power and intervention in the postwar era.

William L. Porter

William L. Porter was Dean of the school from 1971 to 1981. He founded the school's Laboratory of Architecture and Planning to encourage and support field-related research. With Oleg Grabar, professor emeritus of Fine Arts at Harvard, he founded the Aga Khan Program for Islamic Architecture at Harvard and MIT, and served as its co-director until 1985. His research has focused on methods and processes of design of individuals and groups. As architect, Porter worked for Louis I. Kahn in Philadelphia, and on the new city of

Ciudad Guayana with the Harvard-MIT Joint Center for Urban Studies. Porter is a Fellow of the American Institute of Architects, a member of the Boston Society of Architects. He is also past president of the National Architectural Accreditation Board.

Avigail Sachs

Avigail Sachs teaches architecture and landscape architecture history and theory at the University of Tennessee, Knoxville. In 2009, she completed a doctoral degree at the University of California, Berkeley. In her dissertation, *Research and Environmental Design: Building a Discipline and Modernizing the Profession*, she reexamined the inception of modern architecture education in the United States in the mid-20th century and placed architecture education in the context of the housing movement, the building industry, and the American research university. She contributed to Joan Ockman's 2012 edited volume *Architecture School: Three Centuries of Educating Architects in North America*.

Hashim Sarkis

Hashim Sarkis is the Aga Khan Professor of Landscape Architecture and Urbanism in Muslim Societies at the Graduate School of Design, Harvard University. He teaches courses in the history and theory of architecture as well as design studios. Sarkis is a practicing architect between Cambridge and Lebanon. His projects include a housing complex for the fishermen of Tyre, a park in downtown Beirut, two schools in the North Lebanon region, and several urban and landscape projects. He is author of several books and articles including *Circa 1958: Lebanon in the Pictures and Plans of Constantinos Doxiadis* (2003), editor of C*ASE: Le Corbusier's Venice Hospital* (2001), co-editor with Peter G. Rowe of *Projecting Beirut* (1998), and executive editor of the CASE publication series.

Felicity D. Scott

Felicity D. Scott is Associate Professor of Architecture and Director of the program in Critical, Curatorial, and Conceptual Practices in Architecture (CCCP) at the Graduate School of Architecture, Planning, and Preservation, Columbia University. She is also the founding co-editor of *Grey Room*. Her work as an architectural historian and theorist focuses on articulating genealogies of political and theoretical engagement with questions of technological transformation within modern and contemporary architecture, as well as within the discourses and institutions that have shaped and defined the discipline. Scott is the author of *Architecture or Techno-utopia: Politics after Modernism* (2010). She recently completed a manuscript for a book entitled *Cartographies of Drift: Bernard Rudofsky's Encounters with Modernity*, and has undertaken substantial research and writing on her subsequent book-project, *Outlaw Territory*, which investigates architecture's relation to "human unsettlement" and territorial insecurity.

Molly Wright Steenson

Molly Wright Steenson is a PhD candidate at Princeton University's School of Architecture, where her dissertation, "Artificial Intelligence, Architectural Intelligence: Nicholas Negroponte ad the Architecture Machine Group" looks at the intersection of technology and architecture in the 60s and 70s, and how AI and architecture created groundwork for contemporary human-computer interaction. She also researches 19th and early 20th century communication technology at the urban scale. She is interested in the application of these ideas through design pedagogy and digital humanities. In January 2013, Molly will start a position as assistant professor at the University of Wisconsin-Madison in the School of Journalism and Mass Communication. Molly began working with the Web in 1994 at a wide variety of Fortune 500 and smaller, creative companies.

Alise Upitis

Alise Upitis is a Visiting Scholar at the Center for Advanced Visual Studies at MIT, where she is investigating new modes for understanding and disseminating archival productions surrounding time-based artworks. She has curated exhibitions on Cyprien Gaillard and Christoph Draeger; her writing has recently appeared in *Arq* and *Big Red & Shiny*. Upitis holds a PhD in Architecture from MIT and an A.B., summa cum laude, from Smith College.

Anna Vallye

Anna Vallye is the Andrew W. Mellon Postdoctoral Curatorial Fellow in Modern and Contemporary Art at the Philadelphia Museum of Art. She received her PhD in art history at Columbia University. Her dissertation focused on the American careers of Walter Gropius and György Kepes. Her essay "The Reenchantment of the World: Ruth Vollmer's Science" was published in *Thinking the Line: Ruth Vollmer, 1961–1978*, edited by Nadja Rottner and Peter Weibel (2006).

Matthew Wisnioski

Matthew Wisnioski is Associate Professor of Science and Technology in Society at Virginia Tech. He works at the nexus of the history of science & technology, American cultural-intellectual history, engineering studies, and the values of design. His 2012 book *Engineers for Change: Competing Visions of Technology in 1960s America* is the inaugural volume in a new MIT Press Engineering Studies series. It is both a cultural-intellectual history of dominant contemporary assumptions about technology and the first synthetic account of the US engineering profession in the postwar era. He also has written on György Kepes and the collaborative intersections of engineers and artists during the Cold War. He is beginning a second book on the role of innovation discourses and design methods in the making of postwar technoscientific selves.

Illustration Credits

Every reasonable effort has been made to identify owners of copyrights. Errors or omissions will be corrected in subsequent reprints.

Christopher Alexander: 505

American Psychological Association: 410

Stanford O. Anderson: 574-5, 586, 593, 596, 599-601, 604-5, 612, 635--9, 643, 645, 651

Arizona State University, Maria Telkes Archive, 278

Associated Press: 96, 510.

Nishan Bachajian, 181, 211; Abrams Books: 143

Julian Beinart: 722, 733

Boston Architectural College: 130

Boston Redevelopment Authority: 418, 420-4, 426, 428

Steward Brand: 219

George Braziller Inc.: 173-7

Canadian Centre for Architecture: 685

J. Ph. Charbonnier, Courtesy Galerie Agathe Gaillard: 105

Noam Chomsky: 56

Paula Cooper Gallery: 521

William D. Coplin: 462

Douglas Davis: 207

Ann Day: 145

Dover Publications: 155, 157, 161, 164, 166, 170

Arindam Dutta: 518

Peter Eisenman: 47

Olafur Eliasson Studio: 518, 540, 545

Yona Friedman: 370

Andy Gracie: 546

Daniel Gregory: 688

©Hans Haacke/Artists Rights Society: 507, 512-3, 518, 521, 523-4, 533, 535, 538-40, 544, 774-5

N. John Habraken: 56, 816, 819-20

Harvard University Graduate School of Design, Special Collections: 301, 340 (Wilhelm von Moltke), 452, 58-9, 464, 462

Harvard University Press: ©1964 President and Fellows of Harvard College, © renewed 1992 by Christopher Alexander: 56, 503-4

Perry Hoberman: 543

IBM Corporate Archives: 485, 502

© Prof. Dr. Gottfried Jäger/Carl-Strüwe-Archiv Bielefeld/VG Bild-Mark Jarzombek: 47, 553(caption), 556-7, 562, 564, 568-571

Kalman Family: 147

Thessaly Karas: 131-132, 347-9

Julie Kepes Stone and Imre Kepes: 155, 157, 158-9, 161, 164, 166, 168, 170, 173-7, 182, 192, 230

Gyorgy Kepes Papers, Smithsonian Institution, Archives of American Art: 158-9, 192

Kunst Bonn: 164

Los Alamos Scientific Laboratory: 201

The Martin Centre for Architectural and Urban Studies, Department of Architecture, University of Cambridge: 674-5

©The Museum of Modern Art/Licensed by SCALA/Art Resource, NY: 135, 625-7, 629-30

New York University Archives, Records of the New York University College of Engineering, Research Division: 278

©The Royal Society: 880-1

Brain Lee Yung Rowe: 546

Segal Quince Wicksteed: 658-9

Winzen Research Inc.: 202-3

University of Wisconsin Press, Board of Regents of the University of Wisconsin System: 272

Beth Shirk: 78-9

Archive ZERO Foundation: 514

Courtesy Massachusetts Institute of Technology, Cambridge, Massachusetts. All rights reserved.

MIT Libraries, Institute Archives and Special Collections: MIT School of Architecture and Planning, Office of the Dean records: 116-118; 136; 230; Architecture Dean Papers: 236; Albert Farwell Bemis Foundation Records: 233-4, 243, 285, 584; 230, Hoyt Hottel Papers: 255-6, 268, Kevin Lynch Papers: Perceptual Form of the City Series: 397; Planning Office Records: Interior covers, front and back; Rotch Library of Architecture & Planning, Visual Collections: 14, 136

MIT Museum: 52 (Simon Wiltz), 80, 93, 99, 100, 102, 152, 221, 246, 268, 276-7, 382-3, 476-7, 479-80, 486, 489, 734-5, 738-9, 770, 778-9, 788-90, 793; MIT Photo: 381-2

The MIT Press: 194-5, 197, 215, 298-9, 302, 315, 317, 333, 336-8, 399-401, 458-9, 467-9, 471-3, 748-9, 804

MIT School of Architecture & Planning: Department of Architecture: 14, 75, 80, 136, 161, 164, 173-7, 239, 241, 243-5, 248-9, 255-6, 266, 271-2, 274, 283, 285, 347-9, 356, 572-3, 654-5, 682-3, 738-9; Plan: 8, 53-4, 80, 560, 564, 767; William Porter, 7, 75, 220, 345, 559, 695, 719, 740, 756-7, 767-8, 813, 832-3; Program in Art Culture Technology: 221, 225; Department of City & Regional Planning: 415, 417, 439, 441-2, 449; Department of Urban Studies & Planning: 755; Center for Advanced Visual Studies Special Collection: 166, 173-7, 181-2, 184-5, 190-191, 203, 207, 209, 215-6, 528, 782; Nishan Bichajian, 181, 211; Jeanne Coffin, 194; Calvin Campbell, 194, 221; Dietmar Loehrl, 191, 195; Elizabeth Goldring, 195, 197, 215, 222; Walter Lewin, 205; Otto Piene, 202-3, 222; Roger Goldstein, 207; MIT Architecture Machine Group (ArcMac): 207, 360, 363, 364, 366, 371, 373-4, 796-7, 804;

MIT Council for the Arts: 218; MIT School of Engineeering: 492, 495, 500, 501, 661; MIT Technique: 189; MIT's Technology Review: 14, 30, 88, 95, 170, 556-7, 796-7; MIT Tech Talk: 76, 760

Index